Random House
Webster's

Handy
SPANISH
Dictionary

SPANISH • ENGLISH
ENGLISH • SPANISH

ESPAÑOL • INGLÉS
INGLÉS • ESPAÑOL

RANDOM HOUSE
NEW YORK

Random House Webster's Handy Spanish Dictionary

Sale of this book without a front cover may be unauthorized. If this book is coverless, it may have been reported to the publisher as "unsold or destroyed," and the publisher may not have received payment for it.

Copyright © 1999 by Random House, Inc.

Trademarks

This book was edited by Donald F. Solá and is based on the *Random House Spanish–English English–Spanish Dictionary*, edited by David Gold, © 1999.

This book is available for special purchases in bulk by organizations and institutions, not for resale, at special discounts. Please direct all your sales inquiries to Random House Premium Sales, fax 212-572-4961.

Please address all inquiries about electronic licensing of reference products, for use on a network or in software or on CD-ROM, to the Subsidiary Rights Department, Random House Reference, fax 212-940-7352.

Library of Congress Cataloging-in-Publication Data
Random House Webster's Handy Spanish dictionary. -- 1st ed.
    p.   cm.
  ISBN 0-375-70701-8 (pbk.)
  1. Spanish language Dictionaries--English. I. Random House
(Firm) II. Title: Webster's Handy Spanish dictionary. III. Title:
Handy Spanish dictionary.
PC4640.R267   1999
463'.21--dc21   99-31112
                                          CIP

Visit the Random House Reference Web site at www.randomwords.com

Typeset by Random House Reference, a division of Random House, Inc.
Typeset and printed in the United States of America

First Edition
0 9

ISBN: 0-375-70701-8

New York Toronto London Sydney Auckland

Pronunciation Key for Spanish

IPA Symbols	Key Words	Approximate Equivalents
a	alba, banco, cera	father, depart
e	esto, del, parte, mesa	bet; like rain when e ends syllable and is not followed by r, rr, or t
i	ir, fino, adiós, muy	like beet, but shorter
o	oler, flor, grano	like vote, but shorter
u	un, luna, cuento, vergüenza, guarda	fool, group
b	bajo, ambiguo, vaca	by, abet
β	hablar, escribir, lavar	like vehicle, but with lips almost touching
d	dar, desde, andamio, dueña	deal, adept
ð	pedir, edredón, verdad	that, gather
f	fecha, afectar, golf	fan, after
g	gato, grave, gusto, largo, guerra	garden, ugly
h	gemelo, giro, junta, bajo	horse
k	cacao, claro, cura, cuenta, que, quinto	kind, actor
l	lado, lente, habla, papel	lot, altar
ʎ	(in Spain) llama, calle, olla	like million, but with tongue behind teeth
m	mal, amor	more, commit
n	nada, nuevo, mano, bien	not, enter

IPA Symbols	Key Words	Approximate Equivalents
ɲ	ñapa, año	canyon, companion
ŋ	angosto, aunque	ring, anchor
p	peso, guapo	pill, applaud
r	real, faro, deber	like rice, but with single flap of tongue on roof of mouth
rr	perro, sierra	like rice, but with trill, or vibration of tongue, against upper teeth
s	sala, espejo, mas; (in Latin America) cena, hacer, vez	say, clasp
θ	(in Spain) cena, hacer, cierto, cine, zarzuela, lazo, vez	thin, myth
t	tocar, estado, cenit	table, attract
y	ya, ayer; (in Latin America) llama, calle	you, voyage
tʃ	chica, mucho	chill, batch

Diphthongs

ai, ay	baile, hay	high, rye
au	audacia, laudable	out, round
ei, ey	veinte, seis, rey	ray
ie	miel, tambien	fiesta
oi, oy	estoico, hoy	coin, loyal
ua	cuanto	quantity
ue	buena, suerte	sway, quaint

Spanish Stress

In a number of words, spoken stress is marked by an accent ('): *nación, país, médico, día.*

Words which are not so marked are, generally speaking, stressed on the next-to-the-last syllable if they end in a vowel, *n*, or *s;* and on the last syllable if they end in a consonant other than *n* or *s*.

Note: An accent is placed over some words to distinguish them from others having the same spelling and pronunciation but differing in meaning.

Spanish Alphabetization

In Spanish, *ch* and *ll* are no longer considered to be separate letters of the alphabet. They are now alphabetized as they would be in English. However, words with *ñ* are alphabetized after *n*.

Guía de Pronunciación del inglés

Símbolos del AFI	Ejemplos
/æ/	*ingl.* hat; como la **a** de *esp.* paro, pero más cerrada
/ei/	*ingl.* stay; *esp.* reina
/ɛə/ [followed by /r/]	*ingl.* hair; *esp.* ver
/ɑ/	*ingl.* father; similar a las **a**s de *esp.* casa, pero más larga
/ɛ/	*ingl.* bet; *esp.* entre
/i/	*ingl.* bee; como la **i** de *esp.* vida, pero más larga
/ɪə/ [followed by /r/]	*ingl.* hear; como la **i** de *esp.* venir, pero menos cerrada
/ɪ/	*ingl.* sit; como la **i** de *esp.* Chile, pero menos cerrada
/ai/	*ingl.* try; *esp.* hay
/ɒ/	*ingl.* hot; *esp.* poner
/o/	*ingl.* boat; similar a la **o** de *esp.* saco, pero más cerrada
/ɔ/	*ingl.* saw; similar a la **o** de *esp.* corte, pero más cerrada
/ɔi/	*ingl.* toy; *esp.* hoy
/ʊ/	*ingl.* book; como la **u** de *esp.* insulto, pero menos cerrada
/u/	*ingl.* too; como la **u** de *esp.* luna, pero más larga
/au/	*ingl.* cow; *esp.* pausa
/ʌ/	*ingl.* up; entre la **o** de *esp.* borde y la **a** de *esp.* barro
/ɜ/ [followed by /r/]	*ingl.* burn; *fr.* fleur
/ə/	*ingl.* alone; *fr.* demain
/ə/	*ingl.* fire (fiᵊr); *fr.* bastille
/b/	*ingl.* boy; como la **b** de *esp.* boca, pero más aspirada
/tʃ/	*ingl.* child; *esp.* mucho
/d/	*ingl.* dad; *esp.* dar

Símbolos del AFI	Ejemplos
/f/	*ingl.* for; *esp.* fecha
/g/	*ingl.* give; *esp.* gato
/h/	*ingl.* happy; como la j de *esp.* jabón, pero más aspirada y menos aspera
/dʒ/	*ingl.* just; *it.* giorno
/k/	*ingl.* kick; similar a la k de *esp.* kilogramo, pero más aspirada
/l/	*ingl.* love; *esp.* libro
/m/	*ingl.* mother; *esp.* limbo
/n/	*ingl.* now; *esp.* noche
/ŋ/	*ingl.* sing; *esp.* blanco
/p/	*ingl.* pot; como las ps de *esp.* papa, pero más aspirada
/r/	*ingl.* read; como la r de *esp.* para, pero con la lengua elevada hacia el paladar, sin tocarlo
/s/	*ingl.* see; *esp.* hasta
/ʃ/	*ingl.* shop; *fr.* chercher
/t/	*ingl.* ten; similar a la t de *esp.* tomar, pero más aspirada
/θ/	*ingl.* thing; *esp.* (en España) cerdo, zapato
/ð/	*ingl.* father; *esp.* codo
/v/	*ingl.* victory; como la b de *esp.* haba, pero es labiodental en vez de bilabial
/w/	*ingl.* witch; como la u de *esp.* puesto, pero con labios más cerrados
/y/	*ingl.* yes; *esp.* yacer
/z/	*ingl.* zipper; *fr.* zéro
/ʒ/	*ingl.* pleasure; *fr.* jeune

Las consonantes /l̩/, /m̩/, y /n̩/ son similar a las **l**, **m**, y **n** del español, pero alargada y resonante.

English Abbreviations/Abreviaturas inglesas

a.	adjective	*Govt.*	government
abbr.	abbreviation	*Gram.*	grammar
adv.	adverb	*interj.*	interjection
Aero.	aeronautics	*interrog.*	interrogative
Agr.	agriculture	*Leg.*	legal
Anat.	anatomy	*m.*	masculine
art.	article	*Mech.*	mechanics
Auto.	automotive	*Mex.*	Mexico
Biol.	biology	*Mil.*	military
Bot.	botany	*Mus.*	music
Carib.	Caribbean	*n.*	noun
Chem.	chemistry	*Naut.*	nautical
Colloq.	colloquial	*Phot.*	photography
Com.	commerce	*pl.*	plural
conj.	conjunction	*Pol.*	politics
dem.	demonstrative	*prep.*	preposition
Econ.	economics	*pron.*	pronoun
Elec.	electrical	*Punct.*	punctuation
esp.	especially	*rel.*	relative
f.	feminine	*Relig.*	religion
Fig.	figurative	*S.A.*	Spanish America
Fin.	finance	*Theat.*	theater
Geog.	geography	*v.*	verb

Note: If a main entry term is repeated in a boldface subentry in exactly the same form, it is abbreviated. Example: **comedor** *n.m.* dining room. **coche c.,** dining car.

a /a/ *prep.* to; at.

abacería /aβaθe'ria; aβase'ria/ *n. f.* grocery store.

abacero /aβa'θero; aβa'sero/ *n. m.* grocer.

ábaco /'aβako/ *n. m.* abacus.

abad /a'βað/ *n. m.* abbot.

abadía /aβa'ðia/ *n. f.* abbey.

abajar /aβa'har/ *v.* lower; go down.

abajo /a'βaho/ *adv.* down; downstairs.

abandonar /aβando'nar/ *v.* abandon.

abandono /aβan'dono/ *n. m.* abandonment.

abanico /aβa'niko/ *n. m.* fan. —**abanicar,** *v.*

abaratar /aβara'tar/ *v.* cheapen.

abarcar /aβar'kar/ *v.* comprise; clasp.

abastecer /aβaste'θer; aβaste'ser/ *v.* supply, provide.

abatido /aβa'tiðo/ *a.* dejected, despondent.

abatir /aβa'tir/ *v.* knock down; dismantle; depress, dishearten.

abdicación /aβðika'θion; aβðika'sion/ *n. f.* abdication.

abdicar /aβði'kar/ *v.* abdicate.

abdomen /aβ'ðomen/ *n. m.* abdomen.

abdominal /aβðomi'nal/ *a.* **1.** abdominal. —*n.* **2.** *m.* sit-up.

abecé /aβe'θe; aβe'se/ *n. m.* ABCs, rudiments.

abecedario /aβeθe'ðario; aβese'ðario/ *n. m.* alphabet; reading book.

abeja /a'βeha/ *n. f.* bee.

abejarrón /aβeha'rron/ *n. m.* bumblebee.

aberración /aβerra'θion; aβerra'sion/ *n. f.* aberration.

abertura /aβer'tura/ *n. f.* opening, aperture, slit.

abeto /a'βeto/ *n. m.* fir.

abierto /a'βierto/ *a.* open; overt.

abismal /aβis'mal/ *a.* abysmal.

abismo /a'βismo/ *n. m.* abyss, chasm.

ablandar /aβlan'dar/ *v.* soften.

abnegación /aβnega'θion; aβnega'sion/ *n. f.* abnegation.

abochornar /aβotʃor'nar/ *v.* overheat; embarrass.

abogado /aβo'gaðo/ **-da** *n.* lawyer, attorney.

abolengo /aβo'leŋgo/ *n. m.* ancestry.

abolición /aβoli'θion; aβoli'sion/ *n. f.* abolition.

abolladura /aβoʎa'ðura; aβoya'ðura/ *n. f.* dent. —**abollar,** *v.*

abominable /aβomi'naβle/ *a.* abominable.

abominar /aβomi'nar/ *v.* abhor.

abonado /aβo'naðo/ **-da** *n. m. & f.* subscriber.

abonar /aβo'nar/ *v.* pay; fertilize.

abonarse /aβo'narse/ *v.* subscribe.

abono /a'βono/ *n. m.* fertilizer; subscription; season ticket.

aborigen /aβo'rihen/ *a. & n.* aboriginal.

aborrecer /aβorre'θer; aβorre'ser/ *v.* hate, loathe, abhor.

abortar /aβor'tar/ *v.* abort, miscarry.

aborto /a'βorto/ *n. m.* abortion.

abovedar /aβoβe'ðar/ *v.* vault.

abrasar /aβra'sar/ *v.* burn.

abrazar /aβra'θar; aβra'sar/ *v.* embrace; clasp.

abrazo /a'βraθo; a'βraso/ *n. m.* embrace.

abrelatas /aβre'latas/ *n. m.* can opener.

abreviar /aβre'βiar/ *v.* abbreviate, abridge, shorten.

abreviatura /aβreβia'tura/ *n. f.* abbreviation.

abrigar /aβri'gar/ *v.* harbor, shelter.

abrigarse /aβri'garse/ *v.* bundle up.

abrigo /a'βrigo/ *n. m.* overcoat; shelter; *(pl.)* wraps.

abril /a'βril/ *n. m.* April.

abrir /a'βrir/ *v.* open; *Med.* lance.

abrochar /aβro'tʃar/ *v.* clasp.

abrogación /aβroga'θion; aβroga'sion/ *n. f.* abrogation, repeal.

abrogar /aβro'gar/ *v.* abrogate.

abrojo /a'βroho/ *n. m.* thorn.

abrumar /aβru'mar/ *v.* overwhelm, crush, swamp.

absceso /aβs'θeso; aβ'sseso/ *n. m.* abscess.

absolución /aβsolu'θion; aβsolu'sion/ *n. f.* absolution; acquittal.

absoluto /aβso'luto/ *a.* absolute; downright.

absolver /aβsol'βer/ *v.* absolve, pardon.

absorbente /aβsor'βente/ *a.* absorbent.

absorber /aβsor'βer/ *v.* absorb.

absorción /aβsor'θion; aβsor'sion/ *n. f.* absorption.

abstemio /aβs'temio/ *a.* abstemious.

abstenerse /aβste'nerse/ *v.* abstain; refrain.

abstinencia /aβsti'nenθia; aβsti'nensia/ *n. f.* abstinence.

abstracción /aβstrak'θion; aβstrak'sion/ *n. f.* abstraction.

abstracto /aβs'trakto/ *a.* abstract.

abstraer /aβstra'er/ *v.* abstract.

absurdo /aβ'surðo/ a. **1.** absurd. —n. **2.** m. absurdity.

abuchear /aβutʃe'ar/ v. boo.

abuela /a'βuela/ n. f. grandmother.

abuelo /a'βuelo/ n. m. grandfather; (pl.) grandparents.

abultamiento /aβulta'miento/ n. m. bulge. —**abultar**, v.

abundancia /aβun'danθia; aβun'dansia/ n. f. abundance, plenty.

abundante /aβun'dante/ a. abundant, plentiful.

abundar /aβun'dar/ v. abound.

aburrido /aβu'rriðo/ a. boring, tedious.

aburrimiento /aβurri'miento/ n. m. boredom.

aburrir /aβu'rrir/ v. bore.

abusar /aβu'sar/ v. abuse, misuse.

abusivo /aβu'siβo/ a. abusive.

abuso /a'βuso/ n. m. abuse.

abyecto /aβ'yekto/ a. abject, low.

a.C., abbr. **(antes de Cristo)** BC.

acá /a'ka/ adv. here.

acabar /aka'βar/ v. finish. **a. de...**, to have just....

acacia /a'kaθia; a'kasia/ n. f. acacia.

academia /aka'ðemia/ n. f. academy.

académico /aka'ðemiko/ a. academic.

acaecer /akae'θer; akae'ser/ v. happen.

acanalar /akana'lar/ v. groove.

acaparar /akapa'rar/ v. hoard; monopolize.

acariciar /akari'θiar; akari'siar/ v. caress, stroke.

acarrear /akarre'ar/ v. cart, transport; occasion, entail.

acaso /a'kaso/ n. m. chance. **por si a.**, just in case.

acceder /akθe'ðer; akse'ðer/ v accede.

accesible /akθe'siβle; akse'siβle/ a. accessible.

acceso /ak'θeso; ak'seso/ n. m. access, approach.

accesorio /akθe'sorio; akse'sorio/ a. accessory.

accidentado /akθiðen'taðo; aksiðen'taðo/ a. hilly.

accidental /akθiðen'tal; aksiðen'tal/ a. accidental.

accidente /akθi'ðente; aksi'ðente/ n. m. accident, wreck.

acción /ak'θion; ak'sion/ n. f. action, act; Com. share of stock.

accionista /akθio'nista; aksio'nista/ n. m. & f. shareholder.

acechar /aθe'tʃar; ase'tʃar/ v. ambush, spy on.

acedia /a'θeðia; a'seðia/ n. f. heartburn.

aceite /a'θeite; a'seite/ n. m. oil.

aceite de hígado de bacalao /a'θeite de i'gaðo de baka'lao; a'seite/ cod-liver oil.

aceitoso /aθei'toso; asei'toso/ a. oily.

aceituna /aθei'tuna; asei'tuna/ n. f. olive.

aceleración /aθelera'θion; aselera'sion/ n. f. acceleration.

acelerar /aθele'rar; asele'rar/ v. accelerate, speed up.

acento /a'θento; a'sento/ n. m. accent.

acentuar /aθen'tuar; asen'tuar/ v. accent, accentuate, stress.

acepillar /aθepi'ʎar; asepi'yar/ v. brush; plane (wood).

aceptable /aθep'taβle; asep'taβle/ a. acceptable.

aceptación /aθepta'θion; asepta'sion/ n. f. acceptance.

aceptar /aθep'tar; asep'tar/ v. accept.

acequia /a'θekia; ase'kia/ n. f. ditch.

acera /a'θera; a'sera/ n. f. sidewalk.

acerca de /a'θerka de; a'serka de/ prep. about, concerning.

acercar /aθer'kar; aser'kar/ v. bring near.

acercarse /aθer'karse; aser'karse/ v. approach, come near, go near.

acero /a'θero; a'sero/ n. m. steel.

acero inoxidable /a'θero inoksi'ðaβle; a'sero inoksi'ðaβle/ stainless steel.

acertar /aθer'tar; aser'tar/ v. guess right. **a. en,** hit (a mark).

acertijo /aθer'tiho; aser'tiho/ n. m. puzzle, riddle.

achicar /atʃi'kar/ v. diminish, dwarf; humble.

acidez /aθi'ðeθ; asi'ðes/ n. f. acidity.

ácido /'aθiðo; 'asiðo/ a. **1.** sour. —n. **2.** m. acid.

aclamación /aklama'θion; aklama'sion/ n. f. acclamation.

aclamar /akla'mar/ v. acclaim.

aclarar /akla'rar/ v. brighten; clarify, clear up.

acoger /ako'her/ v. welcome, receive.

acogida /ako'hiða/ n. f. welcome, reception.

acometer /akome'ter/ v. attack.

acomodador /akomoða'ðor/ n. m. usher.

acomodar /akomo'ðar/ v. accommodate, fix up.

acompañamiento /akompaɲa'miento/ n. m. accompaniment; following.

acompañar /akompa'ɲar/ v. accompany.

acondicionar /akondiθio'nar; akondisio'nar/ v. condition.

aconsejable /akonse'haβle/ a. advisable.

aconsejar /akonse'har/ v. advise.

acontecer /akonte'θer; akonte'ser/ v. happen.

acontecimiento /akonteθi'miento; akontesi'miento/ n. m. event, happening.

acorazado /akora'θaðo; akora'saðo/ n. **1.**

m. battleship. —*a.* **2.** armor-plated, iron-clad.

acordarse /akor'ðarse/ *v.* remember, recollect.

acordeón /akorðe'on/ *n. m.* accordion.

acordonar /akorðo'nar/ *v.* cordon off.

acortar /akor'tar/ *v.* shorten.

acosar /ako'sar/ *v.* beset, harry.

acostar /ako'star/ *v.* lay down; put to bed.

acostarse /akos'tarse/ *v.* lie down; go to bed.

acostumbrado /akostum'braðo/ *a.* accustomed; customary.

acostumbrar /akostum'brar/ *v.* accustom.

acrecentar /akreðen'tar: akresen'tar/ *v.* increase.

acreditar /akreði'tar/ *v.* accredit.

acreedor /akree'ðor/ **-ra** *n.* creditor.

acróbata /a'kroβata/ *n. m. & f.* acrobat.

acrobático /akro'βatiko/ *a.* acrobatic.

actitud /akti'tuð/ *n. f.* attitude.

actividad /aktiβi'ðað/ *n. f.* activity.

activista /akti'βista/ *a. & n.* activist.

activo /ak'tiβo/ *a.* active.

acto /'akto/ *n. m.* act.

actor /ak'tor/ *n. m.* actor.

actriz /ak'triθ: ak'tris/ *n. f.* actress.

actual /ak'tual/ *a.* present; present day.

actualidades /aktuali'ðaðes/ *n. f.pl.* current events.

actualmente /aktual'mente/ *adv.* at present; nowadays.

actuar /ak'tuar/ *v.* act.

acuarela /akua'rela/ *n. f.* watercolor.

acuario /a'kuario/ *n. m.* aquarium.

acuático /a'kuatiko/ *a.* aquatic.

acuchillar /akutʃi'ʎar: akutʃi'yar/ *v.* slash, knife.

acudir /aku'ðir/ *v.* rally; hasten; be present.

acuerdo /a'kuerðo/ *n. m.* accord, agreement; settlement. **de a.,** in agreement, agreed.

acumulación /akumula'θion: akumula'sion/ *n. f.* accumulation.

acumular /akumu'lar/ *v.* accumulate.

acuñar /aku'ɲar/ *v.* coin, mint.

acupuntura /akupun'tura/ *n. f.* acupuncture.

acusación /akusa'θion: akusa'sion/ *n. f.* accusation, charge.

acusado /aku'saðo/ **-da** *a. & n.* accused; defendant.

acusador /akusa'ðor/ **-ra** *n.* accuser.

acusar /aku'sar/ *v.* accuse; acknowledge.

acústica /a'kustika/ *n. f.* acoustics.

adaptación /aðapta'θion: aðapta'sion/ *n. f.* adaptation.

adaptador /aðapta'ðor/ *n. m.* adapter.

adaptar /aðap'tar/ *v.* adapt.

adecuado /aðe'kuaðo/ *a.* adequate.

adelantado /aðelan'taðo/ *a.* advanced; fast (clock).

adelantamiento /aðelanta'miento/ *n. m.* advancement, promotion.

adelantar /aðelan'tar/ *v.* advance.

adelante /aðe'lante/ *adv.* ahead, forward, onward, on.

adelanto /aðe'lanto/ *n. m.* advancement, progress, improvement.

adelgazar /aðelga'θar: aðelga'sar/ *v.* make thin.

ademán /aðe'man/ *n. m.* attitude; gesture.

además /aðe'mas/ *adv.* in addition, besides, also.

adentro /a'ðentro/ *adv.* in, inside.

adepto /a'ðepto/ *a.* adept.

aderezar /aðere'θar: aðere'sar/ *v.* prepare; trim.

adherirse /aðe'rirse/ *v.* adhere, stick.

adhesivo /aðe'siβo/ *a.* adhesive.

adicción /aðik'θion: aðik'sion/ *n. f.* adiction.

adición /aði'θion: aði'sion/ *n. f.* addition.

adicional /aðiðio'nal: aðisio'nal/ *a.* additional, extra.

adicto /a'ðikto/ **-ta** *a. & n.* addicted; addict.

adinerado /aðine'raðo/ **-a** *a.* wealthy.

adiós /a'ðios/ *n. m. & interj.* good-bye, farewell.

adivinar /aðiβi'nar/ *v.* guess.

adjetivo /aðhe'tiβo/ *n. m.* adjective.

adjunto /að'hunto/ *a.* enclosed.

administración /aðministra'θion: aðministra'sion/ *n. f.* administration.

administrador /aðministra'ðor/ **-ra** *n.* administrator.

administrar /aðminis'trar/ *v.* administer; manage.

administrativo /aðministra'tiβo/ *a.* administrative.

admirable /aðmi'raβle/ *a.* admirable.

admiración. /aðmira'θion: aðmira'sion/ *n. f.* admiration; wonder.

admirar /aðmi'rar/ *v.* admire.

admisión /aðmi'sion/ *n. f.* admission.

admitir /aðmi'tir/ *v.* admit, acknowledge.

ADN, *abbr.* **(ácido deoxirribonucleico)** DNA (deoxyribonucleic acid).

adobar /aðo'βar/ *v.* marinate.

adolescencia /aðoles'θenθia: aðoles'sensia/ *n. f.* adolescence, youth.

adolescente /aðoles'θente: aðoles'sente/ *a. & n.* adolescent.

adónde /a'ðonde/ *adv.* where.

adondequiera /a,ðonde'kiera/ *conj.* wherever.

adopción /aðop'θion: aðop'sion/ *n. f.* adoption.

adoptar /aðop'tar/ *v* adopt.

adoración /aðora'θion; aðora'sion/ n. f. worship, love, adoration. —**adorar**, v.

adormecer /aðorme'θer; aðorme'ser/ v. drowse.

adornar /aðor'nar/ v. adorn; decorate.

adorno /a'ðorno/ n. m. adornment, trimming.

adquirir /aðki'rir/ v. acquire, obtain.

adquisición /aðkisi'θion; aðkisi'sion/ n. f. acquisition, attainment.

aduana /a'ðuana/ n. f. custom house, customs.

adujada /aðu'haða/ n. f. Naut. coil of rope.

adulación /aðula'θion; aðula'sion/ n. f. flattery.

adular /aðu'lar/ v. flatter.

adulterar /aðulte'rar/ v. adulterate.

adulterio /aðul'terio/ n. m. adultery.

adulto /a'ðulto/ **-ta** a. & n. adult.

adusto /a'ðusto/ a. gloomy; austere.

adverbio /að'βerβio/ n. m. adverb.

adversario /aðβer'sario/ n. m. adversary.

adversidad /aðβersi'ðað/ n. f. adversity.

adverso /að'βerso/ a. adverse.

advertencia /aðβer'tenθia; aðβer'tensia/ n. f. warning.

advertir /aðβer'tir/ v. warn; notice.

adyacente /aðya'θente; aðya'sente/ a. adjacent.

aéreo /'aereo/ a. aerial; air.

aerodeslizador /aerodesli'θa'ðor; aerodeslisa'ðor/ n. m. hovercraft.

aeromoza /aero'moθa; aero'mosa/ n. f. stewardess, flight attendant.

aeroplano /aero'plano/ n. m. light plane.

aeropuerto /aero'puerto/ n. m. airport.

aerosol /aero'sol/ n. m. aerosol, spray.

afable /a'faβle/ a. affable, pleasant.

afanarse /afa'narse/ v. toil.

afear /afe'ar/ v. deface, mar, deform.

afectación /afekta'θion; afekta'sion/ n. f. affectation.

afectar /afek'tar/ v. affect.

afecto /a'fekto/ n. m. affection, attachment.

afeitada /afei'taða/ n. f. shave. —**afeitarse**, v.

afeminado /afemi'naðo/ a. effeminate.

afición /afi'θion; afi'sion/ n. f. fondness, liking; hobby.

aficionado /afiθio'naðo; afisio'naðo/ a. fond.

aficionado -da n. fan, devotee; amateur.

aficionarse /afiθio'narse a; afisio'narse a/ v. become fond of.

afilado /afi'laðo/ a. sharp.

afilar /afi'lar/ v. sharpen.

afiliación /afilia'θion; afilia'sion/ n. f. affiliation.

afiliado /afi'liaðo/ **-da** n. affiliate. —**afiliar**, v.

afinar /afi'nar/ v. polish; tune up.

afinidad /afini'ðað/ n. f. relationship, affinity.

afirmación /afirma'θion; afirma'sion/ n. f. affirmation, statement.

afirmar /afir'mar/ v. affirm, assert.

afirmativa /afirma'tiβa/ n. f. affirmative. —**afirmativo**, a.

aflicción /aflik'θion; aflik'sion/ n. f. affliction; sorrow, grief.

afligido /afli'hiðo/ a. sorrowful, grieved.

afligir /afli'hir/ v. grieve, distress.

aflojar /aflo'har/ v. loosen.

afluencia /a'fluenθia; a'fluensia/ n. f. influx.

afortunado /afortu'naðo/ a. fortunate, successful, lucky.

afrenta /a'frenta/ n. f. insult, outrage, affront. —**afrentar**, v.

afrentoso /afren'toso/ a. shameful.

africano /afri'kano/ **-na** a. & n. African.

afuera /a'fuera/ adv. out, outside.

afueras /a'fueras/ n. f.pl. suburbs.

agacharse /aga'tʃarse/ v. squat, crouch; cower.

agarrar /aga'rrar/ v. seize, grasp, clutch.

agarro /a'garro/ n. m. clutch, grasp.

agencia /a'henθia; a'hensia/ n. f. agency.

agencia de colocaciones /a'henθia de koloka'θiones; a'hensia de koloka'siones/ employment agency.

agencia de viajes /a'henθia de 'biahes; a'hensia de 'biahes/ travel agency.

agente /a'hente/ n. m. & f. agent, representative.

agente de aduana /a'hente de a'ðuana/ mf. customs officer.

agente inmobiliario /a'hente imoβi'liario/ **-ria** n. real-estate agent.

ágil /'ahil/ a. agile, spry.

agitación /ahita'θion; ahita'sion/ n. f. agitation, ferment.

agitado /ahi'taðo/ a. agitated; excited.

agitador /ahita'ðor/ n. m. agitator.

agitar /ahi'tar/ v. shake, agitate, excite.

agobiar /ago'βiar/ v. oppress, burden.

agosto /a'gosto/ n. m. August.

agotamiento /a,gota'miento/ n. m. exhaustion.

agotar /ago'tar/ v. exhaust, use up, sap.

agradable /agra'ðaβle/ a. agreeable, pleasant.

agradar /agra'ðar/ v. please.

agradecer /agraðe'θer; agraðe'ser/ v. thank; appreciate, be grateful for.

agradecido /agraðe'θiðo; agraðe'siðo/ a. grateful, thankful.

agradecimiento /agraðeθi'miento; agraðe-si'miento/ *n. m.* gratitude, thanks.

agravar /agra'βar/ *v.* aggravate, make worse.

agravio /a'graβio/ *n. m.* wrong. —**agraviar**, *v.*

agregado /agre'gaðo/ *a. & n.* aggregate; *Pol.* attaché.

agregar /agre'gar/ *v.* add; gather.

agresión /agre'sion/ *n. f.* aggression; *Leg.* battery.

agresivo /agre'siβo/ *a.* aggressive.

agresor /agre'sor/ **-ra** *n.* aggressor.

agrícola /a'grikola/ *a.* agricultural.

agricultor /agrikul'tor/ *n. m.* farmer.

agricultura /agrikul'tura/ *n. f.* agriculture, farming.

agrio /'agrio/ *a.* sour.

agrupar /agru'par/ *v.* group.

agua /'agua/ *n. f.* water. —**aguar**, *v.*

aguacate /agua'kate/ *n. m.* avocado, alligator pear.

aguafuerte /agua'fuerte/ *n. f.* etching.

agua mineral /'agua mine'ral/ mineral water.

aguantar /aguan'tar/ *v.* endure, stand, put up with.

aguardar /aguar'ðar/ *v.* await; expect.

aguardiente /aguar'ðiente/ *n. m.* brandy.

aguas abajo /'aguas a'βaho/ *adv.* downriver, downstream.

aguas arriba /'aguas a'rriβa/ *adv.* upriver, upstream.

agudo /a'guðo/ *a.* sharp, keen, shrill, acute.

agüero /a'guero/ *n. m.* omen.

águila /'agila/ *n. f.* eagle.

aguja /a'guha/ *n. f.* needle.

agujero /agu'hero/ *n. m.* hole.

aguzar /agu'θar; agu'sar/ *v.* sharpen.

ahí /a'i/ *adv.* there.

ahogar /ao'gar/ *v.* drown; choke; suffocate.

ahondar /aon'dar/ *v.* deepen.

ahora /a'ora/ *adv.* now.

ahorcar /aor'kar/ *v.* hang (execute).

ahorrar /ao'rrar/ *v.* save, save up; spare.

ahorros /a'orros/ *n. m.pl.* savings.

ahumar /au'mar/ *v.* smoke.

airado /ai'raðo/ *a.* angry, indignant.

aire /'aire/ *n. m.* air. —**airear**, *v.*

aire acondicionado /'aire akondiθio'naðo; 'aire akondisio'naðo/ air conditioning.

aislamiento /aisla'miento/ *n. m.* isolation.

aislar /ais'lar/ *v.* isolate.

ajedrez /ahe'ðreθ; ahe'ðres/ *n. m.* chess.

ajeno /a'heno/ *a.* alien; someone else's.

ajetreo /ahe'treo/ *n. m.* hustle and bustle.

ají /'ahi/ *n. m.* chili.

ajo /'aho/ *n. m.* garlic.

ajustado /ahus'taðo/ *a.* adjusted; trim; exact.

ajustar /ahus'tar/ *v.* adjust.

ajuste /a'huste/ *n. m.* adjustment, settlement.

al /al/ *contr.* of **a** + **el**.

ala /'ala/ *n. f.* wing; brim (of hat).

alabanza /ala'βanθa; ala'βansa/ *n. f.* praise. —**alabar**, *v.*

alabear /alaβe'ar/ *v.* warp.

ala delta /'ala 'delta/ hang glider.

alambique /alam'bike/ *n. m.* still.

alambre /a'lambre/ *n. m.* wire. **a. de púas**, barbed wire.

alarde /a'larðe/ *n. m.* boasting, ostentation.

alargar /alar'gar/ *v.* lengthen; stretch out.

alarma /a'larma/ *n. f.* alarm. —**alarmar**, *v.*

alba /'alβa/ *n. f.* daybreak, dawn.

albanega /alβa'nega/ *n. f.* hair net.

albañil /alβa'ɲil/ *n. m.* bricklayer; mason.

albaricoque /alβari'koke/ *n. m.* apricot.

alberca /al'βerka/ *n. f.* swimming pool.

albergue /al'βerge/ *n. m.* shelter. —**albergar**, *v.*

alborotar /alβoro'tar/ *v.* disturb, make noise, brawl, riot.

alboroto /alβo'roto/ *n. m.* brawl, disturbance, din, tumult.

álbum /'alβum/ *n. m.* album.

álbum de recortes /'alβum de rre'kortes/ scrapbook.

alcachofa /alka't ʃofa/ *n. f.* artichoke.

alcalde /al'kalde/ *n. m.* mayor.

alcance /al'kanθe; al'kanse/ *n. m.* reach; range, scope.

alcanfor /alkan'for/ *n. m.* camphor.

alcanzar /alkan'θar; alkan'sar/ *v.* reach, overtake, catch.

alcayata /alka'yata/ *n. f.* spike.

alce /'alθe; 'alse/ *n. m.* elk.

alcoba /al'koβa/ *n. f.* bedroom; alcove.

alcoba de huéspedes /al'koβa de 'uespeðes/ guest room.

alcoba de respeto /al'koβa de rres'peto/ guest room.

alcohol /al'kool/ *n. m.* alcohol.

alcohólico /alko'oliko/ **-ca** *a. & n.* alcoholic.

aldaba /al'daβa/ *n. f.* latch.

aldea /al'dea/ *n. f.* village.

alegación /alega'θion; alega'sion/ *n. f.* allegation.

alegar /ale'gar/ *v.* allege.

alegrar /ale'grar/ *v.* make happy, brighten.

alegrarse /ale'grarse/ *v.* be glad.

alegre /a'legre/ *a.* glad, cheerful, merry.

alegría /ale'gria/ *n. f.* gaiety, cheer.

alejarse /ale'harse/ *v.* move away, off.

alemán /ale'man/ **-ana** *a. & n.* German.

Alemania /ale'mania/ *n. f.* Germany.

alentar /alen'tar/ v. cheer up, encourage.

alergia /a'lerhia/ n. f. allergy.

alerta /a'lerta/ adv. on the alert.

aleve /a'leβe/ **alevoso** a. treacherous.

alfabeto /alfa'βeto/ n. m. alphabet.

alfalfa /al'falfa/ n. f. alfalfa.

alfarería /alfare'ria/ n. f. pottery.

alférez /al'fereθ: al'feres/ n. m. (naval) ensign.

alfil /al'fil/ n. m. (chess) bishop.

alfiler /alfi'ler/ n. m. pin.

alfombra /al'fombra/ n. f. carpet, rug.

alforja /al'forha/ n. f. knapsack; saddlebag.

alga /'alga/ n. f. seaweed.

alga marina /'alga ma'rina/ seaweed.

algarabía /algara'βia/ n. f. jargon; din.

álgebra /'alheβra/ n. f. algebra.

algo /'algo/ pron. & adv. something, somewhat; anything.

algodón /algo'ðon/ n. m. cotton.

algodón hidrófilo /algo'ðon i'ðrofilo/ absorbent cotton.

alguien /'algien/ pron. somebody, someone; anybody, anyone.

algún /al'gun/ **-no -na** a. & pron. some; any.

alhaja /al'aha/ n. f. jewel.

aliado /ali'aðo/ **-da** a. & n. allied; ally. —**aliar**, v.

alianza /a'lianθa; a'liansa/ n. f. alliance.

alicates /ali'kates/ n. m.pl. pliers.

aliento /a'liento/ n. m. breath. **dar a.,** encourage.

aligerar /alihe'rar/ v. lighten.

alimentar /alimen'tar/ v. feed, nourish.

alimento /ali'mento/ n. m. nourishment, food.

alinear /aline'ar/ v. line up; Pol. align.

aliñar /ali'ɲar/ v. dress (a salad).

aliño /a'liɲo/ n. m. salad dressing.

alisar /ali'sar/ v. smooth.

alistamiento /alista'miento/ n. m. enlistment.

alistar /alis'tar/ v. make ready, prime.

alistarse /alis'tarse/ v. get ready; Mil. enlist.

aliviar /ali'βiar/ v. alleviate, relieve, ease.

alivio /a'liβio/ n. m. relief.

allá /a'ʎa: a'ya/ adv. there. **más a.,** beyond, farther on.

allanar /aʎa'nar: aya'nar/ v. flatten, smooth, plane.

allí /a'ʎi: a'yi/ adv. there. **por a.,** that way.

alma /'alma/ n. f. soul.

almacén /alma'θen; alma'sen/ n. m. department store; storehouse, warehouse.

almacenaje /almaθe'nahe; almase'nahe/ n. m. storage.

almacenar /almaθe'nar; almase'nar/ v. store.

almanaque /alma'nake/ n. m. almanac.

almeja /al'meha/ n. f. clam.

almendra /al'mendra/ n. f. almond.

almíbar /al'miβar/ n. m. syrup.

almidón /almi'ðon/ n. m. starch. —**almidonar,** v.

almirante /almi'rante/ n. m. admiral.

almohada /almo'aða/ n. f. pillow.

almuerzo /al'muerθo; al'muerso/ n. m. lunch. —**almorzar,** v.

alojamiento /aloha'miento/ n. m. lodging, accommodations.

alojar /alo'har/ v. lodge, house.

alojarse /alo'harse/ v. stay, room.

alquiler /alki'ler/ n. m. rent. —**alquilar,** v.

alrededor /alreðe'ðor/ adv. around.

alrededores /alreðe'ðores/ n. m.pl. environs.

altanero /alta'nero/ a. haughty.

altar /al'tar/ n. m. altar.

altavoz /,alta'βoθ; ,alta'βos/ n. m. loudspeaker.

alteración /altera'θion; altera'sion/ n. f. alteration.

alterar /alte'rar/ v. alter.

alternativa /alterna'tiβa/ n. f. alternative. —**alternativo,** a.

alterno /al'terno/ a. alternate. —**alternar,** v.

alteza /al'teθa; al'tesa/ n. f. highness.

altivo /al'tiβo/ a. proud, haughty; lofty.

alto /'alto/ a. **1.** high, tall; loud. —n. **2.** m. height, story (house).

altura /al'tura/ n. f. height, altitude.

alud /a'luð/ n. m. avalanche.

aludir /alu'ðir/ v. allude.

alumbrado /alum'braðo/ n. m. lighting.

alumbrar /alum'brar/ v. light.

aluminio /alu'minio/ n. m. aluminum.

alumno /a'lumno/ **-na** n. student, pupil.

alusión /alu'sion/ n. f. allusion.

alza /'alθa; 'alsa/ n. f. rise; boost.

alzar /al'θar; al'sar/ v. raise, lift.

ama /'ama/ n. f. housewife, mistress (of house). **a. de llaves,** housekeeper.

amable /a'maβle/ a. kind; pleasant, sweet.

amalgamar /amalga'mar/ v. amalgamate.

amamantar /amaman'tar/ v. suckle, nurse.

amanecer /amane'θer; amane'ser/ v. **1.** m. dawn, daybreak. —v. **2.** dawn; awaken.

amante /a'mante/ n. m. & f. lover.

amapola /ama'pola/ n. f. poppy.

amar /a'mar/ v. love.

amargo /a'margo/ a. bitter.

amargón /amar'gon/ n. m. dandelion.

amargura /amar'gura/ n. f. bitterness.

amarillo /ama'riʎo; ama'riyo/ a. yellow.

amarradero /amarra'ðero/ n. m. mooring.

amarrar /ama'rrar/ v. hitch, moor, tie up.

amartillar /amarti'ʎar; amarti'yar/ *v.* hammer; cock (a gun).

amasar /ama'sar/ *v.* knead, mold.

ámbar /'ambar/ *n. m.* amber.

ambarino /amba'rino/ *a.* amber.

ambición /ambi'θion; ambi'sion/ *n. f.* ambition.

ambicionar /ambiθio'nar; ambisio'nar/ *v.* aspire to.

ambicioso /ambi'θioso; ambi'sioso/ *a.* ambitious.

ambientalista /ambienta'lista/ *n. m. & f.* environmentalist.

ambiente /am'biente/ *n. m.* environment, atmosphere.

ambigüedad /ambigue'ðað/ *n. f.* ambiguity.

ambiguo /am'biguo/ *a.* ambiguous.

ambos /'ambos/ *a. & pron.* both.

ambulancia /ambu'lanθia; ambu'lansia/ *n. f.* ambulance.

amenaza /ame'naθa; ame'nasa/ *n. f.* threat, menace.

amenazar /amena'θar; amena'sar/ *v.* threaten, menace.

ameno /a'meno/ *a.* pleasant.

americana /ameri'kana/ *n. f.* suit coat.

americano /ameri'kano/ **-na** *a. & n.* American.

ametralladora /ametraʎa'ðora; ametraya'ðora/ *n. f.* machine gun.

amigable /ami'gaβle/ *a.* amicable, friendly.

amígdala /a'migðala/ *n. f.* tonsil.

amigo /a'migo/ **-ga** *n.* friend.

aminorar /amino'rar/ *v.* lessen, reduce.

amistad /amis'tað/ *n. f.* friendship.

amistoso /amis'toso/ *a.* friendly.

amniocéntesis /amnioθen'tesis; amniosen'tesis/ *n. m.* amniocentesis.

amo /'amo/ *n. m.* master.

amonestaciones /amonesta'θiones; amonesta'siones/ *n. f.pl.* banns.

amonestar /amones'tar/ *v.* admonish.

amoníaco /amo'niako/ *n. m.* ammonia.

amontonar /amonto'nar/ *v.* amass, pile up.

amor /a'mor/ *n. m.* love. **a. propio,** self-esteem.

amorío /amo'rio/ *n. m.* romance, love affair.

amoroso /amo'roso/ *a.* amorous; loving.

amortecer /amorte'θer; amorte'ser/ *v.* deaden.

amparar /ampa'rar/ *v.* aid, befriend; protect, shield.

amparo /am'paro/ *n. m.* protection.

ampliar /amp'liar/ *v.* enlarge; elaborate.

amplificar /amplifi'kar/ *v.* amplify.

amplio /'amplio/ *a.* ample, roomy.

ampolla /am'poʎa; am'poya/ *n. f.* bubble; bulb; blister.

amputar /ampu'tar/ *v.* amputate.

amueblar /amue'βlar/ *v.* furnish.

analfabeto /analfa'βeto/ **-ta** *a. & n.* illiterate.

analgésico /anal'hesiko/ *n. m.* pain killer.

análisis /a'nalisis/ *n. m.* analysis.

analizar /anali'θar; anali'sar/ *v.* analyze.

analogía /analo'hia/ *n. f.* analogy.

análogo /a'nalogo/ *a.* similar, analogous.

anarquía /anar'kia/ *n. f.* anarchy.

anatomía /anato'mia/ *n. f.* anatomy.

ancho /'antʃo/ *a.* wide, broad.

anchoa /an'tʃoa/ *n. f.* anchovy.

anchura /an'tʃura/ *n. f.* width, breadth.

anciano /an'θiano; an'siano/ **-na** *a. & n.* old, aged (person).

ancla /'ankla/ *n. f.* anchor. **—anclar,** *v.*

anclaje /an'klahe/ *n. m.* anchorage.

andamio /an'damio/ *n. m.* scaffold.

andar /an'dar/ *v.* walk; move, go.

andén /an'den/ *n. m.* (railroad) platform.

andrajoso /andra'hoso/ *a.* ragged, uneven.

anécdota /a'nekðota/ *n. f.* anecdote.

anegar /ane'gar/ *v.* flood, drown.

anestesia /anes'tesia/ *n. f.* anesthetic.

anexar /anek'sar/ *v.* annex.

anexión /anek'sion/ *n. f.* annexation.

anfitrión /anfitri'on/ **-na** *n.* host.

ángel /'anhel/ *n. m.* angel.

angosto /aŋ'gosto/ *a.* narrow.

anguila /aŋ'gila/ *n. f.* eel.

angular /aŋgu'lar/ *a.* angular.

ángulo /'aŋgulo/ *n. m.* angle.

angustia /aŋ'gustia/ *n. f.* anguish, agony.

angustiar /aŋgus'tiar/ *v.* distress.

anhelar /ane'lar/ *v.* long for.

anidar /ani'ðar/ *v.* nest, nestle.

anillo /a'niʎo; a'niyo/ *n. m.* ring; circle.

animación /anima'θion; anima'sion/ *n. f.* animation; bustle.

animado /ani'maðo/ *a.* animated, lively; animate.

animal /ani'mal/ *a. & n.* animal.

ánimo /'animo/ *n. m.* state of mind, spirits; courage.

aniquilar /aniki'lar/ *v.* annihilate, destroy.

aniversario /aniβer'sario/ *n. m.* anniversary.

anoche /a'notʃe/ *adv.* last night.

anochecer /anotʃe'θer; anotʃe'ser/ *n.* **1.** *m.* twilight, nightfall. —*v.* **2.** get dark.

anónimo /a'nonimo/ *a.* anonymous.

anorexia /ano'reksia/ *n. f.* anorexia.

anormal /anor'mal/ *a.* abnormal.

anotación /anota'θion; anota'sion/ *n. f.* annotation.

anotar /ano'tar/ *v.* annotate.

ansia /'ansia/ **ansiedad** *n. f.* anxiety.

ansioso /an'sioso/ *a.* anxious.

antagonismo /antago'nismo/ *n. m.* antagonism.

antagonista /antago'nista/ *n. m. & f.* antagonist, opponent.

anteayer /antea'yer/ *adv.* day before yesterday.

antebrazo /ante'ƀraθo; ante'ƀraso/ *n. m.* forearm.

antecedente /anteθe'ðente; antese'ðente/ *a. & m.* antecedent.

anteceder /anteθe'ðer; antese'ðer/ *v.* precede.

antecesor /anteθe'sor; antese'sor/ *n. m.* ancestor.

antemano /ante'mano/ *de a.,* in advance.

antena /an'tena/ *n. f.* antenna.

antena parabólica /an'tena para'ƀolika/ satellite dish.

anteojos /ante'ohos/ *n. m.pl.* eyeglasses.

antepasado /antepa'saðo/ *n. m.* ancestor.

antepenúltimo /antepe'nultimo/ *a.* antepenultimate.

anterior /ante'rior/ *a.* previous, former.

antes /'antes/ *adv.* before; formerly.

antibala /anti'bala/ *a.* bulletproof.

anticipación /antiθipa'θion; antisipa'sion/ *n. f.* anticipation.

anticipar /antiθi'par; antisi'par/ *v.* anticipate; advance.

anticonceptivo /antikonθep'tiƀo; antikonsep'tiƀo/ *a. & n.* contraceptive.

anticongelante /antikonge'lante/ *n. m.* antifreeze.

anticuado /anti'kuaðo/ *a.* antiquated, obsolete.

antídoto /an'tiðoto/ *n. m.* antidote.

antigüedad /antigue'ðað/ *n. f.* antiquity; antique.

antiguo /an'tiguo/ *a.* former; old; antique.

antihistamínico /antiista'miniko/ *n. m.* antihistamine.

antílope /an'tilope/ *n. m.* antelope.

antinuclear /antinukle'ar/ *a.* antinuclear.

antipatía /antipa'tia/ *n. f.* antipathy.

antipático /anti'patiko/ *a.* disagreeable, nasty.

antiséptico /anti'septiko/ *a. & m.* antiseptic.

antojarse /anto'harse/ *v* **se me antoja...** etc., I desire..., take a fancy to..., etc.

antojo /an'toho/ *n. m.* whim, fancy.

antorcha /an'tortʃa/ *n. f.* torch.

antracita /antra'θita; antra'sita/ *n. f.* anthracite.

anual /a'nual/ *a.* annual, yearly.

anudar /anu'ðar/ *v.* knot; tie.

anular /anu'lar/ *v.* annul, void.

anunciar /anun'θiar; anun'siar/ *v.* announce; proclaim, advertise.

anuncio /a'nunθio; a'nunsio/ *n. m.* announcement; advertisement.

añadir /aɲa'ðir/ *v.* add.

añil /a'ɲil/ *n. m.* bluing; indigo.

año /'aɲo/ *n. m.* year.

apacible /apa'θiƀle; apa'siƀle/ *a.* peaceful, peaceable.

apaciguamiento /a,paθigua'miento; a,pasigua'miento/ *n. m.* appeasement.

apaciguar /apaθi'guar; apasi'guar/ *v.* appease; placate.

apagado /apa'gaðo/ *a.* dull.

apagar /apa'gar/ *v.* extinguish, quench, put out.

apagón /apa'gn/ *n. m.* blackout.

aparador /apara'ðor/ *n. m.* buffet, cupboard.

aparato /apa'rato/ *n. m.* apparatus; machine; appliance, set.

aparcamiento /aparka'miento/ *n. m.* parking lot; parking space.

aparecer /apare'θer; apare'ser/ *v.* appear, show up.

aparejo /apa'reho/ *n. m.* rig. —**aparejar,** *v.*

aparentar /aparen'tar/ *v.* pretend; profess.

aparente /apa'rente/ *a.* apparent.

apariencia /apa'rienθia; apa'riensia/ **aparición** *n. f.* appearance.

apartado /apar'taðo/ *a.* **1.** aloof; separate. —*n.* **2.** *m.* post-office box.

apartamento /aparta'mento/ *n. m.* apartment. **a. en propiedad,** condominium.

apartar /apar'tar/ *v* separate; remove.

aparte /a'parte/ *adv.* apart; aside.

apartheid /apar'teið/ *n. m.* apartheid.

apasionado /apasio'naðo/ *a.* passionate.

apatía /apa'tia/ *n. f.* apathy.

apearse /ape'arse/ *v.* get off, alight.

apedrear /apeðre'ar/ *v.* stone.

apelación /apela'θion; apela'sion/ *n. f.* appeal. —**apelar,** *v.*

apellido /ape'ʎiðo; ape'yiðo/ *n. m.* family name.

apellido materno /ape'ʎiðo ma'terno; ape'yiðo ma'terno/ mother's family name.

apellido paterno /ape'ʎiðo pa'terno; ape'yiðo pa'terno/ father's family name.

apenas /a'penas/ *adv.* scarcely, hardly.

apéndice /a'pendiθe; a'pendise/ *n. m.* appendix.

apercibir /aperθi'ƀir; apersi'ƀir/ *v.* prepare, warn.

aperitivo /aperi'tiƀo/ *n. m.* appetizer.

aperos /a'peros/ *n. m.pl.* implements.

apestar /apes'tar/ *v.* infect; stink.

apetecer /apete'θer; apete'ser/ *v.* desire, have appetite for.

apetito /ape'tito/ *n. m.* appetite.

ápice /'apiθe; 'apise/ *n. m.* apex.

apilar /api'lar/ *v.* stack.

apio /'apio/ *n. m.* celery.

aplacar /apla'kar/ *v.* appease; placate.

aplastar /aplas'tar/ *v.* crush, flatten.

aplaudir /aplau'ðir/ *v.* applaud, cheer.

aplauso /a'plauso/ *n. m.* applause.

aplazar /apla'θar; apla'sar/ *v.* postpone, put off.

aplicable /apli'kaβle/ *a.* applicable.

aplicado /apli'kaðo/ *a.* industrious, diligent.

aplicar /apli'kar/ *v.* apply.

aplomo /a'plomo/ *n. m.* aplomb, poise.

apoderado /apoðe'raðo/ **-da** *n.* attorney.

apoderarse de /apoðe'rarse de/ *v.* get hold of, seize.

apodo /a'poðo/ *n. m.* nickname. **—apodar,** *v.*

apologético /apolo'hetiko/ *a.* apologetic.

apoplejía /apople'hia/ *n. f.* apoplexy.

aposento /apo'sento/ *n. m.* room, flat.

apostar /apos'tar/ *v.* bet, wager.

apóstol /a'postol/ *n. m.* apostle.

apoyar /apo'yar/ *v.* support, prop; lean.

apoyo /a'poyo/ *n. m.* support; prop; aid; approval.

apreciable /apreθia'βle; apresia'βle/ *a.* appreciable.

apreciar /apre'θiar; apre'siar/ *v.* appreciate, prize.

aprecio /a'preθio; a'presio/ *n. m.* appreciation, regard.

apremio /a'premio/ *n. m.* pressure, compulsion.

aprender /apren'der/ *v.* learn.

aprendiz /apren'diθ; apren'dis/ *n. m.* apprentice.

aprendizaje /aprendi'θahe; aprendi'sahe/ *n. m.* apprenticeship.

aprensión /apren'sion/ *n. f.* apprehension.

aprensivo /apren'siβo/ *a.* apprehensive.

apresurado /apresu'raðo/ *a.* hasty, fast.

apresurar /apresu'rar/ *v.* hurry, speed up.

apretado /apre'taðo/ *a.* tight.

apretar /apre'tar/ *v.* squeeze, press; tighten.

apretón /apre'ton/ *n. m.* squeeze.

aprieto /a'prieto/ *n. m.* plight, predicament.

aprobación /aproβa'θion; aproβa'sion/ *n. f.* approbation, approval.

aprobar /apro'βar/ *v.* approve.

apropiación /apropia'θion; apropia'sion/ *n. f.* appropriation.

apropiado /apro'piaðo/ *a.* appropriate. **—apropiar,** *v.*

aprovechar /aproβe'tʃar/ *v.* profit by.

aprovecharse /aproβe'tʃarse/ *v.* take advantage.

aproximado /aproksi'maðo/ *a.* approximate.

aproximarse a /aproksi'marse a/ *v.* approach.

aptitud /apti'tuð/ *n. f.* aptitude.

apto /'apto/ *a.* apt.

apuesta /a'puesta/ *n. f.* bet, wager, stake.

apuntar /apun'tar/ *v.* point, aim; prompt; write down.

apunte /a'punte/ *n. m.* annotation; note; promptings, cue.

apuñalar /apuɲa'lar/ *v.* stab.

apurar /apu'rar/ *v.* hurry; worry.

apuro /a'puro/ *n. m.* predicament, scrape, trouble.

aquel /a'kel/ **aquella** *dem. a.* that.

aquél /a'kel/ **aquélla** *dem. pron.* that (one); the former.

aquello /a'keʎo; a'keyo/ *dem. pron.* that.

aquí /a'ki/ *adv.* here. **por a.,** this way.

aquietar /akie'tar/ *v.* allay; lull, pacify.

ara /'ara/ *n. f.* altar.

árabe /'araβe/ *a. & n.* Arab, Arabic.

arado /a'raðo/ *n. m.* plow. **—arar,** *v.*

arándano /a'randano/ *n. m.* cranberry.

araña /a'raɲa/ *n. f.* spider. **a. de luces,** chandelier.

arbitración /arβitra'θion; arβitra'sion/ *n. f.* arbitration.

arbitrador /arβitra'ðor/ **-ra** *n.* arbitrator.

arbitraje /arβi'trahe/ *n. m.* arbitration.

arbitrar /arβi'trar/ *v.* arbitrate.

arbitrario /arβi'trario/ *a.* arbitrary.

árbitro /'arβitro/ *n. m.* arbiter, umpire, referee.

árbol /'arβol/ *n. m.* tree; mast.

árbol genealógico /'arβol henea'lohiko/ family tree.

arbusto /ar'βusto/ *n. m.* bush, shrub.

arca /'arka/ *n. f.* chest; ark.

arcada /ar'kaða/ *n. f.* arcade.

arcaico /ar'kaiko/ *a.* archaic.

arce /'arθe; 'arse/ *n. m.* maple.

archipiélago /artʃi'pielago/ *n. m.* archipelago.

archivador /artʃiβa'ðor/ *n. m.* file cabinet.

archivo /ar'tʃiβo/ *n. m.* archive; file. **—archivar,** *v.*

arcilla /ar'θiʎa; ar'siya/ *n. f.* clay.

arco /'arko/ *n. m.* arc; arch; (archer's) bow. **a. iris,** rainbow.

arder /ar'ðer/ *v.* burn.

ardid /ar'ðið/ *n. m.* stratagem, cunning.

ardiente /ar'ðiente/ *a.* ardent, burning, fiery.

ardilla /ar'ðiʎa; ar'ðiya/ *n. f.* squirrel.

ardor /ar'ðor/ *n. m.* ardor, fervor.

ardor de estómago /ar'ðor de es'tomago/ heartburn.

arduo /'arðuo/ *a.* arduous.

área /'area/ *n. f.* area.

arena /a'rena/ *n. f.* sand; arena.

arenoso /are'noso/ *a.* sandy.

arenque /a'renke/ *n. m.* herring.

arete /a'rete/ *n.* earring.

argentino /arhen'tino/ **-na** *a.* & *n.* Argentine.

argüir /ar'guir/ *v.* dispute, argue.

árido /'ariðo/ *a.* arid.

aristocracia /aristo'kraθia; aristo'krasia/ *n. f.* aristocracy.

aristócrata /aris'tokrata/ *n. f.* aristocrat.

aristocrático /aristo'kratiko/ *a.* aristocratic.

aritmética /arit'metika/ *n. f.* arithmetic.

arma /'arma/ *n. f.* weapon, arm.

armadura /arma'ðura/ *n. f.* armor; reinforcement; framework.

armamento /arma'mento/ *n. m.* armament.

armar /ar'mar/ *v.* arm.

armario /ar'mario/ *n. m.* cabinet, bureau, wardrobe.

armazón /arma'θon; arma'son/ *n. m.* framework, frame.

armería /arme'ria/ *n. f.* armory.

armisticio /armis'tiθio; armis'tisio/ *n. m.* armistice.

armonía /armo'nia/ *n. f.* harmony.

armonioso /armo'nioso/ *a.* harmonious.

armonizar /armoni'θar; armoni'sar/ *v.* harmonize.

arnés /ar'nes/ *n. m.* harness.

aroma /a'roma/ *n. f.* aroma, fragrance.

aromático /aro'matiko/ *a.* aromatic.

arpa /'arpa/ *n. f.* harp.

arquear /arke'ar/ *v.* arch.

arquitecto /arki'tekto/ *n. m.* architect.

arquitectura /arkitek'tura/ *n. f.* architecture.

arquitectural /arkitektu'ral/ *a.* architectural.

arrabal /arra'βal/ *n. m.* suburb.

arraigar /arrai'gar/ *v.* take root, settle.

arrancar /arran'kar/ *v.* pull out, tear out; start up.

arranque /a'rranke/ *n. m.* dash, sudden start; fit of anger.

arrastrar /arras'trar/ *v.* drag.

arrebatar /arreβa'tar/ *v.* snatch, grab.

arrebato /arre'βato/ *n. m.* sudden attack, fit of anger.

arrecife /arre'θife; arre'sife/ *n. m.* reef.

arreglar /arre'glar/ *v.* arrange; repair, fix; adjust, settle.

arreglárselas /arre'glarselas/ *v.* manage, shift for oneself.

arreglo /a'rreglo/ *n. m.* arrangement, settlement.

arremangarse /arreman'garse/ *v.* roll up one's sleeves; roll up one's pants.

arremeter /arreme'ter/ *v.* attack.

arrendar /arren'dar/ *v.* rent.

arrepentimiento /arrepenti'miento/ *n. m.* repentance.

arrepentirse /arrepen'tirse/ *v.* repent.

arrestar /arres'tar/ *v.* arrest.

arriba /a'rriβa/ *adv.* up; upstairs.

arriendo /a'rriendo/ *n. m.* lease.

arriero /a'rriero/ *n. m.* muleteer.

arriesgar /arries'gar/ *v.* risk.

arrimarse /arri'marse/ *v.* lean.

arrodillarse /arroði'ʎarse; arroði'yarse/ *v.* kneel.

arrogancia /arro'ganθia; arro'gansia/ *n. f.* arrogance.

arrogante /arro'gante/ *a.* arrogant.

arrojar /arro'har/ *v.* throw, hurl; shed.

arrollar /arro'ʎar; arro'yar/ *v.* roll, coil.

arroyo /a'rroyo/ *n. m.* brook; gully; gutter.

arroz /a'rroθ; a'rros/ *n. m.* rice.

arruga /a'rruga/ *n. f.* ridge; wrinkle.

arrugar /arru'gar/ *v.* wrinkle, crumple.

arruinar /arrui'nar/ *v.* ruin, destroy, wreck.

arsenal /arse'nal/ *n. m.* arsenal; armory.

arsénico /ar'seniko/ *n. m.* arsenic.

arte /'arte/ *n. m.* (*f.* in *pl.*) art, craft; wiliness.

arteria /ar'teria/ *n. f.* artery.

artesa /ar'tesa/ *n. f.* trough.

artesano /arte'sano/ **-na** *n.* artisan, craftsman.

ártico /'artiko/ *a.* arctic.

articulación /artikula'θion; artikula'sion/ *n. f.* articulation; joint.

articular /artiku'lar/ *v.* articulate.

artículo /ar'tikulo/ *n. m.* article.

artífice /ar'tifiθe; ar'tifise/ *n. m.* & *f.* artisan.

artificial /artifi'θial; artifi'sial/ *a.* artificial.

artificio /arti'fiθio; arti'fisio/ *n. m.* artifice, device.

artificioso /artifi'θioso; artifi'sioso/ *a.* affected.

artillería /artiʎe'ria; artiye'ria/ *n. f.* artillery.

artista /ar'tista/ *n. m.* & *f.* artist.

artístico /ar'tistiko/ *a.* artistic.

artritis /ar'tritis/ *n. f.* arthritis.

arzobispo /arθo'βispo; arso'βispo/ *n. m.* archbishop.

as /as/ *n. m.* ace.

asado /a'saðo/ *a.* & *n.* roast.

asaltador /asalta'ðor/ **-ra** *n.* assailant.

asaltante /asal'tante/ *n. m.* & *f.* mugger.

asaltar /asal'tar/ *v.* assail, attack.

asalto /a'salto/ *n. m.* assault. **—asaltar,** *v.*

asamblea /asam'βlea/ *n. f.* assembly.

asar /a'sar/ *v.* roast; broil, cook (meat).

asaz /a'saθ; a'sas/ *adv.* enough; quite.

ascender /asθen'der; assen'der/ *v.* ascend, go up; amount.

ascenso /as'θenso; as'senso/ *n. m.* ascent.

ascensor /asθen'sor; assen'sor/ *n. m.* elevator.

ascensorista /asθenso'rista; assenso'rista/ *n. m.* & *f.* (elevator) operator.

asco /'asko/ *n. m.* nausea; disgusting thing. **qué a.,** how disgusting.

aseado /ase'aðo/ *a.* tidy. **—asear,** *v.*

asediar /ase'ðiar/ *v.* besiege.

asedio /a'seðio/ *n. m.* siege.

asegurar /asegu'rar/ *v.* assure; secure.

asegurarse /asegu'rarse/ *v.* make sure.

asemejarse a /aseme'harse a/ *v.* resemble.

asentar /asen'tar/ *v.* settle; seat.

asentimiento /asenti'miento/ *n. m.* assent. **—asentir,** *v.*

aseo /a'seo/ *n. m.* neatness, tidiness.

aseos /a'seos/ *n. m.pl.* restroom.

asequible /ase'kiβle/ *a.* attainable; affordable.

aserción /aser'θion/ *n. f.* assertion.

aserrar /ase'rrar/ *v.* saw.

asesinar /asesi'nar/ *v.* assassinate; murder, slay.

asesinato /asesi'nato/ *n. m.* assassination, murder.

asesino /ase'sino/ **-na** *n.* murderer, assassin.

aseveración /aseβera'θion; aseβera'sion/ *n. f.* assertion.

aseverar /aseβe'rar/ *v.* assert.

asfalto /as'falto/ *n. m.* asphalt.

así /a'si/ *adv.* so, thus, this way, that way. **a. como,** as well as. **a. que,** as soon as.

asiático /a'siatiko/ **-ca** *a. & n.* Asiatic.

asiduo /a'siðuo/ *a.* assiduous.

asiento /a'siento/ *n. m.* seat; chair; site.

asiento delantero /a'siento delan'tero/ front seat.

asiento trasero /a'siento tra'sero/ back seat.

asignar /asig'nar/ *v.* assign; allot.

asilo /a'silo/ *n. m.* asylum, sanctuary.

asimilar /asimi'lar/ *v.* assimilate.

asir /a'sir/ *v.* grasp.

asistencia /asis'tenθia; asistensia/ *n. f.* attendance, presence.

asistir /asis'tir/ *v.* be present, attend.

asno /'asno/ *n. m.* donkey.

asociación /asoθia'θion; asosia'sion/ *n. f.* association.

asociado /aso'θiaðo; aso'siaðo/ *n. m.* associate, partner.

asociar /aso'θiar; aso'siar/ *v.* associate.

asolar /aso'lar/ *v.* desolate; burn, parch.

asoleado /asole'aðo/ *a.* sunny.

asomar /aso'mar/ *v.* appear, loom up, show up.

asombrar /asom'βrar/ *v.* astonish, amaze.

asombro /a'sombro/ *n. m.* amazement, astonishment.

aspa /'aspa/ *n. f.* reel. **—aspar,** *v.*

aspecto /as'pekto/ *n. m.* aspect.

aspereza /aspe'reθa; aspe'resa/ *n. f.* harshness.

áspero /'aspero/ *a.* rough, harsh.

aspiración /aspira'θion; aspira'sion/ *n. f.* aspiration.

aspirador /aspira'ðor/ *n. m.* vacuum cleaner.

aspirar /aspi'rar/ *v.* aspire.

aspirina /aspi'rina/ *n. f.* aspirin.

asqueroso /aske'roso/ *a.* dirty, nasty, filthy.

asta /'asta/ *n. f.* shaft.

asterisco /aste'risko/ *n. m.* asterisk.

astilla /as'tiʎa; as'tiya/ *n. f.* splinter, chip. **—astillar,** *v.*

astillero /asti'ʎero; asti'yero/ *n. m.* dry dock.

astro /'astro/ *n. m.* star.

astronauta /astro'nauta/ *n. m. & f.* astronaut.

astronave /astro'naβe/ *n. f.* spaceship.

astronomía /astrono'mia/ *n. f.* astronomy.

astucia /as'tuθia; as'tusia/ *n. f.* cunning.

astuto /as'tuto/ *a.* astute, sly, shrewd.

asumir /asu'mir/ *v.* assume.

asunto /a'sunto/ *n. m.* matter, affair, business; subject.

asustar /asus'tar/ *v.* frighten, scare, startle.

atacar /ata'kar/ *v.* attack, charge.

atajo /a'taho/ *n. m.* shortcut.

ataque /a'take/ *n. m.* attack, charge; spell, stroke.

ataque cardíaco /a'take kar'ðiako/ heart attack.

atar /a'tar/ *v.* tie, bind, fasten.

atareado /atare'aðo/ *a.* busy.

atascar /atas'kar/ *v.* stall, stop, obstruct.

atasco /a'tasko/ *n. m.* traffic jam.

ataúd /ata'uð/ *n. m.* casket, coffin.

atavío /ata'βio/ *n. m.* dress; gear, equipment.

atemorizar /atemori'θar; atemori'sar/ *v.* frighten.

atención /aten'θion; aten'sion/ *n. f.* attention.

atender /aten'der/ *v.* heed; attend to, wait on.

atenerse a /ate'nerse a/ *v.* count on, depend on.

atentado /aten'taðo/ *n. m.* crime, offense.

atento /a'tento/ *a.* attentive, courteous.

ateo /a'teo/ *n. m.* atheist.

aterrizaje /aterri'θahe; aterri'sahe/ *n. m.* landing (of aircraft).

aterrizaje forzoso /aterri'θahe for'θoso; aterri'sahe for'soso/ emergency landing, forced landing.

aterrizar /aterri'θar; aterri'sar/ *v.* land.

atesorar /ateso'rar/ *v.* hoard.

atestar /ates'tar/ *v.* witness.

atestiguar /atesti'guar/ *v.* attest, testify.

atinar /ati'nar/ *v.* hit upon.

atisbar /atis'βar/ *v.* scrutinize, pry.

Atlántico /at'lantiko/ *n. m.* Atlantic.

atlántico *a.* Atlantic.

atlas /'atlas/ *n. m.* atlas.

atleta /at'leta/ *n. m. & f.* athlete.

atlético /at'letiko/ *a.* athletic.

atletismo /atle'tismo/ *n. m.* athletics.

atmósfera /at'mosfera/ *n. f.* atmosphere.

atmosférico /atmos'feriko/ *a.* atmospheric.

atolladero /atoʎa'ðero; atoya'ðero/ *n. m.* dead end, impasse.

atómico /a'tomiko/ *a.* atomic.

átomo /'atomo/ *n. m.* atom.

atormentar /atormen'tar/ *v.* torment, plague.

atornillar /atorni'ʎar; atorni'yar/ *v.* screw.

atracción /atrak'θion; atrak'sion/ *n. f.* attraction.

atractivo /atrak'tiβo/ *a.* **1.** attractive. —*n.* **2.** *m.* attraction.

atraer /atra'er/ *v.* attract; lure.

atrapar /atra'par/ *v.* trap, catch.

atrás /a'tras/ *adv.* back; behind.

atrasado /atra'saðo/ *a.* belated; backward; slow (clock).

atrasar /atra'sar/ *v.* delay, retard; be slow.

atraso /a'traso/ *n. m.* delay; backwardness; (*pl.*) arrears.

atravesar /atraβe'sar/ *v.* cross.

atreverse /atre'βerse/ *v.* dare.

atrevido /atre'βiðo/ *a.* daring, bold.

atrevimiento /atreβi'miento/ *n. m.* boldness.

atribuir /atri'βuir/ *v.* attribute, ascribe.

atributo /atri'βuto/ *n. m.* attribute.

atrincherar /atrintʃe'rar/ *v.* entrench.

atrocidad /atroθi'ðað; atrosi'ðað/ *n. f.* atrocity, outrage.

atronar /atro'nar/ *v.* deafen.

atropellar /atrope'ʎar; atrope'yar/ *v.* trample; fell.

atroz /a'troθ; a'ntros/ *a.* atrocious.

atún /a'tun/ *n. m.* tuna.

aturdir /atur'ðir/ *v.* daze, stun, bewilder.

audacia /au'ðaθia; au'ðasia/ *n. f.* audacity.

audaz /au'ðaθ; au'ðas/ *a.* audacious, bold.

audible /au'ðiβle/ *a.* audible.

audífono /au'ðifono/ *n. m.* hearing aid.

audiovisual /auðioβi'sual/ *a.* audiovisual.

auditorio /auði'torio/ *n. m.* audience.

aula /'aula/ *n. f.* classroom, hall.

aullar /au'ʎar; au'yar/ *v.* howl, bay.

aullido /au'ʎiðo; au'yiðo/ *n. m.* howl.

aumentar /aumen'tar/ *v.* augment; increase, swell.

aun /aun/ *adv.* still; even. **a. cuando,** even though, even if.

aunque /'aunke/ *conj.* although, though.

áureo /'aureo/ *a.* golden.

aureola /aure'ola/ *n. f.* halo.

auriculares /auriku'lares/ *n. m.pl.* headphones.

aurora /au'rora/ *n. f.* dawn.

ausencia /au'senθia; au'sensia/ *n. f.* absence.

ausentarse /ausen'tarse/ *v.* stay away.

ausente /au'sente/ *a.* absent.

auspicio /aus'piθio; aus'pisio/ *n. m.* auspice.

austeridad /austeri'ðað/ *n. f.* austerity.

austero /aus'tero/ *a.* austere.

austriaco /aus'triako/ **-ca** *a. & n.* Austrian.

auténtico /au'tentiko/ *a.* authentic.

auto /'auto/ **automóvil** *n. m.* auto, automobile.

autobús /auto'βus/ *n. m.* bus.

autocine /auto'θine; auto'sine/ **autocinema** *n. m.* drive-in (movie theater).

automático /auto'matiko/ *a.* automatic.

autonomía /autono'mia/ *n. f.* autonomy.

autopista /auto'pista/ *n. f.* expressway.

autor /au'tor/ *n. m.* author.

autoridad /autori'ðað/ *n. f.* authority.

autoritario /autori'tario/ *a.* authoritarian; authoritative.

autorizar /autori'θar; autori'sar/ *v.* authorize.

autostop /auto'stop/ *n. m.* hitchhiking. **hacer a.,** to hitchhike.

auxiliar /auksi'liar/ *a.* **1.** auxiliary. —*v.* **2.** assist, aid.

auxilio /auk'silio/ *n. m.* aid, assistance.

avaluar /aβa'luar/ *v.* evaluate, appraise.

avance /a'βanθe; a'βanse/ *n. m.* advance. —**avanzar,** *v.*

avaricia /aβa'riθia; aβa'risia/ *n. f.* avarice.

avariento /aβa'riento/ *a.* miserly, greedy.

avaro /a'βaro/ **-ra** *a. & m.* miser; miserly.

ave /'aβe/ *n. f.* bird.

avellana /aβe'ʎana; aβe'yana/ *n. f.* hazelnut.

Ave María /aβema'ria/ *n. m.* Hail Mary.

avena /a'βena/ *n. f.* oat.

avenida /aβe'niða/ *n. f.* avenue; flood.

avenirse /aβe'nirse/ *v.* compromise; agree.

aventajar /aβenta'har/ *v.* surpass, get ahead of.

aventar /aβen'tar/ *v.* fan; scatter.

aventura /aβen'tura/ *n. f.* adventure.

aventurar /aβentu'rar/ *v.* venture, risk, gamble.

aventurero /aβentu'rero/ **-ra** *a. & n.* adventurous; adventurer.

avergonzado /aβergon'θaðo; aβergon'saðo/ *a.* ashamed, abashed.

avergonzar /aβergon'θar; aβergon'sar/ *v.* shame, abash.

avería /aβe'ria/ *n. f.* damage. —**averiar,** *v.*

averiguar /aβeri'guar/ v. ascertain, find out.

aversión /aβer'sion/ n. f. aversion.

avestruz /aβes'truθ; aβes'trus/ n. m. ostrich.

aviación /aβia'θion; aβia'sion/ n. f. aviation.

aviador /aβia'ðor/ -ra n. aviator.

ávido /'aβiðo/ a. avid; eager.

avión /a'βion/ n. m. airplane.

avisar /aβi'sar/ v. notify, let know; warn, advise.

aviso /a'βiso/ n. m. notice, announcement; advertisement; warning.

avispa /a'βispa/ n. f wasp.

avivar /aβi'βar/ v. enliven, revive.

axila /ak'sila/ n. f. armpit.

aya /'aya/ n. f. governess.

ayatolá /aya'tola/ n. m. ayatollah.

ayer /a'yer/ adv. yesterday.

ayuda /a'yuða/ n. f. help, aid. —**ayudar,** v.

ayudante /ayu'ðante/ a. assistant, helper; adjutant.

ayuno /a'yuno/ n. m. fast. —**ayunar,** v.

ayuntamiento /ayunta'miento/ n. m. city hall.

azada /a'θaða; a'saða/ n. f., **azadón,** m. hoe.

azafata /aθa'fata; asa'fata/ n. f. stewardess, flight attendant.

azar /a'θar; a'sar/ n. m. hazard, chance. **al a.,** at random.

azotar /aθo'tar; aso'tar/ v. whip, flog; belabor.

azote /a'θote; a'sote/ n. m. scourge, lash.

azúcar /a'θukar; a'sukar/ n. m. sugar.

azucarero /aθuka'rero; asuka'rero/ n. m. sugar bowl.

azúcar moreno /a'θukar mo'reno; a'sukar mo'reno/ brown sugar.

azul /a'θul; a'sul/ a. blue.

azulado /aθu'laðo; asu'laðo/ a. blue, bluish.

azulejo /aθu'leho; asu'leho/ n. m. tile; bluebird.

azul marino /a'θul ma'rino; a'sul ma'rino/ navy blue.

B

baba /'baβa/ n. f. drivel. —**babear,** v.

babador /baβa'ðor, ba'βero/ n. m. bib.

babucha /ba'βutʃa/ n. f. slipper.

bacalao /baka'lao/ n. m. codfish.

bachiller /batʃi'ʎer; batʃi'yer/ **-ra** n. bachelor (degree).

bacía /ba'θia; ba'sia/ n. f. washbasin.

bacterias /bak'terias/ n. f.pl. bacteria.

bacteriología /bakteriolo'hia/ n. f. bacteriology.

bahía /ba'ia/ n. f. bay.

bailador /baila'ðor/ **-ra** n. dancer.

bailar /bai'lar/ v. dance.

bailarín /baila'rin/ **-ina** n. dancer.

baile /'baile/ n. m. dance.

baja /'baha/ n. f. fall (in price); Mil. casualty.

bajar /ba'har/ v. lower; descend.

bajeza /ba'heθa; ba'hesa/ n. f. baseness.

bajo /'baho/ prep. **1.** under, below. —a. **2.** low; short; base.

bala /'bala/ n. f. bullet; ball; bale.

balada /ba'laða/ n. f. ballad.

balancear /balanθe'ar; balanse'ar/ v. balance; roll, swing, sway.

balanza /ba'lanθa; ba'lansa/ n. f. balance; scales.

balbuceo /balβu'θeo; balβu'seo/ n. m. stammer; babble. —**balbucear,** v.

Balcanes /bal'kanes/ n. m.pl. Balkans.

balcón /bal'kon/ n. m. balcony.

balde /'balde/ n. m. bucket, pail. **de b.,** gratis. **en b.,** in vain.

balística /ba'listika/ n. f. ballistics.

ballena /ba'ʎena; ba'yena/ n. f. whale.

balneario /balne'ario/ n. m. bathing resort; spa.

balompié /balom'pie/ n. m. football.

balón /ba'lon/ n. m. football; balloon tire.

baloncesto /balon'θesto; balon'sesto/ n. m. basketball.

balota /ba'lota/ n. f. ballot, vote. —**balotar,** v.

balsa /'balsa/ n. f. raft.

bálsamo /'balsamo/ n. m. balm.

baluarte /ba'luarte/ n. m. bulwark.

bambolearse /bambole'arse/ v. sway.

bambú /bam'βu/ n. bamboo.

banal /ba'nal/ a. banal, trite.

banana /ba'nana/ n. f. banana.

banano /ba'nano/ n. m. banana tree.

bancarrota /banka'rrota/ n. f. bankruptcy.

banco /'banko/ n. m. bank; bench; school of fish.

banco cooperativo /'banko koopera'tiβo/ credit union.

banda /'banda/ n. f. band.

bandada /ban'daða/ n. f. covey; flock.

banda sonora /'banda so'nora/ n. f. soundtrack.

bandeja /ban'deha/ n. f. tray.

bandera /ban'dera/ *n. f.* flag; banner; ensign.

bandido /ban'diðo/ **-da** *n.* bandit.

bando /'bando/ *n. m.* faction.

bandolero /bando'lero/ **-ra** *n.* bandit, robber.

banquero /ban'kero/ **-ra** *n.* banker.

banqueta /ban'keta/ *n. f.* stool; (Mex.) sidewalk.

banquete /ban'kete/ *n. m.* feast, banquet.

banquillo /ban'kiʎo; ban'kiyo/ *n. m.* stool.

bañar /ba'ɲar/ *v.* bathe.

bañera /ba'ɲera/ *n. f.* bathtub.

baño /'baɲo/ *n. m.* bath; bathroom.

bar /bar/ *n. m.* bar, pub.

baraja /ba'raha/ *n. f.* pack of cards; game of cards.

baranda /ba'randa/ *n. f.* railing, banister.

barato /ba'rato/ *a.* cheap.

barba /'barβa/ *n. f.* beard; chin.

barbacoa /barβa'koa/ *n. f.* barbecue; stretcher.

barbaridad /barβari'ðað/ *n. f.* barbarity; *Colloq.* excess (in anything).

bárbaro /'barβaro/ *a.* barbarous; crude.

barbería /barβe'ria/ *n. f.* barbershop.

barbero /bar'βero/ *n. m.* barber.

barca /'barka/ *n. f.* (small) boat.

barcaza /bar'kaθa; bar'kasa/ *n. f.* barge.

barco /'barko/ *n. m.* ship, boat.

barniz /bar'niθ; bar'nis/ *n. m.* varnish. —**barnizar,** *v.*

barómetro /ba'rometro/ *n. m.* barometer.

barón /ba'ron/ *n. m.* baron.

barquilla /bar'kiʎa; bar'kiya/ *n. f. Naut.* log.

barra /'barra/ *n. f.* bar.

barraca /ba'rraka/ *n. f.* hut, shed.

barrear /barre'ar/ *v.* bar, barricade.

barreno /ba'rreno/ *n. m.* blast; blasting. —**barrenar,** *v.*

barrer /ba'rrer/ *v.* sweep.

barrera /ba'rrera/ *n. f.* barrier.

barricada /barri'kaða/ *n. f.* barricade.

barriga /ba'rriga/ *n. f.* belly.

barril /ba'rril/ *n. m.* barrel; cask.

barrio /'barrio/ *n. m.* district, ward, quarter.

barro /'barro/ *n. m.* clay, mud.

base /'base/ *n. f.* base; basis. —**basar,** *v.*

base de datos /'base de 'datos/ database.

bastante /bas'tante/ *a.* **1.** enough, plenty of. —*adv.* **2.** enough; rather, quite.

bastar /bas'tar/ *v.* suffice, be enough.

bastardo /bas'tarðo/ **-a** *& n.* bastard.

bastear /baste'ar/ *v.* baste.

bastidor /basti'ðor/ *n. m.* wing (in theater).

bastón /bas'ton/ *n. m.* (walking) cane.

bastos /'bastos/ *n. m.pl.* clubs (cards).

basura /ba'sura/ *n. f.* refuse, dirt; garbage; junk.

basurero /basu'rero/ **-ra** *n.* scavenger.

batalla /ba'taʎa; ba'taya/ *n. f.* battle. —**batallar,** *v.*

batallón /bata'ʎon; bata'yon/ *n. m.* battalion.

batata /ba'tata/ *n. f.* sweet potato.

bate /'bate/ *n. m.* bat. —**batear,** *v.*

batería /bate'ria/ *n. f.* battery.

batido /ba'tiðo/ *n. m.* (cooking) batter; milkshake.

batidora /bati'ðora/ *n. f.* mixer (for food).

batir /ba'tir/ *v.* beat; demolish; conquer.

baúl /ba'ul/ *n. m.* trunk.

bautismo /bau'tismo/ *n. m.* baptism.

bautista /bau'tista/ *n. m. & f.* Baptist.

bautizar /bauti'θar; bauti'sar/ *v.* christen, baptize.

bautizo /bau'tiθo; bau'tiso/ *n. m.* baptism.

baya /'baia/ *n. f.* berry.

bayoneta /bayo'neta/ *n. f.* bayonet.

beato /be'ato/ *a.* blessed.

bebé /be'βe/ *n. m.* baby.

beber /be'βer/ *v.* drink.

bebible /be'βiβle/ *a.* drinkable.

bebida /be'βiða/ *n. f.* drink, beverage.

beca /'beka/ *n. f.* grant, scholarship.

becado /be'kaðo/ **-da** *n.* scholar.

becerro /be'θerro; be'serro/ *n. m.* calf; calfskin.

beldad /bel'dað/ *n. f.* beauty.

belga /'belga/ *a. & n.* Belgian.

Bélgica /'belhika/ *n. f.* Belgium.

belicoso /beli'koso/ *a.* warlike.

beligerante /belihe'rante/ *a. & n.* belligerent.

bellaco /be'ʎako; be'yako/ *a.* **1.** sly, roguish. —*n.* **2.** *m.* rogue.

bellas artes /'beʎas 'artes; 'beyas 'artes/ *n. f.pl.* fine arts.

belleza /be'ʎeθa; be'yesa/ *n. f.* beauty.

bello /'beʎo; 'beyo/ *a.* beautiful.

bellota /be'ʎota; be'yota/ *n. f.* acorn.

bendecir /bende'θir; bende'sir/ *v.* bless.

bendición /bendi'θion; bendi'sion/ *n. f.* blessing, benediction.

bendito /ben'dito/ *a.* blessed.

beneficio /bene'fiθio; bene'fisio/ *n. m.* benefit. —**beneficiar,** *v.*

beneficioso /benefi'θioso; benefi'sioso/ *a.* beneficial.

benevolencia /beneβo'lenθia; beneβo'lensia/ *n. f.* benevolence.

benévolo /be'neβolo/ *a.* benevolent.

benigno /be'nigno/ *a.* benign.

beodo /be'oðo/ **-da** *a. & n.* drunk.

berenjena /beren'hena/ *n. f.* eggplant.

beso /'beso/ *n. m.* kiss. —**besar,** *v.*

bestia /'bestia/ *n. f.* beast, brute.

betabel /beta'βel/ n. m. beet.

Biblia /'biβlia/ n. f. Bible.

bíblico /'biβliko/ a. Biblical.

biblioteca /biβlio'teka/ n. f. library.

bicarbonato /bikarβo'nato/ n. m. bicarbonate.

bicicleta /biθi'kleta; bisi'kleta/ n. f. bicycle.

bien /bien/ adv. **1.** well. —n. **2.** good; (pl.) possessions.

bienes inmuebles /'bienes i'mueβles/ n. m.pl. real estate.

bienestar /bienes'tar/ n. m. well-being, welfare.

bienhechor /biene'tʃor/ **-ra** n. benefactor.

bienvenida /biembe'niða/ n. f. welcome.

bienvenido /biembe'niðo/ a. welcome.

biftec /bif'tek/ n. m. steak.

bifurcación /bifurka'θion; bifurka'sion/ n. f. fork. **—bifurcar,** v.

bigamia /bi'gamia/ n. f. bigamy.

bígamo /'bigamo/ **-a** n. bigamist.

bigotes /bi'gotes/ n. m.pl. mustache.

bikini /bi'kini/ n. m. bikini.

bilingüe /bi'lingue/ a. bilingual.

bilingüismo /biliŋ'guismo/ n. m. bilingualism.

bilis /'bilis/ n. f. bile.

billar /bi'ʎar/ n. m. billiards.

billete /bi'ʎete; bi'yete/ n. m. ticket; bank note, bill.

billete de banco /bi'ʎete de 'banko; bi'yete de 'banko/ bank note.

billón /bi'ʎon; bi'yon/ n. m. billion.

bingo /'bingo/ n. m. bingo.

biodegradable /bioðegra'ðaβle/ a. biodegradable.

biografía /biogra'fia/ n. f. biography.

biología /biolo'hia/ n. f. biology.

biombo /'biombo/ n. m. folding screen.

bisabuela /bisa'βuela/ n. f. great-grandmother.

bisabuelo /bisa'βuelo/ n. m. great-grandfather.

bisel /bi'sel/ n. m. bevel. **—biselar,** v.

bisonte /bi'sonte/ n. m. bison.

bisté /bis'te/ **bistec** n. m. steak.

bisutería /bisute'ria/ n. f. costume jewelry.

bizarro /bi'θarro; bi'sarro/ a. brave; generous; smart.

bizco /'biθko/ **-ca** n. **1.** cross-eyed person. —a. **2.** cross-eyed, squinting.

bizcocho /biθ'kotʃo; bis'kotʃo/ n. m. biscuit, cake.

blanco /'blanko/ a. **1.** white; blank. —n. **2.** m. white; target.

blandir /blan'dir/ v. brandish, flourish.

blando /'blando/ a. soft.

blanquear /blanke'ar/ v. whiten; bleach.

blasfemar /blasfe'mar/ v. blaspheme, curse.

blasfemia /blas'femia/ n. f. blasphemy.

blindado /blin'daðo/ a. armored.

blindaje /blin'dahe/ n. m. armor.

bloque /'bloke/ n. m. block. **—bloquear,** v.

bloqueo /blo'keo/ n. m. blockade. **—bloquear,** v.

blusa /'blusa/ n. f. blouse.

bobada /bo'βaða/ n. f. stupid, silly thing.

bobo /'boβo/ **-ba** a. & n. fool; foolish.

boca /'boka/ n. f. mouth.

bocado /bo'kaðo/ n. m. bit; bite, mouthful.

bocanada /boka'naða/ n. f. puff (of smoke); mouthful (of liquor).

bocazas /bo'kaθas/ n. m. & f. Colloq. big-mouth.

bochorno /bo'tʃorno/ n. m. sultry weather; embarrassment.

bocina /bo'θina; bo'sina/ n. f. horn.

boda /'boða/ n. f. wedding.

bodega /bo'ðega/ n. f. wine cellar; Naut. hold; (Carib.) grocery store.

bofetada /bofe'taða/ n. f. **bofetón,** m. slap.

boga /'boga/ n. f. vogue; fad.

bogar /bo'gar/ v. row (a boat).

bohemio /bo'emio/ **-a** a. & n. Bohemian.

boicoteo /boiko'teo/ n. m. boycott. **—boicotear,** v.

boina /'boina/ n. f. beret.

bola /'bola/ n. f. ball.

bola de nieve /bola de 'nieβe/ snowball.

bolas de billar /'bolas de bi'ʎar; 'bolas de bi'yar/ billiard balls.

bolera /bo'lera/ n. f. bowling alley.

boletín /bole'tin/ n. m. bulletin.

boletín informativo /bole'tin informa'tiβo/ news bulletin.

boleto /bo'leto/ n. m. ticket. **b. de embarque,** boarding pass.

boliche /bo'litʃe/ n. m. bowling alley.

bolígrafo /bo'ligrafo/ n. m. ballpoint pen.

boliviano /boli'βiano/ **-a** a. & n. Bolivian.

bollo /'boʎo; 'boyo/ n. m. bun, loaf.

bolos /'bolos/ n. m.pl. bowling.

bolsa /'bolsa/ n. f. purse; stock exchange.

bolsa de agua caliente /'bolsa de 'agua ka'liente/ hot-water bottle.

bolsillo /bol'siʎo; bol'siyo/ n. m. pocket.

bomba /'bomba/ n. f. pump; bomb; gas station.

bombardear /bombarðe'ar/ v. bomb; bombard, shell.

bombear /bombe'ar/ v. pump.

bombero /bom'βero/ n. m. fireman.

bombilla /bom'βiʎa; bom'βiya/ n. f. (light) bulb.

bonanza /bo'nanθa; bo'nansa/ n. f. prosperity; fair weather.

bondad /bon'dað/ n. f. kindness; goodness.

bondadoso /bonda'ðoso/ a. kind, kindly.

bongó /boŋ'goʹ/ n. m. bongo drum.

bonito /boʹnito/ a. pretty.

bono /'bono/ n. m. bonus; Fin. bond.

boqueada /bokeʹaða/ n. f. gasp; gape. —**boquear**, v.

boquilla /boʹkiʎa; boʹkiya/ n. f. cigarette holder.

bordado /borʹðaðo/ n. m., **bordadura**, f. embroidery.

bordar /borʹðar/ v. embroider.

borde /'borðe/ n. m. border, rim, edge, brink, ledge.

borde de la carretera /'borðe de la karreʹtera/ roadside.

borla /'borla/ n. f. tassel.

borracho /boʹrratʃo/ -a & n. drunk.

borrachón /borraʹtʃon/ -na n. drunkard.

borrador /borraʹðor/ n. m. eraser.

borradura /borraʹðura/ n. f. erasure.

borrar /boʹrrar/ v. erase, rub out.

borrasca /boʹrraska/ n. f. squall, storm.

borrico /boʹrriko/ n. m. donkey.

bosque /'boske/ n. m. forest, wood.

bosquejo /bosʹkeho/ n. m. sketch, draft. —**bosquejar**, v.

bostezo /bosʹteθo; bosʹteso/ n. m. yawn. —**bostezar**, v.

bota /'bota/ n. f. boot.

botalón /botaʹlon/ n. m. Naut. boom.

botánica /boʹtanika/ n. f. botany.

botar /boʹtar/ v. throw out, throw away.

bote /'bote/ n. m. boat; can, box.

bote salvavidas /'bote salβaʹβiðas/ lifeboat.

botica /boʹtika/ n. f. pharmacy, drugstore.

boticario /botiʹkario/ n. m. pharmacist, druggist.

botín /boʹtin/ n. m. booty, plunder, spoils.

botiquín /botiʹkin/ n. m. medicine chest.

boto /'boto/ a. dull, stupid.

botón /boʹton/ n. m. button.

botones /boʹtones/ n. m. bellboy (in a hotel).

bóveda /'boβeða/ n. f. vault.

boxeador /bokseaʹðor/ n. m. boxer.

boxeo /bokʹseo/ n. m. boxing. —**boxear**, v.

boya /'boya/ n. f. buoy.

boyante /boʹyante/ a. buoyant.

bozal /boʹθal; boʹsal/ n. m. muzzle.

bragas /'bragas/ n. f.pl. panties.

bramido /braʹmiðo/ n. m. roar, bellow. —**bramar**, v.

brasa /'brasa/ n. f. embers, grill. —**brasear**, v.

brasileño /brasiʹleɲo/ -ña a. & n. Brazilian.

bravata /braʹβata/ n. f. bravado.

bravear /braβeʹar/ v. bully.

braza /'braθa/ n. f. fathom.

brazada /braʹθaða; braʹsaða/ n. f. (swimming) stroke.

brazalete /braθaʹlete; brasaʹlete/ n. m. bracelet.

brazo /'braθo; 'braso/ n. m. arm.

brea /'brea/ n. f. tar, pitch.

brecha /'bretʃa/ n. f. gap, breach.

brécol /'brekol/ n. m. broccoli.

bregar /breʹgar/ v. scramble.

breña /'breɲa/ n. f. rough country with brambly shrubs.

Bretaña /breʹtaɲa/ n. f. Britain.

breve /'breβe/ a. brief, short. **en b.**, shortly, soon.

brevedad /breβeʹðað/ n. f. brevity.

bribón /briʹβon/ -na n. rogue, rascal.

brida /'briða/ n. f. bridle.

brigada /briʹgaða/ n. f. brigade.

brillante /briʹʎante; briʹyante/ a. 1. brilliant, shiny. —n. 2. m. diamond.

brillo /'briʎo; 'briyo/ n. m. shine, glitter. —**brillar**, v.

brinco /'brinko/ n. m. jump; bounce, skip. —**brincar**, v.

brindis /'brindis/ n. m. toast. —**brindar**, v.

brío /'brio/ n. m. vigor.

brioso /briʹoso/ a. vigorous, spirited.

brisa /'brisa/ n. f. breeze.

brisa marina /'brisa maʹrina/ sea breeze.

británico /briʹtaniko/ a. British.

brocado /broʹkaðo/ -da a. & n. brocade.

brocha /'brotʃa/ n. f. brush.

broche /'brotʃe/ n. m. brooch, clasp, pin.

broma /'broma/ n. f. joke. —**bromear**, v.

bronca /'bronka/ n. f. Colloq. quarrel, row, fight.

bronce /'bronθe; 'bronse/ n. m. bronze; brass.

bronceador /bronθeaʹðor; bronseaʹðor/ n. m. suntan lotion, suntan oil.

bronquitis /bronʹkitis/ n. f. bronchitis.

brotar /broʹtar/ v. gush; sprout; bud.

brote /'brote/ n. m. bud, shoot.

bruja /'bruha/ n. f. witch.

brújula /'bruhula/ n. f. compass.

bruma /'bruma/ n. f. mist.

brumoso /bruʹmoso/ a. misty.

brusco /'brusko/ a. brusque; abrupt, curt.

brutal /bruʹtal/ a. savage, brutal.

brutalidad /brutaliʹðað/ n. f. brutality.

bruto /'bruto/ -ta a. 1. brutish; ignorant. —n. 2. blockhead.

bucear /buθeʹar; buseʹar/ v. dive.

bueno /'bueno/ a. good, fair; well (in health).

buey /buei/ n. m. ox, steer.

búfalo /'bufalo/ n. m. buffalo.

bufanda /buʹfanda/ n. f. scarf.

bufón /buʹfon/ -ona a. & n. fool, buffoon, clown.

búho /'buo/ n. m. owl.

buhonero /buoʹnero/ n. m. peddler.

bujía /bu'hia/ n. f. spark plug.
bulevar /bule'βar/ n. m. boulevard.
bulimia /bu'limia/ n. f. bulimia.
bullicio /bu'ʎiθio; bu'yisio/ n. m. bustle, noise.
bullicioso /buʎi'θioso; buyi'sioso/ a. boisterous, noisy.
bulto /'bulto/ n. m. bundle; lump.
buñuelo /bu'ɲuelo/ n. m. bun.
buque /'buke/ n. m. ship.
buque de guerra /'buke de 'gerra/ warship.
buque de pasajeros /'buke de pasa'heros/ passenger ship.
burdo /'burðo/ a. coarse.

burgués /bur'ges/ **-esa** a. & n. bourgeois.
burla /'burla/ n. f. mockery; fun.
burlador /burla'ðor/ **-ra** n. trickster, jokester.
burlar /bur'lar/ v. mock, deride.
burlarse de /bur'larse de/ v. scoff at; make fun of.
burro /'burro/ n. m. donkey.
busca /'buska/ n. f. search, pursuit, quest.
buscar /bus'kar/ v. seek, look for; look up.
busto /'busto/ n. m. bust.
butaca /bu'taka/ n. f. armchair; *Theat.* orchestra seat.
buzo /'buθo; 'buso/ n. m. diver.
buzón /bu'θon; bu'son/ n. m. mailbox.

C

cabal /ka'βal/ a. exact; thorough.
cabalgar /kaβal'ɣar/ v. ride horseback.
caballeresco /kaβaʎe'resko: kaβaye'resko/ a. gentlemanly, chivalrous.
caballería /kaβaʎe'ria; kaβaye'ria/ n. f. cavalry; chivalry.
caballeriza /kaβaʎe'riθa; kaβaye'risa/ n. f. stable.
caballero /kaβa'ʎero; kaβa'yero/ n. m. gentleman; knight.
caballete /kaβa'ʎete; kaβa'yete/ n. m. sawhorse; easel; ridge (of roof).
caballo /ka'βaʎo; ka'βayo/ n. m. horse.
cabaña /ka'βaɲa/ n. f. cabin; booth.
cabaré /kaβa're/ n. m. nightclub.
cabaretero /kaβare'tero/ **-a** n. m. & f. nightclub owner.
cabecear /kaβeθe'ar; kaβese'ar/ v. pitch (as a ship).
cabecera /kaβe'θera; kaβe'sera/ n. f. head (of bed, table).
cabello /ka'βeʎo; ka'βeyo/ n. m. hair.
caber /ka'βer/ v. fit into, be contained in. **no cabe duda,** there is no doubt.
cabeza /ka'βeθa; ka'βesa/ n. f. head; warhead.
cabildo /ka'βildo/ n. m. city hall.
cabildo abierto /ka'βildo a'βierto/ town meeting.
cabizbajo /kaβiθ'βaho; kaβis'βaho/ a. downcast.
cablegrama /kaβle'grama/ n. m. cablegram.
cabo /'kaβo/ n. m. end; *Geog.* cape; *Mil.* corporal. **llevar a c.,** carry out, accomplish.
cabra /'kaβra/ n. f. goat.
cacahuete /kaka'uete/ n. m. peanut.
cacao /ka'kao/ n. m. cocoa; chocolate.
cacerola /kaθe'rola; kase'rola/ n. f. pan, casserole.

cachondeo /katʃon'deo/ n. m. fun, hilarity.
cachondo /ka'tʃondo/ a. funny; *Colloq.* horny.
cachorro /ka'tʃorro/ n. m. cub; puppy.
cada /'kaða/ a. each, every.
cadáver /ka'ðaβer/ n. m. corpse.
cadena /ka'ðena/ n. f. chain.
cadera /ka'ðera/ n. f. hip.
cadete /ka'ðete/ n. m. cadet.
caer /ka'er/ v fall.
café /ka'fe/ n. m. coffee; café.
café exprés /ka'fe eks'pres/ espresso.
café soluble /ka'fe so'luβle/ instant coffee.
cafetal /kafe'tal/ n. m. coffee plantation.
cafetera /kafe'tera/ n. f. coffee pot.
caída /ka'iða/ n. f. fall, drop; collapse.
caimán /kai'man/ n. m. alligator.
caja /'kaha/ n. f. box, case; checkout counter.
caja de ahorros /'kaha de a'orros/ savings bank.
caja de cerillos /'kaha de θe'riʎos; 'kaha de se'riyos/ matchbox.
caja de fósforos /'kaha de 'fosforos/ matchbox.
caja torácica /'kaha to'raθika; 'kaha to'rasika/ rib cage.
cajero /ka'hero/ **-ra** n. cashier.
cajón /ka'hon/ n. m. drawer.
cal /kal/ n. f. lime.
calabaza /kala'βaθa; kala'βasa/ n. f. calabash, pumpkin.
calabozo /kala'βoθo; kala'βoso/ n. m. jail, cell.
calambre /ka'lambre/ n. m. cramp.
calamidad /kalami'ðað/ n. f. calamity, disaster.
calcetín /kalθe'tin; kalse'tin/ n. m. sock.
calcio /'kalθio; 'kalsio/ n. m. calcium.
calcular /kalku'lar/ v. calculate, figure.

cálculo /'kalkulo/ n. m. calculation, estimate.

caldera /kal'dera/ n. f. kettle, caldron; boiler.

caldo /'kaldo/ n. m. broth.

calefacción /kalefak'θion; kalefak'sion/ n. f. heat, heating.

calendario /kalen'dario/ n. m. calendar.

calentar /kalen'tar/ v. heat, warm.

calidad /kali'ðað/ n. f. quality, grade.

caliente /ka'liente/ a. hot, warm.

calificar /kalifi'kar/ v. qualify.

callado /ka'ʎaðo; ka'yaðo/ a. silent, quiet.

callarse /ka'ʎarse; ka'yarse/ v. quiet down; keep still; stop talking.

calle /'kaʎe; 'kaye/ n. f. street.

callejón /kaʎe'hon; kaye'hon/ n. m. alley.

calle sin salida /'kaʎe sin sa'liða; 'kaye sin sa'liða/ dead end.

callo /'kaʎo; 'kayo/ n. m. callus, corn.

calma /'kalma/ n. f. calm, quiet.

calmado /kal'maðo/ a. calm.

calmante /kal'mante/ a. soothing, calming.

calmar /kal'mar/ v. calm, quiet, lull, soothe.

calor /ka'lor/ n. m. heat, warmth. **tener c.,** to be hot, warm; feel hot, warm. **hacer c.,** to be hot, warm (weather).

calorífero /kalo'rifero/ a. 1. heat-producing. —n. 2. m. radiator.

calumnia /ka'lumnia/ n. f. slander. —**calumniar,** v.

caluroso /kalu'roso/ a. warm, hot.

calvario /kal'βario/ n. m. Calvary.

calvo /'kalβo/ a. bald.

calzado /kal'θaðo; kal'saðo/ n. m. footwear.

calzar /kal'θar; kal'sar/ v. wear (as shoes).

calzoncillos /kalθon'θiʎos; kalson'siyos/ n. m.pl. shorts.

calzones /kal'θones; kal'sones/ n. m.pl. trousers.

cama /'kama/ n. f. bed.

cámara /'kamara/ n. f. chamber; camera.

camarada /kama'raða/ n. m. & f. comrade.

camarera /kama'rera/ n. f. chambermaid; waitress.

camarero /kama'rero/ n. m. steward; waiter.

camarón /kama'ron/ n. m. shrimp.

camarote /kama'rote/ n. m. stateroom, berth.

cambiar /kam'βiar/ v. exchange, change, trade; cash.

cambio /'kambio/ n. m. change, exchange. **en c.,** on the other hand.

cambista /kam'βista/ n. m. & f. money changer; banker, broker.

cambur /kam'βur/ n. m. banana.

camello /ka'meʎo; ka'meyo/ n. m. camel.

camilla /ka'miʎa; ka'miya/ n. f. stretcher.

caminar /kami'nar/ v. walk.

caminata /kami'nata/ n. f. tramp, hike.

camino /ka'mino/ n. m. road; way.

camión /ka'mion/ n. m. truck.

camisa /ka'misa/ n. f. shirt.

camisería /kamise'ria/ n. f. haberdashery.

camiseta /kami'seta/ n. f. undershirt; T-shirt.

campamento /kampa'mento/ n. m. camp.

campana /kam'pana/ n. f. bell.

campanario /kampa'nario/ n. m. bell tower, steeple.

campaneo /kampa'neo/ n. m. chime.

campaña /kam'paɲa/ n. f. campaign.

campeón /kampe'on/ **-na** n. champion.

campeonato /kampeo'nato/ n. m. championship.

campesino /kampe'sino/ **-na** n peasant.

campestre /kam'pestre/ a. country, rural.

campo /'kampo/ n. m. field; (the) country.

campo de concentración /'kampo de konθentra'θion; 'kampo de konsentra'sion/ concentration camp.

campo de golf /'kampo de 'golf/ golf course.

Canadá /kana'ða/ n. m. Canada.

canadiense /kana'ðiense/ a. & n. Canadian.

canal /ka'nal/ n. m. canal; channel.

Canal de la Mancha /ka'nal de la 'mantʃa/ n. m. English Channel.

canalla /ka'naʎa; ka'naya/ n. f. rabble.

canario /ka'nario/ n. m. canary.

canasta /ka'nasta/ n. f. basket.

cáncer /'kanθer; 'kanser/ n. m. cancer.

cancha de tenis /'kantʃa de 'tenis/ n. f. tennis court.

canciller /kanθi'ʎer; kansi'yer/ n. m. chancellor.

canción /kan'θion; kan'sion/ n. f. song.

candado /kan'daðo/ n. m. padlock.

candela /kan'dela/ n. f. fire; light; candle.

candelero /kande'lero/ n. m. candlestick.

candidato /kandi'ðato/ **-ta** n. candidate; applicant.

candidatura /kandiða'tura/ n. f candidacy.

canela /ka'nela/ n. f. cinnamon.

cangrejo /kaŋ'greho/ n. m. crab.

caníbal /ka'niβal/ n. m. cannibal.

caniche /ka'nitʃe/ n. m. poodle.

canje /'kanhe/ n. m. exchange, trade. —**canjear,** v.

cano /'kano/ a. gray.

canoa /ka'noa/ n. f. canoe.

cansado /kan'saðo/ a. tired, weary.

cansancio /kan'sanθio; kan'sansio/ n. m. fatigue.

cansar /kan'sar/ v. tire, fatigue, wear out.

cantante /kan'tante/ n. m. & f. singer.

cantar /kan'tar/ n. 1. m. song. —v. 2. sing.

cántaro /'kantaro/ n. m. pitcher.

cantera /kan'tera/ n. f. (stone) quarry.

cantidad /kanti'ðað/ n. f. quantity, amount.

cantina /kan'tina/ n. f. bar, tavern; restaurant.

canto /'kanto/ n. m. chant, song, singing; edge.

caña /'kaɲa/ n. f. cane, reed; sugar cane; small glass of beer.

cañón /ka'ɲon/ n. m. canyon; cannon; gun barrel.

caoba /ka'oβa/ n. f. mahogany.

caos /'kaos/ n. m. chaos.

caótico /ka'otiko/ a. chaotic.

capa /'kapa/ n. f. cape, cloak; coat (of paint).

capacidad /kapaθi'ðað; kapasi'ðað/ n. f. capacity; capability.

capacitar /kapaθi'tar; kapasi'tar/ v. enable.

capataz /kapa'taθ; kapa'tas/ n. m. foreman.

capaz /ka'paθ; ka'pas/ a. capable, able.

capellán /kape'ʎan; kape'yan/ n. m. chaplain.

caperuza /kape'ruθa; kape'rusa/ n. f. hood.

capilla /ka'piʎa; ka'piya/ n. f. chapel.

capital /kapi'tal/ n. **1.** m. capital. **2.** f. capital (city).

capitalista /kapita'lista/ a. & n. capitalist.

capitán /kapi'tan/ n. m. captain.

capitular /kapitu'lar/ v. yield.

capítulo /ka'pitulo/ n. m. chapter.

capota /ka'pota/ n. f. hood.

capricho /ka'pritʃo/ n. m. caprice; fancy, whim.

caprichoso /kapri'tʃoso/ a. capricious.

cápsula /'kapsula/ n. f. capsule.

capturar /kaptu'rar/ v. capture.

capucha /ka'putʃa/ n. f. hood.

capullo /ka'puʎo; ka'puyo/ n. m. cocoon.

cara /'kara/ n. f. face.

caracol /kara'kol/ n. m. snail.

carácter /ka'rakter/ n. m. character.

característica /karakte'ristika/ n. f. characteristic.

característico /karakte'ristiko/ a. characteristic.

caramba /ka'ramba/ mild exclamation.

caramelo /kara'melo/ n. m. caramel; candy.

carátula /ka'ratula/ n. f. dial.

caravana /kara'βana/ n. f. caravan.

carbón /kar'βon/ n. m. carbon; coal.

carbonizar /karβoni'θar; karβoni'sar/ v. char.

carburador /karβura'ðor/ n. m. carburetor.

carcajada /karka'haða/ n. f. burst of laughter.

cárcel /'karθel; 'karsel/ n. f. prison, jail.

carcelero /karθe'lero; karse'lero/ n. m. jailer.

carcinogénico /karθino'heniko; karsino'heniko/ a. carcinogenic.

cardenal /karðe'nal/ n. m. cardinal.

cardiólogo /kar'ðiologo/ **-a** m & f. cardiologist.

carecer /kare'θer; kare'ser/ v. lack.

carestía /kares'tia/ n. f. scarcity; famine.

carga /'karga/ n. f. cargo; load, burden; freight.

cargar /kar'gar/ v. carry; load; charge.

cargo /'kargo/ n. m. load; charge, office.

caricatura /karika'tura/ n. f caricature; cartoon.

caricaturista /karikatu'rista/ n. m. & f. caricaturist; cartoonist.

caricia /ka'riθia; ka'risia/ n. f. caress.

caridad /kari'ðað/ n. f. charity.

cariño /ka'riɲo/ n. m. affection, fondness.

cariñoso /kari'ɲoso/ a. affectionate, fond.

carisma /ka'risma/ n. m. charisma.

caritativo /karita'tiβo/ a. charitable.

carmesí /karme'si/ a. & m. crimson.

carnaval /karna'βal/ n. m. carnival.

carne /'karne/ n. f. meat, flesh; pulp.

carne acecinada /'karne aθeθi'naða; 'karne asesi'naða/ n. f. corned beef.

carnero /kar'nero/ n. m. ram; mutton.

carnicería /karniθe'ria; karnise'ria/ n. f. meat market; massacre.

carnicero /karni'θero; karni'sero/ **-ra** n. butcher.

carnívoro /kar'niβoro/ a. carnivorous.

caro /'karo/ a. dear, costly, expensive.

carpa /'karpa/ n. f. tent.

carpeta /kar'peta/ n. f. folder; briefcase.

carpintero /karpin'tero/ n. m. carpenter.

carrera /ka'rrera/ n. f. race; career.

carrera de caballos /ka'rrera de ka'βaʎos; ka'rrera de ka'βayos/ horse race.

carreta /ka'rreta/ n. f. wagon, cart.

carrete /ka'rrete/ n. m. reel, spool.

carretera /karre'tera/ n. f. road, highway.

carril /ka'rril/ n. m. rail.

carrillo /ka'rriʎo; ka'rriyo/ n. m. cart (for baggage or shopping).

carro /'karro/ n. m. car, automobile; cart.

carroza /ka'rroθa; ka'rrosa/ n. f. chariot.

carruaje /ka'rruahe/ n. m. carriage.

carta /'karta/ n. f. letter; (pl.) cards.

cartel /kar'tel/ n. m. placard, poster; cartel.

cartelera /karte'lera/ n. f. billboard.

cartera /kar'tera/ n. f. pocketbook, handbag, wallet; portfolio.

cartero /kar'tero/ **(-ra)** n. mail carrier.

cartón /kar'ton/ n. m. cardboard.

cartón piedra /kar'ton 'pieðra/ n. m. papier-mâché.

cartucho /kar'tutʃo/ n. m. cartridge; cassette.

casa /'kasa/ n. f. house, dwelling; home.

casaca /ka'saka/ n. f. dress coat.

casa de pisos /'kasa de 'pisos/ apartment house.

casado /ka'saðo/ a. married.

casamiento /kasa'miento/ n. m. marriage.

casar /ka'sar/ v. marry, marry off.

casarse /ka'sarse/ v. get married. **c. con**, marry.

cascabel /kaska'βel/ n. m. jingle bell.

cascada /kas'kaða/ n. f. waterfall, cascade.

cascajo /kas'kaho/ n. m. gravel.

cascanueces /kaska'nueθes; kaska'nueses/ n. m. nutcracker.

cascar /kas'kar/ v. crack, break, burst.

cáscara /'kaskara/ n. f. shell, rind, husk.

casco /'kasko/ n. m. helmet; hull.

casera /ka'sera/ n. f. landlady; housekeeper.

caserío /kase'rio/ n. m. settlement.

casero /ka'sero/ a. **1.** homemade. —n. **2.** m. landlord, superintendent.

caseta /ka'seta/ n. f. cottage, hut.

casi /'kasi/ adv. almost, nearly.

casilla /ka'siʎa; ka'siya/ n. f. booth; ticket office; pigeonhole.

casimir /kasi'mir/ n. m. cashmere.

casino /ka'sino/ n. m. club; clubhouse.

caso /'kaso/ n. m. case. **hacer c. a**, pay attention to.

casorio /ka'sorio/ n. m. informal wedding.

caspa /'kaspa/ n. f. dandruff.

casta /'kasta/ n. f. caste.

castaña /kas'taɲa/ n. f. chestnut.

castaño /kas'taɲo/ a. **1.** brown. —n. **2.** m. chestnut tree.

castañuela /kasta'ɲuela/ n. f. castanet.

castellano /kaste'ʎano; kaste'yano/ -na a. & n. Castilian.

castidad /kasti'ðað/ n. f. chastity.

castigar /kasti'gar/ v. punish, castigate.

castigo /kas'tigo/ n. m. punishment.

castillo /kas'tiʎo; kas'tiyo/ n. m. castle.

castizo /kas'tiθo; kas'tiso/ a. pure, genuine; noble.

casto /'kasto/ a. chaste.

castor /kas'tor/ n. m. beaver.

casual /ka'sual/ adj. accidental, coincidental.

casualidad /kasuali'ðað/ n. f. coincidence. **por c.**, by chance.

casuca /ka'suka/ n. f. hut, shanty, hovel.

cataclismo /kata'klismo/ n. m. cataclysm.

catacumba /kata'kumba/ n. f. catacomb.

catadura /kata'ðura/ n. f. act of tasting; appearance.

catalán /kata'lan/ -na a. & n. Catalonian.

catálogo /ka'talogo/ n. m. catalogue. —**catalogar,** v.

catapulta /kata'pulta/ n. f. catapult.

catar /ka'tar/ v. taste; examine, try.

catarata /kata'rata/ n. f. cataract, waterfall.

catarro /ka'tarro/ n. m. head cold, catarrh.

catástrofe /ka'tastrofe/ n. f. catastrophe.

catecismo /kate'θismo; kate'sismo/ n. m. catechism.

cátedra /'kateðra/ n. f. professorship.

catedral /kate'ðral/ n. f. cathedral.

catedrático /kate'ðratiko/ -ca n. professor.

categoría /katego'ria/ n. f. category.

categórico /kate'goriko/ a. categorical.

catequismo /kate'kismo/ n. m. catechism.

catequizar /kateki'θar; kateki'sar/ v. catechize.

cátodo /'katoðo/ n. m. cathode.

catolicismo /katoli'θismo; katoli'sismo/ n. m. Catholicism.

católico /ka'toliko/ -ca a. & n. Catholic.

catorce /ka'torθe; ka'torse/ a. & pron. fourteen.

catre /'katre/ n. m. cot.

cauce /'kauθe; 'kause/ n. m. riverbed; ditch.

cauchal /kau't ʃal/ n. m. rubber plantation.

caucho /'kautʃo/ n. m. rubber.

caución /kau'θion; kau'sion/ n. f. precaution; security, guarantee.

caudal /kau'ðal/ n. m. means, fortune; (pl.) holdings.

caudaloso /kauða'loso/ a. prosperous, rich.

caudillaje /kauði'ʎahe; kauði'yahe/ n. m. leadership; tyranny.

caudillo /kau'ðiʎo; kau'ðiyo/ n. m. leader, chief.

causa /'kausa/ n. f. cause. —**causar,** v.

cautela /kau'tela/ n. f. caution.

cauteloso /kaute'loso/ n. m. cautious.

cautivar /kauti'βar/ v. captivate.

cautiverio /kauti'βerio/ n. m. captivity.

cautividad /kautiβi'ðað/ n. f. captivity.

cautivo /kau'tiβo/ -va a. & n. captive.

cauto /'kauto/ a. cautious.

cavar /ka'βar/ v. dig.

caverna /ka'βerna/ n. f. cavern, cave.

cavernoso /kaβer'noso/ a. cavernous.

cavidad /kaβi'ðað/ n. f. cavity, hollow.

cavilar /kaβi'lar/ v. criticize, cavil.

cayado /ka'yaðo/ n. m. shepherd's staff.

cayo /'kayo/ n. m. small rocky islet, key.

caza /'kaθa; 'kasa/ n. f. hunting, pursuit, game.

cazador /kaθa'ðor; kasa'ðor/ n. m. hunter.

cazar /ka'θar; ka'sar/ v. hunt.

cazatorpedero /kaθatorpe'ðero; kasatorpe-'ðero/ n. m. torpedo-boat, destroyer.

cazo /'kaθo; 'kaso/ n. m. ladle, dipper; pot.

cazuela /ka'θuela; ka'suela/ n. f. crock.

cebada /θe'βaða; se'βaða/ n. f. barley.

cebiche /θe'bitʃe/ n. m. dish of marinated raw fish.

cebo /'θeβo; 'seβo/ n. m. bait. —**cebar,** v.

cebolla /θe'βoʎa; se'βoya/ n. f. onion.

cebolleta /θeβo'ʎeta; seβo'yeta/ n. f. spring onion.

ceceo /θe'θeo; se'seo/ n. m. lisp. —**cecear,** v.

cecina /θe'θina; se'sina/ n. f. dried beef.

cedazo /θe'ðaθo; se'ðaso/ n. m. sieve, sifter.

ceder /θe'ðer; se'ðer/ v. cede; transfer; yield.

cedro /'θeðro; 'seðro/ n. m. cedar.

cédula /'θeðula; 'seðula/ n. f. decree. **c. personal,** identification card.

céfiro /'θefiro; 'sefiro/ n. m. zephyr.

cegar /θe'gar; se'gar/ v. blind.

ceguedad /θege'ðað, θe'gera; sege'ðað, se-'gera/ **ceguera** n. f. blindness.

ceja /'θeha; 'seha/ n. f. eyebrow.

cejar /θe'har; se'har/ v. go backwards; yield, retreat.

celada /θe'laða; se'laða/ n. f. trap; ambush.

celaje /θe'lahe; se'lahe/ n. m. appearance of the sky.

celar /θe'lar; se'lar/ v. watch carefully, guard.

celda /'θelda; 'selda/ n. f. cell.

celebración /θeleβra'θion; seleβra'sion/ n. f. celebration.

celebrante /θele'βrante; sele'βrante/ n. m. officiating priest.

celebrar /θele'βrar; sele'βrar/ v. celebrate, observe.

célebre /'θeleβre; 'seleβre/ a. celebrated, noted, famous.

celebridad /θeleβri'ðað; seleβri'ðað/ n. f. fame; celebrity; pageant.

celeridad /θeleri'ðað; seleri'ðað/ n. f. speed, rapidity.

celeste /θe'leste; se'leste/ a. celestial.

celestial /θeles'tial; seles'tial/ a. heavenly.

celibato /θeli'βato; seli'βato/ n. m. celibacy.

célibe /'θeliβe; 'seliβe/ a. **1.** unmarried. —n. **2.** m. & f. unmarried person.

celista /θe'lista; se'lista/ n. m. & f. cellist.

cellisca /θe'ʎiska; se'yiska/ n. f. sleet. —**cellisquear,** v.

celo /'θelo; 'selo/ n. m. zeal; (pl.) jealousy.

celofán /θelo'fan; selo'fan/ n. m. cellophane.

celosía /θelo'sia; selo'sia/ n. f. Venetian blind.

celoso /θe'loso; se'loso/ a. jealous; zealous.

céltico /'θeltiko; 'seltiko/ a. Celtic.

célula /'θelula; 'selula/ n. f. Biol. cell.

celuloide /θelu'loiðe; selu'loiðe/ n. m. celluloid.

cementar /θemen'tar; semen'tar/ v. cement.

cementerio /θemen'terio; semen'terio/ n. m. cemetery.

cemento /θe'mento; se'mento/ n. m. cement.

cena /'θena; 'sena/ n. f. supper.

cenagal /θena'gal; sena'gal/ n. m. swamp, marsh.

cenagoso /θena'goso; sena'goso/ a. swampy, marshy, muddy.

cenar /θe'nar; se'nar/ v. dine, eat.

cencerro /θen'θerro; sen'serro/ n. m. cowbell.

cendal /θen'dal; sen'dal/ n. m. thin, light cloth; gauze.

cenicero /θeni'θero; seni'sero/ n. m. ashtray.

ceniciento /θeni'θiento; seni'siento/ a. ashen.

cenit /θe'nit; 'senit/ n. m. zenith.

ceniza /θe'niθa; se'nisa/ n. f. ash, ashes.

censo /'θenso; 'senso/ n. m. census.

censor /θen'sor; sen'sor/ n. m. censor.

censura /θen'sura; sen'sura/ n. f. reproof, censure; censorship.

censurable /θensu'raβle; sensu'raβle/ a. objectionable.

censurar /θensu'rar; sensu'rar/ v. censure, criticize.

centavo /θen'taβo; sen'taβo/ n. m. cent.

centella /θen'teʎa; sen'teya/ n. f. thunderbolt, lightning.

centellear /θenteʎe'ar; senteye'ar/ v. twinkle, sparkle.

centelleo /θente'ʎeo; sente'yeo/ n. m. sparkle.

centenar /θente'nar; sente'nar/ n. m. (a) hundred.

centenario /θente'nario; sente'nario/ n. m. centennial, centenary.

centeno /θen'teno; sen'teno/ n. m. rye.

centígrado /θen'tigraðo; sen'tigraðo/ a. centigrade.

centímetro /θenti'metro; senti'metro/ n. m. centimeter.

céntimo /'θentimo; 'sentimo/ n. m. cent.

centinela /θenti'nela; senti'nela/ n. m. sentry, guard.

central /θen'tral; sen'tral/ a. central.

centralita /θentra'lita; sentra'lita/ n. f. switchboard.

centralizar /θentrali'θar; sentrali'sar/ v. centralize.

centrar /θen'trar; sen'trar/ v. center.

céntrico /'θentriko; 'sentriko/ a. central.

centro /'θentro; 'sentro/ n. m. center.

centroamericano /θentroameri'kano; sentroameri'kano/ **-na** a & n. Central American.

centro de mesa /'θentro de 'mesa; 'sentro de 'mesa/ centerpiece.

ceñidor /θeɲi'ðor; seɲi'ðor/ n. m. belt, sash; girdle.

ceñir /θe'ɲir; se'ɲir/ v. gird.

ceño /'θeɲo; 'seɲo/ n. m. frown.

ceñudo /θe'ɲuðo; se'ɲuðo/ a. frowning, grim.

cepa /'θepa; 'sepa/ n. f stump.

cepillo /θe'piʎo; se'piyo/ n. m. brush; plane. —**cepillar,** v.

cera /'θera; 'sera/ n. f. wax.

cerámica /θe'ramika: se'ramika/ *n. m.* ceramics.

cerámico /θe'ramiko: se'ramiko/ *a.* ceramic.

cerca /'θerka: 'serka/ *adv.* 1. near. —*n.* 2. *f.* fence, hedge.

cercado /θer'kaðo: ser'kaðo/ *n. m.* enclosure; garden.

cercamiento /θerka'miento: serka'miento/ *n. m.* enclosure.

cercanía /θerka'nia: serka'nia/ *n. f.* proximity.

cercano /θer'kano: ser'kano/ *a.* near, nearby.

cercar /θer'kar: ser'kar/ *v.* surround.

cercenar /θerθe'nar: serse'nar/ *v.* clip; lessen, reduce.

cerciorar /θerθio'rar: sersio'rar/ *v.* make sure; affirm.

cerco /'θerko: 'serko/ *n. m.* hoop; siege.

cerda /'θerða: 'serða/ *n. f.* bristle.

cerdo /'θerðo: 'serðo/ **-da** *a.* hog.

cerdoso /θer'ðoso: ser'ðoso/ *a.* bristly.

cereal /θere'al: sere'al/ *a. & m.* cereal.

cerebro /θe'reβro: se'reβro/ *n. m.* brain.

ceremonia /θere'monia: sere'monia/ *n. f.* ceremony.

ceremonial /θeremo'nial: seremo'nial/ *a. & m.* ceremonial, ritual.

ceremonioso /θeremo'nioso: seremo'nioso/ *a.* ceremonious.

cereza /θe're θa: se'resa/ *n. f.* cherry.

cerilla /θe'riʎa: se'riya/ *n. f.*, **cerillo,** *m.* match.

cerner /θer'ner: ser'ner/ *v.* sift.

cero /'θero: 'sero/ *n. m.* zero.

cerrado /θe'rraðo: se'rraðo/ *a.* closed; cloudy; obscure; taciturn.

cerradura /θerra'ðura: serra'ðura/ *n. f.* lock.

cerrajero /θerra'hero: serra'hero/ *n. m.* locksmith.

cerrar /θe'rrar: se'rrar/ *v.* close, shut.

cerro /'θerro: 'serro/ *n. m.* hill.

cerrojo /θe'rroho: se'rroho/ *n. m.* latch, bolt.

certamen /θer'tamen: ser'tamen/ *n. m.* contest; competition.

certero /θer'tero: ser'tero/ *a.* accurate, exact; certain, sure.

certeza /θer'te θa: ser'tesa/ *n. f.* certainty.

certidumbre /θerti'ðumbre: serti'ðumbre/ *n. f.* certainty.

certificado /θertifi'kaðo: sertifi'kaðo/ *n. m.* certificate.

certificado de compra /θertifi'kaðo de 'kompra: sertifi'kaðo de 'kompra/ proof of purchase.

certificar /θertifi'kar: sertifi'kar/ *v.* certify; register (a letter).

cerúleo /θe'ruleo: se'ruleo/ *a.* cerulean, sky-blue.

cervecería /θerβeθe'ria: serβese'ria/ *n. f.* brewery; beer saloon.

cervecero /θerβe'θero: serβe'sero/ *n. m.* brewer.

cerveza /θer'βeθa: ser'βesa/ *n. f.* beer.

cesante /θe'sante: se'sante/ *a.* unemployed.

cesar /θe'sar: se'sar/ *v.* cease.

césped /'θespeð: 'sespeð/ *n. m.* sod, lawn.

cesta /'θesta: 'sesta/ *n. f.*, **cesto,** *m.* basket.

cetrino /θe'trino: se'trino/ *a.* yellow, lemon-colored.

cetro /'θetro: 'setro/ *n. m.* scepter.

chabacano /tʃaβa'kano/ *a.* vulgar.

chacal /tʃa'kal/ *n. m.* jackal.

chacó /tʃa'ko/ *n. m.* shako.

chacona /tʃa'kona/ *n. f.* chaconne.

chacota /tʃa'kota/ *n. f.* fun, mirth.

chacotear /tʃakote'ar/ *v.* joke.

chacra /'tʃakra/ *n. f.* small farm.

chafallar /tʃafa'ʎar: tʃafa'yar/ *v.* mend badly.

chagra /'tʃagra/ *n. m.* rustic; rural person.

chal /tʃal/ *n. m.* shawl.

chalán /tʃa'lan/ *n. m.* horse trader.

chaleco /tʃa'leko/ *n. m.* vest.

chaleco salvavidas /tʃa'leko salβa'βiðas/ life jacket.

chalet /tʃa'le: tʃa'let/ *n. m.* chalet.

challí /tʃa'ʎi: tʃa'yi/ *n. m.* challis.

chamada /tʃa'maða/ *n. f.* brushwood.

chamarillero /tʃamari'ʎero: tʃamari'yero/ *n. m.* gambler.

chamarra /tʃa'marra/ *n. f.* coarse linen jacket.

chambelán /tʃambe'lan/ *n. m.* chamberlain.

champaña /tʃam'paɲa/ *n. m.* champagne.

champú /tʃam'pu/ *n. m.* shampoo.

chamuscar /tʃamus'kar/ *v.* scorch.

chancaco /tʃan'kako/ *a.* brown.

chance /'tʃanθe/ *n. m. & f.* opportunity, break.

chancear /tʃanθe'ar/ *v.* jest, joke.

chanciller /tʃanθi'ʎer: tʃansi'yer/ *n. m.* chancellor.

chancillería /tʃanθiʎe'ria: tʃansiye'ria/ *n. f.* chancery.

chancla /'tʃankla/ *n. f.* old shoe.

chancleta /tʃan'kleta/ *n. f.* slipper.

chanclos /'tʃanklos/ *n. m. pl.* galoshes.

chancro /'tʃankro/ *n. m.* chancre.

changador /tʃaŋga'ðor/ *n. m.* porter; handyman.

chantaje /tʃan'tahe/ *n. m.* blackmail.

chantajista /tʃanta'hista/ *n. m. & f.* blackmailer.

chantejear /tʃantehe'ar/ *v.* blackmail.

chanto /'tʃanto/ *n. m.* flagstone.

chantre /'tʃantre/ *n. m.* precentor.

chanza /'tʃanθa; 'tʃansa/ n. f. joke, jest. —chancear, v.

chanzoneta /tʃanθo'neta; tʃanso'neta/ n. f. chansonnette.

chapa /'tʃapa/ n. f. (metal) sheet, plate; lock.

chapado en oro /tʃa'paðo en 'oro/ a. gold-plated.

chapado en plata /tʃa'paðo en 'plata/ a. silver-plated.

chaparrada /tʃapa'rraða/ n. f. downpour.

chaparral /tʃapa'rral/ n. m. chaparral.

chaparreras /tʃapa'rreras/ n. f.pl. chaps.

chaparrón /tʃapa'rron/ n. m. downpour.

chapear /tʃape'ar/ v. veneer.

chapeo /tʃa'peo/ n. m. hat.

chapero /tʃa'pero/ n. m. Colloq. male homosexual prostitute.

chapitel /tʃapi'tel/ n. m. spire, steeple; (architecture) capital.

chapodar /tʃapo'ðar/ v. lop.

chapón /tʃa'pon/ n. m. inkblot.

chapotear /tʃapote'ar/ v. paddle or splash in the water.

chapoteo /tʃapo'teo/ n. m. splash.

chapucear /tʃapuθe'ar; tʃapuse'ar/ v. fumble, bungle.

chapucero /tʃapu'θero; tʃapu'sero/ a. sloppy, bungling.

chapurrear /tʃapurre'ar/ v. speak (a language) brokenly.

chapuz /tʃa'puθ; tʃa'pus/ n. m. dive; ducking.

chapuzar /tʃapu'θar; tʃapu'sar/ v. dive; duck.

chaqueta /tʃa'keta/ n. f. jacket, coat.

chaqueta deportiva /tʃa'keta depor'tiβa/ sport jacket.

charada /tʃa'raða/ n. f. charade.

charamusca /tʃara'muska/ n. f. twisted candy stick.

charanga /tʃa'ranga/ n. f. military band.

charanguero /tʃaraŋ'guero/ n. m. peddler.

charca /'tʃarka/ n. f. pool, pond.

charco /'tʃarko/ n. m. pool, puddle.

charla /'tʃarla/ n. f. chat; chatter, prattle. —charlar, v.

charladuría /tʃarlaðu'ria/ n. f. chatter.

charlatán /tʃarla'tan/ -ana n. charlatan.

charlatanismo /tʃarlata'nismo/ n. m. charlatanism.

charol /tʃa'rol/ n. m. varnish.

charolar /tʃaro'lar/ v. varnish; polish.

charquear /tʃarke'ar/ v. jerk (beef).

charquí /tʃar'ki/ n. m. jerked beef.

charrán /tʃa'rran/ a. roguish.

chascarillo /tʃaska'riʎo; tʃaska'riyo/ n. risqué story.

chasco /'tʃasko/ n. m. disappointment, blow; practical joke.

chasis /'tʃasis/ n. m. chassis.

chasquear /tʃaske'ar/ v. fool, trick; disappoint; crack (a whip).

chasquido /tʃas'kiðo/ n. m. crack (sound).

chata /'tʃata/ n. f. bedpan.

chatear /tʃate'ar/ v. chat (on the Internet).

chato /'tʃato/ a. flat-nosed, pug-nosed.

chauvinismo /tʃauβi'nismo/ n. m. chauvinism.

chauvinista /tʃauβi'nista/ n. & a. chauvinist.

chelín /tʃe'lin/ n. m. shilling.

cheque /'tʃeke/ n. m. (bank) check.

chica /'tʃika/ n. f. girl.

chicana /tʃi'kana/ n. f. chicanery.

chicha /'tʃitʃa/ n. f. an alcoholic drink.

chícharo /'tʃitʃaro/ n. f. pea.

chicharra /tʃi'tʃarra/ n. f. cicada; talkative person.

chicharrón /tʃitʃa'rron/ n. m. crisp fried scrap of meat.

chichear /tʃitʃe'ar/ v. hiss in disapproval.

chichón /tʃi'tʃon/ n. m. bump, bruise, lump.

chicle /'tʃikle/ n. m. chewing gum.

chico /'tʃiko/ a. **1.** little. —n. **2.** m. boy.

chicote /tʃi'kote/ n. m. cigar; cigar butt.

chicotear /tʃikote'ar/ v. whip, flog.

chifladura /tʃifla'ðura/ n. f. mania; whim; jest.

chiflar /tʃi'flar/ v. whistle; become insane.

chiflido /tʃi'fliðo/ n. m. shrill whistle.

chile /'tʃile/ n. m. chili.

chileno /tʃi'leno/ -na a. & n. Chilean.

chillido /tʃi'ʎiðo; tʃi'yiðo/ n. m. shriek, scream, screech. —chillar, v.

chillón /tʃi'ʎon; tʃi'yon/ a. shrill.

chimenea /tʃime'nea/ n. f. chimney, smokestack; fireplace.

china /'tʃina/ n. f. pebble; maid; Chinese woman.

chinarro /tʃi'narro/ n. m. large pebble, stone.

chinche /'tʃintʃe/ n. f. bedbug; thumbtack.

chincheta /tʃin'tʃeta/ n. f. thumbtack.

chinchilla /tʃin'tʃiʎa; tʃin'tʃiya/ n. f. chinchilla.

chinchorro /tʃin'tʃorro/ n. m. fishing net.

chinela /tʃi'nela/ n. f. slipper.

chinero /tʃi'nero/ n. m. china closet.

chino /'tʃino/ -na a. & n. Chinese.

chipirón /tʃipi'ron/ n. m. baby squid.

chiquero /tʃi'kero/ n. m. pen for pigs, goats, etc.

chiquito /tʃi'kito/ -ta a. **1.** small, tiny. —n. **2.** m. & f. small child.

chiribitil /tʃiriβi'til/ n. m. small room, den.

chirimía /tʃiri'mia/ n. f. flageolet.

chiripa /tʃi'ripa/ n. f. stroke of good luck.

chirla /'tʃirla/ n. f. mussel.

chirle /'tʃirle/ a. insipid.

chirona /tʃi'ronə/ n. f. prison, jail.

chirrido /tʃi'rriðo/ n. m. squeak, chirp. —**chirriar**, v.

chis /tʃis/ interj. hush!

chisgarabís /tʃisgara'βis/ n. meddler; unimportant person.

chisguete /tʃis'gete/ n. m. squirt, splash.

chisme /'tʃisme/ n. m. gossip. —**chismear**, v.

chismero /tʃis'mero/ -**ra** n. gossiper.

chismoso /tʃis'moso/ adj. gossiping.

chispa /'tʃispa/ n. f. spark.

chispeante /tʃispe'ante/ a. sparkling.

chispear /tʃispe'ar/ v. sparkle.

chisporrotear /tʃisporrote'ar/ v emit sparks.

chistar /tʃis'tar/ v. speak.

chiste /'tʃiste/ n. m. joke; witty saying.

chistera /tʃis'tera/ n. f. fish basket; top hat.

chistoso /tʃis'toso/ a. funny, comic, amusing.

chito /'tʃito/ interj. hush!

chiva /'tʃiβa/ n. f. female goat.

chivato /tʃi'βato/ n. m. kid, young goat.

chivo /'tʃiβo/ n. m. male goat.

chocante /tʃo'kante/ a. striking; shocking; unpleasant.

chocar /tʃo'kar/ v. collide, crash; shock.

chocarrear /tʃokarre'ar/ v. joke, jest.

chochear /tʃotʃe'ar/ v. be in one's dotage.

chochera /tʃo'tʃera/ n. f. dotage, senility.

choclo /'tʃoklo/ n. m. clog; overshoe; ear of corn.

chocolate /tʃoko'late/ n. m. chocolate.

chocolate con leche /tʃoko'late kon 'letʃe/ milk chocolate.

chocolatería /tʃokolate'ria/ n. f. chocolate shop.

chofer /'tʃofer/ **chófer** n. m. chauffeur, driver.

chofeta /tʃo'feta/ n. f. chafing dish.

cholo /'tʃolo/ n. m. half-breed.

chopo /'tʃopo/ n. m. black poplar.

choque /'tʃoke/ n. m. collision, clash, crash; shock.

chorizo /tʃo'riθo; tʃo'riso/ n. m. sausage.

chorrear /tʃorre'ar/ v. spout; drip.

chorro /'tʃorro/ n. m. spout; spurt, jet. **llover a chorros**, to pour (rain).

choto /'tʃoto/ n. m. calf, kid.

choza /'tʃoθa; 'tʃosa/ n. f. hut, cabin.

chozno /'tʃoθno; 'tʃosno/ -**na** n. great-great-great-grandchild.

chubasco /tʃu'βasko/ n. m. shower, squall.

chubascoso /tʃuβas'koso/ a. squally.

chuchería /tʃutʃe'ria/ n. f. trinket, knick-knack.

chucho /'tʃutʃo/ n. m. Colloq. mutt.

chulería /tʃule'ria/ n. f. pleasant manner.

chuleta /tʃu'leta/ n. f. chop, cutlet.

chulo /'tʃulo/ n. m. rascal, rogue; joker.

chupa /'tʃupa/ n. f. jacket.

chupada /tʃu'paða/ n. f. suck, sip.

chupado /tʃu'paðo/ a. very thin.

chupaflor /tʃupa'flor/ n. m. hummingbird.

chupar /tʃu'par/ v. suck.

churrasco /tʃu'rrasko/ n. m. roasted meat.

churros /'tʃuros/ n. m.pl. long, slender fritters.

chuscada /tʃus'kaða/ n. f. joke, jest.

chusco /'tʃusko/ a. funny, humorous.

chusma /'tʃusma/ n. f. mob, rabble.

chuzo /'tʃuθo; 'tʃuso/ n. m. pike.

CI, abbr. **(coeficiente intelectual)** IQ (intelligence quotient).

ciberespacio /θiβeres'paθio/ n. m. cyberspace.

cibernauta /θiβer'nauta/ n. m. & f. cybernaut.

cicatero /θika'tero; sika'tero/ a. stingy.

cicatriz /θika'triθ; sika'tris/ n. f. scar.

cicatrizar /θikatri'θar; sikatri'sar/ v. heal.

ciclamato /θi'klamato; si'klamato/ n. m. cyclamate.

ciclista /θi'klista; si'klista/ n. m & f. cyclist.

ciclo /'θiklo; 'siklo/ n. m. cycle.

ciclón /θi'klon; si'klon/ n. m. cyclone.

ciego /'θiego; 'siego/ -**ga** a. **1.** blind. —n. **2.** blind person.

cielo /'θielo; 'sielo/ n. m. heaven; sky, heavens; ceiling.

ciempiés /θiem'pies; siem'pies/ n. m. centipede.

cien /θien; sien/ **ciento** a. & pron. hundred. **por c.,** per cent.

ciénaga /'θienaga; 'sienaga/ n. f. swamp, marsh.

ciencia /'θienθia; 'siensia/ n. f. science.

cieno /'θieno; 'sieno/ n. m. mud.

científico /θien'tifiko; sien'tifiko/ -**ca** a. **1.** scientific. —n. **2.** scientist.

cierre /'θierre; 'sierre/ n. m. fastener, snap, clasp.

cierto /'θierto; 'sierto/ a. certain, sure, true.

ciervo /'θierβo; 'sierβo/ n. m. deer.

cierzo /'θierθo; 'sierso/ n. m. northerly wind.

cifra /'θifra; 'sifra/ n. f. cipher, number. —**cifrar**, v.

cigarra /θi'garra; si'garra/ n. f. locust.

cigarrera /θiga'rrera; siga'rrera/ **cigarrillera** f. cigarette case.

cigarrillo /θiga'rriʎo; siga'rriyo/ n. m. cigarette.

cigarro /θi'garro; si'garro/ n. m. cigar; cigarette.

cigüeña /θi'gueɲa; si'gueɲa/ n. f. stork.

cilíndrico /θi'lindriko; si'lindriko/ a. cylindrical.

cilindro /θi'lindro; si'lindro/ n. m. cylinder.

cima /'θima; 'sima/ *n. f.* summit, peak.

cimarrón /θima'rron; sima'rron/ *a.* **1.** wild, untamed. —*n.* **2.** runaway slave.

címbalo /'θimbalo; 'simbalo/ *n. m.* cymbal.

cimbrar /θim'βrar, θimbre'ar; sim'βrar, simbre'ar/ *v.* shake, brandish.

cimientos /θi'mientos; si'mientos/ *n. m.pl.* foundation.

cinc /θink; sink/ *n. m.* zinc.

cincel /θin'θel; sin'sel/ *n. m.* chisel. —**cincelar,** *v.*

cincha /'θintʃa; 'sintʃa/ *n. f.* (harness) cinch. —**cinchar,** *v.*

cinco /'θinko; 'sinko/ *a.* & *pron.* five.

cincuenta /θin'kuenta; sin'kuenta/ *a.* & *pron.* fifty.

cine /'θine; 'sine/ *n. m.* movies; movie theater.

cíngulo /'θiŋgulo; 'siŋgulo/ *n. m.* cingulum.

cínico /'θiniko; 'siniko/ **-ca** *a.* & *n.* cynical; cynic.

cinismo /θi'nismo; si'nismo/ *n. m.* cynicism.

cinta /'θinta; 'sinta/ *n. f.* ribbon, tape; (movie) film.

cintilar /θinti'lar; sinti'lar/ *v.* glitter, sparkle.

cinto /'θinto; 'sinto/ *n. m.* belt; girdle.

cintura /θin'tura; sin'tura/ *n. f.* waist.

cinturón /θintu'ron; sintu'ron/ *n. m.* belt.

cinturón de seguridad /θintu'ron de seguri'ðað; sintu'ron de seguri'ðað/ safety belt.

ciprés /θi'pres; si'pres/ *n. m.* cypress.

circo /'θirko; 'sirko/ *n. m.* circus.

circuito /θir'kuito; sir'kuito/ *n. m.* circuit.

circulación /θirkula'θion; sirkula'sion/ *n. f.* circulation.

circular /θirku'lar; sirku'lar/ *a.* & *m.* **1.** circular. —*v.* **2.** circulate.

círculo /'θirkulo; 'sirkulo/ *n. m.* circle, club.

circundante /θirkun'dante; sirkun'dante/ *a.* surrounding.

circundar /θirkun'dar; sirkun'dar/ *v.* encircle, surround.

circunferencia /θirkunfe'renθia; sirkunfe'rensia/ *n. f.* circumference.

circunlocución /θirkunloku'θion; sirkunloku'sion/ *n.* circumlocution.

circunscribir /θirkunskri'βir; sirkunskri'βir/ *v.* circumscribe.

circunspección /θirkunspek'θion; sirkunspek'sion/ *n.* decorum, propriety.

circunspecto /θirkuns'pekto; sirkuns'pekto/ *a.* circumspect.

circunstancia /θirkuns'tanθia; sirkuns'tansia/ *n. f.* circumstance.

circunstante /θirkuns'tante; sirkuns'tante/ *n. m.* bystander.

circunvecino /θirkumbe'θino; sirkumbe'sino/ *a.* neighboring, adjacent.

cirio /'θirio; 'sirio/ *n. m.* candle.

cirrosis /θi'rrosis; si'rrosis/ *n. f.* cirrhosis.

ciruela /θi'ruela; si'ruela/ *n. f.* plum; prune.

cirugía /θiru'hia; siru'hia/ *n. f.* surgery.

cirujano /θiru'hano; siru'hano/ *n. m.* surgeon.

cisne /'θisne; 'sisne/ *n. m.* swan.

cisterna /θis'terna; sis'terna/ *n. f.* cistern.

cita /'θita; 'sita/ *n. f.* citation; appointment, date.

citación /θita'θion; sita'sion/ *n. f.* citation; (legal) summons.

citar /θi'tar; si'tar/ *v.* cite, quote; summon; make an appointment with.

cítrico /'θitriko; 'sitriko/ *a.* citric.

ciudad /θiu'ðað; siu'ðað/ *n. f.* city.

ciudadanía /θiuðaða'nia; siuðaða'nia/ *n. f.* citizenship.

ciudadano /θiuða'ðano; siuða'ðano/ **-na** *n.* citizen.

ciudadela /θiuða'ðela; siuða'ðela/ *n. f.* fortress, citadel.

cívico /'θiβiko; 'siβiko/ *a.* civic.

civil /θi'βil; si'βil/ *a.* & *n.* civil; civilian.

civilidad /θiβili'ðað; siβili'ðað/ *n. f.* politeness, civility.

civilización /θiβiliθa'θion; siβilisa'sion/ *n. f.* civilization.

civilizador /θiβiliθa'ðor; siβilisa'ðor/ *a.* civilizing.

civilizar /θiβili'θar; siβili'sar/ *v.* civilize.

cizallas /θi'θaʎas; si'sayas/ *n. f.pl.* shears. —**cizallar,** *v.*

cizaña /θi'θaɲa; si'saɲa/ *n. f.* weed; vice.

clamar /kla'mar/ *v.* clamor.

clamor /kla'mor/ *n. m.* clamor.

clamoreo /klamo'reo/ *n. m.* persistent clamor.

clamoroso /klamo'roso/ *a.* clamorous.

clandestino /klandes'tino/ *a.* secret, clandestine.

clara /'klara/ *n. f.* white (of egg).

claraboya /klara'βoya/ *n. m.* skylight; bull's-eye.

clara de huevo /'klara de 'ueβo/ egg white.

clarear /klare'ar/ *v.* clarify; become light, dawn.

clarete /kla'rete/ *n. m.* claret.

claridad /klari'ðað/ *n. f.* clarity.

clarificar /klarifi'kar/ *v.* clarify.

clarín /kla'rin/ *n. m.* bugle, trumpet.

clarinete /klari'nete/ *n. m.* clarinet.

clarividencia /klariβi'ðenθia; klariβi'ðensia/ *n. f.* clairvoyance.

clarividente /klariβi'ðente/ *a.* clairvoyant.

claro /'klaro/ *a.* clear; bright; light (in color); of course.

clase /'klase/ *n. f.* class; classroom; kind, sort.

clase nocturna /'klase nok'turna/ evening class.

clásico /'klasiko/ *a.* classic, classical.

clasificar /klasifi'kar/ v. classify, rank.

claustro /'klaustro/ n. m. cloister.

claustrofobia /klaustro'foβia/ n. f. claustrophobia.

cláusula /'klausula/ n. f. clause.

clausura /klau'sura/ n. f. cloister; inner sanctum; closing.

clavado /kla'βaðo/ a. 1. nailed. —n. 2. m. & f. dive.

clavar /kla'βar/ v. nail, peg, pin.

clave /'klaβe/ n. f. code; Mus. key.

clavel /kla'βel/ n. m. carnation.

clavetear /klaβete'ar/ v. nail.

clavícula /kla'βikula/ n. f. collarbone.

clavija /kla'βiha/ n. f. pin, peg.

clavo /'klaβo/ n. m. nail, spike; clove.

clemencia /ʌ:le menθia/ kle'mensia/ n. f. clemency.

clemente /kle'mente/ a. merciful.

clementina /klemen'tina/ n. f. tangerine.

clerecía /klere'θia/ klere'sia/ n. f. clergy.

clerical /kleri'kal/ a. clerical.

clérigo /'klerigo/ n. m. clergyman.

clero /'klero/ n. m. clergy.

cliente /'kliente/ n. m. & f. customer, client.

clientela /klien'tela/ n. f. clientele, practice.

clima /'klima/ n. m. climate.

clímax /'klimaks/ n. m. climax.

clínca de reposo /'klinka de rre'poso/ convalescent home.

clínica /'klinika/ n. f. clinic.

clínico /'kliniko/ a. clinical.

clíper /'kliper/ n. m. clipper ship.

cloaca /klo'aka/ n. f. sewer.

cloquear /kloke'ar/ v. cluck, cackle.

cloqueo /klo'keo/ n. m. cluck.

cloro /'kloro/ n. m. chlorine.

club /kluβ/ n. m. club, association.

club juvenil /kluβ huβe'nil/ youth club.

clueca /'klueka/ n. f. brooding hen.

coacción /koak'θion/ koak'sion/ n. compulsion.

coagular /koagu'lar/ v. coagulate, clot.

coágulo /ko'agulo/ n. m. clot.

coalición /koali'θion/ koali'sion/ n. f. coalition.

coartada /koar'taða/ n. f. alibi.

coartar /koar'tar/ v. limit.

cobarde /ko'βarðe/ a. & n. cowardly; coward.

cobardía /koβar'ðia/ n. f. cowardice.

cobayo /ko'βayo/ n. m guinea pig.

cobertizo /koβer'tiθo/ koβer'tiso/ n. m. shed.

cobertor /koβer'tor/ n. m., cobija, f. blanket.

cobertura /koβer'tura/ n. f. cover, wrapping.

cobijar /koβi'har/ v. cover; protect.

cobrador /koβra'ðor/ n. m. collector.

cobranza /ko'βranθa/ ko'βransa/ n. f. collection or recovery of money.

cobrar /ko'βrar/ v. collect; charge; cash.

cobre /'koβre/ n. m. copper.

cobrizo /ko'βriθo/ ko'βriso/ a. coppery.

cobro /'koβro/ n. m. collection or recovery of money.

coca /'koka/ n. f. coca leaves.

cocaína /koka'ina/ n. f. cocaine.

cocal /ko'kal/ n. m. coconut plantation.

cocear /koθe'ar/ kose'ar/ v. kick; resist.

cocer /ko'θer/ ko'ser/ v. cook, boil, bake.

coche /'kotʃe/ n. m. coach; car, automobile.

cochecito de niño /kotʃe'θito de 'niɲo/ kotʃe'sito de 'niɲo/ baby carriage.

coche de choque /'kotʃe de 'tʃoke/ dodgem.

cochera /ko'tʃera/ n. f. garage.

cochero /ko'tʃero/ n. m. coachman; cab driver.

cochinada /kotʃi'naða/ n. f. filth; herd of swine.

cochino /ko'tʃino/ n. m. pig, swine.

cocido /ko'θiðo/ ko'siðo/ n. m. stew.

cociente /ko'θiente/ ko'siente/ n. m. quotient.

cocimiento /koθi'miento/ kosi'miento/ n. m. cooking.

cocina /ko'θina/ ko'sina/ n. f. kitchen.

cocinar /koθi'nar/ kosi'nar/ v. cook.

cocinero /koθi'nero/ kosi'nero/ -ra n. cook.

coco /'koko/ n. m. coconut; coconut tree.

cocodrilo /koko'ðrilo/ n. m. crocodile.

cóctel /kok'tel/ n. m. cocktail.

codazo /ko'ðaθo/ ko'ðaso/ n. m. nudge with the elbow.

codicia /ko'ðiθia/ ko'ðisia/ n. f. avarice, greed; lust.

codiciar /koðiθi'ar/ koðisi'ar/ v. covet.

codicioso /koðiθi'oso/ koðisi'oso/ a. covetous; greedy.

código /'koðigo/ n. m. (law) code.

codo /'koðo/ n. m. elbow.

codorniz /koðor'niθ/ koðor'nis/ n. f. quail.

coeficiente /koefi'θiente/ koefi'siente/ n. m. quotient.

coeficiente intelectual /koefi'θiente intelek'tual/ koefi'siente intelek'tual/ intelligence quotient.

coetáneo /koe'taneo/ a. contemporary.

coexistir /koeksis'tir/ v. coexist.

cofrade /ko'fraðe/ n. m. fellow member of a club, etc.

cofre /'kofre/ n. m. coffer; chest; trunk.

coger /ko'her/ v. catch; pick; take.

cogote /ko'gote/ n. m. nape.

cohecho /ko'etʃo/ n. m. bribe. —cohechar, v.

coheredero /koere'ðero/ **-ra** n. coheir.
coherente /koe'rente/ a. coherent.
cohesión /koe'sion/ n. f. cohesion.
cohete /ko'ete/ n. m. firecracker; rocket.
cohibición /koiβi'θion; koiβi'sion/ n. restraint; repression.
cohibir /koi'βir/ v. restrain; repress.
coincidencia /koinθi'ðenθia; koinsi'ðensia/ n. f. coincidence.
coincidir /koinθi'ðir; koinsi'ðir/ v. coincide.
cojear /kohe'ar/ v. limp.
cojera /ko'hera/ n. m. limp.
cojín /ko'hin/ n. m. cushion.
cojinete /kohi'nete/ n. m. small cushion, pad.
cojo /'koho/ **-a** a. **1.** lame. —n **2.** lame person.
col /kol/ n. f. cabbage.
cola /'kola/ n. f. tail; glue; line, queue. **hacer c.,** stand in line.
colaboración /kolaβora'θion; kolaβora'sion/ n. f. collaboration.
colaborar /kolaβo'rar/ v. collaborate.
cola de caballo /'kola de ka'βaʎo; 'kola de ka'βaʝo/ ponytail.
coladera /kola'ðera/ n. f. strainer.
colador /kola'ðor/ n. m. colander, strainer.
colapso /ko'lapso/ n. m. collapse, prostration.
colar /ko'lar/ v. strain; drain.
colateral /kolate'ral/ a. collateral.
colcha /'koltʃa/ n. f. bedspread, quilt.
colchón /kol'tʃon/ n. m. mattress.
colear /kole'ar/ v. wag the tail.
colección /kolek'θion; kolek'sion/ n. f. collection, set.
coleccionar /kolekθio'nar; koleksio'nar/ v. collect.
colecta /ko'lekta/ n. f. collection; collect (a prayer).
colectivo /kolek'tiβo/ a. collective.
colector /kolek'tor/ n. m. collector.
colega /ko'lega/ n. m. & f. colleague.
colegial /kole'hial/ n. m. college student.
colegiatura /kolehia'tura/ n. f. scholarship; tuition.
colegio /ko'lehio/ n. m. (private) school, college.
colegir /kole'hir/ v. infer, deduce.
cólera /'kolera/ n. **1.** f. rage, wrath. **2.** m. cholera.
colérico /ko'leriko/ adj. angry, irritated.
colesterol /koleste'rol/ n. m. cholesterol.
coleta /ko'leta/ n. f. pigtail; postscript.
coleto /ko'leto/ n. m. leather jacket.
colgado /kol'gaðo/ **-da** n. **1.** crazy person. —a. **2.** hanging, pending.
colgador /kolga'ðor/ n. m. rack, hanger.
colgaduras /kolga'ðuras/ n. f.pl. drapery.
colgante /kol'gante/ a. hanging.

colgar /kol'gar/ v. hang up, suspend.
colibrí /koli'βri/ n. m. hummingbird.
coliflor /koli'flor/ n. f. cauliflower.
coligarse /koli'garse/ v. band together, unite.
colilla /ko'liʎa; ko'liya/ n. f. butt of a cigar or cigarette.
colina /ko'lina/ n. f. hill, hillock.
colinabo /koli'naβo/ n. m. turnip.
colindante /kolin'dante/ a. neighboring, adjacent.
colindar /kolin'dar/ v. neighbor, abut.
coliseo /koli'seo/ n. m. theater; coliseum.
colisión /koli'sion/ n. f. collision.
collado /ko'ʎaðo; ko'yaðo/ n. m. hillock.
collar /ko'ʎar; ko'yar/ n. m. necklace; collar.
colmar /kol'mar/ v. heap up, fill liberally.
colmena /kol'mena/ n. f. hive.
colmillo /kol'miʎo; kol'miyo/ n. m. eyetooth; tusk; fang.
colmo /'kolmo/ n. m. height, peak, extreme.
colocación /koloka'θion; koloka'sion/ n. f. place, position; employment, job; arrangement.
colocar /kolo'kar/ v. place, locate, put, set.
colombiano /kolom'biano/ **-na** a. & n. Colombian.
colon /'kolon/ n. m. colon (of intestines).
colonia /ko'lonia/ n. f. colony; eau de Cologne.
Colonia n. f. Cologne.
colonial /kolo'nial/ a. colonial.
colonización /koloniθa'θion; kolonisa'sion/ n. f. colonization.
colonizador /koloniθa'ðor; kolonisa'ðor/ **-ra** n. colonizer.
colonizar /koloni'θar; koloni'sar/ v. colonize.
colono /ko'lono/ n. m. colonist; tenant farmer.
coloquio /ko'lokio/ n. m. conversation, talk.
color /ko'lor/ n. m. color. —**colorar,** v.
coloración /kolora'θion; kolora'sion/ n. f. coloring.
colorado /kolo'raðo/ a. red, ruddy.
colorar /kolo'rar/ v. color, paint; dye.
colorete /kolo'rete/ n. m. rouge.
colorformo /kolor'formo/ n. m. chloroform.
colorido /kolo'riðo/ n. m. color, coloring. —**colorir,** v.
colosal /kolo'sal/ a. colossal.
columbrar /kolum'brar/ v. discern.
columna /ko'lumna/ n. f. column, pillar, shaft.
columpiar /kolum'piar/ v. swing.
columpio /ko'lumpio/ n. m. swing.

coma /'koma/ *n. f.* coma; comma.

comadre /ko'maðre/ *n. f.* midwife; gossip; close friend.

comadreja /koma'ðreha/ *n. f* weasel.

comadrona /koma'ðrona/ *n. f.* midwife.

comandancia /koman'danθia; koman'dansia/ *n. m.* command; command post.

comandante /koman'dante/ *n. m.* commandant; commander; major.

comandar /koman'dar/ *v.* command.

comandita /koman'dita/ *n. f.* silent partnership.

comanditario /komandi'tario/ **-ra** *n.* silent partner.

comando /ko'mando/ *n. m.* command.

comarca /ko'marka/ *n. f.* region; border, boundary.

comba /'komba/ *n. f.* bulge.

combar /kom'bar/ *v.* bend; bulge.

combate /kom'bate/ *n. m.* combat. **—combatir,** *v.*

combatiente /komba'tiente/ *a. & m.* combatant.

combinación /kombina'θion; kombina'sion/ *n. f.* combination; slip (garment).

combinar /kombi'nar/ *v.* combine.

combustible /kombus'tiβle/ *a.* **1.** combustible. **—n. 2.** *m.* fuel.

combustión /kombus'tion/ *n. f.* combustion.

comedero /kome'ðero/ *n. m.* trough.

comedia /ko'meðia/ *n. f.* comedy; play.

comediante /kome'ðiante/ *n. m.* actor; comedian.

comedido /kome'ðiðo/ *a.* polite, courteous; obliging.

comedirse /kome'ðirse/ *v.* to be polite or obliging.

comedor /kome'ðor/ *n. m.* dining room. **coche c.,** dining car.

comendador /komenda'ðor/ *n. m.* commander.

comensal /komen'sal/ *n. m.* table companion.

comentador /komenta'ðor/ **-ra** *n.* commentator.

comentario /komen'tario/ *n. m.* commentary.

comento /ko'mento/ *n. m.* comment. **—comentar,** *v.*

comenzar /komen'θar; komen'sar/ *v.* begin, start, commence.

comer /ko'mer/ *v.* eat, dine.

comercial /komer'θial; komer'sial/ *a.* commercial.

comercializar /komerθiali'θar; komersiali'sar/ *v.* market.

comerciante /komer'θiante; komer'siante/ **-ta** *n.* merchant, trader, businessperson.

comerciar /komer'θiar; komer'siar/ *v.* trade, deal, do business.

comercio /ko'merθio; ko'mersio/ *n. m.* commerce, trade, business; store.

comestible /komes'tiβle/ *a.* **1.** edible. **—n. 2.** *m. (pl.)* groceries, provisions.

cometa /ko'meta/ *n.* **1.** *m.* comet. **2.** *f.* kite.

cometer /kome'ter/ *v.* commit.

cometido /kome'tiðo/ *n. m.* commission; duty; task.

comezón /kome'θon; kome'son/ *n. f.* itch.

comicios /ko'miθios; ko'misios/ *n. m.pl.* primary elections.

cómico /'komiko/ **-ca** *a. & n.* comic, comical; comedian.

comida /ko'miða/ *n. f.* food; dinner; meal.

comidilla /komi'ðiʎa; komi'ðiya/ *n. f.* light meal; gossip.

comienzo /ko'mienθo; ko'mienso/ *n. m.* beginning.

comilitona /komili'tona/ *n. f.* spread, feast.

comillas /ko'miʎas; ko'miyas/ *n. f.pl.* quotation marks.

comilón /komi'lon/ **-na** *n.* glutton; heavy eater.

comisario /komi'sario/ *n. m.* commissary.

comisión /komi'sion/ *n. f.* commission. **—comisionar,** *v.*

comisionado /komisio'naðo/ **-da** *n.* agent, commissioner.

comisionar /komisio'nar/ *v.* commission.

comiso /ko'miso/ *n. m.* (law) confiscation of illegal goods.

comistrajo /komis'traho/ *n. m.* mess, hodgepodge.

comité /komi'te/ *n. m.* committee.

comitiva /komi'tiβa/ *n. f.* retinue.

como /'komo/ *conj. & adv.* like, as.

cómo *adv.* how.

cómoda /'komoða/ *n. f.* bureau, chest (of drawers).

cómodamente /komoða'mente/ *adv.* conveniently.

comodidad /komoði'ðað/ *n. f.* convenience, comfort; commodity.

comodín /komo'ðin/ *n. m.* joker (playing card).

cómodo /'komoðo/ *a.* comfortable; convenient.

comodoro /komo'ðoro/ *n. m.* commodore.

compacto /kom'pakto/ *a.* compact.

compadecer /kompaðe'θer; kompaðe'ser/ *v.* be sorry for, pity.

compadraje /kompa'ðrahe/ *n. m.* clique.

compadre /kom'paðre/ *n. m.* close friend.

compaginar /kompahi'nar/ *v.* put in order; arrange.

compañerismo /kompaɲe'rismo/ *n. m.* companionship.

compañero /kompa'ɲero/ **-ra** *n.* companion, partner.

compañía /kompa'ɲia/ *n. f.* company.

comparable /kompa'raβle/ *a.* comparable.

comparación /kompara'θion; kompara'sion/ *n. f.* comparison.

comparar /kompa'rar/ *v.* compare.

comparativamente /komparatiβa'mente/ *adv.* comparatively.

comparativo /kompara'tiβo/ *a.* comparative.

comparecer /kompare'θer; kompare'ser/ *v.* appear.

comparendo /kompa'rendo/ *n. m.* summons.

comparsa /kom'parsa/ *n. f.* carnival masquerade; retinue.

compartimiento /komparti'miento/ *n. m.* compartment.

compartir /kompar'tir/ *v.* share.

compás /kom'pas/ *n. m.* compass; beat, rhythm.

compasar /kompa'sar/ *v.* measure exactly.

compasión /kompa'sion/ *n. f.* compassion.

compasivo /kompa'siβo/ *a.* compassionate.

compatibilidad /kompatiβili'ðað/ *n. f.* compatibility.

compatible /kompa'tiβle/ *a.* compatible.

compatriota /kompa'triota/ *n. m. & f.* compatriot.

compeler /kompe'ler/ *v.* compel.

compendiar /kompen'diar/ *v.* summarize; abridge.

compendiariamente /kompendiaria'mente/ *adv.* briefly.

compendio /kom'pendio/ *n. m.* summary; abridgment.

compendiosamente /kompendiosa'mente/ *adv.* briefly.

compensación /kompensa'θion; kompensa'sion/ *n. f.* compensation.

compensar /kompen'sar/ *v.* compensate.

competencia /kompe'tenθia; kompe'tensia/ *n. f.* competence; competition.

competente /kompe'tente/ *a.* competent.

competentemente /kompetente'mente/ *adv.* competently.

competición /kompeti'θion; kompeti'sion/ *n. f.* competition.

competidor /kompeti'ðor/ **-ra** *a. & n.* competitive; competitor.

competir /kompe'tir/ *v.* compete.

compilación /kompila'θion; kompila'sion/ *n. f.* compilation.

compilar /kompi'lar/ *v.* compile.

compinche /kom'pintʃe/ *n. m.* pal.

complacencia /kompla'θenθia; kompla'sensia/ *n. f.* complacency.

complacer /kompla'θer; kompla'ser/ *v.* please, oblige, humor.

complaciente /kompla'θiente; kompla'siente/ *a.* pleasing, obliging.

complejidad /komplehi'ðað/ *n. f.* complexity.

complejo /kom'pleho/ **-ja** *a. & n.* complex.

complemento /komple'mento/ *n. m.* complement; *Gram.* object.

completamente /kompleta'mente/ *adv.* completely.

completamiento /kompleta'miento/ *n. m.* completion, finish.

completar /komple'tar/ *v.* complete.

completo /kom'pleto/ *a.* complete, full, perfect.

complexión /komplek'sion/ *n. f.* nature, temperament.

complicación /komplika'θion; komplika'sion/ *n. f.* complication.

complicado /kompli'kaðo/ *a.* complicated.

complicar /kompli'kar/ *v.* complicate.

cómplice /'kompliθe; 'komplise/ *n. m. & f.* accomplice, accessory.

complicidad /kompliθi'ðað; komplisi'ðað/ *n. f.* complicity.

complot /kom'plot/ *n. m.* conspiracy.

componedor /kompone'ðor/ **-ra** *n.* typesetter.

componenda /kompo'nenda/ *n. f.* compromise; settlement.

componente /kompo'nente/ *a. & m.* component.

componer /kompo'ner/ *v.* compose; fix, repair.

componible /kompo'niβle/ *a.* reparable.

comportable /kompor'taβle/ *a.* endurable.

comportamiento /komporta'miento/ *n. m.* behavior.

comportarse /kompor'tarse/ *v.* behave.

comporte /kom'porte/ *n. m.* behavior.

composición /komposi'θion; komposi'sion/ *n. f.* composition.

compositivo /komposi'tiβo/ *a.* synthetic; composite.

compositor /komposi'tor/ **-ra** *n.* composer.

compost /kom'post/ *n. m.* compost.

compostura /kompos'tura/ *n. f.* composure; repair; neatness.

compota /kom'pota/ *n. f.* (fruit) sauce.

compra /'kompra/ *n. f.* purchase. **ir de compras**, to go shopping.

comprador /kompra'ðor/ **-ra** *n.* buyer, purchaser.

comprar /kom'prar/ *v.* buy, purchase.

comprender /kompren'der/ *v.* comprehend, understand; include, comprise.

comprensibilidad /komprensiβili'ðað/ *n. f.* comprehensibility.

comprensible /kompren'siβle/ *a.* understandable.

comprensión /kompren'sion/ *n. f.* comprehension, understanding.

comprensivo /kompren'siβo/ *n. m.* comprehensive.

compresa /kom'presa/ *n. f.* medical compress.

compresión /kompre'sion/ *n. f.* compression.

comprimir /kompri'mir/ *v.* compress; restrain, control.

comprobación /komproβa'θion; komproβa'sion/ *n. f.* proof.

comprobante /kompro'βante/ *a.* 1. proving. —*n.* 2. *m.* proof.

comprobar /kompro'βar/ *v.* prove; verify, check.

comprometer /komprome'ter/ *v.* compromise.

comprometerse /komprome'terse/ *v.* become engaged.

compromiso /kompro'miso/ *n. m.* compromise; engagement.

compuerta /kom'puerta/ *n. f.* floodgate.

compuesto /kom'puesto/ *n. m.* composition; compound.

compulsión /kompul'sion/ *n. f.* compulsion.

compulsivo /kompul'siβo/ *a.* compulsive.

compunción /kompun'θion; kompun'sion/ *n. f.* compunction.

compungirse /kompuŋ'girse/ *v.* regret, feel remorse.

computación /komputa'θion; komputa'sion/ *n. f.* computation.

computador /komputa'ðor/ *n. m.* computer.

computadora de sobremesa /komputa'ðora de soβre'mesa/ *n. f.* desktop computer.

computadora doméstica /komputa'ðora do'mestika/ *n. f.* home computer.

computar /kompu'tar/ *v.* compute.

cómputo /'komputo/ *n. m.* computation.

comulgar /komul'gar/ *v.* take communion.

comulgatorio /komulga'torio/ *n. m.* communion altar.

común /ko'mun/ *a.* common, usual.

comunal /komu'nal/ *a.* communal.

comunero /komu'nero/ *n. m.* commoner.

comunicable /komuni'kaβle/ *a.* communicable.

comunicación /komunika'θion; komunika'sion/ *n. f.* communication.

comunicante /komuni'kante/ *n. m. & f.* communicant.

comunicar /komuni'kar/ *v.* communicate; convey.

comunicativo /komunika'tiβo/ *a.* communicative.

comunidad /komuni'ðað/ *n. f.* community.

comunión /komu'nion/ *n. f.* communion.

comunismo /komu'nismo/ *n. m.* communism.

comunista /komu'nista/ *a. & n.* communistic; communist.

comúnmente /komu'mente/ *adv.* commonly; usually; often.

con /kon/ *prep.* with.

concavidad /konkaβi'ðað/ *n. f.* concavity.

cóncavo /'konkaβo/ *a.* 1. concave. —*n.* 2. *m.* concavity.

concebible /konθe'βiβle; konse'βiβle/ *a.* conceivable.

concebir /konθe'βir; konse'βir/ *v.* conceive.

conceder /konθe'ðer; konse'ðer/ *v.* concede.

concejal /konθe'hal; konse'hal/ *n. m.* councilman.

concejo /kon'θeho; kon'seho/ *n. m.* city council.

concento /kon'θento; kon'sento/ *n. m.* harmony (of singing voices).

concentración /konθentra'θion; konsentra'sion/ *n. f.* concentration.

concentrar /konθen'trar; konsen'trar/ *v.* concentrate.

concepción /konθep'θion; konsep'sion/ *n. f.* conception.

conceptible /konθep'tiβle; konsep'tiβle/ *a.* conceivable.

concepto /kon'θepto; kon'septo/ *n. m.* concept; opinion.

concerniente /konθer'niente; konser'niente/ *a.* concerning.

concernir /konθer'nir; konser'nir/ *v.* concern.

concertar /konθer'tar; konser'tar/ *v.* arrange.

concertina /konθer'tina; konser'tina/ *n. f.* concertina.

concesión /konθe'sion; konse'sion/ *n. f.* concession.

concha /'kontʃa/ *n. f.* S.A. shell.

conciencia /kon'θienθia; kon'siensia/ *n. f.* conscience; consciousness; conscientiousness.

concienzudo /konθien'θuðo; konsien'suðo/ *a.* conscientious.

concierto /kon'θierto; kon'sierto/ *n. m.* concert.

conciliación /konθilia'θion; konsilia'sion/ *n. f.* conciliation.

conciliador /konθilia'ðor; konsilia'ðor/ **-ra** *n.* conciliator.

conciliar /konθi'liar; konsi'liar/ *v.* conciliate.

concilio /kon'θilio; kon'silio/ *n. m.* council.

concisión /konθi'sion; konsi'sion/ *n. f.* conciseness.

conciso /kon'θiso; kon'siso/ *a.* concise.

concitar /konθi'tar; konsi'tar/ *v.* instigate, stir up.

conciudadano /konθiuða'ðano; konsiuða'ðano/ **-na** *n.* fellow citizen.

concluir /kon'kluir/ *v.* conclude.

conclusión /konklu'sion/ *n. f.* conclusion.

conclusivo /konklu'siβo/ *a.* conclusive.

concluso /kon'kluso/ *a.* concluded; closed.

concluyentemente /konkluyente'mente/ adv. conclusively.

concomitante /konkomi'tante/ a. concomitant, attendant.

concordador /konkor'ðor/ **-ra** n. moderator; conciliator.

concordancia /konkor'ðanθia; konkor'ðansia/ n. f. agreement, concord.

concordar /konkor'ðar/ v. agree; put or be in accord.

concordia /kon'korðia/ n. f. concord, agreement.

concretamente /konkreta'mente/ adv. concretely.

concretar /konkre'tar/ v. summarize; make concrete.

concretarse /konkre'tarse/ v. limit oneself to.

concreto /kon'kreto/ a. & m. concrete.

concubina /konku'βina/ n. f. concubine, mistress.

concupiscente /konkupis'θente; konkupis'sente/ a. lustful.

concurrencia /konku'rrenθia; konku'rrensia/ n. f. assembly; attendance; competition.

concurrente /konku'rrente/ a. concurrent.

concurrido /konku'rriðo/ a. heavily attended or patronized.

concurrir /konku'rrir/ v. concur; attend.

concurso /kon'kurso/ n. m. contest, competition; meeting.

conde /'konde/ n. m. (title) count.

condecente /konde'θente; konde'sente/ a. appropriate, proper.

condecoración /kondekora'θion; kondekora'sion/ n. f. decoration; medal; badge.

condecorar /kondeko'rar/ v. decorate with a medal.

condena /kon'dena/ n. f prison sentence.

condenación /kondena'θion; kondena'sion/ n. f. condemnation.

condenar /konde'nar/ v. condemn; damn; sentence.

condensación /kondensa'θion; kondensa'sion/ n. f. condensation.

condensar /konden'sar/ v. condense.

condesa /kon'desa/ n. f. countess.

condescendencia /kondesθen'denθia; kondessen'densia/ n. f. condescension.

condescender /kondesθen'der; kondessen'der/ v. condescend, deign.

condescendiente /kondesθen'diente; kondessen'diente/ a. condescending.

condición /kondi'θion; kondi'sion/ n. f. condition.

condicional /kondiθio'nal; kondisio'nal/ a. conditional.

condicionalmente /kondiθional'mente; kondisional'mente/ adv. conditionally.

condimentar /kondimen'tar/ v. season, flavor.

condimento /kondi'mento/ n. m. condiment, seasoning, dressing.

condiscípulo /kondis'θipulo; kondis'sipulo/ **-la** n. schoolmate.

condolencia /kondo'lenθia; kondo'lensia/ n. f. condolence, sympathy.

condolerse de /kondo'lerse de/ v. sympathize with.

condominio /kondo'minio/ n. m. condominium.

condómino /kon'domino/ n. m. co-owner.

condonar /kondo'nar/ v. condone.

cóndor /'kondor/ n. m. condor (bird).

conducción /konduk'θion; konduk'sion/ n. f. conveyance.

conducente /kondu'θente; kondu'sente/ a. conducive.

conducir /kondu'θir; kondu'sir/ v. conduct, escort, lead; drive.

conducta /kon'dukta/ n. f. conduct, behavior.

conducto /kon'dukto/ n. m. pipe, conduit; sewer.

conductor /konduk'tor/ **-ra** n. driver; conductor.

conectar /konek'tar/ v. connect.

conejera /kone'hera/ n. f. rabbit warren; place of ill repute.

conejillo de Indias /kone'hiʎo de 'indias; kone'hiyo de 'indias/ guinea pig.

conejo /ko'neho/ **-ja** n. rabbit.

conexión /konek'sion/ n. f. connection; coupling.

conexivo /konek'siβo/ a. connective.

conexo /ko'nekso/ a. connected, united.

confalón /konfa'lon/ n. m. ensign, standard.

confección /konfek'θion; konfek'sion/ n. f. workmanship; ready-made article; concoction.

confeccionar /konfekθio'nar; konfeksio'nar/ v. concoct.

confederación /konfeðera'θion; konfeðera'sion/ n. f. confederation.

confederado /konfeðe'raðo/ **-da** a. & n. confederate.

confederar /konfeðe'rar/ v. confederate, unite, ally.

conferencia /konfe'renθia; konfe'rensia/ n. f. lecture; conference. **c. interurbana**, long-distance call.

conferenciante /konferen'θiante; konferen'siante/ n. m. & f. lecturer, speaker.

conferenciar /konferen'θiar; konferen'siar/ v. confer.

conferencista /konferen'θista; konferen'sista/ n. m. & f. lecturer, speaker.

conferir /konfe'rir/ v. confer.

confesar /konfe'sar/ v. confess.

confesión /konfe'sion/ n. f. confession.

confesionario /konfesio'nario, konfeso'na-rio/ *n. m.* confessional.

confesor /konfe'sor/ **-ra** *n.* confessor.

confeti /kon'feti/ *n. m.pl.* confetti.

confiable /kon'fiaβle/ *a.* dependable.

confiado /kon'fiaðo/ *a.* confident; trusting.

confianza /kon'fianθa; kon'fiansa/ *n. f.* confidence, trust, faith.

confiar /kon'fiar/ *v.* entrust; trust, rely.

confidencia /konfi'ðenθia; konfi'ðensia/ *n. f.* confidence, secret.

confidencial /konfiðen'θial; konfiðen'sial/ *a.* confidential.

confidente /konfi'ðente/ *n. m. & f.* confidant.

confidentemente /konfiðente'mente/ *adv.* confidently.

confín /kon'fin/ *n. m.* confine.

confinamiento /konfina'miento/ *n. m.* confinement.

confinar /konfi'nar/ *v.* confine, imprison; border on.

confirmación /konfirma'θion; konfirma-'sion/ *n. f.* confirmation.

confirmar /konfir'mar/ *v.* confirm.

confiscación /konfiska'θion; konfiska'sion/ *n. f.* confiscation.

confiscar /konfis'kar/ *v.* confiscate.

confitar /konfi'tar/ *v.* sweeten; make into candy or jam.

confite /kon'fite/ *n. m.* candy.

confitería /konfite'ria/ *n. f.* confectionery; candy store.

confitura /konfi'tura/ *n. f.* confection.

conflagración /konflagra'θion; konflagra-'sion/ *n. f.* conflagration.

conflicto /kon'flikto/ *n. m.* conflict.

confluencia /kon'fluenθia; kon'fluensia/ *n. f.* confluence, junction.

confluir /kon'fluir/ *v.* flow into each other.

conformación /konforma'θion; konforma-'sion/ *n. f.* conformation.

conformar /konfor'mar/ *v.* conform.

conforme /kon'forme/ *a.* **1.** acceptable, right, as agreed; in accordance, in agreement. —*conj.* **2.** according, as.

conformidad /konformi'ðað/ *n. f.* conformity; agreement.

conformismo /konfor'mismo/ *n. m.* conformism.

conformista /konfor'mista/ *n. m. & f* conformist.

confortar /konfor'tar/ *v.* comfort.

confraternidad /konfraterni'ðað/ *n. f.* brotherhood, fraternity.

confricar /konfri'kar/ *v.* rub vigorously.

confrontación /konfronta'θion; konfronta-'sion/ *n. f.* confrontation.

confrontar /konfron'tar/ *v.* confront.

confucianismo /konfuθia'nismo; konfu-sia'nismo/ *n. m.* Confucianism.

confundir /konfun'dir/ *v.* confuse; puzzle, mix up.

confusamente /konfusa'mente/ *adv.* confusedly.

confusión /konfu'sion/ *n. f.* confusion, mix-up; clutter.

confuso /kon'fuso/ *a.* confused; confusing.

confutación /konfuta'θion; konfuta'sion/ *n. f.* disproof.

confutar /konfu'tar/ *v.* refute, disprove.

congelable /konge'laβle/ *a.* congealable.

congelación /konhela'θion; konhela'sion/ *n. f.* congealment; deep freeze.

congelado /konge'laðo/ *a.* frozen, congealed.

congelar /konhe'lar/ *v.* congeal, freeze.

congenial /konge'nial/ *a.* congenial; analogous.

congeniar /konhe'niar/ *v.* be congenial.

congestión /konhes'tion/ *n. f.* congestion.

conglomeración /konglomera'θion; konglo-mera'sion/ *n. f.* conglomeration.

congoja /kon'goha/ *n. f.* grief, anguish.

congraciamiento /kongraθia'miento; kon-grasia'miento/ *n. m.* flattery; ingratiation.

congraciar /kongra'θiar; kongra'siar/ *v.* flatter; ingratiate oneself.

congratulación /kongratula'θion; kongratu-la'sion/ *n. f.* congratulation.

congratular /kongratu'lar/ *v.* congratulate.

congregación /kongrega'θion; kongrega-'sion/ *n. f.* congregation.

congregar /kongre'gar/ *v.* congregate.

congresista /kongre'sista/ *n. m. & f.* congressional representative.

congreso /kon'greso/ *n. m.* congress; conference.

conjetura /konhe'tura/ *n. f.* conjecture. —**conjeturar,** *v.*

conjetural /konhetu'ral/ *a.* conjectural.

conjugación /konhuga'θion; konhuga'sion/ *n. f.* conjugation.

conjugar /konhu'gar/ *v.* conjugate.

conjunción /konhun'θion; konhun'sion/ *n. f.* union; conjunction.

conjuntamente /konhunta'mente/ *adv* together, jointly.

conjunto /kon'hunto/ *a.* **1.** joint, unified. —*n.* **2.** *m.* whole.

conjuración /konhura'θion; konhura'sion/ *n. f.* conspiracy, plot.

conjurado /konhu'raðo/ **-da** *n.* conspirator, plotter.

conjurar /konhu'rar/ *v.* conjure.

conjuro /kon'huro/ *n. m.* exorcism; spell; plea.

conllevador /konʎeβa'ðor; konyeβa'ðor/ *n. m.* helper, aide.

conmemoración /komemora'θion; komem-ora'sion/ *n. f.* commemoration; remembrance.

conmemorar /komemo'rar/ *v.* commemorate.

conmemorativo /komemora'tiβo/ *a.* commemorative, memorial.

conmensal /komen'sal/ *n. m.* messmate.

conmigo /ko'migo/ *adv.* with me.

conmilitón /komili'ton/ *n. m.* fellow soldier.

conminación /komina'θion; komina'sion/ *n. f.* threat, warning.

conminar /komi'nar/ *v.* threaten.

conminatorio /komina'torio/ *a.* threatening, warning.

conmiseración /komisera'θion; komisera-'sion/ *n. f.* sympathy.

conmoción /komo'θion: komo'sion/ *n. f.* commotion, stir.

conmovedor /komoβe'ðor/ *a.* moving, touching.

conmover /komo'βer/ *v.* move, affect, touch.

conmutación /komuta'θion; komuta'sion/ *n. f.* commutation.

conmutador /komuta'ðor/ *n. m.* electric switch.

conmutar /komu'tar/ *v.* exchange.

connatural /konnatu'ral/ *a.* innate, inherent.

connotación /konnota'θion; konnota'sion/ *n. f.* connotation.

connotar /konno'tar/ *v.* connote.

connubial /konnu'βial/ *a.* connubial.

connubio /ko'nnuβio/ *n. m.* matrimony.

cono /'kono/ *n. m.* cone.

conocedor /konoθe'ðor; konose'ðor/ **-ra** *n.* expert, connoisseur.

conocer /kono'θer; kono'ser/ *v.* know, be acquainted with; meet, make the acquaintance of.

conocible /kono'θiβle; kono'siβle/ *a.* knowable.

conocido /kono'θiðo; kono'siðo/ **-da** *a.* **1.** familiar, well-known. —*n.* **2.** acquaintance, person known.

conocimiento /konoθi'miento; konosi'miento/ *n. m.* knowledge, acquaintance; consciousness.

conque /'konke/ *conj.* so then; and so.

conquista /kon'kista/ *n. f.* conquest.

conquistador /konkista'ðor/ **-ra** *n.* conqueror.

conquistar /konkis'tar/ *v.* conquer.

consabido /konsa'βiðo/ *a.* aforesaid.

consagración /konsagra'θion; konsagra-'sion/ *n. f.* consecration.

consagrado /konsa'graðo/ *a.* consecrated.

consagrar /konsa'grar/ *v.* consecrate, dedicate, devote.

consanguinidad /konsaŋguini'ðað/ *n. f.* consanguinity.

consciente /kons'θiente; kons'siente/ *a.* conscious, aware.

conscientemente /konsθiente'mente; konssiente'mente/ *adv.* consciously.

conscripción /konskrip'θion; konskrip'sion/ *n. f.* conscription for military service.

consecución /konseku'θion; konseku'sion/ *n. f.* attainment.

consecuencia /konse'kuenθia; konse'kuensia/ *n. f.* consequence.

consecuente /konse'kuente/ *a.* consequent; consistent.

consecuentemente /konsekuente'mente/ *adv.* consequently.

consecutivamente /konsekutiβa'mente/ *adv.* consecutively.

consecutivo /konseku'tiβo/ *a.* consecutive.

conseguir /konse'gir/ *v.* obtain, get, secure; succeed in, manage to.

conseja /kon'seha/ *n. f.* fable.

consejero /konse'hero/ **-ra** *n.* adviser, counselor.

consejo /kon'seho/ *n. m.* council; counsel; (piece of) advice. **c. de redacción**, editorial board.

consenso /kon'senso/ *n. m.* consensus.

consentido /konsen'tiðo/ *a.* spoiled, bratty.

consentimiento /konsenti'miento/ *n. m.* consent.

consentir /konsen'tir/ *v.* allow, permit.

conserje /kon'serhe/ *n. m.* superintendent, keeper.

conserva /kon'serβa/ *n. f.* conserve, preserve.

conservación /konserβa'θion; konserβa-'sion/ *n. f.* conservation.

conservador /konserβa'ðor/ **-ra** *a.* & *n.* conservative.

conservar /konser'βar/ *v.* conserve.

conservativo /konserβa'tiβo/ *a.* conservative, preservative.

conservatorio /konserβa'torio/ *n. m.* conservatory.

considerable /konsiðe'raβle/ *a.* considerable, substantial.

considerablemente /konsiðeraβle'mente/ *adv.* considerably.

consideración /konsiðera'θion; konsiðera-'sion/ *n. f.* consideration.

consideradamente /konsiðeraða'mente/ *adv.* considerably.

considerado /konsiðe'raðo/ *a.* considerate, considered.

considerando /konsiðe'rando/ *conj.* whereas.

considerar /konsiðe'rar/ *v.* consider.

consigna /kon'signa/ *n. f.* watchword.

consignación /konsigna'θion; konsigna-'sion/ *n. f.* consignment.

consignar /konsig'nar/ *v.* consign.

consignatorio /konsigna'torio/ **-ria** n. consignee; trustee.

consigo /kon'sigo/ adv. with herself, with himself, with oneself, with themselves, with yourself, with yourselves.

consiguiente /konsi'giente/ a. **1.** consequent. —n. **2.** m. consequence.

consiguientemente /konsigiente'mente/ adv. consequently.

consistencia /konsis'tenθia; konsis'tensia/ n. f. consistency.

consistente /konsis'tente/ a. consistent.

consistir /konsis'tir/ v. consist.

consistorio /konsis'torio/ n. m. consistory.

consocio /kon'soθio; kon'sosio/ n. m. associate; partner; comrade.

consola /kon'sola/ n. f. console.

consolación /konsola'θion; konsola'sion/ n. f. consolation.

consolar /konso'lar/ v. console.

consolatorio /konsola'tiβo/ a. consolatory.

consolidación /konsoliða'θion; konsoliða-'sion/ n. consolidation.

consolidado /konsoli'ðaðo/ a consolidated.

consolidar /konsoli'ðar/ v. consolidate.

consonancia /konso'nanθia; konso'nansia/ n. f. agreement, accord, harmony.

consonante /konso'nante/ a. & f. consonant.

consonar /konso'nar/ v. rhyme.

consorte /kon'sorte/ n. m. & f. consort, mate.

conspicuo /kons'pikuo/ a. conspicuous.

conspiración /konspira'θion; konspira'sion/ n. f. conspiracy, plot.

conspirador /konspira'ðor/ **-ra** n. conspirator.

conspirar /konspi'rar/ v. conspire, plot.

constancia /kons'tanθia; kons'tansia/ n. f. perseverance; record.

constante /kons'tante/ a. constant.

constantemente /konstante'mente/ adv. constantly.

constar /kons'tar/ v. consist; be clear, be on record.

constelación /konstela'θion; konstela'sion/ n. f. constellation.

consternación /konsterna'θion; konsterna-'sion/ n. f. consternation.

consternar /konster'nar/ v. dismay.

constipación /konstipa'θion; konstipa'sion/ n. f. head cold.

constipado /konsti'paðo/ a. **1.** having a head cold. —n. **2.** m. head cold.

constitución /konstitu'θion; konstitu'sion/ n. f. constitution.

constitucional /konstituθio'nal; konstitusio'nal/ a. constitutional.

constitucionalidad /konstituθionali'ðað; konstitusionali'ðað/ n. f. constitutionality.

constituir /konsti'tuir/ v. constitute.

constitutivo /konstitu'tiβo/ n. m. constituent.

constituyente /konstitu'yente, konstitu'ti-βo/ a. constituent.

constreñidamente /konstreniða'mente/ adv. compulsively; with constraint.

constreñimiento /konstreni'miento/ n. m. compulsion; constraint.

constreñir /konstre'nir/ v. constrain.

constricción /konstrik'θion: konstrik'sion/ n. f. constriction.

construcción /konstruk'θion: konstruk'sion/ n. f. construction.

constructivo /konstruk'tiβo/ a. constructive.

constructor /konstruk'tor/ **-ra** n. builder.

construir /kons'truir/ v. construct, build.

consuelo /kon'suelo/ n. m. consolation.

cónsul /'konsul/ n. m. consul.

consulado /konsu'laðo/ n. m. consulate.

consular /konsu'lar/ a. consular.

consulta /kon'sulta/ n. f. consultation.

consultación /konsulta'θion; konsulta'sion/ n. f. consultation.

consultante /konsul'tante/ n. m. & f. consultant.

consultar /konsul'tar/ v. consult.

consultivo /konsul'tiβo/ a. consultative.

consultor /konsul'tor/ **-ra** n. adviser.

consumación /konsuma'θion; konsuma-'sion/ n. f. consummation; end.

consumado /konsu'maðo/ a. consummate, downright.

consumar /konsu'mar/ v. consummate.

consumidor /konsumi'ðor/ **-ra** n. consumer.

consumir /konsu'mir/ v. consume.

consumo /kon'sumo/ n. m. consumption.

consunción /konsun'θion; konsun'sion/ n. m. consumption, tuberculosis.

contabilidad /kontaβili'ðað/ n. f. accounting, bookkeeping.

contabilista /kontaβi'lista/ **contable** n. m. & f. accountant.

contacto /kon'takto/ n. m. contact.

contado /kon'taðo/ n. m. **al c.,** (for) cash.

contador /konta'ðor/ **-ra** n. accountant, bookkeeper; meter.

contagiar /konta'hiar/ v. infect.

contagio /kon'tahio/ n. m. contagion.

contagioso /konta'hioso/ a. contagious.

contaminación /kontamina'θion; kontamina'sion/ n. f. contamination, pollution. **c. del aire, c. atmosférica,** air pollution.

contaminar /kontami'nar/ v. contaminate, pollute.

contar /kon'tar/ v. count; relate, recount, tell. **c. con,** count on.

contemperar /kontempe'rar/ v. moderate.

contemplación /kontempla'θion; kontempla'sion/ n. f. contemplation.

contemplador /kontempla'ðor/ **-ra** n. thinker.

contemplar /kontem'plar/ v. contemplate.

contemplativamente /kontemplatiβa'mente/ adv. thoughtfully.

contemplativo /kontempla'tiβo/ a. contemplative.

contemporáneo /kontempo'raneo/ **-nea** a. & n. contemporary.

contención /konten'θion; konten'sion/ n. f. contention.

contencioso /konten'θioso; konten'sioso/ a. quarrelsome; argumentative.

contender /konten'der/ v. cope, contend; conflict.

contendiente /konten'diente/ n. m. & f. contender.

contenedor /kontene'ðor/ n. m. container.

contener /konte'ner/ \v. contain; curb, control.

contenido /konte'niðo/ n. m. contents.

contenta /kon'tenta/ n. f. endorsement.

contentamiento /kontenta'miento/ n. m. contentment.

contentar /konten'tar/ v. content, satisfy.

contentible /konten'tiβle/ a. contemptible.

contento /kon'tento/ a. **1.** contented, happy. —n. **2.** m. contentment, satisfaction, pleasure.

contérmino /kon'termino/ a. adjacent, abutting.

contestable /kontes'taβle/ a. disputable.

contestación /kontesta'θion; kontesta'sion/ n. f. answer. —**contestar,** v.

contestador automático /kontesta'ðor auto'matiko/ n. m. answering machine.

contextura /konteks'tura/ n. f. texture.

contienda /kon'tienda/ n. f. combat; match; strife.

contigo /kon'tigo/ adv. with you.

contiguamente /kontigua'mente/ adv. contiguously.

contiguo /kon'tiguo/ a. adjoining, next.

continencia /konti'nenθia; konti'nensia/ n. f. continence, moderation.

continental /konti'nental/ a. continental.

continente /konti'nente/ n. m. continent; mainland.

continentemente /kontinente'mente/ adv. in moderation.

contingencia /kontin'henθia; kontin'hensia/ n. f. contingency.

contingente /kontin'hente/ a. contingent; incidental.

continuación /kontinua'θion; kontinua'sion/ n. f. continuation. **a c.,** thereupon, hereupon.

continuamente /kontinua'mente/ adv. continuously.

continuar /konti'nuar/ v. continue, keep on.

continuidad /kontinui'ðað/ n. f. continuity.

continuo /kon'tinuo/ a. continual; continuous.

contorcerse /kontor'θerse; kontor'serse/ v. writhe, twist.

contorción /kontor'θion; kontor'sion/ n. f. contortion.

contorno /kon'torno/ n. m. contour; profile, outline; neighborhood.

contra /'kontra/ prep. against.

contraalmirante /kontraalmi'rante/ n. m. rear admiral.

contraataque /kontraa'take/ n. m. counterattack.

contrabajo /kontra'βaho/ n. m. double bass.

contrabalancear /kontraβalanθe'ar; kontraβalanse'ar/ v. counterbalance.

contrabandear /kontraβande'ar/ v. smuggle.

contrabandista /kontraβan'dista/ n. m. & f. smuggler.

contrabando /kontra'βando/ n. m. contraband, smuggling.

contracción /kontrak'θion; kontrak'sion/ f. contraction.

contracepción /kontraθep'θion; kontrasep'sion/ n. f. contraception, birth control.

contractual /kontrak'tual/ a. contractual.

contradecir /kontraðe'θir; kontraðe'sir/ v. contradict.

contradicción /kontraðik'θion; kontraðik'sion/ n. f. contradiction.

contradictorio /kontraðik'torio/ adj. contradictory.

contraer /kontra'er/ v. contract; shrink.

contrahacedor /kontraaðe'ðor; kontraase'ðor/ **-ra** n. imitator.

contrahacer /kontraa'θer; kontraa'ser/ v. forge.

contralor /kontra'lor/ n. m. comptroller.

contramandar /kontraman'dar/ v. countermand.

contraorden /kontra'orðen/ n. f. countermand.

contraparte /kontra'parte/ n. f. counterpart.

contrapesar /kontrape'sar/ v. counterbalance; offset.

contrapeso /kontra'peso/ n. m. counterweight.

contraproducente /kontraproðu'θente; kontraproðu'sente/ a. counterproductive.

contrapunto /kontra'punto/ n. m. counterpoint.

contrariamente /kontraria'mente/ adv. contrarily.

contrariar /kontra'riar/ v. contradict; vex; antagonize; counteract.

contrariedad /kontrarie'ðað/ n. f. contrariness; opposition; contradiction; disappointment; trouble.

contrario /kon'trario/ a. & m. contrary, opposite.

contrarrestar /kontrarres'tar/ v. resist; counteract.

contrasol /kontra'sol/ n. m. sunshade.

contraste /kon'traste/ n. m. contrast. —**contrastar,** v.

contratar /kontra'tar/ v. engage, contract.

contratiempo /kontra'tiempo/ n. m. accident; misfortune.

contratista /kontra'tista/ n. m. & f. contractor.

contrato /kon'trato/ n. m. contract.

contribución /kontriβu'θion; kontriβu'sion/ n. f. contribution; tax.

contribuir /kontri'βuir/ v. contribute.

contribuyente /kontriβu'yente/ n. m. & f. contributor; taxpayer.

contrición /kontri'θion; kontri'sion/ n. f. contrition.

contristar /kontris'tar/ v. afflict.

contrito /kon'trito/ a. contrite, remorseful.

control /kon'trol/ n. m. control. —**controlar,** v.

controlador aéreo /kontrola'ðor a'ereo/ n. m. air traffic controller.

controversia /kontro'βersia/ n. f. controversy.

controversista /kontroβer'sista/ n. m. & f. controversialist.

controvertir /kontroβer'tir/ v. dispute.

contumacia /kontu'maθia; kontu'masia/ f. stubbornness.

contumaz /kontu'maθ; kontu'mas/ adj. stubborn.

contumelia /kontu'melia/ n. f. contumely; abuse.

conturbar /kontur'βar/ v. trouble, disturb.

contusión /kontu'sion/ n. f. contusion; bruise.

convalecencia /kombale'θenθia; kombale'sensia/ n. f. convalescence.

convalecer /kombale'θer; kombale'ser/ v. convalesce.

convaleciente /kombale'θiente; kombale'siente/ a. convalescent.

convecino /kombe'θino; kombe'sino/ -na a. **1.** near, close. —n. **2.** neighbor.

convencedor /kombenθe'ðor; kombense'ðor/ adj. convincing.

convencer /komben'θer; komben'ser/ v. convince.

convencimiento /kombenθi'miento; kombensi'miento/ n. m. conviction, firm belief.

convención /komben'θion; komben'sion/ f. convention.

convencional /kombenθio'nal; kombensio'nal/ a. conventional.

conveniencia /kombe'nienθia; kombe'niensia/ n. f. suitability; advantage, interest.

conveniente /kombe'niente/ a. suitable; advantageous, opportune.

convenio /kom'benio/ n. m. pact, treaty; agreement.

convenir /kombe'nir/ v. assent, agree, concur; be suitable, fitting, convenient.

convento /kom'bento/ n. m. convent.

convergencia /komber'henθia; komber'hensia/ n. f. convergence.

convergir /komber'hir/ v. converge.

conversación /kombersa'θion; kombersa'sion/ n. f. conversation.

conversar /komber'sar/ v. converse.

conversión /komber'sion/ n. f. conversion.

convertible /komber'tiβle/ a. convertible.

convertir /komber'tir/ v. convert.

convexidad /kombeksi'ðað/ n. f. convexity.

convexo /kom'bekso/ a. convex.

convicción /kombik'θion; kombik'sion/ n. f. conviction.

convicto /kom'bikto/ a. found guilty.

convidado /kombi'ðaðo/ **-da** n. guest.

convidar /kombi'ðar/ v. invite.

convincente /kombin'θente; kombin'sente/ a. convincing.

convite /kom'bite/ n. m. invitation, treat.

convocación /komboka'θion; komboka'sion/ n. f. convocation.

convocar /kombo'kar/ v. convoke, assemble.

convoy /kom'boi/ n. m. convoy, escort.

convoyar /kombo'yar/ v. convey; escort.

convulsión /kombul'sion/ n. f. convulsion.

convulsivo /kombul'siβo/ a. convulsive.

conyugal /konyu'gal/ a. conjugal.

cónyuge /'konyuhe/ n. m. & f. spouse, mate.

coñac /ko'nak/ n. m. cognac, brandy.

cooperación /koopera'θion; koopera'sion/ n. f. cooperation.

cooperador /koopera'ðor/ a. cooperative.

cooperar /koope'rar/ v. cooperate.

cooperativa /koopera'tiβa/ n. f. (food, etc.) cooperative, co-op.

cooperativo /koopera'tiβo/ a. cooperative.

coordinación /koorðina'θion; koorðina'sion/ n. f. coordination.

coordinar /koorði'nar/ v. coordinate.

copa /'kopa/ n. f. goblet.

copartícipe /kopar'tiθipe; kopar'tisipe/ m & f. partner.

copete /ko'pete/ n. m. tuft; toupee.

copia /'kopia/ n. f. copy. —**copiar,** v.

copiadora /kopia'ðora/ n. f. copier.

copioso /ko'pioso/ a. copious.

copista /ko'pista/ n. m. & f. copyist.

copla /'kopla/ n. f. popular song.

coplero /ko'plero/ n. m. poetaster.

cópula /'kopula/ n. f. connection.

coqueta /ko'keta/ n. f. flirt. **—coquetear,** v.

coraje /ko'rahe/ n. m. courage, bravery; anger.

coral /ko'ral/ a. **1.** choral. **—2.** m. coral.

coralino /kora'lino/ a. coral.

Corán /ko'ran/ n. m. Koran.

corazón /kora'θon; kora'son/ n. m. heart.

corazonada /koraθo'naða; koraso'naða/ n. f. foreboding.

corbata /kor'βata/ n. f. necktie.

corbeta /kor'βeta/ n. f. corvette.

corcho /'kortʃo/ n. m. cork.

corcova /kor'koβa/ n. f. hump, hunchback.

corcovado /korko'βaðo/ **-da** a. & n. hunchback.

cordaje /kor'ðahe/ n. m. rigging.

cordel /kor'ðel/ n. m. string, cord.

cordero /kor'ðero/ n. m. lamb.

cordial /kor'ðial/ a. cordial; hearty.

cordialidad /korðiali'ðað/ n. f. cordiality.

cordillera /korði'ʎera; korði'yera/ n. f. mountain range.

cordón /kor'ðon/ n. m. cord; (shoe) lace.

cordura /kor'ðura/ n. f. sanity.

Corea /ko'rea/ n. f. Korea.

coreano /kore'ano/ **-a** a. & n. Korean.

coreografía /koreogra'fia/ n. f. choreography.

corista /ko'rista/ n. f. chorus girl.

corneja /kor'neha/ n. f. crow.

córneo /'korneo/ a. horny.

corneta /kor'neta/ n. f. bugle, horn, cornet.

corniforme /korni'forme/ a. horn-shaped.

cornisa /kor'nisa/ n. f. cornice.

cornucopia /kornu'kopia/ n. f. cornucopia.

coro /'koro/ n. m. chorus; choir.

corola /ko'rola/ n. f. corolla.

corolario /koro'lario/ n. m. corollary.

corona /ko'rona/ n. f. crown; halo; wreath.

coronación /korona'θion; korona'sion/ n. f. coronation.

coronamiento /korona'miento/ n. m. completion of a task.

coronar /koro'nar/ v. crown.

coronel /koro'nel/ n. m. colonel.

coronilla /koro'niʎa; koro'niya/ n. f. crown, top of the head.

corporación /korpora'θion; korpora'sion/ n. f. corporation.

corporal /korpo'ral/ adj. corporeal, bodily.

corpóreo /kor'poreo/ a. corporeal.

corpulencia /korpu'lenθia; korpu'lensia/ n. f. corpulence.

corpulento /korpu'lento/ a. corpulent, stout.

corpuscular /korpusku'lar/ a. corpuscular.

corpúsculo /kor'puskulo/ n. m. corpuscle.

corral /ko'rral/ n. m. corral, pen, yard.

correa /ko'rrea/ n. f. belt, strap.

correa transportadora /korrea transporta'ðora/ conveyor belt.

corrección /korrek'θion; korrek'sion/ n. f. correction.

correcto /ko'rrekto/ a. correct, proper, right.

corrector /korrek'tor/ **-ra** n. corrector, proofreader.

corredera /korre'ðera/ n. f. race course.

corredizo /korre'ðiθo; korre'ðiso/ a. easily untied.

corredor /korre'ðor/ n. m. corridor; runner.

corregible /korre'hiβle/ a. corrigible.

corregidor /korrehi'ðor/ n. m. corrector; magistrate, mayor.

corregir /korre'hir/ v. correct.

correlación /korrela'θion; korrela'sion/ n. f. correlation.

correlacionar /korrelaθio'nar; korrelasio'nar/ v. correlate.

correlativo /korrela'tiβo/ a. correlative.

correo /ko'rreo/ n. m. mail.

correoso /korre'oso/ a. leathery.

correr /ko'rrer/ v. run.

correría /korre'ria/ n. f. raid; escapade.

correspondencia /korrespon'denθia; korrespon'densia/ n. f. correspondence.

corresponder /korrespon'der/ v. correspond.

correspondiente /korrespon'diente/ a. & m. corresponding; correspondent.

corresponsal /korrespon'sal/ n. m. correspondent.

corretaje /korre'tahe/ n. m. brokerage.

correvedile /korreβe'ðile/ n. m. tale bearer; gossip.

corrida /ko'rriða/ n. f. race. **c. (de toros),** bullfight.

corrido /ko'rriðo/ a. abashed; expert.

corriente /ko'rriente/ a **1.** current, standard. **—n. 2.** f. current, stream. **3.** m. **al c.,** informed, up to date. **contra la c.,** against the current; upriver, upstream.

corroboración /korroβora'θion; korroβora'sion/ n. f. corroboration.

corroborar /korroβo'rar/ v. corroborate.

corroer /korro'er/ v. corrode.

corromper /korrom'per/ v. corrupt.

corrompido /korrom'piðo/ a. corrupt.

corrupción /korrup'θion; korrup'sion/ n. f. corruption.

corruptela /korrup'tela/ n. f. corruption; vice.

corruptibilidad /korruptiβili'ðað/ n. f. corruptibility.

corruptor /korrup'tor/ **-ra** n. corrupter.

corsario /kor'sario/ n. m. corsair.

corsé /kor'se/ n. m. corset.

corso /'korso/ n. m. piracy.

cortacésped /korta'θespeð; korta'sespeð/ n. m. lawnmower.

cortadillo /korta'ðiʎo: korta'ðiyo/ n. m. small glass.

cortado /kor'taðo/ a. cut.

cortadura /korta'ðura/ n. f. cut.

cortante /kor'tante/ a. cutting, sharp, keen.

cortapisa /korta'pisa/ n. f. obstacle.

cortaplumas /korta'plumas/ n. m. penknife.

cortar /kor'tar/ v. cut, cut off, cut out.

corte /'korte/ n. f. court, m. cut.

cortedad /korte'ðað/ n. f. smallness; shyness.

cortejar /korte'har/ v. pay court to, woo.

cortejo /kor'teho/ n. m. court; courtship; sweetheart.

cortés /kor'tes/ a. civil, courteous, polite.

cortesana /korte'sana/ n. f. courtesan.

cortesano. 1. /korte'sano/ a. **1.** courtly, courteous. —n. **2.** m. courtier.

cortesía /korte'sia/ n. f. courtesy.

corteza /kor'teθa; kor'tesa/ n. f. bark; rind; crust.

cortijo /kor'tiho/ n. m. farmhouse.

cortina /kor'tina/ n. f. curtain.

corto /'korto/ a. short.

corva /'korβa/ n. f. back of the knee.

cosa /'kosa/ n. f. thing. **c. de,** a matter of, roughly.

cosecha /ko'setʃa/ n. f. crop, harvest. —**cosechar,** v.

coser /ko'ser/ v. sew, stitch.

cosmético /kos'metiko/ a. & m. cosmetic.

cósmico /'kosmiko/ a. cosmic.

cosmonauta /kosmo'nauta/ n. m. & f. cosmonaut.

cosmopolita /kosmopo'lita/ a. & n. cosmopolitan.

cosmos /'kosmos/ n. m. cosmos.

coso /'koso/ n. m. arena for bull fights.

cosquilla /kos'kiʎa; kos'kiya/ n. f. tickle. —**cosquillar,** v.

cosquilloso /koski'ʎoso; koski'yoso/ a. ticklish.

costa /'kosta/ n. f. coast; cost, expense.

costado /kos'taðo/ n. m. side.

costal /kos'tal/ n. m. sack, bag.

costanero /kosta'nero/ a. coastal.

costar /kos'tar/ v. cost.

costarricense /kostarri'θense; kostarri'sense/ a. & n. Costa Rican.

coste /'koste/ n. m. cost, price.

costear /koste'ar/ v. defray, sponsor; sail along the coast of.

costilla /kos'tiʎa; kos'tiya/ n. f. rib; chop.

costo /'kosto/ n. m. cost, price.

costoso /kos'toso/ a. costly.

costra /'kostra/ n. f. crust.

costumbre /kos'tumbre/ n. f. custom, practice, habit.

costura /kos'tura/ n. f. sewing; seam.

costurera /kostu'rera/ n. f. seamstress, dressmaker.

costurero /kostu'rero/ n. m. sewing basket.

cota de malla /'kota de 'maʎa; 'kota de 'maya/ coat of mail.

cotejar /kote'har/ v. compare.

cotidiano /koti'ðiano/ a. daily; everyday.

cotillón /koti'ʎon: koti'yon/ n. m. cotillion.

cotización /kotiθa'θion: kotisa'sion/ n. f quotation.

cotizar /koti'θar: koti'sar/ v. quote (a price).

coto /'koto/ n. m. enclosure; boundary.

cotón /ko'ton/ n. m. printed cotton cloth.

cotufa /ko'tufa/ n. f. Jerusalem artichoke.

coturno /ko'turno/ n. m. buskin.

covacha /ko'βatʃa/ n. f. small cave.

coxal /kok'sal/ a. of the hip.

coy /koi/ n. m. hammock.

coyote /ko'yote/ n. m. coyote.

coyuntura /koyun'tura/ n. f. joint; juncture.

coz /koθ; kos/ n. f. kick.

crac /krak/ n. m. failure.

cráneo /'kraneo/ n. m. skull.

craniano /kra'niano/ a. cranial.

crapuloso /krapu'loso/ a. drunken.

crasiento /kra'siento/ a. greasy, oily.

craso /'kraso/ a. fat; gross.

cráter /'krater/ n. m. crater.

craza /'kraθa; 'krasa/ n. f. crucible.

creación /krea'θion; krea'sion/ n. f. creation.

creador /krea'ðor/ **-ra** a. & n. creative; creator.

crear /kre'ar/ v. create.

creativo /krea'tiβo/ a. creative.

crébol /'kreβol/ n. m. holly tree.

crecer /kre'θer; kre'ser/ v. grow, grow up; increase.

creces /'kreθes; 'kreses/ n. f.pl. increase, addition.

crecidamente /kreθiða'mente; kresiða'mente/ adv. abundantly.

crecido /kre'θiðo; kre'siðo/ a increased, enlarged; swollen.

creciente /kre'θiente; kre'siente/ a. **1.** growing. —n. **2.** m. crescent.

crecimiento /kreθi'miento; kresi'miento/ n. m. growth.

credenciales /kreðen'θiales; kreðen'siales/ f.pl. credentials.

credibilidad /kreðiβili'ðað/ n. f. credibility.

crédito /'kreðito/ n. m. credit.

credo /'kreðo/ n. m. creed, belief.

crédulamente /kreðula'mente/ adv. credulously, gullibly.

credulidad /kreðuli'ðað/ n. f. credulity.

crédulo /'kreðulo/ a. credulous.

creedero /kree'ðero/ a. credible.

creedor /kree'ðor/ a. credulous, believing.

creencia /kre'enθia; kre'ensia/ n. f. belief.

creer /kre'er/ v. believe; think.

creíble /kre'iβle/ a. credible, believable.

crema /'krema/ n. f. cream.

cremación /krema'θion; krema'sion/ n. f. cremation.

crema dentífrica /'krema den'tifrika/ toothpaste.

cremallera /krema'ʎera; krema'yera/ n. f. zipper.

crémor tártaro /'kremor 'tartaro/ n. m. cream of tartar.

cremoso /kre'moso/ a. creamy.

creosota /kreo'sota/ n. f. creosote.

crepitar /krepi'tar/ v. crackle.

crepuscular /krepusku'lar/ a. of or like the dawn or dusk; crepuscular.

crepúsculo /kre'puskulo/ n. m. dusk, twilight.

crescendo /kres'θendo; kres'sendo/ n. m. crescendo.

crespo /'krespo/ a. curly.

crespón /kres'pon/ n. m. crepe.

cresta /'kresta/ n. f. crest; heraldic crest.

crestado /kres'taðo/ a. crested.

creta /'kreta/ n. f. chalk.

cretáceo /kre'taθeo; kre'taseo/ a. chalky.

cretinismo /kreti'nismo/ n. m. cretinism.

cretino /kre'tino/ **-na** n. & a. cretin.

cretona /kre'tona/ n. f. cretonne.

creyente /kre'yente/ a. **1.** believing. —n. **2.** believer.

creyón /kre'yon/ n. m. crayon.

cría /'kria/ n. f. (stock) breeding; young (of an animal), litter.

criada /kri'aða/ n. f. maid.

criadero /kria'ðero/ n. m. Agr. nursery.

criado /kri'aðo/ **-da** n. servant.

criador /kria'ðor/ a. fruitful, prolific.

crianza /kri'anθa; kri'ansa/ n. f. breeding; upbringing.

criar /kri'ar/ v. raise, rear; breed.

criatura /kria'tura/ n. f. creature; infant.

criba /'kriβa/ n. f. sieve.

cribado /kri'βaðo/ a. sifted.

cribar /kri'βar/ v. sift.

crimen /'krimen/ n. m. crime.

criminal /krimi'nal/ a. & n. criminal.

criminalidad /kriminali'ðað/ n. f. criminality.

criminalmente /kriminal'mente/ adv. criminally.

criminología /kriminolo'hia/ n. f. criminology.

criminoso /krimi'noso/ a. criminal.

crines /'krines/ n. f.pl. mane of a horse.

crinolina /krino'lina/ n. f. crinoline.

criocirugía /krioθiru'hia; kriosiru'hia/ n. f. cryosurgery.

criollo /'krioʎo; 'krioyo/ **-lla** a. & n. native; Creole.

cripta /'kripta/ n. f. crypt.

criptografía /kriptogra'fia/ n. f. cryptography.

crisantemo /krisan'temo/ n. m. chrysanthemum.

crisis /'krisis/ n. f. crisis.

crisis nerviosa /'krisis ner'βiosa/ nervous breakdown.

crisma /'krisma/ n. m. chrism.

crisol /kri'sol/ n. m. crucible.

crispamiento /krispa'miento/ n. m. twitch, contraction.

crispar /kris'par/ v. contract (the muscles); twitch.

cristal /kri'stal/ n. m. glass; crystal; lens.

cristalería /kristale'ria/ n. f. glassware.

cristalino /krista'lino/ a. crystalline.

cristalización /kristaliθa'θion; kristalisa'sion/ n. f. crystallization.

cristalizar /kristali'θar; kristali'sar/ v. crystallize.

cristianar /kristia'nar/ v. baptize.

cristiandad /kristian'dað/ n. f. Christendom.

cristianismo /kristia'nismo/ n. m. Christianity.

cristiano /kris'tiano/ **-na** a. & n. Christian.

Cristo /'kristo/ n. m. Christ.

criterio /kri'terio/ n. m. criterion; judgment.

crítica /'kritika/ n. f. criticism; critique.

criticable /kriti'kaβle/ a. blameworthy.

criticador /kritika'ðor/ a. critical.

criticar /kriti'kar/ v. criticize.

crítico /'kritiko/ **-ca** a. & n. critical; critic.

croar /kro'ar/ v. croak.

crocante /kro'kante/ n. m. almond brittle.

crocitar /kroθi'tar; krosi'tar/ v. crow.

cromático /kro'matiko/ a. chromatic.

cromo /'kromo/ n. m. chromium.

cromosoma /kromo'soma/ n. m. chromosome.

cromotipia /kromo'tipia/ n. f. color printing.

crónica /'kronika/ n. f. chronicle.

crónico /'kroniko/ a. chronic.

cronicón /kroni'kon/ n. m. concise chronicle.

cronista /kro'nista/ n. m & f. chronicler.

cronología /kronolo'hia/ n. f. chronology.

cronológicamente /kronolohika'mente/ adv. chronologically.

cronológico /krono'lohiko/ a. chronologic.

cronometrar /kronome'trar/ v. time.

cronómetro /kro'nometro/ n. m. stopwatch; chronometer.

croqueta /kro'keta/ n. f. croquette.

croquis /'krokis/ n. m. sketch; rough outline.

crótalo /'krotalo/ n. m. rattlesnake; castanet.

cruce /'kruθe; 'kruse/ n. m. crossing, crossroads, junction.

crucero /kru'θero; kru'sero/ n. m. cruiser.

crucífero /kru'θifero; kru'sifero/ a. cross-shaped.

crucificado /kruθifi'kaðo; krusifi'kaðo/ a. crucified.

crucificar /kruθifi'kar; krusifi'kar/ v. crucify.

crucifijo /kruθi'fiho; krusi'fiho/ n. m. crucifix.

crucifixión /kruθifik'sion; krusifik'sion/ n. f. crucifixion.

crucigrama /kruθi'grama; krusi'grama/ n. m. crossword puzzle.

crudamente /kruða'mente/ adv. crudely.

crudeza /kru'ðeθa; kru'ðesa/ n. f. crudeness.

crudo /'kruðo/ a. crude, raw.

cruel /kruel/ a. cruel.

crueldad /kruel'daδ/ n. f. cruelty.

cruelmente /kruel'mente/ adv. cruelly.

cruentamente /kruenta'mente/ adv. bloodily.

cruento /'kruento/ a. bloody.

crujía /kru'hia/ n. f. corridor.

crujido /kru'hiðo/ n. m. creak.

crujir /kru'hir/ v. crackle; creak; rustle.

cruórico /kruoriko/ a. bloody.

crup /krup/ n. m. croup.

crupié /kru'pie/ n. m. & f. croupier.

crustáceo /krus'taθeo; krus'taseo/ n. & a. crustacean.

cruz /kruθ; krus/ n. f. cross.

cruzada /kru'θaða; kru'saða/ n. f. crusade.

cruzado /kru'θaðo; kru'saðo/ -da n. crusader.

cruzamiento /kruθa'miento; krusa'miento/ n. m. crossing.

cruzar /kru'θar; kru'sar/ v. cross.

cruzarse con /kru'θarse kon; kru'sarse kon/ v. to (meet and) pass.

cuaderno /kua'ðerno/ n. m. notebook.

cuadra /'kuaðra/ n. f. block; (hospital) ward.

cuadradamente /kuaðraða'mente/ adv. exactly, precisely; completely, in full.

cuadradillo /kuaðra'ðiλo; kuaðra'ðiyo/ n. m. lump of sugar.

cuadrado /kua'ðraðo/ -da a. & n. square.

cuadrafónico /kuaðra'foniko/ a. quadraphonic.

Cuadragésima /kuaðra'hesima/ n. f. Lent.

cuadragesimal /kuaðrahesi'mal/ a. Lenten.

cuadrángulo /kua'ðraŋgulo/ n. m. quadrangle.

cuadrante /kua'ðrante/ n. m. quadrant; dial.

cuadrar /kua'ðrar/ v. square; suit.

cuadricular /kuaðriku'lar/ a. in squares.

cuadrilátero /kuaðri'latero/ a. quadrilateral.

cuadrilla /kua'ðriλa; kua'ðriya/ n. f. band, troop, gang.

cuadro /'kuaðro/ n. m. picture; painting; frame. **a cuadros,** checked, plaid.

cuadro de servicio /'kuaðro de ser'βiθio; 'kuaðro de ser'βisio/ timetable.

cuadrupedal /kuaðrupe'ðal/ a. quadruped.

cuádruplo /'kuaðruplo/ a. fourfold.

cuajada /kua'haða/ n. f. curd.

cuajamiento /kuaha'miento/ n. m. coagulation.

cuajar /kua'har/ v. coagulate; overdecorate.

cuajo /'kuaho/ n. m. rennet; coagulation.

cual /kual/ rel. pron. which.

cuál a. & pron. what, which.

cualidad /kuali'ðaδ/ n. f. quality.

cualitativo /kualita'tiβo/ a. qualitative.

cualquiera /kual'kiera/ a. & pron. whatever, any; anyone.

cuando /'kuando/ conj. when.

cuando adv. when. **de cuando en cuando,** from time to time.

cuantía /kuan'tia/ n. f. quantity; amount.

cuantiar /kuan'tiar/ v. estimate.

cuantiosamente /kuantiosa'mente/ adv. abundantly.

cuantioso /kuan'tioso/ a. abundant.

cuantitativo /kuantita'tiβo/ a. quantitative.

cuanto /'kuanto/ a, adv. & pron. as much as, as many as; all that which. **en c.,** as soon as. **en c. a,** as for. **c. antes,** as soon as possible. **c. más... tanto más,** the more... the more. **unos cuantos,** a few.

cuánto a. & adv. how much, how many.

cuaquerismo /kuake'rismo/ n. m. Quakerism.

cuáquero /'kuakero/ -ra n. & a. Quaker.

cuarenta /kua'renta/ a. & pron. forty.

cuarentena /kuaren'tena/ n. f. quarantine.

cuaresma /kua'resma/ n. f. Lent.

cuaresmal /kuares'mal/ a. Lenten.

cuarta /'kuarta/ n. f. quarter; quadrant; quart.

cuartear /kuarte'ar/ v. divide into quarters.

cuartel /kuar'tel/ n. m. Mil. quarters; barracks; Naut. hatch. **c. general,** headquarters. **sin c.,** giving no quarter.

cuartelada /kuarte'laða/ n. f. military uprising.

cuarterón /kuarte'ron/ n. & a. quadroon.

cuarteto /kuar'teto/ n. m. quartet.

cuartillo /kuar'tiλo; kuar'tiyo/ n. m. pint.

cuarto /'kuarto/ a. **1.** fourth. —n. **2.** m. quarter; room.

cuarto de baño /'kuarto de 'baɲo/ bathroom.

cuarto de dormir /'kuarto de dor'mir/ bedroom.

cuarto para invitados /'kuarto para imbi'taðos/ guest room.

cuarzo /'kuarθo; 'kuarso/ *n. m.* quartz.

cuasi /'kuasi/ *adv.* almost, nearly.

cuate /'kuate/ *a.* & *n.* twin.

cuatrero /kua'trero/ *n. m.* cattle rustler.

cuatrillón /kuatri'ʎon; kuatri'yon/ *n. m.* quadrillion.

cuatro /'kuatro/ *a.* & *pron.* four.

cuatrocientos /kuatro'θientos; kuatro'sientos/ *a.* & *pron.* four hundred.

cuba /'kuβa/ *n. f.* cask, tub, vat.

cubano /ku'βano/ **-na** *a.* & *n.* Cuban.

cubero /ku'βero/ *n. m.* cooper.

cubeta /ku'βeta/ *n. f.* small barrel, keg.

cúbico /'kuβiko/ *a.* cubic.

cubículo /ku'βikulo/ *n. m.* cubicle.

cubierta /ku'βierta/ *n. f.* cover; envelope; wrapping; tread (of a tire); deck.

cubiertamente /kuβierta'mente/ *adv.* secretly, stealthily.

cubierto /ku'βierto/ *n. m.* place (at table).

cubil /ku'βil/ *n. m.* lair.

cubismo /ku'βismo/ *n. m.* cubism.

cubito de hielo /ku'βito de 'ielo/ *n. m.* ice cube.

cubo /'kuβo/ *n. m.* cube; bucket.

cubo de la basura /'kuβo de la ba'sura/ trash can.

cubrecama /kuβre'kama/ *n. f.* bedspread.

cubrir /ku'βrir/ *v.* cover.

cubrirse /ku'βrirse/ *v.* put on one's hat.

cucaracha /kuka'ratʃa/ *n. f.* cockroach.

cuchara /ku'tʃara/ *n. f.* spoon, tablespoon.

cucharada /kutʃa'raða/ *n. f.* spoonful.

cucharita /kutʃa'rita/ **cucharilla** *n. f.* teaspoon.

cucharón /kutʃa'ron/ *n. m.* dipper, ladle.

cuchicheo /kutʃi'tʃeo/ *n. m.* whisper. —**cuchichear,** *v.*

cuchilla /ku'tʃiʎa; ku'tʃiya/ *n. f.* cleaver.

cuchillada /kutʃi'ʎaða; kutʃi'yaða/ *n. f.* slash.

cuchillería /kutʃiʎe'ria; kutʃiye'ria/ *n. f.* cutlery.

cuchillo /ku'tʃiʎo; ku'tʃiyo/ *n. m.* knife.

cucho /'kutʃo/ *n. m.* fertilizer.

cuchufleta /kutʃu'fleta/ *n. f.* jest.

cuclillo /ku'kliʎo; ku'kliyo/ *n. m.* cuckoo.

cuco /'kuko/ *a.* sly.

cuculla /ku'kuʎa; ku'kuya/ *n. f.* hood, cowl.

cuelga /'kuelga/ *n. f.* cluster, bunch.

cuelgacapas /kuelga'kapas/ *n. m.* coat rack.

cuello /'kueʎo; 'kueyo/ *n. m.* neck; collar.

cuenca /'kuenka/ *n. f.* socket; (river) basin; wooden bowl.

cuenco /'kuenko/ *n. m.* earthen bowl.

cuenta /'kuenta/ *n. f.* account; bill. **darse c.,** to realize. **tener en c.,** to keep in mind.

cuenta bancaria /'kuenta ban'karia/ bank account.

cuenta de ahorros /'kuenta de a'orros/ savings account.

cuentagotas /kuenta'gotas/ *n. m.* dropper (for medicine).

cuentista /kuen'tista/ *n. m.* & *f.* storyteller; informer.

cuento /'kuento/ *n. m.* story, tale.

cuerda /'kuerða/ *n. f.* cord; chord; rope; string; spring (of clock). **dar c. a,** to wind (clock).

cuerdamente /kuerða'mente/ *adv.* sanely; prudently.

cuerdo /'kuerðo/ *a.* sane; prudent.

cuerno /'kuerno/ *n. m.* horn.

cuero /'kuero/ *n. m.* leather; hide.

cuerpo /'kuerpo/ *n. m.* body; corps.

cuervo /'kuerβo/ *n. m.* crow, raven.

cuesco /'kuesko/ *n. m.* pit, stone (of fruit).

cuesta /'kuesta/ *n. f.* hill, slope. **llevar a cuestas,** to carry on one's back.

cuestación /kuesta'θion; kuesta'sion/ *n. f.* solicitation for charity.

cuestión /kues'tion/ *n. f.* question; affair; argument.

cuestionable /kuestio'naβle/ *a.* questionable.

cuestionar /kuestio'nar/ *v.* question; discuss; argue.

cuestionario /kuestio'nario/ *n. m.* questionnaire.

cuete /'kuete/ *n. m.* firecracker.

cueva /'kueβa/ *n. f.* cave; cellar.

cuguar /ku'guar/ *n. m.* cougar.

cugujada /kugu'haða/ *n. f.* lark.

cuidado /kui'ðaðo/ *n. m.* care, caution, worry. **tener c.,** to be careful.

cuidadosamente /kuiðaðosa'mente/ *adv.* carefully.

cuidadoso /kuiða'ðoso/ *a.* careful, painstaking.

cuidante /kui'ðante/ *n.* caretaker, custodian.

cuidar /kui'ðar/ *v.* take care of.

cuita /'kuita/ *n. f.* trouble, care; grief.

cuitado /kui'taðo/ *a.* unfortunate; shy, timid.

cuitamiento /kuita'miento/ *n. m.* timidity.

culata /ku'lata/ *n. f.* haunch, buttock; butt of a gun.

culatada /kula'taða/ *n. f.* recoil.

culatazo /kula'taθo; kula'taso/ *n. m.* blow with the butt of a gun; recoil.

culebra /ku'leβra/ *n. f.* snake.

culero /ku'lero/ *a.* lazy, indolent.

culinario /kuli'nario/ a. culinary.

culminación /kulmina'θion; kulmina'sion/ n. f. culmination.

culminar /kulmi'nar/ v. culminate.

culpa /'kulpa/ n. f. fault, guilt, blame. **tener la c.,** to be at fault. **echar la culpa a,** to blame, culpable.

culpabilidad /kulpaβili'ðað/ n. f. guilt, fault, blame.

culpable /kul'paβle/ a. at fault, guilty, to blame, culpable.

culpar /kul'par/ v. blame, accuse.

cultamente /kulta'mente/ adv. politely, elegantly.

cultivable /kulti'βaβle/ a. arable.

cultivación /kultiβa'θion; kultiβa'sion/ n. f. cultivation.

cultivador /kultiβa'ðor/ **-ra** n. cultivator.

cultivar /kulti'βar/ v. cultivate.

cultivo /kul'tiβo/ n. m. cultivation; (growing) crop.

culto /'kulto/ a. **1.** cultured, cultivated. —n. **2.** m. cult; worship.

cultura /kul'tura/ n. f. culture; refinement.

cultural /kultu'ral/ a. cultural.

culturar /kultu'rar/ v. cultivate.

culturismo /kultu'rismo/ n. m. body building.

culturista /kultu'rista/ n. m. & f. body builder.

cumbre /'kumbre/ n. m. summit, peak.

cumpleaños /kumple'aɲos/ n. m.pl. birthday.

cumplidamente /kumpliða'mente/ adv. courteously, correctly.

cumplido /kum'pliðo/ a. polite, polished.

cumplimentar /kumplimen'tar/ v. compliment.

cumplimiento /kumpli'miento/ n. m. fulfillment; compliment.

cumplir /kum'plir/ v. comply; carry out, fulfill; reach (years of age).

cumulativo /kumula'tiβo/ a. cumulative.

cúmulo /'kumulo/ n. m. heap, pile.

cuna /'kuna/ n. f. cradle.

cundir /kun'dir/ v. spread; expand; propagate.

cuneiforme /kunei'forme/ a. cuneiform, wedge-shaped.

cuneo /ku'neo/ n. m. rocking.

cuña /'kuɲa/ n. f. wedge.

cuñada /ku'ɲaða/ n. f. sister-in-law.

cuñado /ku'ɲaðo/ n. m. brother-in-law.

cuñete /ku'ɲete/ n. m. keg.

cuota /'kuota/ n. f. quota; dues.

cuotidiano /kuoti'ðiano/ a. daily.

cupé /ku'pe/ n. m. coupé.

Cupido /ku'piðo/ n. m. Cupid.

cupo /'kupo/ n. m. share; assigned quota.

cupón /ku'pon/ n. m. coupon.

cúpula /'kupula/ n. f. dome.

cura /'kura/ n. m. priest; f. treatment, (medical) care. **c. de urgencia,** first aid.

curable /ku'raβle/ a. curable.

curación /kura'θion; kura'sion/ n. f. healing; cure; (surgical) dressing.

curado /ku'raðo/ a. cured, healed.

curador /kura'ðor/ **-ra** n. healer.

curandero /kuran'dero/ **-ra** n. healer, medicine man.

curar /ku'rar/ v. cure, heal, treat.

curativo /kura'tiβo/ a. curative, healing.

curia /'kuria/ n. f. ecclesiastical court.

curiosear /kuriose'ar/ v. snoop, pry, meddle.

curiosidad /kuriosi'ðað/ n. f. curiosity.

curioso /ku'rioso/ a. curious.

curro /'kurro/ a. showy, loud, flashy.

cursante /kur'sante/ n. student.

cursar /kur'sar/ v. frequent; attend.

cursi /'kursi/ a. vulgar, shoddy, in bad taste.

curso /'kurso/ n. m. course.

curso por correspondencia /'kurso por korrespon'denθia; 'kurso por korrespon'densia/ n. m. correspondence course.

cursor /kur'sor/ n. m. cursor.

curtidor /kurti'ðor/ n. m. tanner.

curtir /kur'tir/ v. tan.

curva /'kurβa/ n. f. curve; bend.

curvatura /kurβa'tura, kurβi'ðað/ n. f. curvature.

cúspide /'kuspiðe/ n. f. top, peak.

custodia /kus'toðia/ n. f. custody.

custodiar /kusto'ðiar/ v. guard, watch.

custodio /kus'toðio/ n. m. custodian.

cutáneo /ku'taneo/ a. cutaneous.

cutícula /ku'tikula/ n. f. cuticle.

cutis /'kutis/ n. m. or f. skin, complexion.

cutre /'kutre/ a. shoddy.

cuyo /'kuyo/ a. whose.

D

dable /'daβle/ *a.* possible.
dactilógrafo /dakti'lografo/ **-fa** *n.* typist.
dádiva /'daðiβa/ *n. f.* gift.
dadivosamente /daðiβosa'mente/ *adv.* generously.
dadivoso /daði'βoso/ *a.* generous, bountiful.
dado /'daðo/ *n. m.* die.
dador /da'ðor/ **-ra** *n.* giver.
dados /'daðos/ *n. m.pl.* dice.
daga /'daga/ *n. f.* dagger.
dalia /'dalia/ *n f.* dahlia.
dallador /daʎa'ðor; daya'ðor/ *n. m.* lawn mower.
dallar /da'ʎar; da'yar/ *v.* mow.
daltonismo /dalto'nismo/ *n. m.* color blindness.
dama /'dama/ *n. f.* lady.
damasco /da'masko/ *n. m.* apricot; damask.
damisela /dami'sela/ *n. f.* young lady, girl.
danés /da'nes/ **-esa** *a. & n.* Danish, Dane.
danza /'danθa; 'dansa/ *n. f.* (the) dance. **—danzar,** *v.*
danzante /dan'θante; dan'sante/ **-ta** *n.* dancer.
dañable /da'naβle/ *a.* condemnable.
dañar /da'ɲar/ *v.* hurt, harm; damage.
dañino /da'ɲino/ *a.* harmful.
daño /'daɲo/ *n. m.* damage; harm.
dañoso /da'ɲoso/ *a.* harmful.
dar /dar/ *v.* give; strike (clock). **d. a,** face, open on. **d. con,** find, locate. **¡Dalo por hecho!** Consider it done!
dardo /'darðo/ *n. m.* dart.
dársena /'darsena/ *n. f.* dock.
datar /da'tar/ *v.* date.
dátil /'datil/ *n. m.* date (fruit).
dativo /da'tiβo/ *n. m. & a.* dative.
datos /'datos/ *n. m.pl.* data.
de /de/ *prep.* of; from; than.
debajo /de'βaho/ *adv.* underneath. **d. de,** under.
debate /de'βate/ *n. m* debate.
debatir /deβa'tir/ *v* debate, argue.
debe /'deβe/ *n. m.* debit.
debelación /deβela'θion; deβela'sion/ *n. f.* conquest.
debelar /deβe'lar/ *v.* conquer.
deber /de'βer/ *v.* **1.** owe; must; be to, be supposed to. **—n. 2.** *m.* obligation.
deberes /de'βeres/ *n. m.pl.* homework.
debido /de'βiðo/ *a.* due.
débil /'deβil/ *a.* weak, faint.

debilidad /deβili'ðað/ *n. f.* weakness.
debilitación /deβilita'θion; deβilitasion/ *n. f.* weakness.
debilitar /deβili'tar/ *v.* weaken.
débito /'deβito/ *n. m.* debit.
debutar /deβu'tar/ *v.* make a debut.
década /'dekaða/ *n. f.* decade.
decadencia /deka'ðenθia; dekaðensia/ *n. f.* decadence, decline, decay.
decadente /deka'ðente/ *a.* decadent, declining, decaying.
decaer /deka'er/ *v.* decay, decline.
decalitro /deka'litro/ *n. m.* decaliter.
decálogo /de'kalogo/ *n. m. m.* decalogue.
decámetro /de'kametro/ *n. m.* decameter.
decano /de'kano/ *n. m.* dean.
decantado /dekan'taðo/ *a.* much discussed; overexalted.
decapitación /dekapita'θion; dekapitasion/ *n. f.* beheading.
decapitar /dekapi'tar/ *v.* behead.
decencia /de'θenθia; de'sensia/ *n. f.* decency.
decenio /de'θenio; de'senio/ *n. m.* decade.
decente /de'θente; de'sente/ *a.* decent.
decentemente /deθente'mente; desente'mente/ *adv.* decently.
decepción /deθep'θion; desep'sion/ *n. f.* disappointment, letdown; delusion.
decepcionar /deθepθio'nar; desepsio'nar/ *v.* disappoint, disillusion.
dechado /de'tʃaðo/ *n. m.* model; sample; pattern; example.
decibelio /deθi'βelio; desi'βelio/ *n. m.* decibel.
decididamente /deθiðiða'mente; desiðiða'mente/ *adv.* decidedly.
decidir /deθi'ðir; desi'ðir/ *v.* decide.
decigramo /deθi'gramo; desi'gramo/ *n. m.* decigram.
decilitro /deθi'litro; desi'litro/ *n. m.* deciliter.
décima /'deθima; 'desima/ *n. f.* ten-line stanza.
decimal /deθi'mal; desi'mal/ *a.* decimal.
décimo /'deθimo; 'desimo/ *a.* tenth.
decir /de'θir; de'sir/ *v.* tell, say. **es d.,** that is (to say).
decisión /deθi'sion; desi'sion/ *n. f.* decision.
decisivamente /deθisiβa'mente; desisiβa'mente/ *adv.* decisively.
decisivo /deθi'siβo; desi'siβo/ *a.* decisive.
declamación /deklama'θion; deklama'sion/ *n. f.* declamation, speech.
declamar /dekla'mar/ *v.* declaim.

declaración /deklara'θion: deklara'sion/ *n. f.* declaration; statement; plea.

declaración de la renta /deklara'θion de la 'rrenta; deklara'sion de la 'rrenta/ tax return.

declarar /dekla'rar/ *v.* declare, state.

declarativo /deklara'tiβo, deklara'torio/ *a.* declarative.

declinación /deklina'θion; deklina'sion/ *n. f.* descent; decay; decline; declension.

declinar /dekli'nar/ *v.* decline.

declive /de'kliβe./ *n. m.* declivity, slope.

decocción /dekok'θion: dekok'sion/ *n. f.* decoction.

decomiso /deko'miso/ *n. m.* seizure, confiscation.

decoración /dekora'θion; dekora'sion/ *n. f.* decoration, trimming.

decorado /deko'rado/ *n. m. Theat.* scenery, set.

decorar /deko'rar/ *v.* decorate, trim.

decorativo /dekora'tiβo/ *a.* decorative, ornamental.

decoro /de'koro/ *n. m.* decorum; decency.

decoroso /deko'roso/ *a.* decorous.

decrecer /dekre'θer; dekre'ser/ *v.* decrease.

decrépito /de'krepito/ *a.* decrepit.

decreto /de'kreto/ *n. m.* decree. **—decretar,** *v.*

dedal /de'ðal/ *n. m.* thimble.

dédalo /'deðalo/ *n. m.* labyrinth.

dedicación /deðika'θion; deðika'sion/ *n. f.* dedication.

dedicar /deði'kar/ *v.* devote; dedicate.

dedicatoria /deðika'toria/ *n. f.* dedication, inscription.

dedo /'deðo/ *n. m.* finger, toe.

dedo anular /'deðo anu'lar/ ring finger.

dedo corazón /'deðo kora'θon; 'deðo kora'son/ middle finger.

dedo índice /'deðo 'indiθe; 'deðo 'indise/ index finger.

dedo meñique /'deðo me'ɲike/ little finger, pinky.

dedo pulgar /'deðo pul'gar/ thumb.

deducción /deðuk'θion; deðuk'sion/ *n. f.* deduction.

deducir /deðu'θir; deðu'sir/ *v.* deduce; subtract.

defectivo /defek'tiβo/ *a.* defective.

defecto /de'fekto/ *n. m.* defect, flaw.

defectuoso /defek'tuoso/ *a.* defective, faulty.

defender /defen'der/ *v.* defend.

defensa /de'fensa/ *n. f.* defense.

defensivo /defen'siβo/ *a.* defensive.

defensor /defen'sor/ **-ra** *n.* defender.

deferencia /defe'renθia; deferensia/ *n. f.* deference.

deferir /defe'rir/ *v.* defer.

deficiente /defi'θiente; defi'siente/ *a.* deficient.

déficit /'defiθit; 'defisit/ *n. m.* deficit.

definición /defini'θion; defini'sion/ *n. f.* definition.

definido /defi'nido/ *a.* definite.

definir /defi'nir/ *v.* define; establish.

definitivamente /'definitiβa'mente/ *adv.* definitely.

definitivo /defini'tiβo/ *a.* definitive.

deformación /deforma'θion; deforma'sion/ *n. f.* deformation.

deformar /defor'mar/ *v.* deform.

deforme /de'forme/ *a.* deformed; ugly.

deformidad /deformi'ðað/ *n. f.* deformity.

defraudar /defrau'ðar/ *v.* defraud.

defunción /defun'θion; defun'sion/ *n. f.* death.

degeneración /dehenera'θion; dehenera-'sion/ *n. f.* degeneration.

degenerado /dehene'rado/ *a.* degenerate. **—degenerar,** *v.*

deglutir /deglu'tir/ *v.* swallow.

degollar /dego'ʎar; dego'yar/ *v.* behead.

degradación /degraða'θion; degraða'sion/ *n. f.* degradation.

degradar /degra'ðar/ *v.* degrade, debase.

deidad /dei'ðað/ *n. f.* deity.

deificación /deifika'θion; deifika'sion/ *n. f.* deification.

deificar /deifi'kar/ *v.* deify.

deífico /de'ifiko/ *a.* divine, deific.

deísmo /de'ismo/ *n. m.* deism.

dejadez /deha'ðeθ; deha'ðes/ *n. f.* neglect, untidiness; laziness.

dejado /de'haðo/ *a.* untidy; lazy.

dejar /de'har/ *v.* let, allow; leave. **d. de,** stop, leave off. **no d. de,** not fail to.

dejo /'deho/ *n. m.* abandonment; negligence; aftertaste; accent.

del /del/ *contr.* of **de + el.**

delantal /delan'tal/ *n. m.* apron; pinafore. **delantal de niña,** pinafore.

delante /de'lante/ *adv.* ahead, forward; in front.

delantero /delan'tero/ *a.* forward, front, first.

delator /dela'tor/ *n. m.* informer; accuser.

delegación /delega'θion; delega'sion/ *n. f.* delegation.

delegado /dele'gaðo/ **-da** *n.* delegate. **—delegar,** *v.*

deleite /de'leite/ *n. m.* delight. **—deleitar,** *v.*

deleitoso /delei'toso/ *a.* delightful.

deletrear /deletre'ar/ *v.* spell; decipher.

delfín /del'fin/ *n. m.* dolphin; dauphin.

delgadez /delga'ðeθ; delgaðes/ *n. f.* thinness, slenderness.

delgado /del'gaðo/ a. thin, slender, slim, slight.

deliberación /deliβera'θion; deliβera'sion/ n. f. deliberation.

deliberadamente /deliβeraða'mente/ adv. deliberately.

deliberar /deliβe'rar/ v. deliberate.

deliberativo /deliβera'tiβo/ a. deliberative.

delicadamente /delikaða'mente/ adv. delicately.

delicadeza /delika'ðeθa; delika'ðesa/ n. f. delicacy.

delicado /deli'kaðo/ a. delicate, dainty.

delicia /deli'θia; deli'sia/ n. f. delight; deliciousness.

delicioso /deli'θioso; deli'sioso/ a. delicious.

delincuencia /delin'kuenθia; delin'kuensia/ n. f. delinquency.

delincuencia de menores /delin'kuenθia de me'nores; delin'kuensia de me'nores/ **delincuencia juvenil** juvenile delinquency.

delincuente /delin'kuente/ a. & n. delinquent; culprit, offender.

delineación /delinea'θion; delinea'sion/ n. f. delineation, sketch.

delinear /deline'ar/ v. delineate, sketch.

delirante /deli'rante/ a. delirious.

delirar /deli'rar/ v. rave, be delirious.

delirio /de'lirio/ n. m. delirium; rapture, bliss.

delito /de'lito/ n. m. crime, offense.

delta /'delta/ n. m. delta (of river); hang glider.

demacrado /dema'kraðo/ a. emaciated.

demagogia /dema'gohia/ n. f. demagogy.

demagogo /dema'gogo/ n. m. demagogue.

demanda /de'manda/ n. f. demand, claim.

demandador /demanda'ðor/ **-ra** n. plaintiff.

demandar /deman'dar/ v. sue; demand.

demarcación /demarka'θion; demarka'sion/ n. f. demarcation.

demarcar /demar'kar/ v. demarcate, limit.

demás /de'mas/ a. & n. other; (the) rest (of). **por d.,** too much.

demasía /dema'sia/ n. f. excess; audacity; iniquity.

demasiado /dema'siaðo/ a. & adv. too; too much; too many.

demencia /de'menθia; de'mensia/ n. f. dementia; insanity.

demente /de'mente/ a. demented.

democracia /demo'kraθia; demo'krasia/ n. f. democracy.

demócrata /de'mokrata/ n. m. & f. democrat.

democrático /demo'kratiko/ a. democratic.

demoler /demo'ler/ v. demolish, tear down.

demolición /demoli'θion; demoli'sion/ n. f. demolition.

demonio /de'monio/ n. m. demon, devil.

demontre /de'montre/ n. m. devil.

demora /de'mora/ n. f. delay, —**demorar,** v.

demostración /demostra'θion; demostra'sion/ n. f. demonstration.

demostrador /demostra'ðor/ **-ra** n. demonstrator.

demostrar /demos'trar/ v. demonstrate, show.

demostrativo /demostra'tiβo/ a. demonstrative.

demudar /demu'ðar/ v. change; disguise, conceal.

denegación /denega'θion; denega'sion/ n. f. denial; refusal.

denegar /dene'gar/ v. deny; refuse.

dengue /'dengue/ n. m. prudishness; dengue.

denigración /denigra'θion; denigra'sion/ n. f. defamation, disgrace.

denigrar /deni'grar/ v. defame, disgrace.

denodado /deno'ðaðo/ a. brave, dauntless.

denominación /denomina'θion; denomina'sion/ n. f. denomination.

denominar /denomi'nar/ v. name, call.

denotación /denota'θion; denota'sion/ n. f. denotation.

denotar /deno'tar/ v. denote, betoken, express.

densidad /densi'ðað/ n. f. density.

denso /'denso/ a. dense.

dentado /den'taðo/ a. toothed; serrated; cogged.

dentadura /denta'ðura/ n. f. set of teeth.

dentadura postiza /denta'ðura pos'tiθa; denta'ðura pos'tisa/ false teeth, dentures.

dental /den'tal/ a. dental.

dentífrico /den'tifriko/ n. m. dentifrice, toothpaste.

dentista /den'tista/ n. m. & f. dentist.

dentistería /dentiste'ria/ n. f. dentistry.

dentro /'dentro/ adv. within, inside. **d. de poco,** in a short while.

dentudo /den'tuðo/ a. toothy (person).

denuedo /de'nueðo/ n. m. bravery, courage.

denuesto /de'nuesto/ n. m. insult, offense.

denuncia /de'nunθia; de'nunsia/ n. f. denunciation; declaration; complaint.

denunciación /denunθia'θion; denunsia'sion/ n. f. denunciation.

denunciar /denun'θiar; denun'siar/ v. denounce.

deparar /depa'rar/ v. offer; grant.

departamento /departa'mento/ n. m. department, section.

departir /depar'tir/ v. talk, chat.

dependencia /depen'denθia; depen'densia/ n. f. dependence; branch office.

depender /depen'der/ v. depend.

dependiente /depen'diente/ *a. & m.* dependent; clerk.

depilar /depi'lar/ *v.* depilate, pluck.

depilatorio /depila'torio/ *a. & n.* depilatory.

depistar *v.* mislead, put off the track.

deplorable /deplo'raβle/ *a.* deplorable, wretched.

deplorablemente /deploraβle'mente/ *adv.* deplorably.

deplorar /deplo'rar/ *v.* deplore.

deponer /depo'ner/ *v.* depose.

deportación /deporta'θion; deporta'sion/ *n. f.* deportation; exile.

deportar /depor'tar/ *v.* deport.

deporte /de'porte/ *n. m.* sport. —**deportivo,** *a.*

deposición /deposi'θion; deposi'sion/ *n. f.* assertion, deposition; removal; movement.

depositante /deposi'tante/ *n. m. & f.* depositor.

depósito /de'posito/ *n. m.* deposit. —**depositar,** *v.*

depravación /depraβa'θion; depraβa'sion/ *n. f.* depravation; depravity.

depravado /depra'βaðo/ *a.* depraved, wicked.

depravar /depra'βar/ *v.* deprave, corrupt, pervert.

depreciación /depreθia'θion; depresia'sion/ *n. f.* depreciation.

depreciar /depre'θiar; depre'siar/ *v.* depreciate.

depredación /depreða'θion; depreða'sion/ *n. f.* depredation.

depredar /depre'ðar/ *v.* pillage, depredate.

depresión /depre'sion/ *n. f.* depression.

depresivo /depre'siβo/ *a.* depressive.

deprimir /depri'mir/ *v.* depress.

depurar /depu'rar/ *v.* purify.

derecha /de'retʃa/ *n. f.* right (hand, side).

derechera /dere'tʃera/ *n. f.* shortcut.

derecho /de'retʃo/ *a.* **1.** right; straight. —*n.* **2.** *m.* right; (the) law. **derechos,** *Com.* duty.

derechos civiles /de'retʃos θi'βiles; de'retʃos si'βiles/ *n. m.pl.* civil rights.

derechos de aduana /de'retʃos de a'ðuana/ *n. m.pl.* customs duty.

derechura /dere'tʃura/ *n. f.* straightness.

derelicto /dere'likto/ *a.* abandoned, derelict.

deriva /de'riβa/ *n. f. Naut.* drift.

derivación /deriβa'θion; deriβa'sion/ *n. f.* derivation.

derivar /deri'βar/ *v.* derive.

dermatólogo /derma'tologo/ -a *n.* dermatologist, skin doctor.

derogar /dero'gar/ *v.* derogate; repeal, abrogate.

derramamiento /derrama'miento/ *n. m.* overflow.

derramar /derra'mar/ *v.* spill, pour, scatter.

derrame /de'rrame/ *n. m.* overflow; discharge.

derretir /derre'tir/ *v.* melt, dissolve.

derribar /derri'βar/ *v.* demolish, knock down; bowl over, floor, fell.

derrocamiento /derroka'miento/ *n. m.* overthrow.

derrocar /derro'kar/ *v.* overthrow; oust; demolish.

derrochar /derro'tʃar/ *v.* waste.

derroche /de'rrotʃe/ *n. m.* waste.

derrota /de'rrota/ *n. f.* rout, defeat. —**derrotar,** *v.*

derrotismo /derro'tismo/ *n. m.* defeatism.

derrumbamiento /derrumbᴧ'miento/ **derrumbe** *m.* collapse; landslide.

derrumbarse /derrum'βarse/ *v.* collapse, tumble.

derviche /der'βitʃe/ *n. m.* dervish.

desabotonar /desaβoto'nar/ *v.* unbutton.

desabrido /desa'βriðo/ *a.* insipid, tasteless.

desabrigar /desaβri'gar/ *v.* uncover.

desabrochar /desaβro'tʃar/ *v.* unbutton, unclasp.

desacato /desa'kato/ *n. m.* disrespect, lack of respect.

desacierto /desa'θierto; desa'sierto/ *n. m.* error.

desacobardar /desakoβar'ðar/ *v.* remove fear; embolden.

desacomodadamente /desakomoðaða'mente/ *adv.* inconveniently.

desacomodado /desakomo'ðaðo/ *a.* unemployed.

desacomodar /desakomo'ðar/ *v.* molest; inconvenience; dismiss.

desacomodo /desako'moðo/ *n. m.* loss of employment.

desaconsejar /desakonse'har/ *v.* dissuade (someone); advise against (something).

desacordadamente /desakorðaða'mente/ *adv.* unadvisedly.

desacordar /desakor'ðar/ *v.* differ, disagree; be forgetful.

desacorde /desa'korðe/ *a.* discordant.

desacostumbradamente /desakostumbraða'mente/ *adv.* unusually.

desacostumbrado /desakostum'braðo/ *a.* unusual, unaccustomed.

desacostumbrar /desakostum'brar/ *v.* give up a habit or custom.

desacreditar /desakreði'tar/ *v.* discredit.

desacuerdo /desa'kuerðo/ *n. m.* disagreement.

desadeudar /desaðeu'ðar/ *v.* pay one's debts.

desadormecer /desaðorme'θer; desaðorme'ser/ *v.* waken, rouse.

desadornar /desaðor'nar/ v. divest of ornament.

desadvertidamente /desaðβertiða'mente/ adv. inadvertently.

desadvertido /desaðβer'tiðo/ a. imprudent.

desadvertimiento /desaðβerti'miento/ n. m. imprudence, rashness.

desadvertir /desaðβer'tir/ v. act imprudently.

desafección /desafek'θion; desafek'sion/ n. f. disaffection.

desafecto /desa'fekto/ a. disaffected.

desafiar /desa'fiar/ v. defy; challenge.

desafinar /desafi'nar/ v. be out of tune.

desafío /desa'fio/ n. m. defiance; challenge.

desaforar /desafo'rar/ v. infringe one's rights; be outrageous.

desafortunado /desafortu'naðo/ a. unfortunate.

desafuero /desa'fuero/ n. m. violation of the law; outrage.

desagraciado /desagra'θiaðo; desagra'siaðo/ a. graceless.

desagradable /desagra'ðaβle/ a. disagreeable, unpleasant.

desagradablemente /desagraðaβle'mente/ adv. disagreeably.

desagradecido /desagraðe'θiðo; desagraðe'siðo/ a. ungrateful.

desagradecimiento /desagraðeθi'miento; desagraðesimiento/ n. m. ingratitude.

desagrado /desa'graðo/ n. m. displeasure.

desagraviar /desagra'βiar/ v. make amends.

desagregar /desagre'gar/ v. separate, disintegrate.

desagriar /desa'griar/ v. mollify, appease.

desaguadero /desagua'ðero/ n. m. drain, outlet; cesspool; sink.

desaguador /desagua'ðor/ n. m. water pipe.

desaguar /desa'guar/ v. drain.

desaguisado /desagi'saðo/ n. m. offense; injury.

desahogadamente /desaogaða'mente/ adv. impudently; brazenly.

desahogado /desao'gaðo/ a. impudent, brazen; cheeky.

desahogar /desao'gar/ v. relieve.

desahogo /desa'ogo/ n. m. relief; nerve, cheek.

desahuciar /desau'θiar; desau'siar/ v. give up hope for; despair of.

desairado /desai'raðo/ a. graceless.

desaire /des'aire/ n. m. slight; scorn. —**desairar,** v.

desajustar /desahus'tar/ v. mismatch, misfit; make unfit.

desalar /desa'lar/ v. hurry, hasten.

desalentar /desalen'tar/ v. make out of breath; discourage.

desaliento /desa'liento/ n. m. discouragement.

desaliñar /desali'nar/ v. disarrange; make untidy.

desaliño /desa'liño/ n. m. slovenliness, untidiness.

desalivar /desali'βar/ v. remove saliva from.

desalmadamente /desalmaða'mente/ adv. mercilessly.

desalmado /desal'maðo/ a. merciless.

desalojamiento /desaloha'miento/ n. m. displacement; dislodging.

desalojar /desalo'har/ v. dislodge.

desalquilado /desalki'laðo/ a. vacant, unrented.

desamar /desa'mar/ v. cease loving.

desamasado /desama'saðo/ a. dissolved, disunited, undone.

desamistarse /desamis'tarse/ v. quarrel, disagree.

desamor /desa'mor/ n. m. disaffection, dislike; hatred.

desamorado /desamo'raðo/ a. cruel; harsh; rude.

desamparador /desampara'ðor/ n. m. deserter.

desamparar /desampa'rar/ v. desert, abandon.

desamparo /desam'paro/ n. m. desertion, abandonment.

desamueblado /desamue'βlaðo/ a. unfurnished.

desamueblar /desamue'βlar/ v. remove furniture from.

desandrajado /desandra'haðo/ a. shabby, ragged.

desanimadamente /desanimaða'mente/ adv. in a discouraged manner; spiritlessly.

desanimar /desani'mar/ v. dishearten, discourage.

desánimo /des'animo/ n. m. discouragement.

desanudar /desanu'ðar/ v. untie; loosen; disentangle.

desapacible /desapa'θiβle; desapa'siβle/ a. rough, harsh; unpleasant.

desaparecer /desapare'θer; desapare'ser/ v. disappear.

desaparición /desapari'θion; desapari'sion/ n. f. disappearance.

desapasionadamente /desapasionaða'mente/ adv. dispassionately.

desapasionado /desapasio'naðo/ a. dispassionate.

desapego /desa'pego/ n. m. impartiality.

desapercibido /desaperθi'βiðo; desapersi'βiðo/ a. unnoticed; unprepared.

desapiadado /desapia'ðaðo/ *a.* merciless, cruel.

desaplicación /desaplika'θion; desaplika-'sion/ *n. f.* indolence, laziness; negligence.

desaplicado /desapli'kaðo/ *a.* indolent, lazy; negligent.

desaposesionar /desaposesio'nar/ *v.* dispossess.

desapreciar /desapre'θiar; desapre'siar/ *v.* depreciate.

desapretador /desapreta'ðor/ *n. m.* screwdriver.

desapretar /desapre'tar/ *v.* loosen; relieve, ease.

desaprisionar /desaprisio'nar/ *v.* set free, release.

desaprobación /desaproβa'θion; desaproβa-'sion/ *n. f.* disapproval.

desaprobar /desapro'βar/ *v.* disapprove.

desaprovechado /desaproβe'tʃaðo/ *a.* useless, profitless; backward.

desaprovechar /desaproβe'tʃar/ *v.* waste; be backward.

desarbolar /desarβo'lar/ *v.* unmast.

desarmado /desar'maðo/ *a.* disarmed, defenseless.

desarmar /desar'mar/ *v.* disarm.

desarme /de'sarme/ *n. m.* disarmament.

desarraigado /desarrai'gaðo/ *a.* rootless.

desarraigar /desarrai'gar/ *v.* uproot; eradicate; expel.

desarreglar /desarre'glar/ *v.* disarrange, mess up.

desarrollar /desarro'ʎar; desarro'yar/ *v.* develop.

desarrollo /desa'rroʎo; des'arroyo/ *n. m.* development.

desarropar /desarro'par/ *v.* undress; uncover.

desarrugar /desarru'gar/ *v.* remove wrinkles from.

desaseado /desase'aðo/ *a.* dirty; disorderly.

desasear /desase'ar/ *v.* make dirty or disorderly.

desaseo /desa'seo/ *n. m.* dirtiness; disorder.

desasir /desa'sir/ *v.* loosen; disengage.

desasociable /desaso'θiaβle; desaso'siaβle/ *a.* unsociable.

desasosegar /desasose'gar/ *v.* disturb.

desasosiego /desaso'siego/ *n. m.* uneasiness.

desastrado /desas'traðo/ *a.* ragged, wretched.

desastre /de'sastre/ *n. m.* disaster.

desastroso /desas'troso/ *a.* disastrous.

desatar /desa'tar/ *v.* untie, undo.

desatención /desaten'θion; desaten'sion/ *n. f.* inattention; disrespect; rudeness.

desatender /desaten'der/ *v.* ignore; disregard.

desatentado /desaten'taðo/ *a.* inconsiderate; imprudent.

desatinado /desati'naðo/ *a.* foolish; insane, wild.

desatino /desa'tino/ *n. m.* blunder. —**desatinar,** *v.*

desatornillar /desatorni'ʎar; desatorni'yar/ *v.* unscrew.

desautorizado /desautori'θaðo; desautori'saðo/ *a.* unauthorized.

desautorizar /desautori'θar; desautori'sar/ *v.* deprive of authority.

desavenencia /desaβe'nenθia; desaβe'nensia/ *n. f.* disagreement, discord.

desaventajado /desaβenta'haðo/ *a.* disadvantageous.

desayuno /desa'yuno/ *n. m.* breakfast. —**desayunar,** *v.*

desazón /desa'θon; desa'son/ *n. f.* insipidity; uneasiness.

desazonado /desaθo'naðo; desaso'naðo/ *a.* insipid; uneasy.

desbandada /desβan'daða/ *n. f.* disbanding.

desbandarse /desβan'darse/ *v.* disband.

desbarajuste /desβara'huste/ *n. m.* disorder, confusion.

desbaratar /desβara'tar/ *v.* destroy.

desbastar /desβas'tar/ *v.* plane, smoothen.

desbocado /desβo'kaðo/ *a.* foul-spoken, indecent.

desbocarse /desβo'karse/ *v.* use obscene language.

desbordamiento /desβorða'miento/ *n. m.* overflow; flood.

desbordar /desβor'ðar/ *v.* overflow.

desbrozar /desβro'θar; desβro'sar/ *v.* clear away rubbish.

descabal /deska'βal/ *a.* incomplete.

descabalar /deskaβa'lar/ *v.* render incomplete; impair.

descabellado /deskaβe'ʎaðo; deskaβe'yaðo/ *a.* absurd, preposterous.

descabezar /deskaβe'θar; deskaβe'sar/ *v.* behead.

descaecimiento /deskaeθi'miento; deskaesi'miento/ *n. m.* weakness; dejection.

descafeinado /deskafei'naðo/ *a.* decaffeinated.

descalabrar /deskala'βrar/ *v.* injure, wound (esp. the head).

descalabro /deska'laβro/ *n. m.* accident, misfortune.

descalzarse /deskal'θarse; deskal'sarse/ *v.* take off one's shoes.

descalzo /des'kalθo; des'kalso/ *a.* shoeless; barefoot.

descaminado /deskami'naðo/ *a.* wrong, misguided.

descaminar /deskami'nar/ *v.* mislead; lead into error.

descamisado /deskami'saðo/ a. shirtless; shabby.

descansillo /deskan'siʎo; deskan'siyo/ n. m. landing (of stairs).

descanso /des'kanso/ n. m. rest. —**descansar**, v.

descarado /deska'raðo/ a. saucy, fresh.

descarga /des'karga/ n. f. discharge.

descargar /deskar'gar/ v. discharge, unload, dump.

descargo /des'kargo/ n. m. unloading; acquittal.

descarnar /deskar'nar/ v. skin.

descaro /des'karo/ n. m. gall, effrontery.

descarriar /deska'rriar/ v. lead or go astray.

descarrilamiento /deskarrila'miento/ n. m. derailment.

descarrilar /deskarri'lar/ v. derail.

descartar /deskar'tar/ v. discard.

descascarar /deskaska'rar/ v. peel; boast, brag.

descendencia /desθen'denθia; dessen'densia/ n. f. descent, origin; progeny.

descender /desθen'der; dessen'der/ v. descend.

descendiente /desθen'diente; dessen'diente/ n. m. & f. descendant.

descendimiento /desθendi'miento; dessendi'miento/ n. m. descent.

descenso /des'θenso; des'senso/ n. m. descent.

descentralización /desθentraliθa'θion; ssentralisa'sion/ n. f. decentralization.

descifrar /desθi'frar; dessi'frar/ v. decipher, puzzle out.

descoco /des'koko/ n. m. boldness, brazenness.

descolgar /deskol'gar/ v. take down.

descollar /desko'ʎar; desko'yar/ v. stand out; excel.

descolorar /deskolo'rar/ v. discolor.

descolorido /deskolo'riðo/ a. pale, faded.

descomedido /deskome'ðiðo/ a. disproportionate; rude.

descomedirse /deskome'ðirse/ v. be rude.

descomponer /deskompo'ner/ v. decompose; break down, get out of order.

descomposición /deskomposi'θion; deskomposi'sion/ n. f. discomposure; disorder, confusion.

descompuesto /deskom'puesto/ a. impudent, rude.

descomulgar /deskomul'gar/ v. excommunicate.

descomunal /deskomu'nal/ a extraordinary, huge.

desconcertar /deskonθer'tar; deskonser'tar/ v. disconcert, baffle.

desconcierto /deskon'θierto; deskon'sierto/ n. m. confusion, disarray.

desconectar /deskonek'tar/ v. disconnect.

desconfiado /deskon'fiaðo/ a. distrustful.

desconfianza /deskon'fianθa; deskon'fiansa/ n. f. distrust.

desconfiar /deskon'fiar/ v. distrust, mistrust; suspect.

descongelar /deskonǥe'lar/ v. defrost.

descongestionante /deskonǥestio'nante/ n. m. decongestant.

desconocer /deskono'θer; deskono'ser/ v. ignore, fail to recognize.

desconocido /deskono'θiðo; deskonos'iðo/ **-da** n. stranger.

desconocimiento /deskonoθi'miento; deskonosi'miento/ n. m. ingratitude; ignorance.

desconsejado /deskonse'haðo/ a. imprudent, ill advised, rash.

desconsolado /deskonso'laðo/ a. disconsolate, wretched.

desconsuelo /deskon'suelo/ n. m. grief.

descontar /deskon'tar/ v. discount, subtract.

descontentar /deskonten'tar/ v. dissatisfy.

descontento /deskon'tento/ n. m. discontent.

descontinuar /deskonti'nuar/ v. discontinue.

desconvenir /deskombe'nir/ v. disagree.

descorazonar /deskoraθo'nar; deskoraso'nar/ v. dishearten.

descorchar /deskor'tʃar/ v. uncork.

descortés /deskor'tes/ a. discourteous, impolite, rude.

descortesía /deskorte'sia/ n. f. discourtesy, rudeness.

descortezar /deskorte'θar; deskorte'sar/ v. peel.

descoyuntar /deskoyun'tar/ v. dislocate.

descrédito /des'kreðito/ n. m. discredit.

describir /deskri'βir/ v. describe.

descripción /deskrip'θion; deskrip'sion/ n. f. description.

descriptivo /deskrip'tiβo/ a. descriptive.

descuartizar /deskuarti'θar; deskuarti'sar/ v. dismember, disjoint.

descubridor /deskuβri'ðor/ **-ra** n. discoverer.

descubrimiento /deskuβri'miento/ n. m. discovery.

descubrir /desku'βrir/ v. discover; uncover; disclose.

descubrirse /desku'βrirse/ v. take off one's hat.

descuento /des'kuento/ n. m. discount.

descuidado /deskui'ðaðo/ a. reckless, careless; slack.

descuido /des'kuiðo/ n. m. neglect. —**descuidar**, v.

desde /'desðe/ prep. since; from. **d. luego**, of course.

desdén /des'ðen/ n. m. disdain. —**desdeñar**, v.

desdeñoso /desðe'noso/ a. contemptuous, disdainful, scornful.

desdicha /des'ðitʃa/ n. f. misfortune.

deseable /dese'aβle/ a. desirable.

desear /dese'ar/ v. desire, wish.

desecar /dese'kar/ v. dry, desiccate.

desechable /dese'tʃaβle/ a. disposable.

desechar /dese'tʃar/ v. scrap, reject.

desecho /de'setʃo/ n. m. remainder, residue; (pl.) waste.

desembalar /desemba'lar/ v. unpack.

desembarazado /desembara'θaðo; desembara'saðo/ a. free; unrestrained.

desembarazar /desembara'θar; desembara-'sar/ v. free; extricate; unburden.

desembarcar /desembar'kar/ v. disembark, go ashore.

desembocar /desembo'kar/ v. flow into.

desembolsar /desembol'sar/ v. disburse; expend.

desembolso /desem'bolso/ n. m. disbursement.

desemejante /deseme'hante/ a. unlike, dissimilar.

desempacar /desempa'kar/ v. unpack.

desempeñar /desempe'nar/ v. carry out; redeem.

desempeño /desempe'no/ n. m. fulfillment.

desencajar /desenka'har/ v. disjoint; disturb.

desencantar /desenkan'tar/ v. disillusion.

desencanto /desen'kanto/ n. m. disillusion.

desencarcelar /desenkarθe'lar; desenkarse-'lar/ v. set free; release.

desenchufar /desentʃu'far/ v. unplug.

desenfadado /desenfa'ðaðo/ a. free; unembarrassed; spacious.

desenfado /desen'faðo/ n. m. freedom; ease; calmness.

desenfocado /desenfo'kaðo/ a. out of focus.

desengaño /deseŋ'gano/ m. disillusion. —**desengañar** v.

desenlace /desen'laθe; desen'lase/ n. m. outcome, conclusion.

desenredar /desenre'ðar/ v. disentangle.

desensartar /desensar'tar/ v. unthread (pearls).

desentenderse /desenten'derse/ v. overlook; avoid noticing.

desenterrar /desente'rrar/ v. disinter, exhume.

desenvainar /desembai'nar/ v. unsheath.

desenvoltura /desembol'tura/ n. f. confidence; impudence; boldness.

desenvolver /desembol'βer/ v evolve, unfold.

deseo /de'seo/ n. m. wish, desire, urge.

deseoso /dese'oso/ a. desirous.

deserción /deser'θion; deser'sion/ n. f. desertion.

desertar /deser'tar/ v. desert.

desertor /deser'tor/ **-ra** n. deserter.

desesperación /desespera'θion; desespera-'sion/ n. f. despair, desperation.

desesperado /desespe'raðo/ a. desperate; hopeless.

desesperar /desespe'rar/ v. despair.

desfachatez /desfatʃa'teθ; desfatʃa'tes/ n. f. cheek (gall).

desfalcar /desfal'kar/ v. embezzle.

desfase horario /des'fase o'rario/ n. m. jet lag.

desfavorable /desfaβo'raβle/ a. unfavorable.

desfigurar /desfigu'rar/ v. disfigure, mar.

desfiladero /desfila'ðero/ n. m. defile.

desfile /des'file/ n. m. parade. —**desfilar**, v.

desfile de modas /des'file de 'moðas/ fashion show.

desgaire /des'gaire/ n. m. slovenliness.

desgana /des'gana/ n. f. lack of appetite; unwillingness; repugnance.

desgarrar /desga'rrar/ v. tear, lacerate.

desgastar /desgas'tar/ v. wear away; waste; erode.

desgaste /des'gaste/ n. m. wear; erosion.

desgracia /des'graθia; des'grasia/ n. f. misfortune.

desgraciado /desgra'θiaðo; desgra'siaðo/ a. unfortunate.

desgranar /desgra'nar/ v. shell.

desgreñar /desgre'nar/ v. dishevel.

deshacer /desa'θer; desa'ser/ v. undo, take apart, destroy.

deshacerse de /desa'θerse de; desa'serse de/ v. get rid of, dispose of.

deshecho /des'etʃo/ a. undone; wasted.

deshelar /dese'lar/ v. thaw; melt.

desheredamiento /desereða'miento/ n. m. disinheriting.

desheredar /desere'ðar/ v. disinherit.

deshielo /des'ielo/ n. m. thaw, melting.

deshinchar /desin'tʃar/ v. reduce a swelling.

deshojarse /deso'harse/ v. shed (leaves).

deshonestidad /desonesti'ðað/ n. f. dishonesty.

deshonesto /deso'nesto/ a. dishonest.

deshonra /de'sonra/ n. f. dishonor.

deshonrar /deson'rar/ v. disgrace; dishonor.

deshonroso /deson'roso/ a dishonorable.

desierto /de'sierto/ n. m. desert, wilderness.

designar /desig'nar/ v. appoint, name.

designio /de'signio/ n. m. purpose, intent.

desigual /desi'gual/ a. uneven, unequal.

desigualdad /desigual'daδ/ n. f. inequality.

desilusión /desilu'sion/ n. f. disappointment.

desinfección /desinfek'θion; desinfek'sion/ n. f. disinfection.

desinfectar /desinfek'tar/ v. disinfect.

desintegrar /desinte'grar/ v. disintegrate, zap.

desinterés /desinte'res/ n. m. indifference.

desinteresado /desintere'saδo/ a. disinterested, unselfish.

desistir /desis'tir/ v. desist, stop.

desleal /desle'al/ a. disloyal.

deslealtad /desleal'taδ/ n. f. disloyalty.

desleír /desle'ir/ v. dilute, dissolve.

desligar /desli'gar/ v. untie, loosen; free, release.

deslindar /deslin'dar/ v. make the boundaries of.

deslinde /des'linde/ n. m. demarcation.

desliz /des'liθ; des'lis/ n. m. slip; false step; weakness.

deslizarse /desli'θarse; desli'sarse/ v. slide; slip; glide; coast.

deslumbramiento /deslumbra'miento/ n. m. dazzling glare; confusion.

deslumbrar /deslumb'rar/ v. dazzle; glare.

deslustrar /deslus'trar/ n. m. tarnish. —**deslustrar,** v.

desmán /des'man/ n. m. mishap; misbehavior; excess.

desmantelar /desmante'lar/ v. dismantle.

desmañado /desma'ɲaδo/ a. awkward, clumsy.

desmaquillarse /desmaki'ʎarse; desmaki-'yarse/ v. remove one's makeup.

desmayar /desma'yar/ v. depress, dishearten.

desmayo /des'mayo/ n. m. faint. —**desmayarse,** v.

desmejorar /desmeho'rar/ v. make worse; decline.

desmembrar /desmem'brar/ v. dismember.

desmemoria /desme'moria/ n. f. forgetfulness.

desmemoriado /desmemo'riaδo/ a. forgetful.

desmentir /desmen'tir/ v. contradict, disprove.

desmenuzable /desmenu'θaβle; desmenu-'saβle/ a. crisp, crumbly.

desmenuzar /desmenu'θar; desmenu'sar/ v. crumble, break into bits.

desmesurado /desmesu'raδo/ a. excessive.

desmobilizar /desmoβili'θar; desmoβili'sar/ v. demobilize.

desmonetización /desmoneti θa'θion; desmonetisa'sion/ n. f. demonetization.

desmonetizar /desmoneti'θar; desmoneti-'sar/ v. demonetize.

desmontado /desmon'taδo/ a. dismounted.

desmontar /desmon'tar/ v. dismantle.

desmontarse /desmon'tarse/ v. dismount.

desmoralización /desmoraliθa'θion; desmoralisa'sion/ n. f. demoralization.

desmoralizar /desmorali'θar; desmorali'sar/ v. demoralize.

desmoronar /desmoro'nar/ v. crumble, decay.

desmovilizar /desmoβili'θar; desmoβili'sar/ v. demobilize.

desnatar /desna'tar/ v. skim.

desnaturalización /desnaturaliθa'θion; desnaturalisa'sion/ n. f. denaturalization.

desnaturalizar /desnaturali'θar; desnaturali'sar/ v. denaturalize.

desnegamiento /desnega'miento/ n. m. denial, contradiction.

desnervar /desner'βar/ v. enervate.

desnivel /desni'βel/ n. m. unevenness or difference in elevation.

desnudamente /desnuδa'mente/ adv. nakedly.

desnudar /desnu'δar/ v. undress.

desnudez /desnu'δeθ; desnu'δes/ n. f. bareness, nudity.

desnudo /des'nuδo/ a. bare, naked.

desnutrición /desnutri'θion; desnutri'sion/ n. f. malnutrition.

desobedecer /desoβeδe'θer; desoβeδe'ser/ v. disobey.

desobediencia /desoβeδien'θia; desoβe-δien'sia/ n. f. disobedience.

desobediente /desoβe'δiente/ a. disobedient.

desobedientemente /desoβeδiente'mente/ adv. disobediently.

desobligar /desoβli'gar/ v. release from obligation; offend.

desocupado /desoku'paδo/ a. idle, not busy; vacant.

desocupar /desoku'par/ v. vacate.

desolación /desola'θion; desola'sion/ n. f. desolation; ruin.

desolado /deso'laδo/ a. desolate. —**desolar,** v.

desollar /deso'ʎar; deso'yar/ v. skin.

desorden /de'sorδen/ n. m. disorder.

desordenar /desorδe'nar/ v. disarrange.

desorganización /desorganiθa'θion; desorganisa'sion/ n. f. disorganization.

desorganizar /desorgani'θar; desorgani'sar/ v. disorganize.

despabilado /despaβi'laδo/ a. vigilant, watchful; lively.

despachar /despa'tʃar/ v. dispatch, ship, send.

despacho /despa'tʃo/ n. m. shipment; dispatch, promptness; office.

despacio /des'paθio; des'pasio/ adv. slowly.

desparpajo /despar'paho/ *n. m.* glibness; fluency of speech.

desparramar /desparra'mar/ *v.* scatter.

despavorido /despaβo'riðo/ *a.* terrified.

despecho /des'petʃo/ *n. m.* spite.

despedazar /despeða'θar; despeða'sar/ *v.* tear up.

despedida /despe'ðiða/ *n. f.* farewell; leave-taking; discharge.

despedir /despe'ðir/ *v.* dismiss, discharge; see off.

despedirse de /despe'ðirse de/ *v.* say good-bye to, take leave of.

despegar /despe'gar/ *v.* unglue; separate; *Aero.* take off.

despego /des'pego/ *n. m.* indifference; disinterest.

despejar /despe'har/ *v.* clear, clear up.

despejo /des'peho/ *n. m.* sprightliness; clarity; without obstruction.

despensa /des'pensa/ *n. f.* pantry.

despensero /despen'sero/ *n. m.* butler.

despeñar /despe'ɲar/ *v.* throw down.

desperdicio /desper'ðiθio; desper'ðisio/ *n. m.* waste. —**desperdiciar,** *v.*

despertador /desperta'ðor/ *n. m.* alarm clock.

despertar /desper'tar/ *v.* wake, wake up.

despesar /despe'sar/ *n. m.* dislike.

despicar /despi'kar/ *v.* satisfy.

despidida /despi'ðiða/ *n. f.* gutter.

despierto /des'pierto/ *a.* awake; alert, wide-awake.

despilfarrado /despilfa'rraðo/ *a* wasteful, extravagant.

despilfarrar /despilfa'rrar/ *v.* waste, squander.

despilfarro /despil'farro/ *n. m.* waste, extravagance.

despique /des'pike/ *n. m.* revenge.

despistar /despis'tar/ *v.* mislead, put off the track.

desplazamiento /desplaθa'miento; desplasa'miento/ *n. m.* displacement.

desplegar /desple'gar/ *v.* display; unfold.

desplome /des'plome/ *n. m.* collapse. —**desplomarse,** *v.*

desplumar /desplu'mar/ *v.* defeather, pluck.

despoblar /despo'βlar/ *v.* depopulate.

despojar /despo'har/ *v.* strip; despoil, plunder.

despojo /des'poho/ *n. m.* plunder, spoils; (*pl.*) remains, debris.

desposado /despo'saðo/ *a.* newly married.

desposar /despo'sar/ *v.* marry.

desposeer /despose'er/ *v.* dispossess.

déspota /'despota/ *n. m. & f.* despot.

despótico /des'potiko/ *a.* despotic.

despotismo /despo'tismo/ *n. m.* despotism, tyranny.

despreciable /despre'θiaβle; despre'siaβle/ *a.* contemptible.

despreciar /despre'θiar; despre'siar/ *v.* spurn, despise, scorn.

desprecio /des'preθio; des'presio/ *n. m.* scorn, contempt.

desprender /despren'der/ *v.* detach, unfasten.

desprenderse /despren'derse/ *v.* loosen, come apart. **d. de,** part with.

desprendido /despren'diðo/ *a.* disinterested.

despreocupado /despreoku'paðo/ *a.* unconcerned; unprejudiced.

desprevenido /despreβe'niðo/ *a.* unprepared, unready.

desproporción /despropor'θion; despropor'sion/ *n. f.* disproportion.

despropósito /despro'posito/ *n. m.* nonsense.

desprovisto /despro'βisto/ *a.* devoid.

después /des'pues/ *adv.* afterwards, later; then, next. **d. de, d. que,** after.

despuntar /despun'tar/ *v.* blunt; remove the point of.

desquiciar /deski'θiar; deski'siar/ *v.* unhinge; disturb, unsettle.

desquitar /deski'tar/ *v.* get revenge, retaliate.

desquite /des'kite/ *n. m.* revenge, retaliation.

desrazonable /desraθo'naβle; desraso'naβle/ *a.* unreasonable.

destacamento /destaka'mento/ *n. m. Mil.* detachment.

destacarse /desta'karse/ *v.* stand out, be prominent.

destajero /desta'hero/ **-a** *n.* **destajista,** *m. & f.* pieceworker.

destapar /desta'par/ *v.* uncover.

destello /des'teʎo; deste'yo/ *n. m.* sparkle, gleam.

destemplar /destem'plar/ *v. Mus.* untune; disturb, upset.

desteñir /deste'ɲir/ *v.* fade, discolor.

desterrado /deste'rraðo/ **-da** *n.* exile.

desterrar /deste'rrar/ *v.* banish, exile.

destetar /deste'tar/ *v.* wean.

destierro /des'tierro/ *n. m.* banishment, exile.

destilación /destila'θion; destila'sion/ *n. f.* distillation.

destilar /desti'lar/ *v.* distill.

destilería /destile'ria/ *n. f.* distillery.

destilería de petróleo /destile'ria de pe'troleo/ oil refinery.

destinación /destina'θion; destina'sion/ *n. f.* destination.

destinar /desti'nar/ *v.* destine, intend.

destinatario /destina'tario/ **-ria** *n.* addressee (mail); payee (money).

destino /des'tino/ *n. m.* destiny, fate; destination.

destitución /destitu'θion; destitu'sion/ *n. f.* dismissal; abandonment.

destituido /desti'tuiðo/ *a.* destitute.

destorcer /destor'θer; destor'ser/ *v.* undo, straighten out.

destornillado /destorni'ʎaðo; destorni'yaðo/ *a.* reckless, careless.

destornillador /destorniʎa'ðor; destorniya'ðor/ *n. m.* screwdriver.

destraillar /destrai'ʎar; destrai'yar/ *v.* unleash; set loose.

destral /des'tral/ *n. m.* hatchet.

destreza /des'treθa; des'tresa/ *n. f.* cleverness; dexterity, skill.

destripar /destri'par/ *v.* eviscerate, disembowel.

destrísimo /des'trisimo/ *a.* extremely dexterous.

destronamiento /destrona'miento/ *n. m.* dethronement.

destronar /destro'nar/ *v.* dethrone.

destrozador /destroθa'ðor; destrosa'ðor/ *n. m.* destroyer, wrecker.

destrozar /destro'θar; destro'sar/ *v.* destroy, wreck.

destrozo /des'troθo; des'troso/ *n. m.* destruction, ruin.

destrucción /destruk'θion; destruk'sion/ *n. f.* destruction.

destructibilidad /destruktiβili'ðað/ *n. f.* destructibility.

destructible /destruk'tiβle/ *a.* destructible.

destructivamente /destruktiβa'mente/ *adv.* destructively.

destructivo /destruk'tiβo/ *a.* destructive.

destruir /destru'ir/ *v.* destroy; wipe out.

desuello /desu'eʎo; desu'eyo/ *n. m.* impudence.

desunión /desu'nion/ *n. f.* disunion; discord; separation.

desunir /desu'nir/ *v.* disconnect, sever.

desusadamente /desusaða'mente/ *adv.* unusually.

desusado /desu'saðo/ *a.* archaic; obsolete.

desuso /de'suso/ *n. m.* disuse.

desvalido /des'βaliðo/ *a.* helpless; destitute.

desvalijador /desβaliha'ðor/ *n. m.* highwayman.

desván /des'βan/ *n. m.* attic.

desvanecerse /desβane'θerse; desβane-'serse/ *v.* vanish; faint.

desvariado /desβa'riaðo/ *a.* delirious; disorderly.

desvarío /desβa'rio/ *n. m.* raving. —**desvariar**, *v.*

desvedado /desβe'ðaðo/ *a.* free; unrestrained.

desveladamente /desβelaða'mente/ *adv.* watchfully, alertly.

desvelado /desβe'laðo/ *a.* watchful; alert.

desvelar /desβe'lar/ *v.* be watchful; keep awake.

desvelo /des'βelo/ *n. m.* vigilance; uneasiness; insomnia.

desventaja /desβen'taha/ *n. f.* disadvantage.

desventar /desβen'tar/ *v.* let air out of.

desventura /desβen'tura/ *n. f.* misfortune.

desventurado /desβentu'raðo/ *a.* unhappy; unlucky.

desvergonzado /desβergon'θaðo; desβergonsaðo/ *a.* shameless, brazen.

desvergüenza /desβer'guenθa; desβer-'guensa/ *n. f.* shamelessness.

desvestir /desβes'tir/ *v.* undress.

desviación /desβia'θion; desβia'sion/ *n. f.* deviation.

desviado /des'βiaðo/ *a.* deviant; remote.

desviar /des'βiar/ *v.* divert; deviate, detour.

desvío /des'βio/ *n. m.* detour; side track; indifference.

desvirtuar /desβir'tuar/ *v.* decrease the value of.

deszumar /desθu'mar; dessu'mar/ *v.* remove the juice from.

detalle /de'taʎe; de'taye/ *n. m.* detail. —**detallar**, *v.*

detective /de'tektiβe/ *n. m. & f.* detective.

detención /deten'θion; deten'sion/ *n. f.* detention, arrest.

detenedor /detene'ðor/ **-ra** *n.* stopper; catch.

detener /dete'ner/ *v.* detain, stop; arrest.

detenidamente /deteniða'mente/ *adv.* carefully, slowly.

detenido /dete'niðo/ *adv.* stingy; thorough.

detergente /deter'hente/ *a.* detergent.

deterioración /deteriora'θion; deteriora-'sion/ *n. f.* deterioration.

deteriorar /deterio'rar/ *v.* deteriorate.

determinable /determi'naβle/ *a.* determinable.

determinación /determina'θion; determina-'sion/ *n. f.* determination.

determinar /determi'nar/ *v.* determine, settle, decide.

determinismo /determi'nismo/ *n. m.* determinism.

determinista /determi'nista/ *n. & a.* determinist.

detestable /detes'taβle/ *a.* detestable, hateful.

detestablemente /detestaβle'mente/ *adv.* detestably, hatefully, abhorrently.

detestación /detesta'θion; detesta'sion/ *n. f.* detestation, hatefulness.

detestar /detes'tar/ v. detest.

detonación /detona'θion; detona'sion/ n. f. detonation.

detonar /deto'nar/ v. detonate, explode.

detracción /detrak'θion; detrak'sion/ n. f. detraction, defamation.

detractar /detrak'tar/ v. detract, defame, vilify.

detraer /detra'er/ v. detract.

detrás /de'tras/ adv. behind; in back.

detrimento /detri'mento/ n. m. detriment, damage.

deuda /'deuða/ n. f. debt.

deudo /'deuðo/ -da n. relative, kin.

deudor /deu'ðor/ -ra n. debtor.

Deuteronomio /deutero'nomio/ n. m. Deuteronomy.

devalar /deβa'lar/ v. drift off course.

devanar /deβa'nar/ v. to wind, as on a spool.

devanear /deβane'ar/ v. talk deliriously, rave.

devaneo /deβa'neo/ n. m. frivolity; idle pursuit; delirium.

devastación /deβasta'θion; deβasta'sion/ n. f. devastation, ruin, havoc.

devastador /deβasta'ðor/ a. devastating.

devastar /deβas'tar/ v. devastate.

devenir /deβe'nir/ v. happen, occur; become.

devoción /deβo'θion; deβo'sion/ n. f. devotion.

devocionario /deβoθio'nario; deβosio'nario/ n. m. prayer book.

devocionero /deβoθio'nero; deβosio'nero/ a. devotional.

devolver /deβol'βer/ v. return, give back.

devorar /deβo'rar/ v. devour.

devotamente /deβota'mente/ adv. devotedly, devoutly, piously.

devoto /de'βoto/ a. devout; devoted.

deyección /deiek'θion; deiek'sion/ n. f. depression, dejection.

día /'dia/ n. m. day. **buenos días,** good morning.

diabetes /dia'βetes/ n. f. diabetes.

diabético /dia'βetiko/ a. diabetic.

diablear /diaβle'ar/ v. play pranks.

diablo /'diaβlo/ n. m. devil.

diablura /dia'βlura/ n. f. mischief.

diabólicamente /diaβolika'mente/ adv. diabolically.

diabólico /dia'βoliko/ a. diabolic, devilish.

diaconato /diako'nato/ n. m. deaconship.

diaconía /diako'nia/ n. f. deaconry.

diácono /'diakono/ n. m. deacon.

diacrítico /dia'kritiko/ a. diacritic.

diadema /dia'ðema/ n. f. diadem; crown.

diáfano /'diafano/ a. transparent.

diafragma /dia'fragma/ n. m. diaphragm.

diagnosticar /diagnosti'kar/ v. diagnose.

diagonal /diago'nal/ n. f. diagonal.

diagonalmente /diagonal'mente/ adv. diagonally.

diagrama /dia'grama/ n. m. diagram.

dialectal /dialek'tal/ a. dialectal.

dialéctico /dia'lektiko/ a. dialectic.

dialecto /dia'lekto/ n. m. dialect.

diálogo /'dialogo/ n. m. dialogue.

diamante /dia'mante/ n. m. diamond.

diamantista /diaman'tista/ n. m. & f. diamond cutter; jeweler.

diametral /diame'tral/ a. diametric.

diametralmente /diametral'mente/ adv. diametrically.

diámetro /'diametro/ n. m. diameter.

diana /'diana/ n. f. reveille; dartboard.

diapasón /diapa'son/ n. m. standard pitch; tuning fork.

diaplejía /diaple'hia/ n. f. paralysis.

diariamente /diaria'mente/ adv. daily.

diario /'diario/ a. & m. daily; daily paper; diary; journal.

diarrea /dia'rrea/ n. f. diarrhea.

diatriba /dia'triβa/ n. f. diatribe, harangue.

dibujo /di'βuho/ n. m. drawing, sketch. —**dibujar,** v.

dicción /dik'θion; dik'sion/ n. f. diction.

diccionario /dikθio'nario; diksio'nario/ n. m. dictionary.

diccionarista /dikθiona'rista; diksiona'rista/ n. m. & f. lexicographer.

dicha /'ditʃa/ n. f. happiness.

dicho /'ditʃo/ n. m. saying.

dichoso /di'tʃoso/ a. happy; fortunate.

diciembre /di'θiembre; di'siembre/ n. m. December.

dicotomía /dikoto'mia/ n. f. dichotomy.

dictado /dik'taðo/ n. m. dictation.

dictador /dikta'ðor/ -ra n. dictator.

dictadura /dikta'ðura/ n. f. dictatorship.

dictamen /dik'tamen/ n. m. dictate.

dictar /dik'tar/ v. dictate; direct.

dictatorial /diktato'rial/ **dictatorio** a. dictatorial.

didáctico /di'ðaktiko/ a. didactic.

diecinueve /dieθi'nueβe; diesi'nueβe/ a. & pron. nineteen.

dieciocho /die'θiotʃo; die'siotʃo/ a. & pron. eighteen.

dieciseis /dieθi'seis; diesi'seis/ a. & pron. sixteen.

diecisiete /dieθi'siete; diesi'siete/ a. & pron. seventeen.

diente /'diente/ n. m. tooth.

diestramente /diestra'mente/ adv. ably, skillfully; ingeniously.

diestro /'diestro/ a. dexterous, skillful; clever.

dieta /'dieta/ n. f. diet; allowance.

dietética /die'tetika/ *n. f.* dietetics.

dietético /die'tetiko/ *a.* **1.** dietetic; dietary. —*n.* **2.** -**ca.** dietician.

diez /dieθ; dies/ *a. & pron.* ten.

diezmal /dieθ'mal; dies'mal/ *a.* decimal.

diezmar /dieθ'mar; dies'mar/ *v.* decimate.

difamación /difama'θion; difama'sion/ *n. f.* defamation, smear.

difamar /difa'mar/ *v.* defame, smear, libel.

difamatorio /difama'torio/ *a.* defamatory.

diferencia /dife'renθia; dife'rensia/ *n. f.* difference.

diferencial /diferen'θial; diferen'sial/ *a. & f.* differential.

diferenciar /diferen'θiar; diferen'siar/ *v.* differentiate, distinguish.

diferente /dife'rente/ *a.* different.

diferentemente /diferente'mente/ *adv.* differently.

diferir /dife'rir/ *v.* differ; defer, put off.

difícil /di'fiθil; di'fisil/ *a.* difficult, hard.

difícilmente /difiθil'mente; difisil'mente/ *adv.* with difficulty or hardship.

dificultad /difikul'taθ/ *n. f.* difficulty.

dificultar /difikul'tar/ *v.* make difficult.

dificultoso /difikul'toso/ *a.* difficult, hard.

difidencia /difi'ðenθia; difi'ðensia/ *n. f.* diffidence.

difidente /difi'ðente/ *a.* diffident.

difteria /dif'teria/ *n. f.* diphtheria.

difundir /difun'dir/ *v.* diffuse, spread.

difunto /di'funto/ *a.* **1.** deceased, dead, late. —*n.* **2.** -**ta,** deceased person.

difusamente /difusa'mente/ *adv.* diffusely.

difusión /difu'sion/ *n. f.* diffusion, spread.

digerible /dihe'riβle/ *a.* digestible.

digerir /dihe'rir/ *v.* digest.

digestible /dihes'tiβle/ *a.* digestible.

digestión /dihes'tion/ *n. f.* digestion.

digestivo /dihes'tiβo/ *a.* digestive.

digesto /di'hesto/ *n. m.* digest or code of laws.

digitado /dihi'taðo/ *a.* digitate.

digital /dihi'tal/ *a.* **1.** digital. —*n.* **2.** *f.* foxglove, digitalis.

dignación /digna'θion; digna'sion/ *f.* condescension; deigning.

dignamente /digna'mente/ *adv.* with dignity.

dignarse /dig'narse/ *v.* condescend, deign.

dignatario /digna'tario/ -**ra** *n.* dignitary.

dignidad /digni'ðaθ/ *n. f.* dignity.

dignificar /dignifi'kar/ *v.* dignify.

digno /'digno/ *a.* worthy; dignified.

digresión /digre'sion/ *n. f.* digression.

digresivo /digre'siβo/ *a.* digressive.

dij, dije /dih; 'dihe/ *n. m.* trinket, piece of jewelry.

dilación /dila'θion; dila'sion/ *n. f.* delay.

dilapidación /dilapiða'θion; dilapi'ðasion/ *n. f.* dilapidation.

dilapidado /dilapi'ðaðo/ *a.* dilapidated.

dilatación /dilata'θion; dilata'sion/ *n. f.* dilatation, enlargement.

dilatar /dila'tar/ *v.* dilate; delay; expand.

dilatoria /dila'toria/ *n. f.* delay.

dilatorio /dila'torio/ *a.* dilatory.

dilecto /di'lekto/ *a.* loved.

dilema /di'lema/ *n. m.* dilemma.

diligencia /dili'henθia; dili'hensia/ *n. f.* diligence, industriousness.

diligente /dili'hente/ *a.* diligent, industrious.

diligentemente /dilihente'mente/ *adv.* diligently.

dilogía /dilo'hia/ *n. f.* ambiguous meaning.

dilución /dilu'θion; dilu'sion/ *n. f.* dilution.

diluir /di'luir/ *v.* dilute.

diluvial /dilu'βial/ *a.* diluvial.

diluvio /di'luβio/ *n. m.* flood, deluge.

dimensión /dimen'sion/ *n. f.* dimension; measurement.

diminución /diminu'θion; diminu'sion/ *n. f.* diminution.

diminuto /dimi'nuto/ **diminutivo** *a.* diminutive, little.

dimisión /dimi'sion/ *n. f.* resignation.

dimitir /dimi'tir/ *v.* resign.

Dinamarca /dina'marka/ *n. f.* Denmark.

dinamarqués /dinamar'kes/ -**esa** *a. & n.* Danish, Dane.

dinámico /di'namiko/ *a.* dynamic.

dinamita /dina'mita/ *n. f.* dynamite.

dinamitero /dinami'tero/ -**ra** *n.* dynamiter.

dínamo /'dinamo/ *n. m.* dynamo.

dinasta /di'nasta/ *n. m.* dynast, king, monarch.

dinastía /dinas'tia/ *n. f.* dynasty.

dinástico /di'nastiko/ *a.* dynastic.

dinero /di'nero/ *n. m.* money, currency.

dinosauro /dino'sauro/ *n. m.* dinosaur.

diócesis /'dioθesis; 'diosesis/ *n. f.* diocese.

Dios /dios/ *n. m.* God.

dios -**sa** *n.* god, goddess.

diploma /di'ploma/ *n. m.* diploma.

diplomacia /diplo'maθia; diplo'masia/ *n. f.* diplomacy.

diplomado /diplo'maðo/ -**da** *a.* graduate.

diplomarse /diplo'marse/ *v.* graduate (from a school).

diplomática /diplo'matika/ *n. f.* diplomacy.

diplomático /diplo'matiko/ -**ca** *a. & n.* diplomat; diplomatic.

dipsomanía /dipsoma'nia/ *n. f.* dipsomania.

diptongo /dip'toŋgo/ *n. m.* diphthong.

diputación /diputa'θion; diputa'sion/ *n. f.* deputation, delegation.

diputado /dipu'taðo/ -**da** *n.* deputy; delegate.

diputar /dipu'tar/ v. depute, delegate; empower.

dique /'dike/ n. m. dike; dam.

dirección /direk'θion; direk'sion/ n. f. direction; address; guidance; Com. management.

directamente /direkta'mente/ adv. directly.

directo /di'rekto/ a. direct.

director /direk'tor/ -ra n. director; manager.

directorio /direk'torio/ n. m. directory.

dirigente /diri'hente/ a. directing, controlling, managing.

dirigible /diri'hiβle/ n. m. dirigible.

dirigir /diri'hir/ v. direct; lead; manage.

dirigirse a /diri'hirse a/ v. address; approach, turn to; head for.

dirruir /di'rruir/ v. destroy, devastate.

disanto /di'santo/ n. m. holy day.

discantar /diskan'tar/ v. sing (esp. in counterpoint); discuss.

disceptación /disθepta'θion; dissepta'sion/ n. f. argument, quarrel.

disceptar /disθep'tar; dissep'tar/ v. argue, quarrel.

discernimiento /disθerni'miento; disserni'miento/ n. m. discernment.

discernir /disθer'nir; disser'nir/ v. discern.

disciplina /disθi'plina; dissi'plina/ n. f. discipline.

disciplinable /disθipli'naβle; dissipli'naβle/ a. disciplinable.

disciplinar /disθipli'nar; dissipli'nar/ v. discipline, train, teach.

discípulo /dis'θipulo; dis'sipulo/ -la n. disciple, follower; pupil.

disco /'disko/ n. m. disk; (phonograph) record.

disco compacto /'disko kom'pakto/ compact disk.

disco duro /'disko 'duro/ hard disk.

disco flexible /'disko flek'siβle/ floppy disk.

discontinuación /diskontinua'θion; diskontinua'sion/ n. f. discontinuation.

discontinuar /diskonti'nuar/ v. discontinue, break off, cease.

discordancia /diskor'ðanθia; diskor'ðansia/ n. f. discordance.

discordar /diskor'ðar/ v. disagree, conflict.

discordia /dis'korðia/ n. f. discord.

discoteca /disko'teka/ n. f. disco, discotheque.

discreción /diskre'θion; diskre'sion/ n. f. discretion.

discrecional /diskreθio'nal; diskresio'nal/ a. optional.

discrecionalmente /diskreθional'mente; diskresional'mente/ adv. optionally.

discrepancia /diskre'panθia; diskre'pansia/ n. f. discrepancy.

discretamente /diskreta'mente/ adv. discreetly.

discreto /dis'kreto/ a. discreet.

discrimen /dis'krimen/ n. m. risk, hazard.

discriminación /diskrimina'θion; diskrimina'sion/ n. f. discrimination.

discriminar /diskrimi'nar/ v. discriminate.

disculpa /dis'kulpa/ n. f. excuse; apology.

disculpar /diskul'par/ v. excuse; exonerate.

disculparse /diskul'parse/ v. apologize.

discurrir /disku'rrir/ v. roam; flow; think; plan.

discursante /diskur'sante/ n. lecturer, speaker.

discursivo /diskur'siβo/ a. discursive.

discurso /dis'kurso/ n. m. speech, talk.

discusión /disku'sion/ n. f. discussion.

discutible /disku'tiβle/ a. debatable.

discutir /disku'tir/ v. discuss; debate; contest.

disecación /diseka'θion; diseka'sion/ n. f. dissection.

disecar /dise'kar/ v. dissect.

disección /disek'θion; disek'sion/ n. f. dissection.

diseminación /disemina'θion; disemina'sion/ n. f. dissemination.

diseminar /disemi'nar/ v. disseminate, spread.

disensión /disen'sion/ n. f. dissension; dissent.

disenso /di'senso/ n. m. dissent.

disentería /disente'ria/ n. f. dysentery.

disentir /disen'tir/ v. disagree, dissent.

diseñador /diseɲa'ðor/ -ra n. designer.

diseño /di'seɲo/ n. m. design. —**diseñar,** v.

disertación /diserta'θion; diserta'sion/ n. f. dissertation.

disforme /dis'forme/ a. deformed, monstrous, ugly.

disformidad /disformi'ðað/ n. f. deformity.

disfraz /dis'fraθ; dis'fras/ n. m. disguise. —**disfrazar,** v.

disfrutar /disfru'tar/ v. enjoy.

disfrute /dis'frute/ n. m. enjoyment.

disgustar /disgus'tar/ v. displease; disappoint.

disgusto /dis'gusto/ n. m. displeasure; disappointment.

disidencia /disi'ðenθia; disi'ðensia/ n. f. dissidence.

disidente /disi'ðente/ a. & n. dissident.

disímil /di'simil/ a. unlike.

disimilitud /disimili'tuð/ n. f. dissimilarity.

disimulación /disimula'θion; disimula'sion/ n. f. dissimulation.

disimulado /disimu'laðo/ a. dissembling, feigning; sly.

disimular /disimu'lar/ v. hide; dissemble.

disimulo /di'simulo/ n. m. pretense.

disipación /disipa'θion; disipa'sion/ *n. f.* dissipation.

disipado /disi'paðo/ *a.* dissipated; wasted; scattered.

disipar /disi'par/ *v.* waste; scatter.

dislexia /dis'leksia/ *n. f.* dyslexia.

disléxico /dis'leksiko/ *a.* dyslexic.

dislocación /disloka'θion; disloka'sion/ *n. f.* dislocation.

dislocar /dislo'kar/ *v.* dislocate; displace.

disminuir /dismi'nuir/ *v.* diminish, lessen, reduce.

disociación /disoθia'θion; disosia'sion/ *n. f.* dissociation.

disociar /diso'θiar; diso'siar/ *v.* dissociate.

disolubilidad /disoluβili'ðað/ *n. f.* dissolubility.

disoluble /diso'luβle/ *a.* dissoluble.

disolución /disolu'θion; disolu'sion/ *n. f.* dissolution.

disolutamente /disoluta'mente/ *adv.* dissolutely.

disoluto /diso'luto/ *a.* dissolute.

disolver /disol'βer/ *v.* dissolve.

disonancia /diso'nanθia; diso'nansia/ *n. f.* dissonance; discord.

disonante /diso'nante/ *a.* dissonant; discordant.

disonar /diso'nar/ *v.* be discordant; clash in sound.

dísono /di'sono/ *a.* dissonant.

dispar /dis'par/ *a.* unlike.

disparadamente /disparaða'mente/ *adv.* hastily, hurriedly.

disparar /dispa'rar/ *v.* shoot, fire (a weapon).

disparatado /dispara'taðo/ *a.* nonsensical.

disparatar /dispara'tar/ *v.* talk nonsense.

disparate /dispa'rate/ *n. m.* nonsense, tall tale.

disparejo /dispa'reho/ *a.* uneven, unequal.

disparidad /dispari'ðað/ *n. f.* disparity.

disparo /dis'paro/ *n. m.* shot.

dispendio /dis'pendio/ *n. m.* extravagance.

dispendioso /dispen'dioso/ *a.* expensive; extravagant.

dispensa /dis'pensa/ **dispensación** *n. f.* dispensation.

dispensable /dispen'saβle/ *a.* dispensable; excusable.

dispensar /dispen'sar/ *v.* dispense, excuse; grant.

dispensario /dispen'sario/ *n. m.* dispensary.

dispepsia /dis'pepsia/ *n. f.* dyspepsia.

dispéptico /dis'peptiko/ *a.* dyspeptic.

dispersar /disper'sar/ *v.* scatter; dispel; disband.

dispersión /disper'sion/ *n. f.* dispersion, dispersal.

disperso /dis'perso/ *a.* dispersed.

displicente /displi'θente; displi'sente/ *a.* unpleasant.

disponer /dispo'ner/ *v.* dispose. **d. de,** have at one's disposal.

disponible /dispo'niβle/ *a.* available.

disposición /disposi'θion; disposi'sion/ *n. f.* disposition; disposal.

dispuesto /dis'puesto/ *a.* disposed, inclined; attractive.

disputa /dis'puta/ *n. f.* dispute, argument.

disputable /dispu'taβle/ *a.* disputable.

disputador /disputa'ðor/ **-ra** *n.* disputant.

disputar /dispu'tar/ *v.* argue; dispute.

disquete /dis'kete/ *n. m.* diskette.

disquetera /diske'tera/ *n. f.* disk drive.

disquisición /diskisi'θion; diskisi'sion/ *n. f.* disquisition.

distancia /dis'tanθia; dis'tansia/ *n. f.* distance.

distante /dis'tante/ *a.* distant.

distantemente /distante'mente/ *adv.* distantly.

distar /dis'tar/ *v.* be distant, be far.

distender /disten'der/ *v.* distend, swell, enlarge.

distensión /disten'sion/ *n. f.* distension, swelling.

dístico /'distiko/ *n. m.* couplet.

distinción /distin'θion; distin'sion/ *n. f.* distinction, difference.

distingo /dis'tiŋgo/ *n. m.* restriction.

distinguible /distiŋ'guiβle/ *a.* distinguishable.

distinguido /distiŋ'guiðo/ *a.* distinguished, prominent.

distinguir /distiŋ'guir/ *v.* distinguish; make out, spot.

distintamente /distinta'mente/ *adv* distinctly, clearly; differently.

distintivo /distin'tiβo/ *a.* distinctive.

distintivo del país /distin'tiβo del pa'is/ country code.

distinto /dis'tinto/ *a.* distinct; different.

distracción /distrak'θion; distrak'sion/ *n. f.* distraction, pastime; absent-mindedness.

distraer /distra'er/ *v.* distract.

distraídamente /distraiða'mente/ *adv.* absent-mindedly, distractedly.

distraído /distra'iðo/ *a.* absent-minded; distracted.

distribución /distriβu'θion; distriβu'sion/ *n. f.* distribution.

distribuidor /distriβui'ðor/ **-ra** *n.* distributor.

distribuir /distri'βuir/ *v.* distribute.

distributivo /distriβu'tiβo/ *a.* distributive.

distributor /distriβu'tor/ *n. m.* distributor.

distrito /dis'trito/ *n. m.* district.

disturbar /distur'βar/ *v.* disturb, trouble.

disturbio /dis'turβio/ *n. m.* disturbance, outbreak; turmoil.

disuadir /disua'ðir/ *v.* dissuade.

disuasión /disua'sion/ *n. f.* dissuasion; deterrence.

disuasivo /disua'siβo/ *a.* dissuasive.

disyunción /disyun'θion; disyun'sion/ *n. f.* disjunction.

ditirambo /diti'rambo/ *n. m.* dithyramb.

diurno /'diurno/ *a.* diurnal.

diva /'diβa/ *n. f.* diva, prima donna.

divagación /diβaga'θion; diβaga'sion/ *n. f.* digression.

divagar /diβa'gar/ *v.* digress, ramble.

diván /di'βan/ *n. m.* couch.

divergencia /diβer'henθia; diβer'hensia/ *n. f.* divergence.

divergente /diβer'hente/ *a.* divergent, differing.

divergir /diβer'hir/ *v.* diverge.

diversamente /diβersa'mente/ *adv.* diversely.

diversidad /diβersi'ðað/ *n. f.* diversity.

diversificar /diβersifi'kar/ *v.* diversify, vary.

diversión /diβer'sion/ *n. f.* diversion, pastime.

diverso /di'βerso/ *a.* diverse, different; (*pl.*) various, several.

divertido /diβer'tiðo/ *a.* humorous, amusing.

divertimiento /diβerti'miento/ *n. m.* diversion; amusement.

divertir /diβer'tir/ *v.* entertain, amuse.

divertirse /diβer'tirse/ *v.* enjoy oneself, have a good time.

dividendo /diβi'ðendo/ *n. m.* dividend.

dividadero /diβiði'ðero/ *a.* to be divided.

dividido /diβi'ðiðo/ *a.* divided.

dividir /diβi'ðir/ *v.* divide; separate.

divieso /di'βieso/ *n. m. Med.* boil.

divinamente /diβina'mente/ *adv.* divinely.

divinidad /diβini'ðað/ *n. f.* divinity.

divinizar /diβini'θar; diβini'sar/ *v.* deify.

divino /di'βino/ *a.* divine; heavenly.

divisa /di'βisa/ *n. f.* badge, emblem.

divisar /diβi'sar/ *v.* sight, make out.

divisibilidad /diβisiβili'ðað/ *n. f.* divisibility.

divisible /diβi'siβle/ *a.* divisible.

división /diβi'sion/ *n. f.* division.

divisivo /diβi'siβo/ *a.* divisive.

divo /'diβo/ *n. m.* movie star.

divorcio /di'βorθio; di'βorsio/ *n. m.* divorce. —**divorciar,** *v.*

divulgable /diβul'gaβle/ *a.* divulgable.

divulgación /diβulga'θion; diβulga'sion/ *n. f.* divulgation.

divulgar /diβul'gar/ *v.* divulge, reveal.

dobladamente /doβlaða'mente/ *adv.* doubly.

dobladillo /doβla'ðiʎo; doβla'ðiyo/ *n. m.* hem of a skirt or dress.

dobladura /doβla'ðura/ *n. f.* fold; bend.

doblar /do'βlar/ *v.* fold; bend.

doble /'doβle/ *a.* double.

doblegable /doβle'gaβle/ *a.* flexible, foldable.

doblegar /doβle'gar/ *v.* fold, bend; yield.

doblez /do'βleθ; doβles/ *n. m.* fold; duplicity.

doblón /do'βlon/ *n. m.* doubloon.

doce /'doθe; 'dose/ *a. & pron.* twelve.

docena /do'θena; do'sena/ *n. f.* dozen.

docente /do'θente; do'sente/ *a.* educational.

dócil /'doθil; 'dosil/ *a.* docile.

docilidad /doθili'ðað; dosili'ðað/ *n. f.* docility, tractableness.

dócilmente /doθil'mente; dosil'mente/ *adv.* docilely, meekly.

doctamente /dokta'mente/ *adv.* learnedly, profoundly.

docto /'dokto/ *a.* learned, expert.

doctor /dok'tor/ **-ra** *n.* doctor.

doctorado /dokto'raðo/ *n. m.* doctorate.

doctoral /dokto'ral/ *a.* doctoral.

doctrina /dok'trina/ *n. f.* doctrine.

doctrinador /doktrina'ðor/ **-ra** *n.* teacher.

doctrinal /doktri'nal/ *n. m.* doctrinal.

doctrinar /doktri'nar/ *v.* teach.

documentación /dokumenta'θion; dokumenta'sion/ *n. f.* documentation.

documental /dokumen'tal/ *a.* documentary.

documento /doku'mento/ *n. m.* document.

dogal /do'gal/ *n. m.* noose.

dogma /'dogma/ *n. m.* dogma.

dogmáticamente /dog'matikamente/ *adv.* dogmatically.

dogmático /dog'matiko/ *n. m.* dogmatic.

dogmatismo /dogma'tismo/ *n. m.* dogmatism.

dogmatista /dogma'tista/ *n. m. & f.* dogmatist.

dogo /'dogo/ *n. m.* bulldog.

dolar /'dolar/ *v.* cut, chop, hew.

dólar *n m.* dollar.

dolencia /do'lenθia; do'lensia/ *n. f.* pain; disease.

doler /do'ler/ *v.* ache, hurt, be sore.

doliente /do'liente/ *a.* ill; aching.

dolor /do'lor/ *n. m.* pain; grief, sorrow, woe.

dolor de cabeza /do'lor de ka'βeθa; do'lor de ka'βesa/ headache.

dolor de espalda /do'lor de es'palda/ backache.

dolor de estómago /do'lor de es'tomago/ stomachache.

dolorido /dolo'riðo/ *a.* painful, sorrowful.

dolorosamente /dolorosa'mente/ adv. painfully, sorrowfully.

doloroso /dolo'roso/ a. painful, sorrowful.

dolosamente /dolosa'mente/ adv. deceitfully.

doloso /do'loso/ a. deceitful.

domable /do'maβle/ a. that can be tamed or managed.

domar /do'mar/ v. tame; subdue.

dombo /'dombo/ n. m. dome.

domesticable /domesti'kaβle/ a. that can be domesticated.

domesticación /domestika'θion; domestika'sion/ n. f. domestication.

domésticamente /domestika'mente/ adv. domestically.

domesticar /domesti'kar/ v. tame, domesticate.

domesticidad /domestiθi'ðað; domestisi'ðað/ n. f. domesticity.

doméstico /do'mestiko/ a. domestic.

domicilio /domi'θilio; domi'silio/ n. m. dwelling, home, residence, domicile.

dominación /domina'θion; domina'sion/ n. f. domination.

dominador /domina'ðor/ a. dominating.

dominante /domi'nante/ a. dominant.

dominar /domi'nar/ v. rule, dominate; master.

dómine /'domine/ n. m. teacher.

domingo /do'miŋgo/ n. m. Sunday.

dominio /'dominio/ n. m. domain; rule; power.

dominó /domi'no/ n. m. domino.

domo /'domo/ n. m. dome.

Don /don/ title used before a man's first name.

don n. m. gift.

donación /dona'θion; dona'sion/ n. f. donation.

donador /dona'ðor/ -ra n. giver, donor.

donaire /do'naire/ n. m. grace.

donairosamente /donairosa'mente/ adv. gracefully.

donairoso /donai'roso/ a. graceful.

donante /do'nante/ n. giver, donor.

donar /do'nar/ v. donate.

donativo /dona'tiβo/ n. m. donation, contribution; gift.

doncella /don'θeʎa; don'seya/ n. f. lass; maid.

donde /'donde/ **dónde** conj. & adv. where.

dondequiera /donde'kiera/ adv. wherever, anywhere.

donosamente /donosa'mente/ adv. gracefully; wittily.

donoso /do'noso/ a. graceful; witty.

donosura /dono'sura/ n. f. gracefulness; wittiness.

Doña /'doɲa/ title used before a lady's first name.

dopar /do'par/ v. drug, dope.

dorado /do'raðo/ a. gilded.

dorador /dora'ðor/ -ra n. gilder.

dorar /do'rar/ v. gild.

dórico /'doriko/ a. Doric.

dormidero /dormi'ðero/ a. sleep-inducing; soporific.

dormido /dor'miðo/ a. asleep.

dormir /dor'mir/ v. sleep.

dormirse /dor'mirse/ v. fall asleep, go to sleep.

dormitar /dormi'tar/ v. doze.

dormitorio /dormi'torio/ n. m. dormitory; bedroom.

dorsal /dor'sal/ a. dorsal.

dorso /'dorso/ n. m. spine.

dos /dos/ a. & pron. two. **los d.**, both.

dosañal /dosa'ɲal/ a. biennial.

doscientos /dos'θientos; dos'sientos/ a & pron. two hundred.

dosel /do'sel/ n. m. canopy; platform, dais.

dosificación /dosifika'θion; dosifika'sion/ n. f. dosage.

dosis /'dosis/ n. f. dose.

dotación /dota'θion; dota'sion/ n. f. endowment; Naut. crew.

dotador /dota'ðor/ -ra n. donor.

dotar /do'tar/ v. endow; give a dowry to.

dote /'dote/ n. f. dowry; (pl.) talents.

dragaminas /draga'minas/ n. m. mine sweeper.

dragar /dra'gar/ v. dredge; sweep.

dragón /dra'gon/ n. m. dragon; dragoon.

dragonear /dragone'ar/ v. pretend to be.

drama /'drama/ n. m. drama; play.

dramática /dra'matika/ n. f. drama, dramatic art.

dramáticamente /dramatika'mente/ adv. dramatically.

dramático /dra'matiko/ a. dramatic.

dramatizar /dramati'θar; dramati'sar/ v. dramatize.

dramaturgo /drama'turgo/ -ga n. playwright, dramatist.

drástico /'drastiko/ a. drastic.

drenaje /dre'nahe/ n. m. drainage.

dríada /'driaða/ n. f. dryad.

dril /dril/ n. m. denim.

driza /'driθa; 'drisa/ n. f. halyard.

droga /'droga/ n. f. drug.

drogadicto /droga'ðikto/ -ta n. drug addict.

droguería /droge'ria/ n. f. drugstore.

droguero /dro'gero/ n. m. druggist.

dromedario /drome'ðario/ n. m. dromedary.

druida /'druiða/ n. m. & f. Druid.

dualidad /duali'ðað/ n. f. duality.

dubitable /duβi'taβle/ *a.* doubtful.

dubitación /duβita'θion; duβita'sion/ *n. f.* doubt.

ducado /du'kaðo/ *n. m.* duchy.

ducal /du'kal/ *a.* ducal.

ducha /'dutʃa/ *n. f.* shower (bath).

ducharse /du'tʃarse/ *v.* take a shower.

dúctil /'duktil/ *a.* ductile.

ductilidad /duktili'ðað/ *n. f.* ductility.

duda /'duða/ *n. f.* doubt.

dudable /du'ðaβle/ *a.* doubtful.

dudar /du'ðar/ *v.* doubt; hesitate; question.

dudosamente /duðosa'mente/ *adv.* doubtfully.

dudoso /du'ðoso/ *a.* dubious; doubtful.

duela /'duela/ *n. f.* stave.

duelista /due'lista/ *n. m. & f.* duelist.

duelo /'duelo/ *n. m.* duel; grief; mourning.

duende /'duende/ *n. m.* elf, hobgoblin.

dueño /'dueɲo/ **-ña** *n.* owner; landlord -lady; master, mistress.

dulce /'dulθe; dulse/ *a.* **1.** sweet. **agua d.,** fresh water. —*n.* **2.** *m.* piece of candy; (*pl.*) candy.

dulcedumbre /dulθe'ðumbre; dulse'ðumbre/ *n. f.* sweetness.

dulcemente /dulθe'mente; dulse'mente/ *adv.* sweetly.

dulcería /dulθe'ria; dulse'ria/ *n. f.* confectionery; candy shop.

dulcificar /dulθifi'kar; dulsifi'kar/ *v.* sweeten.

dulzura /dul'θura; dul'sura/ *n. f.* sweetness; mildness.

duna /'duna/ *n. f.* dune.

dúo /'duo/ *n. m.* duo, duet.

duodenal /duoðe'nal/ *a.* duodenal.

duplicación /duplika'θion; duplika'sion/ *n. f.* duplication; doubling.

duplicadamente /duplikaða'mente/ *adv.* doubly.

duplicado /dupli'kaðo/ *a. & m.* duplicate.

duplicar /dupli'kar/ *v.* double, duplicate, repeat.

duplicidad /dupliθi'ðað; duplisi'ðað/ *n. f.* duplicity.

duplo /'duplo/ *a.* double.

duque /'duke/ *n. m.* duke.

duquesa /du'kesa/ *n. f.* duchess.

durabilidad /duraβili'ðað/ *n. f.* durability.

durable /du'raβle/ *a.* durable.

duración /dura'θion; dura'sion/ *n. f.* duration.

duradero /dura'ðero/ *a.* lasting, durable.

duramente /dura'mente/ *adv.* harshly, roughly.

durante /du'rante/ *prep.* during.

durar /du'rar/ *v.* last.

durazno /du'raθno; du'rasno/ *n. m.* peach; peach tree.

dureza /du'reθa; du'resa/ *n. f.* hardness.

durmiente /dur'miente/ *a.* sleeping.

duro /'duro/ *a.* hard; stiff; stern; stale.

dux /duks/ *n. m.* doge.

E

e /e/ *conj.* and.

ebanista /eβa'nista/ *n. m. & f.* cabinet-maker.

ebanizar /eβani'θar; eβani'sar/ *v.* give an ebony finish to.

ébano /'eβano/ *n. m.* ebony.

ebonita /eβo'nita/ *n. f.* ebonite.

ebrio /'eβrio/ *a.* drunken, inebriated.

ebullición /eβuʎi'θion; eβuyi'sion/ *n. f.* boiling.

echada /e'tʃaða/ *n. f.* throw.

echadillo /etʃa'ðiʎo; etʃa'ðiyo/ *n. m.* foundling; orphan.

echar /e'tʃar/ *v.* throw, toss; pour. **e. a,** start to. **e. a perder,** spoil, ruin. **e. de menos,** miss.

echarse /e'tʃarse/ *v.* lie down.

eclecticismo /eklekti'θismo; eklekti'sismo/ *n. m.* eclecticism.

ecléctico /e'klektiko/ *n. & a.* eclectic.

eclesiástico /ekle'siastiko/ *a. & m.* ecclesiastic.

eclipse /e'klipse/ *n. m.* eclipse. —**eclipsar,** *v.*

écloga /'ekloga/ *n. f.* eclogue.

eco /'eko/ *n. m.* echo.

ecología /ekolo'hia/ *n. f.* ecology.

ecológico /eko'lohiko/ *n. f.* ecological.

ecologista /ekolo'hista/ *n. m. & f.* ecologist.

economía /ekono'mia/ *n. f.* economy; thrift; economics. **e. política,** political economy.

económicamente /ekonomika'mente/ *adv.* economically.

económico /eko'nomiko/ *a.* economic; economical, thrifty; inexpensive.

economista /ekono'mista/ *n. m. & f.* economist.

economizar /ekonomi'θar; ekonomi'sar/ *v.* save, economize.

ecuación /ekua'θion; ekua'sion/ *n. f.* equation.

ecuador /ekua'ðor/ *n. m.* equator.

ecuanimidad /ekuanimi'ðað/ *n. f.* equanimity.

ecuatorial /ekuato'rial/ *a.* equatorial.

ecuatoriano /ekuato'riano/ **-na** *a.* & *n.* Ecuadorian.

ecuestre /e'kyestre/ *a.* equestrian.

ecuménico. /eku'meniko/ *a.* ecumenical.

edad /e'ðað/ *n. f.* age.

edecán /eðe'kan/ *n. m.* aide-de-camp.

Edén /e'ðen/ *n. m.* Eden.

edición /eði'θion: eði'sion/ *n. f.* edition; issue.

edicto /e'ðikto/ *n. m.* edict, decree.

edificación /eðifika'θion: eðifika'sion/ *n. f.* construction; edification.

edificador /eðifika'ðor/ *n.* constructor; builder.

edificar /eðifi'kar/ *v.* build.

edificio /eði'fiθio: eði'fisio/ *n. m.* edifice, building.

editar /eði'tar/ *v.* publish, issue; edit.

editor /eði'tor/ *n. m.* publisher; editor.

editorial /eðito'rial/ *n. m.* editorial; publishing house.

edredón /eðre'ðon/ *n. m.* quilt.

educación /eðuka'θion: eðuka'sion/ *n. f.* upbringing, breeding; education.

educado /eðu'kaðo/ *a.* well-mannered; educated.

educador /eðuka'ðor/ **-ra** *n.* educator.

educar /eðu'kar/ *v.* educate; bring up; train.

educativo /eðuka'tiβo/ *a.* educational.

educción /eðuk'θion: eðuk'sion/ *n. f.* deduction.

educir /eðu'θir: eðu'sir/ *v.* educe.

efectivamente /efektiβa'mente/ *adv.* actually, really.

efectivo /efek'tiβo/ *a.* effective; actual, real. **en e.,** *Com.* in cash.

efecto /e'fekto/ *n. m.* effect.

efecto invernáculo /e'fekto imber'nakulo/ greenhouse effect.

efectuar /efek'tuar/ *v.* effect; cash.

eferente /efe'rente/ *a.* efferent.

efervescencia /eferβes'θenθia: eferβes'sensia/ *n. f.* effervescence; zeal.

eficacia /efi'kaθia: efi'kasia/ *n. f.* efficacy.

eficaz /efi'kaθ: efi'kas/ *a.* efficient, effective.

eficazmente /efikaθ'mente: efikas'mente/ *adv.* efficaciously.

eficiencia /efi'θienθia: efi'siensia/ *n. f.* efficiency.

eficiente /efi'θiente: efi'siente/ *a.* efficient.

efigie /e'fihie/ *n. f.* effigy.

efímera /efi'mera/ *n. f.* mayfly.

efímero /efi'mero/ *a.* ephemeral, passing.

efluvio /e'fluβio/ *n. m.* effluvium.

efundir /efun'dir/ *v.* effuse; pour out.

efusión /efu'sion/ *n. f.* effusion.

egipcio /e'hipθio: e'hipsio/ **-cia** *a.* & *n.* Egyptian.

Egipto /e'hipto/ *n. m.* Egypt.

egoísmo /ego'ismo/ *n. m.* egoism, egotism, selfishness.

egoísta /ego'ista/ *a.* & *n.* selfish, egoistic; egoist.

egotismo /ego'tismo/ *n. m.* egotism.

egotista /ego'tista/ *n. m. & f.* egotist.

egreso /e'greso/ *n. m.* expense, outlay.

eje /'ehe/ *n. m.* axis; axle.

ejecución /eheku'θion: eheku'sion/ *n. f.* execution; performance; enforcement.

ejecutar /eheku'tar/ *v.* execute; enforce; carry out.

ejecutivo /eheku''tiβo/ **-va** *a.* & *n.* executive.

ejecutor /eheku'tor/ **-ra** *n.* executor.

ejemplar /ehem'plar/ *a.* **1.** exemplary. —*n.* **2.** *m.* copy.

ejemplificación /ehemplifika'θion: ehemplifika'sion/ *n. f.* exemplification.

ejemplificar /ehemplifi'kar/ *v.* illustrate.

ejemplo /e'hemplo/ *n. m.* example.

ejercer /eher'θer: eher'ser/ *v.* exert; practice.

ejercicio /eher'θiθio: eher'sisio/ *n. m.* exercise, drill. **—ejercitar,** *v.*

ejercitación /eherθita'θion: ehersita'sion/ *n. f.* exercise, training, drill.

ejercitar /eherθi'tar: ehersi'tar/ *v.* exercise, train, drill.

ejército /e'herθito: e'hersito/ *n. m.* army.

ejotes /e'hotes/ *n. m.pl.* string beans.

el /el/ *art. & pron.* the; the one.

él *pron.* he, him; it.

elaboración /elaβora'θion: elaβora'sion/ *n. f.* elaboration; working up.

elaborado /elaβo'raðo/ *a.* elaborate.

elaborador /elaβora'ðor/ *n. m.* manufacturer, maker.

elaborar /elaβo'rar/ *v.* elaborate; manufacture; brew.

elación /ela'θion: ela'sion/ *n. f.* elation; magnanimity; turgid style.

elasticidad /elastiθi'ðað: elastisi'ðað/ *n. f.* elasticity.

elástico /e'lastiko/ *n. m.* elastic.

elección /elek'θion: elek'sion/ *n. f.* election; option, choice.

electivo /elek'tiβo/ *a.* elective.

electo /e'lekto/ *a.* elected, chosen, appointed.

electorado /elekto'raðo/ *n. m.* electorate.

electoral /elekto'ral/ *a.* electoral.

electricidad /elektriθi'ðað: elektrisi'ðað/ *n. f.* electricity.

electricista /elektri'θista: elektri'sista/ *n. m. & f.* electrician.

eléctrico /e'lektriko/ *a.* electric.

electrización /elektriθa'θion: elektrisa'sion/ *n. f.* electrification.

electrocardiograma /e,lektrokardio'grama/ *n. m.* electrocardiogram.

electrocución /elektroku'θion; elektroku-'sion/ *n. f.* electrocution.

electrocutar /elektroku'tar/ *v.* electrocute.

electrodo /elek'trodo/ *n. m.* electrode.

electrodoméstico /e,lektrodo'mestiko/ *n. m.* electrical appliance, home appliance.

electroimán /elektroi'man/ *n m.* electromagnet.

electrólisis /elek'trolisis/ *n. f.* electrolysis.

electrólito /elek'trolito/ *n. m.* electrolyte.

electrón /elek'tron/ *n. m.* electron.

electrónico /elek'troniko/ *a.* electronic.

elefante /ele'fante/ *n. m.* elephant.

elegancia /ele'ganθia; ele'gansia/ *n. f.* elegance.

elegante /ele'gante/ *a.* elegant, smart, stylish, fine.

elegantemente /elegante'mente/ *adv.* elegantly.

elegía /ele'hia/ *n. f.* elegy.

elegibilidad /elehiβili'ðað/ *n. f.* eligibility.

elegible /ele'hiβle/ *a.* eligible.

elegir /ele'hir/ *v.* select, choose; elect.

elemental /elemen'tal/ *a.* elementary.

elementalmente /elemental'mente/ *adv.* elementally; fundamentally.

elemento /ele'mento/ *n. m.* element.

elepé /ele'pe/ *n. m.* long-playing (record), LP.

elevación /eleβa'θion; eleβa'sion/ *n. f* elevation; height.

elevador /eleβa'ðor/ *n. m.* elevator.

elevamiento /eleβa'miento/ *n. m.* elevation.

elevar /ele'βar/ *v.* elevate; erect, raise.

elidir /eli'ðir/ *v.* elide.

eliminación /elimina'θion; elimina'sion/ *n. f.* elimination.

eliminar /elimi'nar/ *v.* eliminate.

elipse /e'lipse/ *n. f.* ellipse.

elipsis /e'lipsis/ *n. f.* ellipsis.

elíptico /e'liptiko/ *a.* elliptic.

ella /'eʎa; 'eya/ *pron.* she, her; it.

ello /'eʎo; 'eyo/ *pron.* it.

ellos /'eʎos; 'eyos/ **-as** *pron. pl.* they, them.

elocuencia /elo'kuenθia; elo'kuensia/ *n. f.* eloquence.

elocuente /elo'kuente/ *a.* eloquent.

elocuentemente /elokuente'mente/ *adv.* eloquently.

elogio /e'lohio/ *n. m.* praise, compliment. **—elogiar,** *v.*

elucidación /eluθiða'θion: elusiða'sion/ *n. f.* elucidation.

elucidar /eluθi'ðar; elusi'ðar/ *v.* elucidate.

eludir /elu'ðir/ *v.* elude.

emanar /ema'nar/ *v.* emanate, stem.

emancipación /emanθipa'θion; emansipa-'sion/ *n. f.* emancipation; freeing.

emancipador /emanθipa'ðor; emansipa'ðor/ **-ra** *n.* emancipator.

emancipar /emanθi'par; emansi'par/ *v.* emancipate; free.

embajada /emba'haða/ *n. f.* embassy; legation; *Colloq.* errand.

embajador /embaha'ðor/ **-ra** *n.* ambassador.

embalar /emba'lar/ *v.* pack, bale.

embaldosado /embaldo'saðo/ *n. m.* tile floor.

embalsamador /embalsama'ðor/ *n. m.* embalmer.

embalsamar /embalsa'mar/ *v.* embalm.

embarazada /embara'θaða; embara'saða/ *a.* pregnant.

embarazadamente /embaraθaða'mente; embarasaða'mente/ *adv.* embarrassedly.

embarazar /embara'θar; embara'sar/ *v.* make pregnant; embarrass.

embarazo /emba'raθo; emba'raso/ *n. m.* embarrassment; pregnancy.

embarbascado /embarβas'kaðo/ *a.* difficult; complicated.

embarcación /embarka'θion; embarka'sion/ *n. f.* boat, ship; embarkation.

embarcadero /embarka'ðero/ *n. m.* wharf, pier, dock.

embarcador /embarka'ðor/ *n. m.* shipper, loader, stevedore.

embarcar /embar'kar/ *v.* embark, board ship.

embarcarse /embar'karse/ *v.* embark; sail.

embargador /embarga'ðor/ *n. m.* one who impedes; one who orders an embargo.

embargante /embar'gante/ *a.* impeding, hindering.

embargar /embar'gar/ *v.* impede, restrain; *Leg.* seize, embargo.

embargo /em'bargo/ *n. m.* seizure, embargo. **sin e.,** however, nevertheless.

embarnizar /embarni'θar; embarni'sar/ *v.* varnish.

embarque /em'barke/ *n. m.* shipment.

embarrador /embarra'ðor/ *n. m.* plasterer.

embarrancar /embarran'kar/ *v.* get stuck in mud; *Naut.* run aground.

embarrar /emba'rrar/ *v.* plaster; besmear with mud.

embasamiento /embasa'miento/ *n. m.* foundation of a building.

embastecer /embaste'θer; embaste'ser/ *v.* get fat.

embaucador /embauka'ðor/ **-ra** *n.* impostor.

embaucar /embau'kar/ *v.* deceive, trick, hoax.

embaular /embau'lar/ *v.* pack in a trunk.

embausamiento /embausa'miento/ *n. m.* amazement.

embebecer /embeβe'θer; embeβe'ser/ *v.* amaze, astonish; entertain.

embeber /embe'βer/ *v.* absorb; incorporate; saturate.

embelecador /embeleka'ðor/ **-ra** *n.* impostor.

embeleco /embe'leko/ *n. m.* fraud, perpetration.

embeleñar /embele'ɲar/ *v.* fascinate, charm.

embelesamiento /embelesa'miento/ *n. m.* rapture.

embelesar /embele'sar/ *v.* fascinate, charm.

embeleso /embe'leso/ *n. m.* rapture, bliss.

embellecer /embeʎe'θer; embeye'ser/ *v.* beautify, embellish.

embestida /embes'tiða/ *n. f.* violent assault; attack.

emblandecer /emblande'θer; emblande'ser/ *v.* soften; moisten; move to pity.

emblema /em'blema/ *n. m.* emblem.

emblemático /emble'matiko/ *a.* emblematic.

embocadura /emboka'ðura/ *n. f.* narrow entrance; mouth of a river.

embocar /embo'kar/ *v.* eat hastily; gorge.

embolia /em'bolia/ *n. f.* embolism.

émbolo /'embolo/ *n. m.* piston.

embolsar /embol'sar/ *v.* pocket.

embonar /embo'nar/ *v.* improve, fix, repair.

emborrachador /emborratʃa'ðor/ *a.* intoxicating.

emborrachar /emborra'tʃar/ *v.* get drunk.

emboscada /embos'kaða/ *n. f.* ambush.

emboscar /embos'kar/ *v.* put or lie in ambush.

embotado /embo'taðo/ *a.* blunt, dull (edged). **—embotar,** *v.*

embotadura /embota'ðura/ *n. f.* bluntness; dullness.

embotellamiento /emboteʎa'miento; emboteya'miento/ *n. m.* bottling (liquids); traffic jam.

embotellar /embote'ʎar; embote'yar/ *v.* put in bottles.

embozado /embo'θaðo; embo'saðo/ *v.* muzzled; muffled.

embozar /embo'θar; embo'sar/ *v.* muzzle; muffle.

embozo /em'boθo; em'boso/ *n. m.* muffler.

embrague /em'brage/ *n. m. Auto.* clutch.

embravecer /embraβe'θer; embraβe'ser/ *v.* be or make angry.

embriagado /embria'gaðo/ *a.* drunken, intoxicated.

embriagar /embria'gar/ *v.* intoxicate.

embriaguez /embria'geθ; embria'ges/ *n. f.* drunkenness.

embrión /em'brion/ *n. m.* embryo.

embrionario /embrio'nario/ *a.* embryonic.

embrochado /embro'tʃaðo/ *a.* embroidered.

embrollo /em'broʎo; em'broyo/ *n. m.* muddle. **—embrollar,** *v.*

embromar /embro'mar/ *v.* tease; joke.

embuchado /embu'tʃaðo/ *n. m.* pork sausage.

embudo /em'buðo/ *n. m.* funnel.

embuste /em'buste/ *n. m.* lie, fib.

embustear /embuste'ar/ *v.* lie, fib.

embustero /embus'tero/ **-ra** *n.* liar.

embutir /embu'tir/ *v.* stuff, cram.

emergencia /emer'henθia; emer'hensia/ *n. f.* emergency.

emérito /e'merito/ *a.* emeritus.

emético /e'metiko/ *n. m. & a.* emetic.

emigración /emigra'θion; emigra'sion/ *n. f.* emigration.

emigrante /emi'grante/ *a. & n.* emigrant.

emigrar /emi'grar/ *v.* emigrate.

eminencia /emi'nenθia; emi'nensia/ *n. f.* eminence, height.

eminente /emi'nente/ *a.* eminent.

emisario /emi'sario/ **-ria** *n.* emissary, spy; outlet.

emisión /emi'sion/ *n. f.* issue; emission.

emisor /emi'sor/ *n. m.* radio transmitter.

emitir /emi'tir/ *v.* emit.

emoción /emo'θion: emo'sion/ *n. f.* feeling, emotion, thrill.

emocional /emo'θional; emo'sional/ *a.* emotional.

emocionante /emoθio'nante; emosio'nante/ *a.* exciting.

emocionar /emoθio'nar; emosio'nar/ *v.* touch, move, excite.

emolumento /emolu'mento/ *n. m.* emolument; perquisite.

empacar /empa'kar/ *v.* pack.

empacho /em'patʃo/ *n. m.* shyness, timidity; embarrassment.

empadronamiento /empaðrona'miento/ *n. m.* census; list of taxpayers.

empalizada /empali'θaða; empali'saða/ *n. f.* palisade, stockade.

empanada /empa'naða/ *n. f.* meat pie.

empañar /empa'ɲar/ *v.* blur; soil, sully.

empapar /empa'par/ *v.* soak.

empapelado /empape'laðo/ *n. m.* wallpaper.

empapelar /empape'lar/ *v.* wallpaper.

empaque /em'pake/ *n. m.* packing; appearance, mien.

empaquetar /empake'tar/ *v.* pack, package.

emparedado /empare'ðaðo/ *n. m.* sandwich.

emparejarse /empare'harse/ v. match, pair off; level, even off.

emparentado /emparen'taðo/ a. related by marriage.

emparrado /empa'rraðo/ n. m. arbor.

empastadura /empasta'ðura/ n. f. (dental) filling.

empastar /empas'tar/ v. fill (a tooth); paste.

empate /em'pate/ n. m. tie, draw. —**empatarse**, v.

empecer /empe'θer; empe'ser/ v. hurt, harm, injure; prevent.

empedernir /empeðer'nir/ v. harden.

empeine /em'peine/ n. m. groin; instep; hoof.

empellar /empe'ʎar; empe'yar/ v. shove, jostle.

empellón /empe'ʎon; empe'yon/ n. m. hard push, shove.

empeñar /empe'ɲar/ v. pledge; pawn.

empeñarse en /empe'ɲarse en/ v. persist in, be bent on.

empeño /em'peɲo/ n. m. persistence; pledge; pawning.

empeoramiento /empeora'miento/ n. m. deterioration.

empeorar /empeo'rar/ v. get worse.

emperador /empera'ðor/ n. m. emperor.

emperatriz /empera'triθ; empera'tris/ n. f. empress.

empernar /emper'nar/ v. bolt.

empero /em'pero/ conj. however; but.

emperramiento /emperra'miento/ n. m. stubbornness.

empezar /empe'θar; empe'sar/ v. begin, start.

empinado /empi'naðo/ a. steep.

empinar /empi'nar/ v. raise; exalt.

empíreo /em'pireo/ a. celestial, heavenly; divine.

empíricamente /empirika'mente/ adv. empirically.

empírico /em'piriko/ a. empirical.

empirismo /empi'rismo/ n. m. empiricism.

emplastarse /emplas'tarse/ v. get smeared.

emplasto /em'plasto/ n. m. salve.

emplazamiento /emplaθa'miento; emplasa'miento/ n. m. court summons.

emplazar /empla'θar; empla'sar/ v. summon to court.

empleado /emple'aðo/ **-da** n. employee.

emplear /emple'ar/ v. employ; use.

empleo /em'pleo/ n. m. employment, job; use.

empobrecer /empoβre'θer; empoβre'ser/ v. impoverish.

empobrecimiento /empoβreθi'miento; empoβresi'miento/ n. m. impoverishment.

empollador /empoʎa'ðor; empoya'ðor/ n. m. incubator.

empollar /empo'ʎar; empo'yar/ v. hatch.

empolvado /empol'βaðo/ a. dusty.

empolvar /empol'βar/ v. powder.

emporcar /empor'kar/ v. soil, make dirty.

emporio /em'porio/ n. m. emporium.

emprendedor /emprende'ðor/ a. enterprising.

emprender /empren'der/ v. undertake.

empreñar /empre'ɲar/ v. make pregnant; beget.

empresa /em'presa/ n. f. enterprise, undertaking; company.

empresario /empre'sario/ **-ria** n. businessperson; impresario.

empréstito /em'prestito/ n. m. loan.

empujón /empu'hon/ n. m. push; shove. —**empujar**, v.

empuñar /empu'ɲar/ v. grasp, seize; wield.

emulación /emula'θion; emula'sion/ n. f. emulation; envy; rivalry.

emulador /emula'ðor/ n. m. emulator; rival.

émulo /'emulo/ a. rival. —**emular**, v.

emulsión /emul'sion/ n. f. emulsion.

emulsionar /emulsio'nar/ v. emulsify.

en /en/ prep. in, on, at.

enaguas /e'naguas/ n. f.pl. petticoat; skirt.

enajenable /enahe'naβle/ a. alienable.

enajenación /enahena'θion; enahena'sion/ n. f. alienation; derangement, insanity.

enajenar /enahe'nar/ v. alienate.

enamoradamente /enamoraða'mente/ adv. lovingly.

enamorado /enamo'raðo/ a. in love.

enamorador /enamora'ðor/ n. m. wooer; suitor; lover.

enamorarse /enamo'rarse/ v. fall in love.

enano /e'nano/ **-na** n. midget; dwarf.

enardecer /enarðe'θer; enarðe'ser/ v. inflame.

enastado /enas'taðo/ a. horned.

encabestrar /enkaβes'trar/ v. halter.

encabezado /enkaβe'θaðo; enkaβe'saðo/ n. m. headline.

encabezamiento /enkaβeθa'miento; enkaβesa'miento/ n. m. title; census; tax roll.

encabezar /enkaβe'θar; enkaβe'sar/ v. head.

encachar /enka'tʃar/ v. hide.

encadenamiento /enkaðena'miento/ n. m. connection, linkage.

encadenar /enkaðe'nar/ v. chain; link, connect.

encajar /enka'har/ v. fit in, insert.

encaje /en'kahe/ n. m. lace.

encalar /enka'lar/ v. whitewash.

encallarse /enka'ʎarse; enka'yarse/ v. be stranded.

encallecido /enkaʎe'θiðo; enkaye'siðo/ a. hardened; calloused.

encalvecer /enkalβe'θer; enkalβe'ser/ v. lose one's hair.

encaminar /enkami'nar/ v. guide; direct; be on the way to.

encandilar /enkandi'lar/ v. dazzle; daze.

encantación /enkanta'θion; enkanta'sion/ n. f. incantation.

encantado /enkan'taðo/ a. charmed, fascinated, enchanted.

encantador /enkanta'ðor/ a. charming, delightful.

encante /en'kante/ n. m. public auction.

encanto /en'kanto/ n. m. charm, delight. —encantar, v.

encapillado /enkapi'ʎaðo; enkapi'yaðo/ n. m. clothes one is wearing.

encapotar /enkapo'tar/ v. cover, cloak, muffle.

encaprichamiento /enkapritʃa'miento/ n. m. infatuation.

encaramarse /enkara'marse/ v. perch; climb.

encararse con /enka'rarse kon/ v. face.

encarcelación /enkarθela'θion; enkarsela'sion/ n. f. imprisonment.

encarcelar /enkarθe'lar; enkarse'lar/ v. jail, imprison.

encarecer /enkare'θer; enkare'ser/ v. recommend; extol.

encarecidamente /enkareθiða'mente; enkaresiða'mente/ adv. extremely; ardently.

encargado /enkar'gaðo/ **-da** n. agent; attorney; representative.

encargar /enkar'gar/ v. entrust; order.

encargarse /enkar'garse/ v take charge, be in charge.

encargo /en'kargo/ n. m. errand; assignment; Com. order.

encarnación /enkarna'θion; enkarna'sion/ n. f. incarnation.

encarnado /enkar'naðo/ a. red.

encarnar /enkar'nar/ v. embody.

encarnecer /enkarne'θer; enkarne'ser/ v. grow fat or heavy.

encarnizado /enkarni'θaðo; enkarni'saðo/ a. bloody, fierce.

encarrilar /enkarri'lar/ v. set right; put on the track.

encartar /enkar'tar/ v. ban, outlaw; summon.

encastar /enkas'tar/ v. improve by cross-breeding.

encastillar /enkasti'ʎar; enkasti'yar/ v. be obstinate or unyielding.

encatarrado /enkata'rraðo/ a. suffering from a cold.

encausar /enkau'sar/ v. prosecute; take legal action against.

encauzar /enkau'θar; enkau'sar/ v. channel; direct.

encefalitis /enθefa'litis; ensefa'litis/ n. f. encephalitis.

encelamiento /enθela'miento; ensela'miento/ n. m. envy, jealousy.

encelar /enθe'lar; ense'lar/ v. make jealous.

encenagar /enθena'gar; ensena'gar/ v. wallow in mud.

encendedor /enθende'ðor; ensende'ðor/ n. m. lighter.

encender /enθen'der; ensen'der/ v. light; set fire to, kindle; turn on.

encendido /enθen'diðo; ensen'diðo/ n. m. ignition.

encerado /enθe'raðo; ense'raðo/ n. m. oilcloth; tarpaulin.

encerar /enθe'rar; ense'rar/ v. wax.

encerrar /enθe'rrar; ense'rrar/ v. enclose; confine, shut in.

enchapado /entʃa'paðo/ n. m. veneer.

enchufe /en'tʃufe/ n. m. Elec. plug, socket.

encía /en'θia; en'sia/ n. f. gum.

encíclico /en'θikliko; en'sikliko/ a. **1.** encyclic. —n. **2.** f. encyclical.

enciclopedia /enθiklo'peðia; ensiklo'peðia/ n. f. encyclopedia.

enciclopédico /enθiklo'peðiko; ensiklo'peðiko/ a. encyclopedic.

encierro /en'θierro; en'sierro/ n. m. confinement; enclosure.

encima /en'θima; en'sima/ adv. on top. **e. de,** on. **por e. de,** above.

encina /en'θina; en'sina/ n. f. oak.

encinta /en'θinta; en'sinta/ a. pregnant.

enclavar /enkla'βar/ v. nail.

enclenque /en'klenke/ a. frail, weak, sickly.

encogerse /enko'herse/ v. shrink. **e. de hombros,** shrug the shoulders.

encogido /enko'hiðo/ a. shy, bashful, timid.

encojar /enko'har/ v. make or become lame; cripple.

encolar /enko'lar/ v. glue, paste, stick.

encolerizar /enkoleri'θar; enkoleri'sar/ v. make or become angry.

encomendar /enkomen'dar/ v. commend; recommend.

encomiar /enko'miar/ v. praise, laud, extol.

encomienda /enko'mienda/ n. f. commission, charge; (postal) package.

encomio /en'komio/ n. m. encomium, eulogy.

enconar /enko'nar/ v. irritate, annoy, anger.

encono /en'kono/ n. m. rancor, resentment.

enconoso /enko'noso/ a. rancorous, resentful.

encontrado /enkon'traðo/ a. opposite.

encontrar /enkon'trar/ v. find; meet.

encorajar /enkora'har/ v. encourage; incite.

encornar /enkor'nar/ v. gore.

encorralar /enkorra'lar/ v. corral.

encorvadura /enkorβa'ðura/ n. f. bend, curvature.

encorvar /enkor'βar/ v. arch, bend.

encorvarse /enkor'βarse/ v. stoop.

encrucijada /enkruθi'haða: enkrusi'haða/ n. f. crossroads.

encuadrar /enkuað'rar/ v. frame.

encubierta /enku'βierta/ a. **1.** secret, fraudulent. —n. **2.** f. fraud.

encubrir /enkuβ'rir/ v. hide, conceal.

encuentro /en'kuentro/ n. m. encounter; match, bout.

encurtido /enkur'tiðo/ n. m. pickle.

endeble /en'deβle/ a. rail, weak, sickly.

enderezar /endere'θar; endere'sar/ v. straighten; redress.

endeudarse /endeu'ðarse/ v. get into debt.

endiablado /endia'βlaðo/ a. devilish.

endibia /en'diβia/ n. f. endive.

endiosar /endio'sar/ v. deify.

endorso /en'dorso/ **endoso** n. m. endorsement.

endosador /endosa'ðor/ **-ra** n. endorser.

endosar /endo'sar/ v. endorse.

endosatario /endosa'tario/ **-ria** n. endorsee.

endulzar /endul'θar; endul'sar/ v. sweeten; soothe.

endurar /endu'rar/ v. harden.

endurecer /endure'θer; endure'ser/ v. harden.

enemigo /ene'migo/ **-ga** n. foe, enemy.

enemistad /enemis'tað/ n. f. enmity.

éneo /'eneo/ a. brass.

energía /ener'hia/ n. f. energy.

energía nuclear /ener'hia nukle'ar/ atomic energy, nuclear energy.

energía vital /ener'hia bi'tal/ élan vital, vitality.

enérgicamente /e'nerhikamente/ adv. energetically.

enérgico /e'nerhiko/ a. forceful; energetic.

enero /e'nero/ n. m. January.

enervación /enerβa'θion; enerβa'sion/ n. f. enervation.

enfadado /enfa'ðaðo/ a. angry.

enfadar /enfa'ðar/ v. anger, vex.

enfado /en'faðo/ n. m. anger, vexation.

énfasis /'enfasis/ n. m. or f. emphasis, stress.

enfáticamente /en'fatikamente/ adv. emphatically.

enfático /en'fatiko/ a. emphatic.

enfermar /enfer'mar/ v. make ill; fall ill.

enfermedad /enferme'ðað/ n. f. illness, sickness, disease.

enfermera /enfer'mera/ n. f. nurse.

enfermería /enferme'ria/ n. f. sanatorium.

enfermo /en'fermo/ **-ma** a. & n. ill, sick; sickly; patient.

enfilar /enfi'lar/ v. line up; put in a row.

enflaquecer /enflake'θer; enflake'ser/ v. make thin; grow thin.

enfoque /en'foke/ n. m. focus. —**enfocar**, v.

enfrascamiento /enfraska'miento/ n. m. entanglement.

enfrascar /enfras'kar/ v. bottle; entangle oneself.

enfrenar /enfre'nar/ v. bridle, curb; restrain.

enfrentamiento /enfrenta'miento/ n. m. clash, confrontation.

enfrente /en'frente/ adv. across, opposite; in front.

enfriadera /enfria'ðera/ n. f. icebox; cooler.

enfriar /enf'riar/ v. chill, cool.

enfurecer /enfure'θer; enfure'ser/ v. infuriate, enrage.

engalanar /eŋgala'nar/ v. adorn, trim.

enganchar /eŋgan'tʃar/ v. hook, hitch, attach.

engañar /eŋga'ɲar/ v. deceive, cheat.

engaño /eŋ'gaɲo/ n. m. deceit; delusion.

engañoso /eŋga'ɲoso/ a. deceitful.

engarce /eŋ'garθe; eŋgarse/ n. m. connection, link.

engastar /eŋgas'tar/ v. to put (gems) in a setting.

engaste /eŋ'gaste/ n. m. setting.

engatusar /eŋgatu'sar/ v. deceive, trick.

engendrar /eŋhen'drar/ v. engender, beget, produce.

engendro /eŋ'hendro/ n. m. fetus, embryo.

englobar /eŋglo'βar/ v. include.

engolfar /eŋgol'far/ v. be deeply absorbed.

engolosinar /eŋgolosi'nar/ v. allure, charm, entice.

engomar /eŋgo'mar/ v. gum.

engordador /eŋgor'ðaðor/ a. fattening.

engordar /eŋgor'ðar/ v. fatten; grow fat.

engranaje /eŋgra'nahe/ n. m. Mech. gear.

engranar /eŋgra'nar/ v. gear; mesh together.

engrandecer /eŋgrande'θer; eŋgrande'ser/ v. increase, enlarge; exalt; exaggerate.

engrasación /eŋgrasa'θion; eŋgrasa'sion/ n. f. lubrication.

engrasar /eŋgra'sar/ v. grease, lubricate.

engreído /eŋgre'iðo/ a. conceited.

engreimiento /eŋgrei'miento/ n. m. conceit.

engullidor /eŋguʎi'ðor; eŋguyi'ðor/ **-ra** n. devourer.

engullir /eŋgu'ʎir; eŋgu'yir/ v. devour.

enhebrar /ene'βrar/ v. thread.

enhestadura /enesta'ðura/ n. f. raising.

enhestar /enes'tar/ v. raise, erect, set up.

enhiesto /en'iesto/ a. erect, upright.

enhorabuena /enora'βuena/ n. f. congratulations.

enigma /e'nigma/ n. m. enigma, puzzle.

enigmáticamente /enigmatika'mente/ adv. enigmatically.

enigmático /enig'matiko/ a. enigmatic.

enjabonar /enhaβo'nar/ v. soap, lather.

enjalbegar /enhalβe'gar/ v. whitewash.

enjambradera /enhambra'ðera/ n. f. queen bee.

enjambre /en'hambre/ n. m. swarm. —**enjambrar**, v.

enjaular /enhau'lar/ v. cage, coop up.

enjebe /en'heβe/ n. m. lye.

enjuagar /enhua'gar/ v. rinse.

enjuague bucal /en'huage bu'kal/ n. m. mouthwash.

enjugar /enhu'gar/ v. wipe, dry off.

enjutez /enhu'teθ/ enhu'tes/ n. f. dryness.

enjuto /en'huto/ a. dried; lean, thin.

enlace /en'laθe; en'lase/ n. m. attachment; involvement; connection.

enladrillador /enlaðriʎa'ðor; enlaðriya'ðor/ **-ra** n. bricklayer.

enlardar /enlar'ðar/ v. baste.

enlatado /enla'taðo/ **-da** a. canned (food).

enlatar /enla'tar/ v. can (food).

enlazar /enla'θar; enla'sar/ v. lace; join, connect; wed.

enlodar /enlo'ðar/ v. cover with mud.

enloquecer /enloke'θer; enloke'ser/ v. go insane; drive crazy.

enloquecimiento /enlokeθi'miento; enlokesi'miento/ n. m. insanity.

enlustrecer /enlustre'θer; enlustre'ser/ v. polish, brighten.

enmarañar /emara'ɲar/ v. entangle.

enmendación /emenda'θion; emenda'sion/ n. f. emendation.

enmendador /emenda'ðor/ **-ra** n. emender, reviser.

enmendar /emen'dar/ v. amend, correct.

enmienda /e'mienda/ n. f. amendment; correction.

enmohecer /emoe'θer; emoe'ser/ v. rust; mold.

enmohecido /emoe'θiðo; emoe'siðo/ a. rusty; moldy.

enmudecer /emuðe'θer; emuðe'ser/ v. silence; become silent.

ennegrecer /ennegre'θer; ennegre'ser/ v. blacken.

ennoblecer /ennoβle'θer; ennoβle'ser/ v. ennoble.

enodio /e'noðio/ n. m. young deer.

enojado /eno'haðo/ a. angry, cross.

enojarse /eno'harse/ v. get angry.

enojo /e'noho/ n. m. anger. —**enojar**, v.

enojosamente /enohosa'mente/ adv. angrily.

enorme /e'norme/ a. enormous, huge.

enormemente /enorme'mente/ adv. enormously; hugely.

enormidad /enormi'ðaθ/ n. f. enormity; hugeness.

enraizar /enrai'θar; enrai'sar/ v. take root, sprout.

enramada /enra'maða/ n. f. bower.

enredadera /enreða'ðera/ n. f. climbing plant.

enredado /enre'ðaðo/ a. entangled, snarled.

enredar /enre'ðar/ v. entangle, snarl; mess up.

enredo /en'reðo/ n. m. tangle, entanglement.

enriquecer /enrike'θer; enrike'ser/ v. enrich.

enrojecerse /enrohe'θerse; enrohe'serse/ v. color; blush.

enrollar /enro'ʎar; enro'yar/ v. wind, coil, roll up.

enromar /enro'mar/ v. make dull, blunt.

enronquecimiento /enronkeθi'miento; enronkesi'miento/ n. m. hoarseness.

enroscar /enros'kar/ v. twist, curl, wind.

ensacar /ensa'kar/ v. put in a bag.

ensalada /ensa'laða/ n. f. salad.

ensaladera /ensala'ðera/ n. f. salad bowl.

ensalmo /en'salmo/ n. m. charm, enchantment.

ensalzamiento /ensalθa'miento; ensalsa'miento/ n. m. praise.

ensalzar /ensal'θar; ensal'sar/ v. praise, laud, extol.

ensamblar /ensam'blar/ v. join; unite; connect.

ensanchamiento /ensantʃa'miento/ n. m. widening, expansion, extension.

ensanchar /ensan'tʃar/ v. widen, expand, extend.

ensangrentado /ensaŋgren'taðo/ a. bloody; bloodshot.

ensañar /ensa'ɲar/ v. enrage, infuriate; rage.

ensayar /ensa'yar/ v. try out; rehearse.

ensayista /ensa'yista/ n. m. & f. essayist.

ensayo /ensa'yo/ n. m. attempt; trial; rehearsal.

ensenada /ense'naða/ n. f. cove.

enseña /en'seɲa/ n. f. ensign, standard.

enseñador /enseɲa'ðor/ **-ra** n. teacher.

enseñanza /ense'ɲanθa; ense'ɲansa/ n. f. education; teaching.

enseñar /ense'ɲar/ v. teach, teach; show.

enseres /en'seres/ n. m.pl. household goods.

ensilaje /ensi'lahe/ n. m. ensilage.

ensillar /ensi'ʎar; ensi'yar/ v. saddle.

ensordecedor /ensorðeθe'ðor; ensorðese-'ðor/ *a.* deafening.

ensordecer /ensorðe'θer; ensorðe'ser/ *v.* deafen.

ensordecimiento /ensorðeθi'miento; ensor-ðesi'miento/ *n. m.* deafness.

ensuciar /ensu'θiar; ensu'siar/ *v.* dirty, muddy, soil.

ensueño /en'sueɲo/ *n. m.* illusion, dream.

entablar /enta'βlar/ *v.* board up; initiate, begin.

entallador /entaʎa'ðor; entaya'ðor/ *n. m.* sculptor, carver.

entapizar /entapi'θar; entapi'sar/ *v.* uphol-ster.

ente /'ente/ *n. m.* being.

entenada /ente'naða/ *n. f.* stepdaughter.

entenado /ente'naðo/ *n. m.* stepson.

entender /enten'der/ *v.* understand.

entendimiento /entendi'miento/ *n. m.* un-derstanding.

entenebrecer /enteneβre'θer; enteneβre-'ser/ *v.* darken.

enterado /ente'raðo/ *a.* aware, informed.

enteramente /entera'mente/ *adv.* entirely, completely.

enterar /ente'rar/ *v.* inform.

enterarse /ente'rarse/ *v.* find out.

entereza /ente'reθa; ente'resa/ *n. f.* en-tirety; integrity; firmness.

entero /en'tero/ *a.* entire, whole, total.

enterramiento /enterra'miento/ *n. m.* bur-ial, interment.

enterrar /ente'rrar/ *v.* bury.

entestado /entes'taðo/ *a.* stubborn, willful.

entibiar /enti'βiar/ *v.* to cool; moderate.

entidad /enti'ðað/ *n. f.* entity.

entierro /en'tierro/ *n. m.* interment, burial.

entonación /entona'θion; entona'sion/ *n. f.* intonation.

entonamiento /entona'miento/ *n. m* into-nation.

entonar /ento'nar/ *v.* chant; harmonize.

entonces /en'tonθes; enton'ses/ *adv.* then.

entono /en'tono/ *n. m.* intonation; arro-gance; affectation.

entortadura /entorta'ðura/ *n. f* crooked-ness.

entortar /entor'tar/ *v.* make crooked; bend.

entrada /en'traða/ *n. f.* entrance; admis-sion, admittance.

entrambos /en'trambos/ *a. & pron.* both.

entrante /en'trante/ *a.* coming, next.

entrañable /entra'ɲaβle/ *a.* affectonate.

entrañas /en'traɲas/ *n f pl.* entrails, bow-els; womb.

entrar /en'trar/ *v.* enter, go in, come in.

entre /'entre/ *prep.* among; between.

entreabierto /entrea'βierto/ *a.* ajar, half-open.

entreabrir /entrea'βrir/ *v.* set ajar.

entreacto /entre'akto/ *n. m.* intermission.

entrecejo /entre'θeho; entre'seho/ *n. m.* frown; space between the eyebrows.

entrecuesto /entre'kuesto/ *n. m.* spine, backbone.

entredicho /entre'ðitʃo/ *n. m.* prohibition.

entrega /en'trega/ *n. f.* delivery.

entregar /entre'gar/ *v.* deliver, hand; hand over.

entrelazar /entrela'θar; entrela'sar/ *v.* inter-twine, entwine.

entremedias /entre'meðias/ *adv.* mean-while; halfway.

entremés /entre'mes/ *n. m.* side dish.

entremeterse /entreme'terse/ *v.* meddle, intrude.

entremetido /entreme'tiðo/ *-da* *n.* med-dler.

entrenador /entrena'ðor/ *-ra* *n.* coach. —**entrenar**, *v.*

entrenarse /entre'narse/ *v.* train.

entrepalado /entrepa'laðo/ *a.* variegated; spotted.

entrerenglonar /entrereŋglo'nar/ *v.* inter-line.

entresacar /entresa'kar/ *v.* select, choose; sift.

entresuelo /entre'suelo/ *n. m.* mezzanine.

entretanto /entre'tanto/ *adv.* meanwhile.

entretenedor /entretene'ðor/ *-ra* *n.* enter-tainer.

entretener /entrete'ner/ *v.* entertain, amuse; delay.

entretenimiento /entreteni'miento/ *n. m.* entertainment, amusement.

entrevista /entre'βista/ *n. f.* interview. —**entrevistar**, *v.*

entrevistador /entreβista'ðor/ *-ra* *n.* inter-viewer.

entristecedor /entristeθe'ðor; entristese-'ðor/ *a.* sad.

entristecer /entriste'θer; entriste'ser/ *v.* sadden.

entronar /entro'nar/ *v.* enthrone.

entroncar /entron'kar/ *v.* be related or con-nected.

entronización /entroniθa'θion; entronisa-'sion/ *n. f.* enthronement.

entronque /entron'ke/ *n. m.* relationship; connection.

entumecer /entume'θer; entume'ser/ *v.* be-come or be numb; swell.

entusiasmado /entusias'maðo/ *a.* enthusi-astic.

entusiasmo /entu'siasmo/ *n. m.* enthusi-asm.

entusiasta /entu'siasta/ *n. m. & f.* enthusi-ast.

entusiástico /entu'siastiko/ *a.* enthusiastic.

enumeración /enumera'θion; enumera'sion/ *n. f.* enumeration.

enumerar /enume'rar/ *v.* enumerate.

enunciación /enunθia'θion; enunsia'sion/ *f.* enunciation; statement.

enunciar /enun'θiar; enun'siar/ *v.* enunciate.

envainar /embai'nar/ *v.* sheathe.

envalentonar /embalento'nar/ *v.* encourage, embolden.

envanecimiento /embaneθi'miento: embanesi'miento/ *n. m.* conceit, vanity.

envasar /emba'sar/ *v.* put in a container; bottle.

envase /em'base/ *n. m.* container.

envejecer /embehe'θer; embehe'ser/ *v.* age, grow old.

envejecimiento /embeheθi'miento; embehesi'miento/ *n. m.* oldness, aging.

envenenar /embene'nar/ *v.* poison.

envés /em'bes/ *n. m.* wrong side; back.

envestir /embes'tir/ *v.* put in office; invest.

enviada /em'biaða/ *n. f.* shipment.

enviado /em'biaðo/ **-da** *n.* envoy.

enviar /em'biar/ *v.* send; ship.

envidia /em'biðia/ *n f.* envy. **—envidiar,** *v.*

envidiable /embi'ðiaβle/ *a.* enviable.

envidioso /embi'ðioso/ *a.* envious.

envilecer /embile'θer; embile'ser/ *v.* vilify, debase, disgrace.

envío /em'bio/ *n. m.* shipment.

envión /em'bion/ *n. m.* shove.

envoltura /embol'tura/ *n. f.* wrapping.

envolver /embol'βer/ *v.* wrap, wrap up.

enyesar /enye'sar/ *v.* plaster.

enyugar /enyu'gar/ *v.* yoke.

eperlano /eper'lano/ *n. m.* smelt (fish).

épica /'epika/ *n. f.* epic.

épico /'epiko/ *a.* epic.

epicureísmo /epikure'ismo/ *n. m.* epicureanism.

epicúreo /epi'kureo/ *n. & a.* epicurean.

epidemia /epi'ðemia/ *n. f.* epidemic.

epidémico /epi'ðemiko/ *a.* epidemic.

epidermis /epi'ðermis/ *n. f.* epidermis.

epigrama /epi'grama/ *n. m.* epigram.

epigramático /epigra'matiko/ **-ca** *a.* epigrammatic.

epilepsia /epi'lepsia/ *n. f.* epilepsy.

epiléptico /epi'leptiko/ **-ca** *n. & a.* epileptic.

epílogo /e'pilogo/ *n. m.* epilogue.

episcopado /episko'paðo/ *n. m.* bishopric; episcopate.

episcopal /episko'pal/ *a.* episcopal.

episódico /epi'soðiko/ *a.* episodic.

episodio /epi'soðio/ *n. m.* episode.

epístola /e'pistola/ *n. f.* epistle, letter.

epitafio /epi'tafio/ *n. m.* epitaph.

epitomadamente /epitomaða'mente/ *adv.* concisely.

epitomar /epito'mar/ *v.* epitomize, summarize.

época /'epoka/ *n. f.* epoch, age.

epopeya /epo'peya/ *n. f.* epic.

epsomita /epso'mita/ *n. f.* Epsom salts.

equidad /eki'ðað/ *n. f.* equity.

equilibrado /ekili'βraðo/ *a.* stable.

equilibrio /eki'liβrio/ *n. m.* equilibrium, balance.

equinoccio /eki'nokθio: ekinoksio/ *n. m.* equinox.

equipaje /eki'pahe/ *n. m.* luggage, baggage. **e. de mano,** luggage.

equipar /eki'par/ *v.* equip.

equiparar /ekipa'rar/ *v.* compare.

equipo /e'kipo/ *n. m.* equipment; team.

equitación /ekita'θion; ekita'sion/ *f.* horsemanship; horseback riding, riding.

equitativo /ekita'tiβo/ *a.* fair, equitable.

equivalencia /ekiβa'lenθia; ekiβa'lensia/ *f.* equivalence.

equivalente /ekiβa'lente/ *a.* equivalent.

equivaler /ekiβa'ler/ *v.* equal, be equivalent.

equivocación /ekiβoka'θion; ekiβoka'sion/ *n. f.* mistake.

equivocado /ekiβo'kaðo/ *a.* wrong, mistaken.

equivocarse /ekiβo'karse/ *v.* make a mistake, be wrong.

equívoco /e'kiβoko/ *a.* equivocal, ambiguous.

era /'era/ *n. f.* era, age.

erario /e'rario/ *n. m.* exchequer.

erección /erek'θion; erek'sion/ *n. f.* erection; elevation.

eremita /ere'mita/ *n. m.* hermit.

erguir /er'gir/ *v.* erect; straighten up.

erigir /eri'hir/ *v.* erect, build.

erisipela /erisi'pela/ *n. f.* erysipelas.

erizado /eri'θaðo; eri'saðo/ *a.* bristly.

erizarse /eri'θarse; eri'sarse/ *v.* bristle.

erizo /e'riθo; e'riso/ *n. m.* hedgehog; sea urchin.

ermita /er'mita/ *n. f.* hermitage.

ermitaño /ermi'taɲo/ *n. m.* hermit.

erogación /eroga'θion; eroga'sion/ *n. f.* expenditure. **—erogar,** *v.*

erosión /ero'sion/ *n. f.* erosion.

erótico /e'rotiko/ *a.* erotic.

erradicación /erraðika'θion; erraðika'sion/ *n. f.* eradication.

erradicar /erraði'kar/ *v.* eradicate.

errado /e'rraðo/ *a.* mistaken, erroneous.

errante /e'rrante/ *a.* wandering, roving.

errar /e'rrar/ *v.* be mistaken.

errata /e'rrata/ *n. f.* erratum.

errático /e'rratiko/ *a.* erratic.

erróneamente /erronea'mente/ *adv.* erroneously.

erróneo /e'rroneo/ *a.* erroneous.

error /e'rror/ *n. m.* error, mistake.

eructo /e'rukto/ *n. m.* belch. **—eructar**, *v.*

erudición /eruði'θion; eruði'sion/ *n. f.* scholarship, learning.

eruditamente /eruðita'mente/ *adv.* learnedly.

erudito /eru'ðito/ **-ta** *n.* **1.** scholar. **—a 2.** scholarly.

erupción /erup'θion; erup'sion/ *n. f.* eruption; rash.

eruptivo /erup'tiβo/ *a.* eruptive.

esbozo /es'βoθo: es'βoso/ *n. m.* outline, sketch. **—esbozar**, *v.*

escabechar /eskaβe'tʃar/ *v.* pickle; preserve.

escabeche /eska'βetʃe/ *n. m.* brine.

escabel /eska'βel/ *n. m.* small stool or bench.

escabroso /eska'βroso/ *a.* rough, irregular; craggy; rude.

escabullirse /eskaβu'ʎirse; eskaβu'yirse/ *v.* steal away, sneak away.

escala /es'kala/ *n. f.* scale; ladder. **hacer e.**, to make a stop.

escalada /eska'laða/ *n. f.* escalation.

escalador /eskala'ðor/ **-ra** *n.* climber.

escalar /eska'lar/ *v.* climb; scale.

escaldar /eskal'dar/ *v.* scald.

escalera /eska'lera/ *n. f.* stairs, staircase; ladder.

escalfado /eskal'faðo/ *a.* poached.

escalofriado /eskalo'friaðo/ *a.* chilled.

escalofrío /eskalo'frio/ *n. m.* chill.

escalón /eska'lon/ *n. m.* step.

escalonar /eskalo'nar/ *v.* space out, stagger.

escaloña /eska'loɲa/ *n. f.* scallion.

escalpar /eskal'par/ *v.* scalp.

escalpelo /eskal'pelo/ *n. m.* scalpel.

escama /es'kama/ *n. f.* (fish) scale. **—escamar**, *v.*

escamondar /eskamon'dar/ *v.* trim, cut; prune.

escampada /eskam'paða/ *n. f.* break in the rain, clear spell.

escandalizar /eskandali'θar; eskandali'sar/ *v.* shock, scandalize.

escandalizativo /eskandaliθa'tiβo; eskandalisa'tiβo/ *a.* scandalous.

escándalo /es'kandalo/ *n. m.* scandal.

escandaloso /eskanda'loso/ *a.* scandalous; disgraceful.

escandinavo /eskandi'naβo/ **-va** *n. & a.* Scandinavian.

escandir /eskan'dir/ *v.* scan.

escanear /eskane'ar/ *v.* scan (on a computer).

escáner /es'kaner/ *n. m.* scanner (of a computer).

escanilla /eska'niʎa; eska'niya/ *n. f.* cradle.

escañuelo /eska'ɲuelo/ *n. m.* small footstool.

escapada /eska'paða/ *n. f.* escapade.

escapar /eska'par/ *v.* escape.

escaparate /eskapa'rate/ *n. m.* shop window, store window.

escape /es'kape/ *n. m.* escape; *Auto.* exhaust.

escápula /es'kapula/ *n. f.* scapula.

escarabajo /eskara'βaho/ *n. m.* black beetle; scarab.

escaramucear /eskaramuθe'ar; eskaramuse'ar/ *v.* skirmish; dispute.

escarbadientes /eskarβa'ðientes/ *n. m.* toothpick.

escarbar /eskar'βar/ *v.* scratch; poke.

escarcha /es'kartʃa/ *n. f.* frost.

escardar /eskar'ðar/ *v.* weed.

escarlata /eskar'lata/ *n. f.* scarlet.

escarlatina /eskarla'tina/ *n. f.* scarlet fever.

escarmentar /eskarmen'tar/ *v.* correct severely.

escarnecedor /eskarneθe'ðor; eskarnese'ðor/ **-ra** *n.* scoffer; mocker.

escarnecer /eskarne'θer; eskarne'ser/ *v.* mock, make fun of.

escarola /eska'rola/ *n. f.* endive.

escarpa /es'karpa/ *n. m.* escarpment.

escarpado /eskar'paðo/ *a.* **1.** steep. **—n. 2.** *m.* bluff.

escasamente /eskasa'mente/ *adv.* scarcely; sparingly; barely.

escasear /eskase'ar/ *v.* be scarce.

escasez /eska'seθ; eska'ses/ *n. f.* shortage, scarcity.

escaso /es'kaso/ *a.* scant; scarce.

escatimar /eskati'mar/ *v.* be stingy, skimp; save.

escatimoso /eskati'moso/ *a.* malicious; sly, cunning.

escena /es'θena; es'sena/ *n. f.* scene; stage.

escenario /esθe'nario; esse'nario/ *n. m.* stage (of theater); scenario.

escénico /es'θeniko; es'seniko/ *a.* scenic.

escépticamente /esθeptika'mente; esseptika'mente/ *adv.* skeptically.

escepticismo /esθepti'θismo; essepti'sismo/ *n. m.* skepticism.

escéptico /es'θeptiko; es'septiko/ **-ca** *a. & n.* skeptic; skeptical.

esclarecer /esklare'θer; esklare'ser/ *v.* clear up.

esclavitud /esklaβi'tuð/ *n. f.* slavery; bondage.

esclavizar /esklaβi'θar; esklaβi'sar/ *v.* enslave.

esclavo /es'klaβo/ **-va** *n.* slave.

escoba /es'koβa/ *n. f.* broom.

escocés /esko'θes; esko'ses/ **-esa** *a. & n.* Scotch, Scottish; Scot.

Escocia /es'koθia; eskosia/ *n. f.* Scotland.

escofinar /eskofi'nar/ v. rasp.

escoger /esko'her/ v. choose, select.

escogido /esko'hiðo/ a. chosen, selected.

escogimiento /eskohi'miento/ n. m. choice.

escolar /esko'lar/ a. **1.** scholastic, (of) school. —n. **2.** m.& f. student.

escolasticismo /eskolasti'θismo; eskolasti'sismo/ n. m. scholasticism.

escollo /es'koʎo; es'koyo/ n. m. reef.

escolta /es'kolta/ n. f. escort. —**escoltar,** v.

escombro /es'kombro/ n. m. mackerel.

escombros /es'kombros/ n. m.pl. debris, rubbish.

esconce /es'konθe; es'konse/ n. m. corner.

escondedero /eskonde'ðero/ n. m. hiding place.

esconder /eskon'der/ v. hide, conceal.

escondidamente /eskondiða'mente/ adv. secretly.

escondimiento /eskondi'miento/ n. m. concealment.

escondrijo /eskon'driho/ n. m. hiding place.

escopeta /esko'peta/ n. f. shotgun.

escopetazo /eskope'taθo; eskope'taso/ n. m. gunshot.

escoplo /es'koplo/ n. m. chisel.

escorbuto /eskor'βuto/ n. m. scurvy.

escorpena /eskor'pena/ n. f. grouper.

escorpión /eskor'pion/ n. m. scorpion.

escorzón /eskor'θon; eskor'son/ n. m. toad.

escotado /eskota'ðo/ a. low-cut, with a low neckline.

escote /es'kote/ n. m. low neckline.

escribiente /eskri'βiente/ n. m. & f. clerk.

escribir /eskri'βir/ v. write.

escritor /eskri'tor/ **-ra** n. writer, author.

escritorio /eskri'torio/ n. m. desk.

escritura /eskri'tura/ n. f. writing, handwriting.

escrófula /es'krofula/ n. f. scrofula.

escroto /es'kroto/ n. m. scrotum.

escrúpulo /es'krupulo/ n. m. scruple.

escrupuloso /eskrupu'loso/ a scrupulous.

escrutinio /eskru'tinio/ n. m. scrutiny; examination.

escuadra /es'kuaðra/ n. f. squad; fleet.

escuadrón /eskua'ðron/ n. m. squadron.

escualidez /eskuali'ðeθ; eskuali'ðes/ n. f. squalor; poverty; emaciation.

escuálido /es'kualiðo/ a. squalid.

escualo /es'kualo/ n. m. shark.

escuchar /esku'tʃar/ v. listen; listen to.

escudero /esku'ðero/ n. m. squire.

escudo /es'kuðo/ n. m. shield; protection; coin of certain countries.

escuela /es'kuela/ n. f. school.

escuela nocturna /es'kuela nok'turna/ night school.

escuela por correspondencia /es'kuela por korrespon'denθia; es'kuela por korrespon'densia/ correspondence school.

escuerzo /es'kuerθo; es'kuerso/ n. m. toad.

esculpir /eskul'pir/ v. carve, sculpture.

escultor /eskul'tor/ **-ra** n. sculptor.

escultura /eskul'tura/ n. f sculpture.

escupidera /eskupi'ðera/ n. f. cuspidor.

escupir /esku'pir/ v. spit.

escurridero /eskurri'ðero/ n. m. drain board.

escurridor /eskurri'ðor/ n. m. colander, strainer.

escurrir /esku'rrir/ v. drain off; wring out.

escurrirse /esku'rrirse/ v. slip; sneak away.

ese /'ese/ dem. a. that.

ése, ésa dem. pron. that (one).

esencia /e'senθia; e'sensia/ n. f. essence; perfume.

esencial /esen'θial; esen'sial/ a. essential.

esencialmente /esenθial'mente; esensial'mente/ adv. essentially.

esfera /es'fera/ n. f. sphere.

esfinge /es'finhe/ n. f. sphinx.

esforzar /esfor'θar; esfor'sar/ v. strengthen.

esforzarse /esfor'θarse; esfor'sarse/ v. strive, exert oneself.

esfuerzo /es'fuerθo; es'fuerso/ n. m. effort, attempt; vigor.

esgrima /es'grima/ n. f. fencing.

esguince /es'ginθe; es'ginse/ n. m. sprain.

eslabón /esla'βon/ n. m. link (of a chain).

eslabonar /eslaβo'nar/ v. link, join, connect.

eslavo /es'laβo/ **-va** a. & n. Slavic; Slav.

esmalte /es'malte/ n. m. enamel, polish. —**esmaltar,** v.

esmerado /esme'raðo/ a. careful, thorough.

esmeralda /esme'ralda/ n. f. emerald.

esmerarse /esme'rarse/ v. take pains, do one's best.

esmeril /es'meril/ n. m. emery.

eso /'eso/ dem. pron. that.

esófago /e'sofago/ n. m. esophagus.

esotérico /eso'teriko/ a. esoteric.

espacial /espa'θial; espa'sial/ a. spatial.

espacio /es'paθio; es'pasio/ n. m. space. —**espaciar,** v.

espaciosidad /espaθiosi'ðað; espasiosi'ðað/ n. f. spaciousness.

espacioso /espa'θioso; espa'sioso/ a. spacious.

espada /es'paða/ n. f. sword; spade (in cards).

espadarte /espa'ðarte/ n. m. swordfish.

espaguetis /espa'getis/ n. m.pl. spaghetti.

espalda /es'palda/ n. f. back.

espaldera /espal'dera/ n. f. espalier.

espantar /espan'tar/ v. frighten, scare; scare away.

espanto /es'panto/ *n. m.* fright.

espantoso /espan'toso/ *a.* frightening, frightful.

España /es'paɲa/ *n. f.* Spain.

español /espa'ɲol/ **-ola** *a. & n.* Spanish; Spaniard.

esparcir /espar'θir; espar'sir/ *v* scatter, disperse.

espárrago /es'parrago/ *n. m.* asparagus.

espartano /espar'tano/ **-na** *n. & a.* Spartan.

espasmo /es'pasmo/ *n. m.* spasm.

espasmódico /espas'moðiko/ *a.* spasmodic.

espata /es'pata/ *n. f.* spathe.

espato /es'pato/ *n. m.* spar (mineral).

espátula /es'patula/ *n. f.* spatula.

especia /es'peθia; es'pesia/ *n. f.* spice. **—especiar,** *v*

especial /espe'θial; espe'sial/ *a.* special, especial.

especialidad /espeθiali'ðað; espesiali'ðað/ *n. f.* specialty.

especialista /espeθia'lista; espesia'lista/ *n. m. & f.* specialist.

especialización /espeθialiθa'θion; espesialisa'sion/ *n. f.* specialization.

especialmente /espeθial'mente; espesial'mente/ *adv.* especially.

especie /es'peθie; es'pesie/ *n. f.* species; sort.

especiería /espeθie'ria; espesie'ria/ *n. f.* grocery store; spice store.

especiero /espe'θiero; espe'siero/ **-ra** *n.* spice dealer; spice box.

especificar /espeθifi'kar; espesifi'kar/ *v.* specify.

específico /espe'θifiko; espe'sifiko/ *a.* specific.

espécimen /es'peθimen; es'pesimen/ *n. m.* specimen.

especioso /espe'θioso; espe'sioso/ *a.* neat; polished; specious.

espectacular /espektaku'lar/ *a.* spectacular.

espectáculo /espek'takulo/ *n. m.* spectacle, show.

espectador /espekta'ðor/ **-ra** *n.* spectator.

espectro /es'pektro/ *n. m.* specter, ghost.

especulación /espekula'θion; espekula'sion/ *n. f.* speculation.

especulador /espekula'ðor/ **-ra** *n.* speculator.

especular /espeku'lar/ *v.* speculate.

especulativo /espekula'tiβo/ *a.* speculative.

espejo /es'peho/ *n. m.* mirror.

espelunca /espe'lunka/ *n. f.* dark cave, cavern.

espera /es'pera/ *n. f.* wait.

esperanza /espe'ranθa; espe'ransa/ *n. f.* hope, expectation.

esperar /espe'rar/ *v.* hope; expect; wait, wait for, watch for.

espesar /espe'sar/ *v.* thicken.

espeso /es'peso/ *a.* thick, dense, bushy.

espesor /espe'sor/ *n. m.* thickness, density.

espía /es'pia/ *n. m. & f.* spy. **—espiar,** *v.*

espigón /espi'gon/ *n. m.* bee sting.

espina /es'pina/ *n. f.* thorn.

espinaca /espi'naka/ *n. f.* spinach.

espina dorsal /es'pina dor'sal/ spine.

espinal /espi'nal/ *a.* spinal.

espinazo /espi'naθo; espi'naso/ *n. m.* backbone.

espineta /espi'neta/ *n. f.* spinet.

espino /es'pino/ *n. m.* briar.

espinoso /espi'noso/ *a.* spiny, thorny.

espión /es'pion/ *n. m.* spy.

espionaje /espio'nahe/ *n. m.* espionage.

espiral /espi'ral/ *a. & m.* spiral.

espirar /espi'rar/ *v.* expire; breathe, exhale.

espíritu /es'piritu/ *n. m.* spirit.

espiritual /espiri'tual/ *a.* spiritual.

espiritualidad /espirituali'ðað/ *n. f.* spirituality.

espiritualmente /espiritual'mente/ *adv.* spiritually.

espita /es'pita/ *n. f.* faucet, spigot.

espléndido /es'plendiðo/ *a.* splendid.

esplendor /esplen'dor/ *n. m.* splendor.

espolear /espole'ar/ *v.* incite, urge on.

espoleta /espo'leta/ *n. f.* wishbone.

esponja /es'ponha/ *n. f.* sponge.

esponjoso /espon'hoso/ *a.* spongy.

esponsales /espon'sales/ *n. m.pl.* engagement, betrothal.

esponsalicio /esponsa'liθio; esponsa'lisio/ *a.* nuptial.

espontáneamente /espontanea'mente/ *adv.* spontaneously.

espontaneidad /espontanei'ðað/ *n. f.* spontaneity.

espontáneo /espon'taneo/ *a.* spontaneous.

espora /es'pora/ *n. f.* spore.

esporádico /espo'raðiko/ *a.* sporadic.

esposa /es'posa/ *n. f.* wife.

esposar /espo'sar/ *v.* shackle; handcuff.

esposo /es'poso/ *n. m.* husband.

espuela /es'puela/ *n. f.* spur. **—espolear,** *v.*

espuma /es'puma/ *n. f.* foam. **—espumar,** *v.*

espumadera /espuma'ðera/ *n. f.* whisk; skimmer.

espumajear /espumahe'ar/ *v.* foam at the mouth.

espumajo /espu'maho/ *n. m.* foam.

espumar /espu'mar/ *v.* foam, froth; skim.

espumoso /espu'moso/ *a.* foamy; sparkling (wine).

espurio /es'purio/ *a.* spurious.

esputar /espu'tar/ *v.* spit, expectorate.

esputo /es'puto/ *n. m.* spit, saliva.

esquela /es'kela/ *n. f.* note.

esqueleto /eske'leto/ *n. m.* skeleton.

esquema /es'kema/ *n. m.* scheme; diagram.

esquero /es'kero/ *n. m.* leather sack, leather pouch.

esquiar /es'kiar/ *v.* ski.

esquiciar /eski'θiar: eski'siar/ *v.* outline, sketch.

esquicio /es'kiθio: es'kisio/ *n. m.* rough sketch, rough outline.

esquife /es'kife/ *n. m.* skiff.

esquilar /eski'lar/ *v.* fleece, shear.

esquilmo /es'kilmo/ *n. m.* harvest.

esquimal /eski'mal/ *n. & a.* Eskimo.

esquina /es'kina/ *n. f.* corner.

esquivar /eski'βar/ *v.* evade, shun.

estabilidad /estaβili'ðað/ *n. f.* stability.

estable /es'taβle/ *a.* stable.

establecedor /estaβleθe'ðor; estaβlese'ðor/ *n. m.* founder, originator.

establecer /estaβle'θer; estaβle'ser/ *v.* establish, set up.

establecimiento /estaβleθi'miento: estaβlesi'miento/ *n. m.* establishment.

establero /estaβ'lero/ *n. m.* groom.

establo /es'taβlo/ *n. m.* stable.

estaca /es'taka/ *n. f.* stake.

estación /esta'θion; esta'sion/ *n. f.* station; season.

estacionamiento /estaθiona'miento: estasiona'miento/ *n. m.* parking; parking lot; parking space.

estacionar /estaθio'nar; estasio'nar/ *v.* station; park (a vehicle).

estacionario /estaθio'nario; estasio'nario/ *a.* stationary.

estación de servicio /esta'θion de ser'βiθio; esta'sion de ser'βisio/ service station.

estación de trabajo /esta'θion de tra'βaho; esta'sion de tra'βaho/ work station.

estadista /esta'ðista/ *n. m. &* statesman.

estadística /esta'ðistika/ *n. f.* statistics.

estadístico /esta'ðistiko/ *a.* statistical.

estado /es'taðo/ *n. m.* state; condition; status.

Estados Unidos /es'taðos u'niðos/ *n. m.pl.* United States.

estafa /es'tafa/ *n. f.* swindle, fake. —**estafar,** *v.*

estafeta /esta'feta/ *n. f.* post office.

estagnación /estagna'θion; estagna'sion/ *n. f.* stagnation.

estallar /esta'ʎar: esta'yar/ *v.* explode; burst; break out.

estallido /esta'ʎiðo; esta'yiðo/ *n. m.* crash; crack; explosion.

estampa /es'tampa/ *n. f.* stamp. —**estampar,** *v.*

estampado /estam'paðo/ *n. m.* printed cotton cloth.

estampida /estam'piða/ *n. f.* stampede.

estampilla /estam'piʎa; estam'piya/ *n. f.* (postage) stamp.

estancado /estan'kaðo/ *a.* stagnant.

estancar /estan'kar/ *v.* stanch, stop, check.

estancia /es'tanθia; es'tansia/ *n. f.* stay; (S.A.) small farm.

estanciero /estan'θiero: estan'siero/ **-ra** *n.* small farmer.

estandarte /estan'darte/ *n. m.* banner.

estanque /es'tanke/ *n. m.* pool; pond.

estante /es'tante/ *n. m.* shelf.

estaño /es'taɲo/ *n. m.* tin. —**estañar,** *v.*

estar /es'tar/ *v.* be; stand; look.

estática /es'tatika/ *n. f.* static.

estático /es'tatiko/ *a.* static.

estatua /es'tatua/ *n. f.* statue.

estatura /esta'tura/ *n. f.* stature.

estatuto /esta'tuto/ *n. m.* statute, law.

este /'este/ *n. m.* east.

este, esta *dem. a.* this.

éste, ésta *dem. pron.* this (one); the latter.

estelar /este'lar/ *a.* stellar.

estenografía /estenogra'fia/ *n. f.* stenography.

estenógrafo /este'nografo/ **-fa** *n.* stenographer.

estera /es'tera/ *n. f.* mat, matting.

estereofónico /estereo'foniko/ *a.* stereophonic.

estéril /es'teril/ *a.* barren; sterile.

esterilidad /esterili'ðað/ *n. f.* sterility, fruitlessness.

esterilizar /esterili'θar; esterili'sar/ *v.* sterilize.

esternón /ester'non/ *n. m.* breastbone.

estética /es'tetika/ *n. f.* esthetics.

estético /es'tetiko/ *a.* esthetic.

estetoscopio /esteto'skopio/ *n. m.* stethoscope.

estibador /estiβa'ðor/ *n. m.* stevedore.

estiércol /es'tierkol/ *n. m.* dung, manure.

estigma /es'tigma/ *n. m.* stigma; disgrace.

estilarse /esti'larse/ *v.* be in fashion, be in vogue.

estilo /es'tilo/ *n. m.* style; sort.

estilográfica /estilo'grafika/ *n. f.* (fountain) pen.

estima /es'tima/ *n. f.* esteem.

estimable /esti'maβle/ *a.* estimable, worthy.

estimación /estima'θion: estima'sion/ *n. f.* estimation.

estimar /esti'mar/ *v.* esteem; value; estimate; gauge.

estimular /estimu'lar/ *v.* stimulate.

estímulo /es'timulo/ *n. m.* stimulus.

estío /es'tio/ *n. m.* summer.

estipulación /estipula'θion; estipula'sion/ *n. f.* stipulation.

estipular /estipu'lar/ *v.* stipulate.

estirar /esti'rar/ v. stretch.

estirpe /es'tirpe/ n. m. stock, lineage.

esto /'esto/ dem. pron. this.

estocada /esto'kaða/ n. f. stab, thrust.

estofado /esto'faðo/ n. m. stew. —estofar, v.

estoicismo /estoi'θismo: estoi'sismo/ n. m. stoicism.

estoico /es'toiko/ n. & a. stoic.

estómago /es'tomago/ n. m. stomach.

estorbar /estor'βar/ v. bother, hinder, interfere with.

estorbo /es'torβo/ n. m. hindrance.

estornudo /estor'nuðo/ n. m. sneeze. —estornudar, v.

estrabismo /estra'βismo/ n. m. strabismus.

estrago /es'trago/ n. m. devastation, havoc.

estrangulación /estrangula'θion: estrangula'sion/ n. f. strangulation.

estrangular /estraŋgu'lar/ v. strangle.

estraperlista /estraper'lista/ n. m. & f. black marketeer.

estraperlo /estra'perlo/ n. m. black market.

estratagema /estrata'hema/ n. f. stratagem.

estrategia /estra'tehia/ n. f. strategy.

estratégico /estra'tehiko/ a. strategic.

estrato /es'trato/ n. m. stratum.

estrechar /estre'tʃar/ v. tighten; narrow.

estrechez /estre'tʃeθ; estre'tʃes/ n. f. narrowness; tightness.

estrecho /es'tretʃo/ a. 1. narrow, tight. —n. 2. m. strait.

estregar /estre'gar/ v. scour, scrub.

estrella /es'treʎa: es'treya/ n. f. star.

estrellamar /estreʎa'mar; estreya'mar/ n. f. starfish.

estrellar /estre'ʎar; estre'yar/ v. shatter, smash.

estremecimiento /estremeθi'miento; estremesi'miento/ n. m. shudder. —estremecerse, v.

estrenar /estre'nar/ v. wear for the first time; open (a play).

estreno /es'treno/ n. m. debut, first performance.

estrenuo /es'trenuo/ a. strenuous.

estreñido /estre'niðo/ -da a. constipated.

estreñimiento /estreni'miento/ n. m. constipation.

estreñir /estre'nir/ v. constipate.

estrépito /es'trepito/ n. m. din.

estreptococo /estrepto'koko/ n. m. streptococcus.

estría /es'tria/ n. f. groove.

estribillo /estri'βiʎo; estri'βiyo/ n. m. refrain.

estribo /es'triβo/ n. m. stirrup.

estribor /estri'βor/ n. m. starboard.

estrictamente /estrikta'mente/ adv. strictly.

estrictez /estrik'teθ; estrik'tes/ n. f. strictness.

estricto /es'trikto/ a. strict.

estrofa /es'trofa/ n. f. stanza.

estropajo /estro'paho/ n. m. mop.

estropear /estrope'ar/ v. cripple, damage, spoil.

estructura /estruk'tura/ n. f. structure.

estructural /estruktu'ral/ a. structural.

estruendo /es'truendo/ n. m. din, clatter.

estuario /es'tuario/ n. m. estuary.

estuco /es'tuko/ n. m. stucco.

estudiante /estu'ðiante/ -ta n. student.

estudiar /estu'ðiar/ v. study.

estudio /es'tuðio/ n. m. study; studio.

estudioso /estu'ðioso/ a. studious.

estufa /es'tufa/ n. f. stove.

estufa de aire /es'tufa de 'aire/ fan heater.

estulto /es'tulto/ a. foolish.

estupendo /estu'pendo/ a. wonderful, grand, fine.

estupidez /estupi'ðeθ: estupi'ðes/ n. f. stupidity.

estúpido /es'tupiðo/ a. stupid.

estupor /estu'por/ n. m. stupor.

estuque /es'tuke/ n. m. stucco.

esturión /estu'rion/ n. m. sturgeon.

etapa /e'tapa/ n. f. stage.

éter /'eter/ n. m. ether.

etéreo /e'tereo/ a. ethereal.

eternal /eter'nal/ a. eternal.

eternidad /eterni'ðað/ n. f. eternity.

eterno /e'terno/ a. eternal.

ética /'etika/ n. f. ethics.

ético /'etiko/ a. ethical.

etimología /etimolo'hia/ n. f. etymology.

etiqueta /eti'keta/ n. f. etiquette; tag, label.

étnico /'etniko/ a. ethnic.

etrusco /e'trusko/ -ca n. & a. Etruscan.

eucaristía /eukaris'tia/ n. f. Eucharist.

eufemismo /eufe'mismo/ n. m. euphemism.

eufonía /eufo'nia/ n. f. euphony.

Europa /eu'ropa/ n. f. Europe.

europeo /euro'peo/ -pea a. & n. European.

eutanasia /euta'nasia/ n. f. euthanasia.

evacuación /eβakua'θion; eβakua'sion/ n. f. evacuation.

evacuar /eβa'kuar/ v. evacuate.

evadir /eβa'ðir/ v. evade.

evangélico /eβan'heliko/ a. evangelical.

evangelio /eβan'helio/ n. m. gospel.

evangelista /eβanhe'lista/ n. m. evangelist.

evaporación /eβapora'θion: eβapora'sion/ n. f. evaporation.

evaporarse /eβapo'rarse/ v. evaporate.

evasión /eβa'sion, eβa'siβa/ n. f. evasion.

evasivamente /eβasiβa'mente/ adv. evasively.

evasivo /eβa'siβo/ a. evasive.

evento /e'βento/ n. m. event, occurrence.

eventual /eβen'tual/ a. eventual.

eventualidad /eβentuali'ðað/ n. f. eventuality.

evicción /eβik'θion; eβik'sion/ n. f. eviction.

evidencia /eβi'ðenθia; eβiðensia/ n. f. evidence.

evidenciar /eβiðen'θiar; eβiðen'siar/ v. prove, show.

evidente /eβi'ðente/ a. evident.

evitación /eβita'θion; eβita'sion/ n. f. avoidance.

evitar /eβi'tar/ v. avoid, shun.

evocación /eβoka'θion; eβoka'sion/ n. f. evocation.

evocar /eβo'kar/ v. evoke.

evolución /eβolu'θion; eβolu'sion/ n. f. evolution.

exacerbar /eksaθer'βar; eksaser'βar/ v. irritate deeply; exacerbate.

exactamente /eksakta'mente/ adv. exactly.

exactitud /eksakti'tuð/ n. f. precision, accuracy.

exacto /ek'sakto/ a. exact, accurate.

exageración /eksahera'θion; eksahera'sion/ n. f. exaggeration.

exagerar /eksahe'rar/ v. exaggerate.

exaltación /eksalta'θion; eksalta'sion/ n. f. exaltation.

exaltamiento /eksalta'miento/ n. m. exaltation.

exaltar /eksal'tar/ v. exalt.

examen /ek'samen/ n. m. test, examination.

examen de ingreso /ek'samen de iŋ'greso/ entrance examination.

examinar /eksami'nar/ v. test, examine.

exánime /eksa'nime/ a. spiritless, weak.

exasperación /eksaspera'θion; eksaspera-'sion/ n. f. exasperation.

exasperar /eksaspe'rar/ v. exasperate.

excavación /ekskaβa'θion; ekskaβa'sion/ n. f. excavation.

excavar /ekska'βar/ v. excavate.

exceder /eksθe'ðer; eksse'ðer/ v. exceed, surpass; outrun.

excelencia /eksθe'lenθia; eksse'lensia/ n. f. excellence.

excelente /eksθe'lente; eksse'lente/ a. excellent.

excéntrico /ek'θentriko; eks'sentriko/ a. eccentric.

excepción /eksθep'θion; ekssep'sion/ n. f. exception.

excepcional /eksθepθio'nal; ekssepsio'nal/ a. exceptional.

excepto /eks'θepto; eks'septo/ prep. except, except for.

exceptuar /eksθep'tuar; ekssep'tuar/ v. except.

excesivamente /eksθesiβa'mente; ekssesiβa'mente/ adv. excessively.

excesivo /eksθe'siβo; eksse'siβo/ a. excessive.

exceso /eks'θeso; eks'seso/ n. m. excess.

excitabilidad /eksθitaβili'ðað; ekssitaβili'ðað/ n. f. excitability.

excitación /eksθita'θion; ekssita'sion/ n. f. excitement.

excitar /eksθi'tar; ekssi'tar/ v. excite.

exclamación /eksklama'θion; eksklama-'sion/ n. f. exclamation.

exclamar /ekskla'mar/ v. exclaim.

excluir /eksk'luir/ v. exclude, bar, shut out.

exclusión /eksklu'sion/ n. f. exclusion.

exclusivamente /eksklusiβa'mente/ adv. exclusively.

exclusivo /eksklu'siβo/ a. exclusive.

excomulgar /ekskomul'gar/ v. excommunicate.

excomunión /ekskomu'nion/ n. f. excommunication.

excreción /ekskre'θion; ekskre'sion/ n. f. excretion.

excremento /ekskre'mento/ n. m. excrement.

excretar /ekskre'tar/ v. excrete.

exculpar /ekskul'par/ v. exonerate.

excursión /ekskur'sion/ n. f. excursion.

excursionista /ekskursio'nista/ n m. & f. excursionist; tourist.

excusa /eks'kusa/ n. f. excuse. **—excusar,** v.

excusado /eksku'saðo/ n. m. toilet.

excusarse /eksku'sarse/ v. apologize.

exención /eksen'θion; eksen'sion/ n. f. exemption.

exento /ek'sento/ a. exempt. **—exentar,** v.

exhalación /eksala'θion; eksala'sion/ n. f. exhalation.

exhalar /eksa'lar/ v. exhale, breathe out.

exhausto /ek'sausto/ a. exhausted.

exhibición /eksiβi'θion; eksiβi'sion/ n. f. exhibit, exhibition.

exhibir /eksi'βir/ v. exhibit, display.

exhortación /eksorta'θion; eksorta'sion/ n. f. exhortation.

exhortar /eksor'tar/ v. exhort, admonish.

exhumación /eksuma'θion; eksuma'sion/ n. f. exhumation.

exhumar /eksu'mar/ v. exhume.

exigencia /eksi'henθia; eksi'hensia/ n. f. requirement, demand.

exigente /eksi'hente/ a. exacting, demanding.

exigir /eksi'hir/ v. require, exact, demand.

eximir /eksi'mir/ v. exempt.

existencia /eksis'tenθia: eksis'tensia/ *n. f.* existence; *Econ.* supply.

existente /eksis'tente/ *a.* existent.

existir /eksis'tir/ *v.* exist.

éxito /'eksito/ *n. m.* success.

éxodo /'eksoðo/ *n. m.* exodus.

exoneración /eksonera'θion: eksonera'sion/ *n. f.* exoneration.

exonerar /eksone'rar/ *v.* exonerate, acquit.

exorar /ekso'rar/ *v.* beg, implore.

exorbitancia /eksorβi'tanθia: eksorβi'tansia/ *n. f.* exorbitance.

exorbitante /eksorβi'tante/ *a.* exorbitant.

exorcismo /eksor'θismo; eksor'sismo/ *n. m.* exorcism.

exornar /eksor'nar/ *v.* adorn, decorate.

exótico /ek'sotiko/ *a.* exotic.

expansibilidad /ekspansiβili'ðað/ *n. f.* expansibility.

expansión /ekspan'sion/ *n. f.* expansion.

expansivo /ekspan'siβo/ *a.* expansive; effusive.

expatriación /ekspatria'θion; ekspatria'sion/ *n. f.* expatriation.

expatriar /ekspa'triar/ *v.* expatriate.

expectación /ekspekta'θion; ekspekta'sion/ *n. f.* expectation.

expectorar /ekspekto'rar/ *v.* expectorate.

expedición /ekspeði'θion; ekspeði'sion/ *f.* expedition.

expediente /ekspe'ðiente/ *n. m.* expedient; means.

expedir /ekspe'ðir/ *v.* send off, ship; expedite.

expeditivo /ekspeði'tiβo/ *a.* speedy, prompt.

expedito /ekspe'ðito/ *a.* speedy, prompt.

expeler /ekspe'ler/ *v.* expel, eject.

expendedor /ekspende'ðor/ **-ra** *n.* dealer.

expender /ekspen'der/ *v.* expend.

expensas /ek'spensas/ *n. f.pl.* expenses, costs.

experiencia /ekspe'rienθia; ekspe'riensia/ *n. f* experience.

experimentado /eksperimen'taðo/ *a.* experienced.

experimental /eksperimen'tal/ *a.* experimental.

experimentar /eksperimen'tar/ *v.* experience.

experimento /eksperi'mento/ *n. m.* experiment.

expertamente /eksperta'mente/ *adv.* expertly.

experto /ek'sperto/ **-ta** *a. & n.* expert.

expiación /ekspia'θion; ekspia'sion/ *n. f.* atonement.

expiar /eks'piar/ *v.* atone for.

expiración /ekspira'θion; ekspira'sion/ *n. f.* expiration.

expirar /ekspi'rar/ *v.* expire.

explanación /eksplana'θion; eksplana'sion/ *n. f.* explanation.

explanar /ekspla'nar/ *v.* make level.

expletivo /eksple'tiβo/ *n. & a.* expletive.

explicable /ekspli'kaβle/ *a.* explicable.

explicación /eksplika'θion; eksplika'sion/ *f.* explanation.

explicar /ekspli'kar/ *v.* explain.

explicativo /eksplika'tiβo/ *a.* explanatory.

explícitamente /ekspliθita'mente; eksplisita'mente/ *adv.* explicitly.

explícito /eks'pliθito; eksplisito/ *adj.* explicit.

exploración /eksplora'θion; eksplorasion/ *n. f.* exploration.

explorador /eksplora'ðor/ **-ra** *n.* explorer; scout.

explorar /eksplo'rar/ *v.* explore; scout.

exploratorio /eksplora'torio/ *a.* exploratory.

explosión /eksplo'sion/ *n. f.* explosion; outburst.

explosivo /eksplo'siβo/ *a. & m.* explosive.

explotación /eksplota'θion; eksplota'sion/ *n. f.* exploitation.

explotar /eksplo'tar/ *v.* exploit.

exponer /ekspo'ner/ *v.* expose; set forth.

exportación /eksporta'θion; eksporta'sion/ *n. f.* exportation; export.

exportador /eksporta'ðor/ **-ra** *n.* exporter.

exportar /ekspor'tar/ *v.* export.

exposición /eksposi'θion; eksposi'sion/ *n. f.* exhibit; exposition; exposure.

expósito /eks'posito/ **-ta** *n.* foundling; orphan.

expresado /ekspre'saðo/ *a.* aforesaid.

expresamente /ekspresa'mente/ *adv.* clearly, explicitly.

expresar /ekspre'sar/ *v.* express.

expresión /ekspre'sion/ *n. f.* expression.

expresivo /ekspre'siβo/ *a.* expressive; affectionate.

expreso /eks'preso/ *a. & m.* express.

exprimidera de naranjas /eksprimi'ðera de na'ranhas/ *n. f.* orange squeezer.

exprimir /ekspri'mir/ *v.* squeeze.

expropiación /ekspropia'θion; ekspropia'sion/ *n. f.* expropriation.

expropiar /ekspro'piar/ *v.* expropriate.

expulsar /ekspul'sar/ *v.* expel, eject; evict.

expulsión /ekspul'sion/ *n. f.* expulsion.

expurgación /ekspurga'θion; ekspurga'sion/ *n. f.* expurgation.

expurgar /ekspur'gar/ *v.* expurgate.

exquisitamente /ekskisita'mente/ *adv.* exquisitely.

exquisito /eks'kisito/ *a.* exquisite.

éxtasis /'ekstasis/ *n. m.* ecstasy.

extemporáneo /ekstempo'raneo/ *a.* extemporaneous, impromptu.

extender /eksten'der/ *v.* extend; spread; widen; stretch.

extensamente /ekstensa'mente/ *adv.* extensively.

extensión /eksten'sion/ *n. f.* extension, spread, expanse.

extenso /eks'tenso/ *a.* extensive, widespread.

extenuación /ekstenua'θion; ekstenua'sion/ *n. f.* weakening; emaciation.

extenuar /ekste'nuar/ *v.* extenuate.

exterior /ekste'rior/ *a. & m.* exterior; foreign.

exterminar /ekstermi'nar/ *v.* exterminate.

exterminio /ekster'minio/ *n. m.* extermination, ruin.

extinción /ekstin'θion; ekstin'sion/ *n. f.* extinction.

extinguir /ekstiŋ'guir/ *v.* extinguish.

extinto /eks'tinto/ *a.* extinct.

extintor /ekstin'tor/ *n. m.* fire extinguisher.

extirpar /ekstir'par/ *v.* eradicate.

extorsión /ekstor'sion/ *n. f.* extortion.

extra /'ekstra/ *n.* extra.

extracción /ekstrak'θion: ekstrak'sion/ *n. f.* extraction.

extractar /ekstrak'tar/ *v.* summarize.

extracto /eks'trakto/ *n. m.* extract; summary.

extradición /ekstraði'θion; ekstraði'sion/ *n. f.* extradition.

extraer /ekstra'er/ *v.* extract.

extranjero /ekstran'hero/ **-ra** *a.* **1.** foreign. —*n.* **2.** foreigner; stranger.

extrañar /ekstra'ɲar/ *v.* surprise; miss.

extraño /eks'traɲo/ *a.* strange, queer.

extraordinariamente /ˌekstraorðinaria'mente/ *adv.* extraordinarily.

extraordinario /ekstraorði'nario/ *a.* extraordinary.

extravagancia /ekstraβa'ganθia; ekstraβa'gansia/ *n. f.* extravagance.

extravagante /ekstraβa'gante/ *a.* extravagant.

extraviado /ekstra'βiaðo/ *a.* lost, misplaced.

extraviarse /ekstra'βiarse/ *v.* stray, get lost.

extravío /ekstra'βio/ *n. m.* misplacement; aberration, deviation.

extremadamente /ekstremaða'mente/ *adv.* extremely.

extremado /ekstre'maðo/ *a.* extreme.

extremaunción /ekstremaun'θion; ekstremaun'sion/ *n. f.* extreme unction.

extremidad /ekstremi'ðað/ *n. f.* extremity.

extremista /ekstre'mista/ *n. & a.* extremist.

extremo /eks'tremo/ *a. & m.* extreme, end.

extrínseco /ekstrin'seko/ *a.* extrinsic.

exuberancia /eksuβe'ranθia; eksuβeransia/ *n. f.* exuberance.

exuberante /eksuβe'rante/ *a.* exuberant.

exudación /eksuða'θion; eksuða'sion/ *n. f.* exudation.

exudar /eksu'ðar/ *v.* exude, ooze.

exultación /eksulta'θion; eksulta'sion/ *n. f.* exultation.

eyaculación /eyakula'θion; eyakula'sion/ *n. f.* ejaculation.

eyacular /eyaku'lar/ *v.* ejaculate.

eyección /eyek'θion: eyek'sion/ *n. f.* ejection.

eyectar /eyek'tar/ *v.* eject.

F

fábrica /'faβrika/ *n. f.* factory.

fabricación /faβrika'θion; faβrika'sion/ *n. f.* manufacture, manufacturing.

fabricante /faβri'kante/ *n. m. & f.* manufacturer, maker.

fabricar /faβri'kar/ *v.* manufacture, make.

fabril /fa'βril/ *a.* manufacturing, industrial.

fábula /'faβula/ *n. f.* fable, myth.

fabuloso /faβu'loso/ *a.* fabulous.

facción /fak'θion; fak'sion/ *n. f.* faction, party; (*pl.*) features.

faccioso /fak'θioso; fak'sioso/ *a.* factious.

fachada /fa'tʃaða/ *n. f.* façade, front.

fácil /'faθil; 'fasil/ *a.* easy.

facilidad /faθili'ðað; fasili'ðað/ *n. f.* facility, ease.

facilitar /faθili'tar; fasili'tar/ *v.* facilitate, make easy.

fácilmente /ˌfaθil'mente; ˌfasil'mente/ *adv.* easily.

facsímile /fak'simile/ *n. m.* facsimile.

factible /fak'tiβle/ *a.* feasible.

factor /fak'tor/ *n. m.* factor.

factótum /fak'totum/ *n. m.* factotum; jack of all trades.

factura /fak'tura/ *n. f.* invoice, bill.

facturar /faktu'rar/ *v.* bill; check (baggage).

facultad /fakulta'ð/ *n. f.* faculty; ability.

facultativo /fakulta'tiβo/ *a.* optional.

faena /fa'ena/ *n. f.* task; work.

faisán /fai'san/ *n. m.* pheasant.

faja /'faha/ *n. f.* band; sash; zone.

falacia /fa'laθia; fa'lasia/ *n. f.* fallacy; deceitfulness.

falda /'falda/ *n. f.* skirt; lap.

falibilidad /faliβili'ðað/ *n. f.* fallibility.

falla /'faʎa; 'faya/ *n. f.* failure; fault.

fallar /fa'ʎar; fa'yar/ *v.* fail.

fallecer /faʎe'θer; faye'ser/ *v.* pass away, die.

fallo /'faʎo; 'fayo/ *n. m.* verdict; shortcoming.

falsear /false'ar/ *v.* falsify, counterfeit, forge.

falsedad /false'ðað/ *n. f.* falsehood; lie; falseness.

falsificación /falsifika'θion; falsifika'sion/ *n. f.* falsification; forgery.

falsificar /falsifi'kar/ *v.* falsify, counterfeit, forge.

falso /'falso/ *a.* false; wrong.

falta /'falta/ *n. f.* error, mistake; fault; lack. **hacer f.,** to be lacking, to be necessary. **sin f.,** without fail.

faltar /fal'tar/ *v.* be lacking, be missing; be absent.

faltriquera /faltri'kera/ *n. f.* pocket.

fama /'fama/ *n. f.* fame; reputation; glory.

familia /fa'milia/ *n. f.* family; household.

familiar /fami'liar/ *a.* familiar; domestic; (of) family.

familiaridad /familiari'ðað/ *n. f.* familiarity, intimacy.

familiarizar /familiari'θar; familiari'sar/ *v.* familiarize, acquaint.

famoso /fa'moso/ *a.* famous.

fanal /fa'nal/ *n. m.* lighthouse; lantern, lamp.

fanático /fa'natiko/ **-ca** *a. & n* fanatic.

fanatismo /fana'tismo/ *n. m.* fanaticism.

fanfarria /fan'farria/ *n. f.* bluster. —**fanfarrear,** *v.*

fango /'faŋgo/ *n. m.* mud.

fantasía /fanta'sia/ *n. f.* fantasy; fancy, whim.

fantasma /fan'tasma/ *n. m.* phantom; ghost.

fantástico /fan'tastiko/ *a.* fantastic.

faquín /fa'kin/ *n. m.* porter.

faquir /fa'kir/ *n. m.* fakir.

farallón /fara'ʎon; fara'yon/ *n. m.* cliff.

Faraón /fara'on/ *n. m.* Pharaoh.

fardel /far'ðel/ *n. m.* bag; package.

fardo /far'ðo/ *n. m.* bundle.

farináceo /fari'naθeo; fari'naseo/ *a.* farinaceous.

faringe /fa'rinhe/ *n. f.* pharynx.

fariseo /fari'seo/ *n. m.* pharisee, hypocrite.

farmacéutico /farma'θeutiko; farma'seutiko/ **-ca** *a.* **1.** pharmaceutical. —*n.* **2.** pharmacist.

farmacia /far'maθia; far'masia/ *n. f.* pharmacy.

faro /'faro/ *n. m.* beacon; lighthouse; headlight.

farol /fa'rol/ *n. m.* lantern; (street) light, street lamp.

farra /'farra/ *n. f.* spree.

fárrago /'farrago/ *n. m.* medley; hodgepodge.

farsa /'farsa/ *n. f.* farce.

fascinación /fasθina'θion; fassina'sion/ *n. f.* fascination.

fascinar /fasθi'nar; fassi'nar/ *v.* fascinate, bewitch.

fase /'fase/ *n. f.* phase.

fastidiar /fasti'ðiar/ *v.* disgust; irk, annoy.

fastidio /fasti'ðio/ *n. m.* disgust; annoyance.

fastidioso /fasti'ðioso/ *a.* annoying; tedious.

fasto /'fasto/ *a.* happy, fortunate.

fatal /fa'tal/ *a.* fatal.

fatalidad /fatali'ðað/ *n. f.* fate; calamity, bad luck.

fatalismo /fata'lismo/ *n. m.* fatalism.

fatalista /fata'lista/ *n. & a.* fatalist.

fatiga /fa'tiga/ *n. f.* fatigue. —**fatigar,** *v.*

fauna /'fauna/ *n. f.* fauna.

fauno /'fauno/ *n. m.* faun.

favor /fa'βor/ *n. m.* favor; behalf. **por f.,** please.

¡Favor! Puh-lease!

favorable /faβo'raβle/ *a.* favorable.

favorablemente /faβoraβle'mente/ *adv.* favorably.

favorecer /faβore'θer; faβore'ser/ *v.* favor; flatter.

favoritismo /faβori'tismo/ *n. m.* favoritism.

favorito /faβo'rito/ **-ta** *a. & n.* favorite.

fax /faks/ *n. m.* fax.

faz /faθ; fas/ *n. f.* face.

fe /fe/ *n. f.* faith.

fealdad /feal'dað/ *n. f.* ugliness, homeliness.

febrero /fe'βrero/ *n. m.* February.

febril /fe'βril/ *a.* feverish.

fecha /'fetʃa/ *n. f.* date. —**fechar,** *v.*

fecha de caducidad /'fetʃa de kaðuθi'ðað; 'fetʃa de kaðusi'ðað/ expiration date.

fécula /'fekula/ *n. f.* starch.

fecundar /fekun'dar/ *v.* fertilize.

fecundidad /fekundi'ðað/ *n. f.* fecundity, fertility.

fecundo /fe'kundo/ *a.* fecund, fertile.

federación /feðera'θion; feðera'sion/ *n. f.* federation.

federal /feðe'ral/ *a.* federal.

felicidad /feliθi'ðað; felisi'ðað/ *n. f.* happiness; bliss.

felicitación /feliθita'θion; felisita'sion/ *n. f.* congratulation.

felicitar /feliθi'tar; felisi'tar/ *v.* congratulate.

feligrés /feli'gres/ **-esa** *n.* parishioner.

feliz /fe'liθ; fe'lis/ *a.* happy; fortunate.

felón /fe'lon/ *n. m.* felon.

felonía /felo'nia/ *n. f.* felony.

felpa /'felpa/ *n. f* plush.

felpudo /fel'puðo/ *n. m.* doormat.

femenino /feme'nino/ *a.* feminine.

feminismo /femi'nismo/ *n. m.* feminism.

feminista /femi'nista/ *n. m. & f.* feminist.

fenecer /fene'θer; fene'ser/ *v.* conclude; die.

fénix /'feniks/ *n. m.* phoenix; model.

fenomenal /fenome'nal/ *a.* phenomenal.

fenómeno /fe'nomeno/ *n. m.* phenomenon.

feo /'feo/ *a.* ugly, homely.

feracidad /feraθi'ðað; ferasi'ðað/ *n. f.* feracity, fertility.

feraz /fe'raθ; 'feras/ *a.* fertile, fruitful; copious.

feria /'feria/ *n. f.* fair; market.

feriado /fe'riaðo/ *a.* **día f.,** holiday.

fermentación /fermenta'θion; fermenta-'sion/ *n. f.* fermentation.

fermento /fer'mento/ *n. m.* ferment. **—fermentar,** *v.*

ferocidad /feroθi'ðað; ferosi'ðað/ *n. f.* ferocity, fierceness.

feroz /fe'roθ; fe'ros/ *a.* ferocious, fierce.

férreo /'ferreo/ *a.* of iron.

ferrería /ferre'ria/ *n. f.* ironworks.

ferretería /ferrete'ria/ *n. f.* hardware; hardware store.

ferrocarril /ferroka'rril/ *n. m.* railroad.

fértil /'fertil/ *a.* fertile.

fertilidad /fertili'ðað/ *n. f.* fertility.

fertilizar /fertili'θar; fertili'sar/ *v.* fertilize.

férvido /'ferβiðo/ *a.* fervid, ardent.

ferviente /fer'βiente/ *a.* fervent.

fervor /fer'βor/ *n. m.* fervor, zeal.

fervoroso /ferβo'roso/ *a.* zealous, eager.

festejar /feste'har/ *v.* entertain, fete.

festejo /feste'ho/ *n. m.* feast.

festín /fes'tin/ *n. m.* feast.

festividad /festiβi'ðað/ *n. f.* festivity.

festivo /fes'tiβo/ *a.* festive.

fétido /'fetiðo/ *adj.* fetid.

feudal /feu'ðal/ *a.* feudal.

feudo /'feuðo/ *n. m.* fief; manor.

fiado /'fiaðo, al/ *adj.* on trust, on credit.

fiambrera /fiam'brera/ *n. f.* lunch box.

fianza /'fianθa; 'fiansa/ *n. f.* bail.

fiar /fi'ar/ *v.* trust, sell on credit; give credit.

fiarse de /'fiarse de/ *v.* trust (in), rely on.

fiasco /'fiasko/ *n. m.* fiasco.

fibra /'fiβra/ *n. f.* fiber; vigor.

fibroso /fi'βroso/ *a.* fibrous.

ficción /fik'θion; fik'sion/ *n. f.* fiction.

ficha /'fitʃa/ *n. f.* slip, index card; chip.

fichero /fi'tʃero/ *n. m.* computer file, filing cabinet, card catalog.

ficticio /fik'tiθio; fik'tisio/ *a.* fictitious.

fidedigno /fiðe'ðigno/ *a.* trustworthy.

fideicomisario /fiðeikomi'sario/ **-ria** *n.* trustee.

fideicomiso /fiðeiko'miso/ *n. m.* trust.

fidelidad /fiðeli'ðað/ *n. f.* fidelity.

fideo /fi'ðeo/ *n. m.* noodle.

fiebre /'fieβre/ *n. f.* fever.

fiebre del heno /'fieβre del 'eno/ hayfever.

fiel /fiel/ *a.* faithful.

fieltro /'fieltro/ *n. m.* felt.

fiera /'fiera/ *n. f.* wild animal.

fiereza /fie'reθa; fie'resa/ *n. f.* fierceness, wildness.

fiero /'fiero/ *a.* fierce; wild.

fiesta /'fiesta/ *n. f.* festival, feast; party.

figura /fi'gura/ *n. f.* figure. **—figurar,** *v.*

figurarse /figu'rarse/ *v.* imagine.

figurón /figu'ron/ *n. m.* dummy.

fijar /fi'har/ *v.* fix; set, establish; post.

fijarse en /fi'harse en/ *v.* notice.

fijeza /fi'heθa; fi'hesa/ *n. f.* firmness.

fijo /'fiho/ *a.* fixed, stationary, permanent, set.

fila /'fila/ *n. f.* row, rank, file, line.

filantropía /filantro'pia/ *n. f.* philanthropy.

filatelia /fila'telia/ *n. f.* philately, stamp collecting.

filete /fi'lete/ *n. m.* fillet; steak.

film /film/ *n. m.* film. **—filmar,** *v.*

filo /'filo/ *n. m.* (cutting) edge.

filón /fi'lon/ *n. m.* vein (of ore).

filosofía /filoso'fia/ *n. f.* philosophy.

filosófico /filo'sofiko/ *a.* philosophical.

filósofo /fi'losofo/ **-fa** *n.* philosopher.

filtro /'filtro/ *n. m.* filter. **—filtrar,** *v.*

fin /fin/ *n. m.* end, purpose, goal. **a f. de que,** in order that. **en f.,** in short. **por f.,** finally, at last.

final /fi'nal/ *a.* 1. final. **—n.** 2. *m.* end.

finalidad /finali'ðað/ *n. f.* finality.

finalmente /final'mente/ *adv.* at last.

financiero /finan'θiero; finan'siero/ **-ra** *a.* 1. financial. **—n.** 2. financier.

finca /'finka/ *n. f.* real estate; farm.

finés /fi'nes/ **-esa** *a. & n.* Finnish; Finn.

fineza /fi'neθa; fi'nesa/ *n. f.* courtesy, politeness; fineness.

fingimiento /finhi'miento/ *n. m.* pretense.

fingir /fin'hir/ *v.* feign, pretend.

fino /'fino/ *a.* fine; polite, courteous.

firma /'firma/ *n. f.* signature; *Com.* firm.

firmamento /firma'mento/ *n. m.* firmament, heavens.

firmar /fir'mar/ *v.* sign.

firme /'firme/ *a.* firm, fast, steady, sound.

firmemente /firme'mente/ *adv.* firmly.

firmeza /fir'meθa; fir'mesa/ *n. f.* firmness.

fisco /'fisko/ *n. m.* exchequer, treasury.

física /'fisika/ *n. f.* physics.

físico /'fisiko/ **-ca** *a.* & *n.* physical; physicist.

fisiología /fisiolo'hia/ *n. f.* physiology.

fláccido /'flakθido; 'flaksido/ *a.* flaccid, soft.

flaco /'flako/ *a.* thin, gaunt.

flagelación /flahela'θion; flahela'sion/ *n. f.* flagellation.

flagelar /flahe'lar/ *v.* flagellate, whip.

flagrancia /fla'granθia; fla'gransia/ *n. f.* flagrancy.

flagrante /fla'grante/ *a.* flagrant.

flama /'flama/ *n. f.* flame; ardor, zeal.

flamante /fla'mante/ *a.* flaming.

flamenco /fla'menko/ *n. m.* flamingo.

flan /flan/ *n. m.* custard.

flanco /'flanko/ *n. m.* side; *Mil.* flank.

flanquear /flanke'ar/ *v.* flank.

flaqueza /fla'keθa; fla'kesa/ *n. f.* thinness; weakness.

flauta /'flauta/ *n. f.* flute.

flautín /flau'tin/ *n. m.* piccolo.

flautista /flau'tista/ *n. m.* & *f.* flutist, piper.

flecha /'fletʃa/ *n. f.* arrow.

flechazo /fle'tʃaθo; fle'tʃaso/ *n. m.* love at first sight.

flechero /fle'tʃero/ **-ra** *n.* archer.

fleco /'fleko/ *n. m.* fringe; flounce.

flema /'flema/ *n. f.* phlegm.

flemático /fle'matiko/ *a.* phlegmatic.

flequillo /fle'kiʎo; fle'kiyo/ *n. m.* fringe; bangs (of hair).

flete /'flete/ *n. m.* freight. —**fletar**, *v.*

flexibilidad /fleksiβili'ðað/ *n. f.* flexibility.

flexible /flek'siβle/ *a.* flexible, pliable.

flirtear /flirte'ar/ *v.* flirt.

flojo /'floho/ *a.* limp; loose, flabby, slack.

flor /flor/ *n. f.* flower; compliment.

flora /'flora/ *n. f.* flora.

floral /flo'ral/ *a.* floral.

florecer /flore'θer; flore'ser/ *v.* flower, bloom; flourish.

floreo /flo'reo/ *n. m.* flourish.

florero /flo'rero/ *n. m.* flower pot; vase.

floresta /flo'resta/ *n. f.* forest.

florido /flo'riðo/ *a.* flowery; flowering.

florista /flo'rista/ *n. m.* & *f.* florist.

flota /'flota/ *n. f.* fleet.

flotante /flo'tante/ *a.* floating.

flotar /flo'tar/ *v.* float.

flotilla /flo'tiʎa; flo'tiya/ *n. f.* flotilla, fleet.

fluctuación /fluktua'θion; fluktua'sion/ *n. f.* fluctuation.

fluctuar /fluktu'ar/ *v.* fluctuate.

fluente /'fluente/ *a.* fluent; flowing.

fluidez /flui'ðeθ; flui'ðes/ *n. f.* fluency.

flúido /'fluiðo/ *a.* & *m.* fluid, liquid.

fluir /flu'ir/ *v.* flow.

flujo /'fluho/ *n. m.* flow, flux.

fluor /fluor/ *n. m.* fluorine.

fluorescencia /fluores'θenθia; fluores'sensia/ *n. f.* fluorescence.

fluorescente /fluores'θente; fluores'sente/ *a.* fluorescent.

fobia /'foβia/ *n. f.* phobia.

foca /'foka/ *n. f.* seal.

foco /'foko/ *n. m.* focus, center; floodlight.

fogata /fo'gata/ *n. f.* bonfire.

fogón /fo'gon/ *n. m.* hearth, fireplace.

fogosidad /fogosi'ðað/ *n. f.* vehemence, ardor.

fogoso /fo'goso/ *a.* vehement, ardent.

folclore /fol'klore/ *n. m.* folklore.

follaje /fo'ʎahe; fo'yahe/ *n. m.* foliage.

folleto /fo'ʎeto; fo'yeto/ *n. m.* pamphlet, booklet.

follón /fo'ʎon; fo'yon/ *n. m.* mess, chaos.

fomentar /fomen'tar/ *v.* develop, promote, further, foster.

fomento /fo'mento/ *n. m.* fomentation.

fonda /'fonda/ *n. f.* eating house, inn.

fondo /'fondo/ *n. m.* bottom; back (part); background; (*pl.*) funds; finances. **a f.,** thoroughly.

fonética /fo'netika/ *n. f.* phonetics.

fonético /fo'netiko/ *a.* phonetic.

fonógrafo /fo'nografo/ *n. m.* phonograph.

fontanero /fonta'nero/ **-ra** *n. m.* plumber.

forastero /foras'tero/ **-ra** *a.* **1.** foreign, exotic. —*n.* **2.** stranger.

forjar /for'har/ *v.* forge.

forma /'forma/ *n. f.* form, shape. —**formar**, *v.*

formación /forma'θion; forma''sion/ *n. f.* formation.

formal /for'mal/ *a.* formal.

formaldehido /formalde'iðo/ *n. m.* formaldehyde.

formalidad /formali'ðað/ *n. f.* formality.

formalizar /formali'θar, formali'sar/ *v.* finalize; formulate.

formidable /formi'ðaβle/ *a.* formidable.

formidablemente /formiðaβle'mente/ *adv.* formidably.

formón /for'mon/ *n. m.* chisel.

fórmula /'formula/ *n. f.* formula.

formular /formu'lar/ *v.* formulate, draw up.

formulario /formu'lario/ *n. m.* form.

foro /'foro/ *n. m.* forum.

forrado /fo'rraðo/ *a.* stuffed; *Colloq.* filthy rich.

forraje /fo'rrahe/ *n. m.* forage, fodder.

forrar /fo'rrar/ *v.* line.

forro /'forro/ *n. m.* lining; condom.

fortalecer /fortale'θer; fortale'ser/ *v.* fortify.

fortaleza /forta'leθa; forta'lesa/ *n. f.* fort, fortress; fortitude.

fortificación /fortifika'θion; fortifika'sion/ *n. f.* fortification.

fortitud /forti'tuð/ *n. f.* fortitude.

fortuitamente /fortuita'mente/ *adv.* fortuitously.

fortuito /for'tuito/ *a.* fortuitous.

fortuna /for'tuna/ *n. f.* fortune; luck.

forúnculo /fo'runkulo/ *n. m.* boil.

forzar /for'θar; for'sar/ *v.* force, compel, coerce.

forzosamente /forθosa'mente; forsosa'mente/ *adv.* compulsorily; forcibly.

forzoso /for'θoso; for'soso/ *a.* compulsory; necessary. **paro f.,** unemployment.

forzudo /for'θuðo; for'suðo/ *a.* powerful, vigorous.

fosa /'fosa/ *n. f.* grave; pit.

fósforo /'fosforo/ *n. m.* match; phosphorus.

fósil /'fosil/ *n. m.* fossil.

foso /'foso/ *n. m.* ditch, trench; moat.

fotocopia /foto'kopia/ *n. f.* photocopy.

fotocopiadora /fotokopia'ðora/ *n. f.* photocopier.

fotografía /fotogra'fia/ *n. f.* photograph; photography. **—fotografiar,** *v.*

frac /frak/ *n. m.* dress coat.

fracasar /fraka'sar/ *v.* fail.

fracaso /fra'kaso/ *n. m.* failure.

fracción /frak'θion; frak'sion/ *n. f.* fraction.

fractura /frak'tura/ *n. f.* fracture, break.

fragancia /fra'ganθia; fra'gansia/ *n. f.* fragrance; perfume; aroma.

fragante /fra'gante/ *a.* fragrant.

frágil /'frahil/ *a.* fragile, breakable.

fragilidad /frahili'ðað/ *n. f.* fragility.

fragmentario /fragmen'tario/ *a.* fragmentary.

fragmento /frag'mento/ *n. m.* fragment, bit.

fragor /fra'gor/ *n. m.* noise, clamor.

fragoso /fra'goso/ *a.* noisy.

fragua /'fragua/ *n. f.* forge. **—fraguar,** *v.*

fraile /'fraile/ *n. m.* monk.

frambuesa /fram'buesa/ *n. f.* raspberry.

francamente /franka'mente/ *adv.* frankly, candidly.

francés /fran'θes; fran'ses/ **-esa** *a. & n.* French; Frenchman, Frenchwoman.

Francia /'franθia; 'fransia/ *n. f.* France.

franco /'franko/ *a.* frank.

franela /fra'nela/ *n. f.* flannel.

frangible /fran'giβle/ *a.* breakable.

franqueo /fran'keo/ *n. m.* postage.

franqueza /fran'keθa; fran'kesa/ *n. f.* frankness.

franquicia /fran'kiθia; fran'kisia/ *n. f.* franchise.

frasco /'frasko/ *n. m.* flask, bottle.

frase /'frase/ *n. f.* phrase; sentence.

fraseología /fraseolo'hia/ *n. f.* phraseology; style.

fraternal /frater'nal/ *a.* fraternal, brotherly.

fraternidad /fraterni'ðað/ *n. f.* fraternity, brotherhood.

fraude /'frauðe/ *n. m.* fraud.

fraudulento /frauðu'lento/ *a.* fraudulent.

frazada /fra'θaða; fra'saða/ *n. f.* blanket.

frecuencia /fre'kuenθia; fre'kuensia/ *n. f.* frequency.

frecuente /fre'kuente/ *a.* frequent.

frecuentemente /frekuente'mente/ *adv.* frequently, often.

fregadero /frega'ðero/ *n. m.* sink.

fregadura /frega'ðura/ *n. f.* scouring, scrubbing.

fregar /fre'gar/ *v.* scour, scrub, mop.

fregona /fre'gona/ *n. f.* mop.

freír /fre'ir/ *v.* fry.

fréjol /'frehol/ *n. m.* kidney bean.

frenazo /fre'naθo; fre'naso/ *n. m.* sudden braking, slamming on the brakes.

frenesí /frene'si/ *n. m.* frenzy.

frenéticamente /fre'netikamente/ *adv.* frantically.

frenético /fre'netiko/ *a.* frantic, frenzied.

freno /'freno/ *n. m.* brake. **—frenar,** *v.*

freno de auxilio /'freno de auk'silio/ emergency brake.

freno de mano /'freno de 'mano/ hand brake.

frente /'frente/ *n.* **1.** *f.* forehead. **2.** *m.* front. **en f., al f.,** opposite, across. **f. a,** in front of.

fresa /'fresa/ *n. f.* strawberry.

fresca /'freska/ *n. f.* fresh, cool air.

fresco /'fresko/ *a.* fresh; cool; crisp.

frescura /fres'kura/ *n. f.* coolness, freshness.

fresno /'fresno/ *n. m.* ash tree.

fresquería /freske'ria/ *n. f.* soda fountain.

friabilidad /friaβili'ðað/ *n. f.* brittleness.

friable /'friaβle/ *a.* brittle.

frialdad /frial'dað/ *n. f.* coldness.

fríamente /fria'mente/ *adv.* coldly; coolly.

fricandó /'frikando/ *n. m.* fricandeau.

fricar /fri'kar/ *v.* rub together.

fricción /frik'θion; frik'sion/ *n. f.* friction.

friccionar /frikθio'nar; friksio'nar/ *v.* rub.

friega /'friega/ *n. f.* friction; massage.

frigidez /frihi'ðeθ; frihi'ðes/ *n. f.* frigidity.

frígido /'frihiðo/ *a.* frigid.

frijol /fri'hol/ *n. m.* bean.

frío /'frio/ *a. & n.* cold. **tener f.,** to be cold, feel cold. **hacer f.,** to be cold (weather).

friolento /frio'lento/ **friolero** *a.* chilly; sensitive to cold.

friolera /frio'lera/ *n. f.* trifle, trinket.

friso /'friso/ n. m. frieze.

fritillas /fri'tiʎas; fri'tiyas/ n. f.pl. fritters.

frito /'frito/ a. fried.

fritura /fri'tura/ n. f. fritter.

frívolamente /'friβolamente/ adv. frivolously.

frivolidad /friβoli'ðað/ n. f. frivolity.

frívolo /'friβolo/ a. frivolous.

frondoso /fron'doso/ a. leafy.

frontera /fron'tera/ n. f. frontier; border.

frotar /fro'tar/ v. rub.

fructífero /fruk'tifero/ a. fruitful.

fructificar /fruktifi'kar/ v. bear fruit.

fructuosamente /fruktuosa'mente/ adv. fruitfully.

fructuoso /fruk'tuoso/ a. fruitful.

frugal /fru'gal/ a. frugal; thrifty.

frugalidad /frugali'ðað/ n. f. frugality; thrift.

frugalmente /frugal'mente/ adv. frugally, thriftily.

fruncir /frun'θir; frun'sir/ v. gather, contract. **f. el entrecejo,** frown.

fruslería /frusle'ria/ n. f. trinket.

frustrar /frus'trar/ v. frustrate, thwart.

fruta /'fruta/ n. f. fruit.

frutería /frute'ria/ n. f. fruit store.

fruto /'fruto/ n. m. fruit; product; profit.

fucsia /'fuksia/ n. f. fuchsia.

fuego /'fuego/ n. m. fire.

fuelle /'fueʎe; 'fueye/ n. m. bellows.

fuente /'fuente/ n. f. fountain; source; platter.

fuera /'fuera/ adv. without, outside.

fuero /'fuero/ n. m. statute.

fuerte /'fuerte/ a. **1.** strong; loud. —n. **2.** m. fort.

fuertemente /fuerte'mente/ adv. strongly; loudly.

fuerza /'fuerθa; 'fuersa/ n. f. force, strength.

fuga /'fuga/ n. f. flight, escape.

fugarse /fu'garse/ v. flee, escape.

fugaz /fu'gaθ; fu'gas/ a. fugitive, passing.

fugitivo /fuhi'tiβo/ -va a. & n. fugitive.

fulano /fu'lano/ -na n. Mr., Mrs. so-and-so.

fulcro /'fulkro/ n. m. fulcrum.

fulgor /ful'gor/ n. m. gleam, glow. —**fulgurar,** v.

fulminante /fulmi'nante/ a. explosive.

fumador /fuma'ðor/ -ra n. smoker.

fumar /fu'mar/ v. smoke.

fumigación /fumiga'θion; fumiga'sion/ n. f. fumigation.

fumigador /fumiga'ðor/ -ra n. fumigator.

fumigar /fumi'gar/ v. fumigate.

fumoso /fu'moso/ a. smoky.

función /fun'θion; fun'sion/ n. f. function; performance, show.

funcionar /funθio'nar; funsio'nar/ v. function; work, run.

funcionario /funθio'nario; funsio'nario/ -ria n. official, functionary.

funda /'funda/ n. f. case, sheath, slipcover.

fundación /funda'θion; funda'sion/ n. f. foundation.

fundador /funda'ðor/ -ra n. founder.

fundamental /funda'mental/ a. fundamental, basic.

fundamentalmente /fundamental'mente/ adv. fundamentally.

fundamento /funda'mento/ n. m. base, basis, foundation.

fundar /fun'dar/ v. found, establish.

fundición /fundi'θion; fundi'sion/ n. f. foundry; melting; meltdown.

fundir /fun'dir/ v. fuse; smelt.

fúnebre /'funeβre/ a. dismal.

funeral /fune'ral/ n. m. funeral.

funeraria /fune'raria/ n. f. funeral home, funeral parlor.

funestamente /funesta'mente/ adv. sadly.

fungo /'fungo/ n. m. fungus.

furente /fu'rente/ a. furious, enraged.

furgoneta /furgo'neta/ n. f. van.

furia /'furia/ n. f. fury.

furiosamente /furiosa'mente/ adv furiously.

furioso /fu'rioso/ a. furious.

furor /fu'ror/ n. m. furor; fury.

furtivamente /furtiβa'mente/ adv. furtively.

furtivo /fur'tiβo/ a. furtive, sly.

furúnculo /fu'runkulo/ n. m. boil.

fusibilidad /fusiβili'ðað/ n. f. fusibility.

fusible /fu'siβle/ n. m. fuse.

fusil /fu'sil/ n. m. rifle, gun.

fusilar /fusi'lar/ v. shoot, execute.

fusión /fu'sion/ n. f. fusion; merger.

fusionar /fusio'nar/ v. unite, fuse, merge.

fútbol /'futβol/ n. m. football, soccer.

fútil /'futil/ a. trivial.

futilidad /futili'ðað/ n. f. triviality.

futuro /fu'turo/ a. & m. future.

futurología /futurolo'hia/ n. f futurology.

G

gabán /ga'βan/ n. m. overcoat.

gabardina /gaβar'ðina/ n. f. raincoat.

gabinete /gaβi'nete/ n. m. closet; cabinet; study.

gacela /ga'θela; ga'sela/ n. f. gazelle.

gaceta /ga'θeta; ga'seta/ n. f. gazette, newspaper.

gacetilla /gaθe'tiʎa; gase'tiya/ n. f. personal news section of a newspaper.

gaélico /ga'eliko/ a. Gaelic.

gafas /'gafas/ n. f.pl. eyeglasses.

gaguear /gage'ar/ v. stutter, stammer.

gaita /'gaita/ n. f. bagpipes.

gaje /'gahe/ n. m. salary; fee.

gala /'gala/ n. f. gala, ceremony; (pl.) regalia. **tener a g.**, be proud of.

galán /ga'lan/ n. m. gallant.

galano /ga'lano/ a. stylishly dressed; elegant.

galante /ga'lante/ a. gallant.

galantería /galante'ria/ n. f. gallantry, compliment.

galápago /ga'lapago/ n. m. fresh-water turtle.

galardón /galar'ðon/ n. m. prize; reward.

gáleo /'galeo/ n. m. swordfish.

galera /ga'lera/ n. f. wagon; shed; galley.

galería /gale'ria/ n. f. gallery, *Theat.* balcony.

galés /'gales/ **-esa** a. & n. Welsh; Welshman, Welshwoman.

galgo /'galgo/ n. m. greyhound.

galillo /ga'liʎo; ga'liyo/ n. m. uvula.

galimatías /galima'tias/ n. m. gibberish.

gallardete /gaʎar'ðete; gayar'ðete/ n. m. pennant.

galleta /ga'ʎeta; ga'yeta/ n. f. cracker.

gallina /ga'ʎina; ga'yina/ n. f. hen.

gallinero /gaʎi'nero; gayi'nero/ n. m. chicken coop.

gallo /'ga'ʎo; ga'yo/ n. m. rooster.

galocha /ga'lotʃa/ n. f. galosh.

galón /ga'lon/ n. m. gallon; *Mil.* stripe.

galope /ga'lope/ n. m. gallop. **—galopar,** v.

galopín /galo'pin/ n. m. ragamuffin, urchin (child).

gamba /'gamba/ n. f. prawn.

gamberro /gam'βerro/ **-ra** n. hooligan.

gambito /gam'bito/ n. m. gambit.

gamuza /ga'muθa; ga'musa/ n. f. chamois.

gana /'gana/ n. f. desire, wish, mind (to). **de buena g.**, willingly. **tener ganas de,** to feel like.

ganado /ga'naðo/ n. m. cattle.

ganador /gana'ðor/ **-ra** n. winner.

ganancia /ga'nanθia; ga'nansia/ n. f. gain, profit; (pl.) earnings.

ganapán /gana'pan/ n. m. drudge.

ganar /ga'nar/ v. earn; win; beat.

ganchillo /gan'tʃiʎo; gan'tʃiyo/ n. m. crochet work.

gancho /'gantʃo/ n. m. hook, hanger, clip, hairpin.

gandul /gan'dul/ **-la** n. idler, tramp, hobo.

ganga /'gaŋga/ n. f. bargain.

gangrena /gaŋ'grena/ n. f. gangrene.

gansarón /gansa'ron/ n. m. gosling.

ganso /'ganso/ n. m. goose.

garabato /gara'βato/ n. m. hook; scrawl, scribble.

garaje /ga'rahe/ n. m. garage.

garantía /garan'tia/ n. f. guarantee; collateral, security.

garantizar /garanti'θar; garanti'sar/ v. guarantee, secure, pledge.

garbanzo /gar'βanθo; gar'βanso/ n. m. chickpea.

garbo /'garβo/ n. m. grace.

garboso /gar'βoso/ a. graceful, sprightly.

gardenia /gar'ðenia/ n. f. gardenia.

garfa /'garfa/ n. f. claw, talon.

garfio /'garfio/ n. m. claw, talon.

garganta /gar'ganta/ n. f. throat.

gárgara /'gargara/ n. f. gargle. **—gargarizar,** v.

garita /ga'rita/ n. f. sentry box.

garito /ga'rito/ n. m. gambling house.

garlopa /gar'lopa/ n. f. carpenter's plane.

garra /'garra/ n. f. claw.

garrafa /ga'rrafa/ n. f. decanter, carafe.

garrideza /garri'ðeθa; garri'ðesa/ n. f. elegance, handsomeness.

garrido /ga'rriðo/ a. elegant, handsome.

garrote /ga'rrote/ n. m. club, cudgel.

garrotillo /garro'tiʎo; garro'tiyo/ n. m. croup.

garrudo /ga'rruðo/ a. powerful, brawny.

garza /'garθa; 'garsa/ n. f. heron.

gas /gas/ n. m. gas.

gasa /'gasa/ n. f. gauze.

gaseosa /gase'osa/ n. f. carbonated water.

gaseoso /gase'oso/ a. gaseous.

gasolina /gaso'lina/ n. f. gasoline.

gasolinera /gasoli'nera/ n. f. gas station.

gastar /gas'tar/ v. spend; use up, wear out; waste.

gastritis /gas'tritis/ n. f. gastritis.

gastrómano /gas'tromano/ n. m. glutton.

gastrónomo /gas'tronomo/ -ma n. gourmet, epicure, gastronome.

gatear /gate'ar/ v. creep.

gatillo /ga'tiʎo; ga'tiyo/ n. m. trigger.

gato /'gato/ -ta n. cat.

gaucho /'gautʃo/ n. m. Argentine cowboy.

gaveta /ga'βeta/ n. f. drawer.

gavilla /ga'βiʎa; ga'βiya/ n. f. sheaf.

gaviota /ga'βiota/ n. f. seagull.

gayo /ga'yo/ a. merry, gay.

gayola /ga'yola/ n. m. cage; *Colloq.* prison.

gazapera /gaθa'pera; gasa'pera/ n. f. rabbit warren.

gazapo /ga'θapo; ga'sapo/ n. m. rabbit.

gazmoñada /gaθmo'naða; gasmo'naða/ n. f. prudishness.

gazmoño /gaθ'moɲo; gas'moɲo/ n. m. prude.

gaznate /gaθ'nate; gas'nate/ n. m. windpipe.

gazpacho /gaθ'patʃo; gas'patʃo/ n. m. cold tomato soup; gazpacho.

gelatina /hela'tina/ n. f. gelatine.

gemelo /he'melo/ -la n. twin.

gemelos /he'melos/ n. m.pl. cuff links; opera glasses; **-as,** twins.

gemido /he'miðo/ n. m. moan, groan, wail. **—gemir,** v.

genciana /hen'θiana; hen'siana/ n. f. gentian.

genealogía /henealo'hia/ n. f. genealogy, pedigree.

generación /henera'θion; henera'sion/ n. f. generation.

generador /henera'ðor/ n. m. generator.

general /hene'ral/ a. & m. general.

generalidad /henerali'ðað/ n. f. generality.

generalización /heneraliθa'θion; heneralisa'sion/ n. f. generalization.

generalizar /henerali'θar; henerali'sar/ v. generalize.

generalmente /heneral'mente/ adv. generally.

género /'henero/ n. **1.** m. gender; kind. **2.** (pl.) goods, material.

generosidad /henerosi'ðað/ n. f. generosity.

generoso /hene'roso/ a. generous.

génesis /'henesis/ n. m. genesis.

genético /he'netiko/ a. genetic.

genial /he'nial/ a. genial; brilliant.

genio /'henio/ n. m. genius; temper; disposition.

genitivo /heni'tiβo/ n. m. genitive.

genocidio /heno'θiðio; heno'siðio/ n. m. genocide.

gente /'hente/ n. f. people, folk.

gentil /hen'til/ a. gracious; graceful.

gentileza /henti'leθa; henti'lesa/ n. f. grace, graciousness.

gentío /hen'tio/ n. m. mob, crowd.

genuino /he'nuino/ a. genuine.

geografía /heogra'fia/ n. f. geography.

geográfico /heo'grafiko/ a. geographical.

geométrico /heo'metriko/ a. geometric.

geranio /he'ranio/ n. m. geranium.

gerencia /he'renθia; he'rensia/ n. f. management.

gerente /he'rente/ n. m. & f. manager, director.

germen /'hermen/ n. m. germ.

germinar /hermi'nar/ v. germinate.

gerundio /he'rundio/ n. m. gerund.

gesticulación /hestikula'θion; hestikula'sion/ n. f. gesticulation.

gesticular /hestiku'lar/ v. gesticulate, gesture.

gestión /hes'tion/ n. f. conduct; effort; action.

gesto /'hesto/ n. m. gesture, facial expression.

gigante /hi'gante/ a. & n. gigantic, giant.

gigantesco /higan'tesko/ a. gigantic, huge.

gilipollas /gili'poʎas; gili'poyas/ n. m. & f. *Colloq.* fool, idiot.

gimnasio /him'nasio/ n. m. gymnasium.

gimnástica /him'nastika/ n. f. gymnastics.

gimotear /himote'ar/ v. whine.

ginebra /hi'neβra/ n. f. gin.

ginecólogo /hine'kologo/ -ga n. gynecologist.

gira /'hira/ n. f. tour, trip.

girado /hi'raðo/ -da n. *Com.* drawee.

girador /hira'ðor/ -ra n. *Com.* drawer.

girar /hi'rar/ v revolve, turn, spin, whirl.

giratorio /hira'torio/ a. rotary, revolving.

giro /'hiro/ n. m. whirl, turn, spin; *Com.* draft. **g. postal,** money order.

gitano /hi'tano/ -na a. & n. Gypsy.

glacial /gla'θial; gla'sial/ a. glacial, icy.

glaciar /gla'θiar; gla'siar/ n. m. glacier.

gladiador /glaðia'ðor/ n. m. gladiator.

glándula /'glandula/ n. f. gland.

glándula endocrina /'glandula endo'krina/ endocrine gland.

glándula pituitaria /'glandula pitui'taria/ pituitary gland.

glándula prostática /'glandula pros'tatika/ prostate gland.

glasé /gla'se/ n. m. glacé.

glicerina /gliθe'rina; glise'rina/ n. f. glycerine.

globo /'gloβo/ n. m. globe; balloon.

gloria /'gloria/ n. f. glory.

glorieta /glo'rieta/ n. f. bower.

glorificación /glorifika'θion; glorifika'sion/ n. f. glorification.

glorificar /glorifi'kar/ v. glorify.

glorioso /glo'rioso/ a. glorious.

glosa /'glosa/ n. f. gloss. **—glosar,** v.

glosario /glo'sario/ *n. m.* glossary.

glotón /glo'ton/ **-ona** *a. & n.* gluttonous; glutton.

glucosa /glu'kosa/ *n. f.* glucose.

gluten /'gluten/ *n. m.* gluten; glue.

gobernación /goβerna'θion; goβerna'sion/ *n. f.* government.

gobernador /goβerna'ðor/ **-ra** *n.* governor.

gobernalle /goβer'naʎe; goβer'naye/ *n. m.* rudder, tiller, helm.

gobernante /goβer'nante/ *n. m. & f.* ruler.

gobernar /goβer'nar/ *v.* govern.

gobierno /go'βierno/ *n. m.* government.

goce /'goθe; 'gose/ *n. m.* enjoyment.

gola /'gola/ *n. f.* throat.

golf /golf/ *n. m.* golf.

golfista /gol'fista/ *n. m. & f.* golfer.

golfo /'golfo/ *n. m.* gulf.

gollete /go'ʎete; go'yete/ *n. m.* upper portion of one's throat.

golondrina /golon'drina/ *n. f.* swallow.

golosina /golo'sina/ *n. f.* delicacy.

goloso /go'loso/ *a.* sweet-toothed.

golpe /'golpe/ *n. m.* blow, stroke. **de g.**, suddenly.

golpear /golpe'ar/ *v.* strike, beat, pound.

goma /'goma/ *n. f.* rubber; gum; glue; eraser.

góndola /'gondola/ *n. f.* gondola.

gordo /'gorðo/ *a.* fat.

gordura /gor'ðura/ *n. f.* fatness.

gorila /go'rila/ *n. m.* gorilla.

gorja /'gorha/ *n. f.* gorge.

gorjeo /gor'heo/ *n. m.* warble, chirp. **—gorjear,** *v.*

gorrión /go'rrion/ *n. m.* sparrow.

gorro /'gorro/ *n. m.* cap.

gota /'gota/ *n. f.* drop (of liquid).

gotear /gote'ar/ *v.* drip, leak.

goteo /go'teo/ *n. m.* leak.

gotera /go'tera/ *n. f.* leak; gutter.

gótico /'gotiko/ *a.* Gothic.

gozar /go'θar; go'sar/ *v.* enjoy.

gozne /'goθne; 'gosne/ *n. m.* hinge.

gozo /'goθo; 'goso/ *n. m.* enjoyment, delight, joy.

gozoso /go'θoso; go'soso/ *a.* joyful, joyous.

grabado /gra'βaðo/ *n.* **1.** *m.* engraving, cut, print. **—a. 2.** recorded.

grabador /graβa'ðor/ *n. m.* engraver.

grabadora /graβa'ðora/ *n. f.* tape recorder.

grabar /gra'βar/ *v.* engrave; record.

gracia /'graθia; 'grasia/ *n. f.* grace; wit, charm. **hacer g.,** to amuse, strike as funny. **tener g.,** to be funny, to be witty.

gracias /'graθias; 'grasias/ *n. f.pl.* thanks, thank you.

gracioso /gra'θioso; gra'sioso/ *a.* witty, funny.

grada /'graða/ *n. f.* step.

gradación /graða'θion; graða'sion/ *n. f.* gradation.

grado /'graðo/ *n. m.* grade; rank; degree.

graduado /gra'ðuaðo/ **-da** *n.* graduate.

gradual /gra'ðual/ *a.* gradual.

graduar /gra'ðuar/ *v.* grade; graduate.

gráfico /'grafiko/ *a.* graphic, vivid.

grafito /gra'fito/ *n. m.* graphite.

grajo /'graho/ *n. m.* jackdaw.

gramática /gra'matika/ *n. f.* grammar.

gramo /'gramo/ *n. m.* gram.

gran /gran/ **grande** *a.* big, large; great.

granada /gra'naða/ *n. f.* grenade; pomegranate.

granar /gra'nar/ *v.* seed.

grandes almacenes /'grandes alma'θenes; 'grandes alma'senes/ *n. m.pl.* department store.

grandeza /gran'deθa; gran'desa/ *n. f.* greatness.

grandiosidad /grandiosi'ðað/ *n. f.* grandeur.

grandioso /gran'dioso/ *a.* grand, magnificent.

grandor /gran'dor/ *n. m.* size.

granero /gra'nero/ *n. m.* barn; granary.

granito /gra'nito/ *n. m.* granite.

granizada /grani'θaða; grani'saða/ *n. f.* hailstorm.

granizo /gra'niθo; gra'niso/ *n. m.* hail. **—granizar,** *v.*

granja /'granha/ *n. f.* grange; farm; farmhouse.

granjear /granhe'ar/ *v.* earn, gain; get.

granjero /gran'hero/ **-era** *n.* farmer.

grano /'grano/ *n. m.* grain; kernel.

granuja /gra'nuha/ *n. m.* waif, urchin.

grapa /'grapa/ *n. f.* clamp, clip.

grapadora /grapa'ðora/ *n. f.* stapler.

grasa /'grasa/ *n. f.* grease, fat.

grasiento /gra'siento/ *a.* greasy.

gratificación /gratifika'θion; gratifika'sion/ *n. f.* gratification; reward; tip.

gratificar /gratifi'kar/ *v.* gratify; reward; tip.

gratis /'gratis/ *adv.* gratis, free.

gratitud /grati'tuð/ *n. f.* gratitude.

grato /'grato/ *a.* grateful; pleasant.

gratuito /gra'tuito/ *a.* gratuitous; free.

gravamen /gra'βamen/ *n. m.* tax; burden; obligation.

grave /'graβe/ *a.* grave, serious, severe.

gravedad /graβe'ðað/ *n. f.* gravity, seriousness.

gravitación /graβita'θion; graβita'sion/ *n. f.* gravitation.

gravitar /graβi'tar/ *v.* gravitate.

gravoso /gra'βoso/ *a.* burdensome.

graznido /graθ'niðo; gras'niðo/ *n. m.* croak. **—graznar,** *v.*

Grecia /'greθia; 'gresia/ n. f Greece.

greco /'greko/ **-ca** a. & n. Greek.

greda /'greða/ n. f. clay.

gresca /'greska/ n. f. revelry; quarrel.

griego /'griego/ **-ga** a. & n. Greek.

grieta /'grieta/ n. f. opening; crevice, crack.

grifo /'grifo/ n m. faucet.

grillo /'griʎo: 'griyo/ n. m. cricket.

grima /'grima/ n. f. fright.

gringo /'gringo/ **-ga** n. foreigner (usually North American).

gripa /'gripa/ **gripe** n. f. grippe.

gris /gris/ a. gray.

grito /'grito/ n. m. shout, scream, cry. —**gritar,** v.

grosella /gro'seʎa: gro'seya/ n. f. currant.

grosería /grose'ria/ n. f. grossness; coarseness.

grosero /gro'sero/ a. coarse, vulgar, discourteous.

grotesco /gro'tesko/ a. grotesque.

grúa /'grua/ n. f. crane; tow truck.

gruesa /'gruesa/ n. f. gross.

grueso /'grueso/ a. 1. bulky; stout; coarse, thick. —n. 2. m. bulk.

grulla /'gruʎa; 'gruya/ n. f. crane.

gruñido /gru'ɲiðo/ n. m. growl, snarl, mutter. —**gruñir,** v.

grupo /'grupo/ n. m. group, party.

gruta /'gruta/ n. f. cavern.

guacamol /guaka'mol/ **guacamole** n. m. avocado sauce; guacamole.

guadaña /gua'ðaɲa/ n. f. scythe. —**guadañar,** v.

guagua /'guagua/ n. f. (S.A.) baby; (Carib.) bus.

gualdo /'gualdo/ a. yellow, golden.

guano /'guano/ n. m. guano (fertilizer).

guante /'guante/ n. m. glove.

guantera /guan'tera/ n. f. glove compartment.

guapo /'guapo/ a. handsome.

guarda /'guarða/ n. m. or f. guard.

guardabarros /guarða'βarros/ n. m. fender.

guardacostas /guarða'kostas/ n. m. revenue ship.

guardaespaldas /,guarðaes'paldas/ n. m. & f. bodyguard.

guardameta /guarða'meta/ n. m. & f. goalkeeper.

guardar /guar'ðar/ v. keep, store, put away; guard.

guardarropa /guarða'rropa/ n. f. coat room.

guardarse de /guar'ðarse de/ v. beware of, avoid.

guardia /'guarðia/ n. 1. f. guard; watch. —n. 2. m. policeman.

guardián /guar'ðian/ **-na** n. guardian, keeper, watchman.

guardilla /guar'ðiʎa; guar'ðiya/ n. f. attic.

guarida /gua'riða/ n. f. den.

guarismo /gua'rismo/ n. m. number, figure.

guarnecer /guarne'θer; guarne'ser/ v. adorn.

guarnición /guarni'θion; guarni'sion/ n. f. garrison; trimming.

guasa /'guasa/ n. f. joke, jest.

guayaba /gua'yaβa/ n. f. guava.

gubernativo /guβerna'tiβo/ a. governmental.

guerra /'gerra/ n. f. war.

guerrero /ge'rrero/ **-ra** n. warrior.

guía /'gia/ n. 1. m. & f. guide. 2. f. guidebook, directory.

guiar /giar/ v. guide; steer, drive.

guija /'giha/ n. f. pebble.

guillotina /giʎo'tina; giyo'tina/ n. f. guillotine.

guindar /gin'dar/ v. hang.

guinga /'ginga/ n. f. gingham.

guiñada /gi'ɲaða/ n f., **guiño,** m. wink. —**guiñar,** v.

guión /gi'on/ n. m. dash, hyphen; script.

guirnalda /gir'nalda/ n. f. garland, wreath.

guisa /'gisa/ n. f. guise, manner.

guisado /gi'saðo/ n. m. stew.

guisante /gi'sante/ n. m. pea.

guisar /gi'sar/ v. cook.

guiso /'giso/ n. m. stew.

guita /'gita/ n. f. twine.

guitarra /gi'tarra/ n. f. guitar.

guitarrista /gita'rrista/ n. m. & f. guitarist.

gula /'gula/ n. f. gluttony.

gurú /gu'ru/ n. m. guru.

gusano /gu'sano/ n. m. worm, caterpillar.

gustar /gus'tar/ v. please; taste.

gustillo /gus'tiʎo; gus'tiyo/ n. m. aftertaste, slight pleasure.

gusto /'gusto/ n. m. pleasure; taste; liking.

gustoso /gus'toso/ a. pleasant; tasteful.

gutural /gutu'ral/ a. guttural.

H

haba /'aβa/ *n. f.* bean.

habanera /aβa'nera/ *n. f.* Cuban dance melody.

haber /a'βer/ *v.* have. **h. de,** be to, be supposed to.

haberes /a'βeres/ *n. m.pl.* property; worldly goods.

habichuela /aβi'tʃuela/ *n. f.* bean.

hábil /'aβil/ *a.* skillful; capable; clever.

habilidad /aβili'ðað/ *n. f.* ability; skill; talent.

habilidoso /aβili'ðoso/ *a.* able, skillful, talented.

habilitado /aβili'taðo/ **-da** *n.* paymaster.

habilitar /aβili'tar/ *v.* qualify; supply, equip.

hábilmente /'aβilmente/ *adv.* ably.

habitación /aβita'θion; aβita'sion/ *n. f.* dwelling; room. **h. individual,** single room.

habitante /aβi'tante/ *n. m. & f.* inhabitant.

habitar /aβi'tar/ *v.* inhabit; dwell.

hábito /'aβito/ *n. m.* habit; custom.

habitual /aβi'tual/ *a.* habitual.

habituar /aβi'tuar/ *v.* accustom, habituate.

habla /'aβla/ *n. f.* speech.

hablador /aβla'ðor/ *a.* talkative.

hablar /a'βlar/ *v.* talk, speak.

haca /'aka/ *n. f.* pony.

hacedor /aθe'ðor; ase'ðor/ *n. m.* maker.

hacendado /aθen'daðo; asen'daðo/ **-da** *n.* hacienda owner; farmer.

hacendoso /aθen'doso; asen'doso/ *a.* industrious.

hacer /a'θer; a'ser/ *v.* do; make. **hace dos años,** etc., two years ago, etc.

hacerse /a'θerse; a'serse/ *v.* become, get to be.

hacha /'atʃa/ *n. f.* ax, hatchet.

hacia /'aθia; 'asia/ *prep.* toward.

hacienda /a'θienda; a'sienda/ *n. f.* property; estate; ranch; farm; *Govt.* treasury.

hada /'aða/ *n. f.* fairy.

hado /'aðo/ *n. m.* fate.

halagar /ala'gar/ *v.* flatter.

halar /a'lar/ *v.* haul, pull.

halcón /al'kon/ *n. m.* hawk, falcon.

haleche /a'letʃe/ *n. m.* anchovy.

hallado /a'ʎaðo; a'yaðo/ *a.* found. **bien h.,** welcome. **mal h.,** uneasy.

hallar /a'ʎar; a'yar/ *v.* find, locate.

hallarse /a'ʎarse; a'yarse/ *v.* be located; happen to be.

hallazgo /a'ʎaθgo; a'yasgo/ *n. m.* find, thing found.

hamaca /a'maka/ *n. f.* hammock.

hambre /'ambre/ *n. f.* hunger. **tener h., estar con h.,** to be hungry.

hambrear /ambre'ar/ *v.* hunger; starve.

hambriento /am'briento/ *a.* starving, hungry.

hamburguesa /ambur'gesa/ *n. f.* beefburger, hamburger.

haragán /ara'gan/ **-na** *n.* idler, lazy person.

haraganear /aragane'ar/ *v.* loiter.

harapo /a'rapo/ *n. m.* rag, tatter.

haraposo /ara'poso/ *a.* ragged, shabby.

harén /a'ren/ *n. m.* harem.

harina /a'rina/ *n. f.* flour, meal.

harnero /ar'nero/ *n. m.* sieve.

hartar /ar'tar/ *v.* satiate.

harto /'arto/ *a.* stuffed; fed up.

hartura /ar'tura/ *n. f.* superabundance, glut.

hasta /'asta/ *prep.* **1.** until, till; as far as, up to. **h. luego,** good-bye, so long. —*adv.* **2.** even.

hastío /as'tio/ *n. m.* distaste, loathing.

hato /'ato/ *n. m.* herd.

hay /ai/ *v.* there is, there are. **h. que,** it is necessary to. **no h. de qué,** you're welcome, don't mention it.

haya /'aya/ *n. f.* beech tree.

haz /aθ/ *n. f.* as; *n. f.* bundle, sheaf; face.

hazaña /a'θaɲa; a'saɲa/ *n. f.* deed; exploit, feat.

hebdomadario /eβðoma'ðario/ *a.* weekly.

hebilla /e'βiʎa; e'βiya/ *n. f.* buckle.

hebra /'eβra/ *n. f.* thread, string.

hebreo /e'βreo/ **-rea** *a. & n.* Hebrew.

hechicero /etʃi'θero; etʃi'sero/ **-ra** *n.* wizard, witch.

hechizar /etʃi'θar; etʃi'sar/ *v.* bewitch.

hechizo /e'tʃiθo; e'tʃiso/ *n. m.* spell.

hecho /'etʃo/ *n. m.* fact; act; deed.

hechura /e'tʃura/ *n. f.* workmanship, make.

hediondez /eðion'deθ; eðion'des/ *n. f.* stench.

hégira /'ehira/ *n. f.* hegira.

helada /e'laða/ *n. f.* frost.

heladería /elaðe'ria/ *n. f.* ice-cream parlor.

helado /e'laðo/ *n. m.* ice cream.

helar /e'lar/ *v.* freeze.

helecho /e'letʃo/ *n. m.* fern.

hélice /'eliθe; 'elise/ *n. f.* propeller; helix.

helicóptero /eli'koptero/ *n. m.* helicopter.

helio /'elio/ *n. m.* helium.

hembra /'embra/ *n. f.* female.

hemisferio /emis'ferio/ *n. m.* hemisphere.

hemoglobina /emoglo'βina/ n. f. hemoglobin.

hemorragia /emo'rrahia/ n. f. hemorrhage.

hemorragia nasal /emo'rrahia na'sal/ nosebleed.

henchir /en't∫ir/ v. stuff.

hendedura /ende'ðura/ n. f. crevice, crack.

hendido /en'diðo/ a. cloven, cleft (lip).

heno /'eno/ n. m. hay.

hepática /e'patika/ n. f. liverwort.

hepatitis /epa'titis/ n. f. hepatitis.

heraldo /e'raldo/ n. m. herald.

herbáceo /er'βaθeo; er'βaseo/ a. herbaceous.

herbívoro /er'βiβoro/ a. herbivorous.

heredar /ere'ðar/ v. inherit.

heredero /ere'ðero/ -ra n. heir; successor.

hereditario /ereði'tario/ a. hereditary.

hereje /e'rehe/ n. m. & f. heretic.

herejía /ere'hia/ n. f. heresy.

herencia /e'renθia; e'rensia/ n. f. inheritance; heritage.

herético /e'retiko/ a. heretical.

herida /e'riða/ n. f. wound, injury.

herir /e'rir/ v. wound, injure.

hermafrodita /ermafro'ðita/ a. & n. hermaphrodite.

hermana /er'mana/ n. f. sister.

hermano /er'mano/ n. m. brother.

hermético /er'metiko/ a. airtight.

hermoso /er'moso/ a. beautiful, handsome.

hermosura /ermo'sura/ n. f. beauty.

hernia /'ernia/ n. f. hernia, rupture.

héroe /'eroe/ n. m. hero.

heroico /e'roiko/ a. heroic.

heroína /ero'ina/ n. f. heroine.

heroísmo /ero'ismo/ n. m. heroism.

herradura /erra'ðura/ n. f. horseshoe.

herramienta /erra'mienta/ n. f. tool; implement.

herrería /erre'ria/ n. f. blacksmith's shop.

herrero /e'rrero/ n. m. blacksmith.

herrumbre /e'rrumbre/ n. f. rust.

hertzio /'ertθio; 'ertsio/ n. m. hertz.

hervir /er'βir/ v. boil.

hesitación /esita'θion; esita'sion/ n. f. hesitation.

heterogéneo /etero'heneo/ a. heterogeneous.

heterosexual /eterosek'sual/ a. heterosexual.

hexagonal /eksago'nal/ a. hexagonal.

hexágono /ek'sagono/ n. m. hexagon.

hez /eθ; es/ n. f. dregs, sediment.

híbrido /'iβriðo/ -da n. a. hybrid.

hidalgo /i'ðalgo/ -ga a. & n. noble.

hidalguía /iðal'gia/ n. f. nobility; generosity.

hidráulico /i'ðrauliko/ a. hydraulic.

hidroavión /iðroa'βion/ n. m. seaplane, hydroplane.

hidrofobia /iðro'foβia/ n. f. rabies.

hidrógeno /i'ðroheno/ n. m. hydrogen.

hidropesía /iðrope'sia/ n. f. dropsy.

hiedra /'ieðra/ n. f. ivy.

hiel /iel/ n. f. gall.

hielo /'ielo/ n. m. ice.

hiena /'iena/ n. f. hyena.

hierba /'ierβa/ n. f. grass; herb; marijuana.

hierbabuena /ierβa'βuena/ n. f. mint.

hierro /'ierro/ n. m. iron.

hígado /'igaðo/ n. m. liver.

higiene /i'hiene/ n. f. hygiene.

higiénico /i'hieniko/ a. sanitary, hygienic.

higo /'igo/ n. m. fig.

higuera /i'gera/ n. f. fig tree.

hija /'iha/ n. f. daughter.

hija adoptiva /'iha aðop'tiβa/ adopted daughter.

hijastro /i'hastro/ -tra n. stepchild.

hijo /'iho/ n. m. son.

hijo adoptivo /'iho aðop'tiβo/ n. m. adopted child, adopted son.

hila /'ila/ n. f. line.

hilandero /ilan'dero/ -ra n. spinner.

hilar /i'lar/ v. spin.

hilera /i'lera/ n. f. row, line, tier.

hilo /'ilo/ n. m. thread; string; wire; linen.

himno /'imno/ n. m. hymn.

hincar /in'kar/ v. drive, thrust; sink into.

hincarse /in'karse/ v. kneel. ●

hinchar /in't∫ar/ v. swell.

hindú /in'du/ n. & a. Hindu.

hinojo /i'noho/ n. m. knee.

hiperenlace /iperen'laθe, iperen'lase/ n. m. hyperlink.

hipermercado /ipermer'kaðo/ n. m. hypermarket.

hipertexto /iper'teksto/ n. m. hypertext.

hipnótico /ip'notiko/ a. hypnotic.

hipnotismo /ipno'tismo/ n. m. hypnotism.

hipnotista /ipno'tista/ n. m. & f. hypnotist.

hipnotizar /ipnoti'θar; ipnoti'sar/ v. hypnotize.

hipo /'ipo/ n. m. hiccough.

hipocresía /ipokre'sia/ n. f. hypocrisy.

hipócrita /i'pokrita/ a. & n. hypocritical; hypocrite.

hipódromo /i'poðromo/ n. m. race track.

hipoteca /ipo'teka/ n. f. mortgage. —**hipotecar,** v.

hipótesis /i'potesis/ n. f. hypothesis.

hirsuto /ir'suto/ a. hairy, hirsute.

hispano /is'pano/ a. Hispanic, Spanish American.

Hispanoamérica /ispanoa'merika/ f. Spanish America.

hispanoamericano /ispanoameri'kano/ -na a. & n. Spanish American.

histerectomía /isterekto'mia/ *n. f.* hysterectomy.

histeria /is'teria/ *n. f.* hysteria.

histérico /is'teriko/ *a.* hysterical.

historia /is'toria/ *n. f.* history; story.

historiador /istoria'ðor/ **-ra** *n.* historian.

histórico /is'toriko/ *a.* historic, historical.

histrión /is'trion/ *n. m.* actor.

hocico /o'θiko; o'siko/ *n. m.* snout, muzzle.

hogar /o'gar/ *n. m.* hearth; home.

hoguera /o'gera/ *n. f.* bonfire, blaze.

hoja /'oha/ *n. f.* leaf; sheet (of paper); pane; blade.

hoja de cálculo /'oha de 'kalkulo/ spreadsheet.

hoja de inscripción /'oha de inskrip'θion; 'oha de inskrip'sion/ entry blank.

hoja de pedidos /'oha de pe'ðiðos/ order blank.

hoja informativa /'oha informa'tiβa/ newsletter.

hojalata /oha'lata/ *n. f.* tin.

hojalatero /ohala'tero/ **-ra** *n.* tinsmith.

hojear /ohe'ar/ *v.* scan, skim through.

hola /'ola/ *interj.* hello.

Holanda /o'landa/ *n. f.* Holland, Netherlands.

holandés /olan'des/ **-esa** *a.* & *n.* Dutch; Hollander.

holganza /ol'ganθa; ol'gansa/ *n. f.* leisure; diversion.

holgazán /olga'θan; olga'san/ **-ana** *a.* **1.** idle, lazy. —*n.* **2.** *m.* idler, loiterer, tramp.

holgazanear /olgaθane'ar; olgasane'ar/ *v.* idle, loiter.

hollín /o'ʎin; o'yin/ *n. m.* soot.

holografía /ologra'fia/ *n. f.* holography.

holograma /olo'grama/ *n. m.* hologram.

hombre /'ombre/ *n. m.* man.

hombría /om'βria/ *n. f.* manliness.

hombro /'ombro/ *n. m.* shoulder.

hombruno /om'bruno/ *a.* mannish, masculine (woman).

homenaje /ome'nahe/ *n. m.* homage.

homeópata /ome'opata/ *n. m.* homeopath.

homicidio /omi'θiðio; omi'siðio/ *n. m.* homicide.

homilía /omi'lia/ *n. f.* homily.

homosexual /omose'ksual/ *a.* homosexual, gay.

honda /'onda/ *n. f.* sling.

hondo /'ondo/ *a.* deep.

hondonada /ondo'naða/ *n. f.* ravine.

hondura /on'dura/ *n. f.* depth.

honestidad /onesti'ðað/ *n. f.* modesty, unpretentiousness.

honesto /o'nesto/ *a.* honest; pure; just.

hongo /'oŋgo/ *n. m.* fungus; mushroom.

honor /o'nor/ *n. m.* honor.

honorable /ono'raβle/ *a.* honorable.

honorario /ono'rario/ *a.* **1.** honorary. —*n.* **2.** *m.* honorarium, fee.

honorífico /ono'rifiko/ *a.* honorary.

honra /'onra/ *n. f.* honor. —**honrar,** *v.*

honradez /onra'ðeθ; onra'ðes/ *n. f.* honesty.

honrado /on'raðo/ *a.* honest, honorable.

hora /'ora/ *n. f.* hour; time (of day).

horadar /ora'ðar/ *v.* perforate.

hora punta /'ora 'punta/ rush hour.

horario /o'rario/ *n. m.* timetable, schedule.

horca /'orka/ *n. f.* gallows; pitchfork.

horda /'orða/ *n. f.* horde.

horizontal /oriθon'tal; orison'tal/ *a.* horizontal.

horizonte /ori'θonte; ori'sonte/ *n. m.* horizon.

hormiga /or'miga/ *n. f.* ant.

hormiguear /ormige'ar/ *v.* itch.

hormiguero /ormi'gero/ *n. m.* ant hill.

hornero /or'nero/ **-ra** *n.* baker.

hornillo /or'niʎo; or'niyo/ *n. m.* stove.

horno /'orno/ *n. m.* oven; kiln.

horóscopo /o'roskopo/ *n. m.* horoscope.

horrendo /o'rrendo/ *a.* dreadful, horrendous.

horrible /o'rriβle/ *a.* horrible, hideous, awful.

hórrido /'orriðo/ *a.* horrid.

horror /o'rror/ *n. m.* horror.

horrorizar /orrori'θar; orrori'sar/ *v.* horrify.

horroroso /orro'roso/ *a.* horrible, frightful.

hortelano /orte'lano/ *n. m.* horticulturist.

hospedaje /ospe'ðahe/ *n. m.* lodging.

hospedar /ospe'ðar/ *v.* give or take lodgings.

hospital /ospi'tal/ *n. m.* hospital.

hospitalario /ospita'lario/ *a.* hospitable.

hospitalidad /ospitali'ðað/ *n. f.* hospitality.

hospitalmente /ospital'mente/ *adv.* hospitably.

hostia /'ostia/ *n. f.* host; *Colloq.* hit, blow.

hostil /os'til/ *a.* hostile.

hostilidad /ostili'ðað/ *n. f.* hostility.

hotel /'otel/ *n. m.* hotel.

hoy /oi/ *adv.* today. **h. día, h. en día,** nowadays.

hoya /'oya/ *n. f.* dale, valley.

hoyo /'oyo/ *n. m.* pit, hole.

hoyuelo /o'yuelo/ *n. m.* dimple.

hoz /oθ; os/ *n. f.* sickle.

hucha /'utʃa/ *n. f.* chest, money box; savings.

hueco /'ueko/ *a.* **1.** hollow, empty. —*n.* **2.** *m.* hole, hollow.

huelga /'uelga/ *n. f.* strike.

huelguista /uel'hista/ *n. m.* & *f.* striker.

huella /'ueʎa; 'ueya/ *n. f.* track, trace; footprint.

huérfano /'uerfano/ **-na** *a.* & *n.* orphan.

huero /'uero/ *a.* empty.

huerta /'uerta/ *n. f.* (vegetable) garden.

huerto /'uerto/ *n. m.* orchard.

hueso /'ueso/ *n. m.* bone; fruit pit.

huésped /'uespeð/ *n. m. & f.* guest.

huesudo /ue'sudo/ *a.* bony.

huevo /'ueβo/ *n. m.* egg.

huída /'uiða/ *n. f.* flight, escape.

huir /uir/ *v.* flee.

hule /'ule/ *n. m.* oilcloth.

humanidad /umani'ðað/ *n. f* humanity, mankind; humaneness.

humanista /uma'nista/ *n. m. & f.* humanist.

humanitario /umani'tario/ *a.* humane.

humano /u'mano/ *a.* human; humane.

humareda /uma'reða/ *n. f.* dense cloud of smoke.

humear /ume'ar/ *v.* emit smoke or steam.

humedad /ume'ðað/ *n. f.* humidity, moisture, dampness.

humedecer /umeðe'θer; umeðe'ser/ *v.* moisten, dampen.

húmedo /'umeðo/ *a.* humid, moist, damp.

humildad /umil'dað/ *n. f.* humility, meekness.

humilde /u'milde/ *a.* humble, meek.

humillación /umiʎa'θion; umiya'sion/ *n. f.* humiliation.

humillar /umi'ʎar; umi'yar/ *v.* humiliate.

humo /'umo/ *n. m.* smoke; (*pl.*) airs, affectation.

humor /u'mor/ *n. m.* humor, mood.

humorista /umo'rista/ *n. m. & f.* humorist.

hundimiento /undi'miento/ *n. m.* collapse.

hundir /un'dir/ *v.* sink; collapse.

húngaro /'ungaro/ **-ra** *a. & n.* Hungarian.

Hungría /uŋ'gria/ *n. f.* Hungary.

huracán /ura'kan/ *n. m.* hurricane.

huraño /u'raɲo/ *a.* shy, bashful.

hurgar /ur'gar/ *v.* stir.

hurón /u'ron/ *n. m.* ferret.

hurtadillas /urta'ðiʎas; urta'ðiyas/ *n. f.pl.* **a h.,** on the sly.

hurtador /urta'ðor/ **-ra** *n.* thief.

hurtar /ur'tar/ *v.* steal, rob of; hide.

hurtarse /ur'tarse/ *v.* hide; withdraw.

husmear /usme'ar/ *v.* scent, smell.

huso /'uso/ *n. m.* spindle; bobbin.

huso horario /'uso o'rario/ time zone.

I

ibérico /i'βeriko/ *a.* Iberian.

iberoamericano /iβeroameri'kano/ **-na** *a. & n.* Latin American.

ida /'iða/ *n. f.* departure; trip out. **i. y vuelta,** round trip.

idea /i'ðea/ *n. f.* idea.

ideal /i'ðeal/ *a. & m.* ideal.

idealismo /iðea'lismo/ *n. m.* idealism.

idealista /iðea'lista/ *n. m. & f.* idealist.

idear /iðe'ar/ *v.* plan, conceive.

idéntico /i'ðentiko/ *a.* identical.

identidad /iðenti'ðað/ *n. f.* identity; identification.

identificar /iðentifi'kar/ *v.* identify.

idilio /i'ðilio/ *n. m.* idyll.

idioma /i'ðioma/ *n. m.* language.

idiota /i'ðiota/ *a. & n.* idiotic; idiot.

idiotismo /iðio'tismo/ *n. m.* idiom; idiocy.

idolatrar /iðola'trar/ *v.* idolize, adore.

ídolo /'iðolo/ *n. m.* idol.

idóneo /i'ðoneo/ *a.* suitable, fit, apt.

iglesia /i'glesia/ *n. f.* church.

ignición /igni'θion; igni'sion/ *n. f.* ignition.

ignominia /igno'minia/ *n. f.* ignominy, shame.

ignominioso /ignomi'nioso/ *a.* ignominious, shameful.

ignorancia /igno'ranθia; igno'ransia/ *n. f.* ignorance.

ignorante /igno'rante/ *a.* ignorant.

ignorar /igno'rar/ *v.* be ignorant of, not know.

ignoto /ig'noto/ *a.* unknown.

igual /i'gual/ *a.* equal; the same; (*pl.*) alike. *m.* equal.

igualar /igua'lar/ *v.* equal; equalize; match.

igualdad /igual'dað/ *n. f.* equality; sameness.

ijada /i'haða/ *n. f.* flank (of an animal).

ilegal /ile'gal/ *a.* illegal.

ilegítimo /ile'hitimo/ *a.* illegitimate.

ileso /i'leso/ *a.* unharmed.

ilícito /i'liθito; i'lisito/ *a.* illicit, unlawful.

iluminación /ilumina'θion; ilumina'sion/ *n. f.* illumination.

iluminar /ilumi'nar/ *v.* illuminate.

ilusión /ilu'sion/ *n. f.* illusion.

ilusión de óptica /ilu'sion de 'optika/ optical illusion.

ilusorio /ilu'sorio/ *a.* illusive.

ilustración /ilustra'θion; ilustra'sion/ *n. f.* illustration; learning.

ilustrador /ilustra'ðor/ **-ra** *n.* illustrator.

ilustrar /ilus'trar/ *v.* illustrate.

ilustre /i'lustre/ *a.* illustrious, honorable, distinguished.

imagen /i'mahen/ *n. f.* image.

imaginación /imahina'θion; imahina'sion/ *n. f.* imagination.

imaginar /imahi'nar/ *v.* imagine.

imaginario /imahi'nario/ *a.* imaginary.

imaginativo /imahina'tiβo/ *a.* imaginative.

imán /i'man/ *n. m.* magnet; imam.

imbécil /im'beθil: im'besil/ *a. & n.* imbecile; stupid, foolish; fool.

imbuir /im'buir/ *v.* imbue, instil.

imitación /imita'θion; imita'sion/ *n. f.* imitation.

imitador /imita'ðor/ **-ra** *n.* imitator.

imitar /imi'tar/ *v.* imitate.

impaciencia /impa'θienθia; impa'siensia/ *n. f.* impatience.

impaciente /impa'θiente; impa'siente/ *a.* impatient.

impar /im'par/ *a.* unequal, uneven, odd.

imparcial /impar'θial; impar'sial/ *a.* impartial.

impasible /impa'siβle/ *a.* impassive, unmoved.

impávido /im'paβiðo/ *adj.* fearless, intrepid.

impedimento /impeði'mento/ *n. m.* impediment, obstacle.

impedir /impe'ðir/ *v.* impede, hinder, stop, obstruct.

impeler /impe'ler/ *v.* impel; incite.

impensado /impen'saðo/ *a.* unexpected.

imperar /impe'rar/ *v.* reign; prevail.

imperativo /impera'tiβo/ *a.* imperative.

imperceptible /imperθep'tiβle; impersep'tiβle/ *a.* imperceptible.

imperdible /imper'ðiβle/ *n. m.* safety pin.

imperecedero /impereθe'ðero; imperese'ðero/ *a.* imperishable.

imperfecto /imper'fekto/ *a.* imperfect, faulty.

imperial /impe'rial/ *a.* imperial.

imperialismo /imperia'lismo/ *n. m.* imperialism.

impericia /impe'riθia; impe'risia/ *n. f.* inexperience.

imperio /im'perio/ *n. m.* empire.

imperioso /impe'rioso/ *a.* imperious, domineering.

impermeable /imperme'aβle/ *a.* waterproof. *m.* raincoat.

impersonal /imperso'nal/ *a.* impersonal.

impertinencia /impertinen'θia; impertinen'sia/ *n. f.* impertinence.

ímpetu /'impetu/ *n. m.* impulse; impetus.

impetuoso /impe'tuoso/ *a.* impetuous.

impiedad /impie'ðað/ *n. f.* impiety.

impío /im'pio/ *a.* impious.

implacable /impla'kaβle/ *a.* implacable, unrelenting.

implicar /impli'kar/ *v.* implicate, involve.

implorar /implo'rar/ *v.* implore.

imponente /impo'nente/ *a.* impressive.

imponer /impo'ner/ *v.* impose.

impopular /impopu'lar/ *a.* unpopular.

importación /importa'θion; importa'sion/ *n. f.* importation, importing.

importador /importa'ðor/ **-ra** *n.* importer.

importancia /impor'tanθia; impor'tansia/ *n. f.* importance.

importante /impor'tante/ *a.* important.

importar /impor'tar/ *v.* be important, matter; import.

importe /im'porte/ *n. m.* value; amount.

importunar /importu'nar/ *v.* beg, importune.

imposibilidad /imposiβili'ðað/ *n. f.* impossibility.

imposibilitado /imposiβili'taðo/ *a.* helpless.

imposible /impo'siβle/ *a.* impossible.

imposición /imposi'θion; imposi'sion/ *n. f.* imposition.

impostor /impos'tor/ **-ra** *n.* imposter, faker.

impotencia /impo'tenθia; impo'tensia/ *n. f.* impotence.

impotente /impo'tente/ *a.* impotent.

imprecar /impre'kar/ *v.* curse.

impreciso /impre'θiso; impre'siso/ *adj.* inexact.

impregnar /impreg'nar/ *v.* impregnate.

imprenta /im'prenta/ *n. f.* press; printing house.

imprescindible /impresθin'diβle; impressin'diβle/ *a.* essential.

impresión /impre'sion/ *n. f.* impression.

impresionable /impresio'naβle/ *a.* impressionable.

impresionar /impresio'nar/ *v.* impress.

impresor /impre'sor/ *n. m.* printer.

imprevisión /impreβi'sion/ *n. f.* oversight; thoughtlessness.

imprevisto /impre'βisto/ *a.* unexpected, unforeseen.

imprimir /impri'mir/ *v.* print; imprint.

improbable /impro'βaβle/ *a.* improbable.

ímprobo /im'proβo/ *a.* dishonest.

improductivo /improðuk'tiβo/ *a.* unproductive.

impropio /im'propio/ *n. m.* insult.

impropio /im'propio/ *a.* improper.

improvisación /improβisa'θion; improβisa'sion/ *n. f.* improvisation.

improvisar /improβi'sar/ *v.* improvise.

improviso /impro'βiso, impro'βisto/ *a.* unforeseen.

imprudencia /impru'ðenθia; impru'ðensia/ *n. f.* imprudence.

imprudente /impru'ðente/ *a.* imprudent, reckless.

impuesto /im'puesto/ *n. m.* tax.

impuesto sobre la renta /im'puesto soβre la 'rrenta/ income tax.

impulsar /impul'sar/ v. prompt, impel.

impulsivo /impul'siβo/ a. impulsive.

impulso /im'pulso/ n. m. impulse.

impureza /impu'reθa; impu'resa/ n. f. impurity.

impuro /im'puro/ a. impure.

imputación /imputa'θion; imputa'sion/ n. f. imputation.

imputar /impu'tar/ v. impute, attribute.

inaccesible /inakθe'siβle; inakse'siβle/ a. inaccessible.

inacción /inak'θion; inak'sion/ n. f. inaction; inactivity.

inaceptable /inaθep'taβle; inasep'taβle/ a. unacceptable.

inactivo /inak'tiβo/ a. inactive; sluggish.

inadecuado /inaðe'kuaðo/ a. inadequate.

inadvertencia /inaðβer'tenθia; inaðβer'tensia/ n. f. oversight.

inadvertido /inaðβer'tiðo/ a. inadvertent, careless; unnoticed.

inagotable /inago'taβle/ a. inexhaustible.

inalterado /inalte'raðo/ a. unchanged.

inanición /inani'θion; inani'sion/ n. f. starvation.

inanimado /inani'maðo/ adj. inanimate.

inapetencia /inape'tenθia; inape'tensia/ n. f lack of appetite.

inaplicable /inapli'kaβle/ a. inapplicable; unfit.

inaudito /inau'ðito/ a. unheard of.

inauguración /inaugura'θion; inaugura'sion/ n. f. inauguration.

inaugurar /inaugu'rar/ v. inaugurate, open.

incandescente /inkandes'θente; inkandes'sente/ a. incandescent.

incansable /inkan'saβle/ a. tireless.

incapacidad /inkapaθi'ðað; inkapasi'ðað/ n. f. incapacity.

incapacitar /inkapaθi'tar; inkapasi'tar/ v. incapacitate.

incapaz /inka'paθ; inka'pas/ a. incapable.

incauto /in'kauto/ a. unwary.

incendiar /inθen'diar; insen'diar/ v. set on fire.

incendio /in'θendio; in'sendio/ n. m. fire; conflagration.

incertidumbre /inθerti'ðumbre; inserti'ðumbre/ n. f. uncertainty, suspense.

incesante /inθe'sante; inse'sante/ a. continual, incessant.

incidente /inθi'ðente; insi'ðente/ n. m. incident, event.

incienso /in'θienso; in'sienso/ n. m. incense.

incierto /in'θierto; in'sierto/ a. uncertain, doubtful.

incinerar /inθine'rar; insine'rar/ v. incinerate; cremate.

incisión /inθi'sion; insi'sion/ n. f incision, cut.

incitamiento /inθita'miento; insita'miento/ n. m. incitement, motivation.

incitar /inθi'tar; insi'tar/ v. incite, instigate.

incivil /inθi'βil; insi'βil/ a. impolite, rude.

inclemencia /inkle'menθia; inkle'mensia/ n. f. inclemency.

inclemente /inkle'mente/ a. inclement, merciless.

inclinación /inklina'θion; inklina'sion/ n. f. inclination, bent; slope.

inclinar /inkli'nar/ v. incline; influence.

inclinarse /inkli'narse/ v. slope; lean, bend over; bow.

incluir /in'kluir/ v. include; enclose.

inclusivo /inklu'siβo/ a. inclusive.

incluso /in'kluso/ prep. including.

incógnito /in'kognito/ a. unknown.

incoherente /inkoe'rente/ a. incoherent.

incombustible /inkombus'tiβle/ a. fireproof.

incomible /inko'miβle/ a. inedible.

incomodar /inkomo'ðar/ v. disturb, bother, inconvenience.

incomodidad /inkomoði'ðað/ n. f. inconvenience.

incómodo /in'komoðo/ n. m. uncomfortable; cumbersome; inconvenient.

incomparable /inkompa'raβle/ a. incomparable.

incompatible /inkompa'tiβle/ a. incompatible.

incompetencia /inkompe'tenθia; inkompe'tensia/ n. f. incompetence.

incompetente /inkompe'tente/ a. incompetent.

incompleto /inkom'pleto/ a. incomplete.

incondicional /inkondiθio'nal; inkondisio'nal/ a. unconditional.

inconexo /inkone'kso/ a. incoherent; unconnected.

incongruente /inkoŋgru'ente/ a. incongruous.

inconsciencia /inkon'sθienθia; inkonssiensia/ n. f. unconsciousness.

inconsciente /inkon'sθiente; inkons'siente/ a. unconscious.

inconsecuencia /inkonse'kuenθia; inkonse'kuensia/ n. f. inconsistency.

inconsecuente /inkonse'kuente/ a. inconsistent.

inconsiderado /inkonsiðe'raðo/ a. inconsiderate.

inconstancia /inkons'tanθia; inkons'tansia/ n. f. changeableness.

inconstante /inkons'tante/ a. changeable.

inconveniencia /inkombe'nienθia; inkombe'niensia/ n. f. inconvenience; unsuitability.

inconveniente /inkombe'niente/ a. unsuitable. m. disadvantage; objection.

incorporar /inkorpo'rar/ v. incorporate, embody.

incorporarse /inkorpo'rarse/ v. sit up.

incorrecto /inko'rrekto/ a. incorrect, wrong.

incredulidad /inkreðuli'ðað/ n. f. incredulity.

incrédulo /in'kreðulo/ a. incredulous.

increíble /inkre'iβle/ a. incredible.

incremento /inkre'mento/ n. m. increase.

incubadora /inkuβa'ðora/ n. f. incubator.

incubar /inku'βar/ v. hatch.

inculto /in'kulto/ a. uncultivated.

incumplimiento de contrato /inkumpli'mento de kon'trato/ n. m. breach of contract.

incurable /inku'raβle/ a. incurable.

incurrir /inku'rrir/ v. incur.

indagación /indaga'θion/ n. f. investigation, inquiry.

indagador /indaga'ðor/ -ra n. investigator.

indagar /inda'gar/ v. investigate, inquire into.

indebido /inde'βiðo/ a. undue.

indecencia /inde'θenθia/ n. f. indecency.

indecente /inde'θente/ a. indecent.

indeciso /inde'θiso/ a. undecided.

indefenso /inde'fenso/ a. defenseless.

indefinido /indefi'niðo/ a. indefinite; undefined.

indeleble /inde'leβle/ a. indelible.

indemnización de despido /indemniθa'θion de des'piðo/ n. f. severance pay.

indemnizar /indemni'θar; indemni'sar/ v. indemnify.

independencia /indepen'denθia; independ'ensia/ n. f. independence.

independiente /indepen'diente/ a. independent.

indesmallable /indesma'ʎaβle; indesma'yaβle/ a. runproof.

India /'india/ n. f. India.

indicación /indika'θion; indika'sion/ n. f. indication.

indicar /indi'kar/ v. indicate, point out.

indicativo /indika'tiβo/ a. & m. indicative.

índice /'indiθe; 'indise/ n. m. index; forefinger.

índice de materias /'indiθe de ma'terias; 'indise de ma'terias/ table of contents.

indicio /in'diθio; in'disio/ n. m. hint, clue.

indiferencia /indife'renθia; indife'rensia/ n. f. indifference.

indiferente /indife'rente/ a. indifferent.

indígena /in'dihena/ a. & n. native.

indigente /indi'hente/ a. indigent, poor.

indignación /indigna'θion; indigna'sion/ n. f. indignation.

indignado /indig'naðo/ a. indignant, incensed.

indignar /indig'nar/ v. incense.

indigno /in'digno/ a. unworthy.

indio /'indio/ **-dia** a. & n. Indian.

indirecto /indi'rekto/ a. indirect.

indiscreción /indiskre'θion; indiskre'sion/ n. f. indiscretion.

indiscreto /indis'kreto/ a. indiscreet.

indiscutible /indisku'tiβle/ a. unquestionable.

indispensable /indispen'saβle/ a. indispensable.

indisposición /indisposi'θion; indisposi'sion/ n. f. indisposition, ailment; reluctance.

indistinto /indis'tinto/ a. indistinct, unclear.

individual /indiβi'ðual/ a. individual.

individualidad /indiβiðuali'ðað/ n. f. individuality.

individuo /indi'βiðuo/ a. & m. individual.

índole /'indole/ n. f. nature, character, disposition.

indolencia /indo'lenθia; indo'lensia/ n. f. indolence.

indolente /indo'lente/ a. indolent.

indómito /in'domito/ a. untamed, wild; unruly.

inducir /indu'θir; indu'sir/ v. induce, persuade.

indudable /indu'ðaβle/ a. certain, indubitable.

indulgencia /indul'henθia; indul'hensia/ n. f. indulgence.

indulgente /indul'hente/ a. indulgent.

indultar /indul'tar/ v. free; pardon.

industria /in'dustria/ n. f. industry.

industrial /indus'trial/ a. industrial.

industrioso /indus'trioso/ a. industrious.

inédito /i'neðito/ a. unpublished.

ineficaz /inefi'kaθ; inefi'kas/ a. inefficient.

inepto /i'nepto/ a. incompetent.

inequívoco /ine'kiβoko/ a. unmistakable.

inercia /i'nerθia; i'nersia/ n. f. inertia.

inerte /i'nerte/ a. inert.

inesperado /inespe'raðo/ a. unexpected.

inestable /ines'taβle/ a. unstable.

inevitable /ineβi'taβle/ a. inevitable.

inexacto /ine'ksakto/ a. inexact.

inexperto /ineks'perto/ a. unskilled.

inexplicable /inekspli'kaβle/ a. inexplicable, unexplainable.

infalible /infa'liβle/ a. infallible.

infame /in'fame/ a. infamous, bad.

infamia /in'famia/ n. f. infamy.

infancia /in'fanθia; in'fansia/ *n. f.* infancy; childhood.

infante /in'fante/ **-ta** *n.* infant.

infantería /infante'ria/ *n. f.* infantry.

infantil /infan'til/ *a.* infantile, childish.

infarto (de miocardio) /in'farto de mio-'karðio/ *n. m.* heart attack.

infatigable /infati'gaβle/ *a.* untiring.

infausto /in'fausto/ *a.* unlucky.

infección /infek'θion; infek'sion/ *n. f.* infection.

infeccioso /infek'θioso; infek'sioso/ *a.* infectious.

infectar /infek'tar/ *v.* infect.

infeliz /infe'liθ; infe'lis/ *a.* unhappy, miserable.

inferior /infe'rior/ *a.* inferior; lower.

inferir /infe'rir/ *v.* infer; inflict.

infernal /infer'nal/ *a.* infernal.

infestar /infes'tar/ *v.* infest.

infiel /in'fiel/ *a.* unfaithful.

infierno /in'fierno/ *n. m.* hell.

infiltrar /infil'trar/ *v.* infiltrate.

infinidad /infini'ðað/ *n. f.* infinity.

infinito /infi'nito/ *a.* infinite.

inflación /infla'θion; infla'sion/ *n. f.* inflation.

inflamable /infla'maβle/ *a.* flammable.

inflamación /inflama'θion; inflama'sion/ *n. f.* inflammation.

inflamar /infla'mar/ *v.* inflame, set on fire.

inflar /in'flar/ *v.* inflate, pump up, puff up.

inflexible /infle'ksiβle/ *a.* inflexible, rigid.

inflexión /infle'ksion/ *n. f.* inflection.

infligir /infli'hir/ *v.* inflict.

influencia /influ'enθia; influ'ensia/ *n. f.* influence.

influenza /in'fluenθa; in'fluensa/ *n. f.* influenza, flu.

influir /in'fluir/ *v.* influence, sway.

influyente /influ'yente/ *a.* influential.

información /informa'θion; informa'sion/ *n. f.* information.

informal /infor'mal/ *a.* informal.

informar /infor'mar/ *v.* inform; report.

informática /infor'matika/ *n. f.* computer science; information technology.

informe /in'forme/ *n. m.* report; (*pl.*) information, data.

infortunio /infor'tunio/ *n. m.* misfortune.

infracción /infrak'θion; infrak'sion/ *n. f.* violation.

infracetructura /infraθetruk'tura; infrastruk'tura/ *n. f.* infrastructure.

infrascrito /infras'krito/ **-ta** *n.* signer, undersigned.

infringir /infrin'hir/ *v.* infringe, violate.

infructuoso /infruk'tuoso/ *a.* fruitless.

infundir /infun'dir/ *v.* instil, inspire with.

ingeniería /inhenie'ria/ *n. f.* engineering.

ingeniero /inhe'niero/ **-ra** *n.* engineer.

ingenio /in'henio/ *n. m.* wit; talent.

ingeniosidad /inheniosi'ðað/ *n. f.* ingenuity.

ingenioso /inhe'nioso/ *a.* witty; ingenious.

ingenuidad /inhenui'ðað/ *n. f.* candor; naïveté.

ingenuo /in'henuo/ *a.* ingenuous, naïve, candid.

Inglaterra /ingla'terra/ *n. f.* England.

ingle /'ingle/ *n. f.* groin.

inglés /iŋ'gles/ **-esa** *a. & n.* English; Englishman; Englishwoman.

ingratitud /ingrati'tuð/ *n. f.* ingratitude.

ingrato /iŋ'grato/ *a.* ungrateful.

ingravidez /iŋgraβi'ðeθ; iŋgraβi'ðes/ *n. f.* weightlessness.

ingrávido /iŋ'graβiðo/ *a.* weightless.

ingrediente /iŋgre'ðiente/ *n. m.* ingredient.

ingresar en /iŋgre'sar en/ *v.* enter; join.

ingreso /iŋ'greso/ *n. m.* entrance; (*pl.*) earnings, income.

inhábil /in'aβil/ *a.* unskilled; incapable.

inhabilitar /inaβili'tar/ *v.* disqualify.

inherente /ine'rente/ *a.* inherent.

inhibir /ini'βir/ *v.* inhibit.

inhumano /inu'mano/ *a.* cruel, inhuman.

iniciador /iniθia'ðor; inisia'ðor/ **-ra** *n.* initiator.

inicial /ini'θial; ini'sial/ *a.* initial.

iniciar /ini'θiar; ini'siar/ *v.* initiate, begin.

iniciativa /iniθia'tiβa; inisia'tiβa/ *n. f.* initiative.

inicuo /ini'kuo/ *a.* wicked.

iniquidad /iniki'ðað/ *n. f.* iniquity; sin.

injuria /in'huria/ *n. f.* insult. —**injuriar,** *v.*

injusticia /inhus'tiθia; inhus'tisia/ *n. f.* injustice.

ir.justo /in'husto/ *a.* unjust, unfair.

inmaculado /imaku'laðo/ *a.* immaculate; pure.

inmediato /ime'ðiato/ *a.* immediate.

inmensidad /imensi'ðað/ *n. f.* immensity.

inmenso /i'menso/ *a.* immense.

inmersión /imer'sion/ *n. f.* immersion.

inmigración /imigra'θion; imigra'sion/ *n. f.* immigration.

inmigrante /imi'grante/ *a. & n.* immigrant.

inmigrar /imi'grar/ *v.* immigrate.

inminente /imi'nente/ *a.* imminent.

inmoderado /imoðe'raðo/ *a.* immoderate.

inmodesto /imo'ðesto/ *a.* immodest.

inmoral /imo'ral/ *a.* immoral.

inmoralidad /imorali'ðað/ *n. f.* immorality.

inmortal /imor'tal/ *a.* immortal.

inmortalidad /imortali'ðað/ *n. f.* immortality.

inmóvil /i'moβil/ *a.* immobile, motionless.

inmundicia /imun'diθia; imun'disia/ *n. f.* dirt, filth.

inmune /i'mune/ *a.* immune; exempt.

inmunidad /imuni'ðað/ *n. f.* immunity.

innato /in'nato/ *a.* innate, inborn.

innecesario /inneθe'sario; innese'sario/ *a.* unnecessary, needless.

innegable /inne'gaβle/ *a.* undeniable.

innoble /in'noβle/ *a.* ignoble.

innocuo /inno'kuo/ *a.* innocuous.

innovación /innoβa'θion; innoβa'sion/ *n. f.* innovation.

innumerable /innume'raβle/ *a.* innumerable, countless.

inocencia /ino'θenθia; ino'sensia/ *n. f.* innocence.

inocentada /inoθen'taða; inosen'taða/ *n. f.* practical joke.

inocente /ino'θente; ino'sente/ *a.* innocent.

inocular /inoku'lar/ *v.* inoculate.

inodoro /ino'ðoro/ *n. m.* toilet.

inofensivo /inofen'siβo/ *a.* inoffensive, harmless.

inolvidable /inolβi'ðaβle/ *a.* unforgettable.

inoportuno /inopor'tuno/ *a.* inopportune.

inoxidable /inoksi'ðaβle/ *a.* stainless.

inquietante /inkie'tante/ *a.* disturbing, worrisome, worrying, upsetting.

inquietar /inkie'tar/ *v.* disturb, worry, trouble.

inquieto /in'kieto/ *a.* anxious, uneasy, worried; restless.

inquietud /inkie'tuð/ *n. f.* concern, anxiety, worry; restlessness.

inquilino /inki'lino/ **-na** *n.* occupant, tenant.

inquirir /inki'rir/ *v.* inquire into, investigate.

inquisición /inkisi'θion; inkisi'sion/ *n. f.* inquisition, investigation.

insaciable /insa'θiaβle; insa'siaβle/ *a.* insatiable.

insalubre /insa'luβre/ *a.* unhealthy.

insano /in'sano/ *a.* insane.

inscribir /inskri'βir/ *v.* inscribe; record.

inscribirse /inskri'βirse/ *v.* register, enroll.

inscripción /inskrip'θion; inskrip'sion/ *n. f.* inscription; registration.

insecticida /insekti'θiða; insekti'siða/ *n. m.* insecticide.

insecto /in'sekto/ *n. m.* insect.

inseguro /inse'guro/ *a.* unsure, uncertain; insecure, unsafe.

insensato /insen'sato/ *a.* stupid, senseless.

insensible /insen'siβle/ *a.* unfeeling, heartless.

inseparable /insepa'raβle/ *a.* inseparable.

inserción /inser'θion; inser'sion/ *n. f.* insertion.

insertar /inser'tar/ *v.* insert.

inservible /inser'βiβle/ *a.* useless.

insidioso /insi'ðioso/ *a.* insidious, crafty.

insigne /in'signe/ *a.* famous, noted.

insignia /in'signia/ *n. f.* insignia, badge.

insignificante /insignifi'kante/ *a.* insignificant, negligible.

insincero /insin'θero: insin'sero/ *a.* insincere.

insinuación /insinua'θion; insinua'sion/ *n. f.* insinuation; hint.

insinuar /insi'nuar/ *v.* insinuate, suggest, hint.

insipidez /insipi'ðeθ; insipi'ðes/ *n. f.* insipidity.

insípido /in'sipiðo/ *a.* insipid.

insistencia /insis'tenθia; insis'tensia/ *n. f.* insistence.

insistente /insis'tente/ *a.* insistent.

insistir /insis'tir/ *v.* insist.

insolación /insola'θion; insola'sion/ *n. f.* sunstroke.

insolencia /inso'lenθia; inso'lensia/ *n. f.* insolence.

insolente /inso'lente/ *a.* insolent.

insólito /in'solito/ *a.* unusual.

insolvente /insol'βente/ *a.* insolvent.

insomnio /in'somnio/ *n. m.* insomnia.

insonorizado /insonori'θaðo; insonori'saðo/ *a.* soundproof.

insonorizar /insonori'θar; insonori'sar/ *v.* soundproof.

insoportable /insopor'taβle/ *a.* unbearable.

inspección /inspek'θion; inspek'sion/ *n. f.* inspection.

inspeccionar /inspekθio'nar; inspeksio'nar/ *v.* inspect, examine.

inspector /inspek'tor/ **-ra** *n.* inspector.

inspiración /inspira'θion; inspira'sion/ *n. f.* inspiration.

inspirar /inspi'rar/ *v.* inspire.

instalación /instala'θion; instala'sion/ *n. f.* installation, fixture.

instalar /insta'lar/ *v.* install, set up.

instantánea /instan'tanea/ *n. f.* snapshot.

instantáneo /instan'taneo/ *a.* instantaneous.

instante /ins'tante/ *a. & m.* instant. **al i.,** at once.

instar /ins'tar/ *v.* coax, urge.

instigar /insti'gar/ *v.* instigate, urge.

instintivo /instin'tiβo/ *a.* instinctive.

instinto /ins'tinto/ *n. m.* instinct. **por i.,** by instinct, instinctively.

institución /institu'θion; institu'sion/ *n. f.* institution.

instituto /insti'tuto/ *n. m.* institute. **—instituir,** *v.*

institutriz /institu'triθ; institu'tris/ *n. f.* governess.

instrucción /instruk'θion; instruk'sion/ *n. f.* instruction; education.

instructivo /instruk'tiβo/ *a.* instructive.

instructor /instruk'tor/ **-ra** *n.* instructor.

instruir /ins'truir/ v. instruct, teach.

instrumento /instru'mento/ n. m. instrument.

insuficiente /insufi'θiente; insufi'siente/ a. insufficient.

insufrible /insu'friβle/ a. intolerable.

insular /insu'lar/ a. island, insular.

insulto /in'sulto/ n. m. insult. —**insultar**, v.

insuperable /insupe'raβle/ a. insuperable.

insurgente /insur'hente/ n. & a. insurgent, rebel.

insurrección /insurrek'θion: insurrek'sion/ n. f. insurrection, revolt.

insurrecto /insu'rrekto/ **-ta** a. & n. insurgent.

intacto /in'takto/ a. intact.

integral /inte'gral/ a. integral.

integridad /integri'ðað/ n. f. integrity; entirety.

íntegro /'integro/ a. entire; upright.

intelecto /inte'lekto/ n. m. intellect.

intelectual /intelek'tual/ a. & n. intellectual.

inteligencia /inteli'henθia: inteli'hensia/ n. f. intelligence.

inteligente /inteli'hente/ a. intelligent.

inteligible /inteli'hiβle/ a. intelligible.

intemperie /intem'perie/ n. f. bad weather.

intención /inten'θion; inten'sion/ n. f. intention.

intendente /inten'dente/ n. m manager.

intensidad /intensi'ðað/ n. f. intensity.

intensificar /intensifi'kar/ v. intensify.

intensivo /inten'siβo/ a. intensive.

intenso /in'tenso/ a. intense.

intentar /inten'tar/ v. attempt, try.

intento /in'tento/ n. m. intent; attempt.

intercambiable /interkam'biaβle/ a. interchangeable.

intercambiar /interkam'βiar/ v. exchange, interchange.

interceptar /interθep'tar; intersep'tar/ v. intercept.

intercesión /interθe'sion: interse'sion/ n. f. intercession.

interés /inte'res/ n. m. interest; concern; appeal.

interesante /intere'sante/ a. interesting.

interesar /intere'sar/ v. interest, appeal to.

interfaz /inter'faθ; inter'fas/ n. f. interface.

interferencia /interfe'renθia; interfe'rensia/ n. f. interference.

interino /inte'rino/ a. temporary.

interior /inte'rior/ a. **1.** interior, inner. —n. **2.** m. interior.

interjección /interhek'θion; interhek'sion/ n. f. interjection.

intermedio /inter'meðio/ a. **1.** intermediate. —n. **2.** m. intermediary; intermission.

interminable /intermi'naβle/ a. interminable, endless.

intermisión /intermi'sion/ n. f. intermission.

intermitente /intermi'tente/ a. intermittent.

internacional /internaθio'nal; internasio'nal/ a. international.

internarse en /inter'narse en/ v. enter into, go into.

Internet, el /inter'net/ n. m. the Internet.

interno /in'terno/ a. internal.

interpelar /interpe'lar/ v. ask questions; implore.

interponer /interpo'ner/ v. interpose.

interpretación /interpreta'θion; interpreta'sion/ n. f. interpretation.

interpretar /interpre'tar/ v. interpret; construe.

intérprete /in'terprete/ n. m. & f. interpreter; performer.

interrogación /interroga'θion: interroga'sion/ n. f. interrogation.

interrogar /interro'gar/ v. question, interrogate.

interrogativo /interroga'tiβo/ a. interrogative.

interrumpir /interrum'pir/ v. interrupt.

interrupción /interrup'θion: interrup'sion/ n. f. interruption.

intersección /intersek'θion; intersek'sion/ n. f. intersection.

intervalo /inter'βalo/ n. m. interval.

intervención /interβen'θion; interβen'sion/ n. f. intervention.

intervenir /interβe'nir/ v. intervene, interfere.

intestino /intes'tino/ n. m. intestine.

intimación /intima'θion; intima'sion/ n. f. intimation, hint.

intimar /inti'mar/ v. suggest, hint.

intimidad /intimi'ðað/ n. f. intimacy.

intimidar /intimi'ðar/ v. intimidate.

íntimo /'intimo/ **-ma** a. & n. intimate.

intolerable /intole'raβle/ a. intolerable.

intolerancia /intole'ranθia; intole'ransia/ n. f. intolerance, bigotry.

intolerante /intole'rante/ a. intolerant.

intoxicación alimenticia /intoksika'θion alimen'tiθia; intoksika'sion alimen'tisia/ n. f. food poisoning.

intranquilo /intran'kilo/ a. uneasy.

intravenoso /intraβe'noso/ a. intravenous.

intrepidez /intrepi'ðeθ; intrepi'ðes/ n. f. daring.

intrépido /in'trepiðo/ a. intrepid.

intriga /in'triga/ n. f. intrigue, plot, scheme. —**intrigar**, v.

intrincado /intrin'kaðo/ a. intricate, involved; impenetrable.

introducción /introduk'θion; introduk'sion/ *n. f.* introduction.

introducir /introðu'θir; introðu'sir/ *v.* introduce.

intruso /in'truso/ **-sa** *n.* intruder.

intuición /intui'θion; intui'sion/ *n. f.* intuition.

inundación /inunda'θion; inunda'sion/ *n f.* flood. **—inundar,** *v.*

inútil /i'nutil/ *a.* useless.

invadir /imba'ðir/ *v.* invade.

inválido /im'baliðo/ **-da** *a.* & *n.* invalid.

invariable /imba'riaβle/ *a.* constant.

invasión /imba'sion/ *n. f.* invasion.

invasor /imba'sor/ **-ra** *n.* invader.

invencible /imben'θiβle; imben'siβle/ *a.* invincible.

invención /imben'θion; imben'sion/ *n. f.* invention.

inventar /imben'tar/ *v.* invent; devise.

inventario /imben'tario/ *n. m.* inventory.

inventivo /imben'tiβo/ *a.* inventive.

invento /im'bento/ *n. m.* invention.

inventor /imben'tor/ **-ra** *n.* inventor.

invernáculo /imber'nakulo/ *n. m.* greenhouse.

invernal /imber'nal/ *a.* wintry.

inverosímil /imbero'simil/ *a.* improbable, unlikely.

inversión /imber'sion/ *n. f.* inversion; *Com.* investment.

inverso /im'berso/ *a.* inverse, reverse.

inversor /imber'sor/ **-ra** *n.* investor.

invertir /imber'tir/ *v.* invert; reverse; *Com.* invest.

investigación /imbestiga'θion; imbestiga'sion/ *n. f.* investigation.

investigador /imbestiga'ðor/ **-ra** *n.* investigator; researcher.

investigar /imbesti'gar/ *v.* investigate.

invierno /im'bierno/ *n. m.* winter.

invisible /imbi'siβle/ *a.* invisible.

invitación /imbita'θion; imbita'sion/ *n. f.* invitation.

invitar /imbi'tar/ *v.* invite.

invocar /imbo'kar/ *v.* invoke.

involuntario /imbolun'tario/ *a.* involuntary.

inyección /inyek'θion; inyek'sion/ *n. f.* injection.

inyectar /inyek'tar/ *v.* inject.

ir /ir/ *v.* go. **irse,** go away, leave.

ira /'ira/ *n. f.* anger, ire.

iracundo /ira'kundo/ *a.* wrathful, irate.

iris /'iris/ *n. m.* iris. **arco i.,** rainbow.

Irlanda /ir'landa/ *n. f.* Ireland.

irlandés /irlan'des/ **-esa** *a.* & *n.* Irish; Irishman, Irishwoman.

ironía /iro'nia/ *n. f.* irony.

irónico /i'roniko/ *a.* ironical.

irracional /irraθio'nal; irrasio'nal/ *a.* irrational; insane.

irradiación /irraðia'θion; irraðia'sion/ *n. f.* irradiation.

irradiar /irra'ðiar/ *v.* radiate.

irrazonable /irraθo'naβle; irraso'naβle/ *a.* unreasonable.

irregular /irregu'lar/ *a.* irregular.

irreligioso /irreli'hioso/ *a.* irreligious.

irremediable /irreme'ðiaβle/ *a.* irremediable, hopeless.

irresistible /irresis'tiβle/ *a.* irresistible.

irresoluto /irreso'luto/ *a.* irresolute, wavering.

irrespetuoso /irrespe'tuoso/ *a.* disrespectful.

irreverencia /irreβe'renθia; irreβe'rensia/ *n. f.* irreverence.

irreverente /irreβe'rente/ *adj.* irreverent.

irrigación /irriga'θion; irriga'sion/ *n. f.* irrigation.

irrigar /irri'gar/ *v.* irrigate.

irritación /irrita'θion; irrita'sion/ *n. f.* irritation.

irritar /irri'tar/ *v.* irritate.

irrupción /irrup'θion; irrup'sion/ *n. f.* raid, attack.

isla /'isla/ *n. f.* island.

isleño /is'leɲo/ **-ña** *n.* islander.

israelita /israe'lita/ *n.* & *a.* Israelite.

Italia /i'talia/ *n. f.* Italy.

italiano /ita'liano/ **-na** *a.* & *n.* Italian.

itinerario /itine'rario/ *n. m.* itinerary; timetable.

IVA, *abbrev.* **(impuesto sobre el valor añadido)** VAT (value-added tax).

izar /i'θar; i'sar/ *v.* hoist.

izquierda /iθ'kierða; is'kierða/ *n. f.* left (hand, side).

izquierdista /iθ'kierðista; is'kierðista/ *n.* & *a.* leftist.

izquierdo /iθ'kierðo; is'kierðo/ *a.* left.

jabalí /haβa'li/ *n. m.* wild boar.

jabón /ha'βon/ *n. m.* soap. **j. en polvo,** soap powder.

jabonar /haβo'nar/ *v.* soap.

jaca /'haka/ *n. f.* nag.

jacinto /ha'θinto; ha'sinto/ *n. m.* hyacinth.

jactancia /hak'tanθia; hak'tansia/ *n. f.* boast. **—jactarse,** *v.*

jactancioso /haktan'θioso; haktan'sioso/ *a.* boastful.

jadear /haðe'ar/ *v.* pant, puff.

jaez /ha'eθ; ha'es/ *n. m.* harness; kind.

jalar /ha'lar/ *v.* haul, pull.

jalea /ha'lea/ *n. f.* jelly.

jaleo /ha'leo/ *n. m.* row, uproar; hassle.

jamás /ha'mas/ *adv.* never, ever.

jamón /ha'mon/ *n. m.* ham.

Japón /ha'pon/ *n. m.* Japan.

japonés /hapo'nes/ **-esa** *a. & n.* Japanese.

jaqueca /ha'keka/ *n. f.* headache.

jarabe /ha'raβe/ *n. m.* syrup.

jaranear /harane'ar/ *v.* jest; carouse.

jardín /har'ðin/ *n. m.* garden.

jardín de infancia /har'ðin de in'fanθia; har'ðin de in'fansia/ nursery school.

jardinero /harði'nero/ **-ra** *n.* gardener.

jarra /'harra/ *n. f.* jar; pitcher.

jarro /'harro/ *n. m.* jug, pitcher.

jaspe /'haspe/ *n. m.* jasper.

jaula /'haula/ *n. f.* cage; coop.

jauría /hau'ria/ *n. f.* pack of hounds.

jazmín /haθ'min; has'min/ *n. m.* jasmine.

jefatura /hefa'tura/ *n. f.* headquarters.

jefe /'hefe/ **-fa** *n.* chief, boss.

jefe de comedor /'hefe de kome'ðor/ headwaiter.

jefe de sala /'hefe de 'sala/ maître d'.

jefe de taller /'hefe de ta'ʎer; 'hefe de ta'yer/ foreman.

Jehová /heo'βa/ *n. m.* Jehovah.

jengibre /hen'hiβre/ *n. m.* ginger.

jerez /he'reθ; he'res/ *n. m.* sherry.

jerga /'herga/ *n. f.* slang.

jergón /her'gon/ *n. m.* straw mattress.

jerigonza /heri'gonθa; heri'gonsa/ *n. f.* jargon.

jeringa /he'ringa/ *n. f.* syringe.

jeringar /herin'gar/ *v.* inject; annoy.

jeroglífico /hero'glifiko/ *n. m.* hieroglyph.

jersey /her'sei/ *n. m.* pullover; **j. de cuello alto,** turtleneck sweater.

Jerusalén /herusa'len/ *n. m.* Jerusalem.

jesuita /he'suita/ *n. m.* Jesuit.

Jesús /he'sus/ *n. m.* Jesus.

jeta /'heta/ *n. f.* snout.

jícara /'hikara/ *n. f.* cup.

jinete /hi'nete/ **-ta** *n.* horseman.

jingoísmo /hingo'ismo/ *n. m.* jingoism.

jingoísta /hingo'ista/ *n. & a.* jingoist.

jira /'hira/ *n. f.* picnic; outing.

jirafa /hi'rafa/ *n. f.* giraffe.

jiu-jitsu /hiu'hitsu/ *n. m.* jujitsu.

jocundo /ho'kundo/ *a.* jovial.

jornada /hor'naða/ *n. f.* journey; day's work.

jornal /hor'nal/ *n. m.* day's wage.

jornalero /horna'lero/ *n. m.* day laborer, workman.

joroba /ho'roβa/ *n. f.* hump.

jorobado /horo'βaðo/ *a.* humpbacked.

joven /'hoβen/ *a.* **1.** young. **—***n.* **2.** *m. & f.* young person.

jovial /ho'βial/ *a.* jovial, jolly.

jovialidad /hoβiali'ðað/ *n. f.* joviality.

joya /'hoia/ *n. f.* jewel, gem.

joyas de fantasía /'hoias de fanta'sia/ *n. f.pl.* costume jewelry.

joyelero /hoie'lero/ *n. m.* jewel box.

joyería /hoie'ria/ *n. f.* jewelry; jewelry store.

joyero /ho'iero/ *n. m.* jeweler; jewel case.

juanete /hua'nete/ *n. m.* bunion.

jubilación /huβila'θion; huβila'sion/ *n. f.* retirement; pension.

jubilar /huβi'lar/ *v.* retire, pension.

jubileo /huβi'leo/ *n. m.* jubilee, public festivity.

júbilo /'huβilo/ *n. m.* glee, rejoicing.

jubiloso /huβi'loso/ *a.* joyful, gay.

judaico /hu'ðaiko/ *a.* Jewish.

judaísmo /huða'ismo/ *n. m.* Judaism.

judía /hu'ðia/ *n. f.* bean, string bean.

judicial /huði'θial; huði'sial/ *a.* judicial.

judío /hu'ðio/ **-día** *a. & n.* Jewish; Jew.

juego /'huego/ *n. m.* game; play; gambling; set. **j. de damas,** checkers. **j. limpio,** fair play.

Juegos Olímpicos /huegos o'limpikos/ *n. m.pl.* Olympic Games.

juerga /'huerga/ *n. f.* spree.

jueves /'hueβes/ *n. m.* Thursday.

juez /hueθ; hues/ *n. m.* judge.

jugador /huga'ðor/ **-ra** *n.* player.

jugar /hu'gar/ *v.* play; gamble.

juglar /hug'lar/ *n. m.* minstrel.

jugo /'hugo/ *n. m.* juice. **j. de naranja,** orange juice.

jugoso /hu'goso/ *a.* juicy.

juguete /hu'gete/ *n. m.* toy, plaything.

juguetear /hugete'ar/ *v.* trifle.

juguetón /huge'ton/ *a.* playful.

juicio /'huiθio; 'huisio/ *n m.* sense, wisdom, judgment; sanity; trial.

juicioso /hui'θioso; hui'sioso/ *a.* wise, judicious.

julio /'hulio/ *n. m.* July.

jumento /hu'mento/ *n. m.* donkey.

junco /'hunko/ *n. m.* reed, rush.

jungla /'huŋgla/ *n. f.* jungle.

junio /'hunio/ *n. m.* June.

junípero /hu'nipero/ *n. m.* juniper.

junquillo /hun'kiʎo; hun'kiyo/ *n. m.* jonquil.

junta /'hunta/ *n. f.* board, council; joint, coupling.

juntamente /hunta'mente/ *adv.* jointly.

juntar /hun'tar/ *v.* join; connect; assemble.

junto /'hunto/ *a.* together. **j. a,** next to.

juntura /hun'tura/ *n. f.* joint, juncture.

jurado /hu'raðo/ *n. m.* jury.

juramento /hura'mento/ *n. m.* oath.

jurar /hu'rar/ *v.* swear.

jurisconsulto /huriskon'sulto/ *n. m.* jurist.

jurisdicción /hurisðik'θion; hurisðik'sion/ *n. f.* jurisdiction; territory.

jurisprudencia /hurispru'ðenθia; hurispru-'ðensia/ *n. f.* jurisprudence.

justa /'husta/ *n. f.* joust. —**justar,** *v.*

justicia /hus'tiθia; hus'tisia/ *n. f.* justice, equity.

justiciero /husti'θiero; husti'siero/ *a.* just.

justificación /hustifika'θion; hustifika'sion/ *n. f.* justification.

justificadamente /hustifikaða'mente/ *adv.* justifiably.

justificar /hustifi'kar/ *v.* justify, warrant.

justo /'husto/ *a.* right; exact; just; righteous.

juvenil /huβe'nil/ *a.* youthful.

juventud /huβen'tuð/ *n. f.* youth.

juzgado /huθ'gaðo; hus'gaðo/ *n. m.* court.

juzgar /huθ'gar; hus'gar/ *v.* judge, estimate.

káiser /'kaiser/ *n. m.* kaiser.

karate /ka'rate/ *n. m.* karate.

kepis /'kepis/ *n. m.* military cap.

kerosena /kero'sena/ *n. f.* kerosene.

kilo /'kilo/ **kilogramo** /kilo'gramo/ *n. m.* kilogram.

kilohercio /kilo'erθio; kilo'ersio/ *n. m.* kilohertz.

kilolitro /kilo'litro/ *n. m.* kıloliter.

kilometraje /kilome'trahe/ *n. m.* mileage.

kilómetro /ki'lometro/ *n. m.* kilometer.

kiosco /'kiosko/ *n. m.* newsstand; pavilion.

L

la /la/ *art. & pron.* **1.** the; the one. —*pron.* **2.** her, it, you; (*pl.*) them, you.

laberinto /laβe'rinto/ *n. m.* labyrinth, maze.

labia /'laβia/ *n. f.* eloquence, fluency.

labio /'laβio/ *n. m.* lip.

labor /la'βor/ *n. f.* labor, work.

laborar /laβo'rar/ *v.* work; till.

laboratorio /laβora'torio/ *n. m.* laboratory.

laborioso /laβo'rioso/ *a.* industrious.

labrador /laβra'ðor/ *n. m.* farmer.

labranza /la'βranθa; la'βransa/ *n. f.* farming; farmland.

labrar /la'βrar/ *v.* work, till.

labriego /la'βriego/ **-ga** *n.* peasant.

laca /'laka/ *n. f.* shellac.

lacio /'laθio; 'lasio/ *a.* withered; limp; straight.

lactar /lak'tar/ *v.* nurse, suckle.

lácteo /'lakteo/ *a.* milky.

ladear /laðe'ar/ *v.* tilt, tip; sway.

ladera /la'ðera/ *n. f.* slope.

ladino /la'ðino/ *a.* cunning, crafty.

lado /'laðo/ *n. m.* side. **al l. de,** beside. **de l.,** sideways.

ladra /'laðra/ *n. f.* barking. —**ladrar,** *v.*

ladrillo /la'ðriʎo; la'ðriyo/ *n. m.* brick.

ladrón /la'ðron/ **-ona** *n.* thief, robber.

lagarto /la'garto/ *n. m.* lizard; (Mex.) alligator.

lago /'lago/ *n. m.* lake.

lágrima /'lagrima/ *n. f.* tear.

lagrimear /lagrime'ar/ *v.* weep, cry.

laguna /la'guna/ *n. f.* lagoon; gap.

laico /'laiko/ *a.* lay.

laja /'laha/ *n. f.* stone slab.

lamentable /lamen'taβle/ *a* lamentable.

lamentación /lamenta'θion; lamenta'sion/ *n. f.* lamentation.

lamentar /lamen'tar/ *v.* lament; wail; regret, be sorry.

lamento /la'mento/ *n. m.* lament, wail.

lamer /la'mer/ *v.* lick; lap.

lámina /'lamina/ *n. f.* print, illustration.

lámpara /'lampara/ *n. f.* lamp.

lampiño /lam'piɲo/ *a.* beardless.

lana /'lana/ *n. f.* wool.

lanar /la'nar/ *a.* woolen.

lance /'lanθe; 'lanse/ *n. m.* throw; episode; quarrel.

lancha /'lantʃa/ *n. f.* launch; small boat.

lanchón /lan'tʃon/ *n. m.* barge.

langosta /laŋ'gosta/ n. f. lobster; locust.

langostino /laŋgos'tino/ n. m. king prawn.

languidecer /laŋguiðe'θer: languiðe'ser/ v. languish, pine.

languidez /laŋgui'ðeθ: laŋgui'ðes/ n. f. languidness.

lánguido /'laŋguiðo/ a. languid.

lanza /'lanθa; 'lansa/ n. f. lance, spear.

lanzada /lan'θaða; lan'saða/ n. f. thrust, throw.

lanzar /lan'θar: lan'sar/ v. throw, hurl; launch.

lañar /la'ɲar/ v. cramp; clamp.

lapicero /lapi'θero; lapi'sero/ n. m. mechanical pencil.

lápida /'lapiða/ n. f. stone; tombstone.

lápiz /'lapiθ; 'lapis/ n. m. pencil; crayon.

lápiz de ojos /'lapiθ de 'ohos; 'lapis de 'ohos/ n. m. eyeliner.

lapso /'lapso/ n. m. lapse.

lardo /'larðo/ n. m. lard.

largar /lar'gar/ v. loosen; free.

largo /'largo/ a. **1.** long. **a lo l. de,** along. —n. **2.** m. length.

largometraje /largome'trahe/ n. m. feature film.

largor /lar'gor/ n. m. length.

largueza /lar'geθa; lar'gesa/ n. f. generosity; length.

largura /lar'gura/ n. f. length.

laringe /la'rinhe/ n. f. larynx.

larva /'larβa/ n. f. larva.

lascivia /las'θiβia; las'siβia/ n. f. lasciviousness.

lascivo /las'θiβo; las'siβo/ a. lascivious.

láser /'laser/ n. m. laser.

laso /'laso/ a. weary.

lástima /'lastima/ n. f. pity. **ser l.,** to be a pity, to be too bad.

lastimar /lasti'mar/ v. hurt, injure.

lastimoso /lasti'moso/ a. pitiful.

lastre /'lastre/ n. m. ballast. **—lastrar,** v.

lata /'lata/ n. f. tin can; tin (plate); Colloq. annoyance, bore.

latente /la'tente/ a. latent.

lateral /late'ral/ a. lateral, side.

latigazo /lati'gaθo; lati'gaso/ n. m. lash, whipping.

látigo /'latigo/ n. m. whip.

latín /la'tin/ n. m. Latin (language).

latino /la'tino/ a. Latin.

latir /la'tir/ v. beat, pulsate.

latitud /lati'tuð/ n. f. latitude.

latón /la'ton/ n. m. brass.

laúd /la'uð/ n. m. lute.

laudable /lau'ðaβle/ a. laudable.

láudano /'lauðano/ n. m. laudanum.

laurel /lau'rel/ n. m. laurel.

lava /'laβa/ n. f. lava.

lavabo /la'βaβo/ **lavamanos** n. m. washroom, lavatory.

lavadora /laβa'ðora/ n. f. washing machine.

lavandera /laβan'dera/ n. f. washerwoman, laundress.

lavandería /laβande'ria/ f. laundry; laundromat.

lavaplatos /laβa'platos/ n. **1.** m. dishwasher (machine). —n. **2.** m. & f. dishwasher (person).

lavar /la'βar/ v. wash.

lavatorio /laβa'torio/ n. m. lavatory.

laya /'laia/ n. f. spade. **—layar,** v.

lazar /la'θar; la'sar/ v. lasso.

lazareto /laθa'reto; lasa'reto/ n. m. isolation hospital; quarantine station.

lazo /'laθo; 'laso/ n. m. tie, knot; bow; loop.

le /le/ pron. him, her, you; (pl.) them, you.

leal /le'al/ a. loyal.

lealtad /leal'tað/ n. f. loyalty, allegiance.

lebrel /le'βrel/ n. m. greyhound.

lección /lek'θion; lek'sion/ n. f. lesson.

leche /'letʃe/ n. f. milk.

lechería /letʃe'ria/ n. f. dairy.

lechero /le'tʃero/ n. m. milkman.

lecho /'letʃo/ n. m. bed; couch.

lechón /le'tʃon/ n. m. pig.

lechoso /le'tʃoso/ a. milky.

lechuga /le'tʃuga/ n. f. lettuce.

lechuza /le'tʃuθa; le'tʃusa/ n. f. owl.

lecito /le'θito; le'sito/ n. m. yolk.

lector /lek'tor/ **-ra** n. reader.

lectura /lek'tura/ n. f. reading.

leer /le'er/ v. read.

legación /lega'θion; lega'sion/ n. f. legation.

legado /le'gaðo/ n. m. bequest.

legal /le'gal/ a. legal, lawful.

legalizar /legali'θar; legali'sar/ v. legalize.

legar /le'gar/ v. bequeath, leave, will.

legible /le'hiβle/ a. legible.

legión /le'hion/ n. f. legion.

legislación /lehisla'θion; lehisla'sion/ n. f. legislation.

legislador /lehisla'ðor/ **-ra** n. legislator.

legislar /lehis'lar/ v. legislate.

legislativo /lehisla'tiβo/ a. legislative.

legislatura /lehisla'tura/ n. f. legislature.

legítimo /le'hitimo/ a. legitimate.

lego /'lego/ n. m. layman.

legua /'legua/ n. f. league (measure).

legumbre /le'gumbre/ n. f. vegetable.

lejano /le'hano/ a. distant, far-off.

lejía /le'hía/ n. f. lye.

lejos /'lehos/ adv. far. **a lo l.,** in the distance.

lelo /'lelo/ a. stupid, foolish.

lema /'lema/ n. m. theme; slogan.

lengua /'leŋgua/ n. f. tongue; language.

lenguado /leŋ'guaðo/ n. m. sole, flounder.

lenguaje /leŋ'guahe/ n. m. speech; language.

lenguaraz /leŋgua'raθ; leŋgua'ras/ a. talkative.

lente /'lente/ n. **1.** m. or f. lens. **2.** m.pl. eyeglasses.

lenteja /len'teha/ n. f. lentil.

lentilla /len'tiʎa; len'tiya/ n. f. contact lens.

lentitud /lenti'tuð/ n. f. slowness.

lento /'lento/ a. slow.

leña /'leɲa/ n. f. wood, firewood.

león /le'on/ n. m. lion.

leopardo /leo'parðo/ n. m. leopard.

lerdo /'lerðo/ a. dull-witted.

lesbiana /les'βiana/ n. f. lesbian.

lesión /le'sion/ n. f. wound; damage.

letanía /leta'nia/ n. f. litany.

letárgico /le'tarhiko/ a. lethargic.

letargo /le'targo/ n. m. lethargy.

letra /'letra/ n. f. letter (of alphabet); print; words (of a song).

letrado /le'traðo/ a. **1.** learned. —n. **2.** m. lawyer.

letrero /le'trero/ n. m. sign, poster.

leva /'leβa/ n. f. Mil. draft.

levadura /leβa'ðura/ n. f. yeast, leavening, baking powder.

levantador /leβanta'ðor/ n. m. lifter; rebel, mutineer.

levantar /leβan'tar/ v. raise, lift.

levantarse /leβan'tarse/ v. rise, get up; stand up.

levar /le'βar/ v. weigh (anchor).

leve /'leβe/ a. slight, light.

levita /le'βita/ n. f. frock coat.

léxico /'leksiko/ n. m. lexicon, dictionary.

ley /lei/ n. f. law, statute.

leyenda /le'ienda/ n. f. legend.

lezna /'leθna; 'lesna/ n. f. awl.

libación /liβa'θion; liβa'sion/ n. f. libation.

libelo /li'βelo/ n. m. libel.

libélula /li'βelula/ n. f. dragonfly.

liberación /liβera'θion; liβera'sion/ n. f. liberation, release.

liberal /liβe'ral/ a. liberal.

libertad /liβer'tað/ n. f. liberty, freedom.

libertador /liβerta'ðor/ **-ra** n. liberator.

libertar /liβer'tar/ v. free, liberate.

libertinaje /liβerti'nahe/ n. m. licentiousness.

libertino /liβer'tino/ **-na** n. libertine.

libidine /li'βiðine/ n. f. licentiousness; lust.

libidinoso /liβiði'noso/ a. libidinous; lustful.

libra /'liβra/ n. f. pound.

libranza /li'βranθa; li'βransa/ n. f. draft, bill of exchange.

librar /li'βrar/ v. free, rid.

libre /'liβre/ a. free, unoccupied.

librería /liβre'ria/ n. f. bookstore.

librero /li'βrero/ **-ra** n. bookseller.

libreta /li'βreta/ n. f. notebook; booklet.

libreto /li'βreto/ n. m. libretto.

libro /'liβro/ n. m. book.

libro de texto /'liβro de 'teksto/ textbook.

licencia /li'θenθia; li'sensia/ n. f. permission, license, leave; furlough. **l. de armas,** gun permit.

licenciado /liθen'θiaðo; lisen'siaðo/ **-da** n. graduate.

licencioso /liθen'θioso; lisen'sioso/ a. licentious.

lícito /'liθito; 'lisito/ a. lawful.

licor /li'kor/ n. m. liquor.

licuadora /likua'ðora/ n. f. blender (for food).

lid /lið/ n. f. fight. —**lidiar,** v.

líder /'liðer/ n. m. & f. leader.

liebre /'lieβre/ n. f. hare.

lienzo /'lienθo; 'lienso/ n. m. linen.

liga /'liga/ n. f. league, confederacy; garter.

ligadura /liga'ðura/ n. f. ligature.

ligar /li'gar/ v. tie, bind, join.

ligero /li'hero/ a. light; fast, nimble.

ligustro /li'gustro/ n. m. privet.

lija /'liha/ n. f. sandpaper.

lijar /li'har/ v. sandpaper.

lima /'lima/ n. f. file; lime.

limbo /'limbo/ n. m. limbo.

limitación /limita'θion; limita'sion/ n. f. limitation.

límite /'limite/ n. m. limit. —**limitar,** v.

limo /'limo/ n. m. slime.

limón /li'mon/ n. m. lemon.

limonada /limo'naða/ n. f. lemonade.

limonero /limo'nero/ n. m. lemon tree.

limosna /li'mosna/ n. f. alms.

limosnero /limos'nero/ **-ra** n. beggar.

limpiabotas /limpia'βotas/ n. m. bootblack.

limpiadientes /limpia'ðientes/ n. m. toothpick.

limpiar /lim'piar/ v. clean, wash, wipe.

límpido /'limpiðo/ a. limpid, clear.

limpieza /lim'pieθa; lim'piesa/ n. f. cleanliness.

limpio /'limpio/ n. m. clean.

limusina /limu'sina/ n. f. limousine.

linaje /li'nahe/ n. m. lineage, ancestry.

linaza /li'naθa; li'nasa/ n. f. linseed.

lince /'linθe; 'linse/ a. sharp-sighted, observing.

linchamiento /lintʃa'miento/ n. m. lynching.

linchar /lin'tʃar/ v. lynch.

lindar /lin'dar/ v. border, bound.

linde /'linde/ n. m. boundary; landmark.

lindero /lin'dero/ n. m. boundary.

lindo /'lindo/ a. pretty, lovely, nice.

línea /'linea/ n. f. line.

línea de puntos /'linea de 'puntos/ dotted line.

lineal /line'al/ a. lineal.

linfa /'linfa/ n. f. lymph.

lingüista /liŋ'guista/ n. m. & f. linguist.

lingüístico /liŋ'guistiko/ a. linguistic.

linimento /lini'mento/ n. m. liniment.

lino /'lino/ n. m. linen; flax.

linóleo /li'noleo/ n. m. linoleum.

linterna /lin'terna/ n. f. lantern; flashlight.

lío /'lio/ n. m. pack, bundle; mess, scrape; hassle.

liquidación /likiða'θion; likiða'sion/ n. f. liquidation.

liquidar /liki'ðar/ v. liquidate; settle up.

líquido /'likiðo/ a. & m. liquid.

lira /'lira/ n. f. lyre.

lírico /'liriko/ a. lyric.

lirio /'lirio/ n. m. lily.

lirismo /li'rismo/ n. m. lyricism.

lis /lis/ n. f. lily.

lisiar /li'siar/ v. cripple, lame.

liso /'liso/ a. smooth, even.

lisonja /li'sonha/ n. f. flattery.

lisonjear /lisonhe'ar/ v. flatter.

lisonjero /lison'hero/ **-ra** f. flatterer.

lista /'lista/ n. f. list; stripe; menu.

lista negra /'lista 'negra/ blacklist.

listar /lis'tar/ v. list; put on a list.

listo /'listo/ a. ready; smart, clever.

listón /lis'ton/ n. m. ribbon.

litera /li'tera/ n. f. litter, bunk, berth.

literal /lite'ral/ a. literal.

literario /lite'rario/ a. literary.

literato /lite'rato/ n. m. literary person, writer.

literatura /litera'tura/ n. f. literature.

litigación /litiga'θion; litiga'sion/ n. f. litigation.

litigio /li'tihio/ n. m. litigation; lawsuit.

litoral /lito'ral/ n. m. coast.

litro /'litro/ n. m. liter.

liturgia /li'turhia/ n. f. liturgy.

liviano /li'βiano/ a. light (in weight).

lívido /'liβiðo/ a. livid.

llaga /'ʎaga/ n. f. sore.

llama /'ʎama/ 'yama/ n. f. flame; llama.

llamada /ʎa'maða/ ya'maða/ n. f. call; knock. —**llamar,** v.

llamarse /ʎa'marse/ ya'marse/ v. be called, be named. **se llama...** etc., his name is... etc.

llamativo /ʎama'tiβo/ yama'tiβo/ a. gaudy, showy.

llamear /ʎame'ar/ yame'ar/ v. blaze.

llaneza /ʎa'neθa/ ya'nesa/ n. f. simplicity.

llano /'ʎano/ 'yano/ a. **1.** flat, level; plain. —n. **2.** m. plain.

llanta /'ʎanta/ 'yanta/ n. f. tire.

llanto /'ʎanto; 'yanto/ n. m. crying, weeping.

llanura /ʎa'nura; ya'nura/ n. f. prairie, plain.

llave /'ʎaβe; 'yaβe/ n. f. key; wrench; faucet; *Elec.* switch. **ll. inglesa,** monkey wrench.

llegada /ʎe'gaða; ye'gaða/ n. f. arrival.

llegar /ʎe'gar; ye'gar/ v. arrive; reach. **ll. a ser,** become, come to be.

llenar /ʎe'nar; ye'nar/ v. fill.

lleno /'ʎeno; 'yeno/ a. full.

llenura /ʎe'nura; ye'nura/ n. f. abundance.

llevadero /ʎeβa'ðero; yeβa'ðero/ a. tolerable.

llevar /ʎe'βar; ye'βar/ v. take, carry, bear; wear (clothes); **ll. a cabo,** carry out.

llevarse /ʎe'βarse; ye'βarse/ v. take away, run away with. **ll. bien,** get along well.

llorar /ʎo'rar; yo'rar/ v. cry, weep.

lloroso /ʎo'roso; yo'roso/ a. sorrowful, tearful.

llover /ʎo'βer; yo'βer/ v. rain.

llovido /ʎo'βiðo; yo'βiðo/ n. m. stowaway.

llovizna /ʎo'βiθna; yo'βisna/ n. f. drizzle, sprinkle. —**lloviznar,** v.

lluvia /'ʎuβia; 'yuβia/ n. f. rain.

lluvia ácida /'ʎuβia 'aθiða; 'yuβia 'asiða/ acid rain.

lluvioso /ʎu'βioso; yu'βioso/ a. rainy.

lo /lo/ pron. the; him, it, you; (pl.) them, you.

loar /lo'ar/ v. praise, laud.

lobina /lo'βina/ n. f. striped bass.

lobo /'loβo/ n. m. wolf.

lóbrego /'loβrego/ a. murky; dismal.

local /lo'kal/ a. **1.** local. —n. **2.** m. site.

localidad /lokali'ðað/ n. f. locality; location; seat (in theater).

localizar /lokali'θar; lokali'sar/ v. localize.

loción /lo'θion; lo'sion/ n. f. lotion.

loco /'loko/ **-ca** a. **1.** crazy, insane, mad. —n. **2.** lunatic.

locomotora /lokomo'tora/ n. f. locomotive.

locuaz /lo'kuaθ; lo'kuas/ a. loquacious.

locución /loku'θion; loku'sion/ n. f. locution, expression.

locura /lo'kura/ n. f. folly; madness, insanity.

lodo /'loðo/ n. m. mud.

lodoso /lo'ðoso/ a. muddy.

lógica /'lohika/ n. f. logic.

lógico /'lohiko/ a. logical.

lograr /lo'grar/ v. achieve; succeed in.

logro /'logro/ n. m. accomplishment.

lombriz /lom'βriθ; lom'βris/ n. f. earthworm.

lomo /'lomo/ n. m. loin; back (of an animal).

lona /'lona/ n. f canvas, tarpaulin.

longevidad /lonheβi'ðað/ *n. f.* longevity.

longitud /lonhi'tuð/ *n. f.* longitude; length.

lonja /'lonha/ *n. f.* shop; market.

lontananza /lonta'nanθa; lonta'nansa/ *n. f.* distance.

loro /'loro/ *n. m.* parrot.

losa /'losa/ *n. f.* slab.

lote /'lote/ *n. m.* lot, share.

lotería /lote'ria/ *n. f.* lottery.

loza /'loθa; 'losa/ *n. f.* china, crockery.

lozanía /loθa'nia; losa'nia/ *n. f.* freshness, vigor.

lozano /lo'θano; lo'sano/ *a.* fresh, spirited.

lubricación /luβrika'θion; luβrika'sion/ *n. f.* lubrication.

lubricar /luβri'kar/ *v.* lubricate.

lucero /lu'θero; lu'sero/ *n. m.* (bright) star.

lucha /'lutʃa/ *n. f.* fight, struggle; wrestling.
—**luchar,** *v.*

luchador /lutʃa'ðor/ **-ra** *n.* fighter, wrestler.

lúcido /lu'θiðo; lu'siðo/ *a.* lucid, clear.

luciente /lu'θiente; lu'siente/ *a.* shining, bright.

luciérnaga /lu'θiernaga; lu'siernaga/ *n. f.* firefly.

lucimiento /luθi'miento; lusi'miento/ *n. m.* success; splendor.

lucir /lu'θir; lu'sir/ *v.* shine, sparkle; show off.

lucrativo /lukra'tiβo/ *a.* lucrative, profitable.

luego /'luego/ *adv.* right away; afterwards, next. **l. que,** as soon as. **desde l.,** of course. **hasta l.,** good-bye, so long.

lugar /lu'gar/ *n. m.* place, spot; space, room.

lúgubre /'luguβre/ *a.* gloomy; dismal.

lujo /'luho/ *n. m.* luxury. **de l.,** deluxe.

lujoso /lu'hoso/ *a.* luxurious.

lumbre /'lumbre/ *n. f.* fire; light.

luminoso /lumi'noso/ *a.* luminous.

luna /'luna/ *n. f.* moon.

lunar /lu'nar/ *n. m.* beauty mark, mole; polka dot.

lunático /lu'natiko/ **-ca** *a. & n.* lunatic.

lunes /'lunes/ *n. m.* Monday.

luneta /lu'neta/ *n. f. Theat.* orchestra seat.

lupa /'lupa/ *n. f.* magnifying glass.

lustre /'lustre/ *n. m.* polish, shine.
—**lustrar,** *v.*

lustroso /lus'troso/ *a.* shiny.

luto /'luto/ *n. m.* mourning.

luz /luθ; lus/ *n. f.* light. **dar a l.,** give birth to.

M

maca /'maka/ *n. f.* blemish, flaw.

macaco /ma'kako/ *a.* ugly, horrid.

macareno /maka'reno/ *a.* boasting.

macarrones /maka'rrones/ *n. m.pl.* macaroni.

macear /maθe'ar; mase'ar/ *v.* molest, push around.

macedonia de frutas /maθe'ðonia de 'frutas; mase'ðonia de 'frutas/ *n. f.* fruit salad.

maceta /ma'θeta; ma'seta/ *n. f.* vase; mallet.

machacar /matʃa'kar/ *v.* pound; crush.

machina /mu'tʃina/ *n. f.* derrick.

machista /ma'tʃista/ *a.* macho.

macho /'matʃo/ *n. m.* male.

machucho /ma'tʃutʃo/ *a.* mature, wise.

macizo /ma'θiθo; ma'siso/ *a.* **1.** solid. —*n.* **2.** *m.* bulk; flower bed.

macular /maku'lar/ *v.* stain.

madera /ma'ðera/ *n. f.* lumber; wood.

madero /ma'ðero/ *n. m.* beam, timber.

madrastra /ma'ðrastra/ *n. f.* stepmother.

madre /'maðre/ *n. f.* mother. **m. política,** mother-in-law.

madreperla /maðre'perla/ *n. f.* mother-of-pearl.

madriguera /maðri'gera/ *n. f.* burrow; lair, den.

madrina /ma'ðrina/ *n. f.* godmother.

madroncillo /maðron'θiʎo; maðron'siyo/ *n. m.* strawberry.

madrugada /maðru'gaða/ *n. f.* daybreak.

madrugar /maðru'gar/ *v.* get up early.

madurar /maðu'rar/ *v.* ripen.

madurez /maðu'reθ; maðu'res/ *n. f.* maturity.

maduro /ma'ðuro/ *a.* ripe; mature.

maestría /maes'tria/ *n. f.* mastery; master's degree.

maestro /ma'estro/ *n. m.* master; teacher.

mafia /'mafia/ *n. f.* mafia.

maganto /ma'ganto/ *a.* lethargic, dull.

magia /'mahia/ *n. f.* magic.

mágico /'mahiko/ *a. & m.* magic; magician.

magistrado /mahis'traðo/ *n. m.* magistrate.

magnánimo /mag'nanimo/ *a.* magnanimous.

magnético /mag'netiko/ *a.* magnetic.

magnetismo /magne'tismo/ *n. m.* magnetism.

magnetófono /magne'tofono/ *n. m.* tape recorder.

magnificar /magnifi'kar/ *v.* magnify.

magnificencia /magnifi'θenθia; magnifi'sensia/ *n. f.* magnificence.

magnífico /mag'nifiko/ *a.* magnificent.

magnitud /magni'tuð/ *n. f.* magnitude.

magno /'magno/ *a.* great, grand.

magnolia /mag'nolia/ *n. f.* magnolia.

mago /'mago/ *n. m.* magician; wizard.

magosto /ma'gosto/ *n. m.* chestnut roast; picnic fire for roasting chestnuts.

magro /'magro/ *a.* meager; thin.

magullar /magu'ʎar; magu'yar/ *v.* bruise.

mahometano /maome'tano/ *n. & a.* Mohammedan.

mahometismo /maome'tismo/ *n. m.* Mohammedanism.

maíz /ma'iθ; ma'is/ *n. m.* corn.

majadero /maha'ðero/ **-ra** *a. & n.* foolish; fool.

majar /ma'har/ *v.* mash.

majestad /mahes'tað/ *n. f.* majesty.

majestuoso /mahes'tuoso/ *a.* majestic.

mal /mal/ *adv.* **1.** badly; wrong. —*n.* **2.** *m.* evil, ill; illness.

mala /'mala/ *n. f.* mail.

malacate /mala'kate/ *n. m.* hoist.

malandanza /malan'danθa; malan'dansa/ *n. f.* misfortune.

malaventura /malaβen'tura/ *n. f.* misfortune.

malcomido /malko'miðo/ *a.* underfed; malnourished.

malcontento /malkon'tento/ *a.* disssatisfied.

maldad /mal'dað/ *n. f.* badness; wickedness.

maldecir /malde'θir; malde'sir/ *v.* curse; damn.

maldición /maldi'θion; maldi'sion/ *n. f.* curse.

maldito /mal'dito/ *a.* accursed, damned.

malecón /male'kon/ *n. m.* embankment.

maledicencia /maleði'θenθia; maleði'sensia/ *n. f.* slander.

maleficio /male'fiθio; male'fisio/ *n. m.* spell, charm.

malestar /males'tar/ *n. m.* indisposition.

maleta /ma'leta/ *n. f.* suitcase, valise.

malévolo /ma'leβolo/ *a.* malevolent.

maleza /ma'leθa; ma'lesa/ *n. f.* weeds; underbrush.

malgastar /malgas'tar/ *v.* squander.

malhechor /male'tʃor/ **-ra** *n.* malefactor, evildoer.

malhumorado /malumo'raðo/ *a.* morose, ill-humored.

malicia /ma'liθia; ma'lisia/ *n. f.* malice.

maliciar /mali'θiar; mali'siar/ *v.* suspect.

malicioso /mali'θioso; mali'sioso/ *a.* malicious.

maligno /ma'ligno/ *a.* malignant, evil.

malla /'maʎa, 'maya/ *n. f.* mesh, net.

mallas /'maʎas; 'mayas/ *n. f.pl.* leotard.

mallete /ma'ʎete; ma'yete/ *n. m.* mallet.

malo /'malo/ *a.* bad; evil, wicked; naughty; ill.

malograr /malo'grar/ *v.* miss, lose.

malparto /mal'parto/ *n. m.* abortion, miscarriage.

malquerencia /malke'renθia; malke'rensia/ *n. f.* hatred.

malquerer /malke'rer/ *v.* dislike; bear ill will.

malsano /mal'sano/ *a.* unhealthy; unwholesome.

malsín /mal'sin/ *n. m.* malicious gossip.

malta /'malta/ *n. f.* malt.

maltratar /maltra'tar/ *v.* mistreat.

malvado /mal'βaðo/ **-da** *a.* **1.** wicked. —*n.* **2.** villain.

malversar /malβer'sar/ *v.* embezzle.

malvís /mal'βis/ *n. m.* redwing.

mamá /'mama/ *n. f.* mama, mother.

mamar /ma'mar/ *v.* suckle; suck.

mamífero /ma'mifero/ *n. m.* mammal.

mampara /mam'para/ *n. f.* screen.

mampostería /mamposte'ria/ *n. f.* masonry.

mamut /ma'mut/ *n. m.* mammoth.

manada /ma'naða/ *n. f.* flock, herd, drove.

manantial /manan'tial/ *n. m.* spring (of water).

manar /ma'nar/ *v.* gush, flow out.

mancebo /man'θeβo; man'seβo/ *n. m.* young man.

mancha /'mantʃa/ *n. f.* stain, smear, blemish, spot. —**manchar,** *v.*

mancilla /man'θiʎa; man'siya/ *n. f.* stain; blemish.

manco /'manko/ *a.* armless; one-armed.

mandadero /manda'ðero/ *n. m.* messenger.

mandado /man'daðo/ *n. m.* order, command.

mandamiento /manda'miento/ *n. m.* commandment; command.

mandar /man'dar/ *v.* send; order, command.

mandatario /manda'tario/ *n. m.* attorney; representative.

mandato /man'dato/ *n. m.* mandate, command.

mandíbula /man'diβula/ *n. f.* jaw; jawbone.

mando /'mando/ *n. m.* command, order; leadership.

mando a distancia /'mando a dis'tanθia; 'mando a dis'tansia/ remote control.

mandón /man'don/ *a.* domineering.

mandril /man'dril/ *n. m.* baboon.

manejar /mane'har/ *v.* handle, manage; drive (a car).

manejo /ma'neho/ *n. m.* management; horsemanship.

manera /ma'nera/ *n. f.* way, manner, means. **de m. que**, so, as a result.

manga /'manga/ *n. f.* sleeve.

mangana /man'gana/ *n. f.* lariat, lasso.

manganeso /manga'neso/ *n. m.* manganese.

mango /'mango/ *n. m.* handle; mango (fruit).

mangosta /man'gosta/ *n. f.* mongoose.

manguera /man'guera/ *n. f.* hose.

manguito /man'guito/ *n. m.* muff.

maní /ma'ni/ *n. m.* peanut.

manía /ma'nia/ *n. f.* mania, madness; hobby.

maníaco /ma'niako/ **-ca, maniático -ca** *a.* & *n.* maniac.

manicomio /mani'komio/ *n. m.* insane asylum.

manicura /mani'kura/ *n. f.* manicure.

manifactura /manifak'tura/ *n. f.* manufacture.

manifestación /manifesta'θion; manifesta'sion/ *n. f.* manifestation.

manifestar /manifes'tar/ *v.* manifest, show.

manifiesto /mani'fiesto/ *a.* & *m.* manifest.

manija /ma'niha/ *n. f.* handle; crank.

maniobra /ma'nioβra/ *n. f.* maneuver. —**maniobrar,** *v.*

manipulación /manipula'θion; manipula'sion/ *n. f.* manipulation.

manipular /manipu'lar/ *v.* manipulate.

maniquí /mani'ki/ *n. m.* mannequin.

manivela /mani'βela/ *n. f. Mech.* crank.

manjar /man'har/ *n. m.* food, dish.

manlieve /man'lieβe/ *n. m.* swindle.

mano /'mano/ *n. f.* hand.

manojo /ma'noho/ *n. m.* handful; bunch.

manómetro /ma'nometro/ *n. m.* gauge.

manopla /ma'nopla/ *n. f.* gauntlet.

manosear /manose'ar/ *v.* handle, feel, touch.

manotada /mano'taða/ *n. f.* slap, smack. —**manotear,** *v.*

mansedumbre /manse'ðumbre/ *n. f.* meekness, tameness.

mansión /man'sion/ *n. f.* mansion; abode.

manso /'manso/ *a.* tame, gentle.

manta /'manta/ *n. f.* blanket.

manteca /man'teka/ *n. f.* lard; butter.

mantecado /mante'kaðo/ *n. m.* ice cream.

mantecoso /mante'koso/ *a.* buttery.

mantel /man'tel/ *n. m.* tablecloth.

mantener /mante'ner/ *v.* maintain, keep; sustain; support.

mantenimiento /manteni'miento/ *n. m.* maintenance.

mantequera /mante'kera/ *n. f.* butter dish; churn.

mantequilla /mante'kiʎa; mante'kiya/ *n. f.* butter.

mantilla /man'tiʎa; man'tiya/ *n. f.* mantilla; baby clothes.

mantillo /man'tiʎo; man'tiyo/ *n. m.* humus; manure.

manto /'manto/ *n. m.* mantle, cloak.

manual /ma'nual/ *a.* & *m.* manual.

manubrio /ma'nuβrio/ *n. m.* handle; crank.

manufacturar /manufaktu'rar/ *v.* manufacture; make.

manuscrito /manus'krito/ *n. m.* manuscript.

manzana /man'θana; man'sana/ *n. f.* apple; block (of street).

manzanilla /manθa'niʎa; mansa'niya/ *n. f.* dry sherry.

manzano /man'θano; man'sano/ *n. m.* apple tree.

maña /'maɲa/ *n. f.* skill; cunning; trick.

mañana /ma'ɲana/ *adv.* **1.** tomorrow. —*n.* **2.** *f.* morning.

mañanear /maɲane'ar/ *v.* rise early in the morning.

mañero /ma'ɲero/ *a.* clever; skillful; lazy.

mapa /'mapa/ *n. m.* map, chart.

mapache /ma'patʃe/ *n. m.* raccoon.

mapurito /mapu'rito/ *n. m.* skunk.

máquina /'makina/ *n. f.* machine. **m. de coser,** sewing machine. **m. de lavar,** washing machine.

maquinación /makina'θion; makina'sion/ *n. f.* machination; plot.

maquinador /makina'ðor/ **-ra** *n.* plotter, schemer.

maquinal /maki'nal/ *a.* mechanical.

maquinar /maki'nar/ *v.* scheme, plot.

maquinaria /maki'naria/ *n. f.* machinery.

maquinista /maki'nista/ *n. m.* machinist; engineer.

mar /mar/ *n. m. or f.* sea.

marabú /mara'βu/ *n. m.* marabou.

maraña /ma'raɲa/ *n. f.* tangle; maze; snarl; plot.

maravilla /mara'βiʎa; mara'βiya/ *n. f.* marvel, wonder. —**maravillarse,** *v.*

maravilloso /maraβi'ʎoso; maraβi'yoso/ *a.* marvelous, wonderful.

marbete /mar'βete/ *n. m.* tag, label; check.

marca /'marka/ *n. f.* mark, sign; brand, make.

marcador /marka'ðor/ *n. m.* highlighter.

marcapáginas /marka'pahinas/ *n. m.* bookmark.

marcar /mar'kar/ *v.* mark; observe, note.

marcha /'martʃa/ *n. f.* march; progress. —**marchar,** *v.*

marchante /mar'tʃante/ *n. m.* merchant; customer.

marcharse /mar'tʃarse/ *v.* go away, depart.

marchitable /martʃi'taβle/ *a.* perishable.

marchitar /martʃi'tar/ v. fade, wilt, wither.

marchito /mar'tʃito/ a. faded, withered.

marcial /mar'θial; mar'sial/ a. martial.

marco /'marko/ n. m. frame.

marea /ma'rea/ n. f. tide.

mareado /mare'aðo/ a. seasick.

marearse /mare'arse/ v. get dizzy; be seasick.

mareo /ma'reo/ n. m. dizziness; seasickness.

marfil /mar'fil/ n. m. ivory.

margarita /marga'rita/ n. f. pearl; daisy.

margen /'marhen/ n. m. or f. margin, edge, rim.

marido /ma'riðo/ n. m. husband.

marijuana /mari'huana/ n. f. marijuana.

marimacha /mari'matʃa/ n. f. lesbian.

marimacho /mari'matʃo/ n. m. mannish woman.

marimba /ma'rimba/ n. f. marimba.

marina /ma'rina/ n. f. navy; seascape.

marinero /mari'nero/ n. m. sailor, seaman.

marino /ma'rino/ a. & m. marine, (of) sea; mariner, seaman.

marión /ma'rion/ n. m. sturgeon.

mariposa /mari'posa/ n. f. butterfly.

mariquita /mari'kita/ n. f. ladybird.

mariscal /maris'kal/ n. m. marshal.

marisco /ma'risko/ n. m. shellfish; mollusk.

marital /mari'tal/ a. marital.

marítimo /ma'ritimo/ a. maritime.

marmita /mar'mita/ n. f. pot, kettle.

mármol /'marmol/ n. m. marble.

marmóreo /mar'moreo/ a. marble.

maroma /ma'roma/ n. f. rope.

marqués /mar'kes/ n. m. marquis.

marquesa /mar'kesa/ n. f. marquise.

Marruecos /ma'rruekos/ n. m. Morocco.

Marte /'marte/ n. m. Mars.

martes /'martes/ n. m. Tuesday.

martillo /mar'tiʎo; mar'tiyo/ n. m. hammer. —**martillar,** v.

mártir /'martir/ n. m. & f. martyr.

martirio /mar'tirio/ n. m. martyrdom.

martirizar /martiri'θar; martiri'sar/ v. martyrize.

marzo /'marθo; 'marso/ n. m. March.

mas /mas/ conj. but.

más /mas/ a. & adv. more, most; plus. **no m.,** only; no more.

masa /'masa/ n. f. mass; dough.

masaje /ma'sahe/ n. m. massage.

mascar /mas'kar/ v. chew.

máscara /'maskara/ n. f. mask.

mascarada /maska'raða/ n. f. masquerade.

mascota /mas'kota/ n. f. mascot; good-luck charm.

masculino /masku'lino/ a. masculine.

mascullar /masku'ʎar; masku'yar/ v. mumble.

masón /ma'son/ n. m. Freemason.

masticar /masti'kar/ v. chew.

mástil /'mastil/ n. m. mast; post.

mastín /mas'tin/ n. m. mastiff.

mastín danés /mas'tin da'nes/ Great Dane.

mastuerzo /mas'tuerθo; mas'tuerso/ n. m. fool, ninny.

mata /'mata/ n. f. plant; bush.

matadero /mata'ðero/ n. m. slaughterhouse.

matador /mata'ðor/ **-ra** n. matador.

matafuego /mata'fuego/ n. m. fire extinguisher.

matanza /ma'tanθa; ma'tansa/ n. f. killing, bloodshed, slaughter.

matar /ma'tar/ v. kill, slay; slaughter.

matasanos /mata'sanos/ n. m. quack.

mate /'mate/ n. m. checkmate; Paraguayan tea.

matemáticas /mate'matikas/ n. f.pl. mathematics.

matemático /mate'matiko/ a. mathematical.

materia /ma'teria/ n. f. material; subject (matter).

material /mate'rial/ a. & m. material.

materialismo /materia'lismo/ n. m. materialism.

materializar /materiali'θar; materiali'sar/ v. materialize.

maternal /mater'nal/ **materno** a. maternal.

maternidad /materni'ðað/ n. f. maternity; maternity hospital.

matiné /mati'ne/ n. f. matinee.

matiz /ma'tiθ; ma'tis/ n. m. hue, shade.

matizar /mati'θar; mati'sar/ v. blend; tint.

matón /ma'ton/ n. m. bully.

matorral /mato'rral/ n. m. thicket.

matoso /ma'toso/ a. weedy.

matraca /ma'traka/ n. f. rattle. —**matraquear,** v.

matrícula /ma'trikula/ n. f. registration; tuition.

matricularse /matriku'larse/ v. enroll, register.

matrimonio /matri'monio/ n. m. matrimony, marriage; married couple.

matriz /ma'triθ; ma'tris/ n. f. womb; Mech. die, mold.

matrona /ma'trona/ n. f. matron.

maullar /mau'ʎar; mau'yar/ v. mew.

máxima /'maksima/ n. f. maxim.

máxime /'maksime/ a. principally.

máximo /'maksimo/ a. & m. maximum.

maya /'maya/ n. f. daisy.

mayo /'mayo/ n. m. May.

mayonesa /mayo'nesa/ n. f. mayonnaise.

mayor /ma'yor/ a. larger, largest; greater, greatest; elder, eldest, senior. **m. de edad,**

major, of age. **al por m.,** at wholesale. *m.* major.

mayoral /mayo'ral/ *n. m.* head shepherd; boss; foreman.

mayordomo /mayor'ðomo/ *n. m.* manager; butler, steward.

mayoría /mayo'ria/ *n. f.* majority, bulk.

mayorista /mayo'rista/ *n. m. & f.* wholesaler.

mayúscula /ma'yuskula/ *n. f.* capital letter, upper-case letter.

mazmorra /maθ'morra; mas'morra/ *n. f.* dungeon.

mazorca /ma'θorka; ma'sorka/ *n. f.* ear of corn.

me /me/ *pron.* me; myself.

mecánico /me'kaniko/ **-ca** *a. & n.* mechanical; mechanic.

mecanismo /meka'nismo/ *n. m.* mechanism.

mecanizar /mekani'θar; mekani'sar/ *v.* mechanize.

mecanografía /mekanogra'fia/ *n. f.* typewriting.

mecanógrafo /meka'nografo/ **-fa** *n.* typist.

mecedor /meθe'ðor; mese'ðor/ *n. m.* swing.

mecedora /meθe'ðora; mese'ðora/ *n. f.* rocking chair.

mecer /me'θer; me'ser/ *v.* rock; swing, sway.

mecha /'metʃa/ *n. f.* wick; fuse.

mechón /me'tʃon/ *n. m.* lock (of hair).

medalla /me'ðaʎa; me'ðaya/ *n. f.* medal.

médano /'meðano/ *n. m.* sand dune.

media /'meðia/ *n. f.* stocking.

mediación /meðia'θion; meðia'sion/ *n. f.* mediation.

mediador /meðia'ðor/ **-ra** *n.* mediator.

mediados /me'ðiaðos/ *n. m.pl.* **a m. de,** about the middle of (a period of time).

medianero /meðia'nero/ *n. m.* mediator.

medianía /meðia'nia/ *n. f.* mediocrity.

mediano /me'ðiano/ *a.* medium; moderate; mediocre.

medianoche /meðia'notʃe/ *n. f.* midnight.

mediante /me'ðiante/ *prep.* by means of.

mediar /me'ðiar/ *v.* mediate.

medicamento /meðika'mento/ *n. m.* medicine, drug.

medicastro /meði'kastro/ *n. m.* quack.

medicina /meði'θina; meði'sina/ *n. f.* medicine.

medicinar /meðiθi'nar; meðisi'nar/ *v.* treat (as a doctor).

médico /'meðiko/ *a.* **1.** medical. **—***n.* **2.** *m. & f.* doctor, physician.

medida /me'ðiða/ *n. f* measure, step.

medidor /meði'ðor/ *n. m.* meter.

medieval /meðie'βal/ *a.* medieval.

medio /'meðio/ *a.* **1.** half; mid, middle of. **—**. **2.** *m.* middle; means.

mediocre /me'ðiokre/ *a.* mediocre.

mediocridad /meðiokri'ðað/ *n. f.* mediocrity.

mediodía /meðio'ðia/ *n. m.* midday, noon.

medir /me'ðir/ *v.* measure, gauge.

meditación /meðita'θion; meðita'sion/ *n. f.* meditation.

meditar /meði'tar/ *v.* meditate.

mediterráneo /meðite'rraneo/ *a.* Mediterranean.

medrar /'meðrar/ *v.* thrive; grow.

medroso /me'ðroso/ *a.* fearful, cowardly.

megáfono /me'gafono/ *n. m.* megaphone.

megahercio /mega'erθio; mega'ersio/ *n. f* megahertz.

mejicano /mehi'kano/ **-na** *a. & n.* Mexican.

mejilla /me'hiʎa; me'hiya/ *n. f.* cheek.

mejillón /mehi'ʎon; mehi'yon/ *n. m.* mussel.

mejor /me'hor/ *a. & adv.* better; best. **a lo m.,** perhaps.

mejora /me'hora/ *n. f.,* **mejoramiento,** *m.* improvement.

mejorar /meho'rar/ *v.* improve, better.

mejoría /meho'ria/ *n. f.* improvement; superiority.

melancolía /melanko'lia/ *n. f.* melancholy.

melancólico /melan'koliko/ *a.* melancholy.

melaza /me'laθa; me'lasa/ *n. f.* molasses.

melena /me'lena/ *n. f.* mane; long or loose hair.

melenudo /mele'nuðo/ **-da** *a.* long-haired.

melindroso /melin'droso/ *a.* fussy.

mella /'meʎa; 'meya/ *n. f.* notch; dent. **—mellar,** *v.*

mellizo /me'ʎiθo; me'yiso/ **-za** *n. & a.* twin.

melocotón /meloko'ton/ *n. m.* peach.

melodía /melo'ðia/ *n. f.* melody.

melodioso /melo'ðioso/ *a.* melodious.

melón /me'lon/ *n. m.* melon.

meloso /me'loso/ *a.* like honey.

membrana /mem'brana/ *n. f.* membrane.

membrete /mem'brete/ *n. m.* memorandum; letterhead.

membrillo /mem'briʎo; mem'briyo/ *n. m.* quince.

membrudo /mem'bruðo/ *a.* strong, muscular.

memorable /memo'raβle/ *a.* memorable.

memorándum /memo'randum/ *n. m.* memorandum; notebook.

memoria /me'moria/ *n. f.* memory; memoir; memorandum.

mención /men'θion; men'sion/ *n. f.* mention. **—mencionar,** *v.*

mendigar /mendi'gar/ *v.* beg (for alms).

mendigo /men'digo/ **-a** *n.* beggar.

mendrugo /men'drugo/ *n. m.* (hard) crust, chunk.

menear /mene'ar/ *v.* shake, wag: stir.

menester /menes'ter/ *n. m.* need, want; duty, task. **ser m.,** to be necessary.

menesteroso /meneste'roso/ *a.* needy.

mengua /'meŋgua/ *n. f.* decrease; lack; poverty.

menguar /meŋ'guar/ *v.* abate, decrease.

meningitis /meniŋ'gitis/ *n. f.* meningitis.

menopausia /meno'pausia/ *n. f.* menopause.

menor /me'nor/ *a.* smaller, smallest; lesser, least; younger, youngest, junior. **m. de edad,** minor, under age. **al por m.,** at retail.

menos /'menos/ *a. & adv.* less; least; minus. **a m. que,** unless. **echar de m.,** to miss.

menospreciar /menospre'θiar; menospre'siar/ *v.* cheapen; despise; slight.

mensaje /men'sahe/ *n. m.* message.

mensajero /mensa'hero/ **-ra** *n.* messenger.

menstruar /menstru'ar/ *v.* menstruate.

mensual /men'sual/ *a.* monthly.

mensualidad /mensuali'ðað/ *n. f.* monthly income or allowance; monthly payment.

menta /'menta/ *n. f.* mint, peppermint.

mentado /men'taðo/ *a.* famous.

mental /men'tal/ *a.* mental.

mentalidad /mentali'ðað/ *n. f.* mentality.

menta romana /'menta rro'mana/ spearmint.

mente /'mente/ *n. f.* mind.

mentecato /mente'kato/ *a.* foolish, stupid.

mentir /men'tir/ *v.* lie, tell a lie.

mentira /men'tira/ *n. f.* lie, falsehood. **parece m.,** it seems impossible.

mentiroso /menti'roso/ *a.* lying, untruthful.

mentol /men'tol/ *n. m.* menthol.

menú /me'nu/ *n. m.* menu.

menudeo /menu'ðeo/ *n. m.* retail.

menudo /menu'ðo/ *a.* small, minute. **a m.,** often.

meñique /me'ɲike/ *a.* tiny.

meple /'meple/ *n. m.* maple.

merca /'merka/ *n. f.* purchase.

mercader /merka'ðer/ *n. m.* merchant.

mercaderías /merkaðe'rias/ *n. f.pl.* merchandise, commodities.

mercado /mer'kaðo/ *n. m.* market.

Mercado Común /mer'kaðo ko'mun/ Common Market.

mercado negro /mer'kaðo 'negro/ black market.

mercancía /merkan'θia; merkan'sia/ *n. f.* merchandise; (*pl.*) wares.

mercante /mer'kante/ *a.* merchant.

mercantil /merkan'til/ *a.* mercantile.

merced /mer'θeð; mer'seð/ *n. f.* mercy, grace.

mercenario /merθe'nario; merse'nario/ **-ria** *a. & n.* mercenary.

mercurio /mer'kurio/ *n. m.* mercury.

merecedor /mereθe'ðor; merese'ðor/ *a.* worthy.

merecer /mere'θer; mere'ser/ *v.* merit, deserve.

merecimiento /mereθi'miento; meresi'miento/ *n. m.* merit.

merendar /meren'dar/ *v.* eat lunch; snack.

merendero /meren'dero/ *n. m.* lunchroom.

meridional /meriðio'nal/ *a.* southern.

merienda /me'rienda/ *n. f.* midday meal, lunch; afternoon snack.

mérito /'merito/ *n. m.* merit, worth.

meritorio /meri'torio/ *a.* meritorious.

merla /'merla/ *n. f.* blackbird.

merluza /mer'luθa; mer'lusa/ *n. f.* haddock.

mermelada /merme'laða/ *n. f.* marmalade.

mero /'mero/ *a.* mere.

merodeador /meroðea'ðor/ **-ra** *n.* prowler.

mes /'mes/ *n. m.* month.

mesa /'mesa/ *n. f.* table.

meseta /me'seta/ *n. f.* plateau.

mesón /me'son/ *n. m.* inn.

mesonero /meso'nero/ **-ra** *n.* innkeeper.

mestizo /mes'tiθo; mes'tiso/ **-za** *a. & n.* half-caste.

meta /'meta/ *n. f.* goal, objective.

metabolismo /metaβo'lismo/ *n. m.* metabolism.

metafísica /meta'fisika/ *n. f.* metaphysics.

metáfora /me'tafora/ *n. f.* metaphor.

metal /me'tal/ *n. m.* metal.

metálico /me'taliko/ *a.* metallic.

metalurgia /metalur'hia/ *n. f.* metallurgy.

meteoro /mete'oro/ *n. m.* meteor.

meteorología /meteorolo'hia/ *n. f.* meteorology.

meter /me'ter/ *v.* put (in).

meterse /me'terse/ *v.* interfere, meddle; go into.

metódico /me'toðiko/ *a.* methodic.

método /'metoðo/ *n. m.* method, approach.

metralla /me'traʎa; me'traya/ *n. f.* shrapnel.

métrico /'metriko/ *a.* metric.

metro /'metro/ *n. m.* meter (measure); subway.

metrópoli /me'tropoli/ *n. f.* metropolis.

mexicano /meksi'kano/ **-na** *a. & n.* Mexican.

mezcla /'meθkla; 'meskla/ *n. f.* mixture; blend.

mezclar /meθ'klar; mes'klar/ *v.* mix; blend.

mezcolanza /meθko'lanθa; mesko'lansa/ *n. f.* mixture; hodgepodge.

mezquino /meθ'kino; mes'kino/ *a.* stingy; petty.

mezquita /meθ'kita; mes'kita/ *n. f.* mosque.

mi /'mi/ *a.* my.

mí /'mi/ *pron.* me; myself.

microbio /mi'kroβio/ *n. m.* microbe, germ.

microbús /mikro'βus/ *n. m.* minibus.

microchip /mikro'tʃip/ *n. m.* microchip.

microficha /mikro'fitʃa/ *n. f.* microfiche.

micrófono /mi'krofono/ *n. m.* microphone.

microforma /mikro'forma/ *n. f.* microform.

microscópico /mikros'kopiko/ *a.* microscopic.

microscopio /mikros'kopio/ *n. m.* microscope.

microtaxi /mikro'taksi/ *n. m.* minicab.

miedo /'mieðo/ *n. m.* fear. **tener m.,** fear, be afraid.

miedoso /mie'ðoso/ *a.* fearful.

miel /miel/ *n. f.* honey.

miembro /mi'embro/ *n. m. & f.* member; limb.

mientras /'mientras/ *conj.* while. **m. tanto,** meanwhile. **m. más... más,** the more... the more.

miércoles /'mierkoles/ *n. —.* Wednesday.

miércoles de ceniza /'mierkoles de θe'niθa; 'mierkoles de se'nisa/ Ash Wednesday.

miga /'miga/ **migaja** *n. f.* scrap; crumb.

migración /migra'θion; migra'sion/ *n. f.* migration.

migratorio /migra'torio/ *a.* migratory.

mil /mil/ *a. & pron.* thousand.

milagro /mi'lagro/ *n. m.* miracle.

milagroso /mila'groso/ *a.* miraculous.

milicia /mi'liθia; mi'lisia/ *n. f.* militia.

militante /mili'tante/ *a.* militant.

militar /mili'tar/ *a.* **1.** military. —*n. —. m.* military man.

militarismo /milita'rismo/ *n. m.* militarism.

milla /'miʎa; 'miya/ *n. f.* mile.

millar /mi'ʎar; mi'yar/ *n. m.* (a) thousand.

millón /mi'ʎon; mi'yon/ *n. m.* million.

millonario /miʎo'nario; miyo'nario/ **-ria** *n.* millionaire.

mimar /mi'mar/ *v.* pamper, spoil (a child).

mimbre /'mimbre/ *n. m.* willow; wicker.

mímico /'mimiko/ *a.* mimic.

mimo /'mimo/ *n. m.* mime, mimic.

mina /'mina/ *n. f.* mine. —**minar,** *v.*

mineral /mine'ral/ *a. & m.* mineral.

minero /mi'nero/ **-ra** *n.* miner.

miniatura /minia'tura/ *n. f.* miniature.

miniaturizar /miniaturi'θar; miniaturi'sar/ *v.* miniaturize.

mínimo /'minimo/ *a. & m.* minimum.

ministerio /minis'terio/ *n. m.* ministry; cabinet.

ministro /mi'nistro/ **-a** *n.* Govt. minister, secretary.

minoría /mino'ria/ *n. f.* minority.

minoridad /minori'ðað/ *n. f.* minority (of age).

minucioso /minu'θioso; minu'sioso/ *a.* minute; thorough.

minué /mi'nue/ *n. m.* minuet.

minúscula /mi'nuskula/ *n. f.* lower-case letter, small letter.

minuta /mi'nuta/ *n. f.* draft.

mío /'mio/ *a.* mine.

miopía /mio'pia/ *n. f.* myopia.

mira /'mira/ *n. f.* gunsight.

mirada /mi'raða/ *n. f.* look; gaze, glance.

miramiento /mira'miento/ *n. m.* consideration; respect.

mirar /mi'rar/ *v.* look, look at; watch. **m. a,** face.

miríada /mi'riaða/ *n. f.* myriad.

mirlo /'mirlo/ *n. m.* blackbird.

mirón /mi'ron/ **-ona** *n.* bystander, observer.

mirra /'mirra/ *n. f.* myrrh.

mirto /'mirto/ *n. m.* myrtle.

misa /'misa/ *n. f.* mass, church service.

misceláneo /misθe'laneo; misse'laneo/ *a.* miscellaneous.

miserable /mise'raβle/ *a.* miserable, wretched.

miseria /mi'seria/ *n. f.* misery.

misericordia /miseri'korðia/ *n. f.* mercy.

misericordioso /miserikor'ðioso/ *a.* merciful.

misión /mi'sion/ *n. f.* assignment; mission.

misionario /misio'nario/ **-ria, misionero** **-ra** *n.* missionary.

mismo /'mismo/ *a. & pron.* **1.** same; -self, -selves. —*adv.* **2.** right, exactly.

misterio /mis'terio/ *n. m.* mystery.

misterioso /miste'rioso/ *a.* mysterious, weird.

místico /'mistiko/ **-ca** *a. & n.* mystical, mystic.

mitad /mi'tað/ *n. f.* half.

mítico /'mitiko/ *a.* mythical.

mitigar /miti'gar/ *v.* mitigate.

mitin /'mitin/ *n. m.* meeting; rally.

mito /'mito/ *n. m.* myth.

mitón /mi'ton/ *n. m.* mitten.

mitra /'mitra/ *n. f.* miter (bishop's).

mixto /'miksto/ *a.* mixed.

mixtura /miks'tura/ *n. f.* mixture.

mobiliario /moβi'liario/ *n. m.* household goods.

mocasín /moka'sin/ *n. m.* moccasin.

mocedad /moθe'ðað; mose'ðað/ *n. f.* youthfulness.

mochila /mo'tʃila/ *n. f.* knapsack, backpack.

mocho /'motʃo/ a. cropped, trimmed, shorn.

moción /mo'θion; mo'sion/ n. f. motion.

mocoso /mo'koso/ -sa n. brat.

moda /'moða/ n. f. mode, fashion, style.

modales /mo'ðales/ n. m.pl. manners.

modelo /mo'ðelo/ n. m. model, pattern.

módem /'moðem/ n. m. modem.

moderación /moðera'θion; moðerasion/ n. f. moderation.

moderado /moðe'raðo/ a. moderate. —**moderar,** v.

modernizar /moðerni'θar; moðerni'sar/ v. modernize.

moderno /mo'ðerno/ a. modern.

modestia /mo'ðestia/ n. f. modesty.

modesto /mo'ðesto/ a. modest.

módico /'moðiko/ a. reasonable, moderate.

modificación /moðifi'kaθion; moðifika'sion/ n. f. modification.

modificar /moðifi'kar/ v. modify.

modismo /mo'ðismo/ n. m. Gram. idiom.

modista /mo'ðista/ n. f. dressmaker; milliner.

modo /'moðo/ n. m. way, means.

modular /moðu'lar/ v. modulate.

mofarse /mo'farse/ v. scoff, sneer.

mofletudo /mofle'tuðo/ a. fat-cheeked.

mohín /mo'in/ n. m. grimace.

moho /'moo/ n. m. mold, mildew.

mohoso /mo'oso/ a. moldy.

mojar /mo'har/ v. wet.

mojón /mo'hon/ n. m. landmark; heap.

molde /'molde/ n. m. mold; form, mold.

molécula /mo'lekula/ n. f. molecule.

moler /mo'ler/ v. grind, mill.

molestar /moles'tar/ v. molest, bother, disturb, annoy, trouble.

molestia /mo'lestia/ n. f. bother, annoyance, trouble; hassle.

molesto /mo'lesto/ a. bothersome; annoyed; uncomfortable.

molicie /mo'liθie; mo'lisie/ n. f. softness.

molinero /moli'nero/ n. m. miller.

molino /mo'lino/ n. m. mill. **m. de viento,** windmill.

mollera /mo'ʎera; mo'yera/ n. f. top of the head.

molusco /mo'lusko/ n. m. mollusk.

momentáneo /momen'taneo/ a. momentary.

momento /mo'mento/ n. m. moment.

mona /'mona/ n. f. female monkey.

monarca /mo'narka/ n. m. & f. monarch.

monarquía /monar'kia/ n. f. monarchy.

monarquista /monar'kista/ n. & a. monarchist.

monasterio /mona'sterio/ n. m. monastery.

mondadientes /monda'ðientes/ n. m. toothpick.

moneda /mo'neða/ n. f. coin; money.

monetario /mone'tario/ a. monetary.

monición /moni'θion; moni'sion/ n. m. warning.

monigote /moni'gote/ n. m. puppet.

monja /'monha/ n. f. nun.

monje /'monhe/ n. m. monk.

mono /'mono/ -na a. 1. Colloq. cute. —n. 2. m. & f. monkey.

monólogo /mo'nologo/ n. m. monologue.

monopatín /monopa'tin/ n. m. skateboard.

monopolio /mono'polio/ n. m. monopoly.

monopolizar /monopoli'θar; monopoli'sar/ v. monopolize.

monosílabo /mono'silaβo/ n. m. monosyllable.

monotonía /monoto'nia/ n. f. monotony.

monótono /mo'notono/ a. monotonous, dreary.

monstruo /'monstruo/ n. m. monster.

monstruosidad /monstruosi'ðað/ n. f. monstrosity.

monstruoso /mons'truoso/ a. monstrous.

monta /'monta/ n. f. amount; price.

montaña /mon'taɲa/ n. f. mountain.

montañoso /monta'ɲoso/ a. mountainous.

montar /mon'tar/ v. mount, climb; amount; Mech. assemble. **m. a caballo,** ride horseback.

montaraz /monta'raθ; monta'ras/ a. wild, barbaric.

monte /'monte/ n. m. mountain; forest.

montón /mon'ton/ n. m. heap, pile.

montuoso /mon'tuoso/ a. mountainous.

montura /mon'tura/ n. f. mount; saddle.

monumental /monumen'tal/ a. monumental.

monumento /monu'mento/ n. m. monument.

mora /'mora/ n. f. blackberry.

morada /mo'raða/ n. f. residence, dwelling.

morado /mo'raðo/ a. purple.

moral /mo'ral/ a. 1. moral. —n. 2. f. morale.

moraleja /mora'leha/ n. f. moral.

moralidad /morali'ðað/ n. f. morality, morals.

moralista /mora'lista/ n. m. & f. moralist.

morar /mo'rar/ v. dwell, live, reside.

mórbido /'morβiðo/ a. morbid.

mordaz /mor'ðaθ; mor'ðas/ a. caustic; sarcastic.

mordedura /morðe'ðura/ n. f. bite.

morder /mor'ðer/ v. bite.

moreno /mo'reno/ -na a. & n. brown; dark-skinned; dark-haired, brunette.

morfina /mor'fina/ n. f. morphine.

moribundo /mori'βundo/ a. dying.

morir /mo'rir/ v. die.

morisco /mo'risko/ **-ca, moro -ra** a. & n. Moorish; Moor.

morriña /mo'rriɲa/ n. f. sadness.

morro /'morro/ n. m. bluff; snout.

mortaja /mor'taha/ n. f. shroud.

mortal /mor'tal/ a. & n. mortal.

mortalidad /mortali'ðað/ n. f. mortality.

mortero /mor'tero/ n. m. mortar.

mortífero /mor'tifero/ a. fatal, deadly.

mortificar /mortifi'kar/ v. mortify.

mortuorio /mor'tuorio/ a. funereal.

mosaico /mo'saiko/ a. & m. mosaic.

mosca /'moska/ n. f. fly.

mosquito /mos'kito/ n. m. mosquito.

mostacho /mos'tatʃo/ n. m. mustache.

mostaza /mos'taθa/ mos'tasa/ n. f. mustard.

mostrador /mostra'ðor/ n. m. counter; showcase.

mostrar /mos'trar/ v. show, display.

mote /'mote/ n. m. nickname; alias.

motel /mo'tel/ n. m. motel.

motín /mo'tin/ n. m. mutiny; riot.

motivo /mo'tiβo/ n. m. motive, reason.

motocicleta /motoθi'kleta; motosi'kleta/ n. f. motorcycle.

motociclista /motoθi'klista; motosi'klista/ n. m. & f. motorcyclist.

motor /mo'tor/ n. m. motor.

motorista /moto'rista/ n. m. & f. motorist.

movedizo /moβe'ðiθo; moβe'ðiso/ a. movable; shaky.

mover /mo'βer/ v. move; stir.

movible /mo'βiβle/ a. movable.

móvil /'moβil/ a. mobile.

movilización /moβiliθa'θion; moβilisa'sion/ n. f. mobilization.

movilizar /moβili'θar; moβili'sar/ v. mobilize.

movimiento /moβi'miento/ n. m. movement, motion.

mozo /'moθo; 'moso/ n. m. boy; servant, waiter, porter.

muaré /mua're/ n. m. moiré.

muchacha /mu'tʃatʃa/ n. f. girl, youngster; maid (servant).

muchachez /mutʃa'tʃeθ; mutʃa'tʃes/ n. m. boyhood, girlhood.

muchacho /mu'tʃatʃo/ n. m. boy; youngster.

muchedumbre /mutʃe'ðumbre/ n. f. crowd, mob.

mucho /'mutʃo/ a. **1.** much, many. —adv. **2.** much.

mucoso /mu'koso/ a. mucous.

muda /'muða/ n. f. change.

mudanza /mu'ðanθa; mu'ðansa/ n. f. change; change of residence.

mudar /mu'ðar/ v. change, shift.

mudarse /mu'ðarse/ v. change residence, move.

mudo /'muðo/ **-da** a. & n. mute.

mueble /'mueβle/ n. m. piece of furniture; (pl.) furniture.

mueca /'mueka/ n. f. grimace.

muela /'muela/ n. f. (back) tooth.

muelle /'mueʎe; 'mueye/ n. m. pier, wharf; Mech. spring.

muerte /'muerte/ n. f. death.

muerto /'muerto/ **-ta** a. **1.** dead. —n. **2.** dead person.

muesca /'mueska/ n. f. notch; groove.

muestra /'muestra/ n. f. sample, specimen; sign.

mugido /mu'hiðo/ n. m. lowing; mooing.

mugir /mu'hir/ v. low, moo.

mugre /'mugre/ n. f. filth, dirt.

mugriento /mu'griento/ a. dirty.

mujer /mu'her/ f. woman; wife. **m. de la limpieza,** cleaning lady, charwoman.

mujeril /muhe'ril/ a. womanly, feminine.

mula /'mula/ n. f. mule.

mulato /mu'lato/ **-ta** a. & n. mulatto.

muleta /mu'leta/ n. f. crutch; prop.

mulo /'mulo/ **-la** n. mule.

multa /'multa/ n. f. fine, penalty.

multicolor /multiko'lor/ a. many-colored.

multinacional /multinaθio'nal; multinasio'nal/ a. multinational.

múltiple /'multiple/ a. multiple.

multiplicación /multiplika'θion; multiplika'sion/ n. f. multiplication.

multiplicar /multipli'kar/ v. multiply.

multiplicidad /multipliθi'ðað; multiplisi'ðað/ n. f. multiplicity.

multitud /multi'tuð/ n. f. multitude, crowd.

mundanal /munda'nal/ a. worldly.

mundano /mun'dano/ a. worldly, mundane.

mundial /mun'dial/ a. worldwide; (of the) world.

mundo /'mundo/ n. m. world.

munición /muni'θion; muni'sion/ n. f. ammunition.

municipal /muniθi'pal; munisi'pal/ a. municipal.

municipio /muni'θipio; muni'sipio/ n. m. city hall.

muñeca /mu'ɲeka/ n. f. doll; wrist.

muñeco /mu'ɲeko/ n. m. doll; puppet.

mural /mu'ral/ a. & m. mural.

muralla /mu'raʎa; mu'raya/ n. f. wall.

murciélago /mur'θielago; mur'sielago/ n. m. bat.

murga /'murga/ n. f. musical band.

murmullo /mur'muʎo; mur'muyo/ n. m. murmur; rustle.

murmurar /murmu'rar/ v. murmur; rustle; grumble.

musa /'musa/ *n. f.* muse.
muscular /musku'lar/ *a.* muscular.
músculo /'muskulo/ *n. m.* muscle.
muselina /muse'lina/ *n. f.* muslin.
museo /mu'seo/ *n. m.* museum.
música /'musika/ *n. f.* music.
musical /musi'kal/ *a.* musical.
músico /'musiko/ **-ca** *a. & n.* musical; musician.
muslo /'muslo/ *n. m.* thigh.
mustio /'mustio/ *a.* sad.

musulmano /musul'mano/ **-na** *a. & n.* Muslim.
muta /'muta/ *n. f.* pack of hounds.
mutabilidad /mutaβili'ðað/ *n. f.* mutability.
mutación /muta'θion; muta'sion/ *n. f.* mutation.
mutilación /mutila'θion; mutila'sion/ *n. f.* mutilation.
mutilar /muti'lar/ *v.* mutilate; mangle.
mutuo /'mutuo/ *a.* mutual.
muy /'mui/ *adv.* very.

N Ñ

---

nabo /'naβo/ *n. m.* turnip.
nácar /'nakar/ *n. m.* mother-of-pearl.
nacarado /naka'raðo, na'kareo/ *a.* pearly.
nacer /na'θer; na'ser/ *v.* be born.
naciente /na'θiente; na'siente/ *a.* rising; nascent.
nacimiento /naθi'miento; nasi'miento/ *n. m.* birth.
nación /na'θion; na'sion/ *n. f.* nation.
nacional /naθio'nal; nasio'nal/ *a.* national.
nacionalidad /naθionali'ðað; nasionali'ðað/ *n. f.* nationality.
nacionalismo /naθiona'lismo; nasiona'lismo/ *n. m.* nationalism.
nacionalista /naθiona'lista; nasiona'lista/ *n. & a.* nationalist.
nacionalización /naθionaliθa'θion; nasionalisa'sion/ *n. f.* nationalization.
nacionalizar /naθionali'θar; nasionali'sar/ *v.* nationalize.
Naciones Unidas /na'θiones u'niðas; na'siones u'niðas/ *n. f.pl.* United Nations.
nada /'naða/ *pron.* **1.** nothing; anything. **de n.**, you're welcome. —*adv.* **2.** at all.
nadador /naða'ðor/ **-ra** *n.* swimmer.
nadar /na'ðar/ *v.* swim.
nadie /'naðie/ *pron.* no one, nobody; anyone, anybody.
nafta /'nafta/ *n. f.* naphtha.
naipe /'naipe/ *n. m* (playing) card.
naranja /na'ranha/ *n. f.* orange.
naranjada /naran'haða/ *n. f.* orangeade.
naranjo /na'ranho/ *n. m.* orange tree.
narciso /nar'θiso; nar'siso/ *n. m.* daffodil; narcissus.
narcótico /nar'kotiko/ *a. & m.* narcotic.
nardo /'narðo/ *n. m.* spikenard.
nariz /na'riθ; na'ris/ *n. f.* nose; (*pl.*) nostrils.
narración /narra'θion; narra'sion/ *n. f.* account.
narrador /narra'ðor/ **-ra** *n.* narrator.
narrar /na'rrar/ *v.* narrate.

narrativa /narra'tiβa/ *n. f.* narrative.
nata /'nata/ *n. f.* cream.
nata batida /'nata ba'tiða/ whipped cream.
natación /nata'θion; nata'sion/ *n. f.* swimming.
natal /na'tal/ *a.* native; natal.
natalicio /nata'liθio; nata'lisio/ *n. m.* birthday.
natalidad /natali'ðað/ *n. f.* birth rate.
natillas /na'tiλas; na'tiyas/ *n. f.pl.* custard.
nativo /na'tiβo/ *a.* native; innate.
natural /natu'ral/ *a.* **1.** natural. —*n.* **2.** *m. & f.* native. **3.** *m.* nature, disposition.
naturaleza /natura'leθa; natura'lesa/ *n. f.* nature.
naturalidad /naturali'ðað/ *n. f.* naturalness; nationality.
naturalista /natura'lista/ *a. & n.* naturalistic; naturalist.
naturalización /naturaliθa'θion; naturalisa'sion/ *n. f.* naturalization.
naturalizar /naturali'θar; naturali'sar/ *v.* naturalize.
naufragar /naufra'gar/ *v.* be shipwrecked; fail.
naufragio /nau'frahio/ *n. m.* shipwreck; disaster.
náufrago /'naufrago/ **-ga** *a. & n.* shipwrecked (person).
náusea /'nausea/ *n. f.* nausea.
nausear /nause'ar/ *v.* feel nauseous.
náutico /'nautiko/ *a.* nautical.
navaja /na'βaha/ *n. f.* razor; pen knife.
naval /na'βal/ *a.* naval.
navasca /na'βaska/ *n. f.* blizzard, snow-storm.
nave /'naβe/ *n. f.* ship.
nave espacial /'naβe espa'θial; 'naβe es'pasial/ spaceship.
navegable /naβe'gaβle/ *a.* navigable.
navegación /naβega'θion; naβega'sion/ *n. f.* navigation.
navegador /naβega'ðor/ **-ra** *n.* navigator.

navegante /naβe'gante/ n. m. & f. navigator.

navegar /naβe'gar/ v. sail; navigate.

Navidad /naβi'ðað/ n. f. Christmas.

navío /na'βio/ n. m. ship.

neblina /ne'βlina/ n. f. mist, fog.

nebuloso /neβu'loso/ a. misty; nebulous.

necedad /neθe'ðað/ nese'ðað/ n. f. stupidity; nonsense.

necesario /neθe'sario/ nese'sario/ a. necessary.

necesidad /neθesi'ðað/ nesesi'ðað/ n. f. necessity, need, want.

necesitado /neθesi'taðo/ nesesi'taðo/ a. needy, poor.

necesitar /neθesi'tar/ nesesi'tar/ v. need.

necio /'neθio/ 'nesio/ **-cia** a. **1.** stupid, silly. —n. **2.** fool.

néctar /'nektar/ n. m. nectar.

nectarina /nekta'rina/ n. f. nectarine.

nefando /ne'fando/ a. nefarious.

nefasto /ne'fasto/ a. unlucky, ill-fated.

negable /ne'gaβle/ a. deniable.

negación /nega'θion/ nega'sion/ n. f. denial, negation.

negar /ne'gar/ v. deny.

negarse /ne'garse/ v. refuse, decline.

negativa /nega'tiβa/ n. f. negative, refusal.

negativamente /negatiβa'mente/ adv. negatively.

negativo /nega'tiβo/ a. negative.

negligencia /negli'henθia/ negli'hensia/ n. f. negligence, neglect. ,

negligente /negli'hente/ a. negligent.

negociación /negoθia'θion/ negosia'sion/ n. f. negotiation, deal.

negociador /negoθia'ðor/ negosia'ðor/ **-ra** n. negotiator.

negociante /nego'θiante/ nego'siante/ **-ta** n. businessperson.

negociar /nego'θiar/ nego'siar/ v. negotiate, trade.

negocio /ne'goθio/ ne'gosio/ n. m. trade; business.

negro /'negro/ **-gra** a. **1.** black. —n. **2.** m. Black.

nene /'nene/ **-na** n. baby.

neo /'neo/ **neón** n. m. neon.

nervio /'nerβio/ n. m. nerve.

nerviosamente /nerβiosa'mente/ adv. nervously.

nervioso /ner'βioso/ a. nervous.

nesciencia /nesθien'θia/ nessien'sia/ n. f. ignorance.

nesciente /nes'θiente/ nes'siente/ a. ignorant.

neto /'neto/ a. net.

neumático /neu'matiko/ a. **1.** pneumatic. —n. **2.** m. (pneumatic) tire.

neumático de recambio /neu'matiko de rre'kambio/ spare tire.

neumonía /neumo'nia/ n. f. pneumonia.

neurótico /neu'rotiko/ a. neurotic.

neutral /neu'tral/ a. neutral.

neutralidad /neutrali'ðað/ n. f. neutrality.

neutro /'neutro/ a. neuter; neutral.

neutrón /neu'tron/ n. m. neutron.

nevada /ne'βaða/ n. f. snowfall.

nevado /ne'βaðo/ a. snow-white; snow-capped.

nevar /ne'βar/ v. snow.

nevera /ne'βera/ n. f. icebox.

nevoso /ne'βoso/ a. snowy.

ni /ni/ conj. **1.** nor. **ni... ni**, neither... nor. —adv. **2.** not even.

nicho /'nitʃo/ n. m. recess; niche.

nido /'niðo/ n. m. nest.

niebla /'nieβla/ n. f. fog; mist.

nieto /'nieto/ **-ta** n. grandchild.

nieve /'nieβe/ n. f. snow.

nilón /ni'lon/ n. m. nylon.

nimio /'nimio/ adj. stingy.

ninfa /'ninfa/ n. f. nymph.

ningún /nin'gun/ **-no -na** a. & pron. no, none, neither (one); any, either (one).

niñera /ni'ɲera/ n. f. nursemaid, nanny.

niñez /ni'ɲeθ/ ni'ɲes/ n. f. childhood.

niño /'niɲo/ **-ña 1.** a. **1.** young; childish; childlike. —n. **2.** child.

níquel /'nikel/ n. m. nickel.

niquelado /nike'laðo/ a. nickel-plated.

nítido /'nitiðo/ a. neat, clean, bright.

nitrato /ni'trato/ n. m. nitrate.

nitro /'nitro/ n. m. niter.

nitrógeno /ni'troheno/ n. m. nitrogen.

nivel /ni'βel/ n. m. level; grade. —**nivelar**, v.

no /no/ adv. **1.** not. **no más**, only. —interj. **2.** no.

noble /'noβle/ a. & m. noble; nobleman.

nobleza /no'βleθa/ no'βlesa/ n. f. nobility; nobleness.

noche /'notʃe/ n. f. night; evening.

Nochebuena /notʃe'βuena/ n. f. Christmas Eve.

noción /no'θion/ no'sion/ n. f. notion, idea.

nocivo /no'θiβo/ no'siβo/ a. harmful.

noctiluca /nokti'luka/ n. f. glowworm.

nocturno /nok'turno/ a. nocturnal.

nodriza /no'ðriθa/ no'ðrisa/ n. f. wet nurse.

no fumador /no fuma'ðor/ **-ra** n. m. & f. nonsmoker.

nogal /no'gal/ n. m. walnut.

nombradía /nom'βraðia/ n. f. fame.

nombramiento /nombra'miento/ n. m. appointment, nomination.

nombrar /nom'βrar/ v. name, appoint, nominate; mention.

nombre /'nombre/ n. m. name; noun.

nombre y apellidos /'nombre i ape'ʎiðos: 'nombre i upe'yiðos/ (person's) full name.

nómina /'nomina/ n. f. list; payroll.

nominación /nomina'θion; nomina'sion/ n. f. nomination.

nominal /nomi'nal/ a. nominal.

nominar /nomi'nar/ v. nominate.

non /non/ a. uneven, odd.

nonada /no'naða/ n. f. trifle.

nordeste /nor'ðeste/ n. m. northeast.

nórdico /'norðiko/ a. Nordic; northerly.

norma /'norma/ n. f. norm, standard.

normal /nor'mal/ a. normal, standard.

normalidad /normali'ðað/ n. f. normality.

normalizar /normali'θar; normali'sar/ v. normalize; standardize.

noroeste /noro'este/ n. m. northwest.

norte /'norte/ n. m. north.

norteamericano /norteameri'kano/ **-na** a. & n. North American.

Noruega /no'ruega/ n. f. Norway.

noruego /no'ruego/ **-ga** a. & n. Norwegian.

nos /nos/ pron. us; ourselves.

nosotros /no'sotros, no'sotras/ **-as** pron. we, us; ourselves.

nostalgia /nos'talhia/ n. f. nostalgia, homesickness.

nostálgico /nos'talhiko/ a. nostalgic.

nota /'nota/ n. f. note; grade, mark.

notable /no'taβle/ a. notable, remarkable.

notación /nota'θion; nota'sion/ n. f. notation; note.

notar /no'tar/ v. note, notice.

notario /no'tario/ **-ria** n. notary.

noticia /no'tiθia; no'tisia/ n. f. notice; piece of news; (pl.) news.

noticia de última hora /no'tiθia de 'ultima 'ora; no'tisia de 'ultima 'ora/ news flash.

notificación /notifika'θion; notifika'sion/ n. f. notification.

notificación de reclutamiento /notifika'θion de rrekluta'miento; notifika'sion de rrekluta'miento/ draft notice.

notificar /notifi'kar/ v. notify.

notorio /no'torio/ a. well-known.

novato /no'βato/ **-ta** n. novice.

novecientos /noβe'θientos; noβe'sientos/ a. & pron. nine hundred.

novedad /noβe'ðað/ n. f. novelty; piece of news.

novel /no'βel/ a. new; inexperienced.

novela /no'βela/ n. f. novel.

novelista /noβe'lista/ n. m. & f. novelist.

novena /no'βena/ n. f. novena.

noveno /no'βeno/ a. ninth.

noventa /no'βenta/ a. & pron. ninety.

novia /'noβia/ n. f. bride; sweetheart; fiancée.

noviazgo /no'βiaθgo; no'βiasgo/ n. m. engagement.

novicio /no'βiθio; no'βisio/ **-cia** n. novice, beginner.

noviembre /no'βiembre/ n. m. November.

novilla /no'βiʎa; no'βiya/ n. f. heifer.

novio /'noβio/ n. m. bridegroom; sweetheart; fiancé.

nube /'nuβe/ n. f. cloud.

núbil /'nuβil/ a. marriageable.

nublado /nu'βlaðo/ a. cloudy.

nuclear /nukle'ar/ a. nuclear.

núcleo /'nukleo/ n. m. nucleus.

nudo /'nuðo/ n. m. knot.

nuera /'nuera/ n. f. daughter-in-law.

nuestro /'nuestro/ a. our, ours.

nueva /'nueβa/ n. f. news.

nueve /'nueβe/ a. & pron. nine.

nuevo /'nueβo/ a. new. **de n.,** again, anew.

nuez /nueθ; nues/ n. f. nut; walnut.

nulidad /nuli'ðað/ n. f. nonentity; nullity.

nulo /'nulo/ a. null, void.

numeración /numera'θion; numera'sion/ n. f. numeration.

numerar /nume'rar/ v. number.

numérico /nu'meriko/ a. numerical.

número /'numero/ n. m. number; size (of shoe, etc.) **n. impar,** odd number. **n. par,** even number.

numeroso /nume'roso/ a. numerous.

numismática /numis'matika/ n. f. numismatics.

nunca /'nunka/ adv. never; ever.

nupcial /nup'θial; nup'sial/ a. nuptial.

nupcias /'nupθias; 'nupsias/ n. f.pl. nuptials, wedding.

nutrición /nutri'θion; nutri'sion/ n. f. nutrition.

nutrimento /nutri'mento/ n. m. nourishment.

nutrir /nu'trir/ v. nourish.

nutritivo /nutri'tiβo/ a. nutritious.

nylon /'nilon/ n. m. nylon.

ñame /'ɲame/ n. m. yam.

ñapa /'ɲapa/ n. f. something extra.

ñoñeria /ɲoɲe'ria/ n. f. dotage.

ñoño /'ɲoɲo/ a. feeble-minded, senile.

O

o /o/ *conj.* or. **o... o,** either... or.

oasis /o'asis/ *n. m.* oasis.

obedecer /oβeðe'θer; oβeðe'ser/ *v.* obey, mind.

obediencia /oβe'ðienθia; oβe'ðiensia/ *n. f* obedience.

obediente /oβe'ðiente/ *a.* obedient.

obelisco /oβe'lisko/ *n. m.* obelisk.

obertura /oβer'tura/ *n. f.* overture.

obeso /o'βeso/ *a.* obese.

obispo /o'βispo/ *n. m.* bishop.

obituario /oβi'tuario/ *n. m.* obituary.

objeción /oβhe'θion; oβhe'sion/ *n. f.* objection.

objetivo /oβhe'tiβo/ *a. & m.* objective.

objeto /oβ'heto/ *n. m.* object. **—objetar,** *v.*

objetor de conciencia /oβhe'tor de kon'θienθia; oβhe'tor de kon'siensia/ *n. m* conscientious objector.

oblicuo /o'βlikuo/ *a.* oblique.

obligación /oβliga'θion; oβliga'sion/ *n. f* obligation, duty.

obligar /oβli'gar/ *v.* oblige, require, compel; obligate.

obligatorio /oβliga'torio/ *a.* obligatory, compulsory.

oblongo /o'βloŋgo/ *a.* oblong.

oboe /o'βoe/ *n. m.* oboe.

obra /'oβra/ *n. f.* work. **—obrar,** *v.*

obrero /o'βrero/ **-ra** *n.* worker, laborer.

obscenidad /oβsθeni'ðað; oβsseni'ðað/ *n. f.* obscenity.

obsceno /oβs'θeno; oβs'seno/ *a.* obscene.

obscurecer /oβskure'θer; oβskure'ser/ *v.* obscure; darken.

obscuridad /oβskuri'ðað/ *n. f.* obscurity; darkness.

obscuro /oβs'kuro/ *a.* obscure; dark.

obsequiar /oβse'kiar/ *v.* court; make presents to, fete.

obsequio /oβ'sekio/ *n. m.* obsequiousness; gift; attention.

observación /oβserβa'θion; oβserβa'sion/ *f.* observation.

observador /oβserβa'ðor/ **-ra** *n.* observer.

observancia /oβser'βanθia; oβser'βansia/ *f.* observance.

observar /oβser'βar/ *v.* observe, watch.

observatorio /oβserβa'torio/ *n. m.* observatory.

obsesión /oβse'sion/ *n. f.* obsession.

obstáculo /oβs'takulo/ *n. m.* obstacle.

obstante /oβs'tante/ *adv.* **no o.,** however, yet, nevertheless.

obstar /oβs'tar/ *v.* hinder, obstruct.

obstetricia /oβste'triθia; oβste'trisia/ *n. f.* obstetrics.

obstinación /oβstina'θion; oβstina'sion/ *n.* obstinacy.

obstinado /oβsti'naðo/ *a.* obstinate, stubborn.

obstinarse /oβsti'narse/ *v.* persist, insist.

obstrucción /oβstruk'θion; oβstruk'sion/ *n. f.* obstruction.

obstruir /oβs'truir/ *v.* obstruct, clog, block.

obtener /oβte'ner/ *v.* obtain, get, secure.

obtuso /oβ'tuso/ *a.* obtuse.

obvio /'oββio/ *a.* obvious.

ocasión /oka'sion/ *n. f.* occasion; opportunity, chance. **de o.,** secondhand.

ocasional /okasio'nal/ *a.* occasional.

ocasionalmente /okasio'nal'mente/ *adv.* occasionally.

ocasionar /okasio'nar/ *v.* cause, occasion.

occidental /okθiðen'tal; oksiðen'tal/ *a.* western.

occidente /okθi'ðente; oksi'ðente/ *n. m.* west.

océano /o'θeano; o'seano/ *n. m.* ocean.

Océano Atlántico /o'θeano a'tlantiko; o'seano a'tlantiko/ Atlantic Ocean.

Océano Pacífico /o'θeano pa'θifiko; o'seano pa'sifiko/ Pacific Ocean.

ocelote /oθe'lote; ose'lote/ *n. m.* ocelot.

ochenta /o'tʃenta/ *a. & pron.* eighty.

ocho /'otʃo/ *a. & pron.* eight.

ochocientos /otʃo'θientos; otʃo'sientos/ *a. & pron.* eight hundred.

ocio /'oθio; 'osio/ *n. m.* idleness, leisure.

ociosidad /oθiosi'ðað; osiosi'ðað/ *n. f.* idleness, laziness.

ocioso /o'θioso; o'sioso/ *a.* idle, lazy.

ocre /'okre/ *n. m.* ochre.

octagonal /oktago'nal/ *a.* octagonal.

octava /ok'taβa/ *n. f.* octave.

octavo /ok'taβo/ *a.* eighth.

octubre /ok'tuβre/ *n. m.* October.

oculista /oku'lista/ *n. m. & f.* oculist.

ocultación /okulta'θion; okulta'sion/ *n. f.* concealment.

ocultar /okul'tar/ *v.* hide, conceal.

oculto /o'kulto/ *a.* hidden.

ocupación /okupa'θion; okupa'sion/ *n. f.* occupation.

ocupado /oku'paðo/ *a.* occupied; busy.

ocupante /oku'pante/ *n. m. & f.* occupant.

ocupar /oku'par/ *v.* occupy.

ocuparse de /oku'parse de/ *v.* take care of, take charge of.

ocurrencia /oku'rrenθia; oku'rrensia/ *n. f.* occurrence; witticism.

ocurrente /oku'rrente/ *a.* witty.

ocurrir /oku'rrir/ *v.* occur, happen.

oda /'oða/ *n. f.* ode.

odio /'oðio/ *n. m.* hate. —**odiar,** *v.*

odiosidad /oðiosi'ðað/ *n. f.* odiousness; hatred.

odioso /o'ðioso/ *a.* obnoxious, odious.

odisea /oði'sea/ *n. f.* odyssey.

OEA, *abbr.* (Organización de los Estados Americanos). OAS (**Organization of American States**).

oeste /o'este/ *n. m.* west.

ofender /ofen'der/ *v.* offend, wrong.

ofenderse /ofen'derse/ *v.* be offended, take offense.

ofensa /o'fensa/ *n. f.* offense.

ofensiva /ofen'siβa/ *n. f.* offensive.

ofensivo /ofen'siβo/ *a.* offensive.

ofensor /ofen'sor/ **-ra** *n.* offender.

oferta /o'ferta/ *n. f.* offer, proposal.

ofertorio /ofer'torio/ *n. m.* offertory.

oficial /ofi'θial; ofi'sial/ *a. & m.* official; officer.

oficialmente /ofiθial'mente; ofisial'mente/ *adv.* officially.

oficiar /ofi'θiar; ofi'siar/ *v.* officiate.

oficina /ofi'θina; ofi'sina/ *n. f.* office.

oficio /ofi'θio; ofi'sio/ *n. m.* office; trade; church service.

oficioso /ofi'θioso; ofi'sioso/ *a.* officious.

ofrecer /ofre'θer; ofre'ser/ *v.* offer.

ofrecimiento /ofreθi'miento; ofresi'miento/ *n. m.* offer, offering. **o. de presentación,** introductory offer.

ofrenda /o'frenda/ *n. f.* offering.

oftalmía /oftal'mia/ *n. f.* ophthalmia.

ofuscamiento /ofuska'miento/ *n. m.* obfuscation; bewilderment.

ofuscar /ofus'kar/ *v.* obfuscate; bewilder.

ogro /'ogro/ *n. m.* ogre.

oído /o'iðo/ *n. m.* ear; hearing.

oír /o'ir/ *v.* hear; listen.

ojal /o'hal/ *n. m.* buttonhole.

ojalá /oha'la/ *interj.* expressing wish or hope. **o. que...** would that...

ojeada /ohe'aða/ *n. f.* glance; peep; look.

ojear /ohe'ar/ *v.* eye, look at, glance at, stare at.

ojeriza /ohe'riθa; ohe'risa/ *n. f.* spite; grudge.

ojiva /o'hiβa/ *n. f.* pointed arch, ogive.

ojo /'oho/ *n. m.* eye. **¡Ojo!** Look out!

ola /'ola/ *n. f.* wave.

olaje /o'lahe/ *n. m.* surge of waves.

oleada /ole'aða/ *n. f.* swell.

oleo /'oleo/ *n. m.* oil; holy oil; extreme unction.

oleoducto /oleo'ðukto/ *n. m.* pipeline.

oleomargarina /oleomarga'rina/ *n. f.* oleomargarine.

oleoso /ole'oso/ *a.* oily.

oler /o'ler/ *v.* smell.

olfatear /olfate'ar/ *v.* smell.

olfato /ol'fato/ *n. m.* scent, smell.

oliva /o'liβa/ *n. f.* olive.

olivar /oli'βar/ *n. m.* olive grove.

olivo /o'liβo/ *n. m.* olive tree.

olla /'oʎa; 'oya/ *n. f.* pot, kettle. **o. podrida,** stew.

olmo /'olmo/ *n. m.* elm.

olor /o'lor/ *n. m.* odor, smell, scent.

oloroso /olo'roso/ *a.* fragrant, scented.

olvidadizo /olβiða'ðiθo; olβiða'ðiso/ *a.* forgetful.

olvidar /olβi'ðar/ *v.* forget.

olvido /ol'βiðo/ *n. m.* omission; forgetfulness.

ombligo /om'βligo/ *n. m.* navel.

ominar /omi'nar/ *v.* foretell.

ominoso /omi'noso/ *a.* ominous.

omisión /omi'sion/ *n. f.* omission.

omitir /omi'tir/ *v.* omit, leave out.

ómnibus /'omniβus/ *n. m.* bus.

omnipotencia /omnipo'tenθia; omnipo'tensia/ *n. f.* omnipotence.

omnipotente /omnipo'tente/ *a.* almighty.

omnipresencia /omnipre'senθia; omnipre'sensia/ *n. f.* omnipresence.

omnisciencia /omnis'θienθia; omnis'siensia/ *n. f.* omniscience.

omnívoro /om'niβoro/ *a.* omnivorous.

omóplato /omo'plato/ *n. m.* shoulder blade.

once /'onθe; 'onse/ *a. & pron.* eleven.

onda /'onda/ *n. f.* wave, ripple.

ondear /onde'ar/ *v.* ripple.

ondulación /ondula'θion; ondula'sion/ *n. f.* wave, undulation.

ondular /ondu'lar/ *v.* undulate, ripple.

onza /'onθa; 'onsa/ *n. f.* ounce.

opaco /o'pako/ *a.* opaque.

ópalo /'opalo/ *n. m.* opal.

opción /op'θion; op'sion/ *n. f.* option.

ópera /'opera/ *n. f.* opera.

operación /opera'θion; opera'sion/ *n. f.* operation.

operar /ope'rar/ *v.* operate; operate on.

operario /ope'rario/ **-ria** *n.* operator; (skilled) worker.

operarse /ope'rarse/ *v.* have an operation.

operativo /opera'tiβo/ *a.* operative.

opereta /ope'reta/ *n. f.* operetta.

opiato /o'piato/ *n. m.* opiate.

opinar /opi'nar/ *v.* opine.

opinión /opi'nion/ *n. f.* opinion, view.

opio /'opio/ *n. m.* opium.

oponer /opo'ner/ *v.* oppose.

Oporto /o'porto/ *n. m.* port (wine).

oportunidad /oportuni'ðað/ *n. f.* opportunity.

oportunismo /oportu'nismo/ *n. m.* opportunism.

oportunista /oportu'nista/ *n.* & *a.* opportunist.

oportuno /opor'tuno/ *a.* opportune, expedient.

oposición /oposi'θion; oposi'sion/ *n. f.* opposition.

opresión /opre'sion/ *n. f.* oppression.

opresivo /opre'siβo/ *a.* oppressive.

oprimir /opri'mir/ *v.* oppress.

oprobio /o'proβio/ *n. m.* infamy.

optar /op'tar/ *v.* select, choose.

óptica /'optika/ *n. f.* optics.

óptico /'optiko/ *a.* optic.

optimismo /opti'mismo/ *n. m.* optimism.

optimista /opti'mista/ *a.* & *n.* optimistic; optimist.

óptimo /'optimo/ *a.* best.

opuesto /o'puesto/ *a.* opposite; opposed.

opugnar /opug'nar/ *v.* attack.

opulencia /opu'lenθia; opu'lensia/ *n. f.* opulence, wealth.

opulento /opu'lento/ *a.* opulent, wealthy.

oración /ora'θion; ora'sion/ *n. f.* sentence; prayer; oration.

oráculo /o'rakulo/ *n. m.* oracle.

orador /ora'ðor/ **-ra** *n.* orator, speaker.

oral /o'ral/ *a.* oral.

orangután /oraŋgu'tan/ *n. m.* orangutan.

orar /o'rar/ *v.* pray.

oratoria /ora'toria/ *n. f.* oratory.

oratorio /ora'torio/ *a.* oratorical.

orbe /'orβe/ *n. m.* orb; globe.

órbita /'orβita/ *n. f.* orbit.

orden /'orðen/ *n. m. or f.* order.

ordenador /orðena'ðor/ *n. m.* computer; regulator.

ordenador de sobremesa /orðena'ðor de soβre'mesa/ desktop computer.

ordenador doméstico /orðena'ðor do'mestiko/ home computer.

ordenanza /orðe'nanθa; orðe'nansa/ *n. f.* ordinance.

ordenar /orðe'nar/ *v.* order; put in order; ordain.

ordeñar /orðe'ɲar/ *v.* milk.

ordinal /orði'nal/ *a.* & *m.* ordinal.

ordinario /orði'nario/ *a.* ordinary; common, usual.

oreja /o'reha/ *n. f.* ear.

orejera /ore'hera/ *n. f.* earmuff.

orfanato /orfa'nato/ *n. m.* orphanage.

organdí /organ'di/ *n. m.* organdy.

orgánico /or'ganiko/ *a.* organic.

organigrama /organi'grama/ *n. m.* flow chart.

organismo /orga'nismo/ *n. m.* organism.

organista /orga'nista/ *n. m.* & *f.* organist.

organización /organiθa'θion; organisa'sion/ *n. f.* organization.

organizar /organi'θar; organi'sar/ *v.* organize.

órgano /'organo/ *n. m.* organ.

orgía /or'hia/ *n. f.* orgy, revel.

orgullo /or'guʎo; or'guyo/ *n. m.* pride.

orgulloso /orgu'ʎoso; orgu'yoso/ *a.* proud.

orientación /orienta'θion; orienta'sion/ *n. f.* orientation.

oriental /orien'tal/ *a.* Oriental; eastern.

orientar /orien'tar/ *v.* orient.

oriente /o'riente/ *n. m.* orient, east.

orificación /orifika'θion; orifika'sion/ *n. f.* gold filling (for tooth).

origen /o'rihen/ *n. m.* origin; parentage, descent.

original /orihi'nal/ *a.* original.

originalidad /orihinali'ðað/ *n. f.* originality.

originalmente /orihinal'mente/ *adv.* originally.

originar /orihi'nar/ *v.* originate.

orilla /o'riʎa; o'riya/ *n. f.* shore; bank; edge.

orín /o'rin/ *n. m.* rust.

orina /o'rina/ *n. f.* urine.

orinar /ori'nar/ *v.* urinate.

orines /o'rines/ *n. m.pl.* urine.

oriol /o'riol/ *n. m.* oriole.

orla /'orla/ *n. f.* border; edging.

ornado /or'naðo/ *a.* ornate.

ornamentación /ornamenta'θion; ornamenta'sion/ *n. f.* ornamentation.

ornamento /orna'mento/ *n. m.* ornament. —**ornamentar,** *v.*

ornar /or'nar/ *v.* ornament, adorn.

oro /'oro/ *n. m.* gold.

oropel /oro'pel/ *n. m.* tinsel.

orquesta /or'kesta/ *n. f.* orchestra.

ortiga /or'tiga/ *n. f.* nettle.

ortodoxo /orto'ðokso/ *a.* orthodox.

ortografía /ortogra'fia/ *n. f.* orthography, spelling.

ortóptero /or'toptero/ *a.* orthopterous.

oruga /o'ruga/ *n. f.* caterpillar.

orzuelo /or'θuelo; or'suelo/ *n. m.* sty.

os /os/ *pron.* you (*pl.*); yourselves.

osadía /osa'ðia/ *n. f.* daring.

osar /o'sar/ *v.* dare.

oscilación /osθila'θion; ossila'sion/ *n. f.* oscillation.

oscilar /osθi'lar; ossi'lar/ *v.* oscillate, rock.

ósculo /'oskulo/ *n. m.* kiss.

oscurecer /oskure'θer; oskure'ser/ **oscuridad, oscuro** = obscur-.

oso /'oso/ **osa** *n.* bear.

oso de felpa /'oso de 'felpa/ teddy bear.

ostentación /ostenta'θion: ostenta'sion/ *n. f.* ostentation, showiness.

ostentar /osten'tar/ *v.* show off.

ostentoso /osten'toso/ *a.* ostentatious, flashy.

ostra /'ostra/ *n. f.* oyster.

ostracismo /ostra'θismo; ostra'sismo/ *n. m.* ostracism.

otalgia /o'talhia/ *n. f.* earache.

otero /o'tero/ *n. m.* hill, knoll.

otoño /o'toɲo/ *n. m.* autumn, fall.

otorgar /otor'gar/ *v.* grant, award.

otro /'otro/ *a. & pron.* other, another. **o. vez,** again. **el uno al o.,** one another, each other.

ovación /oβa'θion: oβa'sion/ *n. f.* ovation.

oval /o'βal/ **ovalado** *a.* oval.

óvalo /'oβalo/ *n. m.* oval.

ovario /o'βario/ *n. m.* ovary.

oveja /o'βeha/ *n. f.* sheep.

ovejero /oβe'hero/ *n. m.* sheep dog.

ovillo /o'βiʎo: o'βiyo/ *n. m.* ball of yarn.

OVNI /'oβni/ *abbr.* (objeto volador no identificado) UFO (unidentified flying object).

oxidación /oksiða'θion; oksiða'sion/ *n. f.* oxidation.

oxidar /oksi'ðar/ *v.* oxidize; rust.

óxido /'oksiðo/ *n. m.* oxide.

oxígeno /ok'siheno/ *n. m.* oxygen.

oyente /o'iente/ *n. m. & f.* hearer; (*pl.*) audience.

ozono /o'θono; o'sono/ *n. m.* ozone.

P

pabellón /paβe'ʎon: paβe'yon/ *n. m.* pavilion. **p. de deportes,** sports center.

pabilo /pa'βilo/ *n. m.* wick.

paciencia /pa'θienθia; pa'siensia/ *n. f.* patience.

paciente /pa'θiente; pa'siente/ *a. & n.* patient.

pacificar /paθifi'kar; pasifi'kar/ *v.* pacify.

pacífico /pa'θifiko; pa'sifiko/ *a.* pacific.

pacifismo /paθi'fismo: pasi'fismo/ *n. m.* pacifism.

pacifista /paθi'fista; pasi'fista/ *n. & a.* pacifist.

pacto /'pakto/ *n. m.* pact, treaty.

padecer /paðe'θer; paðe'ser/ *v.* suffer. **p. del corazón,** have heart trouble.

padrastro /pa'ðrastro/ *n. m.* stepfather.

padre /'paðre/ *n. m.* father; priest; (*pl.*) parents.

padrenuestro /paðre'nuestro/ *n. m.* paternoster, Lord's Prayer.

padrino /pa'ðrino/ *n. m.* godfather; sponsor.

paella /pa'eʎa; pa'eya/ *n. f.* dish of rice with meat or chicken.

paga /'paga/ *n. f.* pay, wages. **p. extra** bonus.

pagadero /paga'ðero/ *a.* payable.

pagador /paga'ðor/ **-ra** *n.* payer.

paganismo /paga'nismo/ *n. m.* paganism.

pagano /pa'gano/ **-na** *a. & n.* heathen, pagan.

pagar /pa'gar/ *v.* pay, pay for. **p. en metálico,** pay cash.

página /'pahina/ *n. f.* page.

pago /'pago/ *n. m.* pay, payment.

país /pa'is/ *n. m.* country, nation.

paisaje /pai'sahe/ *n. m.* landscape, scenery, countryside.

paisano /pai'sano/ **-na** *n.* countryman; compatriot; civilian.

paja /'paha/ *n. f.* straw.

pajar /pa'har/ *n. m.* barn.

pajarita /paha'rita/ *n. f.* bow tie.

pájaro /'paharo/ *n. m.* bird.

paje /'pahe/ *n. m.* page (person).

pala /'pala/ *n. f.* shovel, spade.

palabra /pa'laβra/ *n. f.* word.

palabrero /pala'βrero/ *a.* talkative; wordy.

palabrista /pala'βrista/ *n. m. & f.* talkative person.

palacio /pa'laθio; pa'lasio/ *n. m.* palace.

paladar /pala'ðar/ *n. m.* palate.

paladear /palaðe'ar/ *v.* taste; relish.

palanca /pa'lanka/ *n. f.* lever. **p. de cambio,** gearshift.

palangana /palaŋ'gana/ *n. f.* washbasin.

palco /'palko/ *n. m.* theater box.

palenque /pa'lenke/ *n. m.* palisade.

paleta /pa'leta/ *n. f.* mat, pallet.

paletilla /pale'tiʎa; pale'tiya/ *n. f.* shoulder blade.

palidecer /paliðe'θer: paliðe'ser/ *v.* turn pale.

palidez /pali'ðeθ; pali'ðes/ *n. f.* paleness.

pálido /'paliðo/ *a.* pale.

paliza /pa'liθa; pa'lisa/ *n. f.* beating.

palizada /pali'θaða; pali'saða/ *n. m.* palisade.

palma /'palma/ **palmera** *n. f.* palm (tree).

palmada /pal'maða/ *n. f.* slap, clap.

palmear /palme'ar/ *v.* applaud.

palo /'palo/ *n. m.* pole, stick; suit (in cards); *Naut.* mast.

paloma /pa'loma/ *n. f.* dove, pigeon.

palpar /pal'par/ v. touch, feel.

palpitación /palpita'θion; palpita'sion/ n. f. palpitation.

palpitar /palpi'tar/ v. palpitate.

paludismo /palu'ðismo/ n. m. malaria.

pampa /'pampa/ n. f. (S.A.) prairie, plain.

pan /pan/ n. m. bread; loaf. **p. de centeno,** rye bread.

pana /'pana/ n. f. corduroy.

panacea /pana'θea: pana'sea/ n. f. panacea.

panadería /panaðe'ria/ n. f. bakery.

panadero /pana'ðero/ -ra n. baker.

panameño /pana'meɲo/ -ña a. & n. Panamanian, of Panama.

panamericano /panameri'kano/ a. Pan-American.

páncreas /'pankreas/ n. m. pancreas.

pandeo /pan'deo/ n. m. bulge.

pandilla /pan'diʎa; pan'diya/ n. f. band, gang.

panecillo /pane'θiʎo: pane'siyo/ n. m. roll, muffin.

panegírico /pane'hiriko/ n. m. panegyric.

pánico /'paniko/ n. m. panic.

panocha /pa'notʃa/ n. f. ear of corn.

panorama /pano'rama/ n m. panorama.

panorámico /pano'ramiko/ a. panoramic.

pantalla /pan'taʎa; pan'taya/ n. f. (movie) screen; lamp shade.

pantalones /panta'lones/ n. m.pl. trousers, pants.

pantano /pan'tano/ n. m. bog, marsh, swamp.

pantanoso /panta'noso/ a. swampy, marshy.

pantera /pan'tera/ n. f panther.

pantomima /panto'mima/ n. f. pantomime.

pantorrilla /panto'rriʎa; panto'rriya/ n. f. calf (of body).

panza /'panθa; 'pansa/ n. f. belly, paunch.

pañal /pa'ɲal/ n. m. diaper.

paño /'paɲo/ n. m. piece of cloth.

pañuelo /pa'ɲuelo/ n. m. handkerchief.

Papa /'papa/ n. m. Pope.

papa /'papa/ n. f potato.

papá /pa'pa/ n. m. papa, father.

papado /pa'paðo/ n. m. papacy.

papagayo /papa'gaio/ n. m. parrot.

papal /pa'pal/ a. papal.

Papá Noel /pa'pa no'el/ n. m. Santa Claus.

papel /pa'pel/ n. m. paper; role, part.

papel crespón /pa'pel kres'pon/ crepe paper.

papel de aluminio /pa'pel de alu'minio/ aluminum foil.

papel de escribir /pa'pel de eskri'βir/ writing paper.

papel de estaño /pa'pel de es'taɲo/ tin foil.

papel de lija /pa'pel de 'liha/ sandpaper.

papelera /pape'lera/ n. f. file cabinet; wastepaper basket.

papelería /papele'ria/ n. f. stationery store.

papel moneda /pa'pel mo'neða/ paper money.

paperas /pa'peras/ n. f.pl. mumps.

paquete /pa'kete/ n. m. package.

par /par/ a. **1.** even, equal. —n. **2.** m. pair; equal, peer. **abierto de p. en p.,** wide open.

para /'para/ prep. for; in order to. **p. que,** in order that. **estar p.,** to be about to.

parabién /para'βien/ n. m. congratulation.

parabrisa /para'βrisa/ n. m. windshield.

paracaídas /paraka'iðas/ n. m. parachute.

parachoques /para'tʃokes/ n. m. Auto. bumper.

parada /pa'raða/ n. f. stop, halt; stopover; parade.

paradero /para'ðero/ n. m. whereabouts; stopping place.

paradigma /para'ðigma/ n. m. paradigm.

paradoja /para'ðoha/ n. f. paradox.

parafina /para'fina/ n. f. paraffin.

parafrasear /parafrase'ar/ v. paraphrase.

paraguas /pa'raguas/ n. m umbrella.

paraguayano /paragua'yano/ -na n. & a. Paraguayan.

paraíso /para'iso/ n. m. paradise.

paralelo /para'lelo/ a. & m. parallel.

parálisis /pa'ralisis/ n. f. paralysis.

paralizar /parali'θar; parali'sar/ v. paralyze.

paramédico /para'meðiko/ n. m. paramedic.

parámetro /pa'rametro/ n. m. parameter.

parapeto /para'peto/ n. m. parapet.

parar /pa'rar/ v. stop, stem, ward off; stay.

pararse /pa'rarse/ v. stop; stand up.

parasítico /para'sitiko/ a. parasitic.

parásito /pa'rasito/ n. m. parasite.

parcela /par'θela; par'sela/ n. f. plot of ground.

parcial /par'θial; par'sial/ a. partial.

parcialidad /parθiali'ðað; parsiali'ðað/ n f. partiality; bias.

parcialmente /parθial'mente; parsial'mente/ adv. partially.

pardo /'parðo/ a. brown.

parear /pare'ar/ v. pair; match; mate.

parecer /pare'θer; pare'ser/ n. **1.** m. opinion. —v. **2.** seem, appear, look.

parecerse /pare'θerse; pare'serse/ v. look alike. **p. a,** look like.

parecido /pare'θiðo; pare'siðo/ a. similar.

pared /pa'reð/ n. f. wall.

pareja /pa'reha/ n. f. pair, couple; (dancing) partner.

parentela /paren'tela/ n. f. kinfolk.

parentesco /paren'tesko/ n. m. parentage, lineage; kin.

paréntesis /pa'rentesis/ *n. m.* parenthesis.

paria /'paria/ *n. m.* outcast, pariah.

paricipante /pariθi'pante; parisi'pante/ *n. m. & f.* participant.

paridad /pari'ðað/ *n. f.* parity.

pariente /pa'riente/ *n. m. & f.* relative.

parir /pa'rir/ *v.* give birth.

parisiense /pari'siense/ *n. & a.* Parisian.

parlamentario /parlamen'tario/ *a.* parliamentary.

parlamento /parla'mento/ *n. m.* parliament.

paro /'paro/ *n. m.* stoppage; strike. **p. forzoso,** unemployment.

parodia /pa'roðia/ *n. f.* parody.

parodista /paro'ðista/ *n. m. & f.* parodist.

paroxismo /parok'sismo/ *n. m.* paroxysm.

párpado /'parpaðo/ *n. m.* eyelid.

parque /'parke/ *n. m.* park.

parquímetro /par'kimetro/ *n. m.* parking meter.

parra /'parra/ *n. f.* grapevine.

párrafo /'parrafo/ *n. m.* paragraph.

parranda /pa'rranda/ *n. f.* spree.

parrandear /parrande'ar/ *v.* carouse.

parrilla /pa'rriʎa; pa'rriya/ *n. f.* grill; grillroom.

párroco /'parroko/ *n. m.* parish priest.

parroquia /pa'rrokia/ *n. f.* parish.

parroquial /parro'kial/ *a.* parochial.

parsimonia /parsi'monia/ *n. f.* economy, thrift.

parsimonioso /parsimo'nioso/ *a.* economical, thrifty.

parte /'parte/ *n. f.* part. **de p. de,** on behalf of. **alguna p.,** somewhere. **por otra p.,** on the other hand. **dar p. a,** to notify.

partera /par'tera/ *n. f.* midwife.

partición /parti'θion; parti'sion/ *n. f.* distribution.

participación /partiθipa'θion; partisipa'sion/ *n. f.* participation.

participar /partiθi'par; partisi'par/ *v.* participate; announce.

participio /parti'θipio; parti'sipio/ *n. m.* participle.

partícula /par'tikula/ *n. f.* particle.

particular /partiku'lar/ *a.* **1.** particular; private. —*n.* **2.** *m.* particular; detail; individual.

particularmente /partikular'mente/ *adv.* particularly.

partida /par'tiða/ *n. f.* departure; *Mil.* party; (sport) game.

partida de defunción /par'tiða de defun'θion; par'tiða de defun'sion/ death certificate.

partida de matrimonio /par'tiða de matri'monio/ marriage certificate.

partida de nacimiento /par'tiða de naθi-'miento; par'tiða de nasi'miento/ birth certificate.

partidario /parti'ðario/ **-ria** *n.* partisan.

partido /par'tiðo/ *n. m.* side, party, faction; game, match.

partir /par'tir/ *v.* leave, depart; part, cleave, split.

parto /'parto/ *n. m.* delivery, childbirth.

pasa /'pasa/ *n. f.* raisin.

pasado /pa'saðo/ *a.* **1.** past; last. —*n.* **2.** *m.* past.

pasaje /pa'sahe/ *n. m.* passage, fare.

pasajero /pasa'hero/ **-ra** *a.* **1.** passing, transient. —*n.* **2.** passenger.

pasamano /pasa'mano/ *n. m.* banister.

pasaporte /pasa'porte/ *n. m.* passport.

pasar /pa'sar/ *v.* pass; happen; spend (time). **p. por alto,** overlook. **p. lista,** call the roll. **p. sin,** do without.

pasatiempo /pasa'tiempo/ *n. m.* pastime; hobby.

pascua /'paskua/ *n. f.* religious holiday; (*pl.*) Christmas (season). **P. Florida,** Easter.

pase de modelos /'pase de mo'ðelos/ *n. m.* fashion show.

paseo /pa'seo/ *n. m.* walk, stroll; drive. —**pasear,** *v.*

pasillo /pa'siʎo; pa'siyo/ *n. m.* aisle; hallway.

pasión /pa'sion/ *n. f.* passion.

pasivo /pa'siβo/ *a.* passive.

pasmar /pas'mar/ *v.* astonish, astound, stun.

pasmo /'pasmo/ *n. m.* spasm; wonder.

paso /'paso/ *a.* **1.** dried (fruit). —*n.* **2.** *m.* pace, step; (mountain) pass.

paso cebra /'paso 'θeβra; 'paso 'seβra/ crosswalk.

paso de ganso /'paso de 'ganso/ goose step.

paso de peatones /'paso de pea'tones/ pedestrian crossing.

pasta /'pasta/ *n. f.* paste; batter; plastic.

pasta dentífrica /'pasta den'tifrika/ toothpaste.

pastar /pas'tar/ *v.* graze.

pastel /pas'tel/ *n. m.* pastry; pie.

pastelería /pastele'ria/ *n. f.* pastry; pastry shop.

pasteurización /pasteuriθa'θion; pasteurisa'sion/ *n. f.* pasteurization.

pasteurizar /pasteuri'θar; pasteuri'sar/ *v.* pasteurize.

pastilla /pas'tiʎa; pas'tiya/ *n. f.* tablet, lozenge, coughdrop.

pasto /'pasto/ *n. m.* pasture; grass.

pastor /pas'tor/ *n. m.* pastor; shepherd.

pastorear /pastore'ar/ *v.* pasture, tend (a flock).

pastrón /pas'tron/ *n. m.* pastrami.

pastura /pas'tura/ *n. f.* pasture.

pata /'pata/ n. f. foot (of animal).

patada /pa'taða/ n. f. kick.

patán /pa'tan/ n. m. boor.

patanada /pata'naða/ n. f. rudeness.

patata /pa'tata/ n. f. potato. **p. asada**, baked potato.

patear /pate'ar/ v. stamp, tramp, kick.

patente /pa'tente/ a. & m. patent. —**patentar,** v.

paternal /pater'nal/ **paterno** a. paternal.

paternidad /paterni'ðað/ n. f. paternity, fatherhood.

patético /pa'tetiko/ a. pathetic.

patíbulo /pa'tiβulo/ n. m. scaffold; gallows.

patín /pa'tin/ n. m. skate. —**patinar,** v.

patín de ruedas /pa'tin de 'rrueðas/ roller skate.

patio /'patio/ n. m. yard, court, patio.

pato /'pato/ n. m. duck.

patria /'patria/ n. f. native land.

patriarca /patri'arka/ n. m. patriarch.

patrimonio /patri'monio/ n. m. inheritance.

patriota /pa'triota/ n. m. & f. patriot.

patriótico /patri'otiko/ a. patriotic.

patriotismo /patrio'tismo/ n. m. patriotism.

patrocinar /patroθi'nar/ patrosi'nar/ v. patronize, sponsor.

patrón /pa'tron/ **-ona** n. patron; boss; (dress) pattern.

patrulla /pa'truʎa/ pa'truya/ n. f. patrol. —**patrullar,** v.

paulatino /paula'tino/ a. gradual.

pausa /'pausa/ n. f. pause. —**pausar,** v.

pausa para el café /'pausa 'para el ka'fe/ coffee break.

pauta /'pauta/ n. f. guideline.

pavesa /pa'βesa/ n. f. spark, cinder.

pavimentar /paβimen'tar/ v. pave.

pavimento /paβi'mento/ n. m. pavement.

pavo /'paβo/ n. m. turkey. **p. real,** peacock.

pavor /pa'βor/ n. m. terror.

payaso /pa'iaso/ **-sa** n. clown.

paz /paθ/ n. f. peace.

peatón /pea'ton/ **-na** n. pedestrian.

peca /'peka/ n. f. freckle.

pecado /pe'kaðo/ n. m. sin. —**pecar,** v.

pecador /peka'ðor/ **-ra** a. & n. sinful; sinner.

pecera /pe'θera/ pe'sera/ n. f. aquarium, fishbowl.

pechera /pe'tʃera/ n. f. shirt front.

pecho /'petʃo/ n. m. chest; breast; bosom.

pechuga /pe'tʃuɣa/ n. f. breast (of fowl).

pecoso /pe'koso/ a. freckled, freckly.

peculiar /peku'liar/ a. peculiar.

peculiaridad /pekuliari'ðað/ n. f. peculiarity.

pedagogía /peðaɣo'hia/ n. f. pedagogy.

pedagogo /peða'ɣoɣo/ **-ga** n. pedagogue, teacher.

pedal /pe'ðal/ n. m. pedal.

pedantesco /peðan'tesko/ a. pedantic.

pedazo /pe'ðaθo; pe'ðaso/ n. m. piece.

pedernal /peðer'nal/ n. m. flint.

pedestal /peðes'tal/ n. m. pedestal.

pediatra /pe'ðiatra/ n. m. & f. pediatrician.

pediatría /peðia'tria/ n. f. pediatrics.

pedicuro /peði'kuro/ n. m. chiropodist.

pedir /pe'ðir/ v. ask, ask for, request; apply for; order.

pedo /'peðo/ n. m. fart; intoxication.

pedregoso /peðre'goso/ a. rocky.

pegajoso /pega'hoso/ a. sticky.

pegamento /pega'mento/ n. m. glue.

pegar /pe'gar/ v. beat, strike; adhere, fasten, stick.

peinado /pei'naðo/ n. m. coiffure, hairdo.

peine /'peine/ n. m. comb. —**peinar,** v.

peineta /pei'neta/ n. f. (ornamental) comb.

pelagra /pe'lagra/ n. f. pellagra.

pelar /pe'lar/ v. skin, pare, peel.

pelea /pe'lea/ n. f. fight, row. —**pelearse,** v.

pelícano /pe'likano/ n. m. pelican.

película /pe'likula/ n. f. movie, motion picture, film. **p. de terror** horror film.

peligrar /peli'grar/ v. be in danger.

peligro /pe'ligro/ n. m. peril, danger.

peligroso /peli'groso/ a. perilous, dangerous.

pelirrojo /peli'rroho/ **-ja** a. & n. redhead.

pellejo /pe'ʎeho; pe'yeho/ n. m. skin; peel (of fruit).

pellizco /pe'ʎiθko; pe'yisko/ n. m. pinch. —**pellizcar,** v.

pelo /'pelo/ n. m. hair.

pelota /pe'lota/ n. f. ball.

peltre /'peltre/ n. m. pewter.

peluca /pe'luka/ n. f. wig.

peludo /pe'luðo/ a. hairy.

peluquería /peluke'ria/ n. f. hairdresser's shop, beauty parlor.

peluquero /pelu'kero/ **-ra** n. hairdresser.

pena /'pena/ n. f. pain, grief, trouble, woe; penalty. **valer la p.,** to be worthwhile.

penacho /pe'natʃo/ n. m. plume.

penalidad /penali'ðað/ n. f. trouble; penalty.

pender /pen'der/ v. hang, dangle; be pending.

pendiente /pen'diente/ a. **1.** hanging; pending. —n. **2.** m. incline, slope; earring; pendant.

pendón /pen'don/ n. m. pennant, flag.

penetración /penetra'θion; penetra'sion/ n. f. penetration.

penetrar /pene'trar/ v. penetrate, pierce.

penicilina /peniθi'lina; penisi'lina/ n. f. penicillin.

península /pe'ninsula/ n. f. peninsula.

penitencia /peni'tenθia; peni'tensia/ *n. f.* penitence, penance.
penitenciaría /penitenθia'ria; penitensia'ria/ *n. f.* penitentiary.
penoso /pe'noso/ *a.* painful, troublesome, grievous, distressing.
pensador /pensa'ðor/ **-ra** *n.* thinker.
pensamiento /pensa'miento/ *n. m.* thought.
pensar /pen'sar/ *v.* think; intend, plan.
pensativo /pensa'tiβo/ *a.* pensive, thoughtful.
pensión /pen'sion/ *n. f.* pension; boarding-house.
pensionista /pensio'nista/ *n. m. & f.* boarder.
pentagonal /pentago'nal/ *a.* pentagonal.
penúltimo /pe'nultimo/ *a.* next-to-the-last, last but one, penultimate.
penuria /pe'nuria/ *n. f.* penury, poverty.
peña /'peɲa/ *n. f.* rock.
peñascoso /peɲas'koso/ *a.* rocky.
peñón /pe'ɲon/ *n. m.* rock, crag.
Peñón de Gibraltar /pe'ɲon de hiβral'tar/ Rock of Gibraltar.
peón /pe'on/ *n. m.* unskilled laborer; infantryman.
peonada /peo'naða/ *n. f.* group of laborers.
peonía /peo'nia/ *n. f.* peony.
peor /pe'or/ *a.* worse, worst.
pepino /pe'pino/ *n. m.* cucumber.
pepita /pe'pita/ *n. f.* seed (in fruit).
pequeñez /peke'ɲeθ; peke'ɲes/ *n. f.* smallness; trifle.
pequeño /pe'keɲo/ **-ña** *a.* **1.** small, little, short, slight. **—2.** child.
pera /'pera/ *n. f.* pear.
peral /pe'ral/ *n. m.* pear tree.
perca /'perka/ *n. f.* perch (fish).
percal /per'kal/ *n. m.* calico, percale.
percance /per'kanθe; per'kanse/ *n. m.* mishap, snag, hitch.
percepción /perθep'θion; persep'sion/ *n. f.* perception.
perceptivo /perθep'tiβo; persep'tiβo/ *a.* perceptive.
percha /'pertʃa/ *n. f.* perch; clothes hanger, rack.
percibir /perθi'βir; persi'βir/ *v.* perceive, sense; collect.
perder /per'ðer/ *v.* lose; miss; waste. **echar a p.,** spoil. **p. el conocimiento,** lose consciousness.
perdición /perði'θion; perði'sion/ *n. f.* perdition, downfall.
pérdida /'perðiða/ *n. f.* loss.
perdiz /per'ðiθ; per'ðis/ *n. f.* partridge.
perdón /per'ðon/ *n. m.* pardon, forgiveness.
perdonar /perðo'nar/ *v.* forgive, pardon; spare.

perdurable /perðu'raβle/ *a.* enduring, everlasting.
perdurar /perðu'rar/ *v.* endure, last.
perecedero /pereθe'ðero; perese'ðero/ *a.* perishable.
perecer /pere'θer; pere'ser/ *v.* perish.
peregrinación /peregrina'θion; peregrina-'sion/ *n. f.* peregrination; pilgrimage.
peregrino /pere'grino/ **-na** *n.* pilgrim.
perejil /pere'hil/ *n. m.* parsley.
perenne /pe'renne/ *a.* perennial.
pereza /pe'reθa; pe'resa/ *n. f.* laziness.
perezoso /pere'θoso; pere'soso/ *a.* lazy, sluggish.
perfección /perfek'θion; perfek'sion/ *n. f.* perfection.
perfeccionar /perfekθio'nar; perfeksio'nar/ *v.* perfect.
perfeccionista /perfekθio'nista; perfeksio-'nista/ *a. & n.* perfectionist.
perfectamente /perfekta'mente/ *adv.* perfectly.
perfecto /per'fekto/ *a.* perfect.
perfidia /per'fiðia/ *n. f.* falseness, perfidy.
pérfido /'perfiðo/ *a.* perfidious.
perfil /per'fil/ *n. m.* profile.
perforación /perfora'θion; perfora'sion/ *n. f.* perforation.
perforar /perfo'rar/ *v.* pierce, perforate.
perfume /per'fume/ *n. m.* perfume, scent. **—perfumar,** *v.*
pergamino /perga'mino/ *n. m.* parchment.
pericia /pe'riθia; pe'risia/ *n. f.* skill, expertness.
perico /pe'riko/ *n. m.* parakeet.
perímetro /pe'rimetro/ *n. m.* perimeter.
periódico /pe'rioðiko/ *a.* **1.** periodic. **—n. 2.** *m.* newspaper.
periodista /perio'ðista/ *n. m. & f.* journalist.
período /pe'rioðo/ *n. m.* period.
periscopio /peris'kopio/ *n. m.* periscope.
perito /pe'rito/ **-ta** *a. & n.* experienced; expert, connoisseur.
perjudicar /perhuði'kar/ *v.* damage, hurt; impair.
perjudicial /perhuði'θial; perhuði'sial/ *a.* harmful, injurious.
perjuicio /per'huiθio; per'huisio/ *n. m.* injury, damage.
perjurar /perhu'rar/ *v.* commit perjury.
perjurio /per'hurio/ *n. m.* perjury.
perla /'perla/ *n. f.* pearl.
permanecer /permane'θer; permane'ser/ *v.* remain, stay.
permanencia /perma'nenθia; perma'nensia/ *n. f.* permanence; stay.
permanente /perma'nente/ *a.* permanent.
permiso /per'miso/ *n. m.* permission; permit; furlough.

permitir /permi'tir/ v. permit, enable, let, allow.

permuta /per'muta/ n. f. exchange, barter.

pernicioso /perni'θioso; perni'sioso/ a. pernicious.

perno /'perno/ n. m. bolt.

pero /'pero/ conj. but.

peróxido /pe'roksiðo/ n. m. peroxide.

perpendicular /perpendiku'lar/ n. m. & a. perpendicular.

perpetración /perpetra'θion; perpetra'sion/ n. f. perpetration.

perpetrar /perpe'trar/ v. perpetrate.

perpetuar /perpe'tuar/ v. perpetuate.

perpetuidad /perpetui'ðað/ n. f. perpetuity.

perpetuo /per'petuo/ a. perpetual.

perplejo /per'pleho/ a. perplexed, puzzled.

perrito caliente /pe'rrito ka'liente/ n. m. hot dog.

perro /'perro/ **-rra** n. dog.

persecución /perseku'θion; perseku'sion/ f. persecution.

perseguir /perse'gir/ v. pursue; persecute.

perseverancia /perseβe'ranθia; perseβe-'ransia/ n. f. perseverance.

perseverar /perseβe'rar/ v. persevere.

persiana /per'siana/ n. f. shutter, Venetian blind.

persistente /persis'tente/ a. persistent.

persistir /persis'tir/ v. persist.

persona /per'sona/ n. f. person.

personaje /perso'nahe/ n. m. personage; Theat. character.

personal /perso'nal/ a. 1. personal. —n. 2. m. personnel, staff.

personalidad /personali'ðað/ n. f. personality.

personalmente /personal'mente/ adv. personally.

perspectiva /perspek'tiβa/ n. f. perspective; prospect.

perspicaz /perspi'kaθ; perspi'kas/ a. perspicacious, acute.

persuadir /persua'ðir/ v. persuade.

persuasión /persua'sion/ n. f. persuasion.

persuasivo /persua'siβo/ a. persuasive.

pertenecer /pertene'θer; pertene'ser/ v. pertain; belong.

pertinencia /perti'nenθia; perti'nensia/ n. f. pertinence.

pertinente /perti'nente/ a. pertinent; relevant.

perturbar /pertur'βar/ v. perturb, disturb.

peruano /pe'ruano/ **-na** a. & n. Peruvian.

perversidad /perβersi'ðað/ n. f. perversity.

perverso /per'βerso/ a. perverse.

pesadez /pesa'ðeθ; pesa'ðes/ n. f. dullness.

pesadilla /pesa'ðiʎa; pesa'ðiya/ n. f. nightmare.

pesado /pe'saðo/ a. heavy; dull, dreary, boring.

pésame /'pesame/ n. m. condolence.

pesar /pe'sar/ n. m. sorrow; regret. **a p. de,** in spite of. v. weigh.

pesca /'peska/ n. f. fishing; catch (of fish).

pescadería /peskaðe'ria/ n. f. fish store.

pescado /pes'kaðo/ n. m. fish. —**pescar,** v.

pescador /peska'ðor/ n. m. fisherman.

pesebre /pe'seβre/ n. m. stall, manger; crib.

peseta /pe'seta/ n. f. peseta (monetary unit).

pesimismo /pesi'mismo/ n. m. pessimism.

pesimista /pesi'mista/ a. & n. pessimistic; pessimist.

pésimo /'pesimo/ a. awful, terrible, very bad.

peso /'peso/ n. m. weight; load; peso (monetary unit).

pesquera /pes'kera/ n. f. fishery.

pesquisa /pes'kisa/ n. f. investigation.

pestaña /pes'taɲa/ n. f. eyelash.

pestañeo /pesta'ɲeo/ n. m. wink, blink. —**pestañear,** v.

peste /'peste/ n. f. plague.

pesticida /pesti'θiða; pesti'siða/ n. m. pesticide.

pestilencia /pesti'lenθia; pesti'lensia/ n. f. pestilence.

pétalo /'petalo/ n. m. petal.

petardo /pe'tarðo/ n. m. firecracker.

petición /peti'θion; peti'sion/ n. f. petition.

petirrojo /peti'rroho/ n. m. robin.

petrel /pe'trel/ n. m. petrel.

pétreo /'petreo/ a. rocky.

petrificar /petrifi'kar/ v. petrify.

petróleo /pe'troleo/ n. m. petroleum.

petrolero /petro'lero/ n. m. oil tanker.

petunia /pe'tunia/ n. f. petunia.

pez /peθ; pes/ n. 1. m. fish (in the water). —n. 2. f. pitch, tar.

pezuña /pe'θuɲa; pe'suɲa/ n. f. hoof.

piadoso /pia'ðoso/ a. pious; merciful.

pianista /pia'nista/ n. m. & f. pianist.

piano /'piano/ n. m. piano.

picadero /pika'ðero/ n. m. riding school.

picadura /pika'ðura/ n. f. sting, bite, prick.

picamaderos /pikama'ðeros/ n. m. woodpecker.

picante /pi'kante/ a. hot, spicy.

picaporte /pika'porte/ n. m. latch.

picar /pi'kar/ v. sting, bite, prick; itch; chop up, grind up.

pícaro /'pikaro/ **-ra** a. 1. knavish, mischievous. —n. 2. rogue, rascal.

picarse /pi'karse/ v. be offended, piqued.

picazón /pika'θon; pika'son/ n. f. itch.

pícea /'piθea; 'pisea/ n. f. spruce.

pichón /pi'tʃon/ n. m. pigeon, squab.

pico /'piko/ *n. m.* peak; pick; beak; spout; small amount.

picotazo /piko'taθo; piko'taso/ *n. m.* peck. —**picotear,** *v.*

pictórico /pik'toriko/ *a.* pictorial.

pie /pie/ *n. m.* foot. **al p. de la letra,** literally; thoroughly.

piedad /pie'ðað/ *n. f.* piety; pity, mercy.

piedra /'pieðra/ *n. f.* stone.

piel /piel/ *n. f.* skin, hide; fur.

pienso /'pienso/ *n. m.* fodder.

pierna /'pierna/ *n. f.* leg.

pieza /'pieθa; 'piesa/ *n. f.* piece; room; *Theat.* play.

pijama /pi'hama/ *n. m. or m.pl.* pajamas.

pila /'pila/ *n. f.* pile, stack; battery; sink.

pilar /pi'lar/ *n. m.* pillar, column.

píldora /'pildora/ *n. f.* pill.

pillo /'piʎo; 'piyo/ **-a** *n.* thief; rascal.

piloto /pi'loto/ *n. m.* pilot.

pimentón /pimen'ton/ *n. m.* paprika.

pimienta /pi'mienta/ *n. f.* pepper (spice).

pimiento /pi'miento/ *n. m.* pepper (vegetable).

pináculo /pi'nakulo/ *n. m.* pinnacle.

pincel /pin'θel; pin'sel/ *n. m.* (artist's) brush.

pinchadiscos /pintʃa'ðiskos/ *m. & f.* disk jockey.

pinchazo /pin'tʃaθo; pin'tʃaso/ *n. m.* puncture; prick. —**pinchar,** *v.*

pingajo /pin'gaho/ *n. m.* rag, tatter.

pino /'pino/ *n. m.* pine.

pinta /'pinta/ *n. f.* pint.

pintar /pin'tar/ *v.* paint; portray, depict.

pintor /pin'tor/ **-ra** *n.* painter.

pintoresco /pinto'resko/ *a.* picturesque.

pintura /pin'tura/ *n. f.* paint; painting.

pinzas /'pinθas; 'pinsas/ *n. f.pl.* pincers, tweezers; claws.

piña /'piɲa/ *n. f.* pineapple.

pío /'pio/ *a.* pious; merciful.

piojo /'pioho/ *n. m.* louse.

pionero /pio'nero/ **-ra** *n.* pioneer.

pipa /'pipa/ *n. f.* tobacco pipe.

pique /'pike/ *n. m.* resentment, pique. **echar a p.,** sink (ship).

pira /'pira/ *n. f.* pyre.

piragua /pi'ragua/ *n. f.* canoe.

piragüismo /pira'guismo/ *n. m.* canoeing.

piragüista /pira'guista/ *n. m. & f.* canoeist.

pirámide /pi'ramiðe/ *n. f.* pyramid.

pirata /pi'rata/ *n. m. & f.* pirate. **p. de aviones,** hijacker.

pisada /pi'saða/ *n. f.* tread, step. —**pisar,** *v.*

pisapapeles /pisapa'peles/ *n. m.* paperweight.

piscina /pis'θina; pis'sina/ *n. f.* fishpond; swimming pool.

piso /'piso/ *n. m.* floor.

pista /'pista/ *n. f.* trace, clue, track; racetrack.

pista de tenis /'pista de 'tenis/ tennis court.

pistola /pis'tola/ *n. f.* pistol.

pistón /pis'ton/ *n. m.* piston.

pitillo /pi'tiʎo; pi'tiyo/ *n. m.* cigarette.

pito /'pito/ *n. m.* whistle. —**pitar,** *v.*

pizarra /pi'θarra; pi'sarra/ *n. f.* slate; blackboard.

pizca /'piθka; 'piska/ *n. f.* bit, speck; pinch.

pizza /'piθθa; 'pissa/ *n. f.* pizza.

placentero /plaθen'tero; plasen'tero/ *a.* pleasant.

placer /pla'θer; pla'ser/ *n.* **1.** *m.* pleasure. —*v.* **2.** please.

plácido /'plaθiðo; 'plasiðo/ *a.* placid.

plaga /'plaga/ *n. f.* plague, scourge.

plagio /'plahio/ *n. m.* plagiarism; (*S.A.*) kidnapping.

plan /plan/ *n. m.* plan. —**planear,** *v.*

plancha /'plantʃa/ *n. f.* plate; slab, flatiron.

planchar /plan'tʃar/ *v.* iron, press.

planeta /pla'neta/ *n. m.* planet.

planificación /planifika'θion; planifika'sion/ *n. f.* planning.

planificar /planifi'kar/ *v.* plan.

plano /'plano/ *a.* **1.** level, flat. —*n.* **2.** *m.* plan; plane.

planta /'planta/ *n. f.* plant; sole (of foot).

planta baja /'planta 'baha/ *n. f.* ground floor.

plantación /planta'θion; planta'sion/ *n. f.* plantation.

plantar /plan'tar/ *v.* plant.

plantear /plante'ar/ *v.* pose, present.

plantel /plan'tel/ *n. m.* educational institution; *Agr.* nursery.

plasma /'plasma/ *n. m.* plasma.

plástico /'plastiko/ *a. & m.* plastic.

plata /'plata/ *n. f.* silver; *Colloq.* money.

plataforma /plata'forma/ *n. f.* platform.

plátano /'platano/ *n. m.* plantain; banana.

platel /pla'tel/ *n. m.* platter.

plática /'platika/ *n. f.* chat, talk. —**platicar,** *v.*

platillo /pla'tiʎo; pla'tiyo/ *n. m.* saucer.

platillo volante /pla'tiʎo bo'lante; pla'tiyo bo'lante/ flying saucer.

plato /'plato/ *n. m.* plate, dish.

playa /'plaia/ *n. f.* beach, shore.

plaza /'plaθa; 'plasa/ *n. f.* square. **p. de toros,** bullring.

plazo /'plaθo; 'plaso/ *n. m.* term, deadline; installment.

plebe /'pleβe/ *n. f.* common people; masses.

plebiscito /pleβis'θito; pleβis'sito/ *n. m.* plebiscite.

plegable /ple'gaβle/ *a.* foldable, folding.

plegadura /plega'ðura/ n. f. fold, pleat.
—**plegar**, v.

pleito /'pleito/ n. m. lawsuit; dispute.

plenitud /pleni'tuð/ n. f. fullness; abundance.

pleno /'pleno/ a. full. **en pleno...** in the middle of...

pliego /'pliego/ n. m. sheet of paper.

pliegue /'pliege/ n. m. fold, pleat, crease.

plomería /plome'ria/ n. f. plumbing.

plomero /plo'mero/ n. m. plumber.

plomizo /plo'miθo; plo'miso/ a. leaden.

plomo /'plomo/ n. m. lead; fuse.

pluma /'pluma/ n. f. feather; (writing) pen.

pluma estilográfica /'pluma estilo-'grafika/ fountain pen.

plumafuente /pluma'fuente/ n. f. fountain pen.

plumaje /plu'mahe/ n. m. plumage.

plumero /plu'mero/ n. m. feather duster; plume.

plumoso /plu'moso/ a. feathery.

plural /plu'ral/ a. & m. plural.

pluriempleo /pluriem'pleo/ n. m. moonlighting.

PNB, abbr. (producto nacional bruto), GNP (gross national product).

población /poβla'θion; poβla'sion/ n. f. population; town.

poblador /poβla'ðor/ -ra n. settler.

poblar /po'βlar/ v. populate; settle.

pobre /'poβre/ a. n. poor; poor person.

pobreza /po'βreθa; po'βresa/ n. f. poverty, need.

pocilga /po'θilga; po'silga/ n. f. pigpen.

poción /po'θion; po'sion/ n. f. drink; potion.

poco /'poko/ a. & adv. **1.** little, not much, (pl.) few. **por p.,** almost, nearly. —n. **2.** be un p. (de), a little, a bit (of).

poder /po'ðer/ v. **1.** m. power. —v. **2.** be able to; can; be possible, may, might. **no p. menos de,** not be able to help.

poder adquisitivo /po'ðer aðkisi'tiβo/ purchasing power.

poderío /poðe'rio/ n. m. power, might.

poderoso /poðe'roso/ a. powerful, mighty, potent.

podrido /po'ðriðo/ a. rotten.

poema /po'ema/ n. m. poem.

poesía /poe'sia/ n. f. poetry; poem.

poeta /po'eta/ n. m. & f. poet.

poético /po'etiko/ a. poetic.

polaco /po'lako/ -ca a. & n. Polish; Pole.

polar /po'lar/ a. polar.

polaridad /polari'ðað/ n. f. polarity.

polea /po'lea/ n. f. pulley.

polen /'polen/ n. m. pollen.

policía /poli'θia; poli'sia/ n. **1.** f. police. —n. **2.** m. policeman.

polideportivo /poliðepor'tiβo/ n. m. sports center.

poliéster /poli'ester/ n. m. polyester.

poligamia /poli'gamia/ n. f. polygamy.

polígloto /poli'gloto/ -ta n. polyglot.

polígono industrial /po'ligono indus'trial/ n. m. industrial park.

polilla /po'liʎa; po'liya/ n. f. moth.

política /po'litika/ n. f. politics; policy.

político /po'litiko/ -ca a. & n. politic; political; politician.

póliza /'poliθa; 'polisa/ n. f. (insurance) policy; permit, ticket.

polizonte /poli'θonte; poli'sonte/ n. m. policeman.

pollada /po'ʎaða; po'yaða/ n. f. brood.

pollería /poʎe'ria; poye'ria/ n. f. poultry shop.

pollino /po'ʎino; po'yino/ n. m. donkey.

pollo /'poʎo; 'poyo/ n. m. chicken.

polo /'polo/ n. m. pole; polo; popsicle.

polonés /polo'nes/ a. Polish.

Polonia /po'lonia/ n. f. Poland.

polvera /pol'βera/ n. f. powder box; powder puff.

polvo /'polβo/ n. m. powder; dust.

pólvora /'polβora/ n. f. gunpowder.

pompa /'pompa/ n. f. pomp.

pomposo /pom'poso/ a. pompous.

pómulo /'pomulo/ n. m. cheekbone.

ponche /'pontʃe/ n. m. punch (beverage).

ponchera /pon'tʃera/ n. f. punch bowl.

ponderar /ponde'rar/ v. ponder.

ponderoso /ponde'roso/ a. ponderous.

poner /po'ner/ v. put, set, lay, place.

ponerse /po'nerse/ v. put on; become, get; set (sun). **p. a,** start to.

poniente /po'niente/ n. m. west.

pontífice /pon'tifiθe; pon'tifise/ n. m. pontiff.

popa /'popa/ n. f. stern.

popular /popu'lar/ a. popular.

popularidad /populari'ðað/ n. f. popularity.

populazo /popu'laθo; popu'laso/ n. m. populace; masses.

por /por/ prep. by, through, because of; via; for. **p. qué,** why?

porcelana /porθe'lana; porse'lana/ n. f. porcelain, chinaware.

porcentaje /porθen'tahe; porsen'tahe/ n. m. percentage.

porche /'portʃe/ n. m. porch; portico.

porción /por'θion; por'sion/ n. f. portion, lot.

porfiar /por'fiar/ v. persist; argue.

pormenor /porme'nor/ n. m. detail.

pornografía /pornogra'fia/ n. f. pornography.

poro /'poro/ n. m. pore.

poroso /po'roso/ a. porous.

porque /'porke/ *conj.* because.

porqué *n. m.* reason, motive.

porra /'porra/ *n. f.* stick, club.

porrazo /po'rraθo; po'rraso/ *n. m.* blow.

porro /'porro/ *n. m. Colloq.* joint (marijuana).

portaaviones /portaa'βiones/ *n. m.* aircraft carrier.

portador /porta'ðor/ **-ra** *n.* bearer.

portal /por'tal/ *n. m.* portal.

portar /por'tar/ *v.* carry.

portarse /por'tarse/ *v.* behave, act.

portátil /por'tatil/ *a.* portable.

portavoz /porta'βoθ; porta'βos/ *n.* **1.** *m.* megaphone. **2.** *m. & f.* spokesperson.

porte /'porte/ *n. m.* bearing; behavior; postage.

portero /por'tero/ *n. m.* porter; janitor.

pórtico /'portiko/ *n. m.* porch.

portorriqueño /portorri'keɲo/ **-ña** *n. & a.* Puerto Rican.

portugués /portu'ges/ **-esa** *a. & n.* Portuguese.

posada /po'saða/ *n. f.* lodge, inn.

posar /po'sar/ *v.* pose.

posdata /pos'ðata/ *n. f.* postscript.

poseer /pose'er/ *v.* possess, own.

posesión /pose'sion/ *n. f.* possession.

posibilidad /posiβili'ðað/ *n. f.* possibility.

posible /po'siβle/ *a.* possible.

posiblemente /posiβle'mente/ *adv.* possibly.

posición /posi'θion; posi'sion/ *n. f.* position, stand.

positivo /posi'tiβo/ *a.* positive.

posponer /pospo'ner/ *v.* postpone.

postal /pos'tal/ *a.* postal; postcard.

poste /'poste/ *n. m.* post, pillar.

posteridad /posteri'ðað/ *n. f.* posterity.

posterior /poste'rior/ *a.* posterior, rear.

postizo /pos'tiθo; pos'tiso/ *a.* false, artificial.

postrado /pos'traðo/ *a.* prostrate. **—postrar,** *v.*

postre /'postre/ *n. m.* dessert.

póstumo /'postumo/ *a.* posthumous.

postura /pos'tura/ *n. f.* posture, pose; bet.

potable /po'taβle/ *a.* drinkable.

potaje /po'taxe/ *n. m.* porridge; pot stew.

potasa /po'tasa/ *n. f.* potash.

potasio /po'tasio/ *n. m.* potassium.

pote /'pote/ *n. m.* pot, jar.

potencia /po'tenθia; po'tensia/ *n. f.* potency, power.

potencial /poten'θial; poten'sial/ *a. & m.* potential.

potentado /poten'taðo/ *n. m.* potentate.

potente /po'tente/ *a.* potent, powerful.

potestad /potes'tað/ *n. f.* power.

potro /'potro/ *n. m.* colt.

pozo /'poθo; 'poso/ *n. m.* well.

práctica /'praktika/ *n. f.* practice. **—practicar,** *v.*

práctico /'praktiko/ *a.* practical.

pradera /pra'ðera/ *n. f.* prairie, meadow.

prado /'praðo/ *n. m.* meadow; lawn.

pragmatismo /pragma'tismo/ *n. m.* pragmatism.

preámbulo /pre'ambulo/ *n. m.* preamble.

precario /pre'kario/ *a.* precarious.

precaución /prekau'θion; prekau'sion/ *n. f.* precaution.

precaverse /preka'βerse/ *v.* beware.

precavido /preka'βiðo/ *a.* cautious, guarded, wary.

precedencia /preθe'ðenθia; prese'ðensia/ *n. f.* precedence, priority.

precedente /preθe'ðente; prese'ðente/ *a. & m.* preceding; precedent.

preceder /preθe'ðer; prese'ðer/ *v.* precede.

precepto /pre'θepto; pre'septo/ *n. m.* precept.

preciar /pre'θiar; pre'siar/ *v.* value, prize.

preciarse de /pre'θiarse de; pre'siarse de/ *v.* take pride in.

precio /'preθio; 'presio/ *n. m.* price. **p. del billete de avión** air fare. **p. del cubierto** cover charge.

precioso /pre'θioso; pre'sioso/ *a.* precious; beautiful, gorgeous.

precipicio /preθi'piθio; presi'pisio/ *n. m.* precipice, cliff.

precipitación /preθipita'θion; presipita'sion/ *n. f.* precipitation.

precipitar /preθipi'tar; presipi'tar/ *v.* precipitate, rush; throw headlong.

precipitoso /preθipi'toso; presipi'toso/ *a.* precipitous; rash.

precisar /preθi'sar; presi'sar/ *v.* fix, specify; be necessary.

precisión /preθi'sion; presi'sion/ *n. f.* precision; necessity.

preciso /pre'θiso; pre'siso/ *a.* precise; necessary.

precocidad /prekoθi'ðað; prekosi'ðað/ *n. f.* precocity.

precocinado /prekoθi'naðo; prekosi'naðo/ *a.* precooked, ready-cooked.

precoz /pre'koθ; pre'kos/ *a.* precocious.

precursor /prekur'sor/ **-ra** *n.* **1.** preceding. **—n. 2.** precursor, forerunner.

predecesor /preðeθe'sor; preðese'sor/ **-ra** *a. & n.* predecessor.

predecir /preðe'θir; preðe'sir/ *v.* predict, foretell.

predicación /preðika'θion; preðika'sion/ *n. f.* sermon.

predicador /preðika'ðor/ **-ra** *n.* preacher.

predicar /preði'kar/ *v.* preach.

predicción /preðik'θion; preðik'sion/ *n. f.* prediction.

predilecto /preði'lekto/ a. favorite, preferred.

predisponer /preðispo'ner/ v. predispose.

predisposición /preðisposi'θion; preðisposi'sion/ n. f. predisposition; bias.

predominante /preðomi'nante/ a. prevailing, prevalent, predominant.

predominar /preðomi'nar/ v. prevail, predominate.

predominio /preðo'minio/ n. m. predominance, sway.

prefacio /pre'faθio; pre'fasio/ n. m. preface.

preferencia /prefe'renθia; prefe'rensia/ n. f. preference.

preferentemente /preferente'mente/ adv. preferably.

preferible /prefe'riβle/ a. preferable.

preferir /prefe'rir/ v. prefer.

prefijo /pre'fiho/ n. m. prefix; area code, dialing code. —**prefijar**, v.

pregón /pre'gon/ n. m. proclamation; street cry.

pregonar /prego'nar/ v. proclaim; cry out.

pregunta /pre'gunta/ n. f. question, inquiry. **hacer una p.,** to ask a question.

preguntar /pregun'tar/ v. ask, inquire.

preguntarse /pregun'tarse/ v. wonder.

prehistórico /preis'toriko/ a. prehistoric.

prejuicio /pre'huiθio; pre'huisio/ n. m. prejudice.

prelacía /prela'θia; prela'sia/ n. f. prelacy.

preliminar /prelimi'nar/ a. & m. preliminary.

preludio /pre'luðio/ n. m. prelude.

prematuro /prema'turo/ a. premature.

premeditación /premeðita'θion; premeðita-'sion/ n. f. premeditation.

premeditar /premeði'tar/ v. premeditate.

premiar /pre'miar/ v. reward; award a prize to.

premio /'premio/ n. m. prize, award; reward. **p. de consuelo,** consolation prize.

premisa /pre'misa/ n. f. premise.

premura /pre'mura/ n. f. pressure; urgency.

prenda /'prenda/ n. f. jewel; (personal) quality. **p. de vestir,** garment.

prender /pren'der/ v. seize, arrest, catch; pin, clip. **p. fuego a,** set fire to.

prensa /'prensa/ n. f. printing press; (the) press.

prensar /pren'sar/ v. press, compress.

preñado /pre'ɲaðo/ a. pregnant.

preocupación /preokupa'θion; preokupa-'sion/ n. f. worry, preoccupation.

preocupar /preoku'par/ v. worry, preoccupy.

preparación /prepara'θion; prepara'sion/ n. f. preparation.

preparar /prepa'rar/ v. prepare.

preparativo /prepara'tiβo/ n. m. preparation.

preparatorio /prepara'torio/ n. m. preparatory.

preponderante /preponde'rante/ a. preponderant.

preposición /preposi'θion; preposi'sion/ n. f. preposition.

prerrogativa /prerroga'tiβa/ n. f. prerogative, privilege.

presa /'presa/ n. f. capture; (water) dam.

presagiar /presa'hiar/ v. presage, forebode.

presbiteriano /presβite'riano/ **-na** n. & a. Presbyterian.

presbítero /pres'βitero/ n. m. priest.

prescindir de /presθin'dir de; pressin'dir de/ v. dispense with; omit.

prescribir /preskri'βir/ v. prescribe.

prescripción /preskrip'θion; preskrip'sion/ n. f. prescription.

presencia /pre'senθia; pre'sensia/ n. f. presence.

presenciar /presen'θiar; presen'siar/ v. witness, be present at.

presentable /presen'taβle/ a. presentable.

presentación /presenta'θion; presenta'sion/ n. f. presentation; introduction.

presentar /presen'tar/ v. present; introduce.

presente /pre'sente/ a. & m. present.

presentimiento /presenti'miento/ n. m. premonition.

preservación /preserβa'θion; preserβa'sion/ n. f. preservation.

preservar /preser'βar/ v. preserve, keep.

preservativo /preserβa'tiβo/ a. & m. preservative; condom.

presidencia /presi'ðenθia; presi'ðensia/ n. f. presidency.

presidencial /presiðen'θial; presiðen'sial/ a. presidential.

presidente /presi'ðente/ **-ta** n. president.

presidiario /presi'ðiario/ **-ria** n. m. & f. prisoner.

presidio /pre'siðio/ n. m. prison; garrison.

presidir /presi'ðir/ v. preside.

presión /pre'sion/ n. f. pressure.

presión arterial /pre'sion arte'rial/ blood pressure.

preso /'preso/ **-sa** n. prisoner.

presta /'presta/ n. f. mint (plant).

prestador /presta'ðor/ **-ra** n. lender.

prestamista /presta'mista/ n. m. & f. money lender.

préstamo /'prestamo/ n. m. loan.

prestar /pres'tar/ v. lend.

presteza /pres'teθa; pres'tesa/ n. f. haste, promptness.

prestidigitación /prestiðihita'θion; prestiði-hita'sion/ n. f. sleight of hand.

prestigio /pres'tihio/ n. m. prestige.

presto /'presto/ a. **1.** quick, prompt; ready. —adv. **2.** quickly; at once.

presumido /presu'miðo/ a. conceited, presumptuous.

presumir /presu'mir/ v. presume; boast; claim; be conceited.

presunción /presun'θion; presun'sion/ n. f. presumption; conceit.

presunto /pre'sunto/ a. presumed; prospective.

presuntuoso /presun'tuoso/ a. presumptuous.

presupuesto /presu'puesto/ n. m. premise; budget.

pretender /preten'der/ v. pretend; intend; aspire.

pretendiente /preten'diente/ n. m. suitor; pretender (to throne).

pretensión /preten'sion/ n. f. pretension; claim.

pretérito /pre'terito/ a. & m. preterit, past (tense).

pretexto /pre'teksto/ n. m. pretext.

prevalecer /preβale'θer; preβale'ser/ v. prevail.

prevención /preβen'θion; preβen'sion/ n. f. prevention.

prevenir /preβe'nir/ v. prevent; forewarn; prearrange.

preventivo /preβen'tiβo/ a. preventive.

prever /pre'βer/ v. foresee.

previamente /preβia'mente/ adv. previously.

previo /'preβio/ a. previous.

previsible /preβi'siβle/ a. predictable.

previsión /preβi'sion/ n. f. foresight. **p. social**, social security.

prieto /'prieto/ a. blackish, very dark.

primacía /prima'θia; prima'sia/ n. f. primacy.

primario /pri'mario/ a. primary.

primavera /prima'βera/ n. f. spring (season).

primero /pri'mero/ a. & adv. first.

primitivo /primi'tiβo/ a. primitive.

primo /'primo/ -ma n. cousin.

primor /pri'mor/ n. m. beauty; excellence; lovely thing.

primoroso /primo'roso/ a. exquisite, elegant; graceful.

princesa /prin'θesa; prin'sesa/ n. f. princess.

principal /prinθi'pal; prinsi'pal/ a. **1.** principal, main. —n. **2.** m. chief, head, principal.

principalmente /prinθipal'mente; prinsipal'mente/ adv. principally.

príncipe /'prinθipe; 'prinsipe/ n. m. prince.

Príncipe Azul /'prinθipe a'θul; 'prinsipe a'sul/ Prince Charming.

principiar /prinθi'piar; prinsi'piar/ v. begin, initiate.

principio /prin'θipio; prin'sipio/ n. m. beginning, start; principle.

pringado /priŋ'gaðo/ n. m. low-life, loser.

prioridad /priori'ðað/ n. f. priority.

prisa /'prisa/ n. f. hurry, haste. **darse p.**, hurry, hasten. **tener p.**, be in a hurry.

prisión /pri'sion/ n. f. prison; imprisonment.

prisionero /prisio'nero/ -ra n. captive, prisoner.

prisma /'prisma/ n. m. prism.

prismático /pris'matiko/ a. prismatic.

privación /priβa'θion; priβa'sion/ n. f. privation, want.

privado /pri'βaðo/ a. private, secret; deprived.

privar /pri'βar/ v. deprive.

privilegio /priβi'lehio/ n. m. privilege.

pro /pro/ n. m. or f. benefit, advantage. **en p. de**, in behalf of. **en p. y en contra**, pro and con.

proa /'proa/ n. f. prow, bow.

probabilidad /proβaβili'ðað/ n. f. probability.

probable /pro'βaβle/ a. probable, likely.

probablemente /proβaβle'mente/ adv. probably.

probador /proβa'ðor/ n. m. fitting room.

probar /pro'βar/ v. try, sample; taste; test; prove.

probarse /pro'βarse/ v. try on.

probidad /proβi'ðað/ n. f. honesty, integrity.

problema /pro'βlema/ n. m. problem.

probo /'proβo/ a. honest.

procaz /pro'kaθ; pro'kas/ a. impudent, saucy.

proceder /proθe'ðer; prose'ðer/ v. proceed.

procedimiento /proθeði'miento; proseði'miento/ n. m. procedure.

procesar /proθe'sar; prose'sar/ v. prosecute; sue; process.

procesión /proθe'sion; prose'sion/ n. f. procession.

proceso /pro'θeso; pro'seso/ n. m. process; (court) trial.

proclama /pro'klama/ **proclamación** n. f. proclamation.

proclamar /prokla'mar/ v. proclaim.

procreación /prokrea'θion; prokrea'sion/ n. f. procreation.

procrear /prokre'ar/ v. procreate.

procurar /proku'rar/ v. try; see to it; get, procure.

prodigalidad /proðigali'ðað/ n. f. prodigality.

prodigar /proði'gar/ v. lavish; squander, waste.

prodigio /pro'ðihio/ n. m. prodigy.

pródigo /'proðigo/ a. prodigal; profuse; lavish.

producción /proðuk'θion; proðuk'sion/ n. f. production.

producir /produ'θir; produ'sir/ *v.* produce.

productivo /produk'tiβo/ *a.* productive.

producto /pro'δukto/ *n. m.* product.

producto nacional bruto /pro'δukto naθio'nal 'bruto; pro'δukto nasio'nal 'bruto/ gross national product.

proeza /pro'eθa; pro'esa/ *n. f.* prowess.

profanación /profana'θion; profana'sion/ *n. f.* profanation.

profanar /profa'nar/ *v.* defile, desecrate.

profanidad /profani'δaδ/ *n. f.* profanity.

profano /pro'fano/ *a.* profane.

profecía /profe'θia; profe'sia/ *n. f.* prophecy.

proferir /profe'rir/ *v.* utter, express.

profesar /profe'sar/ *v.* profess.

profesión /profe'sion/ *n. f.* profession.

profesional /profesio'nal/ *a.* professional.

profesor /profe'sor/ **-ra** *n.* professor, teacher.

profeta /pro'feta/ *n. m.* prophet.

profético /pro'fetiko/ *a.* prophetic.

profetizar /profeti'θar; profeti'sar/ *v.* prophesy.

proficiente /profi'θiente; profi'siente/ *a.* proficient.

profundamente /profunda'mente/ *adv.* profoundly, deeply.

profundidad /profundi'δaδ/ *n. f.* profundity, depth.

profundizar /profundi'θar; profundi'sar/ *v.* deepen.

profundo /pro'fundo/ *a.* profound, deep.

profuso /pro'fuso/ *a.* profuse.

progenie /pro'henie/ *n. f.* progeny, offspring.

programa /pro'grama/ *n. m.* program; schedule.

programador /programa'δor/ **-ra** *n.* (computer) programmer.

progresar /progre'sar/ *v.* progress, advance.

progresión /progre'sion/ *n. f.* progression.

progresista /progre'sista/ **progresivo** *a.* progressive.

progreso /pro'greso/ *n. m.* progress.

prohibición /proiβi'θion; proiβi'sion/ *n. f.* prohibition.

prohibir /proi'βir/ *v.* prohibit, forbid.

prohibitivo /proiβi'tiβo, proiβi'torio/ *a.* prohibitive.

prole /'prole/ *n. f.* progeny.

proletariado /proleta'riaδo/ *n. m.* proletariat.

proliferación /prolifera'θion; prolifera'sion/ *n. f.* proliferation.

prolijo /pro'liho/ *a.* prolix, tedious; longwinded.

prólogo /'prologo/ *n. m.* prologue; preface.

prolongar /prolon'gar/ *v.* prolong.

promedio /pro'meδio/ *n. m.* average.

promesa /pro'mesa/ *n. f.* promise.

prometer /prome'ter/ *v.* promise.

prometido /prome'tiδo/ *a.* promised; engaged (to marry).

prominencia /promi'nenθia; promi'nensia/ *n. f.* prominence.

promiscuamente /promiskua'mente/ *adv.* promiscuously.

promiscuo /pro'miskuo/ *a.* promiscuous.

promisorio /promi'sorio/ *a.* promissory.

promoción /promo'θion; promo'sion/ *n. f.* promotion.

promocionar /promoθio'nar; promosio'nar/ *v.* advertise, promote.

promover /promo'βer/ *v.* promote, further.

promulgación /promulga'θion; promulga'sion/ *n. f.* promulgation.

promulgar /promul'gar/ *v.* promulgate.

pronombre /pro'nombre/ *n. m.* pronoun.

pronosticación /pronostika'θion; pronostika'sion/ *n. f.* prediction, forecast.

pronosticar /pronosti'kar/ *v.* predict, forecast.

pronóstico /pro'nostiko/ *n. m.* prediction.

prontamente /pronta'mente/ *adv.* promptly.

prontitud /pronti'tuδ/ *n. f.* promptness.

pronto /'pronto/ *a.* **1.** prompt; ready. *—adv.* **2.** soon; quickly. **de p.,** abruptly.

pronunciación /pronunθia'θion; pronunsia'sion/ *n. f.* pronunciation.

pronunciar /pronun'θiar; pronun'siar/ *v.* pronounce.

propagación /propaga'θion; propaga'sion/ *n. f.* propagation.

propaganda /propa'ganda/ *n. f.* propaganda.

propagandista /propagan'dista/ *n. m. & f.* propagandist.

propagar /propa'gar/ *v.* propagate.

propicio /pro'piθio; pro'pisio/ *a.* propitious, auspicious, favorable.

propiedad /propie'δaδ/ *n. f.* property.

propietario /propie'tario/ **-ria** *n.* proprietor; owner; landlord, landlady.

propina /pro'pina/ *n. f.* gratuity, tip.

propio /'propio/ *a.* proper, suitable; typical; (one's) own; -self.

proponer /propo'ner/ *v.* propose.

proporción /propor'θion; propor'sion/ *n. f.* proportion.

proporcionado /proporθio'naδo; proporsio'naδo/ *a.* proportionate.

proporcionar /proporθio'nar; proporsio'nar/ *v.* provide with, supply, afford.

proposición /proposi'θion; proposi'sion/ *n. f.* proposition, offer; proposal.

propósito /pro'posito/ *n. m.* purpose; plan; **a p.,** by the way, apropos; on purpose.

propuesta /pro'puesta/ *n. f.* proposal, motion.

prorrata /pro'rrata/ *n. f.* quota.

prórroga /'prorroga/ *n. f.* renewal, extension.

prorrogar /prorro'gar/ *v.* renew, extend.

prosa /'prosa/ *n. f.* prose.

prosaico /pro'saiko/ *a.* prosaic.

proscribir /proskri'βir/ *v.* prohibit, proscribe, ban.

prosecución /proseku'θion; proseku'sion/ *n. f.* prosecution.

proseguir /prose'gir/ *v.* pursue; proceed, go on.

prosélito /pro'selito/ **-ta** *n.* proselyte.

prospecto /pros'pekto/ *n. m.* prospectus.

prosperar /prospe'rar/ *v.* prosper, thrive, flourish.

prosperidad /prosperi'ðað/ *n. f.* prosperity.

próspero /'prospero/ *a.* prosperous, successful.

prosternado /proster'naðo/ *a.* prostrate.

prostitución /prostitu'θion; prostitu'sion/ *n. f.* prostitution.

prostituir /prosti'tuir/ *v.* prostitute; debase.

prostituta /prosti'tuta/ *n. f.* prostitute.

protagonista /protago'nista/ *n. m. & f.* protagonist, hero, heroine.

protección /protek'θion; protek'sion/ *n. f.* protection.

protector /protek'tor/ **-ra** *a. & n.* protective; protector.

proteger /prote'her/ *v.* protect, safeguard. **p. contra escritura,** write-protect (diskette).

protegido /prote'hiðo/ **-da** *n.* **1.** protégé. —*a.* **2.** protected. **p. contra escritura,** write-protected.

proteína /prote'ina/ *n. f.* protein.

protesta /pro'testa/ *n. f.* protest. —**protestar,** *v.*

protestante /protes'tante/ *a. & n.* Protestant.

protocolo /proto'kolo/ *n. m.* protocol.

protuberancia /protuβe'ranθia; protuβe'ransia/ *n. f.* protuberance, lump.

protuberante /protuβe'rante/ *a.* bulging.

provecho /pro'βetʃo/ *n. m.* profit, gain, benefit. **¡Buen provecho!** May you enjoy your meal!

provechoso /proβe'tʃoso/ *a.* beneficial, advantageous, profitable.

proveer /proβe'er/ *v.* provide, furnish.

provenir de /proβe'nir de/ *v.* originate in, be due to, come from.

proverbial /proβer'βial/ *a.* proverbial.

proverbio /pro'βerβio/ *n. m.* proverb.

providencia /proβi'ðenθia; proβi'ðensia/ *n. f.* providence.

providente /proβi'ðente/ *a.* provident.

provincia /pro'βinθia; pro'βinsia/ *n. f.* province.

provincial /proβin'θial; proβin'sial/ *a.* provincial.

provinciano /proβin'θiano; proβin'siano/ **-na** *a. & n.* provincial.

provisión /proβi'sion/ *n. f.* provision, supply, stock.

provisional /proβisio'nal/ *a.* provisional.

provocación /proβoka'θion; proβoka'sion/ *n. f.* provocation.

provocador /proβoka'ðor/ **-ra** *n.* provoker.

provocar /proβo'kar/ *v.* provoke, excite.

provocativo /proβoka'tiβo/ *a.* provocative.

proximidad /proksimi'ðað/ *n. f.* proximity, vicinity.

próximo /'proksimo/ *a.* next; near.

proyección /proiek'θion; proiek'sion/ *n. f.* projection.

proyectar /proiek'tar/ *v.* plan, project.

proyectil /proyek'til/ *n. m.* projectile, missile, shell.

proyecto /pro'iekto/ *n. m.* plan, project, scheme.

proyector /proiek'tor/ *n. m.* projector.

prudencia /pru'ðenθia; pru'ðensia/ *n. f.* prudence.

prudente /pru'ðente/ *a.* prudent.

prueba /'prueβa/ *n. f.* proof; trial; test.

psicoanálisis /psikoa'nalisis/ *n. m.* psychoanalysis.

psicoanalista /psikoana'lista/ *n. m. & f.* psychoanalyst.

psicodélico /psiko'ðeliko/ *a.* psychedelic.

psicología /psikolo'hia/ *n. f.* psychology.

psicológico /psiko'lohiko/ *a.* psychological.

psicólogo /psi'kologo/ **-ga** *n.* psychologist.

psiquiatra /psi'kiatra/ *n. m. & f.* psychiatrist.

psiquiatría /psikia'tria/ *n. f.* psychiatry.

publicación /puβlika'θion; puβlika'sion/ *n. f.* publication.

publicar /puβli'kar/ *v.* publish.

publicidad /puβliθi'ðað; puβlisi'ðað/ *n. f.* publicity.

publicista /puβli'θista; puβli'sista/ *n. m. & f.* publicity agent.

público /'puβliko/ *a. & m.* public.

puchero /pu'tʃero/ *n. m.* pot.

pudiente /pu'ðiente/ *a.* powerful; wealthy.

pudín /pu'ðin/ *n. m.* pudding.

pudor /pu'ðor/ *n. m.* modesty.

pudoroso /puðo'roso/ *a.* modest.

pudrirse /pu'ðrirse/ *v.* rot.

pueblo /'pueβlo/ *n. m.* town, village; (the) people.

puente /'puente/ *n. m.* bridge.

puente para peatones /'puente para pea'tones/ *n. m.* footbridge.

puerco /'puerko/ **-ca** n. pig.

puericultura /puerikul'tura/ n. f. pediatrics

pueril /pue'ril/ a. childish.

puerilidad /puerili'ðað/ n. f. puerility.

puerta /'puerta/ n. f. door; gate.

puerta giratoria /'puerta hira'toria/ revolving door.

puerta principal /'puerta prinθi'pal; 'puerta prinsi'pal/ front door.

puerto /'puerto/ n. m. port, harbor.

puertorriqueño /puertorri'keɲo/ **-ña** a. & n. Puerto Rican.

pues /'pues/ adv. **1.** well... —conj. **2.** as, since, for.

puesto /'puesto/ n. m. appointment, post, job; place; stand. **p. que,** since.

pugilato /puhi'lato/ n. m. boxing.

pugna /'pugna/ n. f. conflict.

pugnacidad /pugnaθi'ðað: pugnasi'ðað/ n. f. pugnacity.

pugnar /pug'nar/ v. fight; oppose.

pulcritud /pulkri'tuð/ n. f. neatness; exquisiteness.

pulga /'pulga/ n. f. flea.

pulgada /pul'gaða/ n. f. inch.

pulgar /pul'gar/ n. m. thumb.

pulir /pu'lir/ v. polish; beautify.

pulmón /pul'mon/ n. m. lung.

pulmonía /pulmo'nia/ n. f. pneumonia.

pulpa /'pulpa/ n. f. pulp.

púlpito /'pulpito/ n. m. pulpit.

pulque /'pulke/ n. m. pulque (fermented maguey juice).

pulsación /pulsa'θion: pulsa'sion/ n. f. pulsation, beat.

pulsar /pul'sar/ v. pulsate, beat.

pulsera /pul'sera/ n. f. wristband; bracelet.

pulso /'pulso/ n. m. pulse.

pulverizar /pulβeri'θar; pulβeri'sar/ v. pulverize.

puma /'puma/ n. m. puma.

pundonor /pundo'nor/ n. m. point of honor.

punta /'punta/ n. f. point, tip, end.

puntada /pun'taða/ n. f. stitch.

puntapié /punta'pie/ n. m. kick.

puntería /punte'ria/ n. f. (marksman's) aim.

puntiagudo /puntia'guðo/ a. sharppointed.

puntillas /pun'tiʎas; pun'tiyas/ n. f.pl. **de p., en p.,** on tiptoe.

punto /'punto/ n. m. point; period; spot, dot. **dos puntos,** Punct. colon. **a p. de,** about to. **al p.,** instantly.

punto de admiración /'punto de aðmira'θion: 'punto de aðmira'sion/ exclamation mark.

punto de congelación /'punto de koŋgela'θion; 'punto de koŋgela'sion/ freezing point.

punto de ebullición /'punto de eβuʎi'θion: 'punto de eβuyi'sion/ boiling point.

punto de vista /'punto de 'bista/ point of view, viewpoint.

puntuación /puntua'θion; puntua'sion/ n. f. punctuation.

puntual /pun'tual/ a. punctual, prompt.

puntuar /pun'tuar/ v. punctuate.

puñada /pu'ɲaða/ n. f. punch.

puñado /pu'ɲaðo/ n. m. handful.

puñal /pu'ɲal/ n. m. dagger.

puñalada /puɲa'laða/ n. f. stab.

puñetazo /puɲe'taθo; puɲe'taso/ n. m. punch, fist blow.

puño /'puɲo/ n. m. fist; cuff; handle.

pupila /pu'pila/ n. f. pupil (of eye).

pupitre /pu'pitre/ n. m. writing desk, school desk.

pureza /pu'reθa; pu'resa/ n. f. purity; chastity.

purgante /pur'gante/ n. m. laxative.

purgar /pur'gar/ v. purge, cleanse.

purgatorio /purga'torio/ n. m. purgatory.

puridad /puri'ðað/ n. f. secrecy.

purificación /purifika'θion; purifika'sion/ n. f. purification.

purificar /purifi'kar/ v. purify.

purismo /pu'rismo/ n. m. purism.

purista /pu'rista/ n. m. & f. purist.

puritanismo /purita'nismo/ n. m. puritanism.

puro /'puro/ a. **1.** pure. —n. **2.** m. cigar.

púrpura /'purpura/ n. f. purple.

purpúreo /pur'pureo/ a. purple.

purulencia /puru'lenθia; puru'lensia/ n. f. purulence.

purulento /puru'lento/ a. purulent.

pus /pus/ n. m. pus.

pusilánime /pusi'lanime/ a. pusillanimous.

puta /'puta/ **-to** n. prostitute.

putrefacción /putrefak'θion; putrefak'sion/ n. f. putrefaction, rot.

putrefacto /putre'fakto/ a. putrid, rotten.

pútrido /'putriðo/ a. putrid.

puya /'puya/ n. f. goad.

Q R

que /ke/ *rel. pron.* **1.** who, whom; that, which. —*conj.* **2.** than.

qué *a. & pron.* what. **por q., para q.,** why? *adv.* how.

quebrada /ke'βraða/ *n. f.* ravine, gully, gulch; stream.

quebradizo /keβra'ðiθo; keβra'ðiso/ *a.* fragile, brittle.

quebraley /keβra'lei/ *n. m. & f.* lawbreaker, outlaw.

quebrar /ke'βrar/ *v.* break.

queda /'keða/ *n. f.* curfew.

quedar /ke'ðar/ *v.* remain, be located; be left. **q. bien a,** be becoming to.

quedarse /ke'ðarse/ *v.* stay, remain. **q. con,** keep, hold on to; remain with.

quedo /'keðo/ *a.* quiet; gentle.

quehacer /kea'θer; kea'ser/ *n. m.* task; chore.

queja /'keha/ *n. f.* complaint.

quejarse /ke'harse/ *v.* complain, grumble.

quejido /ke'hiðo/ *n. m.* moan.

quejoso /ke'hoso/ *a.* complaining.

quema /'kema/ *n. f.* burning.

quemadura /kema'ðura/ *n. f.* burn.

quemar /ke'mar/ *v.* burn.

querella /ke'reʎa; ke'reya/ *n. f.* quarrel; complaint.

querencia /ke'renθia; ke'rensia/ *n. f.* affection, liking.

querer /ke'rer/ *v.* want, wish; will; love (a person). **q. decir,** mean. **sin q.,** without meaning to; unwillingly.

querido /ke'riðo/ *a.* dear, loved, beloved.

quesería /kese'ria/ *n. f.* dairy.

queso /'keso/ *n. m.* cheese.

queso crema /'keso 'krema/ cream cheese.

quetzal /ket'θal; ket'sal/ *n. m.* quetzal.

quiche /'kitʃe/ *n. f.* quiche.

quiebra /'kieβra/ *n. f* break, fracture; damage; bankruptcy.

quien /kien/ *rel. pron.* who, whom.

quién *interrog. pron.* who, whom.

quienquiera /kien'kiera/ *pron.* whoever, whomever.

quietamente /kieta'mente/ *adv.* quietly.

quieto /'kieto/ *a.* quiet, still.

quietud /kie'tuð/ *n f* quiet, quietude.

quijada /ki'haða/ *n. f.* jaw.

quijotesco /kiho'tesko/ *a.* quixotic.

quilate /ki'late/ *n. m.* carat.

quilla /'kiʎa; 'kiya/ *n. f.* keel.

quimera /ki'mera/ *n. f.* chimera; vision; quarrel.

química /'kimika/ *n. f.* chemistry.

químico /'kimiko/ **-ca** *a. & n.* chemical; chemist.

quimoterapia /kimote'rapia/ *n. f.* chemotherapy.

quincalla /kin'kaʎa; kin'kaya/ *n. f.* (computer) hardware.

quincallería /kinkaʎe'ria; kinkaye'ria/ *n. f.* hardware store.

quince /'kinθe; 'kinse/ *a. & pron.* fifteen.

quinientos /ki'nientos/ *a. & pron.* five hundred.

quinina /ki'nina/ *n. f.* quinine.

quintana /kin'tana/ *n. f.* country home.

quinto /'kinto/ *a.* fifth.

quirúrgico /ki'rurhiko/ *a.* surgical.

quiste /'kiste/ *n. m.* cyst.

quitamanchas /kita'mantʃas/ *n. m.* stain remover.

quitanieves /kita'nieβes/ *n. m.* snowplow.

quitar /ki'tar/ *v.* take away, remove.

quitarse /ki'tarse/ *v.* take off; get rid of.

quitasol /kita'sol/ *n. m.* parasol, umbrella.

quitasueño /kita'sueɲo/ *n. m. Colloq.* nightmare; worry.

quizá /ki'θa; ki'sa/ **quizás** *adv.* perhaps, maybe.

quórum /'korum/ *n. m.* quorum.

rábano /'rraβano/ *n. m.* radish.

rabí /rra'βi/ **rabino** *n. m.* rabbi.

rabia /'rraβia/ *n. f.* rage; grudge; rabies.

rabiar /rra'βiar/ *v.* rage, be furious.

rabieta /rra'βieta/ *n. f.* tantrum.

rabioso /rra'βioso/ *a.* furious; rabid.

rabo /'rraβo/ *n. m.* tail.

racha /'rratʃa/ *n. f.* streak.

racimo /rra'θimo; rra'simo/ *n. m.* bunch, cluster.

ración /rra'θion; rra'sion/ *n. f.* ration. —**racionar,** *v.*

racionabilidad /rraθionaβili'ðað; rrasionaβili'ðað/ *n. f.* rationality.

racional /rraθio'nal; rrasio'nal/ *a.* rational.

racionalismo /rraθiona'lismo; rrasiona'lismo/ *n. m.* rationalism.

racionalmente /rraθional'mente; rrasional'mente/ *adv.* rationally.

radar /rra'ðar/ *n. m.* radar.

radiación /rraðia'θion; rraðia'sion/ *n. f.* radiation.

radiador /rraðia'ðor/ *n. m.* radiator.

radiante /rra'ðiante/ *a.* radiant.

radical /rraði'kal/ *a. & n.* radical.

radicalismo /rraðika'lismo/ *n. m.* radicalism.

radicoso /rraði'koso/ *a.* radical.

radio /'rraðio/ *n. m. or f.* radio.

radioactividad /rraðioaktiβi'ðað/ *n. f.* radioactivity.

radioactivo /rraðioak'tiβo/ *a.* radioactive.

radiocasete /rraðioka'sete/ *n. m.* radio cassette.

radiodifundir /rraðioðifun'dir/ *v.* broadcast.

radiodifusión /rraðioðifu'sion/ *n. f.* (radio) broadcasting.

radiografía /rraðiogra'fia/ *n. f.* X-ray.

radiografiar /rraðiogra'fiar/ *v.* X-ray.

ráfaga /'rrafaga/ *n. f.* gust (of wind).

raíz /rra'iθ; rra'is/ *n. f.* root.

raja /'rraha/ *n. f.* rip; split, crack. —**rajar,** *v.*

ralea /rra'lea/ *n. f.* stock, breed.

ralo /'rralo/ *a.* thin, scattered.

rama /'rrama/ *n. f.* branch, bough.

ramillete /rrami'ʎete; rrami'yete/ *n. m.* bouquet.

ramo /'rramo/ *n. m.* branch, bough; bouquet.

ramonear /rramone'ar/ *v.* browse.

rampa /'rrampa/ *n. f.* ramp.

rana /'rrana/ *n. f.* frog.

ranchero /rran'tʃero/ **-ra** *n.* small farmer.

rancho /'rrantʃo/ *n. m.* ranch.

rancidez /rranθi'ðeθ; rransi'ðes/ *n. f.* rancidity.

rancio /'rranθio; 'rransio/ *a.* rancid, rank, stale, sour.

rango /'rrango/ *n. m.* rank.

ranúnculo /rra'nunkulo/ *n. m.* ranunculus; buttercup.

ranura /rra'nura/ *n. f.* slot.

ranura de expansión /rra'nura de ekspan'sion/ expansion slot.

rapacidad /rrapaθi'ðað; rrapasi'ðað/ *n. f.* rapacity.

rapaz /rra'paθ; rra'pas/ *a.* **1.** rapacious. —*n.* **2.** *m.* young boy.

rapé /'rrape/ *n. m.* snuff.

rápidamente /rrapiða'mente/ *adv.* rapidly.

rapidez /rrapi'ðeθ; rrapi'ðes/ *n. f.* rapidity, speed.

rápido /'rrapiðo/ *a.* **1.** rapid, fast, speedy. —*n.* **2.** *m.* express (train).

rapiña /rra'piɲa/ *n. f.* robbery, plundering.

rapsodia /rrap'soðia/ *n. f.* rhapsody.

rapto /'rrapto/ *n. m.* kidnapping.

raquero /rra'kero/ **-ra** *n.* beachcomber.

raqueta /rra'keta/ *n. f.* (tennis) racket.

rareza /rra'reθa; rra'resa/ *n. f.* rarity; freak.

raridad /rrari'ðað/ *n. f.* rarity.

raro /'rraro/ *a.* rare, strange, unusual, odd, queer.

rasar /rra'sar/ *v.* skim.

rascacielos /rraska'θielos; rraska'sielos/ *n. m.* skyscraper.

rascar /rras'kar/ *v.* scrape; scratch.

rasgadura /rrasga'ðura/ *n. f.* tear, rip. —**rasgar,** *v.*

rasgo /'rrasgo/ *n. m.* trait.

rasgón /rras'gon/ *n. m.* tear.

rasguño /rras'guɲo/ *n. m.* scratch. —**rasguñar,** *v.*

raso /'rraso/ *a.* **1.** plain. **soldado r.,** *Mil.* private. —*n.* **2.** *m.* satin.

raspar /rras'par/ *v.* scrape; erase.

rastra /'rrastra/ *n. f.* trail, track. —**rastrear,** *v.*

rastrillar /rrastri'ʎar; rrastri'yar/ *v.* rake.

rastro /'rrastro/ *n. m.* track, trail, trace; rake; flea market.

rata /'rrata/ *n. f.* rat.

ratificación /rratifika'θion; rratifika'sion/ *n. f.* ratification.

ratificar /rratifi'kar/ *v.* ratify.

rato /'rrato/ *n. m.* while, spell, short time.

ratón /rra'ton/ *n. m.* mouse.

ratonera /rrato'nera/ *n. f.* mousetrap.

raya /'rraya/ *n. f.* dash, line, streak, stripe.

rayar /rra'yar/ *v.* rule, stripe; scratch; cross out.

rayo /'rrayo/ *n. m.* lightning bolt; ray; flash.

rayón /rra'yon/ *n. m.* rayon.

raza /'rraθa; 'rrasa/ *n. f.* race; breed, stock.

razón /rra'θon; rra'son/ *n. f.* reason; ratio. **a r. de,** at the rate of. **tener r.,** to be right.

razonable /rraθo'naβle; rraso'naβle/ *a.* reasonable, sensible.

razonamiento /rraθona'miento; rrasona'miento/ *n. m.* argument.

razonar /rraθo'nar; rraso'nar/ *v.* reason.

reacción /rreak'θion; rreak'sion/ *n. f.* reaction.

reaccionar /rreakθio'nar; rreaksio'nar/ *v.* react.

reaccionario /rreakθio'nario; rreaksio'nario/ **-ria** *a.* & *n.* reactionary.

reacondicionar /rreakondiθio'nar; rreakondisio'nar/ *v.* recondition.

reactivo /rreak'tiβo/ *a.* & *m.* reactive; *Chem.* reagent.

reactor /rreak'tor/ *n. m.* reactor.

real /rre'al/ *a.* royal, regal; real, actual.

realdad /rreal'dað/ *n. f.* royal authority.

realeza /rrea'leθa; rrea'lesa/ *n. f.* royalty.

realidad /rreali'ðað/ *n. f.* reality.

realidad virtual /rreali'ðaeth βir'tual/ virtual reality.

realista /rrea'lista/ *a.* & *n.* realistic; realist.

realización /rrealiθa'θion; rrealisa'sion/ *n. f.* achievement, accomplishment.

realizar /rreali'θar; rreali'sar/ *v.* accomplish; fulfill; effect; *Com.* realize.

realmente /rreal'mente/ *adv.* in reality, really.

realzar /rreal'θar; rreal'sar/ *v.* enhance.

reata /rre'ata/ *n. f.* rope; lasso, lariat.

rebaja /rre'βaha/ *n. f.* reduction.

rebajar /rreβa'har/ *v.* cheapen; reduce (in price); lower.

rebanada /rreβa'naða/ *n. f.* slice. **—rebanar,** *v.*

rebaño /rre'βaɲo/ *n. m.* flock, herd.

rebato /rre'βato/ *n. m.* alarm; sudden attack.

rebelarse /rreβe'larse/ *v.* rebel, revolt.

rebelde /rre'βelde/ *a. & n.* rebellious; rebel.

rebelión /rreβe'lion/ *n. f.* rebellion, revolt.

reborde /rre'βorðe/ *n. m.* border.

rebotar /rreβo'tar/ *v.* rebound.

rebozo /rre'βoθo; rre'βoso/ *n. m.* shawl.

rebuscar /rreβus'kar/ *v.* search thoroughly.

rebuznar /rreβuθ'nar; rreβus'nar/ *v.* bray.

recado /rre'kaðo/ *n. m.* message; errand.

recaída /rreka'iða/ *n. f.* relapse. **—recaer,** *v.*

recalcar /rrekal'kar/ *v.* stress, emphasize.

recalentar /rrekalen'tar/ *v.* reheat.

recámara /rre'kamara/ *n. f.* (Mex.) bedroom.

recapitulación /rrekapitula'θion; rrekapitula'sion/ *n. f.* recapitulation.

recapitular /rrekapitu'lar/ *v.* recapitulate.

recatado /rreka'taðo/ *n. m.* coy; prudent.

recaudador /rrekauða'ðor/ **-ra** *n.* tax collector.

recelar /rreθe'lar; rrese'lar/ *v.* fear, distrust.

receloso /rreθe'loso; rrese'loso/ *a.* distrustful.

recepción /rreθep'θion; rresep'sion/ *n. f.* reception.

recepcionista /rreθepθio'nista; rresepsio'nista/ *n. m. & f.* desk clerk.

receptáculo /rreθep'takulo; rresep'takulo/ *n. m.* receptacle.

receptividad /rreθeptiβi'ðað; rreseptiβi'ðað/ *n. f.* receptivity.

receptivo /rreθep'tiβo; rresep'tiβo/ *a.* receptive.

receptor /rreθep'tor; rresep'tor/ *n. m.* receiver.

receta /rre'θeta; rre'seta/ *n. f.* recipe; prescription.

recetar /rreθe'tar; rrese'tar/ *v.* prescribe.

rechazar /rretʃa'θar; rretʃa'sar/ *v.* reject, spurn, discard.

rechinar /rretʃi'nar/ *v.* chatter.

recibimiento /rreθiβi'miento; rresiβi'miento/ *n. m.* reception; welcome; anteroom.

recibir /rreθi'βir; rresi'βir/ *v.* receive.

recibo /rre'θiβo; rre'siβo/ *n. m.* receipt.

reciclaje /reθi'klahe; resi'klahe/ *n. m.* recycling.

reciclar /rreθi'klar; rresi'klar/ *v.* recycle.

recidiva /rreθi'ðiβa; rresi'ðiβa/ *n. f.* relapse.

recién /rre'θien; rre'sien/ *adv.* recently, newly, just.

reciente /rre'θiente; rre'siente/ *a.* recent.

recinto /rre'θinto; rre'sinto/ *n. m.* enclosure.

recipiente /rreθi'piente; rresi'piente/ *n. m.* recipient.

reciprocación /rreθiproka'θion; rresiproka'sion/ *n. f.* reciprocation.

recíprocamente /rreθiproka'mente; rresiproka'mente/ *adv.* reciprocally.

reciprocar /rreθipro'kar; rresipro'kar/ *v.* reciprocate.

reciprocidad /rreθiproθi'ðað; rresiprosi'ðað/ *n. f.* reciprocity.

recitación /rreθita'θion; rresita'sion/ *n. f.* recitation.

recitar /rreθi'tar; rresi'tar/ *v.* recite.

reclamación /rreklama'θion; rreklama'sion/ *n. f.* claim; complaint.

reclamar /rrekla'mar/ *v.* claim; complain.

reclamo /rre'klamo/ *n. m.* claim; advertisement, advertising; decoy.

reclinar /rrekli'nar/ *v.* recline, repose, lean.

recluta /rre'kluta/ *n. m. & f.* recruit.

reclutar /rreklu'tar/ *v.* recruit, draft.

recobrar /rreko'βrar/ *v.* recover, salvage, regain.

recobro /rre'koβro/ *n. m.* recovery.

recoger /rreko'her/ *v.* gather; collect; pick up. **r. el conocimiento,** regain consciousness.

recogerse /rreko'herse/ *v.* retire (for night).

recolectar /rrekolek'tar/ *v.* gather, assemble; harvest.

recomendación /rrekomenda'θion; rrekomenda'sion/ *n. f.* recommendation; commendation.

recomendar /rrekomen'dar/ *v.* recommend; commend.

recompensa /rrekom'pensa/ *n. f.* recompense; compensation.

recompensar /rrekompen'sar/ *v.* reward; compensate.

reconciliación /rrekonθilia'θion; rrekonsilia'sion/ *n. f.* reconciliation.

reconciliar /rrekonθi'liar; rrekonsi'liar/ *v.* reconcile.

reconocer /rrekono'θer; rrekono'ser/ *v.* recognize; acknowledge; inspect, examine; *Mil.* reconnoiter.

reconocimiento /rrekonoθi'miento; rrekonosi'miento/ *n. m.* recognition; appreciation, gratitude.

reconstituir /rrekonsti'tuir/ *v.* reconstitute.

reconstruir /rrekons'truir/ *v.* reconstruct, rebuild.

record /'rrekorð/ *n. m.* (sports) record.

recordar /rrekor'ðar/ v. recall, recollect; remind.

recorrer /rreko'rrer/ v. go over; read over; cover (distance).

recorte /rre'korte/ n. m. clipping, cutting.

recostarse /rrekos'tarse/ v. recline, lean back, rest.

recreación /rrekrea'θion; rrekrea'sion/ n. f. recreation.

recreo /rre'kreo/ n. m. recreation.

recriminación /rrekrimina'θion; rrekrimina'sion/ n. f. recrimination.

rectangular /rrektaŋgu'lar/ a. rectangular.

rectángulo /rrek'taŋgulo/ n. m. rectangle.

rectificación /rrektifika'θion; rrektifika'sion/ n. f. rectification.

rectificar /rrektifi'kar/ v. rectify.

recto /'rrekto/ a. straight; just, fair. **ángulo r.**, right angle.

recuento /rre'kuento/ n. m. recount.

recuerdo /rre'kuerðo/ n. m. memory; souvenir; remembrance; (pl.) regards.

reculada /rreku'laða/ n. f. recoil. —**recular,** v.

recuperación /rrekupera'θion; rrekupera'sion/ n. f. recuperation.

recuperar /rrekupe'rar/ v. recuperate.

recurrir /rreku'rrir/ v. revert; resort, have recourse.

recurso /rre'kurso/ n. m. resource; recourse.

red /rreð/ n. f. net; trap. **r. local** local area network.

redacción /rreðak'θion; rreðak'sion/ n. f. (editorial) staff; composition (of written material).

redactar /rreðak'tar/ v. draft, draw up; edit.

redactor /rreðak'tor/ -ra n. editor.

redada /rre'ðaða/ n. f. netful, catch, haul.

redargución /rreðargu'θion; rreðargu'sion/ n. f. retort. —**redargüir,** v

redención /rreðen'θion; rreðen'sion/ n. f. redemption, salvation.

redentor /rreðen'tor/ n. m. redeemer.

redimir /rreði'mir/ v. redeem.

redoblante /rreðo'βlante/ n. m. snare drum; snare dummer.

redonda /rre'ðonda/ n. f. neighborhood, vicinity.

redondo /rre'ðondo/ a. round, circular.

reducción /rreðuk'θion; rreðuk'sion/ n. f. reduction.

reducir /rreðu'θir; rreðu'sir/ v. reduce.

reembolso /rreem'βolso/ n. m. refund. —**reembolsar,** v.

reemplazar /rreempla'θar; rreempla'sar/ v. replace, supersede.

reencarnación /rreenkarna'θion; rreenkarna'sion/ n. f. reincarnation.

reexaminar /rreeksami'nar/ v. reexamine.

reexpedir /rreekspe'ðir/ v. forward (mail).

referencia /rrefe'renθia; rrefe'rensia/ n. f. reference.

referéndum /rrefe'rendum/ n. m. referendum.

referir /rrefe'rir/ v. relate, report on.

referirse /rrefe'rirse/ v. refer.

refinamiento /rrefina'miento/ n. m. refinement.

refinar /rrefi'nar/ v. refine.

refinería /rrefine'ria/ n. f. refinery.

reflejar /rrefle'har/ v. reflect; think, ponder.

reflejo /rre'fleho/ n. m. reflection; glare.

reflexión /rreflek'sion/ n. f. reflection, thought.

reflexionar /rrefleksio'nar/ v. reflect, think.

reflujo /rre'fluho/ n. m. ebb; ebb tide.

reforma /rre'forma/ n. f. reform. —**reformar,** v.

reformación /rreforma'θion; rreforma'sion/ n. f. reformation.

reformador /rreforma'ðor/ -ra n. reformer.

reforma tributaria /rre'forma triβu'taria/ tax reform.

reforzar /rrefor'θar; rrefor'sar/ v. reinforce, strengthen; encourage.

refractario /rrefrak'tario/ a. refractory.

refrán /rre'fran/ n. m. proverb, saying.

refrenar /rrefre'nar/ v. curb, rein; restrain.

refrescar /rrefres'kar/ v. refresh, freshen, cool.

refresco /rre'fresko/ n. m. refreshment; cold drink.

refrigeración /rrefrihera'θion; rrefrihera'sion/ n. f. refrigeration.

refrigerador /rrefrihera'ðor/ n. m. refrigerator.

refrigerar /rrefrihe'rar/ v. refrigerate.

refuerzo /rre'fuerθo; rre'fuerso/ n. m. reinforcement.

refugiado /rrefu'hiaðo/ -da n. refugee.

refugiarse /rrefu'hiarse/ v take refuge.

refugio /rre'fuhio/ n. m. refuge, asylum, shelter.

refulgencia /rreful'henθia; rreful'hensia/ n. f. refulgence.

refulgente /rreful'hente/ a. refulgent.

refulgir /rreful'hir/ v. shine.

refunfuñar /rrefunfu'ɲar/ v. mutter, grumble, growl.

refutación /rrefuta'θion; rrefuta'sion/ n. f. refutation; rebuttal.

refutar /rrefu'tar/ v. refute.

regadera /rrega'ðera/ n. f. watering can.

regadizo /rrega'ðiθo; rrega'ðiso/ a. irrigable.

regadura /rrega'ðura/ n. f. irrigation.

regalar /rrega'lar/ v. give (a gift), give away.

regaliz /rrega'liθ; rrega'lis/ n. m. licorice.

regalo /rre'galo/ *n. m.* gift, present, **con r.,** in luxury.

regañar /rrega'ɲar/ *v.* reprove; scold.

regaño /rre'gaɲo/ *n. m.* reprimand; scolding.

regar /rre'gar/ *v.* water, irrigate.

regatear /rregate'ar/ *v.* haggle.

regateo /rrega'teo/ *n. m.* bargaining, haggling.

regazo /rre'gaθo; rre'gaso/ *n. m.* lap.

regencia /rre'henθia; rre'hensia/ *n. f.* regency.

regeneración /rrehenera'θion; rrehenera-'sion/ *n. f.* regeneration.

regenerar /rrehene'rar/ *v.* regenerate.

regente /rre'hente/ **-ta** *a. & n.* regent.

régimen /'rrehimen/ *n. m.* regime; diet.

regimentar /rrehimen'tar/ *v.* regiment.

regimiento /rrehi'miento/ *n. m.* regiment.

región /rre'hion/ *n. f.* region.

regional /rrehio'nal/ *a.* regional, sectional.

regir /rre'hir/ *v.* rule; be in effect.

registrar /rrehis'trar/ *v.* register; record; search.

registro /rre'histro/ *n. m.* register; record; search.

regla /'rregla/ *n. f.* rule, regulation. **en r.,** in order.

reglamento /rregla'mento/ *n. m.* code of regulations.

regocijarse /rregoθi'harse; rregosi'harse/ *v.* rejoice, exult.

regocijo /rrego'θiho; rrego'siho/ *n. f.* rejoicing; merriment, joy.

regordete /rregor'ðete/ *a.* chubby, plump.

regresar /rregre'sar/ *v.* go back, return.

regresión /rregre'sion/ *n. f.* regression.

regresivo /rregre'siβo/ *a.* regressive.

regreso /rre'greso/ *n. m.* return.

regulación /rregula'θion; rregula'sion/ *n. f.* regulation.

regular /rregu'lar/ *a.* 1. regular; fair, middling. —*v.* 2. regulate.

regularidad /rregulari'ðað/ *n. f.* regularity.

regularmente /rregular'mente/ *adv.* regularly.

rehabilitación /rreaβilita'θion; rreaβilita-'sion/ *n. f.* rehabilitation.

rehabilitar /rreaβili'tar/ *v.* rehabilitate.

rehén /rre'en/ *n. m.* hostage.

rehogar /rreo'gar/ *v.* brown.

rehusar /rreu'sar/ *v.* refuse; decline.

reina /'rreina/ *n. f.* queen.

reinado /rrei'naðo/ *n. m.* reign. —**reinar,** *v.*

reino /'rreino/ *n. m.* kingdom; realm; reign.

reír /rre'ir/ *v.* laugh.

reiteración /rreitera'θion; rreitera'sion/ *n. f.* reiteration.

reiterar /rreite'rar/ *v.* reiterate.

reja /'rreha/ *n. f.* grating, grillwork.

relación /rrela'θion; rrela'sion/ *n. f.* relation; account, report.

relacionar /rrelaθio'nar; rrelasio'nar/ *v.* relate, connect.

relajamiento /rrelaha'miento/ *n. m.* laxity, laxness.

relajar /rrela'har/ *v.* relax, slacken.

relámpago /rre'lampago/ *n. m.* lightning; flash (of lightning).

relatador /rrelata'ðor/ **-ra** *n.* teller.

relatar /rrela'tar/ *v.* relate, recount.

relativamente /rrelatiβa'mente/ *adv.* relatively.

relatividad /rrelatiβi'ðað/ *n. f.* relativity.

relativo /rrela'tiβo/ *a.* relative.

relato /rre'lato/ *n. m.* account, story.

relegación /rrelega'θion; rrelega'sion/ *n. f.* relegation.

relegar /rrele'gar/ *v.* relegate.

relevar /rrele'βar/ *v.* relieve.

relicario /rreli'kario/ *n. m.* reliquary; locket.

relieve /rre'lieβe/ *n. m.* (sculpture) relief.

religión /rreli'hion/ *n. f.* religion.

religiosidad /rrelihiosi'ðað/ *n. f.* religiosity.

religioso /rreli'hioso/ **-sa** *a.* 1. religious. —*n.* 2. *m.* member of a religious order.

reliquia /rre'likia/ *n. f.* relic.

rellenar /rreʎe'nar; rreye'nar/ *v.* refill; fill up, stuff.

relleno /rre'ʎeno; rre'yeno/ *n. m.* filling; stuffing.

reloj /rre'loh/ *n. m.* clock; watch.

reloj de pulsera /rre'loh de pul'sera/ wrist watch.

relojería /rrelohe'ria/ *n. f.* watchmaker's shop.

relojero /rrelo'hero/ **-ra** *n.* watchmaker.

relucir /rrelu'θir; rrelu'sir/ *v.* glow, shine; excel.

relumbrar /rrelum'βrar/ *v.* glitter, sparkle.

remache /rre'matʃe/ *n. m.* rivet. —**remachar,** *v.*

remar /rre'mar/ *v.* row (a boat).

rematado /rrema'taðo/ *a.* finished; sold.

remate /rre'mate/ *n. m.* end, finish; auction. **de r.,** utterly.

remedador /rremeða'ðor/ **-ra** *n.* imitator.

remedar /rreme'ðar/ *v.* imitate.

remedio /rre'meðio/ *n. m.* remedy. —**remediar,** *v.*

remendar /rremen'dar/ *v.* mend, patch.

remesa /rre'mesa/ *n. f.* shipment; remittance.

remiendo /rre'miendo/ *n. m.* patch.

remilgado /rremil'gaðo/ *a.* prudish; affected.

reminiscencia /rreminis'θenθia; rreminis-'sensia/ *n. f.* reminiscence.

remitir /rremi'tir/ *v.* remit.

remo /'rremo/ *n. m.* oar.

remolacha /rremo'latʃa/ n. f. beet.

remolcador /rremolka'ðor/ n. m. tug (boat); tow truck.

remolino /rremo'lino/ n. m. whirl; whirlpool; whirlwind.

remolque /rre'molke/ n. m. tow. —**remolcar**, v.

remontar /rremon'tar/ v. ascend, go up.

remontarse /rremon'tarse/ v. get excited; soar. **r. a,** date from; go back to (in time).

remordimiento /rremorði'miento/ n. m. remorse.

remotamente /rremota'mente/ adv. remotely.

remoto /rre'moto/ a. remote.

remover /rremo'βer/ v. remove; stir; shake; loosen.

rempujar /rrempu'har/ v. jostle.

remuneración /rremunera'θion; rremunera'sion/ n. f. remuneration.

remunerar /rremune'rar/ v. remunerate.

renacido /rrena'ðiðo: rrena'siðo/ a. reborn, born-again.

renacimiento /rrenaθi'miento; rrenasi'miento/ n. m. rebirth; renaissance.

rencor /rren'kor/ n. m. rancor, bitterness, animosity; grudge.

rencoroso /rrenko'roso/ a. rancorous, bitter.

rendición /rrendi'θion; rrendi'sion/ n. f. surrender.

rendido /rren'diðo/ a. weary, worn out.

rendir /rren'dir/ v. yield; surrender, give up; win over.

renegado /rrene'gaðo/ **-da** n. renegade.

renglón /rreŋ'glon/ n. m. line; Com. item.

reno /'rreno/ n. m. reindeer.

renombre /rre'nombre/ n. m. renown.

renovación /rrenoβa'θion; rrenoβa'sion/ f. renovation, renewal.

renovar /rreno'βar/ v. renew; renovate.

renta /'rrenta/ n. f. income; rent.

rentar /rren'tar/ v. yield; rent.

renuencia /rre'nuenθia; rre'nuensia/ n. f. reluctance.

renuente /rre'nuente/ a. reluctant.

renuncia /rre'nunθia; rre'nunsia/ n. f. resignation; renunciation.

renunciar /rrenun'θiar; rrenun'siar/ v. resign; renounce, give up.

reñir /rre'ɲir/ v. scold, berate; quarrel, wrangle.

reo /'rreo/ a. & n. criminal; convict.

reorganizar /rreorgani'θar; rreorgani'sar/ v. reorganize.

reparación /rrepara'θion; rrepara'sion/ n. f. reparation, atonement; repair.

reparar /rrepa'rar/ v. repair; mend; stop, stay over. **r. en,** notice; consider.

reparo /rre'paro/ n. m. repair; remark; difficulty; objection.

repartición /rreparti'θion; rreparti'sion/ n. f., **repartimiento, reparto,** m. division, distribution.

repartir /rrepar'tir/ v. divide, apportion, distribute; Theat. cast.

repaso /rre'paso/ n. m. review. —**repasar**, v.

repatriación /rrepatria'θion: rrepatria'sion/ n. f. repatriation.

repatriar /rrepa'triar/ v. repatriate.

repeler /rrepe'ler/ v. repel.

repente /rre'pente/ n. m. **de r.,** suddenly; unexpectedly.

repentinamente /rrepentina'mente/ adv. suddenly.

repentino /rrepen'tino/ a. sudden.

repercusión /rreperku'sion/ n. f. repercussion.

repertorio /rreper'torio/ n. m. repertoire.

repetición /rrepeti'θion; rrepeti'sion/ n. f. repetition; action replay.

repetidamente /rrepetiða'mente/ adv. repeatedly.

repetir /rrepe'tir/ v. repeat.

repisa /rre'pisa/ n. f. shelf.

réplica /'rreplika/ n. f. reply; objection; replica.

replicar /rrepli'kar/ v. reply; answer back.

repollo /rre'poʎo; rre'poyo/ n. m. cabbage.

reponer /rrepo'ner/ v. replace; repair.

reponerse /rrepo'nerse/ v. recover, get well.

reporte /rre'porte/ n. m. report; news.

repórter /rre'porter/ **reportero -ra** n. reporter.

reposado /rrepo'saðo/ a. tranquil, peaceful, quiet.

reposo /rre'poso/ n. m. repose, rest. —**reposar**, v.

reposte /rre'poste/ n. f. pantry.

represalia /rrepre'salia/ n. f. reprisal.

representación /rrepresenta'θion; rrepresenta'sion/ n. f. representation; Theat. performance.

representante /rrepresen'tante/ n. m. & f. representative, agent.

representar /rrepresen'tar/ v. represent; depict; Theat. perform.

representativo /rrepresenta'tiβo/ a. representative.

represión /rrepre'sion/ n. f. repression.

represivo /rrepre'siβo/ a. repressive.

reprimenda /rrepri'menda/ n. f. reprimand.

reprimir /rrepri'mir/ v. repress, quell.

reproche /rre'protʃe/ n. m. reproach. —**reprochar**, v.

reproducción /rreproðuk'θion; rreproðuk-'sion/ n. f. reproduction.

reproducir /rreproðu'θir; rreproðu'sir/ v. reproduce.

reptil /rrep'til/ n. m. reptile.

república /rre'puβlika/ n. f. republic.

republicano /rrepuβli'kano/ **-na** a. & n. republican.

repudiación /rrepuðia'θion: rrepuðia'sion/ n. f. repudiation.

repudiar /rrepu'ðiar/ v. repudiate; disown.

repuesto /rre'puesto/ n. m. spare part. **de r.,** spare.

repugnancia /rrepug'nanθia: rrepug'nansia/ n. f. repugnance.

repugnante /rrepug'nante/ a. disgusting, repugnant, repulsive, revolting.

repugnar /rrepug'nar/ v. disgust.

repulsa /rre'pulsa/ n. f. refusal; repulse.

repulsivo /repul'siβo/ a. repulsive.

reputación /rreputa'θion: rreputa'sion/ n. f. reputation.

reputar /rrepu'tar/ v. repute; appreciate.

requerir /rreke'rir/ v. require.

requesón /rreke'son/ n. m. cottage cheese.

requisición /rrekisi'θion: rrekisi'sion/ n. f. requisition.

requisito /rreki'sito/ n. m. requisite, requirement.

res /rres/ n. f. head of cattle.

resaca /rre'saka/ n. f. hangover.

resbalar /rresβa'lar/ v. slide; slip.

resbaloso /rresβa'loso/ a. slippery.

rescate /rres'kate/ n. m. rescue; ransom. —**rescatar,** v.

rescindir /rresθin'dir; rressin'dir/ v. rescind.

resentimiento /rresenti'miento/ n. m. resentment.

resentirse /rresen'tirse/ v. resent.

reserva /rre'serβa/ n. f. reserve. —**reservar,** v.

reservación /rreserβa'θion; rreserβa'sion/ n. f. reservation.

resfriado /rres'friaðo/ n. m. Med. cold.

resfriarse /rres'friarse/ v. catch cold.

resguardar /rresguar'ðar/ v. guard, protect.

residencia /rresi'ðenθia; rresi'ðensia/ n. f. residence; seat, headquarters.

residente /rresi'ðente/ a. & n. resident.

residir /rresi'ðir/ v. reside.

residuo /rre'siðuo/ n. m. remainder.

resignación /rresigna'θion; rresigna'sion/ n. f. resignation.

resignar /rresig'nar/ v. resign.

resina /rre'sina/ n. f. resin; rosin.

resistencia /rresis'tenθia; rresis'tensia/ n. f. resistance.

resistir /rresis'tir/ v. resist; endure.

resolución /rresolu'θion; rresolu'sion/ n. f. resolution.

resolutivamente /rresolutiβa'mente/ adv. resolutely.

resolver /rresol'βer/ v. resolve; solve.

resonante /rreso'nante/ a. resonant.

resonar /rreso'nar/ v. resound.

resorte /rre'sorte/ n. m. Mech. spring.

respaldar /rrespal'dar/ v. endorse; back.

respaldo /rres'paldo/ n. m. back (of a seat).

respectivo /respek'tiβo/ a. respective.

respecto /rres'pekto/ n. m. relation, proportion; **r. a,** concerning, regarding.

respetabilidad /rrespetaβili'ðað/ n. f. respectability.

respetable /rrespe'taβle/ a. respectable.

respeto /rres'peto/ n. m. respect. —**respetar,** v.

respetuosamente /rrespetuosa'mente/ adv. respectfully.

respetuoso /rrespe'tuoso/ a. respectful.

respiración /rrespira'θion; rrespira'sion/ n. f. respiration, breath.

respirar /rrespi'rar/ v. breathe

resplandeciente /rresplande'θiente; rresplande'siente/ a. resplendent.

resplandor /rresplan'dor/ n. m. brightness, glitter.

responder /rrespon'der/ v. respond, answer.

responsabilidad /rresponsaβili'ðað/ n. f. responsibility.

responsable /rrespon'saβle/ a. responsible.

respuesta /rres'puesta/ n. f. answer, response, reply.

resquicio /rres'kiθio; rres'kisio/ n. m. crack, slit.

resta /'rresta/ n. f. subtraction; remainder.

restablecer /rrestaβle'θer; rrestaβle'ser/ v. restore; reestablish.

restablecerse /rrestaβle'θerse; rrestaβle-'serse/ v. recover, get well.

restar /rres'tar/ v. remain; subtract.

restauración /rrestaura'θion; rrestaura'sion/ n. f. restoration.

restaurante /rrestau'rante/ n. m. restaurant.

restaurar /rrestau'rar/ v. restore.

restitución /rrestitu'θion; rrestitu'sion/ n. f. restitution.

restituir /rresti'tuir/ v. restore, give back.

resto /'rresto/ n. m. remainder; rest; (pl.) remains.

restorán /rresto'ran/ n. m. restaurant.

restregar /rrestre'gar/ v. rub hard; scrub.

restricción /rrestrik'θion; rrestrik'sion/ n. f. restriction.

restrictivo /rrestrik'tiβo/ a. restrictive.

restringir /rrestriŋ'gir/ v. restrict, curtail.

resucitar /rresuθi'tar; rresusi'tar/ v. revive, resuscitate.

resuelto /rre'suelto/ a. resolute.

resultado /rresul'taðo/ n. m. result.

resultar /rresul'tar/ v. result; turn out; ensue.

resumen /rre'sumen/ n. m. résumé, summary, **en r.,** in brief.

resumir /rresu'mir/ v. sum up.

resurgir /rresur'hir/ v. resurge, reappear.

resurrección /rresurrek'θion; rresurrek'sion/ n. f. resurrection.

retaguardia /rreta'guarðia/ n. f. rear guard.

retal /rre'tal/ n. m. remnant.

retardar /rretar'ðar/ v. retard, slow.

retardo /rre'tarðo/ n. m. delay.

retención /rreten'θion; rreten'sion/ n. f. retention.

retener /rrete'ner/ v. retain, keep; withhold.

reticencia /rreti'θenθia; rreti'sensia/ n. f. reticence.

reticente /rreti'θente; rreti'sente/ a. reticent.

retirada /rreti'raða/ n. f. retreat, retirement.

retirar /rreti'rar/ v. retire, retreat, withdraw.

retiro /rre'tiro/ n. m. retirement.

retorcer /rretor'θer; rretor'ser/ v. wring.

retórica /rre'torika/ n. f. rhetoric.

retórico /rre'toriko/ a. rhetorical.

retorno /rre'torno/ n. m. return.

retozo /rre'toθo; rre'toso/ n. m. frolic, romp. —**retozar,** v.

retozón /rreto'θon; rreto'son/ a. frisky.

retracción /rretrak'θion; rretrak'sion/ n. f. retraction.

retractar /rretrak'tar/ v. retract.

retrasar /rretra'sar/ v. delay, set back.

retrasarse /rretra'sarse/ v. be slow.

retraso /rre'traso/ n. m. delay, lag, slowness.

retratar /rretra'tar/ v. portray; photograph.

retrato /rre'trato/ n. m. portrait; picture, photograph.

retreta /rre'treta/ n. f. Mil. retreat.

retrete /rre'trete/ n. m. toilet.

retribución /rretriβu'θion; rretriβu'sion/ n. f. retribution.

retroactivo /rretroak'tiβo/ a. retroactive.

retroalimentación /rretroalimenta'θion; rretroalimenta'sion/ n. f. feedback.

retroceder /rretroθe'ðer; rretrose'ðer/ v. recede, go back, draw back, back up.

retumbar /rretum'βar/ v. resound, rumble.

reumático /rreu'matiko/ a. rheumatic.

reumatismo /rreuma'tismo/ n. m. rheumatism.

reunión /rreu'nion/ n. f. gathering, meeting, party; reunion.

reunir /rreu'nir/ v. gather, collect, bring together.

reunirse /rreu'nirse/ v. meet, assemble, get together.

reutilizar /reutili'zar/ v. reuse.

revelación /rreβela'θion; rreβela'sion/ n. f. revelation.

revelar /rreβe'lar/ v. reveal; betray; Phot. develop.

reventa /rre'βenta/ n. f. resale.

reventar /rreβen'tar/ v. burst; split apart.

reventón /rreβen'ton/ n. m. blowout (of tire).

reverencia /rreβeren'θia; rreβeren'sia/ n. f. reverence.

reverendo /rreβe'rendo/ a. reverend.

reverente /rreβe'rente/ a. reverent.

revertir /rreβer'tir/ v. revert.

revés /rre'βes/ n. m. reverse; back, wrong side. **al r.,** just the opposite; inside out.

revisar /rreβi'sar/ v. revise; review.

revisión /rreβi'sion/ n. f. revision.

revista /rre'βista/ n. f. magazine, periodical; review.

revivir /rreβi'βir/ v. revive.

revocación /rreβoka'θion; rreβoka'sion/ n. f. revocation.

revocar /rreβo'kar/ v. revoke, reverse.

revolotear /rreβolote'ar/ v. hover.

revolución /rreβolu'θion; rreβolu'sion/ n. f. revolution.

revolucionario /rreβoluθio'nario; rreβolusio'nario/ -**ria** a. & n. revolutionary.

revolver /rreβol'βer/ v. revolve; stir, agitate.

revólver n. m. revolver, pistol.

revuelta /rre'βuelta/ n. f. revolt; turn.

rey /rrei/ n. m. king.

reyerta /rre'yerta/ n. f. quarrel, wrangle.

rezar /rre'θar; rre'sar/ v. pray.

rezongar /rreθoŋ'gar; rresoŋ'gar/ v. grumble; mutter.

ría /'rria/ n. f. estuary.

riachuelo /rria't͡fuelo/ n. m. creek.

riba /'rriβa/ n. f. embankment.

rico /'rriko/ a. rich, wealthy; delicious.

ridículamente /rri'ðikulamente/ adv. ridiculously.

ridiculizar /rriðikuli'θar; rriðikuli'sar/ v. ridicule.

ridículo /rri'ðikulo/ a. & m. ridiculous; ridicule.

riego /'rriego/ n. m. irrigation.

rienda /'rrienda/ n. f. rein.

riesgo /'rriesgo/ n. m. risk, gamble.

rifa /'rrifa/ n. f. raffle; lottery; scuffle.

rifle /'rrifle/ n. m. rifle.

rígidamente /'rrihiðamente/ adv. rigidly.

rigidez /rrihi'ðeθ; rrihi'ðes/ n. f. rigidity.

rígido /'rrihiðo/ a. rigid, stiff.

rigor /rri'gor/ n. m. rigor.

riguroso /rrigu'roso/ a. rigorous, strict.

rima /'rrima/ n. f. rhyme. —**rimar,** v.

rimel /rri'mel/ n. f. mascara.

rincón /rrin'kon/ n. m. corner, nook.

rinoceronte /rrinoθe'ronte; rrinose'ronte/ n. m. rhinoceros.

riña /'rriɲa/ n. f. quarrel, feud.

riñón /rri'ɲon/ n. m. kidney.

río /'rrio/ n. m. river. **r. abajo** downstream, downriver. **r. arriba**, upstream, upriver.

ripio /'rripio/ n. m. debris.

riqueza /rri'keθa; rri'kesa/ n. f. wealth.

risa /'rrisa/ n. f. laugh; laughter.

risco /'rrisko/ n. m. cliff.

risibilidad /rrisiβili'ðað/ n. f. risibility.

risotada /rriso'taða/ n. f. peal of laughter.

risueño /rri'sueɲo/ a. cheerful, smiling.

rítmico /'rritmiko/ a. rhythmical.

ritmo /'rritmo/ n. m. rhythm.

rito /'rrito/ n. m. rite.

ritual /rri'tual/ a. & m. ritual.

rivalidad /rriβali'ðað/ n. f. rivalry.

rivera /rri'βera/ n. f. brook.

rizado /rri'θaðo; rri'saðo/ a. curly.

rizo /'rriθo; 'rriso/ n. m. curl. **—rizar,** v.

robar /rro'βar/ v. rob, steal.

roble /'rroβle/ n. m. oak.

roblón /rro'βlon/ n. m. rivet. **—roblar,** v.

robo /'rroβo/ n. m. robbery, theft.

robustamente /rroβusta'mente/ adv. robustly.

robusto /rro'βusto/ a. robust.

roca /'rroka/ n. f. rock; cliff.

rociada /rro'θiaða; rro'siaða/ n. f. spray, sprinkle. **—rociar,** v.

rocío /'rroθio; 'rrosio/ n. m. dew.

rocoso /rro'koso/ a. rocky.

rodar /rro'ðar/ v. roll; roam.

rodear /rroðe'ar/ v. surround, encircle.

rodeo /rro'ðeo/ n. m. turn, winding; roundup.

rodilla /rro'ðiʎa; rro'ðiya/ n. f. knee.

rodillo /rro'ðiʎo; rro'ðiyo/ n. m. roller.

rodio /'rroðio/ n. m. rhodium.

rododendro /rroðo'ðendro/ n. m. rhododendron.

roedor /rroe'ðor/ n. m. rodent.

roer /rro'er/ v. gnaw.

rogación /rroga'θion; rroga'sion/ n. f. request, entreaty.

rogar /rro'gar/ v. beg, plead with, supplicate.

rojizo /rro'hiθo; rro'hiso/ a. reddish.

rojo /'rroho/ a. red.

rollizo /rro'ʎiθo; rro'yiso/ a. chubby.

rollo /'rroʎo; 'rroyo/ n. m. roll; coil.

romadizo /rroma'ðiθo; rroma'ðiso/ n. m. head cold.

romance /rro'manθe; rro'manse/ n. m. romance; ballad.

románico /rro'maniko/ a. Romance.

romano /rro'mano/ **-na** a. & n. Roman.

romántico /rro'mantiko/ a. romantic.

romería /rrome'ria/ n. f. pilgrimage; picnic.

romero /rro'mero/ **-ra** n. pilgrim.

rompecabezas /rrompeka'βeθas: rrompeka-'βesas/ n. m. puzzle (pastime).

romper /rrom'per/ v. break, smash, shatter; sever; tear.

rompible /rrom'piβle/ a. breakable.

ron /rron/ n. m. rum.

roncar /rron'kar/ v. snore.

ronco /'rronko/ a. hoarse.

ronda /'rronda/ n. f. round.

rondar /rron'dar/ v. prowl.

ronquido /rron'kiðo/ n. m. snore.

ronronear /rronrone'ar/ v. purr.

ronzal /rron'θal; rron'sal/ n. m. halter.

roña /'rroɲa/ n. f. scab; filth.

ropa /'rropa/ n. f. clothes, clothing. **r. blanca,** linen. **r. interior,** underwear.

ropa de marca /'rropa de 'marka/ designer clothing.

ropero /rro'pero/ n. m. closet.

rosa /'rrosa/ n. f. rose. **r. náutica,** compass.

rosado /rro'saðo/ a. pink, rosy.

rosal /rro'sal/ n. m. rose bush.

rosario /rro'sario/ n. m. rosary.

rosbif /rros'βif/ n. m. roast beef.

rosca /'rroska/ n. f. thread (of screw).

róseo /'rroseo/ a. rosy.

rostro /'rrostro/ n. m. face, countenance.

rota /'rrota/ n. f. defeat; Naut. course.

rotación /rrota'θion; rrota'sion/ n. f. rotation.

rotatorio /rrota'torio/ a. rotary.

rótula /'rrotula/ n. f. kneecap.

rotulador /rrotula'ðor/ n. m. felt-tipped pen.

rótulo /'rrotulo/ n. m. label. **—rotular,** v.

rotundo /rro'tundo/ a. round; sonorous.

rotura /rro'tura/ n. f. break, fracture, rupture.

rozar /rro'θar; rro'sar/ v. rub against, chafe; graze.

rubí /rru'βi/ n. m. ruby.

rubio /'rruβio/ **-bia** a. & n. blond.

rubor /rru'βor/ n. m. blush; bashfulness.

rúbrica /'rruβrika/ n. f. caption; scroll.

rucho /'rrutʃo/ n. m. donkey.

rudeza /rru'ðeθa; rru'ðesa/ n. f. rudeness; roughness.

rudimentario /rruðimen'tario/ a. rudimentary.

rudimento /rruði'mento/ n. m. rudiment.

rudo /'rruðo/ a. rude, rough.

rueda /'rrueða/ n. f. wheel.

rueda de feria /'rrueða de 'feria/ Ferris wheel.

ruego /'rruego/ n. m. plea; entreaty.

rufián /rru'fian/ n. m. ruffian.

rufo /'rrufo/ a. sandy haired.

rugir /rru'hir/ v. bellow, roar.

rugoso /rru'goso/ a. wrinkled.

ruibarbo /rrui'βarβo/ n. m. rhubarb.

ruido /'rruiðo/ n. m. noise.
ruidoso /rrui'ðoso/ a. noisy.
ruina /'rruina/ n. f. ruin, wreck.
ruinar /rrui'nar/ v. ruin, destroy.
ruinoso /rrui'noso/ a. ruinous.
ruiseñor /rruise'nor/ n. m. nightingale.
ruleta /rru'leta/ n. f. roulette.
rumba /'rrumba/ n. f. rumba (dance or music).
rumbo /'rrumbo/ n m. course, direction.
rumor /rru'mor/ n. m. rumor; murmur.

runrún /rrun'run/ n. m. rumor.
ruptura /rrup'tura/ n. f. rupture, break.
rural /rru'ral/ a. rural.
Rusia /'rrusia/ n. f. Russia.
ruso /'rruso/ **-sa** a. & n. Russian.
rústico /'rrustiko/ **-ca** a. & n. rustic. **en r.,** paperback f.
ruta /'rruta/ n. f. route.
rutina /rru'tina/ n. f. routine.
rutinario /rruti'nario/ a. routine.

S

---

sábado /'saβaðo/ n. m. Saturday.
sábalo /'saβalo/ n. m. shad.
sábana /sa'βana/ n. f. sheet.
sabañon /saβa'ɲon/ n. m. chilblain.
saber /sa'βer/ n. **1.** m. knowledge. —v. **2.** know; learn, find out; know how to; taste. **a s.,** namely, to wit.
sabiduría /saβiðu'ria/ n. f. wisdom; learning.
sabio /'saβio/ **-a 1.** wise; scholarly. —n. **2.** sage; scholar.
sable /'saβle/ n. m. saber.
sabor /sa'βor/ n. m. flavor, taste, savor.
saborear /saβore'ar/ v. savor, relish.
sabotaje /saβo'tahe/ n. m. sabotage.
sabroso /sa'βroso/ a. savory, tasty.
sabueso /sa'βueso/ n. m. hound.
sacacorchos /saka'kortʃos/ n. m. corkscrew.
sacapuntas /saka'puntas/ n. f. pencil sharpener.
sacar /sa'kar/ v. draw out; take out; take.
sacerdocio /saθer'ðoθio; saser'ðosio/ n. m. priesthood.
sacerdote /saθer'ðote; saser'ðote/ n. m. priest.
saciar /sa'θiar; sa'siar/ v. satiate.
saco /'sako/ n. m. sack, bag, pouch; suit coat, jacket.
sacramento /sakra'mento/ n. m. sacrament.
sacrificio /sakri'fiθio; sakri'fisio/ n. m. sacrifice. —**sacrificar,** v.
sacrilegio /sakri'lehio/ n. m. sacrilege.
sacristán /sakris'tan/ n. m. sexton.
sacro /'sakro/ a sacred, holy.
sacrosanto /sakro'santo/ a. sacrosanct.
sacudir /saku'ðir/ v. shake, jerk, jolt.
sádico /'saðiko/ a. sadistic.
sadismo /sa'ðismo/ n. m. sadism.
sagacidad /sagaθi'ðað; sagasi'ðað/ n. f. sagacity.
sagaz /sa'gaθ; sa'gas/ a. sagacious, sage.

sagrado /sa'graðo/ a. sacred, holy.
sal /sal/ n. f. salt; Colloq. wit.
sala /'sala/ n. f. room; living room, parlor; hall, auditorium.
salado /sa'laðo/ a. salted, salty; Colloq. witty.
salar /sa'lar/ v. salt; steep in brine.
salario /sa'lario/ n. m. salary, wages.
salchicha /sal'tʃitʃa/ n. f. sausage.
sal de la Higuera /sal de la i'gera/ Epsom salts.
saldo /'saldo/ n. m. remainder, balance; (bargain) sale.
saldo acreedor /'saldo akree'ðor/ credit balance.
saldo deudor /'saldo deu'ðor/ debit balance.
salero /sa'lero/ n. m. salt shaker.
salida /sa'liða/ n. f. exit, outlet; departure.
salida de urgencia /sa'liða de ur'henθia: sa'liða de ur'hensia/ emergency exit, fire exit.
salir /sa'lir/ v. go out, come out; set out, leave, start; turn out, result.
salirse de /sa'lirse de/ v. get out of. **s. con la suya,** have one's own way.
salitre /sa'litre/ n. m. saltpeter.
saliva /sa'liβa/ n. f. saliva.
salmo /'salmo/ n. m. psalm.
salmón /sal'mon/ n. m. salmon.
salmonete /salmo'nete/ n. m. red mullet.
salmuera /sal'muera/ n. f. pickle; brine.
salobre /sa'loβre/ a. salty.
salón /sa'lon/ n. m. parlor, living room; hall. **s. de baile,** dance hall. **s. de belleza** beauty parlor.
salpicar /salpi'kar/ v. spatter, splash.
salpullido /salpu'ʎiðo; salpu'yiðo/ n. m. rash.
salsa /'salsa/ n. f. sauce; gravy.
saltamontes /salta'montes/ n. m. grasshopper.
salteador /saltea'ðor/ n. m. highwayman.

saltear /salte'ar/ v. hold up, rob; sauté.

salto /'salto/ n. m. jump, leap, spring. **—saltar**, v.

saltón /sal'ton/ n. m. grasshopper.

salubre /sa'luβre/ a. salubrious, healthful.

salubridad /saluβri'ðað/ n. f. health.

salud /sa'luð/ n. f. health.

saludable /salu'ðaβle/ a. healthful, wholesome.

saludar /salu'ðar/ v greet; salute.

saludo /sa'luðo/ n. m. greeting; salutation; salute.

salutación /saluta'θion; saluta'sion/ n. f. salutation.

salva /'salβa/ n. f. salvo.

salvación /salβa'θion; salβa'sion/ n. f. salvation; deliverance.

salvador /salβa'ðor/ **-ra** n. savior; rescuer.

salvaguardia /salβa'guarðia/ n. m. safeguard.

salvaje /sal'βahe/ a. & n. savage, wild (person).

salvamento /salβa'mento/ n. m. salvation; rescue.

salvar /sal'βar/ v. save; salvage; rescue; jump over.

salvavidas /salβa'βiðas/ n. m. life preserver.

salvia /'salβia/ n. f. sage (plant).

salvo /'salβo/ a. 1. safe. **—prep.** 2. except, save (for). **s. que**, unless.

San /san/ title. Saint.

sanar /sa'nar/ v. heal, cure.

sanatorio /sana'torio/ n. m. sanatorium.

sanción /san'θion; san'sion/ n f. sanction. **—sancionar**, v.

sancochar /sanko'tʃar/ v. parboil.

sandalia /san'dalia/ n. f. sandal.

sandez /san'deθ; san'des/ n. f. stupidity.

sandía /san'dia/ n. f. watermelon.

saneamiento /sanea'miento/ n. m. sanitation.

sangrar /saŋ'grar/ v. bleed.

sangre /'saŋgre/ n. f. blood.

sangriento /saŋ'griento/ a. bloody.

sanguinario /saŋgi'nario/ a. bloodthirsty.

sanidad /sani'ðað/ n. f. health.

sanitario /sani'tario/ a. sanitary.

sano /'sano/ a. healthy, sound, sane; healthful, wholesome.

santidad /santi'ðað/ n. f. sanctity, holiness.

santificar /santifi'kar/ v. sanctify.

santo /'santo/ **-ta** a. 1. holy, saintly. **—n.** 2. m. saint.

Santo -ta title. Saint.

santuario /san'tuario/ n. m. sanctuary, shrine.

saña /'saɲa/ n. f. rage, anger.

sapiente /sa'piente/ a. wise.

sapo /'sapo/ n. m. toad.

saquear /sake'ar/ v. sack; ransack; plunder.

sarampión /saram'pion/ n. m. measles.

sarape /sa'rape/ n. m. (Mex.) woven blanket; shawl.

sarcasmo /sar'kasmo/ n. m. sarcasm.

sarcástico /sar'kastiko/ a. sarcastic.

sardina /sar'ðina/ n. f. sardine.

sargento /sar'hento/ n. m. sergeant.

sarna /'sarna/ n. f. itch.

sartén /sar'ten/ n. m. frying pan.

sastre /'sastre/ n. m. tailor.

satánico /sa'taniko/ a. satanic.

satélite /sa'telite/ n. m. satellite.

sátira /'satira/ n. f. satire.

satírico /sa'tiriko/ a. & m. satirical; satirist.

satirizar /satiri'θar; satiri'sar/ v. satirize.

sátiro /'satiro/ n. m. satyr.

satisfacción /satisfak'θion; satisfak'sion/ n. f. satisfaction.

satisfacer /satisfa'θer; satisfa'ser/ v. satisfy.

satisfactorio /satisfak'torio/ a. satisfactory.

saturación /satura'θion; satura'sion/ n. f. saturation.

saturar /satu'rar/ v. saturate.

sauce /'sauθe; 'sause/ n. m. willow.

sauna /'sauna/ n. f. sauna.

savia /'saβia/ n. f. sap.

saxofón /sakso'fon/ **saxófono** n. m. saxophone.

saya /'saya/ n. f. skirt.

sazón /sa'θon; sa'son/ n. f season; seasoning. **a la s.**, at that time.

sazonar /saθo'nar; saso'nar/ v. flavor, season.

se /se/ pron. -self, -selves.

seca /'seka/ n. f. drought.

secador /seka'ðor/ **secador de pelo** n. m. hair dryer.

secante /se'kante/ a. **papel s.**, blotting paper.

secar /se'kar/ v. dry.

sección /sek'θion; sek'sion/ n. f. section.

seco /'seko/ a. dry; curt.

secreción /sekre'θion; sekre'sion/ n. f. secretion.

secretar /sekre'tar/ v. secrete.

secretaría /sekreta'ria/ n. f. secretary's office; secretariat.

secretario /sekre'tario/ **-ra** n. secretary.

secreto /se'kreto/ a. & m. secret.

secta /'sekta/ n. f. denomination; sect.

secuela /se'kuela/ n. f. result; sequel.

secuestrar /sekues'trar/ v. abduct, kidnap; hijack.

secuestro /se'kuestro/ n. m. abduction, kidnapping.

secular /seku'lar/ a. secular.

secundario /sekun'dario/ a. secondary.

sed /seð/ n. f. thirst. **tener s., estar con s.**, to be thirsty.

seda /'seða/ *n. f.* silk.

sedar /se'ðar/ *v.* quiet, allay.

sedativo /seða'tiβo/ *a. & m.* sedative.

sede /'seðe/ *n. f.* seat, headquarters.

sedentario /seðen'tario/ *a.* sedentary.

sedición /seði'θion: seði'sion/ *n. f.* sedition.

sedicioso /seði'θioso; seði'sioso/ *a.* seditious.

sediento /se'ðiento/ *a.* thirsty.

sedimento /seði'mento/ *n. m.* sediment.

sedoso /se'ðoso/ *a.* silky.

seducir /seðu'θir; seðu'sir/ *v.* seduce.

seductivo /seðuk'tiβo/ *a.* seductive, alluring.

segar /se'gar/ *v.* reap, harvest; mow.

seglar /seg'lar/ *n. m. & f.* layman, laywoman.

segmento /seg'mento/ *n. m.* segment.

segregar /segre'gar/ *v.* segregate.

seguida /se'giða/ *n. f.* succession. **en s.,** right away, at once.

seguido /se'giðo/ *a.* consecutive.

seguir /se'gir/ *v.* follow; continue, keep on, go on.

según /se'gun/ *prep.* **1.** according to. —*conj.* **2.** as.

segundo /se'gundo/ *a. & m.* second. —**segundar,** *v.*

seguridad /seguri'ðað/ *n. f.* safety, security; assurance.

seguro /se'guro/ *a.* **1.** safe, secure; sure, certain. —*n.* **2.** *m.* insurance.

seis /seis/ *a. & pron.* six.

seiscientos /seis'θientos; seis'sientos/ *a. & pron.* six hundred.

selección /selek'θion; selek'sion/ *n. f.* selection, choice.

seleccionar /selekθio'nar; seleksio'nar/ *v.* select, choose.

selecto /se'lekto/ *a.* select, choice, elite.

sello /'seʎo; 'seyo/ *n. m.* seal; stamp. —**sellar,** *v.*

selva /'selβa/ *n. f.* forest; jungle.

selvoso /sel'βoso/ *a.* sylvan.

semáforo /se'maforo/ *n. m.* semaphore; traffic light.

semana /se'mana/ *n. f.* week.

semana inglesa /se'mana iŋ'glesa/ five-day work week.

semanal /sema'nal/ *a.* weekly.

semana laboral /se'mana laβo'ral/ work week.

semántica /se'mantika/ *n. f.* semantics.

semblante /sem'βlante/ *n. m.* look, expression.

sembrado /sem'βraðo/ *n. m.* sown field.

sembrar /sem'βrar/ *v.* sow, seed.

semejante /seme'hante/ *a.* **1.** like, similar; such (a). —*n.* **2.** *m.* fellow man.

semejanza /seme'hanθa: seme'hansa/ *n. f.* similarity, likeness.

semejar /seme'har/ *v.* resemble.

semilla /se'miʎa; se'miya/ *n. f.* seed.

seminario /semi'nario/ *n. m.* seminary.

sémola /'semola/ *n. f.* semolina.

senado /se'naðo/ *n. m.* senate.

senador /sena'ðor/ -**ra** *n.* senator.

sencillez /senθi'ʎeθ; sensi'yes/ *n. f.* simplicity; naturalness.

sencillo /sen'θiʎo; sen'siyo/ *a.* simple, natural; single.

senda /'senda/ *n. f.* **sendero,** *m.* path, footpath.

senectud /senek'tuð/ *n. f.* old age.

senil /se'nil/ *a.* senile.

seno /'seno/ *n. m.* breast, bosom.

sensación /sensa'θion; sensa'sion/ *n. f.* sensation.

sensacional /sensaθio'nal; sensasio'nal/ *a.* sensational.

sensato /sen'sato/ *a.* sensible, wise.

sensibilidad /sensiβili'ðað/ *n. f.* sensibility; sensitiveness.

sensible /sen'siβle/ *a.* sensitive; emotional.

sensitivo /sensi'tiβo/ *a.* sensitive.

sensualidad /sensuali'ðað/ *n. f.* sensuality.

sentar /sen'tar/ *v.* seat. **s. bien,** fit well, be becoming.

sentarse /sen'tarse/ *v.* sit, sit down.

sentencia /sen'tenθia; sen'tensia/ *n. f.* (court) sentence.

sentidamente /sentiða'mente/ *adv.* feelingly.

sentido /sen'tiðo/ *n. m.* meaning, sense; consciousness.

sentido común /sen'tiðo ko'mun/ common sense.

sentimental /sentimen'tal/ *a.* sentimental.

sentimiento /senti'miento/ *n. m.* sentiment, feeling.

sentir /sen'tir/ *v.* feel, sense; hear; regret, be sorry.

seña /'sena/ *n. f.* sign, indication; (*pl.*) address.

señal /se'nal/ *n. f.* sign, signal; mark.

señalar /sena'lar/ *v.* designate, point out; mark.

señal de marcar /se'nal de mar'kar/ dial tone.

señor /se'nor/ *n. m.* gentleman; lord; (title) Mr., Sir.

señora /se'nora/ *n. f.* lady; wife; (title) Mrs., Madam.

señora de la limpieza /se'nora de la lim'pieθa; se'nora de la lim'piesa/ cleaning woman.

señorita /seno'rita/ *n. f.* young lady; (title) Miss.

sépalo /'sepalo/ *n. m.* sepal.

separación /separa'θion; separa'sion/ *n. f.* separation, parting.

separadamente /separaða'mente/ *adv.* separately.

separado /sepa'raðo/ *a.* separate; separated. —**separar,** *v.*

septentrional /septentrio'nal/ *a.* northern.

septiembre /sep'tiembre/ *n. m.* September.

séptimo /'septimo/ *a.* seventh.

sepulcro /se'pulkro/ *n. m.* sepulcher.

sepultar /sepul'tar/ *v.* bury, entomb.

sepultura /sepul'tura/ *n. f.* grave.

sequedad /seke'ðað/ *n. f.* dryness.

sequía /se'kia/ *n. f.* drought.

ser /ser/ *v.* be.

serenata /sere'nata/ *n. f.* serenade.

serenidad /sereni'ðað/ *n. f.* serenity.

sereno /se'reno/ *a.* 1. serene, calm. —*n.* 2. *m.* dew; watchman.

ser humano /ser u'mano/ *n.* human being.

serie /'serie/ *n. f.* series, sequence.

seriedad /serie'ðað/ *n. f.* seriousness.

serio /'serio/ *a.* serious. **en s.,** seriously.

sermón /ser'mon/ *n. m.* sermon.

seroso /se'roso/ *a.* watery.

serpiente /ser'piente/ *n. f.* serpent, snake.

serpiente de cascabel /ser'piente de kas-ka'βel/ rattlesnake.

serrano /se'rrano/ *a.* mountaineer.

serrar /se'rrar/ *v.* saw.

serrín /se'rrin/ *n. m.* sawdust.

servicial /serβi'θial; serβi'sial/ *a.* helpful, of service.

servicio /ser'βiθio; ser'βisio/ *n. m.* service; toilet.

servidor /serβi'ðor/ **-ra** *n.* servant.

servidumbre /serβi'ðumbre/ *n. f.* bondage; staff of servants.

servil /ser'βil/ *a.* servile, menial.

servilleta /serβi'ʎeta; serβi'yeta/ *n. f.* napkin.

servir /ser'βir/ *v.* serve. **s. para,** be good for.

servirse /ser'βirse/ *v.* help oneself.

sesenta /se'senta/ *a. & pron.* sixty.

sesgo /'sesgo/ *n. m.* slant. —**sesgar,** *v.*

sesión /se'sion/ *n. f.* session; sitting.

seso /'seso/ *n. m.* brain.

seta /'seta/ *n. f.* mushroom.

setecientos /sete'θientos; sete'sientos/ *a. & pron.* seven hundred.

setenta /se'tenta/ *a. & pron.* seventy.

seto /'seto/ *n. m.* hedge.

severamente /seβera'mente/ *adv.* severely.

severidad /seβeri'ðað/ *n. f.* severity.

severo /se'βero/ *a.* severe, strict, stern.

sexismo /sek'sismo/ *n. m.* sexism.

sexista /sek'sista/ *a. & n.* sexist.

sexo /'sekso/ *n. m.* sex.

sexto /'seksto/ *a.* sixth.

sexual /sek'sual/ *a.* sexual.

si /si/ *conj.* if; whether.

sí *pron.* 1. -self, -selves. —*interj.* 2. yes.

sico-. See **psicoanálisis, psicología,** etc.

sicómoro /siko'moro/ *n. m.* sycamore.

SIDA /'siða/ *n. m.* AIDS.

sidra /'siðra/ *n. f.* cider.

siempre /'siempre/ *adv.* always. **para s.,** forever. **s. que,** whenever; provided that.

sierra /'sierra/ *n. f.* saw; mountain range.

siervo /'sierβo/ **-va** *n.* slave; serf.

siesta /'siesta/ *n. f.* (afternoon) nap.

siete /'siete/ *a. & pron.* seven.

sifón /si'fon/ *n. m.* siphon; siphon bottle.

siglo /'siglo/ *n. m.* century.

signatura /signa'tura/ *n. f. Mus.* signature.

significación /signifika'θion; signifika'sion/ *n. f.* significance.

significado /signifi'kaðo/ *n. m.* meaning.

significante /signifi'kante/ *a.* significant.

significar /signifi'kar/ *v.* signify, mean.

significativo /signifika'tiβo/ *a.* significant.

signo /'signo/ *n. m.* sign, symbol; mark.

siguiente /si'giente/ *a.* following, next.

sílaba /'silaβa/ *n. f.* syllable.

silbar /sil'βar/ *v.* whistle; hiss, boo.

silbato /sil'βato/ **silbido** /sil'βiðo/ *n. m.* whistle.

silencio /si'lenθio; si'lensio/ *n. m.* silence, stillness.

silenciosamente /silenθiosa'mente; silensiosa'mente/ *a.* silently.

silencioso /silen'θioso; silen'sioso/ *a.* silent, still.

silicato /sili'kato/ *n. m.* silicate.

silicio /si'liθio; si'lisio/ *n. m.* silicon.

silla /'siʎa; 'siya/ *n. f.* chair; saddle.

sillón /si'ʎon; si'yon/ *n. m.* armchair.

silueta /si'lueta/ *n. f.* silhouette.

silvestre /sil'βestre/ *a.* wild, uncultivated. **fauna s.,** wildlife.

sima /'sima/ *n. f.* chasm; cavern.

simbólico /sim'boliko/ *a.* symbolic.

símbolo /'simbolo/ *n. m.* symbol.

simetría /sime'tria/ *n. f.* symmetry.

simétrico /si'metriko/ *a.* symmetrical.

símil /'simil/ **similar** *a.* similar, alike.

similitud /simili'tuð/ *n. f.* similarity.

simpatía /simpa'tia/ *n.* congeniality; friendly feeling.

simpático /sim'patiko/ *a.* likeable, nice, congenial.

simple /'simple/ *a.* simple.

simpleza /sim'pleθa; sim'plesa/ *n. f.* silliness; trifle.

simplicidad /simpliθi'ðað; simplisi'ðað/ *n. f.* simplicity.

simplificación /simplifika'θion; simplifika'sion/ *n. f.* simplification.

simplificar /simplifi'kar/ *v.* simplify.

simular /simu'lar/ *v.* simulate.

simultáneo /simul'taneo/ a. simultaneous.

sin /sin/ prep. without. **s. sentido,** meaningless.

sinagoga /sina'goga/ n. f. synagogue.

sinceridad /sinθeri'ðað; sinseri'ðað/ n. f. sincerity.

sincero /sin'θero; sin'sero/ a. sincere.

sincronizar /sinkroni'θar; sinkroni'sar/ v. synchronize.

sindicato /sindi'kato/ n. m. syndicate; labor union.

síndrome /'sindrome/ n. m. syndrome.

sinfonía /sinfo'nia/ n. f. symphony.

sinfónico /sin'foniko/ a. symphonic.

singular /singu'lar/ a. & m. singular.

siniestro /si'niestro/ a. sinister, ominous.

sino /'sino/ conj. but.

sinónimo /si'nonimo/ n. m. synonym.

sinrazón /sinra'θon; sinra'son/ n. f. wrong, injustice.

sinsabor /sinsa'βor/ n. m. displeasure, distaste; trouble.

sintaxis /sin'taksis/ n. f. syntax.

síntesis /'sintesis/ n. f. synthesis.

sintético /sin'tetiko/ a. synthetic.

síntoma /'sintoma/ n. m. symptom.

siquiera /si'kiera/ adv. **ni s.,** not even.

sirena /si'rena/ n. f. siren.

sirviente /sir'βiente/ **-ta** n. servant.

sistema /sis'tema/ n. m. system.

sistemático /siste'matiko/ a. systematic.

sistematizar /sistemati'θar; sistemati'sar/ v. systematize.

sitiar /si'tiar/ v. besiege.

sitio /'sitio/ n. m. site, location, place, spot.

situación /situa'θion; situa'sion/ n. f situation; location.

situar /si'tuar/ v. situate; locate.

smoking /'smoking/ n. m. tuxedo, dinner jacket.

so /so/ prep. under.

soba /'soβa/ n. f. massage. **—sobar,** v

sobaco /so'βako/ n. m. armpit.

sobaquero /soβa'kero/ n. f. armhole.

soberano /soβe'rano/ **-na** a. & n. sovereign.

soberbia /so'βerβia/ n. f. arrogance.

soberbio /so'βerβio/ a. superb; arrogant.

soborno /so'βorno/ n. m. bribe. **—sobornar,** v.

sobra /'soβra/ n. f. excess, surplus. **de sobra,** to spare.

sobrado /so'βrado/ n. m. attic.

sobrante /so'βrante/ a. & m. surplus.

sobras /'soβras/ n. f.pl. leftovers.

sobre /'soβre/ prep. **1.** about; above, over. **—n. 2.** m. envelope.

sobrecama /soβre'kama/ n. f. bedspread.

sobrecargo /soβre'kargo/ n. m. supercargo.

sobredicho /soβre'ðitʃo/ a. aforesaid.

sobredosis /soβre'ðosis/ n. f. overdose.

sobrehumano /soβreu'mano/ a. superhuman.

sobrenatural /soβrenatu'ral/ a. supernatural, weird.

sobrepasar /soβrepa'sar/ v. surpass.

sobresalir /soβresa'lir/ v. excel.

sobretodo /soβre'toðo/ n. m. overcoat.

sobrevivir /soβreβi'βir/ v. survive, outlive.

sobriedad /soβrie'ðað/ n. f. sobriety; moderation.

sobrina /so'βrina/ n. f. niece.

sobrino /so'βrino/ n. m. nephew.

sobrio /'soβrio/ a. sober, temperate.

socarrén /soka'rren/ n. m. eaves.

sociable /so'θiaβle; so'siaβle/ a. sociable.

social /so'θial; so'sial/ a. social.

socialismo /soθia'lismo; sosia'lismo/ n. m. socialism.

socialista /soθia'lista; sosia'lista/ a. & n. socialist.

sociedad /soθie'ðað; sosie'ðað/ n. f. society; association.

sociedad de consumo /soθie'ðað de kon'sumo; sosie'ðað de kon'sumo/ consumer society.

socio /'soθio; 'sosio/ **-cia** n. associate, partner; member.

sociología /soθiolo'hia; sosiolo'hia/ n. f. sociology.

sociológico /soθio'lohiko; sosio'lohiko/ a. sociological.

sociólogo /so'θiologo; so'siologo/ **-ga** n. sociologist.

socorrista /soko'rrista/ n. m. & f. lifeguard.

socorro /so'korro/ n. m. help, aid. **—socorrer,** v.

soda /'soða/ n. f. soda.

sodio /'soðio/ n. m. sodium.

soez /so'eθ; so'es/ a. vulgar.

sofá /so'fa/ n. m. sofa, couch.

sofisma /so'fisma/ n. m. sophism.

sofista /so'fista/ n. m. & f. sophist.

sofocación /sofoka'θion; sofoka'sion/ n. f. suffocation.

sofocar /sofo'kar/ v. smother, suffocate, stifle, choke.

sofrito /so'frito/ n. m. sauce of sautéed tomatoes, peppers, onions, and garlic.

software /'softwer/ n. m. software.

soga /'soga/ n. f. rope.

soja /'soha/ n. f. soya.

sol /sol/ n. m. sun.

solada /so'laða/ n. f. dregs.

solanera /sola'nera/ n. f sunburn.

solapa /so'lapa/ n. f. lapel.

solar /so'lar/ a. **1.** solar. **—n. 2.** m. building lot.

solaz /so'laθ; so'las/ n. m. solace, comfort. **—solazar,** v.

soldado /sol'daðo/ *n. m.* soldier.

soldar /sol'dar/ *v.* solder, weld.

soledad /sole'ðað/ *n. f.* solitude, privacy.

solemne /so'lemne/ *a.* solemn.

solemnemente /solemne'mente/ *adv* solemnly.

solemnidad /solemni'ðað/ *n. f.* solemnity.

soler /so'ler/ *v.* be in the habit of.

solicitador /soliθita'ðor; solisita'ðor/ **-ra** *n.* applicant, petitioner.

solicitar /soliθi'tar; solisi'tar/ *v.* solicit; apply for.

solícito /so'liθito; so'lisito/ *a.* solicitous.

solicitud /soliθi'tuð; solisi'tuð/ *n. f.* solicitude; application.

sólidamente /soliða'mente/ *adv.* solidly.

solidaridad /soliðari'ðað/ *n. f.* solidarity.

solidez /soli'ðeθ; soli'ðes/ *n. f.* solidity.

solidificar /soliðifi'kar/ *v.* solidify.

sólido /'soliðo/ *a. & m.* solid.

soliloquio /soli'lokio/ *n. m.* soliloquy.

solitario /soli'tario/ *a.* solitary, lone.

sollozo /so'ʎoθo; so'yoso/ *n. m.* sob. —**sollozar**, *v.*

solo /'solo/ *a.* **1.** only; single; alone; lonely. **a solas**, alone. —*n.* **2.** *m. Mus.* solo.

sólo *adv.* only, just.

solomillo /solo'miʎo; solo'miyo/ *n. m.* sirloin.

soltar /sol'tar/ *v.* release; loosen.

soltero /sol'tero/ **-ra** *a. & n.* single, unmarried (person).

soltura /sol'tura/ *n. f.* poise, ease, facility.

solubilidad /soluβili'ðað/ *n. f.* solubility.

solución /solu'θion; solu'sion/ *n. f.* solution.

solucionar /soluθio'nar; solusio'nar/ *v.* solve, settle.

solvente /sol'βente/ *a.* solvent.

sombra /'sombra/ *n. f.* shade; shadow. —**sombrear**, *v.*

sombra de ojos /'sombra de 'ohos/ eye shadow.

sombrerera /sombre'rera/ *n. f.* hatbox.

sombrero /som'βrero/ *n. m.* hat.

sombrilla /som'βriʎa; som'βriya/ *n. f.* parasol.

sombrío /som'βrio/ *a.* somber, bleak, gloomy.

sombroso /som'βroso/ *a.* very shady.

someter /some'ter/ *v.* subject; submit.

somnífero /som'nifero/ *n. m.* sleeping pill.

somnolencia /somno'lenθia; somno'lensia/ *n. f.* drowsiness.

son /son/ *n. m.* sound. —**sonar**, *v.*

sonata /so'nata/ *n. f.* sonata.

sondar /son'dar/ *v.* sound, fathom.

sonido /so'niðo/ *n. m.* sound.

sonoridad /sonori'ðað/ *n. f.* sonority.

sonoro /so'noro/ *a.* sonorous.

sonrisa /son'risa/ *n. f.* smile. —**sonreír**, *v.*

sonrojo /son'roho/ *n. m.* flush, blush. —**sonrojarse**, *v.*

soñador /soɲa'ðor/ **-ra** *a. & n.* dreamy; dreamer.

soñar /so'ɲar/ *v.* dream.

soñoliento /soɲo'liento/ *a.* sleepy.

sopa /'sopa/ *n. f.* soup.

soplar /so'plar/ *v.* blow.

soplete /so'plete/ *n. m.* blowtorch.

soplo /'soplo/ *n. m.* breath; puff, gust.

soportar /sopor'tar/ *v.* abide, bear, stand.

soprano /so'prano/ *n. m. & f.* soprano.

sorbete /sor'βete/ *n. m.* sherbet.

sorbo /'sorβo/ *n. m.* sip. —**sorber**, *v.*

sordera /sor'ðera/ *n. f.* deafness.

sórdidamente /sorðiða'mente/ *adv.* sordidly.

sordidez /sorði'ðeθ; sorði'ðes/ *n. f.* sordidness.

sórdido /'sorðiðo/ *a.* sordid.

sordo /'sorðo/ *a.* deaf; muffled, dull.

sordomudo /sorðo'muðo/ **-da** *a. & n.* deafmute.

sorpresa /sor'presa/ *n. f.* surprise. —**sorprender**, *v.*

sorteo /sor'teo/ *n. m.* drawing lots; raffle.

sortija /sor'tiha/ *n. f.* ring.

sosa /'sosa/ *n. f. Chem.* soda.

soso /'soso/ *a.* dull, insipid, tasteless.

sospecha /sos'petʃa/ *n. f.* suspicion.

sospechar /sospe'tʃar/ *v.* suspect.

sospechoso /sospe'tʃoso/ *a.* suspicious.

sostén /sos'ten/ *n. m.* bra, brassiere; support.

sostener /soste'ner/ *v.* hold, support; maintain.

sostenimiento /sosteni'miento/ *n. m.* sustenance.

sota /'sota/ *n. f.* jack (in cards).

sótano /'sotano/ *n. m.* basement, cellar.

soto /'soto/ *n. m.* grove.

soviet /so'βiet/ *n. m.* soviet.

soya /'soya/ *n. f.* soybean.

su /su/ *a.* his, her, its, their, your.

suave /'suaβe/ *a.* smooth; gentle, soft, mild.

suavidad /suaβi'ðað/ *n. f.* smoothness; gentleness, softness, mildness.

suavizar /suaβi'θar; suaβi'sar/ *v.* soften.

subalterno /suβal'terno/ **-na** *a. & n.* subordinate.

subasta /su'βasta/ *n. f.* auction.

subcampeón /suβkampe'on/ **-na** *n.* runner-up.

subconsciencia /suβkons'θienθia; suβkons'siensia/ *n. f.* subconscious.

súbdito /'suβðito/ **-ta** *n.* subject.

subestimar /suβesti'mar/ *v.* underestimate.

subida /su'βiða/ *n. f.* ascent, rise.

subilla /su'βiʎa; su'βiya/ *n. f.* awl.

subir /su'βir/ v. rise, climb, ascend, mount. **s. a,** amount to.

súbito /'suβito/ a. sudden.

subjetivo /suβhe'tiβo/ a. subjective.

subjuntivo /suβhun'tiβo/ a. & m. subjunctive.

sublimación /suβlima'θion; suβlima'sion/ n. f. sublimation.

sublimar /suβli'mar/ v. elevate; sublimate.

sublime /su'βlime/ a. sublime.

submarinismo /suβmari'nismo/ n. m. scuba diving.

submarino /suβma'rino/ a. & m. submarine.

subordinación /suβorðina'θion; suβorðina'sion/ n. f. subordination.

subordinado /suβorði'naðo/ **-da** a. & n. subordinate. —**subordinar,** v.

subrayar /suβra'yar/ v. underline.

subscribirse /suβskri'βirse/ v. subscribe; sign one's name.

subscripción /suβskrip'θion; suβskrip'sion/ n. f. subscription.

subsecuente /suβse'kuente/ a. subsequent.

subsidiario /suβsi'ðiario/ a. subsidiary.

subsiguiente /suβsi'giente/ a. subsequent.

substancia /suβs'tanθia; suβs'tansia/ n. f. substance.

substancial /suβs'tanθial; suβs'tansial/ a. substantial.

substantivo /suβstan'tiβo/ n. m. substantive, noun.

substitución /suβstitu'θion; suβstitu'sion/ n. f. substitution.

substituir /suβsti'tuir/ v. replace; substitute.

substitutivo /suβstitu'tiβo/ a. substitute.

substituto /suβsti'tuto/ **-ta** n. substitute.

substraer /suβstra'er/ v. subtract.

subsuelo /suβ'suelo/ n. m. subsoil.

subterfugio /suβter'fuhio/ n. m. subterfuge.

subterráneo /suβte'rraneo/ a. **1.** subterranean, underground. —n. **2.** m. place underground; subway.

subtítulo /suβ'titulo/ n. m. subtitle.

suburbio /su'βurβio/ n. m. suburb.

subvención /suββen'θion; suββen'sion/ n. f. subsidy, grant.

subversión /suββer'sion/ n. f. subversion.

subversivo /suββer'siβo/ a. subversive.

subvertir /suββer'tir/ v. subvert.

subyugación /suβyuga'θion; suβyuga'sion/ n. f. subjugation.

subyugar /suβyu'gar/ v. subjugate, quell.

succión /suk'θion; suk'sion/ n. f. suction.

suceder /suθe'ðer; suse'ðer/ v. happen, occur, befall. **s. a,** succeed, follow.

sucesión /suθe'sion; suse'sion/ n. f. succession.

sucesivo /suθe'siβo; suse'siβo/ a. successive. **en lo s.,** in the future.

suceso /su'θeso; su'seso/ n. m. event.

sucesor /suθe'sor; suse'sor/ **-ra** n. successor.

suciedad /suθie'ðað; susie'ðað/ n. f. filth, dirt.

sucio /'suθio; 'susio/ a. filthy, dirty.

suculento /suku'lento/ a. succulent.

sucumbir /sukum'βir/ v. succumb.

sud /suð/ n. m. south.

sudadera /suða'ðera/ n. f. sweatshirt.

Sudáfrica /su'ðafrika/ n. f. South Africa.

sudafricano /suðafri'kano/ **-na** a. & n. South African.

sudamericano /suðameri'kano/ **-na** a. & n. South American.

sudar /su'ðar/ v. perspire, sweat.

sudeste /su'ðeste/ n. m. southeast.

sudoeste /suðo'este/ n. m. southwest.

sudor /su'ðor/ n. m. perspiration, sweat.

Suecia /'sueθia; 'suesia/ n. f. Sweden.

sueco /'sueko/ **-ca** a. & n. Swedish; Swede.

suegra /'suegra/ n. f. mother-in-law.

suegro /'suegro/ n. m. father-in-law.

suela /'suela/ n. f. sole.

sueldo /'sueldo/ n. m. salary, wages.

suelo /'suelo/ n. m. soil; floor; ground.

suelto /'suelto/ a. **1.** loose; free; odd, separate. —n. **2.** loose change.

sueño /'sueɲo/ n. m. sleep; sleepiness; dream. **tener s.,** to be sleepy.

suero /'suero/ n. m. serum.

suerte /'suerte/ n. f. luck; chance; lot.

suéter /'sueter/ n. m. sweater.

suficiente /sufi'θiente; sufi'siente/ a. sufficient.

sufragio /su'frahio/ n. m. suffrage.

sufrimiento /sufri'miento/ n. m. suffering, agony.

sufrir /su'frir/ v. suffer; undergo; endure.

sugerencia /suhe'renθia; suhe'rensia/ n. f. suggestion.

sugerir /suhe'rir/ v. suggest.

sugestión /suhes'tion/ n. f. suggestion.

sugestionar /suhestio'nar/ v. influence; hypnotize.

suicida /sui'θiða; sui'siða/ n. m. & f. suicide (person).

suicidarse /suiθi'ðarse; suisi'ðarse/ v. commit suicide.

suicidio /sui'θiðio; sui'siðio/ n. m. (act of) suicide.

Suiza /'suiθa; 'suisa/ n. f. Switzerland.

suizo /'suiθo; 'suiso/ **-za** a. & n. Swiss.

sujeción /suhe'θion; suhe'sion/ n. f. subjection.

sujetador /suheta'ðor/ n. m. bra, brassiere.

sujetapapeles /su'hetapa'peles/ n. m. paper clip.

sujetar /suhe'tar/ v. hold, fasten, clip.

sujeto /su'heto/ a. **1.** subject, liable. —n. **2.** m. Gram. subject.

sulfato /sul'fato/ n. m. sulfate.

sulfuro /sul'furo/ n. m. sulfide.

sultán /sul'tan/ n. m. sultan.

suma /'suma/ n. f. sum, amount. **en s.,** in short. **s. global,** lump sum.

sumar /su'mar/ v. add up.

sumaria /su'maria/ n. f. indictment.

sumario /su'mario/ a. & m. summary.

sumergir /sumer'hir/ v. submerge.

sumersión /sumer'sion/ n. f. submersion.

sumisión /sumi'sion/ n. f. submission.

sumiso /su'miso/ a. submissive.

sumo /'sumo/ a. great, high, utmost.

suntuoso /sun'tuoso/ a. sumptuous.

superar /supe'rar/ v. overcome, surpass.

superficial /superfi'θial; superfi'sial/ a. superficial, shallow.

superficie /super'fiθie; super'fisie/ n. f. surface.

superfluo /su'perfluo/ a. superfluous.

superhombre /super'ombre/ n. m. superman.

superintendente /superinten'dente/ n. m. & f. superintendent.

superior /supe'rior/ a. **1.** superior; upper, higher. —n. **2.** m. superior.

superioridad /superiori'ðað/ n. f. superiority.

superlativo /superla'tiβo/ n. m. & a. superlative.

superstición /supersti'θion; supersti'sion/ n. f. superstition.

supersticioso /supersti'θioso; supersti'sioso/ a. superstitious.

supervisar /superβi'sar/ v. supervise.

supervivencia /superβi'βenθia; superβi'βensia/ n f. survival.

suplantar /suplan'tar/ v. supplant.

suplementario /suplemen'tario/ a. supplementary.

suplemento /suple'mento/ n. m. supplement. —**suplementar,** v.

suplente /su'plente/ a. & n. substitute.

súplica /'suplika/ n. f. request, entreaty, plea.

suplicación /suplika'θion; suplika'sion/ n. f. supplication; request, entreaty.

suplicar /supli'kar/ v. request, entreat; implore.

suplicio /su'pliθio; su'plisio/ n. m torture, ordeal.

suplir /su'plir/ v. supply.

suponer /supo'ner/ v. suppose, pressume, assume.

suposición /suposi'θion; suposi'sion/ n. f. supposition, assumption.

supositorio /suposi'torio/ n. m. suppository.

supremacía /suprema'θia; suprema'sia/ n. f. supremacy.

supremo /su'premo/ a. supreme.

supresión /supre'sion/ n. f. suppression.

suprimir /supri'mir/ v. suppress; abolish.

supuesto /su'puesto/ a. supposed. **por s.,** of course.

sur /sur/ n. m. south.

surco /'surko/ n. m. furrow. —**surcar,** v.

surgir /sur'hir/ v. arise; appear suddenly.

surtido /sur'tiðo/ n. m. assortment; supply, stock.

surtir /sur'tir/ v. furnish, supply.

susceptibilidad /susθeptiβili'ðað; susseptiβili'ðað/ n. f. susceptibility.

susceptible /susθep'tiβle; sussep'tiβle/ a. susceptible.

suscitar /susθi'tar; sussi'tar/ v. stir up.

suscri- = subscri-

suspender /suspen'der/ v. withhold; suspend; fail (in a course).

suspensión /suspen'sion/ n. f. suspension.

suspenso /sus'penso/ n. m. failing grade. **en s.,** in suspense.

suspicacia /suspi'kaθia; suspi'kasia/ n. f. suspicion, distrust.

suspicaz /suspi'kaθ; suspi'kas/ a. suspicious.

suspicazmente /suspikaθ'mente; suspikas'mente/ adv. suspiciously.

suspiro /sus'piro/ n. m. sigh. —**suspirar,** v.

sustan- = substan-

sustentar /susten'tar/ v. sustain, support.

sustento /sus'tento/ n. m. sustenance, support, living.

susti- = substi-

susto /'susto/ n. m. fright, scare.

sustraer /sustra'er/ = substraer.

susurro /su'surro/ n. m. rustle; whisper. —**susurrar,** v.

sutil /'sutil/ a. subtle.

sutileza /suti'leθa, sutili'ðað: suti'lesa, tili'ðað/ **sutilidad** n. f. subtlety.

sutura /su'tura/ n. f. suture.

suyo /'suyo/ a. his, hers, theirs, yours.

T

tabaco /ta'βako/ n. m. tobacco.

tábano /'taβano/ n. m. horsefly.

tabaquería /taβake'ria/ n. f. tobacco shop.

taberna /ta'βerna/ n. f. tavern, bar.

tabernáculo /taβer'nakulo/ n. m. tabernacle.

tabique /ta'βike/ n. m. dividing wall, partition.

tabla /'taβla/ n. f. board, plank; table, list. **t. de planchar,** ironing board.

tablado /ta'βlaðo/ n. m. stage, platform.

tablero /ta'βlero/ n. m. panel.

tableta /ta'βleta/ n. f. tablet.

tablilla /ta'βliʎa; ta'βliya/ n. f. bulletin board.

tabú /ta'βu/ n. m. taboo.

tabular /taβu'lar/ a. tabular.

tacaño /ta'kano/ a. stingy.

tacha /'tatʃa/ n. f. fault, defect.

tachar /ta'tʃar/ v. find fault with; cross out.

tachuela /ta'tʃuela/ n. f. tack.

tácitamente /taθitamente; 'tasitamente/ adv. tacitly.

tácito /'taθito; 'tasito/ a. tacit.

taciturno /taθi'turno; tasi'turno/ a. taciturn.

taco /'tako/ n. m. heel (of shoe); billiard cue.

tacón /ta'kon/ n. m. heel (of shoe).

táctico /'taktiko/ a. tactical.

tacto /'takto/ n. m. (sense of) touch; tact.

tafetán /tafe'tan/ n. m. taffeta.

taimado /tai'maðo/ a. sly.

tajada /ta'haða/ n. cut, slice. —**tajar,** v.

tajea /ta'hea/ n. f. channel.

tal /tal/ a. such. **con t. que.,** provided that. **t. vez,** perhaps.

taladrar /tala'ðrar/ v. drill.

taladro /ta'laðro/ n. m. Mech. drill.

talante /ta'lante/ n. m. humor, disposition.

talco /'talko/ n. m. talc.

talega /ta'lega/ n. f. bag, sack.

talento /ta'lento/ n. m. talent.

talla /'taʎa; 'taya/ n. f. engraving; stature; size (of suit).

tallador /taʎa'ðor; taya'ðor/ **-ra** n. engraver; dealer (at cards).

talle /'taʎe; 'taye/ n. m. figure; waist; fit.

taller /ta'ʎer; ta'yer/ n. m. workshop, factory.

tallo /'taʎo; 'tayo/ n. m. stem, stalk.

talón /ta'lon/ n. m. heel (of foot); (baggage) check, stub.

tamal /ta'mal/ n. m. tamale.

tamaño /ta'mano/ n. m. size.

tambalear /tambale'ar/ v. stagger, totter.

también /tam'bien/ adv. also, too.

tambor /tam'bor/ n. m. drum.

tamiz /ta'miθ; ta'mis/ n. m. sieve, sifter.

tampoco /tam'poko/ adv. neither, either.

tan /tan/ adv. so.

tanda /'tanda/ n. f. turn, relay.

tándem /'tandem/ n. m. tandem; pair.

tangencia /taŋ'genθia; taŋ'gensia/ n. f. tangency.

tangible /taŋ'giβle/ a. tangible.

tango /'taŋgo/ n. m. tango (dance or music).

tanque /'taŋke/ n. m. tank.

tanteo /tan'teo/ n. m. estimate. —**tantear,** v.

tanto /'tanto/ a. & pron. **1.** so much, so many; as much, as many. **entre t., mientras t.,** meanwhile. **por lo t.,** therefore. **un t.,** somewhat, a bit. —n. **2.** point (in games) **3.** (pl.) score. **estar al t.,** to be up to date.

tañer /ta'ner/ v. play (an instrument); ring (bells).

tapa /'tapa/ n. f. cap, cover; snack served in a bar. —**tapar,** v.

tapadero /tapa'ðero/ n. m. stopper, lid.

tápara /'tapara/ n. f. caper.

tapete /ta'pete/ n. m. small rug, mat, cover.

tapia /'tapia/ n. f. wall.

tapicería /tapiθe'ria; tapise'ria/ n. f. tapestry.

tapioca /ta'pioka/ n. f. tapioca.

tapiz /ta'piθ; ta'pis/ n. m. tapestry; carpet.

tapizado (de pared) /tapi'θaðo de pa'reð; tapi'saðo de pa'reð/ n. m. (wall) covering.

tapón /ta'pon/ n. m. plug; cork.

taquigrafía /takigra'fia/ n. f. shorthand.

taquilla /ta'kiʎa; ta'kiya/ n. f. ticket office; box office; ticket window.

tara /'tara/ n. f. hang-up.

tarántula /ta'rantula/ n. f. tarantula.

tararear /tarare'ar/ v. hum.

tardanza /tar'ðanθa; tar'ðansa/ n. f. delay; lateness.

tardar /tar'ðar/ v. delay; be late; take (of time). **a más t.,** at the latest.

tarde /'tarðe/ adv. **1.** late. —n. **2.** f. afternoon.

tardío /tar'ðio/ a. late, belated.

tarea /ta'rea/ n. f. task, assignment.

tarifa /ta'rifa/ n. f. rate; tariff; price list.

tarjeta /tar'heta/ n. f. card.

tarjeta bancaria /tar'heta ban'karia/ bank card.

tarjeta de crédito /tar'heta de 'kreðito/ credit card.

tarjeta de embarque /tar'heta de em'βarke/ boarding pass.

tarta /'tarta/ *n. f.* tart.

tartamudear /tartamuðe'ar/ *v.* stammer, falter.

tasa /'tasa/ *n. f.* rate.

tasación /tasa'θion; tasa'sion/ *n. f.* valuation.

tasar /ta'sar/ *v* assess, appraise.

tasca /'taska/ *n. f.* bar, pub.

tasugo /ta'sugo/ *n. m.* badger.

tatuar /tatu'ar/ *v.* tattoo.

tautología /tautolo'hia/ *n. f.* tautology.

taxi /'taksi/ **taxímetro** *n. m.* taxi.

taxista /tak'sista/ *n. m. & f.* taxi driver.

taxonomía /taksono'mia/ *n. f.* taxonomy.

taza /'taθa; 'tasa/ *n. f.* cup.

te /te/ *pron.* you; yourself.

té *n. m.* tea.

team /tim/ *n. m.* team.

teátrico /te'atriko/ *a.* theatrical.

teatro /te'atro/ *n. m.* theater.

tebeo /te'βeo/ *n. m.* comic book.

techo /'tetʃo/ *n. m.* roof. —**techar,** *v.*

tecla /'tekla/ *n. f.* key (of a piano, etc.).

teclado /te'klaðo/ *n. m.* keyboard.

teclado numérico /te'klaðo nu'meriko/ numeric keypad.

técnica /'teknika/ *n. f.* technique.

técnicamente /'teknikamente/ *adv.* technically.

técnico /'tekniko/ *a.* **1.** technical; —*m.* **2.** repairman, technician.

tecnología /teknolo'hia/ *n. f.* technology.

tedio /'teðio/ *n. m.* tedium, boredom.

tedioso /te'ðioso/ *a.* tedious.

teísmo /te'ismo/ *n. m.* theism.

teja /'texa/ *n. f.* tile.

tejado /te'haðo/ *n. m.* roof.

tejano /te'hano/ **-na** *a. & n.* Texan.

tejanos /te'hanos/ *n. m.pl.* jeans.

tejer /te'her/ *v.* weave; knit.

tejido /te'hiðo/ *n. m.* fabric; weaving.

tejón /te'hon/ *n. m.* badger.

tela /'tela/ *n. f.* cloth, fabric, web. **t. metálica,** screen; screening. **t. vaquera,** denim.

telar /te'lar/ *n. m.* loom.

telaraña /tela'raɲa/ *n. f.* cobweb, spiderweb.

telefonista /telefo'nista/ *n. m. & f.* (telephone) operator.

teléfono /te'lefono/ *n. m.* telephone. —**telefonear,** *v.*

teléfono gratuito /te'lefono gra'tuito/ tollfree number.

teléfono público /te'lefono 'puβliko/ pay phone, public telephone.

teléfono rojo /te'lefono 'rroho/ hotline.

telégrafo /te'legrafo/ *n. m.* telegraph. —**telegrafear,** *v.*

telegrama /tele'grama/ *n. m.* telegram.

telescopio /teles'kopio/ *n. m.* telescope.

televisión /teleβi'sion/ *n. f.* television.

telón /te'lon/ *n. m. Theat.* curtain.

telurio /te'lurio/ *n. m.* tellurium.

tema /'tema/ *n. m.* theme, subject.

temblar /tem'blar/ *v.* tremble, quake; shake, shiver.

temblor /tem'blor/ *n. m.* tremor; shiver.

temer /te'mer/ *v.* fear, be afraid of, dread.

temerario /teme'rario/ *a.* rash.

temeridad /temeri'ðað/ *n. f.* temerity.

temerosamente /temerosa'mente/ *adv.* timorously.

temeroso /teme'roso/ *a.* fearful.

temor /te'mor/ *n. m.* fear.

témpano /'tempano/ *n. m.* kettledrum; iceberg.

temperamento /tempera'mento/ *n. m.* temperament.

temperancia /tempe'ranθia; tempe'ransia/ *n. f.* temperance.

temperatura /tempera'tura/ *n. f.* temperature.

tempestad /tempes'tað/ *n. f.* tempest, storm.

tempestuoso /tempes'tuoso/ *a.* tempestuous, stormy.

templado /tem'plaðo/ *a.* temperate, mild, moderate.

templanza /tem'planθa; tem'plansa/ *n. f.* temperance; mildness.

templar /tem'plar/ *v.* temper; tune (an instrument).

templo /'templo/ *n. m.* temple.

temporada /tempo'raða/ *n. f.* season, time, spell.

temporal /tempo'ral/ **temporáneo** *a.* temporary.

temprano /tem'prano/ *a. & adv.* early.

tenacidad /tenaθi'ðað; tenasi'ðað/ *n. f.* tenacity.

tenaz /te'naθ; te'nas/ *a.* tenacious, stubborn.

tenazmente /tenaθ'mente; tenas'mente/ *adv.* tenaciously.

tendencia /ten'denθia; tendensia/ *n. f.* tendency, trend.

tender /ten'der/ *v.* stretch, stretch out.

tendero /ten'dero/ **-ra** *n.* shopkeeper, storekeeper.

tendón /ten'don/ *n. m.* tendon, sinew.

tenebrosidad /teneβrosi'ðað/ *n. f.* gloom.

tenebroso /tene'βroso/ *a.* dark, gloomy.

tenedor /tene'ðor/ n. **1.** m. & f. keeper; holder. **2.** m. fork.

tener /te'ner/ v. have; own; hold. **t. que,** have to, must.

teniente /te'niente/ n. m. lieutenant.

tenis /'tenis/ n. m. tennis; (pl.) sneakers.

tenor /te'nor/ n. m. tenor.

tensión /ten'sion/ n. f. tension, stress, strain.

tenso /'tenso/ a. tense.

tentación /tenta'θion; tenta'sion/ n. f. temptation.

tentáculo /ten'takulo/ n. m. tentacle.

tentador /tenta'ðor/ a. alluring, tempting.

tentar /ten'tar/ v. tempt, lure; grope, probe.

tentativa /tenta'tiβa/ n. f. attempt.

tentativo /tenta'tiβo/ a. tentative.

teñir /te'ɲir/ v. tint, dye.

teología /teolo'hia/ n. f. theology.

teológico /teo'lohiko/ a. theological.

teoría /teo'ria/ n. f. theory.

teórico /te'oriko/ a. theoretical.

terapéutico /tera'peutiko/ a. therapeutic.

tercero /ter'θero; ter'sero/ a. third.

tercio /'terθio; 'tersio/ n. m. third.

terciopelo /terθio'pelo; tersio'pelo/ n. m. velvet.

terco /'terko/ a. obstinate, stubborn.

termal /ter'mal/ a. thermal.

terminación /termina'θion; termina'sion/ n. f. termination; completion.

terminal aérea /termi'nal 'airea/ n. f. air terminal.

terminar /termi'nar/ v. terminate, finish.

término /'termino/ n. m. term; end.

terminología /terminolo'hia/ n. f. terminology.

termómetro /ter'mometro/ n. m. thermometer.

termos /'termos/ n. m. thermos.

termostato /ter'mostato/ n. m. thermostat.

ternero /ter'nero/ **-ra** n. calf.

ternura /ter'nura/ n. f. tenderness.

terquedad /terke'ðað/ n. f. stubbornness.

terraza /te'rraθa; te'rrasa/ n. f. terrace.

terremoto /terre'moto/ n. m. earthquake.

terreno /te'rreno/ a. **1.** earthly, terrestrial. —n. **2.** m. ground, terrain; lot, plot.

terrible /te'rriβle/ a. terrible, awful.

terrífico /te'rrifiko/ a. terrifying.

territorio /terri'torio/ n. m. territory.

terrón /te'rron/ n. m. clod, lump; mound.

terror /te'rror/ n. m. terror.

terso /'terso/ a. smooth, glossy; terse.

tertulia /ter'tulia/ n. f. social gathering, party.

tesis /'tesis/ n. f. thesis.

tesorería /tesore'ria/ n. f. treasury.

tesorero /teso'rero/ **-ra** n. treasurer.

tesoro /te'soro/ n. m treasure.

testamento /testa'mento/ n. m. will, testament.

testarudo /testa'ruðo/ a. stubborn.

testificar /testifi'kar/ v. testify.

testigo /tes'tigo/ n. m. & f. witness.

testimonial /testimo'nial/ a. testimonal.

testimonio /testi'monio/ n. m. testimony.

teta /'teta/ n. f. teat.

tetera /te'tera/ n. f. teapot.

tétrico /'tetriko/ a. sad; gloomy.

texto /'teksto/ n. m. text.

textura /teks'tura/ n. f. texture.

tez /teθ; tes/ n. f. complexion.

ti /ti/ pron. you; yourself.

tía /'tia/ n. f. aunt.

tibio /'tiβio/ a. lukewarm.

tiburón /tiβu'ron/ n. m. shark.

tiemblo /'tiemblo/ n. m. aspen.

tiempo /'tiempo/ n. m. time; weather; Gram. tense.

tienda /'tienda/ n. f. shop, store; tent.

tientas /'tientas/ n. f.pl. **andar a t.,** to grope (in the dark).

tierno /'tierno/ a. tender.

tierra /'tierra/ n. f. land; ground; earth, dirt, soil.

tieso /'tieso/ a. taut, stiff, hard, strong.

tiesto /'tiesto/ n. m. flower pot.

tiesura /tie'sura/ n. f. stiffness; harshness.

tifo /'tifo/ n. m. typhus.

tifoideo /tifoi'ðeo/ n. m. typhoid fever.

tigre /'tigre/ n. m. tiger.

tijeras /ti'heras/ n. f.pl. scissors.

tila /'tila/ n. f. linden.

timbre /'timbre/ n. m. seal, stamp; tone; (electric) bell.

tímidamente /'timiðamente/ adv. timidly.

timidez /timi'ðeθ; timi'ðes/ n. f. timidity.

tímido /'timiðo/ a. timid, shy.

timón /ti'mon/ n. m. rudder, helm.

tímpano /'timpano/ n. m. kettledrum; eardrum.

tina /'tina/ n. f. tub, vat.

tinaja /ti'naha/ n. f. jar.

tinta /'tinta/ n. f. ink.

tinte /'tinte/ n. m. tint, shade.

tintero /tin'tero/ n. m. inkwell.

tinto /'tinto/ a. wine-colored; red (of wine).

tintorería /tintore'ria/ n. f. dry cleaning shop.

tintorero /tinto'rero/ **-ra** n. dyer; dry cleaner.

tintura /tin'tura/ n. f. tincture; dye.

tiñoso /ti'ɲoso/ a. scabby; stingy.

tío /'tio/ n. m. uncle.

tiovivo /tio'βiβo/ n. m. merry-go-round.

típico /'tipiko/ a. typical.

tipo /'tipo/ n. m. type, sort; (interest) rate; Colloq. guy, fellow.

tipo de cambio /'tipo de 'kambio/ exchange rate.

tipo de interés /'tipo de inte'res/ interest rate.

tira /'tira/ n. f. strip.

tirabuzón /tiraβu'θon; tiraβu'son/ n. m. corkscrew.

tirada /ti'raða/ n. f. edition.

tirado /ti'raðo/ **-da** a. dırt-cheap.

tiranía /tira'nia/ n. f. tyranny.

tiránico /ti'raniko/ a. tyrannical.

tirano /ti'rano/ **-na** n. tyrant.

tirante /ti'rante/ a. **1.** tight, taut; tense. —n. **2.** m.pl. suspenders.⊛

tirar /ti'rar/ v. throw; draw; pull; fire (a weapon).

tiritar /tiri'tar/ v. shiver.

tiro /'tiro/ n. m. throw; shot.

tirón /ti'ron/ n. m. pull. **de un t.,** at a stretch, at one stroke.

tísico /'tisiko/ n. & a. consumptive.

tisis /'tisis/ n. f. consumption, tuberculosıs.

titanio /ti'tanio/ n. m. titanium.

títere /'titere/ n. m. puppet.

titilación /titila'θion; titila'sion/ n. f. twinkle.

titubear /tituβe'ar/ v. stagger; totter; waver.

titulado /titu'laðo/ a. entitled; so-called.

titular /titu'lar/ a. **1.** titular. —v. **2.** entitle.

título /'titulo/ n. m. title, headline.

tiza /'tiθa; 'tisa/ n. f. chalk.

tiznar /tiθ'nar; tis'nar/ v. smudge; stain.

toalla /to'aʎa; to'aya/ n. f. towel. **t. sanitaria,** sanitary napkin.

toalleta /toa'ʎeta; toa'yeta/ n. f. small towel.

tobillo /to'βiʎo; to'βiyo/ n. m. ankle.

tobogán /toβo'gan/ n. m. toboggan.

tocadiscos /toka'ðiskos/ n. m. record player.

tocadiscos compacto /toka'ðiskos kom'pakto/ **tocadiscos digital** CD player.

tocado /to'kaðo/ n. m. hairdo.

tocador /toka'ðor/ n. m. boudoir; dressing table.

tocante /to'kante/ a. touching. **t. a,** concerning, relative to.

tocar /to'kar/ v. touch; play (an instrument). **t. a uno,** be one's turn; be up to one.

tocayo /to'kayo/ **-ya** n. namesake.

tocino /to'θino; to'sino/ n. m. bacon.

tocólogo /to'kologo/ **-ga** n. obstetrician.

todavía /toða'βia/ adv. yet, still.

todo /'toðo/ a. **1.** all, whole. **todos los,** every. —pron. **2.** all, everything. **con t,** still, however. **del t.,** wholly; at all.

todopoderoso /toðopoðe'roso/ a. almighty.

toldo /'toldo/ n. m. awning.

tolerancia /tole'ranθia; tole'ransia/ n. f. tolerance.

tolerante /tole'rante/ a. tolerant.

tolerar /tole'rar/ v. tolerate.

toma /'toma/ n. f. taking, capture, seizure.

tomaína /to'maina/ n. f. ptomaine.

tomar /to'mar/ v. take; drink. **t. el sol,** sunbathe.

tomate /to'mate/ n. m. tomato.

tomillo /to'miʎo; to'miyo/ n. m. thyme.

tomo /'tomo/ n. m. volume.

tonada /to'naða/ n. f. tune.

tonel /to'nel/ n. m. barrel, cask.

tonelada /tone'laða/ n. f. ton.

tonelaje /tone'lahe/ n. m. tonnage.

tónico /'toniko/ a. & m. tonıc.

tono /'tono/ n. m. tone, pitch, shade. **darse t.,** to put on airs.

tonsila /ton'sila/ n. f. tonsil.

tonsilitis /tonsi'litis/ n. f. tonsilitis.

tontería /tonte'ria/ n. f. nonsense, foolishness.

tontifútbol /tonti'futβol/ n. m. excessively defensive strategy (in soccer).

tonto /'tonto/ **-ta** a. & n. foolish, silly; fool.

topacio /to'paθio; to'pasio/ n. m. topaz.

topar /to'par/ v. run into. **t. con,** come upon.

tópico /'topiko/ a **1.** topical. —n. **2.** m. cliché.

topo /'topo/ n. m. mole (animal).

toque /'toke/ n. m. touch.

tórax /'toraks/ n. m. thorax.

torbellino /torβe'ʎino; torβe'yino/ n. m. whirlwind.

torcer /tor'θer; tor'ser/ v. twist; wind; distort.

toreador /torea'ðor/ **-a** n. toreador.

torero /to'rero/ **-ra** n. bullfighter.

torio /'torio/ n. m. thorium.

tormenta /tor'menta/ n. f. storm.

tormento /tor'mento/ n. m. torment.

tornado /tor'naðo/ n. m. tornado.

tornar /tor'nar/ v. return; turn.

tornarse en /tor'narse en/ v. turn into, become.

torneo /tor'neo/ n. m. tournament.

tornillo /tor'niʎo; tor'niyo/ n. m. screw.

toro /'toro/ n. m. bull.

toronja /to'ronha/ n. f. grapefruit.

torpe /'torpe/ a. awkward, clumsy; sluggish.

torpedero /torpe'ðero/ n. m. torpedo boat.

torpedo /tor'peðo/ n. m. torpedo.

torre /'torre/ n. f. tower.

torre de mando /'torre de 'mando/ control tower.

torrente /to'rrente/ n. m. torrent.

tórrido /'torriðo/ a. torrid.

torta /'torta/ n. f. cake; loaf.

tortilla /tor'tiʎa; tor'tiya/ n. f. omelet; (Mex.) tortilla, pancake.

tórtola /'tortola/ n. f. dove.

tortuga /tor'tuga/ n. f. turtle.

tortuoso /tor'tuoso/ a. tortuous.

tortura /tor'tura/ n. f. torture. **—torturar,** v.

tos /tos/ n. m. cough. **—toser,** v.

tosco /'tosko/ a. coarse, rough, uncouth.

tosquedad /toske'ðað/ n. f. coarseness, roughness.

tostador /tosta'ðor/ n. m. toaster.

tostar /'tostar/ v. toast; tan.

total /to'tal/ a. & m. total.

totalidad /totali'ðað/ n. f. totality, entirety, whole.

totalitario /totali'tario/ a. totalitarian.

totalmente /total'mente/ adv. totally; entirely.

tótem /'totem/ n. m. totem.

tóxico /'toksiko/ a. toxic.

toxicómano /toksi'komano/ **-na** n. m. & f. drug addict.

trabajador /traβaha'ðor/ **-ra** a. 1. hardworking. **—n.** 2. worker.

trabajo /tra'βaho/ n. m. work; labor. **—trabajar,** v.

trabar /tra'βar/ v. fasten, shackle; grasp; strike up.

tracción /trak'θion; trak'sion/ n. f. traction.

tracto /'trakto/ n. m. tract.

tractor /trak'tor/ n. m. tractor.

tradición /traði'θion; traði'sion/ n. f. tradition.

tradicional /traðiθio'nal; traðisio'nal/ a. traditional.

traducción /traðuk'θion; traðuk'sion/ n. f. translation.

traducir /traðu'θir; traðu'sir/ v. translate.

traductor /traðuk'tor/ **-ra** n. translator.

traer /tra'er/ v. bring; carry; wear.

tráfico /'trafiko/ n. m. traffic. **—traficar,** v.

tragaperras /traga'perras/ n. f. slot machine, one-armed bandit.

tragar /tra'gar/ v. swallow.

tragedia /tra'heðia/ n. f. tragedy.

trágicamente /'trahikamente/ adv. tragically.

trágico /'trahiko/ **-ca** a. 1. tragic. **—n.** 2. tragedian.

trago /'trago/ n. m. swallow; drink.

traición /trai'θion; trai'sion/ n. f. treason, betrayal.

traicionar /traiθio'nar; traisio'nar/ v. betray.

traidor /trai'ðor/ **-ra** a. & n traitorous; traitor.

traje /'trahe/ n. m. suit; dress; garb, apparel.

traje de baño /'trahe de 'baɲo/ bathing suit.

trama /'trama/ v. plot (of a story).

tramador /trama'ðor/ **-ra** n. weaver; plotter.

tramar /tra'mar/ v. weave; plot, scheme.

trámite /'tramite/ n. m. (business) deal, transaction.

tramo /'tramo/ n. m. span, stretch, section.

trampa /'trampa/ n. f. trap, snare.

trampista /tram'pista/ n. m. & f. cheater; swindler.

trance /'tranθe; 'transe/ n. m. critical moment or stage. **a todo t.,** at any cost.

tranco /'tranko/ n. m. stride.

tranquilidad /trankili'ðað/ n. f. tranquility, calm, quiet.

tranquilizante /trankili'θante; trankili-'sante/ n. m. tranquilizer.

tranquilizar /trankili'θar; trankili'sar/ v. quiet, calm down.

tranquilo /tran'kilo/ a. tranquil, calm.

transacción /transak'θion; transak'sion/ n. f. transaction.

transbordador /transβorða'ðor/ n. m. ferry.

transbordador espacial /transβorða'ðor espa'θial; transβorða'ðor espa'sial/ space, shuttle.

transcribir /transkri'βir/ v. transcribe.

transcripción /transkrip'θion; transkrip-'sion/ n. f. transcription.

transcurrir /transku'rrir/ v. elapse.

transeúnte /tran'seunte/ a. & n. transient; passerby.

transexual /transek'sual/ a. transsexual.

transferencia /transfe'renθia; transfe'rensia/ n. f. transference.

transferir /transfe'rir/ v. transfer.

transformación /transforma'θion; transforma'sion/ n. f. transformation.

transformar /transfor'mar/ v. transform.

transfusión /transfu'sion/ n. f. transfusion.

transgresión /transgre'sion/ n. f. transgression.

transgresor /transgre'sor/ **-ra** n. transgressor.

transición /transi'θion; transi'sion/ n. f. transition.

transigir /transi'hir/ v. compromise, settle; agree.

transistor /transis'tor/ n. m. transistor.

transitivo /transi'tiβo/ a. transitive.

tránsito /'transito/ n. m. transit, passage.

transitorio /transi'torio/ a. transitory.

transmisión /transmi'sion/ n. f. transmission; broadcast.

transmisora /transmi'sora/ n. f. broadcasting station.

transmitir /transmi'tir/ v. transmit; broadcast.

transparencia /transpa'renθia; transpa'ren-sia/ n. f. transparency.

transparente /transpa'rente/ a. **1.** transparent. —n. **2.** m. (window) shade.

transportación /transporta'θion; transporta'sion/ n. f. transportation.

transportar /transpor'tar/ v. transport, convey.

transporte /trans'porte/ n. m. transportation; transport.

tranvía /tram'bia/ n. m. streetcar, trolley.

trapacero /trapa'θero: trapa'sero/ **-ra** n. cheat; swindler.

trapo /'trapo/ n. m. rag.

tráquea /'trakea/ n. f. trachea.

tras /tras/ prep. after; behind.

trasegar /trase'gar/ v. upset, overturn.

trasero /tra'sero/ a. rear, back.

traslado /tras'laðo/ n. m. transfer. —**trasladar,** v.

traslapo /tras'lapo/ n. m. overlap. —**traslapar,** v.

trasnochar /trasno't∫ar/ v. stay up all night.

traspalar /traspa'lar/ v. shovel.

traspasar /traspa'sar/ v. go beyond; cross; violate; pierce.

trasquilar /traski'lar/ v. shear; clip.

trastornar /trastor'nar/ v. overturn, overthrow, upset.

trastorno /tras'torno/ m. overthrow; upheaval.

trastorno mental /tras'torno men'tal/ mental disorder.

trasvasar /trasβa'sar/ v. download; download.

tratado /tra'taðo/ n. m. treaty; treatise.

tratamiento /trata'miento/ n m treatment.

tratar /tra'tar/ v. treat, handle. **t. de,** deal with; try to; call (a name).

tratarse de /tra'tarse de/ v. be a question of.

trato /'trato/ n. m. treatment; manners; Com. deal.

través /tra'βes/ adv. **a t. de,** through, across. **de t.,** sideways.

travesía /traβe'sia/ n. f. crossing; voyage.

travesti /tra'βesti/ n. m. transvestite.

travestido /traβes'tiðo/ a. disguised.

travesura /traβe'sura/ n. f. prank; mischief.

travieso /tra'βieso/ a. naughty, mischievous.

trayectoria /trayek'toria/ n. f. trajectory.

trazar /tra'θar; tra'sar/ v. plan, devise; trace; draw.

trazo /'traθo; 'traso/ n. plan, outline; line, stroke.

trébol /'treβol/ n. m. clover.

trece /'treθe; 'trese/ a. & pron. thirteen.

trecho /'tret∫o/ n. m. space, distance, stretch.

tregua /'tregua/ n. f. truce; respite, lull.

treinta /'treinta/ a & pron. thirty.

tremendo /tre'mendo/ a. tremendous.

tremer /tre'mer/ v. tremble.

tren /tren/ n. m. train.

trenza /'trenθa; 'trensa/ n. f. braid. —**trenzar,** v.

trepar /tre'par/ v. climb, mount.

trepidación /trepiða'θion; trepiða'sion/ n. f. trepidation.

tres /tres/ a. & pron. three.

trescientos /tres'θientos; tres'sientos/ a. & pron. three hundred.

triángulo /tri'aŋgulo/ n. m. triangle.

triar /triar/ v. sort, separate.

tribu /'triβu/ n. f. tribe.

tribulación /triβula'θion; triβula'sion/ n. f. tribulation.

tribuna /tri'βuna/ n. f. rostrum, stand; (pl.) grandstand.

tribunal /triβu'nal/ n. m. court, tribunal.

tributario /triβu'tario/ a. & m. tributary.

tributo /tri'βuto/ n. m. tribute.

triciclo /tri'θiklo; tri'siklo/ n. m. tricycle.

trigo /'trigo/ n. m. wheat.

trigonometría /trigonome'tria/ n. f. trigonometry.

trigueño /tri'geɲo/ a. swarthy, dark.

trilogía /trilo'hia/ n. f. trilogy.

trimestral /trimes'tral/ a. quarterly.

trinchar /trin't∫ar/ v. carve (meat).

trinchera /trin't∫era/ n. f. trench, ditch.

trineo /tri'neo/ n. m. sled; sleigh.

trinidad /trini'ðað/ n. f. trinity.

tripa /'tripa/ n. f. tripe, entrails.

triple /'triple/ a. triple. —**triplicar,** v.

trípode /'tripoðe/ n. m. tripod.

tripulación /tripula'θion; tripula'sion/ n. f. crew.

tripulante /tripu'lante/ m & f. crew member.

tripular /tripu'lar/ v. man.

triste /'triste/ a. sad, sorrowful; dreary.

tristemente /triste'mente/ adv. sadly.

tristeza /tris'teθa; tris'tesa/ n. f. sadness; gloom.

triunfal /triun'fal/ a. triumphal.

triunfante /triun'fante/ a. triumphant.

triunfo /'triunfo/ n. m. triumph; trump. —**triunfar,** v.

trivial /tri'βial/ a. trivial, commonplace.

trivialidad /triβiali'ðað/ n. f. triviality.

trocar /tro'kar/ v. exchange, switch; barter.

trofeo /tro'feo/ n. m. trophy.

trombón /trom'bon/ n. m. trombone.

trompa /'trompa/ **trompeta** n. f. trumpet, horn.

tronada /tro'naða/ n. f. thunderstorm.

tronar /tro'nar/ v. thunder.

tronco /'tronko/ n. m. trunk, stump.

trono /'trono/ n. m. throne.

tropa /'tropa/ n. f. troop.

tropel /tro'pel/ n. m. crowd, throng.

tropezar /trope'θar; trope'sar/ v. trip, stumble. **t. con,** come upon, run into.

trópico /'tropiko/ a. & m. tropical; tropics.

tropiezo /tro'pieθo; tro'pieso/ n. m. stumble; obstacle; slip, error.

trote /'trote/ n. m. trot. —**trotar**, v.

trovador /troβa'ðor/ n. m. troubadour.

trozo /'troθo; 'troso/ n. m. piece, portion, fragment; selection, passage.

trucha /'trutʃa/ n. f. trout.

trueco /'trueko/ **trueque** /n. m. exchange, barter.

trueno /'trueno/ n. m. thunder.

trufa /'trufa/ n. f. truffle.

tu /tu/ a. your.

tú pron. you.

tuberculosis /tuβerku'losis/ n. f. tuberculosis.

tubo /'tuβo/ n. m. tube, pipe.

tubo de ensayo /'tuβo de en'sayo/ test tube.

tubo de escape /'tuβo de es'kape/ exhaust pipe.

tuerca /'tuerka/ n. f. Mech. nut.

tulipán /tuli'pan/ n. m. tulip.

tumba /'tumba/ n. f. tomb, grave.

tumbar /tum'bar/ v. knock down.

tumbarse /tum'βarse/ v. lie down.

tumbo /'tumbo/ n. m. tumble; somersault.

tumbona /tum'βona/ n. f. deck chair.

tumor /tu'mor/ n. m. tumor; growth.

tumulto /tu'multo/ n. m. tumult, commotion.

tumultuoso /tumul'tuoso/ a. tumultuous, boisterous.

tunante /tu'nante/ n. m. rascal, rogue.

tunda /'tunda/ n. f. spanking, whipping.

túnel /'tunel/ n. m. tunnel.

túnel del Canal de la Mancha /'tunel del ka'nal de la 'mantʃa/ Channel Tunnel, Chunnel.

tungsteno /tuŋgs'teno/ n. m. tungsten.

túnica /'tunika/ n. f. tunic, robe.

tupir /tu'pir/ v. pack tight, stuff; stop up.

turbación /turβa'θion; turβa'sion/ n. f. confusion, turmoil.

turbamulta /turβa'multa/ n. f. mob, disorderly crowd.

turbar /tur'βar/ v. disturb, upset; embarrass.

turbina /tur'βina/ n. f. turbine.

turbio /'turβio/ a. turbid; muddy.

turco /'turko/ **-ca** a. & n. Turkish; Turk.

turismo /tu'rismo/ n. m. touring, (foreign) travel, tourism.

turista /tu'rista/ n. m. & f. tourist.

turno /'turno/ n. m. turn; (work) shift.

turquesa /tur'kesa/ n. f. turquoise.

Turquía /tur'kia/ n. f. Turkey.

turrón /tu'rron/ n. m. nougat.

tusa /'tusa/ n. f. corncob; corn.

tutear /tute'ar/ v. use the pronoun **tú**, etc., in addressing a person.

tutela /tu'tela/ n. f. guardianship; aegis.

tutor /tu'tor/ **-ra** n. tutor; guardian.

tuyo /'tuyo/ a. your, yours.

U V

u /u/ conj. or.

ubre /'uβre/ n. f. udder.

Ucrania /u'krania/ n. f. Ukraine.

ucranio /u'kranio/ **-ia** a. & n. Ukrainian.

ufano /u'fano/ a. proud, haughty.

úlcera /'ulθera; 'ulsera/ n. f. ulcer.

ulterior /ulte'rior/ a. ulterior.

último /'ultimo/ a. last, final; ultimate; latest. **por ú.,** finally. **ú. minuto,** last minute, eleventh hour.

ultraje /ul'trahe/ n. m. outrage. —**ultrajar**, v.

ultrasónico /ultra'soniko/ a. ultrasonic.

umbral /um'bral/ n. m. threshold.

umbroso /um'broso/ a. shady.

un /un/ **una** art. & a. a, an; one; (pl.) some.

unánime /u'nanime/ a. unanimous.

unanimidad /unanimi'ðað/ n. f. unanimity.

unción /un'θion; un'sion/ n. f. unction.

ungüento /uŋ'guento/ n. m. ointment.

único /'uniko/ a. only, sole; unique.

unicornio /uni'kornio/ n. m. unicorn.

unidad /uni'ðað/ n. f. unit; unity.

unidad de cuidados intensivos /uni'ðað de kui'ðaðos inten'siβos/ **unidad de vigilancia intensiva** intensive-care unit.

unidad de disco /uni'ðað de 'disko/ disk drive.

unificar /unifi'kar/ v. unify.

uniforme /uni'forme/ a. & m. uniform.

uniformidad /uniformi'ðað/ n. f. uniformity.

unión /u'nion/ n. f. union; joining.

unir /u'nir/ v. unite, join.

universal /uniβer'sal/ a. universal.

universalidad /uniβersali'ðað/ n. f. universality.

universidad /uniβersi'ðað/ n. f. university; college.

universo /uni'βerso/ n. m. universe.

uno /'uno/ **una** pron. one; (pl.) some.

untar /un'tar/ v. spread; grease; anoint.

uña /'uɲa/ n. f. fingernail.

urbanidad /urβani'ðað/ n. f. urbanity; good breeding.

urbanismo /urβa'nismo/ n. m. city planning.

urbano /ur'βano/ a. urban; urbane; wellbred.

urbe /'urβe/ n. f. large city.

urgencia /ur'henθia; ur'hensia/ n. f. urgency.

urgente /ur'hente/ a. urgent, pressing. **entrega u.**, special delivery.

urgir /ur'hir/ v. be urgent.

urna /'urna/ n. f. urn; ballot box; (pl.) polls.

urraca /u'rraka/ n. f. magpie.

usanza /u'sanθa; u'sansa/ n. f. usage, custom.

usar /u'sar/ v. use; wear.

uso /'uso/ n. m. use; usage; wear.

usted /us'teð/ pron. you.

usual /u'sual/ a. usual.

usualmente /usual'mente/ adv. usually.

usura /u'sura/ n. f. usury.

usurero /usu'rero/ **-ra** n. usurer.

usurpación /usurpa'θion; usurpa'sion/ n. f. usurpation.

usurpar /usur'par/ v. usurp.

utensilio /uten'silio/ n. m. utensil.

útero /'utero/ n. m. uterus.

útil /'util/ a. useful, handy.

utilidad /utili'ðað/ n. f. utility, usefulness.

utilizar /utili'θar; utili'sar/ v. use, utilize.

útilmente /util'mente/ adv. usefully.

utópico /u'topiko/ a. utopian.

uva /'uβa/ n. f. grape.

vaca /'baka/ n. f. cow; beef.

vacaciones /baka'θiones; baka'siones/ n. f.pl. vacation, holidays.

vacancia /ba'kanθia; ba'kansia/ n. f. vacancy.

vacante /ba'kante/ a. **1.** vacant. —n. **2.** f. vacancy.

vaciar /ba'θiar; ba'siar/ v. empty; pour out.

vacilación /baθila'θion; basila'sion/ n. f. vacillation, hesitation.

vacilante /baθi'lante; basi'lante/ a. vacillating.

vacilar /baθi'lar; basi'lar/ v. falter, hesitate; waver; stagger.

vacío /ba'θio; ba'sio/ a. **1.** empty. —n. **2.** m. void, empty space.

vacuna /ba'kuna/ n. f. vaccine.

vacunación /bakuna'θion; bakuna'sion/ n. f. vaccination.

vacunar /baku'nar/ v. vaccinate.

vacuo /'bakuo/ a. **1.** empty, vacant. —n. **2.** m. vacuum.

vadear /baðe'ar/ v. wade through, ford.

vado /'baðo/ n. m. ford.

vagabundo /baga'βundo/ **-da** a. & n. vagabond.

vagar /ba'gar/ v. wander, rove, roam; loiter.

vago /'bago/ **-ga** a. **1.** vague, hazy; wandering, vagrant. —n. **2.** vagrant, tramp.

vagón /ba'gon/ n. m. railroad car.

vahído /ba'iðo/ n. m. dizziness.

vaina /'baina/ n. f. sheath; pod.

vainilla /bai'niʎa; bai'niya/ n. f. vanilla.

vaivén /bai'βen/ n. m. vibration, sway.

vajilla /ba'hiʎa; ba'hiya/ n. f. (dinner) dishes.

valentía /balen'tia/ n. f. valor, courage.

valer /ba'ler/ v. **1.** m. worth. —v. **2.** be worth.

valerse de /ba'lerse de/ v. make use of, avail oneself of.

valía /ba'lia/ n. f. value.

validez /bali'ðeθ; bali'ðes/ n. f. validity.

válido /ba'liðo/ a. valid.

valiente /ba'liente/ a. valiant, brave.

valija /ba'liha/ n. f. valise.

valioso /ba'lioso/ a. valuable.

valla /'baʎa; 'baya/ n. f. fence, barrier.

valle /'baʎe; 'baye/ n. m. valley.

valor /ba'lor/ n. m. value, worth; bravery, valor; (pl., Com.) securities.

valoración /balora'θion; balora'sion/ n. f. appraisal.

valorar /balo'rar/ v. value, appraise.

vals /bals/ n. m. waltz.

valsar /bal'sar/ v. waltz.

valuación /balua'θion; balua'sion/ n. f. valuation.

valuar /balu'ar/ v. value; rate.

válvula /'balβula/ n. f. valve.

válvula de seguridad /'balβula de seguri'ðað/ safety valve.

vandalismo /banda'lismo/ n. m. vandalism.

vándalo /'bandalo/ **-la** n. vandal.

vanidad /bani'ðað/ n. f. vanity.

vanidoso /bani'ðoso/ a. vain, conceited.

vano /'bano/ a. vain; inane.

vapor /ba'por/ n. m. vapor; steam; steamer, steamship.

vaquero /ba'kero/ **-ra** n. cowboy.

vara /'bara/ n. f. wand, stick, switch.

varadero /bara'ðero/ n. m. shipyard.

varar /ba'rar/ v. launch; be stranded; run aground.

variable /ba'riaβle/ a. variable.

variación /baria'θion; baria'sion/ n. f. variation.

variar /ba'riar/ v. vary.

varicela /bari'θela; bari'sela/ n. f. chicken pox.

variedad /barie'ðað/ n. f. variety.

varios /'barios/ a. & pron. pl. various; several.

variz /ba'riθ; ba'ris/ n. f. varicose vein.

varón /ba'ron/ n. m. man; male.

varonil /baro'nil/ a. manly, virile.

vasallo /ba'saʎo; ba'sayo/ n. m. vassal.

vasectomía /basekto'mia/ n. f. vasectomy.

vasija /ba'siha/ n. f. bowl, container.

vaso /'baso/ n. m. water glass; vase. **v. de papel,** paper cup.

vástago /'bastago/ n. m. bud, shoot; twig; offspring.

vasto /'basto/ a. vast.

vecindad /beθin'dað; besin'dað/ n. f. **vecindario,** m. neighborhood, vicinity.

vecino /be'θino; be'sino/ **-na** a. & n. neighboring; neighbor.

vedar /be'ðar/ v. forbid; impede.

vega /'bega/ n. f. meadow.

vegetación /beheta'θion; beheta'sion/ n. f. vegetation.

vegetal /behe'tal/ n. m. vegetable.

vehemente /bee'mente/ a. vehement.

vehículo /be'ikulo/ n. m. vehicle.

veinte /'beinte/ a. & pron. twenty.

vejez /be'heθ; be'hes/ n. f. old age.

vejiga /be'higa/ n. f. bladder.

vela /'bela/ n. f. vigil, watch; candle; sail.

velar /be'lar/ v. stay up, sit up; watch over.

vellón /be'ʎon; be'yon/ n. m. fleece.

velloso /be'ʎoso; be'yoso/ a. hairy; fuzzy.

velludo /be'ʎuðo; be'yuðo/ a. downy.

velo /'belo/ n. m. veil.

velocidad /beloθi'ðað; belosi'ðað/ n. f. velocity, speed; rate. **v. máxima,** speed limit.

velomotor /belomo'tor/ n. m. motorbike, moped.

veloz /be'loθ; be'los/ a. speedy, fast, swift.

vena /'bena/ n. f. vein.

venado /be'naðo/ n. m. deer.

vencedor /benθe'ðor; bense'ðor/ **-ra** n. victor.

vencer /ben'θer; ben'ser/ v. defeat, overcome, conquer; *Com.* become due, expire.

vencimiento /benθi'miento; bensi'miento/ n. m. defeat; expiration.

venda /'benda/ n. f. **vendaje,** m. bandage. **—vendar,** v.

vendedor /bende'ðor/ **-ra** n. seller, trader; sales clerk.

vender /ben'der/ v. sell.

vendimia /ben'dimia/ n. f. vintage; grape harvest.

Venecia /be'neθia; be'nesia/ n. f Venice.

veneciano /bene'θiano; bene'siano/ **-na** a. & n. Venetian.

veneno /be'neno/ n. m. poison.

venenoso /bene'noso/ a. poisonous.

veneración /benera'θion; benera'sion/ n. f. veneration.

venerar /bene'rar/ v. venerate, revere.

venero /be'nero/ n. m. spring; origin.

véneto /'beneto/ a. Venetian.

venezolano /beneθo'lano; beneso'lano/ **-na** a. & n. Venezuelan.

vengador /benga'ðor/ **-ra** n. avenger.

venganza /ben'ganθa; ben'gansa/ n. f. vengeance, revenge.

vengar /ben'gar/ v. avenge.

venida /be'niða/ n. f. arrival, advent.

venidero /beni'ðero/ a. future; coming.

venir /be'nir/ v. come.

venta /'benta/ n. f. sale; sales.

ventaja /ben'taha/ n. f. advantage; profit.

ventajoso /benta'hoso/ a. advantageous.

ventana /ben'tana/ n. f. window.

ventero /ben'tero/ **-ra** n. innkeeper.

ventilación /bentila'θion; bentila'sion/ n. m. ventilation.

ventilador /bentila'ðor/ n. m. ventilator, fan.

ventilar /benti'lar/ v. ventilate, air.

ventisquero /bentis'kero/ n. m. snowdrift; glacier.

ventoso /ben'toso/ a. windy.

ventura /ben'tura/ n. f. happiness; luck.

ver /ber/ v. see. **tener que v. con,** have to do with.

vera /'bera/ n. f. edge.

veracidad /beraθi'ðað; berasi'ðað/ n. f. truthfulness, veracity.

verano /be'rano/ n. m. summer. **—veranear,** v.

veras /'beras/ n. f.pl. **de v.,** really, truly.

veraz /be'raθ/ be'ras/ a. truthful.

verbigracia /berβi'graθia; berβi'grasia/ adv. for example.

verbo /'berβo/ n. m. verb.

verboso /ber'βoso/ a. verbose.

verdad /ber'ðað/ n. f. truth. **ser v.,** to be true.

verdadero /berða'ðero/ a. true, real.

verde /'berðe/ a. green; risqué, off-color.

verdor /ber'ðor/ n. m. greenness, verdure.

verdugo /ber'ðugo/ n. m. hangman.

verdura /ber'ðura/ n. f. verdure, vegetation; (pl.) vegetables.

vereda /be'reða/ n. f. path.

veredicto /bere'ðikto/ n. m. verdict.

vergonzoso /bergon'θoso; bergon'soso/ a. shameful, embarrassing; shy, bashful.

vergüenza /ber'guenθa; ber'guensa/ n. f. shame; disgrace; embarrassment.

verificar /berifi'kar/ v. verify, check.

verja /'berha/ n. f. grating, railing.

verosímil /bero'simil/ a. likely, plausible.

verraco /be'rrako/ n. m. boar.

verruga /be'rruga/ n. f. wart.

versátil /ber'satil/ a. versatile.

verse /'berse/ v. look, appear.

versión /ber'sion/ n. f. version.

verso /'berso/ n. m. verse, stanza; line (of poetry).

verter /ber'ter/ v. pour, spill; shed; empty.

vertical /berti'kal/ a. vertical.

vertiente /ber'tiente/ n. f. slope; watershed.

vertiginoso /bertihi'noso/ a. dizzy,

vértigo /'bertigo/ n. m. vertigo, dizziness.

vestíbulo /bes'tiβulo/ n. m. vestibule, lobby.

vestido /bes'tiðo/ n. m. dress; clothing.

vestigio /bes'tihio/ n. m. vestige, trace.

vestir /bes'tir/ v. dress, clothe.

veterano /bete'rano/ **-na** a. & n. veteran.

veterinario /beteri'nario/ **-ria** a. **1.** veterinary. —n. **2.** veterinarian.

veto /'beto/ n. m. veto.

vetusto /be'tusto/ a. ancient, very old.

vez /beθ/ bes/ n. f. time; turn. **tal v.,** perhaps. **a la v.,** at the same time. **en v. de,** instead of. **una v.,** once. **otra v.,** again.

vía /'bia/ n. f. track; route, way.

viaducto /bia'ðukto/ n. m. viaduct.

viajante /bia'hante/ a. & n. traveling; traveler.

viajar /bia'har/ v. travel; journey; tour.

viaje /'biahe/ n. m. trip, journey, voyage; (pl.) travels.

viaje de estudios /'biahe de es'tuðios/ field trip.

viajero /bia'hero/ **-ra** n. traveler; passenger.

viaje todo incluido /'biahe 'toðo in'kluiðo/ package tour.

viandas /'biandas/ n. f.pl. victuals, food.

víbora /'biβora/ n. f. viper.

vibración /biβra'θion; biβra'sion/ n. f. vibration.

vibrar /bi'βrar/ v. vibrate.

vicepresidente /biθepresi'ðente; bisepresi'ðente/ **-ta** n. vice president.

vicio /'biθio; 'bisio/ n. m. vice.

vicioso /bi'θioso; bi'sioso/ a. vicious; licentious.

víctima /'biktima/ n. f. victim.

victoria /bik'toria/ n. f. victory.

victorioso /bikto'rioso/ a. victorious.

vid /bið/ n. f. grapevine.

vida /'biða/ n. f. life; living.

vídeo /'bi'ðeo/ n. m. videotape.

videocámara /biðeo'kamara/ n. f. video camera.

videodisco /biðeo'ðisko/ n. m. videodisc.

videojuego /biðeo'huego/ n. m video game.

vidrio /'biðrio/ n. m. glass.

viejo /'bieho/ **-ja** a. & n. old; old person.

viento /'biento/ n. m. wind. **hacer v.,** to be windy.

vientre /'bientre/ n. m. belly.

viernes /'biernes/ n. m. Friday.

viga /'biga/ n. f beam, rafter.

vigente /bi'hente/ a. in effect (prices, etc.).

vigilante /bihi'lante/ a. & m. vigilant, watchful; watchman.

vigilante nocturno /bihi'lante nok'turno/ night watchman.

vigilar /bihi'lar/ v. guard, watch over.

vigilia /bi'hilia/ n. f. vigil, watchfulness; Relig. fast.

vigor /bi'gor/ n. m. vigor. **en v.,** in effect, in force.

vil /bil/ a. vile, low, contemptible.

vileza /bi'leθa; bi'lesa/ n. f. vileness.

villa /'biʎa; 'biya/ n. f. town; country house.

villancico /biʎan'θiko; biyan'siko/ n. m. Christmas carol.

villanía /biʎa'nia; biya'nia/ n. f. villainy.

villano /bi'ʎano; bi'yano/ n. m. boor.

vinagre /bi'nagre/ n. m. vinegar.

vinagrera /bina'grera/ n. f. cruet.

vínculo /'binkulo/ n. m. link. —**vincular,** v.

vindicar /bindi'kar/ v. vindicate.

vino /'bino/ n. m. wine.

viña /'biɲa/ n. f. vineyard.

violación /biola'θion; biola'sion/ n. f. violation; rape.

violador /biola'ðor/ **-ra** n. m. & f. rapist.

violar /bio'lar/ v. violate; rape.

violencia /bio'lenθia; bio'lensia/ n. f. violence.

violento /bio'lento/ a. violent; impulsive.

violeta /bio'leta/ n. f. violet.

violín /bio'lin/ n. m. violin.

violón /bio'lon/ n. m. bass viol.

virar /bi'rar/ v. veer, change course.

virgen /bir'hen/ n. f. virgin.

viril /bi'ril/ a. virile, manly.

virilidad /birili'ðað/ n. f. virility, manhood.

virtual /bir'tual/ a. virtual.

virtud /bir'tuð/ n. f. virtue; efficacy, power.

virtuoso /bir'tuoso/ a. virtuous.

viruela /bi'ruela/ n. f. smallpox.

viruelas locas /bi'ruelas 'lokas/ n. f.pl. chicken pox.

virus /'birus/ n. m. virus.

visa /'bisa/ n. f. visa.

visaje /bi'sahe/ n. m. grimace.

visera /bi'sera/ n. f. visor.

visible /bi'siβle/ a. visible.

visión /bi'sion/ n. f. vision.

visionario /bisio'nario/ **-ria** *a.* & *n.* visionary.

visita /bi'sita/ *n. f.* visit; *m.* & *f.* visitor, caller. **v. con guía, v. explicada, v. programada,** guided tour.

visitación /bisita'θion: bisita'sion/ *n. f.* visitation.

visitante /bisi'tante/ *a.* & *n.* visiting; visitor.

visitar /bisi'tar/ *v.* visit; inspect, examine.

vislumbrar /bislum'βrar/ *v.* glimpse.

vislumbre /bis'lumbre/ *n. f.* glimpse.

viso /'biso/ *n. m.* looks; outlook.

víspera /'bispera/ *n. f.* eve, day before.

vista /'bista/ *n. f.* view; scene; sight.

vista de pájaro /'bista de 'paharo/ bird's-eye view.

vistazo /bis'taθo; bís'taso/ *n. m.* glance, glimpse.

vistoso /bis'toso/ *a.* beautiful; showy.

visual /bi'sual/ *a.* visual.

vital /bi'tal/ *a.* vital.

vitalidad /bitali'ðað/ *n. f.* vitality.

vitamina /bita'mina/ *n. f.* vitamin.

vitando /bi'tando/ *a.* hateful.

vituperar /bitupe'rar/ *v.* vituperate; revile.

viuda /'biuða/ *n. f.* widow.

viudo /'biuðo/ *n. m.* widower.

vivaz /bi'βaθ; bi'βas/ *a.* vivacious; clever.

víveres /'biβeres/ *n. m.pl.* provisions.

viveza /bi'βeθa; bi'βesa/ *n. f.* animation, liveliness.

vívido /bi'βiðo/ *a.* vivid, bright.

vivienda /bi'βienda/ *n. f.* (living) quarters, dwelling.

vivificar /biβifi'kar/ *v.* vivify, enliven.

vivir /bi'βir/ *v.* live.

vivo /'biβo/ *a.* live, alive, living; vivid; animated, brisk.

vocablo /bo'kaβlo/ *n. m.* word.

vocabulario /bokaβu'lario/ *n. m.* vocabulary.

vocación /boka'θion: boka'sion/ *n. f.* vocation, calling.

vocal /bo'kal/ *a.* **1.** vocal. —*n.* **2.** *f.* vowel.

vocear /boθe'ar; bose'ar/ *v.* vociferate.

vodca /'boðka/ *n. m.* vodka.

vodevil /boðe'βil/ *n. m.* vaudeville.

volante /bo'lante/ *a.* **1.** flying. —*n.* **2.** *m.* memorandum; (steering) wheel.

volar /bo'lar/ *v.* fly; explode.

volcán /bol'kan/ *n. m.* volcano.

volcar /bol'kar/ *v.* upset, capsize.

voltaje /bol'tahe/ *n. m.* voltage.

voltear /bolte'ar/ *v.* turn, whirl; overturn.

voltio /'boltio/ *n. m.* volt.

volumen /bo'lumen/ *n. m.* volume.

voluminoso /bolumi'noso/ *a.* voluminous.

voluntad /bolun'tað/ *n. f.* will. **buena v.** goodwill.

voluntario /bolun'tario/ **-ria** *a.* & *n.* voluntary; volunteer.

voluntarioso /bolunta'rioso/ *a.* willful.

volver /bol'βer/ *v.* turn; return, go back, come back. **v. a hacer** (etc.), do (etc.) again.

volverse /bol'βerse/ *v.* turn around; turn, become.

vómito /'bomito/ *n. m.* vomit. —**vomitar,** *v.*

voracidad /boraθi'ðað; borasi'ðað/ *n. f.* voracity; greed.

voraz /bo'raθ; bo'ras/ *a.* greedy, ravenous.

vórtice /'bortiθe; 'bortise/ *n. m.* whirlpool.

vosotros /bo'sotros, bo'sotras/ **-as** *pron.pl.* you; yourselves.

votación /bota'θion: bota'sion/ *n. f.* voting; vote.

voto /'boto/ *n. m.* vote; vow. —**votar,** *v.*

voz /boθ; bos/ *n. f.* voice; word. **a voces,** by shouting. **en v. alta,** aloud.

vuelco /'buelko/ *n. m.* upset.

vuelo /'buelo/ *n. m.* flight. **v. libre,** hang gliding.

vuelo chárter /'buelo 'tʃarter/ charter flight.

vuelo regular /'buelo rregu'lar/ scheduled flight.

vuelta /'buelta/ *n. f.* turn, bend; return. **a la v. de,** around. **dar una v.,** to take a walk.

vuestro /'buestro/ *a.* your, yours.

vulgar /bul'gar/ *a.* vulgar, common.

vulgaridad /bulgari'ðað/ *n. f.* vulgarity.

vulgo /'bulgo/ *n. m.* (the) masses, (the) common people.

vulnerable /bulne'raβle/ *a.* vulnerable.

Y Z

y /i/ *conj* and.

ya /ya/ *adv.* already; now; at once. **y. no,** no longer, any more. **y. que,** since.

yacer /ya'θer; ya'ser/ *v.* lie.

yacimiento /yaθi'miento; yasi'miento/ *n. m.* deposit.

yanqui /'yanki/ *a. & n.* North American.

yate /'yate/ *n. m.* yacht.

yegua /'yegua/ *n. f.* mare.

yelmo /'yelmo/ *n. m.* helmet.

yema /'yema/ *n. f.* yolk (of an egg).

yerba /'yerβa/ *n. f.* grass; herb.

yerno /'yerno/ *n. m.* son-in-law.

yerro /'yerro/ *n. m.* error, mistake.

yeso /'yeso/ *n. m.* plaster.

yídish /'yiðis/ *n. m.* Yiddish.

yo /yo/ *pron.* I.

yodo /'yoðo/ *n. m.* iodine.

yoduro /jo'ðuro/ *n. m.* iodide.

yonqui /'yonki/ *m. & f. Colloq.* drug addict, junkie.

yugo /'yugo/ *n. m.* yoke.

yunque /'yunke/ *n. m.* anvil.

yunta /'yunta/ *n. f.* team (of animals).

zafarse /θa'farse; sa'farse/ *v.* run away, escape. **z. de,** get rid of.

zafio /'θafio; 'safio/ *a.* coarse, uncivil.

zafiro /θa'firo; sa'firo/ *n. m.* sapphire.

zaguán /θa'guan; sa'guan/ *n. m.* vestibule, hall.

zalamero /θala'mero; sala'mero/ **-ra** *n.* flatterer, wheedler.

zambullir /θambu'ʎir; sambu'yir/ *v.* plunge, dive.

zampar /θam'par; sam'par/ *v. Colloq.* gobble down, wolf down.

zanahoria /θana'oria; sana'oria/ *n. f.* carrot.

zanja /'θanha; 'sanha/ *n. f.* ditch, trench.

zapatería /θapate'ria; sapate'ria/ *n. f.* shoe store; shoemaker's shop.

zapatero /θapa'tero; sapa'tero/ *n. m.* shoemaker.

zapato /θa'pato; sa'pato/ *n. m.* shoe.

zar /θar; sar/ *n. m.* czar.

zaraza /θa'raθa; sa'rasa/ *n. f.* calico; chintz.

zarza /'θarθa; 'sarsa/ *n. f.* bramble.

zarzuela /θar'θuela; sar'suela/ *n. f.* musical comedy.

zodíaco /θo'ðiako; so'ðiako/ *n. m.* zodiac.

zona /'θona; 'sona/ *n. f.* zone.

zoología /θoolo'hia; soolo'hia/ *n. f.* zoology.

zoológico /θoo'lohiko; soo'lohiko/ *a.* zoological.

zorro /'θorro; 'sorro/ **-rra** *n.* fox.

zozobra /θo'θoβra; so'soβra/ *n. f.* worry, anxiety; capsizing.

zozobrar /θoθo'βrar; soso'βrar/ *v.* capsize; worry.

zumba /'θumba; 'sumba/ *n. f.* spanking.

zumbido /θum'βiðo; sum'βiðo/ *n. m.* buzz, hum. **—zumbar,** *v.*

zumo /'θumo; 'sumo/ *n. m.* juice. **z. de naranja,** orange juice.

zurcir /θur'θir; sur'sir/ *v.* darn, mend.

zurdo /'θurðo; 'surðo/ *a.* left-handed.

zurrar /θu'rrar; su'rrar/ *v.* flog, drub.

a /ə, *when stressed* ā/ *art.* un, una.
abacus /'æbəkəs/ *n.* ábaco *m.*
abandon /ə'bændən/ *n.* **1.** desenfreno, abandono *m.* —*v.* **2.** abandonar, desamparar.
abandoned /ə'bændənd/ *a.* abandonado.
abandonment /ə'bændənmənt/ *n.* abandono, desamparo *m.*
abase /ə'beis/ *v.* degradar, humillar.
abasement /ə'beismənt/ *n.* degradación, humillación *f.*
abash /ə'bæʃ/ *v.* avergonzar.
abate /ə'beit/ *v.* menguar, moderarse.
abatement /ə'beitmənt/ *n.* disminución *f.*
abbess /'æbis/ *n.* abadesa *f.*
abbey /'æbi/ *n.* abadía *f.*
abbot /'æbət/ *n.* abad *m.*
abbreviate /ə'brivi,eit/ *v.* abreviar.
abbreviation /ə,brivi'eiʃən/ *n.* abreviatura *f.*
abdicate /'æbdi,keit/ *v.* abdicar.
abdication /,æbdi'keiʃən/ *n.* abdicación *f.*
abdomen /'æbdəmən/ *n.* abdomen *m.*
abdominal /æb'dɒmənļ/ *a.* abdominal.
abduct /æb'dʌkt/ *v.* secuestrar.
abduction /æb'dʌkʃən/ *n.* secuestración *f.*
abductor /æb'dʌktər/ *n.* secuestrador -ra.
aberrant /ə'berənt, 'æbər-/ *a.* aberrante.
aberration /,æbə'reiʃən/ *n.* aberración *f.*
abet /ə'bɛt/ *v.* apoyar, favorecer.
abetment /ə'bɛtmənt/ *n.* apoyo *m.*
abettor /ə'bɛtər/ *n.* cómplice *m. & f.*
abeyance /ə'beiəns/ *n.* suspensión *f.*
abhor /æb'hɔr/ *v.* abominar, odiar.
abhorrence /æb'hɔrəns/ *n.* detestación *f.*; aborrecimiento *m.*
abhorrent /æb'hɔrənt/ *a.* detestable, aborrecible.
abide /ə'baid/ *v.* soportar. **to a. by,** cumplir con.
abiding /ə'baidiŋ/ *a.* perdurable.
ability /ə'bɪliti/ *n.* habilidad *f.*
abject /'æbdʒɛkt/ *a.* abyecto; desanimado.
abjuration /,æbdʒə'reiʃən/ *n.* renuncia *f.*
abjure /æb'dʒʊr/ *v.* renunciar.
ablative /'æblətiv/ *a. & n. Gram.* ablativo *m.*
ablaze /ə'bleiz/ *a.* en llamas.
able /'eibəl/ *a.* capaz; competente. **to be a.,** poder.
able-bodied /'eibəl 'bɒdid/ *a.* robusto.
ablution /ə'bluʃən/ *n.* ablución *f.*
ably /'eibli/ *adv.* hábilmente.
abnegate /'æbni,geit/ *v.* repudiar; negar.

abnegation /,æbni'geiʃən/ *n.* abnegación; repudiación *f.*
abnormal /æb'nɔrməl/ *a.* anormal.
abnormality /,æbnɔr'mæliti/ *n.* anormalidad, deformidad *f.*
abnormally /æb'nɔrməli/ *adv.* anormalmente.
aboard /ə'bɔrd/ *adv.* a bordo.
abode /ə'boud/ *n.* residencia *f.*
abolish /ə'bɒliʃ/ *v.* suprimir.
abolishment /ə'bɒliʃmənt/ *n.* abolición *f.*
abolition /,æbə'liʃən/ *n.* abolición *f.*
abominable /ə'bɒmənəbəl/ *a.* abominable.
abominate /ə'bɒmə,neit/ *v.* abominar, detestar.
abomination /ə,bɒmə'neiʃən/ *n.* abominación *f.*
aboriginal /,æbə'ridʒənļ/ *a. & n.* aborigen *f.*
abortion /ə'bɔrʃən/ *n.* aborto *m.*
abortive /ə'bɔrtiv/ *a.* abortivo.
abound /ə'baund/ *v.* abundar.
about /ə'baut/ *adv.* **1.** como. **about to,** para; a punto de. —*prep.* **2.** de, sobre, acerca de.
about-face /ə'baut,feis, ə'baut'feis/ *n. Mil.* media vuelta.
above /ə'bʌv/ *adv.* **1.** arriba. —*prep.* **2.** sobre; por encima de.
aboveboard /ə'bʌv,bɔrd/ *a. & adv.* sincero, franco.
abrasion /ə'breiʒən/ *n.* raspadura *f.*; *Med.* abrasión *f.*
abrasive /ə'breisiv/ *a.* raspante. *n.* abrasivo *m.*
abreast /ə'brɛst/ *adv.* de frente.
abridge /ə'bridʒ/ *v.* abreviar.
abridgment /ə'bridʒmənt/ *n.* abreviación *f.*; compendio *m.*
abroad /ə'brɔd/ *adv.* en el extranjero, al extranjero.
abrogate /'æbrə,geit/ *v.* abrogar, revocar.
abrogation /,æbrə'geiʃən/ *n.* abrogación, revocación *f.*
abrupt /ə'brʌpt/ *a.* repentino; brusco.
abruptly /ə'brʌptli/ *adv.* bruscamente, precipitadamente.
abruptness /ə'brʌptnis/ *n.* precipitación; brusquedad *f.*
abscess /'æbsɛs/ *n.* absceso *m.*
abscond /æb'skɒnd/ *v.* fugarse.
absence /'æbsəns/ *n.* ausencia, falta *f.*
absent /'æbsənt/ *a.* ausente.
absentee /,æbsən'ti/ *a. & n.* ausente *m. & f.*

absent-minded /'æbsənt 'maindıd/ a. distraído.

absinthe /'æbsınθ/ n. absenta f.

absolute /'æbsə,lut/ a. absoluto.

absolutely /,æbsə'lutli/ adv. absolutamente.

absoluteness /,æbsə'lutnıs/ n. absolutismo m.

absolution /,æbsə'luʃən/ n. absolución f.

absolutism /'æbsəlu,tızəm/ n. absolutismo, despotismo m.

absolve /æb'zɒlv/ v. absolver.

absorb /æb'sɔrb/ v. absorber; preocupar.

absorbed /æb'sɔrbd/ a. absorbido; absorto.

absorbent /æb'sɔrbənt/ a. absorbente.

absorbent cotton algodón hidrófilo m.

absorbing /æb'sɔrbıŋ/ a. interesante.

absorption /æb'sɔrpʃən/ n. absorción; preocupación f.

abstain /æb'stein/ v. abstenerse.

abstemious /æb'stimiəs/ a. abstemio, sobrio.

abstinence /'æbstənəns/ n. abstinencia f.

abstract /a, v æb'strækt, 'æbstrækt; n 'æbstrækt/ a. 1. abstracto. —n. 2. resumen m. —v. 3. abstraer.

abstracted /æb'stræktıd/ a. distraído.

abstraction /æb'strækʃən/ n. abstracción f.

abstruse /æb'strus/ a. abstruso.

absurd /æb'sɜrd/ a. absurdo, ridículo.

absurdity /æb'sɜrdıti/ n. absurdo m.

absurdly /æb'sɜrdli/ adv. absurdamente.

abundance /ə'bʌndəns/ n. abundancia f.

abundant /ə'bʌndənt/ a. abundante.

abundantly /ə'bʌndəntli/ adv. abundantemente.

abuse /n ə'byus; v ə'byuz/ n. 1. abuso m. —v. 2. abusar de; maltratar.

abusive /ə'byusıv/ a. abusivo.

abusively /ə'byusıvli/ adv. abusivamente, ofensivamente.

abutment /ə'bʌtmənt/ n. (building) estribo, contrafuerte m.

abut (on) /ə'bʌt/ v. terminar (en); lindar (con).

abyss /ə'bıs/ n. abismo m.

Abyssinian /,æbə'sınıən/ a. & n. abisinio -nia.

acacia /ə'keiʃə/ n. acacia f.

academic /,ækə'dɛmık/ a. académico.

academy /ə'kædəmi/ n. academia f.

acanthus /ə'kænθəs/ n. Bot. acanto m.

accede /æk'sid/ v. acceder; consentir.

accelerate /æk'sɛlə,reit/ v. acelerar.

acceleration /æk,sɛlə'reiʃən/ n. aceleración f.

accelerator /æk'sɛlə,reitər/ n. Auto. acelerador m.

accent /'æksɛnt/ n. 1. acento m. —v. 2. acentuar.

accentuate /æk'sɛntʃu,eit/ v. acentuar.

accept /æk'sɛpt/ v. aceptar.

acceptability /æk,sɛptə'bılıti/ n. aceptabilidad f.

acceptable /æk'sɛptəbəl/ a. aceptable.

acceptably /æk'sɛptəbli/ adv. aceptablemente.

acceptance /æk'sɛptəns/ n. aceptación f.

access /'æksɛs/ n. acceso m., entrada f.

accessible /æk'sɛsəbəl/ a. accesible.

accessory /æk'sɛsəri/ a. 1. accesorio. —n. 2. cómplice m. & f.

accident /'æksıdənt/ n. accidente m. **by a.,** por casualidad.

accidental /,æksı'dɛntl/ a. accidental.

accidentally /,æksı'dɛntli/ adv. accidentalmente, casualmente.

acclaim /ə'kleim/ v. aclamar.

acclamation /,æklə'meiʃən/ n aclamación f.

acclimate /'æklə,meit/ v. aclimatar.

acclivity /ə'klıvıti/ n. subida f.

accolade /'ækə,leid/ n. acolada f.

accommodate /ə'kɒmə,deit/ v. acomodar.

accommodating /ə'kɒmə,deitıŋ/ a. bondadoso, complaciente.

accommodation /ə,kɒmə'deiʃən/ n. servicio m.; (pl.) alojamiento m.

accompaniment /ə'kʌmpənimənt/ n. acompañamiento m.

accompanist /ə'kʌmpənıst/ n. acompañante m. & f.

accompany /ə'kʌmpəni/ v. acompañar.

accomplice /ə'kɒmplıs/ n. cómplice m. & f.

accomplish /ə'kɒmplıʃ/ v. llevar a cabo; realizar.

accomplished /ə'kɒmplıʃt/ a. acabado, cumplido; culto.

accomplishment /ə'kɒmplıʃmənt/ n. realización f.; logro m.

accord /ə'kɔrd/ n. 1. acuerdo m. —v. 2. otorgar.

accordance /ə'kɔrdns/ n.: **in a. with,** de acuerdo con.

accordingly /ə'kɔrdıŋli/ adv. en conformidad.

according to /ə'kɔrdıŋ/ prep. según.

accordion /ə'kɔrdiən/ n. acordeón m.

accost /ə'kɔst/ v. dirigirse a.

account /ə'kaunt/ n. 1. relato m.; Com. cuenta f. **on a. of,** a causa de. **on no a.,** de ninguna manera. —v. 2. **a. for,** explicar.

accountable /ə'kauntəbəl/ a. responsable.

accountant /ə'kauntıt/ n. contador -ra.

accounting /ə'kauntıŋ/ n. contabilidad f.

accouter /ə'kutər/ v. equipar, ataviar.

accouterments /ə'kutərmənts/ n. equipo, atavío m.

accredit /ə'krɛdıt/ v. acreditar.

accretion /ə'kriʃən/ n. aumento m.

accrual /ə'kruəl/ n. aumento, incremento m.

accrue /ə'kru/ v. provenir; acumularse.

accumulate /ə'kyumyə,leit/ v. acumular.

accumulation /ə,kyumyə'leifən/ n. acumulación f.

accumulative /ə'kyumyə,leitiv/ a. acumulativo.

accumulator /ə'kyumyə,leitər/ n. acumulador m.

accuracy /'ækyərəsi/ n. exactitud, precisión f.

accurate /'ækyərit/ a. exacto.

accursed /ə'kɜrsid, ə'kɜrst/ a. maldito.

accusation /,ækyu'zeifən/ n. acusación f., cargo m.

accusative /ə'kyuzətiv/ a. & n. acusativo m.

accuse /ə'kyuz/ v. acusar.

accused /ə'kyuzd/ a. & n. acusado -da, procesado -da.

accuser /ə'kyuzər/ n. acusador -ra.

accustom /ə'kʌstəm/ v. acostumbrar.

accustomed /ə'kʌstəmd/ a. acostumbrado.

ace /eis/ a. 1. sobresaliente. —n. 2. as m.

acerbity /ə'sɜrbiti/ n. acerbidad, amargura f.

acetate /'æsɪ,teit/ n. Chem. acetato m.

acetic /ə'sitik/ a. acético.

acetylene /ə'setl,in/ a. 1. acetilénico. —n. 2. Chem. acetileno m.

ache /eik/ n. 1. dolor m. —v. 2. doler.

achieve /ə'tʃiv/ v. lograr, llevar a cabo.

achievement /ə'tʃivmənt/ n. realización f.; hecho notable m.

acid /'æsid/ a. & n. ácido m.

acidify /ə'sidə,fai/ v. acidificar.

acidity /ə'siditi/ n. acidez f.

acidosis /,æsi'dousis/ n. Med. acidismo m.

acid rain lluvia ácida f.

acid test prueba decisiva.

acidulous /ə'sidʒələs/ a. agrio, acídulo.

acknowledge /æk'nɒlidʒ/ v. admitir; (receipt) acusar.

acme /'ækmi/ n. apogeo, colmo m.

acne /'ækni/ n. Med. acné m. & f.

acolyte /'ækə,lait/ n. acólito m.

acorn /'eikɔrn/ n. bellota f.

acoustics /ə'kustiks/ n. acústica f.

acquaint /ə'kweint/ v. familiarizar. **to be acquainted with,** conocer.

acquaintance /ə'kweintns/ n. conocimiento m.; (person known) conocido -da. **to make the a. of,** conocer.

acquiesce /,ækwi'es/ v. consentir.

acquiescence /,ækwi'esəns/ n. consentimiento m.

acquire /ə'kwaiǝr/ v. adquirir.

acquirement /ə'kwaiǝrmǝnt/ n. adquisición f.; (pl.) conocimientos m.pl.

acquisition /,ækwə'zifən/ n. adquisición f.

acquisitive /ə'kwizitiv/ a. adquisitivo.

acquit /ə'kwit/ v. exonerar, absolver.

acquittal /ə'kwitl/ n. absolución f.

acre /'eikər/ n. acre m.

acreage /'eikəridʒ/ número de acres.

acrid /'ækrid/ a. acre, punzante.

acrimonious /,ækrə'mouniəs/ a. acrimonioso, mordaz.

acrimony /'ækrə,mouni/ n. acrimonia, aspereza f.

acrobat /'ækrə,bæt/ n. acróbata m. & f.

acrobatic /,ækrə'bætik/ a. acrobático.

across /ə'krɔs/ adv. **1.** a través, al otro lado. —prep. **2.** al otro lado de, a través de.

acrostic /ə'krɔstik/ n. acróstico m.

act /ækt/ n. **1.** acción f; acto m. —v. **2.** actuar, portarse. **act as,** hacer de. **act on,** decidir sobre.

acting /'æktiŋ/ a. **1.** interino. —n. **2.** acción f.; Theat. representación f.

actinism /'æktə,nizəm/ n. actinismo m.

actinium /æk'tiniəm/ n. Chem. actinio m.

action /'ækʃən/ n acción f. **take a.,** tomar medidas.

action replay /'ri,plei/ repetición f.

activate /'æktə,veit/ v. activar.

activation /,æktə'veifən/ n. activación f.

activator /'æktə,veitər/ n. Chem. activador m.

active /'æktiv/ a. activo.

activity /æk'tiviti/ n. actividad f.

actor /'æktər/ n. actor m.

actress /'æktris/ n. actriz f.

actual /'æktʃuəl/ a. real, efectivo.

actuality /,æktʃu'æliti/ n. realidad, actualidad f.

actually /'æktʃuəli/ adv. en realidad.

actuary /'æktʃu,eri/ n. actuario m.

actuate /'æktʃu,eit/ v. impulsar, mover.

acumen /ə'kyumən/ n. cacumen m., perspicacia f.

acupuncture /'ækyu,pʌŋktʃər/ n. acupuntura f.

acute /ə'kyut/ a. agudo; perspicaz.

acutely /ə'kyutli/ adv. agudamente.

acuteness /ə'kyutnis/ n. agudeza f.

adage /'ædidʒ/ n. refrán, proverbio m.

adamant /'ædəmənt/ a. firme.

Adam's apple /'ædəmz/ nuez de la garganta.

adapt /ə'dæpt/ v. adaptar.

adaptability /ə,dæptə'biliti/ n. adaptabilidad f.

adaptable /ə'dæptəbəl/ a. adaptable.

adaptation /,ædəp'teifən/ n. adaptación f.

adapter /ə'dæptər/ n. Elec. adaptador m.; Mech. ajustador m.

adaptive /ə'dæptiv/ a. adaptable, acomodable.

add /æd/ v. agregar, añadir. **a. up,** sumar.

adder /'ædər/ n. víbora; serpiente f.

addict /'ædɪkt/ n. adicto -ta; (fan) aficionado -da.

addition /ə'dɪʃən/ n. adición f. **in a. to,** además de.

additional /ə'dɪʃənl/ a. adicional.

addle /'ædl/ v. confundir.

address /n ə'drɛs, 'ædrɛs; v ə'drɛs/ n. **1.** dirección f.; señas f.pl.; (speech) discurso. —v. **2.** dirigirse a.

addressee /,ædrɛ'si/ n. destinatario -ia.

adduce /ə'dus/ v. aducir.

adenoid /'ædn,ɔɪd/ n. adenoidea.

adept /ə'dɛpt/ a. adepto.

adeptly /ə'dɛptli/ adv diestramente.

adeptness /ə'dɛptnɪs/ n. destreza f.

adequacy /'ædɪkwəsi/ n. suficiencia f.

adequate /'ædɪkwɪt/ a. adecuado.

adequately /'ædɪkwɪtli/ adv. adecuadamente.

adhere /æd'hɪər/ v. adherirse, pegarse.

adherence /æd'hɪərəns/ n. adhesión f.; apego m.

adherent /æd'hɪərənt/ n. adherente m., partidario -ria.

adhesion /æd'hiʒən/ n. adhesión f.

adhesive /æd'hisɪv/ a. adhesivo. **a. tape,** esparadrapo m.

adhesiveness /æd'hisɪvnɪs/ n. adhesividad f.

adieu /ə'du/ interj. **1.** adiós. —n. **2.** despedida f.

adjacent /ə'dʒeɪsənt/ a. adyacente.

adjective /'ædʒɪktɪv/ n. adjetivo m.

adjoin /ə'dʒɔɪn/ v. lindar (con).

adjoining /ə'dʒɔɪnɪŋ/ a. contiguo.

adjourn /ə'dʒɜrn/ v. suspender, levantar.

adjournment /ə'dʒɜrnmənt/ n. suspensión f.; Leg. espera f.

adjunct /'ædʒʌŋkt/ n. adjunto m.; Gram. atributo m.

adjust /ə'dʒʌst/ v. ajustar, acomodar; arreglar.

adjuster /ə'dʒʌstər/ n. ajustador -ra.

adjustment /ə'dʒʌstmənt/ n. ajuste; arreglo m.

adjutant /'ædʒətənt/ n. Mil. ayudante m.

administer /æd'mɪnəstər/ v. administrar.

administration /æd,mɪnə'streɪʃən/ n. administración f.; gobierno m.

administrative /æd'mɪnə,streɪtɪv/ a. administrativo.

administrator /æd'mɪnə,streɪtər/ n. administrador -ra.

admirable /'ædmərəbəl/ a. admirable.

admirably /'ædmərəbli/ adv. admirablemente.

admiral /'ædmərəl/ n. almirante m.

admiralty /'ædmərəlti/ n. Ministerio de Marina.

admiration /,ædmə'reɪʃən/ n. admiración f.

admire /æd'maɪər/ v. admirar.

admirer /æd'maɪərər/ n. admirador -ra; enamorado -da.

admiringly /æd'maɪərɪŋli/ adv. admirativamente.

admissible /æd'mɪsəbəl/ a. admisible, aceptable.

admission /æd'mɪʃən/ n. admisión; entrada f.

admit /æd'mɪt/ v. admitir.

admittance /æd'mɪtns/ n. entrada f.

admittedly /æd'mɪtɪdli/ adv. reconocidamente.

admixture /æd'mɪkstʃər/ n. mezcla f.

admonish /æd'mɒnɪʃ/ v. amonestar.

admonition /,ædmə'nɪʃən/ n. admonición f.

adolescence /,ædl'ɛsəns/ n. adolescencia f.

adolescent /,ædl'ɛsənt/ n. & a. adolescente.

adopt /ə'dɒpt/ v. adoptar.

adopted child /ə'dɒptɪd/ hija adoptiva f., hijo adoptivo m.

adoption /ə'dɒpʃən/ n. adopción f.

adorable /ə'dɔrəbəl/ a. adorable.

adoration /,ædə'reɪʃən/ n. adoración f

adore /ə'dɔr/ v. adorar.

adorn /ə'dɔrn/ v. adornar.

adornment /ə'dɔrnmənt/ n. adorno m.

adrenalin /ə'drɛnlɪn/ n. adrenalina f.

adrift /ə'drɪft/ adv. a la ventura.

adroit /ə'drɔɪt/ a. diestro.

adulate /'ædʒə,leɪt/ v. adular.

adulation /,ædʒə'leɪʃən/ n. adulación f.

adult /ə'dʌlt/ a. & n. adulto -a.

adulterant /ə'dʌltərənt/ a. & n. adulterante m.

adulterate /ə'dʌltə,reɪt/ v. adulterar.

adulterer /ə'dʌltərər/ n. adúltero -ra.

adulteress /ə'dʌltərɪs/ n. adúltera f.

adultery /ə'dʌltəri/ n. adulterio m.

advance /æd'væns/ n. **1.** avance; adelanto m. **in a.,** de antemano, antes. —v. **2.** avanzar, adelantar.

advanced /æd'vænst/ a. avanzado, adelantado.

advancement /æd'vænsmənt/ n. adelantamiento m.; promoción f.

advantage /æd'væntɪdʒ/ n. ventaja f. **take a. of,** aprovecharse de.

advantageous /,ædvən'teɪdʒəs/ a. provechoso, ventajoso.

advantageously /,ædvən'teɪdʒəsli/ adv. ventajosamente.

advent /'ædvɛnt/ n. venida, llegada f.

adventitious /,ædvən'tɪʃəs/ a. adventicio, espontáneo.

adventure /æd'vɛntʃər/ n. aventura f.

adventurer /æd'ventʃərər/ n. aventurero -ra.

adventurous /æd'ventʃərəs/ a. aventurero, intrépido.

adventurously /æd'ventʃərəsli/ adv. arriesgadamente.

adverb /'ædvərb/ n. adverbio m.

adverbial /æd'vərbiəl/ a. adverbial.

adversary /'ædvər,seri/ n. adversario -a.

adverse /æd'vərs/ a. adverso.

adversely /æd'vərsli/ adv. adversamente.

adversity /æd'vərsiti/ n. adversidad f.

advert /æd'vərt/ v. hacer referencia a.

advertise /'ædvər,taiz/ v. avisar, anunciar; (promote) promocionar.

advertisement /,ædvər'taizmənt, æd'vərtismənt/ n. aviso, anuncio m.

advertiser /'ædvər,taizər/ n. anunciante m. & f., avisador -ra.

advertising /'ædvər,taiziŋ/ n. publicidad f.

advice /æd'vais/ n. consejos m.pl.

advisability /æd,vaizə'biliti/ n. prudencia, propiedad f.

advisable /æd'vaizəbəl/ a. aconsejable, prudente.

advisably /æd'vaizəbli/ adv. prudentemente.

advise /æd'vaiz/ v. aconsejar. **a. against,** desaconsejar.

advisedly /æd'vaizidli/ adv. avisadamente, prudentemente.

advisement /æd'vaizmənt/ n. consideración f.; **take under a.,** someter a estudio.

adviser /æd'vaizər/ n. consejero -ra.

advocacy /'ædvəkəsi/ n. abogacía; defensa f.

advocate /n 'ædvəkit; v -,keit/ n. **1.** abogado -da. —v. **2.** apoyar.

aegis /'idʒis/ n. amparo m.

aerate /'eəreit/ v. airear, ventilar.

aeration /,eə'reiʃən/ n. aeración, ventilación f.

aerial /'eəriəl/ a. aéreo.

aerie /'eəri/ n. nido de águila.

aeronautics /,eərə'nɔtiks/ n. aeronáutica f.

aerosol bomb /'eərə,sɔl/ bomba insecticida.

afar /ə'fɑr/ adv. lejos. **from a.,** de lejos, desde lejos.

affability /,æfə'biliti/ n. afabilidad, amabilidad f.

affable /'æfəbəl/ a. afable.

affably /'æfəbli/ adv. afablemente.

affair /ə'feər/ n. asunto m. **love a.,** aventura amorosa.

affect /ə'fekt/ v. afectar; (emotionally) conmover.

affectation /,æfek'teiʃən/ n. afectación f.

affected /ə'fektid/ a. artificioso.

affecting /ə'fektiŋ/ a. conmovedor.

affection /ə'fekʃən/ n. cariño m.

affectionate /ə'fekʃənit/ a. afectuoso, cariñoso.

affectionately /ə'fekʃənitli/ adv. afectuosamente, con cariño.

affiance /ə'faiəns/ v. dar palabra de casamiento; **become affianced,** comprometerse.

affidavit /,æfi'deivit/ n. Leg. declaración, deposición f.

affiliate /n ə'fili,it; v ə'fili,eit/ n. **1.** afiliado -da. —v. **2.** afiliar.

affiliation /ə,fili'eiʃən/ n. afiliación f.

affinity /ə'finiti/ n. afinidad f.

affirm /ə'fərm/ v. afirmar.

affirmation /,æfər'meiʃən/ n. afirmación, aserción f.

affirmative /ə'fərmətiv/ n. **1.** afirmativa f. —a. **2.** afirmativo.

affirmatively /ə'fərmətivli/ adv. afirmativamente, aseveradamente.

affix /n 'æfiks; v ə'fiks/ n. **1.** Gram. afijo m. —v. **2.** fijar, pegar, poner.

afflict /ə'flikt/ v. afligir.

affliction /ə'flikʃən/ n. aflicción f.; mal m.

affluence /'æfluəns/ n. abundancia, opulencia f.

affluent /'æfluənt/ a. opulento, afluente.

afford /ə'fɔrd/ v. proporcionar. **be able to a.,** tener con que comprar.

affordable /ə'fɔrdəbəl/ a. asequible.

affront /ə'frʌnt/ n. **1.** afrenta f. —v. **2.** afrentar, insultar.

afield /ə'fild/ adv. lejos de casa; lejos del camino; lejos del asunto.

afire /ə'faiər/ adv. ardiendo.

afloat /ə'flout/ adv. Naut. a flote.

aforementioned /ə'fɔr,menʃənd/ a. dicho, susodicho.

afraid /ə'freid/ a. **to be a.,** tener miedo, temer.

African /'æfrikən/ n. & a. africano -na.

aft /æft/ adv. Naut. a popa, en popa.

after /'æftər/ prep. **1.** después de. —conj. **2.** después que.

aftermath /'æftər,mæθ/ n. resultados m.pl.; consecuencias f.pl.

afternoon /,æftər'nun/ n. tarde f. **good a.,** buenas tardes.

aftertaste /'æftər,teist/ n. gustillo m.

afterthought /'æftər,θɔt/ n. idea tardía.

afterward(s) /'æftərwərdz/ adv. después.

again /ə'gen/ adv. otra vez, de nuevo. **to do a.,** volver a hacer.

against /ə'genst/ prep. contra; en contra de.

agape /ə'geip/ adv. con la boca abierta.

agate /'ægit/ n. ágata f.

age /eidʒ/ n. **1.** edad f. **of a.,** mayor de edad. **old a.,** vejez f. —v. **2.** envejecer.

aged /eidʒd; 'eidʒid/ a. viejo, anciano, a-ñejo.

ageism /'eidʒizəm/ n. discriminación contra las personas de edad.

ageless /'eidʒlis/ a. sempiterno.

agency /'eidʒənsi/ n. agencia f.

agenda /ə'dʒendə/ n. agenda f., orden m.

agent /'eidʒənt/ n. agente; representante m. & f.

agglutinate /ə'glutn,eit/ v. aglutinar.

agglutination /ə,glutn'eiʃən/ n. aglutinación f.

aggrandize /ə'grændaiz/ v. agrandar; elevar.

aggrandizement /ə'grændizmənt/ n. engrandecimiento m.

aggravate /'ægrə,veit/ v. agravar; irritar.

aggravation /,ægrə'veiʃən/ n. agravamiento; empeoramiento m.

aggregate /'ægrigit, -,geit/ a. & n. agregado m.

aggregation /,ægri'geiʃən/ n. agregación f.

aggression /ə'greʃən/ n. agresión f.

aggressive /ə'gresiv/ a. agresivo.

aggressively /ə'gresivli/ adv. agresivamente.

aggressiveness /ə'gresivnis/ n. agresividad f.

aggressor /ə'gresər/ n. agresor -ra.

aghast /ə'gæst/ a. horrorizado.

agile /'ædʒəl/ a. ágil.

agility /æ'dʒiliti/ n. agilidad f, ligereza, prontitud f.

agitate /'ædʒi,teit/ v. agitar.

agitation /,ædʒi'teiʃən/ n. agitación f.

agitator /'ædʒi,teitər/ n. agitador -ra.

agnostic /æg'nostik/ a. & n. agnóstico -ca.

ago /ə'gou/ adv. hace. **two days a.,** hace dos días.

agonized /'ægə,naizd/ a. angustioso.

agony /'ægəni/ n. sufrimiento m.; angustia f.

agrarian /ə'greəriən/ a. agrario.

agree /ə'gri/ v. estar de acuerdo; convenir. **a. with one,** sentar bien.

agreeable /ə'griəbəl/ a. agradable.

agreeably /ə'griəbli/ adv. agradablemente.

agreement /ə'grimənt/ n. acuerdo m.

agriculture /'ægri,kʌltʃər/ n. agricultura f.

ahead /ə'hed/ adv. adelante.

aid /eid/ n. **1.** ayuda f. —v. **2.** ayudar.

aide /eid/ n. ayudante -ta.

AIDS /eidz/ n. SIDA m.

ailing /'eiliŋ/ adj. enfermo.

ailment /'eilmənt/ n. enfermedad f.

aim /eim/ n. **1.** puntería f.; (purpose) propósito m. —v. **2.** apuntar.

aimless /'eimlis/ a. sin objeto.

air /eər/ n. **1.** aire m. **by a.** por avión. —v. **2.** ventilar, airear.

airbag /'eər,bæg/ n. (in automobiles) saco de aire m.

air-conditioned /'eər kən,diʃənd/ a. con aire acondicionado.

air-conditioning /'eər kən,diʃəniŋ/ acondicionamiento del aire.

aircraft /'eər,kræft/ n. avión m.

aircraft carrier portaaviones m.

airfare /'eər,feər/ n. precio del billete de avión m.

airing /'eəriŋ/ n. ventilación f.

airline /'eər,lain/ n. línea aérea f.

airliner /'eər,lainər/ n. avión de pasajeros.

airmail /'eər,meil/ n. correo aéreo.

airplane /'eər,plein/ n. avión, aeroplano m.

air pollution contaminación atmosférica, contaminación del aire.

airport /'eər,pɔrt/ n. aeropuerto m.

air pressure presión atmosférica.

air raid ataque aéreo.

airsick /'eər,sik/ a. mareado.

air terminal terminal aérea f.

airtight /'eər,tait/ a. hermético.

air traffic controller controlador aéreo m.

aisle /ail/ n. pasillo m.

ajar /ə'dʒar/ a. entreabierto.

akin /ə'kin/ a. emparentado, semejante.

alacrity /ə'lækriti/ n. alacridad, presteza f.

alarm /ə'larm/ n. **1.** alarma f. —v. **2.** alarmar.

alarmist /ə'larmist/ n. alarmista m. & f.

albino /æl'bainou/ n. albino -na.

album /'ælbəm/ n. álbum m.

alcohol /'ælkə,hɔl/ n. alcohol m.

alcoholic /,ælkə'hɔlik/ a. alcohólico.

alcove /'ælkouv/ n. alcoba f.

ale /eil/ n. cerveza inglesa.

alert /ə'lɜrt/ n. **1.** alarma f. **on the a.,** alerta, sobre aviso. —a. **2.** listo, vivo. —v. **3.** poner sobre aviso.

alfalfa /æl'fælfə/ n. alfalfa f.

algebra /'ældʒəbrə/ n. álgebra f.

alias /'eiliəs/ n. alias m.

alibi /'ælə,bai/ n. excusa f.; Leg. coartada f.

alien /'eiliən/ a. **1.** ajeno, extranjero. —n. **2.** extranjero -ra.

alienate /'eiliə,neit/ v. enajenar.

alight /ə'lait/ v. bajar, apearse.

align /ə'lain/ v. alinear.

alike /ə'laik/ a. **1.** semejante, igual. —adv. **2.** del mismo modo, igualmente.

alimentary canal /,ælə'mentəri/ n. tubo digestivo m.

alive /ə'laiv/ a. vivo; animado.

alkali /'ælkə,lai/ n. Chem. álcali, cali m.

alkaline /'ælkə,lain/ a. alcalino.

all /ɔl/ a. & pron. todo. **not at a.,** de ninguna manera, nada.

allay /ə'lei/ v. aquietar.

allegation /,æli'geiʃən/ n. alegación f.

allege /ə'lɛdʒ/ v. alegar; pretender.
allegiance /ə'lidʒəns/ n. lealtad f.; (to country) homenaje m.
allegory /'ælə,gori/ n. alegoría f.
allergy /'ælərdʒi/ n. alergia f.
alleviate /ə'livi,eit/ v. aliviar.
alley /'æli/ n. callejón m. **bowling a.**, bolera f., boliche m.
alliance /ə'laiəns/ n. alianza f.
allied /'ælaid/ a. aliado.
alligator /'ælɪ,geitər/ n. caimán m.; (Mex.) lagarto m. **a. pear**, aguacate m.
allocate /'ælə,keit/ v. colocar, asignar.
allot /ə'lɒt/ v. asignar.
allotment /ə'lɒtmənt/ n. lote, porción f.
allow /ə'lau/ v. permitir, dejar.
allowance /ə'lauəns/ n. abono m.; dieta f. **make a. for**, tener en cuenta.
alloy /'ælɔi/ n. mezcla f.; (metal) aleación f.
all right está bien.
allude /ə'lud/ v. aludir.
allure /ə'lʊr/ n. **1**. atracción f. —v. **2**. atraer, tentar.
alluring /ə'lʊrɪŋ/ a. tentador, seductivo.
allusion /ə'luʒən/ n. alusión f.
ally /n 'ælai, v ə'lai/ n. **1**. aliado -da. —v. **2**. aliar.
almanac /'ɔlmə,næk/ n. almanaque m.
almighty /ɔl'maiti/ a. todopoderoso.
almond /'amənd/ n. almendra f.
almost /'ɔlmoust/ adv. casi.
alms /amz/ n. limosna f.
aloft /ə'lɔft/ adv. arriba, en alto.
alone /ə'loun/ adv. solo, a solas. **to leave a.**, dejar en paz.
along /ə'lɔŋ/ prep. por; a lo largo de. **a. with**, junto con.
alongside /ə'lɔŋ'said/ adv. **1**. al lado. —prep. **2**. junto a.
aloof /ə'luf/ a. apartado.
aloud /ə'laud/ adv en voz alta.
alpaca /æl'pækə/ n. alpaca f.
alphabet /'ælfə,bɛt/ n. alfabeto m.
alphabetical /,ælfə'bɛtɪkəl/ a. alfabético.
alphabetize /'ælfəbɪ,taiz/ v. alfabetizar.
already /ɔl'rɛdi/ adv. ya.
also /'ɔlsou/ adv. también.
altar /'ɔltər/ n. altar m.
alter /'ɔltər/ v. alterar.
alteration /,ɔltə'reiʃən/ n. alteración f.
alternate /a, n 'ɔltərnit; v -,neit/ a. **1**. alterno. —n. **2**. substituto -ta. —v. **3**. alternar.
alternative /ɔl'tɜrnətɪv/ a. **1**. alternativo. —n. **2**. alternativa f.
although /ɔl'ðou/ conj. aunque.
altitude /'ælti,tud/ n. altura f.
alto /'æltou/ n. contralto m.
altogether /,ɔltə'gɛðər/ adv. en junto; enteramente.

altruism /'æltru,izəm/ n. altruismo m.
alum /'æləm/ n. alumbre m.
aluminum /ə'lumənəm/ n. aluminio m.
aluminum foil papel de aluminio m.
always /'ɔlweiz/ adv. siempre.
amalgam /ə'mælgəm/ n. amalgama f.
amalgamate /ə'mælgə,meit/ v. amalgamar.
amass /ə'mæs/ v. amontonar.
amateur /'æmə,tʃʊr/ n. aficionado -da.
amaze /ə'meiz/ v. asombrar; sorprender.
amazement /ə'meizmənt/ n. asombro m.
amazing /ə'meizɪŋ/ a. asombroso, pasmoso.
ambassador /æm'bæsədər/ n. embajador -ra.
amber /'æmbər/ a. **1**. ambarino. —n. **2**. ámbar m.
ambidextrous /,æmbɪ'dɛkstrəs/ a. ambidextro.
ambiguity /,æmbɪ'gyuiti/ n. ambigüedad f.
ambiguous /æm'bɪgyuəs/ a. ambiguo.
ambition /æm'bɪʃən/ n. ambición f.
ambitious /æm'bɪʃəs/ a. ambicioso.
ambulance /'æmbyələns/ n. ambulancia f.
ambush /'æmbuʃ/ n. **1**. emboscada f. —v. **2**. acechar.
ameliorate /ə'milyə,reit/ v. mejorar.
amenable /ə'minəbəl/ a. tratable, dócil.
amend /ə'mɛnd/ v. enmendar.
amendment /ə'mɛndmənt/ n. enmienda f.
amenity /ə'mɛniti/ n. amenidad f.
American /ə'mɛrikən/ a. & n. americano -na, norteamericano -na.
amethyst /'æməθist/ n. amatista f.
amiable /'eimiəbəl/ a. amable.
amicable /'æmikəbəl/ a. amigable.
amid /ə'mid/ prep. entre, en medio de.
amidships /ə'mid,ʃips/ adv. Naut. en medio del navío.
amiss /ə'mis/ adv. mal. **to take a.**, llevar a mal.
amity /'æmiti/ n. amistad f., armonía f.
ammonia /ə'mounyə/ n. amoníaco m.
ammunition /,æmyə'nɪʃən/ n. municiones f.pl.
amnesia /æm'niʒə/ n. amnesia f.
amnesty /'æmnəsti/ n. amnistía f., indulto m.
amniocentesis /,æmniousɛn'tisis/ n. amniocéntesis f.
amoeba /ə'mibə/ n. amiba f.
among /ə'mʌŋ/ prep. entre.
amoral /ei'mɔrəl/ a. amoral.
amorous /'æmərəs/ a. amoroso.
amorphous /ə'mɔrfəs/ a. amorfo.
amortize /'æmər,taiz/ v. Com. amortizar.
amount /ə'maunt/ n. **1**. cantidad, suma f. —v. **2**. **a. to**, subir a.
ampere /'æmpɪər/ n. Elec. amperio m.
amphibian /æm'fɪbiən/ a. & n. anfibio m.

amphitheater /'æmfə,θiətər/ *n.* anfiteatro, circo *m.*

ample /'æmpəl/ *a.* amplio; suficiente.

amplify /'æmplə,fai/ *v.* amplificar.

amputate /'æmpyu,teit/ *v.* amputar.

amuse /ə'myuz/ *v* entretener, divertir.

amusement /ə'myuzmənt/ *n.* diversión *f.*

an /ən, when stressed æn/ *art.* un, una.

anachronism /ə'nækrə,nizəm/ *n.* anacronismo, *m.*

analogous /ə'næləgəs/ *a.* análogo, parecido.

analogy /ə'nælədʒi/ *n.* analogía *f.*

analysis /ə'næləsis/ *n.* análisis *m.*

analyst /'ænlist/ *n.* analista *m. & f.*

analytic /,ænl'itik/ *a.* analítico.

analyze /'ænl,aiz/ *v.* analizar.

anarchy /'ænərki/ *n.* anarquía *f.*

anatomy /ə'nætəmi/ *n.* anatomía *f.*

ancestor /'ænsestər/ *n.* antepasado *m.*

ancestral /æn'sestrəl/ *a.* de los antepasados, hereditario.

ancestry /'ænsestri/ *n.* linaje, abolengo *m.*

anchor /'æŋkər/ *n.* **1.** ancla *f.* **weigh a.,** levar el ancla. —*v.* **2.** anclar.

anchorage /'æŋkərɪdʒ/ *n. Naut.* ancladero, anclaje *m.*

anchovy /'æntʃouvi/ *n.* anchoa *f.*

ancient /'einʃənt/ *a. & n.* antiguo -ua.

and /ænd, ənd/ *conj.* y, (before *i-, hi-*) e.

anecdote /'ænik,dout/ *n.* anécdota *f.*

anemia /ə'nimiə/ *n. Med.* anemia *f.*

anesthetic /,ænəs'θetik/ *n.* anestesia *f.*

anew /ə'nu/ *adv.* de nuevo.

angel /'eindʒəl/ *n.* ángel *m.*

anger /'æŋgər/ *n.* **1.** ira *f.,* enojo *m.* —*v.* **2.** enfadar, enojar.

angle /'æŋgəl/ *n.* ángulo *m.*

angry /'æŋgri/ *a.* enojado, enfadado.

anguish /'æŋgwiʃ/ *n.* angustia *f.*

angular /'æŋgyələr/ *a.* angular.

aniline /'ænlin/ *n. Chem.* anilina *f.*

animal /'ænəməl/ *a. & n.* animal *m.*

animate /*v* 'ænə,meit; *a* -mit/ *v.* **1.** animar. —*a.* **2.** animado.

animated /'ænə,meitid/ *a.* vivo, animado.

animation /,ænə'meiʃən/ *n.* animación, viveza *f.*

animosity /,ænə'mɒsiti/ *n.* rencor *m.*

anise /'ænis/ *n.* anís *m.*

ankle /'æŋkəl/ *n.* tobillo *m.*

annals /'ænlz/ *n.pl.* anales *m.pl.*

annex /*n* 'æneks; *v* ə'neks/ *n.* **1.** anexo *m.,* adición *f.* —*v.* **2.** anexar.

annexation /,ænɪk'seiʃən/ *n.* anexión, adición *f.*

annihilate /ə'naiə,leit/ *v.* aniquilar, destruir.

anniversary /,ænə'vɜrsəri/ *n.* aniversario *m.*

annotate /'ænə,teit/ *v.* anotar.

annotation /,ænə'teiʃən/ *n.* anotación *f.,* apunte *m.*

announce /ə'nauns/ *v.* anunciar.

announcement /ə'naunsmənt/ *n.* anuncio, aviso *m.*

announcer /ə'naunsər/ *n.* anunciador -ra; (radio) locutor -ra.

annoy /ə'nɔi/ *v.* molestar.

annoyance /ə'nɔiəns/ *n.* molestia, incomodidad *f.*

annual /'ænyuəl/ *a.* anual.

annuity /ə'nuiti/ *n.* anualidad, pensión *f.*

annul /ə'nʌl/ *v.* anular, invalidar.

anode /'ænoud/ *n. Elec.* ánodo *m.*

anoint /ə'nɔint/ *v.* untar; *Relig.* ungir.

anomalous /ə'nɒmələs/ *a.* anómalo, irregular.

anonymous /ə'nɒnəməs/ *a.* anónimo.

anorexia /,ænə'rɛksiə/ *n.* anorexia *f.*

another /ə'nʌðər/ *a. & pron.* otro.

answer /'ænsər, 'ɒn-/ *n.* **1.** contestación, respuesta *f.* —*v.* **2.** contestar, responder. **a. for,** ser responsable de.

answerable /'ænsərəbəl/ *a.* discutible, refutable.

answering machine /'ænsəriŋ/ contestador automático *m.*

ant /ænt/ *n.* hormiga *f.*

antacid /ænt'æsid/ *a & n.* antiácido *m.*

antagonism /æn'tægə,nizəm/ *n.* antagonismo *m.*

antagonist /æn'tægənist/ *n.* antagonista *m. & f.*

antagonistic /æn,tægə'nistik/ *a.* antagónico, hostil.

antagonize /æn'tægə,naiz/ *v.* contrariar.

antarctic /ænt'ɑrktik/ *a. & n.* antártico *m.*

antecedent /,æntə'sidnt/ *a.* antecedente *m.*

antedate /'ænti,deit/ *v.* antedatar.

antelope /'æntl,oup/ *n.* antílope *m.,* gacela *f.*

antenna /æn'tenə/ *n.* antena *f.*

antepenultimate /,æntɪpɪ'nʌltəmit/ *a.* antepenúltimo.

anterior /æn'tiəriər/ *a.* anterior.

anteroom /'ænti,rum/ *n.* antecámara *f.*

anthem /'ænθəm/ *n.* himno *m.*; (religious) antífona *f.*

anthology /æn'θɒlədʒi/ *n.* antología *f.*

anthracite /'ænθrə,sait/ *n.* antracita *f.*

anthrax /'ænθræks/ *n. Med.* ántrax *m.*

anthropology /,ænθrə'pɒlədʒi/ *n.* antropología *f.*

antiaircraft /,ænti'eər,kræft, ,æntai-/ *a.* antiaéreo.

antibody /'ænti,bɒdi/ *n.* anticuerpo *m.*

anticipate /æn'tisə,peit/ *v.* esperar, anticipar.

anticipation /æn,tɪsə'peɪʃən/ n. anticipación f.

anticlerical /,ænti'klerɪkəl, ,æntai-/ a. anticlerical.

anticlimax /ænti'klaimæks, ,æntai-/ n. anticlímax m.

antidote /'ænti,dout/ n. antídoto m.

antifreeze /'ænti,friz/ n. anticongelante m.

antihistamine /,ænti'histə,min, -mɪn, ,æntai-/ n. antihistamínico m.

antimony /'æntə,mouni/ n. antimonio m.

antinuclear /,ænti'nukliər, æntai-/ a. antinuclear.

antipathy /æn'tɪpəθi/ n. antipatía f.

antiquated /'ænti,kweitid/ a. antiguado.

antique /æn'tik/ a. **1.** antiguo. —n. **2.** antigüedad f.

antiquity /æn'tikwiti/ n. antigüedad f.

antiseptic /,æntə'septik/ a. & n. antiséptico m.

antisocial /,ænti'souʃəl, ,æntai-/ a. antisocial.

antitoxin /,ænti'tɒksɪn/ n. Med. antitoxina f.

antler /'æntlər/ n. asta f.

anvil /'ænvɪl/ n. yunque m.

anxiety /æŋ'zaiiti/ n. ansia, ansiedad f.

anxious /'æŋkʃəs, 'æŋʃəs/ a. inquieto, ansioso.

any /'eni/ a. alguno; (at all) cualquiera; (after not) ninguno.

anybody /'eni,bɒdi/ pron. alguien; (at all) cualquiera; (after not) nadie.

anyhow /'eni,hau/ adv. de todos modos; en todo caso.

anyone /'eni,wʌn/ pron. = anybody.

anything /'eni,θiŋ/ pron. algo; (at all) cualquier cosa; (after not) nada.

anyway /'eni,wei/ adv. = anyhow.

anywhere /'eni,wɛər/ adv. en alguna parte; (at all) dondequiera; (after not) en ninguna parte.

apart /ə'part/ adv. aparte. **to take a.,** deshacer.

apartheid /ə'partheit, -hait/ n. apartheid m.

apartment /ə'partmənt/ n. apartamento, piso m.

apartment house casa de pisos f.

apathetic /,æpə'θetik/ a. apático.

apathy /'æpəθi/ n. apatía f.

ape /eip/ n. **1.** mono -na. —v. **2.** imitar.

aperture /'æpərtʃər/ n. abertura f.

apex /'eipeks/ n. ápice m.

aphorism /'æfə,rizəm/ n. aforismo m.

apiary /'eipi,ɛri/ n. colmenario, abejar m.

apiece /ə'pis/ adv. por persona; cada uno.

apologetic /ə,pɒlə'dʒetik/ a. apologético.

apologist /ə'pɒlədʒist/ n. apologista m. & f.

apologize /ə'pɒlə,dʒaiz/ v. excusarse, disculparse.

apology /ə'pɒlədʒi/ n. excusa; apología f.

apoplectic /,æpə'plektik/ a. apopléctico.

apoplexy /'æpə,pleksi/ n. apoplejía f.

apostate /ə'pɒsteit/ n. apóstata m. & f.

apostle /ə'pɒsəl/ n. apóstol m.

apostolic /,æpə'stɒlik/ a. apostólico.

appall /ə'pɒl/ v. horrorizar; consternar.

apparatus /,æpə'rætəs/ n. aparato m.

apparel /ə'pærəl/ n. ropa f.

apparent /ə'pærənt/ a. aparente; claro.

apparition /,æpə'rɪʃən/ n. aparición f.; fantasma m.

appeal /ə'pil/ n. **1.** súplica f.; interés m.; Leg. apelación f. —v. **2.** apelar, suplicar; interesar.

appear /ə'piər/ v. aparecer, asomar; (seem) parecer; Leg. comparecer.

appearance /ə'piərəns/ n. apariencia f., aspecto m.; aparición f.

appease /ə'piz/ v. aplacar, apaciguar.

appeasement /ə'pizmənt/ n. apaciguamiento m.

appeaser /ə'pizər/ n. apaciguador -ra, pacificador -ra.

appellant /ə'pelənt/ n. apelante, demandante m. & f.

appellate /ə'pelit/ a. Leg. de apelación.

appendage /ə'pendɪdʒ/ n. añadidura f.

appendectomy /,æpən'dektəmi/ n. apendectomía f.

appendicitis /ə,pendə'saitis/ n. apendicitis f.

appendix /ə'pendiks/ n. apéndice m.

appetite /'æpi,tait/ n. apetito m.

appetizer /'æpi,taizər/ n. aperitivo m.

appetizing /'æpi,taiziŋ/ a. apetitoso.

applaud /ə'plɔd/ v. aplaudir.

applause /ə'plɔz/ n. aplauso m.

apple /'æpəl/ n. manzana f. **a. tree,** manzano m.

applesauce /'æpəl,sɔs/ n. compota de manzana.

appliance /ə'plaiəns/ n. aparato m.

applicable /'æplikəbəl/ a. aplicable.

applicant /'æplikənt/ n. suplicante m. & f.; candidato -ta.

application /,æpli'keiʃən/ n. solicitud f, (computer) programa m.

applied /ə'plaid/ a. aplicado. **a. for,** pedido.

appliqué /,æpli'kei/ n. (sewing) aplicación f.

apply /ə'plai/ v. aplicar. **a. for,** solicitar, pedir.

appoint /ə'point/ v. nombrar.

appointment /ə'pointmənt/ n. nombramiento m.; puesto m.

apportion /ə'pɔrʃən/ v. repartir.

apposition /,æpə'zɪʃən/ n. Gram. aposición f.

appraisal /ə'preizəl/ n. valoración f.

appraise /ə'preiz/ v. evaluar; tasar; estimar.

appreciable /ə'priʃiəbəl/ a. apreciable; notable.

appreciate /ə'priʃi,eit/ v. apreciar, estimar.

appreciation /ə,priʃi'eiʃən/ n. aprecio; reconocimiento m.

apprehend /,æpri'hɛnd/ v. prender, capturar.

apprehension /,æpri'hɛnʃən/ n. aprensión f.; detención f.

apprehensive /,æpri'hɛnsiv/ a. aprensivo.

apprentice /ə'prɛntis/ n. aprendiz -iza.

apprenticeship /ə'prɛntis,ʃip/ n. aprendizaje m.

apprise /ə'praiz/ v. informar.

approach /ə'proutʃ/ n. 1. acceso; método m. —v. 2. acercarse.

approachable /ə'proutʃəbəl/ a. accesible.

approbation /,æprə'beiʃən/ n. aprobación f.

appropriate /a ə'proupriit/ v -,eit/ a. 1. apropiado. —v. 2. apropiar.

appropriation /ə,proupri'eiʃən/ n. apropiación f.

approval /ə'pruvəl/ n. aprobación f.

approve /ə'pruv/ v. aprobar.

approximate /a ə'prɒksəmit/ v -,meit/ a. 1. aproximado. —v. 2. aproximar.

approximately /ə'prɒksəmitli/ adv. aproximadamente.

approximation /ə,prɒksə'meiʃən/ n. aproximación f.

appurtenance /ə'pɜrtnəns/ n. dependencia f.

apricot /'æpri,kɒt/ n. albaricoque, damasco m.

April /'eiprəl/ n. abril m.

apron /'eiprən/ n. delantal m.

apropos /,æprə'pou/ adv. a propósito.

apt /æpt/ a. apto; capaz.

aptitude /'æpti,tud/ n. aptitud; facilidad f.

aquarium /ə'kwɛəriəm/ n. acuario m., pecera f.

aquatic /ə'kwætik/ a. acuático.

aqueduct /'ækwi,dʌkt/ n. acueducto m.

aqueous /'ækwiəs/ a. ácueo, acuoso, aguoso.

aquiline /'ækwə,lain/ a. aquilino, aguileño.

Arab /'ærəb/ a. & n. árabe m. & f.

arable /'ærəbəl/ a. cultivable.

arbitrary /'ɑrbi,trɛri/ a. arbitrario.

arbitrate /'ɑrbi,treit/ v. arbitrar.

arbitration /,ɑrbi'treiʃən/ n. arbitraje m., arbitración f.

arbitrator /'ɑrbi,treitər/ n. arbitrador -ra.

arbor /'ɑrbər/ n. emparrado m.

arboreal /ɑr'bɔriəl/ a. arbóreo.

arc /ɑrk/ n. arco m.

arch /ɑrtʃ/ n. 1. arco m. —v. 2. arquear, encorvar.

archaeology /,ɑrki'ɒlədʒi/ n. arqueología f.

archaic /ɑr'keiik/ a. arcaico.

archbishop /'ɑrtʃ'biʃəp/ n. arzobispo m.

archdiocese /,ɑrtʃ'daiə,sis, -sis/ n. archidiócesis f.

archduke /'ɑrtʃ'duk/ n. archiduque m.

archer /'ɑrtʃər/ n. arquero m.

archery /'ɑrtʃəri/ n. ballestería f.

archipelago /,ɑrkə'pɛlə,gou/ n. archipiélago m.

architect /'ɑrki,tɛkt/ n. arquitecto -ta.

architectural /,ɑrki'tɛktʃərəl/ a. arquitectural.

architecture /'ɑrki,tɛktʃər/ n. arquitectura f.

archive /'ɑrkaiv/ n. archivo m.

archway /'ɑrtʃ,wei/ n. arcada f.

arctic /'ɑrktik, 'ɑrtik/ a. ártico.

ardent /'ɑrdnt/ a. ardiente.

ardor /'ɑrdər/ n. ardor m., pasión f.

arduous /'ɑrdʒuəs/ a. arduo, difícil.

area /'ɛəriə/ n. área; extensión f.

area code prefijo m.

arena /ə'rinə/ n. arena f.

Argentine /'ɑrdʒəntin, -,tain/ a. & n. argentino -na.

argue /'ɑrgyu/ v. disputar; sostener.

argument /'ɑrgyəmənt/ n. disputa f.; razonamiento m.

argumentative /,ɑrgyə'mɛntətiv/ a. argumentoso.

aria /'ɑriə/ n. aria f.

arid /'ærid/ a. árido, seco.

arise /ə'raiz/ v. surgir; alzarse.

aristocracy /,ærə'stɒkrəsi/ n. aristocracia f.

aristocrat /ə'ristə,kræt/ n. aristócrata m.

aristocratic /ə,ristə'krætik/ a. aristocrático.

arithmetic /ə'riθmətik/ n. aritmética f.

ark /ɑrk/ n. arca f.

arm /ɑrm/ n. 1. brazo m.; (weapon) arma f. —v. 2. armar.

armament /'ɑrməmənt/ n. armamento m.

armchair /'ɑrm,tʃɛər/ n. sillón m., butaca f.

armed forces /'ɑrmd 'fɔrsiz/ fuerzas militares.

armful /'ɑrm,fʊl/ n. brazada f.

armhole /'ɑrm,houl/ n. (sew.) sobaquera f.

armistice /'ɑrməstis/ n. armisticio m.

armor /'ɑrmər/ n. armadura f., blindaje m.

armored /'ɑrmərd/ a. blindado.

armory /'ɑrməri/ n. armería f., arsenal m.

armpit /'ɑrm,pit/ n. axila f., sobaco m.

army /'ɑrmi/ n. ejército m.

arnica /'ɑrnikə/ n. árnica f.

aroma /ə'roumə/ n. fragancia f.

aromatic /,ærə'mætik/ a. aromático.

around /ə'raund/ *prep.* alrededor de, a la
vuelta de; cerca de. **a. here,** por aquí.

arouse /ə'rauz/ *v.* despertar; excitar.

arraign /ə'rein/ *v.* Leg. procesar criminalmente.

arrange /ə'reindʒ/ *v.* arreglar; concertar;
Mus. adaptar.

arrangement /ə'reindʒmənt/ *n.* arreglo; orden *m.*

array /ə'rei/ *n.* **1.** orden; adorno *m.* —*v.* **2.**
adornar.

arrears /ə'rɪərz/ *n.* atrasos *m.pl.*

arrest /ə'rɛst/ *n.* **1.** detención *f.* —*v.* **2.** detener, arrestar.

arrival /ə'raivəl/ *n.* llegada *f.*

arrive /ə'raiv/ *v.* llegar.

arrogance /'ærəgəns/ *n.* arrogancia *f.*

arrogant /'ærəgənt/ *a.* arrogante.

arrogate /'ærə,geit/ *v.* arrogarse, usurpar.

arrow /'ærou/ *n.* flecha *f.*

arrowhead /'ærou,hɛd/ *n.* punta de flecha
f.

arsenal /'ɑrsənl/ *n.* arsenal *m.*

arsenic /'ɑrsənɪk/ *n.* arsénico *m.*

arson /'ɑrsən/ *n.* incendio premeditado.

art /ɑrt/ arte *m.* (f. in pl.); (skill) maña *f.*

arterial /ɑr'tɪəriəl/ *a.* arterial.

arteriosclerosis /ɑr,tɪəriousklə'rousɪs/ *n.*
arteriosclerosis *f.*

artery /'ɑrtəri/ *n.* arteria *f.*

artesian well /ɑr'tiʒən/ pozo artesiano.

artful /'ɑrtfəl/ *a.* astuto.

arthritis /ɑr'θraitɪs/ *n.* artritis *f.*

artichoke /'ɑrtɪ,tʃouk/ *n.* alcachofa *f.*

article /'ɑrtɪkəl/ *n.* artículo *m.*

articulate /ɑr'tɪkyə,leit/ *v.* articular.

articulation /ɑr,tɪkyə'leiʃən/ *n.* articulación
f.

artifice /'ɑrtəfɪs/ *n.* artificio *m.*

artificial /,ɑrtə'fɪʃəl/ *a.* artificial.

artificially /,ɑrtə'fɪʃəli/ *adv.* artificialmente.

artillery /ɑr'tɪləri/ *n.* artillería *f.*

artisan /'ɑrtəzən/ *n.* artesano -na.

artist /'ɑrtɪst/ *n.* artista *m.* & *f.*

artistic /ɑr'tɪstɪk/ *a.* artístico.

artistry /'ɑrtɪstri/ *n.* arte *m.* & *f.*

artless /'ɑrtlɪs/ *a.* natural, cándido.

as /æz/ *adv.* & *conj* como; **as... as** tan...
como.

asbestos /æs'bɛstəs/ *n.* asbesto *m.*

ascend /ə'sɛnd/ *v.* ascender.

ascendancy /ə'sɛndənsi/ *n.* ascendiente *m.*

ascendant /ə'sɛndənt/ *a.* ascendente.

ascent /ə'sɛnt/ *n.* subida *f.*, ascenso *m.*

ascertain /,æsər'tein/ *v.* averiguar.

ascetic /ə'sɛtɪk/ *a.* **1.** ascético. —*n.* **2.** as-
ceta *m.* & *f.*

ascribe /ə'skraib/ *v.* atribuir.

ash /æʃ/ *n.* ceniza *f.*

ashamed /ə'ʃeimd/ *a.* avergonzado.

ashen /'æʃən/ *a.* pálido.

ashore /ə'ʃɔr/ *adv.* a tierra. **go a.,** desembarcar.

ashtray /'æʃ,trei/ *n.* cenicero *m.*

Ash Wednesday miércoles de ceniza m.

Asiatic /,eiʒi'ætɪk/ *a.* & *n.* asiático -ca.

aside /ə'said/ *adv.* al lado. **a. from.** aparte
de.

ask /æsk/ *v.* preguntar; invitar; (request)
pedir. **a. for,** pedir. **a. a question,** hacer
una pregunta.

askance /ə'skæns/ *adv.* de soslayo; con recelo.

asleep /ə'slip/ *a.* dormido. **to fall a.,** dormirse.

asparagus /ə'spærəgəs/ *n.* espárrago *m.*

aspect /'æspɛkt/ *n.* aspecto *m.*, apariencia
f.

asperity /ə'spɛrɪti/ *n.* aspereza *f.*

aspersion /ə'spɔrʒən/ *n.* calumnia *f.*

asphalt /'æsfɔlt/ *n.* asfalto *m.*

asphyxia /æs'fɪksiə/ *n.* asfixia *f.*

asphyxiate /æs'fɪksi,eit/ *v.* asfixiar, sofocar.

aspirant /'æspərənt/ *a.* & *n.* aspirante *m.* &
f.

aspirate /'æspə,reit/ *v.* aspirar.

aspiration /,æspə'reiʃən/ *n.* aspiración *f.*

aspirator /'æspə,reitər/ *n.* aspirador *m.*

aspire /ə'spaiᵊr/ *v.* aspirar. **a. to,** ambicionar.

aspirin /'æspərɪn/ *n.* aspirina *f.*

ass /æs/ *n.* asno, burro *m.*

assail /ə'seil/ *v.* asaltar, acometer.

assailant /ə'seilənt/ *n.* asaltador -ra.

assassin /ə'sæsɪn/ *n.* asesino -na.

assassinate /ə'sæsə,neit/ *v.* asesinar.

assassination /ə,sæsə'neiʃən/ *n.* asesinato
m.

assault /ə'sɔlt/ *n.* **1.** asalto *m.* —*v.* **2.** asaltar, atacar.

assay /'æsei/ *v.* examinar; ensayar.

assemblage /ə'sɛmblɪdʒ/ *n.* asamblea *f.*

assemble /ə'sɛmbəl/ *v* juntar, convocar;
(mechanism) montar.

assembly /ə'sɛmbli/ *n.* asamblea, concurrencia *f.*

assent /ə'sɛnt/ *n.* **1.** asentimiento *m.* —*v.* **2.**
asentir, convenir.

assert /ə'sɔrt/ *v.* afirmar, aseverar. **a. oneself,** hacerse sentir.

assertion /ə'sɔrʃən/ *n.* aserción, aseveración *f.*

assertive /ə'sɔrtɪv/ *a.* asertivo.

assess /ə'sɛs/ *v.* tasar, evaluar.

assessor /ə'sɛsər/ *n.* asesor -ra.

asset /'æsɛt/ *n.* ventaja *f.* **assets,** Com. capital *m.*

asseverate /ə'sɛvə,reit/ *v.* aseverar, afirmar.

asseveration /ə,sɛvə'reɪʃən/ n. aseveración f.

assiduous /ə'sɪdjʊəs/ a. asiduo.

assiduously /ə'sɪdjʊəslɪ/ adv. asiduamente.

assign /ə'saɪn/ v. asignar; destinar.

assignable /ə'saɪnəbəl/ a. asignable, transferible.

assignation /,æsɪg'neɪʃən/ n. asignación f.

assignment /ə'saɪnmənt/ n. misión; tarea f.

assimilate /ə'sɪmə,leɪt/ v. asimilar.

assimilation /ə,sɪmə'leɪʃən/ n. asimilación f.

assimilative /ə'sɪmələtɪv/ a. asimilativo.

assist /ə'sɪst/ v. ayudar, auxiliar.

assistance /ə'sɪstəns/ n. ayuda f., auxilio m.

assistant /ə'sɪstənt/ n. ayudante -ta, asistente -ta.

associate /n ə'soʊsiɪt; v -si,eɪt/ n. **1.** socio, socia. —v. **2.** asociar.

association /ə,soʊsi'eɪʃən/ n. asociación; sociedad f.

assonance /'æsənəns/ n. asonancia f.

assort /ə'sɔrt/ v. surtir con variedad.

assorted /ə'sɔrtɪd/ a. variado, surtido.

assortment /ə'sɔrtmənt/ n. surtido m.

assuage /ə'sweɪdʒ/ v. mitigar, aliviar.

assume /ə'sum/ v. suponer; asumir.

assuming /ə'sumɪŋ/ a. presuntuoso. **a. that,** dado que.

assumption /ə'sʌmpʃən/ n. suposición; Relig. asunción f.

assurance /ə'ʃʊrəns/ n. seguridad; confianza f.; garantía f.

assure /ə'ʃʊr/ v. asegurar; dar confianza.

assured /ə'ʃʊrd/ a. **1.** seguro. —a. & n. **2.** Com. asegurado -da.

assuredly /ə'ʃʊrɪdli/ adv. ciertamente.

aster /'æstər/ n. aster f.

asterisk /'æstərɪsk/ n. asterisco m.

astern /ə'stɜrn/ adv. Naut. a popa.

asteroid /'æstə,rɔɪd/ n. asteroide -da.

asthma /'æzmə/ n. Med. asma f.

astigmatism /ə'stɪgmə,tɪzəm/ n. astigmatismo m.

astir /ə'stɜr/ adv. en movimiento.

astonish /ə'stɒnɪʃ/ v. asombrar, pasmar.

astonishment /ə'stɒnɪʃmənt/ n. asombro m., sorpresa f.

astound /ə'staʊnd/ v. pasmar, sorprender.

astral /'æstrəl/ a. astral, estelar.

astray /ə'streɪ/ a. desviado.

astride /ə'straɪd/ adv. a horcajadas.

astringent /ə'strɪndʒənt/ a. & n. astringente m.

astrology /ə'strɒlədʒi/ n. astrología f.

astronaut /'æstrə,nɔt/ n. astronauta m. & f.

astronomy /ə'strɒnəmi/ n. astronomía f.

astute /ə'stut/ a. astuto; agudo.

asunder /ə'sʌndər/ adv. en dos.

asylum /ə'saɪləm/ n. asilo, refugio m.

asymmetry /ei'sɪmɪtri/ n. asimetría f.

at /æt/ prep. a, en; cerca de.

ataxia /ə'tæksiə/ n. Med. ataxia f.

atheist /'eiθiɪst/ n. ateo -tea.

athlete /'æθlit/ n. atleta m. & f.

athletic /æθ'lɛtɪk/ a. atlético.

athletics /æθ'lɛtɪks/ n. atletismo m., deportes m.pl.

athwart /ə'θwɔrt/ prep. a través de.

Atlantic /æt'læntɪk/ a. **1.** atlántico. —n. **2.** Atlántico m.

Atlantic Ocean Océano Atlántico m.

atlas /'ætləs/ n. atlas m.

atmosphere /'ætməs,fiər/ n. atmósfera f.; Fig. ambiente m.

atmospheric /,ætməs'fɛrɪk/ a. atmosférico.

atoll /'ætɒl/ n. atolón m.

atom /'ætəm/ n. átomo m.

atomic /ə'tɒmɪk/ a. atómico.

atomic bomb bomba atómica f.

atomic energy energía atómica, energía nuclear f.

atomic theory teoría atómica. f.

atomic weight peso atómico m.

atonal /ei'toʊnl/ a. Mus. atonal.

atone /ə'toʊn/ v. expiar, compensar.

atonement /ə'toʊnmənt/ n. expiación; reparación f.

atrocious /ə'troʊʃəs/ a. atroz.

atrocity /ə'trɒsɪti/ n. atrocidad f.

atrophy /'ætrəfi/ n. **1.** Med. atrofia f. —v. **2.** atrofiar.

atropine /'ætrə,pin, -pɪn/ n. atropina f.

attach /ə'tætʃ/ v. juntar; prender; (hook) enganchar; Fig. atribuir.

attaché /ætæ'ʃei/ n. agregado -da.

attachment /ə'tætʃmənt/ n. enlace m.; accesorio m.; (emotional) afecto, cariño m.

attack /ə'tæk/ n. **1.** ataque m. —v **2.** atacar.

attacker /ə'tækər/ n. asaltador -ra.

attain /ə'tein/ v. lograr, alcanzar.

attainable /ə'teinəbəl/ a. accesible, realizable.

attainment /ə'teinmənt/ n. logro; (pl.) dotes f.pl.

attempt /ə'tɛmpt/ n. **1.** ensayo; esfuerzo m.; tentativa f. —v. **2.** ensayar, intentar.

attend /ə'tɛnd/ v. atender; (a meeting) asistir a.

attendance /ə'tɛndəns/ n. asistencia; presencia f.

attendant /ə'tɛndənt/ a. **1.** concomitante. —n. **2.** servidor -ra.

attention /ə'tɛnʃən/ n. atención f.; obsequio m. **to pay a. to,** hacer caso a.

attentive /ə'tɛntɪv/ a. atento.

attentively /ə'tɛntɪvli/ adv. atentamente.

attenuate /ə'tɛnyu,eit/ v. atenuar, adelgazar.

attest /ə'tɛst/ v. confirmar, atestiguar.

attic /'ætık/ n. desván m., guardilla f.

attire /ə'taiᵊr/ n. **1.** traje m. —v. **2.** vestir.

attitude /'ætı,tud/ n. actitud f., ademán m.

attorney /ə'tɜrni/ n. abogado -da, apoderado -da.

attract /ə'trækt/ v. atraer. **a. attention**, llamar la atención.

attraction /ə'trækʃən/ n. atracción f., atractivo m.

attractive /ə'træktıv/ a. atractivo; simpático.

attributable /ə'trıbyutəbəl/ a. atribuible, imputable.

attribute /n 'ætrə,byut; v ə'trıbyut/ n. **1.** atributo m. —v. **2.** atribuir.

attrition /ə'trıʃən/ n. roce, desgaste m.; atrición f.

attune /ə'tun/ v. armonizar.

auction /'ɔkʃən/ n. subasta f., S.A. venduta f.

auctioneer /,ɔkʃə'nıᵊr/ n. subastador -ra, S.A. martillero -ra.

audacious /ɔ'deiʃəs/ a. audaz.

audacity /ɔ'dæsıti/ n. audacia f.

audible /'ɔdəbəl/ a. audible.

audience /'ɔdiəns/ n. auditorio, público m.; entrevista f.

audiovisual /,ɔdiou'vıʒuəl/ a. audiovisual.

audit /'ɔdıt/ n. **1.** revisión de cuentas f. —v. **2.** revisar cuentas.

audition /ɔ'dıʃən/ n. audición f.

auditor /'ɔdıtər/ n. interventor -ora, revisor -ora.

auditorium /,ɔdı'tɔriəm/ n. sala f.; teatro m.

auditory /'ɔdı,tɔri/ a. & n. auditorio m.

augment /ɔg'mɛnt/ v. aumentar.

augur /'ɔgər/ v. augurar, pronosticar.

August /'ɔgəst/ n. agosto m.

aunt /ænt, ɑnt/ n. tía f

auspice /'ɔspıs/ n. auspicio m.

auspicious /ɔ'spıʃəs/ a. favorable; propicio.

austere /ɔ'stıᵊr/ a. austero.

austerity /ɔ'stɛrıti/ n. austeridad, severidad f.

Austrian /'ɔstriən/ a. & n. austríaco -ca.

authentic /ɔ'θɛntık/ a. auténtico.

authenticate /ɔ'θɛntı,keit/ v. autenticar.

authenticity /,ɔθɛn'tısıti/ n. autenticidad f.

author /'ɔθər/ n. autor -ra, escritor -ra.

authoritarian /ə,θɔrı'tɛəriən/ a. & n. autoritario -ria.

authoritative /ə'θɔrı,teitıv/ a. autoritativo; autorizado.

authoritatively /ə'θɔrı,teitıvli/ adv. autoritativamente.

authority /ə'θɔrıti/ n. autoridad f.

authorization /,ɔθərə'zeiʃən/ n. autorización f.

authorize /'ɔθə,raiz/ v. autorizar.

auto /'ɔtou/ n. auto, automóvil m.

autobiography /,ɔtəbai'ɔgrəfi/ n. autobiografía f.

autocracy /ɔ'tɒkrəsi/ n. autocracia f.

autocrat /'ɔtə,kræt/ n. autócrata m. & f.

autograph /'ɔtə,græf/ n. autógrafo m.

automatic /,ɔtə'mætık/ a. automático.

automatically /,ɔtə'mætıkəli/ adv. automáticamente.

automobile /,ɔtəmə'bil/ n. automóvil, coche m.

automotive /,ɔtə'moutıv/ a. automotriz.

autonomy /ɔ'tɒnəmi/ n. autonomía f.

autopsy /'ɔtɒpsi/ n. autopsia f.

autumn /'ɔtəm/ n. otoño m.

auxiliary /ɔg'zılyəri/ a. auxiliar.

avail /ə'veil/ n. **1. of no a.,** en vano. —v. **2. a. oneself of,** aprovecharse.

available /ə'veiləbəl/ a. disponible.

avalanche /'ævə,læntʃ/ n. alud m

avarice /'ævərıs/ n. avaricia, codicia f.

avariciously /,ævə'rıʃəsli/ adv. avaramente.

avenge /ə'vɛndʒ/ v vengar.

avenger /ə'vɛndʒər/ n. vengador -ra.

avenue /'ævə,nu/ n. avenida f.

average /'ævərıdʒ/ a. **1.** medio; común. —n. **2.** promedio, término medio m. —v. **3.** calcular el promedio.

averse /ə'vɜrs/ a. **to be a. to,** tener antipatía a, opuesto a.

aversion /ə'vɜrʒən/ n. aversión f.

avert /ə'vɜrt/ v. desviar; impedir.

aviary /'eivi,ɛri/ n. pajarera, avería f.

aviation /,eivi'eiʃən/ n. aviación f.

aviator /'eivi,eitər/ n. aviador -ra.

aviatrix /,eivi'eitrıks/ n. aviatriz f.

avid /'ævıd/ a. ávido.

avocado /,ævə'kɑdou, ,ʌvə-/ n. aguacate m.

avocation /,ævə'keiʃən/ n. pasatiempo f.

avoid /ə'vɔid/ v. evitar.

avoidable /ə'vɔidəbəl/ a. evitable.

avoidance /ə'vɔidns/ n. evitación f.; Leg. anulación f

avow /ə'vau/ v. declarar; admitir.

avowal /ə'vauəl/ n. admisión f.

avowed /ə'vaud/ a. reconocido; admitido.

avowedly /ə'vaudli/ adv. reconocidamente; confesadamente.

await /ə'weit/ v. esperar, aguardar.

awake /ə'weik/ a. despierto.

awaken /ə'weikən/ v. despertar.

award /ə'wɔrd/ n. **1.** premio m. —v. **2.** otorgar.

aware /ə'wɛər/ a. enterado, consciente.

awash /ə'wɒʃ/ a. & adv. Naut. a flor de agua.

away /ə'wei/ adv. (see under verb: **go away, put away, take away,** etc.)

awe /ɔ/ n. pavor m.

awesome /'ɔsəm/ a. pavoroso; aterrador.

awful /'ɔfəl/ a. horrible, terrible, muy malo, pésimo.

awhile /ə'wuil/ adv. por un rato.

awkward /'ɔkwərd/ a. torpe, desmañado; *Fig.* delicado, embarazoso.

awning /'ɔniŋ/ n. toldo m.

awry /ə'rai/ a. oblicuo, torcido.

ax /æks/ n. hacha f.

axiom /'æksiəm/ n. axioma m.

axis /'æksis/ n. eje m.

axle /'æksəl/ n. eje m.

ayatollah /ˌɑyə'toulə/ n. ayatolá m.

azure /'æʒər/ a. azul.

B

babble /'bæbəl/ n. **1.** balbuceo, murmullo m. —v. **2.** balbucear.

babbler /'bæblər/ n. hablador -ra, charlador -ra.

baboon /bæ'bun/ n. mandril m.

baby /'beibi/ n. nene, bebé m.

baby carriage cochecito de niño m.

babyish /'beibiiʃ/ a. infantil.

baby squid /skwid/ chipirón m.

bachelor /'bætʃələr/ n. soltero m.

bacillus /bə'siləs/ n. bacilo, microbio m.

back /bæk/ adv. **1.** atrás. **to be b.,** estar de vuelta. **b. of,** detrás de. —n. **2.** espalda f.; (of animal) lomo m.

backache /'bæk,eik/ n. dolor de espalda m.

backbone /'bæk,boun/ n. espinazo m.; *Fig.* firmeza f.

backer /'bækər/ n. sostenedor -ra.

background /'bæk,graund/ n. fondo m. antecedentes m.pl.

backing /'bækiŋ/ n. apoyo m., garantía f.

backlash /'bæk,læʃ/ n. repercusión negativa.

backlog /'bæk,lɔg/ n. atrasos m.pl.

backpack /'bæk,pæk/ n. mochila f.

back seat asiento trasero m.

backstage /'bæk'steidʒ/ n. entre bastidores m.

backup /'bæk,ʌp/ n. copia de seguridad f.

backward /'bækwərd/ a. **1.** atrasado. —adv. **2.** hacia atrás.

backwardness /'bækwərdnis/ n. atraso m.

backwater /'bæk,wɔtər/ n. parte de río estancada f.

backwoods /'bæk'wudz/ n. región del monte apartada f.

bacon /'beikən/ n. tocino m.

bacteria /bæk'tiəriə/ n. bacterias f.pl.

bacteriologist /ˌbæktiəri'ɔlədʒist/ n. bacteriólogo -a.

bacteriology /ˌbæktiəri'ɔlədʒi/ n. bacteriología f.

bad /bæd/ a. malo.

badge /bædʒ/ n. insignia, divisa f

badger /'bædʒər/ n. **1.** tejón m. —v. **2.** atormentar.

badly /'bædli/ adv. mal.

badness /'bædnis/ n. maldad f.

bad-tempered /'bæd'tɛmpərd/ a. de mal humor.

baffle /'bæfəl/ v. desconcertar.

bafflement /'bæfəlmənt/ n. contrariedad; confusión f.

bag /bæg/ n. **1.** saco m.; bolsa f. —v. **2.** ensacar, cazar.

baggage /'bægidʒ/ n equipaje m. **b. check,** talón m.

baggage cart (airport) carrillo para llevar equipaje.

baggy /'bægi/ a. abotagado; bolsudo; hinchado.

bagpipe /'bæg,paip/ n. gaita f.

bail /beil/ n. **1.** fianza f. —v. **2.** desaguar.

bailiff /'beilif/ n. alguacil m.

bait /beit/ n. **1.** cebo m. —v. **2.** cebar.

bake /beik/ v. cocer en horno.

baked potato /beikt/ patata asada f.

baker /'beikər/ n. panadero -ra, hornero -ra.

bakery /'beikəri, 'beikri/ n. panadería f.

baking /'beikiŋ/ n. hornada f. **b. powder,** levadura f.

balance /'bæləns/ n. balanza f.; equilibrio m.; *Com.* saldo m.

balcony /'bælkəni/ n. balcón m.; *Theat.* galería f.

bald /bɔld/ a. calvo.

baldness /'bɔldnis/ n. calvicie f.

bale /beil/ n. **1.** bala f. —v. **2.** embalar.

balk /bɔk/ v. frustrar; rebelarse.

Balkans /'bɔlkənz/ n.pl. Balcanes m.pl.

balky /'bɔki/ a. rebelón.

ball /bɔl/ n. bola, pelota f.; (dance) baile m.

ballad /'bæləd/ n. romance, m.; balada f.

ballast /'bæləst/ n. **1.** lastre m. —v. **2.** lastrar.

ball bearing cojinete de bolas m.

ballerina /ˌbælə'rinə/ n. bailarina f.

ballet /bæ'lei/ n. danza f.; ballet m.

ballistics /bə'lıstıks/ n. balística f.

balloon /bə'lun/ n. globo m. **b. tire**, neumático de balón.

ballot /'bælət/ n. **1.** balota f., voto m. —v **2.** balotar, votar.

ballpoint pen /'bɔl,pɔint/ bolígrafo m.

ballroom /'bɔl,rum/ n. salón de baile m.

balm /bam/ n. bálsamo; ungüento m.

balmy /'bami/ a. fragante; reparador; calmante.

balsa /'bɔlsə/ n. balsa f.

balsam /'bɔlsəm/ n. bálsamo m.

balustrade /'bælə,streid/ n. barandilla f.

bamboo /bæm'bu/ n. bambú m., caña f.

ban /bæn/ n. **1.** prohibición f. —v. **2.** prohibir; proscribir.

banal /bə'næl/ a. trivial; vulgar.

banana /bə'nænə/ n. banana f., cambur m. **b. tree**, banano, plátano m.

band /bænd/ n. **1.** banda f.; (of men) banda, cuadrilla, partida f. —v. **2.** asociarse.

bandage /'bændıdʒ/ n. **1.** vendaje m. —v. **2.** vendar.

bandanna /bæn'dænə/ n. pañuelo (grande) m.; bandana f.

bandbox /'bænd,bɒks/ n. caja de cartón.

bandit /'bændıt/ n. bandido -da.

bandmaster /'bænd,mæstər/ n. director de una banda musical m.

bandstand /'bænd,stænd/ n. kiosco de música.

bang /bæŋ/ interj. **1.** ¡pum! —n. **2.** ruido de un golpe. —v. **3.** golpear ruidosamente.

banish /'bænıʃ/ v. desterrar.

banishment /'bænıʃmənt/ n. destierro m.

banister /'bænəstər/ n. pasamanos m.pl.

bank /bæŋk/ n. **1.** banco m.; (of a river) margen f. —v. **2.** depositar.

bank account cuenta bancaria f.

bankbook /'bæŋk,bʊk/ n. libreta de depósitos f

bank card tarjeta bancaria f.

banker /'bæŋkər/ n. banquero -ra.

banking /'bæŋkıŋ/ a. bancaria. n. banca f.

bank note billete de banco m.

bankrupt /'bæŋkrʌpt/ a. insolvente.

bankruptcy /'bæŋkrʌptsi/ n. bancarrota f.

banner /'bænər/ n. bandera f.; estandarte m.

banquet /'bæŋkwıt/ n. banquete m.

banter /'bæntər/ n. **1.** choteo m.; zumba; burla f. —v. **2.** chotear; zumbar; burlarse.

baptism /'bæptızəm/ n. bautismo, bautizo m.

baptismal /bæp'tızməl/ a. bautismal.

Baptist /'bæptıst/ n. bautista m. & f.

baptize /bæp'taiz, 'bæptaiz/ v. bautizar.

bar /bar/ n. **1.** barra f.; obstáculo m.; (tav-

ern) taberna f., bar m. —v. **2.** barrear; prohibir, excluir.

barbarian /bar'beəriən/ a. bárbaro. n. bárbaro -ra.

barbarism /'barbə,rızəm/ n. barbarismo m., barbarie f.

barbarous /'barbərəs/ a. bárbaro, cruel.

barbecue /'barbı,kyu/ n. animal asado entero; (Mex.) barbacoa f.

barber /'barbər/ n. barbero m. **b. shop**, barbería f.

barbiturate /bar'bıtʃərıt/ n. barbitúrico m.

bar code código de barras m.

bare /beər/ a. **1.** desnudo; descubierto. —v. **2.** desnudar; descubrir.

bareback /'beər,bæk/ adv. sin silla.

barefoot(ed) /'beər,futıd/ a. descalzo.

barely /'beərli/ adv. escasamente, apenas.

bareness /'beərnıs/ n. desnudez f., pobreza f.

bargain /'bargən/ n. **1.** ganga f., compra ventajosa f.; contrato m —v. **2.** regatear; negociar.

barge /bardʒ/ n. lanchón m., barcaza f

baritone /'bærı,toun/ n. barítono m.

barium /'beəriəm/ n. bario m.

bark /bark/ n. **1.** corteza f.; (of dog) ladrido f. —v. **2.** ladrar.

barley /'barli/ n. cebada f.

barn /barn/ n. granero m.

barnacle /'barnəkəl/ n. lapa f.

barnyard /'barn,yard/ n. corral m.

barometer /bə'rɒmıtər/ n. barómetro m.

barometric /,bærə'metrık/ a. barométrico.

baron /'bærən/ n. barón m.

baroness /'bærənıs/ n. baronesa f.

baronial /bə'rouniəl/ a. baronial.

baroque /bə'rouk/ a. barroco.

barracks /'bærəks/ n. cuartel m.

barrage /bə'ruʒ/ n. cortina de fuego f.

barred /bard/ a. excluido; prohibido.

barrel /'bærəl/ n. barril m.; (of gun) cañón m.

barren /'bærən/ a. estéril.

barrenness /'bærən,nıs/ n. esterilidad f.

barricade /'bærı,keid/ n. barricada, barrera f.

barrier /'bæriər/ n. barrera f.; obstáculo m.

barroom /'bar,rum, -,rʌm/ n. cantina f.

bartender /'bar,tendər/ n. tabernero; cantinero m.

barter /'bartər/ n. **1.** cambio, trueque m. —v. **2.** cambiar, trocar.

base /beis/ a. **1.** bajo, vil. —n. **2.** base f. —v. **3.** basar.

baseball /'beis,bɔl/ n. béisbol m.

baseboard /'beis,bɔrd/ n. tabla de resguardo.

basement /'beismənt/ n. sótano m.

baseness /'beisnıs/ n. bajeza, vileza f.

bashful /'bæʃfəl/ a. vergonzoso, tímido.

bashfully /'bæʃfəli/ adv. tímidamente; vergonzosamente.

bashfulness /'bæʃfəlnɪs/ n. vergüenza; timidez f.

basic /'beɪsɪk/ a. fundamental, básico.

basin /'beɪsən/ n. bacía f.; (of river) cuenca f.

basis /'beɪsɪs/ n. base f.

bask /bæsk/ v. tomar el sol.

basket /'bæskɪt/ n. cesta, canasta f.

bass /bæs/ beis/ n. (fish) lobina f.; Mus. bajo profundo m. **b. viol.** violón m.

bassinet /,bæsə'nɛt/ n. bacinete m.

bassoon /bæ'sun/ n. bajón m.

bastard /'bæstərd/ a. & n. bastardo -da; hijo -a natural.

baste /beɪst/ v. (sew) bastear; (cooking) pringar.

bat /bæt/ n. **1.** (animal) murciélago m.; (baseball) bate m. —v. **2.** batear.

batch /bætʃ/ n. cantidad de cosas.

bath /bæθ/ n. baño m.

bathe /beɪð/ v. bañar, bañarse.

bather /'beɪðər/ n. bañista m. & f.

bathing resort /'beɪðɪŋ/ balneario m.

bathing suit /'beɪðɪŋ/ traje de baño.

bathrobe /'bæθ,roub/ n. bata de baño f.

bathroom /'bæθ,rum, -,rʊm/ n. cuarto de baño.

bathtub /'bæθ,tʌb/ n. bañera f.

baton /bə'tɒn/ n. bastón m.; Mus. batuta f.

battalion /bə'tælyən/ n. batallón m.

batter /'bætər/ n. **1.** (cooking) batido m.; (baseball) voleador m. —v. **2.** batir; derribar.

battery /'bætəri/ n. batería f.; Elec. pila f.

batting /'bætɪŋ/ n. agramaje, moldeaje m.

battle /'bætl/ n. **1.** batalla f.; combate m. —v. **2.** batallar.

battlefield /'bætl,fild/ n. campo de batalla.

battleship /'bætl,ʃɪp/ n. acorazado m.

bauxite /'bɒksaɪt, 'bouzaɪt/ n. bauxita f.

bawl /bɔl/ v. gritar; vocear.

bay /beɪ/ n. bahía f. v. aullar.

bayonet /'beɪənɛt/ n. bayoneta f.

bazaar /bə'zɑr/ n. bazar m., feria f.

BC abbr. (**before Christ**) a.C. (antes de Cristo).

be /bi/ v. ser; estar. (See **hacer; hay; tener** in Sp.-Eng. section.)

beach /bitʃ/ n. playa f.

beachcomber /'bitʃ,koumər/ n. raquero -ra m. & f.

beacon /'bikən/ n. faro m.

bead /bid/ n. cuenta f.; pl. Relig. rosario m.

beading /'bidɪŋ/ n. abalorio m.

beady /'bidi/ a. globuloso; burbujoso.

beak /bik/ n. pico m.

beaker /'bikər/ n. vaso con pico m.

beam /bim/ n. viga f.; (of wood) madero m.; (of light) rayo m.

beaming /'bimɪŋ/ a. radiante.

bean /bin/ n. haba, habichuela f., frijol m.

bear /bɛər/ n. **1.** oso -sa. —v. **2.** llevar; (endure) aguantar.

bearable /'bɛərəbəl/ a. sufrible; soportable.

beard /bɪərd/ n. barba f.

bearded /'bɪərdɪd/ a. barbado; barbudo.

beardless /'bɪərdlɪs/ a. lampiño; imberbe.

bearer /'bɛərər/ n. portador -ra.

bearing /'bɛərɪŋ/ n. porte, aguante m.

bearskin /'bɛər,skɪn/ n. piel de oso f.

beast /bist/ n. bestia f.; bruto -ta.

beat /bit/ v. golpear; batir; pulsar; (in games) ganar, vencer.

beaten /'bitn/ a. vencido; batido.

beatify /bi'ætə,faɪ/ v. beatificar.

beating /'bitɪŋ/ n. paliza f.

beau /bou/ n. novio m.

beautiful /'byutəfəl/ a. hermoso, bello.

beautifully /'byutəfəli/ adv. bellamente.

beautify /'byutə,faɪ/ v. embellecer.

beauty /'byuti/ n. hermosura, belleza f. **b. parlor,** salón de belleza.

beaver /'bivər/ n. castor m.

becalm /bɪ'kɑm/ v. calmar; sosegar; encalmarse.

because /bɪ'kɔz/ conj. porque. **b. of,** a causa de.

beckon /'bɛkən/ v. hacer señas.

become /bɪ'kʌm/ v. hacerse; ponerse.

becoming /bɪ'kʌmɪŋ/ a. propio, correcto; **be b.,** quedar bien, sentar bien.

bed /bɛd/ n. cama f.; lecho m.; (of river) cauce m.

bedbug /'bɛd,bʌg/ n. chinche m.

bedclothes /'bɛd,klouz, -,klouðz/ n. ropa de cama f.

bedding /'bɛdɪŋ/ n. colchones m.pl.

bedfellow /'bɛd,fɛlou/ n. compañero -ra de cama.

bedizen /bɪ'daizən, -'dɪzən/ v. adornar; aderezar.

bedridden /'bɛd,rɪdn/ a. postrado (en cama).

bedrock /'bɛd,rɒk/ n. (mining) lecho de roca m.; Fig. fundamento m.

bedroom /'bɛd,rum/ n. alcoba f.; (Mex.) recámara f.

bedside /'bɛd,said/ n. al lado de una cama m.

bedspread /'bɛd,sprɛd/ n. cubrecama, sobrecama f.

bedstead /'bɛd,stɛd/ n. armadura de cama f.

bedtime /'bɛd,taim/ n. hora de acostarse.

bee /bi/ n. abeja f.

beef /bif/ n. carne de vaca.

beefburger /'bif,bɜrgər/ n. hamburguesa f.

beefsteak /'bif,steik/ n. bistec, bisté m.

beehive /'bi,haiv/ n. colmena f.

beer /biər/ n. cerveza f.

beeswax /'biz,wæks/ n. cera de abejas.

beet /bit/ n. remolacha f.; (Mex.) betabel m.

beetle /'bitl/ n. escarabajo m.

befall /bi'fɔl/ v. suceder, sobrevenir.

befitting /bi'fitiŋ/ a. conveniente; propio; digno.

before /bi'fɔr/ adv. antes. prep. antes de; (in front of) delante de. conj. antes que.

beforehand /bi'fɔr,hænd/ adv. de antemano.

befriend /bi'frɛnd/ v. amparar.

befuddle /bi'fʌdl/ v. confundir; aturdir.

beg /bɛg/ v. rogar, suplicar; (for alms) mendigar.

beget /bi'gɛt/ v. engendrar; producir.

beggar /'bɛgər/ n. mendigo -ga; S.A. limosnero -ra.

beggarly /'bɛgərli/ a. pobre, miserable.

begin /bi'gin/ v. empezar, comenzar, principiar.

beginner /bi'ginər/ n. principiante -ta.

beginning /bi'giniŋ/ n. principio, comienzo m.

begrudge /bi'grʌdʒ/ v. envidiar.

behalf /bi'hæf/ n.: **in, on b. of,** a favor de, en pro de.

behave /bi'heiv/ v. portarse, comportarse.

behavior /bi'heivyər/ n. conducta f.; comportamiento m.

behead /bi'hɛd/ v. decapitar.

behind /bi'haind/ adv. atrás, detrás. prep. detrás de.

behold /bi'hould/ v. contemplar.

beige /beiʒ/ a. beige.

being /'biiŋ/ n. existencia f.; (person) ser m.

bejewel /bi'dʒuəl/ v. adornar con joyas.

belated /bi'leitid/ a. atrasado, tardío.

belch /bɛltʃ/ n. **1.** eructo m. —v. **2.** vomitar; eructar.

belfry /'bɛlfri/ n. campanario m.

Belgian /'bɛldʒən/ a. & n. belga m. & f.

Belgium /'bɛldʒəm/ n. Bélgica f.

belie /bi'lai/ v. desmentir.

belief /bi'lif/ n. creencia f.; parecer m.

believable /bi'livəbəl/ a. creíble.

believe /bi'liv/ v. creer.

believer /bi'livər/ n. creyente m. & f.

belittle /bi'lɪtl/ v. dar poca importancia a.

bell /bɛl/ n. campana f.; (of house) campanilla f.; (electric) timbre m.

bellboy /'bɛl,bɔi/ n. mozo, botones m.

bellicose /'bɛli,kous/ a. guerrero.

belligerence /bə'lidʒərəns/ n. beligerancia f

belligerent /bə'lidʒərənt/ a. & n. beligerante m. & f.

belligerently /bə'lidʒərəntli/ adv. belicosamente.

bellow /'bɛlou/ v. bramar, rugir.

bellows /'bɛlouz/ n. fuelle m.

belly /'bɛli/ n. vientre m.; panza, barriga f.

belong /bi'lɔŋ/ v. pertenecer.

belongings /bi'lɔŋiŋz/ n. propiedad f.

beloved /bi'lʌvid/ a. querido, amado.

below /bi'lou/ adv. **1.** debajo, abajo. —prep. **2.** debajo de.

belt /bɛlt/ n. cinturón m.

bench /bɛntʃ/ n. banco m.

bend /bɛnd/ n. vuelta; curva f. v. encorvar, doblar.

beneath /bi'niθ/ adv. **1.** debajo, abajo. —prep. **2.** debajo de.

benediction /,bɛni'dikʃən/ n. bendición f.

benefactor /'bɛnə,fæktər/ n. bienhechor -ra.

benefactress /'bɛnə,fæktris/ n. bienhechora f.

beneficial /,bɛnə'fiʃəl/ a. provechoso, beneficioso.

beneficiary /,bɛnə'fiʃi,ɛri/ n. beneficiario -ria, beneficiado -da.

benefit /'bɛnəfit/ n. **1.** provecho, beneficio m. —v. **2.** beneficiar.

benevolence /bə'nɛvələns/ n. benevolencia f.

benevolent /bə'nɛvələnt/ a. benévolo.

benevolently /bə'nɛvələntli/ adv. benignamente.

benign /bi'nain/ bi'nignənt/ a. benigno.

benignity /bi'nigniti/ n. benignidad; bondad f.

bent /bɛnt/ a. **1.** encorvado. **b. on,** resuelto a. —n **2.** inclinación f.

benzene /'bɛnzin, bɛn'zin/ n. benceno m.

bequeath /bi'kwið/ v. legar.

bequest /bi'kwɛst/ n. legado m.

berate /bi'reit/ v. reñir, regañar.

bereave /bi'riv/ v. despojar; desolar.

bereavement /bi'rivmənt/ n. privación f.; despojo m.; (mourning) luto m.

berry /'bɛri/ n. baya f.

berth /bɜrθ/ n. camarote m.; Naut. litera f.; (for vessel) amarradero m.

beseech /bi'sitʃ/ v. suplicar; implorar.

beseechingly /bi'sitʃiŋli/ adv. suplicantemente.

beset /bi'sɛt/ v. acosar; rodear.

beside /bi'said/ prep. al lado de.

besides /bi'saidz/ adv. además, por otra parte.

besiege /bi'sidʒ/ v. sitiar; asediar.

besieged /bi'sidʒd/ a. sitiado.

besieger /bi'sidʒər/ n. sitiador -ra.

besmirch /bɪ'smɜrtʃ/ v. manchar; deshonrar.

best /bɛst/ a. & adv. mejor. **at b.**, a lo más.

bestial /'bɛstʃəl/ a. bestial; brutal.

bestir /bɪ'stɜr/ v. incitar; intrigar.

best man n. padrino de boda.

bestow /bɪ'stou/ v. conferir.

bestowal /bɪ'stouəl/ n. dádiva; presentación f.

bet /bɛt/ n. **1.** apuesta f. —v. **2.** apostar.

betoken /bɪ'toukən/ v. presagiar, anunciar.

betray /bɪ'trei/ v. traicionar; revelar.

betrayal /bɪ'treiəl/ n. traición f.

betroth /bɪ'trouð/ v. contraer esponsales; prometerse.

betrothal /bɪ'trouðəl/ n. esponsales m.pl.

better /'bɛtər/ a. & adv. **1.** mejor. —v. **2.** mejorar.

between /bɪ'twin/ prep. entre, en medio de.

bevel /'bɛvəl/ n. **1.** cartabón m. —v. **2.** cortar al sesgo.

beverage /'bɛvərɪdʒ/ n. bebida f.; (cold) refresco m.

bewail /bɪ'weil/ v llorar; lamentar.

beware /bɪ'wɛər/ v. guardarse, precaverse.

bewilder /bɪ'wɪldər/ v. aturdir.

bewildered /bɪ'wɪldərd/ a. descarriado.

bewildering /bɪ'wɪldərɪŋ/ a. aturdente.

bewilderment /bɪ'wɪldərmənt/ n. aturdimiento m.; perplejidad f.

bewitch /bɪ'wɪtʃ/ v. hechizar; embrujar.

beyond /bi'ɒnd/ prep. más allá de.

biannual /bai'ænyuəl/ a. semianual; semestral.

bias /'baiəs/ n. **1.** parcialidad f.; prejuicio m. **on the b.**, al sesgo. —v. **2.** predisponer, influir.

bib /bɪb/ n. babador m.

Bible /'baibəl/ n. Biblia f.

Biblical /'bɪblɪkəl/ a. bíblico.

bibliography /,bɪbli'ɒɡrəfi/ n. bibliografía f.

bicarbonate /bai'kɑrbənɪt/ n. bicarbonato m.

bicentennial /,baisɛn'tɛniəl/ a. & n. bicentenario m.

biceps /'baisɛps/ n. bíceps m.

bicker /'bɪkər/ v. altercar.

bicycle /'baisɪkəl/ n. bicicleta f.

bicyclist /'baisɪklɪst/ n. biciclista m. & f.

bid /bɪd/ n. **1.** proposición, oferta f. —v. **2.** mandar; ofrecer.

bidder /'bɪdər/ n. postor -ra.

bide /baid/ v. aguardar; esperar.

bier /bɪər/ n. ataúd m.

bifocal /bai'foukəl/ a. bifocal.

big /bɪɡ/ a. grande.

bigamist /'bɪɡəmɪst/ n. bígamo -ma.

bigamy /'bɪɡəmi/ n. bigamia f.

bigot /'bɪɡət/ n. persona intolerante.

bigotry /'bɪɡətri/ n. intolerancia f.

bikini /bɪ'kini/ n. bikini m.

bilateral /bai'lætərəl/ a. bilateral.

bile /bail/ n. bilis f.

bilingual /bai'lɪŋgwəl/ a. bilingüe.

bilingualism /bai'lɪŋgwə,lɪzəm/ n. bilingüismo m.

bilious /'bɪlyəs/ a. bilioso.

bill /bɪl/ n. **1.** cuenta, factura f.; (money) billete m.; (of bird) pico m. —v. **2.** facturar.

billboard /'bɪl,bɔrd/ n. cartelera f.

billet /'bɪlɪt/ n. **1.** billete m.; Mil. boleta f. —v. **2.** aposentar.

billfold /'bɪl,fould/ n. cartera f.

billiard balls /'bɪlyərd bɔlz/ bolas de billar.

billiards /'bɪlyərdz/ n. billar m.

billion /'bɪlyən/ n. billón m.

bill of health n. certificado de sanidad.

bill of lading /'leidɪŋ/ n. conocimiento de embarque.

bill of sale n. escritura de venta.

billow /'bɪlou/ n. ola; oleada f.

bimetallic /,baimə'tælɪk/ a. bimetálico.

bimonthly /bai'mʌnθli/ a. & adv. bimestral.

bin /bɪn/ n. hucha f.; depósito m.

bind /baind/ v. atar; obligar; (book) encuadernar.

bindery /'baindəri/ n. taller de encuadernación m.

binding /'baindɪŋ/ n encuadernación f.

bingo /'bɪŋgou/ n. bingo m.

binocular /bə'nɒkyələr/ a. binocular. n.pl. gemelos m.pl.

biochemistry /,baiou'kɛməstri/ n. bioquímica f.

biodegradable /,baioudɪ'greidəbəl/ a. biodegradable.

biofeedback /,baiou'fid,bæk/ n. biofeedback.

biographer /bai'ɒɡrəfər/ n. biógrafo -fa.

biographical /,baiə'ɡræfɪkəl/ a. biográfico.

biography /bai'ɒɡrəfi/ n. biografía f.

biological /,baiə'lɒdʒɪkəl/ a. biológico.

biologically /,baiə'lɒdʒɪkəli/ adv. biológicamente.

biology /bai'ɒlədʒi/ n. biología f.

bipartisan /bai'pɑrtəzən/ a. bipartito.

biped /'baipɛd/ n. bípedo m.

bird /bɜrd/ n. pájaro m.; ave f.

birdie /'bɜrdi/ n. (golf) uno bajo par m.

bird of prey n. ave de rapiña f.

bird's-eye view /'bɜrdz,ai/ n. vista de pájaro f.

birth /bɜrθ/ n. nacimiento m. **give b. to**, dar a luz.

birth certificate partida de nacimiento f.

birth control n. contracepción f.

birthday /'bɜrθ,dei/ n. cumpleaños m.

birthmark /'bərθ,mɑrk/ n. marca de nacimiento f.

birthplace /'bərθ,pleis/ n. natalicio m.

birth rate n. natalidad f.

birthright /'bərθ,rait/ n. primogenitura f.

biscuit /'bɪskɪt/ n. bizcocho m.

bisect /bai'sɛkt/ v. bisecar.

bishop /'bɪʃəp/ n. obispo m.; (chess) alfil m.

bishopric /'bɪʃəprɪk/ n. obispado m.

bismuth /'bɪzməθ/ n. bismuto m.

bison /'baisən/ n. bisonte m.

bit /bɪt/ n. pedacito m.; Mech taladro m.; (for horse) bocado m.; (computer) bit m.

bitch /bɪtʃ/ n. perra f.

bite /bait/ n. **1.** bocado m.; picada f. —v. **2.** morder; picar.

biting /'baitɪŋ/ a. penetrante; mordaz.

bitter /'bɪtər/ a. amargo.

bitterly /'bɪtərli/ adv. amargamente; agriamente.

bitterness /'bɪtərnɪs/ n. amargura f.; rencor m.

bivouac /'bɪvu,æk/ n. **1.** vivaque m. —v. **2.** vivaquear.

biweekly /bai'wikli/ a. quincenal.

black /blæk/ a. negro.

Black /blæk/ n. (person) negro -gra; persona de color.

blackberry /'blæk,bɛri/ n. mora f.

blackbird /'blæk,bərd/ n. mirlo m.

blackboard /'blæk,bɔrd/ n. pizarra f.

blacken /'blækən/ v. ennegrecer.

black eye n. ojo amoratado.

blackguard /'blægɑrd/ n. tunante; pillo m.

blacklist /'blæk,lɪst/ n. lista negra f.

blackmail /'blæk,meil/ n. **1.** chantaje m. —v. **2.** amenazar con chantaje, chantajear.

black market mercado negro, estraperlo m.

black marketeer /,mɑrkɪ'tir/ estraperlista mf.

blackout /'blæk,aut/ n. oscurecimiento, apagamiento m.

blacksmith /'blæk,smɪθ/ n. herrero -ra.

bladder /'blædər/ n. vejiga f.

blade /bleid/ n. (sword) hoja f.; (oar) pala f.; (grass) brizna f.

blame /bleim/ v. culpar, echar la culpa a.

blameless /'bleimlɪs/ a. inculpable.

blanch /blæntʃ/ v. blanquear; escaldar.

bland /blænd/ a. blando.

blank /blæŋk/ a. & n. en blanco.

blanket /'blæŋkɪt/ n. manta f.; cobertor m.

blare /blɛər/ n. sonido de trompeta. v. sonar como trompeta.

blaspheme /blæs'fim/ v. blasfemar.

blasphemer /blæs'fimər/ n. blasfemo -ma, blasfemador -ra.

blasphemous /'blæsfəməs/ a. blasfemo, impío.

blasphemy /'blæsfəmi/ n. blasfemia f.

blast /blæst/ n. **1.** barreno m.; (wind) ráfaga f. —v. **2.** barrenar.

blatant /'bleitnt/ a. bramante; descarado.

blaze /bleiz/ n. **1.** llama, hoguera f. —v. **2.** encenderse en llama.

blazing /'bleizɪŋ/ a. flameante.

bleach /blitʃ/ n. **1.** lejía, blanqueador. —v. **2.** blanquear.

bleachers /'blitʃərz/ n. asientos al aire libre.

bleak /blik/ a. frío y sombrío.

bleakness /'bliknɪs/ n. desolación f.

bleed /blid/ v. sangrar.

blemish /'blɛmɪʃ/ n. **1.** mancha f.; lunar m. —v. **2.** manchar.

blend /blɛnd/ n. **1.** mezcla f. —v. **2.** mezclar, combinar.

blended /'blɛndɪd/ a. mezclado.

blender /'blɛndər/ n. (for food) licuadora f.

bless /blɛs/ v. bendecir.

blessed /'blɛsɪd/ a. bendito.

blessing /'blɛsɪŋ/ n. bendición f.

blight /blait/ n. **1.** plaga f.; tizón m. —v. **2.** atizonar.

blind /blaind/ a. ciego.

blindfold /'blaind,fould/ v. vendar los ojos.

blinding /'blaindɪŋ/ a. deslumbrante; ofuscante.

blindly /'blaindli/ adv. ciegamente.

blindness /'blaindnɪs/ n. ceguedad, ceguera f.

blink /blɪŋk/ n. **1.** guiñada f. —v. **2.** guiñar.

bliss /blɪs/ n. felicidad f.

blissful /'blɪsfəl/ a. dichoso; bienaventurado.

blissfully /'blɪsfəli/ adv. felizmente.

blister /'blɪstər/ n. ampolla f.

blithe /blaið/ a. alegre; jovial; gozoso.

blizzard /'blɪzərd/ n. nevasca f.

bloat /blout/ v. hinchar.

bloc /blɒk/ n. grupo (político); bloc.

block /blɒk/ n. **1.** bloque m.; (street) manzana, cuadra f. —v. **2.** bloquear.

blockade /blɒ'keid/ n. **1.** bloqueo m. —v. **2.** bloquear.

blond /blɒnd/ a. & n. rubio -ia.

blood /blʌd/ n. sangre f.; parentesco, linaje m.

bloodhound /'blʌd,haund/ n. sabueso m.

bloodless /'blʌdlɪs/ a. exangüe; desangrado.

blood poisoning /'pɔizəniŋ/ envenenamiento de sangre.

blood pressure presión arterial.

bloodshed /'blʌd,ʃɛd/ n. matanza f.

bloodthirsty /'blʌd,θərsti/ a. cruel, sanguinario.

bloody /'blʌdi/ a. ensangrentado, sangriento.

bloom /blum/ n. **1.** flor f. —v. **2.** florecer.

blooming /'blumɪŋ/ a. lozano; fresco; floreciente.

blossom /'blɒsəm/ n. **1.** flor f. —v. **2.** florecer.

blot /blɒt/ n. **1.** mancha f. —v. **2.** manchar.

blotch /blɒtʃ/ n. **1.** mancha, roncha f. —v. **2.** manchar.

blotter /'blɒtər/ n. papel secante.

blouse /blaus/ n. blusa f.

blow /blou/ n. **1.** golpe m.; Fig. chasco m. —v. **2.** soplar.

blowout /'blou,aut/ n. reventón de neumático m.

blubber /'blʌbər/ n. grasa de ballena.

bludgeon /'blʌdʒən/ n. porra f. v. apalear.

blue /blu/ a. azul; triste, melancólico.

bluebird /'blu,bɜrd/ n. azulejo m.

blue jeans jeans; vaqueros m.pl.

blueprint /'blu,prɪnt/ n. heliografía f.

bluff /blʌf/ n. risco m. v. alardear; baladronar.

bluing /'bluɪŋ/ n. añil m.

blunder /'blʌndər/ n. **1.** desatino m. —v. **2.** desatinar.

blunderer /'blʌndərər/ n. desatinado -da.

blunt /blʌnt/ a. embotado; descortés. v. embotar.

bluntly /'blʌntli/ a. bruscamente.

bluntness /'blʌntnɪs/ n. grosería f.; brusquedad f.

blur /blɜr/ n. **1.** trazo confuso. —v. **2.** hacer indistinto.

blush /blʌʃ/ n. **1.** rubor, sonrojo m. —v. **2.** sonrojarse.

bluster /'blʌstər/ n. **1.** fanfarria f. —v. **2.** fanfarrear.

boar /bɔr/ n. verraco m. **wild b.,** jabalí.

board /bɔrd/ n. **1.** tabla f.; Govt. consejo m.; junta f. **b. and room,** cuarto y comida, casa y comida. —v. **2.** (ship) abordar.

boarder /'bɔrdər/ n. pensionista m. & f.

boardinghouse /'bɔrdɪŋ/ n. pensión f., casa de huéspedes.

boarding pass /'bɔrdɪŋ/ boleto de embarque m., tarjeta de embarque f.

boast /boust/ n. **1.** jactancia f. —v. **2.** jactarse.

boaster /'boustər/ n. fanfarrón -na.

boastful /'boustfəl/ a. jactancioso.

boastfulness /'boustfəlnɪs/ n. jactancia f.

boat /bout/ n. barco, buque, bote m.

boathouse /'bout,haus/ n. casilla de botes f.

boatswain /'bousən/ n. contramaestre m.

bob /bɒb/ v. menear.

bobbin /'bɒbɪn/ n. bobina f.

bobby pin /'bɒbi/ n. gancho m., horquilla.

bodice /'bɒdɪs/ n. corpiño m.

bodily /'bɒdlji/ a. corporal.

body /'bɒdi/ n. cuerpo m.

body builder culturista mf.

body building culturismo m.

bodyguard /'bɒdi,gɑrd/ n. guardaespaldas.

bog /bɒg/ n. pantano m.

bogey /'bougi/ n. (golf) uno sobre par m.

Bohemian /bou'himiən/ a. & n. bohemio, -mia.

boil /bɔil/ n. **1.** hervor m.; Med. divieso m. —v. **2.** hervir.

boiler /'bɔilər/ n. marmita; caldera f.

boiling point /'bɔilɪŋ/ punto de ebullición m.

boisterous /'bɔistərəs/ a. tumultuoso.

boisterously /'bɔistərəsli/ adv. tumultuosamente.

bold /bould/ a. atrevido, audaz.

boldface /'bould,feis/ n. (type) letra negra.

boldly /'bouldli/ adv. audazmente; descaradamente.

boldness /'bouldnɪs/ n. atrevimiento m.; osadía f.

Bolivian /bou'lɪviən/ a. & n. boliviano -na.

bologna /bə'louni/ n. salchicha f., mortadela.

bolster /'boulstər/ n. **1.** travesero, cojín m. —v. **2.** apoyar, sostener.

bolt /boult/ n. **1.** perno m.; (of door) cerrojo m.; (lightning) rayo m. v. acerrojar.

bomb /bɒm/ n. **1.** bomba f. —v. **2.** bombardear.

bombard /bɒm'bɑrd/ v. bombardear.

bombardier /,bɒmbər'dɪər/ n. bombardero -ra.

bombardment /bɒm'bɑrdmənt/ n. bombardeo m.

bomber /'bɒmər/ n. avión de bombardeo.

bombproof /'bɒm,pruf/ a. a prueba de granadas.

bombshell /'bɒm,ʃel/ n. bomba f.

bonbon /'bɒn,bɒn/ n. dulce, bombón m.

bond /bɒnd/ n. lazo m.; Com. bono m.

bondage /'bɒndɪdʒ/ n. esclavitud, servidumbre f.

bonded /'bɒndɪd/ a. garantizado.

bone /boun/ n. hueso m.

boneless /'bounlɪs/ a. sin huesos.

bonfire /'bɒn,faiər/ n. hoguera, fogata f.

bonnet /'bɒnɪt/ n. gorra f.

bonus /'bounəs/ n. sobrepaga f.

bony /'bouni/ a. huesudo.

boo /bu/ v. abuchear.

book /buk/ n. libro m.

bookbinder /'buk,baindər/ n. encuadernador -ra.

bookcase /'buk,keis/ n. armario para libros.

bookkeeper /'buk,kipər/ n. tenedor -ra de libros.

bookkeeping /'buk,kipiŋ/ n. contabilidad f.

booklet /'buklɪt/ n. folleto m., libreta f.

bookmark /'buk,mɑrk/ n. marcapáginas m.

bookseller /'buk,selər/ n. librero -ra.

bookstore /'buk,stɔr/ n. librería f.

boom /bum/ n. Naut. botalón m.; prosperidad repentina.

boon /bun/ n. dádiva f.

boor /bur/ n. patán, rústico m.

boorish /'burɪʃ/ a. villano.

boost /bust/ n. **1.** alza; ayuda f. —v. **2.** levantar, alzar; fomentar.

booster /'bustər/ n. fomentador m.

boot /but/ n. bota f.

bootblack /'but,blæk/ n. limpiabotas m.

booth /buθ/ n. cabaña; casilla f.

booty /'buti/ n. botín m.

border /'bɔrdər/ n. **1.** borde m.; frontera f. —v. **2. b. on,** lindar con.

borderline /'bɔrdər,laɪn/ a. marginal. n. margen m.

bore /bɔr/ n. lata f.; persona pesada. v. aburrir, fastidiar; Mech. taladrar.

boredom /'bɔrdəm/ n. aburrimiento m.

boric acid /'bɔrɪk/ n. ácido bórico m.

boring /'bɔrɪŋ/ a. aburrido, pesado.

born /bɔrn/ a. nacido. **be born,** nacer.

born-again /'bɔrn ə'gɛn/ a. renacido.

borrow /'bɔrou/ v. pedir prestado.

bosom /'buzəm/ v. seno, pecho m.

boss /bɔs/ n. jefe, patrón m.

botany /'bɒtni/ n. botánica f.

both /bouθ/ pron. & a. ambos, los dos.

bother /'bɒðər/ n. molestia f. v. molestar, incomodar.

bothersome /'bɒðərsəm/ a. molesto.

bottle /'bɒtl/ n. **1.** botella f. —v. **2.** embotellar.

bottling /'bɒtlɪŋ/ n. embotellamiento m.

bottom /'bɒtəm/ n. fondo m.

boudoir /'budwɑr/ n. tocador m.

bough /bau/ n. rama f.

boulder /'bouldər/ n. canto rodado.

boulevard /'bulə,vɑrd/ n. bulevar m.

bounce /bauns/ n. **1.** brinco m. —v. **2.** brincar; hacer saltar.

bound /baund/ n. **1.** salto m. —v. **2.** limitar.

boundary /'baundəri/ n. límite, lindero m.

bouquet /bou'kei. bu-/ n. ramillete de flores.

bourgeois /bur'ʒwɑ/ a. & n. burgués -esa.

bout /baut/ n. encuentro; combate m.

bow /n bau, bou; v bau/ n. **1.** saludo m.; (of ship) proa f.; (archery) arco m.; (ribbon) lazo m. —v. **2.** saludar, inclinar.

bowels /'bauəlz/ n. intestinos m.pl.; entrañas f.pl.

bowl /boul/ n. **1.** vasija f.; platón m. —v. **2.** jugar a los bolos. **b. over,** derribar.

bowlegged /'bou,legɪd/ a. perniabierto.

bowling /'boulɪŋ/ n. bolos m.pl.

bow tie /bou/ pajarita f.

box /bɒks/ n. **1.** caja f.; Theat. palco m. —v. **2.** (sports) boxear.

boxcar /'bɒks,kɑr/ n. vagón m.

boxer /'bɒksər/ n. boxeador -ra, pugilista m. & f.

boxing /'bɒksɪŋ/ n. boxeo m.

box office n. taquilla f.

boy /bɔi/ n. muchacho, chico, niño m.

boycott /'bɔikɒt/ n. **1.** boicoteo m. —v. **2.** boicotear.

boyhood /'bɔihud/ n. muchachez f.

boyish /'bɔiɪʃ/ a. pueril.

boyishly /'bɔiɪʃli/ adv. puerilmente.

bra /brɑ/ n. sujetador, sostén m.

brace /breis/ n. **1.** grapón m.; pl. tirantes m.pl. —v. **2.** reforzar.

bracelet /'breislɪt/ n. brazalete m., pulsera f.

bracket /'brækɪt/ n. ménsula f.

brag /bræg/ v. jactarse.

braggart /'brægərt/ a. **1.** jactancioso. —n. **2.** jaque m.

braid /breid/ n. **1.** trenza f. —v. **2.** trenzar.

brain /brein/ n. cerebro, seso m.

brainy /'breini/ a. sesudo, inteligente.

brake /breik/ n. **1.** freno m. —v. **2.** frenar.

bran /bræn/ n. salvado m.

branch /bræntʃ, brɑntʃ/ n. ramo m.; (of tree) rama f.

brand /brænd/ n. marca f.

brandish /'brændɪʃ/ v. blandir.

brand-new /'bræn'nu/ a. enteramente nuevo.

brandy /'brændi/ n. aguardiente, coñac m.

brash /bræʃ/ a. impetuoso.

brass /bræs/ n. bronce, latón m.

brassiere /brə'zɪər/ n. corpiño, sujetador, sostén m.

brat /bræt/ n. mocoso m.

bravado /brə'vɑdou/ n. bravata f.

brave /breiv/ a. valiente.

bravery /'breivəri/ n. valor m.

brawl /brɔl/ n. alboroto m. v. alborotar.

brawn /brɔn/ n. músculo m.

bray /brei/ v. rebuznar.

brazen /'breizən/ a. desvergonzado.

Brazil /brə'zɪl/ n. Brasil m.

Brazilian /brə'zɪlyən/ a. & n. brasileño -ña.

breach /britʃ/ n. rotura; infracción f.

breach of contract incumplimiento de contrato m.

bread /bred/ n. pan m.

breadth /brɛdθ/ n. anchura f.

break /breik/ n. **1.** rotura; pausa f. —v. **2.** quebrar, romper.

breakable /'breikəbəl/ a. rompible, frágil.

breakage /'breikidʒ/ n. rotura f., destrozo m.

breakfast /'brɛkfəst/ n. **1.** desayuno, almuerzo m. —v. **2.** desayunar, almorzar.

breakneck /'breik,nɛk/ a. rápido, precipitado, atropellado.

breast /brɛst/ n. (of human) pecho, seno m.; (of fowl) pechuga f.

breastbone /'brɛst,boun/ n. esternón m.

breath /brɛθ/ n. aliento; soplo m.

breathe /brið/ v. respirar.

breathless /'brɛθlɪs/ a. desalentado.

breathlessly /'brɛθlɪsli/ adv. jadeante-mente, intensamente.

bred /brɛd/ a. criado; educado.

breeches /'brɪtʃɪz/ n.pl. calzones, pantalones, m.pl.

breed /brid/ n. **1.** raza f. —v. **2.** engendrar; criar.

breeder /'bridər/ n. criador -ra.

breeding /'bridɪŋ/ n. cría f.

breeze /briz/ n. brisa f.

breezy /'brizi/ a.: **it is b.,** hace brisa.

brevity /'brɛvɪti/ n. brevedad f.

brew /bru/ v. fraguar; elaborar.

brewer /'bruər/ n. cervecero m.

brewery /'bruəri/ n. cervecería f.

bribe /braib/ n. **1.** soborno, cohecho m. —v. **2.** sobornar, cohechar.

briber /'braibər/ n. sobornador -ra.

bribery /'braibəri/ n. soborno, cohecho m.

brick /brɪk/ n. ladrillo m.

bricklayer /'brɪk,leiər/ n. albañil m.

bridal /'braidl/ a. nupcial.

bride /braid/ n. novia f.

bridegroom /'braid,grum/ n. novio m.

bridesmaid /'braidz,meid/ n. madrina de boda.

bridge /brɪdʒ/ n. puente m.

bridged /brɪdʒd/ a. conectado.

bridgehead /'brɪdʒ,hɛd/ n. Mil. cabeza de puente.

bridle /'braidl/ n. brida f.

brief /brif/ a. breve.

briefcase /'brif,keis/ n. maletín m.

briefly /'brifli/ adv. brevemente.

briefness /'brifnɪs/ n. brevedad f.

brier /'braiər/ n. zarza f.

brig /brɪg/ n. bergantín m.

brigade /brɪ'geid/ n. brigada f.

bright /brait/ a. claro, brillante.

brighten /'braitn/ v. abrillantar; alegrar.

brightness /'braitnɪs/ n. resplandor m.

brilliance /'brɪlyəns/ n. brillantez f.

brilliant /'brɪlyənt/ a. brillante.

brim /brɪm/ n. borde m.; (of hat) ala f.

brine /brain/ n. escabeche, m. salmuera f.

bring /brɪŋ/ v. traer. **b. about,** efectuar, llevar a cabo.

brink /brɪŋk/ n. borde m.

briny /'braini/ a. salado.

brisk /brɪsk/ a. vivo; enérgico.

briskly /'brɪskli/ adv. vivamente.

briskness /'brɪsknɪs/ n. viveza f.

bristle /'brɪsəl/ n. cerda f.

bristly /'brɪsli/ a. hirsuto.

Britain /'brɪtn/ n. **Great B.,** Gran Bretaña f.

British /'brɪtɪʃ/ a. británico.

British Empire imperio británico m.

British Isles /ailz/ islas británicas f.

Briton /'brɪtn/ n. inglés m.

brittle /'brɪtl/ a. quebradizo, frágil.

broad /brɔd/ a. ancho.

broadcast /'brɔd,kæst/ n. **1.** radiodifusión f. —v. **2.** radiodifundir.

broadcaster /'brɔd,kæstər/ n. locutor -ra.

broadcloth /'brɔd,klɔθ/ n. paño fino.

broaden /'brɔdn/ v. ensanchar.

broadly /'brɔdli/ adv. ampliamente.

broadminded /'brɔd'maindɪd/ a. tolerante, liberal.

brocade /brou'keid/ n. brocado m.

brocaded /brou'keidɪd/ a. espolinado.

broccoli /'brɔkəli/ n. brécol m.

broil /brɔil/ v. asar.

broiler /'brɔilər/ n. parrilla f.

broken /'broukən/ a. roto, quebrado.

broken-hearted /'broukən'hɑrtɪd/ a. angustiado.

broker /'broukər/ n. corredor -ra, bolsista m. & f.

brokerage /'broukərɪdʒ/ n. corretaje m.

bronchial /'brɔŋkiəl/ a. bronquial.

bronchitis /brɔŋ'kaitɪs/ n. bronquitis f.

bronze /brɔnz/ n. bronce m.

brooch /broutʃ/ n. broche m.

brood /brud/ n. **1.** cría, progenie f. —v. **2.** empollar; cobijar.

brook /bruk/ n. arroyo m., quebrada f.

broom /brum/ n. escoba f.

broomstick /'brum,stɪk/ n. palo de escoba.

broth /brɔθ/ n. caldo m.

brothel /'brɔθəl/ n. burdel m.

brother /'brʌðər/ n. hermano m.

brotherhood /'brʌðər,hud/ n. fraternidad f.

brother-in-law /'brʌðər in ,lɔ/ n. cuñado m.

brotherly /'brʌðərli/ a. fraternal.

brow /brau/ n. ceja; frente f.

brown /braun/ a. pardo, moreno; marrón. v. rehogar.

brown sugar azúcar moreno m.

browse /brauz/ v. curiosear; ramonear.

browser /'brauzər/ n. (Internet) nagegador m., visualizador m., visor m.

bruise /bruz/ n. **1.** contusión f. —v. **2.** magullar.

brunette /bru'nɛt/ a. & n. moreno -na. trigueño -ña.

brush /brʌʃ/ n. **1.** cepillo m.; brocha f. —v. **2.** cepillar.

brushwood /'brʌʃ,wud/ n. matorral m.

brusque /brʌsk/ a. brusco.

brusquely /'brʌskli/ adv. bruscamente.

brutal /'brutḷ/ a. brutal.

brutality /bru'tælɪti/ n. brutalidad f.

brutalize /'brutḷ,aiz/ v. embrutecer.

brute /brut/ n. bruto -ta, bestia f.

bubble /'bʌbəl/ n. ampolla f.

bucket /'bʌkɪt/ n. cubo m.

buckle /'bʌkəl/ n. hebilla f.

buckram /'bʌkrəm/ n. bucarán m.

bucksaw /'bʌk'sɔ/ n. sierra de bastidor.

buckshot /'bʌk,ʃɒt/ n. posta f.

buckwheat /'bʌk,wit/ n. trigo sarraceno.

bud /bʌd/ n. **1.** brote m. —v. **2.** brotar.

budding /'bʌdɪŋ/ a. en capullo.

budge /bʌdʒ/ v. moverse.

budget /'bʌdʒɪt/ n. presupuesto m.

buffalo /'bʌfə,lou/ n. búfalo m.

buffer /'bʌfər/ n. parachoques m.

buffet /bə'fei/ n. bufet m.; (furniture) aparador m.

buffoon /bə'fun/ n. bufón m.

bug /bʌg/ n. insecto m.; (computer) error m.

bugle /'byugəl/ n. clarín m.; corneta f.

build /bild/ v. construir.

builder /'bildər/ n. constructor -ra.

building /'bildɪŋ/ n. edificio m.

bulb /bʌlb/ n. bulbo m.; (of lamp) bombilla, ampolla f.

bulge /bʌldʒ/ n. abultamiento m. v. abultar.

bulging /'bʌldʒɪŋ/ a. protuberante.

bulimia /bu'limiə/ n. bulimia f.

bulk /bʌlk/ n. masa f.; grueso m.; mayoría f.

bulkhead /'bʌlk,hed/ n. frontón m.

bulky /'bʌlki/ a. grueso, abultado.

bull /bul/ n. toro m.

bulldog /'bul,dɔg/ n. perro de presa.

bullet /'bulɪt/ n. bala f.

bulletin /'bulɪtn/ n. boletín m.

bulletproof /'bulɪt,pruf/ a. a prueba de bala.

bullfight /'bul,fait/ n. corrida de toros.

bullfighter /'bul,faitər/ n. torero -ra.

bullfinch /'bul,fɪntʃ/ n. pinzón real m.

bully /'buli/ n. **1.** rufián m. —v. **2.** bravear.

bulwark /'bulwərk/ n. baluarte m.

bum /bʌm/ n. holgazán m.

bump /bʌmp/ n. **1.** golpe, choque m. —v. **2. b. into,** chocar contra.

bumper /'bʌmpər/ n. parachoques m.

bun /bʌn/ n. bollo m.

bunch /bʌntʃ/ n. racimo; montón m.

bundle /'bʌndḷ/ n. **1.** bulto m. —v. **2. b. up,** abrigar.

bungalow /'bʌngə,lou/ n. casa de un solo piso.

bungle /'bʌngəl/ v. estropear.

bunion /'bʌnyən/ n. juanete m.

bunk /bʌŋk/ n. litera f.

bunny /'bʌni/ n. conejito -ta.

bunting /'bʌntɪŋ/ n. lanilla; banderas f.

buoy /'bui/ n. boya f.

buoyant /'bɔiənt/ a. boyante; vivaz.

burden /'bɔrdṇ/ n. **1.** carga f. —v. **2.** cargar.

burdensome /'bɔrdṇsəm/ a. gravoso.

bureau /'byurou/ n. (furniture) cómoda f.; departamento m.

burglar /'bɔrglər/ n. ladrón -ona.

burglarize /'bɔrglə,raiz/ v. robar.

burglary /'bɔrgləri/ n. robo m.

burial /'beriəl/ n. entierro m.

burlap /'bɔrlæp/ n. arpillera f.

burly /'bɔrli/ a. corpulento.

burn /bɔrn/ v. quemar; arder.

burner /'bɔrnər/ n. mechero m.

burning /'bɔrnɪŋ/ a. ardiente.

burnish /'bɔrnɪʃ/ v. pulir; acicalar.

burrow /'bɔrou/ v. minar; horadar.

burst /bɔrst/ v. reventar.

bury /'beri/ v. enterrar.

bus /bʌs/ n. autobús m.

bush /buʃ/ n. arbusto m.

bushy /'buʃi/ a. matoso; peludo.

business /'bɪznɪs/ n. negocios m.pl.; comercio m.

businesslike /'bɪznɪs,laik/ a. directo, práctico.

businessman /'bɪznɪs,mæn/ n. hombre de negocios, comerciante m.

businesswoman /'bɪznɪs,wumən/ n. mujer de negocios.

bust /bʌst/ n. busto; pecho m.

bustle /'bʌsəl/ n. bullicio m.; animación f.

busy /'bɪzi/ a. ocupado, atareado.

busybody /'bɪzi,bɒdi/ n. entremetido -da.

but /bʌt/ conj. pero; sino.

butcher /'butʃər/ n. carnicero -ra.

butchery /'butʃəri/ n. carnicería; matanza f.

butler /'bʌtlər/ n. mayordomo m.

butt /bʌt/ n. punta f.; cabo extremo m.

butter /'bʌtər/ n. manteca, mantequilla f.

buttercup /'bʌtər,kʌp/ n. ranúnculo m.

butterfat /'bʌtər,fæt/ n. mantequilla f.

butterfly /'bʌtər,flai/ n. mariposa f.

buttermilk /'bʌtər,mɪlk/ n. suero (de leche) m.

button /'bʌtṇ/ n. botón m.

buttonhole /'bʌtṇ,houl/ n. ojal m.

buttress /'bʌtrɪs/ n. sostén; refuerzo m.

buxom /'bʌksəm/ a. regordete.

buy /bai/ v. comprar.

buyer /'baiər/ n. comprador -ra.

buzz /bʌz/ n. **1.** zumbido m. —v. **2.** zumbar.

buzzard /'bʌzərd/ n. gallinazo m.

buzzer /'bʌzər/ n. zumbador m.; timbre m.

buzz saw n. sierra circular f.

by /bai/ prep. por; (near) cerca de, al lado de; (time) para.

by-and-by /,baiən'bai/ adv. pronto; luego.

bygone /'bai,gɔn/ a. pasado.

bylaw /'bai,lɔ/ n. estatuto, reglamento m.

bypass /'bai,pæs/ n. desvío m.

byproduct /'bai,prɒdəkt/ n. subproducto m.

bystander /'bai,stændər/ n. espectador -ra; mirón -na.

byte /bait/ n. en teoría de la información: ocho bits, byte m.

byway /'bai,wei/ n. camino desviado m.

C

cab /kæb/ n. taxi, coche de alquiler m.

cabaret /,kæbə'rei/ n. cabaret m.

cabbage /'kæbidʒ/ n. repollo m.

cabin /'kæbɪn/ n. cabaña f.

cabinet /'kæbənɪt/ n. gabinete; ministerio m.

cabinetmaker /'kæbənɪt,meikər/ n. ebanista m.

cable /'keibəl/ n. cable m.

cablegram /'keibəl,græm/ n. cablegrama m.

cache /kæʃ/ n. escondite m.

cackle /'kækəl/ n. charla f.; cacareo m. v. cacarear.

cacophony /kə'kɒfəni/ n. cacofonía f.

cactus /'kæktəs/ n. cacto m.

cad /kæd/ n. persona vil.

cadaver /kə'dævər/ n. cadáver m.

cadaverous /kə'dævərəs/ a. cadavérico.

caddie /'kædi/ n. (golf) ayudante m. & f.

cadence /'keidns/ n. cadencia f.

cadet /kə'dɛt/ n. cadete m.

cadmium /'kædmiəm/ n. cadmio m.

cadre /'kædri, 'kɑdrei/ n. núcleo; Mil. cuadro m.

café /kæ'fei/ n. café m., cantina f.

cafeteria /,kæfɪ'tɪəriə/ n. cafetería f.

caffeine /kæ'fin/ n. cafeína f.

cage /keidʒ/ n. jaula f. v. enjaular.

caged /keidʒd/ a. enjaulado.

caisson /'keisɒn, -sən/ n. arcón m.; Mil. furgón m.

cajole /kə'dʒoul/ v. lisonjear; adular.

cake /keik/ n. torta f.; bizcocho m.

calamitous /kə'læmɪtəs/ a. calamitoso.

calamity /kə'læmɪti/ n. calamidad f.

calcify /'kælsə,fai/ v. calcificar.

calcium /'kælsiəm/ n. calcio m.

calculable /'kælkyələbəl/ a. calculable.

calculate /'kælkyə,leit/ v. calcular.

calculating /'kælkyə,leitɪŋ/ a. interesado.

calculation /,kælkyə'leiʃən/ n. calculación f.; cálculo m.

calculus /'kælkyələs/ n. cálculo m.

caldron /'kɔldrən/ n. caldera f.

calendar /'kæləndər/ n. calendario m.

calf /kæf/ n. ternero m. (animal); pantorrilla f. (of the body).

calfskin /'kæf,skɪn/ n. piel de becerro.

caliber /'kælɪbər/ n. calibre m.

calico /'kæli,kou/ n. calicó m.

caliper /'kæləpər/ n. calibrador m.

calisthenics /,kæləs'θɛnɪks/ n. calistenia, gimnasia f.

calk /kɔk/ v. calafatear; rellenar.

calker /'kɔkər/ n. calafate -ta.

call /kɔl/ n. **1.** llamada f. —v. **2.** llamar.

calligraphy /kə'lɪgrəfi/ n. caligrafía f.

calling /'kɔlɪŋ/ n. vocación f.

calling card tarjeta de visita f.

callously /'kæləsli/ adv. insensiblemente.

callow /'kælou/ a. sin experiencia.

callus /'kæləs/ n. callo m.

calm /kɑm/ a. **1.** tranquilo, calmado. —n. **2.** calma f. —v. **3.** calmar.

calmly /'kɑmli/ adv. serenamente.

calmness /'kɑmnɪs/ n. calma f.

caloric /kə'lɔrɪk/ a. calórico.

calorie /'kæləri/ n. caloría f.

calorimeter /,kælə'rɪmɪtər/ n. calorímetro m.

calumniate /kə'lʌmni,eit/ v. calumniar.

calumny /'kæləmni/ n. calumnia f.

Calvary /'kælvəri/ n. Calvario m.

calve /kæv/ v. parir (la vaca).

calyx /'keilɪks/ n. cáliz m.

camaraderie /,kɑmə'rɑdəri/ n. compañerismo m., compadrería f.

cambric /'keimbrɪk/ n. batista f.

camcorder /'kæm,kɔrdər/ n. videocámara f.

camel /'kæməl/ n. camello -lla.

camellia /kə'milyə/ n. camelia f.

camel's hair /'kæməlz/ pelo de camello.

cameo /'kæmi,ou/ n. camafeo m.

camera /'kæmərə/ n. cámara f.

camouflage /'kæmə,flɑʒ/ n. camuflaje m.

camouflaging /'kæmə,flɑʒɪŋ/ n. simulacro, disfraz m.

camp /kæmp/ n. **1.** campamento m. —v. **2.** acampar.

campaign /kæm'pein/ n. campaña f.
camper /'kæmpər/ n. acampado m.
campfire /'kæmp,faiər/ n. fogata de campamento.
camphor /'kæmfər/ n. alcanfor m.
camphor ball bola de alcanfor.
campus /'kæmpəs/ n. campo de colegio (o universidad), campus m.
can /kæn/ v. (be able) poder.
can /kæn/ n. 1. lata f. —v. 2. conservar en latas, enlatar.
Canada /'kænədə/ n. Canadá m.
Canadian /kə'neidiən/ a. & n. canadiense.
canal /kə'næl/ n. canal m.
canalize /'kænl,aiz/ v. canalizar.
canard /kə'nard/ n. embuste m.
canary /kə'nɛəri/ n. canario -ria.
cancel /'kænsəl/ v. cancelar.
cancellation /,kænsə'leiʃən/ n. cancelación f.
cancer /'kænsər/ n. cáncer m.
candelabrum /,kændl'abrəm/ n. candelabro m.
candid /'kændɪd/ a. cándido, sincero.
candidacy /'kændɪdəsi/ n candidatura f.
candidate /'kændɪ,deit/ n. candidato -ta.
candidly /'kændɪdli/ adv. cándidamente.
candidness /'kændɪdnɪs/ n. candidez; sinceridad f.
candied /'kændid/ a. garapiñado.
candle /'kændl/ n. vela f.
candlestick /'kændl,stɪk/ n. candelero m.
candor /'kændər/ n. candor m.; sinceridad f.
candy /'kændi/ n. dulces m.pl.
cane /kein/ n. caña f.; (for walking) bastón m.
canine /'keinain/ a. canino.
canister /'kænəstər/ n. frasco m.; lata f.
canker /'kæŋkər/ n. llaga; úlcera f.
cankerworm /'kæŋkər,wɜrm/ n. oruga f.
canned /kænd/ a. envasado, enlatado.
canner /'kænər/ n. envasador m.
cannery /'kænəri/ n. fábrica de conservas alimenticias f.
cannibal /'kænəbəl/ n. caníbal m. & f.
cannon /'kænən/ n. cañón m.
cannonade /,kænə'neid/ n. cañoneo m.
cannoneer /,kænə'nɪər/ n. cañonero -ra.
canny /'kæni/ a. sagaz; prudente.
canoe /kə'nu/ n. canoa, piragua f.
canoeing /kə'nuɪŋ/ n. piragüismo m.
canoeist /kə'nuɪst/ n. piragüista m. & f.
canon /'kænən/ n. canon m.; Relig. canónigo m.
canonical /kə'nɒnɪkəl/ a. canónico.
canonize /'kænə,naiz/ v. canonizar.
can opener /'oupənər/ abrelatas m.
canopy /'kænəpi/ n. dosel m.
cant /kænt/ n. hipocresía f.

cantaloupe /'kæntl,oup/ n. melón m.
canteen /kæn'tin/ n. cantina f.
canter /'kæntər/ n. 1. medio galope m. —v. 2. galopar.
cantonment /kæn'tɒnmənt/ n. Mil. acuartelamiento m.
canvas /'kænvəs/ n. lona f.
canyon /'kænyən/ n. cañón, desfiladero m.
cap /kæp/ n. 1. tapa f.; (headwear) gorro m. —v. 2. tapar.
capability /,keipə'bılıti/ n. capacidad f.
capable /'keipəbəl/ a. capaz.
capably /'keipəbli/ adv. hábilmente.
capacious /kə'peiʃəs/ a. espacioso.
capacity /kə'pæsiti/ n. capacidad f.
cape /keip/ n. capa f., Geog. cabo m.
caper /'keipər/ n. zapateta f.; Bot. alcaparra f.
capillary /'kæpə,lɛri/ a. capilar.
capital /'kæpɪtl/ n. capital m.; Govt. capital f.
capitalism /'kæpɪtl,ızəm/ n capitalismo m.
capitalist /'kæpɪtlɪst/ n. capitalista m. & f.
capitalistic /,kæpɪtl'ıstık/ a. capitalista.
capitalization /,kæpɪtlə'zeiʃən/ n. capitalización f.
capitalize /'kæpɪtl,aiz/ v. capitalizar.
capital letter n. mayúscula f.
capitulate /kə'pɪtʃə,leit/ v. capitular.
capon /'keipɒn/ n. capón m.
caprice /kə'pris/ n. capricho m.
capricious /kə'prɪʃəs/ a. caprichoso.
capriciously /kə'prɪʃəsli/ adv. caprichosamente.
capriciousness /kə'prɪʃəsnɪs/ n. capricho m.
capsize /'kæpsaiz/ v. zozobrar, volcar.
capsule /'kæpsəl/ n. cápsula f.
captain /'kæptən/ n. capitán m.
caption /'kæpʃən/ n. título m.; (motion pictures) subtítulo m.
captious /'kæpʃəs/ a. capcioso.
captivate /'kæptə,veit/ v. cautivar.
captivating /'kæptə,veitɪŋ/ a. encantador.
captive /'kæptɪv/ n. cautivo -va, prisionero -ra.
captivity /kæp'tɪvɪti/ n. cautividad f.
captor /'kæptər/ n. apresador -ra.
capture /'kæptʃər/ n. 1. captura f. —v. 2. capturar.
car /kar/ n. coche, carro m.; (of train) vagón, coche m. baggage c., vagón de equipajes. parlor c., coche salón.
carafe /kə'ræf/ n. garrafa f.
caramel /'kærəməl/ n. caramelo m.
carat /'kærət/ n. quilate m.
caravan /'kærə,væn/ n. caravana f.
caraway /'kærə,wei/ n. alcaravea f.
carbide /'karbaid/ n. carburo m.
carbine /'karbin/ n. carabina f.

carbohydrate /ˌkɑrbouˈhaidreit/ n. hidrato de carbono.

carbon /ˈkɑrbən/ n. carbón m.

carbon dioxide /daiˈɒksaid/ anhídrido carbónico.

carbon monoxide /mɒnˈɒksaid/ monóxido de carbono.

carbon paper papel carbón m.

carbuncle /ˈkɑrbʌŋkəl/ n. carbúnculo m.

carburetor /ˈkɑrbəˌreitər/ n. carburador m.

carcinogenic /ˌkɑrsənəˈdʒɛnɪk/ a. carcinogénico.

card /kɑrd/ n. tarjeta f. **playing c.,** naipe m.

cardboard /ˈkɑrdˌbɔrd/ n. cartón m.

cardiac /ˈkɑrdiˌæk/ a. cardíaco.

cardigan /ˈkɑrdɪgən/ n. chaqueta de punto.

cardinal /ˈkɑrdnl/ a. **1.** cardinal. —n. **2.** cardenal m.

cardiologist /ˌkɑrdiˈɒlədʒɪst/ n. cardiólogo, -ga m. & f.

care /kɛər/ n. **1.** cuidado. —v. **2. c. for,** cuidar.

careen /kəˈrin/ v. carenar; echarse de costado.

career /kəˈrɪər/ n. carrera f.

carefree /ˈkɛərˌfri/ a. descuidado.

careful /ˈkɛərfəl/ a. cuidadoso. **be. c.,** tener cuidado.

carefully /ˈkɛərfəli/ adv. cuidadosamente.

carefulness /ˈkɛərfəlnɪs/ n. esmero; cuidado m.; cautela f.

careless /ˈkɛərlɪs/ a. descuidado.

carelessly /ˈkɛərlɪsli/ adv. descuidadamente; negligentemente.

carelessness /ˈkɛərlɪsnɪs/ n. descuido m.

caress /kəˈrɛs/ n. **1.** caricia f —v. **2.** acariciar.

caretaker /ˈkɛərˌteikər/ n. guardián -ana.

cargo /ˈkɑrgou/ n. carga f.

caricature /ˈkærɪkətʃər/ n. caricatura f.

caricaturist /ˈkærɪkəˌtʃʊrɪst/ n. caricaturista m. & f.

caries /ˈkɛəriz/ n. caries f.

carjacking /ˈkɑrˌdʒækɪŋ/ n. robo de coche m.

carload /ˈkɑrˌloud/ n. furgonada, vagonada.

carnal /ˈkɑrnl/ a. carnal.

carnation /kɑrˈneiʃən/ n. clavel m.

carnival /ˈkɑrnəvəl/ n. carnaval m.

carnivorous /kɑrˈnɪvərəs/ a. carnívoro.

carol /ˈkærəl/ n. villancico m.

carouse /kəˈrauz/ v. parrandear.

carpenter /ˈkɑrpəntər/ n. carpintero -ra.

carpet /ˈkɑrpɪt/ n. alfombra f.

carpeting /ˈkɑrpɪtɪŋ/ n. alfombrado m.

car pool /ˈkɑrˌpul/ uso habitual, por varias personas, de un automóvil perteneciente a una de ellas.

carriage /ˈkærɪdʒ/ n. carruaje; (bearing) porte m.

carrier /ˈkæriər/ n. portador -ra.

carrier pigeon paloma mensajera.

carrot /ˈkærət/ n. zanahoria f.

carrousel /ˌkærəˈsɛl/ n. volantín, carrusel m.

carry /ˈkæri/ v. llevar, cargar. **c. out,** cumplir, llevar a cabo.

cart /kɑrt/ n. carreta f.

cartage /ˈkɑrtɪdʒ/ n. acarreo, carretaje m.

cartel /kɑrˈtɛl/ n. cartel m.

cartilage /ˈkɑrtlɪdʒ/ n. cartílago m.

carton /ˈkɑrtn/ n. caja de cartón m.

cartoon /kɑrˈtun/ n. caricatura f.

cartoonist /kɑrˈtunɪst/ n. caricaturista m. & f.

cartridge /ˈkɑrtrɪdʒ/ n. cartucho m.

carve /kɑrv/ v. esculpir; (meat) trinchar.

carver /ˈkɑrvər/ n tallador -ra; grabador -ra.

carving /ˈkɑrvɪŋ/ n. entalladura f.; arte de trinchar. **c. knife,** trinchante m.

cascade /kæsˈkeid/ n. cascada f.

case /keis/ n. caso m.; (box) caja f. **in any c.,** sea como sea.

cash /kæʃ/ n. **1.** dinero contante. —v. **2.** efectuar, cambiar.

cashier /kæˈʃɪər/ n. cajero -ra.

cashmere /ˈkæʒmɪər/ n. casimir m.

casino /kəˈsinou/ n. casino m.

cask /kæsk/ n. barril m.

casket /ˈkæskɪt/ n. ataúd m.

casserole /ˈkæsəˌroul/ n. cacerola f.

cassette /kəˈsɛt/ n. cassette m., cartucho m.

cast /kæst/ n. **1.** Theat. reparto de papeles. —v. **2.** echar; Theat. repartir.

castanet /ˌkæstəˈnɛt/ n. castañuela f.

castaway /ˈkæstəˌwei/ n. náufrago -ga.

caste /kæst/ n. casta f.

caster /ˈkæstər/ n. tirador m.

castigate /ˈkæstɪˌgeit/ v. castigar.

Castilian /kæˈstɪlyən/ a. castellano.

cast iron n. hierro colado m.

castle /ˈkæsəl/ n. castillo m.

castoff /ˈkæstˌɔf/ a. descartado.

casual /ˈkæʒuəl/ a. casual.

casually /ˈkæʒuəli/ adv. casualmente.

casualness /ˈkæʒuəlnɪs/ n. casualidad f.

casualty /ˈkæʒuəlti/ n. víctima f.; Mil. baja f.

cat /kæt/ n. gato -ta.

cataclysm /ˈkætəˌklɪzəm/ n. cataclismo m.

catacomb /ˈkætəˌkoum/ n. catacumba f.

catalogue /ˈkætlˌɔg/ n. catálogo m.

catapult /ˈkætəˌpʌlt/ n. catapulta f.

cataract /ˈkætəˌrækt/ n. catarata f.

catarrh /kəˈtɑr/ n. catarro m.

catastrophe /kəˈtæstrəfi/ n. catástrofe f.

catch /kætʃ/ v. alcanzar, atrapar, coger.

catchy /ˈkætʃi/ a. contagioso.

catechism /'kætɪ,kɪzəm/ n. catequismo m.

catechize /'kætɪ,kaɪz/ v. catequizar.

categorical /,kætɪ'gɔrɪkəl/ a. categórico.

category /'kætɪ,gɔri/ n. categoría f.

cater /'keɪtər/ v. abastecer; proveer. **c. to,** complacer.

caterpillar /'kætə,pɪlər/ n. gusano m.

catgut /'kæt,gʌt/ n. cuerda (de tripa).

catharsis /kə'θɑrsɪs/ n. catarsis, purga f.

cathartic /kə'θɑrtɪk/ a. **1.** catártico; purgante. —n. **2.** purgante m.

cathedral /kə'θidrəl/ n. catedral f

cathode /'kæθoʊd/ n. cátodo m.

Catholic /'kæθəlɪk/ a. católico & n. católico -ca.

Catholicism /kə'θɒlə,sɪzəm/ n. catolicismo m.

catnap /'kæt,næp/ n. siesta corta.

catsup /'kætsəp, 'ketʃəp/ n. salsa de tomate.

cattle /'kætl/ n. ganado m.

cattleman /'kætlmən, -,mæn/ n. ganadero m.

cauliflower /'kɔlə,flaʊər/ n. coliflor m.

causation /kɔ'zeɪʃən/ n. causalidad f.

cause /kɔz/ n. causa f.

causeway /'kɔz,weɪ/ n. calzada elevada f., terraplén m.

caustic /'kɔstɪk/ a. cáustico.

cauterize /'kɔtə,raɪz/ v. cauterizar.

cautery /'kɔtəri/ n. cauterio m.

caution /'kɔʃən/ n. cautela f.

cautious /'kɔʃəs/ a. cauteloso.

cavalcade /,kævəl'keɪd/ n. cabalgata f.

cavalier /,kævə'lɪər/ n. caballero m.

cavalry /'kævəlri/ n. caballería f.

cave /keɪv/ **cavern** n. caverna, gruta f.

cave-in /'keɪv ,ɪn/ n. hundimiento m.

caviar /'kævi,ɑr/ n. caviar m.

cavity /'kævɪti/ n. hueco m.

cayman /'keɪmən/ n. caimán m.

CD player tocadiscos compacto, tocadiscos digital m.

cease /sis/ v. cesar.

ceaseless /'sislɪs/ a. incesante.

cedar /'sidər/ n. cedro m.

cede /sid/ v. ceder.

ceiling /'silɪŋ/ n. techo; cielo m.

celebrant /'sɛləbrənt/ n. celebrante -ta.

celebrate /'sɛlə,breɪt/ v. celebrar.

celebration /,sɛlə'breɪʃən/ n. celebración f.

celebrity /sə'lɛbrɪti/ n. celebridad.

celerity /sə'lɛrɪti/ n. celeridad; prontitud f.

celery /'sɛləri/ n. apio m.

celestial /sə'lɛstʃəl/ a. celeste.

celibacy /'sɛləbəsi/ n. celibato -ta.

celibate /'sɛləbɪt/ a. & n. célibe m. & f.

cell /sɛl/ n. celda f.; Biol. célula f.

cellar /'sɛlər/ n. sótano m.

cellist /'tʃɛlɪst/ a. celista m. & f.

cello /'tʃɛloʊ/ n. violonchelo m.

cellophane /'sɛlə,feɪn/ n. celofán m.

cellular /'sɛlyələr/ a. celular.

cellular phone /foʊn/ teléfono móvil m.

celluloid /'sɛlyə,lɔɪd/ n. celuloide m.

cellulose /'sɛlyə,loʊs/ a. **1.** celuloso. —n. **2.** celulosa f.

Celtic /'kɛltɪk, 'sɛl-/ a. céltico.

cement /sɪ'mɛnt/ n. cemento m.

cemetery /'sɛmɪ,tɛri/ n. cementerio m.; campo santo m.

censor /'sɛnsər/ n. censor -ra.

censorious /sɛn'sɔriəs/ a. severo; crítico.

censorship /'sɛnsər,ʃɪp/ n. censura f.

censure /'sɛnʃər/ n. **1.** censura f. —v. **2.** censurar.

census /'sɛnsəs/ n. censo m.

cent /sɛnt/ n. centavo, céntimo m.

centenary /sɛn'tɛnɛri/ a. & n. centenario m.

centennial /sɛn'tɛniəl/ a. & n. centenario m.

center /'sɛntər/ n. centro m.

centerfold /'sɛntər,foʊld/ n. página central desplegable en una revista.

centerpiece /'sɛntər,pis/ n. centro de mesa.

centigrade /'sɛntɪ,greɪd/ a. centígrado.

centigrade thermometer termómetro centígrado.

central /'sɛntrəl/ a. central.

Central American a. & n. centroamericano -na.

centralize /'sɛntrə,laɪz/ v. centralizar.

century /'sɛntʃəri/ n. siglo m.

century plant maguey m.

ceramic /sə'ræmɪk/ a. cerámico.

ceramics /sə'ræmɪks/ n. cerámica f.

cereal /'sɪəriəl/ n. cereal m.

cerebral /sə'ribrəl/ a. cerebral.

ceremonial /,sɛrə'moʊniəl/ a. ceremonial.

ceremonious /,sɛrə'moʊniəs/ a. ceremonioso.

ceremony /'sɛrə,moʊni/ n. ceremonia f.

certain /'sɜrtn/ a. cierto, seguro.

certainly /'sɜrtnli/ adv. sin duda, seguramente.

certainty /'sɜrtnti/ n. certeza f.

certificate /sər'tɪfɪkɪt/ n. certificado m.

certification /,sɜrtəfɪ'keɪʃən, sər,tɪfə-/ n. certificación f.

certified /'sɜrtə,faɪd/ a. certificado.

certify /'sɜrtə,faɪ/ v. certificar.

certitude /'sɜrtɪ,tyud/ n. certeza f.

cessation /sɛ'seɪʃən/ n. cesación, descontinuación f.

cession /'sɛʃən/ n. cesión f.

chafe /tʃeɪf/ v. irritar.

chafing dish /'tʃeɪfɪŋ/ n. escalfador m.

chagrin /ʃə'grɪn/ n. disgusto m.

chain /tʃeɪn/ n. **1.** cadena f. —v. **2.** encadenar.

chair /tʃeər/ n. silla f.

chairman /'tʃeərmən/ n. presidente -ta.

chairperson /'tʃeər,pərsən/ n. presidente -ta; persona que preside.

chalk /tʃɔk/ n. tiza f.

challenge /'tʃælɪndʒ/ n. **1.** desafío m. —v. **2.** desafiar.

challenger /'tʃælɪndʒər/ n. desafiador -ra.

chamber /'tʃeɪmbər/ n. cámara f.

chamberlain /'tʃeɪmbərlɪn/ n. camarero m.

chambermaid /'tʃeɪmbər,meɪd/ n. camarera f.

chameleon /kə'miliən/ n. camaleón m.

chamois /'ʃæmi/ n. gamuza f.

champagne /ʃæm'peɪn/ n. champán m., champaña f.

champion /'tʃæmpiən/ n. **1.** campeón -na —v. **2.** defender.

championship /'tʃæmpiən,ʃɪp/ n. campeonato m.

chance /tʃæns/ n. oportunidad, ocasión f. **by c.,** por casualidad, por acaso. **take a c.,** aventurarse.

chancel /'tʃænsəl/ n. antealtar m.

chancellery /'tʃænsələri/ n. cancillería f.

chancellor /'tʃænsələr/ n. canciller m.

chandelier /,ʃændl'ɪər/ n. araña de luces.

change /tʃeɪndʒ/ n. **1.** cambio; (from a bill) moneda f. —v. **2.** cambiar.

changeability /,tʃeɪndʒə'bɪlɪti/ n. mutabilidad f.

changeable /'tʃeɪndʒəbəl/ a. variable, inconstante.

changer /'tʃeɪndʒər/ n. cambiador -ra.

channel /'tʃænl/ n. **1.** canal m. —v. **2.** encauzar.

Channel Tunnel túnel del Canal de la Mancha m.

chant /tʃænt/ n. **1.** canto llano m. —v. **2.** cantar.

chaos /'keɪɒs/ n. caos m.

chaotic /keɪ'ɒtɪk/ a. caótico.

chap /tʃæp/ n. **1.** Colloq. tipo m. —v. **2.** rajar.

chapel /'tʃæpəl/ n. capilla f.

chaperon /'ʃæpə,roʊn/ n. acompañante -ta de señorita.

chaplain /'tʃæplɪn/ n. capellán m.

chapter /'tʃæptər/ n. capítulo m.

char /tʃɑr/ v. carbonizar.

character /'kærɪktər/ n. carácter m.

characteristic /,kærɪktə'rɪstɪk/ a. **1.** característico. —n. **2.** característica f.

characterization /,kærɪktərə'zeɪʃən/ n. caracterización f.

characterize /'kærɪktə,raɪz/ v. caracterizar.

charcoal /'tʃɑr,koʊl/ n. carbón leña.

charge /tʃɑrdʒ/ n. **1.** acusación f.; ataque m. —v. **2.** cargar; acusar; atacar.

chariot /'tʃæriət/ n. carroza f.

charisma /kə'rɪzmə/ n. carisma m.

charitable /'tʃærɪtəbəl/ a. caritativo.

charitableness /'tʃærɪtəbəlnɪs/ n. caridad f.

charitably /'tʃærɪtəbli/ adv. caritativamente.

charity /'tʃærɪti/ n. caridad f.; (alms) limosna f.

charlatan /'ʃɑrlətn/ n. charlatán -na.

charlatanism /'ʃɑrlətn,ɪzəm/ n. charlatanería f.

charm /tʃɑrm/ n. **1.** encanto m.; (witchcraft) hechizo m. —v. **2.** encantar; hechizar.

charming /'tʃɑrmɪŋ/ a. encantador.

charred /tʃɑrd/ a. carbonizado.

chart /tʃɑrt/ n. tabla, esquema f.

charter /'tʃɑrtər/ n. **1.** carta f. —v. **2.** alquilar.

charter flight vuelo chárter m.

charwoman /'tʃɑr,wʊmən/ n. mujer de la limpieza f.

chase /tʃeɪs/ n. **1.** caza f. —v. **2.** cazar; perseguir.

chaser /'tʃeɪsər/ n. perseguidor -ra.

chasm /'kæzəm/ n. abismo m.

chassis /'tʃæsi/ n. chasis m.

chaste /tʃeɪst/ a. casto.

chasten /'tʃeɪsən/ v. corregir, castigar.

chastise /tʃæs'taɪz/ v. castigar.

chastisement /tʃæs'taɪzmənt/ n. castigo m.

chastity /'tʃæstɪti/ n. castidad, pureza f.

chat /tʃæt/ n. **1.** plática, charla f. —v. **2.** platicar, charlar.

chateau /ʃæ'toʊ/ n. castillo m.

chattels /'tʃætlz/ n.pl. bienes m.

chatter /'tʃætər/ v. **1.** cotorrear; (teeth) rechinar. —n. **2.** cotorreo m.

chatterbox /'tʃætər bɒks/ n. charlador -ra.

chauffeur /'ʃoʊfər/ n. chofer m.

cheap /tʃip/ a. barato.

cheapen /'tʃipən/ v. rebajar, menospreciar.

cheaply /'tʃipli/ adv. barato.

cheapness /'tʃipnɪs/ n. baratura f.

cheat /tʃit/ v. engañar.

cheater /'tʃitər/ n. engañador -ra.

check /tʃɛk/ n. **1.** verificación f.; (bank) cheque m.; (restaurant) cuenta f.; (chess) jaque m. —v. **2.** verificar.

checkers /'tʃɛkərz/ n. juego de damas.

checkmate /'tʃɛk,meɪt/ v. dar mate.

checkout counter /'tʃɛk,aʊt/ caja f.

cheek /tʃik/ n. mejilla f. (of face), desfachatez f. (gall).

cheekbone /'tʃik,boʊn/ n. pómulo m.

cheeky /'tʃiki/ a. fresco, descarado, chulo.

cheer /tʃɪər/ n. **1.** alegría f.; aplauso m. —v. **2.** alegrar; aplaudir.

cheerful /'tʃɪərfəl/ a. alegre.

cheerfully /'tʃɪərfəli/ adv. alegremente.

cheerfulness /'tʃɪərfəlnɪs/ n. alegría f.

cheerless /'tʃɪərlɪs/ a. triste.

cheery /'tʃɪəri/ a. alegre.

cheese /tʃiz/ n. queso m. **cottage c.,** requesón m.

chef /ʃef/ n. cocinero en jefe.

chemical /'kɛmɪkəl/ a. **1.** químico. —n. **2.** reactivo m.

chemically /'kɛmɪkli/ adv. químicamente.

chemist /'kɛmɪst/ n. químico -ca.

chemistry /'kɛməstri/ n. química f.

chemotherapy /ˌkimou'θɛrəpi/ n. quimioterapia f.

chenille /ʃə'nil/ n. felpilla f.

cherish /'tʃerɪʃ/ v. apreciar.

cherry /'tʃeri/ n. cereza f.

cherub /'tʃerəb/ n. querubín m.

chess /tʃes/ n. ajedrez m.

chest /tʃest/ n. arca f.; (physiology) pecho m

chestnut /'tʃes,nʌt/ n. castaña f.

chevron /'ʃevrən/ n. sardineta f.

chew /tʃu/ v. mascar, masticar.

chewer /'tʃuər/ n. mascador -ra.

chic /ʃik/ a. elegante, paquete.

chicanery /ʃɪ'keinəri/ n. trampería f.

chick /tʃɪk/ n. pollito -ta.

chicken /'tʃɪkən/ n. pollo m., gallina f.

chicken-hearted /'tʃɪkən 'hɑrtɪd/ a. cobarde.

chicken pox /pɒks/ viruelas locas, varicela f.

chicle /'tʃɪkəl/ n. chicle m.

chicory /'tʃɪkəri/ n. achicoria f.

chide /tʃaid/ v. regañar, reprender.

chief /tʃif/ a. **1.** principal. —n. **2.** jefe -fa.

chiefly /'tʃifli/ adv. principalmente, mayormente.

chieftain /'tʃiftən/ n. caudillo m.; (Indian c.) cacique m.

chiffon /ʃɪ'fɒn/ n. chifón m., gasa f.

chilblain /'tʃɪlblein/ n. sabañón m.

child /tʃaild/ n. niño -ña; hijo -ja.

childbirth /'tʃaild,bərθ/ n. parto m.

childhood /'tʃaildhud/ n. niñez f.

childish /'tʃaildɪʃ/ a. pueril.

childishness /'tʃaildɪʃnɪs/ n. puerilidad f.

childless /'tʃaildlɪs/ a. sin hijos.

childlike /'tʃaild,laik/ a. infantil.

Chilean /'tʃiliən/ a. & n. chileno -na.

chili /'tʃili/ n. chile, ají m.

chill /tʃil/ n. **1.** frío; escalofrío m. —v. **2.** enfriar.

chilliness /'tʃilinɪs/ n. frialdad f.

chilly /'tʃili/ a. frío; friolento.

chimes /tʃaimz/ n. juego de campanas.

chimney /'tʃɪmni/ n. chimenea f.

chimpanzee /ˌtʃɪmpæn'zi, tʃɪm'pænzi/ n. chimpancé m.

chin /tʃɪn/ n. barba f.

china /'tʃainə/ n. loza f.

chinchilla /tʃɪn'tʃɪlə/ n. chinchilla f.

Chinese /tʃai'niz/ a. & n. chino -na.

chink /tʃɪŋk/ n. grieta f.

chintz /tʃɪnts/ n. zaraza f.

chip /tʃɪp/ n. **1.** astilla f. —v. **2.** astillar.

chiropodist /kɪ'rɒpədɪst/ n. pedicuro -ra.

chiropractor /'kairə,præktər/ n. quiropráctico -ca.

chirp /tʃɜrp/ n. **1.** chirrido m. —v. **2.** chirriar, piar.

chisel /'tʃɪzəl/ n. **1.** cincel m. —v. **2.** cincelar, talar.

chivalrous /'ʃɪvəlrəs/ a. caballeroso.

chivalry /'ʃɪvəlri/ n. caballería f.

chive /tʃaiv/ n. cebollino m.

chloride /'klɔraid/ n. cloruro f.

chlorine /'klɔrin/ n. cloro m.

chloroform /'klɔrə,fɔrm/ n. cloroformo m.

chlorophyll /'klɔrəfɪl/ n. clorofila f.

chock-full /'tʃɒk'ful/ a. repleto, colmado.

chocolate /'tʃɔkəlɪt/ n. chocolate m.

choice /tʃɔis/ a. **1.** selecto, escogido. —n. **2.** selección f.; escogimiento m.

choir /kwaiər/ n. coro m.

choke /tʃouk/ v. sofocar, ahogar.

cholera /'kɒlərə/ n. cólera f.

choleric /'kɒlərɪk/ a. colérico, irascible.

cholesterol /kə'lestə,roul/ n. colesterol m.

choose /tʃuz/ v. elegir, escoger.

chop /tʃɒp/ n. **1.** chuleta, costilla f. —v. **2.** tajar; cortar.

chopper /'tʃɒpər/ n. tajador -ra.

choppy /'tʃɒpi/ a. agitado.

choral /'kɔrəl/ a. coral.

chord /kɔrd/ n. cuerda f.; acorde m.

chore /tʃɔr/ n. tarea f., quehacer m.

choreography /ˌkɔri'ɒgrəfi, ˌkour-/ n. coreografía f.

chorister /'kɔrəstər/ n. corista m.

chorus /'kɔrəs/ n. coro m.

christen /'krɪsən/ v. bautizar.

Christendom /'krɪsəndəm/ n. cristiandad f.

Christian /'krɪstʃən/ a. & n. cristiano -na.

Christianity /ˌkrɪstʃi'ænɪti/ n. cristianismo m.

Christmas /'krɪsməs/ n. Navidad, Pascua f. **Merry C.,** felices Pascuas. **C. Eve,** Nochebuena f.

chromatic /krou'mætɪk/ a. cromático.

chromium /'kroumiəm/ n. cromo m.

chromosome /'kroumə,soum/ n. cromosoma m.

chronic /'krɒnɪk/ a. crónico.

chronicle /'krɒnɪkəl/ n. crónica f.

chronological /ˌkrɒn'ɒdʒɪkəl/ a. cronológico.

chronology /krə'nɒlədʒi/ n. cronología f.

chrysalis /'krɪsəlɪs/ n. crisálida f.

chrysanthemum /krɪ'sænθəməm/ n. crisantemo m.

chubby /'tʃʌbi/ a. regordete, rollizo.

chuck /tʃʌk/ v. (cluck) cloquear; (throw) echar, tirar.

chuckle /'tʃʌkəl/ v. reír entre dientes.

chum /tʃʌm/ n. amigo -ga; compinche m.

chummy /'tʃʌmi/ a. íntimo.

chunk /tʃʌŋk/ n. trozo m.

chunky /'tʃʌŋki/ a. fornido, trabado.

Chunnel /'tʃʌnl/ n. túnel del Canal de la Mancha m.

church /tʃɜrtʃ/ n. iglesia f.

churchman /'tʃɜrtʃmən/ n. eclesiástico m.

churchyard /'tʃɜrtʃ,yard/ n. cementerio m.

churn /tʃɜrn/ n. 1. mantequera f. —v. 2. agitar, revolver.

chute /ʃut/ n. conducto; canal m.

cicada /sɪ'keidə/ n. cigarra, chicharra f.

cider /'saidər/ n. sidra f.

cigar /sɪ'gar/ n. cigarro, puro m.

cigarette /,sɪgə'ret/ n. cigarrillo, cigarro, pitillo m. c. case, cigarrillera f. c. lighter, encendedor m.

cinchona /sɪŋ'kounə/ n. cinchona f.

cinder /'sɪndər/ n. ceniza f.

cinema /'sɪnəmə/ n. cine m.

cinnamon /'sɪnəmən/ n. canela f.

cipher /'saifər/ n. cifra f.

circle /'sɜrkəl/ n. círculo m.

circuit /'sɜrkɪt/ n. circuito m.

circuitous /sər'kyuɪtəs/ a. tortuoso.

circuitously /sər'kyuɪtəsli/ adv. tortuosamente.

circular /'sɜrkyələr/ a. circular, redondo.

circularize /'sɜrkyələ,raiz/ v. hacer circular.

circulate /'sɜrkyə,leit/ v. circular.

circulation /,sɜrkyə'leiʃən/ n. circulación f.

circulator /'sɜrkyə,leitər/ n. diseminador, -ra.

circulatory /'sɜrkyələ,tɔri/ a. circulatorio.

circumcise /'sɜrkəm,saiz/ v. circuncidar.

circumcision /,sɜrkəm'sɪʒən/ n. circuncisión f.

circumference /sər'kʌmfərəns/ n. circunferencia f.

circumlocution /,sɜrkəmlou'kyuʃən/ n. circunlocución f.

circumscribe /'sɜrkəm,skraib/ v. circunscribir; limitar.

circumspect /'sɜrkəm,spekt/ a. discreto.

circumstance /'sɜrkəm,stæns/ n. circunstancia f.

circumstantial /,sɜrkəm'stænʃəl/ a. circunstancial, indirecto.

circumstantially /,sɜrkəm'stænʃəli/ adv. minuciosamente.

circumvent /,sɜrkəm'vent/ v. evadir, evitar.

circumvention /,sɜrkəm'venʃən/ n. trampa f.

circus /'sɜrkəs/ n. circo m.

cirrhosis /sɪ'rousɪs/ n. cirrosis f.

cistern /'sɪstərn/ n. cisterna f.

citadel /'sɪtədl/ n. ciudadela f.

citation /sai'teiʃən/ n. citación f.

cite /sait/ v. citar.

citizen /'sɪtəzən/ n. ciudadano -na.

citizenship /'sɪtəzən,ʃɪp/ n. ciudadanía f.

citric /'sɪtrɪk/ a. cítrico.

city /'sɪti/ n. ciudad f.

city hall ayuntamiento, municipio m.

city planning urbanismo m.

civic /'sɪvɪk/ a. cívico.

civics /'sɪvɪks/ n. ciencia del gobierno civil.

civil /'sɪvəl/ a. civil; cortés.

civilian /sɪ'vɪlyən/ a. & n. civil m. & f.

civility /sɪ'vɪlɪti/ n. cortesía f.

civilization /,sɪvələ'zelʃən/ n. civilización f.

civilize /'sɪvə,laiz/ v. civilizar.

civil rights /raits/ derechos civiles m. pl.

civil service n. servicio civil oficial m.

civil war n. guerra civil f.

clabber /'klæbər/ n. 1. cuajo m. —v. 2. cuajarse.

clad /klæd/ a. vestido.

claim /kleim/ n. 1. demanda; pretensión f. —v. 2. demandar, reclamar.

claimant /'kleimənt/ n. reclamante -ta.

clairvoyance /klɛər'vɔiəns/ n. clarividencia f.

clairvoyant /klɛər'vɔiənt/ a. clarividente.

clam /klæm/ n. almeja f.

clamber /'klæmbər/ v. trepar.

clamor /'klæmər/ n. 1. clamor m. —v. 2. clamar.

clamorous /'klæmərəs/ a. clamoroso.

clamp /klæmp/ n. 1. prensa de sujeción f. —v. 2. asegurar, sujetar.

clan /klæn/ n. tribu f., clan m.

clandestine /klæn'destɪn/ a. clandestino.

clandestinely /klæn'destɪnli/ adv. clandestinamente.

clangor /'klæŋər, 'klæŋgər/ n. estruendo m., estrépito m.

clannish /'klænɪʃ/ a. unido; exclusivista.

clap /klæp/ v. aplaudir.

clapboard /'klæbərd, 'klæp,bɔrd/ n. chilla f.

claque /klæk/ n. claque f.

claret /'klærɪt/ n. clarete m.

clarification /,klærəfə'keiʃən/ n. clarificación f.

clarify /'klærə,fai/ v. clarificar.

clarinet /,klærə'net/ n. clarinete m.

clarinetist /,klærə'netɪst/ n. clarinetista m. & f.

clarity /'klærɪti/ n. claridad f.

clash /klæʃ/ n. 1. choque, enfrentamiento m. —v. 2. chocar.

clasp /klæsp/ n. 1. broche m. —v. 2. abrochar.

class /klæs/ *n.* clase *f.*

classic, /'klæsɪk/ **classical** *a.* clásico.

classicism /'klæsə,sɪzəm/ *n.* clasicismo *m.*

classifiable /'klæsə,faiəbəl/ *a.* clasificable, calificable.

classification /,klæsəfɪ'keiʃən/ *n.* clasificación *f.*

classify /'klæsə,fai/ *v.* clasificar.

classmate /'klæs,meit/ *n.* compañero -ra de clase.

classroom /'klæs,rum, -,rʊm/ *n.* sala de clase.

clatter /'klætər/ *n.* **1.** alboroto *m.* —*v.* **2.** alborotar.

clause /klɔz/ *n.* cláusula *f.*

claustrophobia /,klɔstrə'foubiə/ *n.* claustrofobia *f.*

claw /klɔ/ *n.* garra *f.*

clay /klei/ *n.* arcilla *f.*; barro *m.*

clean /klin/ *a.* **1.** limpio. —*v.* **2.** limpiar.

cleaner /'klinər/ *n.* limpiador -ra.

cleaning lady, cleaning woman /'kliniŋ/ señora de la limpieza, mujer de la limpieza *f.*

cleanliness /'klenlinɪs/ *n.* limpieza *f.*

cleanse /klɛnz/ *v.* limpiar, purificar.

cleanser /'klɛnzər/ *n.* limpiador *m.*, purificador *m.*

clear /klɪər/ *a.* claro.

clearance /'klɪərəns/ *n.* espacio libre. **c. sale,** venta de liquidación.

clearing /'klɪərɪŋ/ *n.* despejo *m.*; desmonte *m.*

clearly /'klɪərli/ *adv.* claramente, evidentemente.

clearness /'klɪərnɪs/ *n.* claridad *f.*

cleavage /'klividʒ/ *n.* resquebradura *f.*

cleaver /'klivər/ *n.* partidor *m.*, hacha *f.*

clef /klɛf/ *n.* clave, llave *f.*

clemency /'klɛmənsi/ *n.* clemencia *f.*

clench /klɛntʃ/ *v.* agarrar.

clergy /'klɜrdʒi/ *n.* clero *m.*

clergyman /'klɜrdʒimən/ *n.* clérigo *m.*

clerical /'klɛrɪkəl/ *a.* clerical. **c. work,** trabajo de oficina.

clericalism /'klɛrɪkə,lɪzəm/ *n.* clericalismo *m.*

clerk /klɜrk/ *n.* dependiente, escribiente *m.*

clerkship /'klɜrkʃɪp/ *n.* escribanía *f.*, secretaría *f.*

clever /'klɛvər/ *a.* diestro, hábil.

cleverly /'klɛvərli/ *adv.* diestramente, hábilmente.

cleverness /'klɛvərnɪs/ *n.* destreza *f.*

cliché /kli'ʃei/ *n.* tópico *m.*

client /'klaiənt/ *n.* cliente -ta.

clientele /,klaiən'tɛl/ *n.* clientela *f.*

cliff /klɪf/ *n.* precipicio, risco *m.*

climate /'klaimɪt/ *n.* clima *m.*

climatic /klai'mætɪk/ *a.* climático.

climax /'klaimæks/ *n.* colmo *m.*, culminación *f.*

climb /klaim/ *v.* escalar; subir.

climber /'klaimər/ *n.* trepador -ra, escalador -ra; *Bot.* enredadera *f.*

climbing plant /'klaimɪŋ/ enredadera *f.*

clinch /klɪntʃ/ *v.* afirmar.

cling /klɪŋ/ *v.* pegarse.

clinic /'klɪnɪk/ *n.* clínica *f.*

clinical /'klɪnɪkəl/ *a.* clínico.

clinically /'klɪnɪkəli/ *adv.* clínicamente.

clip /klɪp/ *n.* **1.** grapa *f.* **paper c.,** gancho *m.* —*v.* **2.** prender; (shear) trasquilar.

clipper /'klɪpər/ *n.* recortador *m.*; *Aero.* clíper *m.*

clipping /'klɪpɪŋ/ *n.* recorte *m.*

clique /klik/ *n.* camarilla *f.*, compadraje *m.*

cloak /klouk/ *n.* capa *f.*, manto *m.*

clock /klɒk/ *n.* reloj *m.* **alarm c.,** despertador *m.*

clod /klɒd/ *n.* terrón *m.*; césped *m.*

clog /klɒg/ *v.* obstruir.

cloister /'klɔistər/ *n.* claustro *m.*

clone /kloun/ *n.* clon *m.* & *f. v.* clonar.

close /a, adv. klous; v klouz/ *a.* **1.** cercano. —*adv.* **2.** cerca. **c. to,** cerca de. —*v.* **3.** cerrar; tapar.

closely /'klousli/ *adv.* (near) de cerca; (tight) estrechamente; (care) cuidadosamente.

closeness /'klousnɪs/ *n.* contiguidad *f.*, apretamiento *m.*; (airless) falta de ventilación *f.*

closet /'klɒzɪt/ *n.* gabinete *m.* **clothes c.,** ropero *m.*

clot /klɒt/ *n.* **1.** coágulo *f.* —*v.* **2.** coagularse.

cloth /klɔθ/ *n.* paño *m.*; tela *f.*

clothe /klouð/ *v.* vestir.

clothes /klouz/ *n.* ropa *f.*

clothing /'klouðiŋ/ *n.* vestidos *m.*, ropa *f.*

cloud /klaud/ *n.* nube *f.*

cloudburst /'klaud,bɜrst/ *n.* chaparrón *m.*

cloudiness /'klaudinɪs/ *n.* nebulosidad *f.*; obscuridad *f.*

cloudless /'klaudlɪs/ *a.* despejado, sin nubes.

cloudy /'klaudi/ *a.* nublado.

clove /klouv/ *n.* clavo *m.*

clover /'klouvər/ *n.* trébol *f.*

clown /klaun/ *n.* bufón -na, payaso -sa.

clownish /'klaunɪʃ/ *a.* grosero; bufonesco.

cloy /klɔi/ *v* saciar, empalagar.

club /klʌb/ *n.* **1.** porra *f.*; (social) círculo, club *m.*; (cards) basto *m.* —*v.* **2.** golpear con una porra.

clubfoot /'klʌb,fʊt/ *n.* pateta *m.*, pie zambo *m.*

clue /klu/ *n.* seña, pista *f.*

clump /klʌmp/ *n.* grupo *m.*, masa *f.*

clumsiness /'klʌmzɪnɪs/ n. tosquedad f.; desmaña f.

clumsy /'klʌmzi/ a. torpe, desmañado.

cluster /'klʌstər/ n. 1. grupo m.; (fruit) racimo m. —v. 2. agrupar.

clutch /klʌtʃ/ n. 1. Auto. embrague m. —v. 2. agarrar.

clutter /'klʌtər/ n. 1. confusión f. —v. 2. poner en desorden.

coach /koutʃ/ n. 1. coche, vagón m.; coche ordinario; (sports) entrenador m. —v. 2. entrenar.

coachman /'koutʃmən/ n. cochero -ra.

coagulate /kou'ægyə,leit/ v. coagular.

coagulation /kou,ægyə'leiʃən/ n. coagulación f.

coal /koul/ n. carbón m.

coalesce /,kouə'lɛs/ v. unirse, soldarse.

coalition /kouə'lɪʃən/ n. coalición f.

coal oil n. petróleo m.

coal tar n. alquitrán m.

coarse /kɔrs/ a. grosero, burdo; (material) tosco, grueso.

coarsen /'kɔrsən/ v. vulgarizar.

coarseness /'kɔrsnɪs/ n. grosería; tosquedad f.

coast /koust/ n. 1. costa f., litoral m. —v. 2. deslizarse.

coastal /'koustl/ a. costanero.

coast guard guardacostas m. & f.

coat /kout/ n. 1. saco m., chaqueta f.; (paint) capa f. —v. 2. cubrir.

coat of arms /armz/ n. escudo m.

coax /kouks/ v. instar.

cobalt /'koubɔlt/ n. cobalto m.

cobbler /'kɔblər/ n. zapatero -ra.

cobblestone /'kɔbəl,stoun/ n. guijarro m.

cobra /'koubrə/ n. cobra f.

cobweb /'kɒb,wɛb/ n. telaraña f.

cocaine /kou'kein/ n. cocaína f.

cock /kɒk/ n. (rooster) gallo m.; (water, etc.) llave f.; (gun) martillo m.

cockfight /'kɒk,fait/ n. riña de gallos f.

cockpit /'kɒk,pɪt/ n. gallera f.; reñidero de gallos m.; Aero. cabina f.

cockroach /'kɒk,routʃ/ n. cucaracha f.

cocktail /'kɒk,teil/ n. cóctel m.

cocky /'kɒki/ a. confiado, atrevido.

cocoa /'koukou/ n. cacao m.

coconut /'koukə,nʌt/ n. coco m.

cocoon /kə'kun/ n. capullo m.

cod /kɒd/ n. bacalao m.

code /koud/ n. código m.; clave f.

codeine /'koudin/ n. codeína f.

codfish /'kɒd,fɪʃ/ n. bacalao m.

codify /'kɒdə,fai/ v. compilar.

cod-liver oil /'kɒd 'lɪvər/ aceite de hígado de bacalao m.

coeducation /,kouɛdʒu'keiʃən/ n. coeducación f.

coequal /kou'ikwəl/ a. mutuamente igual.

coerce /kou'ɜrs/ v. forzar.

coercion /kou'ɜrʃən/ n. coerción f.

coercive /kou'ɜrsɪv/ a. coercitivo.

coexist /,kouɪg'zɪst/ v. coexistir.

coffee /'kɔfi/ n. café m. c. plantation, cafetal m. c. shop, café m.

coffee break pausa para el café f.

coffer /'kɔfər/ n. cofre m.

coffin /'kɔfɪn/ n. ataúd m.

cog /kɒg/ n. diente de rueda m.

cogent /'koudʒənt/ a. convincente.

cogitate /'kɒdʒɪ,teit/ v. pensar, reflexionar.

cognizance /'kɒgnəzəns/ n. conocimiento m., comprensión f.

cognizant /'kɒgnəzənt/ a. conocedor, informado.

cogwheel /'kɒg,wil/ n. rueda dentada f.

cohere /kou'hɪər/ v. pegarse.

coherent /kou'hɪərənt/ a. coherente.

cohesion /kou'hiʒən/ n. cohesión f.

cohesive /kou'hisɪv/ a. cohesivo.

cohort /'kouhɔrt/ n. cohorte f.

coiffure /kwa'fyur/ n. peinado, tocado m.

coil /kɔil/ n. 1. rollo m.; Naut. adujada f. —v. 2. enrollar.

coin /kɔin/ n. moneda f.

coinage /'kɔinɪdʒ/ n. sistema monetario m.

coincide /,kouɪn'said/ v. coincidir.

coincidence /kou'ɪnsɪdəns/ n. coincidencia; casualidad f.

coincident /kou'ɪnsɪdənt/ a. coincidente.

coincidental /kou,ɪnsɪ'dɛntl/ a. coincidental.

coincidentally /kou,ɪnsɪ'dɛntli/ adv. coincidentalmente, al mismo tiempo.

colander /'kɒləndər/ n. colador m.

cold /kould/ a. & n. frío -a; Med. resfriado m. to be c., tener frío; (weather) hacer frío.

coldly /'kouldli/ adv. fríamente.

coldness /'kouldnɪs/ n. frialdad f.

collaborate /kə'læbə,reit/ v. colaborar.

collaboration /kə,læbə'reiʃən/ n. colaboración f.

collaborator /kə'læbə,reitər/ n. colaborador -ra.

collapse /kə'læps/ n. 1. desplome m.; Med. colapso m. —v. 2. desplomarse.

collar /'kɒlər/ n. cuello m.

collarbone /'kɒlər,boun/ n. clavícula f.

collate /kou'leit/ v. comparar.

collateral /kə'lætərəl/ a. 1. colateral. —n. 2. garantía f.

collation /kə'leiʃən/ n. comparación f.; (food) colación f., merienda f.

colleague /'kɒlig/ n. colega m. & f.

collect /'kɒlɛkt/ v. cobrar; recoger; coleccionar.

collection /kə'lɛkʃən/ n. colección f.

collective /kə'lɛktɪv/ a. colectivo.
collectively /kə'lɛktɪvli/ adv. colectivamente, en masa.
collector /kə'lɛktər/ n. colector -ra; coleccionista m. & f.
college /'kɒlɪdʒ/ n. colegio m.; universidad f.
collegiate /kə'lidʒɪt/ n. colegiado m
collide /kə'laid/ v. chocar.
collision /kə'lɪʒən/ n. choque m.
colloquial /kə'loukwiəl/ a. familiar.
colloquially /kə'loukwiəli/ adv. familiarmente.
colloquy /'kɒləkwi/ n. conversación f., coloquio m.
collusion /kə'luʒən/ n. colusión f., connivencia f.
Cologne /kə'loun/ n. Colonia f.
Colombian /kə'lʌmbiən/ a. & n. colombiano -na.
colon /'koulən/ n. colon m.; Punct. dos puntos.
colonel /'kɜrnl/ n. coronel m.
colonial /kə'louniəl/ a. colonial.
colonist /'kɒlənɪst/ n. colono -na.
colonization /,kɒlənə'zeiʃən/ n. colonización f.
colonize /'kɒlə,naiz/ v. colonizar.
colony /'kɒləni/ n. colonia f.
color /'kʌlər/ n. **1.** color; colorido m. —v. **2.** colorar; colorir.
coloration /,kʌlə'reiʃən/ n. colorido m.
colored /'kʌlərd/ a. de color.
colorful /'kʌlərfəl/ a. vívido.
colorless /'kʌlərlɪs/ a. descolorido, sin color.
colossal /kə'lɒsəl/ a. colosal.
colt /koult/ n. potro m.
column /'kɒləm/ n. columna f.
coma /'koumə/ n. coma m.
comb /koum/ n. **1.** peine m. —v. **2.** peinar.
combat /n 'kɒmbæt; v kəm'bæt/ n. **1.** combate m. —v. **2.** combatir.
combatant /kəm'bætənt/ n. combatiente -ta.
combative /kəm'bætɪv/ a. combativo.
combination /,kɒmbə'neiʃən/ n. combinación f.
combine /kəm'bain/ v. combinar.
combustible /kəm'bʌstəbəl/ a. & n. combustible m.
combustion /kəm'bʌstʃən/ n. combustión f.
come /kʌm/ v. venir. **c. back,** volver. **c. in,** entrar. **c. out,** salir. **c. up,** subir. **c. upon,** encontrarse con.
comedian /kə'midiən/ n. cómico -ca.
comedienne /kə,midi'ɛn/ n. cómica f., actriz f.
comedy /'kɒmɪdi/ n. comedia f.
comet /'kɒmɪt/ n. cometa m.

comfort /'kʌmfərt/ n. **1.** confort m.; solaz m. —v. **2.** confortar; solazar.
comfortable /'kʌmftəbəl/ a. cómodo.
comfortably /'kʌmftəbli/ adv. cómodamente.
comforter /'kʌmfərtər/ n. colcha f.
comfortingly /'kʌmfərtɪŋli/ adv. confortantemente.
comfortless /'kɒmfərtlɪs/ a. sin consuelo; sin comodidades.
comic /'kɒmɪk/ **comical** a. cómico.
comic book n. tebeo m.
coming /'kʌmɪŋ/ n. **1.** venida f., llegada f. —a. **2.** próximo, que viene, entrante.
comma /'kɒmə/ n. coma f.
command /kə'mænd/ n. **1.** mando m. —v. **2.** mandar.
commandeer /,kɒmən'dɪər/ v. reclutar forzosamente, expropiar.
commander /kə'mændər/ n. comandante -ta.
commander in chief n. generalísimo, jefe supremo.
commandment /kə'mændmənt/ n. mandato; mandamiento m.
commemorate /kə'mɛmə,reit/ v. conmemorar.
commemoration /kə,mɛmə'reiʃən/ n. conmemoración f.
commemorative /kə'mɛmə,reitɪv/ a. conmemorativo.
commence /kə'mɛns/ v. comenzar, principiar.
commencement /kə'mɛnsmənt/ n. comienzo m.; graduación f.
commend /kə'mɛnd/ v. encomendar; elogiar.
commendable /kə'mɛndəbəl/ a. recomendable.
commendably /kə'mɛndəbli/ adv. loablemente.
commendation /,kɒmən'deiʃən/ n. recomendación f.; elogio m.
commensurate /kə'mɛnsərɪt/ a. proporcionado.
comment /'kɒmɛnt/ n **1.** comentario m. —v. **2.** comentar.
commentary /'kɒmən,tɛri/ n. comentario m.
commentator /'kɒmən,teitər/ n. comentador -ra.
commerce /'kɒmərs/ n. comercio m.
commercial /kə'mɜrʃəl/ a. comercial.
commercialism /kə'mɜrʃə,lɪzəm/ n. comercialismo m.
commercialize /kə'mɜrʃə,laiz/ v. mercantilizar, explotar.
commercially /kə'mɜrʃəli/ a. & adv. comercialmente.
commiserate /kə'mɪzə,reit/ v. compadecerse.

commissary /'kɒmə,seri/ n. comisario m.

commission /kə'mɪʃən/ n. **1.** comisión f. —v. **2.** comisionar.

commissioner /kə'mɪʃənər/ n. comisario -ria.

commit /kə'mɪt/ v. cometer.

commitment /kə'mɪtmənt/ n. compromiso m.

committee /kə'mɪti/ n. comité m.

commodious /kə'moudiəs/ a. cómodo.

commodity /kə'mɒdɪti/ n. mercadería f.

common /'kɒmən/ a. común; ordinario.

commonly /'kɒmənli/ adv. comúnmente, vulgarmente.

Common Market Mercado Común m.

commonplace /'kɒmən,pleɪs/ a. trivial, banal.

common sense sentido común m.

commonwealth /'kɒmən,wɛlθ/ n. estado m.; nación f.

commotion /kə'mouʃən/ n. tumulto m.

communal /kə'myunl/ a. comunal, público.

commune /'kɒmyun/ n. **1.** distrito municipal m.; comuna f. —v. **2.** conversar.

communicable /kə'myunɪkəbəl/ a. comunicable; Med. transmisible.

communicate /kə'myunɪ,keit/ v. comunicar.

communication /kə,myunɪ'keiʃən/ n. comunicación f.

communicative /kə'myunɪ,keitɪv/ a. comunicativo.

communion /kə'myunyən/ n. comunión f. **take c.,** comulgar.

communiqué /kə,myunɪ'kei/ n. comunicación f.

communism /'kɒmyə,nɪzəm/ n. comunismo m.

communist /'kɒmyənɪst/ n. comunista m. & f.

communistic /,kɒmyə'nɪstɪk/ a. comunístico.

community /kə'myunɪti/ n. comunidad f.

commutation /,kɒmyə'teiʃən/ n. conmutación f.

commuter /kə'myutər/ n. empleado que viaja diariamente desde su domicilio hasta la ciudad donde trabaja.

compact /a kəm'pækt; n 'kɒmpækt/ a. **1.** compacto. —n. **2.** pacto m.; (lady's) polvera f.

compact disk disco compacto m.

companion /kəm'pænyən/ n. compañero -ra.

companionable /kəm'pænyənəbəl/ a. sociable.

companionship /kəm'pænyən,ʃɪp/ n. compañerismo m.

company /'kʌmpəni/ n. compañía f.

comparable /'kɒmpərəbəl/ a. comparable.

comparative /kəm'pærətɪv/ a. comparativo.

comparatively /kəm'pærətɪvli/ a. relativamente.

compare /kəm'peər/ v. comparar.

comparison /kəm'pærəsən/ n. comparación f.

compartment /kəm'pɑrtmənt/ n. compartimiento m.

compass /'kʌmpəs/ n. compás m.; Naut. brújula f.

compassion /kəm'pæʃən/ n. compasión f.

compassionate /kəm'pæʃənɪt/ a. compasivo.

compassionately /kəm'pæʃənɪtli/ adv. compasivamente.

compatible /kəm'pætəbəl/ a. compatible.

compatriot /kəm'peitriət/ n. compatriota m. & f.

compel /kəm'pel/ v. obligar.

compensate /'kɒmpən,seit/ v. compensar.

compensation /,kɒmpən'seiʃən/ n. compensación f.

compensatory /kəm'pensə,tɔri/ a. compensatorio.

compete /kəm'pit/ v. competir.

competence /'kɒmpɪtəns/ n. competencia f.

competent /'kɒmpɪtənt/ a. competente, capaz.

competently /'kɒmpɪtəntli/ adv. competentemente.

competition /,kɒmpɪ'tɪʃən/ n. concurrencia f.; concurso m.

competitive /kəm'petitɪv/ a. competidor.

competitor /kəm'petitər/ n. competidor -ra.

compile /kəm'pail/ v. compilar.

complacency /kəm'pleisənsi/ n. complacencia f.

complacent /kəm'pleisənt/ a. complaciente.

complacently /kəm'pleisəntli/ adv. complacientemente.

complain /kəm'plein/ v. quejarse.

complaint /kəm'pleint/ n. queja f.

complement /'kɒmpləmənt/ n. complemento m.

complete /kəm'plit/ a. **1.** completo —v. **2.** completar.

completely /kəm'plitli/ adv. completamente, enteramente.

completeness /kəm'plitnɪs/ n. integridad f.

completion /kəm'pliʃən/ n. terminación f.

complex /kəm'pleks/ a. complejo.

complexion /kəm'plekʃən/ n. tez f.

complexity /kəm'pleksɪti/ n. complejidad f.

compliance /kəm'plaiəns/ n. consentimiento m. **in c. with,** de acuerdo con.

compliant /kəm'plaiənt/ a. dócil; complaciente.

complicate /'kɒmplɪ,keit/ v. complicar.

complicated /'komplɪ,keitɪd/ a. complicado.

complication /,komplɪ'keiʃən/ n. complicación f.

complicity /kəm'plɪsɪti/ n. complicidad f.

compliment /n 'kompləmənt; v -,mɛnt/ n. **1.** elogio m Fig. —v. **2.** felicitar; echar flores.

complimentary /,komplə'mɛntəri/ a. galante, obsequioso, regaloso.

comply /kəm'plai/ v. cumplir.

component /kəm'pounənt/ a. & n. componente m.

comport /kəm'port/ v. portarse.

compose /kəm'pouz/ v. componer.

composed /kəm'pouzd/ a. tranquilo; (made up) compuesto.

composer /kəm'pouzər/ n. compositor -ra.

composite /kəm'pozɪt/ a. compuesto.

composition /,kompə'zɪʃən/ n. composición f.

composure /kəm'pouʒər/ n. serenidad f.; calma f.

compote /'kompout/ n. compota f.

compound /'kompaund/ a. & n. compuesto m.

comprehend /,komprɪ'hɛnd/ v. comprender.

comprehensible /,komprɪ'hɛnsəbəl/ a. comprensible.

comprehension /,komprɪ'hɛnʃən/ n. comprensión f.

comprehensive /,komprɪ'hɛnsɪv/ a. comprensivo.

compress /n 'kompres; v kəm'pres/ n. **1.** cabezal m. —v. **2.** comprimir.

compressed /kəm'prest/ a. comprimido.

compression /kəm'preʃən/ n. compresión f.

compressor /kəm'presər/ n. compresor m.

comprise /kəm'praiz/ v. comprender; abarcar.

compromise /'komprə,maiz/ n. **1.** compromiso m. —v. **2.** comprometer.

compromiser /'komprə,maizər/ n. compromisario m.

compulsion /kəm'pʌlʃən/ n. compulsión f.

compulsive /kəm'pʌlsɪv/ a. compulsivo.

compulsory /kəm'pʌlsəri/ a. obligatorio.

compunction /kəm'pʌŋkʃən/ n. compunción f.; escrúpulo m.

computation /,kompyu'teiʃən/ n. computación f.

compute /kəm'pyut/ v. computar, calcular.

computer /kəm'pyutər/ n. computadora f., ordenador m.

computerize /kəm'pyutə,raiz/ v. procesar en computadora, computerizar.

computer programmer /'prougræmər/ programador -ra de ordenadores.

computer science informática f.

comrade /'komræd/ n. camarada m. & f.; compañero -ra.

comradeship /'komræd,ʃip/ n. camaradería f.

concave /kon'keiv/ a. cóncavo.

conceal /kən'sil/ v. ocultar, esconder.

concealment /kən'silmənt/ n. ocultación f.

concede /kən'sid/ v. conceder.

conceit /kən'sit/ n. amor propio; engreimiento m.

conceited /kən'sitɪd/ a. engreído.

conceivable /kən'sivəbəl/ a. concebible.

conceive /kən'siv/ v. concebir.

concentrate /'konsən,treit/ v. concentrar.

concentration /,konsən'treiʃən/ n. concentración f.

concentration camp campo de concentración m.

concept /'konsept/ n. concepto m.

conception /kən'sepʃən/ n. concepción f.; concepto m.

concern /kən'sərn/ n. **1.** interés m.; inquietud f., Com. negocio m. —v. **2.** concernir.

concerning /kən'sərnɪŋ/ prep. respecto a.

concert /'konsərt/ n. concierto m.

concerted /kən'sərtɪd/ a. convenido.

concession /kən'seʃən/ n. concesión f.

conciliate /kən'sɪli,eit/ v. conciliar.

conciliation /kən,sɪli'eiʃən/ n. conciliación f.

conciliator /kən'sɪli,eitər/ n. conciliador -ra.

conciliatory /kən'sɪliə,tori/ a. conciliatorio.

concise /kən'sais/ a. conciso.

concisely /kən'saisli/ adv. concisamente.

conciseness /kən'saisnɪs/ n. concisión f.

conclave /'konkleiv/ n. conclave m.

conclude /kən'klud/ v. concluir.

conclusion /kən'kluʒən/ n. conclusión f.

conclusive /kən'klusɪv/ a. conclusivo, decisivo.

conclusively /kən'klusɪvli/ adv. concluyentemente.

concoct /kon'kokt/ v. confeccionar.

concomitant /kon'komɪtənt/ n. & a. concomitante m.

concord /'konkord/ n. concordia f.

concordat /kon'kordæt/ n. concordato m.

concourse /'konkors/ n. concurso m.; confluencia f.

concrete /'konkrit/ a. concreto.

concretely /kon'kritli/ adv. concretamente.

concubine /'koŋkyə,bain/ n. concubina, amiga f.

concur /kən'kər/ v. concurrir.

concurrence /kən'kərəns/ n. concurrencia f.; casualidad f.

concurrent /kən'kərənt/ a. concurrente.

concussion /kən'kʌʃən/ n. concusión f.; (c. of the brain) conmoción cerebral f.

condemn /kən'dem/ v. condenar.

condemnable /kən'dɛmnəbəl/ a. culpable, condenable.

condemnation /,kɒndem'neiʃən/ n. condenación f.

condensation /,kɒnden'seiʃən/ n. condensación f.

condense /kən'dens/ v. condensar.

condenser /kən'densər/ n. condensador m.

condescend /,kɒndə'send/ v. condescender.

condescension /,kɒndə'senʃən/ n. condescendencia f.

condiment /'kɒndəmənt/ n. condimento m.

condition /kən'dɪʃən/ n. 1. condición f.; estado m. —v. 2. acondicionar.

conditional /kən'dɪʃənl/ a. condicional.

conditionally /kən'dɪʃənli/ adv. condicionalmente.

condole /kən'doul/ v. condolerse.

condolence /kən'douləns/ n. pésame m.

condom /'kɒndəm/ n. forro, preservativo m

condominium /,kɒndə'mɪniəm/ n. condominio m.

condone /kən'doun/ v. condonar.

conducive /kən'dusɪv, -'dyu-/ a. conducente.

conduct /n 'kɒndʌkt; v kən'dʌkt/ n. 1. conducta f. —v. 2. conducir.

conductivity /,kɒndʌk'tɪvɪti/ n. conductividad f

conductor /kən'dʌktər/ n. conductor m.

conduit /'kɒnduɪt/ n. caño m., canal f.; conducto m.

cone /koun/ n. cono m. **ice-cream c.,** barquillo de helado.

confection /kən'fekʃən/ n. confitura f

confectioner /kən'fekʃənər/ n. confitero m. -ra.

confectionery /kən'fekʃə,neri/ n. dulcería f.

confederacy /kən'fedərəsi/ n. federación f.

confederate /kən'fedərɪt/ a. & n. confederado m.

confederation /kən,fedə'reiʃən/ n. confederación f.

confer /kən'fər/ v. conferenciar; conferir.

conference /'kɒnfərəns/ n. conferencia f.; congreso m.

confess /kən'fes/ v. confesar.

confession /kən'feʃən/ n. confesión f.

confessional /kən'feʃənl/ n. 1. confesionario m. —a. 2. confesional.

confessor /kən'fesər/ n. confesor m.

confetti /kən'feti/ n. confeti m.

confidant /'kɒnfɪ,dænt/ n. confidante n. confidente m. & f.

confide /kən'faid/ v. confiar.

confidence /'kɒnfɪdəns/ n. confianza f.

confident /'kɒnfɪdənt/ a. confiado; cierto.

confidential /,kɒnfɪ'denʃəl/ a. confidencial.

confidentially /,kɒnfɪ'denʃəli/ adv. confidencialmente, en secreto.

confidently /'kɒnfɪdəntli/ adv confiadamente.

confine /kən'fain/ n. 1. confín m. —v. 2. confinar; encerrar.

confirm /kən'fərm/ v. confirmar.

confirmation /,kɒnfər'meiʃən/ n. confirmación f.

confiscate /'kɒnfə,skeit/ v. confiscar.

confiscation /,kɒnfə'skeiʃən/ n. confiscación f.

conflagration /,kɒnflə'greiʃən/ n. incendio m.

conflict /n 'kɒnflɪkt; v kən'flɪkt/ n. 1. conflicto m. —v. 2. oponerse; estar en conflicto.

conform /kən'fɔrm/ v. conformar.

conformation /,kɒnfɔr'meiʃən/ n. conformación f.

conformer /kən'fɔrmər/ n. conformista m. & f.

conformist /kən'fɔrmɪst/ n. conformista m. & f.

conformity /kən'fɔrmɪti/ n. conformidad f.

confound /kɒn'faund/ v. confundir.

confront /kən'frʌnt/ v. confrontar.

confrontation /,kɒnfrən'teiʃən/ n. enfrentamiento m.

confuse /kən'fyuz/ v. confundir.

confusion /kən'fyuʒən/ n. confusión f.

congeal /kən'dʒil/ v. congelar, helar.

congealment /kən'dʒilmənt/ n. congelación f.

congenial /kən'dʒinyəl/ a. congenial.

congenital /kən'dʒenɪtl/ a. congénito.

congenitally /kən'dʒenɪtli/ adv. congenitalmente.

congestion /kən'dʒestʃən/ n. congestión f.

conglomerate /v kən'glɒmə,reit; a, n kən'glɒmərɪt/ v. 1. conglomerar. —a. & n. 2. conglomerado.

conglomeration /kən,glɒmə'reiʃən/ n. conglomeración f.

congratulate /kən'grætʃə,leit/ v. felicitar.

congratulation /kən,grætʃə'leiʃən/ n. felicitación f.

congratulatory /kən'grætʃələ,tɔri/ a. congratulatorio.

congregate /'kɒngrɪ,geit/ v. congregar.

congregation /,kɒngrɪ'geiʃən/ n. congregación f.

congress /'kɒngrɪs/ n. congreso m.

conic /'kɒnɪk/ n. 1. cónica f. —a. 2. cónico.

conjecture /kən'dʒektʃər/ n. 1. conjetura f. —v. 2. conjeturar.

conjugal /'kɒndʒəgəl/ a. conyugal, matrimonial.

conjugate /'kɒndʒə,geit/ v. conjugar.

conjugation /,kɒndʒə'geiʃən/ n. conjugación f.

conjunction /kən'dʒʌŋkʃən/ n. conjunción f.

conjunctive /kən'dʒʌŋktıv/ n. **1.** Gram. conjunción f. —a. **2.** conjuntivo.

conjunctivitis /kən,dʒʌŋktə'vaitıs/ n. conjuntivitis f.

conjure /'kɒndʒər/ v. conjurar.

connect /kə'nɛkt/ v. juntar; relacionar.

connection /kə'nɛkʃən/ n. conexión f.

connivance /kə'naivəns/ n. consentimiento m.

connive /kə'naiv/ v. disimular.

connoisseur /,kɒnə'sɜr/ n. perito -ta.

connotation /,kɒnə'teiʃən/ n. connotación f.

connote /kə'nout/ v. connotar.

connubial /kə'nubiəl/ a. conyugal.

conquer /'kɒŋkər/ v. conquistar.

conquerable /'kɒŋkərəbəl/ a. conquistable, vencible.

conqueror /'kɒŋkərər/ n. conquistador -ra.

conquest /'kɒnkwɛst/ n. conquista f.

conscience /'kɒnʃəns/ n. conciencia f.

conscientious /,kɒnʃi'ɛnʃəs/ a. concienzudo.

conscientiously /,kɒnʃi'ɛnʃəsli/ adv. escrupulosamente.

conscientious objector /ɒb'dʒɛktər/ objetor de conciencia m.

conscious /'kɒnʃəs/ a. consciente.

consciously /'kɒnʃəsli/ adv. con conocimiento.

consciousness /'kɒnʃəsnıs/ n. consciencia f.

conscript /n 'kɒnskrıpt; v kən'skrıpt/ n. **1.** conscripto m., recluta m. —v. **2.** reclutar, alistar.

conscription /kən'skrıpʃən/ n. conscripción f., alistamiento m.

consecrate /'kɒnsı,kreit/ v. consagrar.

consecration /,kɒnsı'kreiʃən/ n. consagración f.

consecutive /kən'sɛkyətıv/ a. consecutivo, seguido.

consecutively /kən'sɛkyətıvli/ adv. consecutivamente, de seguida.

consensus /kən'sɛnsəs/ n. consenso m., acuerdo general m.

consent /kən'sɛnt/ n. **1.** consentimiento m. —v. **2.** consentir.

consequence /'kɒnsı,kwɛns/ n. consecuencia f.

consequent /'kɒnsı,kwɛnt/ a. consiguiente.

consequential /,kɒnsı'kwɛnʃəl/ a. importante.

consequently /'kɒnsı,kwɛntli/ adv. por lo tanto, por consiguiente.

conservation /,kɒnsər'veiʃən/ n. conservación f.

conservatism /kən'sɜrvə,tızəm/ n. conservatismo m.

conservative /kən'sɜrvətıv/ a. conservador, conservativo.

conservatory /kən'sɜrvə,tɔri/ n. (plants) invernáculo m.; (school) conservatorio m.

conserve /kən'sɜrv/ v. conservar.

consider /kən'sıdər/ v. considerar. **C. it done!** ¡Dalo por hecho!

considerable /kən'sıdərəbəl/ a. considerable.

considerably /kən'sıdərəbli/ adv. considerablemente.

considerate /kən'sıdərıt/ a. considerado.

considerately /kən'sıdərıtli/ adv. consideradamente.

consideration /kən,sıdə'reiʃən/ n. consideración f.

considering /kən'sıdərıŋ/ prep. visto que, en vista de.

consign /kən'sain/ v. consignar.

consignment /kən'sainmənt/ n. consignación f., envío m.

consist /kən'sıst/ v consistir.

consistency /kən'sıstənsi/ n. consistencia f.

consistent /kən'sıstənt/ a. consistente.

consolation /,kɒnsə'leiʃən/ n. consolación f.

consolation prize premio de consuelo m.

console /'kɒnsoul/ v. consolar.

consolidate /kən'sɒlı,deit/ v consolidar.

consommé /,kɒnsə'mei/ n. caldo m.

consonant /'kɒnsənənt/ n. consonante f.

consort /n 'kɒnsɔrt, v kən'sɔrt/ n. **1.** cónyuge m. & f.; socio. —v. **2.** asociarse.

conspicuous /kən'spıkyuəs/ a. conspicuo.

conspicuously /kən'spıkyuəsli/ adv. visiblemente, llamativamente.

conspicuousness /kən'spıkyuəsnıs/ n. visibilidad f.; evidencia f.; fama f.

conspiracy /kən'spırəsi/ n. conspiración f.; complot m.

conspirator /kən'spırətər/ n. conspirador -ra.

conspire /kən'spaiər/ v. conspirar.

conspirer /kən'spaiərər/ n. conspirante m. & f.

constancy /'kɒnstənsi/ n. constancia f., lealtad f.

constant /'kɒnstənt/ a. constante.

constantly /'kɒnstəntli/ adv. constantemente, de continuo.

constellation /,kɒnstə'leiʃən/ n. constelación f.

consternation /,kɒnstər'neiʃən/ n. consternación f.

constipate /'kɒnstə,peit/ v. estreñir.

constipated /'kɒnstə,peitıd/ a. estreñido, m.

constipation /,kɒnstə'peiʃən/ n. estreñimiento, m.

constituency /kən'stıtʃuənsi/ n. distrito electoral m.

constituent /kən'stɪtʃuənt/ a. 1. constituyente. —n. 2. elector m.

constitute /'kɒnstɪ,tut/ v. constituir.

constitution /,kɒnstɪ'tuʃən/ n. constitución f.

constitutional /,kɒnstɪ'tuʃənl/ a. constitucional.

constrain /kən'streɪn/ v. constreñir.

constraint /kən'streɪnt/ n. constreñimiento m., compulsión f.

constrict /kən'strɪkt/ v. apretar, estrechar.

construct /kən'strʌkt/ v. construir.

construction /kən'strʌkʃən/ n. construcción f.

constructive /kən'strʌktɪv/ a. constructivo.

constructively /kən'strʌktɪvli/ adv. constructivamente; por deducción.

constructor /kən'strʌktər/ n. constructor m.

construe /kən'stru/ v. interpretar.

consul /'kɒnsəl/ n. cónsul m.

consular /'kɒnsələr/ a. consular.

consulate /'kɒnsəlɪt/ n. consulado m.

consult /kən'sʌlt/ v. consultar.

consultant /kən'sʌltənt/ n. consultor -ora.

consultation /,kɒnsəl'teɪʃən/ n. consulta f.

consume /kən'sum/ v. consumir.

consumer /kən'sumər/ n. consumidor -ra.

consumer society sociedad de consumo f.

consummation /,kɒnsə'meɪʃən/ n. consumación f.

consumption /kən'sʌmpʃən/ n. consumo m.; Med. tisis.

consumptive /kən'sʌmptɪv/ n. 1. tísico m. —a. 2. consuntivo.

contact /'kɒntækt/ n. 1. contacto m. —v. 2. ponerse en contacto con.

contact lens lentilla f.

contagion /kən'teɪdʒən/ n. contagio m.

contagious /kən'teɪdʒəs/ a. contagioso.

contain /kən'teɪn/ v. contener.

container /kən'teɪnər/ n. envase m.

contaminate /kən'tæmə,neɪt/ v. contaminar.

contemplate /'kɒntəm,pleɪt/ v. contemplar.

contemplation /,kɒntəm'pleɪʃən/ n. contemplación f.

contemplative /kən'templətɪv/ a. contemplativo.

contemporary /kən'tempə,reri/ n. & a. contemporáneo -nea.

contempt /kən'tempt/ n. desprecio m.

contemptible /kən'temptəbəl/ a. vil, despreciable.

contemptuous /kən'temptʃuəs/ a. desdeñoso.

contemptuously /kən'temptʃuəsli/ adv. desdeñosamente.

contend /kən'tend/ v. contender; competir.

contender /kən'tendər/ n. competidor -ra.

content /a, v kən'tent; n 'kɒntent/ a. 1. contento. —n. 2. contenido m. —v. 3. contentar.

contented /kən'tentɪd/ a. contento.

contention /kən'tenʃən/ n. contención f.

contentment /kən'tentmənt/ n. contentamiento m.

contest /n 'kɒntest; v kən'test/ n. 1. concurso m. —v. 2. disputar.

contestable /kən'testəbəl/ a. contestable.

context /'kɒntekst/ n. contexto m.

contiguous /kən'tɪgjuəs/ a. contiguo.

continence /'kɒntnəns/ n. continencia f., castidad f.

continent /'kɒntnənt/ n. continente m.

continental /,kɒntn'entl/ a. continental.

contingency /kən'tɪndʒənsi/ n. eventualidad f., casualidad f.

contingent /kən'tɪndʒənt/ a. contingente.

continual /kən'tɪnyuəl/ a. continuo.

continuation /kən,tɪnyu'eɪʃən/ n. continuación f.

continue /kən'tɪnyu/ v. continuar.

continuity /,kɒntn'uɪti/ n. continuidad f.

continuous /kən'tɪnyuəs/ a. continuo.

continuously /kən'tɪnyuəsli/ adv. continuamente.

contour /'kɒntur/ n. contorno m.

contraband /'kɒntrə,bænd/ n. contrabando m.

contraception /,kɒntrə'sepʃən/ n. contracepción f.

contraceptive /,kɒntrə'septɪv/ n. & a. anticeptivo m.

contract /n 'kɒntrækt; v kən'trækt/ n. 1. contrato m. —v. 2. contraer.

contraction /kən'trækʃən/ n. contracción f.

contractor /'kɒntræktər/ n. contratista m. & f.

contradict /,kɒntrə'dɪkt/ v. contradecir.

contradiction /,kɒntrə'dɪkʃən/ n. contradicción f.

contradictory /,kɒntrə'dɪktəri/ a. contradictorio.

contralto /kən'træltou/ n. contralto m.

contrary /'kɒntreri/ a. & n. contrario -ria.

contrast /n 'kɒntræst; v kən'træst/ n. 1. contraste m. —v. 2. contrastar.

contribute /kən'trɪbyut/ v. contribuir.

contribution /,kɒntrə'byuʃən/ n. contribución f.

contributor /kən'trɪbyətər/ n. contribuidor -ra.

contributory /kən'trɪbyə,tɔri/ a. contribuyente.

contrite /kən'traɪt/ a. contrito.

contrition /kən'trɪʃən/ n. contrición f.

contrivance /kən'traɪvəns/ n. aparato m.; estratagema f.

contrive /kən'traiv/ v. inventar, tramar; darse maña.

control /kən'troul/ n. **1.** control m. —v. **2.** controlar.

controllable /kən'troulabəl/ a. controlable, dominable.

controller /kən'troulər/ n. interventor -ra; contralor -ra.

control tower torre de mando f.

controversial /ˌkɒntrə'vərʃəl/ a. contencioso.

controversy /'kɒntrəˌvərsi/ n. controversia f.

contusion /kən'tuʒən/ n. contusión f.

convalesce /ˌkɒnvə'les/ v. convalecer.

convalescence /ˌkɒnvə'lesəns/ n. convalecencia f.

convalescent /ˌkɒnvə'lesənt/ n. convaleciente m. & f.

convalescent home clínica de reposo f.

convene /kən'vin/ v. juntarse; convocar.

convenience /kən'vinyəns/ n. comodidad f.

convenient /kən'vinyənt/ a. cómodo; oportuno.

conveniently /kən'vinyəntli/ adv. cómodamente.

convent /'kɒnvɛnt/ n. convento m.

convention /kən'vɛnʃən/ n. convención f.

conventional /kən'vɛnʃənl/ a. convencional.

conventionally /kən'vɛnʃənli/ adv. convencionalmente.

converge /kən'vərdʒ/ v. convergir.

convergence /kən'vərdʒəns/ n. convergencia f.

convergent /kən'vərdʒənt/ a. convergente.

conversant /kən'vərsənt/ a. versado; entendido (de).

conversation /ˌkɒnvər'seiʃən/ n. conversación, plática f.

conversational /ˌkɒnvər'seiʃənl/ a. de conversación.

conversationalist /ˌkɒnvər'seiʃənlɪst/ n. conversador -ra.

converse /kən'vərs/ v. conversar.

conversely /kən'vərsli/ adv. a la inversa.

convert /n 'kɒnvərt; v kən'vərt/ n. **1.** convertido da-. —v. **2.** convertir.

converter /kən'vərtər/ n. convertidor m.

convertible /kən'vərtəbəl/ a. convertible.

convex /kɒn'vɛks/ a. convexo.

convey /kən'vei/ v. transportar; comunicar.

conveyance /kən'veiəns/ n. transporte; vehículo m.

conveyor /kən'veiər/ n. conductor m.; Mech. transportador m.

conveyor belt correa transportadora f.

convict /n 'kɒnvɪkt; v kən'vɪkt/ n. **1.** reo m. —v. **2.** declarar culpable.

conviction /kən'vɪkʃən/ n. convicción f.

convince /kən'vɪns/ v. convencer.

convincing /kən'vɪnsɪŋ/ a. convincente.

convivial /kən'vɪviəl/ a. convival.

convocation /ˌkɒnvə'keiʃən/ n. convocación; asamblea f.

convoke /kən'vouk/ v. convocar, citar.

convoy /'kɒnvɔi/ n. convoy m.; escolta f.

convulse /kən'vʌls/ v. convulsionar; agitar violentamente.

convulsion /kən'vʌlʃən/ n. convulsión f.

convulsive /kən'vʌlsɪv/ a. convulsivo.

cook /kuk/ n. **1.** cocinero -ra. —v. **2.** cocinar, cocer.

cookbook /'kuk,buk/ n. libro de cocina m.

cookie /'kuki/ n. galleta dulce f.

cool /kul/ a. **1.** fresco. —v. **2.** refrescar.

cooler /'kulər/ n. enfriadera f.

coolness /'kulnɪs/ n. frescura f.

coop /kup/ n. **1.** jaula f. chicken c., gallinero m. —v. **2.** enjaular.

cooperate /kou'ɒpə,reit/ v. cooperar.

cooperation /kou,ɒpə'reiʃən/ n. cooperación f.

cooperative /kou'ɒpərətɪv/ a. cooperativo.

cooperatively /kou'ɒpərətɪvli/ adv. cooperativamente.

coordinate /kou'ɔrdn,eit/ v. coordinar.

coordination /kou,ɔrdn'eiʃən/ n. coordinación f.

coordinator /kou'ɔrdn,eitər/ n. coordinador -ra.

cope /koup/ v. contender. **c. with,** superar, hacer frente a.

copier /'kɒpiər/ n. copiadora f.

copious /'koupiəs/ a. copioso, abundante.

copiously /'koupiəsli/ adv. copiosamente.

copiousness /'koupiəsnɪs/ n. abundancia f.

copper /'kɒpər/ n. cobre m.

copy /'kɒpi/ n. **1.** copia f.; ejemplar m. —v. **2.** copiar.

copyist /'kɒpiɪst/ n. copista m. & f.

copyright /'kɒpi,rait/ n. derechos de propiedad literaria m.pl.

coquetry /'koukɪtri/ n. coquetería f.

coquette /kou'kɛt/ n. coqueta f.

coral /'kɔrəl/ n. coral m.

cord /kɔrd/ n. cuerda f.

cordial /'kɔrdʒəl/ a. cordial.

cordiality /kɔr'dʒælɪti/ n. cordialidad f.

cordially /'kɔrdʒəli/ adv. cordialmente.

cordon off /'kɔrdn/ v. acordonar.

cordovan /'kɔrdəvən/ n. cordobán m.

corduroy /'kɔrdə,rɔi/ n. pana f.

core /kɔr/ n. corazón; centro m.

cork /kɔrk/ n. corcho m.

corkscrew /'kɔrk,skru/ n. tirabuzón f.

corn /kɔrn/ n. maíz m.

cornea /'kɔrniə/ n. córnea f.

corned beef /kɔrnd/ carne acecinada f.

corner /'kɔrnər/ n rincón m.; (of street) esquina f.

cornet /kɔr'net/ n. corneta f.

cornetist /kɔr'netɪst/ n. cornetín m.

cornice /'kɔrnɪs/ n. cornisa f.

cornstarch /'kɔrn.stɑrtʃ/ n. maicena f.

corollary /'kɔrə.leri/ n. corolario m.

coronary /'kɔrə.neri/ a. coronario.

coronation /.kɔrə'neɪʃən/ n. coronación f.

corporal /'kɔrpərəl/ a. 1. corpóreo. —n 2. cabo m.

corporate /'kɔrpərɪt/ a. corporativo.

corporation /.kɔrpə'reɪʃən/ n. corporación f.

corps /kɔr/ n. cuerpo m.

corpse /kɔrps/ n. cadáver m.

corpulent /'kɔrpyələnt/ a. corpulento.

corpuscle /'kɔrpəsəl/ n corpúsculo m.

corral /kə'ræl/ n. 1. corral m. —v. 2. acorralar.

correct /kə'rekt/ a. 1. correcto. —v. 2. corregir.

correction /kə'rekʃən/ n. corrección; enmienda f.

corrective /kə'rektɪv/ n. & a. correctivo.

correctly /kə'rektli/ adv. correctamente.

correctness /kə'rektnɪs/ n. exactitud f.

correlate /'kɔrə.leit/ v. correlacionar.

correlation /.kɔrə'leiʃən/ n. correlación f.

correspond /.kɔrə'spond/ v. corresponder.

correspondence /.kɔrə'spondəns/ n. correspondencia f.

correspondence course curso por correspondencia m.

correspondence school escuela por correspondencia f.

correspondent /.kɔrə'spondənt/ a. & n. correspondiente m. & f.

corresponding /.kɔrə'spondɪŋ/ a. correspondiente.

corridor /'kɔridər/ n. corredor, pasillo m.

corroborate /kə'robə.reit/ v. corroborar.

corroboration /kə.robə'reiʃən/ n. corroboración f.

corroborative /kə'robə.reitɪv/ a. corroborante.

corrode /kə'roud/ v. corroer.

corrosion /kə'rouʒən/ n. corrosión f.

corrugate /'kɔrə.geit/ v. arrugar; ondular.

corrupt /kə'rʌpt/ a. 1. corrompido. —v. 2. corromper.

corruptible /kə'rʌptəbəl/ a. corruptible.

corruption /kə'rʌpʃən/ n. corrupción f.

corruptive /kə'rʌptɪv/ a. corruptivo.

corset /'kɔrsɪt/ n. corsé m., (girdle) faja f.

cortege /kɔr'teʒ/ n. comitiva f., séquito m.

corvette /kɔr'vet/ n. corbeta f.

cosmetic /knz'metɪk/ a. & n. cosmético m.

cosmic /'knzmɪk/ a. cósmico.

cosmonaut /'knzmə.nɔt/ n. cosmonauta m. & f.

cosmopolitan /.knzmə'pnlɪtn/ a. & n. cosmopolita m. & f.

cosmos /'knzməs/ n. cosmos m.

cost /kɔst/ n. 1. coste m.; costa f —v. 2. costar.

Costa Rican /'kɔstə'rikən/ a. & n. costarricense m. & f.

costly /'kɔstli/ a. costoso, caro.

costume /'knstum/ n. traje; disfraz m.

costume jewelry bisutería f., joyas de fantasía f.pl.

cot /knt/ n. catre m.

coterie /'koutəri/ n. camarilla f.

cotillion /kə'tɪlyən/ n. cotillón m.

cottage /'kntidʒ/ n. casita f.

cottage cheese requesón m.

cotton /'kntn/ n. algodón m.

cottonseed /'kntn.sid/ n. semilla del algodón f.

couch /kautʃ/ n. sofá m.

cougar /'kugər/ n. puma m.

cough /kɔf/ n. 1. tos f. —v. 2. toser.

council /'kaunsəl/ n. consejo, concilio m.

counsel /'kaunsəl/ n. 1. consejo; (law) abogado -da. —v. 2. aconsejar. **to keep one's c.,** no decir nada.

counselor /'kaunsələr/ n. consejero -ra; (law) abogado -da.

count /kaunt/ n. 1. cuenta f.; (title) conde m. —v. 2. contar.

countenance /'kauntnəns/ n. 1. aspecto m.; cara f. —v. 2. aprobar.

counter /'kauntər/ adv. 1. **c. to,** contra, en contra de. —n. 2. mostrador m.

counteract /.kauntər'ækt/ v. contrarrestar.

counteraction /.kauntər'ækʃən/ n. neutralización f.

counterbalance /'kauntər.bæləns/ n. 1. contrapeso m. —v. 2. contrapesar.

counterfeit /'kauntər.fit/ a. 1. falsificado. —v. 2. falsear.

countermand /.kauntər'mænd/ v. contramandar.

counteroffensive /.kauntərə'fensiv/ n. contraofensiva f.

counterpart /'kauntər.pɔrt/ n. contraparte f.

counterproductive /.kauntərprə'dʌktiv/ a. contraproducente.

countess /'kauntis/ n. condesa f.

countless /'kauntlis/ a. innumerable.

country /'kʌntri/ n. campo m.; Pol. país m.; (homeland) patria f.

country code distintivo del país m.

countryman /'kʌntrimən/ n. paisano m. **fellow c.,** compatriota m.

countryside /'kʌntri.said/ n. campo, paisaje m.

county /'kaunti/ n. condado m.

coupé /kup/ n. cupé m.

couple /'kʌpəl/ n. **1.** par m. —v. **2.** unir.

coupon /'kupɒn/ n. cupón, talón m.

courage /'kʌrɪdʒ/ n. valor m.

courageous /kə'reɪdʒəs/ a. valiente.

course /kɔrs/ n. curso m. **of c.,** por supuesto, desde luego.

court /kɔrt/ n. **1.** corte f.; cortejo m.; (of law) tribunal m. —v. **2.** cortejar.

courteous /'kɔrtɪəs/ a. cortés.

courtesy /'kɔrtəsi/ n. cortesía f.

courthouse /'kɔrt,haus/ n. palacio de justicia m., tribunal m.

courtier /'kɔrtɪər/ n. cortesano m.

courtly /'kɔrtli/ a. cortés, galante.

courtroom /'kɔrt,rum, -,rʊm/ n. sala de justicia f.

courtship /'kɔrtʃɪp/ n. cortejo m.

courtyard /'kɔrt,yɑrd/ n. patio m.

cousin /'kʌzən/ n. primo -ma.

covenant /'kʌvənənt/ n. contrato, convenio m.

cover /'kʌvər/ n. **1.** cubierta, tapa f. —v. **2.** cubrir, tapar.

cover charge precio del cubierto m.

covet /'kʌvɪt/ v. ambicionar, suspirar por.

covetous /'kʌvɪtəs/ a. codicioso.

cow /kau/ n. vaca f.

coward /'kauərd/ n. cobarde m. & f.

cowardice /'kauərdɪs/ n. cobardía f.

cowardly /'kauərdli/ a. cobarde.

cowboy /'kau,bɔi/ n. vaquero, gaucho m.

cower /'kauər/ v. agacharse (de miedo).

cowhide /'kau,haid/ n. cuero m.

coy /kɔi/ a. recatado, modesto.

coyote /kai'outi/ n. coyote m.

cozy /'kouzi/ a. cómodo y agradable.

crab /kræb/ n. cangrejo m.

crab apple n. manzana silvestre f.

crack /kræk/ n. **1.** hendedura f.; (noise) crujido m. —v. **2.** hender; crujir.

cracker /'krækər/ n. galleta f.

cradle /'kreidl/ n. cuna f.

craft /kræft/ n. arte m.

craftsman /'kræftsmən/ n. artesano -na.

craftsmanship /'kræftsmən,ʃɪp/ n. artesanía f.

crafty /'kræfti/ a. ladino.

crag /kræg/ n. despeñadero m.; peña f.

cram /kræm/ v. rellenar, hartar.

cramp /kræmp/ n. calambre m.

cranberry /'kræn,beri/ n. arándano m.

crane /krein/ n. (bird) grulla f.; Mech. grúa f.

cranium /'kreiniəm/ n. cráneo m.

crank /kræŋk/ n. Mech. manivela f.

cranky /'kræŋki/ a. chiflado, caprichoso.

crash /kræʃ/ n. **1.** choque; estallido m. —v. **2.** estallar.

crate /kreit/ n. canasto m.

crater /'kreitər/ n. cráter m.

crave /kreiv/ v. desear; anhelar.

craven /'kreivən/ a. cobarde.

craving /'kreivɪŋ/ n. sed m., anhelo m.

crawl /krɔl/ v. andar a gatas, arrastrarse.

crayon /'kreiɒn/ n. creyón; lápiz m.

crazy /'kreizi/ a. loco.

creak /krik/ v. crujir.

creaky /'kriki/ a. crujiente.

cream /krim/ n. crema f.

cream cheese queso crema m.

creamery /'kriməri/ n. lechería f.

creamy /'krimi/ a. cremoso.

crease /kris/ n. **1.** pliegue m. —v. **2.** plegar.

create /kri'eit/ v. crear.

creation /kri'eiʃən/ n. creación f.

creative /kri'eitɪv/ a. creativo, creador.

creator /kri'eitər/ n. creador -ra.

creature /'kritʃər/ n. criatura f.

credence /'kridns/ n. creencia f.

credentials /krɪ'dɛnʃəlz/ n. credenciales f.pl.

credibility /,krɛdə'bɪlɪti/ n. credibilidad f.

credible /'krɛdəbəl/ a. creíble.

credit /'krɛdɪt/ n. **1.** crédito m. **on c.,** al fiado. —v. **2.** Com. abonar.

creditable /'krɛdɪtəbəl/ a. fidedigno.

credit balance saldo acreedor.

credit card n. tarjeta de crédito f.

creditor /'krɛdɪtər/ n. acreedor -ra.

credit union banco cooperativo m.

credo /'kridou/ n. credo m.

credulity /krə'dulɪti/ n. credulidad f.

credulous /'krɛdʒələs/ a. crédulo.

creed /krid/ n. credo m.

creek /krik/ n. riachuelo m.

creep /krip/ v. gatear.

cremate /'krimeit/ v. incinerar.

crematory /'krimə,tɔri/ n. crematorio m.

creosote /'kriə,sout/ n. creosota f.

crepe /kreip/ n. crespón m.

crepe paper papel crespón m.

crescent /'krɛsənt/ a. & n. creciente f.

crest /krɛst/ n. cresta; cima f.; (heraldry) timbre m.

cretonne /krɪ'tɒn/ n. cretona f.

crevice /'krɛvɪs/ n. grieta f.

crew /kru/ n. tripulación f.

crew member tripulante m. & f.

crib /krɪb/ n. pesebre m.; cuna f.

cricket /'krɪkɪt/ n. grillo m.

crime /kraim/ n. crimen m.

criminal /'krɪmənl/ a. & n. criminal m. & f.

criminologist /,krɪmə'nɒlədʒɪst/ n. criminólogo, -ga, criminalista m. & f.

criminology /,krɪmə'nɒlədʒi/ n. criminología f.

crimson /'krɪmzən, -sən/ a. & n. carmesí m.

cringe /krɪndʒ/ v. encogerse, temblar.

cripple /'krɪpəl/ n. **1.** lisiado -da. —v. **2.** estropear, lisiar.

crisis /'kraɪsɪs/ n. crisis f.

crisp /krɪsp/ a. crespo, fresco.

crispness /'krɪspnɪs/ n. encrespadura f.

crisscross /'krɪs,krɔs/ a. entrelazado.

criterion /kraɪ'tɪərɪən/ n. criterio m.

critic /'krɪtɪk/ n. crítico -ca.

critical /'krɪtɪkəl/ a. crítico.

criticism /'krɪtə,sɪzəm/ n. crítica; censura f.

criticize /'krɪtə,saɪz/ v. criticar; censurar.

critique /krɪ'tik/ n. crítica f.

croak /krouk/ n. **1.** graznido m. —v. **2.** graznar.

crochet /krou'ʃeɪ/ n. **1.** crochet m. —v. **2.** hacer crochet.

crochet work ganchillo m.

crock /krɒk/ n. cazuela f.; olla de barro.

crockery /'krɒkəri/ n. loza f.

crocodile /'krɒkə,daɪl/ n. cocodrilo m.

crony /'krouni/ n. compinche m.

crooked /'krʊkɪd/ a. encorvado; deshonesto.

croon /krun/ v. canturrear.

crop /krɒp/ n. cosecha f.

croquet /krou'keɪ/ n. juego de croquet m.

croquette /krou'kɛt/ n. croqueta f.

cross /krɔs/ a. **1.** enojado, mal humorado. —n. **2.** cruz f. —v. **3.** cruzar, atravesar.

crossbreed /'krɔs,brid/ n. **1.** mestizo m. —v. **2.** cruzar (animales o plantas).

cross-examine /'krɔs ɪg,zæmɪn/ v. interrogar.

cross-eyed /'krɔs ,aɪd/ a. bizco.

cross-fertilization /'krɔs ,fɜrtələ'zeɪʃən/ n. alogamia f.

crossing /'krɔsɪŋ/ **crossroads** n. cruce m.

cross section corte transversal m.

crosswalk /'krɔs,wɔk/ n. paso cebra m.

crossword puzzle /'krɔs ,wɜrd/ crucigrama m.

crotch /krɒtʃ/ n. bifurcación f.; Anat. bragadura f.

crouch /krautʃ/ v. agacharse.

croup /krup/ n. Med. crup m.

croupier /'krupiər/ n. crupié m. & f.

crow /krou/ n. cuervo m.

crowd /kraud/ n. **1.** muchedumbre f.; tropel m. —v. **2.** apretar.

crowded /'kraudɪd/ a. lleno de gente.

crown /kraun/ n. **1.** corona f. —v. **2.** coronar.

crown prince príncipe heredero m.

crucial /'kruʃəl/ a. crucial.

crucible /'krusəbəl/ n. crisol m.

crucifix /'krusəfɪks/ n. crucifijo m.

crucifixion /,krusə'fɪkʃən/ n. crucifixión f.

crucify /'krusə,faɪ/ v. crucificar.

crude /krud/ a. crudo; (oil) bruto.

crudeness /'krudnɪs/ a. crudeza f.

cruel /'kruəl/ a. cruel.

cruelty /'kruəlti/ n. crueldad f.

cruet /'kruɪt/ n. vinagrera f.

cruise /kruz/ n. **1.** viaje por mar. —v. **2.** navegar.

cruiser /'kruzər/ n. crucero m.

crumb /krʌm/ n. miga; migaja f.

crumble /'krʌmbəl/ v. desmigajar; desmoronar.

crumple /'krʌmpəl/ v. arrugar; encogerse.

crusade /kru'seɪd/ n. cruzada f.

crusader /kru'seɪdər/ n. cruzado m.

crush /krʌʃ/ v. aplastar.

crust /krʌst/ n. costra; corteza f.

crustacean /krʌ'steɪʃən/ n. crustáceo m.

crutch /krʌtʃ/ n. muleta f.

cry /kraɪ/ n. **1.** grito m. —v. **2.** gritar; (weep) llorar.

cryosurgery /,kraɪou'sɜrdʒəri/ n. criocirugía f.

crypt /krɪpt/ n. gruta f., cripta f.

cryptic /'krɪptɪk/ a. secreto.

cryptography /krɪp'tɒgrəfi/ n. criptografía f.

crystal /'krɪstl/ n. cristal m.

crystalline /'krɪstlɪn/ a. cristalino, transparente.

crystallize /'krɪstl,aɪz/ v. cristalizar.

cub /kʌb/ n. cachorro m.

Cuban /'kyubən/ n. & a. cubano -na.

cube /kyub/ n. cubo m.

cubic /'kyubɪk/ a. cúbico.

cubicle /'kyubɪkəl/ n. cubículo m.

cubic measure medida de capacidad f.

cubism /'kyubɪzəm/ n. cubismo m.

cuckoo /'kuku/ n. cuco m.

cucumber /'kyukʌmbər/ n. pepino m.

cuddle /'kʌdl/ v. abrazar.

cudgel /'kʌdʒəl/ n. palo m.

cue /kyu/ n. apunte m.; (billiards) taco m.

cuff /kʌf/ n. puño de camisa. **c. links,** gemelos.

cuisine /kwɪ'zin/ n. arte culinario m.

culinary /'kyulə,nɛri/ a. culinario.

culminate /'kʌlmə,neɪt/ v. culminar.

culmination /,kʌlmə'neɪʃən/ n. culminación f.

culpable /'kʌlpəbəl/ a. culpable.

culprit /'kʌlprɪt/ n. criminal; delincuente m. & f.

cult /kʌlt/ n. culto m.

cultivate /'kʌltə,veɪt/ v. cultivar.

cultivated /'kʌltə,veɪtɪd/ a. cultivado.

cultivation /,kʌltə'veɪʃən/ n. cultivo m.; cultivación f.

cultivator /'kʌltə,veɪtər/ n. cultivador -ra.

cultural /'kʌltʃərəl/ a. cultural.

culture /'kʌltʃər/ n. cultura f.

cultured /'kʌltʃərd/ a. culto.

cumbersome /'kʌmbərsəm/ a. pesado, incómodo.

cumulative /'kyumyələtɪv/ *a.* acumulativo.
cunning /'kʌnɪŋ/ *a.* **1.** astuto. —*n.* **2.** astucia *f.*
cup /kʌp/ *n.* taza, jícara *f.*
cupboard /'kʌbərd/ *n.* armario, aparador *m.*
cupidity /kyu'pɪdɪti/ *n.* avaricia *f.*
curable /'kyurəbəl/ *a.* curable.
curator /kyu'reitər/ *n.* guardián -ana.
curb /kɜrb/ *n.* **1.** freno *m.* —*v.* **2.** refrenar.
curd /kɜrd/ *n.* cuajada *f.*
curdle /'kɜrdl/ *v.* cuajarse, coagularse.
cure /kyur/ *n.* **1.** remedio *m.* —*v.* **2.** curar, sanar.
curfew /'kɜrfyu/ *n.* toque de queda *m.*
curio /'kyuri,ou/ *n.* objeto curioso.
curiosity /,kyuri'ɒsɪti/ *n.* curiosidad *f.*
curious /'kyuriəs/ *a.* curioso.
curl /kɜrl/ *n.* **1.** rizo *m.* —*v.* **2.** rizar.
curly /'kɜrli/ *a.* rizado.
currant /'kɜrənt/ *n.* grosella *f.*
currency /'kɜrənsi/ *n.* circulación *f.*; dinero *m.*
current /'kɜrənt/ *a. & n.* corriente *f.*
current events /ɪ'vɛnts/ actualidades *f.pl.*
currently /'kɜrəntli/ *adv.* corrientemente.
curriculum /kə'rɪkyələm/ *n.* plan de estudio *m.*
curse /kɜrs/ *n.* **1.** maldición *f.* —*v.* **2.** maldecir.
cursor /'kɜrsər/ *n.* cursor *m.*
cursory /'kɜrsəri/ *a.* sumario.
curt /kɜrt/ *a.* brusco.
curtail /kɜr'teil/ *v.* reducir; restringir.
curtain /'kɜrtn̩/ *n.* cortina *f.*; *Theat.* telón *m.*
curtsy /'kɜrtsi/ *n.* **1.** reverencia *f.* —*v.* **2.** hacer una reverencia.
curvature /'kɜrvətʃər/ *n.* curvatura *f.*
curve /kɜrv/ *n.* **1.** curva *f.* —*v.* **2.** encorvar.
cushion /'kuʃən/ *n.* cojín *m.*; almohada *f.*
cuspidor /'kʌspɪ,dɔr/ *n.* escupidera *f.*
custard /'kʌstərd/ *n.* flan *m.*; natillas *f.pl.*

custodian /kʌ'stoudiən/ *n.* custodio *m.*
custody /'kʌstədi/ *n.* custodia *f.*
custom /'kʌstəm/ *n.* costumbre *f.*
customary /'kʌstə,mɛri/ *a.* acostumbrado, usual.
customer /'kʌstəmər/ *n.* cliente *m. & f.*
customhouse /'kʌstəm,haus/ **customs** *n.* aduana *f.*
customs duty /'kʌstəmz/ derechos de aduana *m.pl.*
customs officer /'kʌstəmz/ agente de aduana *m. & f.*
cut /kʌt/ *n.* **1.** corte *m.*; cortada *f.*; tajada *f.*; (printing) grabado *m.* —*v.* **2.** cortar; tajar.
cute /kyut/ *a.* mono, lindo.
cut glass cristal tallado *m.*
cuticle /'kyutɪkəl/ *n.* cutícula *f.*
cutlery /'kʌtləri/ *n.* cuchillería *f.*
cutlet /'kʌtlɪt/ *n.* chuleta *f.*
cutter /'kʌtər/ *n.* cortador -ra; *Naut.* cúter *m.*
cutthroat /'kʌt,θrout/ *n.* asesino -na.
cyberpunk /'saibər,pʌŋk/ *n.* ciberpunk *m. & f.*
cyberspace /'saibər,speis/ *n.* ciberespacio *m.*
cyclamate /'saiklə,meit, 'sɪklə-/ *n.* ciclamato *m.*
cycle /'saikəl/ *n.* ciclo *m.*
cyclist /'saiklɪst/ *n.* ciclista *m. & f.*
cyclone /'saikloun/ *n.* ciclón, huracán *m.*
cyclotron /'saiklə,trɒn, 'sɪklə-/ *n.* ciclotrón *m.*
cylinder /'sɪlɪndər/ *n.* cilindro *m.*
cylindrical /sɪ'lɪndrɪkəl/ *a.* cilíndrico.
cymbal /'sɪmbəl/ *n.* címbalo *m.*
cynic /'sɪnɪk/ *n.* cínico -ca.
cynical /'sɪnɪkəl/ *a.* cínico.
cynicism /'sɪnə,sɪzəm/ *n.* cinismo *m.*
cypress /'saiprəs/ *n.* ciprés *m.* **c. nut,** piñuela *f.*
cyst /sɪst/ *n.* quiste *m.*

D

---

dad /dæd/ *n.* papá *m.*, papito *m.*
daffodil /'dæfədɪl/ *n.* narciso *m.*
dagger /'dægər/ *n.* puñal *m.*
dahlia /'dælyə/ *n.* dalia *f.*
daily /'deili/ *a.* diario, cotidiano.
daintiness /'deintɪnɪs/ *n.* delicadeza *f.*
dainty /'deinti/ *a.* delicado.
dairy /'dɛəri/ *n.* lechería, quesería *f.*
dais /'deɪɪs/ *n.* tablado *m.*
daisy /'deizi/ *n.* margarita *f.*
dale /deil/ *n.* valle *m.*

dally /'dæli/ *v.* holgar; perder el tiempo.
dam /dæm/ *n.* presa *f.*; dique *m.*
damage /'dæmɪdʒ/ *n.* **1.** daño *m.* —*v.* **2.** dañar.
damask /'dæməsk/ *n.* damasco *f.*
damn /dæm/ *v.* condenar.
damnation /dæm'neiʃən/ *n.* condenación *f.*
damp /dæmp/ *a.* húmedo.
dampen /'dæmpən/ *v.* humedecer.
dampness /'dæmpnɪs/ *n.* humedad *f.*
damsel /'dæmzəl/ *n.* doncella *f.*

dance /dæns/ n. 1. baile m.; danza f. —v. 2. bailar.

dance hall salón de baile m.

dancer /'dænsər/ n. bailador -ra; (professional) bailarín -na.

dancing /'dænsɪŋ/ n. baile m.

dandelion /'dændl,aiən/ n. amargón m.

dandruff /'dændrəf/ n. caspa f.

dandy /'dændi/ n. petimetre m.

danger /'deindʒər/ n. peligro m.

dangerous /'deindʒərəs/ a. peligroso.

dangle /'dæŋgəl/ v. colgar.

Danish /'deiniʃ/ a. & n. danés -sa; dinamarqués -sa.

dapper /'dæpər/ a. gallardo.

dare /dɛər/ v. atreverse, osar.

daredevil /'dɛər,dɛvəl/ n. atrevido m., -da f.

daring /'dɛərɪŋ/ a. 1. atrevido. —n. 2. osadía f.

dark /dɑrk/ a. 1. obscuro; moreno. —n. 2. obscuridad f.

darken /'dɑrkən/ v. obscurecer.

darkness /'dɑrknɪs/ n. obscuridad f.

darkroom /'dɑrk,rum, -,rʊm/ n. cámara obscura f.

darling /'dɑrlɪŋ/ a. & n. querido -da, amado -da.

darn /dɑrn/ v. zurcir.

darning needle /'dɑrnɪŋ/ aguja de zurcir m.

dart /dɑrt/ n. dardo m.

dartboard /'dɑrt,bɔrd/ n. diana f.

dash /dæʃ/ n. arranque m.; Punct. guión m.

data /'deitə/ n. datos m.

database /'deitəbeis/ n. base de datos m.

data processing /'prɒsɛsɪŋ/ proceso de datos m.

date /deit/ n. fecha f.; (engagement) cita f.; (fruit) dátil m.

daughter /'dɔtər/ n. hija f.

daughter-in-law /'dɔ,tər ɪn lɔ/ n. nuera f.

daunt /dɔnt, dɑnt/ v. intimidar.

dauntless /'dɔntlɪs/ a. intrépido.

davenport /'dævən,pɔrt/ n. sofá m.

dawn /dɔn/ n. 1. alba, madrugada f. —v. 2. amanecer.

day /dei/ n. día m. **good d.,** buenos días.

daybreak /'dei,breik/ n. alba, madrugada f.

daydream /'dei,drim/ n. fantasía f.

daylight /'dei,lait/ n. luz del día.

daze /deiz/ v. aturdir.

dazzle /'dæzəl/ v. deslumbrar.

deacon /'dikən/ n. diácono m.

dead /dɛd/ a. muerto.

deaden /'dɛdn/ v. amortecer.

dead end atolladero m. (impasse); callejón sin salida m. (street).

deadline /'dɛd,lain/ n. fecha límite f.

deadlock /'dɛd,lɒk/ n. paro m.

deadly /'dɛdli/ a. mortal.

deaf /dɛf/ a. sordo.

deafen /'dɛfən/ v. ensordecer.

deafening /'dɛfənɪŋ/ a. ensordecedor.

deaf-mute /'dɛf 'myut/ n. sordomudo -da.

deafness /'dɛfnɪs/ n. sordera f.

deal /dil/ n. 1. trato m.; negociación f. **a great d., a good d.,** mucho. —v. 2. tratar; negociar.

dealer /'dilər/ n. comerciante m., (at cards) tallador -ra.

dean /din/ n. decano -na.

dear /dɪər/ a. querido; caro.

dearth /dɜrθ/ n. escasez f.

death /dɛθ/ n. muerte f.

death certificate partida de defunción f.

deathless /'dɛθlɪs/ a. inmortal.

debacle /dɪ'bɑkəl/ n. desastre m.

debase /dɪ'beis/ v. degradar.

debatable /dɪ'beitəbəl/ a. discutible.

debate /dɪ'beit/ n. 1. debate m. —v. 2. disputar, deliberar.

debauch /dɪ'bɔtʃ/ v. corromper.

debilitate /dɪ'bɪlɪ,teit/ v. debilitar.

debit /'dɛbɪt/ n. débito m.

debit balance saldo deudor m.

debonair /,dɛbə'nɛər/ a. cortés; alegre, vivo.

debris /dei'bri/ n. escombros m.pl.

debt /dɛt/ n. deuda f. **get into d.** endeudarse.

debtor /'dɛtər/ n. deudor -ra.

debug /di'bʌg/ v. depurar, limpiar.

debunk /dɪ'bʌŋk/ v. desacreditar; desenmascarar.

debut /dei'byu/ n. debut, estreno m.

debutante /'dɛbyu,tɑnt/ n. debutante f.

decade /'dɛkeid/ n. década f.

decadence /'dɛkədəns/ n. decadencia f.

decadent /'dɛkədənt/ a. decadente.

decaffeinated /di'kæfɪ,neitɪd/ a. descafeinado.

decalcomania /dɪ,kælkə'meiniə/ n. calcomanía f.

decanter /dɪ'kæntər/ n. garrafa f.

decapitate /dɪ'kæpɪ,teit/ v. descabezar.

decay /dɪ'kei/ n. 1. descaecimiento m.; (dental) caries f. —v. 2. decaer; (dental) cariarse.

deceased /dɪ'sist/ a. muerto, difunto.

deceit /dɪ'sit/ n. engaño m.

deceitful /dɪ'sitfəl/ a. engañoso.

deceive /dɪ'siv/ v. engañar.

December /dɪ'sɛmbər/ n. diciembre m.

decency /'disənsi/ n. decencia f.; decoro m.

decent /'disənt/ a. decente.

decentralize /di'sɛntrə,laiz/ v. descentralizar.

deception /dɪ'sɛpʃən/ n. decepción f.

deceptive /dɪ'sɛptɪv/ a. deceptivo.

decibel /'desə‚bel/ n. decibelio m.
decide /dɪ'saɪd/ v. decidir.
decimal /'desəməl/ a. decimal.
decipher /dɪ'saɪfər/ v. descifrar.
decision /dɪ'sɪʒən/ n. decisión f.
decisive /dɪ'saɪsɪv/ a. decisivo.
deck /dek/ n. cubierta f.
deck chair tumbona f.
declamation /‚deklə'meɪʃən/ n. declamación f.
declaration /‚deklə'reɪʃən/ n. declaración f.
declarative /dɪ'klærətɪv/ a. declarativo.
declare /dɪ'klɛər/ v. declarar.
declension /dɪ'klenʃən/ n. declinación f.
decline /dɪ'klaɪn/ n. **1.** decadencia f. —v. **2.** decaer; negarse; *Gram.* declinar.
decompose /‚dikəm'pouz/ v. descomponer.
decongestant /‚dikən'dʒestənt/ n. descongestionante m.
decorate /'dekə‚reɪt/ v. decorar, adornar.
decoration /‚dekə'reɪʃən/ n. decoración f.
decorative /'dekərətɪv/ a. decorativo.
decorator /'dekə‚reɪtər/ n. decorador -ra.
decorous /'dekərəs/ a. correcto.
decorum /dɪ'kɔrəm/ n. decoro m.
decrease /dɪ'kris/ v. disminuir.
decree /dɪ'kri/ n. decreto m.
decrepit /dɪ'krepɪt/ a. decrépito.
decry /dɪ'kraɪ/ v. desacreditar.
dedicate /'dedɪ‚keɪt/ v. dedicar; consagrar.
dedication /‚dedɪ'keɪʃən/ n. dedicación; dedicatoria f.
deduce /dɪ'dus/ v. deducir.
deduction /dɪ'dʌkʃən/ n. rebaja; deducción f.
deductive /dɪ'dʌktɪv/ a. deductivo.
deed /did/ n. acción; hazaña f.
deem /dim/ v. estimar.
deep /dip/ a. hondo, profundo.
deepen /'dipən/ v. profundizar, ahondar.
deep freeze congelación f.
deeply /'dipli/ adv. profundamente.
deer /dɪər/ n. venado, ciervo m.
deface /dɪ'feɪs/ v. mutilar.
defamation /‚defə'meɪʃən/ n. calumnia f.
defame /dɪ'feɪm/ v. difamar.
default /dɪ'fɔlt/ n. **1.** defecto m. —v. **2.** faltar.
defeat /dɪ'fit/ n. **1.** derrota f. —v. **2.** derrotar.
defeatism /dɪ'fitɪzəm/ n. derrotismo m.
defect /'difekt, dɪ'fekt/ n. defecto m.
defective /dɪ'fektɪv/ a. defectivo.
defend /dɪ'fend/ v. defender.
defendant /dɪ'fendənt/ n. acusado -da.
defender /dɪ'fendər/ n. defensor -ra.
defense /dɪ'fens/ n. defensa f.
defensive /dɪ'fensɪv/ a. defensivo.
defer /dɪ'fɜr/ v. aplazar; deferir.

deference /'defərəns/ n. deferencia f.
defiance /dɪ'faɪəns/ n. desafío m.
defiant /dɪ'faɪənt/ a. desafiador.
deficiency /dɪ'fɪʃənsi/ n. defecto m.
deficient /dɪ'fɪʃənt/ a. deficiente.
deficit /'defəsɪt/ n. déficit, descubierto m.
defile /dɪ'faɪl/ n. **1.** desfiladero m. —v. **2.** profanar.
define /dɪ'faɪn/ v. definir.
definite /'defənɪt/ a. exacto; definitivo.
definitely /'defənɪtli/ adv. definitivamente.
definition /‚defə'nɪʃən/ n. definición f.
definitive /dɪ'fɪnɪtɪv/ a. definitivo.
deflation /dɪ'fleɪʒən/ n. desinflación f.
deflect /dɪ'flekt/ v. desviar.
deform /dɪ'fɔrm/ v. deformar.
deformity /dɪ'fɔrmɪti/ n. deformidad f.
defraud /dɪ'frɔd/ v. defraudar.
defray /dɪ'freɪ/ v. costear.
defrost /dɪ'frɔst/ v. descongelar.
deft /deft/ a. diestro.
defy /dɪ'faɪ/ v. desafiar.
degenerate /a dɪ'dʒenərɪt; v -‚reɪt/ a. **1.** degenerado. —v. **2.** degenerar.
degeneration /dɪ‚dʒenə'reɪʃən/ n. degeneración f.
degradation /‚degrɪ'deɪʃən/ n. degradación f.
degrade /dɪ'greɪd/ v. degradar.
degree /dɪ'gri/ n. grado m.
deign /deɪn/ v. condescender.
deity /'diɪti/ n. deidad f.
dejected /dɪ'dʒektɪd/ a. abatido.
dejection /dɪ'dʒekʃən/ n. tristeza f.
delay /dɪ'leɪ/ n. **1.** retardo m., demora f. —v. **2.** tardar, demorar.
delegate /n 'delɪgɪt; v -‚geɪt/ n. **1.** delegado -da. —v. **2.** delegar.
delegation /‚delɪ'geɪʃən/ n. delegación f.
delete /dɪ'lit/ v. suprimir, tachar.
deliberate /a dɪ'lɪbərɪt; v -ə‚reɪt/ a. **1.** premeditado. —v. **2.** deliberar.
deliberately /dɪ'lɪbərɪtli/ adv. deliberadamente.
deliberation /dɪ‚lɪbə'reɪʃən/ n. deliberación f.
deliberative /dɪ'lɪbərətɪv/ a. deliberativo.
delicacy /'delɪkəsi/ n. delicadeza f.
delicate /'delɪkɪt/ a. delicado.
delicious /dɪ'lɪʃəs/ a. delicioso.
delight /dɪ'laɪt/ n. deleite m.
delightful /dɪ'laɪtfəl/ a. deleitoso.
delinquency /dɪ'lɪŋkwənsi/ a. delincuencia f.
delinquent /dɪ'lɪŋkwənt/ a. & n. delincuente. m. & f.
delirious /dɪ'lɪəriəs/ a. delirante.
deliver /dɪ'lɪvər/ v. entregar.
deliverance /dɪ'lɪvərəns/ n. liberación; salvación f.

delivery /dɪ'lɪvəri/ n. entrega f.; Med. parto m.

delude /dɪ'lud/ v. engañar.

deluge /'dɛlyudʒ/ n. inundación f.

delusion /dɪ'luʒən/ n. decepción f.; engaño m.

delve /dɛlv/ v. cavar, sondear.

demagogue /'dɛmə,gɒg/ n. demagogo -ga.

demand /dɪ'mænd/ n. **1.** demanda f. —v. **2.** demandar; exigir.

demarcation /,dimɑr'keɪʃən/ n. demarcación f.

demeanor /dɪ'minər/ n. conducta f.

demented /dɪ'mɛntɪd/ a. demente, loco.

demilitarize /di'mɪltə,raɪz/ v. desmilitarizar.

demobilize /di'moubə,laɪz/ v. desmovilizar.

democracy /dɪ'mɒkrəsi/ n. democracia f.

democrat /'dɛmə,kræt/ n. demócrata m. & f.

democratic /,dɛmə'krætɪk/ a. democrático.

demolish /dɪ'mɒlɪʃ/ v. demoler.

demon /'dimən/ n. demonio m.

demonstrate /'dɛmən,streɪt/ v. demostrar.

demonstration /,dɛmən'streɪʃən/ n. demostración f.

demonstrative /də'mɒnstrətɪv/ a. demostrativo.

demoralize /dɪ'mɔrə,laɪz, -'mɒr-/ v. desmoralizar.

demure /dɪ'myʊr/ a. modesto, serio.

den /dɛn/ n. madriguera, caverna f.

denature /di'neɪtʃər/ v. alterar.

denial /dɪ'naɪəl/ n. negación f.

denim /'dɛnəm/ n. dril, tela vaquera.

Denmark /'dɛnmɑrk/ n. Dinamarca f.

denomination /dɪ,nɒmə'neɪʃən/ n. denominación; secta f.

denote /dɪ'nout/ v. denotar.

denounce /dɪ'naʊns/ v. denunciar.

dense /dɛns/ a. denso, espeso; estúpido.

density /'dɛnsɪti/ n. densidad f.

dent /dɛnt/ n. **1.** abolladura f. —v. **2.** abollar.

dental /'dɛntl/ a. dental.

dentist /'dɛntɪst/ n. dentista m & f.

dentistry /'dɛntəstri/ n. odontología f.

denture /'dɛntʃər/ n. dentadura f.

denunciation /dɪ,nʌnsi'eɪʃən/ n. denunciación f.

deny /dɪ'naɪ/ v. negar, rehusar.

deodorant /di'oudərənt/ n. desodorante m.

depart /dɪ'pɑrt/ v. partir; irse, marcharse.

department /dɪ'pɑrtmənt/ n. departamento m.

departmental /dɪ,pɑrt'mɛntl/ a. departamental.

department store grandes almacenes m.pl.

departure /dɪ'pɑrtʃər/ n. salida; desviación f.

depend /dɪ'pɛnd/ v. depender.

dependability /dɪ,pɛndə'bɪlɪti/ n. confiabilidad f.

dependable /dɪ'pɛndəbəl/ a. confiable.

dependence /dɪ'pɛndəns/ n. dependencia f.

dependent /dɪ'pɛndənt/ a. & n. dependiente m. & f.

depict /dɪ'pɪkt/ v. pintar; representar.

deplete /dɪ'plit/ v. agotar.

deplorable /dɪ'plɔrəbəl/ a. deplorable.

deplore /dɪ'plɔr/ v. deplorar.

deport /dɪ'pɔrt/ v. deportar.

deportation /,dipɔr'teɪʃən/ n. deportación f.

deportment /dɪ'pɔrtmənt/ n. conducta f.

depose /dɪ'pouz/ v. deponer.

deposit /dɪ'pɒzɪt/ n. **1.** depósito m. (of money); yacimiento (of ore, etc.) m. —v. **2.** depositar.

depositor /dɪ'pɒzɪtər/ n. depositante m. & f.

depot /'dipou/ n. depósito m.; (railway) estación f.

depravity /dɪ'prævɪti/ n. depravación f.

deprecate /'dɛprɪ,keɪt/ v. deprecar.

depreciate /dɪ'priʃi,eɪt/ v. depreciar.

depreciation /dɪ,priʃi'eɪʃən/ n. depreciación f.

depredation /,dɛprə'deɪʃən/ n. depredación f.

depress /dɪ'prɛs/ v. deprimir; desanimar.

depression /dɪ'prɛʃən/ n. depresión f.

deprive /dɪ'praɪv/ v. privar.

depth /dɛpθ/ n. profundidad, hondura f.

depth charge carga de profundidad f.

deputy /'dɛpyəti/ n. diputado -da.

deride /dɪ'raɪd/ v. burlar.

derision /dɪ'rɪʒən/ n. burla f.

derivation /,dɛrə'veɪʃən/ n. derivación f.

derivative /dɪ'rɪvətɪv/ a. derivativo.

derive /dɪ'raɪv/ v. derivar.

dermatologist /,dɜrmə'tɒlədʒɪst/ n. dermatólogo -ga.

derogatory /dɪ'rɒgə,tɔri/ a. derogatorio.

derrick /'dɛrɪk/ n. grúa f.

descend /dɪ'sɛnd/ v. descender, bajar.

descendant /dɪ'sɛndənt/ n. descendiente m. & f.

descent /dɪ'sɛnt/ n. descenso m.; origen m.

describe /dɪ'skraɪb/ v. describir.

description /dɪ'skrɪpʃən/ n. descripción f.

descriptive /dɪ'skrɪptɪv/ a. descriptivo.

desecrate /'dɛsɪ,kreɪt/ v. profanar.

desert /n /'dɛzərt/ v /dɪ'zɜrt/ n. **1.** desierto m. —v. **2.** abandonar.

deserter /dɪ'zɜrtər/ n. desertor -ra.

desertion /dɪ'zɜrʃən/ n. deserción f.

deserve /dɪ'zɜrv/ v. merecer.

design /dɪ'zaɪn/ n. **1.** diseño m. —v. **2.** diseñar.

designate /'dɛzɪg,neit/ v. señalar, apuntar; designar.

designation /,dɛzɪg'neiʃən/ n. designación f.

designer /dɪ'zainər/ n. diseñador -ra; (technical) proyectista m. & f.

designer clothes, designer clothing ropa de marca f.

desirability /dɪ,zaiərə'bɪliti/ n. conveniencia f.

desirable /dɪ'zaiərəbəl/ a. deseable.

desire /dɪ'zaiər/ n. **1.** deseo m. —v. **2.** desear.

desirous /dɪ'zaiərəs/ a. deseoso.

desist /dɪ'sɪst/ v. desistir.

desk /dɛsk/ n. escritorio m.

desk clerk recepcionista m. & f.

desktop computer /'dɛsk,tɒp/ computadora de sobremesa f., ordenador de sobremesa f.

desolate /a 'dɛsəlɪt; v -,leit/ a. **1.** desolado. —v. **2.** desolar.

desolation /,dɛsə'leiʃən/ n. desolación, ruina f.

despair /dɪ'spɛər/ n. **1.** desesperación f. —v. **2.** desesperar.

despatch /dɪ'spætʃ/ dispatch n. **1.** despacho m.; prontitud f. —v. **2.** despachar.

desperado /,dɛspə'radou/ n. bandido m.

desperate /'dɛspərɪt/ a. desesperado.

desperation /,dɛspə'reiʃən/ n. desesperación f.

despicable /'dɛspɪkəbəl/ a. vil.

despise /dɪ'spaiz/ v. despreciar.

despite /dɪ'spait/ prep. a pesar de.

despondent /dɪ'spɒndənt/ a. abatido; desanimado.

despot /'dɛspət/ n. déspota m & f.

despotic /dɛs'pɒtɪk/ a. despótico.

dessert /dɪ'zərt/ n. postre m.

destination /,dɛstə'neiʃən/ n. destinación f.

destine /'dɛstɪn/ v. destinar.

destiny /'dɛstəni/ n. destino m.

destitute /'dɛstɪ,tut/ a. destituido, indigente.

destitution /,dɛstɪ'tuʃən/ n. destitución f.

destroy /dɪ'strɔi/ v. destrozar, destruir.

destroyer /dɪ'strɔiər/ n. destruidor -ra; (naval) destructor m.

destruction /dɪ'strʌkʃən/ n. destrucción f.

destructive /dɪ'strʌktɪv/ a. destructivo.

desultory /'dɛsəl,tɔri/ a. inconexo; casual.

detach /dɪ'tætʃ/ v. separar, desprender.

detachment /dɪ'tætʃmənt/ n. Mil. destacamento; desprendimiento m.

detail /dɪ'teil/ n. **1.** detalle m. —v. **2.** detallar.

detain /dɪ'tein/ v. detener.

detect /dɪ'tɛkt/ v. descubrir.

detection /dɪ'tɛkʃən/ n. detección f.

detective /dɪ'tɛktɪv/ n. detective m. & f.

détente /dei'tɑnt/ n. distensión f.; Pol. detente.

detention /dɪ'tɛnʃən/ n. detención; cautividad f.

deter /dɪ'tɜr/ v. disuadir.

detergent /dɪ'tɜrdʒənt/ n. & a. detergente m.

deteriorate /dɪ'tɪəriə,reit/ v. deteriorar.

deterioration /dɪ,tɪəriə'reiʃən/ n. deterioración f.

determination /dɪ,tɜrmə'neiʃən/ n. determinación f.

determine /dɪ'tɜrmɪn/ v. determinar.

deterrence /dɪ'tɜrəns/ n. disuasión f.

detest /dɪ'tɛst/ v. detestar.

detonate /'dɛtə,neit/ v. detonar.

detour /'ditur/ n. desvío m. v. desviar.

detract /dɪ'trækt/ v. disminuir.

detriment /'dɛtrəmənt/ n. detrimento m., daño m.

detrimental /,dɛtrə'mɛntl/ a. dañoso.

devaluate /di'vælyu,eit/ v. depreciar.

devastate /'dɛvə,steit/ v. devastar.

develop /dɪ'vɛləp/ v. desarrollar; Phot. revelar.

developing nation /dɪ'vɛləpɪŋ/ nación en desarrollo.

development /dɪ'vɛləpmənt/ n. desarrollo m.

deviate /'divi,eit/ v. desviar.

deviation /,divi'eiʃən/ n. desviación f.

device /dɪ'vais/ n. aparato; artificio m.

devil /'dɛvəl/ n. diablo, demonio m.

devious /'diviəs/ a. desviado.

devise /dɪ'vaiz/ v. inventar.

devoid /dɪ'vɔid/ a. desprovisto.

devote /dɪ'vout/ v. dedicar, consagrar.

devoted /dɪ'voutɪd/ a. devoto.

devotee /,dɛvə'ti/ n. aficionado -da.

devotion /dɪ'vouʃən/ n. devoción f.

devour /dɪ'vaur/ v. devorar.

devout /dɪ'vaut/ a. devoto.

dew /du/ n. rocío, sereno m.

dexterity /dɛk'stɛrɪti/ n. destreza f.

dexterous /'dɛkstrəs/ a. diestro.

diabetes /,daiə'bitis/ n. diabetes f.

diabolic /,daiə'bɒlɪk/ a. diabólico.

diadem /'daiə,dɛm/ n. diadema f.

diagnose /'daiəg,nous/ v. diagnosticar.

diagnosis /,daiəg'nousɪs/ n. diagnóstico m.

diagonal /dai'ægənl/ n. diagonal f.

diagram /'daiə,græm/ n. diagrama m.

dial /'daiəl/ n. **1.** cuadrante m., carátula f. —v. **2.** dial up marcar.

dialect /'daiə,lɛkt/ n. dialecto m.

dialing code /'daiəlɪŋ/ prefijo m.

dialogue /'daiə,lɔg/ n. diálogo m.

dial tone señal de marcar f.

diameter /dai'æmɪtər/ n. diámetro m.

diamond /'daimənd/ n. diamante, brillante m.

diaper /'daipər/ n. pañal m.

diarrhea /,daiə'riə/ n. diarrea f.

diary /'daiəri/ n. diario m.

diathermy /'daiə,θərmi/ n. diatermia f.

dice /dais/ n. dados m.pl.

dictate /'dikteit/ n. **1.** mandato m. —v. **2.** dictar.

dictation /dik'teiʃən/ n. dictado m.

dictator /'dikteitər/ n. dictador -ra.

dictatorship /dik'teitər,ʃip/ n. dictadura f.

diction /'dikʃən/ n. dicción f.

dictionary /'dikʃə,neri/ n. diccionario m.

die /dai/ n. **1.** matriz f.; (game) dado m. —v. **2.** morir.

diet /'daiit/ n. dieta f.

dietary /'daii,teri/ a. dietético.

dietitian /,daii'tiʃən/ n. & a. dietético -ca.

differ /'difər/ v. diferir.

difference /'difərəns/ n. diferencia f. **to make no d.,** no importar.

different /'difərənt/ a. diferente, distinto.

differential /,difə'renʃəl/ n. diferencial f.

differentiate /,difə'renʃi,eit/ v. diferenciar.

difficult /'difi,kʌlt/ a. difícil.

difficulty /'difi,kʌlti/ n. dificultad f.

diffident /'difidənt/ a. tímido.

diffuse /di'fyuz/ v. difundir.

diffusion /di'fyuʒən/ n. difusión f.

dig /dig/ v. cavar.

digest /n 'daidʒest; v di'dʒest, dai-/ n. **1.** extracto m. —v. **2.** digerir.

digestible /di'dʒestəbəl, dai-/ a. digerible.

digestion /di'dʒestʃən, dai-/ n. digestión f.

digestive /di'dʒestiv, dai-/ a. digestivo.

digital /'didʒitl/ a. digital.

digitalis /,didʒi'tælis/ n. digital f.

dignified /'dignə,faid/ a. digno.

dignify /'dignə,fai/ v. dignificar.

dignitary /'digni,teri/ n. dignatario -ria.

dignity /'digniti/ n. dignidad f.

digress /di'gres, dai-/ v. divagar.

digression /di'greʃən, dai-/ n. digresión f.

dike /daik/ n. dique m.

dilapidated /di'læpi,deitid/ a. dilapidado.

dilapidation /di,læpə'deiʃən/ n. dilapidación f.

dilate /dai'leit/ v. dilatar.

dilatory /'dilə,tɔri/ a. dilatorio.

dilemma /di'lemə/ n. dilema m.

dilettante /'dilə,tɑnt/ n. diletante m. & f.

diligence /'dilidʒəns/ n. diligencia f.

diligent /'dilidʒənt/ a. diligente, aplicado.

dilute /di'lut, dai-/ v. diluir.

dim /dim/ a. **1.** oscuro. —v. **2.** oscurecer.

dimension /di'menʃən/ n. dimensión f.

diminish /di'miniʃ/ v. disminuir.

diminution /,dimə'nuʃən/ n. disminución f.

diminutive /di'minyətiv/ a. diminutivo.

dimness /'dimnis/ n. oscuridad f.

dimple /'dimpəl/ n. hoyuelo m.

din /din/ n. alboroto, estrépito m.

dine /dain/ v. comer, cenar.

diner /'dainər/ n. coche comedor m.

dingy /'dindʒi/ a. deslucido, deslustrado.

dining room /'dainiŋ/ comedor m.

dinner /'dinər/ n. comida, cena f.

dinosaur /'dainə,sɔr/ n. dinosauro m.

diocese /'daiəsis/ n. diócesis f.

dip /dip/ v. sumergir, hundir.

diphtheria /dif'θiəriə/ n. difteria f.

diploma /di'ploumə/ n. diploma m.

diplomacy /di'plouməsi/ n. diplomacia f.

diplomat /'diplə,mæt/ n. diplomático -ca.

diplomatic /,diplə'mætik/ a. diplomático.

dipper /'dipər/ n. cucharón m.

dire /daiər/ a. horrendo.

direct /di'rekt, dai-/ a. **1.** directo. —v. **2.** dirigir.

direction /di'rekʃən, 'dai-/ n. dirección f.

directive /di'rektiv, dai-/ n. directiva f.

directly /di'rektli, dai-/ adv. directamente.

director /di'rektər, dai-/ n. director -ra.

directory /di'rektəri, dai-/ n. directorio m., guía f.

dirigible /'diridʒəbəl/ n. dirigible m.

dirt /dərt/ n. basura f.; (earth) tierra f.

dirt-cheap /'dərt 'tʃip/ a. tirado.

dirty /'dərti/ a. sucio.

dis /dis/ v. Colloq. ofender, faltar al respeto.

disability /,disə'biliti/ n. inhabilidad f.

disable /dis'eibəl/ v. incapacitar.

disabuse /,disə'byuz/ v. desengañar.

disadvantage /,disəd'væntidʒ/ n. desventaja f.

disagree /,disə'gri/ v. desconvenir; disentir.

disagreeable /,disə'griəbəl/ a. desagradable.

disagreement /,disə'grimənt/ n. desacuerdo m.

disappear /,disə'piər/ v. desaparecer.

disappearance /,disə'piərəns/ n. desaparición f.

disappoint /,disə'pɔint/ v. disgustar, desilusionar.

disappointment /,disə'pɔintmənt/ n. disgusto m., desilusión f.

disapproval /,disə'pruvəl/ n. desaprobación f.

disapprove /,disə'pruv/ v. desaprobar.

disarm /dis'ɑrm/ v. desarmar.

disarmament /dis'ɑrməmənt/ n. desarme m.

disarrange /,disə'reindʒ/ v. desordenar; desarreglar.

disaster /di'zæstər/ n. desastre m.

disastrous /di'zæstrəs/ a. desastroso.

disavow /,disə'vau/ v. repudiar.

disavowal /ˌdɪsəˈvaʊəl/ n. repudiación f.

disband /dɪsˈbænd/ v. dispersarse.

disbelieve /ˌdɪsbɪˈliv/ v. descreer.

disburse /dɪsˈbɜrs/ v. desembolsar, pagar.

discard /dɪˈskɑrd/ v. descartar.

discern /dɪˈsɜrn/ v. discernir.

discerning /dɪˈsɜrnɪŋ/ a. discernidor, perspicaz.

discernment /dɪˈsɜrnmənt/ n. discernimiento m.

discharge /dɪsˈtʃɑrdʒ/ v. descargar; despedir.

disciple /dɪˈsaɪpəl/ n. discípulo -la.

disciplinary /ˈdɪsəpləˌnɛri/ a. disciplinario.

discipline /ˈdɪsəplɪn/ n. disciplina f.

disclaim /dɪsˈkleɪm/ v. repudiar.

disclaimer /dɪsˈkleɪmər/ n. negación f.

disclose /dɪsˈkloʊz/ v. revelar.

disclosure /dɪsˈkloʊʒər/ n. revelación f.

disco /ˈdɪskoʊ/ n. discoteca f.

discolor /dɪsˈkʌlər/ v. descolorar.

discomfort /dɪsˈkʌmfərt/ n. incomodidad f.

disconcert /ˌdɪskənˈsɜrt/ v. desconcertar.

disconnect /ˌdɪskəˈnɛkt/ v. desunir; desconectar.

disconnected /ˌdɪskəˈnɛktɪd/ a. desunido.

disconsolate /dɪsˈkɒnsəlɪt/ a. desconsolado.

discontent /ˌdɪskənˈtɛnt/ n. descontento m.

discontented /ˌdɪskənˈtɛntɪd/ a. descontento.

discontinue /ˌdɪskənˈtɪnyu/ v descontinuar.

discord /ˈdɪskɔrd/ n. discordia f.

discordant /dɪsˈkɔrdənt/ a. disonante.

discotheque /ˈdɪskəˌtɛk/ n. discoteca f.

discount /ˈdɪskaʊnt/ n. descuento m.

discourage /dɪˈskɜrɪdʒ/ v. desalentar; desanimar.

discouragement /dɪˈskɜrɪdʒmənt/ n. desaliento, desánimo m.

discourse /ˈdɪskɔrs/ n. discurso m.

discourteous /dɪsˈkɜrtiəs/ a. descortés.

discourtesy /dɪsˈkɜrtəsi/ n. descortesía f.

discover /dɪˈskʌvər/ v. descubrir.

discoverer /dɪˈskʌvərər/ n. descubridor -ra.

discovery /dɪˈskʌvəri/ n. descubrimiento m.

discreet /dɪˈskrit/ a. discreto.

discrepancy /dɪˈskrɛpənsi/ n. discrepancia f.

discretion /dɪˈskrɛʃən/ n. discreción f.

discriminate /dɪˈskrɪmˌəneɪt/ v. distinguir. **d. against** discriminar contra.

discrimination /dɪˌskrɪməˈneɪʃən/ n. discernimiento m.; discriminación f.

discuss /dɪˈskʌs/ v. discutir.

discussion /dɪˈskʌʃən/ n. discusión f.

disdain /dɪsˈdeɪn/ n. **1.** desdén m. —v. **2.** desdeñar.

disdainful /dɪsˈdeɪnfəl/ a. desdeñoso.

disease /dɪˈziz/ n. enfermedad f., mal m.

disembark /ˌdɪsɛmˈbɑrk/ v. desembarcar.

disentangle /ˌdɪsɛnˈtæŋgəl/ v. desenredar.

disfigure /dɪsˈfɪgyər/ v. desfigurar.

disgrace /dɪsˈgreɪs/ n. **1.** vergüenza; deshonra f. —v. **2.** deshonrar.

disgraceful /dɪsˈgreɪsfəl/ a. vergonzoso.

disguise /dɪsˈgaɪz/ n. **1.** disfraz m. —v. **2.** disfrazar.

disgust /dɪsˈgʌst/ n. **1.** repugnancia —v **2.** fastidiar; repugnar.

dish /dɪʃ/ n. plato m.

dishearten /dɪsˈhɑrtn/ v. desanimar; descorazonar.

dishonest /dɪsˈɒnɪst/ a. deshonesto.

dishonesty /dɪsˈɒnəsti/ n. deshonestidad f.

dishonor /dɪsˈɒnər/ n. **1.** deshonra f. —v. **2.** deshonrar.

dishonorable /dɪsˈɒnərəbəl/ a. deshonroso.

dishwasher /ˈdɪʃˌwɒʃər/ n. lavaplatos m.

disillusion /ˌdɪsɪˈluʒən/ n. **1.** desengaño m. —v. **2.** desengañar.

disinfect /ˌdɪsɪnˈfɛkt/ v. desinfectar.

disinfectant /ˌdɪsɪnˈfɛktənt/ n. desinfectante m.

disinherit /ˌdɪsɪnˈhɛrɪt/ v. desheredar.

disintegrate /dɪsˈɪntəˌgreɪt/ v. desintegrar.

disinterested /dɪsˈɪntəˌrɛstɪd, -trɪstɪd/ a. desinteresado.

disk /dɪsk/ n. disco m.

disk drive disquetera f.

diskette /dɪˈskɛt/ n. disquete m.

disk jockey pinchadiscos m. & f.

dislike /dɪsˈlaɪk/ n. **1.** antipatía f. —v. **2.** no gustar de.

dislocate /ˈdɪsloʊˌkeɪt/ v. dislocar.

dislodge /dɪsˈlɒdʒ/ v. desalojar; desprender.

disloyal /dɪsˈlɔɪəl/ a. desleal; infiel.

disloyalty /dɪsˈlɔɪəlti/ n. deslealtad f.

dismal /ˈdɪzməl/ a. lúgubre.

dismantle /dɪsˈmæntl/ v. desmantelar, desmontar.

dismay /dɪsˈmeɪ/ n. **1.** consternación f. —v. **2.** consternar.

dismiss /dɪsˈmɪs/ v. despedir.

dismissal /dɪsˈmɪsəl/ n. despedida f.

dismount /dɪsˈmaʊnt/ v. apearse, desmontarse.

disobedience /ˌdɪsəˈbidiəns/ n. desobediencia f.

disobedient /ˌdɪsəˈbidiənt/ a. desobediente.

disobey /ˌdɪsəˈbeɪ/ v. desobedecer.

disorder /dɪsˈɔrdər/ n. desorden m.

disorderly /dɪsˈɔrdərli/ a. desarreglado, desordenado.

disown /dɪsˈoʊn/ v. repudiar.

dispassionate /dɪsˈpæʃənɪt/ a. desapasionado; templado.

dispatch /dɪˈspætʃ/ n. **1.** despacho m. —v. **2.** despachar.

dispel /dɪˈspel/ v. dispersar.

dispensary /dɪˈspensəri/ n. dispensario m.

dispensation /ˌdɪspənˈseɪʃən/ n. dispensación f.

dispense /dɪˈspens/ v. dispensar.

dispersal /dɪˈspɜːrsəl/ n. dispersión f.

disperse /dɪˈspɜːrs/ v. dispersar.

displace /dɪsˈpleɪs/ v. dislocar.

display /dɪˈspleɪ/ n. 1. despliegue m., exhibición f. —v. 2. desplegar, exhibir.

displease /dɪsˈpliz/ v. disgustar; ofender.

displeasure /dɪsˈpleʒər/ n. disgusto, sinsabor m.

disposable /dɪˈspoʊzəbəl/ a. disponible; desechable.

disposal /dɪˈspoʊzəl/ n. disposición f.

dispose /dɪˈspoʊz/ v. disponer.

disposition /ˌdɪspəˈzɪʃən/ n. disposición f.; índole f., genio m.

dispossess /ˌdɪspəˈzes/ v. desposeer.

disproportionate /ˌdɪsprəˈpɔːrʃənɪt/ a. desproporcionado.

disprove /dɪsˈpruv/ v. confutar.

dispute /dɪˈspjut/ n. 1. disputa f. —v. 2. disputar.

disqualify /dɪsˈkwɑːləˌfaɪ/ v. inhabilitar.

disregard /ˌdɪsrɪˈɡɑːrd/ n. 1. desatención f. —v. 2. desatender.

disrepair /ˌdɪsrɪˈpeər/ n. descompostura f.

disreputable /dɪsˈrepjətəbəl/ a. desacreditado.

disrespect /ˌdɪsrɪˈspekt/ n. falta de respeto, f., desacato m.

disrespectful /ˌdɪsrɪˈspektfəl/ a. irrespetuoso.

disrobe /dɪsˈroʊb/ v. desvestir.

disrupt /dɪsˈrʌpt/ v. romper; desbaratar.

dissatisfaction /ˌdɪssætɪsˈfækʃən/ n. descontento m.

dissatisfy /dɪsˈsætɪsˌfaɪ/ v. descontentar.

dissect /dɪˈsekt/ v. disecar.

dissemble /dɪˈsembəl/ v. disimular.

disseminate /dɪˈseməˌneɪt/ v. diseminar.

dissension /dɪˈsenʃən/ n. disensión f.

dissent /dɪˈsent/ n. 1. disensión f. —v. 2. disentir.

dissertation /ˌdɪsərˈteɪʃən/ n. disertación f.

dissimilar /dɪˈsɪmələr/ a. desemejante.

dissipate /ˈdɪsəˌpeɪt/ v. disipar.

dissipation /ˌdɪsəˈpeɪʃən/ n. disipación f.; libertinaje m.

dissolute /ˈdɪsəˌlut/ a. disoluto.

dissolution /ˌdɪsəˈluʃən/ n. disolución f.

dissolve /dɪˈzɒlv/ v. disolver; derretirse.

dissonant /ˈdɪsənənt/ a. disonante.

dissuade /dɪˈsweɪd/ v. disuadir.

distance /ˈdɪstəns/ n. distancia f. **at a d., in the d.,** a lo lejos.

distant /ˈdɪstənt/ a. distante, lejano.

distaste /dɪsˈteɪst/ n. disgusto, sinsabor m.

distasteful /dɪsˈteɪstfəl/ a. desagradable.

distill /dɪˈstɪl/ v. destilar.

distillation /ˌdɪstɪˈleɪʃən/ n. destilación f.

distillery /dɪˈstɪləri/ n. destilería f.

distinct /dɪˈstɪŋkt/ a. distinto.

distinction /dɪˈstɪŋkʃən/ n. distinción f.

distinctive /dɪˈstɪŋktɪv/ a. distintivo; característico.

distinctly /dɪˈstɪŋktli/ adv. distintamente.

distinguish /dɪˈstɪŋɡwɪʃ/ v. distinguir.

distinguished /dɪˈstɪŋɡwɪʃt/ a. distinguido.

distort /dɪˈstɔːrt/ v. falsear; torcer.

distract /dɪˈstrækt/ v. distraer.

distraction /dɪˈstrækʃən/ n. distracción f.

distraught /dɪˈstrɔːt/ a. aturrullado; demente.

distress /dɪˈstres/ n. 1. dolor m. —v. 2. afligir.

distressing /dɪˈstresɪŋ/ a. penoso.

distribute /dɪˈstrɪbjut/ v. distribuir.

distribution /ˌdɪstrəˈbjuʃən/ n. distribución f.; reparto m.

distributor /dɪˈstrɪbjətər/ n. distribuidor -ra.

district /ˈdɪstrɪkt/ n. distrito m.

distrust /dɪsˈtrʌst/ n. 1. desconfianza f. —v. 2. desconfiar.

distrustful /dɪsˈtrʌstfəl/ a. desconfiado; sospechoso.

disturb /dɪˈstɜːrb/ v. incomodar; inquietar.

disturbance /dɪˈstɜːrbəns/ n. disturbio m.

disturbing /dɪˈstɜːrbɪŋ/ a. inquietante.

ditch /dɪtʃ/ n. zanja f.; foso m.

divan /dɪˈvæn/ n. diván m.

dive /daɪv/ n. 1. clavado m.; Colloq. leonera f. —v. 2. echar un clavado; bucear.

diver /ˈdaɪvər/ n. buzo m.

diverge /dɪˈvɜːrdʒ/ v. divergir.

divergence /dɪˈvɜːrdʒəns/ n. divergencia f.

divergent /dɪˈvɜːrdʒənt/ a. divergente.

diverse /dɪˈvɜːrs/ a. diverso.

diversion /dɪˈvɜːrʒən/ n. diversión f.; pasatiempo m.

diversity /dɪˈvɜːrsɪti/ n. diversidad f.

divert /dɪˈvɜːrt/ v. desviar; divertir.

divest /dɪˈvest/ v. desnudar, despojar.

divide /dɪˈvaɪd/ v. dividir.

dividend /ˈdɪvɪˌdend/ n. dividendo m.

divine /dɪˈvaɪn/ a. divino.

divinity /dɪˈvɪnɪti/ n. divinidad f.

division /dɪˈvɪʒən/ n. división f.

divorce /dɪˈvɔːrs/ n. 1. divorcio m. —v. 2. divorciar.

divorcee /dɪvɔːrˈseɪ/ n. divorciado -da.

divulge /dɪˈvʌldʒ/ v. divulgar, revelar.

dizziness /ˈdɪzinəs/ n. vértigo, mareo m.

dizzy /ˈdɪzi/ a. mareado.

DNA abbr. (deoxyribonucleic acid) ADN (ácido deoxirribonucleico) m.

do /du/ v. hacer.

docile /'dɒsəl/ a. dócil.

dock /dɒk/ n. **1.** muelle m. **dry d.,** astillero m. —v. **2.** entrar en muelle.

doctor /'dɒktər/ n. médico m.; doctor -ra.

doctorate /'dɒktərɪt/ n. doctorado m.

doctrine /'dɒktrɪn/ n. doctrina f.

document /'dɒkyəmənt/ n. documento m.

documentary /,dɒkyə'mɛntəri/ a. documental.

documentation /,dɒkyəmən'teiʃən/ n. documentación f.

dodge /dɒdʒ/ n. **1.** evasión f. —v. **2.** evadir.

dodgem /'dɒdʒɪm/ n. coche de choque m.

doe /dou/ n. gama f.

dog /dɔg/ n. perro -a.

dogma /'dɒgmə/ n. dogma m.

dogmatic /dɒg'mætɪk/ a. dogmático.

dogmatism /'dɒgmə,tɪzəm/ n. dogmatismo m.

doily /'dɔili/ n. servilletita f.

doleful /'doulfəl/ a. triste.

doll /dɒl/ n. muñeca -co.

dollar /'dɒlər/ n. dólar m.

dolorous /'doulərəs/ a lastimoso.

dolphin /'dɒlfɪn/ n. delfín m.

domain /dou'mein/ n. dominio m.

dome /doum/ n. domo m.

domestic /də'mɛstɪk/ a. doméstico.

domesticate /də'mɛstɪ,keit/ v. domesticar.

domicile /'dɒmə,sail/ n. domicilio m.

dominance /'dɒmənəns/ n. dominación f.

dominant /'dɒmənənt/ a. dominante.

dominate /'dɒmə,neit/ v. dominar.

domination /,dɒmə'neiʃən/ n. dominación f.

domineer /,dɒmə'nɪər/ v. dominar.

domineering /,dɒmə'nɪərɪŋ/ a. tiránico, mandón.

dominion /də'mɪnyən/ n. dominio; territorio m.

domino /'dɒmə,nou/ n. dominó m.

donate /'douneit/ v. donar; contribuir.

donation /dou'neiʃən/ n. donación f.

donkey /'dɒŋki/ n. asno, burro m.

doom /dum/ n. **1.** perdición, ruina f. —v. **2.** perder, ruinar.

door /dɔr/ n. puerta f.

doorman /'dɔr,mæn, -mən/ n. portero m.

doormat /'dɔr,mæt/ n. felpudo m.

doorway /'dɔr,wei/ n. entrada f.

dope /doup/ n. Colloq. narcótico m.; idiota m.

dormant /'dɔrmənt/ a. durmiente; inactivo.

dormitory /'dɔrmɪ,tɔri/ n. dormitorio m.

dosage /'dousɪdʒ/ n. dosificación f.

dose /dous/ n. dosis f.

dot /dɒt/ n. punto m.

dotted line /'dɒtɪd/ línea de puntos f.

double /'dʌbəl/ a. **1.** doble. —v. **2.** duplicar.

double bass /beis/ contrabajo m.

double-breasted /'dʌbəl 'brɛstɪd/ a. cruzado.

double-cross /'dʌbəl 'krɔs/ v. traicionar.

doubly /'dʌbli/ adv. doblemente.

doubt /daut/ n. **1.** duda f. —v. **2.** dudar.

doubtful /'dautfəl/ a. dudoso, incierto.

doubtless /'dautlɪs/ a. **1.** indudable. —adv. **2.** sin duda.

dough /dou/ n. pasta, masa f.

doughnut /'dounət, -,nʌt/ n. buñuelo m.

dove /duv/ n. paloma f.

dowager /'dauədʒər/ n. viuda (con título) f.

down /daun/ adv. **1.** abajo. —prep. **2. d. the street,** etc. calle abajo, etc.

downcast /'daun,kæst/ a. cabizbajo.

downfall /'daun,fɔl/ n. ruina, perdición f.

downhearted /'daun'hartɪd/ a. descorazonado.

download /'daun,loud/ v. bajar, descargar.

downpour /'daun,pɔr/ n. chaparrón m.

downright /'daun,rait/ a. absoluto, completo.

downriver /'daun'rɪvər/ adv. aguas abajo, río abajo.

downstairs /'daun'stɛərz/ adv. **1.** abajo. —n. **2.** primer piso.

downstream /'daun'strim/ adv. aguas abajo, río abajo.

downtown /'daun'taun/ adv. al centro, en el centro.

downward /'daunwərd/ a. **1.** descendente. —adv. **2.** hacia abajo.

dowry /'dauri/ n. dote f.

doze /douz/ v. dormitar.

dozen /'dʌzən/ n. docena f.

draft /dræft/ n. **1.** dibujo m.; Com. giro m.; Mil. conscripción f. —v. **2.** dibujar; Mil. reclutar.

draftee /dræf'ti/ n. conscripto m.

draft notice notificación de reclutamiento f.

drag /dræg/ v. arrastrar.

dragon /'drægən/ n. dragón m.

drain /drein/ n. **1.** desaguadero m. —v. **2.** desaguar.

drainage /'dreinɪdʒ/ n. drenaje m.

drain board escurridero m.

drama /'drɑmə, 'dræmə/ n. drama m.

dramatic /drə'mætɪk/ a. dramático.

dramatics /drə'mætɪks/ n. dramática f.

dramatist /'dræmətɪst, 'drɑmə-/ n. dramaturgo -ga.

dramatize /'dræmə,taiz, 'drɑmə-/ v. dramatizar.

drape /dreip/ n. cortinas f.pl. v. vestir; adornar.

drapery /'dreipəri/ n. colgaduras f.pl.; ropaje m.

drastic /'dræstɪk/ a. drástico.

draw /drɔ/ v. dibujar; atraer. **d. up**, formular.

drawback /'drɔ,bæk/ n. desventaja f.

drawer /drɔr/ n. cajón m.

drawing /'drɔɪŋ/ n. dibujo m.; rifa f.

dread /drɛd/ n. 1. terror m. —v. 2. temer.

dreadful /'drɛdfəl/ a. terrible.

dreadfully /'drɛdfəli/ adv. horrendamente.

dream /drim/ n. 1. sueño, ensueño m. —v. 2. soñar.

dreamer /'drimər/ n. soñador -ra; visionario -ia.

dreamy /'drimi/ a. soñador, contemplativo.

dreary /'drɪəri/ a. monótono y pesado.

dredge /drɛdʒ/ n. 1. rastra f. —v. 2. rastrear.

dregs /drɛgz/ n. sedimento m.

drench /drɛntʃ/ v. mojar.

dress /drɛs/ n. 1. vestido; traje m. —v. 2. vestir.

dresser /'drɛsər/ n. (furniture) tocador m.

dressing /'drɛsɪŋ/ n. Med. curación f.; (cookery) relleno m.; salsa f.

dressing gown bata f.

dressing table tocador m.

dressmaker /'drɛs,meikər/ n. modista m. & f.

drift /drɪft/ n. 1. tendencia f.; Naut. deriva f. —v. 2. Naut. derivar; (snow) amontonarse.

drill /drɪl/ n. 1. ejercicio m.; Mech. taladro m. —v. 2. Mech. taladrar.

drink /drɪŋk/ n. 1. bebida f. —v. 2. beber, tomar.

drinkable /'drɪŋkəbəl/ a. potable, bebible.

drip /drɪp/ v. gotear.

drive /draiv/ n. 1. paseo m. —v. 2. impeler; Auto. guiar, conducir.

drive-in (movie theater) /'draiv ,ɪn/ n. autocine, autocinema m.

driver /'draivər/ n. conductor -ra; chofer m. **d.'s license**, permiso de conducir.

driveway /'draiv,wei/ n. entrada para coches.

drizzle /'drɪzəl/ n. 1. llovizna f. —v. 2. lloviznar.

dromedary /'drɒmɪ,dɛri/ n. dromedario m.

droop /drup/ v. inclinarse.

drop /drɒp/ n. 1. gota f. —v. 2. soltar; dejar caer.

dropout /'drɒp,aut/ n. joven que abandona sus estudios.

dropper /'drɒpər/ n. cuentagotas f.

dropsy /'drɒpsi/ n. hidropesía f.

drought /draut/ n. sequía f.

drove /drouv/ n. manada f.

drown /draun/ v. ahogar.

drowse /drauz/ v. adormecer.

drowsiness /'drauzɪnɪs/ n. somnolencia f.

drowsy /'drauzi/ a. soñoliento.

drudge /drʌdʒ/ n. ganapán m.

drudgery /'drʌdʒəri/ n. trabajo penoso.

drug /drʌg/ n. 1. droga f. —v. 2. narcotizar.

drug addict drogadicto -ta, toxicómano -na m. & f.

druggist /'drʌgɪst/ n. farmacéutico -ca, boticario -ria.

drugstore /'drʌg,stɔr/ n. farmacia, botica, droguería f.

drum /drʌm/ n. tambor m.

drummer /'drʌmər/ n. tambor m

drumstick /'drʌm,stɪk/ n. palillo m.; Leg. pierna f.

drunk /drʌŋk/ a. & n. borracho, -a.

drunkard /'drʌŋkərd/ n. borrachón m.

drunken /'drʌŋkən/ a. borracho; ebrio.

drunkenness /'drʌŋkənnɪs/ n. embriaguez f.

dry /drai/ a. 1. seco, árido. —v. 2. secar.

dry cell n. pila seca f.

dry cleaner tintorero -ra.

dryness /'drainɪs/ n. sequedad f.

dual /'duəl/ a. doble.

dubious /'dubiəs/ a. dudoso.

duchess /'dʌtʃɪs/ n. duquesa f.

duck /dʌk/ n. 1. pato m. —v. 2. zambullir; (avoid) esquivar.

duct /dʌkt/ n. canal m.

due /du/ a. 1. debido; Com. vencido. —n. 2. **dues** cuota f.

duel /'duəl/ n. duelo m.

duelist /'duəlɪst/ n. duelista f.

duet /du'ɛt/ n. dúo m.

duke /duk/ n. duque m.

dull /dʌl/ a. apagado, desteñido; sin punta; Fig. pesado, soso.

dullness /'dʌlnɪs/ n. estupidez; pesadez f.; deslustre m.

duly /'duli/ adv. debidamente.

dumb /dʌm/ a. mudo; Colloq. estúpido.

dumbwaiter /'dʌm,weitər/ n. montaplatos m.

dumfound /dʌm'faund/ v. confundir.

dummy /'dʌmi/ n. maniquí m.

dump /dʌmp/ n. 1. depósito m. —v. 2. descargar.

dune /dun/ n. duna f.

dungeon /'dʌndʒən/ n. calabozo m.

dunk /dʌŋk/ v. mojar.

dupe /dup/ v. engañar.

duplicate /a, n 'duplɪkɪt: v -,keit/ a. & n. 1. duplicado m. —v. 2. duplicar.

duplication /,duplɪ'keiʃən/ n. duplicación f.

duplicity /du'plɪsɪti/ n. duplicidad f.

durability /,durə'bɪlɪti/ n. durabilidad f.

durable /'durəbəl/ a. durable, duradero.

duration /du'reiʃən/ n. duración f.

duress /du'rɛs/ n. compulsión f.; encierro m.

during /'durɪŋ/ *prep.* durante.
dusk /dʌsk/ *n.* crepúsculo *m.*
dusky /'dʌski/ *a.* oscuro; moreno.
dust /dʌst/ *n.* **1.** polvo *m.* —*v.* **2.** polvorear; despolvorear.
dusty /'dʌsti/ *a.* empolvado.
Dutch /dʌtʃ/ *a.* holandés -sa.
dutiful /'dutəfəl/ *a.* respetuoso.
dutifully /'dutəfəli/ *adv.* respetuosamente, obedientemente.
duty /'duti/ *n.* deber *m.; Com.* derechos *m.pl.*
duty-free /'duti 'fri/ *a.* libre de derechos.
dwarf /dwɔrf/ *n.* **1.** enano -na. —*v.* **2.** achicar.

dwell /dwɛl/ *v.* habitar, residir. **d. on**, espaciarse en.
dwelling /'dwɛlɪŋ/ *n.* morada, casa *f.*
dwindle /'dwɪndl/ *v.* disminuirse.
dye /dai/ *n.* **1.** tintura *f.* —*v.* **2.** teñir.
dyer /'daiər/ *n.* tintorero -ra.
dynamic /dai'næmɪk/ *a.* dinámico.
dynamite /'dainə,mait/ *n.* dinamita *f.*
dynamo /'dainə,mou/ *n.* dínamo *m.*
dynasty /'dainəsti/ *n.* dinastía *f.*
dysentery /'dɪsən,tɛri/ *n.* disentería *f.*
dyslexia /dɪs'lɛksiə/ *n.* dislexia *f.*
dyslexic /dɪs'lɛksɪk/ *a.* disléxico.
dyspepsia /dɪs'pɛpʃə/ *n.* dispepsia *f.*

E

each /itʃ/ *a.* **1.** cada. —*pron.* **2.** cada uno -na. **e. other**, el uno al otro.
eager /'igər/ *a.* ansioso.
eagerly /'igərli/ *adv.* ansiosamente.
eagerness /'igərnɪs/ *n.* ansia *f.*
eagle /'igəl/ *n.* águila *f.*
ear /iər/ *n.* oído *m.;* (outer) oreja *f.;* (of corn) mazorca *f.*
earache /'iər,eik/ *n.* dolor de oído *m.*
earl /ɜrl/ *n.* conde *m.*
early /'ɜrli/ *a.* & *adv.* temprano.
earn /ɜrn/ *v.* ganar.
earnest /'ɜrnɪst/ *a.* serio.
earnestly /'ɜrnɪstli/ *adv.* seriamente.
earnings /'ɜrnɪŋz/ *n.* ganancias *f.pl.; Com.* ingresos *m.pl*
earphone /'iər,foun/ *n.* auricular *m.*
earring /'iər,rɪŋ/ *n.* pendiente, arete *m.*
earth /ɜrθ/ *n.* tierra *f.*
earthquake /'ɜrθ,kweik/ *n.* terremoto *m.*
ease /iz/ *n.* **1.** reposo *m.;* facilidad *f.* —*v* **2.** aliviar.
easel /'izəl/ *n.* caballete *m.*
easily /'izəli/ *adv.* fácilmente.
east /ist/ *n.* oriente, este *m.*
Easter /'istər/ *n.* Pascua Florida.
eastern /'istərn/ *a.* oriental.
eastward /'istwərd/ *adv.* hacia el este.
easy /'izi/ *a.* fácil.
eat /it/ *v.* comer.
eau de Cologne /'ou də kə'loun/ colonia *f.*
eaves /ivz/ *n.* socarrén *m.*
ebb /ɛb/ *n.* **1.** menguante *f.* —*v.* **2.** menguar.
ebony /'ɛbəni/ *n.* ébano *m.*
eccentric /ɪk'sɛntrɪk/ *a.* excéntrico.
eccentricity /,ɛksən'trɪsɪti/ *n.* excentricidad *f.*

ecclesiastic /ɪ,klizi'æstɪk/ *a.* & *n.* eclesiástico *m.*
echelon /'ɛʃə,lɒn/ *n.* escalón *m.*
echo /'ɛkou/ *n.* eco *m.*
eclipse /ɪ'klɪps/ *n.* **1.** eclipse *m.* —*v.* **2.** eclipsar.
ecological /,ɛkə'lɒdʒɪkəl/ *a.* ecológico.
ecology /ɪ'kɒlədʒi/ *n.* ecología *f.*
economic /,ɛkə'nɒmɪk, ,ikə-/ *a.* económico.
economical /,ɛkə'nɒmɪkəl, ,ikə-/ *a.* económico.
economics /,ɛkə'nɒmɪks, ,ikə-/ *n.* economía política.
economist /ɪ'kɒnəmɪst/ *n.* economista *m.* & *f.*
economize /ɪ'kɒnə,maiz/ *v.* economizar.
economy /ɪ'kɒnəmi/ *n.* economía *f*
ecstasy /'ɛkstəsi/ *n.* éxtasis *m.*
Ecuadorian /,ɛkwə'dɔriən/ *a.* & *n.* ecuatoriano -na.
ecumenical /,ɛkyu'mɛnɪkəl/ *a.* ecuménico.
eczema /'ɛksəmə/ *n.* eczema *f.*
eddy /'ɛdi/ *n.* **1.** remolino *m.* —*v.* **2.** remolinar.
edge /ɛdʒ/ *n.* **1.** filo; borde *m.* —*v.* **2. e. one's way**, abrirse paso.
edible /'ɛdəbəl/ *a.* comestible.
edict /'idɪkt/ *n.* edicto *m.*
edifice /'ɛdəfɪs/ *n.* edificio *m.*
edify /'ɛdə,fai/ *v.* edificar.
edition /ɪ'dɪʃən/ *n.* edición *f.*
editor /'ɛdɪtər/ *n.* redactor -ra.
editorial /,ɛdɪ'tɔriəl/ *n.* editorial *m.* **e. board**, consejo de redacción *m.* **e. staff**, redacción *f.*
educate /'ɛdʒə,keit/ *v.* educar.
education /,ɛdʒu'keiʃən/ *n.* instrucción; enseñanza *f.*
educational /,ɛdʒu'keiʃənl/ *a.* educativo.

educator /'ɛdʒʊ,keitər/ n. educador -ra, pedagogo -ga.

eel /il/ n. anguila f.

efface /ɪ'feis/ v. tachar.

effect /ɪ'fɛkt/ n. **1.** efecto m. **in e.**, en vigor. —v. **2.** efectuar, realizar.

effective /ɪ'fɛktɪv/ a. eficaz; efectivo; en vigor.

effectively /ɪ'fɛktɪvli/ adv. eficazmente.

effectiveness /ɪ'fɛktɪvnɪs/ n. efectividad f.

effectual /ɪ'fɛktʃuəl/ a. eficaz.

effeminate /ɪ'fɛmənɪt/ a. afeminado.

efficacy /'ɛfɪkəsi/ n. eficacia f.

efficiency /ɪ'fɪʃənsi/ n. eficiencia f.

efficient /ɪ'fɪʃənt/ a. eficaz.

efficiently /ɪ'fɪʃəntli/ adv. eficazmente.

effigy /'ɛfɪdʒi/ n. efigie f.

effort /'ɛfərt/ n. esfuerzo m.

effrontery /ɪ'frʌntəri/ n. impudencia f.

effusive /ɪ'fyusɪv/ a. efusivo.

egg /ɛg/ n. huevo m. **fried e.**, huevo frito. **soft-boiled e.**, h. pasado por agua. **scrambled eggs**, huevos revueltos.

eggplant /'ɛg,plænt/ n. berenjena f

egg white clara de huevo f.

egoism /'igou,ɪzəm/ **egotism** n. egoísmo m.

egoist /'igouɪst/ **egotist** n. egoísta m. & f.

egotism /'igə,tɪzəm/ n. egotismo m.

egotist /'igətɪst/ n. egotista m. & f.

Egypt /'idʒɪpt/ n. Egipto m.

Egyptian /ɪ'dʒɪpʃən/ a. & n. egipcio -ia.

eight /eit/ a. & pron. ocho.

eighteen /'ei'tin/ a. & pron. dieciocho.

eighth /eitθ, eiθ/ a. octavo.

eightieth /'eitiiθ/ n. octogésimo m.

eighty /'eiti/ a. & pron. ochenta.

either /'iðər/ a. & pron. **1.** cualquiera de los dos. —adv. **2.** tampoco. —conj. **3.** either... or, o... o.

ejaculate /ɪ'dʒækyə,leit/ v. exclamar; eyacular.

ejaculation /ɪ,dʒækyə'leiʃən/ n. eyaculación f.

eject /ɪ'dʒɛkt/ v. expeler; eyectar.

ejection /ɪ'dʒɛkʃən/ n. expulsión f.; eyección f.

elaborate /a ɪ'læbərɪt; v -ə,reit/ v. a. **1.** elaborado. —v. **2.** elaborar; ampliar.

elapse /ɪ'læps/ v. transcurrir; pasar.

elastic /ɪ'læstɪk/ a. & n. elástico m.

elasticity /ɪlæ'stɪsɪti/ n. elasticidad f.

elate /ɪ'leit/ v. exaltar.

elation /ɪ'leiʃən/ n. exaltación f.

elbow /'ɛlbou/ n. codo m.

elder /'ɛldər/ a. **1.** mayor. —n. **2.** anciano -na.

elderly /'ɛldərli/ a. de edad.

eldest /'ɛldɪst/ a. mayor.

elect /ɪ'lɛkt/ v. elegir.

election /ɪ'lɛkʃən/ n. elección f.

elective /ɪ'lɛktɪv/ a. electivo.

electorate /ɪ'lɛktərɪt/ n. electorado m.

electric /ɪ'lɛktrɪk/ **electrical** a. eléctrico.

electrician /ɪlɛk'trɪʃən/ n. electricista m. & f.

electricity /ɪlɛk'trɪsɪti/ n. electricidad f.

electrocardiogram /ɪ,lɛktrou'kardiə,græm/ n. electrocardiograma m.

electrocute /ɪ'lɛktrə,kyut/ v. electrocutar.

electrode /ɪ'lɛktroud/ n. electrodo m.

electrolysis /ɪlɛk'trɒləsɪs/ n. electrólisis f.

electron /ɪ'lɛktrɒn/ n. electrón m.

electronic /ɪlɛk'trɒnɪk/ a. electrónico.

electronics /ɪlɛk'trɒnɪks/ n. electrónica f.

elegance /'ɛlɪgəns/ n. elegancia f.

elegant /'ɛlɪgənt/ a. elegante.

elegy /'ɛlɪdʒi/ n. elegía f.

element /'ɛləmənt/ n. elemento m.

elemental /,ɛlə'mɛntl/ a. elemental.

elementary /,ɛlə'mɛntəri/ a. elemental.

elephant /'ɛləfənt/ n. elefante -ta.

elevate /'ɛlə,veit/ v. elevar.

elevation /,ɛlə'veiʃən/ n. elevación f.

elevator /'ɛlə,veitər/ n. ascensor m.

eleven /ɪ'lɛvən/ a. & pron. once.

eleventh /ɪ'lɛvənθ/ a. undécimo.

eleventh hour último minuto m.

elf /ɛlf/ n. duende m.

elicit /ɪ'lɪsɪt/ v. sacar; despertar.

eligibility /,ɛlɪdʒə'bɪlɪti/ n. elegibilidad f.

eligible /'ɛlɪdʒəbəl/ a. elegible.

eliminate /ɪ'lɪmə,neit/ v. eliminar.

elimination /ɪ,lɪmə'neiʃən/ n. eliminación f.

elixir /ɪ'lɪksər/ n. elixir m.

elk /ɛlk/ n. alce m.. anta m.

elm /ɛlm/ n. olmo m.

elocution /,ɛlə'kyuʃən/ n. elocución f.

elongate /ɪ'lɒŋgeit/ v. alargar.

elope /ɪ'loup/ v. fugarse.

eloquence /'ɛləkwəns/ n. elocuencia f.

eloquent /'ɛləkwənt/ a. elocuente.

eloquently /'ɛləkwəntli/ adv. elocuentemente.

else /ɛls/ adv. más. **someone e.**, otra persona. **something e.**, otra cosa. **or e.**, de otro modo.

elsewhere /'ɛls,wɛər/ adv. en otra parte.

elucidate /ɪ'lusɪ,deit/ v. elucidar.

elude /ɪ'lud/ v. eludir.

elusive /ɪ'lusɪv/ a. evasivo.

emaciated /ɪ'meiʃi,eitɪd/ a. demacrado, enflaquecido.

e-mail /'i,meil/ n. correo electrónico m.

emanate /'ɛmə,neit/ v. emanar.

emancipate /ɪ'mænsə,peit/ v. emancipar.

emancipation /ɪ,mænsə'peiʃən/ n. emancipación f.

emancipator /ɪˈmænsəˌpeɪtər/ *n.* libertador -ra.

embalm /ɛmˈbɑm/ *v.* embalsamar.

embankment /ɛmˈbæŋkmənt/ *n.* malecón, dique *m.*

embargo /ɛmˈbɑrgou/ *n.* embargo *m.*

embark /ɛmˈbɑrk/ *v.* embarcar.

embarrass /ɛmˈbærəs/ *v.* avergonzar; turbar.

embarrassing /ɛmˈbærəsɪŋ/ *a.* penoso, vergonzoso.

embarrassment /ɛmˈbærəsmənt/ *n.* turbación; vergüenza *f.*

embassy /ˈɛmbəsi/ *n.* embajada *f.*

embellish /ɛmˈbɛlɪʃ/ *v.* hermosear, embellecer.

embellishment /ɛmˈbɛlɪʃmənt/ *n.* embellecimiento *m.*

embezzle /ɛmˈbɛzəl/ *v.* desfalcar, malversar.

emblem /ˈɛmbləm/ *n.* emblema *m.*

embody /ɛmˈbɑdi/ *v.* incorporar; personificar.

embrace /ɛmˈbreɪs/ *n.* **1.** abrazo *m.* —*v.* **2.** abrazar.

embroider /ɛmˈbrɔɪdər/ *v.* bordar.

embroidery /ɛmˈbrɔɪdəri, -dri/ *n.* bordado *m.*

embryo /ˈɛmbriˌou/ *n.* embrión *m.*

embryonic /ˌɛmbriˈɒnɪk/ *a.* embrionario.

emerald /ˈɛmərəld/ *n.* esmeralda *f.*

emerge /ɪˈmɜrdʒ/ *v.* salir.

emergency /ɪˈmɜrdʒənsi/ *n.* emergencia *f.*

emergency brake freno de auxilio *m.*

emergency exit salida de urgencia *f.*

emergency landing aterrizaje forzoso *m.*

emergent /ɪˈmɜrdʒənt/ *a.* emergente.

emery /ˈɛməri/ *n.* esmeril *m.*

emetic /ɪˈmɛtɪk/ *n.* emético *m.*

emigrant /ˈɛmɪgrənt/ *a.* & *n.* emigrante *m.* & *f.*

emigrate /ˈɛmɪˌgreɪt/ *v.* emigrar.

emigration /ˌɛməˈgreɪʃən/ *n.* emigración *f.*

eminence /ˈɛmənəns/ *n.* altura; eminencia *f.*

eminent /ˈɛmənənt/ *a.* eminente.

emissary /ˈɛməˌsɛri/ *n.* emisario *m.*

emission /ɪˈmɪʃən/ *n.* emisión *f.*

emit /ɪˈmɪt/ *v.* emitir.

emolument /ɪˈmɒlyəmənt/ *n.* emolumento *m.*

emotion /ɪˈmouʃən/ *n.* emoción *f.*

emotional /ɪˈmouʃənl/ *a.* emocional; sentimental.

emperor /ˈɛmpərər/ *n.* emperador *m.*

emphasis /ˈɛmfəsɪs/ *n.* énfasis *m.* or *f.*

emphasize /ˈɛmfəˌsaɪz/ *v.* acentuar, recalcar.

emphatic /ɛmˈfætɪk/ *a.* enfático.

empire /ˈɛmpaɪᵊr/ *n.* imperio *m.*

empirical /ɛmˈpɪrɪkəl/ *a.* empírico.

employ /ɛmˈplɔɪ/ *v.* emplear.

employee /ɛmˈplɔɪi/ *n.* empleado -da.

employer /ɛmˈplɔɪər/ *n.* patrón -ona.

employment /ɛmˈplɔɪmənt/ *n.* empleo *m.*

employment agency agencia de colocaciones *f.*

empower /ɛmˈpauᵊr/ *v.* autorizar.

emptiness /ˈɛmptinɪs/ *n.* vaciedad; futilidad *f.*

empty /ˈɛmpti/ *a.* **1.** vacío. —*v.* **2.** vaciar.

emulate /ˈɛmyəˌleɪt/ *v.* emular.

emulsion /ɪˈmʌlʃən/ *n.* emulsión *f.*

enable /ɛnˈeɪbəl/ *v.* capacitar; permitir.

enact /ɛnˈækt/ *v.* promulgar, decretar.

enactment /ɛnˈæktmənt/ *n.* ley *f.*, estatuto *m.*

enamel /ɪˈnæməl/ *n.* **1.** esmalte *m.* —*v.* **2.** esmaltar.

enamored /ɪˈnæmərd/ *a.* enamorado.

enchant /ɛnˈtʃænt/ *v.* encantar.

enchantment /ɛnˈtʃæntmənt/ *n.* encanto *m.*

encircle /ɛnˈsɜrkəl/ *v.* circundar.

enclose /ɛnˈklouz/ *v.* encerrar. **enclosed,** (in letter) adjunto.

enclosure /ɛnˈklouʒər/ *n.* recinto *m.*; (in letter) incluso *m.*

encompass /ɛnˈkʌmpəs/ *v.* circundar.

encounter /ɛnˈkaunter/ *n.* **1.** encuentro *m.* —*v.* **2.** encontrar.

encourage /ɛnˈkɜrɪdʒ/ *v.* animar.

encouragement /ɛnˈkɜrɪdʒmənt/ *n.* estímulo *m.*

encroach /ɛnˈkroutʃ/ *v.* usurpar; meterse.

encryption /ɛnˈkrɪpʃən/ *n.* encriptación *f.*, cifrado *m.*

encyclical /ɛnˈsɪklɪkəl/ *n.* encíclica *f.*

encyclopedia /ɛnˌsaɪkləˈpidiə/ *n.* enciclopedia *f.*

end /ɛnd/ *n.* **1.** fin, término, cabo; extremo; (aim) propósito *m.* —*v.* **2.** acabar; terminar.

endanger /ɛnˈdeɪndʒər/ *v.* poner en peligro.

endear /ɛnˈdɪər/ *v.* hacer querer.

endeavor /ɛnˈdɛvər/ *n.* **1.** esfuerzo *m.* —*v.* **2.** esforzarse.

ending /ˈɛndɪŋ/ *n.* conclusión *f.*

endless /ˈɛndlɪs/ *a.* sin fin.

endocrine gland /ˈɛndəkrɪn/ glándula endocrina *f.*

endorse /ɛnˈdɔrs/ *v.* endosar; apoyar.

endorsement /ɛnˈdɔrsmənt/ *n.* endoso *m.*

endow /ɛnˈdau/ *v.* dotar, fundar.

endowment /ɛnˈdaumənt/ *n.* dotación *f.*, fundación *f.*

endurance /ɛnˈdurəns/ *n.* resistencia *f.*

endure /ɛnˈdur/ *v.* soportar, resistir, aguantar.

enema /ˈɛnəmə/ *n.* enema; lavativa *f.*

enemy /'ɛnəmi/ n. enemigo -ga.

energetic /ˌɛnər'dʒɛtɪk/ a. enérgico.

energy /'ɛnərdʒi/ n. energía f.

enervate /'ɛnər,veit/ v. enervar.

enervation /ˌɛnər'veifən/ n. enervación f.

enfold /ɛn'fould/ v. envolver.

enforce /ɛn'fɔrs/ v ejecutar.

enforcement /ɛn'fɔrsmənt/ n. ejecución f.

engage /ɛn'geidʒ/ v. emplear; ocupar.

engaged /ɛn'geidʒd/ a. (to marry) prometido.

engagement /ɛn'geidʒmənt/ n. combate; compromiso; contrato m.; cita f.

engine /'ɛndʒən/ n. máquina f. (railroad) locomotora f.

engineer /ˌɛndʒə'nɪər/ n. ingeniero -ra; maquinista m.

engineering /ˌɛndʒə'nɪrɪŋ/ n. ingeniería f.

England /'ɪŋglənd/ n. Inglaterra f.

English /'ɪŋglɪʃ/ a. & n. inglés -esa.

English Channel Canal de la Mancha m.

Englishman /'ɪŋglɪʃmən/ n. inglés m.

Englishwoman /'ɪŋglɪʃˌwumən/ n. inglesa f.

engrave /ɛn'greiv/ v. grabar.

engraver /ɛn'greivər/ n. grabador m.

engraving /ɛn'greivɪŋ/ n. grabado m.

engross /ɛn'grous/ v. absorber.

enhance /ɛn'hæns/ v. aumentar en valor; realzar.

enigma /ə'nɪgmə/ n. enigma m.

enigmatic /ˌɛnɪg'mætɪk/ a. enigmático.

enjoy /ɛn'dʒɔi/ v. gozar de; disfrutar de. **e. oneself,** divertirse.

enjoyable /ɛn'dʒɔiəbəl/ a. agradable.

enjoyment /ɛn'dʒɔimənt/ n. goce m.

enlarge /ɛn'lɑrdʒ/ v. agrandar; ampliar.

enlargement /ɛn'lɑrdʒmənt/ n. ensanchamiento m., ampliación f.

enlarger /ɛn'lɑrdʒər/ n amplificador m.

enlighten /ɛn'laitn̩/ v. informar.

enlightenment /ɛn'laitn̩mənt/ n. esclarecimiento m.; cultura f.

enlist /ɛn'lɪst/ v. reclutar; alistarse.

enlistment /ɛn'lɪstmənt/ n. alistamiento m.

enliven /ɛn'laivən/ v. avivar.

enmesh /ɛn'mɛʃ/ v. entrampar.

enmity /'ɛnmɪti/ n. enemistad f.

enormity /ɪ'nɔrmɪti/ n. enormidad f.

enormous /ɪ'nɔrməs/ a. enorme.

enough /ɪ'nʌf/ a. & adv. bastante. **to be e.,** bastar.

enrage /ɛn'reidʒ/ v. enfurecer.

enrich /ɛn'rɪtʃ/ v. enriquecer.

enroll /ɛn'roul/ v. registrar; matricularse.

enrollment /ɛn'roulmənt/ n. matriculación f.

ensign /'ɛnsən/ n. bandera f.; (naval) subteniente m.

enslave /ɛn'sleiv/ v. esclavizar.

ensue /ɛn'su/ v. seguir, resultar.

entail /ɛn'teil/ v. acarrear, ocasionar.

entangle /ɛn'tæŋgəl/ v. enredar.

enter /'ɛntər/ v. entrar.

enterprise /'ɛntər,praiz/ n. empresa f.

enterprising /'ɛntər,praizɪŋ/ a. emprendedor.

entertain /ˌɛntər'tein/ v. entretener; divertir.

entertainment /ˌɛntər'teinmənt/ n. entretenimiento m.; diversión f.

enthrall /ɛn'θrɔl/ v. esclavizar; cautivar.

enthusiasm /ɛn'θuzi,æzəm/ n. entusiasmo m.

enthusiast /ɛn'θuzi,æst, -ɪst/ n. entusiasta m. & f.

enthusiastic /ɛn,θuzi'æstɪk/ a. entusiasmado.

entice /ɛn'tais/ v. inducir.

entire /ɛn'taiᵊr/ a. entero.

entirely /ɛn'taiᵊrli/ adv. enteramente.

entirety /ɛn'taiᵊrti/ n. totalidad f.

entitle /ɛn'taitl̩/ v. autorizar; (book) titular.

entity /'ɛntɪti/ n. entidad f.

entrails /'ɛntreilz/ n. entrañas f.pl.

entrance /ɛn'træns/ n. entrada f.

entrance examination examen de ingreso m.

entrant /'ɛntrənt/ n. competidor -ra.

entreat /ɛn'trit/ v. rogar, suplicar.

entreaty /ɛn'triti/ n. ruego m., súplica f.

entrench /ɛn'trɛntʃ/ v. atrincherar.

entrust /ɛn'trʌst/ v. confiar.

entry /'ɛntri/ n. entrada f.; Com. partida f.

entry blank hoja de inscripción f.

enumerate /ɪ'numə,reit/ v. enumerar.

enumeration /ɪ,numə'reifən/ n. enumeración f.

enunciate /ɪ'nʌnsi,eit/ v. enunciar.

enunciation /ɪ,nʌnsi'eifən/ n. enunciación f.

envelop /ɛn'vɛləp/ v. envolver.

envelope /'ɛnvə,loup/ n. sobre m.; cubierta f.

enviable /'ɛnviəbəl/ a. envidiable.

envious /'ɛnviəs/ a. envidioso.

environment /ɛn'vairənmənt/ n. ambiente m.

environmentalist /ɛn,vairən'mɛnt[ɪst/ n. ambientalista, ecologista m. & f.

environmental protection /ɛn,vairən'mɛntəl/ protección del ambiente.

environs /ɛn'vairənz/ n. alrededores m.

envoy /'ɛnvɔi/ n. enviado m.

envy /'ɛnvi/ n. **1.** envidia f. —v. **2.** envidiar.

eon /'iən/ n. eón m.

ephemeral /ɪ'fɛmərəl/ a efímero.

epic /'ɛpɪk/ a. **1.** épico. —n **2.** epopeya f.

epicure /'ɛpɪ,kyor/ n. epicúreo m.

epidemic /ˌɛpɪ'dɛmɪk/ a. **1.** epidémico. —n. **2.** epidemia f.

epidermis /ˌɛpɪ'dɜrmɪs/ n. epidermis f.

epigram /'ɛpɪˌgræm/ n. epigrama m.

epilepsy /'ɛpəˌlɛpsi/ n. epilepsia f.

epilogue /'ɛpəˌlɔg/ n. epílogo m.

episode /'ɛpəˌsoud/ n. episodio m.

epistle /ɪ'pɪsəl/ n. epístola f.

epitaph /'ɛpɪˌtæf/ n. epitafio m.

epithet /'ɛpəˌθɛt/ n. epíteto m.

epitome /ɪ'pɪtəmi/ n. epítome m.

epoch /'ɛpək/ n. época, era f.

Epsom salts /'ɛpsəm/ n.pl. sal de la Higuera f.

equal /'ikwəl/ a. & n. **1.** igual m. —v. **2.** igualar; equivaler.

equality /ɪ'kwɒlɪti/ n. igualdad f.

equalize /'ikwəˌlaiz/ v. igualar.

equanimity /ˌikwə'nɪmɪti/ n. ecuanimidad f.

equate /ɪ'kweit/ v. igualar.

equation /ɪ'kweiʒən/ n. ecuación f.

equator /ɪ'kweitər/ n. ecuador m.

equatorial /ˌikwə'tɔriəl/ a. ecuatorial.

equestrian /ɪ'kwɛstriən/ n. **1.** jinete m. —a. **2.** ecuestre.

equilibrium /ˌikwə'lɪbriəm/ n. equilibrio m.

equinox /'ikwəˌnɒks/ n. equinoccio m.

equip /ɪ'kwɪp/ v. equipar.

equipment /ɪ'kwɪpmənt/ n. equipo m.

equitable /'ɛkwɪtəbəl/ a. equitativo.

equity /'ɛkwɪti/ n. equidad, justicia f.

equivalent /ɪ'kwɪvələnt/ a. & n. equivalente m.

equivocal /ɪ'kwɪvəkəl/ a. equívoco, ambiguo.

era /'ɪərə, 'ɛrə/ n. era, época, edad f.

eradicate /ɪ'rædɪˌkeit/ v. extirpar.

erase /ɪ'reis/ v. borrar.

eraser /ɪ'reisər/ n. borrador m.

erasure /ɪ'reiʒər/ n. borradura f.

erect /ɪ'rɛkt/ a. **1.** derecho, erguido. —v. **2.** erigir.

erection /ɪ'rɛkʃən/ **erectness** n. erección f.

ermine /'ɜrmɪn/ n. armiño m.

erode /ɪ'roud/ v. corroer.

erosion /ɪ'rouʒən/ n. erosión f.

erotic /ɪ'rɒtɪk/ a. erótico.

err /ɜr, ɛr/ v. equivocarse.

errand /'ɛrənd/ n. encargo, recado m.

errant /'ɛrənt/ a. errante.

erratic /ɪ'rætɪk/ a. errático.

erroneous /ə'rouniəs/ a. erróneo.

error /'ɛrər/ n. error m.

erudite /'ɛryuˌdait/ a. erudito.

erudition /ˌɛryu'dɪʃən/ n. erudición f.

eruption /ɪ'rʌpʃən/ n. erupción, irrupción f.

erysipelas /ˌɛrə'sɪpələs/ n. erisipela f.

escalate /'ɛskəˌleit/ v. escalar; intensificarse.

escalator /'ɛskəˌleitər/ n. escalera mecánica f.

escapade /'ɛskəˌpeid/ n. escapada; correría f.

escape /ɪ'skeip/ n. **1.** fuga, huida f. **fire e.,** escalera de salvamento. —v. **2.** escapar; fugarse.

eschew /ɛs'tʃu/ v. evadir.

escort /n 'ɛskɔrt; v ɪ'skɔrt/ n. **1.** escolta f. —v. **2.** escoltar.

escrow /'ɛskrou/ n. plica f.

escutcheon /ɪ'skʌtʃən/ n. escudo de armas m.

esophagus /ɪ'sɒfəgəs/ n. esófago m.

esoteric /ˌɛsə'tɛrɪk/ a. esotérico.

especially /ɪ'spɛʃəli/ adv. especialmente.

espionage /'ɛspiəˌnɒʒ/ n. espionaje m.

espresso /ɛ'sprɛsou/ n. café exprés, m.

essay /'ɛsei/ n. ensayo m.

essayist /'ɛseiɪst/ n. ensayista m. & f.

essence /'ɛsəns/ n. esencia f.; perfume m.

essential /ə'sɛntʃəl/ a. esencial.

essentially /ə'sɛntʃəli/ adv. esencialmente.

establish /ɪ'stæblɪʃ/ v. establecer.

establishment /ɪ'stæblɪʃmənt/ n. establecimiento m.

estate /ɪ'steit/ n. estado m.; hacienda f.; bienes m.pl.

esteem /ɪ'stim/ n. **1.** estima f. —v. **2.** estimar.

estimable /'ɛstəməbəl/ a. estimable.

estimate /n 'ɛstəˌmɪt; v -ˌmeit/ n. **1.** cálculo; presupuesto m. —v. **2.** estimar.

estimation /ˌɛstə'meiʃən/ n. estimación f.; cálculo m.

estrange /ɪ'streindʒ/ v. extrañar; enajenar.

estuary /'ɛstʃuˌɛri/ n. estuario m.

etch /ɛtʃ/ v. grabar al agua fuerte.

etching /'ɛtʃɪŋ/ n. aguafuerte.

eternal /ɪ'tɜrnl/ a. eterno.

eternity /ɪ'tɜrnɪti/ n. eternidad f.

ether /'iθər/ n. éter m.

ethereal /ɪ'θɪəriəl/ a. etéreo.

ethical /'ɛθɪkəl/ a. ético.

ethics /'ɛθɪks/ n. ética f.

ethnic /'ɛθnɪk/ a. étnico.

etiquette /'ɛtɪkɪt/ n. etiqueta f.

etymology /ˌɛtə'mɒlədʒi/ n. etimología f.

eucalyptus /ˌyukə'lɪptəs/ n. eucalipto m.

eugenic /yu'dʒɛnɪk/ a. eugenésico.

eugenics /yu'dʒɛnɪks/ n. eugenesia f.

eulogize /'yuləˌdʒaiz/ v. elogiar.

eulogy /'yulədʒi/ n. elogio m.

eunuch /'yunək/ n. eunuco m.

euphonious /yu'founiəs/ a. eufónico.

Europe /'yurəp/ n. Europa f.

European /ˌyurə'piən/ a. & n. europeo -pea.

euthanasia /ˌyuθə'neiʒə, -ʒiə, -ziə/ n. eutanasia f.

evacuate /ɪ'vækyu,eit/ v. evacuar.
evade /ɪ'veid/ v. evadir.
evaluate /ɪ'vælyu,eit/ v. evaluar.
evaluation /ɪ,vælyu'eiʃən/ n. valoración f.
evangelist /ɪ'vændʒəlɪst/ n. evangelista m. & f.
evaporate /ɪ'væpə,reit/ v. evaporarse.
evaporation /ɪ,væpə'reiʃən/ n. evaporación f.
evasion /ɪ'veiʒən/ n. evasión f.
evasive /ɪ'veisɪv/ a. evasivo.
eve /iv/ n. víspera f.
even /'ivən/ a. 1. llano; igual. —adv. 2. aun; hasta. not e., ni siquiera.
evening /'ivnɪŋ/ n. noche, tarde f. good e.! ¡buenas tardes! ¡buenas noches!
evening class clase nocturna f.
evenness /'ivənnɪs/ n. uniformidad f.
even number número par m.
event /ɪ'vent/ n. acontecimiento, suceso m.
eventful /ɪ'ventfəl/ a. memorable.
eventual /ɪ'ventʃuəl/ a. eventual.
ever /'evər/ adv. alguna vez; (after not) nunca. e. since, desde que.
everlasting /,evər'læstɪŋ/ a. eterno.
every /'evri/ a. cada, todos los.
everybody /'evri,bɒdi, -,bʌdi/ pron. todo el mundo; cada uno.
everyday /'evri,dei/ a. ordinario, de cada día.
everyone /'evri,wʌn/ pron. todo el mundo; cada uno; cada cual.
everything /'evri,θɪŋ/ pron. todo m.
everywhere /'evri,wεər/ adv. por todas partes, en todas partes.
evict /ɪ'vɪkt/ v. expulsar.
eviction /ɪ'vɪkʃən/ n. evicción f.
evidence /'evɪdəns/ n. evidencia f.
evident /'evɪdənt/ a. evidente.
evidently /'evɪdəntli/ adv. evidentemente.
evil /'ivəl/ a. 1. malo; maligno. —n. 2. mal m.
evince /ɪ'vɪns/ v. revelar.
evoke /ɪ'vouk/ v. evocar.
evolution /,evə'luʃən/ n. evolución f.
evolve /ɪ'vɒlv/ v. desenvolver; desarrollar.
ewe /yu/ n. oveja f.
exact /ɪg'zækt/ a. 1. exacto. —v. 2. exigir.
exacting /ɪg'zæktɪŋ/ a. exigente.
exactly /ɪg'zæktli/ adv. exactamente.
exaggerate /ɪg'zædʒə,reit/ v. exagerar.
exaggeration /ɪg,zædʒə'reiʃən/ n. exageración f.
exalt /ɪg'zɔlt/ v. exaltar.
exaltation /,egzɔl'teiʃən/ n. exaltación f.
examination /ɪg,zæmə'neiʃən/ n. examen m.; (legal) interrogatorio m.
examine /ɪg'zæmɪn/ v. examinar.
example /ɪg'zæmpəl/ n. ejemplo m.
exasperate /ɪg'zæspə,reit/ v. exasperar.

exasperation /ɪg,zæspə'reiʃən/ n. exasperación f.
excavate /'ekskə,veit/ v. excavar, cavar.
exceed /ɪk'sid/ v. exceder.
exceedingly /ɪk'sidɪŋli/ adv. sumamente, extremadamente.
excel /ɪk'sel/ v. sobresalir.
excellence /'eksələns/ n. excelencia f.
Excellency /'eksələnsi/ n. (title) Excelencia f.
excellent /'eksələnt/ a. excelente.
except /ɪk'sept/ prep. 1. salvo, excepto. —v. 2. exceptuar.
exception /ɪk'sepʃən/ n. excepción f.
exceptional /ɪk'sepʃənl/ a. excepcional.
excerpt /'eksɜrpt/ n. extracto.
excess /ɪk'ses, 'ekses/ n. exceso m.
excessive /ɪk'sesɪv/ a. excesivo.
exchange /ɪks'tʃeindʒ/ n. 1. cambio; canje m. stock e., bolsa f. telephone e., central telefónica. —v. 2. cambiar, canjear, intercambiar.
exchangeable /ɪks'tʃeindʒəbəl/ a. cambiable.
exchange rate tipo de cambio m.
excise /ɪn 'eksaiz; v ɪk'saiz/ n. 1. sisa f. —v. 2. extirpar.
excite /ɪk'sait/ v. agitar; provocar; emocionar.
excitement /ɪk'saitmənt/ n. agitación, conmoción f.
exciting /ɪk'saitɪŋ/ a. emocionante.
exclaim /ɪk'skleim/ v. exclamar.
exclamation /,eksklə'meiʃən/ n. exclamación f.
exclamation mark punto de admiración m.
exclude /ɪk'sklud/ v. excluir.
exclusion /ɪk'skluʒən/ n. exclusión f.
exclusive /ɪk'sklusɪv/ a. exclusivo.
excommunicate /,ekskə'myunɪ,keit/ v. excomulgar, descomulgar.
excommunication /,ekskə,myunɪ'keiʃən/ n. excomunión f.
excrement /'ekskrəmənt/ n. excremento m.
excruciating /ɪk'skruʃi,eitɪŋ/ a. penosísimo.
exculpate /'ekskʌl,peit/ v. exculpar.
excursion /ɪk'skɜrʒən/ n. excursión, jira f.
excuse /n ɪk'skyus; v ɪk'skyuz/ n. 1. excusa f. —v. 2. excusar, perdonar, disculpar; dispensar.
execrable /'eksɪkrəbəl/ a. execrable.
execute /'eksɪ,kyut/ v. ejecutar.
execution /,eksɪ'kyuʃən/ n. ejecución f.
executioner /,eksɪ'kyuʃənər/ n. verdugo m.
executive /ɪg'zekyətɪv/ a. & n. ejecutivo -va.
executor /ɪg'zekyətər/ n. testamentario m.
exemplary /ɪg'zempləri/ a. ejemplar.
exemplify /ɪg'zemplə,fai/ v. ejemplificar.

exempt /ɪg'zempt/ a. **1.** exento. —v. **2.** exentar.

exercise /'eksər,saiz/ n. **1.** ejercicio m. —v. **2.** ejercitar.

exert /ɪg'zɜrt/ v esforzar.

exertion /ɪg'zɜrʃən/ n. esfuerzo m.

exhale /eks'heil/ v. exhalar.

exhaust /ɪg'zɔst/ n. **1.** Auto. escape m. —v. **2.** agotar.

exhaustion /ɪg'zɔstʃən/ n. agotamiento m.

exhaustive /ɪg'zɔstɪv/ a. exhaustivo.

exhaust pipe tubo de escape m.

exhibit /ɪg'zɪbɪt/ n. **1.** exhibición, exposición f. —v. **2.** exhibir.

exhibition /,eksə'bɪʃən/ n. exhibición f.

exhilarate /ɪg'zɪlə,reit/ v. alegrar; estimular.

exhort /ɪg'zɔrt/ v. exhortar.

exhortation /,egzɔr'teiʃən/ n. exhortación f.

exhume /ɪg'zum/ v. exhumar.

exigency /'eksɪdʒənsi/ n. exigencia f., urgencia f.

exile /'egzail/ n. **1.** destierro m., (person) desterrado m. —v. **2.** desterrar.

exist /ɪg'zɪst/ v. existir.

existence /ɪg'zɪstəns/ n. existencia f.

existent /ɪg'zɪstənt/ a. existente.

exit /'egzɪt, 'eksɪt/ n. salida f.

exodus /'eksədəs/ n éxodo m.

exonerate /ɪg'zɒnə,reit/ v. exonerar.

exorbitant /ɪg'zɔrbɪtənt/ a. exorbitante.

exorcise /'eksɔr,saiz/ v. exorcizar.

exotic /ɪg'zɒtɪk/ a. exótico.

expand /ɪk'spænd/ v. dilatar; ensanchar.

expanse /ɪk'spæns/ n. espacio m.; extensión f.

expansion /ɪk'spænʃən/ n. expansión f.

expansion slot ranura de expansión f.

expansive /ɪk'spænsɪv/ a. expansivo.

expatiate /ɪk'speiʃi,eit/ v. espaciarse.

expatriate /n, a eks'peitriɪt; v eks'peitri,eit/ n. & a. **1.** expatriado m. —v. **2.** expatriar.

expect /ɪk'spekt/ v. esperar; contar con.

expectancy /ɪk'spektənsi/ n. esperanza f.

expectation /,ekspek'teiʃən/ n. esperanza f.

expectorate /ɪk'spektə,reit/ v. expectorar.

expediency /ɪk'spidiənsi/ n. conveniencia f.

expedient /ɪk'spidiənt/ a. **1.** oportuno. —n. **2.** expediente m.

expedite /'ekspɪ,dait/ v. acelerar, despachar.

expedition /,ekspɪ'dɪʃən/ n. expedición f.

expel /ɪk'spel/ v. expeler; expulsar.

expend /ɪk'spend/ v. desembolsar, expender.

expenditure /ɪk'spendɪtʃər/ n. desembolso; gasto m.

expense /ɪk'spens/ n. gasto m.; costa f.

expensive /ɪk'spensɪv/ a. caro, costoso.

expensively /ɪk'spensɪvli/ adv. costosamente.

experience /ɪk'spɪəriəns/ n. **1.** experiencia f. —v. **2.** experimentar.

experienced /ɪk'spɪəriənst/ a. experimentado, perito.

experiment /n ɪk'sperəmənt; v -,ment/ n. **1.** experimento m. —v. **2.** experimentar.

experimental /ɪk,sperə'mentl/ a. experimental.

expert /'ekspɜrt/ a. & n. experto -ta.

expertise /,ekspər'tiz/ n. pericia f.

expiate /'ekspi,eit/ v. expiar.

expiration /,ekspə'reiʃən/ n. expiración f.

expiration date fecha de caducidad f.

expire /ɪk'spaɪər/ v. expirar; Com. vencerse.

explain /ɪk'splein/ v. explicar.

explanation /,eksplə'neiʃən/ n. explicación f.

explanatory /ɪk'splænə,tɔri/ a. explicativo.

expletive /'eksplɪtɪv/ n. **1.** interjección f. —a. **2.** expletivo.

explicit /ɪk'splɪsɪt/ a. explícito, claro.

explode /ɪk'sploud/ v. estallar, volar; refutar.

exploit /ɪk'sploit/ n. **1.** hazaña f. —v. **2.** explotar.

exploitation /,eksplɔi'teiʃən/ n. explotación f.

exploration /,eksplə'reiʃən/ n. exploración f.

exploratory /ɪk'splɔrə,tɔri/ a. exploratorio.

explore /ɪk'splɔr/ v. explorar.

explorer /ɪk'splɔrər/ n. explorador -ra.

explosion /ɪk'splouʒən/ n. explosión f.

explosive /ɪk'splousɪv/ a. explosivo.

export /n 'eksport; v ɪk'sport/ n. **1.** exportación f. —v. **2.** exportar.

exportation /,ekspor'teiʃən/ n. exportación f.

expose /ɪk'spouz/ v. exponer; descubrir.

exposition /,ekspə'zɪʃən/ n. exposición f.

expository /ɪk'spɒzɪ,tɔri/ a. expositivo.

expostulate /ɪk'spɒstʃə,leit/ v. altercar.

exposure /ɪk'spouʒər/ n. exposición f.

expound /ɪk'spaund/ v. exponer, explicar.

express /ɪk'spres/ a. & n. **1.** expreso m. **e. company,** compañía de porteo. —v. **2.** expresar.

expression /ɪk'spreʃən/ n. expresión f.

expressive /ɪk'spresɪv/ a. expresivo.

expressly /ɪk'spresli/ adv. expresamente.

expressman /ɪk'spresmən, -,mæn/ n. empresario de expresos m.

expressway /ɪk'spres,wei/ n. autopista f

expropriate /eks'proupri,eit/ v. expropriar.

expulsion /ɪk'spʌlʃən/ n. expulsión f.

expunge /ɪk'spʌndʒ/ v. borrar, expurgar.

expurgate /'ɛkspər,geit/ v. expurgar.

exquisite /ɪk'skwɪzɪt/ a. exquisito.

extant /'ɛkstənt/ a. existente.

extemporaneous /ɪk,stɛmpə'reiniəs/ a. improvisado.

extend /ɪk'stɛnd/ v. extender.

extension /ɪk'stɛnʃən/ n. extensión f.

extensive /ɪk'stɛnsɪv/ a. extenso.

extensively /ɪk'stɛnsɪvli/ adv. extensamente.

extent /ɪk'stɛnt/ n. extensión f.; grado m. **to a certain e.,** hasta cierto punto.

extenuate /ɪk'stɛnyu,eit/ v. extenuar.

exterior /ɪk'stɪəriər/ a. & n. exterior m.

exterminate /ɪk'stɜrmə,neit/ v. exterminar.

extermination /ɪk,stɜrmə'neiʃən/ n. exterminio m.

external /ɪk'stɜrnl̩/ a. externo, exterior.

extinct /ɪk'stɪŋkt/ a. extinto.

extinction /ɪk'stɪŋkʃən/ n. extinción f.

extinguish /ɪk'stɪŋgwɪʃ/ v. extinguir, apagar.

extol /ɪk'stoul/ v. alabar.

extort /ɪk'stɔrt/ v. exigir dinero sin derecho.

extortion /ɪk'stɔrʃən/ n. extorsión f.

extra /'ɛkstrə/ a. **1.** extraordinario; adicional. —n. **2.** (newspaper) extra m.

extract /n 'ɛkstrækt; v ɪk'strækt/ n. **1.** extracto m. —v. **2.** extraer.

extraction /ɪk'strækʃən/ n. extracción f.

extraneous /ɪk'streiniəs/ a. extraño; ajeno.

extraordinary /ɪk'strɔrdn̩,ɛri/ a. extraordinario.

extravagance /ɪk'strævəgəns/ n. extravagancia f.

extravagant /ɪk'strævəgənt/ a. extravagante.

extreme /ɪk'strim/ a. & n. extremo m.

extremity /ɪk'strɛmɪti/ n. extremidad f.

extricate /'ɛkstrɪ,keit/ v. desenredar.

exuberant /ɪg'zubərənt/ a. exuberante.

exude /ɪg'zud/ v. exudar.

exult /ɪg'zʌlt/ v. regocijarse.

exultant /ɪg'zʌltn̩t/ a. triunfante.

eye /ai/ n. **1.** ojo m. —v. **2.** ojear.

eyeball /'ai,bɔl/ n. globo del ojo.

eyebrow /'ai,brau/ n. ceja f.

eyeglasses /'ai,glæsɪz/ n. lentes m.pl.

eyelash /'ai,læʃ/ n. pestaña f.

eyelid /'ai,lɪd/ n. párpado m.

eyeliner /'ai,lainər/ n. lápiz de ojos m.

eye shadow n. sombra de ojos f.

eyesight /'ai,sait/ n. vista f.

F

fable /'feibəl/ n. fábula; ficción f.

fabric /'fæbrɪk/ n. tejido m., tela f.

fabricate /'fæbrɪ,keit/ v. fabricar.

fabulous /'fæbyələs/ a. fabuloso.

façade /fə'sɑd/ n. fachada f.

face /feis/ n. **1.** cara f. **make faces,** hacer muecas. —v. **2.** encararse con.

facet /'fæsɪt/ n. faceta f.

facetious /fə'siʃəs/ a. chistoso.

facial /'feiʃəl/ n. **1.** masaje facial m. —a. **2.** facial.

facile /'fæsɪl/ a. fácil.

facilitate /fə'sɪlɪ,teit/ v. facilitar.

facility /fə'sɪlɪti/ n. facilidad f.

facsimile /fæk'sɪməli/ n. facsímile m.

fact /fækt/ n. hecho m. **in f.,** en realidad.

faction /'fækʃən/ n. facción f.

factor /'fæktər/ n. factor m.

factory /'fæktəri/ n. fábrica f.

factual /'fæktʃuəl/ a. verdadero.

faculty /'fækəlti/ n. facultad f.

fad /fæd/ n. boga; novedad f.

fade /feid/ v. desteñirse; (flowers) marchitarse.

fail /feil/ n. **1. without f.,** sin falla. —v. **2.** fallar; fracasar. **not to f. to,** no dejar de.

failure /'feilyər/ n. fracaso m.

faint /feint/ a. **1.** débil; vago; pálido. —n. **2.** desmayo m. —v. **3.** desmayarse.

faintly /'feintli/ adv. débilmente; indistintamente.

fair /fɛər/ a. **1.** razonable, justo; (hair) rubio; (weather) bueno. —n. **2.** feria f.

fairly /'fɛərli/ adv. imparcialmente; regularmente; claramente; bellamente.

fairness /'fɛərnɪs/ n. justicia f.

fair play juego limpio m.

fairway /'fɛər,wei/ n. (golf) calle f.

fairy /'fɛəri/ n. hada f., duende m.

faith /feiθ/ n. fe; confianza f.

faithful /'feiθfəl/ a. fiel.

fake /feik/ a. **1.** falso; postizo. —n. **2.** imitación; estafa f. —v. **3.** imitar; fingir.

faker /'feikər/ n. imitador m.; farsante m.

falcon /'fɔlkən/ n. halcón m.

fall /fɔl/ n. **1.** caída; catarata f.; (season) otoño m.; (in price) baja f. —v. **2.** caer; bajar. **f. asleep,** dormirse; **f. in love,** enamorarse.

fallacious /fə'leiʃəs/ a. falaz.

fallacy /'fæləsi/ n. falacia f.

fallible /'fæləbəl/ a falible.

fallout /'fɔl,aut/ *n.* lluvia radiactiva, polvillo radiactivo.

fallow /'fælou/ *a.* sin cultivar; barbecho.

false /fɔls/ *a.* falso; postizo.

falsehood /'fɔlshud/ *n.* falsedad; mentira *f.*

falseness /'fɔlsnɪs/ *n.* falsedad, perfidia *f.*

false teeth /tiθ/ dentadura postiza *f.*

falsetto /fɔl'sɛtou/ *n.* falsete *m.*

falsification /,fɔlsəfɪ'keiʃən/ *n.* falsificación *f.*

falsify /'fɔlsəfai/ *v.* falsificar.

falter /'fɔltər/ *v.* vacilar; (in speech) tartamudear.

fame /feim/ *n.* fama *f.*

familiar /fə'mɪlyər/ *a.* familiar; conocido. **be f. with,** estar familiarizado con.

familiarity /fə,mɪli'ærɪti/ *n.* familiaridad *f.*

familiarize /fə'mɪlyə,raiz/ *v.* familiarizar.

family /'fæməli/ *n.* familia; especie *f.*

family name apellido *m.*

family tree árbol genealógico *m.*

famine /'fæmɪn/ *n.* hambre; carestía *f.*

famished /'fæmɪʃt/ *a.* hambriento.

famous /'feiməs/ *a.* famoso, célebre.

fan /fæn/ *n.* abanico; ventilador *m.* (sports) aficionado -da.

fanatic /fə'nætɪk/ *a.* & *n.* fanático -ca.

fanatical /fə'nætɪkəl/ *a.* fanático.

fanaticism /fə'nætə,sɪzəm/ *n.* fanatismo *m.*

fanciful /'fænsɪfəl/ *a.* caprichoso; fantástico.

fancy /'fænsi/ *a.* **1.** fino, elegante. —*n.* **2.** fantasía *f.*; capricho *m.* —*v.* **3.** imaginar.

fanfare /'fænfɛər/ *n.* fanfarria *f.*

fang /fæŋ/ *n.* colmillo *m.*

fan heater estufa de aire *f.*

fantastic /fæn'tæstɪk/ *a.* fantástico.

fantasy /'fæntəsi/ *n.* fantasía *f.*

FAQ /fæk/ *n.* (Frequently Asked Questions) preguntas más frecuentes *f.pl.*

far /fɑr/ *a.* **1.** lejano, distante. —*adv.* **2.** lejos. **how f.,** a qué distancia. **as f. as,** hasta. **so f., thus f.,** hasta aquí.

farce /fɑrs/ *n.* farsa *f.*

fare /fɛər/ *n.* pasaje *m.*

farewell /,fɛər'wɛl/ *n.* **1.** despedida *f.* **to say f.** despedirse. —*interj.* **2.** ¡adiós!

farfetched /'fɑr'fɛtʃt/ *a.* forzado, inverosímil.

farm /fɑrm/ *n.* **1.** granja; hacienda *f.* —*v.* **2.** cultivar, labrar la tierra.

farmer /'fɑrmər/ *n.* labrador, agricultor *m.*

farmhouse /'fɑrm,haus/ *n.* hacienda, alquería *f.*

farming /'fɑrmɪŋ/ *n.* agricultura *f.*; cultivo *m.*

fart /fɑrt/ *n.* *Colloq.* pedo *m.*

fascinate /'fæsə,neit/ *v.* fascinar.

fascination /,fæsə'neiʃən/ *n.* fascinación *f.*

fascism /'fæʃ,ɪzəm/ *n.* fascismo *m.*

fashion /'fæʃən/ *n.* **1.** moda; costumbre; guisa *f.* **be in f.,** estilarse. —*v.* **2.** formar.

fashionable /'fæʃənəbəl/ *a.* de moda, en boga.

fashion show desfile de modas, pase de modelos *m.*

fast /fæst/ *a.* **1.** rápido, veloz; (watch) adelantado; (color) firme. —*adv.* **2.** ligero, de prisa. —*n.* **3.** ayuno *m.* —*v.* **4.** ayunar.

fasten /'fæsən/ *v.* afirmar; atar; fijar.

fastener /'fæsənər/ *n.* asegurador *m.*

fastidious /fæ'stɪdiəs/ *a.* melindroso.

fat /fæt/ *a.* **1.** gordo. —*n.* **2.** grasa, manteca *f.*

fatal /'feitl/ *a.* fatal.

fatality /fei'tælɪti/ *n.* fatalidad *f.*

fatally /'feitli/ *adv.* fatalmente.

fate /feit/ *n.* destino *m.*; suerte *f.*

fateful /'feitfəl/ *a.* fatal; ominoso.

father /'fɑðər/ *n.* padre *m.*

fatherhood /'fɑðər,hud/ *n.* paternidad *f.*

father-in-law /'fɑ,ðər ɪn lɔ/ *n.* suegro *m.*

fatherland /'fɑðər,lænd/ *n.* patria *f.*

fatherly /'fɑðərli/ *a.* **1.** paternal. —*adv.* **2.** paternalmente.

fathom /'fæðəm/ *n.* **1.** braza *f.* —*v.* **2.** sondar; *Fig.* penetrar en.

fatigue /fə'tig/ *n.* **1.** fatiga *f.*, cansancio *m.* —*v.* **2.** fatigar, cansar.

fatten /'fætn/ *v.* engordar, cebar.

faucet /'fɔsɪt/ *n.* grifo *m.*, llave *f.*

fault /fɔlt/ *n.* culpa *f.*; defecto *m.* **at f.,** culpable.

faultless /'fɔltlɪs/ *a.* sin tacha, perfecto.

faultlessly /'fɔltlɪsli/ *adv.* perfectamente.

faulty /'fɔlti/ *a.* defectuoso, imperfecto.

fauna /'fɔnə/ *n.* fauna *f.*

favor /'feivər/ *n.* **1.** favor *m.* —*v.* **2.** favorecer.

favorable /'feivərəbəl/ *a.* favorable.

favorite /'feivərɪt/ *a.* & *n.* favorito -ta.

favoritism /'feivəri,tɪzəm/ *n.* favoritismo *m.*

fawn /fɔn/ *n.* **1.** cervato *m.* —*v.* **2.** halagar, adular.

fax /fæks/ *n.* **1.** fax *m.* —*v.* **2.** mandar un fax.

faze /feiz/ *v.* desconcertar.

fear /fɪər/ *n.* **1.** miedo, temor *m.* —*v.* **2.** temer.

fearful /'fɪərfəl/ *a.* temeroso, medroso.

fearless /'fɪərlɪs/ *a.* intrépido; sin temor.

fearlessness /'fɪərlɪsnɪs/ *n.* intrepidez *f.*

feasible /'fizəbəl/ *a.* factible.

feast /fist/ *n.* banquete *m.*; fiesta *f.*

feat /fit/ *n.* hazaña *f.*; hecho *m.*

feather /'fɛðər/ *n.* pluma *f.*

feature /'fitʃər/ *n.* **1.** facción *f.*; rasgo *m.*; (movies) película principal *f.*, largometraje *m.* —*v.* **2.** presentar como atracción especial.

February /'fɛbru,ɛri, 'fɛbyu-/ *n.* febrero *m.*

federal /'fɛdərəl/ *a.* federal.

federation /ˌfɛdəˈreiʃən/ n. confederación, federación f.

fee /fi/ n. honorarios m.pl.

feeble /ˈfibəl/ a. débil.

feeble-minded /ˈfibəl ˈmaindɪd/ a. imbécil.

feebleness /ˈfibəlnɪs/ a. debilidad f.

feed /fid/ n. 1. pasto m. —v. 2. alimentar; dar de comer. **fed up with,** harto de.

feedback /ˈfid,bæk/ n. feedback m., retroalimentación f.

feel /fil/ n. 1. sensación f. —v. 2. sentir; palpar. **f. like,** tener ganas de.

feeling /ˈfilɪŋ/ n. sensación; sentimiento.

feign /fein/ v. fingir.

felicitate /fɪˈlɪsɪˌteit/ v. felicitar.

felicitous /fɪˈlɪsɪtəs/ a. feliz.

felicity /fɪˈlɪsɪti/ n. felicidad f., dicha f.

feline /ˈfilain/ a. felino.

fellow /ˈfɛlou/ n. compañero; socio m.; Colloq. tipo m.

fellowship /ˈfɛlou,ʃɪp/ n. compañerismo; (for study) beca f.

felon /ˈfɛlən/ n. reo m. & f., felón -ona.

felony /ˈfɛləni/ n. felonía f.

felt /fɛlt/ n. fieltro m.

felt-tipped pen /ˈfɛlt ,tɪpt/ rotulador m.

female /ˈfimeil/ a. & n. hembra f.

feminine /ˈfɛmənɪn/ a. femenino.

feminist /ˈfɛmənɪst/ a. & n. feminista m.& f.

fence /fɛns/ n. 1. cerca f. —v. 2. cercar.

fender /ˈfɛndər/ n. guardabarros m.pl.

ferment /n. ˈfɜrmɛnt; v. fərˈmɛnt/ n. 1. fermento m.; Fig. agitación f. —v. 2. fermentar.

fermentation /ˌfɜrmɛnˈteiʃən/ n. fermentación f.

fern /fɜrn/ n. helecho m.

ferocious /fəˈrouʃəs/ a. feroz, fiero.

ferociously /fəˈrouʃəsli/ adv. ferozmente.

ferocity /fəˈrɒsɪti/ n. ferocidad, fiereza f.

Ferris wheel /ˈfɛrɪs/ rueda de feria f.

ferry /ˈfɛri/ n. transbordador m., barca de transporte.

fertile /ˈfɜrtl/ a. fecundo; (land) fértil.

fertility /fərˈtɪlɪti/ n. fertilidad f.

fertilization /ˌfɜrtlɪˈzeiʃən/ n. fertilización f.

fertilize /ˈfɜrtl,aiz/ v. fertilizar, abonar.

fertilizer /ˈfɜrtl,aizər/ n. abono m.

fervency /ˈfɜrvənsi/ n. ardor m.

fervent /ˈfɜrvənt/ a. fervoroso.

fervently /ˈfɜrvəntli/ adv. fervorosamente.

fervid /ˈfɜrvɪd/ a. férvido.

fervor /ˈfɜrvər/ n. fervor m.

fester /ˈfɛstər/ v. ulcerarse.

festival /ˈfɛstəvəl/ n. fiesta f.

festive /ˈfɛstɪv/ a. festivo.

festivity /fɛˈstɪvɪti/ n. festividad f.

festoon /fɛˈstun/ n. 1. festón m. —v. 2. festonear.

fetch /fɛtʃ/ v. ir por; traer.

fete /feit/ n. 1. fiesta f. —v. 2. festejar.

fetid /ˈfɛtɪd/ a. fétido.

fetish /ˈfɛtɪʃ/ n. fetiche m.

fetter /ˈfɛtər/ n. 1. grillete m. —v. 2. engrillar.

fetus /ˈfitəs/ n. feto m.

feud /fyud/ n. riña f.

feudal /ˈfyudl/ a. feudal.

feudalism /ˈfyudl,ɪzəm/ n. feudalismo m.

fever /ˈfivər/ n. fiebre f.

feverish /ˈfivərɪʃ/ a. febril.

feverishly /ˈfivərɪʃli/ adv. febrilmente.

few /fyu/ a. pocos. **a. f.,** algunos, unos cuantos.

fiancé, fiancée /ˌfiɑnˈsei/ n. novio -via.

fiasco /fiˈæskou/ n. fiasco m.

fiat /ˈfiɑt/ n. fiat m., orden f.

fib /fɪb/ n. 1. mentira f. —v. 2. mentir.

fiber /ˈfaibər/ n. fibra f.

fibrous /ˈfaibrəs/ a. fibroso.

fickle /ˈfɪkəl/ a. caprichoso.

fickleness /ˈfɪkəlnɪs/ n. inconstancia f.

fiction /ˈfɪkʃən/ n. ficción f.; (literature) novelas f.pl.

fictitious /fɪkˈtɪʃəs/ a. ficticio.

fidelity /fɪˈdɛlɪti/ n. fidelidad f.

fidget /ˈfɪdʒɪt/ v. inquietar.

field /fild/ n. campo m.

field trip viaje de estudios m.

fiend /find/ n. demonio m.

fiendish /ˈfindɪʃ/ a. diabólico, malvado.

fierce /fɪərs/ a. fiero, feroz.

fiery /ˈfaiˀri/ a. ardiente.

fiesta /fiˈestə/ n. fiesta f.

fife /faif/ n. pífano m.

fifteen /ˈfɪfˈtin/ a. & pron. quince.

fifteenth /ˈfɪfˈtinθ/ n. & a. décimoquinto.

fifth /fɪfθ/ a. quinto.

fifty /ˈfɪfti/ a. & pron. cincuenta.

fig /fɪg/ n. higo m. **f. tree,** higuera f.

fight /fait/ n. 1. lucha, pelea f. —v. 2. luchar, pelear.

fighter /ˈfaitər/ n. peleador -ra, luchador -ra.

figment /ˈfɪgmənt/ n. invención f.

figurative /ˈfɪgyərətɪv/ a. metafórico.

figuratively /ˈfɪgyərətɪvli/ adv. figuradamente.

figure /ˈfɪgyər/ n. 1. figura; cifra f. —v. 2. figurar; calcular.

filament /ˈfɪləmənt/ n. filamento m.

file /fail/ n. 1. archivo m.; (instrument) lima f.; (row) fila f. —v. 2. archivar; limar.

file cabinet archivador m.

filial /ˈfɪliəl/ a. filial.

filigree /ˈfɪlə,gri/ n. filigrana f.

fill /fɪl/ v. llenar.

fillet /ˈfɪlɪt/ n. filete m.

filling /ˈfɪlɪŋ/ n. relleno m.; (dental) empastadura f. **f. station,** gasolinera f.

film /fɪlm/ n. 1. película f., film m. —v. 2. filmar.

filter /ˈfɪltər/ n. **1.** filtro m. —v. **2.** filtrar.

filth /fɪlθ/ n. suciedad, mugre f.

filthy /ˈfɪlθi/ a. sucio.

fin /fɪn/ n. aleta f.

final /ˈfaɪnl/ a. **1.** final, último. —n. **2.** examen final. **finals** (sports) final f.

finalist /ˈfaɪnlɪst/ n. finalista m. & f.

finally /ˈfaɪnli/ adv. finalmente.

finances /ˈfaɪnænsəz/ n. recursos, fondos m.pl.

financial /fɪˈnænʃəl/ a. financiero.

financier /ˌfɪnənˈsɪər, ˌfaɪnən-/ n. financiero -ra.

find /faɪnd/ n. **1.** hallazgo m. —v. **2.** hallar; encontrar. **f. out**, averiguar, enterarse, saber.

fine /faɪn/ a. **1.** fino; bueno. —adv. **2.** muy bien. —n. **3.** multa f. —v. **4.** multar.

fine arts /ɑrts/ bellas artes f.pl.

finery /ˈfaɪnəri/ n. gala f., adorno m.

finesse /fɪˈnɛs/ n. **1.** artificio m. —v. **2.** valerse de artificio.

finger /ˈfɪŋɡər/ n. dedo m.

finger bowl n. enjuagatorio m.

fingernail /ˈfɪŋɡərˌneɪl/ n. uña f.

fingerprint /ˈfɪŋɡərˌprɪnt/ n. **1.** impresión digital f. —v. **2.** tomar las impresiones digitales.

finicky /ˈfɪnɪki/ a. melindroso.

finish /ˈfɪnɪʃ/ n. **1.** conclusión f. —v. **2.** acabar, terminar.

finished /ˈfɪnɪʃt/ a. acabado.

finite /ˈfaɪnaɪt/ a. finito.

fir /fɜr/ n. abeto m.

fire /faɪər/ n. **1.** fuego; incendio m. —v. **2.** disparar, tirar; Colloq. despedir.

fire alarm n. alarma de incendio f.

firearm /ˈfaɪərˌɑrm/ n. arma de fuego.

firecracker /ˈfaɪərˌkrækər/ n. triquitraque m., buscapiés m., petardo m.

fire engine bomba de incendios f.

fire escape escalera de incendios f.

fire exit salida de urgencia f.

fire extinguisher /ɪkˈstɪŋɡwɪʃər/ matafuego m.

firefly /ˈfaɪərˌflaɪ/ n. luciérnaga f.

fireman /ˈfaɪərmən/ n. bombero m.; (railway) fogonero m.

fireplace /ˈfaɪərˌpleɪs/ n. hogar, fogón m.

fireproof /ˈfaɪərˌpruf/ a. incombustible.

fireside /ˈfaɪərˌsaɪd/ n. hogar, fogón m.

fireworks /ˈfaɪərˌwɜrks/ n. fuegos artificiales.

firm /fɜrm/ a. **1.** firme. —n. **2.** firma, empresa f.

firmness /ˈfɜrmnɪs/ n. firmeza f.

first /fɜrst/ a. & adv. primero. **at f.**, al principio.

first aid primeros auxilios.

first-class /ˈfɜrst ˈklæs/ a de primera clase.

fiscal /ˈfɪskəl/ a. fiscal.

fish /fɪʃ/ n. **1.** (food) pescado m.; (alive) pez m. —v. **2.** pescar.

fisherman /ˈfɪʃərmən/ n. pescador m.

fishhook /ˈfɪʃˌhʊk/ n. anzuelo m.

fishing /ˈfɪʃɪŋ/ n. pesca f. **go f.**, ir de pesca.

fishmonger /ˈfɪʃˌmʌŋɡər/ n. pescadero m.

fish store pescadería f.

fission /ˈfɪʃən/ n. fisión f.

fissure /ˈfɪʃər/ n. grieta f., quebradura f.; fisura.

fist /fɪst/ n. puño m.

fit /fɪt/ a. **1.** capaz; justo. —n. **2.** corte, talle m.; Med. convulsión f. —v. **3.** caber; quedar bien, sentar bien.

fitful /ˈfɪtfəl/ a. espasmódico; caprichoso.

fitness /ˈfɪtnɪs/ n. aptitud; conveniencia f.

fitting /ˈfɪtɪŋ/ a. **1.** conveniente. **be f.**, convenir. —n. **2.** ajuste m.

fitting room probador m.

five /faɪv/ a. & pron. cinco.

five-day work week /ˈfaɪv ˈdeɪ/ semana inglesa f.

fix /fɪks/ n. **1.** apuro m. —v. **2.** fijar; arreglar; componer, reparar.

fixation /fɪkˈseɪʃən/ n. fijación f.; fijeza f.

fixed /fɪkst/ a. fijo.

fixture /ˈfɪkstʃər/ n. instalación; guarnición f.

flabby /ˈflæbi/ a. flojo.

flaccid /ˈflæksɪd, ˈflæsɪd/ a. flojo; flácido.

flag /flæɡ/ n. bandera f.

flagellant /ˈflædʒələnt/ n. & a. flagelante m.

flagon /ˈflæɡən/ n. frasco m.

flagrant /ˈfleɪɡrənt/ a. flagrante.

flagrantly /ˈfleɪɡrəntli/ adv. notoriamente.

flair /flɛər/ n. aptitud especial f.

flake /fleɪk/ n. **1.** escama f.; copo de nieve. —v. **2.** romperse en láminas.

flamboyant /flæmˈbɔɪənt/ a. flamante, llamativo.

flame /fleɪm/ n. **1.** llama f. —v. **2.** llamear.

flaming /ˈfleɪmɪŋ/ a. llameante, flamante.

flamingo /fləˈmɪŋɡoʊ/ n. flamenco m.

flammable /ˈflæməbəl/ a. inflamable.

flank /flæŋk/ n. **1.** ijada f.; Mil. flanco m. —v. **2.** flanquear.

flannel /ˈflænl/ n. franela f.

flap /flæp/ n. **1.** cartera f. —v. **2.** aletear; sacudirse.

flare /flɛər/ n. **1.** llamarada f. —v. **2.** brillar; Fig. enojarse.

flash /flæʃ/ n. **1.** resplandor m.; (lightning) rayo, relámpago m.; Fig. instante m. —v. **2.** brillar.

flashcube /ˈflæʃˌkyub/ n. cubo de flash m.

flashlight /ˈflæʃˌlaɪt/ n. linterna (eléctrica) f.

flashy /ˈflæʃi/ a. ostentoso.

flask /flæsk/ n. frasco m.

flat /flæt/ *a.* **1.** llano; (tire) desinflado. —*n.* **2.** llanura *f.*; apartamento *m.*

flatness /'flætnɪs/ *n.* llanura *f.*

flatten /'flætṇ/ *v.* aplastar, allanar; abatir.

flatter /'flætər/ *v.* adular, lisonjear.

flatterer /'flætərər/ *n.* lisonjero -ra; zalamero -ra.

flattery /'flætəri/ *n.* adulación, lisonja *f.*

flaunt /flɔnt/ *v.* ostentar.

flavor /'fleɪvər/ *n.* **1.** sabor *m.* —*v.* **2.** sazonar.

flavoring /'fleɪvərɪŋ/ *n.* condimento *m.*

flaw /flɔ/ *n.* defecto *m.*

flax /flæks/ *n.* lino *m.*

flay /fleɪ/ *v.* despellejar; excoriar.

flea /fli/ *n.* pulga *f.*

flea market rastro *m.*

fleck /flɛk/ *n.* **1.** mancha *f.* —*v.* **2.** varetear.

flee /fli/ *v.* huir.

fleece /flis/ *n.* **1.** vellón *m.* —*v.* **2.** esquilar.

fleet /flit/ *a.* **1.** veloz. —*n.* **2.** flota *f.*

fleeting /'flitɪŋ/ *a.* fugaz, pasajero.

flesh /flɛʃ/ *n.* carne *f.*

fleshy /'flɛʃi/ *a.* gordo; carnoso.

flex /flɛks/ *n.* **1.** doblez *m.* —*v.* **2.** doblar.

flexibility /ˌflɛksə'bɪlɪti/ *n.* flexibilidad *f.*

flexible /'flɛksəbəl/ *a.* flexible.

flier /'flaɪər/ *n.* aviador -ra.

flight /flaɪt/ *n.* vuelo *m.*; fuga *f.*

flight attendant *n.* azafata *f.*; ayudante de vuelo *m.*

flimsy /'flɪmzi/ *a.* débil.

flinch /flɪntʃ/ *v.* acobardarse.

fling /flɪŋ/ *v.* lanzar.

flint /flɪnt/ *n.* pedernal *m.*

flip /flɪp/ *v.* lanzar.

flippant /'flɪpənt/ *a.* impertinente.

flippantly /'flɪpəntli/ *adv.* impertinentemente.

flirt /flɜrt/ *n.* **1.** coqueta *f.* —*v.* **2.** coquetear, flirtear.

flirtation /flɜr'teɪʃən/ *n.* coqueteo *m.*

float /floʊt/ *v.* flotar.

flock /flɒk/ *n.* **1.** rebaño *m.* —*v.* **2.** congregarse.

flog /flɒg/ *v.* azotar.

flood /flʌd/ *n.* **1.** inundación *f.* —*v.* **2.** inundar.

floor /flɔr/ *n.* **1.** suelo, piso *m.* —*v.* **2.** derribar.

floppy disk /'flɒpi/ floppy, *m.*, disquete, *m.*

floral /'flɔrəl/ *a.* floral.

florid /'flɔrɪd/ *a.* florido.

florist /'flɔrɪst/ *n.* florista *m. & f.*

flounce /flaʊns/ *n.* **1.** (sewing) volante *m.* —*v* **2.** pernear.

flounder /'flaʊndər/ *n.* rodaballo *m.*

flour /flaʊᵊr/ *n.* harina *f.*

flourish /'flɜrɪʃ/ *n.* **1.** *Mus.* floreo *m.* —*v.* **2.** florecer; prosperar; blandir.

flow /floʊ/ *n.* **1.** flujo *m.* —*v.* **2.** fluir.

flow chart organigrama *m.*

flower /'flaʊər/ *n.* **1.** flor *f.* —*v.* **2.** florecer.

flowerpot /'flaʊər,pɒt/ *n.* maceta *f.*

flowery /'flaʊəri/ *a.* florido.

fluctuate /'flʌktʃu,eɪt/ *v.* fluctuar.

fluctuation /ˌflʌktʃu'eɪʃən/ *n.* fluctuación *f.*

flue /flu/ *n.* humero *m.*

fluency /'fluənsi/ *n.* fluidez *f.*

fluent /'fluənt/ *a.* fluido; competente.

fluffy /'flʌfi/ *a.* velloso.

fluid /'fluɪd/ *a. & n.* fluido *m.*

fluidity /flu'ɪdɪti/ *n.* fluidez *f.*

fluoroscope /'flʊrə,skoʊp/ *n.* fluoroscopio *m.*

flurry /'flɜri/ *n.* agitación *f.*

flush /flʌʃ/ *a.* **1.** bien provisto. —*n.* **2.** sonrojo *m.* —*v.* **3.** limpiar con un chorro de agua; sonrojarse.

flute /flut/ *n.* flauta *f.*

flutter /'flʌtər/ *n.* **1.** agitación *f.* —*v.* **2.** agitarse.

flux /flʌks/ *n.* flujo *m.*

fly /flaɪ/ *n.* **1.** mosca *f.* —*v.* **2.** volar.

flying saucer /'flaɪɪŋ/ platillo volante *m.*

foam /foʊm/ *n.* **1.** espuma *f.* —*v.* **2.** espumar.

focal /'foʊkəl/ *a.* focal.

focus /'foʊkəs/ *n.* **1.** enfoque *m.* —*v.* **2.** enfocar.

fodder /'fɒdər/ *n.* forraje *m.*, pienso *m.*

foe /foʊ/ *n.* adversario -ria, enemigo -ga.

fog /fɒg/ *n.* niebla *f.*

foggy /'fɒgi/ *a.* brumoso.

foil /fɔɪl/ *v.* frustrar.

foist /fɔɪst/ *v.* imponer.

fold /foʊld/ *n.* **1.** pliegue *m.* —*v.* **2.** doblar, plegar.

foldable /'foʊldəbəl/ *a.* plegable.

folder /'foʊldər/ *n.* circular *m.*; (for filing) carpeta *f.*

folding /'foʊldɪŋ/ *a.* plegable.

foliage /'foʊliɪdʒ/ *n.* follaje *m.*

folio /'foʊli,oʊ/ *n.* infolio; folio *m.*

folklore /'foʊk,lɔr/ *n.* folklore *m.*

folks /foʊks/ *n.* gente; familia *f.*

follicle /'fɒlɪkəl/ *n.* folículo *m.*

follow /'fɒloʊ/ *v.* seguir.

follower /'fɒloʊər/ *n.* partidario -ria.

folly /'fɒli/ *n.* locura *f.*

foment /foʊ'mɛnt/ *v.* fomentar.

fond /fɒnd/ *a.* cariñoso, tierno. **be f. of,** ser aficionado a.

fondle /'fɒndl/ *v.* acariciar.

fondly /'fɒndli/ *adv.* tiernamente.

fondness /'fɒndnɪs/ *n.* afición *f.*; cariño *m.*

food /fud/ *n.* alimento *m.*; comida *f.*

foodie /'fudi/ *n. Colloq.* gastrónomo -ma, gourmet *m. & f.*

food poisoning /'pɔizənɪŋ/ intoxicación alimenticia f.

foodstuffs /'fud,stʌfs/ n.pl. comestibles, víveres m.pl.

fool /ful/ **1.** tonto -ta; bobo -ba; bufón -ona. —v. **2.** engañar.

foolhardy /'ful,hardi/ a. temerario.

foolish /'fulɪʃ/ a. bobo, tonto, majadero.

foolproof /'ful,pruf/ a. seguro.

foot /fut/ n. pie m.

footage /'futɪdʒ/ n. longitud en pies.

football /'fut,bɔl/ n. fútbol, balompié m.

footbridge /'fut,brɪdʒ/ n. puente para peatones m.

foothold /'fut,hould/ n. posición establecida.

footing /'futɪŋ/ n. base f., fundamento m.

footlights /'fut,laits/ n.pl. luces del proscenio.

footnote /'fut,nout/ n. nota al pie de una página.

footpath /'fut,pæθ/ n. sendero m.

footprint /'fut,prɪnt/ n. huella f.

footstep /'fut,step/ n. paso m.

footstool /'fut,stul/ n. escañuelo m., banqueta f.

fop /fɒp/ n. petimetre m.

for /fɔr; unstressed fər/ prep. **1.** para; por. **as f.,** en cuanto a. **what f.,** ¿para qué? —conj. **2.** porque, pues.

forage /'fɔrɪdʒ/ n. **1.** forraje m. —v. **2.** forrajear.

foray /'fɔrei/ n. correría f

forbear /fɔr,bear/ v. cesar; abstenerse.

forbearance /fɔr'bearəns/ n. paciencia f.

forbid /fər'bɪd/ v. prohibir.

forbidding /fər'bɪdɪŋ/ a. repugnante.

force /fɔrs/ n. **1.** fuerza f. —v. **2.** forzar.

forced landing /fɔrst/ aterrizaje forzoso m.

forceful /'fɔrsfəl/ a. fuerte; enérgico.

forcible /'fɔrsəbəl/ a. a la fuerza; enérgico.

ford /fɔrd/ n. **1.** vado m. —v. **2.** vadear.

fore /fɔr/ a. **1.** delantero. —n. **2.** delantera f.

fore and aft de popa a proa.

forearm /'fɔr'arm/ n. antebrazo m.

forebears /'fɔr,beərz/ n.pl. antepasados m.pl.

forebode /fɔr'boud/ v. presagiar.

foreboding /fɔr'boudɪŋ/ n. presentimiento m.

forecast /'fɔr,kæst/ n. **1.** pronóstico m.; profecía f. —v. **2.** pronosticar.

forecastle /'fouksəl/ n. Naut. castillo de proa.

forefathers /'fɔr,faðərz/ n. antepasados m.pl.

forefinger /'fɔr,fɪŋgər/ n. índice m.

forego /fɔr'gou/ v. renunciar.

foregone /fɔr'gɔn/ a. predeterminado.

foreground /'fɔr,graund/ n. primer plano.

forehead /'fɔrɪd/ n. frente f.

foreign /'fɔrɪn/ a. extranjero.

foreign aid n. ayuda exterior f.

foreigner /'fɔrɪnər/ n. extranjero -ra; forastero -ra.

foreleg /'fɔr,leg/ n. pierna delantera.

foreman /'fɔrmən/ n. capataz, jefe de taller m.

foremost /'fɔr,moust/ a. **1.** primero. —adv. **2.** en primer lugar.

forenoon /'fɔr,nun/ n. mañana f.

forensic /fə'rensɪk/ a. forense.

forerunner /'fɔr,rʌnər/ n. precursor -ra.

foresee /fɔr'si/ v. prever.

foreshadow /fɔr'ʃædou/ v. prefigurar, anunciar.

foresight /'fɔr,sait/ n. previsión f.

forest /'fɔrɪst/ n. bosque m.; selva f.

forestall /fɔr'stɔl/ v. anticipar; prevenir.

forester /'fɔrəstər/ n. silvicultor -ra; guardamontes m.pl. & f.pl.

forestry /'fɔrəstri/ n. silvicultura f.

foretell /fɔr'tel/ v. predecir.

forever /fɔr'evər/ adv. por siempre, para siempre.

forevermore /fɔr,evər'mɔr/ adv. siempre.

forewarn /fɔr'wɔrn/ v. advertir, avisar.

foreword /'fɔr,wɜrd/ n. prefacio m.

forfeit /'fɔrfɪt/ n. **1.** prenda; multa f. —v. **2.** perder.

forfeiture /'fɔrfɪtʃər/ n. decomiso m., multa f.; pérdida.

forgather /fɔr'gæðər/ v. reunirse.

forge /fɔrdʒ/ n. **1.** fragua f. —v. **2.** forjar; falsear.

forger /'fɔrdʒər/ n. forjador -ra; falsificador -ra.

forgery /'fɔrdʒəri/ n. falsificación f.

forget /fər'get/ v. olvidar.

forgetful /fər'getfəl/ a. olvidadizo.

forgive /fər'gɪv/ v. perdonar.

forgiveness /fər'gɪvnɪs/ n. perdón m.

fork /fɔrk/ n. **1.** tenedor m.; bifurcación f. —v. **2.** bifurcarse.

forlorn /fɔr'lɔrn/ a. triste.

form /fɔrm/ n. **1.** forma f.; (document) formulario m. —v. **2.** formar.

formal /'fɔrməl/ a. formal; ceremonioso. **f. dance,** baile de etiqueta. **f. dress,** traje de etiqueta.

formality /fɔr'mælɪti/ n. formalidad f.

formally /'fɔrməli/ adv. formalmente.

format /'fɔrmæt/ n. formato m.

formation /fɔr'meiʃən/ n. formación f.

formative /'fɔrmətɪv/ a. formativo.

formatting /'fɔrmætɪŋ/ n. formateo m.

former /'fɔrmər/ a. anterior; antiguo. **the f.,** aquél.

formerly /'fɔrmərli/ adv. antiguamente.

formidable /'fɔrmɪdəbəl/ a. formidable.

formless /'fɔrmlɪs/ a. sin forma.

formula /'fɔrmyələ/ n. fórmula f.

formulate /'fɔrmyə,leit/ v. formular.

formulation /,fɔrmy'leiʃən/ n. formulación f.; expresión f.

forsake /fɔr'seik/ v. abandonar.

fort /fɔrt/ n. fortaleza f.; fuerte m.

forte /'fɔrtei/ a. & adv. Mus. forte; fuerte.

forth /fɔrθ/ adv. adelante. **back and f.**, de aquí allá. **and so f.**, etcétera.

forthcoming /fɔrθ'kʌmɪŋ/ a. futuro, próximo.

forthright /'fɔrθ,rait/ a. franco.

forthwith /,fɔrθ'wiθ/ adv. inmediatamente.

fortification /,fɔrtəfɪ'keiʃən/ n. fortificación f.

fortify /'fɔrtə,fai/ v. fortificar.

fortissimo /fɔr'tɪsə,mou/ a. & adv. Mus. fortísimo.

fortitude /'fɔrtɪ,tud/ n. fortaleza; fortitud f.

fortnight /'fɔrt,nait/ n. quincena f.

fortress /'fɔrtrɪs/ n. fuerte m., fortaleza f.

fortuitous /fɔr'tuɪtəs/ a. fortuito.

fortunate /'fɔrtʃənɪt/ a. afortunado.

fortune /'fɔrtʃən/ n. fortuna; suerte f.

fortune-teller /'fɔrtʃən ,tɛlər/ n. sortílego -ga, adivino -na.

forty /'fɔrti/ a. & pron. cuarenta.

forum /'fɔrəm/ n. foro m.

forward /'fɔrwərd/ a. 1. delantero; atrevido. —adv. 2. adelante. —v. 3. trasmitir, reexpedir.

foster /'fɔstər/ n. 1. **f. child**, hijo adoptivo. —v. 2. fomentar; criar.

foul /faul/ a. sucio; impuro.

found /faund/ v. fundar.

foundation /faun'deiʃən/ n. fundación f.; (of building) cimientos m.pl.

founder /'faundər/ n. 1. fundador -ra. —v. 2. irse a pique.

foundry /'faundri/ n. fundición f.

fountain /'fauntn/ n. fuente f.

fountain pen pluma estilográfica, pluma-fuente f.

four /fɔr/ a. & pron. cuatro.

fourteen /'fɔr'tin/ a. & pron. catorce.

fourth /fɔrθ/ a. & n. cuarto m.

fowl /faul/ n. ave f.

fox /fɔks/ n. zorro -rra.

fox-trot /'fɔks,trɒt/ n. foxtrot m.

foxy /'fɔksi/ a. astuto.

foyer /'fɔiər/ n. salón de entrada.

fracas /'freikəs, 'frækəs/ n. riña f.

fraction /'frækʃən/ n. fracción f.

fracture /'fræktʃər/ n. 1. fractura, rotura f. —v. 2. fracturar, romper.

fragile /'frædʒəl/ a. frágil.

fragment /'frægmənt/ n. fragmento, trozo m.

fragmentary /'frægmən,tɛri/ a. fragmentario.

fragrance /'freigrəns/ n. fragancia f.

fragrant /'freigrənt/ a. fragante.

frail /freil/ a. débil, frágil.

frailty /'freilti/ n. debilidad, fragilidad f.

frame /freim/ n. 1. marco; armazón; cuadro; cuerpo m. —v. 2. fabricar; formar; encuadrar.

frame-up /'freim ,ʌp/ n. Colloq. conspiración f

framework /'freim,wɜrk/ n armazón m.

France /fræns/ n. Francia f.

franchise /'fræntʃaiz/ n. franquicia f.

frank /fræŋk/ a. 1. franco. —n. 2. carta franca. —v. 3. franquear.

frankfurter /'fræŋkfɜrtər/ n. salchicha f.

frankly /'fræŋkli/ adv. francamente.

frankness /'fræŋknɪs/ n. franqueza f.

frantic /'fræntɪk/ a. frenético.

fraternal /frə'tɜrnl/ a. fraternal.

fraternity /frə'tɜrnɪti/ n. fraternidad f.

fraternization /,frætərnə'zeiʃən/ n. fraternización f.

fraternize /'frætər,naiz/ v. confraternizar.

fratricide /'frætrɪ,said/ n. fratricida m. & f.; fratricidio m.

fraud /frɔd/ n. fraude m.

fraudulent /'frɔdʒələnt/ a. fraudulento.

fraudulently /'frɔdʒələntli/ adv. fraudulentamente.

fraught /frɔt/ a. cargado.

freak /frik/ n. rareza f.; monstruosidad f.

freckle /'frɛkəl/ n. peca f.

freckled /'frɛkəld/ a. pecoso.

free /fri/ a. 1. libre; gratis. —v. 2. libertar, librar.

freedom /'fridəm/ n. libertad f.

freeze /friz/ v. helar, congelar.

freezer /'frizər/ n. heladora f.

freezing point /'frizɪŋ/ punto de congelación m.

freight /freit/ n. 1. carga f.; flete m. —v. 2. cargar; fletar.

freighter /'freitər/ n. Naut. fletador m.

French /frɛntʃ/ a. & n. francés -esa.

Frenchman /'frɛntʃmən/ n. francés m.

Frenchwoman /'frɛntʃ,wumən/ n. francesa f.

frenzied /'frɛnzid/ a. frenético.

frenzy /'frɛnzi/ n. frenesí m.

frequency /'frikwənsi/ n. frecuencia f.

frequency modulation /,mɒdʒə'leiʃən/ modulación de frecuencia.

frequent /'frikwənt/ a. frecuente.

frequently /'frikwəntli/ adv. frecuentemente.

fresco /'freskou/ n. fresco.

fresh /frɛʃ/ a. fresco. **f. water**, agua dulce.

freshen /'frɛʃən/ v. refrescar.

freshness /'frɛʃnɪs/ n. frescura f.

fret /frɛt/ v. quejarse, irritarse; *Mus.* traste m.

fretful /'frɛtfəl/ a. irritable.

fretfully /'frɛtfəli/ adv. de mala gana.

fretfulness /'frɛtfəlnɪs/ n. mal humor.

friar /'fraɪər/ n. fraile m.

fricassee /ˌfrɪkə'si/ n. fricasé m.

friction /'frɪkʃən/ n. fricción f.

Friday /'fraɪdeɪ/ n. viernes m. **Good F.**, Viernes Santo m.

fried /fraɪd/ a. frito.

friend /frɛnd/ n. amigo -ga.

friendless /'frɛndlɪs/ a. sin amigos.

friendliness /'frɛndlɪnɪs/ n. amistad f.

friendly /'frɛndli/ a. amistoso.

friendship /'frɛndʃɪp/ n. amistad f.

fright /fraɪt/ n. susto m.

frighten /'fraɪtn/ v. asustar, espantar.

frightful /'fraɪtfəl/ a. espantoso.

frigid /'frɪdʒɪd/ a. frígido; frío.

frill /frɪl/ n. (sewing) lechuga f.

fringe /frɪndʒ/ n fleco; borde m.

frisky /'frɪski/ a. retozón.

fritter /'frɪtər/ n. fritura f.

frivolity /frɪ'vɒlɪti/ n. frivolidad f.

frivolous /'frɪvələs/ a. frívolo.

frivolousness /'frɪvələsnɪs/ n. frivolidad f.

frock /frɒk/ n. vestido de mujer. **f. coat**, levita f.

frog /frɒg/ n. rana f.

frolic /'frɒlɪk/ n. **1.** retozo m. —v. **2.** retozar.

from /frʌm, *unstressed* frəm/ prep. de; desde.

front /frʌnt/ n. frente; (of building) fachada f. **in f. of**, delante de.

frontal /'frʌntl/ a. frontal.

front door puerta principal f.

frontier /frʌn'tɪər/ n. frontera f.

front seat asiento delantero m.

frost /frɒst/ n. helada, escarcha f.

frosty /'frɒsti/ a. helado.

froth /frɔθ/ n. espuma f.

frown /fraʊn/ n. **1.** ceño m. —v. **2.** fruncir el entrecejo.

frowzy /'fraʊzi/ a. desaliñado.

frozen /'froʊzən/ a. helado; congelado.

fructify /'frʌktə,faɪ/ v. fructificar.

frugal /'frugəl/ a. frugal.

frugality /fru'gælɪti/ n. frugalidad f.

fruit /frut/ n. fruta f.; (benefits) frutos m.pl. **f. tree**, árbol frutal.

fruitful /'frutfəl/ a. productivo.

fruition /fru'ɪʃən/ n. fruición f.

fruitless /'frutlɪs/ a. inútil, en vano.

fruit salad macedonia de frutas f.

fruit store frutería f.

frustrate /'frʌstreɪt/ v. frustrar.

frustration /frʌ'streɪʃən/ n. frustración f.

fry /fraɪ/ v. freír.

fuel /'fyuəl/ n. combustible m.

fugitive /'fyudʒɪtɪv/ a. & n. fugitivo -va.

fugue /fyug/ n. fuga f.

fulcrum /'fʊlkrəm/ n. fulcro m.

fulfill /fʊl'fɪl/ v. cumplir.

fulfillment /fʊl'fɪlmənt/ n. cumplimiento m.; realización f.

full /fʊl/ a. lleno: completo; pleno.

full name nombre y apellidos.

fullness /'fʊlnɪs/ n. plenitud f.

fulminate /'fʌlmə,neɪt/ v. volar; fulminar.

fulmination /ˌfʌlmə'neɪʃən/ n. fulminación f.; detonación f.

fumble /'fʌmbəl/ v. chapucear.

fume /fyum/ n. **1.** humo m. —v. **2.** humear.

fumigate /'fyumɪ,geɪt/ v. fumigar.

fumigator /'fyumɪ,geɪtər/ n. fumigador m.

fun /fʌn/ n. diversión **f to make f. of**, burlarse de. **to have f.**, divertirse.

function /'fʌŋkʃən/ n. **1.** función f. —v. **2.** funcionar.

functional /'fʌŋkʃənl/ a. funcional.

fund /fʌnd/ n. fondo m.

fundamental /ˌfʌndə'mɛntl/ a. fundamental.

funeral /'fyunərəl/ n. funeral m.

funeral home, funeral parlor funeraria f.

fungus /'fʌŋgəs/ n. hongo m.

funnel /'fʌnl/ n. embudo m.; (of ship) chimenea f.

funny /'fʌni/ a. divertido, gracioso. **to be f.**, tener gracia.

fur /fɜr/ n. piel f.

furious /'fyuriəs/ a. furioso.

furlough /'fɜrloʊ/ n. permiso m.

furnace /'fɜrnɪs/ n. horno m.

furnish /'fɜrnɪʃ/ v surtir, proveer; (a house) amueblar.

furniture /'fɜrnɪtʃər/ n. muebles m.pl.

furrow /'fɜroʊ/ n. **1.** surco m. —v. **2.** surcar.

further /'fɜrðər/ a. & adv. **1.** más. —v. **2.** adelantar, fomentar.

furthermore /'fɜrðər,mɔr/ adv. además.

fury /'fyuri/ n. furor m.; furia f.

fuse /fyuz/ n. **1.** fusible m. —v. **2.** fundir.

fuss /fʌs/ n. **1.** alboroto m. —v. **2.** preocuparse por pequeñeces.

fussy /'fʌsi/ a. melindroso.

futile /'fyutl/ a. fútil.

future /'fyutʃər/ n. **1.** futuro. —n. **2.** porvenir m.

futurology /ˌfyutʃə'rɒlədʒi/ n. futurología f.

fuzzy logic /'fʌzi/ lógica matizada f.

FYI abbr. (For Your Information) para su información.

G

gag /gæg/ n. chiste m.; mordaza f.

gaiety /'geiiti/ n. alegría f.

gain /gein/ n. **1.** ganancia f. —v. **2.** ganar.

gait /geit/ n. paso m.

gale /geil/ n. ventarrón m.

gall /gɔl/ n. hiel f.; Fig. amargura f.; descaro m.

gallant /'gælənt, gə'lænt, -'lunt/ a. **1.** galante. —n. **2.** galán m.

gallery /'gæləri/ n. galería f.; Theat. paraíso m.

gallon /'gælən/ n. galón m.

gallop /'gæləp/ n. **1.** galope m. —v. **2.** galopar.

gallows /'gælouz/ n. horca f.

gamble /'gæmbəl/ v. **1.** riesgo m. —v. **2.** jugar, aventurar.

game /geim/ n. juego m ; (match) partida f.; (hunting) caza f.

gang /gæŋ/ n. cuadrilla; pandilla f.

gangster /'gæŋstər/ n. rufián m.

gap /gæp/ n. raja f.

gape /geip/ v. boquear.

garage /gə'raʒ/ n. garaje m.

garbage /'gɑrbɪdʒ/ n. basura f.

garden /'gɑrdn/ n. jardín m.; (vegetable) huerta f.

gardener /'gɑrdnər/ n. jardinero -ra.

gargle /'gɑrgəl/ n. **1.** gárgara f. —v. **2.** gargarizar.

garland /'gɑrlənd/ n. guirnalda f.

garlic /'gɑrlik/ n. ajo m.

garment /'gɑrmənt/ n. prenda de vestir.

garrison /'gærəsən/ n. guarnición f.

garter /'gɑrtər/ n. liga f.; ataderas f.pl.

gas /gæs/ n. gas m.

gasohol /'gæsə,hɔl, -,hɒl/ n. gasohol m.

gasoline /,gæsə'lin/ n. gasolina f.

gasp /gæsp/ n. **1.** boqueada f. —v. **2.** boquear.

gas station gasolinera f.

gate /geit/ n. puerta; entrada; verja f.

gather /'gæðər/ v. recoger; inferir; reunir.

gaudy /'gɔdi/ a. brillante; llamativo.

gauge /geidʒ/ n. **1.** manómetro, indicador m. —v. **2.** medir; estimar.

gaunt /gɔnt/ a. flaco.

gauze /gɔz/ n. gasa f.

gay /gei/ a. **1.** alegre; homosexual. —n. **2.** homosexual.

gaze /geiz/ n. **1.** mirada f. —v. **2.** mirar con fijeza.

gear /giər/ n. engranaje m. **in g.,** en juego.

gearshift /'giər,ʃift/ n. palanca de cambio f.

gem /dʒɛm/ n. joya f.

gender /'dʒɛndər/ n. género m.

general /'dʒɛnərəl/ a. & n. general m.

generality /,dʒɛnə'ræləti/ n. generalidad f.

generalize /'dʒɛnərə,laiz/ v. generalizar.

generation /,dʒɛnə'reiʃən/ n. generación f.

generator /'dʒɛnə,reitər/ n. generador m.

generosity /,dʒɛnə'rɒsiti/ n. generosidad f.

generous /'dʒɛnərəs/ a. generoso.

genetic /dʒə'nɛtik/ a. genético.

genial /'dʒinyəl/ a. genial.

genius /'dʒinyəs/ n. genio m.

genocide /'dʒɛnə,said/ n. genocidio m.

gentle /'dʒɛntl/ a. suave; manso; benigno.

gentleman /'dʒɛntlmən/ n. señor; caballero m.

gentleness /'dʒɛntlnis/ n. suavidad f.

genuine /'dʒɛnyuin/ a. genuino.

genuineness /'dʒɛnyuinnis/ n. pureza f.

geographical /,dʒiə'græfikəl/ a. geográfico.

geography /dʒi'ɒgrəfi/ n. geografía f.

geometric /,dʒiə'mɛtrik/ a. geométrico.

geranium /dʒə'reiniəm/ n. geranio m.

germ /dʒɜrm/ n. germen; microbio m.

German /'dʒɜrmən/ a. & n. alemán -mana.

Germany /'dʒɜrməni/ n. Alemania f.

gesticulate /dʒɛ'stikyə,leit/ v. gesticular.

gesture /'dʒɛstʃər/ n. **1.** gesto m. —v. **2.** gesticular, hacer gestos.

get /gɛt/ v. obtener; conseguir; (become) ponerse. **go and g.,** ir a buscar; **g. away,** irse; escaparse; **g. together,** reunirse; **g. on,** subirse; **g. off,** bajarse; **g. up,** levantarse; **g. there,** llegar.

ghastly /'gæstli/ a. pálido; espantoso.

ghost /goust/ n. espectro, fantasma m.

giant /'dʒaiənt/ n. gigante m.

gibberish /'dʒibəriʃ/ n. galimatías. m.

gift /gift/ n. regalo, don; talento m.

gigabyte /'giga,bait, 'dʒig-/ n. giga m.

gild /gild/ v. dorar.

gin /dʒin/ n. ginebra f.

ginger /'dʒindʒər/ n. jengibre m.

gingerbread /'dʒindʒər,brɛd/ n. pan de jengibre.

gingham /'giŋəm/ n. guinga f.

gird /gɜrd/ v. ceñir.

girdle /'gɜrdl/ n. faja f.

girl /gɜrl/ n. muchacha, niña, chica f.

give /giv/ v. dar; regalar. **g. back,** devolver. **g. up,** rendirse; renunciar.

giver /'givər/ n. dador -ra; donador -ra.

graham

glacier /'gleɪʃər/ n. glaciar; ventisquero m.

glad /glæd/ a. alegre, contento. **be g.**, alegrarse.

gladly /'glædli/ adj con mucho gusto.

gladness /'glædnɪs/ n. alegría f.; placer m.

glamor /'glæmər/ n. encanto m.; elegancia f.

glamorous /'glæmərəs/ a. encantador; elegante.

glamour /'glæmər/ n. encanto m.; elegancia f.

glance /glæns/ n. **1.** vistazo m., ojeada f. —v. **2.** ojear.

gland /glænd/ n. glándula f.

glare /glɛər/ n. **1.** reflejo; brillo m. —v. **2.** deslumbrar; echar miradas indignadas.

glass /glæs/ n. vidrio; vaso m.; **(eyeglasses)**, lentes, anteojos m.pl.

gleam /glim/ n. **1.** fulgor m. —v. **2.** fulgurar.

glee /gli/ n. alegría f.; júbilo m.

glide /glaɪd/ v. deslizarse.

glimpse /glɪmps/ n. **1.** vislumbre, vistazo m. —v. **2.** vislumbrar, ojear.

glisten /'glɪsən/ n. **1.** brillo m. —v. **2.** brillar.

glitter /'glɪtər/ n. **1.** resplandor m. —v. **2.** brillar.

globe /gloub/ n. globo; orbe m.

gloom /glum/ n. oscuridad; tristeza f.

gloomy /'glumi/ a. oscuro; sombrío, triste.

glorify /'glɔrə,faɪ/ v. glorificar.

glorious /'glɔriəs/ a. glorioso.

glory /'glɔri/ n. gloria, fama f.

glossary /'glɒsəri/ n. glosario m.

glove /glʌv/ n. guante m.

glove compartment guantera f.

glow /glou/ n. **1.** fulgor m. —v. **2.** relucir; arder.

glucose /'glukous/ f. glucosa.

glue /glu/ n. **1.** cola f., pegamento m —v. **2.** encolar, pegar.

glum /glʌm/ a. de mal humor.

glutton /'glʌtn/ n. glotón -ona.

gnaw /nɔ/ v. roer.

GNP (abbr. **gross national product**), **PNB** (producto nacional bruto).

go /gou/ v. ir, irse. **g. away**, irse, marcharse. **g. back**, volver, regresar. **g. down**, bajar. **g. in**, entrar. **g. on**, seguir. **g. out**, salir. **g. up**, subir.

goal /goul/ n. meta f.; objeto m.

goalkeeper /'goul,kipər/ n. guardameta mf.

goat /gout/ n. cabra f.

goblet /'gɒblɪt/ n. copa f.

God /gɒd/ n. Dios m.

gold /gould/ n. oro m.

golden /'gouldən/ a. áureo.

gold-plated /'gould ,pleɪtɪd/ a. chapado en oro.

golf /gɒlf/ n. golf m.

golf course campo de golf m.

golfer /'gɒlfər/ n. golfista m. & f.

good /gʊd/ a. **1.** bueno. —n. **2.** bienes m pl.; Com. géneros m.pl.

good-bye /,gʊd'baɪ/ n. **1.** adiós m. —interj. **2.** ¡adiós!, ¡hasta la vista!, ¡hasta luego! **say g. to**, despedirse de.

goodness /'gʊdnɪs/ n. bondad f.

goodwill /'gʊd'wɪl/ n. buena voluntad. f.

goose /gus/ n. ganso m.

gooseberry /'gus,bɛri/ n. uva crespa f.

gooseneck /'gus,nɛk/ n. **1.** cuello de cisne m. —a. **2.** curvo.

goose step /'gus,stɛp/ paso de ganso m.

gore /gɔr/ n. **1.** sangre f. —v. **2.** acornear.

gorge /gɔrdʒ/ n. **1.** gorja f. —v. **2.** engullir.

gorgeous /'gɔrdʒəs/ a. magnífico; precioso.

gorilla /gə'rɪlə/ n. gorila m.

gory /'gɔri/ a. sangriento.

gosling /'gɒzlɪŋ/ n. gansarón m.

gospel /'gɒspəl/ n. evangelio m.

gossamer /'gɒsəmər/ n. **1.** telaraña f. —a. **2.** delgado.

gossip /'gɒsəp/ n. **1.** chisme m. —v. **2.** chismear.

Gothic /'gɒθɪk/ a. gótico.

gouge /gaudʒ/ n. **1.** gubia f. —v. **2.** escoplear.

gourd /gɔrd/ n. calabaza f.

gourmand /gur'mɒnd/ n. glotón m.

gourmet /gur'meɪ/ a. gastrónomo -ma.

govern /'gʌvərn/ v. gobernar.

governess /'gʌvərnɪs/ n. aya, institutriz f.

government /'gʌvərnmənt, -ərmənt/ n. gobierno m.

governmental /,gʌvərn'mɛntl, ,gʌvər-/ a. gubernamental.

governor /'gʌvərnər/ n. gobernador -ra.

governorship /'gʌvərnər,ʃɪp/ n. gobernatura f.

gown /gaun/ n. vestido m. **dressing g.**, bata f.

grab /græb/ v. agarrar, arrebatar.

grace /greis/ n. gracia; gentileza; merced f.

graceful /'greisfəl/ a. agraciado.

graceless /'greislɪs/ a. réprobo; torpe.

gracious /'greiʃəs/ a. gentil, cortés.

grackle /'grækəl/ n. grajo m.

grade /greid/ n. **1.** grado; nivel m.; pendiente; nota; calidad f. —v. **2.** graduar.

grade crossing n. paso a nivel m.

gradual /'grædʒuəl/ a. gradual, paulatino.

gradually /'grædʒuəli/ adv. gradualmente.

graduate /n 'grædʒuɪt; v -,eɪt/ n. **1.** graduado -da, diplomado -da. —v. **2.** graduar; diplomarse.

graft /græft/ n. **1.** injerto m.; soborno público. —v. **2.** injertar.

graham /'greiəm/ a. centeno; acemita.

grail /greil/ n. grial m.
grain /grein/ n. grano; cereal m.
grain alcohol n. alcohol de madera m.
gram /græm/ n. gramo m.
grammar /'græmər/ n. gramática f.
grammarian /grə'meəriən/ n. gramático -ca.
grammar school n. escuela elemental f.
grammatical /grə'mætɪkəl/ a. gramatical.
gramophone /'græmə,foun/ n. gramófono m.
granary /'greinəri/ n. granero m.
grand /grænd/ a. grande, ilustre; estupendo.
grandchild /'græn,tʃaild/ n. nieto -ta.
granddaughter /'græn,dɔtər/ n. nieta f.
grandee /græn'di/ n. noble m.
grandeur /'grændʒər/ n. grandeza f.
grandfather /'græn,fɑðər/ n. abuelo m.
grandiloquent /græn'dɪləkwənt/ a. grandílocuo.
grandiose /'grændi,ous/ a. grandioso.
grand jury jurado de acusación, jurado de juicio m.
grandly /'grændli/ adv. grandiosamente.
grandmother /'græn,mʌðər/ n abuela f.
grand opera ópera grande f.
grandparents /'grænd,peərənts/ n. abuelos m.pl.
grandson /'græn,sʌn/ n. nieto m.
grandstand /'græn,stænd/ n. andanada f., tribuna f.
grange /greindʒ/ n. granja f.
granger /'greindʒər/ n. labriego m.
granite /'grænɪt/ n. granito m.
granny /'græni/ n. abuelita f.
grant /grænt/ n. 1. concesión; subvención f. —v. 2. otorgar; conceder; conferir. **take for granted,** tomar por cierto.
granular /'grænyələr/ a. granular.
granulate /'grænyə,leit/ v. granular.
granulation /,grænyə'leifən/ n. granulación f.
granule /'grænyul/ n. gránulo m.
grape /greip/ n. uva f.
grapefruit /'greip,frut/ n. toronja f.
grape harvest vendimia f.
grapeshot /'greip,ʃɒt/ n. metralla f.
grapevine /'greip,vain/ n. vid; parra f.
graph /græf/ n. gráfica f.
graphic /'græfɪk/ a. gráfico.
graphite /'græfait/ n. grafito m.
graphology /græ'fɒlədʒi/ n. grafología f.
grapple /'græpəl/ v. agarrar.
grasp /græsp/ n. 1. puño; poder; conocimiento m. —v. 2. empuñar, agarrar; comprender.
grasping /'græspɪŋ/ a. codicioso.
grass /græs/ n. hierba f.; (marijuana) marijuana f.

grasshopper /'græs,hɒpər/ n. saltamontes m.
grassy /'græsi/ a. herboso.
grate /greit/ n. reja f.
grateful /'greitfəl/ a. agradecido.
gratify /'grætə,fai/ v. satisfacer.
grating /'greitɪŋ/ n. 1. enrejado m. —a. 2. discordante.
gratis /'grætɪs/ adv. & a. gratis.
gratitude /'grætɪ,tud/ n. agradecimiento m.
gratuitous /grə'tuɪtəs/ adj. gratuito.
gratuity /grə'tuɪti/ n. propina f.
grave /greiv/ a. 1. grave. —n. 2. sepultura; tumba f.
gravel /'grævəl/ n. cascajo m.
gravely /'greivli/ adv. gravemente.
gravestone /'greiv,stoun/ n. lápida sepulcral f.
graveyard /'greiv,yɑrd/ n. cementerio m.
gravitate /'grævɪ,teit/ v. gravitar.
gravitation /,grævɪ'teiʃən/ n. gravitación f.
gravity /'grævɪti/ n. gravedad: seriedad f.
gravure /grə'vyur/ n. fotograbado m.
gravy /'greivi/ n. salsa f.
gray /grei/ a. gris; (hair) cano.
grayish /'greiʃ/ a. pardusco.
gray matter sustancia gris f.
graze /greiz/ v. rozar; (cattle) pastar.
grazing /'greizɪŋ/ a. pastando.
grease /gris/ n. 1. grasa f. —v. 2. engrasar.
greasy /'grisi/ a. grasiento.
great /greit/ a. grande, ilustre; estupendo.
Great Dane /dein/ mastín danés m.
great-grandfather /,greit 'græn,fɑðər/ n. bisabuelo.
great-grandmother /,greit 'græn,mʌðər/ f. bisabuela.
greatness /'greitnɪs/ n. grandeza f.
Greece /gris/ n. Grecia f.
greed /grid/ **greediness** n. codicia, voracidad f.
greedy /'gridi/ a. voraz.
Greek /grik/ a. & n. griego -ga.
green /grin/ a. & n. verde m. **greens,** n. verduras f.pl.
greenery /'grinəri/ n. verdor m.
greenhouse /'grin,haus/ n. invernáculo m.
greenhouse effect n. efecto invernáculo m.
greet /grit/ v. saludar.
greeting /'gritɪŋ/ n. saludo m.
gregarious /grɪ'geəriəs/ a. gregario; sociable.
grenade /grɪ'neid/ n. granada; bomba f.
greyhound /'grei,haund/ n. galgo m.
grid /grɪd/ n. parrilla f.
griddle /'grɪdl/ n. tortera f.
griddlecake /'grɪdl,keik/ n. tortita de harina f.

gridiron /'grɪd,aɪərn/ n. parrilla f.; campo de fútbol m.

grief /grif/ n. dolor m.; pena f.

grievance /'grivəns/ n. pesar; agravio m.

grieve /griv/ v. afligir.

grievous /'grivəs/ a. penoso.

grill /grɪl/ n. **1.** parrilla f. —v. **2.** asar a la parrilla.

grillroom /'grɪl,rum, -,rʊm/ n. parrilla f.

grim /grɪm/ a. ceñudo.

grimace /'grɪməs/ n. **1.** mueca f. —v. **2.** hacer muecas.

grime /graim/ n. mugre f.

grimy /'graimi/ a. sucio; mugroso.

grin /grɪn/ n. **1.** sonrisa f. —v. **2.** sonreír.

grind /graind/ v. moler; afilar.

grindstone /'graind,stoun/ n. amoladera f.

gringo /'grɪŋgou/ n. gringo; yanqui m.

grip /grɪp/ n. **1.** maleta f. —v. **2.** agarrar.

gripe /graip/ v. **1.** agarrar. —n. **2.** asimiento m., opresión f.

grippe /grɪp/ n. gripe f.

grisly /'grɪzli/ a. espantoso.

grist /grɪst/ n. molienda f.

gristle /'grɪsəl/ n. cartílago m.

grit /grɪt/ n. arena f.; entereza f.

grizzled /'grɪzəld/ a. tordillo.

groan /groun/ n. **1.** gemido m. —v. **2.** gemir.

grocer /'grousər/ n. abacero m.

grocery /'grousəri/ n. tienda de comestibles, abacería; (Carib.) bodega f.

grog /grɒg/ n. brebaje m.

groggy /'grɒgi/ a. medio borracho; vacilante.

groin /grɔin/ n. ingle f.

groom /grum/ n. (of horses) establero; (at wedding) novio m.

groove /gruv/ n. **1.** estría f. —v. **2.** acanalar.

grope /group/ v. tentar; andar a tientas.

gross /grous/ a. **1.** grueso; grosero. —n. **2.** gruesa f.

grossly /'grousli/ adv. groseramente.

gross national product producto nacional bruto m.

grossness /'grousnɪs/ n. grosería f.

grotesque /grou'tɛsk/ a. grotesco.

grotto /'grɒtou/ n. gruta f.

grouch /grautʃ/ n. gruñón; descontento m.

ground /graund/ n. tierra f.; terreno; suelo; campo; fundamento m.

ground floor planta baja f.

groundhog /'graund,hɒg/ n. marmota f.

groundless /'graundlɪs/ a. infundado.

groundwork /'graund,wɜrk/ n. base f., fundamento m.

group /grup/ n. **1.** grupo m. —v. **2.** agrupar.

groupie /'grupi/ n. persona aficionada que acompaña a un grupo de música moderna.

grouse /graus/ v. quejarse

grove /grouv/ n. arboleda f.

grovel /'grɒvəl/ v. rebajarse; envilecerse.

grow /grou/ v. crecer; cultivar.

growl /graul/ n. **1.** gruñido m. —v. **2.** gruñir.

grown /groun/ a. crecido; desarrollado.

grownup /'groun,ʌp/ n. adulto -ta.

growth /grouθ/ n. crecimiento m.; vegetación f.; Med. tumor m.

grub /grʌb/ n. gorgojo m., larva f.

grubby /'grʌbi/ a. gorgojoso, mugriento.

grudge /grʌdʒ/ n. rencor m. **bear a g.,** guardar rencor.

gruel /'gruəl/ n. **1.** atole m. —v. **2.** agotar.

gruesome /'grusəm/ a. horripilante.

gruff /grʌf/ a. ceñudo.

grumble /'grʌmbəl/ v. quejarse.

grumpy /'grʌmpi/ a. gruñón; quejoso.

grunt /grʌnt/ v. gruñir.

guarantee /ˌgærən'ti/ n. **1.** garantía f. —v. **2.** garantizar.

guarantor /'gærən,tɔr/ n. fiador -ra.

guaranty /'gærən,ti/ n. garantía f.

guard /gɑrd/ n. **1.** guardia m. & f. —v. **2.** vigilar.

guarded /'gɑrdɪd/ a. cauteloso.

guardhouse /'gɑrd,haus/ n. prisión militar f.

guardian /'gɑrdiən/ n. guardián -ana.

guardianship /'gɑrdiən,ʃɪp/ n. tutela f.

guardsman /'gɑrdzmən/ n. centinela m.

guava /'gwɑvə/ n. guayaba f.

gubernatorial /ˌgubərnə'tɔriəl/ a. gubernativo.

guerrilla /gə'rɪlə/ n. guerrilla f.; guerrillero -ra.

guess /gɛs/ n. **1.** conjetura f. —v. **2.** adivinar; Colloq. creer.

guesswork /'gɛs,wɜrk/ n. conjetura f.

guest /gɛst/ n. huésped m. & f.

guest room alcoba de huéspedes f., alcoba de respeto f., cuarto para invitados m.

guffaw /gʌ'fɔ/ n. risotada f.

guidance /'gaidns/ n. dirección f.

guide /gaid/ n. **1.** guía m. & f. —v. **2.** guiar.

guidebook /'gaid,bʊk/ n. guía f.

guided tour /'gaidɪd/ visita explicada, visita programada, visita con guía f.

guideline /'gaid,lain/ n. pauta f.

guidepost /'gaid,poust/ n. poste indicador m.

guild /gɪld/ n. gremio m.

guile /gail/ n. engaño m.

guillotine /'gɪlə,tin/ n. **1.** guillotina f. —v. **2.** guillotinar.

guilt /gɪlt/ n. culpa f.

guiltily /'gɪltəli/ adv. culpablemente.

guiltless /'gɪltlɪs/ *a.* inocente.

guilty /'gɪlti/ *a.* culpable.

guinea fowl /'gɪni/ gallina de Guinea *f.*

guinea pig /gɪni/ cobayo *m.*, conejillo de Indias *m.*

guise /gaiz/ *n.* modo *m.*

guitar /gɪ'tɑr/ *n.* guitarra *f.*

guitarist /gɪ'tɑrɪst/ *n.* guitarrista *m. & f.*

gulch /gʌltʃ/ *n.* quebrada *f.*

gulf /gʌlf/ *n.* golfo *m.*

gull /gʌl/ *n.* gaviota *f.*

gullet /'gʌlɪt/ *n.* esófago *m.*; zanja *f.*

gullible /'gʌləbəl/ *a.* crédulo.

gully /'gʌli/ *n.* barranca *f.*

gulp /gʌlp/ *n.* **1.** trago *m.* —*v.* **2.** tragar.

gum /gʌm/ *n.* **1.** goma *f.*; *Anat.* encía *f.* **chewing g.**, chicle *m.* —*v.* **2.** engomar.

gumbo /'gʌmbou/ *n.* quimbombó *m.*

gummy /'gʌmi/ *a.* gomoso.

gun /gʌn/ *n.* fusil, revólver *m.*

gunboat /'gʌn,hout/ *n.* cañonero *m.*

gunman /'gʌnmən/ *n.* bandido *m.*

gunner /'gʌnər/ *n.* artillero *m.*

gun permit licencia de armas *f.*

gunpowder /'gʌn,paudər/ *n.* pólvora *f.*

gunshot /'gʌn,ʃot/ *n.* escopetazo *m.*

gunwale /'gʌnl/ *n.* borda *f.*

gurgle /'gɜrgəl/ *n.* **1.** gorgoteo *m.* —*v.* **2.** gorgotear.

guru /'guru, gu'ru/ *n.* gurú *m.*

gush /gʌʃ/ *n.* **1.** chorro *m.* —*v.* **2.** brotar, chorrear.

gusher /'gʌʃər/ *n.* pozo de petróleo *m.*

gust /gʌst/ *n.* soplo *m.*; ráfaga *f.*

gustatory /'gʌstə,tɔri/ *a.* gustativo.

gusto /'gʌstou/ *n.* gusto; placer *m.*

gusty /'gʌsti/ *a.* borrascoso.

gut /gʌt/ *n.* intestino *m.*, tripa *f.*

gutter /'gʌtər/ *n.* canal; zanja *f.*

guttural /'gʌtərəl/ *a.* gutural.

guy /gai/ *n.* tipo *m.*

guzzle /'gʌzəl/ *v.* engullir; tragar.

gym /dʒɪm/ *n.* gimnasio *m.*

gymnasium /dʒɪm'naziəm/ *n.* gimnasio *m.*

gymnast /'dʒɪmnæst/ *n.* gimnasta *m. & f.*

gymnastic /dʒɪm'næstɪk/ *a.* gimnástico.

gymnastics /dʒɪm'næstɪks/ *n.* gimnasia *f.*

gynecologist /,gainɪ'kɒlədʒɪst/ *n.* ginecólogo, -ga *m. & f.*

gynecology /,gainɪ'kɒlədʒi/ *n.* ginecología *f.*

gypsum /'dʒɪpsəm/ *n.* yeso *m.*

Gypsy /'dʒɪpsi/ *a. & n.* gitano -na.

gyrate /'dʒaireit/ *v.* girar.

gyroscope /'dʒairə,skoup/ *n.* giroscopio *m.*

H

habeas corpus /'heibíəs 'kɔrpəs/ habeas corpus *m.*

haberdasher /'hæbər,dæʃər/ *n.* camisero *m.*

haberdashery /'hæbər,dæʃəri/ *n.* camisería *f.*

habiliment /hə'bɪləmənt/ *n.* vestuario *m.*

habit /'hæbɪt/ *n.* costumbre *f.*, hábito *m.* **be in the h. of**, estar acostumbrado a; soler.

habitable /'hæbɪtəbəl/ *a.* habitable.

habitat /'hæbɪ,tæt/ *n.* habitación *f.*, ambiente *m.*

habitation /,hæbɪ'teiʃən/ *n.* habitación *f.*

habitual /hə'bɪtʃuəl/ *a.* habitual.

habituate /hə'bɪtʃu,eit/ *v.* habituar.

habitué /hə'bɪtʃu,ei/ *n.* parroquiano *m.*

hack /hæk/ *n.* **1.** coche de alquiler. —*v.* **2.** tajar.

hacker /'hækər/ *n.* pirata *m. & f.*

hackneyed /'hæknid/ *a.* trillado.

hacksaw /'hæk,sɔ/ *n.* sierra para cortar metal *f.*

haddock /'hædək/ *n.* merluza *f.*

haft /hæft/ *n.* mango *m.*

hag /hæg, hɑg/ *n.* bruja *f.*

haggard /'hægərd/ *a.* trasnochado.

haggle /'hægəl/ *v.* regatear.

hail /heil/ *n.* **1.** granizo; (greeting) saludo *m.* —*v.* **2.** granizar; saludar.

Hail Mary /'mɛəri/ Ave María *m.*

hailstone /'heil,stoun/ *n.* piedra de granizo *f.*

hailstorm /'heil,stɔrm/ *n.* granizada *f.*

hair /hɛər/ *n.* pelo; cabello *m.*

haircut /'hɛər,kʌt/ *n.* corte de pelo.

hairdo /'hɛər,du/ *n.* peinado *m.*

hairdresser /'hɛər,drɛsər/ *n.* peluquero *m.*

hair dryer /'draiər/ secador de pelo, secador *m.*

hairpin /'hɛər,pɪn/ *n.* horquilla *f.*; gancho *m.*

hair's-breadth /'hɛərz,brɛdθ/ *n.* ancho de un pelo *m.*

hairspray /'hɛərsprei/ *n.* aerosol para cabello.

hairy /'hɛəri/ *a.* peludo.

halcyon /'hælsiən/ *n.* **1.** alcedón *m.* —*a.* **2.** tranquilo.

hale /heil/ *a.* sano.

half /hæf/ *a.* **1.** medio. —*n.* **2.** mitad *f.*

half-and-half /'hæf ən 'hæf/ *a.* mitad y mitad.

half-baked /'hæf 'beikt/ a. medio crudo.

half-breed /'hæf ,brid/ n. mestizo m.

half brother n. medio hermano m.

half-hearted /'hæf'hʊrtid/ a. sin entusiasmo.

half-mast /'hæf 'mæst/ a. & ad. media asta m.

halfpenny /'heipəni/ n. medio penique m.

halfway /'hæf'wei/ adv. a medio camino.

half-wit /'hæf ,wit/ n. bobo m.

halibut /'hæləbət/ n. hipogloso m.

hall /hɔl/ n. corredor m.; (for assembling) sala f. **city h.,** ayuntamiento m.

hallmark /'hɔl,mɑrk/ n. marca del contraste f.

hallow /'hælou/ v. consagrar.

Halloween /,hælə'win/ n. víspera de Todos los Santos f.

hallucination /hə,lusə'neiʃən/ n. alucinación f.

hallway /'hɔl,wei/ n. pasadizo m.

halo /'heilou/ n. halo m.; corona f.

halt /hɔlt/ a. **1.** cojo. —n. **2.** parada f. —v. **3.** parar. —interj. **4.** ¡alto!

halter /'hɔltər/ n. cabestro m.

halve /hæv/ v. dividir en dos partes.

halyard /'hæljərd/ n. driza f.

ham /hæm/ n. jamón m.

hamburger /'hæm,bɑrgər/ n. albóndiga f.

hamlet /'hæmlit/ n. aldea f.

hammer /'hæmər/ n. **1.** martillo m. —v. **2.** martillar.

hammock /'hæmək/ n. hamaca f.

hamper /'hæmpər/ n. canasta f., cesto m.

hamstring /'hæm,strɪŋ/ n. **1.** tendón de la corva m. —v. **2.** desjarretar.

hand /hænd/ n. **1.** mano f. **on the other h.,** en cambio. —v. **2.** pasar. **h. over,** entregar.

handbag /'hænd,bæg/ n. cartera f.

handball /'hænd,bɔl/ n. pelota f.

handbook /'hænd,bʊk/ n. manual m.

handbrake /'hændbreik/ n. freno de mano m.

handcuff /'hænd,kʌf/ n. esposa m. esposar.

handful /'hændfʊl/ n. puñado m.

handicap /'hændi,kæp/ n. desventaja f.

handicraft /'hændi,kræft/ n. artífice m.; destreza manual.

handiwork /'hændi,wɜrk/ n. artefacto m.

handkerchief /'hæŋkərtʃif/ n. pañuelo m.

handle /'hændl/ n. **1.** mango m. —v. **2.** manejar.

hand luggage equipaje de mano m.

handmade /'hænd'meid/ a. hecho a mano.

handmaid /'hænd,meid/ n. criada de mano, sirvienta f.

hand organ organillo m.

handsome /'hænsəm/ a. guapo; hermoso.

hand-to-hand /'hænd tə 'hænd/ adv. de mano a mano.

handwriting /'hænd,raitɪŋ/ n. escritura f.

handy /'hændi/ a. diestro; útil; a la mano.

hang /hæŋ/ v. colgar; ahorcar.

hangar /'hæŋər/ n. hangar m.

hangdog /'hæŋ,dɔg/ a. & n. camastrón m.

hanger /'hæŋər/ n. colgador, gancho m.

hanger-on /'hæŋər 'ɒn/ n. dependiente; mogollón m.

hang glider /'glaidər/ aparato para vuelo libre, delta, ala delta.

hanging /'hæŋɪŋ/ n. **1.** ahorcadura f. —a. **2.** colgante.

hangman /'hæŋmən/ n. verdugo m.

hangnail /'hæŋ,neil/ n. padrastro m.

hang out v. enarbolar.

hangover /'hæŋ,ouvər/ n. resaca f.

hangup /'hæŋʌp/ n. tara (psicológica) f.

hank /hæŋk/ n. madeja f.

hanker /'hæŋkər/ v. ansiar; apetecer.

haphazard. /hæp'hæzərd/ a. casual.

happen /'hæpən/ v. acontecer, suceder, pasar.

happening /'hæpənɪŋ/ n. acontecimiento m.

happiness /'hæpinis/ n. felicidad; dicha f.

happy /'hæpi/ a. feliz; contento; dichoso.

happy-go-lucky /'hæpi gou 'lʌki/ a. & n. descuidado m.

harakiri /hɑrə'kɪəri/ n. harakiri (suicidio japonés) m.

harangue /hə'ræŋ/ n. **1.** arenga f. —v. **2.** arengar.

harass /hə'ræs/ v. acosar; atormentar.

harbinger /'hɑrbɪndʒər/ n. presagio m.

harbor /'hɑrbər/ n. **1.** puerto; albergue m. —v. **2.** abrigar.

hard /hɑrd/ a. **1.** duro; difícil. —adv. **2.** mucho.

hard coal antracita m.

hard disk disco duro m.

harden /'hɑrdn/ v. endurecer.

hard-headed /hɑrd 'hɛdid/ a. terco.

hard-hearted /'hɑrd'hɑrtid/ a. empedernido.

hardiness /'hɑrdinis/ n. vigor m.

hardly /'hɑrdli/ adv. apenas.

hardness /'hɑrdnis/ n. dureza; dificultad f.

hardship /'hɑrdʃip/ n. penalidad f.; trabajo m.

hardware /'hɑrd,wɛər/ n. hardware m.; (computer) quincalla f.

hardwood /'hɑrd,wʊd/ n. madera dura f.

hardy /'hɑrdi/ a. fuerte, robusto.

hare /hɛər/ n. liebre f.

harebrained /'hɛər,breind/ a. tolondro.

harelip /'hɛər,lip/ n. **1.** labio leporino m. —a. **2.** labihendido.

harem /'hɛərəm/ n. harén m.

hark /hɑrk/ v. escuchar; atender.

Harlequin /'hɑrləkwin/ n. arlequín m.

harlot /'hɑrlət/ n. ramera f.

harm /hɑrm/ n. **1.** mal, daño; perjuicio m. —v. **2.** dañar.

harmful /'hɑrmfəl/ a. dañoso.

harmless /'hɑrmlɪs/ a. inocente.

harmonic /hɑr'mɒnɪk/ n. armónico m.

harmonica /hɑr'mɒnɪkə/ n. armónica f.

harmonious /hɑr'moʊniəs/ a. armonioso.

harmonize /'hɑrmə,naɪz/ v. armonizar.

harmony /'hɑrməni/ n. armonía f.

harness /'hɑrnɪs/ n. arnés m.

harp /hɑrp/ n. arpa f.

harpoon /hɑr'pun/ n. arpón m.

harridan /'hʌrɪdn̩/ v. no vieja regañona f.

harrow /'hærου/ n. **1.** rastro m.; grada f. —v. **2.** gradar.

harry /'hæri/ v. acosar.

harsh /hɑrʃ/ a. áspero.

harshness /'hɑrʃnɪs/ n. aspereza f.

harvest /'hɑrvɪst/ n. **1.** cosecha f. —v. **2.** cosechar.

hash /hæʃ/ n. picadillo m.

hashish /'hæʃɪʃ/ n. haxis m.

hasn't /'hæzənt/ v. no tiene (neg. + tener).

hassle /'hæsəl/ n. lío m., molestia f.; controversia f.

hassock /'hæsək/ n. cojín m.

haste /heɪst/ n. prisa f.

hasten /'heɪsən/ v. apresurarse, darse prisa.

hasty /'heɪsti/ a. apresurado.

hat /hæt/ n. sombrero m.

hat box /'hæt,bɒks/ sombrerera f.

hatch /hætʃ/ n. **1.** Naut. cuartel m. —v. **2.** incubar; Fig. tramar.

hatchery /'hætʃəri/ n. criadero m.

hatchet /'hætʃɪt/ n. hacha pequeña.

hate /heɪt/ n. **1.** odio m. —v. **2.** odiar, detestar.

hateful /'heɪtfəl/ a. detestable.

hatred /'heɪtrɪd/ n. odio m.

haughtiness /'hɔtɪnɪs/ n. arrogancia f.

haughty /'hɔti/ a. altivo.

haul /hɔl/ n. **1.** (fishery) redada f. —v. **2.** tirar, halar.

haunch /hɔntʃ/ n. anca f

haunt /hɔnt/ n. **1.** lugar frecuentado. —v. **2.** frecuentar, andar por.

have /hæv: unstressed həv, əv/ v. tener; haber.

haven /'heɪvən/ n. puerto; asilo m.

haven't /'hævənt/ v. no tiene (neg. + tener).

havoc /'hævək/ n. ruina f.

hawk /hɔk/ n. halcón m.

hawker /'hɔkər/ n. buhonero m.

hawser /'hɔzər/ n. cable m.

hawthorn /'hɔ,θɔrn/ n. espino m.

hay /heɪ/ n. heno m.

hay fever n. fiebre del heno f.

hayfield /'heɪfild/ n. henar m.

hayloft /'heɪ,lɔft/ n. henil m.

haystack /'heɪ,stæk/ n. hacina de heno f.

hazard /'hæzərd/ n. **1.** azar m. —v. **2.** aventurar.

hazardous /'hæzərdəs/ a. peligroso.

haze /heɪz/ n. niebla f.

hazel /'heɪzəl/ n. avellano m.

hazelnut /'heɪzəl,nʌt/ avellana f.

hazy /'heɪzi/ a. brumoso.

he /hi/ pron. él m.

head /hɛd/ n. **1.** cabeza f.; jefe m. —v. **2.** dirigir; encabezar.

headache /'hɛd,eɪk/ n. dolor de cabeza m.

headband /'hɛd,bænd/ n. venda para cabeza f.

headfirst /'hɛd'fɜrst/ adv. de cabeza.

headgear /'hɛd,gɪər/ n. tocado m.

headlight /'hɛd,laɪt/ n. linterna delantera f., farol de tope m.

headline /'hɛd,laɪn/ n. encabezado m.

headlong /'hɛd,lɔŋ/ a. precipitoso.

head-on /'hɛd 'ɒn/ adv. de frente.

headphones /'hɛd,foʊnz/ n.pl. auriculares m.pl.

headquarters /'hɛd,kwɔrtərz/ n. jefatura f.; Mil. cuartel general.

headstone /'hɛd,stoʊn/ n. lápida mortuoria f.

headstrong /'hɛd,strɔŋ/ a. terco.

headwaiter /'hɛd'weɪtər/ n. jefe de comedor m. & f.

headwaters /'hɛd,wɔtərz/ n. cabeceras f.pl.

headway /'hɛd,weɪ/ n. avance m., progreso m.

headwork /'hɛd,wɜrk/ n. trabajo mental m.

heady /'hɛdi/ a. impetuoso.

heal /hil/ v. curar, sanar.

health /hɛlθ/ n. salud f.

healthful /'hɛlθfəl/ a. saludable.

healthy /'hɛlθi/ a. sano; salubre.

heap /hip/ n. montón m.

hear /hɪər/ v. oír. **h. from,** tener noticias de. **h. about, h. of,** oír hablar de.

hearing /'hɪərɪŋ/ n. oído m.

hearing aid audífono m.

hearsay /'hɪər,seɪ/ n. rumor m.

hearse /hɜrs/ n. ataúd m.

heart /hɑrt/ n. corazón m.; ánimo m. **by h.,** de memoria. **have h. trouble** padecer del corazón.

heartache /'hɑrt,eɪk/ n. angustia f.

heart attack ataque cardíaco, infarto, infarto de miocardio m.

heartbreak /'hɑrt,breɪk/ n. angustia f.; pesar m.

heartbroken /'hɑrt,broʊkən/ a. acongojado.

heartburn /'hɑrt,bɜrn/ n. acedía f., ardor de estómago m.

heartfelt /'hɑrt,fɛlt/ a. sentido.

hearth /harθ/ n. hogar m., chimenea f.
heartless /'hartlıs/ a. empedernido.
heartsick /'hart,sık/ a. desconsolado.
heart-stricken /'hart 'strıkən/ a. afligido.
heart-to-heart /'hart tə 'hart/ adv. franco; sincero.
hearty /'harti/ a. cordial; vigoroso.
heat /hit/ n. **1.** calor; ardor m.; calefacción f. —v. **2.** calentar.
heated /'hitıd/ a. acalorado.
heater /'hitər/ n. calentador m.
heath /hiθ/ n. matorral m.
heathen /'hiðən/ a. & n. pagano -na.
heather /'hεðər/ n brezo m.
heating /'hitıŋ/ n. calefacción f.
heatstroke /'hit,strouk/ n. insolación f.
heat wave onda de calor f.
heave /hiv/ v. tirar.
heaven /'hεvən/ n. cielo m.
heavenly /'hεvənli/ a. divino.
heavy /'hεvi/ a. pesado; oneroso.
Hebrew /'hibru/ a. & n hebreo -ea.
hectic /'hεktık/ a. turbulento.
hedge /hεdʒ/ n. seto m.
hedgehog /'hεdʒ,hɔg/ n. erizo m.
hedonism /'hidn,ızəm/ n. hedonismo m.
heed /hid/ n. **1.** cuidado m. —v. **2.** atender.
heedless /'hidlıs/ a. desatento; incauto.
heel /hil/ n. talón m.; (of shoe) tacón m.
heifer /'hεfər/ n. novilla f.
height /hait/ n. altura f.
heighten /'haitn/ v. elevar; exaltar.
heinous /'heinəs/ a. nefando.
heir /εər/ n. **heiress** n. heredero -ra.
helicopter /'hεli,kɔptər/ n. helicóptero m.
heliotrope /'hiliə,troup/ n. heliotropo m.
helium /'hiliəm/ n. helio m.
hell /hεl/ n. infierno m.
Hellenism /'hεlə,nızəm/ n. helenismo m.
hellish /'hεlıʃ/ a. infernal.
hello /hε'lou/ interj. ¡hola!; (on telephone) aló; bueno.
helm /hεlm/ n. timón m.
helmet /'hεlmıt/ n. yelmo, casco m.
helmsman /'hεlmzmən/ n. timonel m.
help /hεlp/ n. **1.** ayuda f. **help!** ¡socorro! —v. **2.** ayudar. **h. oneself,** servirse. **can't help (but),** no poder menos de.
helper /'hεlpər/ n. ayudante m.
helpful /'hεlpfəl/ a. útil; servicial.
helpfulness /'hεlpfəlnıs/ n. utilidad f.
helpless /'hεlplıs/ a. imposibilitado.
hem /hεm/ n. **1.** ribete m. —v. **2.** ribetear.
hemisphere /'hεmi,sfıər/ n. hemisferio m.
hemlock /'hεm,lɔk/ n. abeto m.
hemoglobin /'himə,gloubın/ n. hemoglobina f.
hemophilia /,himə'fıliə/ n. hemofilia f.
hemorrhage /'hεmərıdʒ/ n. hemorragia f.

hemorrhoids /'hεmə,rɔidz/ n. hemorroides f.pl.
hemp /hεmp/ n. cáñamo m.
hemstitch /'hεm,stıtʃ/ n. **1.** vainica f. —v. **2.** hacer una vainica.
hen /hεn/ n. gallina f.
hence /hεns/ adv. por lo tanto.
henceforth /,hεns'fɔrθ/ adv. de aquí en adelante.
henchman /'hεntʃmən/ n. paniaguado m.
henna /'hεnə/ n. alheña f.
hepatitis /,hεpə'taitıs/ n. hepatitis f.
her /hər/ unstressed hər, ər/ a. **1.** su. —pron. **2.** ella; la; le.
herald /'hεrəld/ n. heraldo m.
heraldic /hε'rældık/ a. heráldico.
heraldry /'hεrəldri/ n. heráldica f.
herb /ɜrb/ esp. Brit. hɜrb/ n. yerba, hierba f.
herbaceous /hɜr'beiʃəs, ɜr-/ a. herbáceo.
herbarium /hɜr'bεəriəm, ɜr-/ n. herbario m.
herd /hɜrd/ n. **1.** hato, rebaño m. —v. **2.** reunir en hatos.
here /hıər/ adv. aquí; acá.
hereafter /hıər'æftər/ adv. en lo futuro.
hereby /hıər'bai/ adv. por éstas, por la presente.
hereditary /hə'rεdı,tεri/ a. hereditario.
heredity /hə'rεditi/ n. herencia f.
herein /hıər'ın/ adv. aquí dentro; incluso.
heresy /'hεrəsi/ n. herejía f.
heretic /'hεrıtık/ a **1.** herético. —n. **2.** hereje m. & f.
heretical /hə'rεtıkəl/ a. herético.
heretofore /,hıərtə'fɔr/ adv. hasta ahora.
herewith /hıər'wıθ/ adv. con esto, adjunto.
heritage /'hεritıdʒ/ n. herencia f.
hermetic /hər'mεtık/ a. hermético.
hermit /'hɜrmıt/ n. ermitaño m.
hernia /'hɜrniə/ n. hernia f.
hero /'hıərou/ n. héroe m.
heroic /hı'rouık/ a. heroico.
heroically /hı'rouıkəli/ adv. heroicamente.
heroin /'hεrouın/ n. heroína f.
heroine /'hεrouın/ n. heroína f.
heroism /'hεrou,ızəm/ n. heroísmo m.
heron /'hεrən/ n. garza f.
herring /'hεrıŋ/ n. arenque m.
hers /hɜrz/ pron. suyo, de ella.
herself /hər'sεlf/ pron. sí, sí misma, se. **she h.,** ella misma. **with h.,** consigo.
hertz /hɜrts/ n. hertzio m.
hesitancy /'hεzıtənsi/ n. hesitación f.
hesitant /'hεzıtənt/ a. indeciso.
hesitate /'hεzı,teit/ v. vacilar.
hesitation /,hεzı'teiʃən/ n. duda; vacilación f.
heterogeneous /,hεtərə'dʒiniəs/ a. heterogéneo.

heterosexual /,hetərə'sekʃuəl/ a. heterosexual.

hexagon /'heksə,gɒn/ n. hexágono m.

hibernate /'haibər,neit/ v. invernar.

hibernation /,haibər'neiʃən/ n. invernada f.

hibiscus /hai'biskəs/ n. hibisco m.

hiccup /'hikʌp/ n. **1.** hipo m. —v. **2.** tener hipo.

hickory /'hikəri/ n. nogal americano m.

hidden /'hidn/ a. oculto; escondido.

hide /haid/ n. **1.** cuero m.; piel f. —v. **2.** esconder; ocultar.

hideous /'hidiəs/ a. horrible.

hide-out /'haid ,aut/ n. escondite m.

hiding place /'haidiŋ/ escondrijo m.

hierarchy /'haiə,rɑrki/ n. jerarquía f.

high /hai/ a. alto, elevado; (in price) caro.

highbrow /'hai,brau/ a. erudito m.

highfalutin /,haifə'lutn/ a. pomposo, presumido.

high fidelity de alta fidelidad.

highlighter /'hai,laitər/ n. marcador m.

highly /'haili/ adv. altamente; sumamente.

high school escuela secundaria f.

highway /'hai,wei/ n. carretera f.; camino real m.

hijacker /'hai,dʒækər/ n. secuestrador, pirata de aviones m.

hike /haik/ n. caminata f.

hilarious /hi'leəriəs/ a. alegre, bullicioso.

hilarity /hi'læriti/ n. hilaridad f.

hill /hil/ n. colina f.; cerro m.; **down h.**, cuesta abajo. **up h.**, cuesta arriba.

hilly /'hili/ a. accidentado.

hilt /hilt/ n. puño m. **up to the h.**, a fondo.

him /him/ pron. él; lo; le.

himself /him'self/ pron. sí, sí mismo; se. **he h.**, él mismo. **with h.**, consigo.

hinder /'hindər/ v. impedir.

hindmost /'haind,moust/ a. último.

hindquarter /'haind,kwɔrtər/ n. cuarto trasero m.

hindrance /'hindrəns/ n. obstáculo m.

hinge /hindʒ/ n. **1.** gozne m. —v. **2.** engoznar. **h. on,** depender de.

hint /hint/ n. **1.** insinuación f.; indicio m. —v. **2.** insinuar.

hip /hip/ n. cadera f.

hippopotamus /,hipə'pɒtəməs/ n. hipopótamo m.

hire /haiər/ v. alquilar.

his /hiz/ unstressed iz/ a. **1.** su. —pron. **2.** suyo, de él.

Hispanic /hi'spænik/ a. hispano.

hiss /his/ v. silbar, sisear.

historian /hi'stɔriən/ n. historiador m.

historic /hi'stɒrik/ **historical** a. histórico.

history /'histəri/ n. historia f.

histrionic /,histri'ɒnik/ a. histriónico.

hit /hit/ n. **1.** golpe m.; Colloq. éxito m.; (Internet) hit m. —v. **2.** golpear.

hitch /hitʃ/ v. amarrar; enganchar.

hitchhike /'hitʃ,haik/ v. hacer autostop.

hitchhiker /'hitʃ,haikər/ n. autostopista f.

hitchhiking /'hitʃ,haikiŋ/ n. autostop m.

hither /'hiðər/ adv. acá, hacia acá.

hitherto /'hiðər,tu/ adv. hasta ahora.

hive /haiv/ n. colmena f.

hives /haivz/ n. urticaria f.

hoard /hɔrd/ n. **1.** acumulación f. —v. **2.** acaparar; atesorar.

hoarse /hɔrs/ a. ronco.

hoax /houks/ n. **1.** engaño m. —v. **2.** engañar.

hobby /'hɒbi/ n. afición f.; pasatiempo m.

hobgoblin /'hɒb,gɒblin/ n. trasgo m.

hobnob /'hɒb,nɒb/ v. tener intimidad.

hobo /'houbou/ n. vagabundo m.

hockey /'hɒki/ n. hockey m. **ice-h.,** hockey sobre hielo.

hod /hɒd/ n. esparavel m.

hodgepodge /'hɒdʒ,pɒdʒ/ n. baturrillo m.; mezcolanza f.

hoe /hou/ n. **1.** azada f. —v. **2.** cultivar con azada.

hog /hɒg/ n. cerdo, puerco m.

hoist /hɔist/ n. **1.** grúa f., elevador m. —v. **2.** elevar, enarbolar.

hold /hould/ n. **1.** presa f.; agarro m.; Naut. bodega f. **to get h. of,** conseguir, apoderarse de. —v. **2.** tener; detener; sujetar; celebrar.

holder /'houldər/ n. tenedor m. **cigarette h.,** boquilla f.

holdup /'hould,ʌp/ n. salteamiento m.

hole /houl/ n. agujero; hoyo; hueco m.

holiday /'hɒli,dei/ n. día de fiesta.

holiness /'houlinis/ n. santidad f.

Holland /'hɒlənd/ n. Holanda f.

hollow /'hɒlou/ a. **1.** hueco. —n. **2.** cavidad f. —v. **3.** ahuecar; excavar.

holly /'hɒli/ n. acebo m.

hollyhock /'hɒli,hɒk/ n. malva real f.

holocaust /'hɒlə,kɔst/ n. holocausto m.

hologram /'hɒlə,græm/ n. holograma m.

holography /hə'lɒgrəfi/ n. holografía f.

holster /'houlstər/ n. pistolera f.

holy /'houli/ a. santo.

holy day disanto m.

Holy See Santa Sede f.

Holy Spirit Espíritu Santo m.

Holy Week Semana Santa f.

homage /'hɒmidʒ/ n. homenaje m.

home /houm/ n. casa, morada f; hogar m. **at h.,** en casa. **to go h.,** ir a casa.

home appliance electrodoméstica m.

home computer ordenador doméstico m., computadora doméstica f.

homeland /'houm,lænd/ n. patria f.

homely /'houmli/ *a.* feo; casero.

home rule *n.* autonomía *f.*

homesick /'houm,sɪk/ *a.* nostálgico.

homespun /'houm,spʌn/ *a.* casero; tocho.

homeward /'houmwərd/ *adv.* hacia casa.

homework /'houm,wɜrk/ *n.* deberes *m.pl.*

homicide /'hɒmə,said/ *n.* homicida *m. & f.*

homily /'hɒməli/ *n.* homilía *f.*

homogeneous /,houmə'dʒiniəs/ *a.* homogéneo.

homogenize /hə'mɒdʒə,naiz/ *v.* homogeneizar.

homosexual /,houmə'sɛkʃuəl/ *n. & a.* homosexual *m.*

Honduras /hɒn'durəs/ *n.* Honduras *f.*

hone /houn/ *n.* **1.** piedra de afilar *f.* —*v.* **2.** afilar.

honest /'ɒnɪst/ *a.* honrado; honesto; sincero.

honestly /'ɒnɪstli/ *adv.* honradamente; de veras.

honesty /'ɒnəsti/ *n.* honradez, honestidad *f.*

honey /'hʌni/ *n.* miel *f.*

honeybee /'hʌni,bi/ *n.* abeja obrera *f.*

honeymoon /'hʌni,mun/ *n.* luna de miel.

honeysuckle /'hʌni,sʌkəl/ *n.* madreselva *f.*

honor /'ɒnər/ *n.* **1.** honra *f.*; honor *m.* —*v.* **2.** honrar.

honorable /'ɒnərəbəl/ *a.* honorable; ilustre.

honorary /'ɒnə,rɛri/ *a.* honorario.

hood /hud/ *n.* capota *f.*; capucha *f.*; *Auto.* cubierta del motor.

hoodlum /'hudləm/ *n.* pillo *m.*, rufián *m.*

hoodwink /'hud,wɪŋk/ *v.* engañar.

hoof /huf/ *n.* pezuña *f.*

hook /huk/ *n.* **1.** gancho *m.* —*v.* **2.** enganchar.

hooligan /'huligən/ *n.* gamberro -rra.

hoop /hup/ *n.* cerco *m.*

hop /hɒp/ *n.* **1.** salto *m.* —*v.* **2.** saltar.

hope /houp/ *n.* **1.** esperanza *f.* —*v.* **2.** esperar.

hopeful /'houpfəl/ *a.* lleno de esperanzas.

hopeless /'houplɪs/ *a.* desesperado; sin remedio.

horde /hɔrd/ *n.* horda *f.*

horehound /'hɔr,haund/ *n.* marrubio *m.*

horizon /hə'raizən/ *n.* horizonte *m.*

horizontal /,hɔrə'zɒntl/ *a.* horizontal.

hormone /'hɔrmoun/ *n.* hormón *m.*

horn /hɔrn/ *n.* cuerno *m.*; (music) trompa *f.*; *Auto.* bocina *f.*

hornet /'hɔrnɪt/ *n.* avispón *m.*

horny /'hɔrni/ *a.* córneo; calloso.

horoscope /'hɔrə,skoup/ *n.* horóscopo *m.*

horrendous /hə'rɛndəs/ *a.* horrendo.

horrible /'hɒrəbəl/ *a.* horrible.

horrid /'hɒrɪd/ *a.* horrible.

horrify /'hɒrə,fai/ *v.* horrorizar.

horror /'hɔrər/ *n.* horror *m.*

horror film película de terror *f.*

hors d'oeuvre /ɔr 'dɜrv/ *n.* entremés *m.*

horse /hɔrs/ *n.* caballo *m.* **to ride a h.,** cabalgar.

horseback /'hɔrs,bæk/ *n.* **on h.,** a caballo. **to ride h.,** montar a caballo.

horseback riding equitación *f.*

horsehair /'hɔrs,hɛər/ *n.* pelo de caballo *m.*; tela de crin *f.*

horseman /'hɔrsmən/ *n.* jinete *m.*

horsemanship /'hɔrsmən,ʃɪp/ *n.* manejo *m.*, equitación *f.*

horsepower /'hɔrs,pauər/ *n.* caballo de fuerza *m.*

horse race carrera de caballos *f.*

horseradish /'hɔrs,rædɪʃ/ *n.* rábano picante *m.*

horseshoe /'hɔrs,ʃu/ *n.* herradura *f.*

hortatory /'hɔrtə,tɔri/ *a.* exhortatorio.

horticulture /'hɔrtɪ,kʌltʃər/ *n.* horticultura *f.*

hose /houz/ *n.* medias *f.pl*; (garden) manguera *f.*

hosiery /'houʒəri/ *n.* calcetería *f.*

hospitable /'hɒspɪtəbəl/ *a.* hospitalario.

hospital /'hɒspɪtl/ *n.* hospital *m.*

hospitality /,hɒspɪ'tælɪti/ *n.* hospitalidad *f.*

hospitalization /,hɒspɪtl'zeiʃən/ *n.* hospitalización *f.*

hospitalize /'hɒspɪtl,aiz/ *v.* hospitalizar.

host /houst/ *n.* anfitrión *m.*, dueño de la casa; *Relcg.* hostia *f.*

hostage /'hɒstɪdʒ/ *n.* rehén *m.*

hostel /'hɒstl/ *n.* hostería *f.*

hostelry /'hɒstlri/ *n.* fonda *f.*, parador *m.*

hostess /'houstɪs/ *n.* anfitriona *f.*, dueña de la casa.

hostile /'hɒstl/ *a.* hostil.

hostility /hɒ'stɪlɪti/ *n.* hostilidad *f.*

hot /hɒt/ *a.* caliente; (sauce) picante. **to be h.,** tener calor; (weather) hacer calor.

hotbed /'hɒt,bɛd/ *n.* estercolero *m.* *Fig.* foco *m.*

hot dog perrito caliente *m.*

hotel /hou'tɛl/ *n.* hotel *m.*

hotelier /,outɛl'yei, ,hout'ɪər/ *n.* hotelero -ra.

hot-headed /'hɒt 'hɛdɪd/ *a.* turbulento, alborotadizo.

hothouse /'hɒt,haus/ *n.* invernáculo *m.*

hot-water bottle /'hɒt 'wɔtər/ bolsa de agua caliente *f.*

hound /haund/ *n.* **1.** sabueso *m.* —*v.* **2.** perseguir; seguir la pista.

hour /auər/ *n.* hora *f.*

hourglass /'auər,glæs/ *n.* reloj de arena *m.*

hourly /'auərli/ *a.* **1.** por horas. —*adv.* **2.** a cada hora.

house /n haus/ v hauz/ n. **1.** casa f.; *Theat.* público m. —v. **2.** alojar, albergar.

housefly /'haus,flai/ n. mosca ordinaria f.

household /'haus,hould/ n. familia; casa f.

housekeeper /'haus,kipər/ n. ama de llaves.

housemaid /'haus,meid/ n. criada f.; sirvienta f.

housewife /'haus,waif/ n. ama de casa.

housework /'haus,wɜrk/ n. tareas domésticas.

hovel /'hʌvəl/ n. choza f.

hover /'hʌvər/ v. revolotear.

hovercraft /'hʌvər,kræft/ n. aerodeslizador m.

how /hau/ adv. cómo. **h. much,** cuánto. **h. many,** cuántos. **h. far,** a qué distancia.

however /hau'ɛvər/ adv. como quera; sin embargo.

howl /haul/ n. **1.** aullido m. —v. **2.** aullar.

HTML abbr. (HyperText Markup Language) Lenguaje de Marcado de Hipertexto m.

hub /hʌb/ n. centro m.; eje m. **h. of a wheel,** cubo de la rueda m.

hubbub /'hʌbʌb/ n. alboroto m., bulla f.

hue /hyu/ n. matiz; color m.

hug /hʌg/ n. **1.** abrazo m. —v. **2.** abrazar.

huge /hyudʒ/ a. enorme.

hulk /hʌlk/ n. casco de buque m.

hull /hʌl/ n. **1.** cáscara f.; (naval) casco m. —v. **2.** decascarar.

hum /hʌm/ n. **1.** zumbido m. —v. **2.** tararear; zumbar.

human /'hyumən/ a. & n. humano -na.

human being ser humano m.

humane /hyu'mein/ a. humano, humanitario.

humanism /'hyumə,nizəm/ n. humanidad f.; benevolencia f.

humanitarian /hyu,mænɪ'tɛəriən/ a. humanitario.

humanity /hyu'mænɪti/ n. humanidad f.

humanly /'hyumənli/ a. humanamente.

humble /'hʌmbəl/ a. humilde.

humbug /'hʌm,bʌg/ n. farsa f., embaucador m.

humdrum /'hʌm,drʌm/ a. monótono.

humid /'hyumɪd/ a. húmedo.

humidity /hyu'mɪdɪti/ n. humedad f.

humiliate /hyu'mɪli,eit/ v. humillar.

humiliation /hyu,mɪli'eiʃən/ n. mortificación f.; bochorno m.

humility /hyu'mɪlɪti/ n. humildad f.

humor /'hyumər/ n. **1.** humor; capricho m. —v. **2.** complacer.

humorist /'hyumərɪst/ n. humorista f.

humorous /'hyumərəs/ a. divertido.

hump /hʌmp/ n. joroba f.

humpback /'hʌmp,bæk/ n. jorobado m.

humus /'hyuməs/ n. humus m.

hunch /hʌntʃ/ n. giba f.; (idea) corazonada f.

hunchback /'hʌntʃ,bæk/ n. jorobado m.

hundred /'hʌndrɪd/ a. & pron. **1.** cien, ciento. **200,** doscientos. **300,** trescientos. **400,** cuatrocientos. **500,** quinientos. **600,** seiscientos. **700,** setecientos. **800,** ochocientos. **900,** novecientos. —n. **2.** centenar m.

hundredth /'hʌndrɪdθ/ n. & a centésimo m.

Hungarian /hʌŋ'gɛəriən/ a. & n. húngaro -ra.

Hungary /'hʌŋgəri/ Hungría f.

hunger /'hʌŋgər/ n. hambre f.

hunger strike huelga de hambre f.

hungry /'hʌŋgri/ a. hambriento. **to be h.,** tener hambre.

hunt /hʌnt/ n. **1.** caza f. —v. **2.** cazar. **h. up,** buscar.

hunter /'hʌntər/ n. cazador m.

hunting /'hʌntɪŋ/ n. caza f. **to go h.,** ir de caza.

hurdle /'hɜrdl/ n. zarzo m., valla f.; dificultad f.

hurl /hɜrl/ v. arrojar.

hurricane /'hɜri,kein/ n. huracán f.

hurry /'hɜri/ n. **1.** prisa f. **to be in a h.,** tener prisa. —v. **2.** apresurar; darse prisa.

hurt /hɜrt/ n. **1.** daño, perjuicio m. —v. **2.** dañar; lastimar; doler; ofender.

hurtful /'hɜrtfəl/ a. perjudicial, dañino.

hurtle /'hɜrtl/ v. lanzar.

husband /'hʌzbənd/ n marido, esposo m.

husk /hʌsk/ n. **1.** cáscara f. —v. **2.** descascarar.

husky /'hʌski/ a. fornido.

hustle /'hʌsəl/ v. empujar.

hustle and bustle ajetreo m.

hut /hʌt/ n. choza f.

hyacinth /'haiəsɪnθ/ n. jacinto m

hybrid /'haibrid/ a. híbrido.

hydrangea /hai'dreindʒə/ n. hortensia f.

hydraulic /hai'drɔlɪk/ a. hidráulico.

hydroelectric /'haidrou'lɛktrɪk/ a. hidroeléctrico.

hydrogen /'haidrədʒən/ n. hidrógeno m.

hydrophobia /,haidrə'foubiə/ n. hidrofobia. f.

hydroplane /'haidrə,plein/ n. hidroavión m.

hydrotherapy /,haidrə'θɛrəpi/ n. hidroterapia f.

hyena /hai'inə/ n. huena f.

hygiene /'haidʒin/ n. higiene f.

hygienic /,haidʒi'ɛnɪk/ a. higiénico.

hymn /hɪm/ n. himno m.

hymnal /'hɪmnl/ n. himnario m.

hype /haip/ n. Colloq. **1.** bomba publicitario f —v. **2.** promocionar a bombo y platillo.

hypercritical /ˌhaipərˈkrɪtɪkəl/ a. hipercrítico.

hyperlink /ˈhaipərˌlɪŋk/ n. (Internet) hiperenlace m.

hypermarket /ˈhaipərˌmɑrkɪt/ n. hipermercado m.

hypertension /ˌhaipərˈtɛnʃən/ n. hipertensión f.

hypertext /ˈhaipərˌtɛkst/ n. (Internet) hipertexto m.

hyphen /ˈhaifən/ n. guión m.

hyphenate /ˈhaifəˌneit/ v. separar con guión.

hypnosis /hɪpˈnousɪs/ n. hipnosis f.

hypnotic /hɪpˈnɒtɪk/ a. hipnótico.

hypnotism /ˈhɪpnəˌtɪzəm/ n. hipnotismo m.

hypnotize /ˈhɪpnəˌtaiz/ v. hipnotizar.

hypochondria /ˌhaipəˈkɒndriə/ n. hipocondría f.

hypochondriac /ˌhaipəˈkɒndriˌæk/ n. & a. hipocondríaco m.

hypocrisy /hɪˈpɒkrəsi/ n. hipocresía f.

hypocrite /ˈhɪpəkrɪt/ n. hipócrita m. & f.

hypocritical /ˌhɪpəˈkrɪtɪkəl/ a. hipócrita.

hypodermic /ˌhaipəˈdɜrmɪk/ a. hipodérmico.

hypotenuse /haiˈpɒtnˌus/ n. hipotenusa f.

hypothesis /haiˈpɒθəsɪs/ n. hipótesis f.

hypothetical /ˌhaipəˈθɛtɪkəl/ a. hipotético.

hysterectomy /ˌhɪstəˈrɛktəmi/ n. histerectomía f.

hysteria /hɪˈstɛriə/ **hysterics** n. histeria f.

hysterical /hɪˈstɛrɪkəl/ a. histérico.

I

I /ai/ pron. yo.

iambic /aiˈæmbɪk/ a. yámbico.

ice /ais/ n. hielo m.

iceberg /ˈaisbɜrg/ n. iceberg m.

icebox /ˈaisˌbɒks/ n. refrigerador m.

ice cream helado, mantecado m.; **i.-c. cone**, barquillo de helado; **i.-c. parlor** heladería f.

ice cube cubito de hielo m.

ice skate patín de cuchilla m.

icon /ˈaiknɒ/ n. icón m.

icy /ˈaisi/ a. helado; indiferente.

idea /aiˈdiə/ n. idea f.

ideal /aiˈdiəl/ a. ideal.

idealism /aiˈdiəˌlɪzəm/ n. idealismo m.

idealist /aiˈdiəlɪst/ n. idealista m. & f.

idealistic /aiˌdiəˈlɪstɪk/ a. idealista.

idealize /aiˈdiəˌlaiz/ v. idealizar.

ideally /aiˈdiəli/ adv. idealmente.

identical /aiˈdɛntɪkəl/ a. idéntico.

identifiable /aiˌdɛntɪˈfaiəbəl/ a. identificable.

identification /aiˌdɛntɪfɪˈkeiʃən/ n. identificación f. **i. papers**, cédula de identidad f.

identify /aiˈdɛntəˌfai/ v. identificar.

identity /aiˈdɛntɪti/ n. identidad f.

ideology /ˌaidiˈɒlədʒi/ n. ideología f.

idiocy /ˈɪdiəsi/ n. idiotez f.

idiom /ˈɪdiəm/ n. modismo m.; idioma m.

idiot /ˈɪdiət/ n. idiota m. & f.

idiotic /ˌɪdiˈɒtɪk/ a. idiota, tonto.

idle /ˈaidl/ a. desocupado; perezoso.

idleness /ˈaidlnɪs/ n. ociosidad, pereza f.

idol /ˈaidl/ n. ídolo m.

idolatry /aiˈdɒlətri/ n. idolatría f.

idolize /ˈaidlˌaiz/ v. idolatrar.

idyl /ˈaidl/ n. idilio m.

idyllic /aiˈdɪlɪk/ a. idílico.

if /ɪf/ conj. si. **even if**, aunque.

ignite /ɪgˈnait/ v. encender.

ignition /ɪgˈnɪʃən/ n. ignición f.

ignoble /ɪgˈnoubəl/ a. innoble, indigno.

ignominious /ˌɪgnəˈmɪniəs/ a. ignominioso.

ignoramus /ˌɪgnəˈreiməs/ n. ignorante m.

ignorance /ˈɪgnərəns/ n. ignorancia f.

ignorant /ˈɪgnərənt/ a. ignorante. **to be i. of**, ignorar.

ignore /ɪgˈnɔr/ v. desconocer, pasar por alto.

ill /ɪl/ a. enfermo, malo.

illegal /ɪˈligəl/ a. ilegal.

illegible /ɪˈlɛdʒəbəl/ a. ilegible.

illegibly /ɪˈlɛdʒəbli/ a. ilegiblemente.

illegitimacy /ˌɪlɪˈdʒɪtəməsi/ n. ilegitimidad f.

illegitimate /ˌɪlɪˈdʒɪtəmɪt/ a. ilegítimo; desautorizado.

illicit /ɪˈlɪsɪt/ a. ilícito.

illiteracy /ɪˈlɪtərəsi/ n. analfabetismo m.

illiterate /ɪˈlɪtərɪt/ a. & n. analfabeto -ta.

illness /ˈɪlnɪs/ n. enfermedad, maldad f.

illogical /ɪˈlɒdʒɪkəl/ a. ilógico.

illuminate /ɪˈluməˌneit/ v. iluminar.

illumination /ɪˌluməˈneiʃən/ n. iluminación f.

illusion /ɪˈluʒən/ n. ilusión f.; ensueño m.

illusive /ɪˈlusɪv/ a. ilusivo.

illustrate /ˈɪləˌstreit/ v. ilustrar; ejemplificar.

illustration /ˌɪləˈstreiʃən/ n. ilustración f.; ejemplo; grabado m.

illustrative /ɪˈlʌstrətɪv/ a. ilustrativo.

illustrious /ɪˈlʌstriəs/ a. ilustre.

ill will n. malevolencia f.

image /'ımıdʒ/ n. imagen, estatua f.
imagery /'ımıdʒrı/ n. imaginación f.
imaginable /ı'mædʒənəbəl/ a. imaginable.
imaginary /ı'mædʒə,nɛri/ a. imaginario.
imagination /ı,mædʒə'neıʃən/ n. imaginación f.
imaginative /ı'mædʒənətıv/ a. imaginativo.
imagine /ı'mædʒın/ v. imaginarse, figurarse.
imam /ı'mɑm/ n. imán m.
imbecile /'ımbəsıl/ n. & a. imbécil m.
imitate /'ımı,teıt/ v. imitar.
imitation /,ımı'teıʃən/ n. imitación f.
imitative /'ımı,teıtıv/ a. imitativo.
immaculate /ı'mækyəlıt/ a. inmaculado.
immanent /'ımənənt/ a. inmanente.
immaterial /,ımə'tıərıəl/ a. inmaterial; sin importancia.
immature /,ımə'tʃʊr/ a. inmaturo.
immediate /ı'midııt/ a. inmediato.
immediately /ı'midııtlı/ adv. inmediatamente.
immense /ı'mɛns/ a. inmenso.
immerse /ı'mɜrs/ v. sumergir.
immigrant /'ımıgrənt/ n. & a. inmigrante m. & f.
immigrate /'ımı,greıt/ v. inmigrar.
imminent /'ımənənt/ a. inminente.
immobile /ı'moubəl/ a. inmóvil.
immoderate /ı'mɒdərıt/ a. inmoderado.
immodest /ı'mɒdıst/ a. inmodesto; atrevido.
immoral /ı'mɔrəl/ a. inmoral.
immorality /,ımə'rælıtı/ n. inmoralidad f.
immorally /ı'mɔrəlı/ adv. licenciosamente.
immortal /ı'mɔrtl/ a. inmortal.
immortality /,ımɔr'tælıtı/ n. inmortalidad f.
immortalize /ı'mɔrtl,aız/ v. inmortalizar.
immune /ı'myun/ a. inmune.
immunity /ı'myunıtı/ n. inmunidad f.
immunize /'ımyə,naız/ v. inmunizar.
impact /'ımpækt/ n. impacto m.
impair /ım'pɛər/ v. empeorar, perjudicar.
impale /ım'peıl/ v. empalar.
impart /ım'pɑrt/ v. impartir, comunicar.
impartial /ım'pɑrʃəl/ a. imparcial.
impatience /ım'peıʃəns/ n. impaciencia f.
impatient /ım'peıʃənt/ a. impaciente.
impede /ım'pid/ v. impedir, estorbar.
impediment /ım'pɛdəmənt/ n. impedimento m.
impel /ım'pɛl/ v. impeler.
impenetrable /ım'pɛnıtrəbəl/ a. impenetrable.
impenitent /ım'pɛnıtənt/ n. & a. impenitente m.
imperative /ım'pɛrətıv/ a. imperativo.
imperceptible /,ımpər'sɛptəbəl/ a. imperceptible.
imperfect /ım'pɜrfıkt/ a. imperfecto.

imperfection /,ımpər'fɛkʃən/ n. imperfección f.
imperial /ım'pıərıəl/ a. imperial.
imperialism /ım'pıərıə,lızəm/ n. imperialismo m.
imperious /ım'pıərıəs/ a. imperioso.
impersonal /ım'pɜrsənl/ a. impersonal.
impersonate /ım'pɜrsə,neıt/ v. personificar; imitar.
impersonation /ım,pɜrsə'neıʃən/ n. personificación f.; imitación f.
impertinence /ım'pɜrtnəns/ n. impertinencia f.
impervious /ım'pɜrvıəs/ a. impermeable.
impetuous /ım'pɛtʃuəs/ a. impetuoso.
impetus /'ımpıtəs/ n. ímpetu m., impulso m.
impinge /ım'pındʒ/ v. tropezar; infringir.
implacable /ım'plækəbəl/ a. implacable.
implant /ım'plænt/ v. implantar; inculcar.
implement /'ımpləmənt/ n. herramienta f.
implicate /'ımplı,keıt/ v. implicar; embrollar.
implication /,ımplı'keıʃən/ n. inferencia f.; complicidad f.
implicit /ım'plısıt/ a. implícito.
implied /ım'plaıd/ a. implícito.
implore /ım'plɔr/ v. implorar.
imply /ım'plaı/ v. significar; dar a entender.
impolite /,ımpə'laıt/ a. descortés.
import /n 'ımpɔrt; v ım'pɔrt/ n. **1.** importación f. —v. **2.** importar.
importance /ım'pɔrtns/ n. importancia f.
important /ım'pɔrtnt/ a. importante.
importation /,ımpɔr'teıʃən/ n. importación f.
importune /,ımpɔr'tun/ v. importunar.
impose /ım'pouz/ v. imponer.
imposition /,ımpə'zıʃən/ n. imposición f.
impossibility /ım,pɒsə'bılıtı/ n. imposibilidad f.
impossible /ım'pɒsəbəl/ a. imposible.
impotence /'ımpətəns/ n. impotencia f.
impotent /'ımpətənt/ a. impotente.
impregnable /ım'prɛgnəbəl/ a. impregnable.
impregnate /ım'prɛgneıt/ v. impregnar; fecundizar.
impresario /,ımprə'sɑri,ou/ n. empresario m.
impress /ım'prɛs/ v. impresionar.
impression /ım'prɛʃən/ n. impresión f.
impressive /ım'prɛsıv/ a. imponente.
imprison /ım'prızən/ v. encarcelar.
imprisonment /ım'prızənmənt/ n. prisión, encarcelación f.
improbable /ım'prɒbəbəl/ a. improbable.
impromptu /ım'prɒmptu/ a. extemporáneo.
improper /ım'prɒpər/ a. impropio.
improve /ım'pruv/ v. mejorar; progresar.

improvement /ɪm'pruːvmənt/ n. mejoramiento; progreso m.

improvise /'ɪmprə,vaiz/ v. improvisar.

impudent /'ɪmpjədənt/ a. descarado.

impugn /ɪm'pjuːn/ v. impugnar.

impulse /'ɪmpʌls/ n. impulso m.

impulsive /ɪm'pʌlsɪv/ a. impulsivo.

impunity /ɪm'pjuːnɪti/ n. impunidad f.

impure /ɪm'pjʊr/ a. impuro.

impurity /ɪm'pjʊrɪti/ n. impureza f.; deshonestidad f

impute /ɪm'pjut/ v. imputar.

in /ɪn/ prep. **1.** en; dentro de. —adv. **2.** adentro.

inadvertent /,ɪnəd'vɜrtn̩t/ a. inadvertido.

inalienable /ɪn'eiljənəbəl/ a. inalienable.

inane /ɪ'nein/ a. mentecato.

inaugural /ɪn'ɔgyərəl/ a. inaugural.

inaugurate /ɪn'ɔgyə,reit/ v. inaugurar.

inauguration /ɪn,ɔgyə'reiʃən/ n. inauguración f.

Inca /'ɪŋkə/ n. inca m.

incandescent /,ɪnkən'dɛsənt/ a. incandescente.

incantation /,ɪnkæn'teiʃən/ n. encantación f., conjuro m.

incapacitate /,ɪnkə'pæsɪ,teit/ v. incapacitar.

incarcerate /ɪn'kɑrsə,reit/ v. encarcelar.

incarnate /ɪn'kɑrnɪt/ a. encarnado; personificado.

incarnation /,ɪnkɑr'neiʃən/ n. encarnación f.

incendiary /ɪn'sɛndi,ɛri/ a. incendiario.

incense /ɪn'sɛns/ n. **1.** incienso m. —v. **2.** indignar.

incentive /ɪn'sɛntɪv/ n. incentivo m.

inception /ɪn'sɛpʃən/ n. comienzo m.

incessant /ɪn'sɛsənt/ a. incesante.

incest /'ɪnsɛst/ n. incesto m.

inch /ɪntʃ/ n. pulgada f.

incidence /'ɪnsɪdəns/ n. incidencia f.

incident /'ɪnsɪdənt/ n. incidente m.

incidental /,ɪnsɪ'dɛntl/ a. incidental.

incidentally /,ɪnsɪ'dɛntli/ adv. incidentalmente; entre paréntesis.

incinerate /ɪn'sɪnə,reit/ v. incinerar.

incinerator /ɪn'sɪnə,reitər/ n. incinerador m.

incipient /ɪn'sɪpiənt/ a. incipiente.

incision /ɪn'sɪʒən/ n. incisión f.; cortadura f.

incisive /ɪn'saisɪv/ a. incisivo; mordaz.

incisor /ɪn'saizər/ n. incisivo m.

incite /ɪn'sait/ v. incitar, instigar.

inclination /,ɪnklə'neiʃən/ n. inclinación f.; declive m.

incline /n 'ɪnklain; v ɪn'klain/ n. **1.** pendiente m. —v. **2.** inclinar.

inclose /ɪn'klouz/ v. incluir.

include /ɪn'klud/ v. incluir, englobar.

including /ɪn'kludɪŋ/ prep. incluso.

inclusive /ɪn'klusɪv/ a. inclusivo.

incognito /,ɪnkɔg'nitou/ n. & adv. incógnito m.

income /'ɪnkʌm/ n. renta f.; ingresos m.pl.

income tax impuesto sobre la renta m.

incomparable /ɪn'kɒmpərəbəl/ a. incomparable.

inconvenience /,ɪnkən'vinyəns/ n. **1.** incomodidad f. —v. **2.** incomodar.

inconvenient /,ɪnkən'vinyənt/ a. incómodo.

incorporate /ɪn'kɔrpə,reit/ v. incorporar; dar cuerpo.

incorrigible /ɪn'kɔrɪdʒəbəl/ a. incorregible.

increase /ɪn'kris/ v. crecer; aumentar.

incredible /ɪn'krɛdəbəl/ a. increíble.

incredulity /,ɪnkrɪ'dulɪti/ n. incredulidad f.

incredulous /ɪn'krɛdʒələs/ a. incrédulo.

increment /'ɪnkrəmənt/ n. incremento m., aumento m.

incriminate /ɪn'krɪmə,neit/ v. incriminar.

incrimination /ɪn,krɪmə'neiʃən/ n. incriminación f.

incrust /ɪn'krʌst/ v. incrustar.

incubator /'ɪnkyə,beitər/ n. incubadora f.

inculcate /ɪn'kʌlkeit/ v. inculcar.

incumbency /ɪn'kʌmbənsi/ n. incumbencia f.

incumbent /ɪn'kʌmbənt/ a. obligatorio; colocado sobre.

incur /ɪn'kɜr/ v. incurrir.

incurable /ɪn'kyurəbəl/ a. incurable.

indebted /ɪn'dɛtɪd/ a. obligado; adeudado.

indeed /ɪn'did/ adv. verdaderamente, de veras. **no i.,** de ninguna manera.

indefatigable /,ɪndɪ'fætɪgəbəl/ a. incansable.

indefinite /ɪn'dɛfənɪt/ a. indefinido.

indefinitely /ɪn'dɛfənɪtli/ adv. indefinidamente.

indelible /ɪn'dɛləbəl/ a. indeleble.

indemnify /ɪn'dɛmnə,fai/ v. indemnizar.

indemnity /ɪn'dɛmnɪti/ n. indemnificación f.

indent /ɪn'dɛnt/ n. **1.** diente f., mella f. —v. **2.** indentar, mellar.

indentation /,ɪndɛn'teiʃən/ n. indentación f.

independence /,ɪndɪ'pɛndəns/ n. independencia f.

independent /,ɪndɪ'pɛndənt/ a. independiente.

in-depth /'ɪn 'dɛpθ/ adj. en profundidad.

index /'ɪndɛks/ n. índice m.; (of book) tabla f.

index card ficha f.

index finger dedo índice m.

India /'ɪndiə/ n. India f.

Indian /'ɪndiən/ a. & n. indio -dia.

indicate /'ɪndɪ,keit/ v. indicar.

indication /ˌɪndɪˈkeɪʃən/ *n.* indicación *f.*

indicative /ɪnˈdɪkətɪv/ *a.* & *n.* indicativo *m.*

indict /ɪnˈdaɪt/ *v.* encausar.

indictment /ɪnˈdaɪtmənt/ *n.* (law) sumaria; denuncia *f.*

indifference /ɪnˈdɪfərəns/ *n.* indiferencia *f.*

indifferent /ɪnˈdɪfərənt/ *a.* indiferente.

indigenous /ɪnˈdɪdʒənəs/ *a.* indígena.

indigent /ˈɪndɪdʒənt/ *a.* indigente, pobre.

indigestion /ˌɪndɪˈdʒestʃən/ *n.* indigestión *f.*

indignant /ɪnˈdɪgnənt/ *a.* indignado.

indignation /ˌɪndɪgˈneɪʃən/ *n.* indignación *f.*

indignity /ɪnˈdɪgnɪti/ *n.* indignidad *f.*

indirect /ˌɪndəˈrekt/ *a.* indirecto.

indiscreet /ˌɪndɪˈskriːt/ *a.* indiscreto.

indiscretion /ˌɪndɪˈskreʃən/ *n.* indiscreción *f.*

indiscriminate /ˌɪndɪˈskrɪmənɪt/ *a.* promiscuo.

indispensable /ˌɪndɪˈspensəbəl/ *a.* indispensable.

indisposed /ˌɪndɪˈspouzd/ *a.* indispuesto.

individual /ˌɪndəˈvɪdʒuəl/ *a.* & *n.* individuo *m.*

individuality /ˌɪndəˌvɪdʒuˈælɪti/ *n.* individualidad *f.*

individually /ˌɪndəˈvɪdʒuəli/ *adv.* individualmente.

indivisible /ˌɪndəˈvɪzəbəl/ *a.* indivisible.

indoctrinate /ɪnˈdɒktrəˌneɪt/ *v.* doctrinar, enseñar.

indolent /ˈɪndələnt/ *a.* indolente.

indoor /ˈɪnˌdɔr/ *a.* **1.** interior. **indoors** —*adv.* **2.** en casa; bajo techo.

indorse /ɪnˈdɔrs/ *v.* endosar.

induce /ɪnˈdus/ *v.* inducir, persuadir.

induct /ɪnˈdʌkt/ *v.* instalar, iniciar.

induction /ɪnˈdʌkʃən/ *n.* introducción *f.*; instalación *f.*

inductive /ɪnˈdʌktɪv/ *a.* inductivo; introductor.

indulge /ɪnˈdʌldʒ/ *v.* favorecer. **i. in**, entregarse a.

indulgence /ɪnˈdʌldʒəns/ *n.* indulgencia *f.*

indulgent /ɪnˈdʌldʒənt/ *a.* indulgente.

industrial /ɪnˈdʌstriəl/ *a.* industrial.

industrialist /ɪnˈdʌstriəlɪst/ *n.* industrial *m.*

industrial park polígono industrial *m.*

industrious /ɪnˈdʌstriəs/ *a.* industrioso, trabajador.

industry /ˈɪndəstri/ *n.* industria *f.*

inedible /ɪnˈedəbəl/ *a.* incomible.

ineligible /ɪnˈelɪdʒəbəl/ *a.* inelegible.

inept /ɪnˈept/ *a.* inepto.

inert /ɪnˈɜrt/ *a.* inerte.

inertia /ɪnˈɜrʃə/ *n.* inercia *f.*

inevitable /ɪnˈevɪtəbəl/ *a.* inevitable.

inexpensive /ˌɪnɪkˈspensɪv/ *a.* económico.

inexplicable /ɪnˈeksplɪkəbəl/ *a.* inexplicable.

infallible /ɪnˈfæləbəl/ *a.* infalible.

infamous /ˈɪnfəməs/ *a.* infame.

infamy /ˈɪnfəmi/ *n.* infamia *f.*

infancy /ˈɪnfənsi/ *n.* infancia *f.*

infant /ˈɪnfənt/ *n.* nene *m.*; criatura *f.*

infantile /ˈɪnfənˌtaɪl/ *a.* infantil.

infantry /ˈɪnfəntri/ *n.* infantería *f.*

infatuated /ɪnˈfætʃuˌeɪtəd/ *a.* infatuado.

infatuation /ɪnˌfætʃuˈeɪʃən/ *n.* encaprichamiento *m.*

infect /ɪnˈfekt/ *v.* infectar.

infection /ɪnˈfekʃən/ *n.* infección *f.*

infectious /ɪnˈfekʃəs/ *a.* infeccioso.

infer /ɪnˈfɜr/ *v.* inferir.

inference /ˈɪnfərəns/ *n.* inferencia *f.*

inferior /ɪnˈfɪriər/ *a.* inferior.

infernal /ɪnˈfɜrnl/ *a.* infernal.

inferno /ɪnˈfɜrnou/ *n.* infierno *m.*

infest /ɪnˈfest/ *v.* infestar.

infidel /ˈɪnfɪdl/ *n.* **1.** infiel *m.* & *f.*; pagano -na. —*a.* **2.** infiel.

infidelity /ˌɪnfɪˈdelɪti/ *n.* infidelidad *f.*

infiltrate /ɪnˈfɪltreɪt/ *v.* infiltrar.

infinite /ˈɪnfənɪt/ *a.* infinito.

infinitesimal /ˌɪnfɪnɪˈtesəməl/ *a.* infinitesimal.

infinitive /ɪnˈfɪnɪtɪv/ *n.* & *a.* infinitivo *m.*

infinity /ɪnˈfɪnɪti/ *n.* infinidad *f.*

infirm /ɪnˈfɜrm/ *a.* enfermizo.

infirmary /ɪnˈfɜrməri/ *n.* hospital *m.*, enfermería *f.*

infirmity /ɪnˈfɜrmɪti/ *n.* enfermedad *f.*

inflame /ɪnˈfleɪm/ *v.* inflamar.

inflammable /ɪnˈflæməbəl/ *a.* inflamable.

inflammation /ˌɪnfləˈmeɪʃən/ *n.* inflamación *f.*

inflammatory /ɪnˈflæməˌtɔri/ *a.* inflamante; *Med.* inflamatorio.

inflate /ɪnˈfleɪt/ *v.* inflar.

inflation /ɪnˈfleɪʃən/ *n.* inflación *f.*

inflection /ɪnˈflekʃən/ *n.* inflexión *f.*; (of the voice) modulación de la voz *f.*

inflict /ɪnˈflɪkt/ *v.* infligir.

infliction /ɪnˈflɪkʃən/ *n.* imposición *f.*

influence /ˈɪnfluəns/ *n.* **1.** influencia *f.* —*v.* **2.** influir en.

influential /ˌɪnfluˈenʃəl/ *a.* influyente.

influenza /ˌɪnfluˈenzə/ *n.* gripe *f.*

influx /ˈɪnˌflʌks/ *n.* afluencia *f.*

inform /ɪnˈfɔrm/ *v.* informar. **i. oneself**, enterarse.

informal /ɪnˈfɔrməl/ *a.* informal.

information /ˌɪnfərˈmeɪʃən/ *n.* informaciones *f.pl.*

information technology *n.* informática *f.*

infrastructure /ˈɪnfrəˌstrʌktʃər/ *n.* infraestructura *f.*

infringe /ɪnˈfrɪndʒ/ *v.* infringir.

infuriate /ɪnˈfyuri,eit/ v. enfurecer.
ingenious /ɪnˈdʒinyəs/ a. ingenioso.
ingenuity /,ɪndʒəˈnuiti/ n. ingeniosidad; destreza f.
ingredient /ɪnˈgridiənt/ n. ingrediente m.
inhabit /ɪnˈhæbɪt/ v. habitar.
inhabitant /ɪnˈhæbɪtənt/ n. habitante m. & f.
inhale /ɪnˈheil/ v. inhalar.
inherent /ɪnˈhɪərənt/ a. inherente.
inherit /ɪnˈherɪt/ v. heredar.
inheritance /ɪnˈherɪtəns/ n. herencia f.
inhibit /ɪnˈhɪbɪt/ v. inhibir.
inhibition /,ɪnɪˈbɪʃən/ n. inhibición f.
inhuman /ɪnˈhyumən/ a. inhumano.
inimical /ɪˈnɪmɪkəl/ a. hostil.
inimitable /ɪˈnɪmɪtəbəl/ a. inimitable.
iniquity /ɪˈnɪkwɪti/ n. iniquidad f.
initial /ɪˈnɪʃəl/ a. & n. inicial f.
initiate /ɪˈnɪʃi,eit/ v. iniciar.
initiation /ɪ,nɪʃiˈeiʃən/ n. iniciación f.
initiative /ɪˈnɪʃiətɪv/ n. iniciativa f.
inject /ɪnˈdʒekt/ v. inyectar.
injection /ɪnˈdʒekʃən/ n. inyección f.
injunction /ɪnˈdʒʌŋkʃən/ n. mandato m.; (law) embargo m.
injure /ˈɪndʒər/ v. herir; lastimar; ofender.
injurious /ɪnˈdʒuriəs/ a. perjudicial.
injury /ˈɪndʒəri/ n. herida; afrenta f.; perjuicio m.
injustice /ɪnˈdʒʌstɪs/ n. injusticia f.
ink /ɪŋk/ n. tinta f.
inland /ˈɪnlænd/ a. **1.** interior. —adv. **2.** tierra adentro.
inlet /ˈɪnlet/ n. entrada f.; ensenada f.; estuario m.
inmate /ˈɪn,meit/ n. residente m. & f.; (of a prison) preso -sa.
inn /ɪn/ n. posada f.; mesón m.
inner /ˈɪnər/ a. interior. **i. tube,** cámara de aire.
innocence /ˈɪnəsəns/ n. inocencia f.
innocent /ˈɪnəsənt/ a. inocente.
innocuous /ɪˈnɒkyuəs/ a. innocuo.
innovation /,ɪnəˈveiʃən/ n. innovación f.
innuendo /,ɪnyuˈendou/ n. insinuación f.
innumerable /ɪˈnumərəbəl/ a. innumerable.
inoculate /ɪˈnɒkyə,leit/ v. inocular.
inoculation /ɪ,nɒkyəˈleiʃən/ n. inoculación f.
input /ˈɪn,put/ n. aducto m., ingreso m., entrada f.
inquest /ˈɪnkwest/ n. indagación f.
inquire /ɪnˈkwaiᵊr/ v. preguntar; inquirir.
inquiry /ɪnˈkwaiᵊri/ n. pregunta; investigación f.
inquisition /,ɪnkwəˈzɪʃən/ n. escudriñamiento m.; (church) Inquisición f.
insane /ɪnˈsein/ a. loco. **to go i.,** perder la razón; volverse loco.

insanity /ɪnˈsæniti/ n. locura f., demencia f.
inscribe /ɪnˈskraib/ v. inscribir.
inscription /ɪnˈskrɪpʃən/ n. inscripción; dedicatoria f.
insect /ˈɪnsekt/ n. insecto m.
insecticide /ɪnˈsektə,said/ n. & a. insecticida m.
inseparable /ɪnˈsepərəbəl/ a. inseparable.
insert /ɪnˈsɜrt/ v. insertar, meter.
insertion /ɪnˈsɜrʃən/ n. inserción f.
inside /ɪnˈsaid/ a. & n. **1.** interior m. —adv. **2.** adentro, por dentro. **i. out,** al revés. —prep. **3.** dentro de.
insidious /ɪnˈsɪdiəs/ a. insidioso.
insight /ˈɪn,sait/ n. perspicacia f.; comprensión f.
insignia /ɪnˈsɪɡniə/ n. insignias f.pl.
insignificance /,ɪnsɪɡˈnɪfɪkəns/ n. insignificancia f.
insignificant /,ɪnsɪɡˈnɪfɪkənt/ a. insignificante.
insinuate /ɪnˈsɪnyu,eit/ v. insinuar.
insinuation /ɪn,sɪnyuˈeiʃən/ n. insinuación f.
insipid /ɪnˈsɪpɪd/ a. insípido.
insist /ɪnˈsɪst/ v. insistir.
insistence /ɪnˈsɪstəns/ n. insistencia f.
insistent /ɪnˈsɪstənt/ a. insistente.
insolence /ˈɪnsələns/ n. insolencia f.
insolent /ˈɪnsələnt/ a. insolente.
insomnia /ɪnˈsɒmniə/ n. insomnio m.
inspect /ɪnˈspekt/ v. inspeccionar, examinar.
inspection /ɪnˈspekʃən/ n. inspección f.
inspector /ɪnˈspektər/ n. inspector -ora.
inspiration /,ɪnspəˈreiʃən/ n. inspiración f.
inspire /ɪnˈspaiᵊr/ v. inspirar.
install /ɪnˈstɔl/ v. instalar.
installation /,ɪnstəˈleiʃən/ n. instalación f.
installment /ɪnˈstɔlmənt/ n. plazo m.
instance /ˈɪnstəns/ n. ocasión f. **for i.,** por ejemplo.
instant /ˈɪnstənt/ a. & n. instante m.
instantaneous /,ɪnstənˈteiniəs/ a. instantáneo.
instant coffee café soluble m.
instantly /ˈɪnstəntli/ adv. al instante.
instead /ɪnˈsted/ adv. en lugar de eso. **i. of,** en vez de, en lugar de.
instigate /ˈɪnstɪ,geit/ v. instigar.
instill /ɪnˈstɪl/ v. instilar.
instinct /ˈɪnstɪŋkt/ n. instinto m. **by i.,** por instinto.
instinctive /ɪnˈstɪŋktɪv/ a. instintivo.
instinctively /ɪnˈstɪŋktɪvli/ adv. por instinto.
institute /ˈɪnstɪ,tut/ n. **1.** instituto m. —v. **2.** instituir.
institution /,ɪnstɪˈtuʃən/ n. institución f.
instruct /ɪnˈstrʌkt/ v. instruir.

instruction /ɪnˈstrʌkʃən/ n. instrucción f.

instructive /ɪnˈstrʌktɪv/ a. instructivo.

instructor /ɪnˈstrʌktər/ n. instructor -ora.

instrument /ˈɪnstrəmənt/ n. instrumento m.

instrumental /ˌɪnstrəˈmentl/ a. instrumental.

insufficient /ˌɪnsəˈfɪʃənt/ a. insuficiente.

insular /ˈɪnsələr/ a. insular; estrecho de miras.

insulate /ˈɪnsəˌleɪt/ v. aislar.

insulation /ˌɪnsəˈleɪʃən/ n. aislamiento m.

insulator /ˈɪnsəˌleɪtər/ n. aislador m.

insulin /ˈɪnsəlɪn/ n. insulina f.

insult /n. ˈɪnsʌlt; v. ɪnˈsʌlt/ n. **1.** insulto m. —v. **2.** insultar.

insuperable /ɪnˈsupərəbəl/ a. insuperable.

insurance /ɪnˈʃʊrəns/ n. seguro m.

insure /ɪnˈʃʊr, -ˈʃɜr/ v. asegurar.

insurgent /ɪnˈsɜrdʒənt/ a. & n. insurgente m. & f.

insurrection /ˌɪnsəˈrekʃən/ n. insurrección f.

intact /ɪnˈtækt/ a. intacto.

intangible /ɪnˈtændʒəbəl/ a. intangible, impalpable.

integral /ˈɪntɪɡrəl/ a. íntegro.

integrate /ˈɪntɪˌɡreɪt/ v. integrar.

integrity /ɪnˈtɛɡrɪti/ n. integridad f.

intellect /ˈɪntlˌɛkt/ n. intelecto m.

intellectual /ˌɪntlˈɛktʃuəl/ a. & n. intelectual m. & f.

intelligence /ɪnˈtɛlɪdʒəns/ n. inteligencia f.

intelligence quotient /ˈkwoʊʃənt/ coeficiente intelectual m.

intelligent /ɪnˈtɛlɪdʒənt/ a. inteligente.

intelligible /ɪnˈtɛlɪdʒəbəl/ a. inteligible.

intend /ɪnˈtɛnd/ v. pensar; intentar; destinar.

intense /ɪnˈtɛns/ a. intenso.

intensify /ɪnˈtɛnsəˌfaɪ/ v. intensificar.

intensity /ɪnˈtɛnsɪti/ n. intensidad f.

intensive /ɪnˈtɛnsɪv/ a. intensivo.

intensive-care unit /ɪnˈtɛnsɪvˈkɛər/ unidad de cuidados intensivos, unidad de vigilancia intensiva f.

intent /ɪnˈtɛnt/ n. intento m.

intention /ɪnˈtɛnʃən/ n. intención f.

intentional /ɪnˈtɛnʃənl/ a. intencional.

intercede /ˌɪntərˈsid/ v. interceder.

intercept /ˌɪntərˈsɛpt/ v. interceptar; detener.

interchange /ˌɪntərˈtʃeɪndʒ/ v. intercambiar.

interchangeable /ˌɪntərˈtʃeɪndʒəbəl/ a. intercambiable.

intercourse /ˈɪntərˌkɔrs/ n. tráfico m.; comunicación f.; coito m.

interest /ˈɪntərɪst/ n. **1.** interés m. —v. **2.** interesar.

interesting /ˈɪntərəstɪŋ/ a. interesante.

interest rate n. tipo de interés m.

interface /ˈɪntərˌfeɪs/ n. interfaz.

interfere /ˌɪntərˈfɪər/ v. entrometerse, intervenir. i. **with,** estorbar.

interference /ˌɪntərˈfɪərəns/ n. intervención f.; obstáculo m.

interior /ɪnˈtɪəriər/ a. interior.

interject /ˌɪntərˈdʒɛkt/ v. interponer; intervenir.

interjection /ˌɪntərˈdʒɛkʃən/ n. interjección f.; interposición f.

interlude /ˈɪntərˌlud/ n. intervalo m.; Theat. intermedio m.; (music) interludio m.

intermediary /ˌɪntərˈmidiˌɛri/ n. intermediario -ria.

intermediate /ˌɪntərˈmidiˌeɪt/ a. intermedio.

interment /ɪnˈtɜrmənt/ n. entierro m.

intermission /ˌɪntərˈmɪʃən/ n. intermisión f.; Theat. entreacto m.

intermittent /ˌɪntərˈmɪtn̩t/ a. intermitente.

intern /ɪnˈtɜrn/ n. **1.** interno -na, internado -da. —v. **2.** internar.

internal /ɪnˈtɜrnl/ a. interno.

international /ˌɪntərˈnæʃənl/ a. internacional.

internationalism /ˌɪntərˈnæʃənlˌɪzəm/ n. internacionalismo m.

Internet, the /ˈɪntərˌnɛt/ n. el Internet m.

interpose /ˌɪntərˈpoʊz/ v. interponer.

interpret /ɪnˈtɜrprɪt/ v. interpretar.

interpretation /ɪnˌtɜrprɪˈteɪʃən/ n. interpretación f.

interpreter /ɪnˈtɜrprɪtər/ n. intérprete m. & f.

interrogate /ɪnˈtɛrəˌɡeɪt/ v. interrogar.

interrogation /ɪnˌtɛrəˈɡeɪʃən/ n. interrogación; pregunta f.

interrogative /ˌɪntəˈrɒɡətɪv/ a. interrogativo.

interrupt /ˌɪntəˈrʌpt/ v. interrumpir.

interruption /ˌɪntəˈrʌpʃən/ n. interrupción f.

intersect /ˌɪntərˈsɛkt/ v. cortar.

intersection /ˌɪntərˈsɛkʃən/ n. intersección f.; (street) bocacalle f.

intersperse /ˌɪntərˈspɜrs/ v. entremezclar.

interval /ˈɪntərvəl/ n. intervalo m.

intervene /ˌɪntərˈvin/ v. intervenir.

intervention /ˌɪntərˈvɛnʃən/ n. intervención f.

interview /ˈɪntərˌvyu/ n. **1.** entrevista f. —v. **2.** entrevistar.

interviewer /ˈɪntərˌvyuər/ n. entrevistador -ora m. & f.

intestine /ɪnˈtɛstɪn/ n. intestino m.

intimacy /ˈɪntəməsi/ n. intimidad; familiaridad f.

intimate /ˈɪntəmɪt/ a. **1.** íntimo, familiar.

—*n.* **2.** amigo -ga íntimo -ma. —*v.* **3.** insinuar.

intimidate /ɪn'tɪmɪ,deɪt/ *v.* intimidar.

intimidation /ɪn,tɪmɪ'deɪʃən/ *n.* intimidación *f.*

into /'ɪntu; *unstressed* -tʊ, -tə/ *prep.* en, dentro de.

intonation /,ɪntou'neɪʃən/ *n.* entonación *f.*

intone /ɪn'toun/ *v.* entonar.

intoxicate /ɪn'tɒksɪ,keɪt/ *v.* embriagar.

intoxication /ɪn,tɒksɪ'keɪʃən/ *n.* embriaguez *f.*

intravenous /,ɪntrə'vinəs/ *a.* intravenoso.

intrepid /ɪn'trɛpɪd/ *a.* intrépido.

intricacy /'ɪntrɪkəsi/ *n.* complejidad *f.*; enredo *m.*

intricate /'ɪntrɪkɪt/ *a.* intrincado; complejo.

intrigue /ɪn'trig; *n. also* 'ɪntrig/ *n.* **1.** intriga *f.* —*v.* **2.** intrigar.

intrinsic /ɪn'trɪnsɪk/ *a.* intrínseco.

introduce /,ɪntrə'dus/ *v.* introducir; (a person) presentar.

introduction /,ɪntrə'dʌkʃən/ *n.* presentación; introducción *f.*

introductory /,ɪntrə'dʌktəri/ *a.* introductor; preliminar. **i. offer,** ofrecimiento de presentación *m.*

introvert /'ɪntrə,vɜrt/ *n. & a.* introvertido -da.

intrude /ɪn'trud/ *v.* entremeterse.

intruder /ɪn'trudər/ *n.* intruso -sa.

intuition /,ɪntu'ɪʃən/ *n.* intuición *f.*

intuitive /ɪn'tuɪtɪv/ *a.* intuitivo.

inundate /'ɪnən,deɪt/ *v.* inundar.

invade /ɪn'veɪd/ *v.* invadir.

invader /ɪn'veɪdər/ *n.* invasor -ra.

invalid /ɪn'vælɪd/ *a. & n.* inválido -da.

invariable /ɪn'vɛəriəbəl/ *a.* invariable.

invasion /ɪn'veɪʒən/ *n.* invasión *f.*

invective /ɪn'vɛktɪv/ *n.* **1.** invectiva *f.* —*a.* **2.** ultrajante.

inveigle /ɪn'veɪgəl/ *v.* seducir.

invent /ɪn'vɛnt/ *v.* inventar.

invention /ɪn'vɛnʃən/ *n.* invención *f.*

inventive /ɪn'vɛntɪv/ *a.* inventivo.

inventor /ɪn'vɛntər/ *n.* inventor -ra.

inventory /'ɪnvən,tɔri/ *n.* inventario *m.*

invertebrate /ɪn'vɜrtəbrɪt/ *n. & a.* invertebrado *m.*

invest /ɪn'vɛst/ *v.* investir; *Com.* invertir.

investigate /ɪn'vɛstɪ,geɪt/ *v.* investigar.

investigation /ɪn,vɛstɪ'geɪʃən/ *n.* investigación *f.*

investment /ɪn'vɛstmənt/ *n.* inversión *f.*

investor /ɪn'vɛstər/ *n.* inversor, -ra.

inveterate /ɪn'vɛtərɪt/ *a.* inveterado.

invidious /ɪn'vɪdiəs/ *a.* abominable, odioso, injusto.

invigorate /ɪn'vɪgə,reɪt/ *v.* vigorizar, fortificar.

invincible /ɪn'vɪnsəbəl/ *a.* invencible.

invisible /ɪn'vɪzəbəl/ *a.* invisible.

invitation /,ɪnvɪ'teɪʃən/ *n.* invitación *f.*

invite /ɪn'vaɪt/ *v.* invitar, convidar.

invocation /,ɪnvə'keɪʃən/ *n.* invocación *f.*

invoice /'ɪnvɔɪs/ *n.* factura *f.*

invoke /ɪn'vouk/ *v.* invocar.

involuntary /ɪn'vɒlən,tɛri/ *a.* involuntario.

involve /ɪn'vɒlv/ *v.* envolver; implicar.

involved /ɪn'vɒlvd/ *a.* complicado.

invulnerable /ɪn'vʌlnərəbəl/ *a.* invulnerable.

inward /'ɪnwərd/ *adv.* hacia adentro.

inwardly /'ɪnwərdli/ *adv.* interiormente.

iodine /'aiə,daɪn/ *n.* iodo *m.*

IQ *abbr.* CI (coeficiente intelectual) *m.*

irate /aɪ'reɪt/ *a.* encolerizado.

Ireland /'aiᵊrlənd/ *n.* Irlanda *f.*

iris /'aɪrɪs/ *n. Anat.* iris *m.*; (botany) flor de lis *f.*

Irish /'aɪrɪʃ/ *a.* irlandés.

irk /ɜrk/ *v.* fastidiar.

iron /'aɪərn/ *n.* **1.** hierro *m.*; (appliance) plancha *f.* —*v.* **2.** planchar.

ironical /aɪ'rɒnɪkəl/ *a.* irónico.

ironing board /'aiərnɪŋ/ tabla de planchar *f.*

irony /'aɪrəni/ *n.* ironía *f.*

irrational /ɪ'ræʃənl/ *a.* irracional; ilógico.

irregular /ɪ'rɛgyələr/ *a.* irregular.

irregularity /ɪ,rɛgyə'lærɪti/ *n.* irregularidad *f.*

irrelevant /ɪ'rɛləvənt/ *a.* ajeno.

irresistible /,ɪrɪ'zɪstəbəl/ *a.* irresistible.

irresponsible /,ɪrɪ'spɒnsəbəl/ *a.* irresponsable.

irreverent /ɪ'rɛvərənt/ *a.* irreverente.

irrevocable /ɪ'rɛvəkəbəl/ *a.* irrevocable.

irrigate /'ɪrɪ,geɪt/ *v.* regar; *Med.* irrigar.

irrigation /,ɪrɪ'geɪʃən/ *n.* riego *m.*

irritability /,ɪrɪtə'bɪlɪti/ *n.* irritabilidad *f.*

irritable /'ɪrɪtəbəl/ *a.* irritable.

irritant /'ɪrɪtənt/ *n. & a.* irritante *m.*

irritate /'ɪrɪ,teɪt/ *v.* irritar.

irritation /,ɪrɪ'teɪʃən/ *n.* irritación *f.*

island /'aɪlənd/ *n.* isla *f.*

isolate /'aisə,leɪt/ *v.* aislar.

isolation /,aisə'leɪʃən/ *n.* aislamiento *m.*

isosceles /aɪ'sɒsə,liz/ *a.* isósceles.

issuance /'ɪʃuəns/ *n.* emisión *f.*; publicación *f.*

issue /'ɪʃu/ *n.* **1.** emisión; edición; progenie *f.*; número *m.*; punto en disputa. —*v.* **2.** emitir; publicar.

isthmus /'ɪsməs/ *n.* istmo *m.*

it /ɪt/ *pron.* ello; él, ella; lo, la.

Italian /ɪ'tælyən/ *a. & n.* italiano -na.

Italy /'ɪtli/ *n.* Italia *f.*

itch /ɪtʃ/ *n.* **1.** picazón *f.* —*v.* **2.** picar.

item /'aitəm/ n. artículo; detalle m.; inserción f.; Com. renglón m.

itemize /'aitə,maiz/ v. detallar.

itinerant /ai'tinərənt/ n. **1.** viandante m. —a. **2.** ambulante.

itinerary /ai'tinə'reri/ n. itinerario m.

its /its/ a. su.

itself /it'self/ pron. sí; se.

ivory /'aivəri/ n. marfil m.

ivy /'aivi/ n. hiedra f.

J

jab /dʒæb/ n. **1.** pinchazo m. —v. **2.** pinchar.

jack /dʒæk/ n. (for lifting) gato m.; (cards) sota f.

jackal /'dʒækəl/ n. chacal m.

jackass /'dʒæk,æs/ n. asno m.

jacket /'dʒækit/ n. chaqueta f.; saco m.

jack-of-all-trades /'dʒæk əv 'ɔl 'treidz/ n. estuche f.

jade /dʒeid/ n. (horse) rocín m.; (woman) picarona f.; (mineral) jade m.

jaded /'dʒeidid/ a. rendido.

jagged /'dʒægid/ a. mellado.

jaguar /'dʒægwur/ n. jaguar m.

jail /dʒeil/ n. cárcel f.

jailer /'dʒeilər/ n. carcelero m.

jam /dʒæm/ n. **1.** conserva f.; aprieto, apretón m. —v. **2.** apiñar, apretar; trabar.

janitor /'dʒænitər/ n. portero m.

January /'dʒænyu,eri/ n. enero m.

Japan /dʒə'pæn/ n. Japón m.

Japanese /,dʒæpə'niz/ a. & n. japonés -esa.

jar /dʒur/ n. **1.** jarro m. —v. **2.** chocar; agitar.

jargon /'dʒurgən/ n. jerga f.

jasmine /'dʒæzmin/ n. jazmín m.

jaundice /'dʒɔndis/ n. ictericia f.

jaunt /dʒɔnt/ n. paseo m.

javelin /'dʒævlin/ n. jabalina f.

jaw /dʒɔ/ n. quijada f.

jay /dʒei/ n. grajo m.

jazz /dʒæz/ n. jazz m.

jealous /'dʒɛləs/ a. celoso. **to be j.**, tener celos.

jealousy /'dʒɛləsi/ n. celos m.pl.

jeans /dʒinz/ n. vaqueros, tejanos m pl.

jeer /dʒiər/ n. **1.** burla f., mofa f. —v. **2.** burlar, mofar.

jelly /'dʒɛli/ n. jalea f.

jellyfish /'dʒɛli,fiʃ/ n. aguamar m.

jeopardize /'dʒɛpər,daiz/ v. arriesgar.

jeopardy /'dʒɛpərdi/ n. riesgo m.

jerk /dʒɜrk/ n. **1.** sacudida f. —v. **2.** sacudir.

jerky /'dʒɜrki/ a. espasmódico.

Jerusalem /dʒɪ'rusələm/ n. Jerusalén m.

jest /dʒɛst/ n. **1.** broma f. —v. **2.** bromear.

jester /'dʒɛstər/ n. bufón -ona; burlón -ona.

Jesuit /'dʒɛʒuit/ a. & n. jesuíta m.

Jesus Christ /'dʒizəs 'kraist/ n. Jesucristo m.

jet /dʒɛt/ n. chorro m.; (gas) mechero m.

jet lag n. defase horario m., inadaptación horaria f.

jetsam /'dʒɛtsəm/ n. echazón f.

jettison /'dʒɛtəsən/ v. echar al mar.

jetty /'dʒɛti/ n. muelle m.

Jew /dʒu/ n. judío -día.

jewel /'dʒuəl/ n. joya f.

jeweler /'dʒuələr/ n. joyero -ra.

jewelry /'dʒuəlri/ n. joyas f.pl. **j. store**, joyería f.

Jewish /'dʒuiʃ/ a. judío.

jib /dʒib/ n. Naut. foque m.

jiffy /'dʒifi/ n. instante m.

jig /dʒig/ n. jiga f. **j-saw**, sierra de vaivén f.

jilt /dʒilt/ v. dar calabazas.

jingle /'dʒingəl/ n. **1.** retintín m.; rima pueril f. —v. **2.** retiñir.

jinx /dʒiŋks/ n. **1.** aojo m. —v. **2.** aojar.

jittery /'dʒitəri/ a. nervioso.

job /dʒɒb/ n. empleo m.

jobber /'dʒɒbər/ n. destajista m. & f., corredor m.

jockey /'dʒɒki/ n. jockey m.

jocular /'dʒɒkyələr/ a. jocoso.

jog /dʒɒg/ n. empujoncito m. v. empujar; estimular. **j. along**, ir a un trote corto.

join /dʒɔin/ v. juntar; unir.

joiner /'dʒɔinər/ n. ebanista m.

joint /dʒɔint/ n. juntura f.

jointly /'dʒɔintli/ adv. conjuntamente.

joke /dʒouk/ n. **1.** broma, chanza f.; chiste m. —v. **2.** bromear.

joker /'dʒoukər/ n. bromista m. & f.; comodín m.

jolly /'dʒɒli/ a. alegre, jovial.

jolt /dʒoult/ n. **1.** sacudido m. —v. **2.** sacudir.

jonquil /'dʒɒŋkwil/ n. junquillo m.

jostle /'dʒɒsəl/ v. empujar.

journal /'dʒɜrnl/ n. diario m.; revista f.

journalism /'dʒɜrnl,izəm/ n. periodismo m.

journalist /'dʒɜrnlist/ n. periodista m. & f.

journey /'dʒɜrni/ n. **1.** viaje m.; jornada f. —v. **2.** viajar.

journeyman /'dʒɜrnimən/ n. jornalero m., oficial m.

jovial /'dʒouviəl/ *a.* jovial.

jowl /dʒaul/ *n.* carrillo *m.*

joy /dʒɔi/ *n.* alegría *f.*

joyful /'dʒɔifəl/ **joyous** *a.* alegre, gozoso.

jubilant /'dʒubələnt/ *a.* jubiloso.

jubilee /'dʒubə,li/ *n.* jubileo *m.*

Judaism /'dʒudi,ɪzəm/ *n.* judaísmo *m.*

judge /dʒʌdʒ/ *n.* **1.** juez *m.* & *f.* —*v.* **2.** juzgar.

judgment /'dʒʌdʒmənt/ *n.* juicio *m.*

judicial /dʒu'dɪʃəl/ *a.* judicial.

judiciary /dʒu'dɪʃi,cri/ *a.* judiciario.

judicious /dʒu'dɪʃəs/ *a.* juicioso.

jug /dʒʌg/ *n.* jarro *m.*

juggle /'dʒʌgəl/ *v.* escamotear.

juice /dʒus/ *n.* jugo, zumo *m.*

juicy /'dʒusi/ *a.* jugoso.

July /dʒu'lai/ *n.* julio *m.*

jumble /'dʒʌmbəl/ *n.* **1.** revoltillo *m.* —*v.* **2.** arrebujar, revolver.

jump /dʒʌmp/ *n.* **1.** salto *m.* —*v.* **2.** saltar, brincar.

junction /'dʒʌŋkʃən/ *n.* confluencia *f.*; (railway) empalme *m.*

juncture /'dʒʌŋktʃər/ *n.* juntura *f.*; coyuntura *f.*

June /dʒun/ *n.* junio *m.*

jungle /'dʒʌŋgəl/ *n.* jungla, selva *f.*

junior /'dʒunyər/ *a.* menor; más joven. **Jr.**, hijo.

juniper /'dʒunəpər/ *n.* enebro *m.*

junk /dʒʌŋk/ *n.* basura *f.*

junket /'dʒʌŋkɪt/ *n.* **1.** leche cuajada *f.* —*v.* **2.** festejar.

junkie /'dʒʌŋki/ *n. Colloq.* yonqui *m.* & *f.*, toxicómano -na.

junk mail *n.* porpaganda indeseada *f.*, correo basura *m.*

jurisdiction /,dʒurɪs'dɪkʃən/ *n.* jurisdicción *f.*

jurisprudence /,dʒurɪs'prudns/ *n.* jurisprudencia *f.*

jurist /'dʒurɪst/ *n.* jurista *m.* & *f.*

juror /'dʒurər/ *n.* jurado -da.

jury /'dʒuri/ *n.* jurado *m.*

just /dʒʌst/ *a.* **1.** justo; exacto. —*adv.* **2.** exactamente; (only) sólo. **j. now**, ahora mismo. **to have j.**, acabar de.

justice /'dʒʌstɪs/ *n.* justicia *f.*; (person) juez *m.* & *f.*

justifiable /'dʒʌstə,faiəbəl/ *a.* justificable.

justification /,dʒʌstəfi'keiʃən/ *n.* justificación *f.*

justify /'dʒʌstə,fai/ *v.* justificar.

jut /dʒʌt/ *v.* sobresalir.

jute /dʒut/ *n.* yute *m.*

juvenile /'dʒuvənl/ *a.* juvenil.

juvenile delinquency delincuencia de menores, delincuencia juvenil *f.*

K

kaleidoscope /kə'laidə,skoup/ *n.* calidoscopio *m.*

kangaroo /,kæŋgə'ru/ *n.* canguro *m.*

karakul /'kærəkəl/ *n.* caracul *m.*

karat /'kærət/ *n.* quilate *m.*

karate /kə'rɑti/ *n.* karate *m.*

keel /kil/ *n.* **1.** quilla *f.* —*v.* **2. to k. over**, volcarse.

keen /kin/ *a.* agudo; penetrante.

keep /kip/ *v.* mantener, retener; guardar; preservar. **k. on**, seguir, continuar.

keeper /'kipər/ *n.* guardián *m.*

keepsake /'kip,seik/ *n.* recuerdo *m.*

keg /keg/ *n.* barrilito *m.*

kennel /'kɛnl/ *n.* perrera *f.*

kerchief /'kɔrtʃif/ *n.* pañuelo *m.*

kernel /'kɔrnl/ *n.* pepita *f.*; grano *m.*

kerosene /'kɛrə,sin/ *n.* kerosén *m.*

ketchup /'kɛtʃəp/ *n.* salsa de tomate *f.*

kettle /'kɛtl/ *n.* caldera, olla *f.*

kettledrum /'kɛtl,drʌm/ *n.* tímpano *m.*

key /ki/ *n.* llave *f.*; (music) clave *f.*; (piano) tecla *f.*

keyboard /'ki,bɔrd/ *n.* teclado *m.*

keyhole /'ki,houl/ *n.* bocallave *f.*

keypad /'ki,pæd/ *n.* teclado *m.*

khaki /'kæki/ *a.* caqui.

kick /kɪk/ *n.* **1.** patada *f.* —*v.* **2.** patear; *Colloq.* quejarse.

kid /kɪd/ *n.* **1.** cabrito *m.*; *Colloq.* niño -ña, chico -ca. —*v.* **2.** *Colloq.* bromear.

kidnap /'kɪdnæp/ *v.* secuestrar.

kidnaper /'kɪdnæpər/ *n.* secuestrador -ora.

kidnaping /'kɪdnæpɪŋ/ *n.* rapto, secuestro *m.*

kidney /'kɪdni/ *n.* riñón *m.*

kidney bean *n.* frijol *m.*

kill /kɪl/ *v.* matar.

killer /'kɪlər/ *n.* matador -ora.

killjoy /'kɪldʒɔi/ *n.* aguafiestas *m.* & *f.*

kiln /kɪl/ *n.* horno *m.*

kilogram /'kɪlə,græm/ *n.* kilogramo *m.*

kilohertz /'kɪlə,hɑrts/ *n.* kilohercio *m.*

kilometer /'kɪlɒmɪtər/ *n.* kilómetro *m.*

kilowatt /'kɪlə,wɒt/ *n.* kilovatio *m.*

kin /kɪn/ *n.* parentesco *m.*; parientes *m.pl.*

kind /kaind/ *a.* **1.** bondadoso, amable. —*n.* **2.** género *m.*; clase *f.* **k. of**, algo, un poco.

kindergarten /'kɪndər,gɑrtn/ n. kindergarten m.

kindle /'kɪndl/ v. encender.

kindling /'kɪndlɪŋ/ n. encendimiento m. **k.-wood**, leña menuda f.

kindly /'kaindlɪ/ a. bondadoso.

kindness /'kaindnɪs/ n. bondad f.

kindred /'kɪndrɪd/ n. parentesco m.

kinetic /kɪ'nɛtɪk/ a. cinético.

king /kɪŋ/ n. rey m.

kingdom /'kɪŋdəm/ n. reino m.

king prawn langostino m.

kink /kɪŋk/ n. retorcimiento m.

kinky /'kɪŋkɪ/ a. Colloq. pervertidillo; (hair) rizado.

kiosk /'kinsk/ n. kiosco m.

kiss /kɪs/ n. 1. beso m. —v. 2. besar.

kitchen /'kɪtʃən/ n. cocina f.

kite /kait/ n. cometa f.

kitten /'kɪtn/ n. gatito -ta.

kleptomania /,klɛptə'meiniə/ n. cleptomanía f.

kleptomaniac /,klɛptə'meiniæk/ n. cleptómano -na.

klutz /klʌts/ n. Colloq. torpe, patoso -sa.

knack /næk/ n. don m., destreza f.

knapsack /'næp,sæk/ n. alforja f.

knead /nid/ v. amasar.

knee /ni/ n. rodilla f.

kneecap /'ni,kæp/ n. rodillera, rótula f.

kneel /nil/ v. arrodillarse.

knickers /'nikərz/ n. calzón corto m., pantalones m.pl.

knife /naif/ n. cuchillo m.

knight /nait/ n. caballero m.; (chess) caballo m.

knit /nɪt/ v. tejer.

knob /nɒb/ n. tirador m.

knock /nɒk/ n. 1. golpe m.; llamada f. —v. 2. golpear; tocar, llamar.

knot /nɒt/ n. 1. nudo; lazo m. —v. 2. anudar.

knotty /'nɒtɪ/ a. nudoso.

know /nou/ v. saber: (a person) conocer.

knowledge /'nɒlɪdʒ/ n. conocimiento, saber m.

knuckle /'nʌkəl/ n. nudillo m. **k. bone**, jarrete m. **to k. under**, ceder a.

Koran /kə'run/ n. Corán m.

Korea /kə'riə/ n. Corea f.

Korean /kə'riən/ a. & n. coreano.

L

---

label /'leibəl/ n. 1. rótulo m. —v. 2. rotular; designar.

labor /'leibər/ n. 1. trabajo m ; la clase obrera. —v. 2. trabajar.

laboratory /'læbrə,tɔri/ n. laboratorio m.

laborer /'leibərər/ n. trabajador, obrero m.

laborious /lə'bɔriəs/ a. laborioso, difícil.

labor union gremio obrero, sindicato m.

labyrinth /'læbərɪnθ/ n. laberinto m.

lace /leis/ n. 1. encaje m.; (of shoe) lazo m. —v. 2. amarrar.

lacerate /'læsə,reit/ v. lacerar, lastimar.

laceration /,læsə'reiʃən/ n. laceración f., desgarro m.

lack /læk/ n. 1. falta f. **l. of respect**, desacato m. —v. 2. faltar, carecer.

lackadaisical /,lækə'deizɪkəl/ a. indiferente; soñador.

laconic /lə'kɒnɪk/ a. lacónico.

lacquer /'lækər/ n. 1. laca f., barniz m. —v. 2. laquear, barnizar.

lactic /'læktɪk/ a. láctico.

lactose /'læktous/ n. lactosa f.

ladder /'lædər/ n. escalera f.

ladle /'leidl/ n. 1. cucharón m. —v. 2. servir con cucharón.

lady /'leidɪ/ n. señora, dama f.

ladybug /'leidɪ,bʌg/ n. mariquita f.

lag /læg/ n. 1. retraso m. —v. 2. quedarse atrás.

lagoon /lə'gun/ n. laguna f.

laid-back /'leid 'bæk/ a. de buen talante, ecuánime, pacífico.

laity /'leiti/ n. laicado m.

lake /leik/ n. lago m.

lamb /læm/ n. cordero m.

lame /leim/ a. 1. cojo; estropeado. —v. 2. estropear, lisiar; incapacitar.

lament /lə'mɛnt/ n. 1. lamento m. —v. 2. lamentar.

lamentable /lə'mɛntəbəl/ a. lamentable.

lamentation /,læmən'teiʃən/ n. lamento m.; lamentación f.

laminate /'læmə,neit/ a. laminado. v. laminar.

lamp /læmp/ n. lámpara f.

lampoon /læm'pun/ n. 1. pasquín m. —v. 2. pasquinar.

lance /læns/ n. 1. lanza f. —v. 2. Med. abrir.

land /lænd/ n. 1. país m.; tierra f. **native l.**, patria f. —v. 2. desembarcar; (plane) aterrizar.

landholder /'lænd,houldər/ n. hacendado -da.

landing /'lændɪŋ/ n. (of stairs) descanso,

descansillo *m.*; (ship) desembarcadero *m.*; (airplane) aterrizaje *m.*

landlady /'lænd,leidi/ **landlord** *n.* propietario -ria.

landmark /'lænd,mɑrk/ *n.* mojón *m.*, señal *f.*; rasgo sobresaliente *m.*

landscape /'lænd,skeip/ *n.* paisaje *m.*

landslide /'lænd,slaid/ *n.* derrumbe *m.*

lane /lein/ *n.* senda *f.*

language /'læŋgwɪdʒ/ *n.* lengua *f.*, idioma; lenguaje *m.*

languid /'læŋgwɪd/ *a.* lánguido.

languish /'læŋgwɪʃ/ *v.* languidecer.

languor /'læŋgər/ *n.* languidez *f.*

lanky /'læŋki/ *a.* larguirucho; desgarbado.

lanolin /'lænlɪn/ *n.* lanolina *f.*

lantern /'læntərn/ *n.* linterna *f.*; farol *m.*

lap /læp/ *n.* **1.** regazo *m.*; falda *f.* —*v.* **2.** lamer.

lapel /lə'pɛl/ *n.* solapa *f.*

lapse /læps/ *n.* **1.** lapso *m.* —*v.* **2.** pasar; decaer; caer en error.

laptop computer /'læp,tɒp/ ordenador portátil *m.*

larceny /'lɑrsəni/ *n.* ratería *f.*

lard /lɑrd/ *n.* manteca de cerdo *f.*

large /lɑrdʒ/ *a.* grande.

largely /'lɑrdʒli/ *adv.* ampliamente; mayormente; muy.

largo /'lɑrgou/ *n. & a. Mus.* largo *m.*

lariat /'læriət/ *n.* lazo *m.*

lark /lɑrk/ *n.* (bird) alondra *f.*

larva /'lɑrvə/ *n.* larva *f.*

laryngitis /,lærən'dʒaitis/ *n.* laringitis *f.*

larynx /'læriŋks/ *n.* laringe *f.*

lascivious /lə'sɪviəs/ *a.* lascivo.

laser /'leizər/ *n.* láser *m.*

lash /læʃ/ *n.* **1.** azote, latigazo *m.* —*v.* **2.** azotar.

lass /læs/ *n.* doncella *f.*

lassitude /'læsɪ,tud/ *n.* lasitud *f.*

lasso /'læsou/ *n.* **1.** lazo *m.* —*v.* **2.** enlazar.

last /læst/ *a.* **1.** pasado; (final) último. **at l.**, por fin. **l. but one**, penúltimo. **l. but two**, antepenúltimo. —*v.* **2.** durar.

lasting /'læstɪŋ/ *a.* duradero.

latch /lætʃ/ *n.* aldaba *f.*

late /leit/ *a.* **1.** tardío; (deceased) difunto. **to be l.**, llegar tarde. —*adv.* **2.** tarde.

lately /'leitli/ *adv.* recientemente.

latent /'leitnt/ *a.* latente.

lateral /'lætərəl/ *a.* lateral.

lather /'læðər/ *n.* **1.** espuma de jabón. —*v.* **2.** enjabonar.

Latin /'lætɪn/ *a.* latín *m.*

Latin America /ə'mɛrikə/ Hispanoamérica, América Latina *f.*

Latin American hispanoamericano -na.

latitude /'læti,tud/ *n.* latitud *f.*

latrine /lə'trin/ *n.* letrina *f.*

latter /'lætər/ *a.* posterior. **the l.**, éste.

lattice /'lætɪs/ *n.* celosía *f.*

laud /lɔd/ *v.* loar.

laudable /'lɔdəbəl/ *a.* laudable.

laudanum /'lɔdnəm/ *n.* láudano *m.*

laudatory /'lɔdə,tɔri/ *a.* laudatorio.

laugh /læf/ *n.* **1.** risa, risotada *f.* —*v.* **2.** reír. **l. at**, reírse de.

laughable /'læfəbəl/ *a.* risible.

laughter /'læftər/ *n.* risa *f.*

launch /lɔntʃ/ *n.* **1.** *Naut.* lancha *f.* —*v.* **2.** lanzar.

launder /'lɔndər/ *v.* lavar y planchar la ropa.

laundry /'lɔndri/ *n.* lavandería *f.*

laundryman /'lɔndri,mæn/ *n.* lavandero -ra.

laureate /'lɔriit/ *n. & a.* laureado -da.

laurel /'lɔrəl/ *n.* laurel *m.*

lava /'lɑvə/ *n.* lava *f.*

lavatory /'lævə,tɔri/ *n.* lavatorio *m.*

lavender /'lævəndər/ *n.* lavándula *f.*

lavish /'lævɪʃ/ *a.* **1.** pródigo. —*v.* **2.** prodigar.

law /lɔ/ *n.* ley *f.*; derecho *m.*

lawful /'lɔfəl/ *a.* legal.

lawless /'lɔlɪs/ *a.* sin ley.

lawn /lɔn/ *n.* césped; prado *m.*

lawn mower /'mouər/ *n.* cortacésped *m. & f.*

lawsuit /'lɔ,sut/ *n.* pleito *m.*

lawyer /'lɔyər/ *n.* abogado *m. & f.*

lax /læks/ *a.* flojo, laxo.

laxative /'læksətɪv/ *n.* purgante *m.*

laxity /'læksɪti/ *n.* laxidad *f.*; flojedad *f.*

lay /lei/ *a.* **1.** secular. —*v.* **2.** poner.

layer /'leiər/ *n.* capa *f.*

layman /'leimən/ *n.* lego, seglar *m.*

lazy /'leizi/ *a.* perezoso.

lead /lɛd , lid/ *n.* **1.** plomo *m.*; *Theat.* papel principal. **to take the l.**, tomar la delantera. —*v.* **2.** conducir; dirigir.

leaden /'lɛdn/ *a.* plomizo; pesado; abatido.

leader /'lidər/ *n.* líder *m. & f.*; jefe *m. & f.*; director -ora.

leadership /'lidər,ʃip/ *n.* dirección *f.*

leaf /lif/ *n.* hoja *f.*

leaflet /'liflɪt/ *n. Bot.* hojilla *f.*; folleto *m.*

league /lig/ *n.* liga; (measure) legua *f.*

leak /lik/ *n.* **1.** escape; goteo *m.* —*v.* **2.** gotear; *Naut.* hacer agua.

leakage /'likɪdʒ/ *n.* goteo *m.*, escape *m.*, pérdida *f.*

leaky /'liki/ *a.* llovedizo, resquebrajado.

lean /lin/ *a.* **1.** flaco, magro. —*v.* **2.** apoyarse, arrimarse.

leap /lip/ *n.* **1.** salto *m.* —*v.* **2.** saltar.

leap year *n.* año bisiesto *m.*

learn /lɜrn/ *v.* aprender; saber.

learned /'lɜrnɪd/ *a.* erudito.

learning /'lərnɪŋ/ n. erudición f., instrucción f.

lease /lis/ n. **1.** arriendo m. —v. **2.** arrendar.

leash /liʃ/ n. **1.** correa f. —v. **2.** atraillar.

least /list/ a. menor; mínimo. **the l.,** lo menos. **at l.,** por lo menos.

leather /'lɛðər/ n. cuero m.

leathery /'lɛðəri/ a. coriáceo.

leave /liv/ n. **1.** licencia f. **to take l.,** despedirse. —v. **2.** dejar; (depart) salir, irse. **l. out,** omitir.

leaven /'lɛvən/ n. **1.** levadura f. —v. **2.** fermentar, imbuir.

lecherous /'lɛtʃərəs/ a. lujurioso.

lecture /'lɛktʃər/ n. conferencia f.

lecturer /'lɛktʃərər/ n. conferencista m. & f.; catedrático -ca.

ledge /lɛdʒ/ n. borde m.; capa f.

ledger /'lɛdʒər/ n. libro mayor m.

lee /li/ n. sotavento m.

leech /litʃ/ n. sanguijuela f.

leek /lik/ n. puerro m.

leer /lɪər/ v. mirar de soslayo.

leeward /'liwərd/ a. sotavento.

left /lɛft/ a. izquierdo. **the l.,** la izquierda. **to be left,** quedarse.

left-handed /'lɛft 'hændɪd/ a. zurdo.

leftist /'lɛftɪst/ n. izquierdista m. & f.

leftovers /'lɛft,ouvərz/ n. sobras f.pl.

leg /lɛg/ n. pierna f.

legacy /'lɛgəsi/ n. legado m., herencia f.

legal /'ligəl/ a. legal.

legalize /'ligə,laiz/ v. legalizar.

legation /lɪ'geiʃən/ n. legación, embajada f.

legend /'lɛdʒənd/ n. leyenda f.

legendary /'lɛdʒən,dɛri/ a. legendario.

legible /'lɛdʒəbəl/ a. legible.

legion /'lidʒən/ n. legión f.

legislate /'lɛdʒɪs,leit/ v. legislar.

legislation /,lɛdʒɪs'leiʃən/ n. legislación f.

legislator /'lɛdʒɪs,leitər/ n. legislador -ra.

legislature /'lɛdʒɪs,leitʃər/ n. legislatura f.

legitimate /lɪ'dʒɪtəmɪt/ a. legítimo.

legume /'lɛgyum/ n. legumbre f.

leisure /'liʒər/ n. desocupación f.; horas libres.

leisurely /'liʒərli/ a. **1.** deliberado. —adv. **2.** despacio.

lemon /'lɛmən/ n. limón m.

lemonade /,lɛmə'neid/ n. limonada f.

lend /lɛnd/ v. prestar.

length /lɛŋkθ/ n. largo m.; duración f.

lengthen /'lɛŋkθən/ v. alargar.

lengthwise /'lɛŋkθ,waiz/ adv. a lo largo.

lengthy /'lɛŋkθi/ a. largo.

lenient /'liniənt/ a. indulgente.

lens /lɛnz/ n. lente m. or f.

Lent /lɛnt/ n. cuaresma f.

Lenten /'lɛntɪn/ a. cuaresmal.

lentil /'lɛntɪl/ n. lenteja f.

leopard /'lɛpərd/ n. leopardo m.

leotard /'liə,tɑrd/ n. mallas f.pl.

leper /'lɛpər/ n. leproso -sa.

leprosy /'lɛprəsi/ n. lepra f.

lesbian /'lɛzbiən/ n. lesbiana f.

lesion /'liʒən/ n. lesión f.

less /lɛs/ a. & adv. menos.

lessen /'lɛsən/ v. disminuir.

lesser /'lɛsər/ a. menor; más pequeño.

lesson /'lɛsən/ n. lección f.

lest /lɛst/ conj. para que no.

let /lɛt/ v. dejar; permitir; arrendar.

letdown /'lɛt,daun/ n. decepción f.

lethal /'liθəl/ a. letal.

lethargic /lə'θɑrdʒɪk/ a. letárgico.

lethargy /'lɛθərdʒi/ n. letargo m.

letter /'lɛtər/ n. carta; (of alphabet) letra f.

letterhead /'lɛtər,hɛd/ n. membrete m.

lettuce /'lɛtɪs/ n. lechuga f.

leukemia /lu'kimiə/ n. leucemia f.

levee /'lɛvi, lɛ'vi/ n. recepción f.

level /'lɛvəl/ a. **1.** llano, nivelado. —n. **2.** nivel m.; llanura f. —v. **3.** allanar; nivelar.

lever /'lɛvər/ n. palanca f.

levity /'lɛvɪti/ n. levedad f.

levy /'lɛvi/ n. **1.** leva f. —v. **2.** imponer.

lewd /lud/ a. lascivo.

lexicon /'lɛksɪ,kɒn/ n. léxico m.

liability /,laiə'bɪlɪti/ n. riesgo m.; obligación f.

liable /'laiəbəl/ a. sujeto; responsable.

liaison /li'eizən/ n. vinculación f., enlace m.; concubinaje m.

liar /'laiər/ n. embustero -ra.

libel /'laibəl/ n. **1.** libelo m. —v. **2.** difamar.

libelous /'laibələs/ a. difamatorio.

liberal /'lɪbərəl/ a. liberal; generoso.

liberalism /'lɪbərə,lɪzəm/ n. liberalismo m.

liberality /,lɪbə'rælɪti/ n. liberalidad f.

liberate /'lɪbə,reit/ v. libertar.

liberty /'lɪbərti/ n. libertad f.

libidinous /lɪ'bɪdnəs/ a. libidinoso.

librarian /lai'brɛəriən/ n. bibliotecario -ria.

library /'lai,brɛri/ n. biblioteca f.

libretto /lɪ'brɛtou/ n. libreto m.

license /'laisəns/ n. licencia f.; permiso m.

licentious /lai'sɛnʃəs/ a. licencioso.

lick /lɪk/ v. lamer.

licorice /'lɪkərɪʃ, 'lɪkrɪʃ, 'lɪkərɪs/ n. regaliz m.

lid /lɪd/ n. tapa f.

lie /lai/ n. **1.** mentira f. —v. **2.** mentir. **l. down,** acostarse, echarse.

lieutenant /lu'tɛnənt/ n. teniente m

life /laif/ n. vida f.

lifeboat /'laif,bout/ n. bote salvavidas m.

life buoy boya f.

lifeguard /'laif,gɑrd/ n. socorrista m. & f.

life insurance seguro de vida *m*.
life jacket chaleco salvavidas *m*.
lifeless /'laiflıs/ *a*. sin vida.
life preserver /prı'zɜrvər/ salvavidas *m*.
lifestyle /'laifstail/ *n*. modo de vida *m*.
lift /lıft/ *v*. levantar, alzar, elevar.
ligament /'lıgəmənt/ *n*. ligamento *m*.
ligature /'lıgətʃər/ *n*. ligadura *f*.
light /lait/ *a*. **1.** ligero; liviano; (in color) claro. —*n*. **2.** luz; candela *f*. —*v*. **3.** encender; iluminar.
light bulb bombilla *f*.
lighten /'laitn/ *v*. aligerar; aclarar; iluminar.
lighter /'laitər/ *n*. encendedor *m*.
lighthouse /'lait,haus/ *n*. faro *m*.
lightness /'laitnıs/ *n*. ligereza; agilidad *f*.
lightning /'laitnıŋ/ *n*. relámpago *m*.
like /laik/ *a*. **1.** semejante. —*prep.* **2.** como. —*v*. **3.** I like... me gusta, me gustan... I should like, quisiera.
likeable /'laikəbəl/ *a*. simpático, agradable.
likelihood /'laikli,hud/ *n*. probabilidad *f*.
likely /'laikli/ *a*. probable; verosímil.
liken /'laikən/ *v*. comparar; asemejar.
likeness /'laiknıs/ *n*. semejanza *f*.
likewise /'laik,waiz/ *adv.* igualmente.
lilac /'lailək/ *n*. lila *f*.
lilt /lılt/ *n*. **1.** cadencia alegre *f*. —*v*. **2.** cantar alegremente.
lily /'lıli/ *n*. lirio *m*.
lily of the valley muguete *m*.
limb /lım/ *n*. rama *f*.
limber /'lımbər/ *a*. flexible. **to l. up,** ponerse flexible
limbo /'lımbou/ *n*. limbo *m*.
lime /laim/ *n*. cal *f*.; (fruit) limoncito *m*., lima *f*.
limestone /'laim,stoun/ *n*. piedra caliza *f*.
limewater /'laim,wɔtər/ *n*. agua de cal *f*.
limit /'lımıt/ *n*. **1.** límite *m*. —*v*. **2.** limitar.
limitation /,lımı'teiʃən/ *n*. limitación *f*.
limitless /'lımıtlıs/ *a*. ilimitado.
limousine /'lımə,zin/ *n*. limusina *f*.
limp /lımp/ *n*. **1.** cojera *f*. —*a*. **2.** flojo. —*v*. **3.** cojear.
limpid /'lımpıd/ *a*. límpido.
line /lain/ *n*. **1.** línea; fila; raya *f*.; (of print) renglón *m*. —*v*. **2.** forrar; rayar.
lineage /'lınıdʒ/ *n*. linaje *m*.
lineal /'lınial/ *a*. lineal.
linear /'lınıər/ *a*. linear, longitudinal.
linen /'lınən/ *n*. lienzo, lino *m*.; ropa blanca.
liner /'lainər/ *n*. vapor *m*.
linger /'lıŋgər/ *v*. demorarse.
lingerie /,lɑnʒə'rei/ *n*. ropa blanca *f*.
linguist /'lıŋgwıst/ *n*. lingüista *m*. & *f*.
linguistic /lıŋ'gwıstık/ *a*. lingüístico.
liniment /'lınəmənt/ *n*. linimento *m*.
lining /'lainıŋ/ *n*. forro *m*.

link /lıŋk/ *n*. **1.** eslabón; vínculo *m*. —*v*. **2.** vincular.
linoleum /lı'nouliəm/ *n*. linóleo *m*.
linseed /'lın,sid/ *n*. linaza *f*.; simiente de lino *f*.
lint /lınt/ *n*. hilacha *f*.
lion /'laiən/ *n*. león *m*.
lip /lıp/ *n*. labio *m*.
liposuction /'lıpə,sʌkʃən, 'laipə-/ *n*. liposucción *f*.
lipstick /'lıp,stık/ *n*. lápiz de labios.
liqueur /lı'kɜr/ *n*. licor *m*.
liquid /'lıkwıd/ *a*. & *n*. líquido *m*.
liquidate /'lıkwı,deit/ *v*. liquidar.
liquidation /,lıkwı'deiʃən/ *n*. liquidación *f*.
liquor /'lıkər/ *n*. licor *m*.
lisp /lısp/ *n*. **1.** ceceo *m*. —*v*. **2.** cecear.
list /lıst/ *n*. **1.** lista *f*. —*v*. **2.** registrar.
listen (to) /'lısən/ *v*. escuchar.
listless /'lıstlıs/ *ad*. indiferente.
litany /'lıtṇi/ *n*. letanía *f*.
liter /'litər/ *n*. litro *m*.
literal /'lıtərəl/ *a*. literal.
literary /'lıtə,reri/ *a*. literario.
literate /'lıtərıt/ *a*. alfabetizado.
literature /'lıtərətʃər/ *n*. literatura *f*.
litigant /'lıtıgənt/ *n*. & *a*. litigante *m*. & *f*.
litigation /,lıtı'geiʃən/ *n*. litigio, pleito *m*.
litter /'lıtər/ *n*. **1.** litera *f*.; cama de paja. —*v*. **2.** poner en desorden.
little /'lıtl/ *a*. pequeño; (quantity) poco.
little finger meñique *m*.
liturgical /lı'tɜrdʒıkəl/ *a*. litúrgico.
liturgy /'lıtərdʒi/ *n*. liturgia *f*.
live /*a*. laiv; *v* lıv/ *a*. **1.** vivo. —*v*. **2.** vivir.
livelihood /'laivli,hud/ *n*. subsistencia *f*.
lively /'laivli/ *a*. vivo; rápido; animado.
liver /'lıvər/ *n*. hígado *m*.
livery /'lıvəri/ *n*. librea *f*.
livestock /'laiv,stɒk/ *n*. ganadería *f*.
livid /'lıvıd/ *a*. lívido.
living /'lıvıŋ/ *a*. **1.** vivo. —*n*. **2.** sustento *m*. **to earn (make) a living,** ganarse la vida.
living room salón *m*.
lizard /'lızərd/ *n*. lagarto *m*., lagartija *f*.
llama /'lɑmə/ *n*. llama *f*.
load /loud/ *n*. **1.** carga *f*. —*v*. **2.** cargar.
loaf /louf/ *n*. **1.** pan *m*. —*v*. **2.** holgazanear.
loam /loum/ *n*. marga *f*.
loan /loun/ *n*. **1.** préstamo *m*. —*v*. **2.** prestar.
loathe /louð/ *v*. aborrecer, detestar.
loathsome /'louðsəm/ *a*. repugnante.
lobby /'lɒbi/ *n*. vestíbulo *m*.
lobe /loub/ *n*. lóbulo *m*.
lobster /'lɒbstər/ *n*. langosta *f*.
local /'loukəl/ *a*. local.
local area network red local *f*.
locale /lou'kæl/ *n*. localidad *f*.

locality /lou'kælıti/ *n.* localidad *f.*, lugar *m.*

localize /'loukə,laiz/ *v.* localizar.

locate /'loukeit/ *v.* situar; hallar.

location /lou'keiʃən/ *n.* sitio *m.*; posición *f.*

lock /lɒk/ *n.* **1.** cerradura *f.*; (*pl.*) cabellos *m.pl.* —*v.* **2.** cerrar con llave.

locker /'lɒkər/ *n.* cajón *m.*; ropero *m.*

locket /'lɒkɪt/ *n.* guardapelo *m.*; medallón *m.*

lockjaw /'lɒk,dʒɔ/ *n.* trismo *m.*

locksmith /'lɒk,smɪθ/ *n.* cerrajero -ra.

locomotive /,loukə'moutɪv/ *n.* locomotora *f.*

locust /'loukəst/ *n.* cigarra *f.*, saltamontes *m.*

locution /lou'kyuʃən/ *n.* locución *f*

lode /loud/ *n.* filón *m.*, veta *f.*

lodge /lɒdʒ/ *n.* **1.** logia; (inn) posada *f.* —*v.* **2.** fijar; alojar, morar.

lodger /'lɒdʒər/ *n.* inquilino *m.*

lodging /'lɒdʒɪŋ/ *n.* alojamiento *m.*

loft /lɒft/ *n.* desván, sobrado *m.*

lofty /'lɒfti/ *a.* alto; altivo.

log /lɔg/ *n.* tronco de árbol; *Naut.* barquilla *f.*

loge /louʒ/ *n.* palco *m.*

logic /'lɒdʒɪk/ *n.* lógica *f*

logical /'lɒdʒɪkəl/ *a.* lógico.

loin /lɔin/ *n.* lomo *m.*

loincloth /'lɔin,klɔθ/ *n.* taparrabos *m.*

loiter /'lɔitər/ *v.* haraganear.

lone /loun/ *a.* solitario.

loneliness /'lounlinıs/ *n.* soledad *f.*

lonely, /'lounli/ lonesome *a.* solo y triste.

lonesome /'lounsəm/ *a.* solitario, aislado.

long /lɔŋ/ *a.* **1.** largo. **a l. time,** mucho tiempo. **how l.,** cuánto tiempo. **no longer,** ya no. —*v.* **3. l. for,** anhelar.

long-distance call /'lɔŋ 'dıstəns/ conferencia interurbana *f.*

longevity /lɒn'dʒevıti/ *n.* longevidad *f.*

long-haired /'lɔŋ 'hɛərd/ *a.* melenudo.

longing /'lɔŋɪŋ/ *n.* anhelo *m.*

longitude /'lɒndʒı,tud/ *n.* longitud *m.*

look /lʊk/ *n.* **1.** mirada *f.*; aspecto *m.* —*v.* **2.** parecer; mirar. **l. at,** mirar. **l. for,** buscar. **l. like,** parecerse a. **l. out!,** ¡cuidado! **l. up,** buscar; ir a ver, venir a ver.

looking glass /'lʊkıŋ/ espejo *m.*

loom /lum/ *n.* **1.** telar *m.* —*v.* **2.** asomar.

loop /lup/ *n.* vuelta *f.*

loophole /'lup,houl/ *n.* aspillera *f.*; *Fig.* callejuela, evasiva *f.*, efugio *m.*

loose /lus/ *a.* suelto; flojo.

loose change suelto *m.*

loosen /'lusən/ *v.* soltar; aflojar.

loot /lut/ *n.* **1.** botín *m.*, saqueo *m.* —*v.* **2.** saquear.

lopsided /lɒp'saidıd/ *a.* desequilibrado.

loquacious /lou'kweiʃəs/ *a.* locuaz.

lord /lɔrd/ *n.* señor *m.*; (Brit. title) lord *m.*

lordship /'lɔrdʃıp/ *n.* señorío *m.*

lose /luz/ *v.* perder. **l. consciousness,** perder el conocimiento.

loss /lɔs/ *n.* pérdida *f.*

lost /lɔst/ *a.* perdido.

lot /lɒt/ *n.* suerte *f.* **building l.,** solar *m.* **a lot (of), lots of,** mucho.

lotion /'louʃən/ *n.* loción *f.*

lottery /'lɒtəri/ *n.* lotería *f.*

loud /laud/ *a.* **1.** fuerte; ruidoso. —*adv.* **2.** alto.

loudspeaker /'laud,spikər/ *n.* altavoz *m.*

lounge /laundʒ/ *n.* sofá *m.*; salón de fumar *m.*

louse /laus/ *n.* piojo *m.*

love /lʌv/ *n.* **1.** amor *m.* **in l.,** enamorado. **to fall in l.,** enamorarse. **l. at first sight,** flechazo *m.* —*v.* **2.** querer; amar; adorar.

lovely /'lʌvli/ *a.* hermoso.

lover /'lʌvər/ *n.* amante *m.* & *f.*

low /lou/ *a.* bajo; vil.

low-cut /'lou 'kʌt/ *a.* escotado.

lower /'louər/ *v.* bajar; (in price) rebajar.

lower-case letter /'louər 'keis/ minúscula *f.*

lowly /'louli/ *a.* humilde.

low neckline /'nɛk,lain/ escote *m.*

loyal /'lɔiəl/ *a.* leal, fiel.

loyalist /'lɔiəlıst/ *n.* lealista *m.* & *f.*

loyalty /'lɔiəlti/ *n.* lealtad *f.*

lozenge /'lɒzındʒ/ *n.* pastilla *f.*

lubricant /'lubrıkənt/ *n.* lubricante *m.*

lubricate /'lubrı,keit/ *v.* engrasar, lubricar.

lucid /'lusıd/ *a.* claro, lúcido.

luck /lʌk/ *n.* suerte; fortuna *f.*

lucky /'lʌki/ *a.* afortunado. **to be l.,** tener suerte.

lucrative /'lukrətıv/ *a.* lucrativo.

ludicrous /'ludıkrəs/ *a.* rídiculo.

luggage /'lʌgıdʒ/ *n.* equipaje *m.*

lukewarm /'luk'wɔrm/ *a.* tibio.

lull /lʌl/ *n.* **1.** momento de calma. —*v.* **2.** calmar.

lullaby /'lʌlə,bai/ *n.* arrullo *m.*

lumbago /lʌm'beigou/ *n.* lumbago *m.*

lumber /'lʌmbər/ *n.* madera *f.*

luminous /'lumənəs/ *a.* luminoso.

lump /lʌmp/ *n.* protuberancia *f.*; (of sugar) terrón *m.*

lump sum suma global *f.*

lunacy /'lunəsi/ *n.* locura *f.*

lunar /'lunər/ *a.* lunar.

lunatic /'lunətık/ *a.* & *n.* loco -ca.

lunch, luncheon /lʌntʃ; 'lʌntʃən/ *n.* **1.** merienda *f.*, almuerzo *m.* —*v.* **2.** merendar, almorzar.

lunch box /'lʌntʃ,bɒks/ fiambrera *f.*

lung /lʌŋ/ *n.* pulmón *m.*

lunge /lʌndʒ/ n. **1.** estocada, arremetida f.
—v. **2.** dar un estocada, arremeter.
lure /lur/ v. atraer.
lurid /ˈlorɪd/ a. sensacional; espeluznante.
lurk /lɜrk/ v. esconderse; espiar.
luscious /ˈlʌʃəs/ a. sabroso, delicioso.
lust /lʌst/ n. sensualidad; codicia f.
luster /ˈlʌstər/ n. lustre m.
lustful /ˈlʌstfəl/ a. sensual, lascivo.
lusty /ˈlʌsti/ a. vigoroso.
lute /lut/ n. laúd m.

Lutheran /ˈluθərən/ n. & a. luterano -na.
luxuriant /lʌgˈʒuriənt/ a. exuberante, frondoso.
luxurious /lʌgˈʒuriəs/ a. lujoso.
luxury /ˈlʌkʃəri/ n. lujo m.
lying /ˈlaiɪŋ/ a. mentiroso.
lymph /lɪmf/ n. linfa f.
lynch /lɪntʃ/ v. linchar.
lyre /laiər/ n. lira f.
lyric /ˈlɪrɪk/ a. lírico.
lyricism /ˈlɪrəˌsɪzəm/ n. lirismo m.

M

macabre /məˈkubrə/ a. macabro.
macaroni /ˌmækəˈrouni/ n. macarrones m.
machine /məˈʃin/ n. máquina f.
machine gun ametralladora f.
machinery /məˈʃinəri/ n. maquinaria f.
machinist /məˈʃinɪst/ n. maquinista m. & f., mecánico m.
macho /ˈmɑtʃou/ a. machista.
mackerel /ˈmækərəl/ n. escombro m.
macro /ˈmækrou/ n. (computer) macro m.
mad /mæd/ a. loco; furioso.
madam /ˈmædəm/ n. señora f.
mafia /ˈmɑfiə/ n. mafia f.
magazine /ˌmægəˈzin/ n. revista f.
magic /ˈmædʒɪk/ a. **1.** mágico. —n. **2.** magia f.
magician /məˈdʒiʃən/ n. mágico m.
magistrate /ˈmædʒəˌstreit/ n. magistrado -da.
magnanimous /mægˈnænəməs/ a. magnánimo.
magnate /ˈmægneit/ n. magnate m.
magnesium /mægˈniziəm/ n. magnesio m.
magnet /ˈmægnɪt/ n. imán m.
magnetic /mægˈnetɪk/ a. magnético.
magnificence /mægˈnɪfəsəns/ n. magnificencia f.
magnificent /mægˈnɪfəsənt/ a. magnífico.
magnify /ˈmægnəˌfai/ v. magnificar.
magnifying glass /ˈmægnəˌfaiɪŋ/ lupa f.
magnitude /ˈmægnɪˌtud/ n. magnitud f.
magpie /ˈmægˌpai/ n. hurraca f.
mahogany /məˈhogəni/ n. caoba f.
maid /meid/ n. criada f. **old m.,** solterona f.
maiden /ˈmeidn/ a. soltera.
mail /meil/ n. **1.** correo m. **air m.,** correo aéreo. **by return m.,** a vuelta de correo. —v. **2.** echar al correo.
mailbox /ˈmeilˌbɒks/ n. buzón m.
mailman /ˈmeilˌmæn/ n. cartero m.
maim /meim/ v. mutilar.
main /mein/ a. principal.

mainframe /ˈmeinˌfreim/ n. componente central de una computadora.
mainland /ˈmeinˌlænd/ n. continente m.
maintain /meinˈtein/ v. mantener; sostener.
maintenance /ˈmeintənəns/ n. mantenimiento; sustento m.; conservación f.
maître d' /ˌmeiˈtər di, ˌmeitrə, ˌmetrə/ n. jefe de sala m. & f.
maize /meiz/ n. maíz m.
majestic /məˈdʒestɪk/ a. majestuoso.
majesty /ˈmædʒəsti/ n. majestad f.
major /ˈmeidʒər/ a. **1.** mayor. —n. **2.** Mil. comandante m.; (study) especialidad f.
majority /məˈdʒoriti/ n. mayoría f.
make /meik/ n. **1.** marca f. —v. **2.** hacer; fabricar; (earn) ganar.
maker /ˈmeikər/ n. fabricante m.
makeshift /ˈmeikˌʃift/ a. provisional.
make-up /ˈmeikˌʌp/ n. cosméticos m.pl.
malady /ˈmælədi/ n. mal m., enfermedad f.
malaria /məˈleariə/ n. paludismo m.
male /meil/ a. & n. macho m.
malevolent /məˈlevələnt/ a. malévolo.
malice /ˈmælɪs/ n. malicia f.
malicious /məˈliʃəs/ a. malicioso.
malign /məˈlain/ v. **1.** difamar. —a. **2.** maligno.
malignant /məˈlignənt/ a. maligno.
malnutrition /ˌmælnuˈtriʃən/ n. desnutrición f.
malt /mɒlt/ n. malta f.
mammal /ˈmæməl/ n. mamífero m.
man /mæn/ n. hombre; varón m. v. tripular.
manage /ˈmænɪdʒ/ v. manejar; dirigir; administrar; arreglárselas m. **to,** lograr.
management /ˈmænɪdʒmənt/ n. dirección, administración f.
manager /ˈmænɪdʒər/ n. director -ora.
mandate /ˈmændeit/ n. mandato m.
mandatory /ˈmændəˌtori/ a. obligatorio.
mandolin /ˈmændlɪn/ n. mandolina f.
mane /mein/ n. crines f.pl.

maneuver /mə'nuvər/ n. 1. maniobra f. —v. 2. maniobrar.

manganese /'mæŋgə,nis. -,niz/ n. manganeso m.

manger /'meindʒər/ n. pesebre m.

mangle /'mæŋgəl/ n. 1. rodillo, exprimidor m. —v. 2. mutilar.

manhood /'mænhud/ n. virilidad f.

mania /'meiniə/ n. manía f.

maniac /'meini,æk/ a. & n. maniático -ca; maníaco -ca.

manicure /'mæni,kyur/ n. manicura f.

manifest /'mænə,fɛst/ a. & n 1. manifiesto m. —v. 2. manifestar.

manifesto /,mænə'fɛstou/ n. manifiesto m.

manifold /'mænə,fould/ a. 1. muchos. —n. 2. Auto. múltiple.

manipulate /mə'nɪpyə,leit/ v. manipular.

mankind /'mæn'kaind/ n. humanidad f.

manly /'mænli/ a. varonil.

manner /'mænər/ n. manera f., modo m. **manners**, modales m.pl.

mannerism /'mænə,rɪzəm/ n. manerismo m.

mansion /'mænʃən/ n. mansión f.

mantel /'mæntl/ n. manto de chimenea.

mantle /'mæntl/ n. manto m.

manual /'mænyuəl/ a. & n. manual m.

manufacture /,mænyə'fæktʃər/ v. fabricar.

manufacturer /,mænyə'fæktʃərər/ n. fabricante m.

manufacturing /,mænyə'fæktʃərɪŋ/ n. fabricación f.

manure /mə'nur/ n. abono, estiércol m.

manuscript /'mænyə,skrɪpt/ n. manuscrito m.

many /'mɛni/ a. muchos. **how m.,** cuántos. **so m.,** tantos. **too m.,** demasiados. **as m. as,** tantos como.

map /mæp/ n. mapa m.

maple /'meipəl/ n. arce m.

mar /mar/ v. estropear; desfigurar.

marble /'marbəl/ n. mármol m.

march /martʃ/ n. 1. marcha f. —v. 2. marchar.

March /martʃ/ n. marzo m.

mare /mɛər/ n. yegua f.

margarine /'mardʒərɪn/ n. margarina f.

margin /'mardʒɪn/ n. margen m. or f.

marijuana /,mærə'wanə/ n. marijuana f.

marine /mə'rin/ a. 1. marino. —n. 2. soldado de marina.

mariner /'mærənər/ n. marinero m.

marionette /,mæriə'nɛt/ n. marioneta f.

marital /'mærɪtl/ a. marital.

maritime /'mærɪ,taim/ a. marítimo.

mark /mark/ n. 1. marca f. —v. 2. marcar.

market /'markɪt/ n. mercado m. **meat m.,** carnicería f. **stock m.,** bolsa f. v. comercializar.

marmalade /'marmə,leid/ n. mermelada f

maroon /mə'run/ a. & n. color rojo oscuro. v. dejar abandonado.

marquis /'markwɪs/ n. marqués m.

marriage /'mærɪdʒ/ n. matrimonio m.

marriage certificate partida de matrimonio f.

married /'mærid/ a. casado. **to get m.,** casarse.

marrow /'mærou/ n. médula f.; substancia f.

marry /'mæri/ v. casarse con; casar.

marsh /marʃ/ n. pantano m.

marshal /'marʃəl/ n. mariscal m.

marshmallow /'marʃ,mɛlou/ n. malvarisco m.; bombón de altea m.

martial /'marʃəl/ a. marcial. **m. law,** gobierno militar.

martyr /'martər/ n. mártir m. & f.

martyrdom /'martərdəm/ n. martirio m.

marvel /'marvəl/ n. 1. maravilla f. —v. 2. maravillarse.

marvelous /'marvələs/ a. maravilloso.

mascara /mæ'skɛrə/ n. rimel m.

mascot /'mæskot/ n. mascota f.

masculine /'mæskyəlɪn/ a. masculino.

mash /mæʃ/ v. majar. **mashed potatoes,** puré de papas m.

mask /mæsk/ n. máscara f.

mason /'meisən/ n. albañil m.

masquerade /,mæskə'reid/ n. mascarada f.

mass /mæs/ n. masa f.; Relig. misa f. **to say m.,** cantar misa. **m. production,** producción en serie.

massacre /'mæsəkər/ n. 1. carnicería, matanza f. —v. 2. matar atrozmente, destrozar.

massage /mə'saʒ/ n. 1. masaje m.; soba f. —v. 2. sobar.

masseur /mə'sɜr/ n. masajista m & f.

massive /'mæsɪv/ a. macizo, sólido.

mast /mæst/ n. palo, árbol m.

master /'mæstər/ n. 1. amo; maestro m. —v. 2. domar, dominar.

masterpiece /'mæstər,pis/ n. obra maestra f.

master's degree /'mæstərz/ maestría f.

mastery /'mæstəri/ n. maestría f.

mat /mæt/ n. 1. estera; palleta f. —v. 2. enredar.

match /mætʃ/ n. 1. igual m; fósforo m., (sport) partida, contienda f.; (marriage) noviazgo; casamiento. —v. 2. ser igual a; igualar.

matchbox /'mætʃ,boks/ n. caja de cerillas, caja de fósforos f.

mate /meit/ n. 1. consorte m. & f.; compañero -ra. —v. 2. igualar; casar.

material /mə'tɪəriəl/ a. & n. material m. **raw materials,** materias primas.

materialism /mə'tɪəriə,lɪzəm/ n. materialismo m.

materialize /mə'tɪərɪə,laɪz/ v. materializar.

maternal /mə'tɜrnl/ a. materno.

maternity /mə'tɜrnɪti/ n. maternidad f.

maternity hospital maternidad f.

mathematical /,mæθə'mætɪkəl/ a. matemático.

mathematics /,mæθə'mætɪks/ n. matemáticas f.pl.

matinee /,mætn'eɪ/ n. matiné f.

matrimony /'mætrə,mouni/ n. matrimonio m.

matron /'meɪtrən/ n. matrona; directora f.

matter /'mætər/ n. **1.** materia f.; asunto m. **what's the m.?**, ¿qué pasa? —v. **2.** importar.

mattress /'mætrɪs/ n. colchón m.

mature /mə'tʃʊr/ a. **1.** maduro. —v. **2.** madurar.

maturity /mə'tʃʊrɪti/ n. madurez f.

maudlin /'mɔdlɪn/ a. sentimental en exceso; sensiblero.

maul /mɔl/ v. aporrear.

maxim /'mæksɪm/ n. máxima f.

maximum /'mæksəməm/ a. & n. máximo.

may /meɪ/ v. poder.

May /meɪ/ n. mayo m.

maybe /'meɪbi/ adv. quizá, quizás, tal vez.

mayonnaise /,meɪə'neɪz/ n. mayonesa f.

mayor /'meɪər/ n. alcalde m. alcaldesa f.

maze /meɪz/ n. laberinto m.

me /mi/ pron. mí; me. **with me,** conmigo.

meadow /'mɛdoʊ/ n. prado m.; vega f.

meager /'migər/ a. magro; pobre.

meal /mil/ n. comida; (flour) harina f.

mean /min/ a. **1.** bajo; malo. —n. **2.** medio (see also **means**). —v. **3.** significar; querer decir.

meander /mi'ændər/ v. (river) serpentear; (person) deambular.

meaning /'minɪŋ/ n. sentido, significado m.

meaningless /'minɪŋlɪs/ a. sin sentido.

means /minz/ n.pl. medios, recursos m. **by all m.,** sin falta. **by no m.,** de ningún modo. **by m. of,** por medio de.

meanwhile /'min,waɪl/ adv. mientras tanto.

measles /'mizəlz/ n. sarampión m.

measure /'mɛʒər/ n. **1.** medida f.; (music) compás m. —v. **2.** medir.

measurement /'mɛʒərmənt/ n. medida, dimensión f.

meat /mit/ n. carne f.

mechanic /mə'kænɪk/ n. mecánico m. & f.

mechanical /mə'kænɪkəl/ a. mecánico.

mechanism /'mɛkə,nɪzəm/ n. mecanismo m.

mechanize /'mɛkə,naɪz/ v. mecanizar.

medal /'mɛdl/ n. medalla f.

meddle /'mɛdl/ v. meterse, entremeterse.

mediate /'midi,eɪt/ v. mediar.

medical /'mɛdɪkəl/ a. médico.

medicine /'mɛdəsɪn/ n. medicina f.

medicine chest botiquín m.

medieval /,midi'ivəl/ a. medieval.

mediocre /,midi'oukər/ a. mediocre.

mediocrity /,midi'ɒkrɪti/ n. mediocridad f.

meditate /'mɛdɪ,teɪt/ v. meditar.

meditation /,mɛdɪ'teɪʃən/ n. meditación f.

Mediterranean /,mɛdɪtə'reɪniən/ n. Mediterráneo m.

medium /'midiəm/ a. **1.** mediano, medio. —n. **2.** medio m.

medley /'mɛdli/ n. mezcla f., ensalada f.

meek /mik/ a. manso; humilde.

meekness /'miknɪs/ n. modestia; humildad f.

meet /mit/ a. **1.** apropiado. —n. **2.** concurso m. —v. **3.** encontrar; reunirse; conocer.

meeting /'mitɪŋ/ n. reunión f.; mitin m.

megahertz /'mɛgə,hɜrts/ n. megahercio m.

megaphone /'mɛgə,foʊn/ n. megáfono m.

melancholy /'mɛlən,koli/ a. **1.** melancólico. —n. **2.** melancolía f.

mellow /'mɛloʊ/ a. suave; blando; maduro.

melodious /mə'loudiəs/ a. melodioso.

melodrama /'mɛlə,dramə/ n. melodrama m.

melody /'mɛlədi/ n. melodía f.

melon /'mɛlən/ n. melón m.

melt /mɛlt/ v. derretir.

meltdown /'mɛlt,daʊn/ n. fundición resultante de un accidente en un reactor nuclear.

member /'mɛmbər/ n. socio -ia; miembro m. **m. of the crew,** tripulante m. & f.

membership /'mɛmbər,ʃɪp/ n. número de miembros.

membrane /'mɛmbreɪn/ n. membrana f.

memento /mə'mɛntoʊ/ n. recuerdo m.

memoir /'mɛmwɑr/ n. memoria f.

memorable /'mɛmərəbəl/ a. memorable.

memorandum /,mɛmə'rændəm/ n. memorándum, volante m.

memorial /mə'mɔriəl/ a. **1.** conmemorativo. —n. **2.** memorial m.

memorize /'mɛmə,raɪz/ v. aprender de memoria.

memory /'mɛməri/ n. memoria f.; recuerdo m.

menace /'mɛnɪs/ n. **1.** amenaza f. —v. **2.** amenazar.

mend /mɛnd/ v. reparar, remendar.

menial /'miniəl/ a. **1.** servil. —n. **2.** sirviente -ta.

meningitis /,mɛnɪn'dʒaɪtɪs/ n. meningitis f.

menopause /'mɛnə,pɔz/ n. menopausia f.

menstruation /,mɛnstru'eɪʃən/ n. menstruación f.

menswear /'mɛnz,wɛər/ n. ropa de caballeros f.

mental /'mentl/ a. mental.

mental disorder trastorno mental m.

mentality /men'tæliti/ n. mentalidad f.

menthol /'menθɒl/ n. mentol m.

mention /'menʃən/ n. **1.** mención f. —v. **2.** mencionar.

menu /'menyu/ n. menú m., lista f.

mercantile /'mərkən,til/ a. mercantil.

mercenary /'mərsə,neri/ a. & n. mercenario -ria.

merchandise /'mərtʃən,daiz/ n. mercancía f.

merchant /'mərtʃənt/ a. **1.** mercante. —n. **2.** comerciante m.

merciful /'mərsifəl/ a. misericordioso, compasivo.

merciless /'mərsilis/ a. cruel, inhumano.

mercury /'mərkyəri/ n. mercurio m.

mercy /'mərsi/ n. misericordia; merced f.

mere /miər/ a. mero, puro.

merely /'miərli/ adv. solamente; simplemente.

merge /mərdʒ/ v. unir, combinar.

merger /'mərdʒər/ n. consolidación, fusión f.

meringue /mə'ræŋ/ n. merengue m.

merit /'merit/ n. **1.** mérito m. —v. **2.** merecer.

meritorious /,meri'tɔriəs/ a. meritorio.

mermaid /'mər,meid/ n. sirena f.

merriment /'merimənt/ n. regocijo m.

merry /'meri/ a. alegre, festivo.

merry-go-round /'meri gou ,raund/ n. caballitos m. pl.; tiovivo m.

mesh /meʃ/ n. malla f.

mess /mes/ n. **1.** lío m.; confusión f.; Mil. salón comedor; rancho m. —v. **2. m. up,** ensuciar; enredar.

message /'mesidʒ/ n. mensaje, recado m.

messenger /'mesəndʒər/ n. mensajero -ra.

messy /'mesi/ a. confuso; desarreglado.

metabolism /mə'tæbə,lizəm/ n. metabolismo m.

metal /'metl/ n. metal m.

metallic /mə'tælik/ a. metálico.

metaphysics /,metə'fiziks/ n. metafísica f.

meteor /'mitiər/ n. meteoro m.

meteorology /,mitiə'rɒlədʒi/ n. meteorología f.

meter /'mitər/ n. contador, medidor m. (measure) metro m.

method /'meθəd/ n. método m.

meticulous /mə'tikyələs/ a. meticuloso.

metric /'metrik/ a. métrico.

metropolis /mi'trɒpəlis/ n. metrópoli f.

metropolitan /,metrə'pɒlitṇ/ a. metropolitano.

Mexican /'meksikən/ a. & n. mexicano -na.

Mexico /'meksi,kou/ n. México m.

mezzanine /'mezə,nin/ n. entresuelo m.

microbe /'maikroub/ n. microbio m.

microchip /'maikrou,tʃip/ n. microchip m.

microfiche /'maikrə,fiʃ/ n. microficha f

microfilm /'maikrə,film/ n. microfilm m.

microform /'maikrə,fɔrm/ n. microforma f.

microphone /'maikrə,foun/ n. micrófono m.

microscope /'maikrə,skoup/ n. microscopio m.

microscopic /,maikrə'skɒpik/ a. microscópico.

mid /mid/ a. medio.

middle /'midl/ a. & n. medio m. **in the m. of,** en medio de, a mediados de.

middle-aged /eidʒd/ a. de edad madura.

Middle East Medio Oriente m.

middle finger dedo corazón m.

midget /'midʒit/ n. enano -na.

midnight /'mid,nait/ n. medianoche f.

midwife /'mid,waif/ n. comadrona, partera f.

might /mait/ n. poder m., fuerza f.

mighty /'maiti/ a. poderoso.

migraine /'maigrein/ n. migraña f.; jaqueca f.

migrate /'maigreit/ v. emigrar.

migration /mai'greiʃən/ n. emigración f.

migratory /'maigrə,tɔri/ a. migratorio.

mild /maild/ a. moderado, suave; templado.

mildew /'mil,du/ n. añublo m., moho m.

mile /mail/ n. milla f.

mileage /'mailidʒ/ n. kilometraje m.

militant /'militənt/ a. militante.

militarism /'militə,rizəm/ n. militarismo m.

military /'mili,teri/ a. militar.

militia /mi'liʃə/ n. milicia f.

milk /milk/ n. **1.** leche f. —v. **2.** ordeñar.

milk chocolate chocolate con leche m.

milkman /'milk,mæn/ n. lechero m.

milk shake batido m.

milky /'milki/ a. lácteo; lechoso.

mill /mil/ n. **1.** molino m.; fábrica f. —v. **2.** moler.

miller /'milər/ n. molinero -ra.

millimeter /'milə,mitər/ n. milímetro m.

milliner /'milənər/ n. sombrerero -ra.

millinery /'milə,neri/ n. sombrerería f.

million /'milyən/ n. millón m.

millionaire /,milyə'nɛər/ n. millonario -ria.

mimic /'mimik/ n. **1.** mimo -ma. —v. **2.** imitar.

mind /maind/ n. **1.** mente; opinión f. —v. **2.** obedecer. **never m.,** no se ocupe.

mindful /'maindfəl/ a. atento.

mine /main/ pron. **1.** mío. —n. **2.** mina f. —v. **3.** minar.

miner /'mainər/ n. minero m.

mineral /'minərəl/ a. & n. mineral m.

mineral water agua mineral f.

mine sweeper /'main,swipər/ dragaminas f.

mingle /'mɪŋgəl/ v. mezclar.

miniature /'mɪniətʃər/ n. miniatura f.

miniaturize /'mɪniətʃə,raiz/ v. miniaturizar.

minibus /'mɪni,bʌs/ n. microbús m.

minicab /'mɪni,kæb/ n. microtaxi m.

minimize /'mɪnə,maiz/ v. menospreciar.

minimum /'mɪnəməm/ a. & n. mínimo m.

mining /'mainɪŋ/ n. minería f.

minister /'mɪnəstər/ n. **1.** ministro -tra; *Relig.* pastor m. —v. **2.** ministrar.

ministry /'mɪnəstri/ n. ministerio m.

mink /mɪŋk/ n. visón m.; (fur) piel de visón m.

minor /'mainər/ a. **1.** menor. —n. **2.** menor de edad.

minority /mɪ'nɔriti/ n. minoría f.

minstrel /'mɪnstrəl/ n. juglar m.

mint /mɪnt/ n. **1.** menta f.; casa de moneda. —v. **2.** acuñar.

minus /'mainəs/ prep. menos.

minute /'mai'nut/ a. **1.** minucioso. —n. **2.** minuto, momento m.

miracle /'mɪrəkəl/ n. milagro m.

miraculous /mɪ'rækyələs/ a. milagroso.

mirage /mɪ'rɑʒ/ n. espejismo m.

mire /mai³r/ n. lodo m.

mirror /'mɪrər/ n. espejo m.

mirth /mɜrθ/ n. alegría; risa f.

misbehave /,mɪsbɪ'heiv/ v. portarse mal.

miscellaneous /,mɪsə'leiniəs/ a. misceláneo.

mischief /'mɪstʃɪf/ n. travesura, diablura f.

mischievous /'mɪstʃəvəs/ a. travieso, dañino.

miser /'maizər/ n. avaro -ra.

miserable /'mɪzərəbəl/ a. miserable; infeliz.

miserly /'maizərli/ a. avariento, tacaño.

misfortune /mɪs'fɔrtʃən/ n. desgracia f., infortunio, revés m.

misgiving /mɪs'gɪvɪŋ/ n. recelo m., desconfianza f.

mishap /'mɪshæp/ n. desgracia f., contratiempo m.

mislay /mɪs'lei/ v. perder.

mislead /mɪs'lid/ v. extraviar, despistar; pervertir.

misplaced /mɪs'pleist/ a. extraviado.

mispronounce /,mɪsprə'nouns/ v. pronunciar mal.

miss /mɪs/ n. **1.** señorita f. —v. **2.** perder; echar de menos, extrañar. **be missing**, faltar.

missile /'mɪsəl/ n. proyectil m.

mission /'mɪʃən/ n. misión f.

missionary /'mɪʃə,neri/ n. misionero -ra.

mist /mɪst/ n. niebla, bruma f.

mistake /mɪ'steik/ n. equivocación f.; error m. **to make a m.,** equivocarse.

mistaken /mɪ'steikən/ a. equivocado.

mister /'mɪstər/ n. señor m.

mistletoe /'mɪsəl,tou/ n. muérdago m.

mistreat /mɪs'trit/ v. maltratar.

mistress /'mɪstrɪs/ n. ama; señora; concubina f.

mistrust /mɪs'trʌst/ v. desconfiar; sospechar.

misty /'mɪsti/ a. nebuloso, brumoso.

misunderstand /,mɪsʌndər'stænd/ v. entender mal.

misuse /mɪs'yuz/ v. maltratar; abusar.

mite /mait/ n. pizca f., blanca f.

mitten /'mɪtn/ n. mitón, confortante m.

mix /mɪks/ v. mezclar. **m. up,** confundir.

mixer /'mɪksər/ (for food), n. batidora f.

mixture /'mɪkstʃər/ n. mezcla, mixtura f.

mix-up /'mɪks,ʌp/ n. confusión f.

moan /moun/ n. **1.** quejido, gemido m. —v. **2.** gemir.

mob /mɒb/ n. muchedumbre f.; gentío m.

mobilization /,moubələ'zeiʃən/ n. movilización f.

mobilize /'moubə,laiz/ v. movilizar.

mock /mɒk/ v. burlar.

mockery /'mɒkəri/ n. burla f.

mod /mɒd/ a. a la última; en boga.

mode /moud/ n. modo m.

model /'mɒdl/ n. **1.** modelo m. —v. **2.** modelar.

modem /'moudəm/ n. módem m.

moderate /'mɒdərɪt; v -ə,reit/ a. **1.** moderado. —v. **2.** moderar.

moderation /,mɒdə'reiʃən/ n. moderación; sobriedad f.

modern /'mɒdərn/ a. moderno.

modernize /'mɒdər,naiz/ v. modernizar.

modest /'mɒdɪst/ a. modesto.

modesty /'mɒdəsti/ n. modestia f.

modify /'mɒdə,fai/ v. modificar.

modulate /'mɒdʒə,leit/ v. modular.

moist /mɔist/ a. húmedo.

moisten /'mɔisən/ v. humedecer.

moisture /'mɔistʃər/ n. humedad f.

moisturize /'mɔistʃə,raiz/ v. hidratar.

molar /'moulər/ n. molar m.

molasses /mə'læsɪz/ n. melaza f.

mold /mould/ n. **1.** molde; moho m. —v. **2.** moldar, formar; enmohecerse.

moldy /'mouldi/ a. mohoso.

mole /moulei/ n. lunar m.; (animal) topo m.

molecule /'mɒlɪ,kyul/ n. molécula f.

molest /mə'lest/ v. molestar.

mollify /'mɒlə,fai/ v. molificar.

moment /'moumənt/ n. momento m.

momentary /'moumən,teri/ a. momentáneo.

momentous /mou'mɛntəs/ a. importante.

monarch /'mɒnərk/ n. monarca m. & f.

monarchy /'mɒnərki/ n. monarquía f.

monastery /'mɒnə,steri/ n. monasterio m.

Monday /'mʌndei/ n. lunes m.

monetary /'mɒnɪ,teri/ a. monetário.

money /'mʌni/ n. dinero m. **m. order,** giro postal.

mongrel /'mʌŋgrəl/ n. **1.** mestizo m. —a. **2.** mestizo, cruzado.

monitor /'mɒnɪtər/ n. amonestador m.; (computer) consola f., pantalla f.

monk /mʌŋk/ n. monje m.

monkey /'mʌŋki/ n. mono -na.

monocle /'mɒnəkəl/ n. monóculo m.

monologue /'mɒnə,lɔg/ n. monólogo m.

monopolize /mə'nɒpə,laiz/ v. monopolizar.

monopoly /mə'nɒpəli/ n. monopolio m.

monosyllable /'mɒnə,sɪləbəl/ n. monosílabo m.

monotone /'mɒnə,toun/ n. monotonía f.

monotonous /mə'nɒtnəs/ a. monótono.

monotony /mə'nɒtni/ n. monotonía f.

monsoon /mɒn'sun/ n. monzón m.

monster /'mɒnstər/ n. monstruo m.

monstrosity /mɒn'strɒsɪti/ n. monstruosidad f.

monstrous /'mɒnstrəs/ a. monstruoso.

month /mʌnθ/ n. mes m.

monthly /'mʌnθli/ a. mensual.

monument /'mɒnyəmənt/ n. monumento m.

monumental /,mɒnyə'mɛntḷ/ a. monumental.

mood /mud/ n. humor m.; Gram. modo m.

moody /'mudi/ a. caprichoso, taciturno.

moon /mun/ n. luna f.

moonlight /'mun,lait/ n. luz de la luna.

moonlighting /'mun,laitɪŋ/ n. pluriempleo m.

moor /mʊr/ n. **1.** páramo m. —v. **2.** anclar.

Moor /mʊr/ n. moro -ra.

mop /mɒp/ n. **1.** fregasuelos m., fregona f., (S.A.) trapeador m. —v. **2.** fregar, (S.A.) trapear.

moped /'mou,pɛd/ n. (vehicle) velomotor m.

moral /'mɔrəl/ a. **1.** moral. —n. **2.** moraleja f. **morals,** moralidad f.

morale /mə'ræl/ n. espíritu m.

moralist /'mɔrəlɪst/ n. moralista m. & f.

morality /mə'rælɪti/ n. moralidad, ética f.

morbid /'mɔrbɪd/ a. mórbido.

more /mɔr/ a. & adv. más. **m. and m.,** cada vez más.

moreover /mɔr'ouvər/ adv. además.

morgue /mɔrg/ n. necrocomio m.

morning /'mɔrnɪŋ/ n. mañana f. **good m.,** buenos días.

Morocco /mə'rɒkou/ n. Marruecos m.

morose /mə'rous/ a. malhumorado.

morphine /'mɔrfin/ n. morfina f.

morsel /'mɔrsəl/ n. bocado m.

mortal /'mɔrtḷ/ a. & n. mortal m. & f.

mortality /mɔr'tælɪti/ n. mortalidad f.

mortar /'mɔrtər/ n. mortero m.

mortgage /'mɔrgɪdʒ/ n. **1.** hipoteca f. —v **2.** hipotecar.

mortify /'mɔrtə,fai/ v. mortificar.

mosaic /mou'zeiɪk/ n. & a. mosaico m.

mosque /mɒsk/ n. mezquita f.

mosquito /mə'skitou/ n. mosquito m.

moss /mɔs/ n. musgo m.

most /moust/ a. **1.** más. —adv. **2.** más; sumamente. —pron. **3.** m. of, la mayor parte de.

mostly /'moustli/ adv. principalmente; en su mayor parte.

motel /mou'tɛl/ n. motel m.

moth /mɔθ/ n. polilla f.

mother /'mʌðər/ n. madre f.

mother-in-law /'mʌðər ɪn ,lɔ/ n. suegra f.

motif /mou'tif/ n. tema m.

motion /'mouʃən/ n. **1.** moción f.; movimiento m. —v. **2.** hacer señas.

motionless /'mouʃənlɪs/ a. inmóvil.

motion picture película f.

motivate /'moutə,veit/ v. motivar.

motive /'moutɪv/ n. motivo m.

motor /'moutər/ n. motor m.

motorboat /'moutər,bout/ n. lancha motora f., autobote, motorbote m., gasolinera f.

motorcycle /'moutər,saikəl/ n. motocicleta f.

motorcyclist /'moutər,saiklɪst/ n. motociclista m. & f.

motorist /'moutərɪst/ n. motorista m. & f.

motto /'mɒtou/ n. lema m.

mound /maund/ n. terrón; montón m.

mount /maunt/ n. **1.** monte m.; (horse) montura f. —v. **2.** montar; subir.

mountain /'mauntṇ/ n. montaña f.

mountaineer /,mauntṇ'ɪər/ n. montañés m.

mountainous /'mauntṇəs/ a. montañoso.

mourn /mɔrn/ v. lamentar, llorar; llevar luto.

mournful /'mɔrnfəl/ a. triste.

mourning /'mɔrnɪŋ/ n. luto; lamento m.

mouse /maus/ n. ratón, ratoncito m.

mouth /mauθ/ n. boca f.; (of river) desembocadura f.

mouthwash /'mauθ,wɒʃ/ n. enjuague bucal m.

movable /'muvəbəl/ a. móvible, movedizo.

move /muv/ n. **1.** movimiento m.; mudanza f. —v. **2.** mover; mudarse; emocionar, conmover. **m. away,** quitar; alejarse; mudarse.

movement /'muvmənt/ n. movimiento m.

movie /'muvi/ n. película f. **m. theater, movies,** cine m.

moving /'muvɪŋ/ a. conmovedor; persuasivo.

mow /mou/ v. guadañar, segar.

Mr. /'mɪstər/ title. Señor (Sr.).

Mrs. /'mɪsəz/ title. Señora (Sra.).

much /mʌtʃ/ a. & adv. mucho. **how m.,** cuánto. **so m.,** tanto. **too m.,** demasiado. **as m. as,** tanto como.

mucilage /'myusəlɪdʒ/ n. mucílago m.

mucous /'myukəs/ a. mucoso.

mucous membrane n. membrana mucosa f.

mud /mʌd/ n. fango, lodo m.

muddy /'mʌdi/ a. **1.** lodoso; turbio. —v. **2.** ensuciar; enturbiar.

muff /mʌf/ n. manguito m.

muffin /'mʌfɪn/ n. panecillo m.

mug /mʌg/ n. cubilete m.

mugger /'mʌgər/ n. asaltante m. & f.

mulatto /mə'lætou/ n. mulato m.

mule /myul/ n. mula f.

mullah /'mʌlə/ n. mullah m.

multicultural /,mʌlti'kʌltʃərəl, ,mʌltaɪ-/ a. multicultural.

multinational /,mʌlti'næʃənl, ,mʌltaɪ-/ a. multinacional.

multiple /'mʌltəpəl/ a. múltiple.

multiplication /,mʌltəplɪ'keɪʃən/ n. multiplicación f.

multiplicity /,mʌltə'plɪsɪti/ n. multiplicidad f.

multiply /'mʌltəpli/ v. multiplicar.

multitasking /,mʌlti'tæskɪŋ, ,mʌltaɪ-/ n. multitarea f.

multitude /'mʌltɪ,tud/ n. multitud f.

mummy /'mʌmi/ n. momia f.

mumps /mʌmps/ n. paperas f.pl.

municipal /myu'nɪsəpəl/ a. municipal.

munificent /myu'nɪfəsənt/ a. munífico.

munitions /myu'nɪʃənz/ n. municiones m.pl.

mural /'myʊrəl/ a. & n. mural m.

murder /'mɜrdər/ n. **1.** asesinato; homicidio m. —v. **2.** asesinar.

murderer /'mɜrdərər/ n. asesino -na.

murmur /'mɜrmər/ n. **1.** murmullo m. —v. **2.** murmurar.

muscle /'mʌsəl/ n. músculo m.

muscular /'mʌskyələr/ a. muscular.

muse /myuz/ n. **1.** musa f. —v. **2.** meditar.

museum /myu'ziəm/ n. museo m.

mushroom /'mʌʃrum/ n. seta f., hongo m.

music /'myuzɪk/ n. música f.

musical /'myuzɪkəl/ a. musical; melodioso.

musician /myu'zɪʃən/ n. músico -ca.

Muslim /'mʌzlɪm/ a. & n. musulmán.

muslin /'mʌzlɪn/ n. muselina f.; percal m.

mussel /'mʌsəl/ n. mejillón m.

must /mʌst/ v. deber; tener que.

mustache /'mʌstæʃ/ n. bigotes m.pl.

mustard /'mʌstərd/ n. mostaza f.

muster /'mʌstər/ n. **1.** Mil. revista f. —v. **2.** reunir, juntar.

mute /myut/ a. & n. mudo -da.

mutilate /'myut],eɪt/ v. mutilar.

mutiny /'myutṇi/ n. **1.** motín m. —v. **2.** amotinarse.

mutt /mʌt/ n. Colloq. chucho m.

mutter /'mʌtər/ v. refunfuñar, gruñir.

mutton /'mʌtṇ/ n. carnero m.

mutual /'myutʃuəl/ a. mutuo.

muzzle /'mʌzəl/ n. **1.** hocico m.; bozal m. —v. **2.** embozar.

my /maɪ/ a. mi.

myriad /'mɪriəd/ n. miríada f.

myrtle /'mɜrtl/ n. mirto m.

myself /maɪ'sɛlf/ pron. mí, mí mismo; me. **I m.,** yo mismo.

mysterious /mɪ'stɪəriəs/ a. misterioso.

mystery /'mɪstəri/ n. misterio m.

mystic /'mɪstɪk/ a. místico.

mystify /'mɪstə,faɪ/ v. confundir.

myth /mɪθ/ n. mito m.

mythical /'mɪθɪkəl/ a. mítico.

mythology /mɪ'θɒlədʒi/ n. mitología f.

N

nag /næg/ n. **1.** jaca f. —v. **2.** regañar; sermonear.

nail /neɪl/ n. **1.** clavo m.; (finger) uña f. **n. polish,** esmalte para las uñas. —v. **2.** clavar.

naïve /nɑ'iv/ a. ingenuo.

naked /'neɪkɪd/ a. desnudo.

name /neɪm/ n. **1.** nombre m.; reputación f. —v. **2.** nombrar, mencionar.

namely /'neɪmli/ adv. a saber; es decir.

namesake /'neɪm,seɪk/ n. tocayo m.

nanny /'næni/ n. niñera f.

nap /næp/ n. siesta f. **to take a n.,** echar una siesta.

naphtha /'næfθə, 'næp-/ n. nafta f.

napkin /'næpkɪn/ n. servilleta f.

narcissus /nɑr'sɪsəs/ n. narciso m.

narcotic /nɑr'kɒtɪk/ a. & n. narcótico m.

narrate /'næreɪt/ v. narrar.

narrative /'nærətɪv/ a. **1.** narrativo. —n. **2.** cuento, relato m.

narrow /'nærou/ a. estrecho, angosto. **n.-minded,** intolerante.

nasal /'neizəl/ a. nasal.

nasty /'næsti/ a. desagradable.

nation /'neiʃən/ n. nación f.

national /'næʃənl/ a. nacional.

nationalism /'næʃənl,ızəm/ n. nacionalismo m.

nationality /,næʃə'næliti/ n. nacionalidad f.

nationalization /,næʃənlə'zeiʃən/ n. nacionalización f.

nationalize /'næʃənl,aiz, 'næʃnə,laiz/ v. nacionalizar.

native /'neitiv/ a. **1.** nativo. —n. **2.** natural; indígena m. & f.

nativity /nə'tiviti/ n. natividad f.

natural /'nætʃərəl/ a. natural.

naturalist /'nætʃərəlıst/ n. naturalista m. & f.

naturalize /'nætʃərə,laiz/ v. naturalizar.

naturalness /,nætʃərəlnıs/ n. naturalidad f.

nature /'neitʃər/ n. naturaleza f.; índole f.; humor m.

naughty /'nɔti/ a. travieso, desobediente.

nausea /'nɔziə, -ʒə/ n. náusea f.

nauseous /'nɔʃəs/ a. nauseoso.

nautical /'nɔtikəl/ a. náutico.

naval /'neivəl/ a. naval.

nave /neiv/ n. nave f.

navel /'neivəl/ n. ombligo m.

navigable /'nævɪɡəbəl/ a. navegable.

navigate /'nævɪ,ɡeit/ v. navegar.

navigation /,nævɪ'ɡeiʃən/ n. navegación f.

navigator /'nævɪ,ɡeitər/ n. navegante m. & f.

navy /'neivi/ n. marina f.

navy blue azul marino m.

near /nɪər/ a. **1.** cercano, próximo. —adv. **2.** cerca. —prep. **3.** cerca de.

nearby /'nɪər'bai/ a. **1.** cercano. —adv **2.** cerca.

nearly /'nɪərli/ adv. casi.

nearsighted /'nɪər,saitid/ a. corto de vista.

neat /nit/ a. aseado; ordenado.

neatness /'nitnıs/ n. aseo m.

nebulous /'nebyələs/ a. nebuloso.

necessary /'nesə,seri/ a. necesario.

necessity /nə'sesiti/ n. necesidad f.

neck /nɛk/ n. cuello m.

necklace /'nɛklıs/ n. collar m.

necktie /'nɛk,tai/ n. corbata f.

nectar /'nɛktər/ n. néctar m.

nectarine /,nɛktə'rin/ n. nectarina f.

need /nid/ n. **1.** necesidad; (poverty) pobreza f. —v. **2.** necesitar.

needle /'nidl/ n. aguja f.

needless /'nidlıs/ a. innecesario, inútil.

needy /'nidi/ a. indigente, necesitado, pobre.

nefarious /nɪ'fɛəriəs/ a. nefario.

negative /'nɛɡətiv/ a. negativo. n. negativa f.

neglect /nɪ'ɡlɛkt/ n. **1.** negligencia f.; descuido m. —v. **2.** descuidar.

negligee /,nɛɡlɪ'ʒei/ n. negligé m., bata de casa f.

negligent /'nɛɡlɪdʒənt/ a. negligente, descuidado.

negligible /'nɛɡlɪdʒəbəl/ a. insignificante.

negotiate /nɪ'ɡouʃi,eit/ v. negociar.

negotiation /nɪ,ɡouʃi'eiʃən/ n. negociación f.

Negro /'nigrou/ n. negro -ra.

neighbor /'neibər/ n. vecino -na.

neighborhood /'neibər,hud/ n. vecindad f.

neither /'niðər, 'nai-/ a. & pron. **1.** ninguno de los dos. —adv. **2.** tampoco. —conj. **3.** neither... nor, ni... ni.

neon /'nion/ n. neón m. **n. light,** tubo neón m.

nephew /'nɛfyu/ n. sobrino m.

nerve /nɜrv/ n. nervio m.; Colloq. audacia f.

nervous /'nɜrvəs/ a. nervioso.

nervous breakdown /'breik,daun/ crisis nerviosa f.

nest /nɛst/ n. nido m.

net /nɛt/ a. **1.** neto. —n. **2.** red f. **hair n.,** albanega, redecilla f. v. redar; Com. ganar.

netiquette /'nɛtikıt/ n. etiqueta de la red f.

netting /'nɛtiŋ/ n. red m.; obra de malla f.

network /'nɛt,wɜrk/ n. (radio) red radiodifusora.

neuralgia /nu'rældʒə/ n. neuralgia f.

neurology /nu'rolədʒi/ n. neurología f.

neurotic /nu'rotik/ a. neurótico.

neutral /'nutrəl/ a. neutral.

neutrality /nu'træliti/ n. neutralidad f.

neutron /'nutron/ n. neutrón m.

neutron bomb bomba de neutrones f.

never /'nɛvər/ adv. nunca, jamás; **n. mind,** no importa.

nevertheless /,nɛvərðə'lɛs/ adv. no obstante, sin embargo.

new /nu/ a. nuevo.

newbie /'nubi/ n. Colloq. novato -ta, inexperto -ta.

news /nuz/ n. noticias f.pl.

newsboy /'nuz,boi/ n. vendedor -ra de periódicos.

news bulletin boletín informativo m.

news flash n. noticia de última hora f.

newsgroup /'nuz,grup/ n. grupo de discusión m.

newsletter /'nuz,lɛtər/ n. hoja informativa f.

newspaper /'nuz,peipər/ n. periódico m.

New Testament Nuevo Testamento m.

new year n. año nuevo m.

next /nɛkst/ a. **1.** próximo; siguiente; contiguo. —*adv.* **2.** luego, después. **n. door,** al lado. **n. to,** al lado de.

next-to-the-last /'nɛkst tə ðə 'læst/ *a.* penúltimo.

nibble /'nɪbəl/ *v.* picar.

nice /nis/ *a.* simpático, agradable; amable; hermoso; exacto.

nick /nɪk/ *n.* muesca *f.*, picadura *f.* **in the n. of time,** a punto.

nickel /'nɪkəl/ *n.* níquel *m.*

nickname /'nɪk,neim/ *n.* **1.** apodo, mote *m.* —*v.* **2.** apodar.

nicotine /'nɪkə,tin/ *n.* nicotina *f.*

niece /nis/ *n.* sobrina *f.*

niggardly /'nɪgərdli/ *a.* mezquino.

night /nait/ *n.* noche *f.* **good n.,** buenas noches. **last n.,** anoche. **n. club,** cabaret *m.*

nightclub /'nait,klʌb/ *n.* cabaret *m.*

nightclub owner cabaretero -ra *m. & f.*

nightgown /'nait,gaun/ *n.* camisa de dormir.

nightingale /'naitṇ,geil, 'naitɪŋ-/ *n.* ruiseñor *m.*

nightly /'naitli/ *adv.* todas las noches.

nightmare /'nait,mɛər/ *n.* pesadilla *f.*

night school escuela nocturna *f.*

night watchman vigilante nocturno *m.*

nimble /'nɪmbəl/ *a.* ágil.

nine /nain/ *a. & pron.* nueve.

nineteen /'nain'tin/ *a. & pron.* diecinueve.

ninety /'nainti/ *a. & pron.* noventa.

ninth /nainθ/ *a.* noveno.

nipple /'nɪpəl/ *n.* teta *f.*; pezón *m.*

nitrogen /'naitrədʒən/ *n.* nitrógeno *m.*

no /nou/ *a.* **1.** ninguno. **no one,** nadie. —*adv.* **2.** no.

nobility /nou'bɪlɪti/ *n.* nobleza *f.*

noble /'noubəl/ *a. & n.* noble *m.*

nobleman /'noubəlmən/ *n.* noble *m.*

nobody /'nou,bɒdi/ *pron.* nadie.

nocturnal /nɒk'tɜrnl/ *a.* nocturno.

nocturne /'nɒktɜrn/ *n.* nocturno *m.*

nod /nɒd/ *n.* **1.** seña con la cabeza. —*v.* **2.** inclinar la cabeza; (doze) dormitar.

no-frills /'nou 'frɪlz/ *a.* sin extras.

noise /nɔiz/ *n.* ruido *m.*

noiseless /'nɔizlɪs/ *a.* silencioso.

noisy /'nɔizi/ *a.* ruidoso.

nominal /'nɒmənl/ *a.* nominal.

nominate /'nɒmə,neit/ *v.* nombrar.

nomination /,nɒmə'neiʃən/ *n.* nombramiento *m.*, nominación *f.*

nominee /,nɒmə'ni/ *n.* candidato -ta.

nonaligned /,nɒnə'laind/ (in political sense), *a.* no alineado.

nonchalant /,nɒnʃə'lɒnt/ *a.* indiferente.

noncombatant /,nɒnkəm'bætnt/ *n.* no combatiente *m.*

noncommittal /,nɒnkə'mɪtl/ *a.* evasivo; reservado.

nondescript /,nɒndɪ'skrɪpt/ *a.* difícil de describir.

none /nʌn/ *pron.* ninguno.

nonentity /nɒn'ɛntɪti/ *n.* nulidad *f.*

nonpartisan /nɒn'pɑrtəzən/ *a.* sin afiliación.

non-proliferation /,nɒnprə,lɪfə'reiʃən/ *n.* no proliferación *f.*

nonsense /'nɒnsɛns/ *n.* tontería *f.*

nonsmoker /nɒn'smoukər/ *n.* no fumador -dora.

noodle /'nudl/ *n.* fideo *m.*

noon /nun/ *n.* mediodía *m.*

noose /nus/ *n.* lazo corredizo *m.*; dogal *m.*

nor /nɔr; unstressed nər/ conj. ni.

normal /'nɔrməl/ *a.* normal.

north /nɔrθ/ *n.* norte *m.*

North America /ə'mɛrɪkə/ Norte América *f.*

North American *a. & n.* norteamericano -na.

northeast /,nɔrθ'ist/ *Naut.* ,nɔr-/ *n.* nordeste *m.*

northern /'nɔrðərn/ *a.* septentrional.

North Pole *n.* Polo Norte *m.*

northwest /,nɔrθ'wɛst/ *Naut.* ,nɔr-/ *n.* noroeste *m.*

Norway /'nɔrwei/ *n.* Noruega *f.*

Norwegian /nɔr'widʒən/ *a. & n.* noruego -ga.

nose /nouz/ *n.* nariz *f.*

nosebleed /'nouz,blid/ *n.* hemorragia nasal *f.*

nostalgia /nɒ'stældʒə/ *n.* nostalgia *f*

nostril /'nɒstrəl/ *n.* ventana de la nariz; (pl.) narices *f.pl.*

not /nɒt/ *adv.* no. **n. at all,** de ninguna manera. **n. even,** ni siquiera.

notable /'noutəbəl/ *a.* notable.

notary /'noutəri/ *n.* notario *m.*

notation /nou'teiʃən/ *n.* notación *f.*

notch /nɒtʃ/ *n.* muesca *f.*; corte *m.*

note /nout/ *n.* **1.** nota *f.*; apunte *m.* —*v.* **2.** notar.

notebook /'nout,buk/ *n.* libreta *f.*, cuaderno *m.*

noted /'noutɪd/ *a.* célebre.

notepaper /'nout,peipər/ *n.* papel de notas *m.*

noteworthy /'nout,wɜrði/ *a.* notable.

nothing /'nʌθɪŋ/ *pron.* nada.

notice /'noutɪs/ *n.* **1.** aviso *m.*; noticia *f.* —*v.* **2.** observar, fijarse en.

noticeable /'noutɪsəbəl/ *a.* notable.

notification /,noutəfɪ'keiʃən/ *n.* notificación *f.*

notify /'noutə,fai/ *v.* notificar.

notion /'nouʃən/ *n.* noción; idea *f.*; (pl.) novedades *f.pl.*

notoriety /ˌnoutəˈraiti/ n. notoriedad f.

notorious /nouˈtɔriəs/ a. notorio.

noun /naun/ n. nombre, sustantivo m.

nourish /ˈnɔriʃ/ v. nutrir, alimentar.

nourishment /ˈnɔriʃmənt/ n. nutrimento; alimento m.

novel /ˈnɒvəl/ a. **1.** nuevo, original. —n. **2.** novela f.

novelist /ˈnɒvəlɪst/ n. novelista m. & f.

novelty /ˈnɒvəlti/ n. novedad f.

November /nouˈvɛmbər/ n. noviembre m.

novena /nouˈvinə/ n. novena f.

novice /ˈnɒvɪs/ n. novicio -cia, novato -ta.

novocaine /ˈnouvəˌkein/ n. novocaína f.

now /nau/ adv. ahora. **n. and then,** de vez en cuando. **by n.,** ya. **from n. on,** de ahora en adelante. **just n.,** ahorita. **right n.,** ahora mismo.

nowadays /ˈnauəˌdeiz/ adv. hoy día, hoy en día, actualmente.

nowhere /ˈnouˌwɛər/ adv. en ninguna parte.

nozzle /ˈnɒzəl/ n. boquilla f.

nuance /ˈnuɑns/ n. matiz m.

nuclear /ˈnukliər/ a. nuclear.

nuclear energy energía nuclear f.

nuclear warhead /ˈwɔrˌhɛd/ cabeza nuclear f.

nuclear waste desechos nucleares m.pl.

nucleus /ˈnukliəs/ n. núcleo m.

nude /nud/ a. desnudo.

nuisance /ˈnusəns/ n. molestia f.

nuke /nuk/ n. bomba atómica f.

nullify /ˈnʌləˌfai/ v. anular.

number /ˈnʌmbər/ n. **1.** número m.; cifra f. **license n.,** matrícula f. —v. **2.** numerar, contar.

numeric /nuˈmɛrɪk/ **numerical** a. numérico.

numeric keypad /nuˈmɛrɪk/ teclado numérico m.

numerous /ˈnumərəs/ a. numeroso.

nun /nun/ n. monja f.

nuptial /ˈnʌpʃəl/ a. nupcial.

nurse /nɜrs/ n. **1.** enfermera f.; (child's) ama, niñera f. —v. **2.** criar, alimentar, amamantar; cuidar.

nursery /ˈnɜrsəri/ n. cuarto destinado a los niños; Agr. plantel, criadero m.

nursery school jardín de infancia m.

nurture /ˈnɜrtʃər/ v. nutrir.

nut /nʌt/ n. nuez f.; Mech. tuerca f.

nutcracker /ˈnʌtˌkrækər/ n. cascanueces m.

nutrition /nuˈtrɪʃən/ n. nutrición f.

nutritious /nuˈtrɪʃəs/ a. nutritivo.

nylon /ˈnailɒn/ n. nilón m.

nymph /nɪmf/ n. ninfa f.

O

oak /ouk/ n. roble m.

oar /ɔr/ n. remo m.

OAS abbr. (Organization of American States) OEA (Organización de los Estados Americanos) f.

oasis /ouˈeisɪs/ n. oasis m.

oat /out/ n. avena f.

oath /ouθ/ n. juramento m.

oatmeal /ˈoutˌmil/ n. harina de avena f.

obedience /ouˈbidiəns/ n. obediencia f.

obedient /ouˈbidiənt/ a. obediente.

obese /ouˈbis/ a. obeso, gordo.

obey /ouˈbei/ v. obedecer.

obituary /ouˈbɪtʃuˌɛri/ n obituario m.

object /n ˈɒbdʒɪkt; v əbˈdʒɛkt/ n. **1.** objeto m.; Gram. complemento m. —v. **2.** oponerse; objetar.

objection /əbˈdʒɛkʃən/ n. objeción f.

objectionable /əbˈdʒɛkʃənəbəl/ a. censurable.

objective /əbˈdʒɛktɪv/ a. & n. objetivo m.

obligation /ˌɒblɪˈgeiʃən/ n. obligación f.

obligatory /əˈblɪgəˌtɔri/ a. obligatorio.

oblige /əˈblaidʒ/ v. obligar; complacer.

oblique /əˈblik/ a. oblicuo.

obliterate /əˈblɪtəˌreit/ v. borrar; destruir.

oblivion /əˈblɪviən/ n. olvido m.

oblong /ˈɒbˌlɔŋ/ a. oblongo.

obnoxious /əbˈnɒkʃəs/ a. ofensivo, odioso.

obscene /əbˈsin/ a. obsceno, indecente.

obscure /əbˈskyur/ a. **1.** obscuro. —v. **2.** obscurecer.

observance /əbˈzɜrvəns/ n. observancia; ceremonia f.

observation /ˌɒbzərˈveiʃən/ n. observación f.

observatory /əbˈzɜrvəˌtɔri/ n. observatorio m.

observe /əbˈzɜrv/ v. observar; celebrar.

observer /əbˈzɜrvər/ n. observador -ra.

obsession /əbˈsɛʃən/ n. obsesión f.

obsolete /ˌɒbsəˈlit/ a. anticuado.

obstacle /ˈɒbstəkəl/ n. obstáculo m.

obstetrician /ˌɒbstɪˈtrɪʃən/ n. obstétrico, -ca, tocólogo, -ga m. & f.

obstinate /ˈɒbstənɪt/ a. obstinado, terco.

obstruct /əbˈstrʌkt/ v. obstruir, impedir.

obstruction /əbˈstrʌkʃən/ n. obstrucción f.

obtain /əbˈtein/ v. obtener, conseguir.

obtuse /əbˈtus/ a. obtuso.

obviate /ˈɒbviˌeit/ v. obviar.

obvious /ˈɒbviəs/ a. evidente, obvio.

occasion /əˈkeiʒən/ n. **1.** ocasión f. —v. **2.** ocasionar.

occasional /əˈkeiʒənl/ a. ocasional.

occult /əˈkʌlt/ a. oculto.

occupant /ˈɒkyəpənt/ n. ocupante m. & f.; inquilino -na.

occupation /ˌɒkyəˈpeiʃən/ n. ocupación f.; empleo m.

occupy /ˈɒkyəˌpai/ v. ocupar; emplear.

occur /əˈkɜr/ v. ocurrir.

occurrence /əˈkɜrəns/ n. ocurrencia f.

ocean /ˈouʃən/ n. océano m.

o'clock /əˈklɒk/ it's one o., es la una. it's two o., son las dos, etc. at... o., a las...

octagon /ˈɒktəˌgɒn/ n. octágono m.

octave /ˈɒktɪv/ n. octava f.

October /ɒkˈtoubər/ n. octubre m.

octopus /ˈɒktəpəs/ n. pulpo m.

oculist /ˈɒkyəlɪst/ n. oculista m. & f.

odd /ɒd/ a. impar; suelto; raro.

odd number número impar m.

odious /ˈoudiəs/ a. odioso.

odor /ˈoudər/ n. olor m.; fragancia f.

of /əv/ prep. de.

off /ɔf/ adv. (see under verb: stop off, take off, etc.)

offend /əˈfend/ v. ofender.

offender /əˈfendər/ n. ofensor -ra; delincuente m. & f.

offense /əˈfens/ n. ofensa f.; crimen m.

offensive /əˈfensɪv/ a. **1.** ofensivo. —n. **2.** ofensiva f.

offer /ˈɔfər/ n. **1.** oferta f. —v. **2.** ofrecer.

offering /ˈɔfərɪŋ/ n. oferta f.

office /ˈɔfɪs/ n. oficina f.; despacho m.; oficio, cargo m.

officer /ˈɔfəsər/ n. oficial m. & f. police o., agente de policía m. & f.

official /əˈfiʃəl/ a. **1.** oficial. —n. **2.** oficial m. & f., funcionario -ria.

officiate /əˈfiʃiˌeit/ v. oficiar.

officious /əˈfiʃəs/ a. oficioso.

offspring /ˈɔfˌsprɪŋ/ n. hijos m.pl.; progenie f.

often /ˈɔfən/ adv. muchas veces, a menudo. how o., con qué frecuencia.

oil /ɔil/ n. **1.** aceite; óleo; petróleo m. —v. **2.** aceitar; engrasar.

oil refinery /rɪˈfainəri/ destilería de petróleo f.

oil tanker /ˈtæŋkər/ petrolero m.

oily /ˈɔili/ a. aceitoso.

ointment /ˈɔintmənt/ n. ungüento m.

okay /ˈouˈkei, ˌouˈkei/ adv. bien; de acuerdo.

old /ould/ a. viejo; antiguo. o. man, o. woman, viejo -ja.

old-fashioned /ˈould ˈfæʃənd/ a. fuera de moda, anticuado.

Old Testament Antiguo Testamento m.

olive /ˈɒlɪv/ n. aceituna, oliva f.

ombudsman /ˈɒmbədzmən/ n. ombudsman m.

omelet /ˈɒmlɪt/ n. tortilla de huevos.

omen /ˈoumən/ n. agüero m.

ominous /ˈɒmənəs/ a. ominoso, siniestro.

omission /ouˈmiʃən/ n. omisión f.; olvido m.

omit /ouˈmɪt/ v. omitir.

omnibus /ˈɒmnəˌbʌs/ n. ómnibus m.

omnipotent /ɒmˈnipətənt/ a. omnipotente.

on /ɒn/ prep. **1.** en, sobre, encima de. —adv. **2.** adelante.

once /wʌns/ adv. una vez. at o., en seguida. o. in a while, de vez en cuando.

one /wʌn/ a. & pron. uno -na.

one-armed bandit /ˈwʌn ˌɑrmd/ tragaperras f.

oneself /wʌnˈsɛlf/ pron. sí mismo -ma; se. with o., consigo.

onion /ˈʌnyən/ n. cebolla f.

on-line /ˈɒn ˈlain/ a. conectado.

only /ˈounli/ a. **1.** único, solo. —adv. **2.** sólo, solamente.

onward /ˈɒnwərd/ adv. adelante.

opal /ˈoupəl/ n. ópalo m.

opaque /ouˈpeik/ a. opaco.

open /ˈoupən/ a. **1.** abierto; franco. o. air, aire libre. —v. **2.** abrir.

opening /ˈoupənɪŋ/ n. abertura f.

opera /ˈɒpərə/ n. ópera f. o. glasses, anteojos de ópera; gemelos m.pl.

operate /ˈɒpəˌreit/ v. operar.

operation /ˌɒpəˈreiʃən/ n. operación f. to have an o., operarse, ser operado.

operative /ˈɒpərətɪv/ a. eficaz, operativo.

operator /ˈɒpəˌreitər/ n. operario -ria. elevator o., ascensorista m. & f. telephone o., telefonista m. & f.

operetta /ˌɒpəˈretə/ n. opereta f.

ophthalmic /ɒfˈθælmɪk, ɒp-/ a. oftálmico.

opinion /əˈpinyən/ n. opinión f.

opponent /əˈpounənt/ n. antagonista m. & f.

opportunism /ˌɒpərˈtunizəm/ n. oportunismo m.

opportunity /ˌɒpərˈtuniti/ n. ocasión, oportunidad f.

oppose /əˈpouz/ v. oponer.

opposite /ˈɒpəzɪt/ a. **1.** opuesto, contrario. —prep. **2.** al frente de. —n. **3.** contrario m.

opposition /ˌɒpəˈziʃən/ n. oposición f.

oppress /əˈpres/ v. oprimir.

oppression /əˈpreʃən/ n. opresión f.

oppressive /əˈpresɪv/ a. opresivo.

optic /ˈɒptɪk/ a. óptico.

optical disc /ˈɒptɪkəl ˈdɪsk/ disco óptico m.

optical illusion /'ɒptɪkəl/ ɪlusión de óptica f.

optician /ɒp'tɪʃən/ n. óptico -ca.

optics /'ɒptɪks/ n. óptica f.

optimism /'ɒptə,mɪzəm/ n. optimismo.

optimistic /,ɒptə'mɪstɪk/ a. optimista.

option /'ɒpʃən/ n. opción, elección f.

optional /'ɒpʃənl/ a. discrecional, facultativo.

optometry /ɒp'tɒmɪtri/ n. optometría f.

opulent /'ɒpyələnt/ a. opulento.

or /ɔr/ conj. o, (before o-, ho-) u.

oracle /'ɔrəkəl/ n. oráculo m.

oral /'ɔrəl/ a. oral, vocal.

orange /'ɔrɪndʒ/ n. naranja f.

orange juice jugo de naranja, zumo de naranja m.

orange squeezer /'skwizər/ n. exprimidora de naranjas f.

oration /ɔ'reɪʃən/ n. discurso m.; oración f.

orator /'ɔrətər/ n. orador -ra.

oratory /'ɔrə,tɔri/ n. oratoria f.; (church) oratorio m.

orbit /'ɔrbɪt/ n. órbita f.

orchard /'ɔrtʃərd/ n. huerto m.

orchestra /'ɔrkəstrə/ n. orquesta f. **o. seat,** butaca f.

orchid /'ɔrkɪd/ n. orquídea f.

ordain /ɔr'deɪn/ v. ordenar.

ordeal /ɔr'dil/ n. prueba f.

order /'ɔrdər/ n. orden, m. or f.; clase f.; Com. pedido m. **in o. that,** para que. v. ordenar; mandar; pedir.

order blank hoja de pedidos f.

orderly /'ɔrdərli/ a. ordenado.

ordinance /'ɔrdnəns/ n. ordenanza f.

ordinary /'ɔrdn,ɛri/ a. ordinario.

ordination /,ɔrdn'eɪʃən/ n. ordenación f.

ore /ɔr/ n. mineral m.

organ /'ɔrgən/ n. órgano m.

organdy /'ɔrgəndi/ n. organdí m.

organic /ɔr'gænɪk/ a. orgánico.

organism /'ɔrgə,nɪzəm/ n. organismo m.

organist /'ɔrgənɪst/ n. organista m. & f.

organization /,ɔrgənə'zeɪʃən/ n. organización f.

organize /'ɔrgə,naɪz/ v. organizar.

orgy /'ɔrdʒi/ n. orgía f.

orient /'ɔriənt/ n. **1.** oriente m. —v. **2.** orientar.

Orient /'ɔriənt/ n. Oriente m.

Oriental /,ɔri'ɛntl/ a. oriental.

orientation /,ɔriən'teɪʃən/ n. orientación f.

origin /'ɔrɪdʒɪn/ n. origen m.

original /ə'rɪdʒənl/ a. & n. original m.

originality /ə,rɪdʒə'nælɪti/ n. originalidad f.

ornament /n 'ɔrnəmənt; v -,mɛnt/ n. **1.** ornamento m. —v. **2.** ornamentar.

ornamental /,ɔrnə'mɛntl/ a. ornamental, decorativo.

ornate /ɔr'neɪt/ a. ornado.

ornithology /,ɔrnə'θɒlədʒi/ n. ornitología f.

orphan /'ɔrfən/ a. & n. huérfano -na.

orphanage /'ɔrfənɪdʒ/ n. orfanato m.

orthodox /'ɔrθə,dɒks/ a. ortodoxo.

ostentation /,ɒstɛn'teɪʃən/ n. ostentación f.

ostentatious /,ɒstɛn'teɪʃəs/ a. ostentoso.

ostrich /'ɒstrɪtʃ/ n. avestruz f.

other /'ʌðər/ a. & pron. otro. **every o. day,** un día sí otro no.

otherwise /'ʌðər,waɪz/ adv. de otra manera.

ought /ɔt/ v. deber.

ounce /aʊns/ n. onza f.

our /aʊ³r; unstressed ɑr/ **ours** a. & pron. nuestro.

ourselves /ʊr'sɛlvz/ pron. nosotros, -as; mismos, -as; nos.

oust /aʊst/ v. desalojar.

ouster /'aʊstər/ n. desahucio m.

out /aʊt/ adv. **1.** fuera, afuera. **out of,** fuera de. —prep. **2.** por.

outbreak /'aʊt,breɪk/ n. erupción f.

outcast /'aʊt,kæst/ n. paria m. & f.

outcome /'aʊt,kʌm/ n. resultado m.

outdoors /,aʊt'dɔrz/ adv. fuera de casa; aire libre.

outer /'aʊtər/ a. exterior, externo.

outfit /'aʊt,fɪt/ n. **1.** equipo; traje m. —v. **2.** equipar.

outgrowth /'aʊt,groʊθ/ n. resultado m.

outing /'aʊtɪŋ/ n. paseo m.

outlaw /'aʊt,lɔ/ n. **1.** bandido m. —v. **2.** proscribir.

outlet /'aʊtlɛt/ n. salida f.

outline /'aʊt,laɪn/ n. **1.** contorno; esbozo m.; silueta f. —v. **2.** esbozar.

outlive /,aʊt'lɪv/ v. sobrevivir.

out-of-court settlement /'aʊtəv,kɔrt/ arreglo pacífico m.

out-of-date /'aʊt əv 'deɪt/ a. anticuado.

out of focus a. desenfocado.

outpost /'aʊt,poʊst/ n. puesto avanzado m.

output /'aʊt,pʊt/ n. capacidad f.; producción f.

outrage /'aʊtreɪdʒ/ n. **1.** ultraje m.; atrocidad f. —v. **2.** ultrajar.

outrageous /aʊt'reɪdʒəs/ a. atroz.

outrun /,aʊt'rʌn/ v. exceder.

outside /a. prep. adv 'aʊt'saɪd; n 'aʊt'saɪd/ a. & n. **1.** exterior m. —adv. **2.** afuera, por fuera. —prep. **3.** fuera de.

outskirt /'aʊt,skɜrt/ n. borde m.

outward /'aʊtwərd/ adv. hacia afuera.

outwardly /'aʊtwərdli/ adv. exteriormente.

oval /'oʊvəl/ a. **1.** oval, ovalado. —n. **2.** óvalo m.

ovary /'oʊvəri/ n. ovario m.

ovation /oʊ'veɪʃən/ n. ovación f.

oven /'ʌvən/ n. horno m.

over /'ouvər/ *prep.* **1.** sobre, encima de; por. —*adv.* **2. o. here,** aquí. **o. there,** allí, por allí. **to be o.,** estar terminado.

overcoat /'ouvər,kout/ *n.* abrigo, sobretodo *m.*

overcome /,ouvər'kʌm/ *v.* superar, vencer.

overdose /'ouvər,dous/ *n.* sobredosis *f.*

overdue /,ouvər'du/ *a.* retrasado.

overflow /n 'ouvər,flou; v ,ouvər'flou/ *n.* **1.** inundación *f.* —*v.* **2.** inundar.

overhaul /,ouvər'hɔl/ *v.* repasar.

overhead /'ouvər'hed/ *adv.* arriba, en lo alto.

overkill /'ouvər,kɪl/ *n.* efecto mayor que el pretendido.

overlook /,ouvər'luk/ *v.* pasar por alto.

overnight /'ouvər'nait/ *adv.* **to stay or stop o.,** pasar la noche.

overpower /,ouvər'pauər/ *v.* vencer.

overrule /,ouvər'rul/ *v.* predominar.

overrun /,ouvər'rʌn/ *v.* invadir.

oversee /,ouvər'si/ *v.* superentender.

oversight /'ouvər,sait/ *n.* descuido *m.*

overt /ou'vərt/ *a.* abierto.

overtake /,ouvər'teik/ *v.* alcanzar.

overthrow /n 'ouvər,θrou; v ,ouvər'θrou/ *n.* **1.** trastorno *m.* —*v.* **2.** trastornar.

overture /'ouvərtʃər/ *n. Mus.* obertura *f.*

overturn /,ouvər'tərn/ *v.* trastornar.

overview /'ouvər,vyu/ *n.* visión de conjunto *f.*

overweight /'ouvər,weit/ *a.* demasiado pesado.

overwhelm /,ouvər'welm/ *v.* abrumar.

overwork /,ouvər'wərk/ *v.* trabajar demasiado.

owe /ou/ *v.* deber. **owing to,** debido a.

owl /aul/ *n.* búho *m.*, lechuza *f.*

own /oun/ *a* **1.** propio. —*v.* **2.** poseer.

owner /'ounər/ *n.* dueño -ña.

ox /ɒks/ *n.* buey *m.*

oxygen /'ɒksɪdʒən/ *n.* oxígeno *m.*

oxygen tent tienda de oxígeno *f.*

oyster /'ɔistər/ *n.* ostra *f.*

P

pace /peis/ *n.* **1.** paso *m.* —*v.* **2.** pasearse. **p. off,** medir a pasos.

pacific /pə'sɪfɪk/ *a.* pacífico.

Pacific Ocean Océano Pacífico *m.*

pacifier /'pæsə,faiər/ *n.* pacificador *m.*; (baby p.) chupete *m.*

pacifism /'pæsə,fɪzəm/ *n.* pacifismo *m.*

pacifist /'pæsəfɪst/ *n.* pacifista *m.* & *f.*

pacify /'pæsə,fai/ *v.* pacificar.

pack /pæk/ *n.* **1.** fardo; paquete *m.*; (animals) muta *f.* **p. of cards,** baraja *f.* —*v.* **2.** empaquetar; (baggage) empacar.

package /'pækɪdʒ/ *n.* paquete, bulto *m.*

package tour viaje todo incluido *m.*

pact /pækt/ *n.* pacto *m.*

pad /pæd/ *n.* **1.** colchoncillo *m.* **p. of paper,** bloc de papel. —*v.* **2.** rellenar.

paddle /'pædl/ *n.* **1.** canalete *m.* —*v.* **2.** remar.

padlock /'pæd,lɒk/ *n.* candado *m.*

pagan /'peigən/ *a.* & *n.* pagano -na.

page /peidʒ/ *n.* página *f.*; (boy) paje *m.*

pageant /'pædʒənt/ *n.* espectáculo *m.*; procesión *f.*

pail /peil/ *n.* cubo *m.*

pain /pein/ *n.* dolor *m.* **to take pains,** esmerarse.

painful /'peinfəl/ *a.* doloroso; penoso.

pain killer /'pein,kɪlər/ analgésico *m.*

paint /peint/ *n.* **1.** pintura *f.* —*v.* **2.** pintar.

painter /'peintər/ *n.* pintor -ra.

painting /'peintɪŋ/ *n.* pintura *f.*; cuadro *m.*

pair /peər/ *n.* **1.** par *m.*; pareja *f.* —*v.* **2.** parear. **p. off,** emparejarse.

pajamas /pə'dʒɑməz, -'dʒæməz/ *n.* pijama *m.*

palace /'pælɪs/ *n.* palacio *m.*

palatable /'pælətəbəl/ *a.* sabroso, agradable.

palate /'pælɪt/ *n.* paladar *m.*

palatial /pə'leifəl/ *a.* palaciego, suntuoso.

pale /peil/ *a.* pálido. **to turn pale,** palidecer.

paleness /'peilnɪs/ *n.* palidez *f.*

palette /'pælɪt/ *n.* paleta *f.*

pallbearer /'pɔl,beərər/ *n.* portador del féretro, portaféretro *m.*

pallid /'pælɪd/ *a.* pálido.

palm /pɑm/ *n.* palma *f.* **p. tree,** palmera *f.*

palpitate /'pælpɪ,teit/ *v.* palpitar.

paltry /'pɔltri/ *a.* miserable.

pamper /'pæmpər/ *v.* mimar.

pamphlet /'pæmflɪt/ *n.* folleto *m.*

pan /pæn/ *n.* cacerola *f.*

panacea /,pænə'siə/ *n.* panacea *f.*

Pan-American /,pænə'merɪkən/ *a.* panamericano.

pane /pein/ *n.* hoja de vidrio *f.*, cuadro *m.*

panel /'pænl/ *n.* tablero *m.*

pang /pæŋ/ *n.* dolor; remordimiento *m.*

panic /'pænɪk/ *n.* pánico *m.*

panorama /,pænə'ræmə, -'rɑmə/ *n.* panorama *m.*

pant /pænt/ *v.* jadear.

panther /'pænθər/ n. pantera f.

pantomine /'pæntə,maim/ n. pantomima f.; mímica f.

pantry /'pæntri/ n. despensa f.

pants /pænts/ n. pantalones, m.pl.

panty hose /'pænti,houz/ n. pantys, pantimedias f.pl. (medias hasta la cintura).

papal /'peipəl/ a. papal.

paper /'peipər/ n. papel; periódico; artículo m.

paperback /'peipər,bæk/ n. libro en rústica m.

paper clip sujetapapeles m.

paper cup vaso de papel m.

paper hanger /'peipər,hæŋər/ empapelador -ra.

paper money papel moneda m.

paperweight /'peipər,weit/ pisapapeles m.

papier-mâché /,peipərmə'ʃei, pɑ,pyei-/ n. cartón piedra m.

paprika /pæ'prikə, pə-, pɑ-, 'pæprikə/ n. pimentón m.

par /pɑr/ n. paridad f.; Com. par f.

parable /'pærəbəl/ n. parábola f.

parachute /'pærə,ʃut/ n. paracaídas m.

parade /pə'reid/ n. 1. desfile m., procesión f. —v. 2. desfilar.

paradise /'pærə,dais/ n. paraíso m.

paradox /'pærə,dɒks/ n. paradoja f.

paraffin /'pærəfin/ n. parafina f.

paragraph /'pærə,græf/ n. párrafo m.

parakeet /'pærə,kit/ n. perico m.

parallel /'pærə,lel/ a. 1. paralelo. —v. 2. correr parejas con.

paralysis /pə'ræləsis/ n. parálisis f.

paralyze /'pærə,laiz/ v. paralizar.

paramedic /,pærə'medik/ n. paramédico -ca.

parameter /pə'ræmitər/ n. parámetro m.

paramount /'pærə,maunt/ a. supremo.

paraphrase /'pærə,freiz/ n. 1. paráfrasis f. —v. 2. parafrasear.

paraplegic /pærə'plidʒik/ n. parapléjico -ca.

parasite /'pærə,sait/ n. parásito m.

parboil /'pɑr,bɔil/ v. sancochar.

parcel /'pɑrsəl/ n. paquete m. **p. of land,** lote de terreno.

parchment /'pɑrtʃmənt/ n. pergamino m.

pardon /'pɑrdn/ n. 1. perdón m. —v. 2. perdonar.

pare /pɛər/ v. pelar.

parentage /'pɛərəntidʒ, 'pær-/ n. origen m.; extracción f.

parenthesis /pə'renθəsis/ n. paréntesis m.

parents /'pɛərənts/ n. padres m.pl.

parish /'pæriʃ/ n. parroquia f.

Parisian /pə'riʒən, -'riʒən, -'riziən/ a. & n. parisiense m & f.

parity /'pæriti/ n. igualdad, paridad f.

park /pɑrk/ n. 1. parque m. —v. 2. estacionar.

parking lot /'pɑrkiŋ/ n. estacionamiento, aparcamiento m.

parking meter /'pɑrkiŋ/ parquímetro m.

parking space /'pɑrkiŋ/ estacionamiento, aparcamiento m.

parkway /'pɑrk,wei/ n. bulevar m.; autopista f.

parley /'pɑrli/ n. conferencia f.; Mil. parlamento m.

parliament /'pɑrləmənt/ n. parlamento m.

parliamentary /,pɑrlə'mentəri, -tri; sometimes ,pɑrlyə-/ a. parlamentario.

parlor /'pɑrlər/ n. sala f., salón m.

parochial /pə'roukiəl/ a. parroquial.

parody /'pærədi/ n. 1. parodia f. —v. 2. parodiar.

parole /pə'roul/ n. 1. palabra de honor f.; Mil. santo y seña. —v. 2. poner en libertad bajo palabra.

paroxysm /'pærək,sizəm/ n. paroxismo m.

parrot /'pærət/ n. loro, papagayo m.

parsimony /'pɑrsə,mouni/ n. parsimonia f.

parsley /'pɑrsli/ n. perejil m.

parson /'pɑrsən/ n. párroco m.

part /pɑrt/ n. 1. parte f.; Theat. papel m. —v. 2. separarse, partirse. **p. with,** desprenderse de.

partake /pɑr'teik/ v. tomar parte.

partial /'pɑrʃəl/ a. parcial.

participant /pɑr'tisəpənt/ n. participante m. & f.

participate /pɑr'tisə,peit/ v. participar.

participation /pɑr,tisə'peiʃən/ n. participación f.

participle /'pɑrtə,sipəl, -səpəl/ n. participio m.

particle /'pɑrtikəl/ n. partícula f.

particular /pɑr'tikyələr/ a. & n. particular m.

parting /'pɑrtiŋ/ n. despedida f.

partisan /'pɑrtəzən, -sən/ a. & n. partidario -ria.

partition /pɑr'tiʃən, pər-/ n. tabique m. v. dividir, partir.

partly /'pɑrtli/ adv. en parte.

partner /'pɑrtnər/ n. socio -cia; compañero -ra.

partridge /'pɑrtridʒ/ n. perdiz f.

party /'pɑrti/ n. tertulia, fiesta f.; grupo m.; (political) partido m.

pass /pæs/ n. 1. pase; (mountain) paso m. —v. 2. pasar. **p. away,** fallecer.

passable /'pæsəbəl/ a. transitable; regular.

passage /'pæsidʒ/ n. pasaje; (corridor) pasillo m.

passé /pæ'sei/ a. anticuado.

passenger /'pæsəndʒər/ n. pasajero -ra.

passenger ship buque de pasajeros m.

passerby /'pæsər'bai/ n. transeúnte m. & f.

passion /'pæʃən/ n. pasión f.

passionate /'pæʃənit/ a. apasionado.

passive /'pæsɪv/ a. pasivo.

passport /'pæsport/ n. pasaporte m.

password /'pæs,wərd/ n. código m., clave m., contraseña f.

past /pæst/ a. & n. **1.** pasado m. —prep. **2.** más allá de; después de.

paste /peist/ n. **1.** pasta f. —v. **2.** empastar; pegar.

pasteurize /'pæstʃə,raiz/ v. pasteurizar.

pastime /'pæs,taim/ n. pasatiempo m.; diversión f.

pastor /'pæstər/ n. pastor m.

pastrami /pə'strɑmi/ n. pastrón m.

pastry /'peistri/ n. pastelería f.

pasture /'pæstʃər/ n. **1.** pasto m.; pradera f. —v. **2.** pastar.

pat /pæt/ n. **1.** golpecillo m. **to stand p.,** mantenerse firme. —v. **2.** dar golpecillos.

patch /pætʃ/ n. **1.** remiendo m. —v. **2.** remendar.

patent /'pætnt/ a & n. **1.** patente m. —v. **2.** patentar.

patent leather /'pætnt. 'pætṇ/ charol m.

paternal /pə'tɜrnḷ/ a. paterno, paternal.

paternity /pə'tɜrnɪti/ n. paternidad f.

path /pæθ/ n. senda f.

pathetic /pə'θɛtɪk/ a. patético.

pathology /pə'θnlədʒi/ n. patología f.

pathos /'peiθns/ n. rasgo conmovedor m.

patience /'peiʃəns/ n. paciencia f.

patient /'peiʃənt/ a. **1.** paciente —n. **2.** enfermo -ma, paciente m. & f.

patio /'pæti,ou/ n. patio m.

patriarch /'peitri,urk/ n. patriarca m.

patriot /'peitriət/ n. patriota m. & f.

patriotic /,peitri'ɒtɪk/ a. patriótico.

patriotism /'peitriə,tɪzəm/ n. patriotismo m.

patrol /pə'troul/ n. **1.** patrulla f. —v. **2.** patrullar.

patrolman /pə'troulmən/ n. vigilante m.; patrullador m.

patron /'peitrən/ n. patrón m.

patronize /'peitrə,naiz/ v. condescender; patrocinar; ser cliente de.

pattern /'pætərn/ n. modelo m.

pauper /'pɔpər/ n. indigente m. & f.

pause /pɔz/ n. **1.** pausa f. —v. **2.** pausar.

pave /peiv/ v. pavimentar. **p. the way,** preparar el camino.

pavement /'peivmənt/ n. pavimento m.

pavilion /pə'vɪlyən/ n. pabellón m.

paw /pɔ/ n. **1.** pata f. —v. **2.** patear.

pawn /pɔn/ n. **1.** prenda f.; (chess) peón de ajedrez m. —v. **2.** empeñar.

pay /pei/ n. **1.** pago m.; sueldo, salario m.; —v. **2.** pagar. **p. back,** pagar; vengarse de. **p. cash,** pagar en metálico.

payee /pei'i/ n. destinatario -ria m. & f.

payment /'peimənt/ n. pago m.; recompensa f.

pay phone teléfono público m.

pea /pi/ n. guisante m.

peace /pis/ n. paz f.

peaceable /'pisəbəl/ a. pacífico.

peaceful /'pisfəl/ a. tranquilo.

peach /pitʃ/ n. durazno, melocotón m.

peacock /'pi,kɒk/ n. pavo real m.

peak /pik/ n. pico, cumbre; máximo m.

peal /pil/ n. repique; estruendo m. **p. of laughter,** risotada f.

peanut /'pi,nʌt/ n. maní, cacahuete m

pear /pɛər/ n. pera f.

pearl /pɜrl/ n. perla f.

peasant /'pɛzənt/ n. campesino -na.

pebble /'pɛbəl/ n. guija f.

peck /pɛk/ n. **1.** picotazo m. —v. **2.** picotear.

peckish /'pɛkɪʃ/ a. tener un poco de hambre.

peculiar /pɪ'kyulyər/ a. peculiar.

pecuniary /pɪ'kyuni,ɛri/ a. pecuniario.

pedagogue /'pɛdə,gɒg/ n. pedagogo -ga.

pedagogy /'pɛdə,goudʒi, -,gɒdʒi/ n. pedagogía f.

pedal /'pɛdḷ/ n. pedal m.

pedant /'pɛdnt/ n. pedante m & f.

peddler /'pɛdlər/ n. buhonero m.

pedestal /'pɛdəstḷ/ n. pedestal m.

pedestrian /pə'dɛstriən/ n. peatón -na.

pedestrian crossing paso de peatones m.

pediatrician /,pidiə'trɪʃən/ n. pediatra m. & f.

pediatrics /,pidi'ætrɪks/ n. puericultura f.

pedigree /'pɛdɪ,gri/ n. genealogía f.

peek /pik/ n. **1.** atisbo m. —v. **2.** atisbar.

peel /pil/ n. **1.** corteza f.; (fruit) pellejo m. —v. **2.** descortezar; pelar.

peep /pip/ n. **1.** ojeada f. —v **2.** mirar, atisbar.

peer /pɪər/ n. **1.** par m. —v. **2.** mirar fijamente.

peg /pɛg/ n. clavija; estaquilla f.; gancho m.

pelt /pɛlt/ n. **1.** pellejo m. —v. **2.** apedrear; (rain) caer con fuerza.

pelvis /'pɛlvɪs/ n. pelvis f.

pen /pɛn/ n. pluma f.; corral m. **fountain p.,** pluma fuente.

penalty /'pɛnḷti/ n. pena; multa f., castigo m.

penance /'pɛnəns/ n. penitencia f. **to do p.,** penar.

penchant /'pɛntʃənt/ n. propensión f

pencil /'pɛnsəl/ n. lápiz m.

pencil sharpener /'ʃɑrpənər/ sacapuntas *m.*

pending /'pɛndɪŋ/ *a.* pendiente. **to be p.,** pender.

penetrate /'pɛnɪ,treit/ *v.* penetrar.

penetration /,pɛnɪ'treiʃən/ *n.* penetración *f.*

penicillin /,pɛnə'sɪlɪn/ *n.* penicilina *f.*

peninsula /pə'nɪnsələ, -'nɪnsyələ/ *n.* península *f.*

penitent /'pɛnɪtənt/ *n. & a.* penitente *m. & f.*

penknife /'pɛn,naif/ *n.* cortaplumas *f.*

penniless /'pɛnɪlɪs/ *a.* indigente.

penny /'pɛni/ *n.* penique *m.*

pension /'pɛnʃən/ *n.* pensión *f.*

pensive /'pɛnsɪv/ *a.* pensativo.

penultimate /pɪ'nʌltəmɪt/ *a.* penúltimo.

penury /'pɛnyəri/ *n.* penuria *f.*

people /'pipəl/ *n.* **1.** gente *f.;* (of a nation) pueblo *m.* —*v.* **2.** poblar.

pepper /'pɛpər/ *n.* pimienta *f.;* (plant) pimiento *m.*

per /pər; *unstressed* pər/ *prep.* por.

perambulator /pər'æmbyə,leitər/ *n.* cochecillo de niño *m.*

perceive /pər'siv/ *v.* percibir.

percent /pər'sɛnt/ *adv.* por ciento.

percentage /pər'sɛntɪdʒ/ *n.* porcentaje *m.*

perceptible /pər'sɛptəbəl/ *a.* perceptible.

perception /pər'sɛpʃən/ *n.* percepción *f.*

perch /pɜrtʃ/ *n.* percha *f.;* (fish) perca *f.*

perdition /pər'dɪʃən/ *n.* perdición *f.*

peremptory /pə'rɛmptəri/ *a.* perentorio, terminante.

perennial /pə'rɛniəl/ *a.* perenne.

perfect /*a.* 'pɜrfɪkt; *v.* pər'fɛkt/ *a.* **1.** perfecto. —*v.* **2.** perfeccionar.

perfection /pər'fɛkʃən/ *n.* perfección *f.*

perfectionist /pər'fɛkʃənɪst/ *a. & n.* perfeccionista *m. & f.*

perforation /,pɜrfə'reiʃən/ *n.* perforación *f.*

perform /pər'fɔrm/ *v.* hacer; ejecutar; *Theat.* representar.

performance /pər'fɔrməns/ *n.* ejecución *f.;* *Theat.* representación *f.*

perfume /*n.* 'pɜrfyum; *v.* pər'fyum/ *n.* **1.** perfume *m.;* fragancia *f.* —*v.* **2.** perfumar.

perfunctory /pər'fʌŋktəri/ *a.* perfunctorio, superficial.

perhaps /pər'hæps/ *adv.* quizá, quizás, tal vez.

peril /'pɛrəl/ *n.* peligro *m.*

perilous /'pɛrələs/ *a.* peligroso.

perimeter /pə'rɪmɪtər/ *n.* perímetro *m.*

period /'pɪəriəd/ *n.* período *m.;* *Punct.* punto *m.*

periodic /,pɪəri'ɒdɪk/ *a.* periódico.

periodical /,pɪəri'ɒdɪkəl/ *n.* revista *f.*

periphery /pə'rɪfəri/ *n.* periferia *f.*

perish /'pɛrɪʃ/ *v.* perecer.

perishable /'pɛrɪʃəbəl/ *a.* perecedero.

perjury /'pɜrdʒəri/ *n.* perjurio *m.*

permanent /'pɜrmənənt/ *a.* permanente. **p. wave,** ondulado permanente.

permeate /'pɜrmi,eit/ *v.* penetrar.

permissible /pər'mɪsəbəl/ *a.* permisible.

permission /pər'mɪʃən/ *n.* permiso *m.*

permit /*n.* 'pɜrmɪt; *v.* pər'mɪt/ *n.* **1.** permiso *m.* —*v.* **2.** permitir.

pernicious /pər'nɪʃəs/ *a.* pernicioso.

perpendicular /,pɜrpən'dɪkyələr/ *n. & a.* perpendicular *f.*

perpetrate /'pɜrpɪ,treit/ *v.* perpetrar.

perpetual /pər'pɛtʃuəl/ *a.* perpetuo.

perplex /pər'plɛks/ *v.* confundir.

perplexity /pər'plɛksɪti/ *n.* perplejidad *f.*

persecute /'pɜrsɪ,kyut/ *v.* perseguir.

persecution /,pɜrsɪ'kyuʃən/ *n.* persecución *f.*

perseverance /,pɜrsə'vɪərəns/ *n.* perseverancia *f.*

persevere /,pɜrsə'vɪər/ *v.* perseverar.

persist /pər'sɪst/ *v.* persistir.

persistent /pər'sɪstənt/ *a.* persistente.

person /'pɜrsən/ *n.* persona *f.*

personage /'pɜrsənɪdʒ/ *n.* personaje *m.*

personal /'pɜrsənl/ *a.* personal.

personality /,pɜrsə'nælɪti/ *n.* personalidad *f.*

personnel /,pɜrsə'nɛl/ *n.* personal *m.*

perspective /pər'spɛktɪv/ *n.* perspectiva *f.*

perspiration /,pɜrspə'reiʃən/ *n.* sudor *m.*

perspire /pər'spaiər/ *v.* sudar.

persuade /pər'sweid/ *v.* persuadir.

persuasive /pər'sweisɪv/ *a.* persuasivo.

pertain /pər'tein/ *v.* pertenecer.

pertinent /'pɜrtnənt/ *a.* pertinente.

perturb /pər'tɜrb/ *v.* perturbar.

peruse /pə'ruz/ *v.* leer con cuidado.

pervade /pər'veid/ *v.* penetrar; llenar.

perverse /pər'vɜrs/ *a.* perverso.

perversion /pər'vɜrʒən/ *n.* perversión *f.*

pessimism /'pɛsə,mɪzəm/ *n.* pesimismo *m.*

pester /'pɛstər/ *v.* molestar; fastidiar.

pesticide /'pɛstə,said/ *n.* pesticida *m.*

pestilence /'pɛstləns/ *n.* pestilencia *f.*

pet /pɛt/ *n.* **1.** favorito ·ta.; animal doméstico *m.* —*v.* **2.** mimar.

petal /'pɛtl/ *n.* pétalo *m.*

petition /pə'tɪʃən/ *n.* **1.** petición, súplica *f.* —*v.* **2.** pedir, suplicar.

petrify /'pɛtrə,fai/ *v.* petrificar.

petroleum /pə'trouliəm/ *n.* petróleo *m.*

petticoat /'pɛti,kout/ *n.* enagua *f.*

petty /'pɛti/ *a.* mezquino, insignificante.

petulant /'pɛtʃələnt/ *a.* quisquilloso.

pew /pyu/ *n.* banco de iglesia *m.*

pewter /'pyutər/ *n.* peltre *m.*

phantom /'fæntəm/ n. espectro, fantasma m.

pharmacist /'furməsist/ n. farmacéutico, -ca, boticario, -ria.

pharmacy /'furməsi/ n. farmacia, botica f.

phase /feiz/ n. fase f.

pheasant /'fezənt/ n. faisán m.

phenomenal /fɪ'nomənl/ a. fenomenal.

phenomenon /fɪ'nomə,non/ n. fenómeno f.

philanthropy /fɪ'lænθrəpi/ n. filantropía f.

philately /fɪ'lætli/ n. filatelia f.

philosopher /fɪ'losəfər/ n. filósofo -fa.

philosophical /,fɪlə'sofɪkəl/ a. filosófico.

philosophy /fɪ'losəfi/ n. filosofía f.

phlegm /flem/ n. flema f.

phlegmatic /fleg'mætɪk/ a. flemático.

phobia /'foubiə/ n. fobia f.

phone /foun/ n. teléfono m.

phonetic /fə'nɛtɪk/ a. fonético.

phonograph /'founə,græf/ n. fonógrafo m.

phosphorus /'fosfərəs/ n. fósforo m.

photocopier /'foutə,kɒpiər/ n. fotocopiadora f.

photocopy /'foutə,kɒpi/ n. **1.** fotocopia f. —v. **2.** fotocopiar.

photoelectric /,foutoui'lɛktrɪk/ a. fotoeléctrico.

photogenic /,foutə'dʒɛnɪk/ a. fotogénico.

photograph /'foutə,græf/ n. **1.** fotografía f. —v. **2.** fotografiar; retratar.

photography /fə'tɒgrəfi/ n. fotografía f.

phrase /freiz/ n. **1.** frase f. —v. **2.** expresar.

physical /'fɪzɪkəl/ a. físico.

physician /fɪ'zɪʃən/ n. médico m. & f.

physics /'fɪzɪks/ n. física f.

physiology /,fɪzi'ɒlədʒi/ n. fisiología f.

physiotherapy /,fɪziou'θɛrəpi/ n. fisioterapia f.

physique /fɪ'zik/ n. físico m.

pianist /pi'ænɪst, 'piənɪst/ n. pianista m. & f.

piano /pi'ænou/ n. piano m.

picayune /,pɪkə'yun/ a. insignificante.

piccolo /'pɪkə,lou/ n. flautín m.

pick /pɪk/ n. **1.** pico m. —v. **2.** escoger. **p. up,** recoger.

picket /'pɪkɪt/ n. piquete m.

pickle /'pɪkəl/ n. **1.** salmuera f.; encurtido m. —v. **2.** escabechar.

pickpocket /'pɪk,pɒkɪt/ n. cortabolsas m. & f.

picnic /'pɪknɪk/ n. picnic m.

picture /'pɪktʃər/ n. **1.** cuadro; retrato m.; fotografía f.; (movie) película f. —v. **2.** imaginarse.

picturesque /,pɪktʃə'rɛsk/ a. pintoresco.

pie /pai/ n. pastel m

piece /pis/ n. pedazo m.; pieza f.

pieceworker /'pis,wɜrkər/ n. destajero -ra, destajista m. & f.

pier /pɪər/ n. muelle m.

pierce /pɪərs/ v. perforar; pinchar; traspasar.

piety /'paiɪti/ n. piedad f.

pig /pɪg/ n. puerco, cerdo, lechón m.

pigeon /'pɪdʒən/ n. paloma f.

pigeonhole /'pɪdʒən,houl/ n. casilla f.

pigment /'pɪgmənt/ n. pigmento m.

pile /pail/ n. **1.** pila f., montón m.; Med. hemorroides f.pl. —v. **2.** amontonar.

pilfer /'pɪlfər/ v. ratear.

pilgrim /'pɪlgrɪm/ n peregrino -na, romero -ra.

pilgrimage /'pɪlgrəmɪdʒ/ n. romería f.

pill /pɪl/ n. píldora f.

pillage /'pɪlɪdʒ/ n. **1.** pillaje m. —v. **2.** pillar.

pillar /'pɪlər/ n. columna f.

pillow /'pɪlou/ n. almohada f.

pillowcase /'pɪlou,keis/ n. funda de almohada f.

pilot /'pailət/ n. **1.** piloto m. & f. —v. **2.** pilotar.

pimple /'pɪmpəl/ n. grano m.

pin /pɪn/ n. **1.** alfiler; broche m.; Mech. clavija f. —v. **2.** prender. **p. up,** fijar.

pinafore /'pɪnə,fɔr/ n. delantal (de niña) m.

pinch /pɪntʃ/ n. **1.** pellizco m. —v. **2.** pellizcar.

pine /pain/ n. **1.** pino m. —v. **2.** **p. away,** languidecer. **p. for,** anhelar.

pineapple /'pai,næpəl/ n. piña f., ananás m.pl.

pink /pɪŋk/ a. rosado.

pinky /'pɪŋki/ n. meñique m

pinnacle /'pɪnəkəl/ n. pináculo m.; cumbre f.

pint /paint/ n. pinta f.

pioneer /,paiə'nɪər/ n. pionero -ra.

pious /'paiəs/ a. piadoso.

pipe /paip/ n. pipa f.; tubo; (of organ) cañón m.

pipeline /'paip,lain/ n. oleoducto m.

piper /'paipər/ n. flautista m. & f.

piquant /'pikənt/ a. picante.

pirate /'pairət/ n. pirata m.

pistol /'pɪstl/ n. pistola f.

piston /'pɪstən/ n. émbolo, pistón m.

pitch /pɪtʃ/ n. **1.** brea f.; grado de inclinación; (music) tono m.; —v. **2.** lanzar; (ship) cabecear

pitchblende /'pɪtʃ,blɛnd/ n. pechblenda f.

pitcher /'pɪtʃər/ n. cántaro m.; (baseball) lanzador -ra.

pitchfork /'pɪtʃ,fɔrk/ n. horca f.; tridente m.

pitfall /'pɪt,fɔl/ n. trampa f., hoya cubierta f.

pitiful /'pɪtɪfəl/ a. lastimoso.

pitiless /'pɪtɪlɪs/ a. cruel.

pituitary gland /pɪ'tuɪˌteri/ glándula pituitaria f.

pity /'pɪti/ n. **1.** compasión, piedad f. **to be a p.,** ser lástima. —v. **2.** compadecer.

pivot /'pɪvət/ n. **1.** espiga f., pivote m.; punto de partida m. —v. **2.** girar sobre un pivote.

pizza /'pitsə/ n. pizza f.

placard /'plækɑrd/ n. **1.** cartel m. —v. **2.** fijar carteles.

placate /'pleikeit/ v. aplacar.

place /pleis/ n. **1.** lugar, sitio, puesto m. —v. **2.** colocar, poner.

placid /'plæsɪd/ a. plácido.

plagiarism /'pleidʒəˌrɪzəm/ n. plagio m.

plague /pleig/ n. **1.** plaga, peste f. —v. **2.** atormentar.

plain /plein/ a. **1.** sencillo; puro; evidente. —n. **2.** llano m.

plaintiff /'pleintɪf/ n. demandante m. & f.

plan /plæn/ n. **1.** plan, propósito m. —v. **2.** planear; pensar; planificar. **p. on,** contar con.

plane /plein/ n. **1.** plano m.; (tool) cepillo m. —v. **2.** allanar; acepillar.

planet /'plænɪt/ n. planeta m.

planetarium /ˌplænɪ'tɛəriəm/ n. planetario m.

plank /plæŋk/ n. tablón m.

planning /'plænɪŋ/ n. planificación f.

plant /plænt/ n. **1.** mata, planta f. —v. **2.** sembrar, plantar.

plantation /plæn'teiʃən/ n. plantación f. **coffee p.,** cafetal m.

planter /'plæntər/ n. plantador; hacendado m.

plasma /'plæzmə/ n. plasma m.

plaster /'plæstər/ n. **1.** yeso; emplasto m. —v. **2.** enyesar; emplastar.

plastic /'plæstɪk/ a. plástico.

plate /pleit/ n. **1.** plato m.; plancha de metal. —v. **2.** planchear.

plateau /plæ'tou/ n. meseta f.

platform /'plætfɔrm/ n. plataforma f.

platinum /'plætnəm/ n. platino m.

platitude /'plætɪˌtud/ n. perogrullada f.

platter /'plætər/ n. fuente f., platel m.

plaudit /'plɔdɪt/ n. aplauso m.

plausible /'plɔzəbəl/ a. plausible.

play /plei/ n. **1.** juego m.; Theat. pieza f. —v. **2.** jugar; (music) tocar; Theat. representar. **p. a part,** hacer un papel.

player /'pleiər/ n. jugador -ra; (music) músico -ca.; Theat. actor m., actriz f.

playful /'pleifəl/ a. juguetón.

playground /'pleiˌgraund/ n. campo de deportes; patio de recreo.

playmate /'pleiˌmeit/ n. compañero -ra de juego.

playwright /'pleiˌrait/ n. dramaturgo -ga.

plea /pli/ n. ruego m.; súplica f.; (legal) declaración f.

plead /plid/ v. suplicar; declararse. **p. a case,** defender un pleito.

pleasant /'plɛzənt/ a. agradable.

please /pliz/ v. **1.** gustar, agradar. **Pleased to meet you,** Mucho gusto en conocer a Vd. —adv. **2.** por favor. **Please...** Haga el favor de..., Tenga la bondad de..., Sírvase...

pleasure /'plɛʒər/ n. gusto, placer m.

pleat /plit/ n. **1.** pliegue m. —v. **2.** plegar.

plebiscite /'plɛbəˌsait/ n. plebiscito m.

pledge /plɛdʒ/ n. **1.** empeño m. —v. **2.** empeñar.

plentiful /'plɛntɪfəl/ a. abundante.

plenty /'plɛnti/ n. abundancia f. **p. of,** bastante. **p. more,** mucho más.

pleurisy /'plʊrəsi/ n. pleuritis f.

pliable, pliant /'plaiəbəl; 'plaiənt/ a. flexible.

pliers /'plaiərz/ n.pl. alicates m.pl.

plight /plait/ n. apuro, aprieto m.

plot /plɒt/ n. **1.** conspiración; (of a story) trama; (of land) parcela f. —v. **2.** conspirar; tramar.

plow /plau/ n. **1.** arado m. —v. **2.** arar.

pluck /plʌk/ n. **1.** valor m. —v. **2.** arrancar; desplumar.

plug /plʌg/ n. **1.** tapón m.; Elec. enchufe m. **spark p.,** bujía f. —v. **2.** tapar.

plum /plʌm/ n. ciruela f.

plumage /'plumɪdʒ/ n. plumaje m.

plumber /'plʌmər/ n. fontanero -era, plomero -era.

plume /plum/ n. pluma f.

plump /plʌmp/ a. regordete.

plunder /'plʌndər/ n. **1.** botín m.; despojos m.pl. —v. **2.** saquear.

plunge /plʌndʒ/ v. zambullir; precipitar.

plural /'plʊrəl/ a. & n. plural m.

plus /plʌs/ prep. más.

plutocrat /'plutəˌkræt/ n. plutócrata m. & f.

pneumatic /nʊ'mætɪk/ a. neumático.

pneumonia /nʊ'mounyə/ n. pulmonía f.

poach /poutʃ/ v. (eggs) escalfar; invadir; cazar en vedado.

pocket /'pɒkɪt/ n. **1.** bolsillo m. —v. **2.** embolsar.

pocketbook /'pɒkɪtˌbuk/ n. cartera f.

podiatry /pə'daiətri/ n. podiatría f.

poem /'pouəm/ n. poema m.

poet /'pouɪt/ n. poeta m. & f.

poetic /pou'ɛtɪk/ a. poético.

poetry /'pouɪtri/ n. poesía f.

poignant /'pɔinyənt/ a. conmovedor.

point /pɔint/ n. **1.** punta f.; punto m. —v. **2.** apuntar. **p. out,** señalar.

pointed /'pɔintɪd/ a. puntiagudo; directo.

pointless /'pɔintlɪs/ a. inútil.

poise /pɔiz/ n. **1.** equilibrio m.; serenidad f. —v. **2.** equilibrar; estar suspendido.

poison /'pɔizən/ n. **1.** veneno m. —v. **2.** envenenar.

poisonous /'pɔizənəs/ a. venenoso.

poke /pouk/ n. **1.** empuje m., hurgonada f. —v. **2.** picar; haronear.

Poland /'poulənd/ n. Polonia f.

polar /'poulər/ a. polar.

pole /poul/ n. palo; Geog. polo m.

polemical /pə'lemikəl/ a. polémico.

police /pə'lis/ n. policía f.

policeman /pə'lismən/ n. policía m.

policy /'pɔləsi/ n. política f. **insurance p.,** póliza de seguro.

Polish /'poulɪʃ/ a. & n. polaco -ca.

polish /'pɒlɪʃ/ n. **1.** lustre m. —v. **2.** pulir, lustrar.

polite /pə'lait/ a. cortés.

politic /'pɒlɪtɪk/ **political** a. político.

politician /pɒlɪ'tɪʃən/ n. político -ca.

politics /'pɒlɪtɪks/ n. política f.

poll /poul/ n. encuesta f.; (pl.) urnas f.pl.

pollen /'pɒlən/ n. polen m.

pollute /pə'lut/ v. contaminar.

pollution /pə'luʃən/ n. contaminación f.

polo /'poulou/ n. polo m.

polyester /ˌpɒli'estər/ n. poliéster m.

polygamy /pə'lɪgəmi/ n. poligamia f.

polygon /'pɒlɪˌgɒn/ n. polígono m.

pomp /pɒmp/ n. pompa f.

pompous /'pɒmpəs/ a. pomposo.

poncho /'pɒntʃou/ n. poncho m.

pond /pɒnd/ n. charca f.

ponder /'pɒndər/ v. ponderar, meditar.

ponderous /'pɒndərəs/ a. ponderoso, pesado.

pontiff /'pɒntɪf/ n. pontífice m.

pontoon /pɒn'tun/ n. pontón m.

pony /'pouni/ n. caballito m.

ponytail /'pouniˌteil/ n. cola de caballo f.

poodle /'pudl/ n. caniche m.

pool /pul/ n. charco m. **swimming p.,** piscina f.

poor /pur/ a. pobre; (not good) malo.

pop /pɒp/ n. chasquido m.

popcorn /'pɒpˌkɔrn/ n. rosetas de maíz, palomitas de maíz f.pl.

pope /poup/ n. papa m.

poppy /'pɒpi/ n. amapola f.

popsicle /'pɒpsɪkəl/ n. polo m.

popular /'pɒpyələr/ a. popular.

popularity /ˌpɒpyə'lærɪti/ n. popularidad f.

population /ˌpɒpyə'leiʃən/ n. población f.

porcelain /'pɔrsəlɪn/ n. porcelana f.

porch /pɔrtʃ/ n. pórtico m.; galería f.

pore /pɔr/ n. poro m.

pork /pɔrk/ n. carne de puerco.

pornography /pɔr'nɒgrəfi/ n. pornografía f.

porous /'pɔrəs/ a. poroso, esponjoso.

port /pɔrt/ n. puerto; Naut. babor m. **p. wine,** oporto m.

portable /'pɔrtəbəl/ a. portátil.

portal /'pɔrtl/ n. portal m.

portend /pɔr'tend/ v. pronosticar.

portent /'pɔrtent/ n. presagio m., portento m.

porter /'pɔrtər/ n. portero m.

portfolio /pɔrt'fouliˌou/ n. cartera f.

porthole /'pɔrtˌhoul/ n. porta f.

portion /'pɔrʃən/ n. porción f.

portly /'pɔrtli/ a. corpulento.

portrait /'pɔrtrɪt/ n. retrato m.

portray /pɔr'trei/ v. pintar.

Portugal /'pɔrtʃəgəl/ n. Portugal m.

Portuguese /ˌpɔrtʃə'giz/ a. & n. portugués -esa.

pose /pouz/ n. **1.** postura; actitud f. —v. **2.** posar. **p. as,** pretender ser.

position /pə'zɪʃən/ n. posición f.

positive /'pɒzɪtɪv/ a. positivo.

possess /pə'zɛs/ v. poseer.

possession /pə'zɛʃən/ n. posesión f.

possessive /pə'zɛsɪv/ a. posesivo.

possibility /ˌpɒsə'bɪlɪti/ n. posibilidad f.

possible /'pɒsəbəl/ a. posible.

post /poust/ n. **1.** poste; puesto m. —v. **2.** fijar; situar; echar al correo.

postage /'poustɪdʒ/ n. porte de correo. **p. stamp,** sello m.

postal /'poustl/ a. postal.

post card tarjeta postal.

poster /'poustər/ n. cartel, letrero m.

posterior /pɒ'stiəriər/ a. posterior.

posterity /pɒ'stɛrɪti/ n. posteridad f.

postgraduate /poust'grædʒuit/ a. & n. postgraduado -da.

postmark /'poustˌmɑrk/ n. matasellos m.

post office correos m.pl.

postpone /poust'poun/ v. posponer, aplazar.

postscript /'poustˌskrɪpt/ n. posdata f.

posture /'pɒstʃər/ n. postura f.

pot /pɒt/ n. olla, marmita; (marijuana) marijuana, hierba f. **flower p.,** tiesto m.

potassium /pə'tæsiəm/ n. potasio m.

potato /pə'teitou/ n. patata, papa f. **sweet p.,** batata f.

potent /'poutnt/ a. potente, poderoso.

potential /pə'tɛnʃəl/ a. & n. potencial f.

potion /'pouʃən/ n. poción, pócima f.

pottery /'pɒtəri/ n. alfarería f.

pouch /pautʃ/ n. saco m.; bolsa f.

poultry /'poultri/ n. aves de corral.

pound /paund/ n. **1.** libra f. —v. **2.** golpear.

pour /pɔr/ v. echar; verter; llover a cántaros.

poverty /'pɒvərti/ n. pobreza f.

powder /'paudər/ n. **1.** polvo m.; (gun) pólvora f. —v. **2.** empolvar; pulverizar.

power /'pauər/ n. poder m.; potencia f.

powerful /'pauərfəl/ a. poderoso, fuerte.

powerless /'pauərlıs/ a. impotente.

practical /'præktıkəl/ a. práctico.

practical joke inocentada f.

practically /'præktıkli/ adv. casi; prácticamente.

practice /'præktıs/ n. **1.** práctica; costumbre; clientela f. —v. **2.** practicar; ejercer.

practiced /'præktıst/ a. experto.

practitioner /præk'tıʃənər/ n. practicante m. & f.

pragmatic /præg'mætık/ a. pragmático.

prairie /'prɛəri/ n. llanura; S.A. pampa f.

praise /preiz/ n. **1.** alabanza f. —v. **2.** alabar.

prank /præŋk/ n. travesura f.

prawn /prɔn/ n. gamba f.

pray /prei/ v. rezar; (beg) rogar.

prayer /'preiər/ n. oración; súplica f., ruego m.

preach /pritʃ/ v. predicar; sermonear.

preacher /'pritʃər/ n. predicador m.

preamble /'pri,æmbəl/ n. preámbulo m.

precarious /prı'kɛəriəs/ a. precario.

precaution /prı'kɔʃən/ n. precaución f.

precede /prı'sid/ v. preceder, anteceder.

precedent /n. 'prɛsıdənt; a. prı'sıdnt/ n. & a. precedente m.

precept /'prisɛpt/ n. precepto m.

precinct /'prisıŋkt/ n. recinto m

precious /'prɛʃəs/ a. precioso.

precipice /'prɛsəpıs/ n. precipicio m.

precipitate /prı'sıpı,teit/ v. precipitar.

precise /prı'sais/ a. preciso, exacto.

precision /prı'sıʒən/ n. precisión f.

preclude /prı'klud/ v. evitar.

precocious /prı'kouʃəs/ a. precoz.

precooked /pri'kukt/ a. precocinado.

predatory /'prɛdə,tɔri/ a. de rapiña, rapaz.

predecessor /'prɛdə,sɛsər/ n. predecesor -ra, antecesor -ra.

predicament /prı'dıkəmənt/ n. dificultad f.; apuro m.

predict /prı'dıkt/ v. pronosticar, predecir.

predictable /prı'dıktəbəl/ a. previsible.

predilection /,prɛdl'ɛkʃən/ n. predilección f.

predispose /,pridı'spouz/ v. predisponer.

predominant /prı'dɒmənənt/ a. predominante.

prefabricate /pri'fæbrı,keit/ v. fabricar de antemano.

preface /'prɛfıs/ n. prefacio m.

prefer /prı'fзr/ v. preferir.

preferable /'prɛfərəbəl/ a. preferible.

preference /'prɛfərəns/ n. preferencia f.

prefix /'prifıks/ n. **1.** prefijo m —v. **2.** prefijar.

pregnant /'prɛgnənt/ a. preñada.

prehistoric /,prih'stɔrık/ a. prehistórico.

prejudice /'prɛdʒədıs/ n. prejuicio m.

prejudiced /'prɛdʒədıst/ a. (S.A.) prejuiciado.

preliminary /prı'lımə,nɛri/ a. preliminar.

prelude /'prɛlyud/ n. preludio m.

premature /,primə'tʃur/ a. prematuro.

premeditate /pri'mɛdı,teit/ v. premeditar.

premier /prı'mıər/ n. primer ministro.

première /prı'mıər/ n. estreno m.

premise /'prɛmıs/ n. premisa f.

premium /'primiəm/ n. premio m.

premonition /,primə'nıʃən/ n. presentimiento m.

prenatal /pri'neitl/ a. prenatal.

preparation /,prɛpə'reiʃən/ n. preparativo m.; preparación n.

preparatory /prı'pærə,tɔri/ a. preparatorio. **p. to,** antes de.

prepare /prı'pɛər/ v. preparar.

preponderant /prı'pɒndərənt/ a. preponderante.

preposition /,prıpə'zıʃən/ n. preposición f.

preposterous /prı'pɒstərəs/ a. prepóstero, absurdo.

prerequisite /prı'rɛkwəzıt/ n. requisito previo.

prerogative /prı'rogətıv/ n. prerrogativa f.

prescribe /prı'skraib/ v. prescribir; Med. recetar.

prescription /prı'skrıpʃən/ n. prescripción f.; Med. receta f.

presence /'prɛzəns/ n. presencia f.; porte m.

present /a, n 'prɛzənt; v prı'zɛnt/ a. **1.** presente. **to be present at,** asistir a. —n. **2.** presente; (gift) regalo m. **at p.,** ahora, actualmente. **for the p.,** por ahora. —v. **3.** presentar.

presentable /prı'zɛntəbəl/ a. presentable.

presentation /,prɛzən'teiʃən/ n. presentación; introducción f.; Theat. representación f.

presently /'prɛzəntli/ adv. luego; dentro de poco.

preservative /prı'zзrvətıv/ a. & n. preservativo m.

preserve /prı'zзrv/ n. **1.** conserva f.; (hunting) vedado m. —v. **2.** preservar.

preside /prı'zaid/ v. presidir.

presidency /'prɛzıdənsi/ n. presidencia f.

president /'prɛzıdənt/ n. presidente -ta.

press /prɛs/ n. **1.** prensa f. —v. **2.** apretar; urgir; (clothes) planchar.

pressing /'prɛsıŋ/ a. urgente.

pressure /'prɛʃər/ n. presión f.

pressure cooker /'kukər/ cocina de presión f.

prestige /prɛ'stiʒ/ n. prestigio m.

presume /prɪ'zum/ v. presumir, suponer.

presumptuous /prɪ'zʌmptʃuəs/ a. presuntuoso.

presuppose /ˌprisə'pouz/ v. presuponer.

pretend /prɪ'tɛnd/ v. fingir. **p. to the throne,** aspirar al trono.

pretense /prɪ'tɛns, 'pritɛns/ n. pretensión f.; fingimiento m.

pretension /prɪ'tɛnʃən/ n. pretensión f.

pretentious /prɪ'tɛnʃəs/ a. presumido.

pretext /'pritɛkst/ n. pretexto m.

pretty /'prɪti/ a. **1.** bonito, lindo. —adv. **2.** bastante.

prevail /prɪ'veil/ v. prevalecer.

prevailing /prɪ'veilɪŋ/ **prevalent** a. predominante.

prevent /prɪ'vɛnt/ v. impedir; evitar.

prevention /prɪ'vɛnʃən/ n. prevención f.

preventive /prɪ'vɛntɪv/ a. preventivo.

preview /'pri,vyu/ n. vista anticipada f.

previous /'priviəs/ a. anterior, previo.

prey /prei/ n. presa f.

price /prais/ n. precio m.

priceless /'praisləs/ a. sin precio.

prick /prɪk/ n. **1.** punzada f. —v. **2.** punzar.

pride /praid/ n. orgullo m.

priest /prist/ n. sacerdote, cura m.

prim /prɪm/ a. estirado, remilgado.

primary /'praimɛri/ a. primario, principal.

prime /praim/ a. **1.** primero. —n. **2.** flor f. —v. **3.** alistar.

prime minister primer ministro m. & f.

primitive /'prɪmɪtɪv/ a. primitivo.

prince /prɪns/ n. príncipe m.

Prince Charming Príncipe Azul m.

princess /'prɪnsɪs/ n. princesa f.

principal /'prɪnsəpəl/ a. **1.** principal. —n. **2.** principal m. & f.; director -ra.

principle /'prɪnsəpəl/ n. principio m.

print /prɪnt/ n. **1.** letra de molde f.; (art) grabado m. —v. **2.** imprimir, estampar.

printer /'prɪntər/ n. impresora f.

printing /'prɪntɪŋ/ n. impresión; **p. office,** imprenta f.

printing press prensa f.

printout /'prɪnt,aut/ n. impreso producido por una computadora, impresión f.

priority /prai'ɔrɪti/ n. prioridad, precedencia f.

prism /'prɪzəm/ n. prisma m.

prison /'prɪzən/ n. prisión, cárcel f.

prisoner /'prɪzənər/ n. presidiario -ria, prisionero -ra, preso -sa.

pristine /'prɪstin/ a. inmaculado.

privacy /'praivəsi/ n. soledad f.

private /'praivɪt/ a. **1.** particular. —n. **2.** soldado raso. **in p.,** en particular.

privation /prai'veiʃən/ n. privación f.

privet /'prɪvɪt/ n. ligustro m.

privilege /'prɪvəlɪdʒ/ n. privilegio m.

privy /'prɪvi/ n. letrina f.

prize /praiz/ n. **1.** premio m. —v. **2.** apreciar, estimar.

probability /ˌprɒbə'bɪlɪti/ n. probabilidad f.

probable /'prɒbəbəl/ a. probable.

probate /'proubeit/ a. testamentario.

probation /prou'beiʃən/ n. prueba f.; probación f.; libertad condicional f.

probe /proub/ n. **1.** indagación f. —v. **2.** indagar; tentar.

probity /'proubɪti/ n. probidad f.

problem /'prɒbləm/ n. problema m.

procedure /prə'sidʒər/ n. procedimiento m.

proceed /prə'sid/ v. proceder; proseguir.

process /'prɒsɛs/ n. proceso m.

procession /prə'sɛʃən/ n. procesión f.

proclaim /prou'kleim/ v. proclamar, anunciar.

proclamation /ˌprɒklə'meiʃən/ n. proclamación f.; decreto m.

procrastinate /prou'kræstə,neit/ v. dilatar.

procure /prou'kyur/ v. obtener, procurar.

prodigal /'prɒdɪgəl/ n. & a. pródigo -ga.

prodigy /'prɒdɪdʒi/ n. prodigio m.

produce /prə'dus/ v. producir.

product /'prɒdʌkt/ n. producto m.

production /prə'dʌkʃən/ n. producción f.

productive /prə'dʌktɪv/ a. productivo.

profane /prə'fein/ a. **1.** profano. —v. **2.** profanar.

profanity /prə'fænɪti/ n. profanidad f.

profess /prə'fɛs/ v. profesar; declarar.

profession /prə'fɛʃən/ n. profesión f.

professional /prə'fɛʃənl/ a. & n. profesional m. & f.

professor /prə'fɛsər/ n. profesor -ra; catedrático -ca.

proficient /prə'fɪʃənt/ a. experto, proficiente.

profile /'proufail/ n. perfil m.

profit /'prɒfɪt/ n. **1.** provecho m.; ventaja f.; Com. ganancia f. —v. **2.** aprovechar; beneficiar.

profitable /'prɒfɪtəbəl/ a. provechoso, ventajoso, lucrativo.

profiteer /ˌprɒfɪ'tɪər/ n. **1.** explotador -ra —v. **2.** explotar.

profound /prə'faund/ a. profundo, hondo.

profuse /prə'fyus/ a. pródigo; profuso.

prognosis /prɒg'nousɪs/ n. pronóstico m.

program /'prougræm/ n. programa m.

progress /n. 'progrɛs; v. prə'grɛs/ n. **1.** progresos m.pl. **in p.,** en marcha. —v. **2.** progresar; marchar.

progressive /prə'grɛsɪv/ a. progresivo; progresista.

prohibit /prou'hɪbɪt/ v. prohibir.

prohibition /ˌprouə'bɪʃən/ n. prohibición f.

prohibitive /prou'hɪbɪtɪv/ a. prohibitivo.

project / n. 'prɒdʒɛkt/ v. prə'dʒɛkt/ n. **1.** proyecto m. —v. **2.** proyectar.

projectile /prə'dʒɛktɪl/ n. proyectil m.

projection /prə'dʒɛkʃən/ n. proyección f.

projector /prə'dʒɛktər/ n. proyector m.

proliferation /prə,lɪfə'reɪʃən/ n. proliferación f.

prolific /prə'lɪfɪk/ a. prolífico.

prologue /'proulɔg/ n. prólogo m.

prolong /prə'lɔŋ/ v. prolongar.

prominent /'prɒmənənt/ a. prominente, eminente.

promiscuous /prə'mɪskyuəs/ a. promiscuo.

promise /'prɒmɪs/ n. **1.** promesa f. —v. **2.** prometer.

promote /prə'mout/ v. fomentar; estimular; adelantar; promocionar.

promotion /prə'mouʃən/ n. promoción f.; adelanto m.

prompt /prɒmpt/ a. **1.** puntual. —v. **2.** impulsar; *Theat.* apuntar. —adv. **3.** pronto.

promulgate /'prɒməl,geit/ v. promulgar.

pronoun /'prou,naun/ n. pronombre m.

pronounce /prə'nauns/ v. pronunciar.

pronunciation /prə,nʌnsi'eiʃən/ n. pronunciación f.

proof /pruf/ n. prueba f.

proof of purchase certificado de compra m.

proofread /'pruf,rid/ v. corregir pruebas.

prop /prɒp/ n. **1.** apoyo, m. —v. **2.** sostener.

propaganda /,prɒpə'gændə/ n. propaganda f.

propagate /'prɒpə,geit/ v. propagar.

propel /prə'pɛl/ v. propulsar.

propeller /prə'pɛlər/ n. hélice f.

propensity /prə'pɛnsɪti/ n. tendencia f.

proper /'prɒpər/ a. propio; correcto.

property /'prɒpərti/ n. propiedad f.

prophecy /'prɒfəsi/ n. profecía f.

prophesy /'prɒfə,sai/ v. predecir, profetizar.

prophet /'prɒfɪt/ n. profeta m.

prophetic /prə'fɛtɪk/ a. profético.

propitious /prə'pɪʃəs/ a. propicio.

proponent /prə'pounənt/ n. & a. proponente m.

proportion /prə'pɔrʃən/ n. proporción f.

proportionate /prə'pɔrʃənɪt/ a. proporcionado.

proposal /prə'pouzəl/ n. propuesta; oferta f.; (marriage) declaración f.

propose /prə'pouz/ v. proponer; pensar; declararse.

proposition /,prɒpə'zɪʃən/ n. proposición f.

proprietor /prə'praiɪtər/ n. propietario -ria, dueño -ña.

propriety /prə'praiɪti/ n. corrección f., decoro m.

prosaic /prou'zeiɪk/ a. prosaico.

proscribe /prou'skraib/ v. proscribir.

prose /prouz/ n. prosa f.

prosecute /'prɒsɪ,kyut/ v. acusar, procesar.

prospect /'prɒspɛkt/ n. perspectiva; esperanza f.

prospective /prə'spɛktɪv/ a. anticipado, presunto.

prosper /'prɒspər/ v. prosperar.

prosperity /prɒ'spɛrɪti/ n. prosperidad f.

prosperous /'prɒspərəs/ a. próspero.

prostate gland /'prɒsteit/ glándula prostática f.

prostitute /'prɒstɪ,tut/ n. **1.** prostituta f. —v. **2.** prostituir.

prostrate /'prɒstreit/ a. **1.** postrado. —v. **2.** postrar.

protect /prə'tɛkt/ v. proteger; amparar.

protection /prə'tɛkʃən/ n. protección f.; amparo m.

protective /prə'tɛktɪv/ a. protector.

protector /prə'tɛktər/ n. protector -ora.

protégé /'proutə,ʒei/ n. protegido -da.

protein /'proutin, -tiin/ n. proteína f.

protest /n. 'proutɛst; v. prə'tɛst, 'proutɛst/ n. **1.** protesta f. —v. **2.** protestar.

Protestant /'prɒtəstənt/ a. & n. protestante m. & f.

protocol /'proutə,kɔl/ n. protocolo m.

proton /'prouton/ n. protón m.

protract /prou'trækt/ v. alargar, demorar.

protrude /prou'trud/ v. salir fuera.

protuberance /prou'tubərəns/ n. protuberancia f.

proud /praud/ a. orgulloso.

prove /pruv/ v. comprobar.

proverb /'prɒvərb/ n. proverbio, refrán m.

provide /prə'vaid/ v. proporcionar; proveer.

provided /prə'vaidɪd/ conj. con tal que.

providence /'prɒvɪdəns/ n. providencia f.

province /'prɒvɪns/ n. provincia f.

provincial /prə'vɪnʃəl/ a. **1.** provincial. —n. **2.** provinciano -na.

provision /prə'vɪʒən/ n. **1.** provisión f.; (pl.) comestibles m.pl. —v. **2.** abastecer.

provocation /,prɒvə'keiʃən/ n. provocación f.

provoke /prə'vouk/ v. provocar.

prowess /'prauɪs/ n. proeza f

prowl /praul/ v. rondar.

prowler /'praulər/ n. merodeador -dora m. & f.

proximity /prɒk'sɪmɪti/ n. proximidad f.

proxy /'prɒksi/ n. delegado -da. **by p.,** mediante apoderado.

prudence /'prudns/ n. prudencia f.

prudent /'prudnt/ a. prudente, cauteloso.

prune /prun/ n. ciruela pasa f.

pry /prai/ v. atisbar; curiosear; *Mech.* alzaprimar.

pyromania

psalm /sɑm/ n. salmo m.

pseudonym /'sudnɪm/ n. seudónimo m.

psychedelic /ˌsaɪkɪ'dɛlɪk/ a. psiquedélico.

psychiatrist /sɪ'kaɪətrɪst, saɪ-/ n. psiquiatra m. & f.

psychiatry /sɪ'kaɪətri, saɪ-/ n. psiquiatría f

psychoanalysis /ˌsaɪkouə'næləsɪs/ n. psicoanálisis m.

psychoanalyst /ˌsaɪkou'ænlɪst/ n. psicoanalista m. & f.

psychological /ˌsaɪkə'lɒdʒɪkəl/ a. psicológico.

psychology /saɪ'kɒlədʒi/ n. psicología f.

psychosis /saɪ'kousɪs/ n. psicosis f.

ptomaine /'toumeɪn/ n. tomaína f.

pub /pʌb/ n. bar m.

public /'pʌblɪk/ a. & n. público m.

publication /ˌpʌblɪ'keɪʃən/ n. publicación; revista f.

publicity /pʌ'blɪsɪti/ n. publicidad f.

publicity agent publicista m. & f.

publish /'pʌblɪʃ/ v. publicar.

publisher /'pʌblɪʃər/ n. editor -ora.

pudding /'pudɪŋ/ n. pudín m.

puddle /'pʌdl/ n. charco, lodazal m.

Puerto Rican /'pwɛrtə 'rikən, 'pɔr-/ a. & n. puertorriqueño -ña.

Puerto Rico /'pwɛr'tə rikou, 'pɔrtə/ Puerto Rico m.

puff /pʌf/ n. **1.** soplo m.; (of smoke) bocanada f. **powder p.**, polvera f. —v. **2.** jadear; echar bocanadas. **p. up**, hinchar; Fig. engreír.

pugnacious /pʌg'neɪʃəs/ a. pugnaz.

puh-lease! /pʌ 'liz/ ¡Favor!

pull /pul/ n. **1.** tirón m.; Colloq. influencia f. —v. **2.** tirar; halar.

pulley /'puli/ n. polea f., motón m.

pulmonary /'pʌlmə,nɛri/ a. pulmonar.

pulp /pʌlp/ n. pulpa; (of fruit) carne f.

pulpit /'pulpɪt, 'pʌl-/ n. púlpito m.

pulsar /'pʌlsɑr/ n. pulsar m.

pulsate /'pʌlseɪt/ v. pulsar.

pulse /pʌls/ n. pulso m.

pump /pʌmp/ n. **1.** bomba f. —v. **2.** bombear. **p. up**, inflar.

pumpkin /'pʌmpkɪn/ n. calabaza f.

pun /pʌn/ n. juego de palabras.

punch /pʌntʃ/ n. **1.** puñetazo; Mech. pun-

zón; (beverage) ponche m. —v. **2.** dar puñetazos; punzar.

punch bowl ponchera f.

punctual /'pʌŋktʃuəl/ a. puntual.

punctuate /'pʌŋktʃu,eɪt/ v. puntuar.

puncture /'pʌŋktʃər/ n. **1.** pinchazo m., perforación f. —v. **2.** pinchar, perforar.

pungent /'pʌndʒənt/ a. picante, pungente.

punish /'pʌnɪʃ/ v. castigar.

punishment /'pʌnɪʃmənt/ n. castigo m

punitive /'pyunɪtɪv/ a. punitivo.

puny /'pyuni/ a. encanijado.

pupil /'pyupəl/ n. alumno -na; Anat. pupila f.

puppet /'pʌpɪt/ n. muñeco m.

puppy /'pʌpi/ n. perrito -ta.

purchase /'pɜrtʃəs/ n. **1.** compra f. —v. **2.** comprar.

purchasing power /'pɜrtʃəsɪŋ/ poder adquisitivo m

pure /pyur/ a. puro.

purée /pyu'reɪ/ n. puré m.

purge /pɜrdʒ/ v. purgar.

purify /'pyurə,faɪ/ v. purificar.

puritanical /ˌpyurɪ'tænɪkəl/ a. puritano.

purity /'pyurɪti/ n. pureza f.

purple /'pɜrpəl/ a. **1.** purpúreo. —n. **2.** púrpura f.

purport /n. 'pɜrpɔrt; v. pər'pɔrt/ n. **1.** significación f. —v. **2.** significar.

purpose /'pɜrpəs/ n. propósito m. **on p.**, de propósito.

purr /pɜr/ v. ronronear.

purse /pɜrs/ n. bolsa f.

pursue /pər'su/ v. perseguir.

pursuit /pər'sut/ n. caza; busca; ocupación f. **p. plane**, avión de caza m.

push /puʃ/ n. **1.** empuje; impulso m. —v. **2.** empujar.

put /put/ v. poner, colocar. **p. away**, guardar. **p. in**, meter. **p. off**, dejar. **p. on**, ponerse. **p. out**, apagar. **p. up with**, aguantar.

putrid /'pyutrɪd/ a. podrido.

putt /pʌt/ n. (golf) golpe corto m.

puzzle /'pʌzəl/ n. **1.** enigma; rompecabezas m. —v. **2.** dejar perplejo. **p. out**, descifrar.

pyramid /'pɪrəmɪd/ n. pirámide f.

pyromania /ˌpaɪrə'meɪniə/ n. piromanía f.

Q R

quack /kwæk/ *n.* **1.** (doctor) curandero -ra; (duck) graznido *m.* —*v.* **2.** graznar.

quadrangle /'kwɒd,ræŋgəl/ *n.* cuadrángulo *m.*

quadraphonic /,kwɒdrə'fɒnɪk/ *a.* cuatrifónico.

quadruped /'kwɒdrʊ,ped/ *a.* & *n.* cuadrúpedo *m.*

quail /kweil/ *n.* **1.** codorniz *f.* —*v.* **2.** descorazonarse.

quaint /kweint/ *a* curioso.

quake /kweik/ *n.* **1.** temblor *m.* —*v.* **2.** temblar.

qualification /,kwɒləfɪ'keiʃən/ *n.* requisito *m.*; (pl.) preparaciones *f.pl.*

qualified /'kwɒlə,faid/ *a.* calificado, competente; preparado.

qualify /'kwɒlə,fai/ *v.* calificar, modificar; llenar los requisitos.

quality /'kwɒlɪti/ *n.* calidad *f.*

quandary /'kwɒndəri, -dri/ *n.* incertidumbre *f.*

quantity /'kwɒntɪti/ *n.* cantidad *f.*

quarantine /'kwɔrən,tin, 'kwɒr-, ,kwɔrən'tin, ,kwɒr-/ *n.* cuarentena *f.*

quarrel /'kwɔrəl, 'kwɒr-/ *n.* **1.** riña, disputa *f.* —*v.* **2.** reñir, disputar.

quarry /'kwɔri, 'kwɒri/ *n.* cantera; (hunting) presa *f.*

quarter /'kwɔrtər/ *n.* cuarto *m.*; (pl.) vivienda *f.*

quarterly /'kwɔrtərli/ *a.* **1.** trimestral. —*adv.* **2.** por cuartos.

quartet /kwɔr'tet/ *n.* cuarteto *m.*

quartz /kwɔrts/ *n.* cuarzo *m.*

quasar /'kweizɑr/ *n.* cuasar *m.*

quaver /'kweivər/ *v.* temblar.

queen /kwin/ *n.* reina *f.*; (chess) dama *f.*

queer /kwɪər/ *a.* extraño, raro.

quell /kwel/ *v.* reprimir.

quench /kwentʃ/ *v.* apagar.

query /'kwɪəri/ *n.* **1.** pregunta *f.* —*v.* **2.** preguntar.

quest /kwest/ *n.* busca *f.*

question /'kwestʃən/ *n.* **1.** pregunta; cuestión *f* **q. mark,** signo de interrogación. —*v.* **2.** preguntar; interrogar; dudar.

questionable /'kwestʃənəbəl/ *a.* dudoso.

questionnaire /,kwestʃə'nɛər/ *n.* cuestionario *m.*

quiche /kiʃ/ *n.* quiche *f.*

quick /kwɪk/ *a.* rápido.

quicken /'kwɪkən/ *v.* acelerar.

quicksand /'kwɪk,sænd/ *n.* arena movediza.

quiet /'kwaiit/ *a.* **1.** quieto, tranquilo; callado. **be q., keep q.,** callarse. —*n.* **2.** calma; quietud *f.* —*v.* **3.** tranquilizar. **q. down,** callarse; calmarse.

quilt /kwɪlt/ *n.* colcha *f.*

quinine /'kwainain/ *n.* quinina *f.*

quintet /kwɪn'tet/ *n. Mus* quinteto *m.*

quip /kwɪp/ *n.* **1.** pulla *f.* —*v.* **2.** echar pullas.

quit /kwɪt/ *v.* dejar; renunciar a. **q. doing** (etc.) dejar de hacer (etc.).

quite /kwait/ *adv.* bastante; completamente. **not q.,** no precisamente; no completamente.

quiver /'kwɪvər/ *n.* **1.** aljaba *f.*; temblor *m.* —*v.* **2.** temblar.

quixotic /kwɪk'sɒtɪk/ *a.* quijotesco.

quorum /'kwɔrəm/ *n.* quórum *m.*

quota /'kwoutə/ *n.* cuota *f.*

quotation /kwou'teiʃən/ *n.* citación; *Com.* cotización *f.* **q. marks,** comillas *f.pl.*

quote /kwout/ *v.* citar; *Com.* cotizar.

rabbi /'ræbai/ *n.* rabí, rabino *m.*

rabbit /'ræbɪt/ *n.* conejo *m.*

rabble /'ræbəl/ *n.* canalla *f.*

rabid /'ræbɪd/ *a.* rabioso.

rabies /'reibiz/ *n.* hidrofobia *f.*

race /reis/ *n.* **1.** raza; carrera *f.* —*v.* **2.** echar una carrera; correr de prisa.

race track /reis,træk/ hipódromo *m.*

rack /ræk/ *n.* **1.** (cooking) pesebre *m.*; (clothing) colgador *m.* —*v.* **2.** atormentar.

racket /'rækɪt/ *n.* (noise) ruido *m.*; (tennis) raqueta *f.*; (graft) fraude organizado.

radar /'reidɑr/ *n.* radar *m.*

radiance /'reidiəns/ *n.* brillo *m.*

radiant /'reidiənt/ *a.* radiante.

radiate /'reidi,eit/ *v.* irradiar.

radiation /,reidi'eiʃən/ *n.* irradiación *f.*

radiator /'reidi,eitər/ *n.* calorífero *m.*; *Auto.* radiador *m.*

radical /'rædɪkəl/ *a.* & *n.* radical *m.*

radio /'reidi,ou/ *n.* radio *m. or f.* **r. station,** estación radiodifusora *f.*

radioactive /,reidiou'æktɪv/ *a.* radioactivo.

radio cassette radiocasete *m.*

radish /'rædɪʃ/ *n.* rábano *m.*

radium /'reidiəm/ *n.* radio *m.*

radius /'reidiəs/ *n.* radio *m.*

raffle /'ræfəl/ *n.* **1.** rifa, lotería *f.* —*v.* **2.** rifar.

raft /ræft/ *n.* balsa *f.*

rafter /'ræftər/ *n.* viga *f.*

rag /ræg/ *n.* trapo *m.*

ragamuffin /'rægə,mʌfɪn/ *n.* galopín *m.*

rage /reidʒ/ n. **1.** rabia f. —v. **2.** rabiar.

ragged /'rægɪd/ a. andrajoso; desigual.

raid /reid/ n. Mil. correría f.

rail /reil/ n. baranda f.; carril m. **by r.**, por ferrocarril.

railroad /'reil,roud/ n. ferrocarril m.

rain /rein/ n. **1.** lluvia f. —v. **2.** llover.

rainbow /'rein,bou/ n. arco iris m.

raincoat /'rein,kout/ n. impermeable m.; gabardina f.

rainfall /'rein,fɔl/ n. precipitación f.

rainy /'reini/ a. lluvioso.

raise /reiz/ n. **1.** aumento m. —v. **2.** levantar, alzar; criar.

raisin /'reizɪn/ n. pasa f.

rake /reik/ n. **1.** rastro m. —v. **2.** rastrillar.

rally /'ræli/ n. **1.** reunión f. —v. **2.** reunirse.

ram /ræm/ n. carnero m.

ramble /'ræmbəl/ v. vagar.

ramp /ræmp/ n. rampa f.

rampart /'ræmpɑrt/ n. terraplén m.

ranch /ræntʃ/ n. rancho m.

rancid /'rænsɪd/ a. rancio.

rancor /'ræŋkər/ n. rencor m.

random /'rændəm/ a. fortuito. **at r.**, a la ventura.

range /reindʒ/ n. **1.** extensión f.; alcance m.; estufa; sierra f.; terreno de pasto. —v. **2.** recorrer; extenderse.

rank /ræŋk/ a. **1.** espeso; rancio. —n. **2.** fila f.; grado m. —v. **3.** clasificar.

ransack /'rænsæk/ v. saquear.

ransom /'rænsəm/ n. **1.** rescate m. —v. **2.** rescatar.

rap /ræp/ n. **1.** golpecito m. —v. **2.** golpear.

rapid /'ræpɪd/ a. rápido.

rapist /'reipɪst/ n. violador -dora m. & f.

rapport /ræ'pɔr/ n. armonía f.

rapture /'ræptʃər/ n. éxtasis m.

rare /rɛər/ a. raro; (of food) a medio cocer.

rascal /'ræskəl/ n. pícaro, bribón m.

rash /ræʃ/ a. **1.** temerario. —n. **2.** erupción f.

raspberry /'ræz,bɛri/ n. frambuesa f.

rat /ræt/ n. rata f.

rate /reit/ n. **1.** velocidad; tasa f.; precio m.; (of exchange; of interest) tipo m. **at any r.**, de todos modos. —v. **2.** valuar.

rather /'ræðər/ adv. bastante; más bien, mejor dicho.

ratify /'rætə,fai/ v. ratificar.

ratio /'reiʃou/ n. razón; proporción f.

ration /'ræʃən, 'reiʃən/ n. ración f. —v. **2.** racionar.

rational /'ræʃənl/ a. racional.

rattle /'rætl/ n. **1.** ruido m.; matraca f. **r. snake**, culebra f., serpiente de cascabel f. —v. **2.** matraquear; rechinar.

raucous /'rɔkəs/ a. ronco.

ravage /'rævɪdʒ/ v. pillar; destruir; asolar.

rave /reiv/ v. delirar; entusiasmarse.

ravel /'rævəl/ v. deshilar.

raven /'reivən/ n. cuervo m.

ravenous /'rævənəs/ a. voraz.

raw /rɔ/ a. crudo; verde.

ray /rei/ n. rayo m.

rayon /'reinn/ n. rayón m.

razor /'reizər/ n. navaja de afeitar. **r. blade**, hoja de afeitar.

reach /ritʃ/ n. **1.** alcance m. —v. **2.** alcanzar.

react /ri'ækt/ v. reaccionar.

reaction /ri'ækʃən/ n. reacción f.

reactionary /ri'ækʃə,nɛri/ a. **1.** reaccionario. —n. **2.** Pol. retrógrado m.

read /rid/ v. leer.

reader /'ridər/ n. lector -ra; libro de lectura m.

readily /'rɛdli/ adv. fácilmente.

reading /'ridɪŋ/ n. lectura f.

ready /'rɛdi/ a. listo, preparado; dispuesto.

ready-cooked /'rɛdi ,kukt/ a. precocinado.

real /'reiʊl/ a. verdadero; real.

real estate bienes inmuebles, m.pl.

real-estate agent /'riəl ɪ'steit/ agente inmobiliario m., agente inmobiliaria f.

realist /'riəlɪst/ n. realista m. & f.

realistic /,riə'lɪstɪk/ a. realista.

reality /ri'ælɪti/ n. realidad f.

realization /,riələ'zeiʃən/ n. comprensión; realización f.

realize /'riə,laiz/ v. darse cuenta de; realizar.

really /'riəli/ adv. de veras; en realidad.

realm /rɛlm/ n. reino; dominio m.

reap /rip/ v. segar, cosechar.

rear /rɪər/ a. **1.** posterior. —n. **2.** parte posterior. —v. **3.** criar; levantar.

reason /'rizən/ n. **1.** razón; causa f.; motivo m. —v. **2.** razonar.

reasonable /'rizənəbəl/ a. razonable.

reassure /,riə'ʃʊr/ v. calmar, tranquilizar.

rebate /'ribeit/ n. rebaja f.

rebel /n. 'rɛbəl; v. rɪ'bɛl/ n. **1.** rebelde m. & f. —v. **2.** rebelarse.

rebellion /rɪ'bɛlyən/ n. rebelión f.

rebellious /rɪ'bɛlyəs/ a. rebelde.

rebirth /rɪ'bɜrθ/ n. renacimiento m.

rebound /rɪ'baund/ v. repercutir; resaltar.

rebuff /rɪ'bʌf/ n. **1.** repulsa f. —v. **2.** rechazar.

rebuke /rɪ'byuk/ v. **1.** reprensión f. —v. **2.** reprender.

rebuttal /rɪ'bʌtl/ n. refutación f.

recalcitrant /rɪ'kælsɪtrənt/ a. recalcitrante.

recall /rɪ'kɔl/ v. recordar; acordarse de; hacer volver.

recapitulate /,rikə'pɪtʃə,leit/ v. recapitular.

recede /rɪ'sid/ v. retroceder.

receipt /rɪ'siːt/ n. recibo m.; (com., pl.) ingresos m pl.

receive /rɪ'siːv/ v. recibir.

receiver /rɪ'siːvər/ n. receptor m.

recent /'riːsənt/ a. reciente.

recently /'riːsəntlɪ/ adv. recién.

receptacle /rɪ'sɛptəkəl/ n. receptáculo m.

reception /rɪ'sɛpʃən/ n. acogida; recepción f.

receptionist /rɪ'sɛpʃənɪst/ n. recepcionista m. & f.

receptive /rɪ'sɛptɪv/ a. receptivo.

recess /rɪ'sɛs, 'riːsɛs/ n. nicho; retiro; recreo m.

recipe /'rɛsəpɪ/ n. receta f.

recipient /rɪ'sɪpɪənt/ n. recibidor -ra, recipiente m. & f.

reciprocate /rɪ'sɪprə,keɪt/ v. corresponder; reciprocar.

recite /rɪ'saɪt/ v. recitar.

reckless /'rɛklɪs/ a. descuidado; imprudente.

reckon /'rɛkən/ v. contar; calcular.

reclaim /rɪ'kleɪm/ v. reformar; Leg. reclamar.

recline /rɪ'klaɪn/ v. reclinar; recostar.

recognition /,rɛkəg'nɪʃən/ n. reconocimiento m.

recognize /'rɛkəg,naɪz/ v. reconocer.

recoil /n. 'riːkɔɪl; v. rɪ'kɔɪl/ n. 1. culatada f. —v. 2. recular.

recollect /,rɛkə'lɛkt/ v. recordar, acordarse de.

recommend /,rɛkə'mɛnd/ v. recomendar.

recommendation /,rɛkəmən'deɪʃən/ n. recomendación f.

recompense /'rɛkəm,pɛns/ n. 1. recompensa f. —v. 2. recompensar.

reconcile /'rɛkən,saɪl/ v. reconciliar.

recondition /,rikən'dɪʃən/ v. reacondicionar.

reconsider /,rikən'sɪdər/ v. considerar de nuevo.

reconstruct /,rikən'strʌkt/ v. reconstruir.

record /n. 'rɛkərd, v. rɪ'kɔrd/ n. 1. registro m.; (sports) record m. **phonograph r.**, disco m. —v. 2. registrar.

record player tocadiscos m.

recount /rɪ'kaʊnt/ v. relatar; contar.

recover /rɪ'kʌvər/ v. recobrar; restablecerse.

recovery /rɪ'kʌvərɪ/ n. recobro m.; recuperación f.

recruit /rɪ'kruːt/ n. 1. recluta m. —v. 2. reclutar.

rectangle /'rɛk,tæŋgəl/ n. rectángulo m.

rectify /'rɛktə,faɪ/ v. rectificar.

recuperate /rɪ'kupə,reɪt/ v. recuperar.

recur /rɪ'kɜr/ v. recurrir.

recycle /ri'saɪkəl/ v. reciclar.

red /rɛd/ a. rojo, colorado.

redeem /rɪ'diːm/ v. redimir, rescatar.

redemption /rɪ'dɛmpʃən/ n. redención f.

redhead /'rɛd,hɛd/ n. pelirrojo -ja.

red mullet /'mʌlɪt/ salmonete m.

reduce /rɪ'duːs/ v. reducir.

reduction /rɪ'dʌkʃən/ n. reducción f.

reed /rid/ n. caña f., S.A. bejuco m.

reef /rif/ n. arrecife, escollo m.

reel /ril/ n. 1. aspa f., carrete m. —v. 2. aspar.

refer /rɪ'fɜr/ v. referir.

referee /,rɛfə'ri/ n. árbitro m. & f.

reference /'rɛfərəns/ n. referencia f.

refill /n. 'ri,fɪl; v. ri'fɪl/ n. 1. relleno m. —v. 2. rellenar.

refine /rɪ'faɪn/ v. refinar.

refinement /rɪ'faɪnmənt/ n. refinamiento m.; cultura f.

reflect /rɪ'flɛkt/ v. reflejar; reflexionar.

reflection /rɪ'flɛkʃən/ n. reflejo m.; reflexión f.

reflex /'riflɛks/ a. reflejo.

reform /rɪ'fɔrm/ n. 1. reforma f. —v. 2. reformar.

reformation /,rɛfər'meɪʃən/ n. reformación f.

refractory /rɪ'fræktərɪ/ a. refractario.

refrain /rɪ'freɪn/ n. 1. estribillo m. —v. 2. abstenerse.

refresh /rɪ'frɛʃ/ v. refrescar.

refreshment /rɪ'frɛʃmənt/ n. refresco m.

refrigerator /rɪ'frɪdʒə,reɪtər/ n. refrigerador m.

refuge /'rɛfyudʒ/ n. refugio m.

refugee /,rɛfyu'dʒi/ n. refugiado -da.

refund /n 'ri,fʌnd; v ri'fʌnd/ n. 1. reembolso m. —v. 2. reembolsar.

refusal /rɪ'fyuzəl/ n. negativa f.

refuse /n 'rɛfyus; v rɪ'fyuz/ n. 1. basura f. —v. 2. negarse, rehusar.

refute /rɪ'fyut/ v. refutar.

regain /rɪ'geɪn/ v. recobrar. **r. consciousness**, recobrar el conocimiento.

regal /'rigəl/ a. real.

regard /rɪ'gɑrd/ n. 1. aprecio; respeto m. **with r. to**, con respecto a. —v. 2. considerar; estimar.

regarding /rɪ'gɑrdɪŋ/ prep. en cuanto a, acerca de.

regardless (of) /rɪ'gɑrdlɪs/ a pesar de.

regent /'ridʒənt/ n. regente m. & f.

regime /rə'ʒim, rei-/ n. régimen m.

regiment /n. 'rɛdʒəmənt; v. -,mɛnt/ n. 1. regimiento m. —v. 2. regimentar.

region /'ridʒən/ n. región f.

register /'rɛdʒəstər/ n. 1. registro m. **cash r.**, caja registradora f. —v. 2. registrar; matricularse; (a letter) certificar.

registration /,rɛdʒə'streiʃən/ n. registro m.; matrícula f.

regret /rɪ'grɛt/ n. **1.** pena f. —v. **2.** sentir, lamentar.

regular /'rɛgyələr/ a. regular; ordinario.

regularity /ˌrɛgyə'lærɪtɪ/ n. regularidad f.

regulate /'rɛgyə,leɪt/ v. regular.

regulation /ˌrɛgyə'leɪʃən/ n. regulación f.

regulator /'rɛgyə,leɪtər/ n. regulador m.

rehabilitate /ˌrihə'bɪlɪ,teɪt, ˌriə-/ v. rehabilitar.

rehearse /rɪ'hɜrs/ v. repasar; Theat. ensayar.

reheat /ri'hit/ v. recalentar.

reign /reɪn/ n. **1.** reino, reinado m. —v. **2.** reinar.

reimburse /ˌriɪm'bɜrs/ v. reembolsar.

rein /reɪn/ n. **1.** rienda f. —v. **2.** refrenar.

reincarnation /ˌriɪnkɑr'neɪʃən/ n. reencarnación f.

reindeer /'reɪn,dɪər/ n. reno m.

reinforce /ˌriɪn'fɔrs, -'fours/ v. reforzar.

reinforcement /ˌriɪn'fɔrsmənt, -'fours-/ n. refuerzo m.; armadura f.

reiterate /ri'ɪtə,reɪt/ v. reiterar.

reject /rɪ'dʒɛkt/ v. rechazar.

rejoice /rɪ'dʒɔɪs/ v. regocijarse.

rejoin /rɪ'dʒɔɪn/ v. reunirse con; replicar.

rejuvenate /rɪ'dʒuvə,neɪt/ v. rejuvenecer.

relapse /v. rɪ'læps; n. also 'rilæps/ v. **1.** recaer. —n. **2.** recaída f.

relate /rɪ'leɪt/ v. relatar, contar; relacionar. **r. to,** llevarse bien con.

relation /rɪ'leɪʃən/ n. relación f.; pariente m. & f.

relative /'rɛlətɪv/ a. **1.** relativo. —n. **2.** pariente m. & f.

relativity /ˌrɛlə'tɪvɪtɪ/ n. relatividad f.

relax /rɪ'læks/ v. descansar; relajar.

relay /'rilei; v. also rɪ'lei/ n. **1.** relevo m. —v. **2.** retransmitir.

release /rɪ'lis/ n. **1.** liberación f. —v. **2.** soltar.

relent /rɪ'lɛnt/ v. ceder.

relevant /'rɛləvənt/ a. pertinente.

reliability /rɪˌlaɪə'bɪlɪtɪ/ n. veracidad f.

reliable /rɪ'laɪəbəl/ a. responsable; digno de confianza.

relic /'rɛlɪk/ n. reliquia f.

relief /rɪ'lif/ n. alivio; (sculpture) relieve m.

relieve /rɪ'liv/ v. aliviar.

religion /rɪ'lɪdʒən/ n. religión f.

religious /rɪ'lɪdʒəs/ a. religioso.

relinquish /rɪ'lɪŋkwɪʃ/ v. abandonar.

relish /'rɛlɪʃ/ n. **1.** sabor; condimento m. —v. **2.** saborear.

reluctant /rɪ'lʌktənt/ a. renuente.

rely /rɪ'laɪ/ v. **r. on,** confiar en; contar con; depender de.

remain /rɪ'mein/ n. **1.** (pl.) restos m.pl. —v. **2.** quedar, permanecer.

remainder /rɪ'meɪndər/ n. resto m.

remark /rɪ'mɑrk/ n. **1.** observación f —v. **2.** observar.

remarkable /rɪ'mɑrkəbəl/ a. notable.

remedial /rɪ'midiəl/ a. reparador.

remedy /'rɛmɪdi/ n. **1.** remedio m. —v. **2.** remediar.

remember /rɪ'mɛmbər/ v. acordarse de, recordar.

remembrance /rɪ'mɛmbrəns/ n. recuerdo m.

remind /rɪ'maɪnd/ v. **r. of,** recordar.

reminisce /ˌrɛmə'nɪs/ v. pensar en o hablar de cosas pasadas.

remiss /rɪ'mɪs/ a. remiso; flojo.

remit /rɪ'mɪt/ v. remitir.

remorse /rɪ'mɔrs/ n. remordimiento m.

remote /rɪ'mout/ a. remoto.

remote control mando a distancia m.

removal /rɪ'muvəl/ n. alejamiento m.; eliminación f.

remove /rɪ'muv/ v. quitar; remover.

renaissance /ˌrɛnə'sɑns/ n. renacimiento m.

rend /rɛnd/ v. hacer pedazos; separar.

render /'rɛndər/ v. dar; rendir; Theat. interpretar.

rendezvous /'rɑndə,vu, -dei-/ n. cita f.

rendition /rɛn'dɪʃən/ n. interpretación, rendición f.

renege /rɪ'nɪg, -'nɛg/ v. renunciar; faltar a su palabra, no cumplir una promesa.

renew /rɪ'nu, -'nyu/ v. renovar.

renewal /rɪ'nuəl, -'nyu-/ n. renovación; Com. prórroga f.

renounce /rɪ'naʊns/ v. renunciar a.

renovate /'rɛnə,veɪt/ v. renovar.

renown /rɪ'naʊn/ n. renombre m., fama f.

rent /rɛnt/ n. **1.** alquiler m. —v. **2.** arrendar, alquilar.

repair /rɪ'pɛər/ n. **1.** reparo m. —v. **2.** reparar.

repairman /rɪ'pɛər,mæn/ n. técnico m.

repatriate /ri'peɪtri,eɪt/ v. repatriar.

repay /rɪ'peɪ/ v. pagar; devolver.

repeat /rɪ'pit/ v. repetir.

repel /rɪ'pɛl/ v. repeler, repulsar.

repent /rɪ'pɛnt/ v. arrepentirse.

repentance /rɪ'pɛntns, -'pɛntəns/ n. arrepentimiento m.

repercussion /ˌripər'kʌʃən, ˌrɛpər-/ n. repercusión f.

repertoire /'rɛpər,twɑr/ n. repertorio m.

repetition /ˌrɛpɪ'tɪʃən/ n. repetición f.

replace /rɪ'pleɪs/ v. reemplazar.

replenish /rɪ'plɛnɪʃ/ v. rellenar; surtir de nuevo.

reply /rɪ'plaɪ/ n. **1.** respuesta f. —v. **2.** replicar; contestar.

report /rɪ'pɔrt, -'pourt/ n. **1.** informe m.

—v. **2.** informar, contar; denunciar; presentarse.

reporter /rɪ'pɔrtər, -'pour-/ n. repórter m. & f., reportero -ra.

repose /rɪ'pouz/ n. **1.** reposo m. —v. **2.** reposar; reclinar.

reprehensible /,reprɪ'hensəbəl/ a. reprensible.

represent /,reprɪ'zent/ v. representar.

representation /,reprizen'teiʃən, -zən-/ n. representación f.

representative /,reprɪ'zentətɪv/ a. **1.** representativo. —n. **2.** representante m. & f.

repress /rɪ'pres/ v. reprimir.

reprimand /'reprə,mænd, -,mɑnd/ n. **1.** regaño m. —v. **2.** regañar.

reprisal /rɪ'praizəl/ n. represalia f.

reproach /rɪ'proutʃ/ n. **1.** reproche m. —v. **2.** reprochar.

reproduce /,riprə'dus, -'dyus/ v. reproducir.

reproduction /,riprə'dʌkʃən/ n. reproducción f.

reproof /rɪ'pruf/ n. censura f.

reprove /rɪ'pruv/ v. censurar, regañar.

reptile /'reptil, -tail/ n. reptil m.

republic /rɪ'pʌblɪk/ n. república f.

republican /rɪ'pʌblɪkən/ a. & n. republicano -na.

repudiate /rɪ'pyudi,eit/ v. repudiar.

repulsive /rɪ'pʌlsɪv/ a. repulsivo, repugnante.

reputation /,repyə'teiʃən/ n. reputación f., fama f.

repute /rɪ'pyut/ n. **1.** reputación f. —v. **2.** reputar.

request /rɪ'kwest/ n. **1.** súplica f., ruego m. —v. **2.** pedir; rogar, suplicar.

require /rɪ'kwaiᵊr/ v. requerir; exigir.

requirement /rɪ'kwaiᵊrmənt/ n. requisito m.

requisite /'rekwəzit/ a. **1.** necesario. —n. **2.** requisito m.

requisition /,rekwə'zɪʃən/ n. requisición f.

rescind /rɪ'sɪnd/ v. rescindir, anular.

rescue /'reskyu/ n. **1.** rescate m. —v. **2.** rescatar.

research /rɪ'sɜrtʃ, 'risɜrtʃ/ n. investigación f.

researcher /rɪ'sɜrtʃər/ n. investigador, -dora.

resemble /rɪ'zembəl/ v. parecerse a, asemejarse a.

resent /rɪ'zent/ v. resentirse de.

reservation /,rezər'veiʃən/ n. reservación f.

reserve /rɪ'zɜrv/ n. **1.** reserva f. —v. **2.** reservar.

reservoir /'rezər,vwar, -,vwɔr, -,vɔr, 'rezə-/ n. depósito; tanque m.

reside /rɪ'zaid/ v. residir, morar.

residence /'rezɪdəns/ n. residencia, morada f.

resident /'rezɪdənt/ n. residente m. & f.

residue /'rezɪ,du/ n. residuo m.

resign /rɪ'zain/ v. dimitir; resignar.

resignation /,rezɪg'neiʃən/ n. dimisión; resignación f.

resist /rɪ'zɪst/ v. resistir.

resistance /rɪ'zɪstəns/ n. resistencia f.

resolute /'rezə,lut/ a. resuelto.

resolution /,rezə'luʃən/ n. resolución f.

resolve /rɪ'zɒlv/ v. resolver.

resonant /'rezənənt/ a. resonante.

resort /rɪ'zɔrt/ n. **1.** recurso; expediente m. **summer r.,** lugar de veraneo. —v. **2.** acudir, recurrir.

resound /rɪ'zaund/ v. resonar.

resource /'risɔrs/ n. recurso m.

respect /rɪ'spekt/ n. **1.** respeto m. **with r. to,** con respecto a. —v. **2.** respetar.

respectable /rɪ'spektəbəl/ a. respetable.

respectful /rɪ'spektfəl/ a. respetuoso.

respective /rɪ'spektɪv/ a. respectivo.

respiration /,respə'reiʃən/ n. respiración f.

respite /'respɪt/ n. pausa, tregua f.

respond /rɪ'spɒnd/ v. responder.

response /rɪ'spɒns/ n. respuesta f.

responsibility /rɪ,spɒnsə'bɪlɪti/ n. responsabilidad f.

responsible /rɪ'spɒnsəbəl/ a. responsable.

responsive /rɪ'spɒnsɪv/ a. sensible a.

rest /rest/ n. **1.** descanso; reposo m.; (music) pausa f. **the r.,** el resto, lo demás; los demás. —v. **2.** descansar; recostar.

restaurant /'restərənt, -tə,rɑnt, -trɑnt/ n. restaurante m.

restful /'restfəl/ a. tranquilo.

restitution /,restɪ'tuʃən, -'tyu-/ n. restitución f.

restless /'restlɪs/ a. inquieto.

restoration /,restə'reiʃən/ n. restauración f.

restore /rɪ'stɔr, -'stour/ v. restaurar.

restrain /rɪ'strein/ v. refrenar.

restraint /rɪ'streint/ n. limitación, restricción f.

restrict /rɪ'strɪkt/ v. restringir, limitar.

rest room aseos m.pl.

result /rɪ'zʌlt/ n. **1.** resultado m. —v. **2.** resultar.

resume /rɪ'zum/ v. reasumir; empezar de nuevo.

résumé /'rezʊ,mei/ n. resumen f.

resurgent /rɪ'sɜrdʒənt/ a. resurgente.

resurrect /,rezə'rekt/ v. resucitar.

resuscitate /rɪ'sʌsɪ,teit/ v. resucitar.

retail /'riteil/ n. **at r.,** al por menor.

retain /rɪ'tein/ v. retener.

retaliate /rɪ'tæli,eit/ v. vengarse.

retard /rɪ'tɑrd/ v. retardar.

retention /rɪ'tenʃən/ n. retención f.

reticent /'retəsənt/ a. reticente.

retire /rɪ'taiᵊr/ v. retirar.

retirement /rɪˈtaiᵊrmənt/ *n.* jubilación *f.*

retort /rɪˈtɔrt/ *n.* **1.** réplica; *Chem.* retorta *f.* —*v.* **2.** replicar.

retreat /rɪˈtrit/ *n.* **1.** retiro *m.*; *Mil.* retirada, retreta *f.* —*v.* **2.** retirarse.

retribution /ˌretrəˈbyuʃən/ *n.* retribución *f.*

retrieve /rɪˈtriv/ *v.* recobrar.

return /rɪˈtɜrn/ *n.* **1.** vuelta *f.*, regreso; retorno *m.* **by r. mail,** a vuelta de correo. —*v.* **2.** volver, regresar; devolver.

reunion /riˈyunyən/ *n.* reunión *f.*

rev /rev/ *n.* **1.** revolución *f.* —*v.* **2.** (motor) acelerar.

reveal /rɪˈvil/ *v.* revelar.

revelation /ˌrevəˈleiʃən/ *n.* revelación *f.*

revenge /rɪˈvendʒ/ *n.* venganza *f.* **to get r.,** vengarse.

revenue /ˈrevənˌyu, -əˌnu/ *n.* renta *f.*

revere /rɪˈvɪər/ *v.* reverenciar, venerar.

reverence /ˈrevərəns, ˈrevrəns/ *n.* **1.** reverencia *f.* —*v.* **2.** reverenciar.

reverend /ˈrevərənd, ˈrevrənd/ *a.* **1.** reverendo. —*n.* **2.** pastor *m.*

reverent /ˈrevərənt, ˈrevrənt/ *a.* reverente.

reverse /rɪˈvɜrs/ *a.* **1.** inverso. —*n.* **2.** revés, inverso *m.* —*v.* **3.** invertir; revocar.

revert /rɪˈvɜrt/ *v.* revertir.

review /rɪˈvyu/ *n.* **1.** repaso *m.*; revista *f.* —*v.* **2.** repasar; *Mil.* revistar.

revise /rɪˈvaiz/ *v.* revisar.

revision /rɪˈvɪʒən/ *n.* revisión *f.*

revival /rɪˈvaivəl/ *n.* reavivamiento *m.*

revive /rɪˈvaiv/ *v.* avivar; revivir, resucitar.

revoke /rɪˈvouk/ *v.* revocar.

revolt /rɪˈvoult/ *n.* **1.** rebelión *f.* —*v.* **2.** rebelarse.

revolting /rɪˈvoultɪŋ/ *a.* repugnante.

revolution /ˌrevəˈluʃən/ *n.* revolución *f.*

revolutionary /ˌrevəˈluʃəˌneri/ *a. & n.* revolucionario -ria.

revolve /rɪˈvɒlv/ *v.* girar; dar vueltas.

revolver /rɪˈvɒlvər/ *n.* revólver *m.*

revolving door /rɪˈvɒlvɪŋ/ puerta giratoria *f.*

reward /rɪˈwɔrd/ *n.* **1.** pago *m.*; recompensa *f.* —*v.* **2.** recompensar.

rhetoric /ˈretərɪk/ *n.* retórica *f.*

rheumatism /ˈrumə,tɪzəm/ *n.* reumatismo *m.*

rhinoceros /raiˈnɒsərəs/ *n.* rinoceronte *m.*

rhubarb /ˈrubɑrb/ *n.* ruibarbo *m.*

rhyme /raim/ *n.* **1.** rima *f.* —*v.* **2.** rimar.

rhythm /ˈrɪðəm/ *n.* ritmo *m.*

rhythmical /ˈrɪðmɪkəl/ *a.* rítmico.

rib /rɪb/ *n.* costilla *f.*

ribbon /ˈrɪbən/ *n.* cinta *f.*

rib cage caja torácica *f.*

rice /rais/ *n.* arroz *m.*

rich /rɪtʃ/ *a.* rico.

rid /rɪd/ *v.* librar. **get r. of,** deshacerse de, quitarse.

riddle /ˈrɪdl/ *n.* enigma; rompecabezas *m.*

ride /raid/ *n.* **1.** paseo (a caballo, en coche, etc.) *m.* —*v.* **2.** cabalgar; ir en coche.

ridge /rɪdʒ/ *n.* cerro *m.*; arruga *f.*; (of a roof) caballete *m.*

ridicule /ˈrɪdɪˌkyul/ *n.* **1.** ridículo *m.* —*v.* **2.** ridiculizar.

ridiculous /rɪˈdɪkyələs/ *a.* ridículo.

riding /ˈraidɪŋ/ *n.* equitación *f.*

riding school picadero *m.*

rifle /ˈraifəl/ *n.* **1.** fusil *m.* —*v.* **2.** robar.

right /rait/ *a.* **1.** derecho; correcto. **to be r.,** tener razón. —*adv.* **2.** bien, correctamente. **r. here,** etc., aquí mismo, etc. **all r.,** está bien, muy bien. —*n.* **3.** derecho *m.*; justicia *f.* **to the r.,** a la derecha. —*v.* **4.** corregir; enderezar.

righteous /ˈraitʃəs/ *a.* justo.

rigid /ˈrɪdʒɪd/ *a.* rígido.

rigor /ˈrɪgər/ *n.* rigor *m.*

rigorous /ˈrɪgərəs/ *a.* riguroso.

rim /rɪm/ *n.* margen *m.* or *f.*; borde *m.*

ring /rɪŋ/ *n.* **1.** anillo *m.*; sortija *f.*, círculo; campaneo *m.* —*v.* **2.** cercar; sonar; tocar.

ring finger dedo anular *m.*

rinse /rɪns/ *v.* enjuagar, lavar.

riot /ˈraiət/ *n.* motín; alboroto *m.*

rip /rɪp/ *n.* **1.** rasgadura *f.* —*v.* **2.** rasgar; descoser.

ripe /raip/ *a.* maduro.

ripen /ˈraipən/ *v.* madurar.

ripoff /ˈrɪpˌɔf/ *n.* robo, atraco *m.*

ripple /ˈrɪpəl/ *n.* **1.** onda *f.* —*v.* **2.** ondear.

rise /raiz/ *n.* **1.** subida *f.* —*v.* **2.** ascender; levantarse; (moon) salir.

risk /rɪsk/ *n.* **1.** riesgo *m.* —*v.* **2.** arriesgar.

rite /rait/ *n.* rito *m.*

ritual /ˈrɪtʃuəl/ *a. & n.* ritual *m.*

rival /ˈraivəl/ *n.* rival *m. & f.*

rivalry /ˈraivəlri/ *n.* rivalidad *f.*

river /ˈraivər/ *n.* río *m.*

rivet /ˈrɪvɪt/ *n.* **1.** remache, roblón *m.* —*v.* **2.** remachar, roblar.

road /roud/ *n.* camino *m.*; carretera *f.*

roadside /ˈroudˌsaid/ *n.* borde de la carretera *m.*

roam /roum/ *v.* vagar.

roar /rɔr, rour/ *n.* **1.** rugido, bramido *m.* —*v.* **2.** rugir, bramar.

roast /roust/ *n.* **1.** asado *m.* —*v.* **2.** asar.

rob /rɒb/ *v.* robar.

robber /ˈrɒbər/ *n.* ladrón -na.

robbery /ˈrɒbəri/ *n.* robo *m.*

robe /roub/ *n.* manto *m.*

robin /ˈrɒbɪn/ *n.* petirrojo *m.*

robust /rouˈbʌst, ˈroubʌst/ *a.* robusto.

rock /rɒk/ *n.* **1.** roca, peña *f.*; (music) rock

m., música (de) rock *f.* —*v.* **2.** mecer; oscilar.

rocker /'rɒkər/ *n.* mecedora *f.*

rocket /'rɒkɪt/ *n.* cohete *m.*

rocking chair /'rɒkɪŋ/ mecedora *f.*

Rock of Gibraltar /dʒɪ'brɔːltər/ Peñón de Gibraltar *m.*

rocky /'rɒki/ *a.* pedregoso.

rod /rɒd/ *n.* varilla *f.*

rodent /'roudnt/ *n.* roedor *m.*

rogue /roug/ *n.* bribón, pícaro *m.*

roguish /'rougɪʃ/ *a.* pícaro.

role /roul/ *n.* papel *m.*

roll /roul/ **1.** rollo *m.;* lista *f.;* panecillo *m.* **to call the r.,** pasar lista. —*v.* **2.** rodar. **r. up,** enrollar. **r. up one's sleeves,** arremangarse.

roller /'roulər/ *n.* rodillo, cilindro *m.*

roller skate patín de ruedas *m.*

Roman /'roumən/ *a. & n.* romano -na.

romance /rou'mæns, 'roumæns/ *a.* **1.** románico. —*n.* **2.** romance *m.;* amorío *m.*

romantic /rou'mæntɪk/ *a.* romántico.

romp /rɒmp/ *v.* retozar; jugar.

roof /ruːf, rʊf/ *n.* **1.** techo *m.;* —*v.* **2.** techar.

room /rum, rʊm/ *n.* **1.** cuarto *m.,* habitación *f.;* lugar *m.* —*v.* **2.** alojarse.

roommate /'rum,meit, 'rʊm-/ *n.* compañero -ra de cuarto.

rooster /'rustər/ *n.* gallo *m.*

root /rut/ *n.* raíz *f.* **to take r.,** arraigar.

rootless /'rutlɪs/ *a.* desarraigado.

rope /roup/ *n.* cuerda, soga *f.*

rose /rouz/ *n.* rosa *f.*

rosy /'rouzi/ *a.* róseo, rosado.

rot /rɒt/ *n.* **1.** putrefacción *f.* —*v.* **2.** pudrirse.

rotary /'routəri/ *a.* giratorio; rotativo.

rotate /'routeit/ *v.* girar; alternar.

rotation /rou'teiʃən/ *n.* rotación *f.*

rotten /'rɒtn/ *a.* podrido.

rouge /ruʒ/ *n.* colorete *m.*

rough /rʌf/ *a.* áspero; rudo; grosero; aproximado.

round /raund/ *a.* **1.** redondo. **r. trip,** viaje de ida y vuelta. —*n.* **2.** ronda *f.;* (boxing) asalto *m.*

rouse /rauz/ *v.* despertar.

rout /raut, rut/ *n.* **1.** derrota *f.* —*v.* **2.** derrotar.

route /rut, raut/ *n.* ruta, vía *f.*

routine /ru'tin/ *a.* **1.** rutinario. —*n.* **2.** rutina *f.*

rove /rouv/ *v.* vagar.

rover /'rouvər/ *n.* vagabundo -da.

row /rou/ *n.* **1.** fila *f.* —*v.* **2.** *Naut.* remar.

rowboat /'rou,bout/ *n.* bote de remos.

rowdy /'raudi/ *a.* alborotado.

royal /'rɔiəl/ *a.* real.

royalty /'rɔiəlti/ *n.* realeza *f.,* (pl.) regalías *f.pl.*

rub /rʌb/ *v.* frotar. **r. against,** rozar. **r. out,** borrar.

rubber /'rʌbər/ *n.* goma *f.;* caucho *m.;* (pl.) chanclos *m.pl.,* zapatos de goma.

rubbish /'rʌbɪʃ/ *n.* basura *f.;* (nonsense) tonterías *f.pl.*

ruby /'rubi/ *n.* rubí *m.*

rudder /'rʌdər/ *n.* timón *m.*

ruddy /'rʌdi/ *a.* colorado.

rude /rud/ *a.* rudo; grosero; descortés.

rudiment /'rudəmənt/ *n.* rudimento *m.*

rudimentary /,rudə'mɛntəri, -tri/ *a.* rudimentario.

rue /ru/ *v.* deplorar; lamentar.

ruffian /'rʌfiən, 'rʌfyən/ *n.* rufián, bandolero *m.*

ruffle /'rʌfəl/ *n.* **1.** volante fruncido. —*v.* **2.** fruncir; irritar.

rug /rʌg/ *n.* alfombra *f.*

rugged /'rʌgɪd/ *a.* áspero; robusto.

ruin /'ruɪn/ *n.* **1.** ruina *f.* —*v.* **2.** arruinar.

ruinous /'ruənəs/ *a.* ruinoso.

rule /rul/ *n.* **1.** regla *f.* **as a r.,** por regla general. —*v.* **2.** gobernar; mandar; rayar.

ruler /'rulər/ *n.* gobernante *m. & f.;* soberano -na; regla *f.*

rum /rʌm/ *n.* ron *m.*

rumble /'rʌmbəl/ *v.* retumbar.

rumor /'rumər/ *n.* rumor *m.*

rumpus /'rʌmpəs/ *n.* lío, jaleo, escandalo *m*

run /rʌn/ *v.* correr; hacer correr. **r. away,** escaparse. **r. into,** chocar con.

runner /'rʌnər/ *n.* corredor -ra; mensajero -ra.

runner-up /'rʌnər 'ʌp/ *n.* subcampeón, -ona.

runproof /'rʌnpruf/ *a.* indesmallable.

rupture /'rʌptʃər/ *n.* **1.** rotura; hernia *f.* —*v.* **2.** reventar.

rural /'rʊrəl/ *a.* rural, campestre.

rush /rʌʃ/ *n.* **1.** prisa *f.;* *Bot.* junco *m.* —*v.* **2.** ir de prisa.

rush hour hora punta *f.*

Russia /'rʌʃə/ *n.* Rusia *f.*

Russian /'rʌʃən/ *a. & n.* ruso -sa.

rust /rʌst/ *n.* **1.** herrumbre *f.* —*v.* **2.** aherrumbrarse.

rustic /'rʌstɪk/ *a.* rústico.

rustle /'rʌsəl/ *n.* **1.** susurro *m.* —*v.* **2.** susurrar.

rusty /'rʌsti/ *a.* mohoso.

rut /rʌt/ *n.* surco *m.*

ruthless /'ruθlɪs/ *a.* cruel, inhumano.

rye /rai/ *n.* centeno *m.*

rye bread pan de centeno *m.*

S

saber /'seibər/ n. sable m.

sable /'seibəl/ n. cebellina f.

sabotage /'sæbə,taʒ/ n. sabotaje m.

sachet /sæ'ʃei/ n. perfumador m.

sack /sæk/ n. 1. saco m. —v. 2. Mil. saquear.

sacred /'seikrid/ a. sagrado, santo.

sacrifice /'sækrə,fais/ n. 1. sacrificio m. —v. 2. sacrificar.

sacrilege /'sækrəlidʒ/ n. sacrilegio m.

sad /sæd/ a. triste.

saddle /'sædl/ n. 1. silla de montar. —v. 2. ensillar.

sadness /'sædnis/ n. tristeza f.

safe /seif/ a. 1. seguro; salvo. —n. 2. caja de caudales.

safeguard /'seif,gard/ n. 1. salvaguardia m. —v. 2. proteger, poner a salvo.

safety /'seifti/ n. seguridad, protección f.

safety belt cinturón de seguridad m.

safety pin imperdible m.

safety valve /vælv/ válvula de seguridad f.

sage /seidʒ/ a. 1. sabio, sagaz. —n. 2. sabio m.; Bot. salvia f.

sail /seil/ n. 1. vela f.; paseo por mar. —v. 2. navegar; embarcarse.

sailboat /'seil,bout/ n. barco de vela.

sailor /'seilər/ n. marinero m.

saint /seint/ n. santo -ta.

sake /seik/ n. **for the s. of**, por; por el bien de.

salad /'sæləd/ n. ensalada f. **s. bowl**, ensaladera f.

salad dressing aliño m.

salary /'sæləri/ n. sueldo, salario m.

sale /seil/ n. venta f.

salesman /'seilzmən/ n. vendedor m.; viajante de comercio.

sales tax /seilz/ impuesto sobre la venta.

saliva /sə'laivə/ n. saliva f.

salmon /'sæmən/ n. salmón m.

salt /sɔlt/ a. 1. salado. —n. 2. sal f. —v. 3. salar.

salute /sə'lut/ n. 1. saludo m. —v. 2. saludar.

salvage /'sælvidʒ/ v. salvar; recobrar.

salvation /sæl'veiʃən/ n. salvación f.

salve /sæv/ n. emplasto, ungüento m.

same /seim/ a. & pron. mismo. **it's all the s.**, lo mismo da.

sample /'sæmpəl/ n. 1. muestra f. —v. 2. probar.

sanatorium /,sænə'tɔriəm/ n. sanatorio m.

sanctify /'sæŋktə,fai/ v. santificar.

sanction /'sæŋkʃən/ n. 1. sanción f. —v. 2. sancionar.

sanctity /'sæŋktiti/ n. santidad f.

sanctuary /'sæŋktʃu,eri/ n. santuario, asilo m.

sand /sænd/ n. arena f.

sandal /'sændl/ n. sandalia f.

sandpaper /'sænd,peipər/ n. papel de lija m.

sandwich /'sændwitʃ, 'sæn-/ n. emparedado, sándwich m.

sandy /'sændi/ a. arenoso; (color) rufo.

sane /sein/ a. cuerdo; sano.

sanitary /'sæni,teri/ a. higiénico, sanitario. **s. napkin**, toalla sanitaria.

sanitation /,sæni'teiʃən/ n. saneamiento m.

sanity /'sæniti/ n. cordura f.

Santa Claus /'sæntə klɔz/ Papá Noel m.

sap /sæp/ n. 1. savia f.; Colloq. estúpido, bobo m. —v. 2. agotar.

sapphire /'sæfaiᵊr/ n. zafiro m.

sarcasm /'sarkæzəm/ n. sarcasmo m.

sardine /sar'din/ n. sardina f.

sash /sæʃ/ n. cinta f.

satellite /'sætl,ait/ n. satélite m.

satellite dish antena parabólica f.

satin /'sætn/ n. raso m.

satire /'sætaiᵊr/ n. sátira f.

satisfaction /,sætis'fækʃən/ n. satisfacción; recompensa f.

satisfactory /,sætis'fæktəri/ a. satisfactorio.

satisfy /'sætis,fai/ v. satisfacer. **be satisfied that...**, estar convencido de que.

saturate /'sætʃə,reit/ v. saturar.

Saturday /'sætər,dei/ n. sábado m.

sauce /sɔs/ n. salsa; compota f.

saucer /'sɔsər/ n. platillo m.

saucy /'sɔsi/ a. descarado, insolente.

sauna /'sɔnə/ n. sauna f.

sausage /'sɔsidʒ/ n. salchicha f.

savage /'sævidʒ/ a. & n. salvaje m. & f.

save /seiv/ v. 1. salvar; guardar; ahorrar; economizar. —prep. 2. salvo, excepto.

savings /'seiviŋz/ n. ahorros m.pl.

savings account cuenta de ahorros m.

savings bank caja de ahorros f.

savior /'seivyər/ n. salvador -ora.

savor /'seivər/ n. 1. sabor m. —v. 2. saborear.

savory /'seivəri/ a. sabroso.

saw /sɔ/ n. 1. sierra f. —v. 2. aserrar.

saxophone /'sæksə,foun/ n. saxofón, saxófono, m.

say /sei/ v. decir; recitar.

saying /'seiŋ/ n. dicho, refrán m.

scaffold /'skæfəld/ n. andamio; (gallows) patíbulo m.

scald /skɔld/ v. escaldar.

scale /skeil/ n. 1. escala; (of fish) escama f.; (pl.) balanza f. —v. 2. escalar; escamar.

scalp /skælp/ n. pericráneo m. v. escalpar.

scan /skæn/ v. hojear, repasar; (poetry) escandir; (computer) escanear, digitalizar.

scandal /'skændl/ n. escándalo m.

scanner /'skænər/ n. escáner m.

scant /skænt/ a. escaso.

scar /skɑr/ n. cicatriz f.

scarce /skeərs/ a. escaso; raro.

scarcely /'skeərsli/ adv. & conj. apenas.

scare /skeər/ n. 1. susto m. —v. 2. asustar. **s. away,** espantar.

scarf /skɑrf/ n. pañueleta, bufanda f.

scarlet /'skɑrlit/ n. escarlata f.

scarlet fever escarlatina f.

scatter /'skætər/ v. esparcir; dispersar.

scavenger /'skævɪndʒər/ n. basurero m.

scenario /sɪ'neəri,ou, -'nɑr-/ n. escenario m.

scene /sin/ n. vista f., paisaje m.; Theat. escena f. **behind the scenes,** entre bastidores.

scenery /'sinəri/ n. paisaje m.; Theat. decorado m.

scent /sent/ n. 1. olor, perfume; (sense) olfato m. —v. 2. perfumar; Fig. sospechar.

schedule /'skedʒul, -ʊl, -uəl/ n. 1. programa, horario m. —v. 2. fijar la hora para.

scheme /skim/ n. 1. proyecto; esquema m. —v. 2. intrigar.

scholar /'skɑlər/ n. erudito -ta; becado -da.

scholarship /'skɑlər,ʃɪp/ n. beca; erudición f.

school /skul/ n. 1. escuela f.; colegio m.; (of fish) banco m. —v. 2. enseñar.

sciatica /sai'ætɪkə/ n. ciática f.

science /'saiəns/ n. ciencia f.

science fiction ciencia ficción.

scientific /,saiən'tɪfɪk/ a. científico.

scientist /'saiəntɪst/ n. científico -ca.

scissors /'sɪzərz/ n. tijeras f.pl.

scoff /skɔf, skɒf/ v. mofarse, burlarse.

scold /skould/ v. regañar.

scoop /skup/ n. 1. cucharón m.; cucharada f. —v. 2. **s. out,** recoger, sacar.

scope /skoup/ n. alcance; campo m.

score /skɔr/ n. 1. tantos m.pl.; (music) partitura f. —v. 2. marcar, hacer tantos.

scorn /skɔrn/ n. 1. desprecio m. —v. 2. despreciar.

scornful /'skɔrnfəl/ a. desdeñoso.

Scotland /'skɒtlənd/ n. Escocia f.

Scottish /'skɒtɪʃ/ a. escocés.

scour /skauᵊr/ v. fregar, estregar.

scourge /skɜrdʒ/ n. azote m.; plaga f.

scout /skaut/ n. 1. explorador -ra. —v. 2. explorar, reconocer.

scramble /'skræmbəl/ n. 1. rebatiña f. —v. 2. bregar. **scrambled eggs,** huevos revueltos.

scrap /skræp/ n. 1. migaja f.; pedacito m.; Colloq. riña f. **s. metal,** hierro viejo m. **s. paper,** papel borrador. —v. 2. desechar; Colloq. reñir.

scrapbook /'skræp,bʊk/ n. álbum de recortes m.

scrape /skreip/ n. 1. lío, apuro m. —v. 2. raspar; (feet) restregar.

scratch /skrætʃ/ n. 1. rasguño m. —v. 2. rasguñar; rayar.

scream /skrim/ n. 1. grito, chillido m. —v. 2. gritar, chillar.

screen /skrin/ n. biombo m.; (for window) tela metálica; (movie) pantalla f.

screw /skru/ n. 1. tornillo m. —v. 2. atornillar.

screwdriver /'skru,draivər/ n. destornillador m.

scribble /'skrɪbəl/ v. hacer garabatos.

scroll /skroul/ n. rúbrica f.; rollo de papel.

scroll bar n. barra de enrollar f.

scrub /skrʌb/ v. fregar, estregar.

scruple /'skrupəl/ n. escrúpulo m.

scrupulous /'skrupyələs/ a. escrupuloso.

scuba diving /'skubə 'daiviŋ/ submarinismo m.

sculptor /'skʌlptər/ n. escultor -ra.

sculpture /'skʌlptʃər/ n. 1. escultura f. —v. 2. esculpir.

scythe /saið/ n. guadaña f.

sea /si/ n. mar m. or f.

seabed /'si,bed/ n. lecho marino m.

sea breeze brisa marina f.

seafood /'si,fud/ n. mariscos m.pl.

seal /sil/ n. 1. sello m.; (animal) foca f. —v. 2. sellar.

seam /sim/ n. costura f.

seamy /'simi/ a. sórdido.

seaplane /'si,plein/ n. hidroavión m.

seaport /'si,pɔrt/ n. puerto de mar.

search /sɜrtʃ/ n. 1. registro m. **in s. of,** en busca de. —v. 2. registrar. **s. for,** buscar.

search engine motor de búsqueda m., buscador m., indexador de información m.

seasick /'si,sɪk/ a. mareado. **to get s.,** marearse.

season /'sizən/ n. 1. estación; sazón; temporada f. —v. 2. sazonar.

seasoning /'sizənɪŋ/ n. condimento m.

season ticket abono m.

seat /sit/ n. 1. asiento m.; residencia, sede f.; Theat. localidad f **s. belt,** cinturón de seguridad. —v. 2. sentar. **be seated,** sentarse.

seaweed /'si,wid/ n. alga, alga marina f.

second /sɪ'kɒnd/ a. & n. **1.** segundo m. —v. **2.** apoyar, segundar.

secondary /'sɛkən,deri/ a. secundario.

secret /'sikrɪt/ a. & n. secreto m.

secretary /'sɛkrɪ,teri/ n. secretario -ria; Govt. ministro -tra; (furniture) papelera f.

sect /sɛkt/ n. secta f.; partido m.

section /'sɛkʃən/ n. sección, parte f.

sectional /'sɛkʃənl/ a. regional, local.

secular /'sɛkyələr/ a. secular.

secure /sɪ'kyur/ a. **1.** seguro. —v **2.** asegurar; obtener; Fin. garantizar.

security /sɪ'kyurɪti/ n. seguridad; garantía f.

sedative /'sɛdətɪv/ a. & n. sedativo m.

seduce /sɪ'dus/ v. seducir.

see /si/ v. ver; comprender. **s. off**, despedirse de. **s. to**, encargarse de.

seed /sid/ n. **1.** semilla f. —v. **2.** sembrar.

seek /sik/ v. buscar. **s. to**, tratar de.

seem /sim/ v. parecer.

seep /sip/ v. colarse.

segment /'sɛgmənt/ n. segmento m.

segregate /'sɛgrɪ,geit/ v. segregar.

seize /siz/ v. agarrar; apoderarse de.

seldom /'sɛldəm/ adv. rara vez.

select /sɪ'lɛkt/ a. **1.** escogido, selecto. —v. **2.** elegir, seleccionar.

selection /sɪ'lɛkʃən/ n. selección f.

selective /sɪ'lɛktɪv/ a. selectivo.

selfish /'sɛlfɪʃ/ a. egoísta.

selfishness /'sɛlfɪʃnɪs/ n. egoísmo m.

sell /sɛl/ v. vender.

semester /sɪ'mɛstər/ n. semestre m.

semicircle /'sɛmi,sɜrkəl/ n. semicírculo m.

semolina /,sɛmə'linə/ n. sémola f.

senate /'sɛnɪt/ n. senado m.

senator /'sɛnətər/ n. senador -ra.

send /sɛnd/ v. mandar, enviar; (a wire) poner. **s. away**, despedir. **s. back**, devolver. **s. for**, mandar buscar. **s. off**, expedir. **s. word**, mandar recado.

senile /'sinail/ a. senil.

senior /'sinyər/ a. mayor; más viejo. **Sr.**, padre.

senior citizen persona de edad avanzada.

sensation /sɛn'seiʃən/ n. sensación f.

sensational /sɛn'seiʃənl/ a. sensacional.

sense /sɛns/ n. **1.** sentido; juicio m. —v. **2.** percibir; sospechar.

sensible /'sɛnsəbəl/ a. sensato, razonable.

sensitive /'sɛnsɪtɪv/ a. sensible; sensitivo.

sensual /'sɛnʃuəl/ a. sensual.

sentence /'sɛntəns/ n. **1.** frase; Gram. oración; Leg. sentencia f. —v. **2.** condenar.

sentiment /'sɛntəmənt/ n. sentimiento m.

sentimental /,sɛntə'mɛntl/ a. sentimental.

separate /a. 'sɛpərɪt; v. -,reit/ a. **1.** separado; suelto. —v. **2.** separar, dividir.

separation /,sɛpə'reiʃən/ n. separación f.

September /sɛp'tɛmbər/ n. septiembre m.

sequence /'sikwəns/ n. serie f. **in s.**, seguidos.

serenade /,sɛrə'neid/ n. **1.** serenata f. —v. **2.** dar serenata a.

serene /sə'rin/ a. sereno; tranquilo.

sergeant /'sɑrdʒənt/ n. sargento m.

serial /'stɔriəl/ a. en serie, de serie.

series /'stɔriz/ n. serie f.

serious /'stɔriəs/ a. serio; grave.

sermon /'sɜrmən/ n. sermón m.

serpent /'sɜrpənt/ n. serpiente f.

servant /'sɜrvənt/ n. criado -da; servidor -ra.

serve /sɜrv/ v. servir.

server /'sɜrvər/ n. servidor m.

service /'sɜrvɪs/ n. **1.** servicio m. **at the s. of**, a las órdenes de. **be of s.**, servir; ser útil. —v. **2.** Auto. reparar.

service station estación de servicio f.

session /'sɛʃən/ n. sesión f.

set /sɛt/ a. **1.** fijo. —n. **2.** colección f.; (of a game) juego; Mech. aparato; Theat. decorado m. —v. **3.** poner, colocar; fijar; (sun) ponerse. **s. forth**, exponer. **s. off**, out, salir. **s. up**, instalar; establecer.

settle /'sɛtl/ v. solucionar; arreglar; establecerse.

settlement /'sɛtlmənt/ n. caserío; arreglo; acuerdo m.

settler /'sɛtlər/ n. poblador -ra.

seven /'sɛvən/ a. & pron. siete.

seventeen /'sɛvən'tin/ a. & pron. diecisiete.

seventh /'sɛvənθ/ a. séptimo.

seventy /'sɛvənti/ a. & pron. setenta.

sever /'sɛvər/ v. desunir; romper.

several /'sɛvərəl/ a. & pron. varios.

severance pay /'sɛvərəns/ indemnización de despido.

severe /sə'vɪər/ a. severo; grave.

severity /sə'vɛrɪti/ n. severidad f.

sew /sou/ v. coser.

sewer /'suər/ n. cloaca f.

sewing /'souɪŋ/ n. costura f.

sewing basket costurero m.

sewing machine máquina de coser f.

sex /sɛks/ n. sexo m.

sexism /'sɛksɪzəm/ n. sexismo m.

sexist /'sɛksɪst/ a. & n. sexista m. & f.

sexton /'sɛkstən/ n. sacristán f.

sexual /'sɛkʃuəl/ a. sexual.

shabby /'ʃæbi/ a. haraposo, desaliñado.

shade /ʃeid/ n. **1.** sombra f.; tinte m.; (window) transparente m. —v. **2.** sombrear.

shadow /'ʃædou/ n. sombra f.

shady /'ʃeidi/ a. sombroso; sospechoso.

shaft /ʃæft/ n. (columna) fuste m.; Mech. asta f.

shake /ʃeik/ v. sacudir; agitar; temblar. **s. hands with,** dar la mano a.

shallow /'ʃælou/ a. poco hondo; superficial.

shame /ʃeim/ n. **1.** vergüenza f. **be a s.,** ser una lástima. —v. **2.** avergonzar.

shameful /'ʃeimfəl/ a. vergonzoso.

shampoo /ʃæm'pu/ n. champú m.

shape /ʃeip/ n. **1.** forma f.; estado m. —v. **2.** formar.

share /ʃeər/ n. **1.** parte; (stock) acción f. 2 —v. **2.** compartir.

shareholder /'ʃeər,houldər/ n. accionista m. & f.

shareware /'ʃeər,weər/ n. programas compartidos m.pl.

shark /ʃark/ n. tiburón m.

sharp /ʃarp/ a. agudo; (blade) afilado.

sharpen /'ʃarpən/ v. aguzar; afilar.

shatter /'ʃætər/ v. estrellar; hacer pedazos.

shave /ʃeiv/ n. **1.** afeitada f. —v. **2.** afeitarse.

shawl /ʃɔl/ n. rebozo, chal m.

she /ʃi/ pron. ella f.

sheaf /ʃif/ n. gavilla f.

shear /ʃiər/ v. cizallar.

shears /ʃiərz/ n. cizallas f.pl.

sheath /ʃiθ/ n. vaina f.

shed /ʃed/ n. **1.** cobertizo m. —v. **2.** arrojar, quitarse.

sheep /ʃip/ n. oveja f.

sheet /ʃit/ n. sábana f.; (of paper) hoja f.

shelf /ʃelf/ n. estante, m., repisa f.

shell /ʃel/ n. **1.** cáscara; (sea) concha f.; Mil. proyectil m. —v. **2.** desgranar; bombardear.

shellac /ʃə'læk/ n. laca f.

shelter /'ʃeltər/ n. **1.** albergue; refugio m. —v. **2.** albergar; amparar.

shepherd /'ʃepərd/ n. pastor m.

sherry /'ʃeri/ n. jerez m.

shield /ʃild/ n. **1.** escudo m. —v. **2.** amparar.

shift /ʃift/ n. **1.** cambio; (work) turno m. —v. **2.** cambiar, mudar. **s. for oneself,** arreglárselas.

shine /ʃain/ n. **1.** brillo, lustre m. —v. **2.** brillar; (shoes) lustrar.

shiny /'ʃaini/ a. brillante, lustroso.

ship /ʃip/ n. **1.** barco m., nave f —v. **2.** embarcar; Com. enviar.

shipment /'ʃipmənt/ n. envío; embarque m.

shirk /ʃɜrk/ v. faltar al deber.

shirt /ʃɜrt/ n. camisa f.

shiver /'ʃivər/ n. **1.** temblor m. —v. **2.** temblar.

shock /ʃɒk/ n. **1.** choque m. —v. **2.** chocar.

shoe /ʃu/ n. zapato m.

shoelace /'ʃu,leis/ n. lazo m.; cordón de zapato.

shoemaker /'ʃu,meikər/ n. zapatero m.

shoot /ʃut/ v. tirar; (gun) disparar. **s. away, s. off,** salir disparado.

shop /ʃɒp/ n. tienda f.

shopping /'ʃɒpiŋ/ n. **to go s.,** hacer compras. ir de compras.

shop window escaparate m.

shore /ʃɔr/ n. orilla; playa f.

short /ʃɔrt/ a. corto; breve; (in stature) pequeño, bajo. **a s. time,** poco tiempo. **in s.,** en suma.

shortage /'ʃɔrtidʒ/ n. escasez; falta f.

shorten /'ʃɔrtn/ v. acortar, abreviar.

shortly /'ʃɔrtli/ adv. en breve, dentro de poco.

shorts /ʃɔrts/ n. calzoncillos m.pl.

shot /ʃɒt/ n. tiro, disparo m.

shoulder /'ʃouldər/ n. **1.** hombro m. —v. **2.** asumir; cargar con.

shoulder blade n. omóplato m., paletilla f.

shout /ʃaut/ n. **1.** grito m. —v. **2.** gritar.

shove /ʃʌv/ n. **1.** empujón m. —v. **2.** empujar.

shovel /'ʃʌvəl/ n. **1.** pala f. —v. **2.** traspalar.

show /ʃou/ n. **1.** ostentación f.; Theat. función f.; espectáculo m. —v. **2.** enseñar, mostrar; verse. **s. up,** destacarse; Colloq. asomar.

shower /'ʃauər/ n. chubasco m.; (bath) ducha f. v. ducharse.

shrapnel /'ʃræpnl/ n. metralla f.

shrewd /ʃrud/ a. astuto.

shriek /ʃrik/ n. **1.** chillido m. —v. **2.** chillar.

shrill /ʃril/ a. chillón, agudo.

shrimp /ʃrimp/ n. camarón m.

shrine /ʃrain/ n. santuario m.

shrink /ʃriŋk/ v. encogerse, contraerse. **s. from,** huir de.

shroud /ʃraud/ n. **1.** mortaja f. —v. **2.** Fig. ocultar.

shrub /ʃrʌb/ n. arbusto m.

shudder /'ʃʌdər/ n. **1.** estremecimiento m. —v. **2.** estremecerse.

shun /ʃʌn/ v. evitar, huir de.

shut /ʃʌt/ v. cerrar. **s. in,** encerrar. **s. up,** Colloq. callarse.

shutter /'ʃʌtər/ n. persiana f.

shy /ʃai/ a. tímido, vergonzoso.

sick /sik/ a. enfermo. **s. of,** aburrido de, cansado de.

sickness /'siknis/ n. enfermedad f.

side /said/ n. **1.** lado; partido m.; parte f.; Anat. costado m. —v. **2. s. with,** ponerse del lado de.

sidewalk /'said,wɔk/ n. acera, vereda f.

siege /sidʒ/ n. asedio m.

sieve /siv/ n. cedazo m.

sift /sɪft/ v. cerner.

sigh /sai/ n. **1.** suspiro m. —v. **2.** suspirar.

sight /sait/ n. **1.** vista f.; punto de interés m. **lose s. of,** perder de vista. —v. **2.** divisar.

sign /sain/ n. **1.** letrero; señal, seña f. —v. **2.** firmar. **s. up,** inscribirse.

signal /'sɪgnl/ n. **1.** señal f. —v. **2.** hacer señales.

signature /'sɪgnətʃər/ n. firma f.

significance /sɪg'nɪfɪkəns/ n. significación f.

significant /sɪg'nɪfɪkənt/ a. significativo.

significant other pareja m. & f.

signify /'sɪgnə,fai/ v. significar.

silence /'sailəns/ n. **1.** silencio m. —v. **2.** hacer callar.

silent /'sailənt/ a. silencioso; callado.

silk /sɪlk/ n. seda f.

silken /'sɪlkən/ **silky** a. sedoso.

sill /sɪl/ n. umbral de puerta m., solera f.

silly /'sɪli/ a. necio, tonto.

silo /'sailou/ n. silo m.

silver /'sɪlvər/ n. plata f.

silver-plated /'sɪlvər 'pleitɪd/ a. chapado en plata.

silverware /'sɪlvər,wɛər/ n. vajilla de plata f.

similar /'sɪmələr/ a. semejante, parecido.

similarity /,sɪmə'lærɪti/ n. semejanza f.

simple /'sɪmpəl/ a. sencillo, simple.

simplicity /sɪm'plɪsɪti/ n. sencillez f.

simplify /'sɪmplə,fai/ v. simplificar.

simulate /'sɪmyə,leit/ v. simular.

simultaneous /,saiməl'teiniəs/ a. simultáneo.

sin /sɪn/ n. **1.** pecado m. —v. **2.** pecar.

since /sɪns/ adv. **1.** desde entonces. —prep. **2.** desde. —conj. **3.** desde que; puesto que.

sincere /sɪn'sɪər/ a. sincero.

sincerely /sɪn'sɪərli/ adv. sinceramente.

sincerity /sɪn'scrɪti/ n. sinceridad f.

sinew /'sɪnyu/ n. tendón m.

sinful /'sɪnfəl/ a. pecador.

sing /sɪŋ/ v. cantar.

singe /sɪndʒ/ v. chamuscar.

singer /'sɪŋər/ n. cantante m. & f.

single /'sɪŋgəl/ a. solo; (room) sencillo; (unmarried) soltero. **s. room,** habitación individual.

singular /'sɪŋgyələr/ a. & n. singular m.

sinister /'sɪnəstər/ a. siniestro.

sink /sɪŋk/ n. **1.** fregadero m. —v **2.** hundir; Fig. abatir.

sinner /'sɪnər/ n. pecador -ra.

sinuous /'sɪnyuəs/ a. sinuoso.

sinus /'sainəs/ n. seno m.

sip /sɪp/ n. **1.** sorbo m. —v. **2.** sorber.

siphon /'saifən/ n. sifón m.

sir /sɜr/ title. señor.

siren /'sairən/ n. sirena f.

sirloin /'sɜrloin/ n. solomillo m.

sisal /'saisəl, 'sɪsəl/ n. henequén m.

sister /'sɪstər/ n. hermana f.

sister-in-law /'sɪstərɪn,lɔ/ n. cuñada f.

sit /sɪt/ v. sentarse; posar. **be sitting,** estar sentado. **s. down,** sentarse. **s. up,** incorporarse; quedar levantado.

site /sait/ n. sitio, local m.

sitting /'sɪtɪŋ/ n. sesión f. a. sentado.

situate /'sɪtʃu,eit/ v. situar.

situation /,sɪtʃu'eiʃən/ n situación f.

sit-up /'sɪt ,ʌp/ n. abdominal m.

six /sɪks/ a. & pron. seis.

sixteen /'sɪks'tin/ a. & pron. dieciseis.

sixth /sɪksθ/ a. sexto.

sixty /'sɪksti/ a. & pron. sesenta.

size /saiz/ n. tamaño; (of shoe, etc.) número m.; talla f

sizing /'saizɪŋ/ n. upreso m.; sisa, cola de retazo f.

skate /skeit/ n. **1.** patín m. —v. **2.** patinar.

skateboard /'skeit,bɔrd/ n. monopatín m.

skein /skein/ n. madeja f.

skeleton /'skɛlɪtn/ n. esqueleto m

skeptic /'skɛptɪk/ n. escéptico -ca.

skeptical /'skɛptɪkəl/ a. escéptico.

sketch /skɛtʃ/ n. **1.** esbozo m. —v. **2.** esbozar.

ski /ski/ n. **1.** esquí m. —v. **2.** esquiar.

skid /skɪd/ v. **1.** resbalar. —n. **2.** varadera f.

skill /skɪl/ n. destreza, habilidad f.

skillful /'skɪlfəl/ a. diestro, hábil.

skim /skɪm/ v. rasar; (milk) desnatar. **s. over, s. through,** hojear.

skin /skɪn/ n. **1.** piel; (of fruit) corteza f. —v. **2.** desollar.

skin doctor dermatólogo -ga m. & f.

skip /skɪp/ n. **1.** brinco m. —v. **2.** brincar. **s. over,** pasar por alto.

skirmish /'skɜrmɪʃ/ n. escaramuza f.

skirt /skɜrt/ n. falda f.

skull /skʌl/ n. cráneo m.

skunk /skʌŋk/ n. zorrillo m.

sky /skai/ n. cielo m.

skylight /'skai,lait/ n. tragaluz m.

skyscraper /'skai,skreipər/ n. rascacielos m.

slab /slæb/ n. tabla f.

slack /slæk/ a. flojo; descuidado.

slacken /'slækən/ v. relajar.

slacks /slæks/ n. pantalones flojos.

slam /slæm/ n. **1.** portazo m. —v. **2.** cerrar de golpe. **slamming on the brakes,** frenazo m.

slander /'slændər/ n. **1.** calumnia f. —v. **2.** calumniar.

slang /slæŋ/ n. jerga f.

slant /slænt/ n. **1.** sesgo m. —v. **2.** sesgar.

slap /slæp/ n. **1.** bofetada, palmada f. —v. **2.** dar una bofetada.

slash /slæʃ/ n. **1.** cuchillada f. —v. **2.** acuchillar.

slat /slæt/ n. **1.** tablilla f. —v. **2.** lanzar.

slate /sleit/ n. **1.** pizarra f.; lista de candidatos. —n. **2.** destinar.

slaughter /'slɔtər/ n. **1.** matanza f. —v. **2.** matar.

slave /sleiv/ n. esclavo -va.

slavery /'sleivəri/ n. esclavitud f

Slavic /'slɑvɪk/ a. eslavo.

slay /slei/ v. matar, asesinar.

sled /slɛd/ n. trineo m.

sleek /slik/ a. liso y brillante.

sleep /slip/ n. **1.** sueño m. **to get much s.,** dormir mucho. —v. **2.** dormir.

sleeping car /'slipɪŋ/ coche cama.

sleeping pill /'slipɪŋ/ pastilla para dormir, somnífero m.

sleepy /'slipi/ a. soñoliento. **to be s.,** tener sueño.

sleet /slit/ n. **1.** cellisca f. —v. **2.** cellisquear.

sleeve /sliv/ n. manga f.

slender /'slɛndər/ a. delgado.

slice /slais/ n. **1.** rebanada f.; (of meat) tajada f. —v. **2.** rebanar; tajar.

slide /slaid/ v. resbalar, deslizarse.

slide rule regla de cálculo f.

slight /slait/ n. **1.** desaire m. —a. **2.** pequeño; leve. —v. **3.** desairar.

slim /slɪm/ a. delgado.

slime /slaim/ n. lama f.

sling /slɪŋ/ n. **1.** honda f.; Med. cabestrillo m. —v. **2.** tirar.

slink /slɪŋk/ v. escabullirse.

slip /slɪp/ n. **1.** imprudencia; (garment) combinación f.; (of paper) trozo m.; ficha f. —v. **2.** resbalar; deslizar. **s. up,** equivocarse.

slipper /'slɪpər/ n. chinela f.

slippery /'slɪpəri/ a. resbaloso.

slit /slɪt/ n. **1.** abertura f. —v. **2.** cortar.

slogan /'slougən/ n. lema m.

slope /sloup/ n. **1.** declive m. —v. **2.** inclinarse.

sloppy /'slɑpi/ a. desaliñado, chapucero.

slot /slɑt/ n. ranura f.

slot machine tragaperras f.

slouch /slautʃ/ n. **1.** patán m. —v. **2.** estar gacho.

slovenly /'slʌvənli/ a. desaliñado.

slow /slou/ a. **1.** lento; (watch) atrasado. —v. **2. s. down, s. up,** retardar; ir más despacio.

slowly /'slouli/ adv. despacio.

slowness /'slounɪs/ n. lentitud f.

sluggish /'slʌgɪʃ/ a. perezoso, inactivo.

slum /slʌm/ n. barrio bajo m.

slumber /'slʌmbər/ v. dormitar.

slur /slɜr/ n. **1.** estigma m. —v. **2.** menospreciar.

slush /slʌʃ/ n. fango m.

sly /slai/ a. taimado. **on the s.** a hurtadillas.

smack /smæk/ n. **1.** manotada f. —v. **2.** manotear.

small /smɔl/ a. pequeño.

small letter minúscula f

smallpox /'smɔl,pɑks/ n. viruela f.

smart /smɑrt/ a. **1.** listo; elegante. —v. **2.** escocer.

smash /smæʃ/ v. aplastar; hacer pedazos.

smear /smɪr/ n. **1.** mancha; difamación f. —v. **2.** manchar; difamar.

smell /smɛl/ n. **1.** olor; (sense) olfato m. —v. **2.** oler.

smelt /smɛlt/ n. **1.** eperlano m. —v. **2.** fundir.

smile /smail/ n. **1.** sonrisa f. —v. **2.** sonreír.

smite /smait/ v. afligir; apenar.

smock /smɑk/ n. camisa de mujer f.

smoke /smouk/ n. **1.** humo m. —v. **2.** fumar; (food) ahumar.

smokestack /'smouk,stæk/ n. chimenea f.

smolder /'smouldər/ v. arder sin llama.

smooth /smuð/ a. **1.** liso; suave; tranquilo. —v. **2.** alisar.

smother /'smʌðər/ v. sofocar.

smug /smʌg/ a. presumido.

smuggle /'smʌgəl/ v. pasar de contrabando.

snack /snæk/ n. bocadillo m.

snag /snæg/ n. nudo; obstáculo m.

snail /sneil/ n. caracol m.

snake /sneik/ n. culebra, serpiente f.

snap /snæp/ n. **1.** trueno m. —v. **2.** tronar; romper.

snapshot /'snæp,ʃɑt/ n. instantánea f.

snare /snɛr/ n. trampa f.

snarl /snɑrl/ n. **1.** gruñido m. —v. **2.** gruñir; (hair) enredar.

snatch /snætʃ/ v. arrebatar.

sneak /snik/ v. ir, entrar, salir (etc.) a hurtadillas.

sneaker /'snikər/ n. sujeto ruín m. zapatilla de tenis.

sneer /snɪr/ n. **1.** mofa f. —v. **2.** mofarse.

sneeze /sniz/ n. **1.** estornudo m. —v. **2.** estornudar.

snicker /'snɪkər/ n. risita m.

snob /snɑb/ n. esnob m.

snore /snɔr/ n. **1.** ronquido m. —v. **2.** roncar.

snow /snou/ n. **1.** nieve f. —v. **2.** nevar.

snowball /'snou,bɔl/ n. bola de nieve f.

snowdrift /'snou,drɪft/ n. ventisquero m.

snowplow /'snou,plau/ n. quitanieves m.

snowstorm /'snou,stɔrm/ n. nevasca f.

snub /snʌb/ v. desairar.

snug /snʌg/ a. abrigado y cómodo.

so /sou/ *adv.* **1.** así; (also) también. **so as to**, para. **so that**, para que. **so... as**, tan... como. **so... that**, tan... que. —*conj.* **2.** así es que.

soak /souk/ *v.* empapar.

soap /soup/ *n.* **1.** jabón *m.* —*v.* **2.** enjabonar.

soap powder jabón en polvo *m.*

soar /sɔr/ *v.* remontarse.

sob /sɒb/ *n.* **1.** sollozo *m.* —*v.* **2.** sollozar.

sober /'soubər/ *a.* sobrio; pensativo.

sociable /'souʃəbəl/ *a.* sociable.

social /'souʃəl/ *a.* **1.** social. —*n.* **2.** tertulia *f.*

socialism /'souʃə,lɪzəm/ *n.* socialismo *m.*

socialist /'souʃəlɪst/ *a.* & *n.* socialista *m.* & *f.*

society /sə'saɪɪti/ *n.* sociedad; compañía *f.*

sociological /,sousiə'lɒdʒɪkəl/ *a.* sociológico.

sociologist /,sousi,ɒlədʒɪst/ *n.* sociólogo -ga *m.* & *f.*

sociology /,sousi'ɒlədʒi/ *n.* sociología *f.*

sock /sɒk/ *n.* **1.** calcetín; puñetazo *m.* —*v.* **2.** dar un puñetazo a.

socket /'sɒkɪt/ *n.* cuenca *f.*; *Elec.* enchufe *m.*

sod /sɒd/ *n.* césped *m.*

soda /'soudə/ *n.* soda; *Chem.* sosa *f.*

sodium /'soudiəm/ *n.* sodio *m.*

sofa /'soufə/ *n.* sofá *m.*

soft /sɔft/ *a.* blando; fino; suave.

soft drink bebida no alcohólica.

soften /'sɔfən/ *v.* ablandar; suavizar.

software /'sɔft,wɛər/ *n.* software *m.*, programa *m.*

soil /sɔɪl/ *n.* **1.** suelo *m.* —*v.* **2.** ensuciar.

sojourn /'soudʒɜrn/ *n.* morada *f.*, estancia *f.*

solace /'sɒlɪs/ *n.* **1.** solaz *m.* —*v.* **2.** solazar.

solar /'soulər/ *a.* solar.

solar system sistema solar *m.*

solder /'sɒdər/ *v.* **1.** soldar. —*n.* **2.** soldadura *f.*

soldier /'souldʒər/ *n.* soldado *m.* & *f.*

sole /soul/ *n.* **1.** suela; (of foot) planta *f.*; (fish) lenguado *m.* —*a.* **2.** único.

solemn /'sɒləm/ *a.* solemne.

solemnity /sə'lɛmnɪti/ *n.* solemnidad *f.*

solicit /sə'lɪsɪt/ *v.* solicitar.

solicitous /sə'lɪsɪtəs/ *a.* solícito.

solid /'sɒlɪd/ *a.* & *n.* sólido *m.*

solidify /sə'lɪdə,faɪ/ *v.* solidificar.

solidity /sə'lɪdɪti/ *n.* solidez *f.*

solitary /'sɒlɪ,tɛri/ *a.* solitario.

solitude /'sɒlɪ,tud/ *n.* soledad *f.*

solo /'soulou/ *n.* solo *m.*

soloist /'soulouɪst/ *n.* solista *m.* & *f.*

soluble /'sɒlyəbəl/ *a.* soluble.

solution /sə'luʃən/ *n.* solución *f.*

solve /sɒlv/ *v.* solucionar; resolver.

solvent /'sɒlvənt/ *a.* solvente.

somber /'sɒmbər/ *a.* sombrío.

some /sʌm; *unstressed* səm/ *a.* & *pron.* algo (de), un poco (de); alguno; (pl.) algunos, unos.

somebody, someone /'sʌmbɒdi; 'sʌm,wʌn/ *pron.* alguien.

somehow /'sʌm,hau/ *adv.* de algún modo.

someone /'sʌm,wʌn/ *n.* alguien o alguno

somersault /'sʌmər,sɔlt/ *n.* salto mortal *m.*

something /'sʌm,θɪŋ/ *pron.* algo, alguna cosa.

sometime /'sʌm,taɪm/ *adv.* alguna vez.

sometimes /'sʌm,taɪmz/ *adv.* a veces, algunas veces.

somewhat /'sʌm,wʌt/ *adv.* algo, un poco.

somewhere /'sʌm,wɛər/ *adv.* en (or a) alguna parte.

son /sʌn/ *n.* hijo *m.*

song /sɔŋ/ *n.* canción *f.*

son-in-law /'sʌn ɪn ,lɔ/ *n.* yerno *m.*

soon /sun/ *adv.* pronto. **as s. as possible**, cuanto antes. **sooner or later**, tarde o temprano. **no sooner... than**, apenas... cuando.

soot /sut/ *n.* hollín *m.*

soothe /suð/ *v.* calmar.

soothingly /'suðɪŋli/ *adv.* tiernamente.

sophisticated /sə'fɪstɪ,keitɪd/ *a.* sofisticado.

sophomore /'sɒfə,mɔr/ *n.* estudiante de segundo año *m.*

soprano /sə'prænou/ *n.* soprano *m.* & *f.*

sorcery /'sɔrsəri/ *n.* encantamiento *m.*

sordid /'sɔrdɪd/ *a.* sórdido.

sore /sɔr/ *n.* **1.** llaga *f.* —*a.* **2.** lastimado; *Colloq.* enojado. **to be s.**, doler.

sorority /sə'rɔrɪti, -'rɒr-/ *n.* hermandad de mujeres *f.*

sorrow /'sɒrou/ *n.* pesar, dolor *m.*, aflicción *f.*

sorrowful /'sɒrəfəl/ *a.* doloroso; afligido.

sorry /'sɒri/ *a.* **to be s.**, sentir, lamentar. **to be s. for**, compadecer.

sort /sɔrt/ *n.* **1.** tipo *m.*; clase, especie *f.* **s. of**, algo, un poco. —*v.* **2.** clasificar.

soul /soul/ *n.* alma *f.*

sound /saund/ *a.* **1.** sano; razonable; firme. —*n.* **2.** sonido *m.* —*v.* **3.** sonar; parecer.

soundproof /'saund,pruf/ *a.* insonorizado. *v.* insonorizar.

soundtrack /'saund,træk/ *n.* banda sonora *f.*

soup /sup/ *n.* sopa *f.*

sour /sau³r/ *a.* agrio; ácido; rancio.

source /sɔrs/ *n.* fuente; causa *f.*

south /sauθ/ *n.* sur *m.*

South Africa /'æfrɪkə/ Sudáfrica *f.*

South African *a.* & *n.* sudafricano.

South America /ə'mɛrıkə/ Sud América, América del Sur.

South American a. & n. sudamericano -na.

southeast /,sauθ'ist/ Naut. ,sau-/ n. sudeste m.

southern /'sʌðərn/ a. meridional.

South Pole n. Polo Sur m.

southwest /,sauθ'wɛst/ Naut. ,sau-/ n. sudoeste m.

souvenir /,suvə'nıər/ n. recuerdo m.

sovereign /'sɒvrın/ n. soberano -na.

sovereignty /'sɒvrınti/ n. soberanía f.

Soviet Russia Rusia Soviética f.

sow /sau/ n. 1. puerca f. —v. 2. sembrar.

space /speis/ n. 1. espacio m. —v. 2. espaciar.

space out v. escalonar.

spaceship /'speis,ʃıp/ n. nave espacial, astronave f.

space shuttle /'ʃʌtl/ transbordador espacial m.

spacious /'speiʃəs/ a. espacioso.

spade /speid/ n. 1. laya; (cards) espada f. —v. 2. layar.

spaghetti /spə'gɛti/ n. espaguetis m.pl.

Spain /spein/ n. España f.

span /spæn/ n. 1. tramo m. —v. 2. extenderse sobre.

Spaniard /'spænyərd/ n. español -ola.

Spanish /'spænıʃ/ a. & n. español -ola.

spank /spæŋk/ v. pegar.

spanking /'spæŋkıŋ/ n. tunda, zumba f.

spar /spɑr/ v. altercar.

spare /spɛər/ a. 1. de repuesto. —v. 2. perdonar; ahorrar; prestar. **have... to s.,** tener... de sobra.

spare tire neumático de recambio m.

spark /spɑrk/ n. chispa f.

sparkle /'spɑrkəl/ n. 1. destello m. —v. 2. chispear. **sparkling wine,** vino espumoso.

spark plug /'spɑrk,plʌg/ n. bujía f.

sparrow /'spærou/ n. gorrión m.

sparse /spɑrs/ a. esparcido.

spasm /'spæzəm/ n. espasmo m.

spasmodic /spæz'mɒdık/ a. espasmódico.

spatter /'spætər/ v. salpicar; manchar.

speak /spik/ v. hablar.

speaker /'spikər/ n. conferencista m. & f.

spear /spıər/ n. lanza f.

spearmint /'spıər,mınt/ n. menta romana f.

special /'spɛʃəl/ a. especial. **s. delivery,** entrega inmediata, entrega urgente.

specialist /'spɛʃəlıst/ n. especialista m. & f.

specialty /'spɛʃəlti/ n. especialidad f.

species /'spiʃiz, -siz/ n. especie f.

specific /spı'sıfık/ a. específico.

specify /'spɛsə,fai/ v. especificar.

specimen /'spɛsəmən/ n. espécimen m.; muestra f.

spectacle /'spɛktəkəl/ n. espectáculo m.; (pl.) lentes, anteojos m.pl.

spectacular /spɛk'tækyələr/ a. espectacular, aparatoso.

spectator /'spɛkteitər/ n. espectador -ra.

spectrum /'spɛktrəm/ n. espectro m.

speculate /'spɛkyə,leit/ v. especular.

speculation /,spɛkyə'leiʃən/ n. especulación f.

speech /spitʃ/ n. habla f.; lenguaje; discurso m. **part of s.,** parte de la oración.

speechless /'spitʃlıs/ a. mudo.

speed /spid/ n. 1. velocidad; rapidez f. —v. 2. **s. up,** acelerar, apresurar.

speed limit velocidad máxima f.

speedometer /spı'dɒmıtər/ n. velocímetro m.

speedy /'spidi/ a. veloz, rápido.

spell /spɛl/ n. 1. hechizo; rato; Med. ataque m. —v. 2. escribir; relevar.

spelling /'spɛlıŋ/ n. ortografía f.

spend /spɛnd/ v. gastar; (time) pasar.

spendthrift /'spɛnd,θrıft/ a. & n. pródigo; manirroto m.

sphere /sfıər/ n. esfera f.

spice /spais/ n. 1. especia f. —v. 2. especiar.

spider /'spaidər/ n. araña f.

spider web telaraña f.

spike /spaik/ n. alcayata f.; punta f., clavo m.

spill /spıl/ v. derramar. n. caída f., vuelco m.

spillway /'spıl,wei/ n. vertedero m.

spin /spın/ v. hilar; girar.

spinach /'spınıtʃ/ n. espinaca f.

spine /spain/ n. espina dorsal f.

spinet /'spınıt/ n. espineta m.

spinster /'spınstər/ n. solterona f.

spiral /'spairəl/ a. & n. espiral f.

spire /spaiər/ n. caracol m., espiral f.

spirit /'spırıt/ n. espíritu; ánimo m.

spiritual /'spırıtʃuəl/ a. espiritual.

spiritualism /'spırıtʃuə,lızəm/ n. espiritismo m.

spirituality /,spırıtʃu'ælıti/ n. espiritualidad f.

spit /spıt/ v. escupir.

spite /spait/ n. despecho m. **in s. of,** a pesar de.

splash /splæʃ/ n. 1. salpicadura f. —v. 2. salpicar.

splendid /'splɛndıd/ a. espléndido.

splendor /'splɛndər/ n. esplendor m.

splice /splais/ v. 1. empalmar. —n. 2. empalme m.

splint /splınt/ n. tablilla f.

splinter /'splıntər/ n. 1. astilla f. —v. 2. astillar.

split /split/ n. **1.** división f. —v. **2.** dividir, romper en dos.

splurge /splɜrdʒ/ v. **1.** fachendear. —n. **2.** fachenda f.

spoil /spɔil/ n. **1.** (pl.) botín m. —v. **2.** echar a perder; (a child) mimar.

spoke /spouk/ n. rayo (de rueda) m.

spokesman /'spouksmən/ n. portavoz m. & f.

spokesperson /'spouks,pɜrsən/ n. portavoz m. & f.

sponge /spʌndʒ/ n. esponja f.

sponsor /'spɒnsər/ n. **1.** patrocinador m. —v. **2.** patrocinar; costear.

spontaneity /,spɒntə'niiti, -'nei-/ n. espontaneidad f.

spontaneous /spɒn'teiniəs/ a. espontáneo.

spool /spul/ n. carrete m.

spoon /spun/ n. cuchara f.

spoonful /'spunful/ n. cucharada f.

sporadic /spə'rædɪk/ a. esporádico.

sport /spɔrt/ n. deporte m.

sport jacket chaqueta deportiva f.

sports center /spɔrts/ pabellón de deportes, polideportivo m.

sportsman /'spɔrtsmən/ a. **1.** deportivo. —n. **2.** deportista m. & f.

spot /spɒt/ n. **1.** mancha f.; lugar, punto m. —v. **2.** distinguir.

spouse /spaus/ n. esposo -sa.

spout /spaut/ n. **1.** chorro m.; (of teapot) pico m. —v. **2.** correr a chorro.

sprain /sprein/ n. **1.** torcedura f., esguince m. —v. **2.** torcerse.

sprawl /sprɔl/ v. tenderse.

spray /sprei/ n. **1.** rociada f. —v. **2.** rociar.

spread /spred/ n. **1.** propagación; extensión; (for bed) colcha f. —v. **2.** propagar; extender.

spreadsheet /'spred,ʃit/ n. hoja de cálculo f.

spree /spri/ n. parranda f.

sprig /sprɪg/ n. ramita f.

sprightly /'spraitli/ a. garboso.

spring /sprɪŋ/ n. resorte, muelle m.; (season) primavera f.; (of water) manantial m.

springboard /'sprɪŋ,bɔrd/ n. trampolín f.

spring onion cebolleta f.

sprinkle /'sprɪŋkəl/ v. rociar; (rain) lloviznar.

sprint /sprɪnt/ n. carrera f.

sprout /spraut/ n. retoño m.

spry /sprai/ a. ágil.

spun /spʌn/ a. hilado.

spur /spɜr/ n. **1.** espuela f. **on the s. of the moment,** sin pensarlo. —v. **2.** espolear.

spurious /'spyuriəs/ a. espurio.

spurn /spɜrn/ v. rechazar, despreciar.

spurt /spɜrt/ n. **1.** chorro m.; esfuerzo supremo. —v. **2.** salir en chorro.

spy /spai/ **1.** espía m. & f. —v. **2.** espiar.

squabble /'skwɒblɪŋ/ n. **1.** riña f. —v. **2.** reñir.

squad /skwɒd/ n. escuadra f.

squadron /'skwɒdrən/ n. escuadrón m.

squalid /'skwɒlɪd/ a. escuálido.

squall /skwɔl/ n. borrasca f.

squalor /'skwɒlər/ n. escualidez f.

squander /'skwɒndər/ v. malgastar.

square /skwɛər/ a. **1.** cuadrado. —n. **2.** cuadrado m.; plaza f.

square dance n. contradanza f.

squat /skwɒt/ v. agacharse.

squeak /skwik/ n. **1.** chirrido m. —v. **2.** chirriar.

squeamish /'skwimɪʃ/ a. escrupuloso.

squeeze /skwiz/ n. **1.** apretón m. —v. **2.** apretar; (fruit) exprimir.

squirrel /'skwɜrəl// n. ardilla f.

squirt /skwɜrt/ n. **1.** chisguete m. —v. **2.** jeringar.

stab /stæb/ n. **1.** puñalada f. —v. **2.** apuñalar.

stability /stə'bɪliti/ n. estabilidad f.

stabilize /'steibə,laiz/ v. estabilizar.

stable /'steibəl/ a. **1.** estable, equilibrado. —n. **2.** caballeriza f.

stack /stæk/ n. **1.** pila f. —v. **2.** apilar.

stadium /'steidiəm/ n. estadio m.

staff /stæf/ n. personal m. **editorial s.,** cuerpo de redacción. **general s.,** estado mayor.

stag /stæg/ n. ciervo m.

stage /steidʒ/ n. **1.** etapa; Theat. escena f. —v. **2.** representar.

stagflation /stæg'fleiʃən/ n. estagflación.

stagger /'stægər/ v. (teeter) tambalear; (space out) escalonar.

stagnant /'stægnənt/ a. estancado.

stagnate /'stægneit/ v. estancarse.

stain /stein/ n. **1.** mancha f. —v. **2.** manchar.

stainless steel /'steinlɪs/ acero inoxidable m.

staircase /'stɛər,keis/ **stairs** n. escalera f.

stake /steik/ n. estaca; (bet) apuesta f. **at s.,** en juego; en peligro.

stale /steil/ a. rancio.

stalemate /'steil,meit/ n. estancación f.; tablas f.pl.

stalk /stɔk/ n. caña f.; (of flower) tallo m. v. acechar.

stall /stɔl/ n. **1.** tenderete; (for horse) pesebre m. —v. **2.** demorar; (motor) atascar.

stallion /'stælyən/ n. S.A. garañón m.

stalwart /'stɔlwərt/ a. fornido.

stamina /'stæmənə/ n. vigor m.

stammer /'stæmər/ v. tartamudear.

stamp /stæmp/ n. **1.** sello m., estampilla f. —v. **2.** sellar.

stamp collecting /kə'lɛktɪŋ/ filatelia f.

stampede /stæm'pid/ n. estampida f.

stand /stænd/ n. **1.** puesto m.; posición; (speaker's) tribuna; (furniture) mesita f. —v. **2.** estar; estar de pie; aguantar. **s. up**, pararse, levantarse.

standard /'stændərd/ a. **1.** normal, corriente. —n. **2.** norma f. **s. of living**, nivel de vida.

standardize /'stændər,daɪz/ v. uniformar.

standing /'stændɪŋ/ a. fijo; establecido.

standpoint /'stænd,pɔɪnt/ n. punto de vista m.

staple /'steɪpəl/ n. materia prima f.; grapa f.

stapler /'steɪplər/ n. grapadora f.

star /stɑr/ n. estrella f.

starboard /'stɑrbərd/ n. estribor m.

starch /stɑrtʃ/ n. **1.** almidón m.; (in diet) fécula f. —v. **2.** almidonar.

stare /stɛər/ v. mirar fijamente.

stark /stɑrk/ a. **1.** severo. —adv. **2.** completamente.

start /stɑrt/ n. **1.** susto; principio m. —v. **2.** comenzar, empezar; salir; poner en marcha; causar.

startle /'stɑrtl/ v. asustar.

starvation /stɑr'veɪʃən/ n. hambre f.

starve /stɑrv/ v. morir de hambre.

state /steɪt/ n. **1.** estado m. —v. **2.** declarar, decir.

statement /'steɪtmənt/ n. declaración f.

stateroom /'steɪt,rum/ n. camarote m.

statesman /'steɪtsmən/ n. estadista m.

static /'stætɪk/ a. **1.** estático. —n. **2.** estática f.

station /'steɪʃən/ n. estación f.

stationary /'steɪʃə,nɛri/ a. estacionario, fijo.

stationery /'steɪʃə,nɛri/ n. papel de escribir.

statistics /stə'tɪstɪks/ n. estadística f.

statue /'stætʃu/ n. estatua f.

stature /'stætʃər/ n. estatura f.

status /'steɪtəs, 'stætəs/ n. condición, estado m.

statute /'stætʃut/ n. ley f.

staunch /stɔntʃ/ a. fiel; constante.

stay /steɪ/ n. **1.** estancia; visita f. —v. **2.** quedar, permanecer; parar, alojarse. **s. away**, ausentarse. **s. up**, velar.

steadfast /'stɛd,fæst/ a. inmutable.

steady /'stɛdi/ a. **1.** firme; permanente; regular. —v. **2.** sostener.

steak /steɪk/ n. biftec, bistec m.

steal /stil/ v. robar. **s. away**, escabullirse.

stealth /stɛlθ/ n. cautela f.

steam /stim/ n. vapor m.

steamboat /'stim,bout/ **steamer, steamship** n. vapor m.

steel /stil/ n. **1.** acero m. —v. **2. s. oneself**, fortalecerse.

steep /stip/ a. escarpado, empinado.

steeple /'stipəl/ n. campanario m.

steer /stɪər/ n. **1.** buey m. —v. **2.** guiar, manejar.

stellar /'stɛlər/ a. astral.

stem /stɛm/ n. **1.** tallo m. —v. **2.** parar. **s. from**, emanar de.

stencil /'stɛnsəl/ n. **1.** estarcido. —v. **2.** estarcir.

stenographer /stə'nɒgrəfər/ n. estenógrafo m.

stenography /stə'nɒgrəfi/ n. taquigrafía f.

step /stɛp/ n. **1.** paso m.; medida f.; (stairs) escalón m. —v. **2.** pisar. **s. back**, retirarse.

stepladder /'stɛp,lædər/ n. escalera de mano f.

stereophonic /,stɛriə'fɒnɪk/ a. estereofónico.

stereotype /'stɛriə,taɪp/ n. **1.** estereotipo m. —v. **2.** estereotipar.

sterile /'stɛrɪl/ a. estéril.

sterilize /'stɛrə,laɪz/ v. esterilizar.

sterling /'stɜrlɪŋ/ a. esterlina, genuino.

stern /stɜrn/ n. **1.** popa f. —a. **2.** duro, severo.

stethoscope /'stɛθə,skoup/ n. estetoscopio m.

stevedore /'stivɪ,dɔr/ n. estibador m.

stew /stu/ n. **1.** guisado m. —v. **2.** estofar.

steward /'stuərd/ n. camarero m.

stewardess /'stuərdɪs/ n. azafata f., aeromoza f.

stick /stɪk/ n. **1.** palo, bastón m. —v. **2.** pegar; (put) poner, meter.

sticky /'stɪki/ a. pegajoso.

stiff /stɪf/ a. tieso; duro.

stiffness /'stɪfnɪs/ n. tiesura f.

stifle /'staɪfəl/ v. sofocar; Fig. suprimir.

stigma /'stɪgmə/ n. estigma m.

still /stɪl/ a. **1.** quieto; silencioso. **to keep s.**, quedarse quieto. —adv. **2.** todavía, aún; no obstante. —n. **3.** alambique m.

stillborn /'stɪl,bɔrn/ n. & a. nacido -da muerto -ta.

still life n. naturaleza muerta f.

stillness /'stɪlnɪs/ n. silencio m.

stilted /'stɪltɪd/ a. afectado, artificial.

stimulant /'stɪmyələnt/ a. & n. estimulante m.

stimulate /'stɪmyə,leɪt/ v. estimular.

stimulus /'stɪmyələs/ n. estímulo m.

sting /stɪŋ/ n. **1.** picadura f. —v. **2.** picar.

stingy /'stɪndʒi/ a. tacaño.

stipulate /'stɪpyə,leɪt/ v. estipular.

stir /stɜr/ n. **1.** conmoción f. —v. **2.** mover. **s. up**, conmover; suscitar.

stitch /stɪtʃ/ n. **1.** puntada f. —v. **2.** coser.

stock /stɒk/ n. surtido f.; raza f.; (finance)

acciones. *f.pl.* **in s.,** en existencia. **to take s.´in,** tener fe en.

stock exchange bolsa *f.*

stockholder /'stɒk,houldər/ *n.* accionista *m. & f.*

stocking /'stɒkɪŋ/ *n.* media *f.*

stockyard /'stɒk,yɑrd/ *n.* corral de ganado *m.*

stodgy /'stɒdʒi/ *a.* pesado.

stoical /'stouikəl/ *a.* estoico.

stole /stoul/ *n.* estola *f.*

stolid /'stɒlɪd/ *a.* impasible.

stomach /'stʌmək/ *n.* estómago *m.*

stomachache /'stʌmək,eik/ *n.* dolor de estómago *m.*

stone /stoun/ *n.* piedra *f.*

stool /stul/ *n.* banquillo *m.*

stoop /stup/ *v.* encorvar; *Fig.* rebajarse. espaldas encorvadas *f.pl.*

stop /stɒp/ *n* **1.** parada *f.* **to put a s. to,** poner fin a. —*v.* **2.** parar; suspender; detener; impedir. **s. doing** (etc.), dejar de hacer (etc.).

stopgap /'stɒp,gæp/ *n.* recurso provisional *m.*

stopover /'stɒp,ouvər/ *n.* parada *f.*

stopwatch /'stɒp,wɒtʃ/ *n.* cronómetro *m.*

storage /'stɔrɪdʒ/ *n.* almacenaje *m.*

store /stɔr/ *n.* **1.** tienda; provisión *f.* **department s.,** almacén *m.* —*v.* **2.** guardar; almacenar.

store window escaparate *m.*

stork /stɔrk/ *n.* cigüeña *f.*

storm /stɔrm/ *n.* tempestad, tormenta *f.*

stormy /'stɔrmi/ *a.* tempestuoso.

story /'stɔri/ *n.* cuento; relato *m.; historia f.* **short s.,** cuento.

stout /staut/ *a.* corpulento.

stove /stouv/ *n.* hornilla; estufa *f.*

straight /streit/ *a.* **1.** recto; derecho. —*adv.* **2.** directamente.

straighten /'streitn/ *v.* enderezar. **s. out,** poner en orden.

straightforward /,streit'fɔrwərd/ *a.* recto, sincero.

strain /strein/ *n.* **1.** tensión *f.* —*v.* **2.** colar.

strainer /'streinər/ *n.* colador *m.*

strait /streit/ *n.* estrecho *m.*

strand /strænd/ *n.* **1.** hilo *m.* —*v.* **2.** **be stranded,** encallarse.

strange /streindʒ/ *a.* extraño; raro.

stranger /'streindʒər/ *n.* extranjero -ra; forastero -ra; desconocido -da.

strangle /'stræŋgəl/ *v.* estrangular.

strap /stræp/ *n.* correa *f.*

stratagem /'strætədʒəm/ *n.* estratagema *f.*

strategic /strə'tidʒɪk/ *a.* estratégico.

strategy /'strætɪdʒi/ *n.* estrategia *f.*

stratosphere /'strætə,sfɪər/ *n.* estratosfera *f.*

straw /strɔ/ *n.* paja *f.*

strawberry /'strɔ,beri/ *n.* fresa *f.*

stray /strei/ *a.* **1.** vagabundo. —*v.* **2.** extraviarse.

streak /strik/ *n.* **1.** racha; raya *f.;* lado *m.* —*v.* **2.** rayar.

stream /strim/ *n.* corriente *f.;* arroyo *m.*

street /strit/ *n.* calle *f.*

streetcar /'strit,kɑr/ *n.* tranvía *m.*

street lamp /'strit,læmp/ *n.* farol *m.*

strength /strɛŋkθ/ *n.* fuerza *m.*

strengthen /'strɛŋkθən. 'strɛn–/ *v.* reforzar.

strenuous /'strɛnyuəs/ *a.* estrenuo.

streptococcus /,strɛptə'kɒkəs/ *n.* estreptococo *m.*

stress /strɛs/ *n.* **1.** tensión *f.;* énfasis *m.* —*v.* **2.** recalcar; acentuar.

stretch /strɛtʃ/ *n.* **1.** trecho *m.* **at one s.,** de un tirón. —*v.* **2.** tender; extender; estirarse.

stretcher /'strɛtʃər/ *n.* camilla *f.*

strew /stru/ *v.* esparcir.

stricken /'strɪkən/ *a.* agobiado.

strict /strɪkt/ *a.* estricto; severo.

stride /straid/ *n.* **1.** tranco *m.;* (fig., pl.) progresos. —*v.* **2.** andar a trancos.

strife /straif/ *n.* contienda *f.*

strike /straik/ *n.* **1.** huelga *f.* —*v.* **2.** pegar; chocar con; (clock) dar.

striker /'straikər/ *n.* huelguista *m. & f.*

string /strɪŋ/ *n.* cuerda *f.;* cordel *m.*

string bean *n.* habichuela *f.*

stringent /'strɪndʒənt/ *a.* estricto.

strip /strɪp/ *n.* **1.** tira *f.* —*v.* **2.** despojar; desnudarse.

stripe /straip/ *n.* raya *f.; Mil.* galón *m.*

strive /straiv/ *v.* esforzarse.

stroke /strouk/ *n.* golpe *m.;* (swimming) brazada *f.; Med.* ataque *m.* **s. of luck,** suerte *f.*

stroll /stroul/ *n.* **1.** paseo *m.* —*v.* **2.** pasearse.

stroller /'stroulər/ *n.* vagabundo *m.;* cochecito (de niño).

strong /strɔŋ/ *a.* fuerte.

stronghold /'strɔŋ,hould/ *n.* fortificación *f.*

structure /'strʌktʃər/ *n.* estructura *f.*

struggle /'strʌgəl/ *n.* **1.** lucha *f.* —*v.* **2.** luchar.

strut /strʌt/ *n.* **1.** pavonada *f.* —*v.* **2.** pavonear.

stub /stʌb/ *n.* **1.** cabo; (ticket) talón *m.* —*v.* **2. s. on one's toes,** tropezar con.

stubborn /'stʌbərn/ *a.* testarudo.

stucco /'stʌkou/ *n.* **1.** estuco *m.* —*v.* **2.** estucar.

student /'studnt/ *n.* alumno -na, estudiante -ta.

studio /'studi,ou/ *n.* estudio *m.*

studious /'studiəs/ *a.* aplicado; estudioso.

study /'stʌdi/ n. **1.** estudio m. —v. **2.** estudiar.

stuff /stʌf/ n. **1.** cosas f.pl. —v. **2.** llenar; rellenar.

stuffing /'stʌfɪŋ/ n. relleno m.

stumble /'stʌmbəl/ v. tropezar.

stump /stʌmp/ n. cabo; tocón; muñón m.

stun /stʌn/ v. aturdir.

stunt /stʌnt/ n. **1.** maniobra sensacional f. —v. **2.** impedir crecimiento.

stupendous /stu'pendəs/ a. estupendo.

stupid /'stupid/ a. estúpido.

stupidity /stu'pɪdɪti/ n. estupidez f.

stupor /'stupər/ n. estupor m.

sturdy /'stɜrdi/ a. robusto.

stutter /'stʌtər/ v. **1.** tartamudear. —n. **2.** tartamudeo m.

sty /stai/ n. pocilga f.; Med. orzuelo.

style /stail/ n. estilo m.; moda f.

stylish /'stailɪʃ/ a. elegante; a la moda.

suave /swɑv/ a. afable, suave.

subconscious /sʌb'kɒnʃəs/ a. subconsciente.

subdue /səb'du/ v. dominar.

subject /n. 'sʌbdʒɪkt; v. səb'dʒɛkt/ n. **1.** tema m.; (of study) materia f.; Pol. súbdito -ta; Gram. sujeto m. —v. **2.** someter.

subjugate /'sʌbdʒə,geit/ v. sojuzgar, subyugar.

subjunctive /səb'dʒʌŋktɪv/ a. & n. subjuntivo m.

sublimate /'sʌblə,meit/ v. sublimar.

sublime /sə'blaim/ a. sublime.

submarine /,sʌbmə'rin/ a. & n. submarino m.

submerge /səb'mɜrdʒ/ v. sumergir.

submission /səb'mɪʃən/ n. sumisión f.

submit /səb'mɪt/ v. someter.

subnormal /sʌb'nɔrməl/ a. subnormal.

subordinate /a, n sə'bɔrdnɪt; v -dn,eit/ a. & n. **1.** subordinado -da. —v. **2.** subordinar.

subscribe /səb'skraib/ v. aprobar; abonarse.

subscriber /səb'skraibər/ n. abonado -da m. & f.

subscription /səb'skrɪpʃən/ n. abono m.

subsequent /'sʌbsɪkwənt/ a. subsiguiente.

subservient /səb'sɜrviənt/ a. servicial.

subside /səb'said/ v. apaciguarse, menguar.

subsidy /'sʌbsɪdi/ n. subvención f.

subsoil /'sʌb,sɔil/ n. subsuelo m.

substance /'sʌbstəns/ n. substancia f.

substantial /səb'stænʃəl/ a. substancial; considerable.

substitute /'sʌbstɪ,tut/ a. **1.** substitutivo. —n. **2.** substituto -ta. —v. **3.** substituir.

substitution /,sʌbstɪ'tuʃən/ n. substitución f.

subterfuge /'sʌbtər,fyudʒ/ n. subterfugio m.

subtitle /'sʌb,taitl/ n. subtítulo m.

subtle /'sʌtl/ a. sutil.

subtract /səb'trækt/ v. substraer.

suburb /'sʌbɜrb/ n. suburbio m.; (pl.) afueras f.pl.

subversive /səb'vɜrsiv/ a. subversivo.

subway /'sʌb,wei/ n. metro m.

succeed /sək'sid/ v. lograr, tener éxito; (in office) suceder a.

success /sək'sɛs/ n. éxito m.

successful /sək'sɛsfəl/ a. próspero; afortunado.

succession /sək'sɛʃən/ n. sucesión f.

successive /sək'sɛsɪv/ a. sucesivo.

successor /sək'sɛsər/ n. sucesor, -ra; heredero, -ra.

succor /'sʌkər/ n. **1.** socorro m. —v. **2.** socorrer.

succumb /sə'kʌm/ v. sucumbir.

such /sʌtʃ/ a. tal.

suck /sʌk/ v. chupar.

suction /'sʌkʃən/ n. succión f.

sudden /'sʌdn/ a. repentino, súbito. **all of a s.,** de repente.

suds /sʌdz/ n. jabonaduras f.pl

sue /su/ v. demandar.

suffer /'sʌfər/ v. sufrir; padecer.

suffice /sə'fais/ v. bastar.

sufficient /sə'fɪʃənt/ a. suficiente.

suffocate /'sʌfə,keit/ v. sofocar.

sugar /'ʃʊgər/ n. azúcar m.

sugar bowl azucarero m.

suggest /səg'dʒɛst/ v. sugerir.

suggestion /səg'dʒɛstʃən/ n. sugerencia f.

suicide /'suə,said/ n. suicidio m.; (person) suicida m. & f. **to commit s.,** suicidarse.

suit /sut/ n. **1.** traje; (cards) palo; (law) pleito m. —v. **2.** convenir a.

suitable /'sutəbəl/ a. apropiado; que conviene.

suitcase /'sut,keis/ n. maleta f.

suite /swit/ n. serie f., séquito m.

suitor /'sutər/ n. pretendiente m.

sullen /'sʌlən/ a. hosco.

sum /sʌm/ n. **1.** suma f. —v. **2. s. up,** resumir.

summarize /'sʌmə,raiz/ v. resumir.

summary /'sʌməri/ n. resumen m.

summer /'sʌmər/ n. verano m.

summon /'sʌmən/ v. llamar; (law) citar.

summons /'sʌmənz/ n. citación f.

sumptuous /'sʌmptʃuəs/ a. suntuoso.

sun /sʌn/ n. **1.** sol m. —v. **2.** tomar el sol.

sunbathe /'sʌn,beið/ v. tomar el sol.

sunburn /'sʌn,bɜrn/ n. quemadura de sol.

sunburned /'sʌn,bɜrnd/ a. quemado por el sol.

Sunday /'sʌndei/ n. domingo m.

sunken /'sʌŋkən/ a. hundido.

sunny /'sʌni/ a. asoleado. **s. day**, día de sol. **to be s.**, (weather) hacer sol.

sunshine /'sʌn,fain/ n. luz del sol.

suntan /'sʌn,tæn/ n. bronceado m. **s. lotion**, loción bronceadora f., bronceador m.

superb /su'pɜrb/ a. soberbio.

superficial /,supər'fiʃəl/ a. superficial.

superfluous /su'pɜrfluəs/ a. superfluo.

superhuman /,supər'hyumən/ a. sobrehumano.

superintendent /,supərin'tɛndənt/ n. superintendente m. & f.; (of building) conserje m.; (of school) director -ra general.

superior /sə'piəriər/ a. & n. superior m.

superiority /sə,piəri'ɔriti/ n. superioridad f.

superlative /sə'pɜrlətiv/ a. superlativo.

supernatural /,supər'nætʃərəl/ a. sobrenatural.

supersede /,supər'sid/ v. reemplazar.

superstar /'supər,star/ n. superestrella m. & f.

superstition /,supər'stiʃən/ n. superstición f.

superstitious /,supər'stiʃəs/ a. supersticioso.

supervise /'supər,vaiz/ v. supervisar.

supper /'sʌpər/ n. cena f.

supplement /'sʌpləmənt/ n. **1.** suplemento m. —v. **2.** suplementar.

supply /sə'plai/ n. **1.** provisión f; Com. surtido m.; Econ. existencia f. —v. **2.** suplir; proporcionar.

support /sə'pɔrt/ n. **1.** sustento; apoyo m. —v. **2.** mantener; apoyar.

suppose /sə'pouz/ v. suponer. **be supposed to,** deber.

suppository /sə'pɒzi,tɔri/ n. supositorio m.

suppress /sə'prɛs/ v. suprimir.

suppression /sə'prɛʃən/ n. supresión f.

supreme /sə'prim/ a. supremo.

sure /ʃur, ʃɜr/ a. seguro, cierto. **for s.,** con seguridad. **to make s.,** asegurarse.

surety /'ʃurti, 'ʃɜr-/ n. garantía f

surf /sɜrf/ n. **1.** oleaje m. —v. **2.** (Internet) navegar; (sport) surfear.

surface /'sɜrfis/ n. superficie f.

surfboard /'sɜrf,bɔrd/ n. tabla de surf f.

surfer /'sɜrfər/ n. (Internet) usuario -ria, navegante m. & f.; (sport) surfero -ra.

surge /sɜrdʒ/ v. surgir.

surgeon /'sɜrdʒən/ n. cirujano -na.

surgery /'sɜrdʒəri/ n. cirugía f.

surmise /sər'maiz/ v. suponer.

surmount /sər'maunt/ v. vencer.

surname /'sɜr,neim/ n. apellido m.

surpass /sər'pæs/ v. superar.

surplus /'sɜrpləs/ a. & n. sobrante m.

surprise /sər'praiz, sə-/ n. **1.** sorpresa —v. **2.** sorprender. **I am surprised...,** me extraña...

surrender /sə'rɛndər/ n. **1.** rendición f. —v. **2.** rendir.

surround /sə'raund/ v. rodear, circundar.

surveillance /sər'veiləns/ n. vigilancia f.

survey /n. 'sɜrvei; v. sər'vei/ n. **1.** examen; estudio m. —v. **2.** examinar; (land) medir.

survival /sər'vaivəl/ n. supervivencia f.

survive /sər'vaiv/ v. sobrevivir.

susceptible /sə'sɛptəbəl/ a. susceptible.

suspect /v. sə'spɛkt; n. 'sʌspɛkt/ v. **1.** sospechar. —n. **2.** sospechoso -sa.

suspend /sə'spɛnd/ v. suspender.

suspense /sə'spɛns/ n. incertidumbre f. **in s.,** en suspenso.

suspension /sə'spɛnʃən/ n. suspensión f.

suspension bridge n. puente colgante m.

suspicion /sə'spiʃən/ n. sospecha f.

suspicious /sə'spiʃəs/ a. sospechoso.

sustain /sə'stein/ v. sustentar; mantener.

swallow /'swɒlou/ n. **1.** trago m.; (bird) golondrina f. —v. **2.** tragar.

swamp /swɒmp/ n. **1.** pantano m. —v. **2.** Fig. abrumar.

swan /swɒn/ n. cisne m.

swap /swɒp/ n. **1.** trueque m. —v. **2.** cambalachear.

swarm /swɔrm/ n. enjambre m.

swarthy /'swɔrði/ a. moreno.

sway /swei/ v. **1.** predominio m. —v. **2.** bambolearse; Fig. influir en.

swear /swɛər/ v. jurar. **s. off,** renunciar a.

sweat /swɛt/ n. **1.** sudor m. —v. **2.** sudar.

sweater /'swɛtər/ n. suéter m.

sweatshirt /'swɛt,ʃɜrt/ n. sudadera f.

Swede /swid/ n. sueco -ca.

Sweden /'swidn/ n. Suecia f.

Swedish /'swidiʃ/ a. sueco.

sweep /swip/ v. barrer.

sweet /swit/ a. **1.** dulce; amable, simpático. —n. **2.** (pl.) dulces m.pl.

sweetheart /'swit,hɑrt/ n. novio -via.

sweetness /'switnis/ n. dulzura f.

sweet-toothed /'swit ,tuθt/ a. goloso.

swell /swɛl/ a. **1.** Colloq. estupendo, excelente. —n. **2.** (of the sea) oleada f. —v. **3.** hincharse; aumentar.

swelter /'swɛltər/ v. sofocarse de calor.

swift /swift/ a. rápido, veloz.

swim /swim/ n. **1.** nadada f. —v. **2.** nadar.

swimming /'swimiŋ/ n. natación f.

swimming pool n. alberca, piscina f.

swindle /'swindl/ n. **1.** estafa f. —v. **2.** estafar.

swine /swain/ n. puercos m.pl.

swing /swiŋ/ n. **1.** columpio m. **in full s.,** en plena actividad. —v. **2.** mecer; balancear.

swirl /swɜrl/ n. **1.** remolino m. —v. **2.** arremolinar.

Swiss /swis/ a. & n. suizo -za.

switch /swɪtʃ/ n. **1.** varilla f.; *Elec.* llave f., conmutador m.; (railway) cambiavía m. —v. **2.** cambiar; trocar.

switchboard /'swɪtʃˌbɔrd/ n. cuadro conmutador m., centralita f.

Switzerland /'swɪtsərlənd/ n. Suiza f.

sword /sɔrd/ n. espada f.

syllable /'sɪləbəl/ n. sílaba f.

symbol /'sɪmbəl/ n. símbolo m.

sympathetic /ˌsɪmpə'θɛtɪk/ a. compasivo. **to be s.,** tener simpatía.

sympathy /'sɪmpəθi/ n. lástima; condolencia f.

symphony /'sɪmfəni/ n. sinfonía f.

symptom /'sɪmptəm/ n. síntoma m.

synagogue /'sɪnəˌgɒg/ n. sinagoga f.

synchronize /'sɪŋkrəˌnaɪz/ v. sincronizar.

syndicate /'sɪndɪkɪt/ n. sindicato m.

syndrome /'sɪndroum. -drəm/ n. síndrome m.

synonym /'sɪnənɪm/ n. sinónimo m.

synthetic /sɪn'θɛtɪk/ a. sintético.

syringe /sə'rɪndʒ/ n. jeringa f.

syrup /'sɪrəp. 'sɜr-/ n. almíbar; *Med.* jarabe m.

system /'sɪstəm/ n. sistema m.

systematic /ˌsɪstə'mætɪk/ a. sistemático.

T

---

tabernacle /'tæbərˌnækəl/ n. tabernáculo m.

table /'teibəl/ n. mesa; (list) tabla f.

tablecloth /'teibəlˌklɔθ/ n. mantel m.

table of contents /'kɒntɛnts/ índice de materias m.

tablespoon /'teibəlˌspun/ n. cuchara f.

tablespoonful /'teibəlspunˌfʊl/ n. cucharada f.

tablet /'tæblɪt/ n. tableta; *Med.* pastilla f.

tack /tæk/ n. tachuela f.

tact /tækt/ n. tacto m.

tag /tæg/ n. etiqueta f., rótulo m.

tail /teil/ n. cola f., rabo m.

tailor /'teilər/ n. sastre m.

take /teik/ v. tomar; llevar. **t. a bath,** bañarse. **t. a shower,** ducharse. **t. away,** quitar. **t. off,** quitarse. **t. out,** sacar. **t. long,** tardar mucho.

tale /teil/ n. cuento m.

talent /'tælənt/ n. talento m.

talk /tɔk/ n. **1.** plática, habla f.; discurso m. —v. **2.** hablar.

talkative /'tɔkətɪv/ a. locuaz.

tall /tɔl/ a. alto.

tame /teim/ a. **1.** manso, domesticado. —v. **2.** domesticar.

tamper /'tæmpər/ v. **t. with,** entremeterse en.

tampon /'tæmpɒn/ n. tampón m.

tan /tæn/ a. **1.** color de arena. —v. **2.** curtir; tostar. n. bronceado m.

tangerine /ˌtændʒə'rin/ n. clementina f.

tangible /'tændʒəbəl/ a. tangible.

tangle /'tæŋgəl/ n. **1.** enredo m. —v. **2.** enredar.

tank /tæŋk/ n. tanque m.

tap /tæp/ n. **1.** golpe ligero. —v. **2.** golpear ligeramente; decentar.

tape /teip/ n. cinta f.

tape recorder /rɪ'kɔrdər/ magnetófono m., grabadora f.

tapestry /'tæpəstri/ n. tapiz m.; tapicería f.

tar /tur/ n. **1.** brea f. —v. **2.** embrear.

target /'turgɪt/ n. blanco m.

tarnish /'turnɪʃ/ n. **1.** deslustre m. —v. **2.** deslustrar.

tarpaulin /tur'pɔlɪn, 'turpəlɪn/ n. lona f.

task /tæsk/ n. tarea f.

taste /teist/ n. **1.** gusto; sabor m. —v. **2.** gustar; probar. **t. of,** saber a.

tasty /'teisti/ a. sabroso.

tattoo /tæ'tu/ v. tatuar.

taut /tɔt/ a. tieso.

tavern /'tævərn/ n. taberna f.

tax /tæks/ n. **1.** impuesto m. —v. **2.** imponer impuestos.

tax collector n. recaudador -ra m. & f.

taxi /'tæksi/ n. taxi, taxímetro m. **t. driver,** taxista m. & f.

taxpayer /'tæksˌpeiər/ n. contribuyente m. & f.

tax reform reforma tributaria f.

tax return declaración de la renta f.

tea /ti/ n. té m.

teach /titʃ/ v. enseñar.

teacher /'titʃər/ n. maestro -tra, profesor -ra.

team /tim/ n. equipo m.; pareja f.

tear /tɪər/ n. **1.** rasgón m.; lágrima f. —v. **2.** rasgar, lacerar. **t. apart,** separar.

tease /tiz/ v. atormentar; embromar.

teaspoon /'tiˌspun/ n. cucharita f.

technical /'tɛknɪkəl/ a. técnico.

technician /tɛk'nɪʃən/ n. técnico -ca m. & f.

technique /tɛk'nik/ n. técnica f.

technology /tɛk'nɒlədʒi/ n. tecnología f.

teddy bear /'tɛdi/ oso de felpa m.

tedious /'tidiəs/ a. tedioso.

telegram /'tɛlɪ,græm/ n. telegrama m.

telegraph /'tɛlɪ,græf/ n. **1.** telégrafo m. —v. **2.** telegrafiar.

telephone /'tɛlə,foun/ n. **1.** teléfono m. **t. book,** directorio telefónico. —v. **2.** telefonear; llamar por teléfono.

telescope /'tɛlə,skoup/ n. **1.** telescopio m. —v. **2.** enchufar.

television /'tɛlə,vɪʒən/ n. televisión f.

tell /tɛl/ v. decir; contar; distinguir.

temper /'tɛmpər/ n. **1.** temperamento, genio m. —v. **2.** templar.

temperament /'tɛmpərəmənt, -prəmənt/ n. temperamento.

temperamental /,tɛmpərə'mɛntl/, -prə'mɛn-/ a. sensitivo, emocional.

temperance /'tɛmpərəns/ n. moderación; sobriedad f.

temperate /'tɛmpərɪt/ a. templado.

temperature /'tɛmpərətʃər/ n. temperatura f.

tempest /'tɛmpɪst/ n. tempestad f.

tempestuous /tɛm'pɛstʃuəs/ a. tempestuoso.

temple /'tɛmpəl/ n. templo m.

temporary /'tɛmpə,rɛri/ a. temporal, temporario.

tempt /tɛmpt/ v. tentar.

temptation /tɛmp'teiʃən/ n. tentación f.

ten /tɛn/ a. & pron. diez.

tenant /'tɛnənt/ n. inquilino -na.

tend /tɛnd/ v. tender. **t. to,** atender.

tendency /'tɛndənsi/ n. tendencia f.

tender /'tɛndər/ a. **1.** tierno. —v. **2.** ofrecer.

tenderness /'tɛndərnɪs/ n. ternura f.

tennis /'tɛnɪs/ n. tenis m.

tennis court cancha de tenis, pista de tenis f.

tenor /'tɛnər/ n. tenor m.

tense /tɛns/ a. **1.** tenso. —n. **2.** Gram. tiempo m.

tent /tɛnt/ n. tienda, carpa f.

tenth /tɛnθ/ a. décimo.

term /tɜrm/ n. **1.** término; plazo m. —v. **2.** llamar.

terminal /'tɜrmənl/ n. terminal f.

terrace /'tɛrəs/ n. terraza f.

terrible /'tɛrəbəl/ a. terrible, espantoso; pésimo.

territory /'tɛrɪ,tɔri/ n. territorio m.

terror /'tɛrər/ n. terror, espanto, pavor m.

test /tɛst/ n. **1.** prueba f.; examen m. —v. **2.** probar; examinar.

testament /'tɛstəmənt/ n. testamento m.

testify /'tɛstə,fai/ v. atestiguar, testificar.

testimony /'tɛstə,mouni/ n. testimonio m.

test tube tubo de ensayo m.

text /tɛkst/ n. texto; tema m.

textbook /'tɛkst,buk/ n. libro de texto.

textile /'tɛkstail/ a. **1.** textil. —n. **2.** tejido m.

texture /'tɛkstʃər/ n. textura f.; tejido m.

than /ðæn, ðɛn; unstressed ðən, ən/ conj. que; de.

thank /θæŋk/ v. agradecer, dar gracias; **thanks, th. you,** gracias.

thankful /'θæŋkfəl/ a. agradecido; grato.

that /ðæt: unstressed ðət/ a. **1.** ese, aquel. —dem. pron. **2.** ése, aquél; eso, aquello. —rel. pron. & conj. **3.** que.

the /stressed ði; unstressed before a consonant ðə, unstressed before a vowel ði/ art. el, la, los, las; lo.

theater /'θiətər/ n. teatro m.

theft /θɛft/ n. robo m.

their /ðɛər; unstressed ðər/ a. su.

theirs /ðɛərz/ pron. suyo, de ellos.

them /ðɛm: unstressed ðəm, əm/ pron. ellos, ellas; los, las; les.

theme /θim/ n. tema; Mus. motivo m.

themselves /ðəm'sɛlvz, ,ðɛm-/ pron. sí, sí mismos -as. **they th.,** ellos mismos, ellas mismas. **with th.,** consigo.

then /ðɛn/ adv. entonces, después; pues.

thence /ðɛns/ adv. de allí.

theology /θi'ɒlədʒi/ n. teología f.

theory /'θiəri/ n. teoría f.

there /ðɛər; unstressed ðər/ adv. allí, allá, ahí. **there is, there are,** hay.

therefore /'ðɛər,fɔr/ adv. por lo tanto, por consiguiente.

thermometer /θər'mɒmɪtər/ n. termómetro m.

thermostat /'θɜrmə,stæt/ n. termostato m.

they /ðei/ pron. ellos, ellas.

thick /θɪk/ a. espeso, grueso, denso; torpe.

thicken /'θɪkən/ v. espesar, condensar.

thief /θif/ n. ladrón -na.

thigh /θai/ n. muslo m.

thimble /'θɪmbəl/ n. dedal m.

thin /θɪn/ a. **1.** delgado; raro; claro; escaso. —v. **2.** enrarecer; adelgazar.

thing /θɪŋ/ n. cosa f.

thingamabob /'θɪŋəmə,bɒb/ n. Colloq. chisme m.

think /θɪŋk/ v. pensar; creer.

thinker /'θɪŋkər/ n. pensador -ra.

third /θɜrd/ a. tercero.

Third World Tercer Mundo m.

thirst /θɜrst/ n. sed f.

thirsty /'θɜrsti/ a. sediento. **to be th.,** tener sed.

thirteen /'θɜr'tin/ a. & pron. trece.

thirty /'θɜrti/ a. & pron. treinta.

this /ðɪs/ a. **1.** este. —pron. **2.** éste; esto.

thoracic cage /θə'ræsɪk/ n. caja torácica f.

thorn /θɔrn/ n. espina f.

thorough /'θɜrou/ a. completo; cuidadoso.

though /ðou/ adv. **1.** sin embargo. —conj. **2.** aunque. **as th.,** como si.

thought /θɔt/ n. pensamiento m.

thoughtful /'θɔtfəl/ a. pensativo; considerado.

thousand /'θauzənd/ a. & pron. mil.

thread /θrɛd/ n. hilo m.; (of screw) rosca f.

threat /θrɛt/ n. amenaza f.

threaten /'θrɛtn/ v. amenazar.

three /θri/ a. & pron. tres.

thrift /θrɪft/ n. economía, frugalidad f.

thrill /θrɪl/ n. **1.** emoción f. —v. **2.** emocionar.

thrive /θraiv/ v. prosperar.

throat /θrout/ n. garganta f.

throne /θroun/ n. trono m.

through /θru/ prep **1.** por; a través de; por medio de. —a. **2.** continuo. **th. train,** tren directo. **to be th.,** haber terminado.

throughout /θru'aut/ prep. **1.** por todo, durante todo. —adv. **2.** en todas partes; completamente.

throw /θrou/ n. **1.** tiro m. —v. **2.** tirar, lanzar. **th. away,** arrojar. **th. out,** echar.

thrust /θrʌst/ n. **1.** lanzada f. —v. **2.** empujar.

thumb /θʌm/ n. dedo pulgar, pulgar m.

thumbtack /'θʌm,tæk/ n. chincheta f.

thunder /'θʌndər/ n. **1.** trueno m. —v. **2.** tronar.

Thursday /'θɜrzdei/ n. jueves m.

thus /ðʌs/ adv. así, de este modo.

thwart /θwɔrt/ v. frustrar.

ticket /'tɪkɪt/ n. billete, boleto m. **t. window,** taquilla f. **round trip t.,** billete de ida y vuelta.

tickle /'tɪkəl/ n. **1.** cosquilla f. —v. **2.** hacer cosquillas a.

ticklish /'tɪklɪʃ/ a. cosquilloso.

tide /taid/ n. marea f.

tidy /'taidi/ a. **1.** limpio, ordenado. —v. **2.** poner en orden.

tie /tai/ n. **1.** corbata f.; lazo; (game) empate m. —v. **2.** atar; anudar.

tier /'tɪər/ n. hilera f.

tiger /'taigər/ n. tigre m.

tight /tait/ a. apretado; tacaño.

tighten /'taitn/ v. estrechar, apretar.

tile /tail/ n. teja f.; azulejo m.

till /tɪl/ prep. **1.** hasta. —conj. **2.** hasta que. —n. **3.** cajón m. —v. **4.** cultivar, labrar.

tilt /tɪlt/ n. **1.** inclinación; justa f. —v. **2.** inclinar; justar.

timber /'tɪmbər/ n. madera f.; (beam) madero m.

time /taim/ n. tiempo m.; vez f.; (of day) hora f.; v. cronometrar.

timetable /'taim,teibəl/ n. horario, itinerario m.

time zone huso horario m.

timid /'tɪmɪd/ a. tímido.

timidity /tɪ'mɪdɪti/ n. timidez f.

tin /tɪn/ n. estaño m.; hojalata f. **t. can,** lata f.

tin foil papel de estaño m.

tint /tɪnt/ n. **1.** tinte m. —v. **2.** teñir.

tiny /'taini/ a. chiquito, pequeñito.

tip /tɪp/ n. **1.** punta; propina f. —v. **2.** inclinar; dar propina a.

tire /taiər/ n. **1.** llanta, goma f., neumático m. —v. **2.** cansar.

tired /taiərd/ a. cansado.

tissue /'tɪʃu/ n. tejido m. **t. paper,** papel de seda.

title /'taitl/ n. **1.** título m. —v. **2.** titular.

to /tu/ unstressed tʊ, tə/ prep. a; para.

toast /toust/ n. **1.** tostada f.; (drink) brindis m. —v. **2.** tostar; brindar.

toaster /'toustər/ n. tostador m.

tobacco /tə'bækou/ n. tabaco m. **t. shop,** tabaquería f.

toboggan /tə'bɒgən/ n. tobogán m.

today /tə'dei/ adv. hoy.

toe /tou/ n. dedo del pie.

together /tə'gɛðər/ a. **1.** juntos. —adv. **2.** juntamente.

toil /tɔil/ n. **1.** trabajo m. —v. **2.** afanarse.

toilet /'tɔilɪt/ n. tocado; excusado, retrete m. **t. paper,** papel higiénico.

token /'toukən/ n. señal f.

tolerance /'tɒlərəns/ n. tolerancia f.

tolerate /'tɒlə,reit/ v. tolerar.

toll-free number /'toul 'fri/ teléfono gratuito m.

tomato /tə'meitou/ n. tomate m.

tomb /tum/ n. tumba f.

tomorrow /tə'mɔrou/ adv. mañana. **day after t.,** pasado mañana.

ton /tʌn/ n. tonelada f.

tone /toun/ n. tono m.

tongue /tʌŋ/ n. lengua f.

tonic /'tɒnɪk/ n. tónico m.

tonight /tə'nait/ adv. esta noche.

tonsil /'tɒnsəl/ n. amígdala f.

too /tu/ adv. también. **t. much,** demasiado. **t. many,** demasiados.

tool /tul/ n. herramienta f.

tooth /tuθ/ n. diente m.; (back) muela f.

toothache /'tuθ,eik/ n. dolor de muela.

toothbrush /'tuθ,brʌʃ/ n. cepillo de dientes.

toothpaste /'tuθ,peist/ n. crema dentífrica, pasta dentífrica.

top /tɒp/ n. **1.** parte de arriba. —v. **2.** cubrir; sobrepasar.

topic /'tɒpɪk/ n. S.A. tópico m.

topical /'tɒpɪkəl/ a. tópico.

torch /tɔrtʃ/ n. antorcha f.

torment /n. 'tɔrment/ n. tɔr'ment/ n. **1.** tormento m. —v. **2.** atormentar.

torrent /'tɔrənt/ n. torrente m.

torture /'tɔrtʃər/ n. **1.** tortura f. —v. **2.** torturar.

toss /tɔs/ v. tirar; agitar.

total /'toutl/ a. **1.** total, entero. —n. **2.** total m.

touch /tʌtʃ/ n. **1.** tacto m. **in t.,** en comunicación. —v. **2.** tocar; conmover.

tough /tʌf/ a. tosco; tieso; fuerte.

tour /tʊr/ n. **1.** viaje m. —v. **2.** viajar.

tourist /'tʊrɪst/ n. turista m. & f. a. turístico.

tournament /'tʊrnəmənt/ n. torneo m.

tow /tou/ v. **1.** remolque m. —v. **2.** remolcar.

toward /tɔrd, tə'wɔrd/ prep. hacia.

towel /'tauəl/ n. toalla f.

tower /'tauər/ n. torre f.

town /taun/ n. pueblo m.

town meeting cabildo abierto m.

tow truck grúa f.

toy /tɔi/ n. **1.** juguete m. —v. **2.** jugar.

trace /treis/ n. **1.** vestigio; rastro m. —v. **2.** trazar; rastrear; investigar.

track /træk/ n. **1.** huella, pista f. **race t.,** hipódromo m. —v. **2.** rastrear.

tract /trækt/ n. trecho; tracto m.

tractor /'træktər/ n. tractor m.

trade /treid/ n. **1.** comercio, negocio; oficio; canje m. —v. **2.** comerciar, negociar; cambiar.

trader /'treidər/ n. comerciante m.

tradition /trə'dɪʃən/ n. tradición f.

traditional /trə'dɪʃənl/ a. tradicional.

traffic /'træfɪk/ n. **1.** tráfico m. —v. **2.** traficar.

traffic jam atasco, embotellamiento m.

traffic light semáforo m.

tragedy /'trædʒɪdi/ n. tragedia f.

tragic /'trædʒɪk/ a. trágico.

trail /treil/ n. **1.** sendero; rastro m. —v. **2.** rastrear; arrastrar.

train /trein/ n. **1.** tren m. —v. **2.** enseñar; disciplinar; (sport) entrenarse.

traitor /'treitər/ n. traidor -ora.

tramp /træmp/ n. **1.** caminata f.; vagabundo m. —v. **2.** patear.

tranquil /'træŋkwɪl/ a. tranquilo.

tranquilizer /'træŋkwə,laizər/ n. tranquilizante m.

tranquillity /træŋ'kwɪlɪti/ n. tranquilidad f.

transaction /træn'sækʃən/ n. transacción f.

transfer /n. 'trænsfər, v. træns'fɜr/ n. **1.** traslado m.; boleto de transbordo. —v. **2.** trasladar, transferir.

transform /træns'fɔrm/ v. transformar.

transfusion /træns'fyuʒən/ n. transfusión f.

transistor /træn'zɪstər/ n. transistor m.

transition /træn'zɪʃən/ n. transición f.

translate /træns'leit/ v. traducir.

translation /træns'leiʃən/ n. traducción f.

transmit /træns'mɪt/ v. transmitir.

transparent /træns'pɛərənt/ a. transparente.

transport /n. 'trænspɔrt, v. træns'pɔrt/ n. **1.** transporte m. —v. **2.** transportar.

transportation /ˌtrænspər'teiʃən/ n. transporte m.

transsexual /træns'sɛkʃuəl/ a. & n. transexual m. & f.

transvestite /træns'vɛstait/ n. travestí m. & f.

trap /træp/ n. **1.** trampa f. —v. **2.** atrapar.

trash /træʃ/ n. desecho m.; basura f.

trash can cubo de la basura m.

travel /'trævəl/ n. **1.** tráfico m.; (pl.) viajes m.pl. —v. **2.** viajar.

travel agency agencia de viajes f.

traveler /'trævələr/ n. viajero -ra.

traveler's check /'trævələrz/ cheque de viaje m.

tray /trei/ n. bandeja f.

tread /trɛd/ n. **1.** pisada f.; (of a tire) cubierta f. —v. **2.** pisar.

treason /'trizən/ n. traición f.

treasure /'trɛʒər/ n. tesoro m.

treasurer /'trɛʒərər/ n. tesorero -ra.

treasury /'trɛʒəri/ n. tesorería f.

treat /trit/ v. tratar; convidar.

treatment /'tritmənt/ n. trato, tratamiento m.

treaty /'triti/ n. tratado, pacto m.

tree /tri/ n. árbol m.

tremble /'trɛmbəl/ v. temblar.

tremendous /trɪ'mɛndəs/ a. tremendo.

trench /trɛntʃ/ n. foso m.; Mil. trinchera f.

trend /trɛnd/ n. **1.** tendencia f. —v. **2.** tender.

trespass /'trɛspəs, -pæs/ v. traspasar; violar.

triage /tri'ɑʒ/ n. clasificación de los heridos después del combate.

trial /'traiəl/ n. prueba f.; Leg. proceso, juicio m.

triangle /'trai,æŋgəl/ n. triángulo m.

tribulation /ˌtrɪbyə'leiʃən/ n. tribulación f.

tributary /'trɪbyə,tɛri/ a. & n. tributario m.

tribute /'trɪbyut/ n. tributo m.

trick /trɪk/ n. **1.** engaño m.; maña f.; (cards) baza f. —v. **2.** engañar.

trifle /'traifəl/ n. **1.** pequeñez f. —v. **2.** juguetear.

trigger /'trɪgər/ n. gatillo m.

trim /trɪm/ a. **1.** ajustado; acicalado. —n. **2.** adorno m. —v. **3.** adornar; ajustar; cortar un poco.

trinket /'trɪŋkɪt/ n. bagatela, chuchería f.

trip /trɪp/ n. **1.** viaje m. —v. **2.** tropezar.

triple /'trɪpəl/ a. **1.** triple. —v. **2.** triplicar.

tripod /'traipɒd/ n. trípode m.

trite /traɪt/ a. banal.

triumph /'traɪəmf/ n. **1.** triunfo m. —v. **2.** triunfar.

triumphant /traɪ'ʌmfənt/ a. triunfante.

trivial /'trɪvɪəl/ a. trivial.

trolley /'trɒli/ n. tranvía m.

trombone /trɒm'boun/ n. trombón m.

troop /trup/ n. tropa f.

trophy /'troufi/ n. trofeo m.

tropical /'trɒpɪkəl/ a. trópico.

tropics /'trɒpɪks/ n. trópico m.

trot /trɒt/ n. **1.** trote m. —v. **2.** trotar.

trouble /'trʌbəl/ n. **1.** apuro m.; congoja, aflicción f. —v. **2.** molestar; afligir.

troublesome /'trʌbəlsəm/ a. penoso, molesto.

trough /trɒf/ n. artesa f.

trousers /'trauzərz/ n. pantalones, calzones m.pl.

trout /traut/ n. trucha f.

truce /trus/ n. tregua f.

truck /trʌk/ n. camión m.

true /tru/ a. verdadero, cierto, verdad.

truffle /'trʌfəl/ n. trufa f.

trumpet /'trʌmpɪt/ n. trompeta, trompa f.

trunk /trʌŋk/ n. baúl m.; (of a tree) tronco m.

trust /trʌst/ n. **1.** confianza f. —v. **2.** confiar.

trustworthy /'trʌst,wərði/ a. digno de confianza.

truth /truθ/ n. verdad f.

truthful /'truθfəl/ a. veraz.

try /traɪ/ n. **1.** prueba f.; ensayo m. —v. **2.** tratar; probar; ensayar; Leg. juzgar. **t. on,** probarse.

T-shirt /'ti,ʃərt/ n. camiseta f.

tub /tʌb/ n. tina f.

tube /tub/ n. tubo m.

tuberculosis /tu,bərkyə'lousɪs/ n. tuberculosis f.

tuck /tʌk/ n. **1.** recogido m. —v. **2.** recoger.

Tuesday /'tuzdeɪ/ n. martes m.

tug /tʌg/ n. tirada f.; (boat) remolcador m. —v. **2.** tirar de.

tuition /tu'ɪʃən/ n. matrícula, colegiatura f.

tumble /'tʌmbəl/ n. **1.** caída f. —v. **2.** caer, tumbar; voltear.

tumult /'tumʌlt/ n. tumulto, alboroto m.

tuna /'tʌni/ n. atún m.

tune /tun/ n. **1.** tono m.; melodía, canción f. —v. **2.** templar.

tunnel /'tʌnl/ n. túnel m.

turf /tərf/ n. césped m.

Turkey /'tərki/ n. Turquía f.

Turkish /'tərkɪʃ/ a. turco.

turmoil /'tərmoɪl/ n. disturbio m.

turn /tərn/ n. **1.** vuelta f.; giro; turno m. —v. **2.** volver, tornear, girar; **t. into,** transformar. **t. around,** volverse. **t. on,** encender; abrir. **t. off, t. out,** apagar.

turnip /'tərnɪp/ n. nabo m.

turret /'tərɪt/ n. torrecilla f.

turtle /'tərtl/ n. tortuga f.

turtleneck sweater /'tərtl,nɛk/ jersey de cuello alto m.

tutor /'tutər/ n. **1.** tutor -ra. —v. **2.** enseñar.

tweezers /'twizərz/ n.pl. pinzas f.pl.

twelve /twɛlv/ a. & pron. doce.

twenty /'twɛnti/ a. & pron. veinte.

twice /twaɪs/ adv. dos veces.

twig /twɪg/ n. varita; ramita f.; vástago m.

twilight /'twaɪ,laɪt/ n. crepúsculo m.

twin /twɪn/ n. gemelo -la.

twine /twaɪn/ n. **1.** guita f. —v. **2.** torcer.

twinkle /'twɪŋkəl/ v. centellear.

twist /twɪst/ v. torcer.

two /tu/ a. & pron. dos.

type /taɪp/ n. **1.** tipo m. —v. **2.** escribir a máquina.

typewriter /'taɪp,raɪtər/ n. máquina de escribir.

typhoid fever /'taɪfoɪd/ fiebre tifoidea.

typical /'tɪpɪkəl/ a. típico.

typist /'taɪpɪst/ n. mecanógrafo -fa.

tyranny /'tɪrəni/ n. tiranía f.

tyrant /'taɪrənt/ n. tirano -na.

U V

---

udder /'ʌdər/ n. ubre f.

UFO abbr. (unidentified flying object) OVNI m. (objeto volador no identificado).

ugly /'ʌgli/ a. feo.

Ukraine /yu'kreɪn/ n. Ucrania f.

Ukrainian /yu'kreɪniən/ a. & n. ucranio.

ulcer /'ʌlsər/ n. úlcera f.

ulterior /ʌl'tɪriər/ a. ulterior.

ultimate /'ʌltəmɪt/ a. último.

ultrasonic /,ʌltrə'sɒnɪk/ a. ultrasónico.

umbrella /ʌm'brɛlə/ n. paraguas m. **sun u.,** quitasol m.

umpire /'ʌmpaɪr/ n. árbitro m.

unable /ʌn'eɪbəl/ a. incapaz. **to be u.,** no poder.

unanimous /yu'nænəməs/ a. unánime.

uncertain /ʌn'sərtn/ a. incierto, inseguro.

uncle /'ʌŋkəl/ n. tío m.

unconscious /ʌn'kɒnʃəs/ a. inconsciente; desmayado.

uncover /ʌn'kʌvər/ v. descubrir.

undeniable /ˌʌndɪ'naɪəbəl/ a. innegable.

under /'ʌndər/ adv. **1.** debajo, abajo. —prep. **2.** bajo, debajo de.

underestimate /ˌʌndər'ɛstə,meit/ v. menospreciar; subestimar.

undergo /ˌʌndər'gou/ v. sufrir.

underground /'ʌndər,graund/ a. subterráneo; clandestino.

underline /ʌndər,lain/ v. subrayar.

underneath /ˌʌndər'niθ/ adv **1.** por debajo. —prep. **2.** debajo de.

undershirt /'ʌndər,ʃɜrt/ n. camiseta f.

understand /ˌʌndər'stænd/ v. entender, comprender.

undertake /ˌʌndər'teik/ v. emprender.

underwear /'ʌndər,wɛər/ n. ropa interior.

undo /ʌn'du/ v. deshacer; desatar.

undress /ʌn'drɛs/ v. desnudar, desvestir.

uneasy /ʌn'izi/ a. inquieto.

uneven /ʌn'ivən/ a. desigual.

unexpected /ˌʌnɪk'spɛktɪd/ a. inesperado.

unfair /ʌn'fɛər/ a. injusto.

unfit /ʌn'fɪt/ a. incapaz; inadecuado.

unfold /ʌn'fould/ v. desplegar; revelar.

unforgettable /ˌʌnfər'gɛtəbəl/ a. inolvidable.

unfortunate /ʌn'fɔrtʃənɪt/ a. desafortunado, desgraciado.

unfurnished /ʌn'fɜrnɪʃt/ a. desamueblado.

unhappy /ʌn'hæpi/ a. infeliz.

uniform /'yunə,fɔrm/ a. & n. uniforme m.

unify /'yunə,fai/ v. unificar.

union /'yunyən/ n. unión f. **labor u.,** sindicato de obreros.

unique /yu'nik/ a. único.

unisex /'yunə,sɛks/ a. unisex.

unit /'yunɪt/ n. unidad f.

unite /yu'nait/ v. unir.

United Nations /yu'naitɪd 'neiʃənz/ Naciones Unidas f.pl.

United States /yu'naitɪd 'steits/ Estados Unidos m.pl.

unity /'yunɪti/ n. unidad f.

universal /ˌyunə'vɜrsəl/ a. universal.

universe /'yunə,vɜrs/ n. universo m.

university /ˌyunə'vɜrsɪti/ n. universidad f.

unleaded /ʌn'lɛdɪd/ a. sin plomo.

unless /ʌn'lɛs/ conj. a menos que, si no es que.

unlike /ʌn'laik/ a. disímil.

unload /ʌn'loud/ v. descargar.

unlock /ʌn'lɒk/ v. abrir.

unplug /ʌn'plʌg/ v. desenchufar.

unpopular /ʌn'pɒpyələr/ a. impopular.

unreasonable /ʌn'rizənəbəl/ a. desrazonable.

unscrew /ʌn'skru/ v. desatornillar.

untie /ʌn'tai/ v. desatar; soltar.

until /ʌn'tɪl/ prep. **1.** hasta. —conj. **2.** hasta que.

unusual /ʌn'yuʒuəl/ a. raro, inusitado.

up /ʌp/ adv. **1.** arriba. —prep. **2. u. the street,** etc. calle arriba, etc.

uphold /ʌp'hould/ v. apoyar; defender.

upholster /ʌp'houlstər, ə'poul-/ v. entapizar.

upload /ʌp,loud/ n. **1.** ascenso de archivos m. —v. **2.** subir, cargar.

upon /ə'pɒn/ prep. sobre, encima de.

upper /'ʌpər/ a. superior.

upper-case letter /'ʌpər 'keis/ mayúscula f.

upright /'ʌp,rait/ a. derecho, recto.

upriver /'ʌp'rɪvər/ adv. río arriba.

uproar /'ʌp,rɔr/ n. alboroto, tumulto m.

upset /n. 'ʌp,sɛt; v. ʌp'sɛt/ n. **1.** trastorno m. —v. **2.** trastornar.

upsetting /ʌp'sɛtɪŋ/ a. inquietante.

upstream /'ʌp'strim/ adv. aguas arriba, contra la corriente, río arriba.

uptight /'ʌp'tait/ a. (psicológicamente) tenso, tieso.

upward /'ʌpwərd/ adv. hacia arriba.

urge /ɜrdʒ/ n. **1.** deseo m. —v. **2.** instar.

urgency /'ɜrdʒənsi/ n. urgencia f.

urgent /'ɜrdʒənt/ a. urgente. **to be u.,** urgir.

us /ʌs/ pron. nosotros -as; nos.

use /n. yus; v. yuz/ n. **1.** uso m. —v. **2.** usar, emplear. **u. up,** gastar, agotar. **be used to,** estar acostumbrado a.

useful /'yusfəl/ a. útil.

useless /'yuslɪs/ a. inútil, inservible.

user-friendly /'yuzər 'frɛndli/ a. amigable.

username /'yuzər'neim/ n. nombre de usuario m.

usher /'ʌʃər/ n. **1.** acomodador -ora. —v. **2.** introducir.

usual /'yuʒuəl/ a. usual.

utensil /yu'tɛnsəl/ n. utensilio m.

utmost /'ʌt,moust/ a. sumo, extremo.

utter /'ʌtər/ a. **1.** completo. —v. **2.** proferir; dar.

utterance /'ʌtərəns/ n. expresión f.

vacancy /'veikənsi/ n. vacante f.

vacant /'veikənt/ a. desocupado, libre.

vacation /vei'keiʃən/ n. vacaciones f.pl.

vaccinate /'væksə,neit/ v. vacunar.

vacuum /'vækyum/ n. vacío, vacío m. **v. cleaner,** aspiradora f.

vagrant /'veigrənt/ n. & a. vagabundo- da.

vague /veig/ a. vago.

vain /vein/ a. vano; vanidoso. **in v.,** en vano.

valiant /'vælyənt/ a. valiente.

valid /'vælɪd/ a. válido.

valley /'væli/ n. valle m.

valor /'vælər/ *n.* valor *m.*, valentía *f.*

valuable /'vælyuəbəl/ *a.* valioso.

value /'vælyu/ *n.* **1.** valor, importe *m.* —*v.* **2.** valorar; estimar.

van /væn/ *n.* furgoneta *f.*

vandal /'vændļ/ *n.* vándalo *m.*

vandalism /'vændļˌizəm/ *n.* vandalismo *m.*

vanish /'vænɪʃ/ *v.* desaparecer.

vanity /'vænɪti/ *n.* vanidad *f.* **v. case**, polvera *f.*

vanquish /'væŋkwɪʃ/ *v.* vencer.

vapor /'veipər/ *n.* vapor *m.*

variation /ˌveəri'eiʃən/ *n.* variación *f.*

varicose vein /'væriˌkous/ variz *f.*

variety /və'raiiti/ *n.* variedad *f.*

various /'veəriəs/ *a.* varios; diversos.

varnish /'varnɪʃ/ *n.* **1.** barniz *m.* —*v.* **2.** barnizar.

vary /'veəri/ *v.* variar; cambiar.

vase /veis, veiz, vaz/ *n.* florero; jarrón *m.*

vasectomy /væ'sɛktəmi/ *n.* vasectomía *f.*

vassal /'væsəl/ *n.* vasallo *m.*

vast /væst/ *a.* vasto.

vat /væt/ *n.* tina *f.*, tanque *m.*

VAT /væt/ *n.* IVA (impuesto sobre el valor añadido).

vault /vɔlt/ *n.* bóveda *f.*

vegetable /'vɛdʒtəbəl/ *a. & n.* vegetal *m.*; (*pl.*) legumbres, verduras *f.pl.*

vehement /'viəmənt/ *a.* vehemente.

vehicle /'viːkəl or, sometimes,* 'vihɪ-/ *n.* vehículo *m.*

veil /veil/ *n.* **1.** velo *m.* —*v.* **2.** velar.

vein /vein/ *n.* vena *f.*

velocity /və'lɒsɪti/ *n.* velocidad *f.*

velvet /'vɛlvɪt/ *n.* terciopelo *m.*

Venetian /və'niʃən/ *a. & n.* veneciano.

vengeance /'vɛndʒəns/ *n.* venganza *f.*

Venice /'vɛnɪs/ *n.* Venecia *f.*

vent /vɛnt/ *n.* apertura *f.*

ventilate /'vɛntļˌeit/ *v.* ventilar.

venture /'vɛntʃər/ *n.* ventura *f.*

verb /vɜrb/ *n.* verbo *m.*

verbose /vər'bous/ *a.* verboso.

verdict /'vɜrdɪkt/ *n.* veredicto, fallo *m.*

verge /vɜrdʒ/ *n.* borde *m.*

verify /'vɛrəˌfai/ *v.* verificar.

versatile /'vɜrsətļ/ *a.* versátil.

verse /vɜrs/ *n.* verso *m.*

version /'vɜrʒən/ *n.* versión *f.*

vertical /'vɜrtɪkəl/ *a.* vertical.

very /'vɛri/ *a.* **1.** mismo. —*adv.* **2.** muy.

vessel /'vɛsəl/ *n.* vasija *f.*; barco *m.*

vest /vɛst/ *n.* chaleco *m.*

veteran /'vɛtərən/ *a. & n.* veterano -na.

veto /'vitou/ *n.* veto *m.*

vex /vɛks/ *v.* molestar.

via /'vaiə, 'viə/ *prep.* por la vía de; por.

viaduct /'vaiəˌdʌkt/ *n.* viaducto *m.*

vibrate /'vaibreit/ *v.* vibrar.

vibration /vai'breiʃən/ *n.* vibración *f.*

vice /vais/ *n.* vicio *m.*

vicinity /vɪ'sɪnɪti/ *n.* vecindad *f.*

vicious /'vɪʃəs/ *a.* vicioso.

victim /'vɪktəm/ *n.* víctima *f.*

victor /'vɪktər/ *n.* vencedor -ora.

victorious /vɪk'tɔriəs/ *a.* victorioso.

victory /'vɪktəri/ *n.* victoria *f.*

video camera /'vɪdiˌou/ videocámara *f.*

videoconference /'vɪdiouˌkɒnfərəns/ videoconferencia *f.*

videodisc /'vɪdiouˌdɪsk/ *n.* videodisco *m.*

video game /'vɪdiˌou/ videojuego *m.*

videotape /'vɪdiouˌteip/ *n.* vídeo *m.*, magnetoscopio *m.*

view /vyu/ *n.* **1.** vista *f.* —*v.* **2.** ver.

viewpoint /'vyuˌpɔint/ *n.* punto de vista *m.*

vigil /'vɪdʒəl/ *n.* vigilia, vela *f.*

vigilant /'vɪdʒələnt/ *a.* vigilante.

vigor /'vɪgər/ *n.* vigor *m.*

vile /vail/ *a.* vil, bajo.

village /'vɪlɪdʒ/ *n.* aldea *f.*

villain /'vɪlən/ *n.* malvado -da.

vindicate /'vɪndɪˌkeit/ *v.* vindicar.

vine /vain/ *n.* parra, vid *f.*

vinegar /'vɪnɪgər/ *n.* vinagre *m.*

vintage /'vɪntɪdʒ/ *n.* vendimia *f.*

violate /'vaiəˌleit/ *v.* violar.

violation /ˌvaiə'leiʃən/ *n.* violación *f.*

violence /'vaiələns/ *n.* violencia *f.*

violent /'vaiələnt/ *a.* violento.

violin /ˌvaiə'lɪn/ *n.* violín *m.*

virgin /'vɜrdʒɪn/ *n.* virgen *f.*

virile /'vɪrəl/ *a.* viril.

virtual /'vɜrtʃuəl/ *a.* virtual.

virtual memory memoria virtual *f.*

virtual reality realidad virtual *f.*

virtue /'vɜrtʃu/ *n.* virtud *f.*

virtuous /'vɜrtʃuəs/ *a.* virtuoso.

virus /'vairəs/ *n.* virus *m.*

visa /'vizə/ *n.* visa *f.*

visible /'vɪzəbəl/ *a.* visible.

vision /'vɪʒən/ *n.* visión *f.*

visit /'vɪzɪt/ *n.* **1.** visita *f.* —*v.* **2.** visitar.

visitor /'vɪzɪtər/ *n.* visitante *m. & f.*

visual /'vɪʒuəl/ *a.* visual.

vital /'vaitļ/ *a.* vital.

vitality /vai'tælɪti/ *n.* vitalidad *f.*

vitamin /'vaitəmɪn/ *n.* vitamina *f.*

vivacious /vɪ'veiʃəs, vai-/ *a.* vivaz.

vivid /'vɪvɪd/ *a.* vivo; gráfico.

vocabulary /vou'kæbyəˌlɛri/ *n.* vocabulario *m.*

vocal /'voukəl/ *a.* vocal.

vodka /'vɒdkə/ *n.* vodca *m.*

vogue /voug/ *n.* boga; moda *f.* **be in vogue** estilarse.

voice /vɔis/ *n.* **1.** voz *f.* —*v.* **2.** expresar.

voice mail correo de voz *m.*
voice recognition reconocimiento de voz *m.*
void /vɔid/ *a.* **1.** vacío. —*n.* **2.** vacío *m.* —*v.* **3.** invalidar.
voltage /'voultidʒ/ *n.* voltaje *m.*
volume /'volyum/ *n.* volumen; tomo *m.*
voluntary /'volən,teri/ *a.* voluntario.
volunteer /,volən'tiər/ *n.* **1.** voluntario -ria. —*v.* **2.** ofrecerse.

vomit /'vomit/ *v.* vomitar.
vote /vout/ *n.* **1.** voto *m.* —*v.* **2.** votar.
voter /'voutər/ *n.* votante *m. & f.*
vouch /vautʃ/ *v.* **v. for,** garantizar.
vow /vau/ *n.* **1.** voto *m.* —*v.* **2.** jurar.
vowel /'vauəl/ *n.* vocal *f.*
voyage /'vɔidʒ/ *n.* viaje *m.*
vulgar /'vʌlgər/ *a.* vulgar; común; soez.
vulnerable /'vʌlnərəbəl/ *a.* vulnerable.

W

---

wade /weid/ *v.* vadear.
wag /wæg/ *v.* menear.
wage /weidʒ/ *n.* **1.** (pl.) sueldo, salario *m.* —*v.* **2. w. war,** hacer guerra.
wagon /'wægən/ *n.* carreta *f.*
wail /weil/ *n.* **1.** lamento, gemido *m.* —*v.* **2.** lamentar, gemir.
waist /weist/ *n.* cintura *f.*
wait /weit/ *n.* **1.** espera *f.* —*v.* **2.** esperar. **w. for,** esperar. **w. on,** atender.
waiter /'weitər/ **waitress** *n.* camarero -ra.
waiting room /'weitiŋ/ sala de espera.
wake /weik/ *v.* **w. up,** despertar.
walk /wɔk/ *n.* **1.** paseo *m.*; vuelta; caminata *f.*; modo de andar. —*v.* **2.** andar; caminar; ir a pie.
wall /wɔl/ *n.* pared; muralla *f.*
wallcovering /'wɔl,kʌvəriŋ/ *n.* tapizado de pared *m.*
wallet /'wɔlit/ *n.* cartera *f.*
wallpaper /'wɔl,peipər/ *n.* empapelado *m.*
walnut /'wɔl,nʌt/ *n.* nuez *f.*
waltz /wɔlts/ *n.* vals *m.*
wander /'wɔndər/ *v.* vagar.
want /wɔnt/ *n.* **1.** necesidad *f.* —*v.* **2.** querer.
war /wɔr/ *n.* guerra *f.*
ward /wɔrd/ *n.* **1.** *Pol.* barrio *m.*; (hospital) cuadra *f.* —*v.* **2. w. off,** parar.
warehouse /'wɛər,haus/ *n.* almacén *m.*
wares /wɛərz/ *n.* mercancías *f.pl.*
warlike /'wɔr,laik/ *a.* belicoso.
warm /wɔrm/ *a.* **1.** caliente; *Fig.* caluroso. **to be w.,** tener calor; (weather) hacer calor. —*v.* **2.** calentar.
warmth /wɔrmθ/ *n.* calor *m.*
warn /wɔrn/ *v.* advertir.
warning /'wɔrniŋ/ *n.* aviso *m.*
warp /wɔrp/ *v.* alabear.
warrant /'wɔrənt, 'wɔr-/ *v.* justificar.
warrior /'wɔriər/ *n.* guerrero -ra.
warship /'wɔr,ʃip/ *n.* navío de guerra, buque de guerra *m.*
wash /wɔʃ/ *v.* lavar.

washing machine /'wɔʃiŋ/ máquina de lavar, lavadora *f.*
wasp /wɒsp/ *n.* avispa *f.*
waste /weist/ *n.* **1.** gasto *m.*; desechos *m.pl.* —*v.* **2.** gastar; perder.
watch /wɒtʃ/ *n.* **1.** reloj *m.*; *Mil.* guardia *f.* —*v.* **2.** observar, mirar. **w. for,** esperar. **w. out for,** tener cuidado con. **w. over,** guardar; velar por.
watchful /'wɒtʃfəl/ *a.* desvelado.
watchmaker /'wɒtʃ,meikər/ *n.* relojero -ra.
watchman /'wɒtʃmən/ *n.* sereno *m.*
water /'wɔtər/ *n.* **1.** agua *f.* **w. color,** acuarela *f.* —*v.* **2.** aguar.
waterbed /'wɔtər,bed/ *n.* cama de agua *f.*
waterfall /'wɔtər,fɔl/ *n.* catarata *f.*
watering can /'wɔtəriŋ/ regadera *f.*
waterproof /'wɔtər,pruf/ *a.* impermeable.
wave /weiv/ *n.* **1.** onda; ola *f.* —*v.* **2.** ondear; agitar; hacer señas.
waver /'weivər/ *v.* vacilar.
wax /wæks/ *n.* **1.** cera *f.* —*v.* **2.** encerar.
way /wei/ *n.* camino; modo *m.*, manera *f.* **in a w.,** hasta cierto punto. **a long w.,** muy lejos. **by the w.,** a propósito. **this w.,** por aquí. **that w.,** por allí.
we /wi/ *pron.* nosotros -as.
weak /wik/ *a.* débil.
weaken /'wikən/ *v.* debilitar.
weakness /'wiknis/ *n.* debilidad *f.*
wealth /welθ/ *n.* riqueza *f.*
wealthy /'welθi/ *a.* adinerado.
wean /win/ *v.* destetar.
weapon /'wepən/ *n.* arma *f.*
wear /wɛər/ *n.* **1.** uso; desgaste *m.*; (clothes) ropa *f.* —*v.* **2.** usar, llevar. **w. out,** gastar; cansar.
weary /'wiəri/ *a.* cansado, rendido.
weather /'wɛðər/ *n.* tiempo *m.*
weave /wiv/ *v.* tejer.
weaver /'wivər/ *n.* tejedor -ra.
web /web/ *n.* tela *f.*
Web /web/ *n.* (Internet) malla *f.*, telaraña *f.*, web *m.*

wedding /'wɛdɪŋ/ n. boda f.

wedge /wɛdʒ/ n. cuña f.

Wednesday /'wɛnzdei/ n. miércoles m.

weed /wid/ n. maleza f.

week /wik/ n. semana f.

weekday /'wik,dei/ n. día de trabajo.

weekend /'wik,ɛnd/ n. fin de semana.

weekly /'wikli/ a. semanal.

weep /wip/ v llorar.

weigh /wei/ v. pesar.

weight /weit/ n. peso m.

weightless /'weitlɪs/ a. ingrávido.

weightlessness /'weitlɪsnɪs/ n. ingravidez f.

weird /wɪərd/ a. misterioso, extraño.

welcome /'wɛlkəm/ a. 1. bienvenido. **you're w.**, de nada, no hay de qué. —n. 2. acogida, bienvenida f. —v. 3. acoger, recibir bien.

welfare /'wɛl,fɛər/ n. bienestar m.

well /wɛl/ a. 1. sano, bueno. —adv. 2. bien; pues. —n. 3. pozo m.

well-done /'wɛl 'dʌn/ a. (food) bien cocido.

well-known /'wɛl 'noun/ a. bien conocido.

west /wɛst/ n. oeste, occidente m.

western /'wɛstərn/ a. occidental.

westward /'wɛstwərd/ adv. hacia el oeste.

wet /wɛt/ a. 1. mojado. **to get w.,** mojarse. —v. 2. mojar.

whale /weil/ n. ballena f.

what /wʌt; unstressed wət/ a. 1. qué; cuál. —interrog. pron. 2. qué. —rel. pron. 3. lo que.

whatever /wʌt'ɛvər/ a. 1. cualquier. —pron. 2. lo que; todo lo que.

wheat /wit/ n. trigo m.

wheel /wil/ n. rueda f. **steering w.,** volante m.

when /wɛn; unstressed wən/ adv. 1. cuándo. —conj. 2. cuando.

whenever /wɛn'ɛvər/ conj. siempre que, cuando quiera que.

where /wɛər/ adv. 1. dónde, adónde. —conj. 2. donde.

wherever /wɛər'ɛvər/ conj. dondequiera que, adondequiera que.

whether /'wɛðər/ conj. si.

which /wɪtʃ/ a. 1. qué. —interrog. pron. 2. cuál. —rel. pron. 3. que; el cual; lo cual.

whichever /wɪtʃ'ɛvər/ a. & pron. cualquiera que.

while /wail/ conj. 1. mientras; mientras que. —n. 2. rato m.

whip /wɪp/ n. 1. látigo m. —v. 2. azotar.

whipped cream /wɪpt/ nata batida f.

whirl /wɜrl/ v. girar.

whirlpool /'wɜrl,pul/ n. vórtice m.

whirlwind /'wɜrl,wɪnd/ n. torbellino m.

whisk broom /wɪsk/ escobilla f.

whisker /'wɪskər/ n. bigote m.

whiskey /'wɪski/ n. whisky m.

whisper /'wɪspər/ n. 1. cuchicheo m. —v. 2. cuchichear.

whistle /'wɪsəl/ n. 1. pito; silbido m. —v. 2. silbar.

white /wait/ a. 1. blanco. —n. 2. (of egg) clara f.

who /hu/ **whom** interrog. pron. 1. quién. —rel. pron. 2. que; quien.

whoever /hu'ɛvər/ **whomever** pron. quienquiera que.

whole /houl/ a. 1. entero. **the wh.,** todo el. —n. 2. totalidad f. **on the wh.,** por lo general.

wholesale /'houl,seil/ n. **at wh.,** al por mayor.

wholesaler /'houl,seilər/ n. mayorista m. & f.

wholesome /'houlsəm/ a. sano, saludable.

wholly /'houli/ adv. enteramente.

whose /huz/ interrog. adj. 1. de quién. —rel. adj. 2. cuyo.

why /wai/ adv. por qué; para qué.

wicked /'wɪkɪd/ a. malo, malvado.

wickedness /'wɪkɪdnɪs/ n. maldad f.

wide /waid/ a. 1. ancho; extenso. —adv. 2. **w. open,** abierto de par en par.

widen /'waidn/ v. ensanchar; extender.

widespread /'waid'sprɛd/ a. extenso.

widow /'wɪdou/ n. viuda f.

widower /'wɪdouər/ n. viudo m.

width /wɪdθ/ n. anchura f.

wield /wild/ v. manejar, empuñar.

wife /waif/ n. esposa, señora, mujer f.

wig /wɪg/ n. peluca f.

wild /waild/ a. salvaje; bárbaro.

wilderness /'wɪldərnɪs/ n. desierto m.

wildlife /'waild,laif/ n. fauna silvestre f.

will /wɪl/ n. 1. voluntad f.; testamento m. —v. 2. querer; determinar; Leg. legar.

willful /'wɪlfəl/ a. voluntarioso; premeditado.

willing /'wɪlɪŋ/ a. **to be w.,** estar dispuesto.

willingly /'wɪlɪŋli/ adv. de buena gana.

wilt /wɪlt/ v. marchitar.

win /wɪn/ v. ganar.

wind /wɪnd/ n. 1. viento m. —v. 2. torcer; dar cuerda a.

windmill /'wɪnd,mɪl/ n. molino de viento m.

window /'wɪndou/ n. ventana f.; (of car) ventanilla f.; (of shop or store) escaparate m.

windshield /'wɪnd,ʃild/ n. parabrisas m.

windy /'wɪndi/ a. ventoso. **to be w.,** (weather) hacer viento.

wine /wain/ n. vino m.

wing /wɪŋ/ n. ala f.; Theat. bastidor m.

wink /wɪŋk/ n. 1. guiño m. —v. 2. guiñar.

winner /'wɪnər/ n. ganador -ra.

winter /'wɪntər/ n. invierno m.

wipe /waip/ v. limpiar; (dry) secar. **w. out,** destruir.

wire /wai⁹r/ n. **1.** alambre; hilo; telegrama m. —v. **2.** telegrafiar.

wireless /ˈwai⁹rlɪs/ n. telégrafo sin hilos.

wisdom /ˈwɪzdəm/ n. juicio m.; sabiduría f.

wise /waiz/ a. sensato, juicioso; sabio.

wish /wɪʃ/ n. **1.** deseo; voto m. —v. **2.** desear; querer.

wit /wɪt/ n. ingenio m., sal f.

witch /wɪtʃ/ n. bruja f.

with /wɪθ, wɪð/ prep. con.

withdraw /wɪð'drɔ, wɪθ-/ v. retirar.

wither /ˈwɪðər/ v. marchitar.

withhold /wɪθ'hould, wɪð-/ v. retener, suspender.

within /wɪð'ɪn, wɪθ-/ adv **1.** dentro, por dentro. —prep. **2.** dentro de; en.

without /wɪð'aut, wɪθ-/ adv. **1.** fuera, por fuera. —prep. **2.** sin.

witness /ˈwɪtnɪs/ n. **1.** testigo; testimonio m. & f. —v. **2.** presenciar; atestar.

witty /ˈwɪti/ a. ingenioso, gracioso.

wizard /ˈwɪzərd/ n. hechicero m.

woe /wou/ n. dolor m.; pena f.

wolf /wulf/ n. lobo -ba.

woman /ˈwumən/ n. mujer f.

womb /wum/ n. entrañas f.pl., matriz f.

wonder /ˈwʌndər/ n. **1.** maravilla; admiración f. **for a w.,** por milagro. **no w.,** no es extraño. —v. **2.** preguntarse; maravillarse.

wonderful /ˈwʌndərfəl/ a. maravilloso.

woo /wu/ v. cortejar.

wood /wud/ n. madera; (for fire) leña f.

wooden /ˈwudn̩/ a. de madera.

wool /wul/ n. lana f. -ba.

word /wərd/ n. **1.** palabra f. **the words** (of a song), la letra. —v. **2.** expresar.

word processing /ˈprɒsɛsɪŋ/ procesamiento de textos m.

word processor /ˈprɒsɛsər/ procesador de textos m.

work /wərk/ n. **1.** trabajo m.; (of art) obra f. —v. **2.** trabajar; obrar; funcionar.

worker /ˈwərkər/ n. trabajador, -ra; obrero, -ra.

workman /ˈwərkmən/ n. obrero m.

work station estación de trabajo f.

work week /ˈwərk,wik/ semana laboral f.

world /wərld/ n. mundo m. **w. war,** guerra mundial.

worldly /ˈwərldli/ a. mundano.

worldwide /ˈwərld'waid/ a. mundial.

worm /wərm/ n. gusano m.

worn /wɔrn/ a. usado. **w. out,** gastado; cansado, rendido.

worrisome /ˈwərisəm/ a. inquietante.

worry /ˈwəri/ n. **1.** preocupación f. —v. **2.** preocupar.

worrying /ˈwəriɪŋ/ a inquietante.

worse /wərs/ a. peor. **to get w.,** empeorar.

worship /ˈwərʃɪp/ n. **1.** adoración f. —v. **2.** adorar.

worst /wərst/ a. peor.

worth /wərθ/ a. **1. to be w.,** valer. —n. **2.** valor m.

worthless /ˈwərθlɪs/ a sin valor.

worthy /ˈwərði/ a. digno.

wound /wund/ n. **1.** herida f. —v. **2.** herir.

wrap /ræp/ n. **1.** (pl.) abrigos m.pl. —n. **2.** envolver.

wrapping /ˈræpɪŋ/ n. cubierta f

wrath /ræθ/ n. ira, cólera f.

wreath /riθ/ n. guirnalda; corona f.

wreck /rɛk/ n. **1.** ruina f.; accidente m. —v. **2.** destrozar, arruinar.

wrench /rɛntʃ/ n. llave f. **monkey w.,** llave inglesa.

wrestle /ˈrɛsəl/ v. luchar.

wretched /ˈrɛtʃɪd/ a. miserable.

wring /rɪŋ/ v. retorcer.

wrinkle /ˈrɪŋkəl/ n. **1.** arruga f. —v. **2.** arrugar.

wrist /rɪst/ n. muñeca f. **w. watch,** reloj de pulsera.

write /rait/ v. escribir. **w. down,** apuntar.

writer /ˈraitər/ n. escritor -ra.

writhe /raið/ v. contorcerse.

writing paper /ˈraitɪŋ/ papel de escribir m.

wrong /rɒŋ/ a. **1.** equivocado; incorrecto. **to be w.,** equivocarse; no tener razón. —adv. **2.** mal, incorrectamente. —n. **3.** agravio m. **right and w.,** el bien y el mal. —v. **4.** agraviar, ofender.

WWW abbr. (World Wide Web) malla mundial f.

X Y Z

x-ray /'ɛks,rei/ *n.* **1.** rayo X *m.*, radiografía, *f.* —*v.* **2.** radiografiar.

xylophone /'zailə,foun/ *n.* xilófono *m.*

yacht /yɒt/ *n.* yate *m.*

yard /yɑrd/ *n.* patio, corral *m.*; (measure) yarda *f.*

yarn /yɑrn/ *n.* hilo.

yawn /yɔn/ *n.* **1.** bostezo *m.* —*v.* **2.** bostezar.

year /yɪər/ *n.* año *m.*

yearly /'yɪərli/ *a.* anual.

yearn /yɜrn/ *v.* anhelar.

yell /yɛl/ *n.* **1.** grito *m.* —*v.* **2.** gritar.

yellow /'yɛlou/ *a.* amarillo.

yes /yɛs/ *adv.* sí.

yesterday /'yɛstər,dei/ *adv.* ayer.

yet /yɛt/ *adv.* todavía, aún.

Yiddish /'yɪdɪʃ/ *n.* yídish *m.*

yield /yild/ *v.* producir; ceder.

yogurt /'yougərt/ *n.* yogur *m.*

yoke /youk/ *n.* yugo *m.*

yolk /youk/ *n.* yema *f.*

you /yu; *unstressed* yʊ, yə/ *pron.* usted, (pl.) ustedes; lo, la, los, las; le, les; (familiar) tú, (pl.) vosotros -as; ti; te, (pl.) os. **with y.**, contigo, con usted.

young /yʌŋ/ *a.* joven.

youngster /'yʌŋstər/ *n.* muchacho -cha *m. & f.*

your /yʊr, yər; *unstressed* yər/ *a.* su; (familiar) tu; (pl.) vuestro.

yours /yʊrz, yɔrz/ *pron.* suyo; (familiar) tuyo; (pl.) vuestro.

yourself -selves /yʊr'sɛlf, yər- yər-/ *pron.* sí; se; (familiar) ti; te. **with y.**, consigo; contigo. **you y.**, usted mismo, ustedes mismos; tú mismo, vosotros mismos.

youth /yuθ/ *n.* juventud *f.*; (person) joven *m. & f.*

youth club club juvenil *m.*

youthful /'yuθfəl/ *a.* juvenil.

yuppie /'yʌpi/ *n.* yuppie *m. & f.*

zap /zæp/ *v.* desintegrar, aniquilar.

zeal /zil/ *n.* celo, fervor *m.*

zealous /'zɛləs/ *a.* celoso, fervoroso.

zero /'zɪərou/ *n.* cero *m.*

zest /zɛst/ *n.* gusto *m.*

zip code /zɪp/ número de distrito postal.

zipper /'zɪpər/ *m.* cremallera *f.*

zone /zoun/ *n.* zona *f.*

zoo /zu/ *n.* jardín zoológico.

Spanish Irregular Verbs

Infinitive	Present	Future	Preterit	Past Part.
andar	ando	andaré	anduve	andado
caber	quepo	cabré	cupe	cabido
caer	caigo	caeré	caí	caído
conducir	conduzco	conduciré	conduje	conducido
dar	doy	daré	di	dado
decir	digo	diré	dije	dicho
estar	estoy	estaré	estuve	estado
haber	he	habré	hube	habido
hacer	hago	haré	hice	hecho
ir	voy	iré	fui	ido
jugar	juego	jugaré	jugué	jugado
morir	muero	moriré	morí	muerto
oir	oigo	oiré	oí	oído
poder	puedo	podré	pude	podido
poner	pongo	pondré	puse	puesto
querer	quiero	querré	quise	querido
saber	sé	sabré	supe	sabido
salir	salgo	saldré	salí	salido
ser	soy	seré	fui	sido
tener	tengo	tendré	tuve	tenido
traer	traigo	traeré	traje	traído
valer	valgo	valdré	valí	valido
venir	vengo	vendré	vine	venido
ver	veo	veré	vi	visto

Las formas del verbo inglés

1. Se forma la 3ª persona singular del tiempo presente exactamente al igual que el plural de los sustantivos, añadiendo **-es** o **-s** a la forma sencilla según las mismas reglas, así:

(1)   teach   pass   wish   fix   buzz

        teaches   passes   wishes   fixes   buzzes

(2) place   change judge   please   freeze
    places   changes judges   pleases   freezes

(3a) find   sell   clean   hear   love   buy   know
     finds sells cleans hears loves buys knows

(3b) think   like   laugh   stop   hope   meet   want
     thinks likes laughs stops hopes meets wants

(4) cry   try   dry   carry   deny
    cries   tries   dries   carries denies

Cinco verbos muy comunes tienen 3ª persona singular irregular:

(5) go   do   say   have   be
    goes   does   says   has   is

2. Se forman el tiempo pasado y el participio de modo igual, añadiendo a la forma sencilla la terminación **-ed** o **-d** según las reglas que siguen:

(1) Si la forma sencilla termina en **-d** o **-t,** se le pone **-ed** como sílaba aparte:

    end   fold   need   load
    ended   folded   needed   loaded

    want   feast   wait   light
    wanted   feasted waited   lighted

(2) Si la forma sencilla termina en cualquier otra consonante, se añade también **-ed** pero sin hacer sílaba aparte:

(2a) bang   sail   seem   harm   earn   weigh
     banged sailed seemed harmed earned weighed

(2b) lunch   work   look   laugh   help   pass
      lunched worked looked laughed helped passed

(3)   Si la forma sencilla termina en **-e**, se le pone sólo **-d**:

(3a) hate   taste   waste   guide   fade   trade
      hated   tasted   wasted   guided   faded   traded

(3b) free   judge   rule   name   dine   scare
      freed   judged   ruled   named   dined   scared

(3c) place   force   knife   like   hope   base
      placed   forced   knifed   liked   hoped   based

(4) Una **-y** final que sigue a cualquier consonante se cambia en **-ie** al añadir la **-d** del pasado/participio:

   cry   try   dry   carry   deny
   cried   tried   dried   carried   denied

3. Varios verbos muy comunes forman el tiempo pasado y el participio de manera irregular. Pertenecen a tres grupos.

(1) Los que tienen una sola forma irregular para tiempo pasado y participio, como los siguientes:

   bend   bleed   bring   build   buy   catch   creep deal
   bent   bled   brought built   bought caught crept dealt

   dig   feed   feel   fight   find   flee   get   hang
   dug   fed   felt   fought found fled   got   hung

   have   hear   hold   keep   lead   leave   lend   lose
   had   heard   held   kept   led   left   lent   lost

make	mean	meet	say	seek	sell	send	shine
made	meant	met	said	sought	sold	sent	shone

shoot	sit	sleep	spend	stand	strike	sweep	teach
shot	sat	slept	spent	stood	struck	swept	taught

(2) Los que tienen una forma irregular para el tiempo pasado y otra forma irregular para el participio, como los siguientes:

be	beat	become	begin	bite
was	beat	became	began	bit
been	beaten	become	begun	bitten

blow	break	choose	come	do
blew	broke	chose	came	did
blown	broken	chosen	come	done

draw	drink	drive	eat	fall
drew	drank	drove	ate	fell
drawn	drunk	driven	eaten	fallen

fly	forget	freeze	give	go
flew	forgot	froze	gave	went
flown	forgotten	frozen	given	gone

grow	hide	know	ride	ring
grew	hid	knew	rode	rang
grown	hidden	known	ridden	rung

rise	run	see	shake	shrink
rose	ran	saw	shook	shrank
risen	run	seen	shaken	shrunk

sing	sink	speak	steal	swear
sang	sank	spoke	stole	swore
sung	sunk	spoken	stolen	sworn

swim	tear	throw	wear	write
swam	tore	threw	wore	wrote
swum	torn	thrown	worn	written

(3) Los que no varían del todo, la forma sencilla funcionando también como pasado/participio; entre éstos son de mayor frecuencia:

bet	burst	cast	cost	cut
hit	hurt	let	put	quit
read	set	shed	shut	slit
spit	split	spread	thrust	wet

El plural del sustantivo inglés

A la forma singular se añade la terminación **-es** o **-s** de acuerdo con las reglas siguientes.

(1) Si el singular termina en **-ch, -s, -sh, -x** o **-z**, se le pone **-es** como sílaba aparte:

match	glass	dish	box	buzz
matches	glasses	dishes	boxes	buzzes

(2) Si el singular termina en **-ce, -ge, -se** o **-ze**, se le pone una **-s** que con la vocal precedente forma sílaba aparte:

face	page	house	size
faces	pages	houses	sizes

(3) Una **-y** final que sigue a cualquier consonante se cambia en **-ie** a ponérsele la **-s** del plural:

sky	city	lady	ferry	penny
skies	cities	ladies	ferries	pennies

(4) Los siguientes sustantivos comunes tienen plural irregular:

man	woman	child	foot	mouse	goose
men	women	children	feet	mice	geese
wife	knife	life	half	leaf	deer
wives	knives	lives	halves	leaves	deer

Days of the Week/Días de la Semana

Sunday	domingo	**Thursday**	jueves
Monday	lunes	**Friday**	viernes
Tuesday	martes	**Saturday**	sábado
Wednesday	miércoles		

Months/Meses

January	enero	**July**	julio
February	febrero	**August**	agosto
March	marzo	**September**	septiembre
April	abril	**October**	octubre
May	mayo	**November**	noviembre
June	junio	**December**	diciembre

Weights and Measures/Pesos y Medidas

1 centímetro	=	.3937 inches
1 kilolitro	=	264.18 gallons
1 metro	=	39.37 inches
1 inch	=	2.54 centímetros
1 kilómetro	=	.621 mile
1 foot	=	.305 metros
1 centigramo	=	.1543 grain
1 mile	=	1.61 kilómetros
1 gramo	=	15.432 grains
1 grain	=	.065 gramos
1 kilogramo	=	2.2046 pounds
1 pound	=	.455 kilogramos
1 tonelada	=	2.204 pounds
1 ton	=	.907 toneladas
1 centilitro	=	.338 ounces
1 ounce	=	2.96 centilitros
1 litro	=	1.0567 quart (liquid); .908 quart (dry)
1 quart	=	1.13 litros
1 gallon	=	4.52 litros